social psychology

social psychology

social psychology

seventh edition

Saul Kassin | **Steven Fein** | **Hazel Rose Markus**

John Jay College
of Criminal Justice

Williams College

Williams College

Stanford University

Houghton Mifflin Company   Boston   New York

Executive Publisher: George Hoffman
Senior Sponsoring Editor: Jane Potter
Marketing Manager: Amy Whitaker
Senior Development Editor: Rita Lombard
Senior Project Editor: Bob Greiner
Art and Design Manager: Jill Haber
Cover Design Director: Anthony L. Saizon
Senior Photo Editor: Jennifer Meyer Dare
Editorial Associate: Henry Cheek
New Title Project Manager: James Lonergan
Senior Composition Buyer: Chuck Dutton
Marketing Assistant: Samantha Abrams
Editorial Production Assistant: Emily Meyer

Cover art: Blend Images/Alamy

Printed in the U.S.A.

Library of Congress Catalog Number: 2007926779

ISBN-10: 0-618-86846-1
ISBN-13: 978-0-618-86846-9

3 4 5 6 7 8 9-CRK-11 10 09 08

We dedicate this book to our families,
friends, students, and colleagues.

Brief Contents

CONTENTS

PART 3 Social Relations

9 Attraction and Close Relationships 300

10 Helping Others 344

PREFACE

Twenty years ago, Sharon Brehm conceived of this textbook, brought it to life, and nurtured it into full form. Now, after six editions, and as president of the American Psychological Association, she has passed the torch to her friends and co-authors. The field of social psychology has grown substantially over these many years, and our coverage in this edition fully reflects that growth. Nevertheless, while Sharon's name may no longer appear on the cover, every page carries her imprint.

We used to think of social psychology as a discipline that is slow to change. As in other sciences, we thought that knowledge accumulates in small increments, one step at a time. Social psychology has no "critical" experiments, no single study can "prove" a theory or hypothesis, and future social psychologists will stand firmly on the shoulders of their predecessors. While all this remains true, the process of revising this textbook has shown us how dynamic and responsive our field can be. As the world around us rapidly changes—socially, politically, technologically, and in other areas of science—so too does social psychology.

As always, we had two main goals for this revision. Our first was to present the most important and exciting perspectives in the field as a whole. To communicate the depth of social psychology, we have self-consciously expanded our coverage in ways that we will soon describe. Second, we wanted this book to serve as a good teacher outside the classroom. While speaking the student's language, we wanted it to connect social psychology to current events in politics, sports, business, law, entertainment, the Internet, and other life domains.

WHAT'S NEW IN THIS EDITION

As in the past, we have tried to capture some subtle but important shifts within the field so that the reader can feel the pulse of social psychology *today* in the pages of this textbook.

The Content

■ **Comprehensive, Up-to-Date Scholarship**   Like its predecessors, the seventh edition offers a broad, balanced, mainstream look at social psychology. Thus, it includes detailed descriptions of classic studies from social psychology's historical warehouse as well as the latest research findings from hundreds of new references. In particular, we draw your attention to the following topics, which are either new to this edition or have received expanded coverage:

- How social context affects judgments on important issues (Chapter 1)
- Uses in research of brain-imaging technologies (Chapter 1)
- The challenges of doing research across cultures (Chapter 2)
- Costs and benefits in the pursuit of self-esteem (Chapter 3)
- Psychological consequences of terrorism (Chapter 3)
- Cultural influences on thought and attribution (Chapter 4)
- Motivational factors in the automaticity and inhibition of stereotyping (Chapter 5)
- Implicit stereotypes and prejudice effects on interracial perceptions and behaviors (Chapter 5)
- Brain-imaging studies of people's reactions to black and white faces (Chapter 5)
- Race effects on police officers' decisions on whether to shoot a crime suspect (Chapter 5)

▶ Classical conditioning of implicit attitudes (Chapter 6)

▶ PAST model of ambivalence in attitudes (Chapter 6)

▶ Cultural influences on cognitive dissonance (Chapter 6)

▶ "Automatic" social mimicry (Chapter 7)

▶ Conformity, deviance, and ostracism in online interactions (Chapter 7)

▶ fMRI images of conformity and exclusion (Chapter 7)

▶ Keys to successful negotiation between groups (Chapter 8)

▶ Effects of diversity on group performance (Chapter 8)

▶ Process gain in groups (Chapter 8)

▶ "I-sharing" and attraction (Chapter 9)

▶ Roots of sexual orientation (Chapter 9)

▶ Cultural influences on attraction and love (Chapter 9)

▶ Implicit bystander effects (Chapter 10)

▶ Evolutionary approaches to helping (Chapter 10)

▶ Helping among chimpanzees and human infants (Chapter 10)

▶ Gender and relational aggression (Chapter 11)

▶ Effects of violent video games (Chapter 11)

▶ Race effects in jury decision making (Chapter 12)

▶ The "CSI effect" in juries (Chapter 12)

▶ Cultural perspectives on law and justice (Chapter 12)

▶ Attitudes toward affirmative action and organizational diversity (Chapter 13)

▶ 360-degree performance assessments (Chapter 13)

▶ The human capacity for resilience (Chapter 14)

▶ Cultural differences in coping styles (Chapter 14)

This list shows that we have paid close attention to four relatively recent developments. The first concerns social neuroscience and the fMRI brain-imaging studies that are poised to enlighten our understanding of the human social experience. Social neuroscience has not fully arrived, and researchers do not know how to interpret the newly observed links between brain activity and self-referential thoughts, social perceptions, motives, emotions, and behavior. While we acknowledge the current limitations, we wanted to provide students with a glimpse of this exciting new fusion of psychology and neuroscience.

Second, we have sought to integrate the far more developed distinction between implicit and explicit processes. In matters relating to the unconscious, psychology owes a debt of gratitude to Freud. After some resistance, social psychologists have also come to realize the importance of the conscious-unconscious distinction when it comes to self-esteem, priming, stereotyping, prejudice, attitudes, ambivalence, social influence, and other core topics. Hence, we describe recent work involving the Implicit Association Test, or IAT, and the ongoing debate about what it measures, what it means, and what it predicts.

Third, we continue to represent biological perspectives on human nature, at the heart of which is the notion that we humans, like other species, have an ancestral past that predisposes us to behave in ways that are adapted to promote survival and reproduction. Evolutionary psychologists seek to explain a wide range of social behaviors, such as helping, aggression, mate selection, and romantic jealousy. We realize that this perspective is controversial. Still, respected journals are filled with studies and critiques of evolutionary psychology. This edition discusses the evolutionary approach, particularly in chapters pertaining to social relations.

A fourth development concerns the interplay of cognitive and affective factors. When the cognitive revolution swept through psychology, it spawned an important social-cognitive perspective that suggested, for example, that people are like naïve scientists; that attitudes change through central-route processes; and that prejudices arise as an innocent byproduct of the way people think. Today the warm-blooded social animal has reemerged, fully motivated and filled with emotion. This animal sees the world through a screen of positive illusions, changes attitudes to satisfy self-serving motives, and harbors hatred born of pride, insecurity, and a need for dominance. It is now clear that both perspectives are necessary, and both are discussed throughout this book.

■ **Cultural Perspectives**   Social psychologists have long been fascinated by similarity and difference—among cultural groups and between racial and ethnic groups within cultures. As the people of the world have come into closer contact through high-speed air travel, international trade, satellite TV, and the Internet, researchers have broadened their scope from the situational snapshot to a fuller consideration of people in their cultural milieu. Cultural phenomena, once marginalized within the field, are now fully integrated into the social psychology family. This new team of authors is thus fully committed to bringing cultural practices, values, ideas, and context from the margins into the mainstream. This exploration reveals some universals in human social behavior as well as local influences that distinguish the different peoples of the world.

Unique to this seventh edition, every chapter—from the basics of the self, attitudes, social cognition, interpersonal behavior, and group dynamics, to the applied areas of law, business, and health—now contains one, two, or three sections on the role of culture. These sections appear within the body of the text and are richly accompanied by photographs, not boxed or set apart. Moreover, because social psychology has become a truly international discipline, this book includes many new citations to research conducted throughout Europe, Asia, Australia, and other parts of the world. We believe that the study of human diversity—from the perspectives of researchers who themselves are a diverse lot—can help students become more informed about interpersonal relations as well as about ethics and values.

■ **Connections with Current Events**   To cover social psychology is one thing; to use its principles to explain events in the real world is quite another. The events of 9/11 changed the world. More than ever, we remain convinced that connecting theory to real life is the single best way to heighten student interest and involvement. Over the years, teachers and students alike have told us how much they value the "newsy" feature of our book.

The seventh edition, like other editions, is committed to making social psychology *relevant*. Almost every page includes a passage, a quote, a figure, a table, a photo, or a cartoon that refers to people, places, events, and issues that are prominent in contemporary culture. The reader will find stories about 9/11 and its aftermath; Italy's 2006 World Cup Soccer Championship; the events surrounding Hurricane Katrina; the devastating tsunamis in Asia; the war in Lebanon; the Abu Ghraib Prison scandal in Iraq; the charitable works of actress Angelina Jolie, U2's Bono, and basketball star Dikembe Mutombo; John Mark Karr's false confession to the JonBenet Ramsey murder; the popular TV show *American Idol*; the ongoing debates over immigration, affirmative action, and gay marriage; the trial of former Enron executives; the popularity of social networking Internet sites such as facebook.com and myspace.com and the video-sharing site Youtube; Mel Gibson's anti-Semitic and sexist outburst after being arrested; the controversy over remarks made by Larry Summers, then-president of Harvard University, on the abilities of women in math and science; media portrayals of Martha Stewart, Hillary Clinton, and Condoleeza Rice; professional athletes who take steroids; and the use of hidden cameras in TV news magazine shows like *20/20* and *Dateline*.

As in our last edition, you will also find—within the margins—various quotations, song lyrics, public opinion poll results, "factoids," and Web site addresses. These high-interest items are designed to further illustrate the connectedness of social psychology to a world that extends beyond the borders of a college campus.

■ **Social Psychology and Common Sense**   In a prior edition, we introduced a feature that we remain excited about. Building on a discussion in Chapter 1 about the links between social psychology and common sense, each substantive chapter opens with *Putting Common Sense to the Test,* a set of true-false questions designed to assess the student's intuitive beliefs about material later contained in that chapter. Some examples: "Sometimes the harder you try to control a thought, feeling, or behavior, the less likely you are to succeed," "People often come to like what they suffer for," "Opposites attract," and "Groups are less likely than individuals to invest more in a project that is failing." The answers to these questions are revealed in a marginal box after the topic is presented in the text. These answers are then explained at the end of each chapter. We think that students will find this exercise engaging. It will also enable them, as they read, to check their intuitive beliefs against the findings of social psychology and to notice the discrepancies that exist.

The Organization

Of all the challenges faced by teachers and textbooks, perhaps the greatest is to put information together in a way that is accurate and easy to understand. A strong organizational framework helps in meeting this challenge. There is nothing worse for a student than having to wade through a "laundry list" of endless studies whose interconnections remain a profound mystery. A strong structure thus facilitates the development of conceptual understanding.

But the tail should not wag the dog. Since organizational structure is a means to an end, not an end in itself, we wanted to keep it simple and unobtrusive. Continuing in the tradition of previous editions, we present social psychology in four major parts, a heuristic structure that instructors and students have found sensible and easy to follow. As before, we start with an intraindividual focus on *Social Perception* (Part One), shift outward to *Social Influence* (Part Two) and *Social Relations* (Part Three), and conclude with *Applying Social Psychology* (Part Four). We realize that some instructors like to reshuffle the deck to develop a chapter order that better fits their own approach. There is no problem in doing this. Each chapter stands on its own and does not require that others be read first.

The Presentation

Even when the content of a textbook is accurate and up-to-date, and even when its organization is sound, there is still the matter of presentation. As the teacher outside the classroom, a good textbook should facilitate learning. Thus, every chapter comes complete with the following pedagogical features:

▶ A narrative preview, chapter outline, and common-sense quiz (beginning with Chapter 3).

▶ Key terms highlighted in the text, defined in the margin, listed at the end of the chapter, and reprinted in an alphabetized glossary at the end of the book. Both the list and the glossary provide page numbers for easy location of each term.

▶ Numerous bar graphs, line graphs, tables, sketches, photographs, flow charts, and cartoons that illustrate, extend, enhance, and enliven material in the text. Some of these depict classic images and studies from social psychology's history; others, new to the seventh edition, are contemporary and often "newsy."

▶ At the end of each chapter, a comprehensive bulleted review summarizing the major sections and points.

TEACHING AND LEARNING SUPPORT PACKAGE

For the Instructor

Instructor's Resource Manual This manual contains learning objectives, detailed chapter outlines, discussion ideas, classroom activities, handouts, and audiovisual resource suggestions. The classroom exercises feature a unique and popular "What If This Bombs?" section that offers tips for making the most of every activity—even if it does not work.

Test Bank Available in print on demand or within a testing software program *(HMTesting)*, this test bank features an extensive set of multiple-choice questions and essay questions with sample answers. Three types of objective questions are provided—factual, conceptual, and applied—and all answers are keyed to learning objectives and text pages.

PowerPoint Slides The seventh edition includes a revised set of PowerPoint slides that include lecture outlines, and tables and figures from the text. The slides are available on the instructor Web site.

■ **New!** ***Classroom Response System (CRS)***   The *Classroom Response System (CRS)* content, available on the instructor Web site allows instructors to perform "on-the-spot" assessments, deliver quick quizzes, gauge students' understanding of a particular question or concept, conduct anonymous polling for class discussion purposes and take their class roster easily. Students receive immediate feedback on how well they understand concepts covered in the text, and where they need to improve. Answer slides provide the correct answer and an explanation of why the answer is correct.

New! ***HMTesting CD-ROM*** HMTesting (powered by Diploma) is a flexible testing program that allows instructors to create, edit, customize, and deliver multiple types of tests via print, network server, or the Web on either the MAC or Windows platform. The test bank contains over 1,700 multiple-choice and 70 essay questions. For convenience, Word files of the test bank are also included on the CD-ROM.

Textbook Web Site On the full-service, interactive Web site accompanying the seventh edition, instructors have access to the PowerPoint slides, a downloadable version of the *Instructor's Resource Manual,* content for Classroom Response Systems (clickers), PDFs of overhead transparencies, and teaching tips and other lecture material for our new *Revealing Psychology* video. To access the site, go to college.hmco .com/pic/kassin7e.

New! ***Eduspace*** ® (powered by Blackboard™) This is a powerful course management system that enables instructors to create all or part of their courses online using the widely recognized tools of Blackboard™ and text-specific content from Kassin/Fein/Markus, *Social Psychology, 7/e.* Instructors and students have access to automatically graded online homework, *Revealing Psychology* video clips with quizzes, and tutorials with accompanying pedagogy. Instructor presentation tools include PowerPoint presentations, CRS content, downloadable PDFs of overhead transparencies, and select art from the textbook.

Course Management Software *Blackboard* and *Web CT* course cartridges allow instructors to use text-specific material to create an online course on their own campus course management system. The cartridges feature interactive tutorials and other student materials and key instructor presentation tools, including PowerPoint slides, CRS content (clicker), and the *Instructor's Resource Manual,* all correlated to each chapter in the new edition of the text. The seventh edition cartridges feature all of the content described in the Eduspace course described above.

New! ***Revealing Psychology*** This feature provides a series of social psychology video segments that are informative, engaging and fun. Hidden cameras reveal people's surprising and amusing reactions when social forces conspire against them. How do you behave when people invade your personal space? Do you help a person who lies sprawled on a busy street? How often do you lie in a ten-minute conversation? These real-world vignettes reveal human foibles and at the same time dramatically illustrate underlying psychological principles. They are available to instructors on DVD for classroom presentation and to students via the Eduspace® course.

Houghton Mifflin's Social Psych in Film DVD/VHS This DVD,with closed captioning, contains over twenty-five clips from popular films and classic experiments that illustrate key concepts in social psychology. Clips from films like *Apollo 13, Schindler's List, Snow Falling on Cedars, In the Name of the Father,* and many others are combined with overviews and discussion questions to help bring psychology alive for students and to demonstrate its relevance to contemporary life and culture.

New! An *on-demand package* of the student text and Houghton Mifflin's trade title *The Namesake* by Jhumpa Lahiri is available. *The Namesake* can be used as an additional case study, and supplementary instructor material including discussion questions are available online. Contact your Houghton Mifflin sales representative for more details.

For the Student

Readings in Social Psychology: The Art and Science of Research, Fourth Edition This item contains original articles, each with a brief introduction, and questions to stimulate critical thinking about "doing" social psychology. The articles represent some of the most creative and accessible research, both classic and contemporary, on topics of interest to students.

New! *Research Companion.* This printed booklet shows students how to do research in social psychology and includes case study experiments.

Online Study Guide Available on the student Web site, the *Online Study Guide* facilitates student learning through the use of a chapter outline, learning objectives, a review of key terms and concepts, multiple-choice questions with explanations for why the correct answer is the best choice, and a practice essay questions with sample answers.

Textbook Web Site The text-specific Web site offers students a wide range of independent study resources, including interactive tutorials, Thinking Critically and Evaluating Research exercises, ACE self-quizzes, Flashcards and recommended Web links, and articles on current events, books, and movies. To access the site, go to college.hmco.com/pic/kassin7e.

Our Commitment to You

We are committed to the highest standards of customer support and service. Please don't hesitate to contact us with any questions or queries you may have.

For technical questions related to Web site access and our HMTesting CD-ROM, please call Houghton Mifflin's Software Support line at (800) 732-3223 (Monday through Thursday 9-8 EST, Friday 9-5 EST) or go to college.hmco.com/how/how_techsupp.html to submit an online help form. To learn more about Eduspace, please go to www.eduspace.com. You can contact your sales representative through our Sales Representative Locator at http:college.hmco.com/instructors/index.html.

ACKNOWLEDGMENTS

Textbooks are the product of a team effort. As always, we are grateful to Houghton Mifflin Company for its commitment to quality as the first priority. First, we want to thank Rita Lombard, our Editor, whose common sense, energy, and persistence kept us on task and on time. We also want to express our gratitude to Lisa Jelly Smith, our Photo Editor, who has helped to make this book so photographically interesting. Finally, we want to thank all those whose considerable talents and countless hours of hard work can be seen on every page: Bob Greiner, Senior Project Editor; Susan Zorn, Copyeditor; and Emily Meyer, Editorial Assistant. We also thank Senior Sponsoring Editor Jane Potter, Marketing Manager Amy Whitaker, and Marketing Assistant Samantha Abrams.

Several colleagues have guided us through their feedback on this and all prior editions. Every one of these teachers and scholars has helped to make this a better book. We are particularly grateful to Nicole M. Stephens and MarYam G. Hamedani, both of Stanford University, for their reviews and insights on recent cultural research. For their invaluable insights, comments, and suggestions, we also thank:

Shelley N. Aikman, *Syracuse University*

Scott Allison, *University of Richmond*

Thomas William Altermatt, *Hanover College*

Sowmya Anand, *The Ohio State University*

Craig A. Anderson, *Iowa State University*

Robin A. Anderson, *St. Ambrose University*

C. Daniel Batson, *University of Kansas*

Arnold James Benjamin, Jr., *Oklahoma Panhandle State University*

Lisa M. Bohon, *California State University*

Bryan Bonner, *The University of Utah*

Jennifer K. Bosson, *The University of Oklahoma*

Martin Bourgeois, *University of Wyoming*

Nyla Branscombe, *University of Kansas*

Brad J. Bushman, *University of Michigan*

Melissa A. Cahoon, *University of Dayton*

Nathaniel Carter, *Lane College*

Serena Chen, *University of California, Berkeley*

James E. Collins, *Carson Newman College*

Eric Cooley, *Western Oregon University*

Keith E. Davis, *University of South Carolina*

Richard Ennis, *University of Waterloo*

Leandre R. Fabrigar, *Queen's University*

Mark A. Ferguson, *University of Kansas*

Joseph R. Ferrari, *DePaul University*

J.H. Forthman, *San Antonio College*

Timothy M. Franz, *St. John Fisher College*

Traci Giuliano, *Southwestern University*

Diana Odom Gunn, *McNeese State University*

Karen L. Harris, *Western Illinois University*

Lora D. Haynes, *University of Louisville*

James Hobbs, *Ulster County Community College*

L. Rowell Huesmann, *University of Michigan*

Karen Huxtable-Jester, *University of Texas at Dallas*

Robert D. Johnson, *Arkansas State University*

Warren H. Jones, *University of Tennessee*

Cheryl Kaiser, *Michigan State University*

Steven J. Karau, *Southern Illinois University*

Suzanne C. Kieffer, *University of Houston*

William M. Klein, *University of Pittsburgh*

LaRue Kobrin, *College of the Redwoods*

Vladimir J. Konecni, *University of California, San Diego*

Doug Krull, *Northern Kentucky University*

Kevin Lanning, *Florida Atlantic University*

Patrick Laughlin, *University of Illinois*

Herbert L. Leff, *University of Vermont*

Margaret A. Lloyd, *Georgia Southern University*

David C. Lundgren, *University of Cincinnati*

Judith McIlwee, *Mira Costa College*

Roque V. Mendez, *Southwest Texas State University*

Daniel Molden, *Northwestern University*

Margo J. Monteith, *Purdue University*

Cynthia R. Nordstrom, *Illinois State University*

Randall E. Osborne, *Indiana University East*

Patricia A. Oswald, *Iona College*

Carol K. Oyster, *University of Wisconsin–La Crosse*

Paul Paulus, *University of Texas at Arlington*

David Pillow, *University of Texas at San Antonio*

Louis H. Porter, *Westchester University of Pennsylvania*

Margaret M. Pulsifer, *Psychology Assessment Center at Massachusetts General Hospital, and Psychiatry Department, Harvard Medical School*

Sally Radmacher, *Missouri Western State University*

Chris Robert, *University of Missouri*

Todd K. Shackelford, *Florida Atlantic University*

Laura S. Sidorowicz, *Nassau Community College*

Paul Silvia, *University of North Carolina at Greensboro*

Anthony Stahelski, *Central Washington University*

Charles Stangor, *University of Maryland*

Jeffrey Stone, *University of Arizona*

JoNell Strough, *West Virginia University*

Courtney von Hippel, *University of Queensland*

William von Hippel, *University of Queensland*

Kipling D. Williams, *Purdue University*

Ann Zak, *College of St. Rose*

Finally, we are very grateful to Fred Whitford, Montana State University, for helping to create a top-of-the-line *Study Guide and ACE Practice Tests*. We are also deeply indebted to Sam Sommers, Tufts University, author of the excellent *Test Bank*; Billa Reiss, St. John's University, author of the *Instructor's Resource Manual*; Mary Inman, Hope College, author of the *Research Companion*; and Carla Grayson, University of Michigan, for authoring the *Classroom Response* (clicker) material. These works have added a whole new dimension to this text.

Saul Kassin
Steven Fein
Hazel Rose Markus

ABOUT THE AUTHORS

Saul Kassin is Distinguished Professor of Psychology at John Jay College of Criminal Justice and Massachusetts Professor of Psychology at Williams College. Born and raised in Brooklyn, he received his Ph.D. from the University of Connecticut followed by a postdoctoral fellowship at the University of Kansas. He was later awarded a U.S. Supreme Court Judicial Fellowship and a research fellowship at Stanford University. He is an author of textbooks and has co-authored and edited *Confessions in the Courtroom, The Psychology of Evidence and Trial Procedure, The American Jury on Trial,* and *Developmental Social Psychology.* Several years ago, Kassin pioneered the scientific study of false confessions, an interest that continues to this day. He has also studied the impact of this and other evidence on the attributions, social perceptions, and verdicts of juries. Kassin is a Fellow of APS, APA, and Divisions 8 and 41. He has testified as an expert witness; lectures frequently to judges, lawyers, and law enforcement groups; and has appeared as a media consultant on national and syndicated news programs.

Steven Fein is Professor of Psychology at Williams College, Williamstown, Massachusetts. Born and raised in Bayonne, New Jersey, he received his A.B. from Princeton University and his Ph.D. in social psychology from the University of Michigan. He has been teaching at Williams College since 1991, with time spent teaching at Stanford University in 1999. His edited books include *Emotion: Interdisciplinary Perspectives, Readings in Social Psychology: The Art and Science of Research,* and *Motivated Social Perception: The Ontario Symposium.* He has served on the executive committee of the Society of Personality and Social Psychology and as the social and personality psychology representative at the American Psychological Association. His research interests concern stereotyping and prejudice, suspicion and attributional processes, social influence, and self-affirmation theory.

Hazel Rose Markus is the Davis-Brack Professor in the Behavioral Sciences at Stanford University. She also co-directs the Stanford Center for Comparative Studies in Race and Ethnicity. Before moving to Stanford in 1994, she was a professor at the University of Michigan, where she received her Ph.D. Her work focuses on how the self-system, including current conceptions of self and possible selves, structures and lends meaning to experience. Born in England of English parents and raised in San Diego, California, she has been persistently fascinated by how nation of origin, region of the country, gender, ethnicity, race, religion, and social class shape self and identity. With her colleague Shinobu Kitayama at the University of Michigan, she has pioneered the experimental study of how culture and self influence one another. Markus was elected to the American Academy of Arts and Sciences in 1994 and is a Fellow of APS, APA, and Division 8. Some of her recent co-edited books include *Culture and Emotion: Empirical Studies of Mutual Influence, Engaging Cultural Differences: The Multicultural Challenge in Liberal Democracies,* and *Just Schools: Pursuing Equal Education in Societies of Difference.*

social psychology

1

Introduction

PREVIEW

This chapter introduces you to the study of *social psychology*. We begin by defining social psychology and identifying how it is distinct from but related to some other areas of study, both outside and within psychology. Next, we review the *history of the field*. We conclude by looking forward, with a discussion of the important themes and perspectives that are propelling *social psychology into a new century*.

A few years from now, you may receive a letter in the mail inviting you to a high school or college reunion. You'll probably feel a bit nostalgic, and you'll begin to think about those old school days. What thoughts will come to mind first? Will you remember the poetry you finally began to appreciate in your junior year? Will you think about the excitement you felt when you completed your first chemistry lab? Will a tear form in your eye as you remember how inspiring your social psychology class was?

Perhaps. But what will probably dominate your thoughts are the people you knew in school and the interactions you had with them—the long and intense discussions about everything imaginable; the loves you had, lost, or wanted so desperately to experience; the time you made a fool of yourself at a party; the effort of trying to be accepted by a fraternity, sorority, or clique of popular people; the day you sat in the pouring rain with your friends while watching a football game.

We focus on these social situations because we are social beings. We forge our individual identities not alone but in the context of other people. We work, play, and live together. We hurt and help each other. We define happiness and success for each other. And we don't fall passively into social interactions; we actively seek them. We visit family, make friends, give parties, build networks, go on dates, pledge an enduring commitment, decide to have children. We watch others, speculate about them, and predict who will wind up with whom, whether in real life or on "reality" TV shows like *The Real World* and *Survivor*. Many of us log in frequently to Web sites such as *facebook* or *myspace* to interact with countless peers from around the world, adding hundreds or even thousands of "friends" to our social networks.

You've probably seen the movie *It's a Wonderful Life*. When the hero, George Bailey, was about to kill himself, the would-be angel Clarence didn't save him by showing him how much personal happiness he'd miss if he ended his life. Instead, he showed George how much his life had touched the lives of others and how many people would be hurt if he were not a part of their world. It was these social relationships that saved George's life, just as they define our own.

One of the exciting aspects of learning about social psychology is discovering how basic and profoundly important these social relationships are to the human animal. And research continues to find new evidence for and point to new implications of our social nature. Consider, for example, this set of conclusions from recent research:

● Having close friends and staying in contact with family members is associated with health benefits such as protecting against the effects of Alzheimer's disease, having lower blood pressure, and living longer (Bennett et al., 2006; Giles et al., 2005; Hawkley et al., 2006, 2007).

Strangers quickly become celebrities as millions of people tune in to watch them relate to each other on "reality" shows, such as this cast from a recent season of MTV's The Real World. *The enormous popularity of shows like these illustrates part of the appeal of social psychology—people are fascinated with how we relate to one another.*

"Man is a social animal."

—Benedict Spinoza, *Ethics*

● Children who are socially excluded from activities by their peers are more likely than other children to suffer academically, as well as socially, in school several years later (Buhs et al., 2006).

● Experiencing a social rejection is so painful that it produces activity in the same part of the brain—the anterior cingulate cortex—as when we feel physical pain, and people feel this pain of social rejection even when the rejection comes from a group they dislike (Eisenberger et al., 2003; Gonsalkorale & Williams, 2007).

Precisely because we need and care so much about social interactions and relationships, the social contexts in which we find ourselves can influence us profoundly. You can find many examples of this kind of influence in your own life. Have you ever laughed at a joke you didn't get just because those around you were laughing? Do you present yourself in one way with one group of people and in quite a different way with another group? The power of the situation can also be much more subtle, and yet more powerful, than in these examples, as when another's unspoken expectations about you literally seem to cause you to become a different person.

The relevance of social psychology is evident in everyday life, of course, such as when two people become attracted to each other, or when a group tries to coordinate its efforts on a project. Dramatic events can heighten its significance all the more, as is evident in people's behavior during and after war, terrorist attacks, or natural disasters such as tsunamis and hurricanes. In these traumatic times a spotlight shines on how people help or exploit each other, and we witness some of the worst and best that human relations have to offer. These events invariably call attention to the kinds of questions that social psychologists study—questions about hatred and violence, about intergroup conflict and suspicion, as well as about heroism, cooperation, and the capacity for understanding across cultural, ethnic, racial, religious, and geographic divides. We are reminded of the need for a better understanding of social psychological issues as we read the latest tragic news coming out of the Middle East, see footage of death and destruction in the Persian Gulf or the Congo, or are confronted with the reality of an all-too-violent world as nearby as our own neighborhoods and campuses. We also appreciate the majesty and power of social connections as we recognize the courage of a firefighter, read about the charity of a donor, or see the glow in the eyes of a new parent. These are all—the bad and the good, the mundane and the extraordinary—part of the fascinating landscape of social psychology.

The relevance of social psychology is evident in everyday situations, but dramatic, life-changing events such as the terrorist attacks of September 11, 2001 (left), or the shootings at Virginia Tech University on April 16, 2007 (right), make all the more clear how important it is to better understand human relations and the kinds of questions that social psychologists study.

You will see evidence of these points throughout this book. What's more, you will learn *how* social psychologists have discovered this evidence. It is an exciting process, and one that we are enthusiastic about sharing with you. The purpose of this first

BREAKING NEWS
POLICE: "AT LEAST 20 FATALITIES" IN VIRGINIA TECH SHOOTINGS
WDBJ/BLACKSBURG, VA
DOW 100.69

chapter is to provide you with a broad overview of the field of social psychology. By the time you finish it, you should be ready and (we hope) eager for what lies ahead.

What Is Social Psychology?

We begin by previewing the new territory you're about to enter. Then we define social psychology and map out its relationship to sociology and some other disciplines within the field of psychology.

Defining Social Psychology

Social psychology is the scientific study of how individuals think, feel, and behave in a social context. Let's look at each part of this definition.

Scientific Study   There are many approaches to understanding how people think, feel, and behave. We can learn about human behavior from novels, films, history, and philosophy—to name just a few possibilities. What makes social psychology different from these artistic and humanistic endeavors is that social psychology is a science. It applies the *scientific method* of systematic observation, description, and measurement to the study of the human condition. How, and why, social psychologists do this is explained in Chapter 2.

How Individuals Think, Feel, and Behave   Social psychology concerns an amazingly diverse set of topics. People's private, even nonconscious beliefs and attitudes, their most passionate emotions, their heroic, cowardly, or merely mundane public behaviors—these all fall within the broad scope of social psychology. In this way, social psychology differs from other social sciences such as economics and political science. Research on attitudes (see Chapter 6) offers a good illustration. Whereas economists and political scientists may be interested in people's economic and political attitudes, respectively, social psychologists investigate a wide variety of attitudes and contexts, such as individuals' attitudes toward particular groups of people, or how their attitudes are affected by their peers or their mood. In doing so, social psychologists strive to establish general principles of attitude formation and change that apply in a variety of situations, rather than exclusively to particular domains.

Note the word *individuals* in our definition of social psychology. This word points to another important way in which social psychology differs from some other social sciences. Sociology, for instance, typically classifies people in terms of their nationality, race, socioeconomic class, and other *group factors*. In contrast,

Our social relationships and interactions are extremely important to us. Most people seek out and are profoundly affected by other people. This social nature of the human animal is what social psychology is all about.

Social psychology   The scientific study of how individuals think, feel, and behave in a social context.

A well-liked celebrity like Oprah Winfrey can influence the attitudes and behaviors of millions of people. When Oprah recommends a book, for example, sales of the book are likely to skyrocket.

social psychology typically focuses on the psychology of the *individual*. Even when social psychologists study groups of people, they usually emphasize the behavior of the individual in the group context.

A Social Context Here is where the "social" in social psychology comes into play and how social psychology is distinguished from other branches of psychology. As a whole, the discipline of psychology is an immense, sprawling enterprise, the 800-pound gorilla of the social sciences, concerned with everything from the actions of neurotransmitters in the brain to the actions of music fans in a mosh pit. What makes social psychology unique is its emphasis on the social nature of individuals.

However, the "socialness" of social psychology varies. In attempting to establish general principles of human behavior, social psychologists sometimes examine nonsocial factors that affect people's thoughts, emotions, motives, and actions. For example, they may study whether heat causes people to behave more aggressively (Anderson et al., 2000; Bushman et al., 2005). What is social about this is the behavior: people hurting each other. In addition, social psychologists sometimes study people's thoughts or feelings about nonsocial things, such as people's attitudes toward Nike versus New Balance basketball shoes. How can attitudes toward basketball shoes be of interest to social psychologists? One way is if these attitudes are influenced by something social, such as whether Tiger Woods's endorsement of Nike makes people like Nike. Both examples, determining whether heat causes an increase in aggression or whether Tiger Woods causes an increase in sales of Nike shoes, are *social* psychological pursuits because the thoughts, feelings, or behaviors either (a) *concern other people* or (b) *are influenced by other people*.

The "social context" referred to in the definition of *social psychology* does not have to be real or present. Even the implied or imagined presence of others can have important effects on individuals (Allport, 1985). For example, if people imagine receiving positive or negative reactions from others, their self-esteem can be affected significantly (Leary et al., 2004). And if young people are asked to imagine living a day in the life of a particular older man, their ratings of the elderly on a number of traits can become more positive (Galinsky & Ku, 2004).

 ## Social Psychological Questions and Applications

For those of us fascinated by social behavior, social psychology is a dream come true. Just look at Table 1.1 and consider a small sample of the questions you'll explore in this textbook. As you can see, the social nature of the human animal is what social psychology is all about. Learning about social psychology is learning about ourselves and our social worlds. And because social psychology is scientific rather than anecdotal, systematic rather than haphazard, it provides insights that would be impossible to gain through intuition or experience alone.

The value of social psychology's perspective on human behavior is widely recognized. Courses in social psychology are often required for undergraduate majors in business, education, and journalism as well as in psychology and sociology. Although most advanced graduates with a Ph.D. in social psychology hold faculty appointments in colleges or universities, they also work in medical centers, law firms, government agencies, and a variety of business settings involving investment banking, marketing, advertising, human resources, negotiating, and e-commerce.

TABLE 1.1
Examples of Social Psychological Questions

Social Perception: What Affects the Way We Perceive Ourselves and Others?

- Why do people sometimes sabotage their own performance, making it more likely that they will fail? (Ch. 3)
- How do people in East Asia often differ from North Americans in the way they explain people's behavior? (Ch. 4)
- Where do stereotypes come from, and why are they so resistant to change? (Ch. 5)

Social Influence: How Do We Influence Each Other?

- Why do we often like what we suffer for? (Ch. 6)
- How do salespeople sometimes trick us into buying things we never really wanted? (Ch. 7)
- Why do people often perform worse in groups than they would have alone? (Ch. 8)

Social Interaction: What Causes Us to Like, Love, Help, and Hurt Others?

- How similar or different are the sexes in what they look for in an intimate relationship? (Ch. 9)
- When is a bystander more or less likely to help you in an emergency? (Ch. 10)
- Does exposure to TV violence, or to pornography, trigger aggressive behavior? (Ch. 11)

Applying Social Psychology: How Does Social Psychology Help Us Understand Questions About Law, Business, and Health?

- Why do people sometimes confess to crimes they did not commit? (Ch. 12)
- How can business leaders most effectively motivate their employees? (Ch. 13)
- How does stress affect one's health, and what are the most effective ways of coping with stressful experiences? (Ch. 14)

The number and importance of these applications continue to grow. Judges are drawing on social psychological research to render landmark decisions, and lawyers are depending on it to select juries and to support or refute evidence. Businesses are utilizing cross-cultural social psychological research to operate in the global marketplace and group-dynamics research to foster the best conditions for their work forces. Health professionals are increasingly aware of the role of social psychological factors in the prevention and treatment of disease. Indeed, we can think of no other field of study that offers expertise that is more clearly relevant to so many different career paths.

The Power of the Social Context: An Example of a Social Psychology Experiment

The social nature of people runs so deep that our perceptions of something can be influenced more by the reactions of others to it than by the thing itself. This point is illustrated in recent research conducted by one of the authors of this text (Fein et al., 2007). In one experiment college students watched a tape of a 1984 debate between Ronald Reagan and Walter Mondale, two candidates for the presidency of the United States. During that debate Reagan fired off a pair of one-liners that elicited a great deal of laughter from the audience. Political analysts have wondered whether those one-liners may have won the debate, and possibly the election, for Reagan. The one-liners comprised only seconds of a ninety-minute debate concerning the most important issues of the day. Could these few seconds have made such a difference?

To study this issue, we had students watch the debate under one of three conditions. One-third of the students saw the debate as it was, without any editing. One-third of the students saw the debate with the one-liners and the ensuing audience reaction edited out. By comparing these two conditions, we could see whether the presence versus absence of this pair of jokes could make a large difference in people's impressions of Reagan from the debate. However, there was also a third condition. One-third of the students saw the debate with the one-liners intact but the audience reaction edited out. That is, Reagan told his jokes, but there appeared to be no audience response, and the debate continued uninterrupted.

After watching the debate, the students judged the performance of the candidates on a scale ranging from 0 (*terrible*) to 100 (*excellent*). As you can see from the first two bars in Figure 1.1, the students who saw the entire unedited tape did not rate Reagan much more positively than did the students who saw the debate without the one-liners. This suggests that Reagan's jokes did not have much impact on these

FIGURE 1.1

Influence of Others' Reactions

This graph shows the results of research in which participants saw different versions of a tape of a 1984 presidential debate between Ronald Reagan and Walter Mondale. During the debate, Reagan had delivered a pair of witty one-liners that elicited a positive audience reaction. Participants who saw an unedited version of the tape and participants who saw a version with the jokes and the audience reaction edited out judged Reagan's performance similarly. Participants who saw a version with the jokes left in but the audience reaction edited out (suggesting that the audience didn't find the jokes funny) rated Reagan much more negatively. (Adapted from Fein et al., 2007).

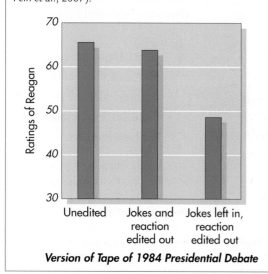

Version of Tape of 1984 Presidential Debate

viewers' perceptions of him. But look at the third bar in the figure. It illustrates that the students who saw the version of the debate with the one-liners kept in but the audience reaction edited out rated Reagan much less positively than did either of the other groups. What could explain their negativity toward Reagan's debate performance? Perhaps when Reagan's jokes appeared to elicit no reaction, the students unknowingly used the lack of reaction as an indication that Reagan's attempts at wit were inept, and this conclusion caused them to see Reagan in a much less positive light.

What is interesting about these results from a social psychological standpoint is that the students' judgments were influenced more by other people's *reactions* to what Reagan said (that is, whether or not the audience appeared to laugh) than by the *content* of what he said (that is, whether or not the one-liners were edited out of the tape). And it is important to note that these "other people" were not in the room with the students; they were simply sounds on a videotape recorded many years before. Findings such as this demonstrate that the "social context" can be very subtle and yet can have very powerful effects on our thoughts, feelings, and behaviors.

 ## Social Psychology and Related Fields: Distinctions and Intersections

Social psychology is sometimes confused with certain other fields of study. Before we go on, it is important to clarify how social psychology is distinct from these other fields. At the same time, it is important to illustrate some of the ways in which interesting and significant questions can be addressed through interactions between social psychology and these other fields (see Table 1.2).

Social Psychology and Sociology Sociologists and social psychologists share an interest in many issues, such as violence, prejudice, cultural differences, and marriage. As noted, however, sociology tends to focus on the group level, whereas social psychology tends to focus on the individual level. For example, sociologists might track the racial attitudes of the middle class in the United States, whereas social psychologists might examine some of the specific factors that make individuals more or less likely to behave in a racist way toward members of some group.

In addition, sociologists most often study the relation between people's behaviors and *societal* variables, such as social class. In contrast, social psychologists are more likely to study the relation between people's behaviors and more specific, immediate variables, such as manipulations of mood and exposure to particular models of behavior. Finally, although there are many exceptions, social psychologists are more likely than sociologists to conduct experiments in which they manipulate some variable and determine the effects of this manipulation using precise, quantifiable measures.

Despite these differences, sociology and social psychology are clearly related. Indeed, many sociologists and social psychologists share the same training and publish in the same journals. When these two fields intersect, the result can be a more complete understanding of important issues. For example, interdisciplinary research on stereotyping and prejudice has examined the dynamic roles of both societal and immediate factors, such as how particular social systems or institutional norms and beliefs affect individuals' attitudes and behaviors (Haley & Sidanius, 2005; Hogg et al., 2006; Jost, 2007; Wood & Eagly, 2007).

TABLE 1.2

Distinctions Between Social Psychology and Related Fields: The Case of Research on Prejudice

To see the differences between social psychology and related fields, consider an example of how researchers in each field might conduct a study of prejudice.

Field of Study	Example of How a Researcher in the Field Might Study Prejudice
Sociology	Track how Americans' prejudice toward Japanese has changed since World War II
Clinical psychology	Test various therapies for people with antisocial personalities who exhibit great degrees of prejudice
Personality psychology	Develop a questionnaire to identify men who are very high or low in degree of prejudice toward women
Cognitive psychology	Manipulate exposure to a member of some category of people and measure the thoughts and concepts that are automatically activated (*A study of prejudice in this field would, by definition, be at the intersection of cognitive and social psychology.*)
Social psychology	Manipulate various kinds of contact between individuals of different groups and examine the effect of these manipulations on the degree of prejudice exhibited

Social Psychology and Clinical Psychology Tell people not very familiar with psychology that you are taking a social psychology class, and they are likely to say things like "Oh, great, now you're going to start psychoanalyzing me" or "Finally, maybe you can tell me why everyone in my family is so messed up." The assumption underlying these reactions, of course, is that you are studying clinical, or abnormal, psychology. Clinical psychologists seek to understand and treat people with psychological difficulties or disorders. Social psychologists do not focus on disorders; rather, they focus on the more typical ways in which individuals think, feel, behave, and influence each other.

There are, however, many fascinating ways in which clinical and social psychology intersect. Both, for example, may address how people cope with anxiety or pressure in social situations; how depressed and non-depressed individuals differ in the way they perceive or act toward other people; or how being bullied or stereotyped by others can affect individuals' health and feelings of self-worth (Chu et al., 2007; Inzlicht et al., 2006; Ledley et al., 2006; Miller, 2006; Swann & Bosson, 2007).

Social Psychology and Personality Psychology Both personality psychology and social psychology are concerned with individuals and their thoughts, feelings, and behaviors. However, personality psychology seeks to understand differences between individuals that remain relatively stable across a variety of situations, whereas social psychology seeks to understand how social factors affect most individuals, *regardless* of their different personalities.

In other words, personality psychologists are interested in cross-situational consistency. They may ask, "Is this person outgoing and friendly almost all the time, in just about any setting?" Social psychologists are interested in how different situations cause different behaviors. They may ask, "Are people in general more likely to seek out companionship when they are made anxious by a situation than when they are made to feel relaxed?"

These examples show the contrast between the fields; but in fact, personality psychology and social psychology are very closely linked. The American Psychological Association has more than fifty different divisions, and yet personality psychologists and social psychologists share the same division. Many of these scholars belong to an organization called the Society of Personality and Social Psychology, attend the same conferences, and publish their research in the same journals. So personality and social psychologists see a lot of each other.

The reason for the high degree of connection between social psychology and personality psychology is that the two areas complement each other so well. For example, some social psychologists examine how receiving negative feedback (a situational factor) can have different effects on people as a function of whether their self-esteem is high or low (an individual-difference factor), or whether playing violent video games (a situational factor) is especially likely to trigger aggressiveness in

Do provocative, sexualized images in advertisings, such as on the billboard seen here (near the sign about "student body cards"), make people more sexist or prone to sexual aggression? This is one of the questions that social psychology addresses.

particular types of children (an individual-difference factor) (Anderson et al., 2007; Kernis, 2007; Lambird & Mann, 2006).

Social Psychology and Cognitive Psychology Cognitive psychologists study mental processes such as thinking, learning, remembering, and reasoning. Social psychologists are often interested in these same processes. More specifically, though, social psychologists are interested in how people think, learn, remember, and reason with respect to social information and in how these processes are relevant to social behavior.

The last two decades have seen an explosion of interest in the intersection of cognitive and social psychology. The study of *social cognition* is discussed in more detail later in this chapter, and it is a focus throughout this text, especially in Part I on Social Perception.

Social Psychology and Common Sense

After reading about a theory or finding of social psychology, you may sometimes think, "Of course. I knew that all along. Anyone could have told me that." This "knew-it-all-along" phenomenon often causes people to question how social psychology is different from common sense, or traditional folk wisdom. After all, why would any of the following social psychological findings be surprising?

- Beauty and brains don't mix: Physically attractive people tend to be seen as less smart than physically unattractive people.

- People will like an activity more if you offer them a large reward for doing it, causing them to associate the activity with the positive reinforcement.

- People think that they're more distinctive than they really are: They tend to underestimate the extent to which others share the same opinions or interests.

- Playing contact sports or violent video games releases aggression and makes people less likely to vent their anger in violent ways.

In a minute we will have more to say about each of these statements.

Common sense may seem to explain many social psychological findings after the fact. The problem is distinguishing common-sense fact from common-sense myth. After all, for most common-sense notions, there is an equally sensible-sounding notion that says the opposite. Is it "Birds of a feather flock together" or "Opposites attract"? Is it "Two heads are better than one" or "Too many cooks spoil the broth"? Which are correct? We have no reliable way to answer such questions through common sense or intuition alone.

Social psychology, unlike common sense, uses the scientific method to put its theories to the test. How it does so will be discussed in greater detail in the next chapter. But before we leave this section, one word of caution: Those four "findings" listed above? *They are all false.* Although there may be sensible reasons to believe each of the statements to be true, research indicates otherwise. Therein lies another problem with relying on common sense: Despite offering very compelling predictions and explanations, it is sometimes wildly inaccurate. And even when it is not completely wrong, common sense can be misleading in its simplicity. Often there is no simple answer to a question such as "Does absence make the heart grow fonder?" In reality, the answer is more complex than common sense would suggest, and social psychological research reveals how such an answer depends on a variety of factors.

To emphasize these points, and to encourage you to think critically about social psychological issues *before* as well as after learning about them, this textbook contains a feature called "Putting Common Sense to the Test." Beginning with Chapter 3, each chapter opens with a few statements about social psychological issues that will be covered in that chapter. Some of the statements are true, and some are false. As you read each statement, make a prediction about whether it is true or false, and think about why this is your prediction. Marginal notes throughout the chapter will tell you whether the statements are true or false. In reading the chapter, check not only whether your prediction was correct but also whether your reasons for the prediction were appropriate. If your intuition wasn't quite on the mark, think about what the right answer is and how the evidence supports that answer. There are few better ways of learning and remembering than through this kind of critical thinking.

From Past to Present: A Brief History of Social Psychology

People have probably been asking social psychological questions for as long as humans could think about each other. Certainly, early philosophers such as Plato offered keen insights into many social psychological issues. But no systematic and scientific study of social psychological issues developed until the end of the nineteenth century. The field of social psychology is therefore a very young one. As a testament to this youth, the social psychologist Dorwin Cartwright said in 1979 that 90 percent of social psychologists who had ever lived were still alive at that time. Recent years have marked a tremendous interest in social psychology and an injection of many new scholars into the field. As social psychology is now early in its second century, it is instructive to look back to see how the field today has been shaped by the people and events of its first century.

The Birth and Infancy of Social Psychology: 1880s–1920s

"Psychology has a long past, but only a short history."

— Herman Ebbinghaus, *Summary of Psychology*

Like most such honors, the title "founder of social psychology" has many potential recipients, and not everyone agrees on who should prevail. Most point to the American psychologist Norman Triplett, who is credited with having published the first research article in social psychology at the end of the nineteenth century (1897–1898). Triplett's work was noteworthy because, after observing that bicyclists tended to race faster when racing in the presence of others than when simply racing against a clock, he designed an experiment to study this phenomenon in a carefully controlled, precise way. This scientific approach to studying the effects of the social context on individuals' behavior can be seen as marking the birth of social psychology.

A case can also be made for the French agricultural engineer Max Ringelmann. Ringelmann's research was conducted in the 1880s but wasn't published until 1913. In an interesting twist of fate, Ringelmann also studied the effects of the presence of others on the performance of individuals. In contrast to Triplett, however, Ringelmann noted that individuals often performed worse on simple tasks such as pulling rope when they performed the tasks with other people. The issues addressed by these two early researchers continue to be of vital interest, as will be seen later in Chapter 8 on Group Processes.

Despite their place in the history of social psychology, neither Triplett nor Ringelmann actually established social psychology as a distinct field of study. Credit for this creation goes to the writers of the first three textbooks in social psychology: the English psychologist William McDougall (1908) and two Americans, Edward

Racers sprint to the finish line of one of the stages of the Tour de France in July 2006. Would these cyclists have raced faster or slower if they were racing individually against the clock rather than racing simultaneously along with their competitors? More generally, what effect does the presence of others have on an individual's performance? The earliest social psychology experiments ever done sought to answer questions such as these. Chapter 8 on Group Processes brings you up to date on the latest research in this area.

Ross (1908) and Floyd Allport (1924). Allport's book in particular, with its focus on the interaction of individuals and their social context and its emphasis on the use of experimentation and the scientific method, helped establish social psychology as the discipline it is today. These authors announced the arrival of a new approach to the social aspects of human behavior. Social psychology was born.

A Call to Action: 1930s–1950s

What one person would you guess has had the strongest influence on the field of social psychology? Various social psychologists, as well as psychologists of other areas, might be mentioned in response to this question. But someone who was not a psychologist at all may have had the most dramatic impact on the field: Adolf Hitler.

Hitler's rise to power and the ensuing turmoil caused people around the world to become desperate for answers to social psychological questions about what causes violence, prejudice and genocide, conformity and obedience, and a host of other social problems and behaviors. In addition, many social psychologists living in Europe in the 1930s fled to the United States and helped establish a critical mass of social psychologists who would give shape to the rapidly maturing field. The years just before, during, and soon after World War II marked an explosion of interest in social psychology.

In 1936, Gordon Allport (younger brother of Floyd, author of the 1924 textbook) and a number of other social psychologists formed the Society for the Psychological Study of Social Issues. The name of the society illustrates these psychologists' concern for making important, practical contributions to society. Also in 1936, a social psychologist named Muzafer Sherif published groundbreaking experimental research on social influence. As a youth in Turkey, Sherif had witnessed groups of Greek soldiers brutally killing his friends. After immigrating to the United States, Sherif drew on this experience and began to conduct research on the powerful influences groups can exert on their individual members. Sherif's research was crucial for the development of social psychology because it demonstrated that it is possible to study complex social processes such as conformity and social influence in a rigorous, scientific manner. This innovation laid the foundation for what was to become one of the major topics in social psychology. Research and theory on social influence are discussed throughout this text, particularly in Part II on Social Influence.

Another great contributor to social psychology, Kurt Lewin, fled the Nazi onslaught in Germany and immigrated to the United States in the early 1930s. Lewin was a bold and creative theorist whose concepts have had lasting effects on the field. Among the fundamental principles of social psychology that Lewin (1935, 1947) helped establish were the following:

- *What we do depends to a large extent on how we perceive and interpret the world around us.* Different people can see the same situation differently, and their behavior will vary accordingly. This theme continues to be important in social psychology. You will encounter it throughout this textbook, especially in Part I on Social Perception.

- *Behavior is a function of the interaction between the person and the environment.* Lewin's conviction that both internal and external factors affect behavior helped create a unified view that was distinct from the other major psychological paradigms during his lifetime: psychoanalysis, with its emphasis on internal motives and fantasies; and behaviorism, with its focus on external rewards

What determines whether people are likely to act to conserve their environment, as these individuals did by volunteering their time to clean up a beach in Great Britain? Built on the legacy of Kurt Lewin, one of the leading figures in the development of the field, applied social psychology contributes to the solution of numerous social problems, such as environmental conservation.

interactionist perspective
An emphasis on how both an individual's personality and environmental characteristics influence behavior.

and punishments. Lewin's position was an early version of what today is known as the **interactionist perspective** (Blass, 1991). This approach combines personality psychology (stressing internal, psychological differences among individuals) with social psychology (stressing differences among external situations). Throughout this book, we examine the impact of both individual and situational differences, alone and together.

● *Social psychological theories should be applied to important, practical issues.* Lewin researched a number of practical issues, such as how to persuade Americans at home during the war to conserve materials to help the war effort; how to promote more economical and nutritious eating habits; and what kinds of leaders elicit the best work from group members. Through these studies, Lewin showed how social psychology could enlarge our understanding of social problems and contribute to their solution. Built on Lewin's legacy, applied social psychology flourishes today in areas such as advertising, business, education, environmental protection, health, law, politics, public policy, religion, and sports. Throughout this text, we draw on the findings of applied social psychology to illustrate the implications of social psychological principles for our daily lives. In Part IV, three prominent areas of applied social psychology are discussed in detail: law, business, and health. One of Lewin's statements can be seen as a call to action for the entire field: "No research without action, no action without research."

During World War II, many social psychologists answered Lewin's call as they worked for the U.S. government to investigate how to protect soldiers from the propaganda of the enemy, how to persuade citizens to support the war effort, how to select officers for various positions, and other practical issues. During and after the war, social psychologists sought to understand the prejudice, aggression, and conformity the war had brought to light. The 1950s saw many major contributions to the field of social psychology. For example, Gordon Allport (1954) published *The Nature of Prejudice*, a book that continues to inspire research on stereotyping and prejudice more than a half century later. Solomon Asch's (1951) demonstration of how willing people are to conform to an obviously wrong majority amazes students even today. Leon Festinger (1954, 1957) introduced two important theories—one concerning how people try to learn about themselves by comparing themselves to other people, and one about how people's attitudes can be changed by their own behavior—that remain among the most influential theories in the field. These are just a sample of a long list of landmark contributions made during the 1950s. With this remarkable burst of activity and impact, social psychology was clearly, and irrevocably, on the map.

Confidence and Crisis: 1960s–Mid-1970s

In spectacular fashion, Stanley Milgram's research in the early and middle 1960s linked the post–World War II era with the coming era of social revolution. Milgram's research was inspired by the destructive obedience demonstrated by Nazi officers and ordinary citizens in World War II, but it also looked ahead to the civil disobedience that was beginning to challenge institutions in many parts of the world. Milgram's experiments, which demonstrated individuals' vulnerability to the destructive commands of authority, became the most famous research in the history of social psychology. This research is discussed in detail in Chapter 7.

With its foundation firmly in place, social psychology entered a period of expansion and enthusiasm. The sheer range of its investigations was staggering. Social

This World War II poster featuring "Rosie the Riveter" was part of the United States government's campaign to encourage American women to take jobs in traditionally male-dominated occupations, such as in welding. When the war was over and the men who had served in the military returned to the work force, new advertisements were designed to encourage women to leave these jobs and concentrate on raising families.

psychologists considered how people thought and felt about themselves and others. They studied interactions in groups and social problems, such as why people fail to help others in distress. They also examined aggression, physical attractiveness, and stress. For the field as a whole, it was a time of great productivity.

Ironically, it was also a time of crisis and heated debate. Many of the strong disagreements during this period can be understood as a reaction to the dominant research method of the day: the laboratory experiment. The social psychologists who questioned this type of research maintained that certain practices were unethical (Kelman, 1967), that experimenters' expectations influenced their participants' behavior (Orne, 1962; Rosenthal, 1976), and that the theories being tested in the laboratory were historically and culturally limited (Gergen, 1973). Those who favored laboratory experimentation, on the other hand, contended that their procedures were ethical, their results valid, and their theoretical principles widely applicable (McGuire, 1967). For a while, social psychology seemed split in two.

An Era of Pluralism: Mid-1970s–1990s

Fortunately, both sides won. As we will see in the next chapter, more rigorous ethical standards for research were instituted, more stringent procedures to guard against bias were adopted, and more attention was paid to possible cross-cultural differences in behavior. But the baby was not thrown out with the bath water. Laboratory experiments continued. They did, however, get some company, as a single-minded attachment to one research method evolved into a broader acceptance of many methods. The logic behind a pluralistic approach is compelling (Carr & MacLachlan, 1998; Houts et al., 1986; Van Lange, 2006):

- Because different topics require different kinds of investigations, a range of research techniques is needed.

- Because no research method is perfect, a *multimethod* investigation of a topic increases our confidence that the results obtained do not simply reflect the peculiar characteristics of any one approach.

The various research methods used by today's social psychologists are described in the next chapter.

Pluralism in social psychology extends far beyond its methods. There are also important variations in what aspects of human behavior are emphasized. Some social psychology research takes what we might call a "hot" perspective, focusing on *emotion* and *motivation* as determinants of our thoughts and actions. Other research in this field takes a "cold" perspective that emphasizes the role of *cognition*, examining the ways in which people's thoughts affect how they feel, what they want, and what they do. Of course, some social psychologists examine behavior from both perspectives separately as well as interactively. Integrating such different perspectives is characteristic of the pluralism that the field has come to embrace in recent years.

Another source of pluralism in social psychology is its development of international and multicultural perspectives. Although, as we have seen, individuals from many countries helped establish the field, social psychology achieved its greatest professional recognition in the United States and Canada. At one point, it was estimated that 75 to 90 percent of social psychologists lived in North America (Smith & Bond, 1993; Triandis, 1994). Indeed, some called social psychology "culture-bound" (Berry et al., 1992) and "largely monocultural" (Moghaddam et al., 1993). However, this aspect of social psychology began to change rapidly in the 1990s, reflecting not

Social psychologists are becoming increasingly interested in cross-cultural research, which helps us break out of our culture-bound perspective. Many of our behaviors differ across cultures. In some cultures, for example, people are expected to negotiate about the price of the products they buy, as in this market in Tunisia. In other cultures, such bargaining would be highly unusual and cause confusion and distress.

only the different geographic and cultural backgrounds of its researchers and participants but also the recognition that many social psychological phenomena once assumed to be universal may actually vary dramatically as a function of culture. You can find evidence of this new appreciation of the role of culture in every chapter of this book.

Social Psychology in a New Century

As we began the twenty-first century, social psychology began its second hundred years. The field today continues to grow in numbers and diversity of researchers and research topics, areas of the world in which research is conducted, and industries that hire social psychologists and apply their work.

Throughout this text, we emphasize the most current, cutting-edge research in the field, along with the classic findings of the past. In the remainder of the chapter we focus on a few of the exciting themes and perspectives emerging from current research—research that is helping to shape the social psychology of the new century.

Integration of Emotion, Motivation, and Cognition

If any one perspective dominated the final quarter of social psychology's first century, it may have been **social cognition**, the study of how we perceive, remember, and interpret information about ourselves and others. Social psychologists demonstrated that these social-cognitive processes are critically important to virtually every area in the field. Social-cognitive explanations were so powerful that the roles of "hotter" influences, such as emotions and motivations, often took a back seat. Social cognition continues to flourish, but one of the more exciting developments in the field is the re-emergence of interest in how individuals' emotions and motivations influence their thoughts and actions. Especially exciting is the fact that the social-cognitive approach is not necessarily seen as being at odds with approaches that emphasize motivations and emotions. Instead, there is a new push to integrate these perspectives, as in research investigating how people's motivations influence nonconscious cognitive processes, and vice versa (Forgas, 2006; Maner et al., 2005; Moskowitz, 2005; Smith & Semin, 2006; Spencer et al., 2003; von Hippel et al., 2005).

social cognition The study of how people perceive, remember, and interpret information about themselves and others.

"On the one hand, eliminating the middleman would result in lower costs, increased sales, and greater consumer satisfaction; on the other hand, we're the middleman."

Our desire to be accurate in our judgments can sometimes interfere with our desire to feel good about ourselves.

One issue illustrating the integration of "hot" and "cold" variables concerns the conflict between wanting to be right and wanting to feel good about oneself. Most of us hold two very different motivations simultaneously: On the one hand, we want to be accurate in our judgments about ourselves and others. On the other hand, we don't want to be accurate if it means we will learn something bad about ourselves or those closest to us. These goals can pull our cognitive processes in very different directions. How we perform the required mental gymnastics is an ongoing concern for social psychologists.

Another theme running through many chapters of this book is the growing interest in distinguishing between automatic and controllable processes and in understanding the dynamic relationship between them (Bargh & Williams, 2006; Hassin et al., 2005; Olson & Fazio, 2006). For example, there is a great deal of new evidence concerning whether and when stereotypes can be activated in one's mind automatically—that is, quickly and spontaneously, with no awareness, intention, or effort, and possibly even against one's will. Participants in many social psychology experiments are often surprised—to their great dismay—when they learn that their reactions to someone during the study were biased by negative stereotypes (such as about the person's race, gender, age, or sexual orientation) that they in fact did not believe in. On the other hand, there also is growing evidence that even such automatic reactions can be controlled under particular conditions. The automatic and controlled nature of a variety of processes and behaviors relevant to social psychology will no doubt continue to be an exciting area of research in the coming years.

Biological and Evolutionary Perspectives

As the technology available to researchers evolves, biological perspectives are increasingly being integrated into all branches of psychology, and this integration should continue to grow in social psychology. We are, of course, biological organisms, and it is clear that our brains and bodies influence, and are influenced by, our social experiences. This dynamic can be seen in a great deal of contemporary research, such as in studies demonstrating the cardiovascular effects of being the target of racism, or research illustrating that the manner in which people respond to stress can influence their athletic performance (Blascovich et al., 2004; Harris et al., 2006; Merritt et al., 2006).

Social psychologists have been concerned with physiological influences and responses for many years. Examples of this interest can be found throughout the textbook. A particularly exciting recent development is the emergence of the subfield of **social neuroscience**—the study of the relationship between neural and social processes. Social neuroscience is part of a flourishing set of research that explores how the social world affects the brain and biology, and vice versa. Recent research has investigated such issues as how a person's likelihood of acting aggressively may be influenced by his or her neurological responses to social rejection, gender differences in neuroendocrine reaction to stress, and the relationship between activity in the amygdala (a structure in the brain) and how one responds to observing black versus white faces (Eisenberger et al., 2007; Lieberman, 2007; Ochsner, 2007; van Anders & Watson, 2006).

Recent advances in **behavioral genetics**—a subfield of psychology that examines the effects of genes on behavior—has triggered new research to investigate such matters as the extent to which aggression is an inherited trait and the roles

social neuroscience The study of the relationship between neural and social processes.
behavioral genetics A subfield of psychology that examines the role of genetic factors in behavior.

that genes play in individuals' sexual orientation or identity (James, 2005; Vierikko et al., 2006).

Evolutionary psychology, which uses the principles of evolution to understand human behavior, is another growing area that is sparking new research in social psychology. According to this perspective, to understand a social psychological issue such as jealousy, we should ask how the psychological mechanisms underlying jealousy today may have evolved from the natural-selection pressures our ancestors faced. Evolutionary psychological theories can then be used to explain and predict gender differences in jealousy, the situational factors most likely to trigger jealousy, and so on (Buss, 2007; Forgas et al., 2007). This perspective is discussed in many places in the textbook, especially in Part III on Social Relations.

Cultural Perspectives

Because of the fantastic advancements in communication technologies in recent years and the globalization of the world's economies, it is faster, easier, and more necessary than ever before for people from vastly different cultures to interact with one another. Thus, our need and desire to understand how we are similar to and different from one another are greater than ever as well. Social psychology is currently experiencing tremendous growth in research designed to give us a better understanding and appreciation of the role of culture in all aspects of social psychology.

What is meant by "culture" is not easy to pin down, as many researchers think of culture in very different ways. Broadly speaking, **culture** may be considered to be a system of enduring meanings, beliefs, values, assumptions, institutions, and practices shared by a large group of people and transmitted from one generation to the next. Whatever the specific definition, it is clear that how individuals perceive and derive meaning from their world are influenced profoundly by the beliefs, norms, and practices of the people and institutions around them.

Increasing numbers of social psychologists are evaluating the universal generality or cultural specificity of their theories and findings by conducting **cross-cultural research**, in which they examine similarities and differences across a variety of cultures. More and more social psychologists are also conducting **multicultural research**, in which they examine racial and ethnic groups within cultures.

These developments are already profoundly influencing our view of human behavior. For example, a rapidly growing body of cross-cultural research has revealed important distinctions between the collectivist cultures typically found in Africa, Asia, and Latin America and the individualistic ones more commonly found in North America and Europe. The implications of these differences can be seen throughout the textbook. Consider, for instance, our earlier discussion of the integration of "hot" and "cold" variables in contemporary social psychology, in which we mentioned the conflict people have between wanting to be right and wanting to feel good about themselves. Cross-cultural research has shown that how people try to juggle these two goals can differ dramatically across cultures. Several researchers have found, for example, that people from individualistic cultures are more likely than people from collectivist cultures to seek out or focus on information that makes them feel good about themselves rather than information that points to the need for improvement (Heine, 2007). Figure 1.2 illustrates the results of an experiment by Michael Ross and others (2005) in which individuals from Japan and Canada were asked to write brief descriptions of themselves. The Canadian participants tended to write mostly positive self-descriptions, but the Japanese participants wrote self-descriptions that were much more balanced between favorable and unfavorable elements.

Within a particular society, people are often treated differently as a function of social categories such as gender, race, physical appearance, and so on. Boys and girls, for example, may be raised differently by their parents, confronted with different expectations by teachers, exposed to different types of advertising and marketing, and offered different kinds of jobs. In a sense, then, despite their frequent

evolutionary psychology
A subfield of psychology that uses the principles of evolution to understand human social behavior.

culture A system of enduring meanings, beliefs, values, assumptions, institutions, and practices shared by a large group of people and transmitted from one generation to the next.

cross-cultural research
Research designed to compare and contrast people of different cultures.

multicultural research
Research designed to examine racial and ethnic groups within cultures.

FIGURE 1.2

Self-descriptions Across Cultures

Research participants from Japan and Canada were asked to write descriptions of themselves. The self-descriptions written by the Canadians (the two bars on the left) included more favorable than unfavorable elements, but the self-descriptions written by the Japanese (the two bars on the right) were much more evenly balanced between favorable and unfavorable. These results are consistent with other research illustrating that people from collectivist cultures like Japan tend to be less self-promotional in how they present themselves to others than are people from individualist cultures like Canada.

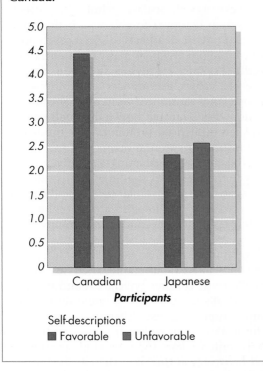

and intimate contact, women and men may develop and live in distinct subcultures. Social psychologists have studied the role of sociocultural factors in a variety of domains, such as conformity, leadership style, and aggression. Recent research is not only extending this tradition; it is also sometimes turning it on its ear by illustrating that many previous research programs were flawed as a result of taking a male-dominated approach. New research on aggression, for example, illustrates that most of the older research focused almost exclusively on the forms of aggression typical of boys, thereby failing to recognize important issues relevant to aggression among girls.

These are but a few examples of the cultural research taking place today. In this text, we describe studies conducted in dozens of countries, representing every continent on earth. As our knowledge expands, we should be able to see much more clearly both the behavioral differences among cultures and the similarities we all share.

Some social psychology textbooks devote a separate chapter to culture or to culture and gender. We chose not to do so. Because we believe that sociocultural influences are inherent in all aspects of social psychology, we chose instead to integrate discussions of the role of culture and gender in every chapter of the textbook.

New Technologies

Advances in technologies that allow researchers to see images of the brain at work, through noninvasive procedures, have had a profound effect on several areas of psychology, including social psychology. A growing number of social psychologists are using techniques such as *positron emission tomography (PET)* and *functional magnetic resonance imaging (fMRI)* to study the interplay of the brain and discrete thoughts, feelings, and behaviors. Social psychology research today benefits from other technological advances as well, such as new and better techniques to measure hormone levels, to code people's everyday dialogue into quantifiable units, and to present visual stimuli to research participants at fractions of a second and then record the number of milliseconds it takes the participants to respond to these stimuli. Researchers are beginning to use virtual reality technology to examine a number of social psychological questions. James Blascovich and others have created the Research Center for Virtual Environments and Behavior at the University of California at Santa Barbara and have been conducting fascinating research on issues such as conformity, group dynamics, aggression and altruism, and eyewitness testimony (e.g., Bailenson et al., 2005). Because participants in these experiments are immersed in a virtual reality that the experimenters create for them, the researchers can test questions that would be impractical, impossible, or unethical without this technology.

Awesome is an overused word, but it surely describes the revolution that is taking place in how we access information and communicate with each other. The waves of this revolution have carried social psychology research along with it. Social psychologists around the world can now not only communicate and collaborate much more easily but can also gain access to research participants from populations that would otherwise never have been available. These developments have sparked the field's internationalization, perhaps its most exciting course in this new century. World War II triggered an explosion of social psychological research in the United States; the Internet is extending this research to the rest of the world.

The Internet itself is also becoming a provocative topic of study. As more people interact with each other through e-mail and social networking sites, there is growing

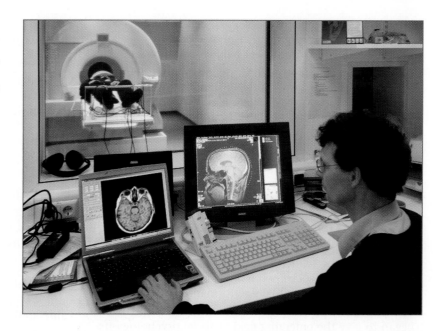

Advances in technology enable social psychologists to extend their research in exciting new directions, such as by using functional magnetic resonance imaging (fMRI) to study activation in the brain in response to various thoughts or stimuli.

interest in studying how attraction, prejudice, group dynamics, and a host of other social psychological phenomena unfold online versus offline (Bargh et al., 2003; Gibbs et al., 2006).

We would be presumptuous, and probably naive, to try to predict how new communication and new technologies will influence the ways in which people interact in the coming years; but it probably is safe to predict that their influence will be great. As more and more people fall in love online, or fall into social isolation, or react with anxiety or violence to the loss of individual privacy, social psychology will explore these issues. We expect that some of the students reading this textbook today will be among those explorers in the coming years.

REVIEW

What Is Social Psychology?

Defining Social Psychology

- Social psychology is the scientific study of how individuals think, feel, and behave in a social context.

- Like other sciences, social psychology relies on the systematic approach of the scientific method.

- Distinctive characteristics of social psychology include a focus on the individual as well as a broad perspective on a variety of social contexts and behaviors.

- The "socialness" of social psychology varies, as social psychologists sometimes examine how nonsocial factors affect social thoughts, feelings, and behaviors and sometimes study how social factors influence nonsocial thoughts, feelings, and behaviors.

Social Psychological Questions and Applications

- Social psychologists study a large variety of fascinating questions about people and their social worlds, and the scope and relevance of these questions to so many important aspects of our lives make social psychology applicable to many careers and interests.

The Power of the Social Context: An Example of a Social Psychology Experiment

- In one experiment that illustrates the power of the social context, participants' judgments of a political candidate's performance in a debate were influenced more by the reactions of other people to some remarks made by the candidate than by the remarks themselves.

Social Psychology and Related Fields: Distinctions and Intersections

- Social psychology is related to a number of different areas of study, including sociology, clinical psychology, personality psychology, and cognitive psychology. Important work is being done at the intersection of social psychology and each of these fields.

- Social psychology tends to focus on individuals, whereas sociology tends to focus on groups. In addition, social psychology is less likely than sociology to study the relation between broad societal variables and people's behaviors and is more likely to use experimentation.

- In contrast to clinical psychology, social psychology focuses not on disorders but, rather, on the more typical ways in which individuals think, feel, behave, and interact.
- Personality psychology focuses on differences between individuals that remain relatively stable across a variety of situations; social psychology focuses on how social factors affect most individuals, regardless of their different personalities.
- Cognitive and social psychologists share an interest in mental processes such as thinking, learning, remembering, and reasoning; but social psychologists focus on the relevance of these processes to social behavior.

Social Psychology and Common Sense

- Many social psychological theories and findings appear to be like common sense. One problem with common sense, however, is that it may offer conflicting explanations and provide no way to test which is correct. Another problem is that common sense is often oversimplified and therefore misleading.

From Past to Present: A Brief History of Social Psychology

The Birth and Infancy of Social Psychology: 1880s–1920s

- Early research by Triplett and Ringelmann established an enduring topic in social psychology: how the presence of others affects an individual's performance.
- The first social psychology textbooks in 1908 and 1924 began to give the emerging field of social psychology its shape.

A Call to Action: 1930s–1950s

- Social psychology began to flourish because the world needed an explanation for the violence of war and solutions to it.
- Sherif's work laid the foundation for later studies of social influence, and the legacy of Kurt Lewin is still evident throughout much of social psychology.

- The 1940s and 1950s saw a burst of activity in social psychology that firmly established it as a major social science.

Confidence and Crisis: 1960s–Mid-1970s

- Stanley Milgram's experiments demonstrated individuals' vulnerability to the destructive commands of authority.
- While social psychology was expanding in many new directions, there was also intense debate about the ethics of research procedures, the validity of research results, and the generalizability of conclusions drawn from research.

An Era of Pluralism: Mid-1970s–1990s

- During the 1970s, social psychology began to take a pluralistic approach to its research methods, views on human behavior, and development of international and multicultural perspectives; this approach continues today.

Social Psychology in a New Century

- Several exciting themes and perspectives are helping to shape the beginning of social psychology's second century.

Integration of Emotion, Motivation, and Cognition

- Researchers are becoming more interested in how emotion, motivation, and cognition can operate together in influencing individuals' thoughts, feelings, and behaviors.
- A great deal of recent social psychological research has explored the automatic versus controllable nature of a number of processes, such as stereotyping.

Biological and Evolutionary Perspectives

- Biological perspectives, including perspectives based on neuroscience, genetics, and evolutionary principles, are being applied to the study of social psychological issues such as gender differences, relationships, and aggression.

Cultural Perspectives

- Increasing numbers of social psychologists are evaluating the universal generality or cultural specificity of their theories and findings by examining similarities and differences across cultures as well as between racial and ethnic groups within cultures.

- For example, in one experiment Canadian participants used more favorable than unfavorable statements in describing themselves, whereas Japanese participants used a balance of favorable and unfavorable descriptions.

New Technologies

- Advances in technology, such as improved brain-imaging techniques, have given rise to groundbreaking research in social psychology.
- Virtual reality technology enables researchers to test questions that otherwise would be impractical, impossible, or unethical.
- The Internet has fostered communication and collaboration among researchers around the world, enabled researchers to study participants from diverse populations, and inspired researchers to investigate whether various social psychological phenomena are similar or different online versus offline.
- As rapidly advancing technologies change how individuals communicate and access information, the ways in which they interact are also likely to change. The social psychology of the next era will explore these issues.

KEY TERMS

behavioral genetics (16)

cross-cultural research (17)

culture (17)

evolutionary psychology
  (17)

interactionist perspective
  (13)

multicultural research (17)

social cognition (15)

social neuroscience (16)

social psychology (5)

2

Doing Social Psychology Research

PREVIEW

This chapter examines how social psychologists do their research. We begin by asking, *"Why should you learn about research methods?"* We answer this question by discussing how learning about research methods can benefit you both in this course and beyond. Then we consider how researchers come up with and *develop ideas and begin the research process*. Next, we provide an overview of the *research designs* that social psychologists use to *test their ideas*. Finally, we turn to important questions about *ethics and values in social psychology*.

t's a familiar situation. You're starting a new semester or quarter at school, and you're just beginning to settle into a new schedule and routine. You're looking forward to your new courses. In general, it's an exciting time. But there's one major catch: As you spend more and more time with your new classmates and new responsibilities, you're leaving someone behind. It could be a boyfriend or girlfriend, a spouse, or a close friend—someone who is not involved in what you are doing now. You may now live far apart from each other, or your new commitments in school may be keeping you apart from each other much more than you'd like. The romantic in you says, "Together forever." Or at least, "No problem." But the realist in you worries a bit. Will your love or friendship be the same? Can it survive the long distance, or the new demands on your time, or the new people in your respective environments? Your friends or family may have advice to offer in this situation. Some might smile and reassure you, "Don't worry. Remember what they say, 'Absence makes the heart grow fonder.' This will only strengthen your relationship." Others might call you aside and whisper, "Don't listen to them. Everybody knows, 'Out of sight, out of mind.' You'd better be careful."

Taking your mind off this problem, you begin to work on a class project. You have the option of working alone or as part of a group. Which should you do? You consult the wisdom of common sense. Maybe you should work in a group. After all, everyone knows that "two heads are better than one." As some members of your group begin to miss meetings and shirk responsibilities, though, you remember that "too many cooks spoil the broth." Will you regret having been so quick to decide to join this group? After all, haven't you been taught to "look before you leap"? Then again, if you had waited and missed the chance to join the group, you might have regretted your inaction, recalling that "he who hesitates is lost."

Questions about the course of relationships, the efficiency of working in groups, and the regret from action versus inaction are social psychological questions. And because we all are interested in predicting and explaining people's behaviors and their thoughts and feelings about each other, we all have our own opinions and intuitions about social psychological matters. If the discipline of social psychology were built on the personal experiences, observations, and intuitions of everyone who is interested in social psychological questions, it would be chock full of interesting theories and ideas; but it would also be a morass of contradictions, ambiguities, and relativism. Instead, social psychology is built on the scientific method.

Scientific? It's easy to see how chemistry is scientific. When you mix two specific compounds in the lab, you can predict exactly what will happen. The compounds will act the same way every time you mix them if the general conditions in the lab are the same. But what happens when you mix together two chemists, or any two people, in a social context? Sometimes you get great chemistry between them; other times you get apathy or even repulsion. How, then, can social behavior, which seems so variable, be studied scientifically?

To many of us in the field, that's the great excitement and challenge of social psychology—the fact that it *is* so dynamic and diverse. Furthermore, in spite of these characteristics, social psychology can, and should, be studied according to scientific principles. Social psychologists develop specific, quantifiable hypotheses that can be tested empirically. If these hypotheses are wrong, they can be proven wrong. In addition, social scientists report the details of how they conduct their tests so

"The most exciting phrase to hear in science, the one that heralds new discoveries, is not 'Eureka!' (I found it!) but 'That's funny. . . .'"
—Isaac Asimov

that others can try to replicate their findings. They integrate evidence from across time and place. And slowly but steadily, they build a consistent and ever more precise understanding of human nature. How social psychologists investigate social psychological questions scientifically is the focus of this chapter. Before we explain the methodology they use, we first explain why it's important and interesting for you to learn about these matters.

Why Should You Learn About Research Methods?

One very practical reason for learning about research methods is that it will help you better understand and learn the material in this book, which will in turn help you on tests and in subsequent courses. Let's look more closely at why this is so. Because social psychology is so relevant to our everyday lives, and because there are so many common-sense notions about social psychological questions, separating myths from truths can be difficult. Most of us don't have an intuition about particular questions concerning quantum mechanics, but we do have intuitions about, say, whether people work better alone or in groups. If you simply read a list of social psychological findings about issues such as this, without knowing and understanding the evidence that social psychologists have produced to support the findings, you may discover later that the task of remembering which were the actual findings and which were merely your own intuitions is difficult. This task is sometimes especially challenging in multiple-choice exams. The right answer might seem very plausible; but then again, so might some of the wrong answers, just as there are good reasons to believe both that "two heads are better than one" and that "too many cooks spoil the broth." Learning about the evidence on which the true research findings and theories are based should help you distinguish the correct from the plausible but incorrect answers.

But the benefits of learning about research methods go far beyond the academic. Training in research methods in psychology can improve your reasoning about real-life events (Lehman et al., 1988; VanderStoep & Shaughnessy, 1997). It can make you a better, more sophisticated consumer of information in general. We are constantly bombarded with "facts" from the media, from sales pitches, and from other people. Much of this information turns out to be wrong or, at best, oversimplified and misleading. We are told about the health benefits of eating certain kinds

We are bombarded with information in our everyday lives, such as in the countless advertisements designed to persuade us to buy particular products or adopt particular opinions or attitudes. Learning the methods used in social psychology research can help students become more sophisticated consumers of this information.

of food, the college entrance exam score benefits of certain preparation courses, or the social status benefits of driving a certain kind of car or wearing a certain kind of shoe. To each of these pronouncements, we should say, "Prove it." What is the evidence? What alternative explanations might there be? For example, a commercial tells us that most doctors prefer a particular (and relatively expensive) brand of aspirin. So should we buy this brand? Think about what it was compared with. Perhaps the doctors didn't prefer that brand of aspirin over other (and cheaper) brands of aspirin but, rather, were asked to compare that brand of aspirin with several non-aspirin products for a particular problem. In that event, the doctors may have preferred any brand of aspirin over non-aspirin products for that need. Thinking like a scientist while reading this text will foster a healthy sense of doubt about claims like these. You will be in a better position to critically evaluate the information to which you're exposed and separate fact from fiction.

Developing Ideas: Beginning the Research Process

The research process involves coming up with ideas, refining them, testing them, and interpreting the meaning of the results obtained. This section describes the first stage of research, coming up with ideas. It also discusses the role of hypotheses and theories and of basic and applied research.

 ## Asking Questions

"Education is not the filling of a pail, but the lighting of a fire."

—William Butler Yeats

Every social psychology study begins with a question. And the questions come from everywhere. As discussed in Chapter 1, the first social psychology experiment published was triggered by the question "Why do bicyclists race faster in the presence of other bicyclists?" (Triplett, 1897–1898). Questions can come from a variety of sources, from something distressing, such as a gruesome murder and the inaction of witnesses to that murder, to something amusing, such as the lyrics of a country song suggesting that female patrons seem prettier to the men in a bar as closing time approaches (Latané & Darley, 1970; Pennebaker et al., 1979).

Questions also come from reading about research that has already been done. Solomon Asch (1946), for example, read about Muzafer Sherif's (1936) demonstration of how individuals in a group conform to others in the group when making judgments about a very ambiguous stimulus (mentioned in Chapter 1 and described in Chapter 7 on Conformity). Asch questioned whether people would conform to

A day after a mass shooting at an Amish schoolhouse in Pennsylvania in October 2006 (discussed in Chapter 11), people in a nearby town mourn the tragedy at a candle light prayer vigil. Over the years, tragic incidents like this one have inspired social psychologists to conduct research on violence and a wide variety of other important social problems.

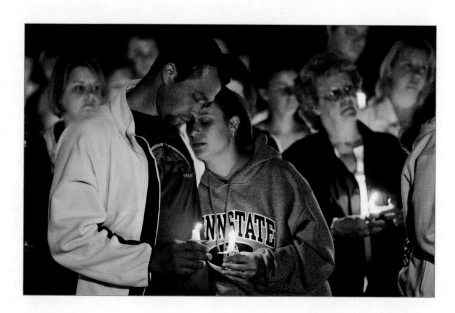

"Give people facts and you feed their minds for an hour. Awaken curiosity and they feed their own minds for a lifetime."

—Ian Russell

the opinions of others in a group even when it was quite clear that the group was wrong. He tested this question, and the results surprised him and the rest of the field: People often did conform even though it was clear that the group was wrong. Thus, one of the most famous experiments in the field inspired an even more famous experiment.

Searching the Literature

Once the researcher has an idea, whether it came from personal observation, folk wisdom, a news story, or previous findings, it is important to see what research has already been done on this topic and related topics. Textbooks such as this one offer a starting point. One of the best ways to search for published materials on topics of interest is by using an electronic database. Some of these databases, such as PsycLIT and PsycINFO, are specific to the psychology literature; others are more general. When you use an electronic database, you can search hundreds of thousands of published articles and books in seconds. You can type in names of authors, key words or phrases, years, or the like and instantly receive summaries of articles that fit your search criteria. In addition to searching databases specific to the psychology literature, you can learn about other research by searching more generally, such as by *googling* particular terms or looking in databases that contain references to newspaper and magazine articles. Once you have found some relevant articles, there is a good chance that they will refer to other articles that are also relevant. Going from article to article, sometimes called *treeing*, can prove very valuable in tracking down information about the research question.

More often than not, the researcher's original question is changed in one way or another during the course of searching the literature. The question should become more precise, more specific to particular sets of conditions that are likely to have different effects, and more readily testable.

Hypotheses and Theories

An initial idea for research may be so vague that it amounts to little more than a hunch or an educated guess. Some ideas vanish with the break of day. But others can be shaped into a **hypothesis**—an explicit, testable prediction about the conditions under which an event will occur. Based on observation, existing theory, or previous research findings, one might test a hypothesis such as "Teenage boys are more likely to be aggressive toward others if they have just played a violent video game for an hour than if they played a nonviolent video game for an hour." This is a specific prediction, and it can be tested empirically. Formulating a hypothesis is a critical step toward planning and conducting research. It allows us to move from the realm of common sense to the rigors of the scientific method.

As hypotheses proliferate and data are collected to test the hypotheses, a more advanced step in the research process may take place: the proposal of a **theory**—an organized set of principles used to explain observed phenomena. Theories are usually evaluated in terms of three criteria: simplicity, comprehensiveness, and generativity. All else being equal, the best theories are elegant and precise; encompass all of the relevant information; and lead to new hypotheses, further research, and better understanding.

In social psychology, there are many theories. Social psychologists do not attempt the all-encompassing grand theory, such as those of Freud or Piaget, which you may have studied in introductory psychology. Instead, they rely on more precise "mini-theories" that address limited and specific aspects of the way people behave, make explicit predictions about behavior, and allow meaningful empirical investigation. Consider, for example, Daryl Bem's (1967, 1972) self-perception theory, which is discussed in Chapter 3 on the Social Self. Bem proposed that when people's internal states, such as a feeling or attitude, are difficult for them to interpret, they infer this feeling or attitude by observing their own behavior and the situation in which it takes place. This theory did not apply to all situations; rather, it

"The currency of science is not truth, but doubt."

—Dennis Overbye

hypothesis A testable prediction about the conditions under which an event will occur.

theory An organized set of principles used to explain observed phenomena.

was specific to situations in which people make inferences about their own actions when their own internal states are somewhat ambiguous. Though more limited in scope than a grand theory of personality or development, self-perception theory did generate numerous specific, empirically testable hypotheses.

Good social psychological theories inspire subsequent research. Specifically, they stimulate systematic studies designed to test various aspects of the theories and the specific hypotheses that are derived from them. A theory may be quite accurate and yet have little worth if it cannot be tested. Conversely, a theory may make an important contribution to the field even if it turns out to be wrong. The research it inspires may prove more valuable than the theory itself, as the results shed light on new truths that might not have been discovered without the directions suggested by the theory.

Indeed, when Bem introduced self-perception theory to the field, it generated a great deal of attention and controversy. Part of its value as a good theory was that it helped organize and make sense of evidence that had been found in previous studies. Furthermore, it generated testable new hypotheses. Many scholars doubted the validity of the theory, however, and conducted research designed to prove it wrong. In short, both supporters and doubters of the theory launched a wave of studies, which ultimately led to a greater understanding of the processes described in Bem's theory.

Beginning students of social psychology are often surprised by the lack of consensus in the field. In part, such disagreement reflects the fact that social psychology is a relatively young science (Kruglanski, 2001). At this stage in its development, premature closure is a worse sin than contradiction or even confusion. But debate is an essential feature of even the most mature science. It is the fate of all scientific theories to be criticized and, eventually, surpassed.

> "[Close cooperation between theoretical and applied psychology] can be accomplished . . . if the theorist does not look toward applied problems with highbrow aversion or with a fear of social problems, and if the applied psychologist realizes that there is nothing so practical as a good theory."
>
> —Kurt Lewin

Basic and Applied Research

Is testing a theory the purpose of research in social psychology? For some researchers, yes. **Basic research** seeks to increase our understanding of human behavior and is often designed to test a specific hypothesis from a specific theory. **Applied research** has a different purpose: to make use of social psychology's theories or methods to enlarge our understanding of naturally occurring events and to contribute to the solution of social problems.

Despite their differences, basic and applied research are closely connected in social psychology. Some researchers switch back and forth between the two—today basic, tomorrow applied. Some studies test a theory and examine a real-world phenomenon simultaneously. As a pioneer in both approaches, Kurt Lewin (1951) set the tone when he encouraged basic researchers to be concerned with complex social problems and urged applied researchers to recognize how important and practical good theories are.

Refining Ideas: Defining and Measuring Social Psychological Variables

basic research Research whose goal is to increase the understanding of human behavior, often by testing hypotheses based on a theory.

applied research Research whose goals are to enlarge the understanding of naturally occurring events and to find solutions to practical problems.

No matter what method researchers plan to use to test their hypotheses, they always must decide how they will define and measure the variables in which they are interested. This is sometimes a straightforward process. For example, if you are interested in comparing how quickly people run a 100-meter dash when alone and when racing against another person, you can rely on well-established ways to define and measure the variables in question. Many other times, however, the process is less straightforward. If you are interested in studying the effects of self-esteem on altruistic behavior, you must first define self-esteem and altruistic behavior. There may be countless ways to do this. Which ones should you pick?

Conceptual Variables and Operational Definitions: From the Abstract to the Specific

When a researcher first develops a hypothesis, the variables typically are in an abstract, general form. These are *conceptual variables*. Examples of conceptual variables include prejudice, conformity, attraction, love, violence, group pressure, and social anxiety. In order to test specific hypotheses, we must then transform these conceptual variables into variables that can be manipulated or measured in a study. The specific way in which a conceptual variable is manipulated or measured is called the **operational definition** of the variable. For example, a researcher might operationally define "conformity" in a particular study as the number of times a participant indicated agreement with the obviously wrong judgments made by a group of confederates. Part of the challenge and fun of designing research in social psychology is taking an abstract conceptual variable such as love or group pressure and deciding how to operationally define it so as to manipulate or measure it.

From this picture, we can guess that the boy sitting by himself on the playground is lonely, but how do researchers precisely define and measure conceptual variables like loneliness? Researchers may use any of a number of approaches, such as asking people how they feel or observing their behavior.

Often, there is no single best way to transform a variable from the abstract (conceptual) to the specific (operational). A great deal of trial and error may be involved. However, sometimes there are systematic, statistical ways of checking how valid various manipulations and measures are, and researchers spend a great deal of time fine-tuning their operational definitions to best capture the conceptual variables they wish to study.

Researchers evaluate the manipulation and measurement of variables in terms of their **construct validity**. Construct validity refers to the extent to which (1) the manipulations in an experiment really manipulate the conceptual variables they were designed to manipulate and (2) the measures used in a study (experimental or otherwise) really measure the conceptual variables they were designed to measure. Imagine, for example, wanting to conduct an experiment on the effects of alcohol on aggression. One of the conceptual variables might be whether or not participants are intoxicated. There are several ways of measuring this variable, most of which are relatively straightforward: assessing participants' blood alcohol concentration, measuring their ability to perform simple motor tasks, or asking them how drunk they feel, for example. Thus, one researcher might operationally define intoxication as when a participant has a blood alcohol level of .10 or more, while another might define it as when a participant says that he or she feels drunk. A second conceptual variable in this study would be aggression. Measuring aggression in experiments is particularly difficult because of ethical and practical issues—researchers can't let participants in their studies attack each other. Researchers interested in measuring aggression are thus often forced to measure relatively unusual behaviors, such as administering shocks to another person as part of a specific task. Does this really measure aggression? It's hard to tell. Some researchers say that such measures often are valid; others say they often aren't (Anderson et al., 1999; Tedeschi & Quigley, 2000).

operational definition   The specific procedures for manipulating or measuring a conceptual variable.

construct validity   The extent to which the measures used in a study measure the variables they were designed to measure and the manipulations in an experiment manipulate the variables they were designed to manipulate.

The importance of well-designed questions and response options may never have been more evident than in the aftermath of the U.S. presidential election of November 2000. The positioning of the choices on this "butterfly" ballot design confused countless voters in Palm Beach County, Florida, apparently causing thousands of people to mistakenly vote for Pat Buchanan when they had intended to vote for Al Gore. This confusion may well have caused Gore to lose the presidency to George W. Bush.

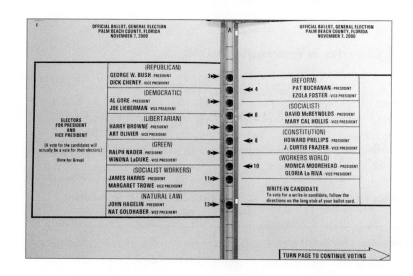

Measuring Variables: Using Self-Reports, Observations, and Technology

Social psychologists measure variables in many ways, but most can be placed into one of two categories: self-reports and observations. We discuss each of these methods in the next sections, along with how advances in technology are enabling social psychologists to measure variables in new ways.

Self-Reports   Collecting *self-reports*—in which participants disclose their thoughts, feelings, desires, and actions—is a widely used measurement technique in social psychology. Self-reports can consist of individual questions or sets of questions that together measure a single conceptual variable. One popular self-report measure, the Rosenberg Self-Esteem Scale, consists of a set of questions that measures individuals' overall self-esteem. For example, respondents are asked the extent to which they agree with statements such as "I feel that I have a number of good qualities," and "All in all, I am inclined to feel that I'm a failure." This scale is used in a wide variety of settings, and many researchers consider it to have good construct validity (Griffiths et al., 1999; Heatherton & Wyland, 2003; Robins et al., 2001).

Self-reports give the researcher access to an individual's beliefs and perceptions. But self-reports are not always accurate and can be misleading. For example, the desire to look good to ourselves and others can influence how we respond. As Shakespeare put it in the play *Measure for Measure*, "It oft falls out, to have what we would have, we speak not what we mean." Research using a procedure called the "bogus pipeline" indicates that participants who are led to believe that their responses will be verified by an infallible lie-detector report facts about themselves more accurately and endorse socially unacceptable opinions more frequently than those not told about such a device. The bogus pipeline is, in fact, bogus; no such infallible device exists. But belief in its powers discourages people from lying (Alexander & Fisher, 2003; Derakshan & Eysenck, 2005; Plant et al., 2003; Roese & Jamieson, 1993).

Self-reports are also affected by the way in which questions are asked, such as how they are worded or in what order or context they are asked (Schwarz, 1999, 2007; Schwarz & Oyserman, 2001). For instance, when UCLA freshmen were asked on a survey,

"Clemson here. How may I disappoint you?"

This person would probably score low on Rosenberg's Self-Esteem Scale.

TABLE 2.1
Are Condoms Effective in Preventing AIDS?

Participants were asked whether they thought condoms were effective in preventing the spread of AIDS. Some participants were told that condoms had a "95% success rate," whereas other participants were told that they had a "5% failure rate." Even though these two rates are functionally the same thing, this difference in wording caused a dramatic difference in participants' responses. (*Linville et al., 1992.*)

Statement Given to Participants	Percent Who Said Condoms Were Effective
"Condoms have a 95% success rate."	88
"Condoms have a 5% failure rate."	42

"How much special consideration should black students receive in college admissions?" more than 70 percent said that at least some special consideration should be given. However, when asked, "Should affirmative action be abolished?" 50 percent said yes (Shea, 1996). In another study, a large majority of participants indicated that they thought condoms were effective in stopping AIDS when condoms were said to have a "95 percent success rate" (see Table 2.1). However, when condoms were said to have a "5 percent failure rate" (which is merely another way of saying the same thing as a 95 percent success rate), less than half of the participants indicated that they thought condoms were effective (Linville et al., 1992).

Another reason self-reports can be inaccurate is that they often ask participants to report on thoughts or behaviors from the past, and people's memory of their thoughts or behaviors is very prone to error. To minimize this problem, psychologists have developed ways to reduce the time that elapses between an actual experience and the person's report of it. For example, some use *interval-contingent* self-reports, in which respondents report their experiences at regular intervals, usually once a day. Researchers may also collect *signal-contingent* self-reports. Here, respondents report their experiences as soon as possible after being signaled to do so, usually by means of a beeper. Finally, some researchers collect *event-contingent* self-reports, in which respondents report on a designated set of events as soon as possible after such events have occurred. For example, the Rochester Interaction Record (RIR) is an event-contingent self-report questionnaire used by respondents to record every social interaction lasting ten minutes or more that occurs during the course of the study, usually a week or two (Nezlek & Leary, 2002; Nezlek & Smith, 2005).

Whatever their differences, most self-report methods require participants to provide specific answers to specific questions. In contrast, *narrative studies* collect lengthy responses on a general topic. Narrative materials can be generated by participants at the researcher's request or taken from other sources (such as diaries, speeches, books, or chatroom discussions). These accounts are then analyzed in terms of a coding scheme developed by the researcher. For example, the researcher might code descriptions of an event for the use of particular stereotypes, diaries for evidence of the writers' personality styles, and sports articles in newspapers for athletes' explanations for winning or losing (Fink & Kensicki, 2002; Mehl & Pennebaker, 2003; Roesch & Amirkhan, 1997; Salzer, 2000).

Observations   Self-reports are but one tool social psychologists use to measure variables. Researchers can also observe people's actions. Sometimes these observations are very simple, as when a researcher notes which of two items a person selects. At other times, however, the observations are more elaborate and (like the coding of narrative accounts) require that interrater reliability be established. **Interrater reliability** refers to the level of agreement among multiple observers of the same behavior. Only when different observers agree can the data be trusted.

The advantage of observational methods is that they avoid our sometimes faulty recollections and distorted interpretations of our own behavior. Actions can speak louder than words. But if individuals know they are being observed, some observational methods are as vulnerable as self-reports to people's desire to present themselves in a favorable light.

interrater reliability
The degree to which different observers agree on their observations.

Observational methods provide a useful alternative to self-reports. Here an experimenter behind a one-way mirror observes and records notes from a conversation between two research participants in a psychology lab.

Technology Social psychologists use more than merely their eyes and ears to observe their subjects, of course. Advances in technology offer researchers exciting new tools that enable them to make extremely precise, subtle, and complex observations that were beyond the dreams of social psychologists just a generation or so ago. Various kinds of equipment are used to measure physiological responses such as changes in heart rate, levels of particular hormones, and sexual arousal. Computers are used to record the speed with which participants respond to stimuli, such as how quickly they can identify the race of people in photographs or the presence of a weapon in the hands of a white or black man (Correll et al., 2002; Hugenberg & Bodenhausen, 2004). Eye-tracking technology is used to measure exactly where and for how long participants look at particular parts of a stimulus, such as an advertisement or a video (Day et al., 2006; Eberhardt et al., 2007).

Most recently, social psychologists have begun opening a window into the live human brain—fortunately, without having to lift a scalpel. Brain-imaging technologies take and combine thousands of images of the brain in action. As mentioned in Chapter 1, two of the most common imaging techniques in social psychology research today are PET (positron emission tomography) and fMRI (functional magnetic resonance imaging) scans. Both types of scanning provide researchers with visual images of activity in parts of the brain while the research subject is thinking, making decisions, responding to audio or visual stimuli, and so on. These images can show researchers what parts of the brain seem to "light up"—or show increased activity—in response to a particular stimulus or situation. For example, although participants in a study of racism may show no signs of any racial biases on their self-reports or through easily observable behavior in the lab, these same participants may show increased activity in parts of their brain associated with feelings of threat or strong emotion when they see pictures of people from a particular racial group (Cunningham et al., 2004; Lieberman et al., 2005).

Testing Ideas: Research Designs

Social psychologists use several different methods to test their research hypotheses and theories. Although methods vary, the field generally emphasizes objective, systematic, and quantifiable approaches. Social psychologists do not simply seek out evidence that supports their ideas; rather, they test their ideas in ways that could very clearly prove them wrong.

The most popular and preferred research method in social psychology is experimentation, in which researchers can test cause-and-effect relationships, such as whether exposure to a violent television program causes viewers to behave more aggressively. We emphasize the experimental approach in this book. In addition, we report the results of many studies that use another popular approach: correlational research, which looks for associations between two variables without establishing cause and effect. We also report the results of studies that use a relatively new technique called meta-analysis, which integrates the research findings of many different studies. Before describing these approaches, though, we turn to an approach with which we all are very familiar: descriptive research. This is the approach used in opinion polls, ratings of the popularity of TV shows, box scores in the sports section, and the like.

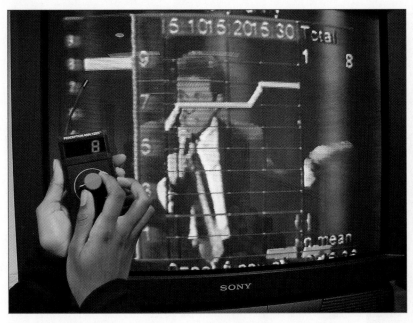

Computerized video technology, such as this Perception Analyzer™, allows researchers to track participants' moment-by-moment reactions to events on the screen (in this case, a comedian's performance). It can also simultaneously display the average ratings of groups of participants in a graph superimposed over the video. This technology can help researchers study the dynamics of social influence.

 ## Descriptive Research: Discovering Trends and Tendencies

One obvious way of testing ideas about people is simply to record how frequently or how typically people think, feel, or behave in particular ways. The goal of *descriptive research* in social psychology is, as the term implies, to describe people and their thoughts, feelings, and behaviors. This method can test questions such as: Do most people support capital punishment? What percentage of people who encounter a person lying on the sidewalk would offer to help that person? What do men and women say are the things most likely to make them jealous of their partner? Particular methods of doing descriptive research include observing people, studying records of past events and behaviors, and surveying people. We discuss each of these methods in this section.

Observational Studies   We can learn about other people simply by observing them, of course, and some social psychological questions can be addressed through observational studies. For example, a team of researchers (Hawkins et al., 2001; Pepler & Craig, 1995) wanted to know how common bullying is among schoolchildren in Canada, and how often peers step in to help those who are being bullied. Is bullying an infrequent occurrence, revolving around a handful of bullies, or is it a widespread problem? Are there gender differences in bullying or in peer interventions? To investigate these questions, the researchers used hidden cameras and microphones to record the incidents of bullying and peer interventions in a number of schools in Canada (with the permission of the schools and parents). This peek into the schoolyard enabled the researchers to discover that the problem of bullying is much more pervasive than many people believe, and they were able to report the frequency with which particular forms of aggression, and helping, occurred. This research could be used to suggest strategies for reducing the prevalence and harmful impact of bullying among schoolchildren.

TV newsmagazine shows like *20/20* and *Dateline* often use hidden cameras to record people's behaviors. The ethics of this can be troublesome; we return to the issue of ethics in research later in the chapter. In addition to ethical matters, though, questions of accuracy may arise in connection with these news programs. TV reporters and journalists often are more interested in telling a good story than in being scientifically sound, so we should be careful when drawing general conclusions from their presentations. A news program may show footage that is consistent with the point of view of their overall story—for example, footage demonstrating that certain kinds of people are treated worse by car salespeople or auto mechanics than others—but may not show footage that is inconsistent with this point of view. Social psychologists are trained to be systematic and unbiased in their observations and to report all of the data that are relevant to the research question, not just the data that support a particular hypothesis.

Archival Studies   Archival research involves examining existing records of past events and behaviors, such as newspaper articles, medical records, diaries, sports statistics, personal ads, crime statistics, or hits on a Web page. A major advantage of archival measures is that, because the researchers are observing behavior secondhand, they can be sure that they did not influence the behavior by their presence. A limitation of this approach is that available records are not always complete or sufficiently detailed, and they may have been collected in a nonsystematic manner.

"Just as we suspected—they're beginning to form a boy band."

Observational research can reveal some fascinating—and sometimes disturbing!—insights into social behavior.

Archival measures are particularly valuable for examining cultural and historical trends. In Chapter 11 on Aggression, for example, we report a number of trends concerning the rate of violent crime in the United States and how it has changed in recent years, and we report differences in homicide rates in countries around the world. These data come from archival records, such as the records of police stations, the Federal Bureau of Investigation (FBI), and the United Nations. Other examples of archival research include a study that tracked the proportion of *New Yorker* cartoons over the years that featured black men and women in various roles (Thibodeau, 1989) and a study that examined the waist-to-hip ratio of Miss America winners and *Playboy* playmates over the past several decades (Singh, 1993).

Surveys It seems that nobody in politics these days sneezes without first conducting an opinion poll. Surveys have become increasingly popular in recent years, and they are conducted on everything from politics, to attitudes about social issues, to the percentages of women and men who squeeze the toothpaste tube from the bottom (O.K., we'll tell you: 37 percent of women and 18 percent of men; Weiss, 1991). Conducting surveys involves asking people questions about their attitudes, beliefs, and behaviors. Surveys can be conducted in person, over the phone, by mail, or via the Internet. Many social psychological questions can be addressed only with surveys because they involve variables that are impossible or unethical to observe directly or manipulate, such as people's sexual behaviors or their optimism about the future.

Although anyone can conduct a survey (and sometimes it seems that everyone does), there is a science to designing, conducting, and interpreting the results of surveys. Like other self-report measures, surveys can be affected strongly by subtle aspects of the wording and context of questions, and survey researchers are trained to consider these issues and to test various kinds of wording and question ordering before conducting their surveys.

One of the most important issues that survey researchers face is how to select the people who will take part in the survey. The researchers first must identify the *population* in which they are interested. Is this survey supposed to tell us about the

Many social psychological questions are addressed using surveys, which can be conducted over the phone, by mail, via the Internet, or face-to-face in field settings such as at this shopping center.

In the 1948 U.S. presidential election, pollsters nationwide predicted that Thomas Dewey would defeat Harry Truman by a wide margin. As Truman basked in his victory, pollsters realized that their predictions were based on nonrandom samples of voters. Random sampling would have led to much more accurate predictions.

attitudes of North Americans in general, shoppers at Wal-Mart, or students in Introduction to Social Psychology at University X, for example? From this general population, the researchers select a subset, or *sample*, of individuals. For a survey to be accurate, the sample must be similar to, or representative of, the population on important characteristics such as age, sex, race, income, education, and cultural background. The best way to achieve this representativeness is to use **random sampling**, a method of selection in which everyone in a population has an equal chance of being selected for the sample. Survey researchers use randomizing procedures, such as tables of randomly distributed numbers generated by computers, to decide how to select individuals for their samples.

To see the importance of random sampling, consider a pair of U.S. presidential elections (Rosnow & Rosenthal, 1993). Just before the 1936 election, a magazine called the *Literary Digest* predicted that Alfred Landon, the Republican governor of Kansas, would win by 14 percentage points over Franklin Roosevelt. The *Digest* based its prediction on a survey of more than 2 million Americans. In fact, though, Landon *lost* the election by 24 percentage points. The magazine, which had been in financial trouble before the election, declared bankruptcy soon after.

Twenty years later, the Gallup survey's prediction of Dwight Eisenhower's victory was almost perfect—it was off by less than 2 percent. The size of its sample? Only about 8,000. How could the 1936 survey, with its much larger sample, be so wrong and the 1956 survey be so right? The answer is that the 1936 sample was not randomly selected. The *Digest* contacted people through sources such as phone books and club membership lists. In 1936, many people could not afford to have telephones or belong to clubs. The people in the sample, therefore, tended to be wealthier than much of the population, and wealthier people preferred Landon. In 1956, by contrast, Gallup pollsters randomly selected election districts throughout the country and then randomly selected households within those districts. Today, because of improved sampling procedures, surveys conducted on little more than 1,000 Americans can be used to make accurate predictions about the entire U.S. population.

Correlational Research: Looking for Associations

Although there is much to learn from descriptive research, social psychologists typically want to know more. Most research hypotheses in social psychology concern the relationship between variables. For example, is there a relationship between people's gender and their willingness to ask for help from others, or between how physically attractive people are and how much money they make?

One way to test such hypotheses is with correlational research. Like descriptive research, **correlational research** can be conducted using observational, archival, or survey methods. Unlike descriptive research, however, correlational approaches measure the *relationship* between different variables. The extent to which variables relate to each other, or correlate, can suggest how similar or distinct two different measures are (for example, how related people's self-esteem and popularity are) and how well one variable can be used to predict another (for example, how well we can predict academic success in college from college entrance exam scores). It is important to note that researchers doing correlational research typically do not manipulate the variables they study; they simply measure them.

random sampling A method of selecting participants for a study so that everyone in a population has an equal chance of being in the study.

correlational research Research designed to measure the association between variables that are not manipulated by the researcher.

Similarity is correlated with attraction—the more similar two people are, the more attractive they are likely to find each other. But a correlation cannot identify the cause of this association. Chapter 9 on Attraction and Close Relationships discusses both correlational and experimental research on the role of similarity in the attraction process.

Correlation Coefficient   When researchers examine the relationship between variables that vary in quantity (such as temperature or degree of self-esteem), they can measure the strength and direction of the relationship between the variables and calculate a statistic called a **correlation coefficient**. Correlation coefficients can range from +1.0 to –1.0. The absolute value of the number (the number itself, without the positive or negative sign) indicates how strongly the two variables are associated. The larger the absolute value of the number, the stronger the association between the two variables, and thus the better either of the variables is as a predictor of the other. Whether the coefficient is positive or negative indicates the direction of the relationship. A positive correlation coefficient indicates that as one variable increases, so does the other. For example, college entrance exam scores correlate positively with grades. The positive direction of this relationship indicates that higher entrance exam scores are associated with higher grades and lower entrance exam scores are associated with lower grades. This correlation is not perfect; some people with high entrance exam scores have poor grades, and vice versa. Therefore, the correlation is less than +1.0; but it is greater than 0, because there is some association between the two. A negative coefficient indicates that the two variables go in opposite directions: As one goes up, the other tends to go down. For example, number of classes missed and GPA are likely to be negatively correlated. And a correlation close to 0 indicates that there is no consistent relationship at all. These three types of patterns are illustrated in Figure 2.1. Because few variables are perfectly related to each other, most correlation coefficients do not approach +1.0 or –1.0 but have more moderate values, such as +.39 or –.57.

Some correlational studies involve a variable that does not vary in quantity, such as race, gender, political affiliation, or whether Italian, Mexican, or Thai food is their favorite. In this case, researchers cannot compute a typical correlation coefficient. Nevertheless, such studies can reveal relationships between variables. For example, some research indicates that students who study Latin and take the Latin Achievement Test do more than 100 points better on verbal and math SATs than other students (Costa, 1982). This research indicates a relationship between whether or not a student studies Latin (which is an either/or variable that does not vary in quantity—a student either does or does not study Latin) and students' success on the SAT (which is a variable that does vary in quantity from zero points to a perfect score). Does this correlation mean that studying Latin causes students to do better on the SAT? Think about it; we'll return to this question later.

Advantages and Disadvantages of Correlational Research   Correlational research has many advantages. It can study the associations of naturally occurring variables that cannot be manipulated or induced—such as gender, race, ethnicity, and age. It can examine phenomena that would be difficult or unethical to create for research purposes, such as love, hate, and abuse. And it offers researchers a great deal of freedom in where variables are measured. Participants can be brought into a laboratory specially constructed for research purposes, or they can be approached in a real-world setting (often called "the field") such as a shopping mall or airport.

Despite these advantages, however, correlational research has one very serious disadvantage. And here it is in bold letters: **Correlation is not causation.**

In other words, a correlation cannot demonstrate a cause-and-effect relationship. Instead of revealing a specific causal pathway from one variable, A, to another variable, B, a correlation between variables A and B contains within it three possible causal effects: A could cause B; B could cause A; or a third variable, C, could cause both A and B. For example, imagine learning that the number of hours per night

correlation coefficient   A statistical measure of the strength and direction of the association between two variables.

FIGURE 2.1

Correlations: Positive, Negative, and None

Correlations reveal a systematic association between two variables. Positive correlations indicate that variables are in sync: Increases in one variable are associated with increases in the other, decreases with decreases. Negative correlations indicate that variables go in opposite directions: Increases in one variable are associated with decreases in the other. When two variables are not systematically associated, there is no correlation.

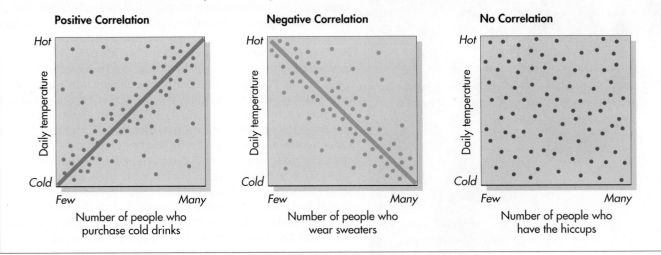

one sleeps is negatively correlated with the number of colds one gets. This means that as the amount of sleep increases, colds decrease in frequency; conversely, as sleep decreases, colds become more frequent. One reasonable explanation for this relationship is that lack of sleep (variable A) causes people to become more vulnerable to colds (variable B). Another reasonable explanation, however, is that people who have colds can't sleep well, and so colds (variable B) cause lack of sleep (variable A). A third reasonable explanation is that some other variable (C) causes both lack of sleep and greater frequency of colds. This third variable could be stress. Indeed, stress has many effects on people, as will be discussed in Chapter 14 on Health. Figure 2.2 describes another correlation that can be explained in many ways—the correlation between TV watching and aggression.

As sure as death and taxes, there will be many, many times in your life when you'll encounter reports in the media that suggest cause-and-effect relationships based on correlational research. One of the great benefits of learning and gaining experience with the material in this chapter is that you can see the flaws in media reports like these and not be taken in by them. Correlation is not causation.

To illustrate how even such respected representatives of the media as the *New York Times* make this mistake, let's return to the Latin and SAT correlation discussed above. This relationship was reported in an op-ed piece in the *Times* entitled "Latin and Greek Are Good for You" (Costa, 1982). The author cited the SAT figures indicating that students who took the Latin Achievement Test did much better on their SATs than other students and concluded that "Latin is good for you." So why is this conclusion wrong? It *is* possible that studying Latin caused an improvement in SAT scores, but other causal explanations are possible as well. In terms of Figure 2.2, A (Latin) might have caused B (elevated SAT scores). Although B could not have caused A, because the students took the SATs only after they had been studying Latin, it is very possible that some other variable (C) caused both A and B. For example, high school students who decide to study Latin may in general be more intelligent than students who show no interest in the subject, or schools that offer study in languages such as Latin and Greek may in general be better academically than schools that do not. So, it is possible that studying Latin had no effect on the students' SAT scores, despite the correlation between these two variables (Lehman et al., 1988).

FIGURE 2.2

Explaining Correlations: Three Possibilities

The correlation between one variable (A) and another variable (B) could be explained in three ways. Variable A could cause changes in variable B, or variable B could cause changes in variable A, or a third variable (C) could cause similar changes in both A and B, even if A and B did not influence each other. For example, a correlation between how much TV children watch and how aggressively they behave could be explained in the following ways:

(1) TV watching causes aggressive behavior;

(2) children who behave aggressively like to watch a lot of TV; or

(3) children who have family troubles, such as parents who are not very involved in the children's development, tend both to watch a lot of TV and to behave aggressively.

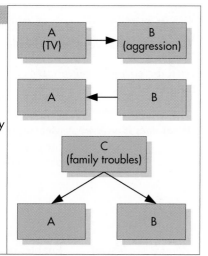

Do we learn nothing, then, from correlations? To say that would be to take caution too far. Correlations tell researchers about the strength and direction of relationships between variables, thus helping them understand these variables better and allowing them to use one variable to predict the other. Correlations can be extremely useful in developing new hypotheses to guide future research. And by gathering large sets of correlations and using complicated statistical techniques to crunch the data, we can develop highly accurate predictions of future events. But still, correlation is not causation.

Experiments: Looking for Cause and Effect

Social psychologists often do want to examine cause-and-effect relationships. Although it is informative to know, for example, that watching a lot of TV is correlated with violent behavior in real life, the inevitable next question is whether watching a lot of TV *causes* an increase in violent behavior. If we want to examine cause-and-effect relationships, we need to conduct an **experiment**. Experiments in social psychology range from the very simple to the incredibly elaborate. All of them, however, share two essential characteristics.

1. The researcher has *control* over the experimental procedures, manipulating the variables of interest while ensuring uniformity elsewhere. In other words, all participants in the research are treated in exactly the same manner—except for the specific differences the experimenter wants to create. By exercising control, the researcher attempts to ensure that differences obtained after the experimental manipulation are produced only by that manipulation and are not affected by other events in the experiment.

2. Participants in the study are *randomly* assigned to the different manipulations (called "conditions") included in the experiment. If there are two conditions, who goes where may be determined by simply flipping a coin. If there are many conditions, a computer program may be used. But however it's done, **random assignment** means that participants are not assigned to a condition on the basis of their personal or behavioral characteristics. Through random assignment, the experimenter attempts to ensure a level playing field: *On average, the participants randomly assigned to one condition are no different from those assigned to another condition.* Differences that appear between conditions after an experimental manipulation can therefore be attributed to the impact of that manipulation and not to any pre-existing differences between participants.

experiment A form of research that can demonstrate causal relationships because (1) the experimenter has control over the events that occur and (2) participants are randomly assigned to conditions.

random assignment A method of assigning participants to the various conditions of an experiment so that each participant in the experiment has an equal chance of being in any of the conditions.

TABLE 2.2
Correlations Versus Experiments

	Correlational Research	Experimental Research
What does it involve?	Measuring variables and the degree of association between them	Random assignment to conditions and control over the events that occur; determining the effects of manipulations of the independent variable(s) on changes in the dependent variable(s)
What is the biggest advantage of using this method?	Enables researchers to study naturally occurring variables, including variables that would be too difficult or unethical to manipulate	Enables researchers to determine cause-and-effect relationships—that is, whether the independent variable can cause a change in the dependent variable

Because of experimenter control and random assignment of participants, an experiment is a powerful technique for examining cause and effect. Both characteristics serve the same goal: to eliminate the influence of any factors other than the experimental manipulation. By ruling out alternative explanations for research results, we become more confident that we understand just what has, in fact, caused a certain behavior to occur. Table 2.2 summarizes the distinctions between correlational and experimental research.

Random Sampling Versus Random Assignment You may recall that we mentioned random sampling earlier, in connection with surveys. It's important to remember the differences between random *sampling* and random *assignment*. Table 2.3 summarizes these differences. Random sampling concerns how individuals are selected to be in a study; it is important for generalizing the results obtained from a sample to a broader population, and it is therefore very important for survey research. Random assignment concerns not who is selected to be in the study but, rather, how participants in the study are assigned to different conditions, as explained above. Random assignment is essential to experiments because it is necessary for determining cause-and-effect relationships; without it, there is always the possibility that any differences found between the conditions in a study were caused by pre-existing differences among participants. Random sampling, in contrast, is not necessary for establishing causality. For that reason, and because random sampling is difficult and expensive, very few experiments use random sampling. We consider the implications of this fact later in the chapter.

Laboratory and Field Experiments Most experiments in social psychology are conducted in a *laboratory* setting, usually located in a university, so that the environment can be controlled and the participants carefully studied. Social psychology labs do not necessarily look like stereotypical laboratories with liquid bubbling in beakers or expensive equipment everywhere (although many social psychology labs are indeed very "high-tech"). They can resemble ordinary living rooms or even game rooms. The key point here is that the laboratory setting enables researchers to have control over the setting, measure participants' behaviors precisely, and keep conditions identical for participants.

Field research is conducted in real-world settings outside of the laboratory. Researchers interested in studying helping behavior, for example, might conduct an experiment in a public park. The advantage of field experiments is that people are more likely to act naturally in a natural setting than in a laboratory in which they know they are being studied. The disadvantage of field settings is that the experimenter often has less control and cannot ensure that the participants in the various conditions of the experiment will be exposed to the same things.

Independent and Dependent Variables In an experiment, researchers manipulate one or more **independent variables** and examine the effect of these

independent variable
In an experiment, a factor that experimenters manipulate to see if it affects the dependent variable.

TABLE 2.3
Random Sampling Versus Random Assignment

	Random Sampling	Random Assignment
What does it involve?	Selecting participants to be in the study so that everyone from a population has an equal chance of being a participant in the study	Assigning participants (who are already in the study) to the various conditions of the experiment so that each participant has an equal chance of being in any of the conditions
What is the biggest advantage of using this procedure?	Enables researchers to collect data from samples that are representative of the broader population; important for being able to generalize the results to the broader population	Equalizes the conditions of the experiment so that it is very unlikely that the conditions differ in terms of pre-existing differences among the participants; essential to determine that the independent variable(s) caused an effect on the dependent variable(s)

manipulations on one or more **dependent variables**. For example, consider an experiment by Emily Pronin and others (2004) that was designed to examine how being the targets of negative stereotypes about their abilities in math could affect women's self-perceptions and identity. In this study, some female students read an article reporting that boys tended to perform better on a standardized math test than did girls, whereas other female students read an article unrelated to gender and math. Which article a student read was determined by random assignment. Therefore, which article the students read was the independent variable in this study; that is, the researchers manipulated this variable to determine its effects on another variable, the dependent variable. In this study, one of the dependent variables was the students' ratings of how strongly they personally identified with each of a series of feminine characteristics. The ratings were the dependent variable because the researchers were interested in seeing if they would *depend* on (that is, be influenced by) the manipulation of the independent variable. The researchers found that the manipulation did have a significant effect on the dependent variable: The students who read the article indicating that boys outperformed girls in math rated themselves as identifying less with the feminine characteristics than did the students who had not read this article.

Subject Variables   Some experiments include variables that are neither dependent nor truly independent. In many experiments, some of the participants are male and some are female. Some participants may be politically conservative, some politically liberal, and some neither. The sex or political leanings of the participants cannot be manipulated and randomly assigned, so they are not true independent variables; and they are not influenced by the independent variables, so they are not a dependent variable. Variables such as these are called **subject variables**, because they characterize pre-existing differences among the subjects, or participants, in the experiment. If a study includes subject variables but no true, randomly assigned independent variable, it is not a true experiment. But experiments often include subject variables along with independent variables so that researchers can test whether the independent variables have the same or different effects on different kinds of participants.

Main Effects and Interactions   Some experiments include multiple independent variables. Researchers can then examine the separate effects of each independent variable on the dependent variable and can also study how the different independent variables combine to create interactive effects. In such cases, researchers can examine (1) the **main effect** of each independent variable—the overall effect of the independent variable on the dependent variable, ignoring all other independent variables, and (2) the **interaction** between independent variables—the change in the effect of each independent variable as a function of other independent variables.

dependent variable   In an experiment, a factor that experimenters measure to see if it is affected by the independent variable.

subject variable   A variable that characterizes pre-existing differences among the participants in a study.

main effect   A statistical term indicating the overall effect that an independent variable has on the dependent variable, ignoring all other independent variables.

interaction   A statistical term indicating the change in the effect of each independent variable as a function of other independent variables.

In field research, people are observed in real-world settings. Field researchers may observe children in a schoolyard, for example, to study any of a variety of social psychological issues, such as friendship patterns, group dynamics, conformity, helping, aggression, and cultural differences.

By way of illustration, let's consider an experiment by Joseph Vandello and Dov Cohen (2003). Vandello and Cohen were interested in cultural differences concerning gender roles, particularly in how a man is perceived as a function of whether his wife is faithful or not to him. As we will see in Chapter 11 on Aggression, researchers have been examining cultural differences in the degree to which a man's honor and status are emphasized, which has implications for how men are expected to protect or reclaim their honor and status. Vandello and Cohen conducted an experiment to test one particular hypothesis stemming from this body of research: A wife's infidelity would have stronger effects on the husband's reputation in *cultures of honor* than in less honor-focused cultures.

In one study, the researchers had college students from either the northern United States or Brazil read a story either about a man whose wife was faithful to him or about a man whose wife was unfaithful to him by having an affair. The variation in culture—northern United States versus Brazil—was a *subject variable* in this study; that is, the participants' culture was a pre-existing condition that they brought with them to the study, rather than a condition to which they were randomly assigned. The researchers treated this subject variable as an independent variable in the analysis, but if this had been the only variation in the study, it would not have been a true experiment because it would have lacked random assignment. (Another subject variable in this study was the gender of the participants—some were male and some female. We'll ignore that variable in this discussion, in part because it did not make a difference in any of the results that Vandello and Cohen found.)

The *independent variable* in this study was the version of the story the students read—participants were randomly assigned to read either the story in which the wife did not cheat on her husband, or the story in which she was unfaithful to him. Table 2.4 summarizes the design of the experiment.

TABLE 2.4
Female Infidelity, Male Honor, and Culture: The Conditions

In Vandello and Cohen's experiment, participants from either Brazil or the northern United States read about a man whose wife was either faithful or unfaithful to him. Combining these two variables—culture and the wife's behavior—creates the four conditions displayed here. (*Based on Vandello & Cohen, 2003.*)

	Northern United States	**Brazil**
	Condition 1	Condition 2
Wife is faithful	U.S./Faithful	Brazil/Faithful
	Condition 3	Condition 4
Wife is unfaithful	U.S./Unfaithful	Brazil/Unfaithful

FIGURE 2.3

Female Infidelity, Male Honor, and Culture: The Results

This graph shows how U.S. and Brazilian students rated a man's manliness when his wife was either faithful or unfaithful. In general, students rated a man as less manly if his wife was unfaithful to him than if his wife was faithful. Also in general, students from the northern United States tended to rate the man as more manly than did students from Brazil. But the *interaction* between these two variables is most relevant for this study: The effect of the wife's unfaithfulness on ratings of the man's reputation was much stronger among Brazilian students than among American students.   (Based on Vandello & Cohen, 2003, 2005.)

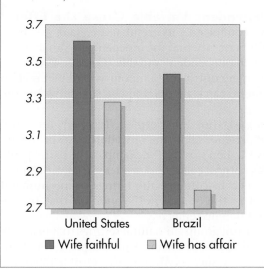

United States   Brazil

■ Wife faithful   ▢ Wife has affair

One of the outcomes studied in this research (a *dependent variable*) was the students' ratings of the man's "manliness." Vandello and Cohen took an average of each student's ratings on several dimensions related to the construct of manliness, such as masculinity, courage, and strength. The higher the average rating (on a 5-point scale), the more they saw him as "manly."

What were the researchers looking for in this study? They wanted to test the hypothesis that the students from the more honor-focused culture (i.e., Brazil) would be more affected by the wife's behavior in their ratings of the man than would the students from the less honor-based culture.

Figure 2.3 depicts the results of this study. One question we might ask at this point is whether there was a main effect for the independent variable concerning the wife's behavior. In other words, did the students who read that she cheated on her husband tend to rate the husband as being less manly than did the students who read that she was faithful? Remember, for a main effect, you look at the effect of one independent variable but ignore the effect of any other independent (or subject) variables, so for now we ignore the difference between American and Brazilian participants. If you look closely at the figure, comparing just the average scores of the students in the "faithful" conditions with those in the "unfaithful" conditions (ignoring the variable of culture), you should see that the man did tend to be rated as more manly if his wife was faithful than if she was unfaithful. That is, the teal bars tend to be higher than the gold bars. In short, there is a main effect for the manipulation of the wife's behavior.

Next, we can examine if there is a main effect for culture. Although it is a subject variable, we can treat it as an independent variable in these analyses, to see if there is a difference in the ratings of the man as a function of the students' culture. The figure suggests there is a main effect for culture, since the students from the United States tended to rate the man as more manly than did the students from Brazil. Again, to assess the main effect, we ignore other independent variables, so here we ignore whether the story was about the faithful or unfaithful wife. It does appear, then, that there is a main effect for culture in this study.

Why would the U.S. students rate the husband as more manly than the students from Brazil? If you look closely at the graph, you can see that the difference between the U.S. sample and the Brazil sample was pretty small when the wife was described as faithful; the difference was large only if the wife was described as unfaithful. This illustrates why it is important to look for the *interaction* between the two independent variables.

To look for the interaction, ask yourself, "Does the effect of one independent variable change as a function of the other independent variable?" To the extent that it does, there is an interaction between the two variables. So, in this study, did the *effect* of the manipulation of the wife's infidelity change as a function of whether the students were from the United States or Brazil? Yes. That is, although *in general* students rated the husband as less manly if his wife was unfaithful, this difference was especially great among students from Brazil. Similarly, although *in general* students from Brazil rated the husband as less manly than did the students from the United States, this difference was especially great if his wife was unfaithful.

So, the researchers' hypothesis was supported by the data. The wife's fidelity did have more of an impact on the man's reputation in Brazil than in the United States, which is consistent with the theory and research concerning cultures of honor. Vandello and Cohen believe that these results have implications for the issue of domestic violence, and we will return to this issue in Chapter 11.

Statistical Significance   Another close look at the results in Figure 2.3 reveals that the average scores in the four conditions in Vandello and Cohen's experiment differed by only fractions of a point on a 5-point scale. Are such differences large enough to be meaningful, or could they simply be due to chance? After all, if you flip a coin ten times, you might get six tails and four heads. Is the difference between 6 and 4 a meaningful difference? Surely it isn't—one could expect differences like this from random luck alone. Results obtained in an experiment are examined with statistical analyses that allow the researcher to determine how likely it is that the results could have occurred by chance. The standard convention is that if the results could have occurred by chance 5 or fewer times in 100 possible outcomes, then the result is *statistically significant* and should be taken seriously.

The fact that results are statistically significant does not mean that they are absolutely certain. In essence, statistical significance is an attractive betting proposition. The odds are quite good (at least 95 out of 100) that the effects obtained in the study were due to the experimental manipulation of the independent variable. But there is still the possibility (as high as 5 out of 100) that the findings occurred by chance. This is one reason why it is important to try to *replicate* the results of an experiment—to repeat the experiment and see if similar results are found. If similar results are found, the probability that these results could have occurred by chance both times is 5 percent times 5 percent, or one-quarter of 1 percent (which equals 1 time in 400 possible outcomes).

Internal Validity: Did the Independent Variable Cause the Effect?

When an experiment is properly conducted, its results are said to have **internal validity**: There is reasonable certainty that the independent variable did, in fact, cause the effects obtained on the dependent variable (Cook & Campbell, 1979). As noted earlier, both experimenter control and random assignment seek to rule out alternative explanations of the research results, thereby strengthening the internal validity of the research.

Experiments also include *control groups* for this purpose. Typically, a control group consists of participants who experience all of the procedures except the experimental treatment. In Vandello and Cohen's study, for example, the participants in the condition in which the wife was faithful could be considered a control group, which provided a baseline against which to compare the ratings of the husband when the wife was unfaithful. It was in the "unfaithful" condition that the researchers expected to see the cultural difference emerge.

Outside the laboratory, creating control groups in natural settings that examine real-life events raises many practical and ethical problems. For example, research on new medical treatments for deadly diseases, such as AIDS, faces a terrible dilemma. Individuals randomly assigned to the control group receive the standard treatment, but they are excluded for the duration of the study from what could turn out to be a life-saving new intervention. Yet without such a comparison, it is extremely difficult to determine which new treatments are effective and which are useless. Although some AIDS activists oppose including control groups in treatment research, others have become more supportive of this approach (Gorman, 1994; Rothman & Rothman, 2006).

In assessing internal validity, researchers need to consider their own role as well. Unwittingly, they can sometimes sabotage their own research. For example, imagine you are a researcher and you know what conditions the participants in your study have been assigned to. You will no doubt have expectations, and possibly even fervent hopes, about how your participants will respond differently between conditions. Without realizing it, then, because of these expectations, you may treat the participants a little differently between conditions. It turns out that even very subtle differences in an experimenter's behavior can influence participants' behavior (Rosenthal, 1976). Therefore, the results you find in your experiment may be produced by *your own* actions rather than by the independent variable!

The best way to protect an experiment from the influence of experimenters' expectations—called **experimenter expectancy effects**—is to keep experimenters uninformed about assignments to conditions. If they do not know the condition to which a participant has been assigned, they cannot treat participants

internal validity   The degree to which there can be reasonable certainty that the independent variables in an experiment caused the effects obtained on the dependent variables.

experimenter expectancy effects   The effects produced when an experimenter's expectations about the results of an experiment affect his or her behavior toward a participant and thereby influence the participant's responses.

differently as a function of their condition. Of course, there may be times when keeping experimenters uninformed is impossible or impractical. In such cases, the opportunity for experimenter expectancy effects to occur can at least be reduced—specifically, by minimizing the interaction between experimenters and participants. For example, rather than receiving instructions directly from an experimenter, participants can be asked to read the instructions on a computer screen.

External Validity: Do the Results Generalize?   In addition to guarding internal validity, researchers are concerned about **external validity**, the extent to which the results obtained under one set of circumstances would also occur in a different set of circumstances (Berkowitz & Donnerstein, 1982). When an experiment has external validity, its findings can be assumed to generalize to other people and to other situations. Both the participants in the experiment and the setting in which it takes place affect external validity.

Because social psychologists often seek to establish universal principles of human behavior, their ideal sample of participants should be representative of all human beings all over the world. Such an all-inclusive representative sample has never been seen and probably never will be. Representative samples of more limited populations do exist and can be achieved by random sampling of a population, which was discussed earlier in the chapter. But, as also mentioned earlier, social psychologists rarely study representative samples. Usually, they rely on convenience samples drawn from populations that are readily available to them, which explains why so much of social psychological research is conducted on college students.

There are very practical reasons for the use of convenience samples. Representative samples are fine for surveys requiring short answers to a short list of questions. But what about complex, time-consuming experiments? The expense of bringing participants from diverse geographic areas into the lab would be staggering. And various extraneous variables (travel fatigue, disruptions in regular routines) could distort the results. Advocates of convenience samples also contend that there is no contradiction between universal principles and particular participants. Indeed, the more basic the principle, the less it matters who participates in the research. For example, various people or cultures might differ in the *form* of aggression they typically exhibit when angry; but the situational factors that cause people to be *more likely to* aggress—in whatever way that aggression is expressed—may be similar for most individuals across time and place. Yet in spite of these arguments, the drawbacks to convenience samples are clear—an important consideration given the need for social psychology to become more inclusive. The growing interest in cross-cultural research in the field is certainly one step in the right direction.

External validity is also affected by the setting in which the research is conducted. Because field research occurs in real-life natural settings rather than in the artificial arrangements of a laboratory, aren't its results more generalizable to actual behavior? The answer depends on where you stand on the issue of mundane versus experimental realism (Aronson & Carlsmith, 1968).

Mundane realism refers to the extent to which the research setting resembles the real-world setting of interest. In order to study interpersonal attraction, Theodore Newcomb (1961) set up an entire college dormitory—a striking example of mundane realism. Advocates of mundane realism contend that if research procedures are more realistic, research findings are more likely to reveal what really goes on.

In contrast, **experimental realism** refers to the degree to which the experimental setting and procedures are real and involving to the participant, regardless of whether they resemble real life or not. According to those who favor experimental realism, if the experimental situation is compelling and real to the participants while they are participating in the study, their behavior in the lab—even if the lab is in the basement of the psychology building—will be as natural and spontaneous as their behavior in the real world. The majority of social psychologists who conduct experiments emphasize experimental realism.

external validity The degree to which there can be reasonable confidence that the results of a study would be obtained for other people and in other situations.

mundane realism The degree to which the experimental situation resembles places and events in the real world.

experimental realism The degree to which experimental procedures are involving to participants and lead them to behave naturally and spontaneously.

The settings in which children attend school can vary dramatically across cultures. Here students sit outside in a class in Imbabura, Ecuador. Recognizing cultural variation has become increasingly important in social psychology today, and social psychologists are conducting their research across a wider range of cultures and contexts than ever before.

Deception in Experiments Researchers who strive to create a highly involving experience for participants often rely on **deception**, providing participants with false information about experimental procedures. Toward this end, social psychologists sometimes employ **confederates**, who act as though they are participants in the experiment but are really working for the experimenter. For example, in Solomon Asch's (1956) classic research on conformity, research participants made judgments about the lengths of lines while in the midst of a number of confederates—pretending to be ordinary participants—who at various times all gave wrong answers. The researchers wanted to see if the real participants would conform to the confederates and give the obviously wrong answer that the confederates had given. Although it was a very odd setting, the situation was a very real one to the participants, many of whom clearly struggled with the decision about whether or not to conform.

Deception not only strengthens experimental realism but also confers other benefits: It allows the experimenter to manufacture situations in the laboratory that would be difficult to find in a natural setting, such as a regulated, safe environment in which to study a potentially harmful behavior like aggression. Studies have shown that participants are rarely bothered by deception and often particularly enjoy studies that use it (Smith & Richardson, 1983). Nevertheless, the use of deception creates some serious ethical concerns, which we examine later in this chapter.

🔵 Meta-Analysis: Combining Results Across Studies

We have seen that social psychologists conduct original descriptive, correlational, and experimental studies to test their hypotheses. Another way to test hypotheses in social psychology is to use a set of statistical procedures to examine, in a new way, relevant research that has already been conducted and reported. This technique is called **meta-analysis**. By "meta-analyzing" the results of a number of studies that have been conducted in different places and by different researchers, a social psychologist can measure precisely how strong and reliable particular effects are. For example, studies published concerning the effects of alcohol on aggression may sometimes contradict each other. Sometimes alcohol increases aggression; sometimes it doesn't. By combining the data from all the studies that are relevant to this hypothesis and conducting a meta-analysis, a researcher can determine what effect alcohol typically has, how strong that effect typically is, and perhaps under what specific conditions that effect is most likely to occur. This technique, which was developed relatively recently, is being used with increasing frequency in social psychology today, and we report the results of many meta-analyses in this textbook.

deception In the context of research, a method that provides false information to participants.

confederate Accomplice of an experimenter who, in dealing with the real participants in an experiment, acts as if he or she is also a participant.

meta-analysis A set of statistical procedures used to review a body of evidence by combining the results of individual studies to measure the overall reliability and strength of particular effects.

Culture and Research Methods

Earlier in this chapter we described an experiment that examined the reactions of students from the northern United States and Brazil to a story about a woman who did or did not cheat on her husband (Vandello & Cohen, 2003). This study is but one example of the growing interest in studying culture in social psychology. One of the advantages of this approach is that it provides better tests of the external validity of the research that has been conducted in any one setting. By examining whether the results of an experiment generalize to a very different culture, social psychologists can begin to answer questions about the universality or cultural specificity of their research. It is important to keep in mind that when a finding in one culture does not generalize well to another culture, this should be seen not simply as a failure to replicate but also as an opportunity to learn about potentially interesting and important cultural differences, and how and why these differences affect the issue being studied.

As important and exciting as these cultural investigations are, however, they offer special challenges to researchers. For one thing, there are important cultural differences in the assumptions individuals make and the information they tend to give as they respond to questions on a survey (Schwarz, 2007). Susanne Haberstroh and others (2002), for example, found that individuals from a culture that promotes interdependent, collectivistic values and self-concepts (such as China) are more likely to take into account question context when completing a questionnaire than are respondents from cultures associated with a more independent, individualistic orientation (such as Germany). Another difference between cultures concerns how willing people are to answer personal questions as part of a research study. North Americans are used to answering personal questions, for example, but people in some cultures feel much more uncomfortable talking about themselves (Fiske, 2002). It can also be difficult for researchers to translate materials from one language into another. Although it is relatively easy to create literal translations, it can be surprisingly challenging to create translations that have the same meaning to people from various cultures. Table 2.5 presents examples—from signs displayed around the world—of what can go wrong when simple sentences are poorly translated.

TABLE 2.5

Lost in Translation

- "Drop your trousers here for best results." *(a dry cleaner in Thailand)*
- "You are invited to take advantage of the chambermaid." *(a hotel in Japan)*
- "Ladies are requested not to have children in the bar." *(a cocktail lounge in Mexico)*
- "Take one of our horse-driven city tours—we guarantee no miscarriages." *(a tourist agency in the former Czechoslovakia)*
- "We take your bags and send them in all directions." *(an airline in Denmark)*

Source: **Triandis (1994).**

Ethics and Values in Social Psychology

Regardless of where research is conducted and what method is used, ethical issues must always be considered. Researchers in all fields have a moral and legal responsibility to abide by ethical principles. In social psychology, the use of deception has caused particular concern (Bersoff, 2003; Lawson, 2001; Ortmann & Hertwig, 1997), and several studies have provoked fierce debate about whether they went beyond the bounds of ethical acceptability. For example, Stanley Milgram (1963) designed a series of experiments to address the question "Would people obey orders to harm an innocent person?" To test this question, he put volunteers into a situation in which an experimenter commanded them to administer painful electric shocks to someone they thought was another volunteer participant (in fact, the other person was a confederate who was not actually receiving any shocks). The experiment had extremely high experimental realism—many of the participants experienced a great deal of anxiety and stress as they debated whether they should disobey the experimenter or continue to inflict pain on another person. The details and results of this experiment will be discussed in Chapter 7 on Conformity, but suffice it to say that the results of the study made people realize how prevalent and powerful obedience can be.

Milgram's research was inspired by the obedience displayed by Nazi officers in World War II. No one disputes the importance of his research question. What has been debated, however, is whether the significance of the research topic justified exposing participants to possibly harmful psychological consequences. Under today's provisions for the protection of human participants, Milgram's classic experiments probably could not be conducted in their original form. (In an interesting twist, while conducting an experiment like Milgram's might be impossible now, in popular culture today individuals are put through far greater stress and even humiliation in numerous unscripted TV shows such as *Fear Factor* and *Punk'd*.)

Milgram's research was by no means the only social psychological research to trigger debates about ethics. Several studies in the history of social psychology have sparked a great deal of controversy. And it is not only the controversial studies that receive scrutiny. Today, virtually every prospective social psychology study is evaluated for its ethics by other people before the study can be conducted. In the following sections, we describe current policies and procedures as well as continuing concerns about ethics and values in social psychological research.

Institutional Review Boards and Informed Consent: Protecting Research Participants

In 1974, the agency then called the United States Department of Health, Education, and Welfare established regulations for the protection of human participants in research. These regulations created institutional review boards (IRBs) at all institutions seeking federal funding for research involving human participants. Charged with the responsibility for reviewing research proposals to ensure that the welfare of participants was adequately protected, IRBs were to be the "watchdogs" of research.

Besides submitting their research to government-mandated IRBs, researchers must also abide by their profession's code of ethics. The statement of ethics of the American Psychological Association (APA), called *Ethical Principles of Psychologists and Code of Conduct* (1992), considers a wide range of ethical issues, including those related to research procedures and practices. The APA code stipulates that researchers are obligated to guard the rights and welfare of all those who participate in their studies.

One such obligation is to obtain **informed consent**. Individuals must be asked whether they wish to participate in the research project and must be given enough information to make an informed decision. Deceiving research participants about "significant aspects that would affect their willingness to participate, such as physical risks, discomfort, or unpleasant emotional experiences," is explicitly prohibited, although withholding less vital information is presumably allowed. Participants must also know that they are free to withdraw from participation in the research at any point. The APA code also recognizes that research "involving only anonymous questionnaires, naturalistic observations, or certain kinds of archival research" may not require informed consent.

Debriefing: Telling All

Have you ever participated in psychological research? If so, what was your reaction to this experience? Have you ever been deceived about the hypothesis or procedures of a study in which you were a participant? If so, how did you feel about it? Most research on participants' reactions indicates that they have positive attitudes about their participation, even when they were deceived about some aspects of a study (Christensen, 1988; Epley & Huff, 1998). Indeed, deceived participants sometimes have expressed more favorable opinions than those who have not been deceived, presumably because studies involving deception are often interesting and creative (Smith & Richardson, 1983).

informed consent An individual's deliberate, voluntary decision to participate in research, based on the researcher's description of what will be required during such participation.

"What if these guys in white coats who bring us food are, like, studying us and we're part of some kind of big experiment?"

One reason for the use of deception in an experiment is so that the participants will act more naturally when they are not aware of what is being studied. In these cases it is especially important for the researchers to provide a full and thorough debriefing.

These findings are reassuring, but they do not remove the obligation of researchers to use deception only when non-deceptive alternatives are not feasible. In addition, whenever deception has been used, there is a special urgency to the requirement that, once the data have been collected, researchers fully inform their participants about the nature of the research in which they have participated. This process of disclosure is called **debriefing**. During a debriefing, the researcher goes over all procedures, explaining exactly what happened and why. Deceptions are revealed, the purpose of the research is discussed, and the researcher makes every effort to help the participant feel good about having participated. A skillful debriefing takes time and requires close attention to the individual participant.

Values and Science: Points of View

Ethical principles are based on moral values. These values set standards for and impose limits on the conduct of research, just as they influence individuals' personal behavior. Ethical issues are an appropriate focus for moral values in science, but do values affect science in other ways as well? Although many people hold science to a standard of complete objectivity, science can probably never be completely unbiased and objective because it is a human enterprise. Scientists choose what to study and how to study it; their choices are affected by personal values as well as by professional rewards. Indeed, some think that values *should* fuel scientific research, and scientists would be not only naïve but also irresponsible to try to keep values out of the picture.

Most—although certainly not all—social psychologists would probably agree with a position offered by Stanley Parkinson (1994): "Scientists are not necessarily more objective than other people; rather, they use methods that have been developed to minimize self-deception" (p. 137). By scrutinizing their own behavior and adopting the rigors of the scientific method, scientists attempt to free themselves of their preconceptions and, thereby, to see reality more clearly, even if never perfectly.

As you read about the research reported throughout this book, you might stop every now and then to consider what *you* think about the role of values in science. Do you think values influence the work done by social psychologists? Do you think values *should* affect scientific inquiry?

Your introduction to the field of social psychology is now complete. In these first two chapters, you have gone step by step through a definition of social psychology, a review of its history and discussion of its future, an overview of its research methods, and a consideration of ethics and values. As you study the material presented in the coming chapters, the three of us who wrote this book invite you to share our enthusiasm. You can look forward to information that overturns common-sense assumptions, to lively debate and heated controversy, and to a better understanding of yourself and other people. Welcome to the world according to social psychology. We hope you enjoy it!

"[Objectivity in science] is willingness (even the eagerness in truly honorable practitioners) to abandon a favored notion when testable evidence disconfirms key expectations."

—Stephen Jay Gould

debriefing A disclosure, made to participants after research procedures are completed, in which the researcher explains the purpose of the research, attempts to resolve any negative feelings, and emphasizes the scientific contribution made by the participants' involvement.

REVIEW

Why Should You Learn About Research Methods?

- Because common sense and intuitive ideas about social psychological issues can be misleading and contradictory, it is important to understand the scientific evidence on which social psychological theories and findings are based.

- Studying research methods in psychology improves people's reasoning about real-life events and information presented by the media and other sources.

Developing Ideas: Beginning the Research Process

Asking Questions

- Ideas for research in social psychology come from everywhere—personal experiences and observations, events in the news, and other research.

Searching the Literature

- Before pursuing a research idea, it is important to see what research has already been done on this and related topics.
- Electronic databases provide access to a wealth of information, both in the psychology literature and in more general sources.

Hypotheses and Theories

- Formulating a hypothesis is a critical step toward planning and conducting research.

- Theories in social psychology are specific rather than comprehensive and generate research that can support or disconfirm them. They should be revised and improved as a result of the research they inspire.

Basic and Applied Research

- The goal of basic research is to increase understanding of human behavior.
- The goal of applied research is to increase understanding of real-world events and contribute to the solution of social problems.

Refining Ideas: Defining and Measuring Social Psychological Variables

Conceptual Variables and Operational Definitions: From the Abstract to the Specific

- Researchers often must transform abstract, conceptual variables into specific operational definitions that indicate exactly how the variables are to be manipulated or measured.
- Construct validity is the extent to which the operational definitions successfully manipulate or measure the conceptual variables to which they correspond.

Measuring Variables: Using Self-Reports, Observations, and Technology

- In self-reports, participants indicate their thoughts, feelings, desires, and actions.
- Self-reports can be distorted by efforts to make a good impression, as well as by the effects of the wording and context of questions.

- To increase the accuracy of self-reports, some approaches emphasize the need to collect self-reports as soon as possible after participants experience the relevant thoughts, feelings, or behaviors.
- Narrative studies analyze the content of lengthy responses on a general topic.
- Observations are another way for social psychologists to measure variables.
- Interrater reliability, or the level of agreement among multiple observers of the same behavior, is important when measuring variables using observation.
- New and improved technologies enable researchers to measure physiological responses, reaction times, eye movements, and activity in regions of the brain.

Testing Ideas: Research Designs

- Most social psychologists test their ideas by using objective, systematic, and quantifiable methods.

Descriptive Research: Discovering Trends and Tendencies

- In descriptive research, social psychologists record how frequently or typically people think, feel, or behave in particular ways.
- One form of descriptive research is observational research, in which researchers observe individuals systematically, often in natural settings.
- In archival research, researchers examine existing records and documents such as newspaper articles, diaries, and published crime statistics.
- Surveys involve asking people questions about their attitudes, beliefs, and behaviors.
- Survey researchers identify the population to which they want the results of the survey to generalize, and they select a sample of people from that population to take the survey.
- To best ensure a sample that is representative of the broader population, researchers should randomly select people from the population to be in the survey.

Correlational Research: Looking for Associations

- Correlational research examines the association between variables.
- A correlation coefficient is a measure of the strength and direction of the association between two variables.
- Positive correlations indicate that as scores on one variable increase, scores on the other variable increase; and that as scores on one variable decrease, scores on the other decrease.
- Negative correlations indicate that as scores on one variable increase, scores on the other decrease.
- Correlation does not indicate causation; the fact that two variables are correlated does not necessarily mean that one causes the other.
- Correlations can be used for prediction and for generating hypotheses.

Experiments: Looking for Cause and Effect

- Experiments require (1) control by the experimenter over events in the study and (2) random assignment of participants to conditions.
- Random sampling concerns how people are selected to be in a study, whereas random assignment concerns how people who are in the study are assigned to the different conditions of the study.

- Experiments are often conducted in a laboratory so that the researchers can have control over the context and can measure variables precisely.
- Field experiments are conducted in real-world settings outside the laboratory.
- Experiments examine the effects of one or more independent variables on one or more dependent variables.
- Subject variables are variables that characterize pre-existing differences among the participants.
- In a main effect, the levels of a single independent variable produce differences in the dependent variable; this effect is independent of (not related to) the effects of any other independent variables.
- In an interaction, the effect of one independent variable on the dependent variable changes as a function of another independent variable; thus, the independent variables jointly affect the dependent variable.
- Results that are statistically significant could have occurred by chance 5 or fewer times in 100 possible outcomes.
- Experimental findings have internal validity to the extent that changes in the dependent variable can be attributed to the independent variables.
- Control groups strengthen internal validity; experimenter expectancy effects weaken it.
- Research results have external validity to the extent that they can be generalized to other people and other situations.
- A representative sample strengthens external validity; a convenience sample weakens it.
- Mundane realism is the extent to which the research setting seems similar to real-world situations.
- Experimental realism is the extent to which the participants experience the experimental setting and procedures as real and involving.
- Deception is sometimes used to increase experimental realism.
- Confederates act as though they are participants in an experiment but actually work for the experimenter.

Meta-Analysis: Combining Results Across Studies

- Meta-analysis uses statistical techniques to integrate the quantitative results of different studies.

Culture and Research Methods

- There is growing interest in studying the role of culture in social psychology.
- As important and exciting as these cultural investigations are, they offer special challenges to researchers.

Ethics and Values in Social Psychology

- Ethical issues are particularly important in social psychology because of the use of deception in some research.

Institutional Review Boards and Informed Consent: Protecting Research Participants

- Established by the federal government, IRBs are responsible for reviewing research proposals to ensure that the welfare of participants is adequately protected.
- The American Psychological Association's code of ethics requires psychologists to secure informed consent from research participants.

Debriefing: Telling All

- Most participants have positive attitudes about their participation in research, even if they were deceived about some aspects of the study.

- Whenever deception has been used in a study, a full debriefing is essential; the researchers must disclose the facts about the study and make sure that the participant does not experience any distress.

Values and Science: Points of View

- Moral values set standards for and impose limits on the conduct of research.
- There are various views on the relation between values and science. Few believe that there can be a completely value-free science, but some advocate trying to minimize the influence of values on science, whereas others argue that values should be recognized and encouraged as an important factor in science.

KEY TERMS

applied research (27)

basic research (27)

confederate (44)

construct validity (28)

correlation coefficient (35)

correlational research (34)

debriefing (47)

deception (44)

dependent variables (39)

experiment (37)

experimental realism (43)

experimenter expectancy
  effects (42)

external validity (43)

hypothesis (26)

independent variables (38)

informed consent (46)

interaction (39)

internal validity (42)

interrater reliability (30)

main effect (39)

meta-analysis (44)

mundane realism (43)

operational definition (28)

random assignment (37)

random sampling (34)

subject variables (39)

theory (26)

3

The Social Self

PREVIEW

This chapter examines three interrelated aspects of the "social self."
First, it considers the *self-concept* and the question of how people come
to understand their own actions, emotions, and motivations. Second, it
considers *self-esteem*, the affective component, and the question of how
people evaluate themselves and defend against threats to their self-
esteem. Third, it considers *self-presentation*, a behavioral manifestation of
the self, and the question of how people present themselves to others.
As we will see, the self is complex and multifaceted.

PUTTING COMMON SENSE TO THE TEST

T/F

_____ Humans are the only animals who recognize themselves in the mirror.

_____ Smiling can make you feel happier.

_____ Sometimes the harder you try to control a thought, feeling, or behavior, the less likely you are to succeed.

_____ People often sabotage their own performance in order to protect their self-esteem.

_____ It's more adaptive to alter one's behavior than to stay consistent from one social situation to the next.

Can you imagine living a meaningful or coherent life without a clear sense of who you are? In *The Man Who Mistook His Wife for a Hat*, neurologist Oliver Sacks (1985) described such a person—a patient named William Thompson. According to Sacks, Thompson suffered from an organic brain disorder that impairs a person's memory of recent events. Unable to recall anything for more than a few seconds, Thompson was always disoriented and lacked a sense of inner continuity. The effect on his behavior was startling. Trying to grasp a constantly vanishing identity, Thompson would construct one tale after another to account for who he was, where he was, and what he was doing. From one moment to the next, he would improvise new identities—a grocery store clerk, minister, or medical patient, to name just a few. In social settings, Thompson's behavior was especially intriguing. As Sacks (1985) observed,

> The presence of others, other people, excite and rattle him, force him into an endless, frenzied, social chatter, a veritable delirium of identity-making and -seeking; the presence of plants, a quiet garden, the nonhuman order, making no social demands upon him, allow this identity-delirium to relax, to subside. (p. 110)

Thompson's plight is unusual, but it highlights two important points—one about the private "inner" self, the other about the "outer" self we show to others. First, the capacity for self-reflection is necessary for people to feel as if they understand their own motives and emotions and the causes of their behavior. Unable to ponder his own actions, Thompson appeared vacant and without feeling—"desouled," as Sacks put it. Second, the self is heavily influenced by social factors. Thompson himself seemed compelled to put on a face for others and to improvise characters for the company he kept. We all do, to some extent. We may not create a kaleidoscope of multiple identities as Thompson did, but the way we manage ourselves is influenced by the people around us.

This chapter examines the ABCs of the self: *affect*, *behavior*, and *cognition*. First, we ask the cognitive question: How do people come to know themselves, develop a self-concept, and maintain a stable sense of identity? Second, we explore an affective, or emotional, question: How do people evaluate themselves, enhance their self-images, and defend against threats to their self-esteem? Third, we confront a behavioral question: How do people regulate their own actions and present themselves to others according to interpersonal demands? As we'll see, the self is a topic that in recent years has attracted unprecedented interest among social psychologists (Leary & Tangney, 2003; Tesser et al., 2005; Vohs & Finkel, 2006).

The Self-Concept

Have you ever been at a noisy gathering—holding a drink in one hand and a spring roll in the other, struggling to have a conversation over music and the chatter of voices—and yet managed to hear someone at the other end of the room mention your name? If so, then you have experienced the "cocktail party effect"—the tendency of people to pick a personally relevant stimulus, like a name, out of a complex and noisy environment (Cherry, 1953; Wood & Cowan, 1995). Even infants who are too young to walk or talk exhibit this tendency (Newman, 2005). To the cognitive psychologist, this phenomenon shows that human beings are selective in their attention. To the social psychologist, it also shows that the self is an important object of our own attention.

The term **self-concept** refers to the sum total of beliefs that people have about themselves. But what, specifically, does the self-concept consist of? According to Hazel Markus (1977), the self-concept is made up of cognitive molecules called **self-schemas**: beliefs about oneself that guide the processing of self-relevant information. Self-schemas are to an individual's total self-concept what hypotheses are to a theory, or what books are to a library. You can think of yourself as masculine or feminine, as independent or dependent, as liberal or conservative, as introverted or extroverted. Indeed, any specific attribute may have relevance to the self-concept for some people but not for others. The self-schema for body weight is a good example. Men and women who regard themselves as extremely overweight or underweight, or for whom body image is a conspicuous aspect of the self-concept, are considered *schematic* with respect to weight. For body-weight schematics, a wide range of otherwise mundane events—a trip to the supermarket, new clothing, dinner at a restaurant, a day at the beach, or a friend's eating habits—may trigger thoughts about the self. In contrast, those who do not regard their own weight as extreme or as an important part of their lives are *aschematic* on that attribute (Markus et al., 1987).

Rudiments of the Self-Concept

Clearly, the self is a special object of our attention. Whether you are mentally focused on a memory, a conversation, a foul odor, the song in your head, your growling stomach, or this sentence, consciousness is like a "spotlight." It can shine on only one object at a point in time, but it can shift rapidly from one object to another and process information outside of awareness. In this spotlight, the self is front and center. But is the self so special that it is uniquely represented in the neural circuitry of the brain? And is the self a uniquely human concept, or do other animals also distinguish the self from everything else?

Is the Self Specially Represented in the Brain? As illustrated by the opening story of William Thompson, our sense of identity is biologically rooted. In *The Synaptic Self: How Our Brains Become Who We Are*, neuroscientist Joseph LeDoux (2002) argues that the synaptic connections within the brain provide the biological base for memory, which makes possible the sense of continuity that is needed for a normal identity. In *The Lost Self: Pathologies of the Brain and Identity*, Todd Feinberg and Julian Keenan (2005) describe how the self can be transformed, and even destroyed, by severe head injuries, brain tumors, diseases, and exposure to toxic substances that damage the brain and nervous system.

Social neuroscientists are just now starting to explore these possibilities. Using PET scans, fMRI, and other imaging techniques that can photograph the brain in action, these researchers are finding that certain areas become more active when laboratory participants see a picture of themselves rather than a picture of others (Platek et al., 2006), when they try to judge whether trait words are descriptive of themselves rather than of others (Kelley et al., 2002), and when they take a first-

self-concept The sum total of an individual's beliefs about his or her own personal attributes.

self-schema A belief people hold about themselves that guides the processing of self-relevant information.

Infants begin to recognize them-selves in the mirror at eighteen to twenty-four months of age.

person perspective while playing a video game as opposed to a third-person perspective (David et al., 2006). As we will see throughout this chapter, the self is a frame of reference that powerfully influences our thoughts, feelings, and behaviors in complex ways. Not all aspects of the self are housed in a single structure of the brain. However, the bulk of research does seem to suggest that various self-based processes can be traced to activities occurring in certain areas of the brain (Northoff & Bermpohl, 2004; Northoff et al., 2006).

Do Nonhuman Animals Show Self-Recognition? When you stand in front of a mirror, you recognize the image as a reflection of yourself. But what about dogs, cats, and other animals—how can we possibly know what nonhumans think about mirrors? In a series of studies, Gordon Gallup (1977) placed different species of animals in a room with a large mirror. At first, they greeted their own images by vocalizing, gesturing, and making other social responses. After several days, only great apes (chimpanzees, gorillas, and orangutans)—but not other animals—seemed capable of self-recognition, using the mirror to pick food out of their teeth, groom themselves, blow bubbles, and make faces for their own entertainment. From all appearances, the apes recognized themselves.

In other studies, Gallup anesthetized the animals, then painted an odorless red dye on their brows and returned them to the mirror. Upon seeing the red spot, only the apes spontaneously reached for their own brows—proof that they perceived the image as their own (Povinelli et al., 1997; Keenan et al., 2003). Among apes, this form of self-recognition emerges in young adolescence and is stable across the life span, at least until old age (de Veer et al., 2003). By using a similar red dye test (without anesthetizing the infants), developmental psychologists have found that most human infants begin to recognize themselves in the mirror between the ages of eighteen and twenty-four months (Lewis & Brooks-Gunn, 1979). Today, many researchers believe that self-recognition among great apes and human infants is the first clear expression of the concept "me" (Boysen & Himes, 1999). In an interesting recent study, researchers at the New York Aquarium found that two bottlenose dolphins marked with black ink also exhibited self-recognition, often stopping to examine themselves in a mirror (Reiss & Marino, 2001).

What Makes the Self a Social Concept? The ability to see yourself as a distinct entity in the world is a necessary first step in the evolution and development of a self-concept. The second step involves social factors. Sociologist Charles Horton Cooley (1902) introduced the term *looking-glass self* to suggest that other people serve as a mirror in which we see ourselves. Expanding on this idea, George Herbert Mead (1934) added that we often come to know ourselves by imagining what significant others think of us and then incorporating these perceptions into our self-concepts.

Picking up where the classic sociologists left off, Susan Andersen and Serena Chen (2002) theorized that the self is "relational"—that we draw our sense of who we are from our past and current relationships with the significant others in our lives. It is interesting that when Gallup tested his apes, those that had been raised in isolation—without exposure to peers—did not recognize themselves in the mirror. Only after such exposure did they begin to show signs of self-recognition. Among human beings, our self-concepts match our *perceptions* of what others think of us.

But there's an important hitch: What we think of ourselves often does not match what specific others *actually* think of us (Kenny & DePaulo, 1993; Shrauger & Schoeneman, 1979; Tice & Wallace, 2003).

In recent years, social psychologists have broken new ground in the effort to understand the social self. People are not born thinking of themselves as reckless, likable, shy, or outgoing. So where do their self-concepts come from? In the coming pages, five sources are considered: introspection, perceptions of our own behavior, the influences of other people, autobiographical memories, and the cultures in which we live.

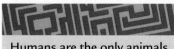

Humans are the only animals who recognize themselves in the mirror. **False.**

Introspection

Let's start at the beginning: How do people achieve insight into their own beliefs, attitudes, emotions, and motivations? Common sense makes this question seem ludicrous. After all, don't you know what you think because *you* think it? And don't you know how you feel because *you* feel it? Look through popular books on how to achieve self-insight, and you'll find the unambiguous answers to these questions to be yes. Whether the prescribed technique is yoga, meditation, psychotherapy, religion, dream analysis, or hypnosis, the advice is basically the same: Self-knowledge is derived from introspection, a looking inward at one's own thoughts and feelings.

If these how-to books are correct, it stands to reason that no one can know you as well as you know yourself. Thus, people tend to assume that for others to know you at all, they would need information about your private thoughts, feelings, and other inner states—not just your behavior. But is this really the case? Most social psychologists are not sure that this faith in introspection is justified. Several years ago, Richard Nisbett and Timothy Wilson (1977) found that research participants often cannot accurately explain the causes or correlates of their own behavior. This observation forced researchers to confront a thorny question: Does introspection provide a direct pipeline to self-knowledge?

In *Strangers to Ourselves*, Wilson (2002) argues that it does not. In fact, he finds that introspection can sometimes impair self-knowledge. In a series of studies, he found that the attitudes people reported having about different objects corresponded closely to their behavior toward those objects. The more participants said they enjoyed a task, the more time they spent on it; the more attractive they found a scenic landscape, the more pleasure they revealed in their facial expressions; the happier they said they were with a current dating partner, the longer the relationship with that partner ultimately lasted. Yet after participants were told to analyze the reasons for how they felt, the attitudes that they reported no longer corresponded to their behavior. There are two problems. The first, as described by Wilson, is that human beings are mentally busy processing information, which is why we so often fail to understand our own thoughts, feelings, and behaviors. Apparently, it is possible to think too much, and be too analytical, only to get confused.

In *Self-Insight: Roadblocks and Detours on the Path to Knowing Thyself*, David Dunning (2005) points to a second type of problem in self-assessment: that people overestimate the positives. Most people, most of the time, think they are better than average, even though it is statistically impossible for this to happen. As we will see in our later discussion of self-enhancement, people from all walks of life tend to overrate their own skills, their prospects for success, the accuracy of their

In some ways, our sense of self is malleable and subject to change.

"Look, babe. At this point, you've reinvented yourself so many times you're back to who you were at the start."

opinions, and the impressions they form of others—sometimes with dire consequences for their health and well-being.

People also have difficulty projecting forward and predicting how they would feel in response to future emotional events—a process referred to as **affective forecasting**. Imagine that you have a favorite candidate in an upcoming political campaign. Can you anticipate how happy you would be one month after the election if this candidate were to win? How unhappy would you be if he or she were to lose? Closer to home, how happy would you be six months after winning a million-dollar lottery? Or, how unhappy would you be if injured in an automobile accident?

In a series of studies, Timothy Wilson and Daniel Gilbert (2003, 2005) asked research participants to predict how they would feel after various positive and negative life events and compared their predictions to how others experiencing those events said they actually felt. Consistently, they found that people overestimate the strength and duration of their emotional reactions, a phenomenon they call the impact or durability bias. In one study, junior professors predicted that receiving tenure would increase their happiness levels for several years, yet professors who actually received tenure were no happier at that later point than those not granted tenure. In a second study, voters predicted they would be happier a month after an election if their candidate won than if he or she lost. In actuality, supporters of the winning and losing candidates did not differ in their happiness levels one month after the election. In a third study, subway passengers anticipated that they would experience more regret and self-blame if they missed their train by a short minute than by a wider margin. Yet when actual subway riders who missed a train were questioned, they did *not*, as predicted, report feeling intensely regretful in this close situation (Gilbert et al., 2004).

There are two possible reasons for the impact bias in affective forecasting. First, when it comes to negative life events—such as an injury, illness, or financial loss—people do not fully appreciate the extent to which our psychological coping mechanisms help us to cushion the blow. In the face of adversity, human beings can be remarkably resilient—and not as devastated as we fear we will be (Gilbert et al., 1998). A second reason for these overestimates is that when we introspect about the emotional impact on us of a future event—say, the breakup of a close relationship—we become so focused on that single event that we neglect to take into account the effects of other life experiences. To become more accurate in our predictions, then, we need to force ourselves to think more broadly, about *all* the events that impact us. In one study, college students were asked to predict their emotional reactions to their school football team's winning or losing an important game. As usual, they tended to overestimate how long it would take them to recover from the victory or defeat. This bias disappeared, however, when the students first completed a "prospective diary" in which they estimated the amount of future time they will spend on everyday activities like going to class, talking to friends, studying, and eating meals (Wilson et al., 2000).

Perceptions of Our Own Behavior

Regardless of what we can learn from introspection, Daryl Bem (1972) believes that people can learn about themselves the same way outside observers do—by watching their own behavior. Bem's **self-perception theory** is simple yet profound. To the extent that internal states are weak or difficult to interpret, people infer what they think or how they feel by observing their own behavior and the situation in which that behavior takes place. Have you ever listened to yourself arguing with someone, only to realize with amazement how angry you were? Have you ever devoured a sandwich in record time, only then to conclude that you must have been incredibly hungry? In each case, you made an inference about yourself by watching your own actions.

There are limits to self-perception, of course. According to Bem, people do not infer their own internal states from behavior that occurred in the presence of compelling situational pressures such as reward or punishment. If you argued vehemently or wolfed down a sandwich because you were paid to do so, you probably would not assume that you were angry or hungry. In other words, people learn

affective forecasting The process of predicting how one would feel in response to future emotional events.

self-perception theory The theory that when internal cues are difficult to interpret, people gain self-insight by observing their own behavior.

"I don't sing because I am happy. I am happy because I sing."

As suggested by self-perception theory, we sometimes infer how we feel by observing our own behavior.

facial feedback hypothesis
The hypothesis that changes in facial expression can lead to corresponding changes in emotion.

about themselves through self-perception only when the situation alone seems insufficient to have caused their behavior.

A good deal of research supports self-perception theory. When people are gently coaxed into saying or doing something, and when they are not otherwise certain about how they feel, they often come to view themselves in ways that are consistent with their public statements and behavior (Chaiken & Baldwin, 1981; Schlenker & Trudeau, 1990; Kelly & Rodriguez, 2006). Thus, research participants induced to describe themselves in flattering terms scored higher on a later test of self-esteem than did those who were led to describe themselves more modestly (Jones et al., 1981; Rhodewalt & Agusts-dottir, 1986). Similarly, those who were maneuvered by leading questions into describing themselves as introverted or extroverted—whether or not they really were—came to define themselves as such later on, unless they were certain of this aspect of their personality (Fazio et al., 1981; Swann & Ely, 1984). British author E. M. Forster long ago anticipated the theory when he asked, "How can I tell what I think 'til I see what I say?"

Self-Perceptions of Emotion   Draw the corners of your mouth back and up and tense your eye muscles. Okay, relax. Now raise your eyebrows, open your eyes wide, and let your mouth drop open slightly. Relax. Now pull your brows down and together and clench your teeth. Relax. If you followed these directions, you would have appeared to others to be feeling first happy, then fearful, and finally angry. The question is, How would you have appeared to yourself?

Social psychologists who study emotion have asked precisely that question. Viewed within the framework of self-perception theory, the **facial feedback hypothesis** states that changes in facial expression can trigger corresponding changes in the subjective experience of emotion. In the first test of this hypothesis, James Laird (1974) told participants that they were taking part in an experiment on activity of the facial muscles. After attaching electrodes to their faces, he showed them a series of cartoons. Before each one, the participants were instructed to contract certain facial muscles in ways that created either a smile or a frown. As Laird predicted, participants rated what they saw as funnier, and reported feeling happier, when they were smiling than when they were frowning. In follow-up research, people were similarly induced through posed expressions to experience fear, anger, sadness, and disgust (Duclos et al., 1989)—and even a reduction in racial bias (Ito et al., 2006).

Facial feedback can evoke and magnify certain emotional states. It's important to note, however, that the face is not *necessary* to the subjective experience of emotion. When neuropsychologists recently tested a young woman who suffered from bilateral facial paralysis, they found that despite her inability to outwardly *show* emotion, she reported *feeling* various emotions in response to positive and negative visual images (Keillor et al., 2003).

How does facial feedback work? With eighty muscles in the human face, which can create over 7,000 expressions, can we actually vary our own emotions by contracting certain muscles and wearing different expressions? Research suggests that we can, though it is not clear what the results mean. Laird argues that facial expressions affect emotion through a process of self-perception: "If I'm smiling, I must be happy." Consistent with this hypothesis, Chris Kleinke and others (1998) asked people to emulate either the happy or angry facial expressions that were depicted in a series of photographs. Half the participants saw themselves in a mirror during the task; the others did not. Did these manipulations affect mood states? Yes. Compared to participants in a no-expression control group, those who put on happy faces felt better—and those who put on angry faces felt worse. As predicted by self-perception theory, the differences were particularly pronounced among participants who saw themselves in a mirror.

Other researchers maintain that facial movements spark emotion by producing physiological changes in the brain (Izard, 1990). For example, Robert Zajonc (1993) argues that smiling causes facial muscles to increase the flow of air-cooled blood to the brain, a process that produces a pleasant state by lowering brain temperature. Conversely, frowning decreases blood flow, producing an unpleasant state by raising temperature. To demonstrate, Zajonc and his colleagues (1989) conducted a study in which they asked participants to repeat certain vowels twenty times each, including the sounds *ah, e, u,* and the German vowel *ü.* In the meantime, temperature changes in the forehead were measured and participants reported on how they felt. As it turned out, *ah* and *e* (sounds that cause people to mimic smiling) lowered forehead temperature and elevated mood, whereas *u* and *ü* (sounds that cause us to mimic frowning) increased temperature and dampened mood. In short, people need not infer how they feel. Rather, facial expressions evoke physiological changes that produce an emotional experience.

Other expressive behaviors, like body posture, can also provide us with sensory feedback and influence the way we feel. When people feel proud, they stand erect with their shoulders raised, chest expanded, and head held high (*expansion*). When dejected, however, people slump over with their shoulders drooping and head bowed (*contraction*). Clearly, your emotional state is revealed in the way you carry yourself. But is it also possible that the way you carry yourself affects your emotional state? Can people lift their spirits by expansion or lower their spirits by contraction? Yes. Sabine Stepper and Fritz Strack (1993) arranged for people to sit in either a slumped or an upright position by varying the height of the table they had to write on. Those forced to sit upright reported feeling more pride after succeeding at a task than did those who were placed in a slumped position. In another study, participants who were instructed to lean forward with their fists clenched during the experiment reported feeling anger, while those who sat slumped with their heads down said they felt sadness (Duclos et al., 1989; Flack et al., 1999).

Self-Perceptions of Motivation   Without quite realizing it, Mark Twain was a self-perception theorist. In *The Adventures of Tom Sawyer*, written in the late 1800s, he quipped, "There are wealthy gentlemen in England who drive four-horse passenger coaches twenty or thirty miles on a daily line, in the summer, because the privilege costs them considerable money; but if they were offered wages for the service that would turn it into work then they would resign." Twain's hypothesis—that reward for an enjoyable activity can undermine interest in that activity—seems to contradict both our intuition and the results of psychological research. After all, aren't we all motivated by reward, as declared by B. F. Skinner and other behaviorists? The answer depends on how *motivation* is defined.

As a keen observer of human behavior, Twain anticipated a key distinction between intrinsic and extrinsic motivation. *Intrinsic motivation* originates in factors within a person. People are said to be intrinsically motivated when they engage in an activity for the sake of their own interest, the challenge, or sheer enjoyment. Eating a fine meal, listening to music, spending time with friends, and having a hobby are among the activities that you might find intrinsically motivating. In contrast, *extrinsic motivation* originates in factors outside the person. People are said to be extrinsically motivated when they engage in an activity as a means to an end, for tangible benefits. It might be for money, grades, or recognition; to fulfill obligations; or to avoid punishment. As the behaviorists have always said, people do strive for reward. The question is, what happens to the intrinsic motivation once that reward is no longer available?

From the standpoint of self-perception theory, Twain's hypothesis makes sense. When someone is rewarded for listening to music, playing a game, or eating a tasty food, his or her behavior becomes *over*justified, or *over*rewarded, which means that it can be attributed to extrinsic as well as intrinsic motives. This **overjustification effect** can be dangerous: Observing that their own efforts have paid off, people begin to wonder if the activity was ever worth pursuing in its own right.

Research shows that when people start getting "paid" for a task they already enjoy, they sometimes lose interest in it. In an early demonstration of this phenomenon, Mark Lepper and his colleagues (1973) gave preschool children an opportunity to play with colorful felt-tipped markers—an opportunity most could not resist. By observing how much time the children spent on the activity, the researchers were

Smiling can make you feel happier. **True.**

overjustification effect
The tendency for intrinsic motivation to diminish for activities that have become associated with reward or other extrinsic factors.

able to measure their intrinsic motivation. Two weeks later, the children were divided into three groups, all about equal in terms of initial levels of intrinsic motivation. In one, the children were simply asked to draw some pictures with the markers. In the second, they were told that if they used the markers they would receive a "Good Player Award," a certificate with a gold star and a red ribbon. In a third group, the children were not offered a reward for drawing pictures, but—like those in the second group—they received a reward when they were done.

About a week later, the teachers placed the markers and paper on a table in the classroom while the experimenters observed through a one-way mirror. Since no rewards were offered on this occasion, the amount of free time the children spent playing with the markers reflected their intrinsic motivation. As predicted, those who had expected and received a reward for their efforts were no longer as interested in the markers as they had been. Children who had not received a reward were not adversely affected, nor were those who had received the unexpected reward. Having played with the markers without the promise of tangible benefit, these children remained intrinsically motivated (see Figure 3.1).

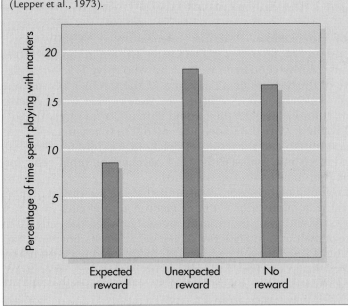

FIGURE 3.1

Paradoxical Effects of Reward on Intrinsic Motivation

In this study, an expected reward undermined children's intrinsic motivation to play with felt-tipped markers. Children who received an unexpected reward or no reward did not lose interest.

(Lepper et al., 1973).

The paradox that reward can undermine rather than enhance intrinsic motivation has been observed in many settings and with both children and adults (Deci & Ryan, 1985; Enzle & Anderson, 1993; Pittman & Heller, 1987; Tang & Hall, 1995). Accept money for a leisure activity, and before you know it, what used to be "play" comes to feel more like "work." In the long run, this can have negative effects on the quality of your performance. In a series of studies, Teresa Amabile (1996) and others had participants write poems, draw or paint pictures, make paper collages, and generate creative solutions to business dilemmas. Consistently, they found that people are more creative when they feel interested and challenged by the work itself than when they feel pressured to make money, fulfill obligations, meet deadlines, win competitions, or impress others. In one study, Amabile had art experts rate the works of professional artists and found that the artists' commissioned work (art they were contracted for) was judged as lower in quality than their noncommissioned work. People are likely to be more creative when they are intrinsically motivated in relation to the task, not compelled by outside forces.

But wait. If extrinsic benefits serve to undermine intrinsic motivation, should teachers and parents *not* offer rewards to their children? Are the employee incentive programs that are so often used to motivate workers in the business world doomed to fail, as some have suggested? (Kohn, 1993). It all depends on how the reward is perceived—and by whom. If a reward is presented in the form of verbal praise that is perceived to be sincere, or as a special "bonus" for superior performance, then it can actually *enhance* intrinsic motivation by providing positive feedback about competence—as when people win competitions, scholarships, or a pat on the back from people they respect (Cameron & Pierce, 1994; Covington, 2000; Eisenberger & Cameron, 1996; Henderlong & Lepper, 2002).

Individual differences in people's motivational orientation toward work must also be considered. For intrinsically oriented people who say, "What matters most to me is enjoying what I do" and "I seldom think about salary and promotions," reward may be unnecessary—and may even be detrimental (Amabile et al., 1994). Yet for people who are highly focused on the achievement of certain goals—whether at school, at work, or in sports—extrinsic inducements such as grades, scores, bonuses, awards, trophies, and the sheer thrill of competition, as in team sports, tend to boost intrinsic motivation (Harackiewicz & Elliot, 1993; Sansone & Harackiewicz, 2000; Tauer & Harackiewicz, 2004).

 ## Influences of Other People

As we noted earlier, Cooley's (1902) theory of the looking-glass self emphasized that other people help us define ourselves. In this section, we will see the importance of this proposition to our self-concepts.

Social Comparison Theory   Suppose a stranger were to ask, "Who are you?" If you had only a minute or two to answer, would you mention your ethnic or religious background? What about your hometown? Would you describe your talents and your interests or your likes and dislikes? When asked this question, people tend to describe themselves in ways that set them apart from others in their immediate vicinity (McGuire & McGuire, 1988). Among children, boys are more likely to cite their gender when they grow up in families that are predominantly female; girls do the same when living in families that are predominantly male (McGuire et al., 1979). Similarly, on the college campus, "nontraditional" older students are more likely to mention age than are traditional younger students (Kite, 1992). Regardless of whether the unique attribute is gender, age, height, or eye color, this pattern is basically the same. The implication is intriguing: Change someone's social surroundings, and you can change that person's spontaneous self-description.

This reliance on distinguishing features in self-description indicates that the self is "relative," a social construct, and that each of us defines ourself in part by using family members, friends, acquaintances, and others as a benchmark (Mussweiler & Rüter, 2003; Mussweiler & Strack, 2000). Temporarily, our standards of self-comparison can even be influenced by our fleeting, everyday exposures to strangers (Mussweiler et al., 2004). Indeed, that is what Leon Festinger (1954) proposed in his **social comparison theory**. Festinger argued that when people are uncertain of their abilities or opinions—that is, when objective information is not readily available—they evaluate themselves through comparisons with similar others. The theory seems reasonable, but is it valid? Over the years, social psychologists have put social comparison theory to the test, focusing on two key questions: (1) *When* do we turn to others for comparative information? (2) Of all the people who inhabit the earth, *with whom* do we choose to compare ourselves? (Suls & Wheeler, 2000).

As Festinger proposed, the answer to the "when" question appears to be that people engage in social comparison in states of uncertainty, when more objective means of self-evaluation are not available. In fact, recent studies suggest that Festinger may have understated the importance of social comparison processes—that people may judge themselves in relation to others even when more objective standards are available. For example, William Klein (1997) asked college students to make a series of judgments of artwork. Giving false feedback, he then told the students that 60 percent or 40 percent of their answers were correct—and that this was 20 percent higher or lower than the average among students. When they later rated their own skill at the task, the participants were influenced not by their absolute scores, but by where they stood in relation to their peers. For them, it was better to have had a 40 percent score that was above average than a 60 percent score that was below average.

The "with whom" question has also been the subject of many studies. The answer seems to be that when we evaluate our own taste in music, value on the job market, or athletic ability, we look to others who are similar to us in relevant ways (Goethals & Darley, 1977; Wheeler et al., 1982)—a choice that we make automatically, without thinking or necessarily being aware of it (Gilbert et al., 1995). If you are curious about your flair for writing, for example, you're more likely to compare yourself with other college students than with high schoolers or best-selling authors. There are exceptions to this rule, of course. Later in this chapter, we will see that people often cope with personal inadequacies by focusing on others who are *less* able or *less* fortunate than themselves.

social comparison theory The theory that people evaluate their own abilities and opinions by comparing themselves to others.

Two-Factor Theory of Emotion   People seek social comparison information to evaluate their abilities and opinions. Do they also turn to others to determine something as personal and subjective as their own emotions? In classic experiments on affiliation, Stanley Schachter (1959) found that when people were frightened into thinking they would receive painful electric shocks, most sought the company of others who were in the same predicament. Nervous and uncertain about how they should be feeling, participants wanted to affiliate with similar others, presumably for the purpose of comparison. Yet when they were not fearful, and expected only mild shocks, or when the "others" were not taking part in the same experiment, participants preferred to be alone. As Schachter put it, "Misery doesn't just love any kind of company; it loves only miserable company" (p. 24).

Intrigued by the possibilities, Schachter and his research team took the next step. Could it be, they wondered, that when people are uncertain about how they feel, their emotional state is actually determined by the reactions of others around them? In answer to this question, the researchers proposed that two factors are necessary to feel a specific emotion. First, the person must experience the symptoms of physiological arousal—like a racing heart, perspiration, rapid breathing, and tightening of the stomach. Second, the person must make a *cognitive interpretation* that explains the source of the arousal. And that is where the people around us come in: Their reactions help us interpret our own arousal.

To test this provocative **two-factor theory of emotion**, Schachter and Jerome Singer (1962) injected male volunteers with epinephrine, a drug that heightens physiological arousal. Although one group was forewarned about the drug's effects, a second group was not. Members of a third group were injected with a harmless placebo. Before the drug (which was described as a vitamin supplement) actually took effect, participants were left alone with a male confederate introduced as another participant who had received the same injection. In some sessions, the confederate behaved in a euphoric manner. For twenty minutes, he bounced around happily, doodling on scratch paper, sinking jump shots into the wastebasket, flying paper airplanes across the room, and playing with a hula-hoop. In other sessions, the confederate displayed anger, ridiculing a questionnaire they were filling out and, in a fit of rage, ripping it up and hurling it into the wastebasket.

Think for a moment about these various situations. As the drug takes effect, participants in the *drug-informed* group begin to feel their hearts pound, their hands shake, and their faces flush. Having been told to expect these symptoms, however, they need not search for an explanation. Participants in the *placebo* group do not become aroused in the first place, so they have no symptoms to explain. But now consider the plight of those in the *drug-uninformed* group, who suddenly become aroused without knowing why. Trying to identify the sensations, these participants, according to the theory, should take their cues from someone else in the same predicament—namely, the confederate.

In general, the experimental results supported Schachter and Singer's line of reasoning. Drug-uninformed participants reported feeling relatively happy or angry depending on the confederate's performance. In many instances, they even exhibited similar kinds of behavior. One participant, for example, "threw open the window and, laughing, hurled paper basketballs at passersby." In the drug-informed and placebo groups, however, participants were, as expected, less influenced by these social cues.

Schachter and Singer's two-factor theory has attracted a good deal of controversy, as some studies have corroborated their findings but others have not. In one experiment, for example, participants who were injected with epinephrine and not forewarned about the symptoms later exhibited more fear in response to a scary film, but they were not more angry or amused while seeing films that tend to elicit these other emotions (Mezzacappa et al., 1999). Overall, it now appears that one limited but important conclusion can safely be drawn: When people are unclear about their own emotional states, they sometimes interpret how they feel by watching others (Reisenzein, 1983). The "sometimes" part of the conclusion is important. For others to influence your emotion, your level of physiological arousal cannot be too intense, or else it will be experienced as aversive—regardless of the situation (Maslach,

two-factor theory of emotion   The theory that the experience of emotion is based on two factors: physiological arousal and a cognitive interpretation of that arousal.

Although adults recall more events from the recent than distant past, people are filled with memories from late adolescence and early adulthood. These formative years are nicely captured by high school yearbook photos—such as those of American actresses Angelina Jolie (left) and Jennifer Aniston (right).

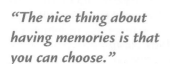

"The nice thing about having memories is that you can choose."

—William Trevor

1979; Zimbardo et al., 1993). Also, research shows that other people must be present as a possible explanation for arousal *before* its onset. Once people are aroused, they turn for an explanation to events that preceded the change in their physiological state (Schachter & Singer, 1979; Sinclair et al., 1994).

In subsequent chapters, we will see that the two-factor theory of emotion has far-reaching implications for passionate love, anger and aggression, and other affective experiences.

Autobiographical Memories

Philosopher James Mill once said, "The phenomenon of the Self and that of Memory are merely two sides of the same fact." If the story of patient William Thompson at the start of this chapter is any indication, Mill was right. Without autobiographical memories—recollections of the sequences of events that have touched your life (Fivush et al., 2003; Rubin, 1996; Thompson et al., 1998)—you would have no coherent self-concept. After all, who would you be if you could not remember your parents or your childhood playmates, your successes and failures, the places you lived, the schools you attended, the books you read, and the teams you played for? Clearly, memories shape the self-concept. In this section, we'll see that the self-concept shapes our personal memories as well (Conway & Pleydell-Pearce, 2000).

When people are prompted to recall their own experiences, they typically report more events from the recent past than from the distant past. There are, however, two consistent exceptions to this simple recency rule. The first is that older adults retrieve a large number of personal memories from their adolescence and early adulthood years—a "reminiscence peak" that may occur because these are busy and formative years in one's life (Fitzgerald, 1988; Jansari & Parkin, 1996; Schroots et al., 2004). A second exception is that people tend to remember transitional "firsts." Reflect for a moment on your own college career. What events pop to mind—and when did they occur? Did you come up with the day you arrived on campus or the first time you met your closest friend? What about notable classes, parties, or sports events? When David Pillemer and his colleagues (1996) asked juniors and seniors to recount the most memorable experiences of their first year, 32 percent of all recollections were from the transitional month of September. When college graduates were given the same task, they, too, cited a disproportionate number of events from the opening two months of their first year—followed by the next major transitional period, the last month of their senior year. Among students, these busy transitional periods are important regardless of whether their schools follow a semester calendar or some other academic schedule (Kurbat et al., 1998).

Obviously, not all experiences leave the same impression. Ask people old enough to remember November 22, 1963, and they probably can tell you exactly where they were, whom they were with, and what was happening the moment they heard the news that President John F. Kennedy had been shot. Roger Brown and James Kulik (1977) coined the term *flashbulb memories* to describe these enduring, detailed, high-resolution recollections and speculated that humans are biologically equipped for survival purposes to "print" dramatic events in memory. These flashbulb memories are not necessarily accurate or even consistent over time. When asked, for example, how he heard about the infamous September 11, 2001, terrorist attacks, President George W. Bush gave different accounts on three occasions when asked what he was doing and who told him the news (Greenberg, 2004). Accurate or not, these recollections "feel" special and serve as prominent landmarks in the biographies that we tell about ourselves (Conway, 1995; Ross, 1989).

By linking the present to the past and providing us with an inner sense of continuity, autobiographical memory is a vital part of—and can be shaped by—

FIGURE 3.2

Distortions in Memory of High School Grades

College students were asked to recall their high school grades, which were then checked against their actual transcripts. These comparisons revealed that most errors in memory were grade inflations. Lower grades were recalled with the least accuracy (and the most inflation). It appears that people sometimes revise their own past to suit their current self-image.

(Bahrick et al., 1996.)

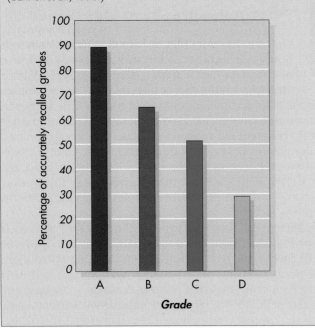

our identity. In particular, people are often motivated to distort the past in ways that are self-inflated. According to Anthony Greenwald (1980), "The past is remembered as if it were a drama in which the self was the leading player" (p. 604). To illustrate this bias, let's turn the clock back to a momentous event in American history: the Senate Watergate hearings of 1973. The witness was John Dean, former counsel to President Richard Nixon. Dean had submitted a 245-page statement in which he recounted word for word the details of many conversations. Dean's memory seemed so impressive that he was called "the human tape recorder." But then, in an ironic twist of fate, investigators discovered that Nixon had taped the meetings that Dean recalled. Was Dean accurate? A comparison of his testimony with the actual tapes revealed that although he correctly remembered the gist of his White House meetings, he consistently exaggerated his own role and importance in these events. Cognitive psychologist Ulric Neisser (1981), who analyzed Dean's testimony, wondered, "Are we all like this? Is everyone's memory constructed, staged, self-centered?" The answer is yes—there is a bit of John Dean in all of us (Ross & Sicoly, 1979).

In other ways, too, people tend to revise their fading personal histories to reflect favorably on the self. In one study, George Goethals and Richard Reckman (1973) found that people whose attitudes about school busing were changed by a persuasive speaker later assumed that they had held their new attitude all along. In a second study, Harry Bahrick and others (1996) had ninety-nine college students try to recall all of their high school grades and then checked their reports against the actual transcripts. Overall, the majority of grades were recalled correctly. But most of the errors in memory were grade *inflations*—and most of these were made when the actual grades were *low* (see Figure 3.2). In a third study, Simone Schlagman and others (2006) talked to young and old volunteers for a period of one week and then analyzed the autobiographical memories that they spontaneously recounted—about births, deaths, holidays, accidents, school events, special occasions, and the like. Both groups recalled plenty of positive events, but older adults recalled fewer negative memories. Together, these findings bring to mind sociologist George Herbert Mead's (1934) contention that our visions of the past are like pure "escape fancies . . . in which we rebuild the world according to our hearts' desires" (pp. 348–349).

Cultural Influences on the Self-Concept

The self-concept is also influenced by cultural factors. In America, it is said that "the squeaky wheel gets the grease"; in Japan, it is said that "the nail that stands out gets pounded down." Thus American parents try to raise their children to be independent, self-reliant, and assertive (a "cut above the rest"), whereas Japanese children are raised to fit into their groups and community.

The preceding example illustrates two contrasting cultural orientations. One values *individualism* and the virtues of independence, autonomy, and self-reliance. The other orientation values *collectivism* and the virtues of interdependence, cooperation, and social harmony. Under the banner of individualism, one's personal goals take priority over group allegiances. In collectivist cultures, by contrast, a person is first and foremost a loyal member of a family, team, company, church, and state, motivated to be part of a group—not different, better, or worse (Triandis, 1994). In what countries are these orientations the most extreme? In a worldwide study of 116,000 employees of IBM, Geert Hofstede (1980) found that the most fiercely individualistic people were from the United States, Australia, Great Britain, Canada, and the Netherlands—in that order. The most collectivist people were from Venezuela, Colombia, Pakistan, Peru, Taiwan, and China.

It's also important to realize that individualism and collectivism are not simple opposites on a continuum and that the similarities and differences between countries do not fit a simple pattern. Daphna Oyserman and others (2002) conducted a meta-analysis of many thousands of respondents in eighty-three studies. Within the United States, they found that African Americans were the most individualistic subgroup and that Asian and Latino Americans were the most collectivistic. Comparing nations, they found that collectivist orientations varied within Asia, as the Chinese were more collectivistic than Japanese and Korean respondents.

Individualism and collectivism are so deeply ingrained in a culture that they mold our very self-conceptions and identities. According to Hazel Markus and Shinobu Kitayama (1991), most North Americans and Europeans have an *independent* view of the self. In this view, the self is an entity that is distinct, autonomous, self-contained, and endowed with unique dispositions. Yet in much of Asia, Africa, and Latin America, people hold an *interdependent* view of the self. Here, the self is part of a larger social network that includes one's family, co-workers, and others with whom one is socially connected. People with an independent view say that "the only person you can count on is yourself" and "I enjoy being unique and different from others." In contrast, those with an interdependent view are more likely to agree that "I'm partly to blame if one of my family members or co-workers fails" and "my happiness depends on the happiness of those around me" (Rhee et al., 1995; Singelis, 1994; Triandis et al., 1998). These contrasting orientations—one focused on the personal self, the other on a collective self—are depicted in Figure 3.3.

Research confirms that there is a close link between cultural orientation and conceptions of the self. David Trafimow and his colleagues (1991) had North American and Chinese college students complete twenty sentences beginning with "I am. . . ." The Americans were more likely to fill in the blank with trait descriptions ("I am shy"), whereas the Chinese were more likely to identify themselves by group affiliations ("I am a college student"). It's no wonder that in China, one's family name comes *before* one's personal name. Similar differences are found between Australians and Malaysians (Bochner, 1994).

Our cultural orientations can influence the way we perceive, evaluate, and present ourselves in relation to others. Markus and Kitayama (1991) identified two particularly interesting differences between East and West. The first is that people in individualistic cultures strive for personal achievement, while those living in collectivist cultures derive more satisfaction from the status of a valued group. Thus, whereas North Americans tend to overestimate their own contributions to a team effort, seize the credit for success, and blame others for failure, people from collectivist cultures tend to underestimate their own role and present themselves in more modest, self-effacing terms in relation to other members of the group (Akimoto & Sanbonmatsu, 1999; Heine et al., 2000).

A second consequence of these differing conceptions of the self is that American college students see themselves as less similar to others than do Asian Indian

Reflecting an interdependent view of the self, children in Japan are taught to fit into the community. Reflecting a more independent view of the self, children in the United States are encouraged to express their individuality.

FIGURE 3.3

Cultural Conceptions of Self

As depicted here, different cultures foster different conceptions of the self. Many westerners have an *independent* view of the self as an entity that is distinct, autonomous, and self-contained. Yet many Asians, Africans, and Latin Americans hold an *interdependent* view of the self that encompasses others in a larger social network.

(Markus & Kitayama, 1991.)

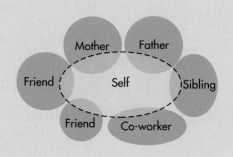

A. Independent View of Self

B. Interdependent View of Self

students. This difference reinforces the idea that individuals with independent conceptions of the self believe they are unique. In fact, our cultural orientations toward conformity or independence may lead us to favor similarity or uniqueness in all things. In a fascinating study that illustrates the point, Heejung Kim and Hazel Markus (1999) showed abstract figures to subjects from the United States and Korea. Each figure contained nine parts. Most of the parts were identical in shape, position, and direction. One or more were different. Look at Figure 3.4. Which of the nine subfigures within each group do you like most? The American subjects liked the subfigures that were unique or in the minority, while Korean subjects preferred those that "fit in" as part of the group. In another study, these same researchers approached pedestrians of American and East Asian heritage at San Francisco's airport and asked them to fill out a questionnaire. Afterward, as a gift, they offered all the participants a choice of one pen from a handful of pens, three or four of which had the same color barrel, green or orange. The result: 74 percent of the Americans chose a uniquely colored pen, and 76 percent of the East Asians selected one of the commonly colored pens. It seems that our culturally ingrained orientations to conformity and independence leave a mark on us, leading us to form preferences for things that "fit in" or "stand out."

Are people from disparate cultures locked into thinking about the self in either personal or collective terms, or are both aspects of the self present in everyone, to be expressed according to the situation? Reconsider the study noted above, where American students described themselves more in terms of personal traits and Chinese students cited more group affiliations. In a fascinating follow-up to that study, Trafimow and others (1997) tested students from Hong Kong, all of whom spoke English as a second language. One half of the students were given the "Who am I?" test in Chinese, and the other half took the test in English. Did this variation influence the results? Yes. Students who took the test in English focused more on personal traits, while those who took the test in Chinese focused more on group affiliations. It appears that each of us have both personal and collective aspects of the

FIGURE 3.4

What's Your Preference: Similarity or Uniqueness?

Which subfigure within each set do you prefer? Kim and Markus (1999) found that Americans tend to like subfigures that "stand out" as unique or in the minority, while Koreans tend to like subfigures that "fit in" with the surrounding group.

(Kim & Markus, 1999).

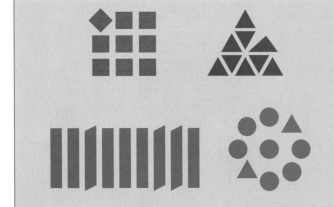

self to draw on—and that the part that comes to mind depends on the situation we are in.

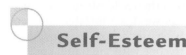

Self-Esteem

How do you feel about yourself? Are you generally satisfied with the way you look, your personality, academic and athletic abilities, accomplishments, and friendships? Are you optimistic about your future? When it comes to the self, people are not cool, objective, dispassionate observers. Rather, we are judgmental, motivated, emotional, and highly protective of our **self-esteem**—an affectively charged component of the self.

The word *esteem* comes from the Latin *aestimare*, which means "to estimate or appraise." Self-esteem thus refers to our positive and negative evaluations of ourselves (Coopersmith, 1967). Some individuals have a higher self-esteem than others do—an attribute that can have a profound impact on the way they think about, feel about, and present themselves. It's important to keep in mind, however, that although some of us have higher self-esteem than others, a feeling of self-worth is not a single trait etched permanently in stone. Rather, it is a state of mind that fluctuates in response to success, failure, ups and downs in fortune, social relations, and other life experiences (Heatherton & Polivy, 1991). Also, because the self-concept is made up of many self-schemas, people typically view parts of the self differently: Some parts they judge more favorably, or see more clearly or as important, than other parts (Pelham, 1995; Pelham & Swann, 1989). Indeed, just as individuals differ according to how high or low their self-esteem is, they also differ in the extent to which their self-esteem is stable or unstable. As a general rule, self-esteem has some stability from childhood through old age (Trzesniewski et al., 2003). Yet for some people in particular, self-esteem seems to fluctuate in response to daily experiences—which makes them highly responsive to praise and overly sensitive to criticism (Baldwin & Sinclair, 1996; Kernis & Waschull, 1995; Schimel et al., 2001).

The Need for Self-Esteem

You, me, and just about everyone else on the planet seem to have a need for self-esteem, wanting to see ourselves in a positive light. As a result of who we are and the culture we live in, each of us may value different attributes and pursue this need in different ways. Some people derive a sense of worth from their appearance; others value physical strength, professional accomplishments, wealth, people skills, or group affiliations. Whatever the source, it is clear that the pursuit of self-worth is an aspect of human motivation that runs deep. But let's step back for a moment and ask, why? Why do we seem to need self-esteem the way we need food, air, sleep, and water?

At present, there are two social psychological answers to this basic question. One theory, proposed by Mark Leary and Roy Baumeister (2000), is that people are inherently social animals and that the desire for self-esteem is driven by this more primitive need to connect with others and gain their approval. In this way, our sense of self-esteem serves as a "sociometer," a rough indicator of how we're doing in the eyes of others. The threat of social rejection thus lowers self-esteem, which activates the need to regain approval and acceptance.

Alternatively, Jeff Greenberg, Sheldon Solomon, and Thomas Pyszczynski (1997) proposed **Terror Management Theory** to help explain our relentless need for self-esteem. According to this theory, we humans are biologically programmed for life and self-preservation. Yet we are conscious of—and terrified by—the inevitability of our own death. To cope with this paralyzing, deeply rooted fear, we construct and accept cultural worldviews about how, why, and by whom the earth was created; religious explanations of the purpose of our existence; and a sense of history filled with heroes, villains, and momentous events. These worldviews provide meaning and purpose and a buffer against anxiety. In a series of experiments, these investigators found that people react to graphic scenes of death, or to the thought of their own

self-esteem An affective component of the self, consisting of a person's positive and negative self-evaluations.

terror management theory The theory that humans cope with the fear of their own death by constructing worldviews that help to preserve their self-esteem.

death, with intense defensiveness and anxiety. When given positive feedback on a test, however, which boosts their self-esteem, that reaction is muted. As we'll see in later chapters, this theory has been used to explain how Americans are likely to cope with the trauma of 9/11 and the terror that it triggered (Pyszczynski et al., 2003).

As for the need for self-esteem, Pyszczynski and his colleagues (2004) put it this way:

Self-esteem is a protective shield designed to control the potential for terror that results from awareness of the horrifying possibility that we humans are merely transient animals groping to survive in a meaningless universe, designed only to die and decay. From this perspective, each individual human's name and identity, family and social identifications, goals and aspirations, occupation and title, and humanly created adornments are draped over an animal that, in the cosmic scheme of things, may be no more significant or enduring than any individual potato, pineapple, or porcupine. (p. 436)

Confirming folk wisdom, a good deal of research suggests that high self-esteem colors our outlook on life. People with positive self-images tend to be happy, healthy, productive, and successful. They also tend to be confident, bringing to new challenges a winning attitude that leads them to persist longer at difficult tasks, sleep better at night, maintain their independence in the face of peer pressure, and suffer from fewer ulcers. In contrast, people with negative self-images tend to be more depressed, pessimistic about the future, and prone to failure. Lacking confidence, they bring to new tasks a losing attitude that traps them in a vicious, self-defeating cycle. Expecting to fail, and fearing the worst, they become anxious, exert less effort, and "tune out" on important challenges. People with low self-esteem don't trust their own positive self-appraisals (Josephs et al., 2003). And when they fail, they tend to blame themselves, which makes them feel even less competent (Brockner, 1983; Brown & Dutton, 1995). Low self-esteem may even be hazardous to your health. Indeed, some research suggests that becoming aware of one's own negative attributes adversely affects the activity of certain white blood cells in the immune system, thus compromising the body's capacity to ward off disease (Strauman et al., 1993, 2004).

Does high self-esteem ensure desirable life outcomes? Not necessarily. Based on extensive reviews of the research, two recent perspectives suggest that the presumed links between self-esteem and life outcomes are somewhat more complicated. In one article, Baumeister and his colleagues (2003) find that although high self-esteem leads people to feel good, take on new challenges, and persist through failure, the correlational evidence does not clearly support the strong conclusion that boosting self-esteem *causes* people to perform well in school or at work, to be socially popular, or to behave in ways that foster physical health. In a second article, Jennifer Crocker and Lora Park (2004) argue that the process of pursuing self-esteem itself is costly. Specifically, they point to research showing that in trying hard to boost and maintain their self-esteem, people often become anxious, avoid activities that risk failure, neglect the needs of others, and suffer from stress-related health problems. Self-esteem has its benefits, but striving for it can also be costly.

Are There Gender and Race Differences?

Just as individuals differ in their self-esteem, so, too, do social and cultural groups. If you were to administer a self-esteem test to thousands of people all over the world, would you find that some segments of the population score higher than others? Would you expect to see differences in the averages of men and women, Blacks and

FIGURE 3.5

Self-Esteem in U.S. Minorities

Through a meta-analysis, Twenge and Crocker (2002) found that African Americans score higher on self-esteem tests relative to Whites, but that Hispanic-, Asian-, and Native-American minorities score lower.

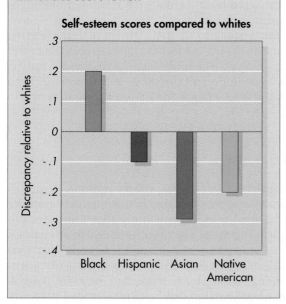

Self-esteem scores compared to whites

Whites, or inhabitants of different cultures? Believing that self-esteem promotes health, happiness, and success, and concerned that some groups are disadvantaged in this regard, researchers have indeed made these types of comparisons.

Are there gender differences in self-esteem? Over the years, a lot has been written in the popular press about the inflated but fragile "male ego," the low self-regard among adolescent girls and young women, and the resulting gender-related "confidence gap" (Orenstein, 1994). So, does the research support this assumption? To find out, Kristin Kling and others (1999) statistically combined the results of 216 studies involving 97,000 respondents and then analyzed the surveys of 48,000 American students conducted by the National Center for Education Statistics. The result: Among adolescents and adults, males outscored females on various general measures of self-esteem. Contrary to popular belief, however, the difference was very small, particularly among older adults.

Researchers have also wondered if low self-esteem is a problem for members of stigmatized minority groups—historically, victims of prejudice and discrimination. Does membership in a minority group, such as African Americans, deflate one's sense of self-worth? Based on the combined results of studies involving more than half a million respondents, Bernadette Gray-Little and Adam Hafdahl (2000) reported that black American children, adolescents, and adults consistently score higher—not lower—than their white counterparts on measures of self-esteem.

In a meta-analysis of hundreds of studies that compared all age groups and different American minorities, Jean Twenge and Jennifer Crocker (2002) confirmed the African American advantage in self-esteem relative to whites but found that Hispanic, Asian, and Native American minorities have lower self-esteem scores. This self-esteem advantage, as illustrated in Figure 3.5, is not easy to interpret. Surprised by the high African American scores, some researchers have suggested that perhaps African Americans—more than other minorities—are able to preserve their self-esteem in the face of adversity by attributing negative outcomes to the forces of discrimination and using this adversity to build a sense of group pride. In this regard, Twenge and Crocker found that self-esteem scores of black Americans, relative to those of Whites, have risen over time—from the pre–civil rights days of the 1950s to the present.

Self-Discrepancy Theory

What determines how people feel about themselves? According to E. Tory Higgins (1989), our self-esteem is defined by the match or mismatch between how we see ourselves and how we want to see ourselves. To demonstrate, try the following exercise. On a blank sheet of paper, write down ten traits that describe the kind of person you think you *actually* are (smart? easygoing? sexy? excitable?). Next, list ten traits that describe the kind of person you think you *ought* to be, characteristics that would enable you to meet your sense of duty, obligation, and responsibility. Then make a list of traits that describe the kind of person you *would like* to be, an *ideal* that embodies your hopes, wishes, and dreams. If you follow these instructions, you should have three lists: your actual self, your ought self, and your ideal self.

Research has shown that these lists can be used to predict your self-esteem and your emotional well-being. The first list is your self-concept. The others represent your personal standards, or *self-guides*. To the extent that you fall short of these standards, you will experience lowered self-esteem, negative emotion, and, in extreme cases, a serious affective disorder. The specific consequence depends on which self-guide you fail to achieve. If there's a discrepancy between your actual and ought selves, you will feel guilty, ashamed, and resentful. You might even suffer from excessive fears and anxiety-related disorders. If the mismatch is between your actual and ideal selves, you'll feel disappointed, frustrated, unfulfilled, and sad. In the worst-case scenario you might even become depressed (Boldero & Francis, 2000; Higgins, 1999; Strauman, 1992). Our self-discrepancies may even set into motion a self-perpetuating process. Participating in a study of body images, college women with high rather than low self-ideal discrepancies were more likely to compare themselves with thin models in TV commercials, which further increased their body dissatisfaction and depression (Bessenoff, 2006).

It's clear that every one of us must cope with some degree of self-discrepancy. Nobody is perfect. Yet we do not all suffer from the emotional consequences. The reason, according to Higgins, is that self-esteem depends on a number of factors. One is simply the amount of discrepancy. The more of it there is, the worse we feel. Another is the importance of the discrepancy to the self. The more important the domain in which we fall short, again, the worse we feel. A third factor is the extent to which we focus on our self-discrepancies. The more focused we are, the greater the harm. This last observation raises an important question: What causes us to be more or less focused on our personal shortcomings? For an answer, we turn to self-awareness theory.

The Self-Awareness "Trap"

If you carefully review your daily routine—classes, work, chores at home, leisure activities, social interactions, and meals—you will probably be surprised at how little time you actually spend thinking about yourself. In a study that illustrates this point, more than a hundred people, ranging in age from nineteen to sixty-three, were equipped for a week with electronic beepers that sounded every two hours or so between 7:30 A.M. and 10:30 P.M. Each time the beepers went off, participants interrupted whatever they were doing, wrote down what they were thinking at that moment, and filled out a brief questionnaire. Out of 4,700 recorded thoughts, only 8 percent were about the self. For the most part, attention was focused on work and other activities. In fact, when participants were thinking about themselves, they reported feeling relatively unhappy and wished they were doing something else (Csikszentmihalyi & Figurski, 1982).

Self-Focusing Situations   The finding that people may be unhappy while they think about themselves is interesting, but what does it mean? Does self-reflection bring out our personal shortcomings the way staring into a mirror draws our gaze to every blemish on the face? Is self-awareness an unpleasant mental state from which we need to retreat?

Many years ago, Robert Wicklund and his colleagues theorized that the answer is yes (Duval & Wicklund, 1972; Wicklund, 1975; Silvia & Duval, 2001). According to their **self-awareness theory**, people are not usually self-focused, but certain situations predictably force us to turn inward and become the objects of our own attention. When we talk about ourselves, glance in a mirror, stand before an audience or camera, watch ourselves on videotape, or behave in a conspicuous manner, we enter into a state of heightened self-awareness that leads us naturally to compare our behavior to some standard. This comparison often results in a negative discrepancy and a temporary reduction in self-esteem as we discover that we fall short. Thus, research participants who are seated in front of a mirror tend to react more negatively to their self-discrepancies, often slipping into a negative mood state (Fejfar & Hoyle, 2000; Hass & Eisenstadt, 1990; Phillips & Silvia, 2005). In fact, the more self-focused people are in general, the more likely they are to find themselves in a bad mood (Flory et al., 2000) or depressed (Pyszczynski & Greenberg, 1987). People who are self-absorbed are also more likely to suffer from alcoholism, anxiety, and other clinical disorders (Ingram, 1990; Mor & Winquist, 2002).

Is there a solution? Self-awareness theory suggests two basic ways of coping with such discomfort: (1) "Shape up" by behaving in ways that reduce our self-discrepancies or (2) "ship out" by withdrawing from self-awareness. According to Charles Carver and Michael Scheier (1981), the solution chosen depends on whether people think they can reduce their self-discrepancy and whether they're pleased with the progress they make once they try (Duval et al., 1992). If so, they

"I have the true feeling of myself only when I am unbearably unhappy."

—Franz Kafka

self-awareness theory
The theory that self-focused attention leads people to notice self-discrepancies, thereby motivating either an escape from self-awareness or a change in behavior.

tend to match their behavior to personal or societal standards; if not, they tune out, look for distractions, and turn attention away from the self. This process is depicted in Figure 3.6.

In general, research supports the prediction that when people are self-focused, they are more likely to behave in ways that are consistent either with their own personal values or with socially accepted ideals (Gibbons, 1990). Two interesting field studies illustrate this point. In one, Halloween trick-or-treaters—children with masks, costumes, and painted faces—were greeted at a researcher's door and left alone to help themselves from a bowl of candy. Although the children were asked to take only one piece, 34 percent violated the request. When a full-length mirror was placed behind the candy bowl, however, that number dropped to 12 percent. Apparently, the mirror forced the children to become self-focused, leading them to behave in a way that was consistent with public standards of desirable conduct (Beaman et al., 1979). In a second study, conducted in England, customers at a lunch counter were trusted to pay for their coffee, tea, and milk by depositing money into an unsupervised "honesty box." Hanging on the wall behind the counter was a poster that featured a picture of flowers or a pair of eyes. By calculating the ratio of money deposited to drinks consumed, researchers observed that people paid nearly three times more money in the presence of the eyes (Bateson et al., 2006).

Self-awareness theory states that if a successful reduction of self-discrepancy seems unlikely, individuals will take a second route: escape from self-awareness. Roy Baumeister (1991) speculates that drug abuse, sexual masochism, spiritual ecstasy, binge eating, and suicide all serve this escapist function. Even television may serve as a form of escape. In one study, Sophia Moskalenko and Steven Heine (2003) brought college students into a laboratory and tested their actual-ideal self-discrepancies twice. Half watched a brief TV show on nature before the second test. In a second study, students were sent home with the questionnaire and instructed to fill it out either before or after watching TV. In both cases, those who watched TV had lower self-discrepancies on the second measure. In yet a third study, students who were told they had done poorly on an IQ test spent more time watching TV while waiting in the lab than those who were told they had succeeded. Perhaps TV and other forms of entertainment enable people to "watch their troubles away."

One particularly disturbing health implication concerns the use of alcohol. According to Jay Hull, people often drown their sorrows in a bottle as a way to escape the negative implications of self-awareness. To test this hypothesis, Hull and Richard Young (1983) administered what was supposed to be an IQ test to male participants and gave false feedback suggesting that they had either succeeded or failed. Supposedly as part of a separate study, those participants were then asked to taste and rate different wines. As they did so, experimenters kept track of how much they

FIGURE 3.6

The Causes and Effects of Self-Awareness

Self-awareness pressures people to reduce self-discrepancies either by matching their behavior to personal or societal standards or by withdrawing from self-awareness.

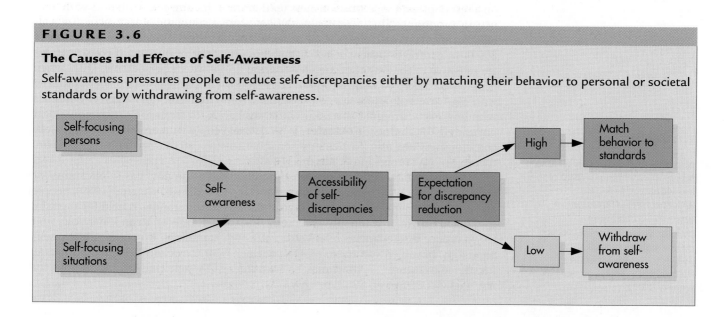

TABLE 3.1

How Self-Conscious Are You?

These sample items appear in the Self-Consciousness Scale. How would you describe yourself on the public and the private aspects of self-consciousness?

(Fenigstein et al., 1975.)

Items That Measure Private Self-Consciousness

- I'm always trying to figure myself out.
- I'm constantly examining my motives.
- I'm often the subject of my fantasies.
- I'm alert to changes in my mood.
- I'm aware of the way my mind works when I work on a problem.

Items That Measure Public Self-Consciousness

- I'm concerned about what other people think of me.
- I'm self-conscious about the way I look.
- I'm concerned about the way I present myself.
- I usually worry about making a good impression.
- One of the last things I do before leaving my house is look in the mirror.

drank during a fifteen-minute tasting period. As predicted, participants who were prone to self-awareness drank more wine after failure than after success, presumably to dodge the blow to their self-esteem. Among participants not prone to self-awareness, there was no difference in alcohol consumption. These results come as no surprise. Indeed, many of us expect alcohol to grant this form of relief (Leigh & Stacy, 1993) and help us manage our emotional highs and lows (Cooper et al., 1995).

Claude Steele and Robert Josephs (1990) believe that alcoholic intoxication offers more than just a means of tuning out on the self. By causing people to lose touch with reality and shed their inhibitions, it also evokes a state of "drunken self-inflation." In one study, for example, participants rated their actual and ideal selves on various traits—some important to self-esteem, others not important. After drinking either an 80-proof vodka cocktail or a harmless placebo, they re-rated themselves on the same traits. As measured by the perceived discrepancy between actual and ideal selves, participants who were drinking expressed inflated views of themselves on traits they considered important (Banaji & Steele, 1989).

Self-Focusing Persons   Just as *situations* evoke a state of self-awareness, some *individuals* are generally more self-focused than others. Research has revealed an important distinction between **private self-consciousness**—the tendency to introspect about our inner thoughts and feelings—and **public self-consciousness**—the tendency to focus on our outer public image (Buss, 1980; Fenigstein et al., 1975). Table 3.1 presents a sample of items used to measure these traits.

Private and public self-consciousness are distinct traits. People who score high on a test of private self-consciousness tend to fill in incomplete sentences with first-person pronouns. They also make self-descriptive statements and recognize self-relevant words more quickly than other words (Mueller, 1982; Eichstaedt & Silvia, 2003). In contrast, those who score high on a measure of public self-consciousness are sensitive to the way they are viewed from an outsider's perspective. Thus, when people were asked to draw a capital letter E on their foreheads, 43 percent of those with high levels of public self-consciousness, compared with only 6 percent of those with low levels, oriented the E so that it was backward from their own standpoint but correct for an outside observer (Hass, 1984). People who are high in public self-consciousness are also particularly sensitive to the extent to which others share their opinions (Fenigstein & Abrams, 1993).

The distinction between private and public self-awareness has implications for the ways in which we reduce self-discrepancies. According to Higgins (1989), people are motivated to meet either their own standards or the standards held for them by significant others. If you're privately self-conscious, you listen to an inner voice and try to reduce discrepancies relative to your own standards; if you're publicly self-conscious, however, you try to match your behavior to socially accepted norms. As illustrated in Figure 3.7, there may be "two sides of the self: one for you and one for me" (Scheier & Carver, 1983, p. 123).

private self-consciousness
A personality characteristic of individuals who are introspective, often attending to their own inner states.

public self-consciousness
A personality characteristic of individuals who focus on themselves as social objects, as seen by others.

FIGURE 3.7

Revolving Images of Self

According to self-awareness theory, people try to meet either their own standards or standards held for them by others—depending, perhaps, on whether they are in a state of private or public self-consciousness. As Scheier and Carver (1983, p. 123) put it, there are "two sides of the self: one for you and one for me."

(Snyder et al., 1983.)

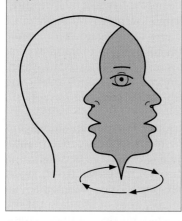

"The highest possible stage in moral culture is when we recognize that we ought to control our thoughts."

—Charles Darwin

Self-Regulation and Its Limits

To this point, we have seen that self-focused attention can motivate us to control our behavior and strive toward personal or social ideals. To achieve these goals—which enables us to reduce the self-discrepancies that haunt us—we must constantly engage in self-regulation, the processes by which we seek to control or alter our thoughts, feelings, behaviors, and urges. From lifting ourselves out of bed in the morning to dieting, running the extra mile, smiling politely at people we really don't like, and working when we have more exciting things to do, the exercise of self-control is something we do all the time (Carver & Scheier, 1998; Baumeister & Vohs, 2004).

Mark Muraven and Roy Baumeister (2000) theorize that self-control is a limited inner resource that can temporarily be depleted by usage. There are two components to their theory. The first is that all self-control efforts draw from a single common reservoir. The second is that exercising self-control is like flexing a muscle: Once used, it becomes fatigued and loses strength, making it more difficult to re-exert self-control—at least for a while, until the resource is replenished. Deny yourself the ice-cream sundae that tickles your sweet tooth and you'll find it more difficult to hold your temper when angered. Try to conceal your stage fright as you stand before an audience and you'll find it harder to resist the urge to watch TV when you should be studying.

Thus far, research has supported this provocative hypothesis. In one study, for example, Muraven and Baumeister (1998) had participants watch a brief clip from an upsetting film that shows scenes of sick and dying animals exposed to radioactive waste. Some of the participants were instructed to stifle their emotional responses to the clip, including their facial expressions; others were told to amplify or exaggerate their facial responses; a third group received no special instructions. Both before and after the movie, self-control was measured by the length of time participants were able to squeeze a handgrip exerciser without letting go. As predicted, those who had to inhibit or amplify their emotions during the film—but not those in the third group—lost their willpower in the handgrip task from the first time they tried it and the second (see Figure 3.8). Other studies have since confirmed the point: After people exert self-control in one task, their capacity for self-regulation is weakened—causing them to talk too much, disclose too much, or brag too much in a later social situation (Vohs et al., 2005).

It appears that we can control ourselves only so much before self-regulation fatigue sets in, causing us to "lose it." What might this mean, then, for people who are constantly regulating their behavior? To find out, Kathleen Vohs and Todd Heatherton (2000) showed a brief and dull documentary to individual female college students, half of whom were chronic dieters. Placed in the viewing room—either within arm's reach (high temptation) or ten feet away (low temptation)—was a bowl filled with Skittles, M&Ms, Doritos, and salted peanuts that participants were free to sample. After watching the movie, they were taken to another room for an ice-cream taste test and told they could eat as much as they wanted. How much ice cream did they consume? The researchers predicted that dieters seated within reach of the bowl would have to fight the hardest to avoid snacking—an act of self-control that would cost them later. The prediction was confirmed. As measured by the amount of ice cream consumed in the taste test, dieters in the high-temptation condition ate more ice cream than did all non-dieters and dieters in the low-temptation situation. What's more, a second study showed that dieters who had to fight the urge in the high-temptation situation were later less persistent—and quicker to give up—on a set of impossible cognitive problems they were asked to solve.

There's another possible downside to self-control that is often seen in sports when athletes become so self-focused under pressure that they stiffen up and "choke." While many athletes rise to the occasion, the pages of sports history are filled with stories of basketball players who lose their touch in the final minute of a championship game, of golfers who lose the pin while putting for tournament victory, and of tennis players who lose their serve, double-faulting when it matters

FIGURE 3.8

Self-Control as a Limited Inner Resource

Participants were shown an upsetting film and told to amplify or suppress their emotional responses to it (a third group received no self-control instruction). Before and afterward, self-control was measured by persistence at squeezing a handgrip exerciser. As shown, the two groups that had to control their emotions during the film—but not those in the third group—later lost their willpower on the handgrip.

(Muraven & Baumeister, 1998.)

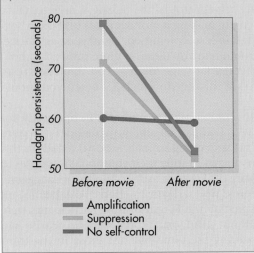

Sometimes the harder you try to control a thought, feeling, or behavior, the less likely you are to succeed. **True.**

most. "Choking" in these ways seems to be a paradoxical type of failure caused by trying too hard and thinking too much. When you learn a new motor activity, like how to throw a curve ball or land a jump, you must think through the mechanics in a slow and cautious manner. As you get better, however, your movements become automatic, so you do not have to think about timing, breathing, the position of your head and limbs, or the distribution of your weight. You relax and just do it. Unless trained to perform while self-focused, athletes under pressure often try their hardest not to fail, become self-conscious, and think too much—all of which disrupts the fluid and natural flow of their performance (Baumeister, 1984; Beilock & Carr, 2001; Gray, 2004; Lewis & Linder, 1997).

The paradoxical effects of attempted self-control are evident in other situations, too. Studying what he calls *ironic processes*, Daniel Wegner (1994) has found that, at times, the harder you try to inhibit a thought, feeling, or behavior, the less likely you are to succeed. Try not to think about a white bear for the next thirty seconds, he finds, and that very image intrudes upon consciousness with remarkable frequency. Instruct the members of a jury to disregard inadmissible evidence, and the censored material is sure to pop to mind as they deliberate. Try not to worry about how long it's taking to fall asleep, and you'll stay awake. Try not to laugh in class, think about the chocolate cake in the fridge, or scratch the itch on your nose—well, you get the idea.

According to Wegner, every conscious effort at maintaining control is met by a concern about failing to do so. This concern automatically triggers an "ironic operating process" as the person, trying hard *not* to fail, searches his or her mind for the unwanted thought. The ironic process will not necessarily prevail, says Wegner. Sometimes we can put the imaginary white bear out of mind. But if the person is cognitively busy, tired, distracted, hurried, or under stress, then the ironic process, because it "just happens," will prevail over the intentional process, which requires conscious attention and effort. Thus, Wegner (1997) notes that "any attempt at mental control contains the seeds of its own undoing" (p. 148).

Ironic processes have been observed in a wide range of behaviors. In an intriguing study of this effect on the control of motor behavior, Wegner and his colleagues (1998) had participants hold a pendulum (a crystalline pendant suspended from a nylon fishing line) over the center of two intersecting axes on a glass grid, which formed a +. Some participants were instructed simply to keep the pendulum steady, while others were pointedly told not to allow it to swing back and forth along the horizontal axis. Try this yourself, and you'll see that it's not easy to prevent all movement. In this experiment, however, the pendulum was more likely to swing horizontally when this direction was specifically forbidden. To further examine the role of mental distraction, the researchers instructed some participants to count backward from a thousand by sevens while controlling the pendulum. In this situation, the ironic effect was even greater. Among those who tried to prevent horizontal movement but could not concentrate fully on the task, the pendulum swayed freely back and forth—in the forbidden direction (see Figure 3.9). Applying this logic to keeping secrets, other researchers have found that instructing word-game players to conceal hidden clues from a fellow player increased rather than decreased their tendency to leak that information (Lane et al., 2006). It may seem both comic and tragic, but at times our efforts at self-control backfire, thwarting even the best of intentions.

Mechanisms of Self-Enhancement

We have seen that self-awareness can create discomfort and lower self-esteem by focusing attention on discrepancies. We have seen that people often avoid focusing on themselves and turn away from unpleasant truths, but that such avoidance is

Why do some athletes choke under pressure and others rise to the occasion? Heading into the 2006 Winter Olympics in Turin, Italy, American downhill racer Bode Miller, a daredevil from New Hampshire, was favored to win several gold medals. Yet after slipping, falling, and missing gates, he failed to win a single medal, gold or otherwise (left). In contrast, Japan's unassuming figure skater Shizuka Arakawa was not favored to win a medal. But then, as if feeling no pressure, she skated a strong and fluid final program, landed her triple jump combinations cleanly, and won the gold (right).

"We don't see things as they are, we see them as we are."

—Anais Nin

implicit egotism
A nonconscious form of self-enhancement.

not always possible. And we have seen that efforts at self-regulation often fail and sometimes even backfire. How, then, does the average person cope with his or her faults, inadequacies, and uncertain future?

At least in Western cultures, most people think highly of themselves most of the time. Consistently, and across a broad range of life domains, research has shown that participants see positive traits as more self-descriptive than negative traits, evaluate themselves more highly than they do others, rate themselves more highly than they are rated *by* others, exaggerate their control over life events, and predict that they have a bright future (Taylor, 1989; Dunning et al., 2004).

Research shows that people overrate their effectiveness as speakers to an audience (Keysar & Henly, 2002) and overestimate their contributions to a group and the extent to which they would be missed if absent (Savitsky et al., 2003). People also overestimate their intellectual and social abilities across a wide range of domains. What's particularly interesting about this tendency is that those who are least competent are the most likely to overrate their own performance. In a series of studies, Justin Kruger and David Dunning (1999) found that college students with the lowest scores on tests of logic, grammar, and humor were the ones who most grossly overjudged their own abilities (on average, their scores were in the lowest 12 percent among peers, yet they estimated themselves to be in the 62nd percentile). These investigators found that when the low-scorers were trained to be more competent in these areas, they became more realistic in their self-assessments. Ignorance, as they say, is bliss.

Other research, too, shows that people exhibit **implicit egotism**, an unconscious and subtle form of self-enhancement. This is well illustrated in the finding that people rate the letters contained within their name more favorably than the other letters of the alphabet (Hoorens & Nuttin, 1993). In an article entitled "Why Susie Sells Seashells by the Seashore," Brett Pelham and his colleagues (2002) argue that people form positive associations to the sight and sound of their own name and thus are drawn to other people, places, and entities that share this most personal aspect of "self." In a thought-provoking series of studies, these researchers examined several important life choices that we make and found that people exhibit small but statistically detectable preferences for things that contain the letters of their own first or last name. For example, men and women are more likely than would be predicted by chance to live in places (Michelle in Michigan, George in Georgia), attend schools (Kari from the University of Kansas, Preston from Penn State University), and choose careers (Dennis and Denise as dentists) whose names resemble their own. Indeed, marriage records found on various genealogical Web sites reveal that people are disproportionately likely to marry others whose first or last names resemble their

FIGURE 3.9

Ironic Effects of Mental Control

In this study, participants tried to hold a pendulum motion-less over a grid. As illustrated in the tracings shown here, they were better at the task when simply instructed to keep the pendulum steady (*a*) than when specifically told to prevent horizontal movement (*c*). Among participants who were mentally distracted during the task, this ironic effect was even greater (*b* and *d*).

(Wegner et al., 1998).

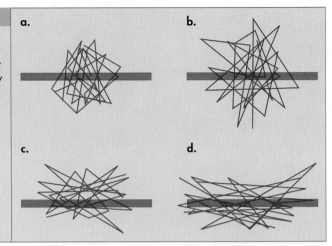

own (Jones et al., 2004). In a subtle but remarkable way, we unconsciously seek out reflections of the self in our surroundings.

This recent research on implicit egotism shows that people hold themselves in high regard. It's not that we consciously or openly flatter ourselves. The response is more like a reflex. Indeed, when research participants are busy or distracted as they make self-ratings, their judgments are quicker and even more favorable (Hixon & Swann, 1993; Paulhus et al., 1989). We can't all be perfect, nor can we all be better than average. So what supports this common illusion? In this section, we examine four methods that people use to rationalize or otherwise enhance their self-esteem: self-serving cognitions, self-handicapping, basking in the glory of others, and downward social comparisons.

Self-Serving Cognitions   How well did you do on the Scholastic Assessment Test (SAT)? When James Shepperd (1993b) asked college students about their performance on this infamous test, he uncovered two interesting patterns. First, the students overestimated their actual scores by an average of 17 points. This inflationary distortion was most pronounced among those with relatively low scores, and it persisted somewhat even when students knew that the experimenter would check their academic files. Second, a majority of students whose SAT scores were low described their scores as inaccurate and the test in general as invalid. In fact, the SATs for the group as a whole were predictive of their grade point averages.

When students receive exam grades, those who do well take credit for the success; those who do poorly complain about the instructor or test questions. When researchers have articles accepted for publication, they credit the quality of their work; when articles are rejected, they blame the editors and reviewers. When gamblers win a bet, they marvel at their skillfulness; when they lose, they blame fluke events that transformed near victory into defeat. Whether people have high or low self-esteem, explain their own outcomes publicly or in private, and try to be honest or to make a good impression, there is bias. Across a range of cultures, people tend to take credit for success and distance themselves from failure (Mezulis et al., 2004; Schlenker et al., 1990)—all while seeing themselves as objective, not biased (Pronin et al., 2004).

Most of us are also unrealistically optimistic. College students who were asked to predict their own future compared with that of the average peer believed that they would graduate higher in their class, get a better job, have a happier marriage, and bear a gifted child. They also believed that they were less likely to get fired or divorced, have a car accident, become depressed, be victimized by crime, or suffer a heart attack (Weinstein, 1980). In sports, politics, health, and social issues, people exhibit an optimistic bias about their own future (Helweg-Larsen & Shepperd, 2001).

Obviously, the future is not always bright, so what supports this unwavering optimism? Ziva Kunda (1987) found that people bolster their rosy outlook with elaborate theories that link their own personal attributes to desirable outcomes. In

In casinos, racetracks, and lotteries, gamblers lose billions of dollars a year. This self-defeating behavior persists in part because people exaggerate their control over random events. For example, many slot machine addicts mistakenly think that they can find "hot" machines that have not recently surrendered a jackpot.

one study, for example, people who had been involved in a serious high school relationship said they believed that such an experience promotes a stable marriage. Yet those who had not been romantically involved said they believed that a *lack* of experience promotes a happy-ever-after ending. It is no wonder that those who participated in Kunda's study predicted there was only a 20 percent chance that their own future marriages would end in divorce—despite knowing that the population divorce rate is 50 percent.

Perhaps one reason that people are eternally optimistic is that they harbor illusions of control, overestimating the extent to which they can influence personal outcomes that are not, in fact, within their power to control (Thompson, 1999). In a series of classic experiments on the illusion of control, Ellen Langer (1975) found that college students bet more money in a chance game of high-card when their opponent seemed nervous rather than confident and were more reluctant to sell a lottery ticket if they'd chosen the number themselves than if it was assigned. Emily Pronin and others (2006) tested the related hypothesis that imagining an event before it occurs can lead people to think they had influenced it. In one study, for example, participants watched a trained confederate shoot hoops on a basketball court. Before each shot, they were instructed to visualize his success ("the shooter releases the ball and it swooshes through the net") or an irrelevant event ("the shooter's arm curls to lift a dumbbell"). After the confederate's successful shooting spree, spectators rated the extent of their influence over his performance. As if linking thoughts to outcomes, they exhibited an illusion of mental causation—taking more credit for influence when they had visualized the shooter's success than when they had not.

Self-Handicapping "My dog ate my homework." "I had a flat tire." "My alarm didn't go off." "My computer crashed." "I had a bad headache." "The referee blew the call." On occasion, people make excuses for their past performance. Sometimes they even come up with excuses in anticipation of future performance. Particularly when people are afraid that they might fail in an important situation, they use illness, shyness, anxiety, pain, trauma, and other complaints as excuses (Kowalski, 1996; Snyder & Higgins, 1988). The reason people do this is simple: By admitting to a limited physical or mental weakness, they can shield themselves from what could be the most shattering implication of failure—a lack of ability.

One form of excuse-making that many of us can relate to is *procrastination*— a purposive delay in starting or completing a task that is due at a particular time (Ferrari et al., 1995). Some people procrastinate chronically, while others do so only in certain situations. There are many reasons why someone might put off what needs to get done—whether it's studying for a test, shopping for Christmas, or preparing for the April 15 tax deadline. According to Joseph Ferrari (1998), one "benefit" of procrastinating is that it helps to provide an excuse for possible failure.

Making verbal excuses is one way to cope with the threatening implications of failure. Under certain conditions, this strategy is taken one step further, as when people actually sabotage their own performance. It seems like the ultimate paradox, but there are times when we purposely set *our*selves up for failure in order to preserve our precious self-esteem. As first described by Stephen Berglas and Edward Jones (1978), **self-handicapping** refers to actions people take to handicap their own performance in order to build an excuse for anticipated failure. To demonstrate, Berglas and Jones recruited college students for an experiment supposedly concerning the effects of drugs on intellectual performance. All the participants worked on a twenty-item test of analogies and were told that they had done well, after which they expected to work on a second, similar test. For one group, the problems in the first test were relatively easy, leading participants to expect more success in the second

self-handicapping
Behaviors designed to sabotage one's own performance in order to provide a subsequent excuse for failure.

test; for a second group, the problems were insoluble, leaving participants confused about their initial success and worried about possible failure. Before seeing or taking the second test, participants were given a choice of two drugs: Actavil, which was supposed to improve performance, and Pandocrin, which was supposed to impair it.

Although no drugs were actually administered, most participants who were confident about the upcoming test selected the Actavil. In contrast, most males (but not females) who feared the outcome of the second test chose the Pandocrin. By handicapping themselves, these men set up a convenient excuse for failure—an excuse, we should add, that may have been intended more for the experimenter's benefit than for the benefit of the participants themselves. Indeed, a follow-up study showed that although self-handicapping occurs when the experimenter witnesses the participants' drug choice, it is reduced when the experimenter is not present while that choice is being made (Kolditz & Arkin, 1982).

Some people use self-handicapping as a defense more than others do (Rhodewalt, 1990), and there are different ways to use it. For example, some men self-handicap by taking drugs (Higgins & Harris, 1988) or neglecting to practice (Hirt et al., 1991), while women tend to report stress and physical symptoms (Smith et al., 1983). Another tactic is to set one's goals too high, as perfectionists like to do, which sets up failure—but not because of a lack of ability (Hewitt et al., 2003; Schultheiss & Brunstein, 2000). Yet another paradoxical tactic used to reduce performance pressure is to play down our own ability, lower expectations, and predict for everyone to hear that we will fail—a self-presentation strategy known as "sandbagging" (Gibson & Sachau, 2000). People also differ in their reasons for self-handicapping. Dianne Tice (1991) found that people who are low in self-esteem use self-handicapping to set up a defensive, face-saving excuse in case they fail, while those who are high in self-esteem use it as an opportunity to claim extra credit if they succeed.

Whatever the tactics and whatever the goal, self-handicapping appears to be an ingenious strategy: With the odds seemingly stacked against us, the self is insulated from failure and enhanced by success. By easing the pressure to succeed, self-handicapping might even enable us to enjoy what we're doing without worrying so much about how well we do it (Deppe & Harackiewicz, 1996). Of course, this strategy is not without a cost. Sabotaging ourselves—by not practicing, or by drinking too much, using drugs, faking illness, or setting goals too high—objectively increases the risk of failure. What's worse, it does not exactly endear us to others. Frederick Rhodewalt and his colleagues (1995) found that participants did not like their partners in an experiment when they thought that these partners had self-handicapped by claiming they did not care, were anxious, or were medically impaired. Women in particular are suspicious and critical of people who self-handicap (Hirt et al., 2003).

People often sabotage their own performance in order to protect their self-esteem. **True.**

Basking in the Glory of Others To some extent, your self-esteem is influenced by individuals and groups with whom you identify. According to Robert Cialdini and his colleagues (1976), people often **bask in reflected glory (BIRG)** by showing off their connections to successful others. Cialdini's team first observed BIRGing on the university campuses of Arizona State, Louisiana State, Notre Dame, Michigan, Pittsburgh, Ohio State, and Southern California. On the Monday mornings after football games, they counted the number of school sweatshirts worn on campus and found that more of them were worn if the team had won its game on the previous Saturday. In fact, the larger the margin of victory was, the more school shirts were counted.

To evaluate the effects of self-esteem on BIRGing, Cialdini gave students a general-knowledge test and rigged the results so half would succeed and half would fail. The students were then asked to describe in their own words the outcome of a recent football game. In these descriptions, students who thought they had just failed a test were more likely than those who thought they had succeeded to share in their team's victory by exclaiming that "*we* won" and to distance themselves from defeat by lamenting how "*they* lost." In another study, participants coming off a recent failure were quick to point out that they had the same birth date as someone known to be successful—thus BIRGing by a merely coincidental association (Cialdini & De Nicholas, 1989).

bask in reflected glory (BIRG) To increase self-esteem by associating with others who are successful.

When Vietnam veterans returned in defeat more than twenty-five years ago, they were neglected, even scorned, by the American public. It seems that the tendency to bask in reflected glory is matched by an equally powerful need to cut off reflected failure.

If self-esteem is influenced by our links to others, how do we cope with friends, family members, teammates, and co-workers of low status? Again, consider sports fans, an interesting breed. As loudly as they cheer in victory, they often turn and jeer their teams in defeat. This behavior seems fickle, but it is consistent with the notion that people derive part of their self-esteem from associations with others. In one study, participants took part in a problem-solving team that then succeeded, failed, or received no feedback about its performance. Participants were later offered a chance to take home a team badge. In the success and no-feedback groups, 68 and 50 percent, respectively, took badges; in the failure group, only 9 percent did (Snyder et al., 1986). It seems that the tendency to bask in reflected glory is matched by an equally powerful tendency to CORF—that is, to "cut off reflected failure."

Additional research confirms that the failures of others with whom we identify can influence our own sense of well-being. Edward Hirt and his colleagues (1992) found that avid sports fans temporarily lost faith in their own mental and social abilities after a favorite team suffered defeat. Reflected failure may even have physiological effects on the body. Paul Bernhardt and others (1998) took saliva samples from male college students before and after they watched a basketball or soccer game between their favorite team and an arch-rival. By measuring pre- to post-game changes in testosterone levels, these investigators found that men who witnessed their teams in defeat—compared to those who enjoyed victory—had lowered levels of testosterone, the male sex hormone.

Downward Social Comparisons   Earlier, we discussed Festinger's (1954) theory that people evaluate themselves by social comparison with similar others. But let's contemplate the implications. If the people around us achieve more than we do, what does that do to our self-esteem? Perhaps adults who shy away from class reunions in order to avoid having to compare themselves with former classmates are acting out an answer to that question.

Festinger fully realized that people don't always seek out objective information and that social comparisons are sometimes made in self-defense. When a person's self-esteem is at stake, he or she often benefits from making **downward social comparisons** with others who are less successful, less happy, or less fortunate (Hakmiller, 1966; Wills, 1981; Wood, 1989). Research shows that people who suffer some form of setback or failure adjust their social comparisons in a downward direction (Gibbons et al., 2002)—and these comparisons have an uplifting effect on their mood and on their outlook for the future (Aspinwall & Taylor, 1993; Gibbons & McCoy, 1991).

Although Festinger never addressed the issue, Anne Wilson and Michael Ross (2000) note that in addition to making social comparisons between ourselves and similar others, we make *temporal* comparisons between our past and present selves. In one study, these investigators had college students describe themselves; in another, they analyzed the autobiographical accounts of celebrities appearing in popular magazines. In both cases, they counted the number of times the self-descriptions contained references to past selves, to future selves, and to others. The result: People made more comparisons to their own past selves than to others, and most of these temporal comparisons were favorable. Keenly aware of how "I'm better today than when I was younger," people use downward temporal comparisons the way they use downward social comparisons as a means of self-enhancement.

Whether people make upward or downward social comparisons can have striking implications for health-related issues. When victimized by tragic life events (perhaps a crime, an accident, a disease, or the death of a loved one) people like to *affiliate* with others in the same predicament who have adjusted well, role models who offer hope and guidance. But they tend to *compare* themselves with others who are worse off, a form of downward social comparison (Taylor & Lobel, 1989). Clearly, it helps

downward social comparison   The defensive tendency to compare ourselves with others who are worse off than we are.

to know that life could be worse, which is why most cancer patients compare themselves with others in the same predicament but who are adjusting less well than they are. In a study of 312 women who had early-stage breast cancer and were in peer support groups, Laura Bogart and Vicki Helgeson (2000) had the patients report every week for seven weeks on instances in which they talked to, heard about, or thought about another patient. They found that 53 percent of all the social comparisons made were downward, to others who were worse off, while only 12 percent were upward, to others who were better off. (The remainder were "lateral" comparisons to similar or dissimilar others.) Bogart and Helgeson also found that the more often patients made these social comparisons, the better they felt.

Interviews of women with breast cancer tell the story. One woman who had only a lump removed wondered, "How awful it must be for women who have had a full mastectomy." An older woman who had a mastectomy said: "The people I really feel sorry for are these young gals. To lose a breast when you're so young must be awful." Yet a young mastectomy patient derived comfort from the fact that "if I hadn't been married, this thing would have really gotten to me" (Taylor, 1989, p. 171). As these quotes poignantly illustrate, there's often someone else with whom we can favorably compare—and this downward comparison makes us feel better (VanderZee et al., 1996). In the words of a terminally ill patient shown on the CBS documentary *A Time to Die*, "It's not the worst thing that could happen."

Unfortunately, it's not always possible to defend the self via downward social comparison. Think about it. When a sibling, spouse, or close friend has more success than you do, what happens to your self-esteem? Abraham Tesser (1988) predicted two possible reactions. On the one hand, you might feel proud of your association with this successful other, as in the process of basking in reflected glory. If you've ever bragged about the achievements of a loved one as if they were your own, you know how "reflection" can bolster self-esteem. On the other hand, you may feel overshadowed by the success of this other person and experience social comparison jealousy—a mixture of emotions that include resentment, envy, and a drop in self-esteem. According to Tesser, the key to whether one feels the pleasure of reflection or the pain of jealousy is whether the other person's success is self-relevant. When close friends surpass us in ways that are vital to our self-concepts, we become jealous and distance ourselves from them in order to keep up our own self-esteem. When intimate others surpass us in ways that are not important, however, we take pride in their triumphs through a process of reflection (Tesser & Collins, 1988; Tesser et al., 1989).

Personal and cultural factors may also influence the way people react to the success of others. For some people—as in those from collectivist cultures, whose concept of self is expanded to include friends, relatives, co-workers, classmates, and others with whom they identify—the success of another may bolster, not threaten, self-esteem. To test this hypothesis, Wendi Gardner and her colleagues (2002) brought pairs of friends into the laboratory together for a problem-solving task. They found that when they led the friends to think in collectivist terms, each derived pleasure, not jealousy and threat, from the other's greater success.

 ## Are Positive Illusions Adaptive?

Psychologists used to maintain that an accurate perception of reality is vital to mental health. In recent years, however, this view has been challenged by research on the mechanisms of self-defense. Consistently, as we have seen, people preserve their self-esteem by deluding themselves and others with biased cognitions, self-handicapping, BIRGing, and downward comparisons. Are these strategies a sign of health and well-being, or are they symptoms of disorder?

When Shelley Taylor and Jonathon Brown (1988) reviewed the relevant research, they found that individuals who are depressed or low in self-esteem actually have more realistic views of themselves than do most others who are better adjusted. Their self-appraisals are more likely to match appraisals of them made by neutral observers; they make fewer self-serving attributions to account for success and failure; they are less likely to exaggerate their control over uncontrollable events; and they make more balanced predictions about their future. Based on these results, Taylor and Brown reached the provocative conclusion that positive illusions promote happiness, the desire to care for others, and the ability to engage in productive work—hallmark attributes of mental health: "These illusions help make each individual's world a warmer and more active and beneficent place in which to live" (p. 205). People with high self-esteem thus appear to be better adjusted in personality tests and in interviews rated by friends, strangers, and mental health professionals (Taylor et al., 2003).

Not everyone agrees with the notion that it is adaptive in the long run to wear rose-colored lenses. Roy Baumeister and Steven Scher (1988) warned that positive illusions can give rise to chronic patterns of self-defeating behavior, as when people escape from self-awareness through alcohol and other drugs, self-handicap themselves into failure and underachievement, deny health-related problems until it's too late for treatment, and rely on the illusion of control to protect them from the tender mercies of the gambling casino. Others have similarly noted that people sometimes need to be self-critical in order to improve. In a study on success and failure feedback, Heine and others (2001) found that whereas North American college students persisted less on a task after an initial failure than after success, Japanese students persisted more in this situation. Sometimes we have to face up to our shortcomings in order to correct them.

From an interpersonal standpoint, C. Randall Colvin and others (1995) found that people with inflated rather than realistic views of themselves were rated less favorably on certain dimensions by their own friends. In their studies, self-enhancing men were seen as boastful, condescending, hostile, and less considerate of others; self-enhancing women were seen as more hostile, more defensive and sensitive to criticism, more likely to overreact to minor setbacks, and less well liked. People with inflated self-images may make a good first impression on others, but they are liked less and less as time wears on (Paulhus, 1998).

In a study that illustrates this dark side of high self-esteem, Todd Heatherton and Kathleen Vohs (2000) administered a standard self-esteem test to pairs of unacquainted college students and then brought them together for a brief conversation. Just before meeting, one student within each pair took a "Remote Associates Test," which involved finding one word that connects sets of three seemingly unrelated words (for example, *lick, sprinkle,* and *mines* were linked by the word *salt*). For half of these target students, the test was pitched as experimental and the problems given to them were easy to solve. Others were told that the test measured achievement potential and were given very difficult problems—leading them to perform, supposedly, worse than average. Did this ego-threatening feedback affect the students' behavior—and the impressions they made on their interaction partners? In the no-ego-threat group, the high and low self-esteem students were equally well liked. In the ego-threat situation, however, students with high self-esteem became less likable; in fact, they were rated by their partners as rude, unfriendly, and arrogant.

Realism or illusion, which orientation is more adaptive? As social psychologists debate the short-term and long-term effects of positive illusions, it's clear that there is no simple answer. For now, the picture that has emerged is this: People who harbor positive illusions of themselves are likely to enjoy the benefits and achievements of high self-esteem. But these same individuals may pay a price in other ways—as in their relations with others. So what are we to conclude? Do positive illusions motivate personal achievement but alienate us socially from others? Is it adaptive to see oneself in slightly inflated terms, but maladaptive to take a view that is too biased? It will be interesting to see how this thorny debate is resolved in the years to come.

Culture and Self-Esteem

Earlier we saw that inhabitants of individualistic cultures tend to view themselves as distinct and autonomous, whereas those in collectivist cultures view the self as part of an interdependent social network. Do these different orientations have implications for self-esteem? This turns out to be tricky question.

Steven Heine and his colleagues (1999) have argued that cultures have differing effects on the pursuit of self-esteem. Comparing the distribution of self-esteem test scores in Canada and Japan, they found that whereas most Canadians' scores clustered in the high-end range, the majority of Japanese respondents scored in the center of that same range. In other studies, they also observed that Japanese respondents can sometimes be quite self-critical, being willing to talk about themselves in negative, self-effacing terms.

Do Japanese people really have a less positive self-esteem compared to North Americans? Or do Japanese respondents, high in their self-esteem, simply feel compelled to present themselves modestly *to others* (as a function of the collectivist need to "fit in" rather than "stand out")? To answer this question, some researchers have tried to develop indirect, subtle, "implicit" tests that would enable them to measure a person's self-esteem without his or her awareness. In a timed word-association study, researchers found that despite their lower scores on overt self-esteem tests, Asian Americans—just like their European American counterparts—are quicker to associate themselves with positive words like *happy* and *sunshine* than with negative words such as *vomit* and *poison* (Greenwald & Farnham, 2000; Kitayama & Uchida, 2003).

Drawing on these results, Constantine Sedikides and his colleagues (2003) maintain that people from individualist and collectivist cultures are similarly motivated to think highly of themselves—that the burning need for positive self-regard is universal, or "pancultural." The observed differences, they argue, stem from the fact that cultures influence *how* we seek to fulfill that need: Individualists present themselves as unique and self-confident, while collectivists present themselves as modest, equal members of a group. From this perspective, people are tactical in their self-enhancements, exhibiting self-praise or humility depending on what is desirable within their cultural surroundings (J. D. Brown, 2003; Lalwani et al., 2006; Sedikides et al., 2005).

Heine and his colleagues agree only in part with this interpretation of the research. They too argue that all people have a need for positive self-regard, wanting to become "good selves" within their own culture. They note, however, that in the effort to achieve this goal, Westerners and other individualists tend to use self-enhancement tactics to stand out, confirm, and express themselves, while East Asians and other collectivists tend to maintain face in order to fit in, improve the self, and adjust to the standards set by their groups. In short, the basic need for positive self-regard is universal but the specific drive toward self-enhancement is culturally ingrained (Heine, 2005; Heine et al., in press).

Self-Presentation

The human quest for self-knowledge and self-esteem tells us about the inner self. The portrait is not complete, however, until we paint in the outermost layer, the behavioral expression of the social self. Most people are acutely concerned about the image they present to others. The fashion industry, diet centers, cosmetic surgeries designed to reshape everything from eyelids to breasts, and the endless search for miracle drugs that grow hair, remove hair, whiten teeth, freshen breath, and smooth out wrinkles all exploit our preoccupation with physical appearance. Similarly, we are concerned about the impressions we convey through our public behavior. What, as they say, will the neighbors think?

Thomas Gilovich and others (2000) found that people are so self-conscious in public settings that they are often subject to the *spotlight effect*, a tendency to believe that the social spotlight shines more brightly on them than it really does. In one set of studies, participants were asked to wear a T-shirt with a flattering or embarrassing image into a room full of strangers, after which they estimated how many of those strangers would be able to identify the image. Demonstrating that people self-consciously feel as if all eyes are upon them, the T-shirted participants overestimated by 23–40 percent the number of observers who had noticed and could recall what they were wearing. Follow-up studies have similarly shown that when people commit a public social blunder, they later overestimate the negative impact of their behavior on those who had observed them (Savitsky et al., 2001).

In *As You Like It*, William Shakespeare wrote, "All the world's a stage, and all the men and women merely players." This insight was first put into social science terms by sociologist Erving Goffman (1959), who argued that life is like a theater and that each of us acts out certain *lines*, as if from a script. Most important, said Goffman, is that each of us assumes a certain *face*, or social identity, that others politely help us to maintain. Inspired by Goffman's theory, social psychologists study **self-presentation**: the process by which we try to shape what other people think of us and what we think of ourselves (Schlenker, 2003). An act of self-presentation may take many different forms. It may be conscious or unconscious, accurate or misleading, intended for an external audience or for ourselves. In this section, we look at the various goals of self-presentation and the ways in which people try to achieve these goals.

 ## Strategic Self-Presentation

There are basically two types of self-presentation, each serving a different motive. *Strategic self-presentation* consists of our efforts to shape others' impressions in specific ways in order to gain influence, power, sympathy, or approval. Prominent examples of strategic self-presentation are everywhere: in personal ads, in online message boards, in political campaign promises, in defendants' appeals to the jury. The specific goals vary and include the desire to be seen as likable, competent, moral, dangerous, or helpless. Whatever the goal may be, people find it less effortful to present themselves in ways that are accurate rather than contrived (Vohs et al., 2005).

To illustrate this point, Beth Pontari and Barry Schlenker (2000) instructed research participants who were introverted or extroverted to present themselves to a job interviewer in a way that was consistent or inconsistent with their true personality. Without distraction, all participants successfully presented themselves as introverted or extroverted, depending on the task they were given. But could they present themselves as needed if, during the interview, they also had to keep an eight-digit number in mind for a memorization test? In this situation, cognitively busy participants self-presented successfully when asked to convey their true personalities but not when asked to portray themselves in a way that was out of character.

The specific identities that people try to present may vary from one person and situation to another. There are, however, two strategic self-presentation goals that are very common. The first is *ingratiation*, a term used to describe acts that are motivated by the desire to "get along" with others and be liked. The other is *self-promotion*, a term used to describe acts that are motivated by a desire to "get ahead" and gain respect for one's competence (Arkin, 1981; Jones & Pittman, 1982). As shown in Table 3.2, observations of employment interviews reveal that ingratiation and self-promotion are the most common self-presentation tactics that job applicants use (Stevens & Kristof, 1995)—and that these tactics lead recruiters to form positive impressions (Higgins & Judge, 2004).

On the surface, it seems easy to achieve these goals. When people want to be liked, they put their best foot forward, smile a lot, nod their heads, express agreement, and, if necessary, use favors, compliments, and apple-polishing flattery. When people want to be admired for their competence, they try to impress others by talking about themselves and immodestly showing off their status, knowledge, and exploits. In both cases, there are tradeoffs. As the term *brown-nosing* graphically suggests, ingratiation tactics need to be subtle or else they will backfire (Jones, 1964). People also do not like those who relentlessly trumpet and brag about their own achievements (Godfrey et al., 1986) or who exhibit a "slimy" pattern of being friendly to

self-presentation Strategies people use to shape what others think of them.

TABLE 3.2
Strategic Self-Presentation in the Employment Interview

In studies of the influence tactics that job applicants report using in employment interviews, the following uses of ingratiation and self-promotion were commonly reported.

(Higgins & Judge, 2004; Stevens & Kristof, 1995.)

Ingratiation

- I complimented the interviewer or organization.
- I discussed interests I shared in common with the recruiter.
- I indicated my interest in the position and the company.
- I indicated my enthusiasm for working for this organization.
- I smiled a lot or used other friendly nonverbal behaviors.

Self-Promotion

- I played up the value of positive events that I took credit for.
- I described my skills and abilities in an attractive way.
- I took charge during the interview to get my main points across.
- I took credit for positive events even if I was not solely responsible.
- I made positive events I was responsible for appear better than they actually were.

their superiors but not to subordinates (Vonk, 1998).

Self-presentation may give rise to other problems as well. Suggesting that "Self-Presentation Can Be Hazardous to Your Health," Mark Leary and his colleagues (1994) reviewed evidence suggesting that the need to project a favorable public image can lure us into unsafe patterns of behavior. For example, self-presentation concerns can increase the risk of AIDS (as when men are too embarrassed to buy condoms and talk openly with their sex partners), skin cancer (as when people bake under the sun to get an attractive tan), eating disorders (as when women over-diet or use amphetamines, laxatives, and forced vomiting to stay thin), drug abuse (as when teenagers smoke, drink, and use drugs to impress their peers), and accidental injury (as when young men drive recklessly to look fearless to others).

 ## Self-Verification

In contrast to strategic self-presentation is a second motive, *self-verification:* the desire to have others perceive us as we truly perceive ourselves. According to William Swann (1987), people are highly motivated in their social encounters to confirm or verify their existing self-concept in the eyes of others. Swann and his colleagues have gathered a great deal of evidence for this hypothesis—and have found, for example, that people selectively elicit, recall, and accept personality feedback that confirms their self-conceptions. In fact, people sometimes bend over backward to correct others whose impressions are positive but mistaken. In one study, participants interacted with a confederate who later said that they seemed dominant or submissive. When the comment was consistent with the participant's self-concept, it was accepted at face value. Yet when it was inconsistent, participants went out of their way to prove the confederate wrong: Those who perceived themselves as dominant but were labeled submissive later behaved more assertively than usual; those who viewed themselves as submissive but were labeled dominant subsequently became even more docile (Swann & Hill, 1982).

Self-verification seems desirable, but wait: Do people who harbor a negative self-concept want others to share that impression? Nobody is perfect, and everyone has some faults. But do we really want to verify these faults in the eyes of others? Do those of us who feel painfully shy, socially awkward, or insecure about an ability want others to see these weaknesses? Or would we prefer to present ourselves in public as bold, graceful, or com-

Ingratiation is a strategy often used to curry favor.

"Great-looking tie!"

petent? What happens when the desire for self-verification clashes with the need for self-enhancement?

Seeking to answer this question, Swann and his colleagues (Stein-Seroussi and Giesler, 1992) asked each student participant in a laboratory study to fill out a self-concept questionnaire and then choose an interaction partner from two other participants—one who supposedly had evaluated them favorably; the other, unfavorably. The result? Although participants with a positive self-concept chose partners who viewed them in a positive light, a majority of those with a negative self-concept preferred partners who confirmed their admitted shortcomings. In a later study, 64 percent of participants with low self-esteem, compared with only 25 percent of those with high self-esteem, sought clinical feedback about their weaknesses rather than strengths when given a choice (Giesler et al., 1996). Indeed, research suggests that people also prefer to interact with others who verify their group memberships, an aspect of their collective self (Chen et al., 2004).

If people seek self-verification from laboratory partners, it stands to reason that they would want the same from their close relationships. In a study of married couples, husbands and wives separately answered questions about their self-concepts, spouses, and commitment to the marriage. As predicted, people who had a positive self-concept expressed more commitment to partners who appraised them favorably, while those with a negative self-concept felt more committed to partners who appraised them *un*favorably (Swann, Hixon, and De La Ronde, 1992).

On important aspects of the self-concept, research shows that people would rather reflect on and learn more about their positive qualities than negative ones (Sedikides, 1993). Still, it appears that the desire for self-verification is powerful— and can even, at times, trump the need for self-enhancement. We all want to make a good impression, but we also want others in our lives to have an accurate impression, one that is compatible with our own self-concept (Swann, 1999).

Individual Differences in Self-Monitoring

Although self-presentation is a way of life for all of us, it differs considerably among individuals. Some people are generally more conscious of their public image than others. Also, some people are more likely to engage in strategic self-presentation, while others seem to prefer self-verification. According to Mark Snyder (1987), these differences are related to a personality trait he called **self-monitoring**: the tendency to regulate one's own behavior to meet the demands of social situations.

Individuals who are high in self-monitoring appear to have a repertoire of selves from which to draw. Sensitive to strategic self-presentation concerns, they are poised, ready, and able to modify their behavior as they move from one setting to another. As measured by the Self-Monitoring Scale (Snyder, 1974; Snyder & Gangestad, 1986), they are likely to agree with such statements as "I would probably make a good actor" and "In different situations and with different people, I often act like very different persons." In contrast, low self-monitors are self-verifiers by nature, appearing less concerned about the propriety of their behavior. Like character actors always cast in the same role, they express themselves in a consistent manner from one situation to the next, exhibiting what they regard as their true and honest self. On the Self-Monitoring Scale, low self-monitors say that "I can only argue for ideas which I already believe" and "I have never been good at games like charades or improvisational acting" (see Table 3.3).

Social psychologists disagree on whether the Self-Monitoring Scale measures one global trait or a combination of two or more specific traits. They also disagree about whether high and low self-monitors represent two discrete types of people or just points along a continuum. Either way, the test scores do appear to predict important social behaviors (Gangestad & Snyder, 2000).

Concerned with public image, high self-monitors go out of their way to learn about others with whom they might interact and about the rules for appropriate conduct. Then, once they have the situation sized up, they modify their behavior accordingly. If a situation calls for conformity, high self-monitors conform; if the same situation calls for autonomy, they refuse to conform. Unconsciously adapting to

self-monitoring The tendency to change behavior in response to the self-presentation concerns of the situation.

TABLE 3.3
Self-Monitoring Scale

Are you a high or low self-monitor? For each statement, answer True or False. When you are done, give yourself one point if you answered T to items 4, 5, 6, 8, 10, 12, 17, and 18. Then give yourself one point if you answered F to items 1, 2, 3, 7, 9, 11, 13, 14, 15, and 16. Count your total number of points. This total represents your Self-Monitoring Score. Among North American college students, the average score is about 10 or 11.

(Snyder & Gangestad, 1986.)

1. I find it hard to imitate the behavior of other people.
2. At parties and social gatherings, I do not attempt to do or say things that others will like.
3. I can only argue for ideas which I already believe.
4. I can make impromptu speeches even on topics about which I have almost no information.
5. I guess I put on a show to impress or entertain others.
6. I would probably make a good actor.
7. In a group of people I am rarely the center of attention.
8. In different situations and with different people, I often act like very different persons.
9. I am not particularly good at making other people like me.
10. I'm not always the person I appear to be.
11. I would not change my opinions (or the way I do things) in order to please someone or win their favor.
12. I have considered being an entertainer.
13. I have never been good at games like charades or improvisational acting.
14. I have trouble changing my behavior to suit different people and different situations.
15. At a party I let others keep the jokes and stories going.
16. I feel a bit awkward in company and do not show up quite as well as I should.
17. I can look anyone in the eye and tell a lie with a straight face (if for a right end).
18. I may deceive people by being friendly when I really dislike them.

It's more adaptive to alter one's behavior than to stay consistent from one social situation to the next. **False.**

social situations, high self-monitors are likely to mimic the demeanor of others in subtle ways that facilitate smooth social interactions (Cheng & Chartrand, 2003). By contrast, low self-monitors maintain a relatively consistent posture across a range of situations (Snyder & Monson, 1975). As they are highly attuned to their own inner dispositions, low self-monitors may adjust their behavior in response to feedback about their own characteristics (DeMarree et al., 2005). Consistent with the finding that high self-monitors are more concerned than lows about what *other people* think of them, research conducted in work settings shows that high self-monitors receive higher performance ratings and more promotions, and they are more likely to emerge as leaders (Day et al., 2002).

In the coming chapters, we will see that because so much of our behavior is influenced by social norms, self-monitoring is relevant to many aspects of social psychology. There are also interesting developmental implications. A survey of eighteen- to seventy-three-year-olds revealed that self-monitoring scores tend to drop with age—presumably because people become more settled and secure about their personal identities as they get older (Reifman et al., 1989). For now, however, ponder this question: Is it better to be a high or low self-monitor? Is one orientation inherently more adaptive than the other?

The existing research does not enable us to make this kind of value judgment. Consider high self-monitors. Quite accurately, they regard themselves as *pragmatic*, flexible, and adaptive and as able to cope with the diversity of life's roles. But they could also be described as fickle or phony opportunists, more concerned with appearances than with reality and willing to change colors like the reptile chameleon just to fit in. Now think about low self-monitors. They describe themselves as *principled* and forthright; they are without pretense, always speaking their minds so others know where they stand. Of course, they could also be viewed as stubborn, insensitive to their surroundings, and unwilling to compromise in order to get along. Concerning the relative value of these two orientations, then, it is safe to conclude that neither high nor low self-monitoring is necessarily undesirable—unless carried to the extreme. Goffman (1955) made the same point many years ago, when he wrote:

> Too little perceptiveness, too little savoir faire, too little pride and considerateness, and the person ceases to be someone who can be trusted to take a hint about himself or give a hint that will save others embarrassment. . . . Too much savoir faire or too much considerateness and he becomes someone who is too socialized, who leaves others with the feeling that they do not know how they really stand with him, nor what they should do to make an effective long-term adjustment. (p. 227)

Epilogue: The Multifaceted Self

Throughout human history, writers, poets, philosophers, and personality theorists have portrayed the self as an enduring aspect of personality, as an invisible "inner core" that is stable over time and slow to change. The struggle to "find yourself" and "be true to yourself" is based on this portrait. Indeed, when people over eighty-five years old were asked to reflect on their lives, almost all said that despite having changed in certain ways, they had remained essentially the same person (Troll & Skaff, 1997). In recent years, however, social psychologists have focused on change. In doing so, they have discovered that at least part of the self is malleable—molded by life experiences and varying from one situation to the next. From this perspective, the self has many different faces.

When you look into the mirror, what do you see, one self or many? Do you see a person whose self-concept is enduring or one whose identity seems to change from time to time? Do you see a person whose strengths and weaknesses are evaluated with an objective eye or one who is insulated from unpleasant truths by mechanisms of self-defense? Do you see a person who has an inner, hidden self that is different from the face shown to others?

Based on the material presented in this chapter, the answer to such questions seems always to be the same: The self has all these characteristics. More than a hundred years ago, William James (1890) said that the self is not simple but complex and multifaceted. Based on current theories and research, we can now appreciate just how right James was. Sure, there's an aspect of the self-concept that we come to know only through introspection and that is stable over time. But there's also an aspect that changes with the company we keep and the information we get from others. When it comes to self-esteem, there are times when we are self-focused enough to become acutely aware of our shortcomings. Yet there are also times when we guard ourselves through self-serving cognitions, self-handicapping, BIRGing, and downward social comparisons. Then there is the matter of self-presentation. It's clear that each of us has a private self that consists of our inner thoughts, feelings, and memories. But it is equally clear that we also have an outer self, portrayed by the roles we play and the masks we wear in public. As you read through the pages of this text, you will see that the cognitive, affective, and behavioral components of the self are not separate and distinct but interrelated. They are also of great significance for the rest of social psychology.

REVIEW

The Self-Concept

- The self-concept is the sum total of a person's beliefs about his or her own attributes. It is the cognitive component of the self.

Rudiments of the Self-Concept

- Using brain scans, social neuroscientists find that certain areas become relatively more active when people process self-relevant information.
- Recognizing oneself as a distinct entity is the first step in the development of a self-concept.
- Human beings and apes are the only animals to recognize their mirror-image reflections as their own.
- Cooley's "looking-glass" self suggests that social factors are a necessary second step.

Introspection

- People believe that introspection is a key to knowing the true self.
- But research shows that introspection sometimes diminishes the accuracy of self-reports.
- People also tend to overestimate their emotional reactions to future positive and negative events.

Perceptions of Our Own Behavior

- Bem's self-perception theory holds that when internal states are difficult to interpret, we infer our inner states by observing our own behavior and the surrounding situation.
- Based on self-perception theory, the facial feedback hypothesis states that facial expressions can produce, not just reflect, an emotion state (smiling can cause us to feel happy).
- But it's unclear if the emotion occurs via self-perception or because facial expressions trigger physiological changes that produce the emotional response.
- Also derived from self-perception theory, studies of the overjustification effect show that people sometimes lose interest in activities for which they are rewarded.

- But if a reward is seen as a "bonus" for superior performance, then it can enhance intrinsic motivation by providing positive feedback.

Influences of Other People

- According to social comparison theory, people often evaluate their own opinions and abilities by comparing themselves to similar others.
- Schachter and Singer proposed that the experience of emotion is based on two factors: physiological arousal and a cognitive label for that arousal.
- Under certain conditions, people interpret their own arousal by watching others in the same situation.

Autobiographical Memories

- Memory of one's life events is critical to the self-concept.
- When people recall life experiences, they typically report more events from the recent past than from the distant past, though some types of memories are generally more vivid and lasting than others.
- Autobiographical memories are shaped by self-serving motives, as people overemphasize their own roles in past events.

Cultural Influences on the Self-Concept

- Cultures foster different conceptions of self.
- Many Europeans and North Americans hold an independent view of the self that emphasizes autonomy.
- People in certain Asian, African, and Latin American cultures hold an interdependent view of the self that encompasses social connections.
- These cultural differences influence the way we perceive, feel about, and present ourselves in relation to others.

Self-Esteem

- Self-esteem refers to a person's positive and negative evaluations of the self.

The Need for Self-Esteem

- People have a need for high self-esteem and want to see themselves in a positive light.
- People with low self-esteem often find themselves caught in a vicious cycle of self-defeating behavior.

Are there Gender and Race Differences?

- Among adolescents and young adults, males have higher self-esteem than females do, though the difference is very small, particularly among older adults.
- African Americans outscore white Americans on self-esteem tests, indicating, perhaps, that stigmatized minorities focus on their positive attributes.

Self-Discrepancy Theory

- Self-esteem can be defined by the match between how we see ourselves and how we want to see ourselves. Large self-discrepancies are associated with negative emotional states.
- Discrepancies between the actual and ideal selves are related to feelings of disappointment and depression.
- Discrepancies between the actual and the ought selves are related to shame, guilt, and anxiety.
- These emotional effects depend on the amount of discrepancy and whether we are consciously focused on it.

The Self-Awareness "Trap"

- In general, people spend little time actually thinking about themselves.
- But certain situations (mirrors, cameras, audiences) increase self-awareness, and certain people are generally more self-conscious than others.
- Self-awareness forces us to notice self-discrepancies and can produce a temporary reduction in self-esteem.
- To cope, we either adjust our behavior to meet our standards or withdraw from the self-focusing situation.
- Heavy drinking can be viewed as a means of escaping from self-awareness.

Self-Regulation and Its Limits

- Self-control can temporarily be depleted by usage.
- Due to the operation of ironic processes, our efforts at self-control may also backfire, causing us to think, feel, and act in ways that are opposite to our intentions.

Mechanisms of Self-Enhancement

- Most people think highly of themselves and have unconscious positive associations with things related to the self.
- People protect their self-esteem in four major ways: through self-serving cognitions, such as taking credit for success and denying the blame for failure; self-handicapping, in order to excuse anticipated failure; basking in reflected glory, which boosts their self-esteem through associations with successful others; and downward social comparisons to others who are less well off.
- When others surpass us in ways that are important to us, we become jealous and distance ourselves from them. When surpassed in ways that are not self-relevant, we feel pride and seek closeness.

Are Positive Illusions Adaptive?

- Recent research suggests that certain positive illusions may foster high self-esteem and mental health.
- An alternative view is that such illusions promote self-defeating behavior patterns and that people with inflated views of themselves are liked less by others.

Culture and Self-Esteem

- Cross-cultural comparisons indicate that people from collectivist cultures present themselves as modest in their self-esteem relative to people from individualistic cultures.
- Researchers are seeking to determine whether collectivists have a less inflated self-esteem or simply feel compelled to present themselves modestly *to others*.
- Everyone has a need for positive self-regard; individualists and collectivists seek to achieve that need in different ways.

Self-Presentation

- We care deeply about what others think of us and often believe that the social spotlight shines more brightly on us than it really does.
- Self-presentation is the process by which we try to shape what others think of us and even what we think of ourselves. There are two general motives in self-presentation: strategic self-presentation and self-verification.

Strategic Self-Presentation

- Strategic self-presentation is the process by which we try to shape others' impressions of us.
- In social encounters, people often try to get others to see them in a positive light, as likable or competent

Self-Verification

- Apart from the motive to be seen in a positive light, people seek self-verification, a process by which we try to get others to perceive us "accurately," as we see ourselves.

- Research shows that self-verification motives often trump the desire to be seen in a positive light.

Individual Differences in Self-Monitoring

- Individuals differ in the tendency to regulate their behavior to meet the demands of social situations.
- High self-monitors modify their behavior, as appropriate, from one situation to the next.
- Low self-monitors express themselves in a more consistent manner, exhibiting at all times what they see as their true self.

Epilogue: The Multifaceted Self

- As this chapter has shown, the self is not simple but complex and multifaceted.

KEY TERMS

affective forecasting (57)

bask in reflected glory (BIRG) (78)

downward social comparisons (79)

facial feedback hypothesis (58)

implicit egotism (75)

overjustification effect (59)

private self-consciousness (72)

public self-consciousness (72)

self-awareness theory (70)

self-concept (54)

self-esteem (67)

self-handicapping (77)

self-monitoring (85)

self-perception theory (57)

self-presentation (83)

self-schemas (54)

social comparison theory (61)

terror management theory (67)

two-factor theory of emotion (62)

PUTTING COMMON SENSE TO THE TEST

Humans are the only animals who recognize themselves in the mirror.

False. Studies have shown that the great apes (chimpanzees, gorillas, and orangutans) are also capable of self-recognition.

Smiling can make you feel happier.

True. Consistent with the facial feedback hypothesis, facial expressions can trigger or amplify the subjective experience of emotion.

Sometimes the harder you try to control a thought, feeling, or behavior, the less likely you are to succeed.

True. Research on ironic processes in mental control have revealed that trying to inhibit a thought, feeling, or behavior often backfires.

People often sabotage their own performance in order to protect their self-esteem.

True. Studies have shown that people often handicap their own performance in order to build an excuse for anticipated failure.

It's more adaptive to alter one's behavior than to stay consistent from one social situation to the next.

True. High and low self-monitors differ in the extent to which they alter their behavior to suit the situation they are in, but neither style is inherently more adaptive.

4

Perceiving Persons

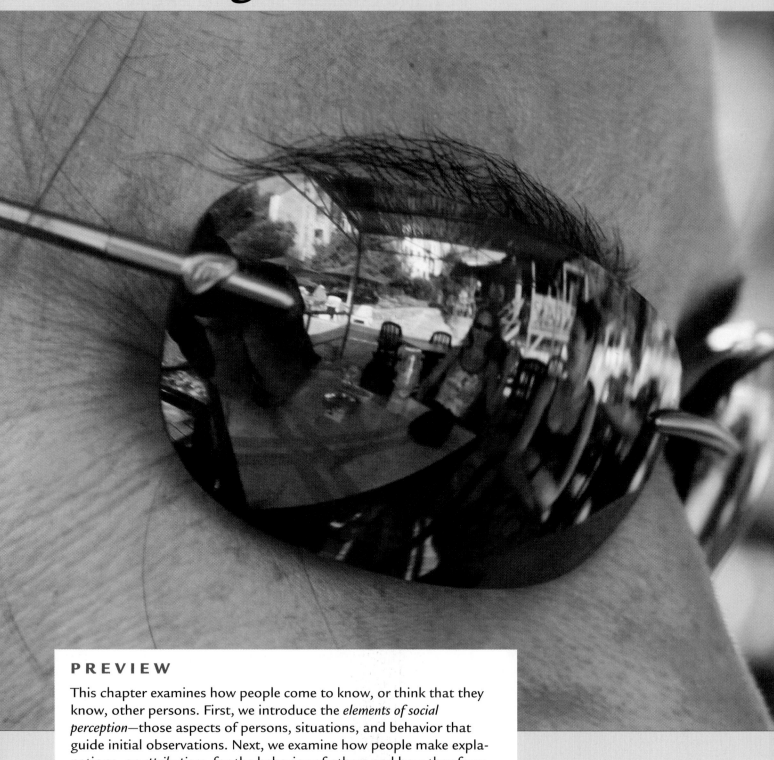

PREVIEW

This chapter examines how people come to know, or think that they know, other persons. First, we introduce the *elements of social perception*—those aspects of persons, situations, and behavior that guide initial observations. Next, we examine how people make explanations, or *attributions*, for the behavior of others and how they form *integrated impressions* based on initial perceptions and attributions. We then consider *confirmation biases*, the subtle ways in which initial impressions lead people to distort later information, setting in motion a self-fulfilling prophecy.

T/F

_____ The impressions we form of others are influenced by superficial aspects of their appearance.

_____ Adaptively, people are skilled at knowing when someone is lying rather than telling the truth.

_____ Like social psychologists, people are sensitive to situational causes when explaining the behavior of others.

_____ People are slow to change their first impressions on the basis of new information.

_____ The notion that we can create a "self-fulfilling prophecy" by getting others to behave in ways we expect is a myth.

_____ People are more accurate at judging the personality of friends and acquaintances than of strangers.

O n July 9, 2006, in front of the 66,000 flag-draped, face-painted fans that filled Olympic Stadium in Berlin, Italy and France squared off for the World Cup soccer final. To get to this point, Italy had most recently defeated Australia, Ukraine, and Germany; France had beaten Spain, Brazil, and Portugal. Tied 1–1 and in overtime, the coveted World Cup championship was still in doubt. Suddenly, France's Zinedine Zidane, voted the most valuable player of the tournament, lowered his head and rammed Italy's Marco Materazzi in the chest, knocking him to the ground. Zidane was ejected from the game, and Italy won on penalty kicks. Why did Zidane head-butt his opponent at this time? Does he have a violent streak he cannot control? Was he overly aroused by the competition and frustrated by Italy's defense? Was he provoked by something Materazzi said? Sports fans wanted to know: What caused this World Cup soccer star to erupt?

One month later, the world's attention shifted to the Middle East. Just as war had broken out between Israel and the Iran-supported Hezbollah militia in Lebanon, Iranian president Mahmoud Ahmadinejad proclaimed to the United Nations, and in several TV appearances, that Iran would not curtail its pursuit of nuclear power. Rejecting U.N. threats and incentives to stop the enrichment of uranium, Ahmadinejad argued that his intentions were peaceful, that he sought to produce nuclear power, not weapons. Yet coming on the heels of remarks he had made that Israel should be "wiped off the map" and that the Holocaust was a "myth," western leaders were apprehensive. Which portrait of Ahmadinejad is correct? Can he be trusted, or do his nuclear ambitions pose a threat to world peace?

Moving from the Middle East to Thailand, U.S. police picked up forty-one-year-old John Mark Karr on suspicion that he had murdered six-year-old beauty contestant JonBenet Ramsey—a high-profile crime committed in Boulder, Colorado, ten years earlier that was never solved. In August 2006, Karr, who had just started to teach a second-grade class in Bangkok, confessed. According to investigators, Karr said he had drugged Ramsey and sexually assaulted her before killing her. In front of TV cameras, he then admitted: "I loved JonBenet, and she died accidentally." Two weeks later, tests on the DNA left on the girl's underwear suggested that Karr was not the killer. So, why would an innocent Karr confess? Was he merely seeking attention? Was he delusional, truly believing that he committed a crime that captured his imagination? Or, was Karr coerced into confessing under the pressure of his Bangkok interrogations?

Whatever the topic—sports, world politics, law, or even personal events closer to home—we are all active and interested participants in **social perception**, the processes by which people come to understand one another. This chapter is divided into four sections. First we look at the "raw data" of social perception: persons, situations,

social perception A general term for the processes by which people come to understand one another.

In the World Cup soccer final of 2006, France's Zinedine Zidane head-butted Italy's Marco Materazzi. Zidane was ejected from the game, and Italy went on to win the championship. What caused Zidane to erupt? Is he a violent person by nature, was he aroused by the intensity of the competition, or was he provoked by his opponent? As social perceivers, this is the type of question we often ask ourselves in trying to understand people.

and behavior. Second, we examine how people explain and analyze behavior. Third, we consider how people integrate their observations into a coherent impression of other persons. Fourth, we discuss some of the subtle ways in which our impressions create a distorted picture of reality, often setting in motion a self-fulfilling prophecy. As you read this chapter, you will notice that the various processes are considered from a perceiver's vantage point. Keep in mind, however, that in the events of life, you are both a *perceiver* and a *target* of others' perceptions.

Observation: The Elements of Social Perception

As our opening examples suggest, understanding others may be difficult, but it's a common and vital part of everyday life. How do we do it? What kinds of evidence do we use? We cannot actually "see" someone's mental or emotional state, or his or her motives or intentions, any more than a detective can see a crime that has already been committed. So, like a detective who tries to reconstruct events by turning up witnesses, fingerprints, blood samples, and other evidence, the social perceiver comes to know others by relying on indirect clues—the elements of social perception. These clues arise from an interplay of three sources: persons, situations, and behavior.

Persons: Judging a Book by Its Cover

Have you ever met someone for the first time and formed a quick impression based only on a quick "snapshot" of information? As children, we were told that we should not judge a book by its cover, that things are not always what they seem, that appearances are deceptive, and that all that glitters is not gold. Yet as adults we can't seem to help ourselves.

To illustrate the rapid-fire nature of the process, Janine Willis and Alexander Todorov (2006) showed college students photographs of unfamiliar faces for one-tenth of a second, half a second, or a full second. Whether the students judged the faces for how attractive, likable, competent, trustworthy, or aggressive they were, their ratings—even at the briefest exposure—were quick and highly correlated with judgments that other observers made without time exposure limits (see Table 4.1). Flip quickly through the pages of an illustrated magazine, and you may see for yourself that it takes a mere fraction of a second to form an impression of a stranger from his or her face.

If first impressions are quick to form, on what are they based? In 500 B.C.E., the mathematician Pythagoras looked into the eyes of prospective students to determine if they were gifted. At about the same time, Hippocrates, the founder of modern medicine, used facial features to make diagnoses of life and death. In the nineteenth century, Viennese physician Franz Gall introduced a carnival-like science called phrenology and claimed that he could assess people's character by the shape of their skulls. And in 1954, psychologist William Sheldon concluded from flawed studies of adult men that there is a strong link between physique and personality.

TABLE 4.1
First Impressions in a Fraction of a Second

Participants rated unfamiliar faces based on pictures they saw for one-tenth of a second, half a second, or a full second. Would their impressions stay the same or change with unlimited time? As measured by the correlations of these ratings with those made by observers who had no exposure time limits, the results showed that ratings were highly correlated even at the briefest exposure times. Giving participants more time did not increase these correlations.

(Willis & Todorov, 2006.)

Traits being judged	.10 sec	.50 sec	1 sec
Trustworthy	.73	.66	.74
Competent	.52	.67	.59
Likeable	.59	.57	.63
Aggressive	.52	.56	.59
Attractive	.69	.57	.66

In the 2000 U.S. presidential election between Bush and Gore, the Florida vote was too close to call. As the world watched, local election officials manually recounted thousands of punch-card ballots previously rejected by machine in order to determine each voter's "intent." What if a cardboard chad was punctured but not dislodged, the so-called hanging chad? Did that signal intent? What about the dimpled or "pregnant" chad, or one that was scratched but not pushed in? These now historic images of social perception in action show how tricky it can be to judge another person's state of mind from strictly behavioral evidence.

People may not measure each other by bumps on the head, as phrenologists used to do, but first impressions are influenced in subtle ways by a person's height, weight, skin color, hair color, tattoos, piercings, eyeglasses, and other aspects of physical appearance. As social perceivers, we also form impressions of people, often accurate, based on a host of indirect cues such as personal offices and dormitory bedrooms (Gosling et al., 2002), the identity claims made on personal Web sites (Vazire & Gosling, 2004), and the type of music that inhabits the iPod (Rentfrow & Gosling, 2006). In one study, crime suspects were seen as more aggressive when dressed in black, a color that is associated with evil and death in many cultures, than when they wore lighter clothing (Vrij, 1997). In another study, both men and women were seen as more feminine when they spoke in high-pitched voices than in lower-pitched voices (Ko et al., 2006). We can even be influenced by a person's name. Hence, in one study fictional characters with "old-generation" names such as Harry, Walter, Dorothy, and Edith were judged less popular and intelligent than those with younger-generation names such as Kevin, Michael, Lisa, and Michelle (Young et al., 1993).

The human face in particular attracts more than its share of attention. Since the time of ancient Greece, human beings have attended to physiognomy—the art of reading character from faces. Although we may not realize it, this tendency persists today. For example, Ran Hassin and Yaacov Trope (2000) found that people prejudge others in photographs as kind-hearted rather than mean-spirited based on such features as a full, round face, curly hair, long eyelashes, large eyes, a short nose, full lips, and an upturned mouth. Interestingly, these researchers also found that just as people read traits from *faces*, at times they read traits *into* faces based on prior information. In one study, for example, participants who were told that a man was kind—compared to those told he was mean—later judged his face to be fuller, rounder, and more attractive.

In social perception studies of the human face, researchers have found that adults who have baby-faced features—large, round eyes, high eyebrows, round cheeks, a large forehead, smooth skin, and a rounded chin—tend to be seen as warm, kind,

In the nineteenth century, Franz Gall introduced phrenology, the pseudo-scientific theory that personality traits and abilities could be "seen" in the bumps on the skull.

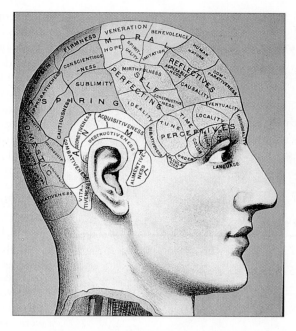

The impressions we form of others are influenced by superficial aspects of their appearance. **True.**

"Our faces, together with our language, are social tools that help us navigate the social encounters that define our 'selves' and fashion our lives."

—Alan J. Fridlund

naive, weak, honest, and submissive. In contrast, adults who have mature features—small eyes, low brows and a small forehead, wrinkled skin, and an angular chin—are seen as stronger, more dominant, and more competent (Berry & Zebrowitz-McArthur, 1986). Thus, in small claims court, judges are more likely to favor baby-faced defendants who are accused of intentional wrongdoing, but they tend to rule against baby-faced individuals accused of negligence (Zebrowitz & McDonald, 1991). And in the work setting, baby-faced job applicants are more likely to be recommended for employment as day-care teachers, whereas mature-faced adults are considered to be better suited for work as bankers (Zebrowitz et al., 1991). Results like these have been found in so many contexts that Leslie Zebrowitz and Joann Montepare (2005) recently concluded that baby-facedness "profoundly affects human behavior in the blink of an eye" (p. 1565).

What accounts for these findings? And why, in general, are people so quick to judge others by appearances? There are three possible explanations. One is that humans are genetically programmed to respond gently to infantile features so that real babies are treated with tender loving care. Another possibility is that we simply learn to associate infantile features with helplessness and then generalize this expectation to baby-faced adults. Third, maybe there is an actual link between physical appearance and behavior, a possibility suggested by the fact that research participants exposed only to photos or brief videotapes of strangers formed impressions that correlated with the self-descriptions of these same strangers (Kenny et al., 1992; Zebrowitz et al., 2003).

Situations: The Scripts of Life

In addition to the beliefs we hold about persons, each of us has preset notions about certain types of situations—"scripts" that enable people to anticipate the goals, behaviors, and outcomes likely to occur in a particular setting (Abelson, 1981; Read, 1987). Based on past experience, people can easily imagine the sequences of events likely to unfold in a typical greeting or at the shopping mall, the dinner table, or a tennis match. The more experience you have in a given situation, the more detail your scripts will contain. As described in Roger Axtell's (1993) *Do's and Taboos Around the World*, many scripts are culture-specific. In Bolivia, dinner guests clean their plates to prove that they enjoyed the meal. Eat in an Indian home, however, and you'll see that many native guests leave some food on the plate to show the host that they had enough to eat. Such scripts can influence perceptions and behavior. As we'll see in Chapter 11 on Aggression, in "cultures of honor," in which men are expected to defend against insult while their women remain modest and loyal, indications of female infidelity can trigger domestic violence (Vandello & Cohen, 2003).

Behavioral scripts can be quite elaborate. Studying the "first date" script, John Pryor and Thomas Merluzzi (1985) asked U.S. college students to list the sequence of events that take place in this situation. From these lists, a picture of a typical American first date emerged. Sixteen steps were identified, including: (1) male arrives; (2) female greets male at door; (3) female introduces date to parents or roommate; (4) male and female discuss plans and make small talk; (5) they go to a movie; (6) they get something to eat or drink; (7) male takes female home; (8) if interested, he remarks about a future date; (9) they kiss; (10) they say good night. Sound familiar? Pryor and Merluzzi then randomized their list of events and asked participants to arrange them into the appropriate order. They found that those with extensive dating experience were able to organize the statements more quickly than those who had less dating experience. For people who are familiar with a script, the events fall into place like the pieces of a puzzle.

Knowledge of social settings provides an important context for understanding other people's verbal and nonverbal behavior. For example, this knowledge leads us to expect someone to be polite during a job interview, playful at a picnic, and rowdy at a keg party. Scripts influence social perceptions in two ways. First, we sometimes see what we expect to see in a particular situation. In one study, participants looked at photographs of human faces that had ambiguous expressions. When told that the person in the photo was being threatened by a vicious dog, they saw the expression as fearful; when told that the individual had just won money, participants interpreted the *same* expression as a sign of happiness (Trope, 1986). Second, people use what they know about social situations to explain the causes of human behavior. As described later in this chapter, an action seems to offer more information about a person when it departs from the norm than when it is common. In other words, you would learn more about someone who is rowdy during a job interview or polite at a keg party than if it were the other way around.

Behavioral Evidence

An essential first step in social perception is to recognize what someone is doing at a given moment. Identifying actions from movement is surprisingly easy. Even when actors dressed in black move about in a dark room with point lights attached only to the joints of their bodies, people quickly and easily recognize such complex acts as walking, running, jumping, exercising, and falling (Johansson et al., 1980). This ability is found in people of all cultures (Barrett et al., 2005).

More interesting, perhaps, is that people derive *meaning* from their observations by dividing the continuous stream of human behavior into discrete "units." By having participants observe someone on videotape and press a button whenever they

Can you tell how these individuals are feeling? If you are like most people, regardless of your culture, you will have little trouble recognizing the emotions portrayed.

detect a meaningful action, Darren Newtson and his colleagues (1987) found that some perceivers break the behavior stream into a large number of fine units, whereas others break it into a small number of gross units. While watching a baseball game, for example, you might press the button after each pitch, after each batter, after every inning, or only after runs are scored. The manner in which people divide a stream of behavior can influence their perceptions in important ways. Research participants who were told to break an event into fine units rather than gross units attended more closely, detected more meaningful actions, and remembered more details about the actor's behavior than did gross-unit participants (Lassiter et al., 1988). More recent research shows that social perceivers who identify another's actions in high-level terms rather than low-level terms (for example, by describing "painting a house" as trying to make a house look new, not just applying brush strokes) are more likely to attribute humanizing thoughts, intentions, emotions, and other mental states to that actor (Kozak et al., 2006).

The Silent Language of Nonverbal Behavior   Behavioral cues are used not only to identify someone's physical actions but also to determine his or her inner states. Knowing how another person is feeling can be tricky because people often try to hide their true emotions. Have you ever had to suppress your rage at someone, mask your disappointment after failure, feign surprise, make excuses, or pretend to like something just to be polite? Sometimes people come right out and tell us how they feel. At other times, however, they do not tell us, they are themselves not sure, or they actively try to conceal their true feelings. For these reasons, we often tune in to the silent language of **nonverbal behavior**.

What kinds of nonverbal cues do people use in judging how someone else is feeling? In *The Expression of the Emotions in Man and Animals*, Charles Darwin (1872) proposed that the face expresses emotion in ways that are innate and understood by people all over the world. Contemporary research supports this notion. Numerous studies have shown that when presented with photographs similar to those on page 97, people can reliably identify at least six "primary" emotions: happiness, sadness, anger, fear, surprise, and disgust. In one study, participants from ten different countries—Estonia, Germany, Greece, Hong Kong, Italy, Japan, Scotland, Sumatra, Turkey, and the United States—exhibited high levels of agreement in their recognition of these emotions (Ekman et al., 1987).

From one end of the world to the other, it is clear that a smile is a smile and a frown is a frown, and that just about everyone knows what they mean—even when these expressions are "put on" by actors and not genuinely felt. But do the results fully support the claim that basic emotions are "universally" recognized from the face, or is the link culturally specific? (Russell, 1994). To answer this question, Hillary Elfenbein and Nalini Ambady (2002) meta-analyzed ninety-seven studies involving a total of 22,148 social perceivers from forty-two different countries. As shown in Figure 4.1, they found support for both points of view. On the one hand, people all over the world are able to recognize the primary emotions from photographs of facial expressions. On the other hand, people are 9 percent more accurate at judging faces from their own national, ethnic, or regional groups than from members of less familiar groups—indicating that we enjoy an "in-group advantage" when it comes to knowing how those who are closest to us are feeling. In a study that illustrates the point, Elfenbein and Ambady (2003) showed pictures of American faces to groups with varying degrees of exposure to Americans. As predicted, more life exposure was associated with greater accuracy, from a low of 60 percent among Chinese participants living in China, up to 83 percent among Chinese living in the United States, 87 percent among Chinese Americans, and 93 percent among non-Chinese Americans. When it comes to recognizing emotions in the face, it appears that familiarity breeds accuracy.

Darwin believed that the ability to recognize emotion in others has survival value for all members of a species. This hypothesis suggests that it is more important to identify some emotions than others. For example, it may be more adaptive to beware of someone who is angry, and hence prone to lash out in violence, than of someone who is happy, a nonthreatening emotion. Indeed, studies have shown that angry faces arouse us and cause us to frown even when presented subliminally and

Many animals communicate nonverbally. For example, ants send chemical signals to indicate food, and vervet monkeys give off loud alarm calls that differ depending on whether the predator they see is a snake, eagle, or leopard.

nonverbal behavior
Behavior that reveals a person's feelings without words—through facial expressions, body language, and vocal cues.

FIGURE 4.1

How Good Are People at Identifying Emotions in the Face?

A meta-analysis of emotion recognition studies involving 22,148 participants from forty-two countries confirmed that people all over the world can recognize the six basic emotions from posed facial expressions.

(Elfenbein & Ambady, 2002.)

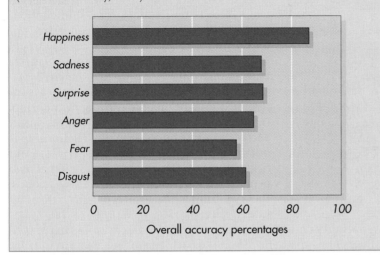

without our awareness (Dimberg & Ohman, 1996; Dimberg et al., 2000). Illustrating what Christine and Ranald Hansen (1988) called the "anger superiority effect," researchers have found that people are quicker to spot—and slower to look away from—angry faces in a crowd than faces with neutral and less threatening emotions (Fox et al., 2002; Horstmann & Bauland, 2006). As to what the face of anger looks like, Joel Aronoff and others (1992) note that anger is universally "seen" in certain geometric patterns in the face, such as triangular eyes that point toward the nose and other hard downward lines in the forehead, cheeks, mouth, and chin.

Disgust is another basic emotion that has adaptive significance. When confronted with an offensive stimulus such as a foul odor, spoiled food, feces, rotting flesh, or the sight of mutilation, people react with an aversion that shows in the way they wrinkle the nose, raise the upper lip, and gape. This visceral reaction is often accompanied by nausea and can facilitate the expulsion of bad food from the mouth (Rozin & Fallon, 1987). In nature, food poisoning is a real threat, so it is adaptive for us to recognize disgust in the face of others. In a recent study, Bruno Wicker and others (2003) had fourteen men watch video clips of people smelling pleasant, disgusting, or neutral odors. Afterward, these same men were exposed to the odors themselves. If you've ever inhaled the sweet, floury aroma of a bakery or inserted your nose into a carton of soured milk, you'll appreciate the different reactions that would appear on your face. Using fMRI, researchers monitored activity in the participants' brains throughout the experiment. They found that a structure in the brain known as the *insula* was activated not only when participants sniffed the disgusting odor but also when they watched *others* sniffing it. This result suggests that people more than recognize the face of disgust; they experience it at a neural level.

The social value of the human face is evident to those who communicate online. When e-mail first became popular, the written word was often misinterpreted, especially when the writer tried to be funny, because it lacked the nonverbal cues that normally animate and clarify live interactions. To fill in this gap, e-mailers created smiley faces and other "emoticons" (emotion icons) from standard keyboard characters. A sampling of routinely used emoticons, which are meant to be viewed with one's head tilted 90 degrees to the left, are shown in Figure 4.2 (Sanderson, 1997).

Other nonverbal cues can also influence social perception, enabling us to make quick and often accurate judgments of others based on "thin slices" of their expressive behavior (Ambady & Rosenthal, 1993). "Thin slicing is not an exotic gift," notes Malcom Gladwell (2005), author of the best-seller *Blink*. "It is a central part of what it means to be human" (p. 43). In one study, for example, research participants were able to judge the intelligence of strangers accurately, as measured by standardized test scores, based only on hearing them read short sentences (Borkenau et al., 2004). Other studies show that social perceivers are often fluent readers of *body language*—the ways in which people stand, sit, walk, and gesture. Thus, men and women who have a youthful walking style—who sway their hips, bend their knees, lift their feet, and swing their arms—are seen as happier and more powerful than those who walk slowly, take shorter steps, and stiffly drag their feet (Montepare & McArthur, 1988).

Eye contact, or *gaze*, is another powerful form of nonverbal communication. People are highly attentive to eyes, often following the gaze of others. Look up, down, left, or right, and someone observing you will likely follow the direction of your eyes (Langton et al., 2000). Controlled studies show that even one-year-old

FIGURE 4.2

Some Common E-mail "Emoticons"

In order to clarify meaning of their written words, e-mailers often add smiles, winks, and other face-like symbols, or emoticons, to their electronic messages. One set of emoticons is shown here; you may be familiar with others.

(Sanderson, 1997.)

Wink	Smirk	Said smiling	Said frowning	Sardonic incredulity
'-)	:-,	:-)	:-(	;-)

Disgusted	Kiss, kiss	Clowning around	Said late at night	Said tongue-in-cheek
:-|	:-X	:*)	|-(	:-J

infants tend to follow gaze, looking toward or pointing at the object of an adult researcher's attention (Brooks & Meltzoff, 2002).

Eyes have been called the "windows of the soul." In many cultures, people tend to assume that someone who avoids eye contact is evasive, cold, fearful, shy, or indifferent; that frequent gazing signals intimacy, sincerity, self-confidence, and respect; and that the person who stares is tense, angry, and unfriendly. If you've ever conversed with someone who kept looking away, as if uninterested, then you would understand why people might form negative impressions from "gaze disengagement" (Mason et al., 2005). Sometimes eye contact is interpreted in light of a pre-existing relationship. If a relationship is friendly, frequent eye contact elicits a positive impression. If a relationship is not friendly, that same eye contact is seen in negative terms. Hence, it is said that if two people lock eyes for more than a few seconds, they will either make love or kill each other (Kleinke, 1986).

Another powerful and primitive form of nonverbal signal is *touch*—as in the congratulatory high-five, the sympathetic pat on the back, the joking elbow in the ribs, the painfully strong handshake, and the lingering loving embrace. Physical touching has long been regarded as an expression of friendship, nurturance, and sexual interest. But it may also serve other functions. Many years ago, Nancy Henley (1977) observed that men, older persons, and those of high socioeconomic status were more likely to touch women, younger persons, and individuals of lower status than the other way around. Henley's interpretation: that touching may be an expression not only of intimacy but also of dominance and control. Is social touching reserved for those in power? It appears that the answer is no. After an exhaustive review of past research, Judith Hall and her colleagues (2005) found that although we tend to believe that people touch others more when they are dominant than when they are subordinate, there is no behavioral support for this hypothesis (though dominant people are more facially expressive, encroach more on others' personal space, speak louder, and are more likely to interrupt).

As described by Axtell (1993), nonverbal communication norms vary from one culture to the next. So watch out! In Bulgaria, nodding your head means "no" and shaking your head sideways means "yes." In Germany and Brazil, the American "okay" sign (forming a circle with your thumb and forefinger) is an obscene gesture. Personal-space habits also vary across cultures. Japanese people like to maintain a comfortable distance while interacting. But in Puerto Rico and much of Latin America, people stand very close and backing off is considered an insult. Also beware of what you do with your eyes. In Latin America, locking eyes is a must; yet in Japan, too much eye contact shows a lack of respect. If you're in the habit of stroking your cheek, you should know that in Italy, Greece, and Spain it means that you find the person you're talking to attractive. And whatever you do, don't ever touch someone's head in Buddhist countries, especially Thailand. The head is sacred there.

Different cultures also have vastly different rules for the common greeting. In Finland, you should give a firm handshake; in France, you should loosen the grip; in Zambia, you should use your left hand to support the right; and in Bolivia, you should extend your arm if your hand is dirty. In Japan, people bow; in Thailand, they put both hands together in a praying position on the chest; and in Fiji, they smile and raise their eyebrows. In certain parts of Latin America, it is common for people to hug, embrace, and kiss upon meeting. And in most Arab countries, men greet

Greg "Fossilman" Raymer was the 2004 World Series of Poker Champion, winning $5 million for his first-place finish. So that his eyes would not betray his inner thoughts and feelings, Raymer, like many other poker players, wore reflective sunglasses for the entire tournament.

"I knew the suspect was lying because of certain telltale discrepancies between his voice and nonverbal gestures. Also his pants were on fire."

one another by saying *salaam alaykum*, then shaking hands, saying *kaif halak*, and kissing each other on the cheek.

Distinguishing Truth from Deception

Social perception is tricky because people often try to hide or stretch the truth about themselves. Poker players bluff to win money, witnesses lie to protect themselves, public officials make campaign promises they don't intend to keep, and acquaintances pass compliments to each other to be polite and supportive. On occasion, everyone tells something less than "the truth, the whole truth, and nothing but the truth." Can social perceivers tell the difference? Can *you* tell when someone is lying?

Sigmund Freud, the founder of psychoanalysis, once said that "no mortal can keep a secret. If his lips are silent, he chatters with his fingertips; betrayal oozes out of him at every pore" (1905, p. 94). Paul Ekman and Wallace Friesen (1974) later revised Freud's observation by pointing out that some pores "ooze" more than others. Ekman and Friesen proposed that some channels of communication are difficult for deceivers to control, while others are relatively easy. To test this hypothesis, they showed a series of films—some pleasant, others disgusting—to a group of female nurses. While watching, the nurses were instructed either to report their honest impressions of these films or to conceal their true feelings. Through the use of hidden cameras, these participants were videotaped. Others, acting as observers, then viewed the tapes and judged whether the participants had been truthful or deceptive. The results showed that judgment accuracy rates were influenced by which types of nonverbal cues the observers were exposed to. Observers who watched tapes that focused on the body were better at detecting deception than were those who saw tapes focused on the face. The face can communicate emotion, but it is relatively easy for deceivers to control, unlike nervous movements of the hands and feet. Clearly, there is nothing like the wooden Pinocchio's nose to reveal whether someone is lying or telling the truth.

This study was the first of hundreds. In all the studies, one group of participants makes truthful or deceptive statements while another group reads the transcripts, listens to audiotapes or watches videotapes, and then tries to evaluate the statements. This research shows that people frequently make mistakes in their judgments of truth and deception and too often accept what others say at face value. Even more sobering is that people don't have a good sense of their own lie-detection skills, being confident in their judgments regardless of whether they are correct or incorrect (DePaulo et al., 1997).

As you might expect, some people are better lie detectors than others (Frank & Ekman, 1997). Surprisingly, however, professionals who are specially trained and who regularly make these kinds of judgments for a living—such as police detectives, trial judges, psychiatrists, customs inspectors, and those who administer lie-detector tests for the CIA, FBI, and military—are, like the rest of us, highly prone to error (Ekman & O'Sullivan, 1991; Granhag & Strömwall, 2004; Vrij, 2000; see Table 4.2).

What seems to be the problem? Many years ago, Miron Zuckerman and others (1981) argued that there's a *mismatch* between the behavioral cues that actually signal

TABLE 4.2
Can the "Experts" Distinguish Truth and Deception?

Lie-detection experts with experience at making judgments of truth and deception were shown brief videotapes of ten women telling the truth or lying about their feelings. Considering that there was a fifty-fifty chance of guessing correctly, the accuracy rates were remarkably low. Only a sample of U.S. Secret Service agents posted a better-than-chance performance.

(Ekman & O'Sullivan, 1991.)

Observer Groups	Accuracy Rates %
College students	52.82
CIA, FBI, and military	55.67
Police investigators	55.79
Trial judges	56.73
Psychiatrists	57.61
U.S. Secret Service agents	64.12

deception and those used by perceivers to detect deception. This conclusion is generally supported by a more recent meta-analysis of results from 120 studies involving thousands of research participants (DePaulo et al., 2003). The problem is this: There are four channels of communication that provide potentially relevant information: the spoken word, the face, the body, and the voice. When people have a reason to lie, the *words* they choose cannot be trusted. The *face* is also controllable. We tend to think that people do not smile when they lie, but it is common for deceivers to mask their real feelings with false smiles that do not stretch up into the eye muscles. Indeed, psychophysiological research confirms that there are two distinct types of smiles, one more genuine than the other. The *body* may be somewhat more revealing than the face because deception is sometimes accompanied by fidgeting and restless movements of the hands and feet. Finally, the *voice* is the leakiest, most revealing cue. When people lie, especially when they are highly motivated to do so, their voices rise in pitch, and the number of speech hesitations increases.

In the wake of the September 11 terrorist attacks and heightened worldwide concerns for security, the ability to distinguish truths and lies is essential, a matter of life and death. Yet research shows that social perceivers tune in to the wrong channels of communication. Too easily seduced by the silver tongue and the smiling face, we often fail to notice the restless body and quivering voice. Hence, perceivers are more accurate when instructed to pay more attention to the telltale vocal cues than to the face and when they report having based their judgments on auditory cues rather than verbal or visual information (Bond & DePaulo, 2006).

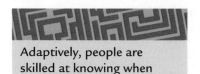

 Adaptively, people are skilled at knowing when someone is lying rather than telling the truth. **False.**

Attribution: From Elements to Dispositions

To interact effectively with others, we need to know how they feel and when they can be trusted. But to understand people well enough to predict their future behavior, we must also identify their inner *dispositions:* stable characteristics such as personality traits, attitudes, and abilities. Since we cannot actually see dispositions, we infer them indirectly from what a person says and does. In this section, we look at the processes that lead us to make these inferences.

Attribution Theories

Do you ever think about the influence that you have on other people? What about the roles of heredity, childhood experiences, and social forces? Do you wonder why some people succeed while others fail? Individuals differ in the extent to which they feel a need to explain the uncertain events of human behavior (Weary & Edwards, 1994). Among college students, for example, psychology majors are more curious about people than are natural-science majors (Fletcher et al., 1986). Although there are vast differences among us, people in general tend to ask "why?" when they confront events that are important, negative, or unexpected (Hastie, 1984; Weiner, 1985) and when understanding these events has personal relevance (Malle & Knobe, 1997).

To make sense of our social world, we try to understand the causes of other people's behavior. But what kinds of explanations do we make, and how do we go about making them? In a classic book entitled *The Psychology of Interpersonal Relations*, Fritz Heider (1958) took the first step toward answering these questions. To Heider, we are all scientists of a sort. Motivated to understand others well enough to manage our social lives, we observe, analyze, and explain their behavior. The explanations we come up with are called *attributions*, and the theory that

People make personal and situational attributions all the time in an effort to make sense of their social world. But what kind of attribution is being made here?

"It's not you, Frank, it's me—I don't like you."

FIGURE 4.3

What Does This Speechwriter Really Believe?

As predicted by correspondent inference theory, participants who read a student's speech (behavior) were more likely to assume that it reflected the student's true attitude (disposition) when the position taken was freely chosen (left) rather than assigned (right). But also note the evidence for the fundamental attribution error. Even participants who thought the student had been assigned a position inferred the student's attitude from the speech.

(Jones & Harris, 1967.)

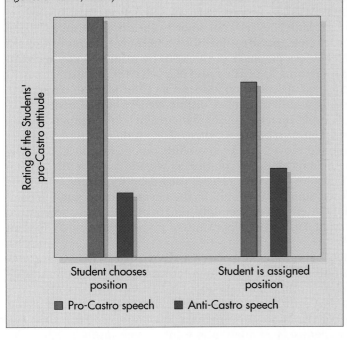

Rating of the Students' pro-Castro attitude

Student chooses position   Student is assigned position

■ Pro-Castro speech   ■ Anti-Castro speech

describes the process is called **attribution theory**. The questions posed at the beginning of the chapter regarding French soccer star Zinedine Zidane, Iranian president Mahmoud Ahmadinejad, and confessor John Mark Karr are questions of attribution.

Ask people to explain why their fellow human beings behave as they do—why they succeed or fail, laugh or cry, work or play, or help or hurt others—and you'll see that they come up with complex explanations often focused on whether the behavior is intentional or unintentional (Malle et al., 2000). Interested in how people answer these *why* questions, Heider found it particularly useful to group the explanations people give into two categories: *personal* and *situational*. In the 2006 World Soccer Cup example, everyone wanted to know: What caused Zidane to lash out, forcefully head-butting his Italian opponent to the ground? Immediately, some observers pointed the finger of blame at Zidane, an aggressive player with a short temper (a **personal attribution**). Yet others speculated that his actions were provoked by an accumulation of frustration or something his opponent said (a **situational attribution**). (Materazzi later admitted to making an insulting remark about Zidane's sister; Zidane later apologized for his outburst.) The task for the attribution theorist is not to determine the true *causes* of such an event but, rather, to understand people's *perceptions* of causality. For now, two major attribution theories are described.

Jones's Correspondent Inference Theory According to Edward Jones and Keith Davis (1965), each of us tries to understand other people by observing and analyzing their behavior. Jones and Davis's *correspondent inference theory* predicts that people try to infer from an action whether the act itself corresponds to an enduring personal characteristic of the actor. Is the person who commits an act of aggression a beast? Is the person who donates money to charity an altruist? To answer these kinds of questions, people make inferences on the basis of three factors.

The first factor is a person's degree of *choice*. Behavior that is freely chosen is more informative about a person than behavior that is coerced. In one study, participants read a speech, presumably written by a college student, that either favored or opposed Fidel Castro, the communist leader of Cuba. Some participants were told that the student had freely chosen this position, and others were told that the student had been assigned the position by a professor. When asked to determine the student's true attitude, participants were more likely to assume a correspondence between his or her essay (behavior) and attitude (disposition) when the student had had a choice than when he or she had been assigned to the role (Jones & Harris, 1967; see Figure 4.3). Keep this study in mind. It supports correspondent inference theory; but, as we will see later, it also demonstrates one of the most tenacious biases of social perception.

The second factor that leads people to make dispositional inferences is the *expectedness* of behavior. As previously noted, an action tells us more about a person when it departs from the norm than when it is typical, part of a social role, or otherwise expected under the circumstances (Jones et al., 1961). Thus, people think they know more about a student who wears three-piece suits to class or a citizen who openly refuses to pay taxes than about a student who wears blue jeans to class or a citizen who files tax returns on April 15.

Third, social perceivers take into account the intended *effects* or consequences of someone's behavior. Acts that produce many desirable outcomes do not reveal a person's specific motives as clearly as acts that produce only a single desirable outcome

attribution theory A group of theories that describe how people explain the causes of behavior.

personal attribution Attribution to internal characteristics of an actor, such as ability, personality, mood, or effort.

situational attribution Attribution to factors external to an actor, such as the task, other people, or luck.

(Newtson, 1974). For example, you are likely to be uncertain about exactly why a person stays on a job that is enjoyable, high paying, and in an attractive location—three desirable outcomes, each sufficient to explain the behavior. In contrast, you may feel more certain about why a person stays on a job that is tedious and low paying but is in an attractive location—only one desirable outcome.

Kelley's Covariation Theory Correspondent inference theory seeks to describe how perceivers try to discern an individual's personal characteristics from a slice of behavioral evidence. However, behavior can be attributed not only to personal factors but to situational factors as well. How is this distinction made? In the opening chapter, we noted that the causes of human behavior can be derived only through experiments. That is, one has to make more than a single observation and compare behavior in two or more settings in which everything stays the same except for the independent variables. Like Heider, Harold Kelley (1967) believes that people are much like scientists in this regard. They may not observe others in a controlled laboratory, but they too search for clues, make comparisons, and think in terms of "experiments." According to Kelley, people make attributions by using the **covariation principle**: In order for something to be the cause of a behavior, it must be present when the behavior occurs and absent when it does not. Three kinds of covariation information are particularly useful: consensus, distinctiveness, and consistency.

To illustrate these concepts, imagine you are standing on a street corner one hot, steamy evening minding your own business, when all of a sudden a stranger comes out of a cool air-conditioned movie theater and blurts out, "Great flick!" Looking up, you don't recognize the movie title, so you wonder what to make of this "recommendation." Was the behavior (the rave review) caused by something about the person (the stranger), the stimulus (the film), or the circumstances (say, the comfortable theater)? Possibly interested in spending a night at the movie, how would you proceed to explain what happened? What kinds of information would you want to obtain?

Thinking like a scientist, you might seek out *consensus information* to see how different persons react to the same stimulus. In other words, what do other moviegoers think about this film? If others also rave about it, then this stranger's behavior is high in consensus and is attributed to the stimulus. If others are critical of this film, however, then the behavior is low in consensus and is attributed to the person.

Still thinking like a scientist, you might also want to have *distinctiveness information* to see how the same person reacts to different stimuli. In other words, what does this moviegoer think of other films? If the stranger is generally critical of other films, then the target behavior is high in distinctiveness and is attributed to the stimulus. If the stranger raves about everything he or she sees, however, then the behavior is low in distinctiveness and is attributed to the person.

Finally, you might seek *consistency information* to see what happens to the behavior at another time when the person and the stimulus both remain the same. How does this moviegoer feel about this film on other occasions? If the stranger raves about the film on video as well as in the theater, regardless of surroundings, then the behavior is high in consistency. If the stranger does not always enjoy the film, the behavior is low in consistency. According to Kelley, behavior that is consistent is attributed to the stimulus when consensus and distinctiveness are also high and to the person when they are low. In contrast, behavior that is low in consistency is attributed to transient circumstances, such as the temperature of the movie theater.

Kelley's theory and the predictions it makes are represented in Figure 4.4. Does this model describe the kinds of information you seek when you try to determine what causes people to behave as they do? Often it does. Research shows that people who are instructed to make attributions for various events do, in general, follow the logic of covariation (Cheng & Novick, 1990; Fosterling, 1992; McArthur, 1972). However, this research also shows that individuals have their own attributional styles, so people often disagree about what caused a particular behavior (Robins et al., 2004). There are two ways in which they differ. First, individuals vary in the extent to which they believe that human behaviors are caused by personal characteristics that are fixed ("Everyone is a certain kind of person, and there is not much that can be done to really change that") or malleable ("People can change even their most basic

covariation principle A principle of attribution theory holding that people attribute behavior to factors that are present when a behavior occurs and absent when it does not.

FIGURE 4.4

Kelley's Covariation Theory

For behaviors that are high in consistency, people make personal attributions when there is low consensus and distinctiveness (top row) and stimulus attributions when there is high consensus and distinctiveness (bottom row). Behaviors that are low in consistency (not shown) are attributed to passing circumstances.

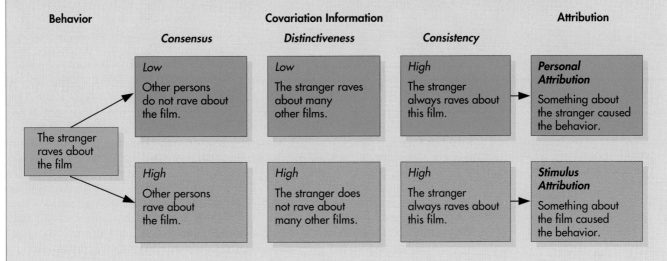

qualities") (Dweck et al., 1995; Levy et al., 2001). Second, some individuals are more likely than others to process information in ways that are colored by self-serving motivations (von Hippel et al., 2005).

Attribution Biases

When the theories of attribution were first proposed, they were represented by such elaborate flow charts, formulas, and diagrams that many social psychologists began to wonder: Do people really analyze behavior in the way that one might expect of computers? Do people have the time, the motivation, or the cognitive capacity for such elaborate and mindful processes? The answer is sometimes yes, sometimes no. As social perceivers, we are limited in our ability to process all relevant information, or we may lack the kinds of training needed to employ fully the principles of attribution theory. More important, we often don't make an effort to think carefully about our attributions. With so much to explain and not enough time in a day, people take mental shortcuts, cross their fingers, hope for the best, and get on with life. The problem is that speed brings bias and perhaps even a loss of accuracy. In this section, we examine some of these shortcuts and their consequences.

Cognitive Heuristics   According to Daniel Kahneman, Amos Tversky, and others, people often make attributions and other types of social judgments by using certain cognitive heuristics: information-processing rules of thumb that enable us to think in ways that are quick and easy but that frequently lead to error (Gilovich et al., 2002; Kahneman et al., 1982; Nisbett & Ross, 1980).

One rule of thumb that has particularly troublesome effects on attribution is the **availability heuristic**, a tendency to estimate the odds that an event will occur by how easily instances of it pop to mind. To demonstrate this phenomenon, Tversky and Kahneman (1973) asked research participants: Which is more common, words that start with the letter *r* or words that contain *r* as the third letter? In actuality, the English language has many more words with *r* as the third letter than as the first. Yet most people guessed that more words begin with *r*. The reason? It's easier to bring to mind words in which *r* appears first. Apparently, our estimates of likelihood are

availability heuristic   The tendency to estimate the likelihood that an event will occur by how easily instances of it come to mind.

TABLE 4.3
The False-Consensus Effect

In this study, participants who did vs. did not rate various personality traits as descriptive of themselves estimated the percentage of other people who had these traits. As shown below, participants' estimates of the population consensus were biased by their own self-perceptions.

(Krueger, 2000.)

Traits	Self-Yes (%)	Self-No (%)
Alert	75	65
Discontented	48	33
Loud	46	43
Meticulous	52	41
Sly	36	28
Smug	41	33

false-consensus effect The tendency for people to overestimate the extent to which others share their opinions, attributes, and behaviors.

base-rate fallacy The finding that people are relatively insensitive to consensus information presented in the form of numerical base rates.

counterfactual thinking The tendency to imagine alternative events or outcomes that might have occurred but did not.

heavily influenced by events that are readily available in memory (MacLeod & Campbell, 1992).

The availability heuristic can lead us astray in two ways. First, it gives rise to the **false-consensus effect**, a tendency for people to overestimate the extent to which others share their opinions, attributes, and behaviors. This bias is pervasive. Regardless of whether people are asked to predict how others feel about military spending, abortion, gun control, Campbell's soup, certain types of music, or norms for appropriate behavior, they exaggerate the percentage of others who behave similarly or share their views (Krueger, 1998; Ross, Greene, & House, 1977).

To illustrate the effect, Joachim Krueger (2000) asked participants in a study to indicate whether or not they had certain personality traits. Then they were asked to estimate the percentage of people in general who have these same traits. As shown in Table 4.3, participants' beliefs about other people's personalities were biased by their own self-perceptions. In part, the false-consensus bias is a byproduct of the availability heuristic. We tend to associate with others who are like us in important ways, so we are more likely to notice and recall instances of similar rather than dissimilar behavior (Deutsch, 1989). Interestingly, people do *not* exhibit this bias when asked to predict the behavior of groups other than their own (Mullen et al., 1992). People also do not exhibit this bias when predicting aspects of others for which they see themselves as distinct rather than typical (Karniol, 2003).

A second consequence of the availability heuristic is that social perceptions are influenced more by one vivid life story than by hard statistical facts. Have you ever wondered why so many people buy lottery tickets despite the astonishingly low odds or why so many travelers are afraid to fly even though they are more likely to perish in a car accident? These behaviors are symptomatic of the **base-rate fallacy**—the fact that people are relatively insensitive to numerical base rates, or probabilities, being influenced more by graphic, dramatic events such as the sight of a multimillion-dollar lottery winner celebrating on TV or a photograph of bodies being pulled from the wreckage of a plane crash. The base-rate fallacy can thus lead to various misperceptions of risk. Indeed, people overestimate the number of those who die in shootings, fires, floods, and terrorist bombings and underestimate the death toll caused by heart attacks, strokes, diabetes, and other mundane events. Made relevant by newly acquired fears of terrorism, research shows that perceptions of risk are affected more by fear, anxiety, and other emotions than by cold probabilities (Loewenstein et al., 2001; Slovic, 2000).

Every day, we are besieged by both types of information: We read about the unemployment rate, and we watch personal interviews with frustrated job seekers; we read the casualty figures of war, and we witness the agony of a parent who has lost a child in combat. Logically, statistics that summarize the experiences of large numbers of people are more informative than a single and perhaps atypical case, but perceivers march to a different drummer. As long as the personal anecdote is seen as relevant (Schwarz, Strack, Hilton, & Naderer, 1991) and the source as credible (Hinsz et al., 1988), it seems that one good image is worth a thousand numbers.

People can also be influenced by how easy it is to imagine events that did *not* occur. As thoughtful and curious beings, we often are not content to accept what happens to us or to others without wondering, at least in private, "What if . . . ?" According to Daniel Kahneman and Dale Miller (1986), people's emotional reactions to events are often colored by **counterfactual thinking**, the tendency to imagine alternative outcomes that might have occurred but did not. There are different types of counterfactual thoughts. If we imagine a result that is better than the actual result, then we're likely to experience disappointment, regret, and frustration. If the imagined result is worse, then we react with emotions that range from relief and satisfaction to elation. Thus, the psychological impact of positive and negative events depends on the way we think about "what might have been" (Roese, 1997; Roese & Olson, 1995).

What domains of life trigger the most counterfactual thinking—and the regret that often follows? Summarizing past research, Neal Roese and Amy Summerville (2005) found that people's top three regrets center, in order, on education ("I should have stayed in school"), career ("If only I had applied for that job"), and romance ("If only I had asked her out")—all domains that present us with opportunities that we may or may not realize.

Obviously, people don't immerse themselves in counterfactual thought after every experience. Research shows that we are more likely to think about what might have been—often with feelings of regret—after negative outcomes that result from actions we take rather than from actions we don't take (Byrne & McEleney, 2000). Consider an experience that may sound all too familiar: You take a multiple-choice test and after reviewing an item you had struggled over, you want to change the answer. What do you do? Over the years, research has shown that most test answer changes are from incorrect to correct. Yet most college students harbor the "first instinct fallacy" that it is best to stick with one's original answer. Why? Justin Kruger and his colleagues (2005) found that this myth arises from counterfactual thinking: that students are more likely to react with regret and frustration ("If only I had . . .") after changing a correct answer than after failing to change an incorrect answer.

According to Victoria Medvec and Kenneth Savitsky (1997), certain situations— such as being on the *verge* of a better or worse outcome, just above or below some cut-off point—also make it especially easy to conjure up images of what might have been. The implications are intriguing. Imagine, for example, that you are an Olympic athlete and have just won a silver medal—a remarkable feat. Now imagine that you have just won the bronze medal. Which situation would make you feel better? Rationally speaking, you should feel more pride and satisfaction with a silver medal. But what if your achievement had prompted you to engage in counterfactual thinking? What alternative would haunt your mind if you had finished in second place? Where would your focus be if you had placed third? Is it possible that the athlete who is better off objectively will feel worse?

To examine this question, Medvec and others (1995) videotaped forty-one athletes in the 1992 summer Olympic Games at the moment they realized that they had won a silver or a bronze medal and again, later, during the medal ceremony. Then they showed these tapes, without sound, to people who did not know the order of finish. These participants were asked to observe the medalists and rate their emotional states on a scale ranging from "agony" to "ecstasy." The intriguing result, as you might expect, was that the bronze medalists, on average, seemed happier than the silver medalists. Was there any more direct evidence of counterfactual thinking? In a second study, participants who watched interviews with many of these same athletes rated the silver medalists as more negatively focused on finishing second rather than first and the bronze medalists as more positively focused on finishing third rather than fourth. For these world-class athletes, feelings of satisfaction were based more on their thoughts of what might have been than on the reality of what was.

The Fundamental Attribution Error By the time you finish reading this textbook, you will know the cardinal lesson of social psychology: People are profoundly influenced by the *situational* contexts of behavior. This point is not as obvious as it may seem. For instance, parents are often surprised to hear that their mischievous child, the family monster, is a perfect angel in the classroom. And students are often surprised to observe that their favorite professor, so eloquent in the lecture hall, may stumble over words in less formal gatherings. These reactions are symptomatic of a well-documented aspect of social perception. When people explain the behavior of others, they tend to overestimate the role of personal factors and overlook the impact of situations. Because this bias is so pervasive, and sometimes so misleading, it has been called the **fundamental attribution error** (Ross, 1977).

During the 1996 summer Olympics, Nike ran this counterfactual— and controversial— advertisement: "You don't win silver, you lose gold."

fundamental attribution error The tendency to focus on the role of personal causes and underestimate the impact of situations on other people's behavior.

Evidence of the fundamental attribution error was first reported in the Jones and Harris (1967) study described earlier, in which participants read an essay presumably written by a student. In that study, participants were more likely to infer the student's true attitude when the position taken had been freely chosen than when they thought that the student had been assigned to it. But look again at Figure 4.3, and you'll notice that even when participants thought that the student had no choice but to assert a position, they still used the speech to infer his or her attitude. This finding has been repeated many times. Whether the essay topic is nuclear power, abortion, drug laws, or the death penalty, the results are essentially the same (Jones, 1990).

People fall prey to the fundamental attribution error even when they are fully aware of the situation's impact on behavior. In one experiment, the participants were themselves assigned to take a position, whereupon they swapped essays and rated each other. Remarkably, they still jumped to conclusions about each other's attitudes (Miller et al., 1981). In another experiment, participants inferred attitudes from a speech even when they were the ones who had assigned the position to be taken (Gilbert & Jones, 1986).

A fascinating study by Lee Ross and his colleagues (1977) demonstrates the fundamental attribution error in a familiar setting, the TV quiz show (Ross, Amabile, & Steinmetz, 1977). By a flip of the coin, participants in this study were randomly assigned to play the role of either the questioner or the contestant in a quiz game while spectators looked on. In front of the contestant and spectators, the experimenter instructed the questioner to write ten challenging questions from his or her own store of general knowledge. If you are a trivia buff, you can imagine how esoteric such questions can be: Who was the founder of e-Bay? What team won the NHL Stanley Cup in 1968? It is no wonder that contestants correctly answered only about 40 percent of the questions asked. When the game was over, all participants rated the questioner's and contestant's general knowledge on a scale of 0 to 100.

Picture the events that transpired. The questioners appeared more knowledgeable than the contestants. After all, they knew all the answers. But a moment's reflection should remind us that the situation put the questioner at a distinct advantage (there were no differences between the two groups on an objective test of general knowledge). Did participants take the questioner's advantage into account, or did they assume that the questioners actually had greater knowledge? The results were startling. Spectators rated the questioners as above average in their general knowledge and the contestants as below average. The contestants even rated themselves as inferior to their partners. Like the spectators, they too were fooled by the loaded situation (see Figure 4.5).

What's going on here? Why do social perceivers consistently make assumptions about persons and fail to appreciate the impact of situations? According to Daniel Gilbert and Patrick Malone (1995), the problem stems in part from *how* we make attributions. Attribution theorists used to assume that people survey all the evidence and then decide on whether to make a personal or a situational attribution. Instead, it appears that social perception is a two-step process: First we identify

FIGURE 4.5

Fundamental Attribution Error and the TV Quiz Show

Even though the simulated quiz show situation placed questioners in an obvious position of advantage over contestants, observers rated the questioners as more knowledgeable (right). Questioners did not overrate their general knowledge (left); but contestants rated themselves as inferior (middle) and observers rated them as inferior as well. These results illustrate the fundamental attribution error.

(Ross, Amabile, and Steinmetz, 1977.)

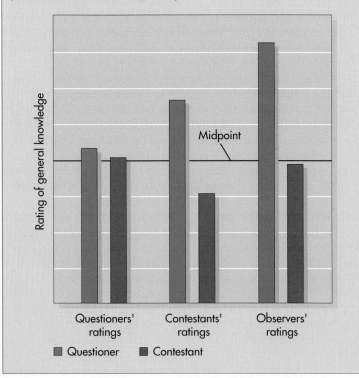

Rating of general knowledge

Midpoint

Questioners' ratings   Contestants' ratings   Observers' ratings

■ Questioner   ■ Contestant

How knowledgeable is this man? Alex Trebek has hosted the TV quiz show Jeopardy! since 1984. As host, Trebek reads questions to contestants and then reveals the correct answers. In light of the quiz show study by Ross and others (1977), which illustrates the fundamental attribution error, viewers probably see Trebek as highly knowledgeable, despite knowing that the answers he recites are provided to him as part of his job.

the behavior and make a quick personal attribution; then we correct or adjust that inference to account for situational influences. At least for those raised in a western culture, the first step is simple and automatic, like a reflex; the second requires attention, thought, and effort (see Figure 4.6). At present, social neuroscience researchers are beginning to use neuroimaging to probe the brain for evidence of this model (Lieberman et al., 2004).

Several research findings support this hypothesis. First, without realizing it, people often form impressions of others based on a quick glimpse at a face or sample of behavior (Newman & Uleman, 1989; Todorov & Uleman, 2004). Second, perceivers are *more* likely to commit the fundamental attribution error when they are cognitively busy, or distracted, as they observe the target person than when they pay full attention (Gilbert et al., 1992; Trope & Alfieri, 1997). Since the two-step model predicts that personal attributions are automatic but that the later adjustment for situational factors requires conscious thought, it makes sense to suggest that when attention is divided, when the attribution is made hastily, or when perceivers lack motivation, the second step suffers more than the first. As Gilbert and his colleagues (1988) put it, "The first step is a snap, but the second one's a doozy" (p. 738).

Why is the first step such a snap, and why does it seem so natural for people to assume a link between acts and personal dispositions? One possible explanation is based on Heider's (1958) insight that people see dispositions in behavior because of a perceptual bias, something like an optical illusion. When you listen to a speech or watch a quiz show, the actor is the conspicuous *figure* of your attention; the situation fades into the *background* ("out of sight, out of mind," as they say). According to Heider, people attribute events to factors that are perceptually conspicuous, or *salient*. To test this hypothesis, Shelley Taylor and Susan Fiske (1975) varied the seating arrangements of observers who watched as two actors engaged in a carefully staged conversation. In each session, the participants were seated so that they faced actor A, actor B, or both actors. When later questioned about their observations, they rated the actor they faced as the more dominant member of the pair, the one who set the tone and direction.

People may commit the fundamental attribution error when they explain the behavior of others, but do they exhibit the same bias in explaining their own behavior? Think about yourself. Are you shy or outgoing, or does your behavior depend on the situation? Are you calm or intense, quiet or talkative, lenient or firm? Or, again, does your behavior in these respects depend primarily on the situation? Now think of a friend, and answer the same questions about his or her behavior. Do you notice

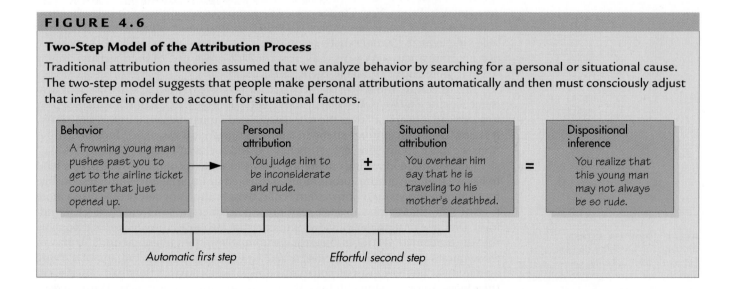

FIGURE 4.6

Two-Step Model of the Attribution Process

Traditional attribution theories assumed that we analyze behavior by searching for a personal or situational cause. The two-step model suggests that people make personal attributions automatically and then must consciously adjust that inference in order to account for situational factors.

Behavior	Personal attribution		Situational attribution		Dispositional inference
A frowning young man pushes past you to get to the airline ticket counter that just opened up.	You judge him to be inconsiderate and rude.	±	You overhear him say that he is traveling to his mother's deathbed.	=	You realize that this young man may not always be so rude.

Automatic first step   Effortful second step

a difference? Chances are, you do. Research shows that people are more likely to say "It depends on the situation" to describe themselves than to describe others. When Lewis Goldberg (1978) administered 2,800 English trait words to fourteen groups, each containing 100 people, he found that 85 percent checked off more traits for others than for themselves.

The tendency to make personal attributions for the behavior of others and situational attributions for ourselves is called the **actor-observer effect** and has been widely demonstrated (Jones & Nisbett, 1972; Watson, 1982). In one study, sixty prison inmates and their counselors were asked to explain why the inmates had committed their offenses. The counselors cited enduring personal characteristics; the prisoners referred to transient situational factors (Saulnier & Perlman, 1981). In a second study, an analysis of "Dear Abby" letters appearing in a newspaper revealed that people seeking advice explained the behavior of others in terms more dispositional than the terms they used to explain their own actions (Schoeneman & Rubanowitz, 1985). In a third study, young drivers who were asked about some of the risks that they and their friends take while behind the wheel made more personal attributions for friends, such as showing off, and more situational attributions for themselves, such as being late and in a hurry (Harré et al., 2004).

Cultural Influences on Attribution

In the fifth century B.C.E., Herodotus, a Greek historian, argued that the Greeks and Egyptians thought differently because the Greeks wrote from left to right and the Egyptians from right to left. Many years later, inspired by anthropologist Edward Sapir, Benjamin Lee Whorf (1956) theorized that the language people speak—the words, the rules, and so on—determines the way they conceptualize the world. To illustrate, he pointed to cultural variations in the use of words to represent reality. He noted that the Hanunoo of the Philippines have ninety-two different terms for rice, in contrast to the crude distinction North Americans make between "white rice" and "brown rice." Similarly, while English speakers have one word for snow, Eskimos have several words, which, Whorf argued, enables them to make distinctions that others may miss between "falling snow, snow on the ground, snow packed hard like ice, slushy snow, wind-driven flying snow—whatever the situation may be" (p. 216).

As a result of many years of research, it is now clear that language and culture can influence the way people think about time, space, objects, and other aspects of the physical world around them (Bloom, 1981; Hardin & Banaji, 1993). Consider our perceptions of color. The rainbow is a continuum of light varying smoothly between the shortest and longest wavelengths of the visible spectrum. Yet when we look at it, we see distinct categories of color that correspond to "red," "orange," "yellow," "green," "blue," and so on. Languages differ in the parts of the color spectrum that are named. In Papua, New Guinea, where Berinmo speakers distinguish between green and brown (they single out a form of "khaki" as the color of dead leaves), an object reflecting light at 450 nanometers would be called green. Yet many English speakers, distinguishing between colors that cross the blue-green part of the spectrum, might see that same object as blue (Özgen, 2004).

Just as culture influences the way people perceive the physical world, so it also influences the way we view social events. Hence, although attribution researchers used to assume that people all over the world explained human behavior in the same ways, it is now clear that cultures shape in subtle but profound ways the kinds of attributions we make about people, their behavior, and social situations (Nisbett, 2003).

Consider the contrasting orientations between western cultures (where people tend to believe that persons are autonomous, motivated by internal forces, and responsible for their own actions) and nonwestern "collectivist" cultures (where people take a more holistic view that emphasizes the relationship between persons and their surroundings). Do these differing worldviews influence the attributions we make? Is it possible that the fundamental attribution error is a uniquely western phenomenon? To answer these questions, Joan Miller (1984) asked Americans and Asian Indians of varying ages to describe the causes of positive and negative behaviors they had observed in their lives. Among young children, there were no cultural differences. With increas-

---

Like social psychologists, people are sensitive to situational causes when explaining the behavior of others. **False.**

---

actor-observer effect The tendency to attribute our own behavior to situational causes and the behavior of others to personal factors.

FIGURE 4.7

Fundamental Attribution Error: A Western Bias?

American and Asian Indian participants of varying ages described the causes of negative actions they had observed. Among young children, there were no cultural differences. With increasing age, however, Americans made more personal attributions, and Indian participants made more situational attributions. Explanations for positive behaviors followed a similar pattern. This finding suggests that the fundamental error is a western phenomenon.

(J. G. Miller, 1984.)

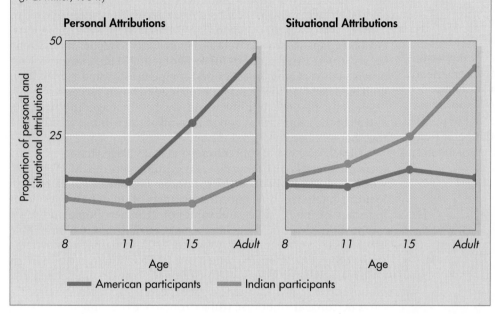

ing age, however, the American participants made more personal attributions, while the Indians made more situational attributions (see Figure 4.7). Testing this hypothesis in different ways, other studies as well have revealed that people form habits of thought, learning to make attributions according to culturally formed beliefs about the causes of human behavior (Lieberman et al., 2005; Masuda & Kitayama, 2004; Miyamoto & Kitayama, 2002).

On this point, Ara Norenzayan and Richard Nisbett (2000) argue that cultural differences in attribution are founded on varying folk theories about human causality. Western cultures, they note, emphasize the individual person and his or her attributes, whereas East Asian cultures focus on the background or field that surrounds that person. To test this hypothesis, they showed American and Japanese college students underwater scenes featuring a cast of small fish, small animals, plants, rocks, and coral—and one or more large, fast-moving *focal* fish, the stars of the show. Moments later, when asked to recount what they had seen, both groups recalled details about the focal fish to a nearly equal extent, but the Japanese reported far more details about the supporting cast in the background. Other researchers have also observed cultural differences in the extent to which people notice, think

Look at this tropical underwater scene; then turn away and try to recount as much of it as you can. What did you notice? What did you forget? When researchers showed American and Japanese students underwater scenes, they found that while both groups recalled the focal fish (like the large blue one shown here), the Japanese recalled more about the elements of the background.

FIGURE 4.8

Attributions Within Cultural Frames

When one fish swims ahead of the others in a group, Americans see that fish as *leading* the others (a personal attribution), while Chinese see it as being *chased* by the others (a situational attribution). In a study of bicultural Chinese students attending college in California, Ying-yi Hong and others (2000) displayed visual images that symbolized the United States or China before administering the fish test. As you can see, compared to students who were not shown any images (center), the tendency to make situational attributions was more common among those exposed to Chinese images (right) and less common among those exposed to American images (left). For people familiar with both worldviews, it appears that social perceptions are fluid—and depend on which culture is brought to mind.

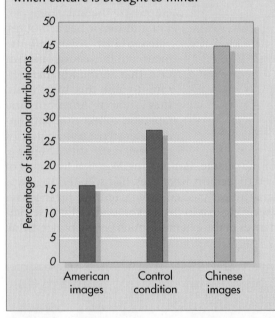

about, and remember the details of focal objects and their contexts (Ishii et al., 2003; Kitayama et al., 2003; Masuda & Nisbett, 2001).

These cultural differences can also be observed in naturally occurring settings outside a psychology laboratory. In an article entitled "Going for the Gold," Hazel Rose Markus and her colleagues (2006) compared the way Olympic performances were described in the United States and Japan. By analyzing the newspaper and TV coverage in these countries, these researchers discovered that although everyone attributed victory and defeat to the athletes, American media were more likely to focus on each athlete's unique personal attributes (such as strength, speed, health, and determination). "I just stayed focused," said Misty Hyman, American gold medalist swimmer. "It was time to show the world what I could do." In addition to reflecting on personal attributes, Japanese media were also more likely to report more wholly on an athlete's background, his or her mental state, and the role of others such as parents, coaches, and competitors. Woman's marathon gold medalist Naoko Takahashi explained her own success this way: "Here is the best coach in the world, the best manager in the world, and all of the people who support me—all of these things were getting together and became a gold medal."

Clearly, the world is becoming a global village characterized by increasing racial and ethnic diversity within countries. Many people who migrate from one country to another become *bicultural* in their identity, retaining some ancestral manners of thought while adopting some of the lifestyles and values of their new homeland. How might these bicultural individuals make attributions for human behavior? Is it possible that they view people through one cultural frame or the other, depending on which one is brought to mind? It's interesting that when shown a picture of one fish swimming ahead of a group, and asked why, Americans see the lone fish as *leading* the others (a personal attribution), while Chinese see the same fish as being *chased* by the others (a situational attribution). But what about bicultural social perceivers? In a study of China-born students attending college in California, researchers presented images symbolizing one of the two cultures (such as the U.S. and Chinese flags), administered the fish test, and found that compared to students exposed to the American images, those who saw the Chinese images made more situational attributions, seeing the lone fish as being chased rather than as leading (see Figure 4.8). Apparently, it is possible for us to hold differing cultural worldviews at the same time and to perceive others through either lens, depending on which culture is brought to mind (Hong et al., 2000; Peng & Knowles, 2003).

 Motivational Biases

As objective as we try to be, our social perceptions are sometimes colored by personal needs, wishes, and preferences. This tendency showed itself in the officiating controversies of the 2002 Winter Olympics. Canadian figure skating pair Jamie Sale and David Pelletier had skated a flawless program and beamed smiles to the cheering crowd. They "knew" they had won the gold medal over Russia's Elena Berezhnaya and Anton Sikharulidze. Yet when the judges' scores came up moments later, the Russian pair was granted first place, unleashing a torrent of disapproval from the Salt Lake Ice Center crowd. Soon, a French judge admitted that she was pressured in her vote, leading the International Olympic Committee to award a second gold to the Canadian skaters. Canadian fans saw the revised decision as fair and just; but many Russians were outraged, insisting that Berezhnaya and Sikharulidze had won outright. This conflict illustrates a powerful bias in social perception: sometimes we see what we want to see.

Canadian figure skating pair Jamie Sale and David Pelletier (left) look at Russian skaters Elena Berezhnaya and Anton Sikharulidze (right) during the initial award ceremony at the 2002 Winter Olympics. Because of a judging scandal, the International Olympic Committee later granted gold medals to both pairs. Showing that people tend to see what they want to see, most Canadian fans saw the double gold as just; most Russian fans did not.

People have a strong need for self-esteem, and this motive can lead us to make favorable, self-serving, and one-sided attributions for our own behavior. In Chapter 3, we saw that research with students, teachers, parents, workers, athletes, and others shows that people tend to take more credit for success than for failure. Similarly, people seek more information about their strengths than about weaknesses, overestimate their contributions to group efforts, exaggerate their control, and predict a rosy future. The false-consensus effect described earlier also has a self-serving side to it. It seems that we overestimate the extent to which others think, feel, and behave as we do, in part to reassure ourselves that our ways are correct, normal, and socially appropriate (Alicke & Largo, 1995). The positivity bias in attributions is ubiquitous. Through a meta-analysis of 266 studies involving thousands of participants, Amy Mezulis and others (2004) found that except in some Asian cultures, "the self-serving bias is pervasive in the general population" (p. 711).

According to David Dunning (2005), the need for self-esteem can bias our social perceptions in other subtle ways, too, even when we don't realize that the self is implicated. For example, do you consider yourself to be a "people-person," or are you more of a "task-oriented" type? And which of the two styles do you think makes for great leadership? It turns out that students who describe themselves as people-oriented see social skills as necessary for good leadership, while those who are more task-focused see a task orientation as better for leadership. Hence, people tend to judge favorably others who are similar to themselves, rather than different, on key characteristics (McElwee et al., 2001).

Sometimes ideological motives can color our attributions for the behavior of others. In the United States, it is common for political conservatives to blame poverty, crime, and other social problems on an "underclass" of people who are uneducated, lazy, immoral, or self-indulgent; in contrast, liberals often attribute these same problems to social and economic institutions that favor some groups over others. Do conservatives and liberals think differently about the causes of human behavior, or do the attributions they make depend on whether the particular behavior they're trying to explain fits with their ideology? In a series of studies, Linda Skitka and others (2002) had college students who identified themselves as conservative or liberal make attributions for various events. They found that while participants in general made dispositional attributions, as westerners reflexively tend to do, they corrected for situational factors when ideologically motivated to do so. To explain why a prisoner was paroled, conservatives were more likely to believe that the facility was overcrowded (a situational attribution) than that the prisoner had reformed (a personal attribution); to explain why a man lost his job, liberals were more likely to blame the company's finances (a situational attribution) than the worker's poor performance (a personal attribution).

At times, personal defensive motives lead us to blame others for their misfortunes. Consider the following classic experiment. Participants thought they were taking part in an emotion-perception study. One person, actually a confederate, was selected randomly to take a memory test while the others looked on. Each time the confederate made a mistake, she was jolted by a painful electric shock (actually, there was no shock; what participants saw was a staged videotape). Since participants knew that only the luck of the draw had kept them off the "hot seat," you might think they would react with sympathy and compassion. Not so. In fact, they belittled the hapless confederate (Lerner & Simmons, 1966).

Melvin Lerner (1980) argues that the tendency to be critical of victims stems from our deep-seated **belief in a just world**. According to Lerner, people need to view the world as a just place in which we "get what we deserve" and "deserve what

belief in a just world The belief that individuals get what they deserve in life, an orientation that leads people to disparage victims.

we get"—a world where hard work and clean living always pay off and where laziness and a sinful lifestyle are punished. To believe otherwise is to concede that we, too, are vulnerable to the cruel twists and turns of fate. Research suggests that the belief in a just world can help victims cope and serves as a buffer against stress. But how might this belief system influence our perceptions of *others*? If people cannot help or compensate the victims of misfortune, they turn on them. Thus, it is often assumed that poor people are lazy, that crime victims are careless, that battered wives provoke their abusive husbands, and that gay men and women with AIDS are promiscuous. As you might expect, cross-national comparisons reveal that people in poorer countries are less likely than those in more affluent countries to believe in a just world (Furnham, 2003).

The tendency to disparage victims may seem like just another symptom of the fundamental attribution error: too much focus on the person and not enough on the situation. But the conditions that trigger this tendency suggest there is more to it. Studies have shown that accident victims are held more responsible for their fate when the consequences of the accident are severe rather than mild (Walster, 1966), when the victim's situation is similar to the perceiver's (Shaver, 1970), and when the perceiver is generally anxious about threats to the self (Thornton, 1992). The more threatened we feel by an apparent injustice, the greater is the need to protect ourselves from the dreadful implication that it could happen to us, an implication we defend by disparaging the victim. Ironically, recent research shows that people may also satisfy their belief in a just world by *enhancing* members of disadvantaged groups—for example, by inferring that poor people are happy and that obese people are sociable, both attributes that restore justice by compensation (Kay & Jost, 2003; Kay et al., 2005).

In a laboratory experiment that reveals part of this process at work, participants watched a TV news story about a boy who was robbed and beaten. Some were told that the boy's assailants were captured, tried, and sent to prison. Others were told that the assailants fled the country, never to be brought to trial—a story that strains one's belief in a just world. Afterward, participants were asked to name as quickly as they could the colors in which various words in a list were typed (for example, the word *chair* may have been written in blue, *floor* in yellow, and *wide* in red). When the words themselves were neutral, all participants—regardless of which story they had seen—were equally fast at naming the colors. But when the words pertained to justice (words such as *fair* and *unequal*), those who had seen the justice-threatened version of the story were more distracted by the words and, hence, slower to name the colors. In fact, the more distracted they were, the more they derogated the victim. With their cherished belief in a just world threatened, these participants became highly sensitive to the concept of "justice" and quick to disparage the innocent victim (Hafer, 2000).

Integration: From Dispositions to Impressions

When behavior is attributed to situational factors, we do not generally make inferences about the actor. However, personal attributions often lead us to infer that a person has a certain disposition—that the leader of a failing business is incompetent, for example, or that the enemy who extends the olive branch seeks peace. Human beings are not one-dimensional, however, and one trait does not a person make. To have a complete picture of someone, social perceivers must assemble the various bits and pieces into a unified impression.

Information Integration: The Arithmetic

impression formation The process of integrating information about a person to form a coherent impression.

Once personal attributions are made, how are they combined into a single coherent picture of a person? How do we approach the process of **impression formation**? Do we simply add up all of a person's traits and calculate a mental average, or do we combine the information in more complicated ways? Anyone who has written or

"And see that you place the blame where it will do the most good."

Attributions of blame are often biased by self-serving motivations.

received letters of recommendation will surely appreciate the practical implications. Suppose you're told that an applicant is friendly and intelligent, two highly favorable qualities. Would you be more or less impressed if you then learned that this applicant was also prudent and even-tempered, two moderately favorable qualities? If you are more impressed, then you are intuitively following a *summation* model of impression formation: The more positive traits there are, the better. If you are less impressed, then you are using an *averaging* model: The higher the average value of all the various traits, the better.

To quantify the formation of impressions, Norman Anderson (1968) had research participants rate the desirability of 555 traits on a 7-point scale. By calculating the average ratings, he obtained a *scale value* for each trait (*sincere* had the highest scale value; *liar* had the lowest). In an earlier study, Anderson (1965) used similar values and compared the summation and averaging models. Specifically, he asked a group of participants to rate how much they liked a person described by two traits with extremely high scale values (H, H). A second group received a list of four traits, including two that were high and two that were moderately high in their scale values (H, H, M1, M1). In a third group, participants received two extremely low, negative traits (L, L). In a fourth group, they received four traits, including two that were low and two that were moderately low (L, L, M2, M2). What effect did the moderate traits have on impressions? As predicted by an averaging model, the moderate traits diluted from rather than added to the impact of the highly positive and negative traits. The practical implication for those who write letters of recommendation is clear. Applicants are better off if their letters include only the most glowing comments and omit favorable remarks that are somewhat more guarded in nature.

After extensive amounts of research, it appears that although people tend to combine traits by averaging, the process is somewhat more complicated. Consistent with Anderson's (1981) **information integration theory**, impressions formed of others are based on a combination, or integration, of (1) personal dispositions of the perceiver and (2) a *weighted* average, not a simple average, of the target person's characteristics (Kashima & Kerekes, 1994). Let's look more closely at these two sets of factors.

Deviations from the Arithmetic

Like other aspects of our social perceptions, impression formation does not follow the rules of cold logic. Weighted averaging may describe the way most people combine different traits, but the whole process begins with a warm-blooded human perceiver, not a computer. Thus, certain deviations from the "arithmetic" are inevitable.

Perceiver Characteristics   To begin with, perceivers differ in the kinds of impressions they form of others. Some people seem to measure everyone with an intellectual yardstick; others look for physical beauty, a warm smile, a good sense of humor, or a firm handshake. Whatever the attribute, each of us is more likely to notice and recall certain traits than others (Bargh et al., 1988; Higgins et al., 1982). Thus, when people are asked to describe a group of target individuals, there's typically more overlap between the various descriptions provided *by* the same *perceiver* than there is between those provided *for* the same *target* (Dornbusch et al., 1965; Park, 1986). Part of the reason for differences among perceivers is that we tend to use ourselves as a standard, or frame of reference, when evaluating others. Compared with the inert couch potato, for example, the serious jock is more likely to see others as less active and athletic (Dunning & Hayes, 1996). As we saw earlier, people also tend to see their own skills and traits as particularly desirable for others to have (McElwee et al., 2001).

information integration theory   The theory that impressions are based on (1) perceiver dispositions and (2) a weighted average of a target person's traits.

A perceiver's current, temporary *mood* can also influence the impressions formed of others (Forgas, 2000). For example, Joseph Forgas and Gordon Bower (1987) told research participants that they had performed very well or poorly on a test of social adjustment. As expected, this feedback altered their moods; it also affected their outlook on others. When presented with behavioral information about various characters, participants spent more time attending to positive facts and formed more favorable impressions when they were happy than when they were sad. Follow-up research shows that people who are induced into a happy mood are also more optimistic, more lenient, and less critical in the attributions they make for others who succeed or fail (Forgas & Locke, 2005). In short, the combined effects of perceiver differences and fluctuating moods point to an important conclusion: that to some extent, impression formation is in the eye of the beholder.

Priming Effects The characteristics we tend to notice in other people also change from time to time, depending on recent experiences. Have you ever noticed that once a seldom-used word slips into a conversation, it is often repeated over and over again? If so, you have observed **priming**, the tendency for frequently or recently used concepts to come to mind easily and influence the way we interpret new information.

The effect of priming on person impressions was first demonstrated by E. Tory Higgins and others (1977). Research participants were presented with a list of trait words, ostensibly as part of an experiment on memory. In fact, the task was designed as a priming device to plant certain ideas in their minds. Some participants read words that evoked a positive image: *brave, independent, adventurous*. Others read words that evoked a more negative image: *reckless, foolish, careless*. Later, in what they thought to be an unrelated experiment, participants read about a man who climbed mountains, drove in a demolition derby, and tried to cross the Atlantic Ocean in a sailboat. As predicted, their impressions were shaped by the trait words they had earlier memorized. Those exposed to positive words later formed more favorable impressions of the character than those exposed to negative words. All the participants read exactly the same description, yet they formed different impressions depending on what was already on their minds. In fact, priming seems to work best when the prime words are presented so rapidly that people are not even aware of the exposure (Bargh & Pietromonaco, 1982).

Additional research has shown that our motivation and even our social behavior are also subject to the automatic effects of priming without awareness. In one provocative study, John Bargh and Tanya Chartrand (1999) gave participants a "word search" puzzle that contained either neutral words or words associated with achievement motivation (*strive, win, master, compete, succeed*). Afterward, the participants were left alone and given three minutes to write down as many words as they could from a set of Scrabble letter tiles. When the three-minute limit was up, they were signaled over an intercom to stop. Did these participants, driven to obtain a high score, stop on cue or continue to write? Through the use of hidden cameras, the experimenters observed that 57 percent of those primed with achievement-related words continued to write after the stop signal—compared to only 22 percent in the control group.

Looking at priming effects on social behavior, Bargh, Chen, and Burrows (1996) gave people thirty sets of words presented in scrambled order ("he it hides finds instantly") and told them to use some of the words in each set to form grammatical sentences. After explaining the test, which would take five minutes, the experimenter told participants to locate him down the hall when they were finished so he could administer a second task. So far so good. But when participants found the experimenter, he was in the hallway immersed in conversation, and he stayed in that conversation for ten full minutes without acknowledging their presence. What's a person to do, wait patiently or interrupt? The participants didn't know it, but some had worked on a scrambled word test that contained many "politeness" words (*yield, respect, considerate, courteous*), while others had been exposed to words related to rudeness (*disturb, intrude, bold, bluntly*). Would these test words secretly prime participants, a few minutes later, to behave in one way or the other? Yes. Compared with those given the neutral words to unscramble, participants primed for rudeness were more likely—and those primed for politeness were less likely—to break in and interrupt the experimenter (see Figure 4.9).

priming The tendency for recently used or perceived words or ideas to come to mind easily and influence the interpretation of new information.

FIGURE 4.9

The Priming of Social Behavior Without Awareness

Would waiting participants interrupt the busy experimenter? Compared with those who had previously been given neutral words to unscramble (center), participants given polite-ness words were less likely to cut in (left) and those given rudeness words were more likely to cut in (right). These results show that priming can influence not only our social judgments but our behavior as well.

(Bargh, Chen, & Burrows, 1996.)

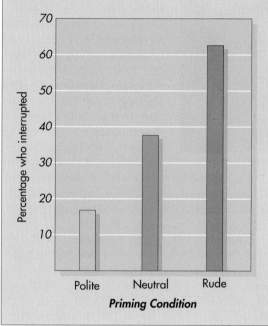

What accounts for this effect of priming, not only on our social perceptions but also on our behavior? Clearly the link between perception and behavior is automatic; it happens like a mindless reflex. Present scrambled words that prime the "elderly" stereotype (*old, bingo*) and research participants walk out of the experiment more slowly, as if mimicking an elderly person (Dijksterhuis & Bargh, 2001). But why? Joseph Cesario and others (2006) suggest that the automatic priming of behavior is an adaptive social mechanism that helps us to prepare for upcoming encounters with a primed target—if we are so motivated. After measuring participants' attitudes toward the elderly, these researchers predicted and found that those who liked old people walked more slowly after priming (as if synchronizing with a slow friend), while those who disliked old people walked more quickly (as if fleeing from such an interaction).

Target Characteristics   Just as not all social perceivers are created equal, neither are all traits created equal. In recent years, personality researchers have discovered, across cultures, that individuals can reliably be distinguished from one another along five broad traits, or factors: extroversion, emotional stability, openness to experience, agreeableness, and conscientiousness (De Raad, 2000; McCrae & Costa, 2003; Wiggins, 1996). Some of these factors are easier to judge than others. Based on their review of thirty-two studies, David Kenny and others (1994) found that social perceivers are most likely to agree in their judgments of a target's extroversion: that is, the extent to which he or she is sociable, friendly, fun-loving, outgoing, and adventurous. It seems that this characteristic is easy to spot, and different perceivers often agree on it even when rating a target person whom they are seeing for the first time.

The valence of a trait—whether it is considered good or bad—also affects its impact on our final impressions. Specifically, research shows that people exhibit a *trait negativity bias*, the tendency for negative information to weigh more heavily than positive information (Rozin & Royzman, 2001; Skowronski & Carlston, 1989). This means that we form more extreme impressions of a person who is said to be dishonest than of one who is said to be honest. It seems that we tend to view others favorably, so we are quick to take notice and pay more careful attention when this expectation is violated (Pratto & John, 1991). One bad trait may well be enough to destroy a person's reputation—regardless of other qualities. Research on American political campaigns confirms the point: Public opinion is shaped more by a candidate's "negatives" than by positive information (Klein, 1991; Lau, 1985). In light of all this research, Baumeister and others (2001) have concluded that bad is stronger than good in a "disappointingly relentless pattern" (p. 362).

When you think about it, it's probably adaptive for people to stay alert for and pay particularly close attention to negative information. Recent research suggests that people are quicker to sense their exposure to subliminally presented negative words such as *bomb, thief, shark,* and *cancer* than to positive words such as *baby, sweet, friend,* and *beach* (Dijksterhuis & Aarts, 2003). This sensitivity to negative information can even be "seen" in the brain (N. K. Smith et al., 2003). In one study, for example, Tiffany Ito and others (1998) exposed research participants to slides that depicted images that were positive (a red Ferrari, people enjoying a roller coaster), negative (a mutilated face, a handgun pointed at the camera), or neutral (a plate, a hair dryer). Using electrodes attached to participants' scalps, these researchers recorded electrical activity in different areas of the brain during the slide presentation. Sure enough, they observed that certain types of activity were more pronounced when participants saw negative images than when they saw stimuli that were positive or neutral. It appears, as these researchers commented, that "negative information weighs more heavily on the brain" (p. 887).

The impact of trait information on our impressions of others ends not only on characteristics of the perceiver and target but on context as well. Two contextual factors are particularly important in this regard: (1) implicit theories of personality and (2) the order in which we receive information about one trait relative to other traits.

Implicit Personality Theories   Years ago, when O. J. Simpson was charged with brutally murdering his ex-wife Nicole and her friend Ron Goldman, everyone was shocked. Simpson was a national hero: athletic, attractive, charming, intelligent, and successful. Once the premier running back in the National Football League, Simpson went on to become a sports broadcaster, Hollywood actor, and father of four children.

It's easy to understand why people initially reacted to the charges with disbelief. Simpson just didn't seem like *the kind of person* who would commit a cold-blooded murder. That reaction was based on an **implicit personality theory**—a network of assumptions that we hold about relationships among various types of people, traits, and behaviors. Knowing that someone has one trait thus leads us to infer that he or she has other traits as well (Bruner & Tagiuri, 1954; Schneider, 1973; Sedikides & Anderson, 1994). For example, you might assume that a person who is unpredictable is probably also dangerous or that someone who speaks slowly is also slow-witted. You might also assume that certain traits and behaviors are linked together (Reeder, 1993; Reeder & Brewer, 1979)—that a beloved sports hero like O. J. Simpson, for example, could not possibly stab two people to death.

Brain research shows that when people are exposed to negative emotional images—such as the car bomb on the right as opposed to the beach scene on the left—activity in certain parts of the brain is more pronounced.

Solomon Asch (1946) was the first to discover that the presence of one trait often implies the presence of other traits. Asch told one group of research participants that an individual was "intelligent, skillful, industrious, warm, determined, practical and cautious." Another group read an identical list of traits, except that the word *warm* was replaced by *cold*. Only the one term was changed, but the two groups formed very different impressions. Participants inferred that the warm person was also happier and more generous, good-natured, and humorous than the cold person. When two other words were varied (*polite and blunt*), however, the differences were less pronounced. Why? Asch concluded that *warm* and *cold* are **central traits**, meaning that they imply the presence of certain other traits and exert a powerful influence on final impressions. Other researchers have observed similar effects (Stapel & Koomen, 2000). In fact, the impact of central traits is not limited to studies using trait lists. When college students in different classes were led to believe that a guest lecturer was a warm or cold person, their impressions after the lecture were consistent with these beliefs, even though he gave the same lecture to everyone (Kelley, 1950; Widmeyer & Loy, 1988).

The Primacy Effect   The order in which a trait is discovered can also influence its impact. It is often said that first impressions are critical, and social psychologists are quick to agree. Studies show that information often has greater impact when presented early in a sequence rather than late, a common phenomenon known as the **primacy effect**.

In another of Asch's (1946) classic experiments, one group of participants learned that a person was "intelligent, industrious, impulsive, critical, stubborn, and envious." A second group received exactly the same list but in reverse order. Rationally speaking, the two groups should have felt the same way about the person. But

implicit personality theory A network of assumptions people make about the relationships among traits and behaviors.

central traits Traits that exert a powerful influence on overall impressions.

primacy effect The tendency for information presented early in a sequence to have more impact on impressions than information presented later.

instead, participants who heard the first list in which the more positive traits came first formed more favorable impressions than did those who heard the second list. Similar findings were obtained among participants who watched a videotape of a woman taking an SAT-like test. In all cases, she correctly answered fifteen out of thirty multiple-choice questions. But participants who observed a pattern of initial success followed by failure perceived the woman as more intelligent than did those who observed the opposite pattern of failure followed by success (Jones et al., 1968). There are exceptions, but as a general rule, people tend to be more heavily influenced by the "early returns."

What accounts for this primacy effect? There are two basic explanations. The first is that once perceivers think they have formed an accurate impression of someone, they tend to pay less attention to subsequent information. Thus, when research participants read a series of statements about a person, the amount of time they spent reading each of the items declined steadily with each succeeding statement (Belmore, 1987).

Does this mean we are doomed to a life of primacy? Not at all. If unstimulated, or mentally tired, our attention may wane. But if perceivers are sufficiently motivated to avoid tuning out and are not pressured to form a quick first impression, then primacy effects are diminished (Anderson & Hubert, 1963; Kruglanski & Freund, 1983). In one study, college students "leaped to conclusions" about a target person on the basis of preliminary information when they were mentally fatigued from having just taken a two-hour exam, but not when they were fresh, alert, and motivated to pay attention (Webster et al., 1996). In addition, Arie Kruglanski and Donna Webster (1996) found that some people are more likely than others to "seize" upon and "freeze" their first impressions. Apparently, individuals differ in their **need for closure**, the desire to reduce ambiguity. People who are low in this regard are open-minded, deliberate, and perhaps even reluctant to draw firm conclusions about others. In contrast, those who are high in the need for closure tend to be impulsive and impatient and to form quick and lasting judgments of others.

More unsettling is the second reason for primacy, known as the *change-of-meaning hypothesis*. Once people have formed an impression, they start to interpret inconsistent information in light of that impression. Asch's research shows just how malleable the meaning of a trait can be. When people are told that a kind person is *calm*, they assume that he or she is gentle, peaceful, and serene. When a cruel person is said to be *calm*, however, the same word is interpreted to mean cool, shrewd, and calculating. There are many examples to illustrate the point. Based on your first impression, the word *proud* can mean self-respecting or conceited, *critical* can mean astute or picky, and *impulsive* can mean spontaneous or reckless.

It is remarkable just how creative we are in our efforts to transform a bundle of contradictions into a coherent, integrated impression. For example, the person who is said to be "good" but also "a thief" can be viewed as a Robin Hood character (Burnstein & Schul, 1982). Asch and Henri Zukier (1984) presented people with inconsistent trait pairs and found that they used different strategies to reconcile the conflicts. For example, a brilliant-foolish person may be seen as "very bright on abstract matters, but silly about day-to-day practical tasks," a sociable-lonely person has "many superficial ties but is unable to form deep relations," and a cheerful-gloomy person may simply be someone who is "moody."

Confirmation Biases: From Impressions to Reality

"Please your majesty," said the knave, "I didn't write it and they can't prove I did; there's no name signed at the end." "If you didn't sign it," said the King, "that only makes the matter worse. You must have meant some mischief, or else you'd have signed your name like an honest man."

need for closure   The desire to reduce cognitive uncertainty, which heightens the importance of first impressions.

This exchange, taken from Lewis Carroll's *Alice's Adventures in Wonderland*, illustrates the power of existing impressions. It is striking but often true: Once people

"It is a capital mistake to theorize before you have all the evidence. It biases the judgment."

—Arthur Conan Doyle

make up their minds about something—even if they have incomplete information—they become more and more unlikely to change their minds when confronted with new evidence.

In his book, *State of Denial,* journalist Bob Woodward (2006) argued that the Bush administration would not alter its projections about the war in Iraq despite military intelligence warnings. This type of stubbornness is hardly unique. Political leaders often refuse to withdraw support for government programs that don't work, just as scientists steadfastly defend their pet theories in the face of contradictory research data. All these instances are easy to explain. Presidents, politicians, and scientists have personal stakes in their opinions, as votes, pride, funding, and reputation may be at risk. But what about people who more innocently fail to revise their opinions, often to their own detriment? What about the baseball manager who clings to old strategies that are ineffective or the trial lawyer who consistently selects juries according to false stereotypes? Why are they often slow to face the facts? As we will see, people are subject to various **confirmation biases**—tendencies to interpret, seek, and create information in ways that verify existing beliefs.

Perseverance of Beliefs

Imagine you are looking at a slide that is completely out of focus. Gradually, it becomes focused enough so that the image is less blurry. At this point, the experimenter wants to know if you can recognize the picture. The response you're likely to make is interesting. Participants in experiments of this type have more trouble making an identification if they watch the gradual focusing procedure than if they simply view the final, blurry image. In the mechanics of the perceptual process, people apparently form early impressions that interfere with their subsequent ability to "see straight" once presented with improved evidence (Bruner & Potter, 1964). As we will see in this section, social perception is subject to the same kind of interference, which is another reason why first impressions often stick like glue even after we are forced to confront information that discredits them.

Consider what happens when you're led to expect something that does not materialize. In one study, John Darley and Paget Gross (1983) asked participants to evaluate the academic potential of a nine-year-old girl named Hannah. One group was led to believe that Hannah came from an affluent community in which both parents were well-educated professionals (high expectations). A second group thought that she was from a run-down urban neighborhood and that both parents were uneducated blue-collar workers (low expectations). As shown in Figure 4.10, participants in the first group were slightly more optimistic in their ratings of Hannah's potential than were those in the second group. In each of these groups, however, half the participants then watched a videotape of Hannah taking an achievement test. Her performance on the tape seemed average. She correctly answered some difficult questions but missed others that were relatively easy. Look again at Figure 4.10 and you'll see that even though all participants saw the same tape, Hannah now received much lower ratings of ability from those who thought she was poor and higher ratings from those who thought she was affluent. Apparently, presenting an identical body of mixed evidence did not extinguish the biasing effects of beliefs; it *fueled* these effects.

Events that are ambiguous enough to support contrasting interpretations are like inkblots: We see in them what we want or expect to see. Illustrating the point, researchers had people rate from photographs the extent to which pairs of adults and children resembled each other. Interestingly, the participants did not see more resemblance in parents and offspring than in random pairs of adults and children. Yet when told that certain pairs were related, they did "see" a resemblance, even when the relatedness information was false (Bressan & Martello, 2002).

What about information that plainly disconfirms our beliefs? What then happens to our first impressions? Craig Anderson and his colleagues (1980) addressed this question by supplying participants with false information. After they had time to think about it, they were told that it was untrue. In one experiment, half the participants read case studies suggesting that people who take risks make better firefighters

confirmation bias The tendency to seek, interpret, and create information that verifies existing beliefs.

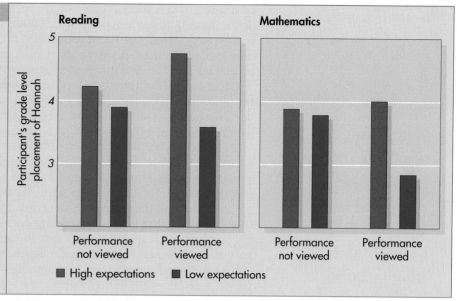

FIGURE 4.10

Mixed Evidence: Does It Extinguish or Fuel First Impressions?

Participants evaluated the potential of a schoolgirl. Without seeing her test performance, those with high expectations rated her slightly higher than did those with low expectations. Among the participants who watched a tape of the girl taking a test, the expectations effect was even greater.

(Darley & Gross, 1983.)

than do those who are cautious. The others read cases suggesting the opposite conclusion. Next, participants were asked to come up with a theory for the suggested correlation. The possibilities are easy to imagine: "He who hesitates is lost" supports risk-taking, whereas "You have to look before you leap" supports caution. Finally, participants were led to believe that the session was over and were told that the information they had received was false, manufactured for the sake of the experiment. Participants, however, did not abandon their firefighter theories. Instead they exhibited **belief perseverance**, sticking to initial beliefs even after these had been discredited. Apparently, it's easier to get people to build a theory than to convince them to tear it down. Thus, five full months after the terrorist attack on the World Trade Center, the Gallup Organization interviewed some ten thousand residents of nine Muslim countries and found that 61 percent did *not* believe—despite hard evidence—that the attacks were carried out by Arab men (Gallup Poll Editors, 2002).

Why do beliefs often outlive the evidence on which they are supposed to be based? The reason is that when people conjure up explanations that make sense, those explanations take on a life of their own. In fact, once people form an opinion, that opinion becomes strengthened when they merely *think* about the topic, even if they do not articulate the reasons for it (Tesser, 1978). And therein lies a possible solution. By asking people to consider why an *alternative* theory might be true, we can reduce or eliminate the belief perseverance effects to which they are vulnerable (Anderson & Sechler, 1986).

People are slow to change their first impressions on the basis of new information. **True.**

Confirmatory Hypothesis Testing

Social perceivers are not passive recipients of information. Like detectives, we ask questions and actively search for clues. But do we seek information objectively, or are we inclined to confirm the suspicions we already hold?

Mark Snyder and William Swann (1978) addressed this question by having pairs of participants who were strangers to one another take part in a getting-acquainted interview. In each pair, one participant was supposed to interview the other. But first, that participant was falsely led to believe that his or her partner was either introverted or extroverted (actually, participants were assigned to these conditions on a random basis) and was then told to select questions from a prepared list. Those who thought they were talking to an introvert chose mostly introvert-oriented questions ("Have you ever felt left out of some social group?"), while those who thought they were talking to an extrovert asked extrovert-oriented questions ("How do you liven

belief perseverance The tendency to maintain beliefs even after they have been discredited.

up a party?"). Expecting a certain kind of person, participants unwittingly sought evidence that would confirm their expectations. By asking loaded questions, in fact, the interviewers actually gathered support for their beliefs. Thus, neutral observers who later listened to the tapes were also left with the mistaken impression that the interviewees really were as introverted or extroverted as the interviewers had assumed.

This last part of the study is powerful but, in hindsight, not all that surprising. Imagine yourself on the receiving end of an interview. Asked about what you do to liven up parties, you would probably talk about organizing group games, playing dance music, and telling jokes. On the other hand, if you were asked about difficult social situations, you might talk about being nervous before oral presentations or about what it feels like to be the new kid on the block. In other words, simply by going along with the questions that are asked, you supply evidence confirming the interviewer's beliefs. Thus, perceivers set in motion a vicious cycle: Thinking someone has a certain trait, they engage in a one-sided search for information; and in doing so, they create a reality that ultimately supports their beliefs (Zuckerman et al., 1995).

Are people so blinded by their existing beliefs that they cannot manage an open and objective search for evidence? It depends. In the type of task devised by Snyder and Swann, different circumstances produce less biasing results. Specifically, when people are not certain of their beliefs and are concerned about the accuracy of their impressions (Kruglanski & Mayseless, 1988), when they are allowed to prepare their own interviews (Trope et al., 1984), or when available nonconfirmatory questions are better than the confirmatory questions (Skov & Sherman, 1986), they tend to pursue a more balanced search for information.

Let's stop for a moment and contemplate what this research means for the broader question of why we often seem to resist changing our negative but mistaken impressions of others more than our positive but mistaken impressions. Jerker Denrell (2005) argues that even when we form a negative first impression on the basis of all available evidence, and even when we interpret that evidence accurately, our impression may be misleading. The reason: *biased experience sampling*. Meet someone who seems likable and you may interact with that person again. Then if he or she turns out to be twisted, dishonest, or self-centered, you'll be in a position to observe these traits and revise your impression. But if you meet someone you don't like, you will try to avoid that person in the future, cutting yourself off from new information and limiting the opportunity to revise your opinion. Attraction breeds interaction, which is why our negative first impressions in particular tend to stick like glue.

The Self-Fulfilling Prophecy

In 1948, sociologist Robert Merton told a story about Cartwright Millingville, president of the Last National Bank during the Depression. Although the bank was solvent, a rumor began to spread that it was floundering. Within hours, hundreds of depositors were lined up to withdraw their savings before no money was left to withdraw. The rumor was false, but the bank eventually failed. Using stories such as this, Merton proposed what seemed like an outrageous hypothesis: that a perceiver's expectation can actually lead to its own fulfillment, a **self-fulfilling prophecy**.

Merton's hypothesis lay dormant within psychology until Robert Rosenthal and Lenore Jacobson (1968) published the results of a study in a book entitled *Pygmalion in the Classroom*. Noticing that teachers had higher expectations for better students, they wondered if teacher expectations *influenced* student performance rather than the other way around. To address the question, they told teachers in a San Francisco elementary school that certain pupils were on the verge of an intellectual growth spurt. The results of an IQ test were cited, but, in fact, the pupils had been randomly selected. Then eight months later, when real tests were administered, the "late bloomers" exhibited an increase in their IQ scores compared with children assigned to a control group. They were also evaluated more favorably by their classroom teachers.

When the Pygmalion study was first published, it was greeted with chagrin. If positive teacher expectations can boost student performance, can negative expectations have the opposite effect? What about the social implications? Could it be that affluent children are destined for success and disadvantaged children are doomed to

self-fulfilling prophecy
The process by which one's expectations about a person eventually lead that person to behave in ways that confirm those expectations.

failure because educators hold different expectations for them? Many researchers were critical of the study itself and skeptical about the generality of the results. Unfortunately, though, these findings cannot be swept under the proverbial rug. In a review of additional studies, Rosenthal (1985) found that teachers' expectations significantly predicted their students' performance 36 percent of the time. Mercifully, the predictive value of teacher expectancies seems to wear off, not accumulate, as children graduate from one grade to the next (A. Smith et al., 1999).

How might teacher expectations be transformed into reality? There are two points of view. According to Rosenthal (2002), the process involves covert communication. The teacher forms an initial impression of students early in the school year based, perhaps, on their background or reputation, physical appearance, initial classroom performance, and standardized-test scores. The teacher then alters his or her behavior in ways that are consistent with that impression. If initial expectations are high rather than low, the teacher gives the student more praise, attention, challenging homework, and better feedback. In turn, the student adjusts his or her own behavior. If the signals are positive, the student may become energized, work hard, and succeed. If negative, there may be a loss of interest and self-confidence. The cycle is thus complete and the expectations confirmed.

While recognizing that this effect can occur, Lee Jussim and his colleagues (1996; Jussim & Harber, 2005) question whether teachers in real life are so prone in the first place to form erroneous impressions of their students. It's true, in many naturalistic studies, that the expectations teachers have at the start of a school year are ultimately confirmed by their students—a result that is consistent with the notion that the teachers had a hand in producing that outcome. But wait. That same result is also consistent with a more innocent possibility: that perhaps the expectations that teachers form of their students are *accurate*. There are times, Jussim admits, when teachers may stereotype a student and, without realizing it, behave in ways that create a self-fulfilling prophecy. But there are also times when teachers can predict how their students will perform without necessarily influencing that performance (Alvidrez & Weinstein, 1999).

Addressing this question in a longitudinal study of mothers and their children, Stephanie Madon and others (2003) found that underage adolescents are more likely to drink when their mothers had earlier expected them to. Statistical analyses revealed that this prophecy was fulfilled in part because the mothers *influence* their sons and daughters, as Rosenthal's work would suggest, and in part because the mothers are able to *predict* their children's behavior, as Jussim's model would suggest. In fact, a follow-up study suggests that the link between a mother's expectations and her adolescent's later alcohol consumption did not strengthen or weaken over time, remaining stable as the child moved from the seventh grade through the twelfth (Madon et al., 2006).

It's clear that self-fulfilling prophecies are at work in many settings—not only schools but also a wide range of organizations, including the military (Kierein & Gold, 2000; McNatt, 2000). In a study of a thousand men assigned to twenty-nine platoons in the Israeli Defense Forces, Dov Eden (1990) led some platoon leaders but not others to expect that the groups of trainees they were about to receive had great potential (in fact, these groups were of average ability). After ten weeks, the trainees assigned to the high-expectation platoons scored higher than the others on written exams and on the ability to operate a weapon.

The process may also be found in the criminal justice system, where police interrogate suspects. To illustrate, Kassin and others (2003) had some college students but not others commit a mock crime, stealing $100 from a laboratory. All suspects were then questioned by student interrogators who were led to believe that their suspect was probably guilty or innocent. Interrogators who presumed guilt asked more incriminating questions, conducted more coercive interrogations, and tried harder to get the suspect to confess. In turn, this more aggressive style made the suspects sound defensive and led observers who later listened to the tapes to judge them guilty, even when they were innocent. Still other self-fulfilling prophecy studies have shown that judges unwittingly bias juries (Hart, 1995) and that negotiators settle for lesser outcomes if they believe that their counterparts are highly competitive (Diekmann et al., 2003).

The self-fulfilling prophecy is a powerful phenomenon (Darley & Fazio, 1980; Harris & Rosenthal, 1985; Rosenthal, 2002). But how does it work? How do social perceivers

FIGURE 4.11

The Self-fulfilling Prophecy as a Three-Step Process

How do people transform their expectations into reality? (1) A perceiver has expectations of a target person, (2) The perceiver then behaves in a manner consistent with those expectations, (3) The target unwittingly adjusts his or her behavior according to the perceiver's actions.

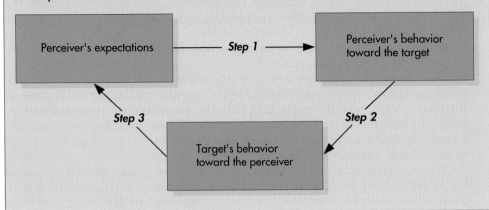

transform their expectations of others into reality? Research indicates that the phenomenon occurs as a three-step process. First, a perceiver forms an impression of a target person—an impression that may be based on interactions with the target or on other information. Second, the perceiver behaves in a manner that is consistent with that first impression. Third, the target person unwittingly adjusts his or her behavior to the perceiver's actions. The net result: behavioral confirmation of the first impression (see Figure 4.11).

But now let's straighten out this picture. It would be a sad commentary on human nature if each of us were so easily molded by others' perceptions into appearing brilliant or stupid, introverted or extroverted, competitive or cooperative, warm or cold. The effects are well established, but there are limits. By viewing the self-fulfilling prophecy as a three-step process, social psychologists can identify the links in the chain that can be broken to prevent the vicious cycle.

Consider the first step, the link between one's expectations and one's behavior toward the target person. In the typical study, perceivers try to get to know the target on only a casual basis and are not necessarily driven to form an accurate impression. But when perceivers are highly motivated to seek the truth (as when they are considering the target as a possible teammate or opponent), they become more objective and often do not confirm prior expectations (Harris & Perkins, 1995; Hilton & Darley, 1991).

The link between expectations and behavior depends in other ways as well on a perceiver's goals and motivations in the interaction (Snyder & Stukas, 1999). In one study, John Copeland (1994) put either the perceiver or the target into a position of relative power. In all cases, the perceiver interacted with a target who was said to be introverted or extroverted. In half the pairs, the perceiver was given the power to accept or reject the target as a teammate for a money-winning game. In the other half, it was the target who was empowered to choose a teammate. The two participants interacted, the interaction was recorded, and neutral observers listened to the tapes and rated the target person. So, did perceivers cause the targets to behave as introverted or extroverted, depending on initial expectations? Yes and no. Illustrating what Copeland called "prophecies of power," the results showed that high-power perceivers triggered the self-fulfilling prophecy, as in past research, but that low-power perceivers did not. In the low-power situation, the perceivers spent less time getting to know the target person and more time trying to be liked.

Now consider the second step, the link between a perceiver's behavior and the target's response. In much of the past research, as in much of life, target persons are not aware of the false impressions held by others. Thus, it is unlikely that Rosenthal and Jacobson's (1968) "late bloomers" knew of their teachers' high expectations or that Snyder and Swann's (1978) "introverts" and "extroverts" knew of their interviewers' misconceptions. But what if they had known? How would *you* react if you found yourself being cast in a particular light? When it happened to participants in one experiment, they managed to overcome the effect by behaving in ways that forced the perceivers to abandon their expectations (Hilton & Darley, 1985).

As you may recall from the discussion of self-verification in Chapter 3, this result is most likely to occur when perceiver expectations clash with a target person's

The notion that we can create a "self-fulfilling prophecy" by getting others to behave in ways we expect is a myth. **False.**

self-concept. When targets who viewed themselves as extroverted were interviewed by perceivers who believed they were introverted (and vice versa), what changed as a result of the interaction were the perceivers' beliefs, not the targets' behavior (Swann & Ely, 1984). Social perception is a two-way street; the persons we judge have their own prophecies to fulfill.

Social Perception: The Bottom Line

Trying to understand people—whether they are professional athletes, world leaders, trial lawyers, or loved ones closer to home—is no easy task. As you reflect on the material in this chapter, you will notice that there are two radically different views of social perception. One suggests that the process is quick and relatively automatic. At the drop of a hat, without much thought, effort, or awareness, people make rapid-fire snap judgments about others based on physical appearance, preconceptions, or just a hint of behavioral evidence. According to a second view, however, the process is relatively mindful. People observe others carefully and reserve judgment until their analysis of the target person, behavior, and situation is complete. As suggested by theories of attribution and information integration, the process is eminently logical. In light of recent research, it is now safe to conclude that both accounts of social perception are correct. Sometimes, our judgments are made instantly; at other times, they are based on a more painstaking analysis of behavior. Either way, we often steer our interactions with others along a path that is narrowed by first impressions, a process that can set in motion a self-fulfilling prophecy. The various aspects of social perception, as described in this chapter, are summarized in Figure 4.12.

At this point, we must confront an important question: How *accurate* are people's impressions of each other? For years, this question has proved provocative but hard to answer (Cronbach, 1955; Kenny, 1994). Granted, people often depart from the ideals of logic and exhibit bias in their social perceptions. In this chapter alone, we have seen that perceivers typically focus on the wrong cues to judge if someone is lying; use cognitive heuristics without regard for numerical base rates; overlook the situational influences on behavior; disparage victims whose misfortunes threaten their sense of justice; form premature first impressions; and interpret, seek, and create evidence in ways that support these impressions.

FIGURE 4.12

The Processes of Social Perception

Summarizing Chapter 4, this diagram depicts the processes of social perception. As shown, it begins with the observation of persons, situations, and behavior. Sometimes we make snap judgments from these cues. At other times, we form impressions only after making attributions and integrating these attributions. Either way, our impressions are subject to confirmation biases and the risk of a self-fulfilling prophecy.

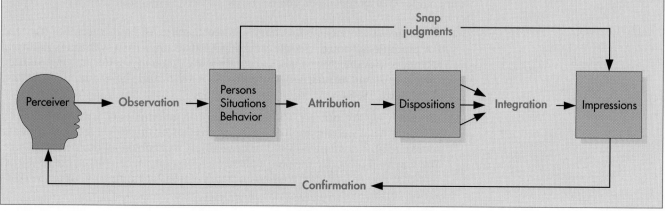

To make matters worse, we often have little awareness of our limitations, leading us to feel *overconfident* in our judgments. In a series of studies, David Dunning and his colleagues (1990) asked college students to predict how a target person would react in various situations. Some made predictions about a fellow student whom they had just met and interviewed, and others made predictions about their roommates. In both cases, participants reported their confidence in each prediction, and accuracy was determined by the responses of the target persons themselves. The results were clear: Regardless of whether they judged a stranger or a roommate, the students consistently overestimated the accuracy of their predictions. In fact, Kruger and Dunning (1999) found that people who scored low on tests of spelling, logic, grammar, and humor appreciation were later the most likely to overestimate their own performance. Apparently, poor performers are doubly cursed: They don't know what they don't know (Dunning et al., 2003), and they don't know they are biased (Ehrlinger et al., 2005).

Standing back from the material presented in this chapter, you may find the list of shortcomings, punctuated by the problem of overconfidence, to be long and depressing. So, how can this list be reconciled with the triumphs of civilization? Or to put it another way, "If we're so dumb, how come we made it to the moon?" (Nisbett & Ross, 1980, p. 249).

A number of years ago, Herbert Simon (1956) coined the term *satisficing* (by combining *satisfying* and *sufficing*) to describe the way people make judgments that, while not logically perfect, are good enough. Today, many psychologists believe that people operate by a principle of "bounded rationality"—that we are rational *within bounds* depending on our abilities, motives, available time, and other factors. In a book entitled *Simple Heuristics That Make Us Smart*, Gerd Gigerenzer and others (1999) noted that people seldom compute intricate probabilities to make decisions; rather, they "reach into an adaptive toolbox filled with fast and frugal heuristics" (p. 5). They also note that these heuristics often serve us well enough. As an example, consider a simple heuristic: that people, objects, or places we recognize have greater value than those we don't recognize. In a study of investment decision making in the stock market, Bernhard Borges and others (1999) asked people to indicate which publicly traded companies they had heard of such as Kodak, Ford Motors, Coca-Cola, Intel, and American Express. These researchers then created two stock portfolios, one containing high-recognition companies and the other, low-recognition companies. After six months, the group of high-recognition stocks actually made more money than did the low-recognition stocks. In general, it even outperformed the market. So, can a naive and ignorant investor pick winning stocks based on name recognition? The heuristic in question is not perfect, but it may be good enough.

It is true that people fall prey to the biases identified by social psychologists and probably even to some that have not yet been noticed. It is also true that we often get fooled by con artists, misjudge our partners in marriage, and hire the wrong job applicants. As Thomas Gilovich (1991) points out, more Americans believe in ESP than in evolution, and there are twenty times more astrologers in the world than astronomers. The problem is, these biases can have harmful consequences and give rise, as we'll see in Chapter 5, to stereotypes, prejudice, and discrimination.

Despite our imperfections, there are four reasons to be guardedly optimistic about our competence as social perceivers:

1. The more experience people have with each other, the more accurate they are. For example, although people have a limited ability to assess the personality of strangers they meet in a laboratory, they are generally better at judging their own friends and acquaintances (Kenny & Acitelli, 2001; Levesque, 1997; Malloy & Albright, 1990).

2. Although we are not good at making global judgments of others (that is, at knowing what people are like across a range of settings), we are able to make more circumscribed predictions of how others will behave in our own presence. You may well misjudge the personality of a roommate or co-worker, but to the extent that you can predict your roommate's actions at home or your co-worker's actions on the job, the mistakes may not matter (Swann, 1984).

3. Social perception skills can be improved in people who are taught the rules of probability and logic (Kosonen & Winne, 1995; Nisbett et al., 1987). For example, graduate students in psychology—because they take courses in statistics—tend to improve in their ability to reason about everyday social events (Lehman et al., 1988).

4. People can form more accurate impressions of others when motivated by concerns for accuracy and open-mindedness (Kruglanski & Webster, 1996). Many studies described in this chapter have shown that people exhibit less bias when there is an incentive for accuracy within the experiment, as when the perceiver judges a prospective teammate's ability to facilitate success in a future task (Fiske & Neuberg, 1990) or a future dating partner's *social* competence (Goodwin et al., 2002).

To summarize, research on the accuracy of social perceptions offers a valuable lesson: To the extent that we observe others with whom we have had time to interact, make judgments that are reasonably specific, have some knowledge of the rules of logic, and are sufficiently motivated to form an accurate impression, the problems that plague us can be minimized. Indeed, just being aware of the biases described in this chapter may well be a necessary first step toward a better understanding of others.

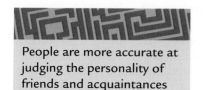

People are more accurate at judging the personality of friends and acquaintances than of strangers. **True.**

REVIEW

Observation: The Elements of Social Perception

- To understand others, social perceivers rely on indirect clues—the elements of social perception.

Persons: Judging a Book by Its Cover

- People often make snap judgments of others based on physical appearances (for example, adults with baby-faced features are seen as having childlike qualities).

Situations: The Scripts of Life

- People have preconceptions, or "scripts," about certain types of situations. These scripts guide our interpretations of behavior.

Behavioral Evidence

- People derive meaning from behavior by dividing it into discrete, meaningful units.

- Nonverbal behaviors are often used to determine how others are feeling.

- From facial expressions, people all over the world can identify the emotions of happiness, fear, sadness, surprise, anger, and disgust.

- Body language, gaze, and touch are also important forms of nonverbal communication.

- People use nonverbal cues to detect deception but are often not accurate in making these judgments because they pay too much attention to the face and neglect cues that are more revealing.

Attribution: From Elements to Dispositions

- Attribution is the process by which we explain people's behavior.

Attribution Theories

- People begin to understand others by making personal or situational attributions for their behavior.

- Correspondent inference theory states that people learn about others from behavior that is freely chosen, that is unexpected, and that results in a small number of desirable outcomes.

- From multiple behaviors, we base our attributions on three kinds of covariation information: consensus, distinctiveness, and consistency.

Attribution Biases

- People depart from the logic of attribution theory in two major ways.

- First, we use cognitive heuristics—rules of thumb that enable us to make judgments that are quick but often in error.

- Second, we tend to commit the fundamental attribution error, overestimating the role of personal factors and underestimating the impact of situations.

Cultural Influences on Attribution

- Cultures differ in their implicit theories about the causes of human behavior.

- Studies show, for example, that East Asians are more likely than Americans to consider the impact of the social and situational contexts of which they are a part.

Motivational Biases

- Our attributions for the behavior of others are often biased by our own self-esteem motives.
- Needing to believe in a just world, people often criticize victims and blame them for their fate.

Integration: From Dispositions to Impressions

Information Integration: The Arithmetic

- The impressions we form are usually based on an averaging of a person's traits, not on a summation.
- According to information integration theory, impressions are based on perceiver predispositions and a weighted average of individual traits.

Deviations from the Arithmetic

- Perceivers differ in their sensitivity to certain traits and in the impressions they form.
- Differences stem from stable perceiver characteristics, priming from recent experiences, implicit personality theories, and the primacy effect.

Confirmation Biases: From Impressions to Reality

- Once an impression is formed, people become less likely to change their minds when confronted with nonsupportive evidence.
- People tend to interpret, seek, and create information in ways that confirm existing beliefs.

Perseverance of Beliefs

- First impressions may survive in the face of inconsistent information.
- Ambiguous evidence is interpreted in ways that bolster first impressions.
- The effect of evidence that is later discredited perseveres because people formulate theories to support their initial beliefs.

Confirmatory Hypothesis Testing

- Once perceivers have beliefs about someone, they seek further information in ways that confirm those beliefs.

The Self-Fulfilling Prophecy

- As shown by the effects of teacher expectancies on student achievement, first impressions set in motion a self-fulfilling prophecy.
- This is the product of a three-step process: (1) A perceiver forms an expectation of a target person, (2) the perceiver behaves accordingly, and (3) the target adjusts to the perceiver's actions.
- This self-fulfilling prophecy effect is powerful but limited in important ways.

Social Perception: The Bottom Line

- Sometimes, people make snap judgments; at other times, they evaluate others by carefully analyzing their behavior.
- Research suggests that our judgments are often biased and that we are overconfident.
- Still, there are conditions under which we are more competent as social perceivers.

KEY TERMS

PUTTING COMMON SENSE TO THE TEST

The impressions we form of others are influenced by superficial aspects of their appearance.

True. Research shows that first impressions are influenced by height, weight, clothing, facial characteristics, and other aspects of appearance.

Adaptively, people are skilled at knowing when someone is lying rather than telling the truth.

False. People frequently make mistakes in their judgments of truth and deception, too often accepting what others say at face value.

Like social psychologists, people are sensitive to situational causes when explaining the behavior of others.

False. In explaining the behavior of others, people overestimate the importance of personal factors and overlook the impact of situations, a bias known as the "fundamental attribution error."

People are slow to change their first impressions on the basis of new information.

True. Studies have shown that once people form an impression of someone, they become resistant to change even when faced with contradictory new evidence.

The notion that we can create a "self-fulfilling prophecy" by getting others to behave in ways we expect is a myth.

False. In the laboratory and in the classroom, a perceiver's expectation can actually lead to its own fulfillment.

People are more accurate at judging the personality of friends and acquaintances than of strangers.

True. People often form erroneous impressions of strangers but tend to be more accurate in their judgments of friends and acquaintances.

5

Stereotypes, Prejudice, and Discrimination

PREVIEW

This chapter considers how people think, feel, and behave toward members of social groups. We begin by examining *stereotypes*, beliefs about groups that influence our judgments of individuals. Next, we examine *prejudice*, negative feelings toward others based on their group membership. To illustrate these problems, we then focus on *sexism* and *racism*, forms of discrimination based on a person's gender and racial background. After considering some of the effects of being the targets of these biases, we discuss some ways to *reduce stereotypes, prejudice, and discrimination* today and in the future.

T/F

_____ Very brief exposure to a member of a stereotyped group does not lead to biased judgments or responses, but longer exposure typically does.

_____ Being reminded of one's own mortality makes people put things into greater perspective, thereby tending to reduce ingroup-outgroup distinctions and hostilities.

_____ Even brief exposure to sexist television commercials can significantly influence the behaviors of men and women.

_____ An African American student is likely to perform worse on an athletic task if the task is described as one reflecting sports intelligence than if it is described as reflecting natural athletic ability.

_____ Groups with a history of prejudice toward each other tend to become much less prejudiced soon after they are made to interact with each other in a desegregated setting.

On September 2, 2005, during a televised benefit concert for Hurricane Katrina relief, rap/hip-hop star Kanye West and movie star Mike Myers appeared together on camera to appeal to viewers to contribute to the relief efforts. When West ignored the prepared script, looked straight at the camera, and said, "George Bush doesn't care about black people," the look of shock, confusion, and anxiety on Myers's face was so evident and raw that it would become a target for jokes and parodies for weeks to come. But the emotions behind both Myers's reactions and West's charged words were deadly serious at the time, and they reflect important issues and lessons concerning stereotypes, prejudice, and discrimination.

West, an African American, was asserting that racism and discrimination were behind what he saw as the government's insufficient support for the people hit hardest by Hurricane Katrina in and around New Orleans, a predominately poor and black group of people. Myers, who is white and from Canada, may have felt especially uncomfortable responding to West's unscripted remarks against the U.S. president and government. Indeed, it is very common for people to feel anxiety and confusion about how to even talk about issues of stereotyping, prejudice, and discrimination. Because of this anxiety, as well as a lack of understanding, such issues are often ignored until a dramatic event like Hurricane Katrina thrusts them back into the spotlight.

Both the discomfort and the lack of understanding can be seen in the controversy triggered several years before by the words of another popular musician. In the middle of a sold-out concert in Atlanta, Georgia, in the summer of 2000, Bruce Springsteen debuted a new song he had recently written. The song began with Springsteen plaintively chanting, "forty-one shots" about ten times. From those words alone, most of the audience instantly understood what the song was about. Just hours later, word

Mike Myers looks on awkwardly as Kanye West ignores the script in their televised appearance and criticizes U.S. president George Bush for not caring about black people in the aftermath of Hurricane Katrina, in September 2005.

41 shots, cut through
* the night*
you're kneeling over his
body in a vestibule
Praying for his life

Is it a gun, is it a knife
Is it a wallet, this is your life
It ain't no secret, no secret
* my friend*
You can get killed just for
* living in your American*
* skin*

Some of the lyrics from Bruce
Springsteen's song, "American
Skin (41 Shots)," which was in-
spired by the Amadou Diallo
tragedy.

of this unreleased song had spread to New York City, setting off a firestorm of controversy. Heads of two police unions called for a boycott of Springsteen's upcoming con-
certs in New York. One called him "a dirtbag" and "a floating fag" for singing a song
about this issue. Fans and activists called the song "brilliant" and "compassionate."

What was so incendiary about the words "forty-one shots"? As the concertgoers
in Atlanta, the police in New York, and many people around the world quickly inferred, the words alluded to the tragic death a year earlier of a West African immigrant in New York City who was killed in a hail of forty-one bullets in the vestibule
of his apartment building.

On February 4, 1999, just after midnight, Amadou Diallo entered his apartment
building. He was spotted by members of the Street Crime Unit, an elite unit of officers
who patrolled crime-ridden areas of the city. The unit had been extraordinarily successful in reducing crime, but its methods were often criticized for being too aggressive. In particular, critics charged that it singled out African American and Hispanic
men. Thousands had been routinely stopped, frisked, and searched. That winter night
in 1999, Amadou Diallo would have been one more. Four white police officers from
the unit spotted Diallo. He matched the general description of a suspected rapist they
were searching for. The police thought that Diallo looked suspicious as he appeared
to duck into his building to avoid them. As they approached, he reached into his
pocket and began pulling out a black object. Thinking that the object was a gun, the
police opened fire. Forty-one shots. Nineteen of them hit Diallo, and he lay dead in
the vestibule. The police removed the black object from his hand. It was a wallet.
Diallo did not have a weapon.

Protesters held rallies in the days that followed, chanting "forty-one shots" and
holding up wallets. "Racial profiling," the controversial use of race as a factor in
determining whom to stop and search for possible criminal activities, came under
renewed attack. The Street Crime Unit was disbanded. Many politicians, columnists,
and citizens defended the police officers, noting how difficult it is to make life-or-death
decisions in the blink of an eye. In March 2000, all four officers were found not guilty
of any criminal charges.

Springsteen's song was fair and balanced, neither condemning nor condoning
the police's actions but instead highlighting the tragic consequences of living in a
violent, dangerous society. However, it did raise the critical question of whether the
officers' perception of a gun rather than a wallet involved their "eyes" or their
"heart." The implied question was whether stereotypes associated with the color of
Diallo's skin made the officers more likely to misperceive the wallet as a gun. Although none of us can ever know whether this was the case in the Diallo tragedy,
the research discussed in this chapter—including experiments inspired directly by

Protesters against police violence
walk down Broadway in New York
City on April 5, 2000. At the center
is a photo of Amadou Diallo, an
unarmed African immigrant who
was killed in a burst of forty-one
gunshots by New York City police.

FIGURE 5.1

Multiple Paths

There are two paths to discrimination: one based on stereotypes, the other on prejudice. Note also that there are other links among these variables. Discriminatory practices may support stereotypes and prejudice; stereotypes may cause people to become prejudiced; and prejudiced people may use stereotypes to justify their feelings.

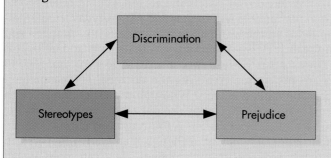

the Diallo tragedy—will make it clear that such an effect is possible. Perception of others is profoundly influenced by the act of perceiving them as a member of a group.

Race is but one kind of group membership that can influence perceivers' thoughts, feelings, and actions. Others include gender, sexual orientation, age, physical appearance, and economic class. Indeed, stereotypes, prejudice, and discrimination are problems worldwide. Watch the news and you might see stories about genocide in Darfur, terror and war fueled by ethnic and religious divisions in the Middle East, neo-Nazi violence in Germany and France, race riots on the beaches of Australia, and hate crimes against gay men in the United States. And for every bit of violence, there are countless other, more subtle ways in which people hurt others as a result of viewing them through the lenses of group identity.

For the purposes of this chapter, a **group** is defined as two or more people perceived as having at least one of the following characteristics: (1) direct interactions with each other over a period of time; (2) joint membership in a social category based on sex, race, or other attributes; (3) a shared, common fate, identity, or set of goals. We see people in fundamentally different ways if we consider them to constitute a group rather than simply an aggregate of individuals. How does this happen, and why? How are people's thoughts, feelings, and behaviors affected? Examining these questions is the focus of this chapter.

The chapter is divided into five parts. First, we consider the causes and effects of **stereotypes**—beliefs that associate a whole group of people with certain traits. Second, we examine **prejudice**, which consists of negative feelings about others because of their connection to a social group. To put these problems in concrete terms, we then focus specifically on sexism and racism, two historically common forms of **discrimination**—negative behaviors directed against persons because of their membership in a particular group. Next, we shift the focus from the perceivers to the perceived: What are some of the ways in which people are affected by being the targets of stereotypes, prejudice, and discrimination? The chapter concludes with a discussion of some ways in which stereotypes, prejudice, and discrimination can be reduced. Although this chapter discusses stereotypes, prejudice, and discrimination in separate sections, it is clear that they are related to each other. Our beliefs and feelings influence each other, they both give rise to discrimination, and discriminatory behavior, in turn, fuels stereotypes and prejudices (see Figure 5.1).

Stereotypes

group Two or more persons perceived as related because of their interactions, membership in the same social category, or common fate.

stereotype A belief that associates a group of people with certain traits.

prejudice Negative feelings toward persons based on their membership in certain groups.

discrimination Behavior directed against persons because of their membership in a particular group.

When you stop to think about it, the list of well-known stereotypes seems endless. Consider some examples: The Japanese are sneaky, athletes are brainless, librarians are quiet, Italians are emotional, accountants are dull, Californians are laid back, white men can't jump, and used-car salesmen can't be trusted as far as you can throw them. Stereotypes are so universal and frequently experienced that they seem almost an essential part of the human condition. For this reason, it may be difficult to consider where they come from and why they are so difficult to extinguish. But to understand stereotypes, it is critical to trace their roots. In this section, we focus on a variety of factors that give rise to, and help maintain, stereotypes.

How Stereotypes Form

The origins of stereotypes can be traced to a number of sources, including historical, economic, and political origins. Social psychologists pose an additional question: Regardless of the original sources of stereotypes within a culture, how do they grow and operate in the minds of individuals? We will focus on three factors. The first focuses on a cultural perspective, examining how people learn associations, beliefs, values, and ways of making sense of the world from their culture. Next, we will examine two related processes concerning how people perceive other people: the process of *categorization,* in which we sort people into groups, and the process by which people perceive groups to which we belong (*ingroups*) as being different from groups to which we do not belong (*outgroups*). These two processes reflect basic cognitive operations, but they in turn are influenced by variations in culture, motivation, and individuals' theories about groups.

Culture and Cognition   Where do our beliefs and attitudes about other people come from? Some come from our families and friends and our everyday social interactions. Others come from living in the world and noticing how it is arranged and organized. The movies and reality TV we watch, the advertisements and billboards we see, and the blogs and newspapers we read expose us to stereotypic images and ideas about people. Who are the nurses? Who are the doctors? The elementary school teachers? The political and military leaders? Who attends the best schools with the state-of-the art facilities? Who gets stopped by the police on campus? Noticing these patterns in our social world is inevitable, as is forming associations between groups of people and certain kinds of behavior. Although it could be otherwise, in today's society, gender, ethnicity, and race organize our lives. These categories predict the quality of your neighborhood and school, as well as your future educational attainment, income, occupation, and health.

Stereotyping arises when we try to explain the associations and patterns that we see in the world. For example, there are relatively few women professors in mathematics and physics. Is this because women are less good at math and physics than men? Or is it because people in our culture do not expect women to become mathematicians and physicists, the climate in these fields is not hospitable to women, and there are few women scientists represented in the media to serve as role models for young girls? Our shared history and culture influence the types of explanations we give for the associations we see in the world.

Just as individuals' tastes in fashion, hairstyles, and music are influenced by the people around them, so too is their adoption of particular stereotypes and prejudices. It may become more or less fashionable for movies or TV comedies to present gays in a particular way, for example, and these representations can influence viewers' own attitudes and beliefs. Closer to home, the beliefs and attitudes expressed by peers, family, and other social contacts often have profound effects on individuals. Jeff Greenberg and Thomas Pyszczynski (1985) found that merely overhearing someone utter a racial slur can increase one's own expressions of prejudice. One author of this textbook recalls a time when he was about eight years old and his two best friends suddenly called him a "Jew ball." They had never thought of him as different from them or categorized him as Jewish before, and yet on this day, suddenly Jewishness was relevant—and negative to them. But why *then,* and how did they come up with "Jew ball"?! Only much later did it become clear that they had misheard their father say "Jew boy." Trying to model their father's values, they used an approximation of this expression against their friend, and they would thereafter see him in a different way. The biased lens through which the father saw people was passed down to the next generation.

Social Categorization   Although it was surprising at the time, the fact that these boys saw their friend not merely as an individual but as a member of some category is not shocking. As perceivers, we routinely sort single objects into groups rather than think of each as unique. Biologists classify animals into species; archaeologists divide time into eras; geographers split the earth into regions. Likewise, people sort each other into groups on the basis of gender, race, and other common attributes in a process called **social categorization**. In some ways, social categorization is natural and adaptive. By grouping people the way we group foods, animals, and other objects, we form impressions quickly and use past experience to guide new interactions. With so many things to pay attention to in our social worlds, we can save time and effort by using people's group memberships to make inferences about them

social categorization The classification of persons into groups on the basis of common attributes.

(Bodenhausen et al., 2003; Hall & Crisp, 2005; Sherman et al., 2004; Wigboldus et al., 2004).

There is, however, a serious drawback to the time and energy saved through social categorization. Like lumping apples and oranges together because both are fruit, categorizing people leads us to overestimate the differences between groups and to underestimate the differences within groups (Ford & Tonander, 1998; Krueger et al., 1989; Spears, 2002; Stangor & Lange, 1994; Wyer et al., 2002). Aware of the social categories to which individuals belong, we can fail even to *perceive* information about these individuals that does not conform to our stereotypes about their groups (von Hippel et al., 1995). And we may come to believe that the distinctions between social categories are more rigid, even more biologically rooted, than they are. Many people assume, for example, that there is a clear genetic basis for classifying people by race. The fact is, however, that how societies make distinctions between races can change dramatically as a function of historical contexts. For instance, it was fairly common for Americans in the early part of the twentieth century to consider Irish Americans as distinct from Whites, but today such thinking is quite rare. Moreover, biologists, anthropologists, and psychologists have noted that there is more genetic variation within races than between them (Eberhardt & Goff, 2004; Marks, 1995; Ore, 2000). The categories we apply to others often say more about ourselves than about them.

Why are some categorizations—such as race, gender, and sexual preference—more likely to dominate our perceptions than others? Why, and when, are people quicker to categorize a black male firefighter as black than as a man or as a firefighter? Cognitive factors can determine this; if perceivers have recently been primed to think about one of the categories, that category becomes more likely to dominate perceptions. But, as we have indicated earlier, cultural factors also play important roles, such as how people are represented in various institutions, by the popular media, or by peers and family. For example, D. Conor Seyle and Matthew Newman (2006) argue that the frequent distinction made by political commentators in the American media between politically conservative "red states" and politically liberal "blue states" calls so much attention to this categorization that it becomes a kind of self-fulfilling prophecy. An exaggerated cultural difference becomes more and more real.

Whether people are likely to immediately categorize this person by his race, gender, or occupation depends on a combination of cognitive, cultural, and motivational factors.

In addition, our own immediate needs and motivations can affect how we categorize others. If your house is on fire, you are much more likely to categorize a black male firefighter as a firefighter than as black or male (Bodenhausen & Macrae, 1998). More abstract goals can also affect us. For example, people in powerful positions in society may be motivated to categorize others in ways that help them maintain the status quo and justify their feelings of superiority (Jost, 2008; Operario & Fiske, 2001).

Ingroups Versus Outgroups Although grouping humans is much like grouping objects, there is a key difference. When it comes to social categorization, perceivers themselves are members or nonmembers of the categories they use. Groups that you identify with—your country, your religion, your political party, even your hometown sports team—are called **ingroups**, whereas groups other than your own are called **outgroups**. This strong tendency to carve the world into "us" and "them" has important consequences.

One consequence is that we exaggerate the differences between our ingroup and other outgroups. Ingroup members often care a great deal about preserving distinctions between their ingroup and outgroups (Castano et al., 2002). Indeed, Robert Kurzban and Mark Leary (2001) propose that this vigilance has evolutionary origins; that is, it was adaptive for humans to avoid contact with outsiders, who might have posed health or safety risks, and to work in groups that would compete with and possibly exploit other groups.

Another consequence is a phenomenon known as the **outgroup homogeneity effect**, whereby perceivers assume that there is a greater similarity among members

ingroups Groups with which an individual feels a sense of membership, belonging, and identity.

outgroups Groups with which an individual does not feel a sense of membership, belonging, or identity.

outgroup homogeneity effect The tendency to assume that there is greater similarity among members of outgroups than among members of ingroups.

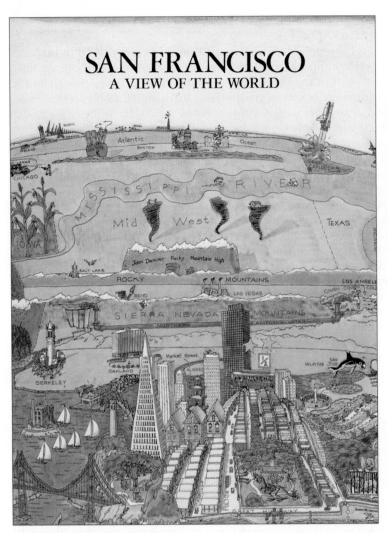

SAN FRANCISCO
A VIEW OF THE WORLD

People often have a great deal of detailed, diverse information about their own groups, and much less information about other groups. This situation can contribute to the outgroup homogeneity effect, in which people assume that "they" are all alike.

of outgroups than among members of one's own group. In other words, there may be fine and subtle differences among "us," but "they" are all alike (Linville & Jones, 1980).

Research shows that outgroup homogeneity effects are common and evident around the world (Bartsch et al., 1997; Linville, 1998; Read & Urada, 2003). Indeed, there are many real-life examples. People from China, Korea, Taiwan, and Vietnam see themselves as different from one another, of course, but to many western eyes they are all Asian. Business majors like to talk about engineering types; engineers talk about business types; liberals lump together all conservatives; teenagers lump together all old people; and as the natives of California proclaim their cultural and ethnic diversity, outsiders talk of the typical Californian. To people outside the group, outgroup members can even seem to look alike: People are less accurate in distinguishing and recognizing the faces of members of racial outgroups, especially if they are unfamiliar with those other groups (Hills & Lewis, 2006; Meissner et al., 2005; Pezdek et al., 2003; Wright et al., 2003).

There are two reasons for the tendency to perceive outgroups as homogeneous. First, we often do not notice subtle differences among outgroups because we have little personal contact with them. Think about your family or your favorite sports team, and specific individuals come to mind. Think about an unfamiliar outgroup, however, and you are likely to think in abstract terms about the group as a whole. Indeed, the more familiar people are with an outgroup, the less likely they are to perceive it as homogeneous. A second problem is that people often do not encounter a representative sample of outgroup members. A student from one school who encounters students from a rival school only when they cruise into town for a Saturday football game, screaming at the top of their lungs, sees only the most avid rival fans—hardly a diverse lot (Linville et al., 1989; Quattrone, 1986). People sometimes perceive their own group to be homogeneous when they first join it, but over time, as they become more familiar with fellow group members, they see their group as more diverse relative to outgroups (Ryan & Bogart, 1997).

Cultures differ in how they make ingroup-outgroup distinctions. For example, Darío Páez and others (1998) have noted that people from collectivistic cultures, which value group harmony, are more likely to perceive ingroup homogeneity than are people from individualistic cultures, which value the distinctiveness of the individual. Motivational factors also influence perceptions of ingroups and outgroups. People who are motivated to protect or affirm their group identity—for example, when they feel that their group's status is under threat—become more likely to see their ingroup as relatively *homogeneous* (Brewer & Brown, 1998; Lorenzi-Cioldi et al., 1998; Pickett & Brewer, 2001).

Implicit Personality Theories About Groups Researchers develop theories about stereotypes, of course, but all of us are likely to develop ideas about how our social worlds work. Chapter 4 discussed *implicit personality theories:* networks of assumptions that people hold about the relationships among traits and behaviors. People also have implicit theories about social groups. For example, individuals may vary in the extent to which they think of social groups as relatively fixed, static entities or as dynamic and malleable (Levy et al., 2001). **Entity theorists** tend to see groups in terms of traits and to expect more similarity and consistency within groups. They may think of a group as having a core essence, and when they perceive

entity theorists People who tend to see social groups as relatively fixed, static entities and the borders between groups as relatively clear and rigid.

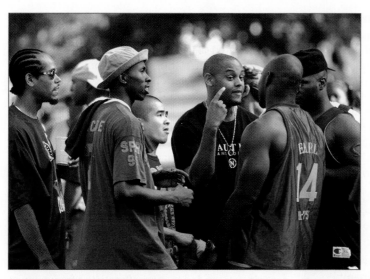

The extent to which individuals see groups as distinct entities can influence their perceptions of group members. For example, entity theorists are more likely than incremental theorists to see this group of fraternity members as similar to each other and distinct from outgroups, and to take information learned about one group member and apply it to all group members.

and evaluate groups, they process information about them almost as they would about a single person. **Incremental theorists**, in contrast, expect less consistency within a social group, are less likely to see a group in trait terms or as having a core essence, and see the boundaries between groups as fuzzy and changeable.

These differences in implicit theories have numerous implications for stereotyping (Brewer et al., 2004; Haslam & Levy, 2006; Hong et al., 2004; Demoulin et al., 2006; McConnell, 2001). Sheri Levy and her colleagues (1998), for example, found that although entity theorists and incremental theorists were equally aware of common stereotypes in their culture, entity theorists believed and used them more. A related difference in people's implicit theories concerns whether they see differences between groups as due to genetic differences. These kinds of beliefs can strongly affect how people see their ingroups and outgroups. For example, Toby Jayaratne and others (2006) found that white participants who believed that perceived racial differences could be explained by genetic differences exhibited greater prejudice toward Blacks than did white participants who did not have these genetic-based theories.

Are Stereotypes Ever Accurate?   So many stereotypes are so widespread that one may wonder if they are accurate. Like people, stereotypes are not all alike. Some are more accurate than others. And some researchers have argued that the field has overstated the inaccuracy of stereotypes (Jussim et al., 2005; Madon et al., 1998). Although many stereotypes are based on completely illusory information or perceptions, some do stem from a kernel of truth, and still others may be fairly accurate. Even when they are based on reality, though, they often exaggerate differences and understate similarities between groups (e.g., Diekman et al., 2002; Krueger et al., 2003).

But the question of accuracy is more complicated than it may appear. First, what is meant by "accurate" can be debated. "Accurate" could mean that stereotypes reflect universal, stable, possibly genetic differences; or it could mean that stereotypes reflect differences that exist under particular sets of societal and historic conditions, although with the recognition that these differences may well change if these conditions change. Most social psychologists focus on the latter meaning.

Second, imagine that you believe that members of some social category tend to be rude. If you encounter a member of this group and anticipate that she is likely to be rude, you may react to her in a cold, unfriendly way. This in turn may cause her to act rudely back to you. Was your expectation of that person accurate? In a sense, it was: She *was* rude to you, just as you expected. But clearly your own behavior may have caused the rudeness. As we will see in the paragraphs to follow, there are a variety of ways in which people perceive others, explain their behavior, and act toward them in ways that can reinforce stereotypes, often making stereotypes seem more accurate than they really are. Moreover, to the extent that many people, or an entire culture, treats a group of people in this way, the effects on the targets of these stereotypes can be profound, potentially causing what may appear to be confirmation of these stereotypes.

How Stereotypes Survive and Self-Perpetuate

incremental theorists
People who tend to see social groups as relatively dynamic and changeable, with less consistency within groups and more malleability between groups.

Stereotypes offer us quick and convenient summaries of social groups. It is clear, however, that they often cause us to overlook the diversity within categories and to form mistaken impressions of specific individuals. Given their shortcomings, why do stereotypes endure? We turn now to some of the mechanisms that help perpetuate stereotypes.

Illusory Correlations One way in which stereotypes endure is through the illusory correlation, a tendency for people to overestimate the link between variables that are only slightly or not at all correlated (Berndsen et al., 2002; Meiser & Hewstone, 2006; Stroessner & Plaks, 2001). Illusory correlations result from two different processes. First, people tend to overestimate the association between variables that are *distinctive*: variables that capture attention simply because they are novel or deviant. When two relatively unusual events happen together, that may stick in people's minds, and this can lead them to overestimate an association between them. Table 5.1 gives an example of how this occurs. The implications for stereotyping are important: Unless otherwise motivated, people overestimate the joint occurrence of distinctive variables such as minority groups and deviant acts. Even children in second grade may perceive these false associations (Johnston & Jacobs, 2003).

Second, people tend to overestimate the association between variables that they already expect to go together. For example, in one study, participants were presented with lists of paired words, such as *lion-tiger, lion-eggs, bacon-tiger,* and *bacon-egg*. The participants tended to overestimate the frequency of pairings that had meaningful, expected associations (*lion-tiger, bacon-eggs*), even if such pairings actually occurred no more frequently than less expected pairings (*lion-eggs, bacon-tiger*) (Chapman, 1967). David Hamilton and Terrence Rose (1980) found that stereotypes can lead people to expect social groups and traits to fit together like bacon and eggs and to overestimate the frequency with which they've actually observed these associations. The implications for stereotyping are important here as well: People overestimate the joint occurrence of variables they expect to be associated with each other, such as stereotyped groups and stereotypic behaviors. Here again research has found children as young as second grade exhibiting this kind of illusory correlation (Susskind, 2003).

TABLE 5.1
The Illusory Correlation

Perceivers often overestimate the frequency with which distinctive variables co-occur, such as when minority group members (group Y) behave in a relatively rare, negative way. Although the proportion of group X members who behave negatively is the same as the proportion of group Y members who do, perceivers see group Y members as more likely to behave negatively.

Reality	Perception
100 Group X People	*100 Group X People*
75 positive behaviors (75%)	75 positive behaviors (75%)
25 negative behaviors (25%)	25 negative behaviors (25%)
20 Group Y People	*20 Group Y People*
15 positive behaviors (75%)	10 positive behaviors (50%)
5 negative behaviors (25%)	10 negative behaviors (50%)

Attributions People also maintain their stereotypes through how they explain others' behaviors. Chapter 4 on Perceiving Persons discusses how perceivers make attributions, or explanations, about the causes of other people's behaviors, and how these attributions can sometimes be flawed. These flaws can help perpetuate stereotypes. For example, although discrimination certainly can impair the performance of stereotyped individuals, perceivers may fail to take this effect into account when explaining this underperformance and instead see it as evidence supporting the negative stereotype. In this way, perceivers may see confirmation of the stereotype rather than recognize the consequences of discrimination.

On the other hand, when people see others acting in ways that seem to contradict a stereotype, they may be *more* likely to think about situational factors in order to explain the surprising behavior. Rather than accept a stereotype-disconfirming behavior at face value, such as a woman defeating a man in an athletic contest, perceivers imagine the situational factors that might explain away this apparent exception to the rule, such as random luck, ulterior motives, or other special circumstances. In this way, perceivers can more easily maintain their stereotypes of these groups (Karpinski & von Hippel, 1996; Philippot, 2005; Sekaquaptewa et al., 2003; Seta et al., 2003; Sherman et al., 2005).

Subtyping and Contrast Effects Have you ever noticed that people often manage to hold negative views about a social group even when they like individual members of that group? Gordon Allport (1954) recognized this phenomenon more than half a century ago. He wrote, "There is a common mental device that permits people to hold prejudgments even in the face of much contradictory evidence. It is the device of admitting exceptions. . . . By excluding a few favored cases, the nega-

illusory correlation An overestimate of the association between variables that are only slightly or not at all correlated.

Women who play rough contact sports—such as these members of the Canadian women's hockey team, which won the Olympic gold medal in 2006—defy gender stereotypes. But rather than change their gender stereotypes, many perceivers subtype these women and dismiss them as exceptions.

tive rubric is kept intact for all other cases" (p. 23). Confronted with a woman who does not seem particularly warm and nurturing, for example, people can either develop a more diversified image of females or toss the mismatch into a special subtype—say, "career women." To the extent that people create this subtype, their existing image of women-in-general will remain relatively intact (Hewstone & Lord, 1998; Weber & Crocker, 1983; Wilder et al., 1996).

Indeed, exceptions to the rule sometimes can be seen in particularly extreme ways. As a general rule, when something differs only slightly from expectations, the difference is barely noticed, if at all. But when it varies considerably from expectations, the perceived difference may be magnified, a biased perception known as the **contrast effect**. An ambitious, assertive businesswoman may be perceived as more extremely ambitious and assertive than a comparable man. Successful but demanding women like Martha Stewart or Hilary Clinton are often portrayed in very extreme, superaggressive ways for actions that they and others have argued would hardly be noticed if not for stereotypes about women.

Confirmation Biases and Self-Fulfilling Prophecies Imagine learning that a mother yelled at a sixteen-year-old girl, that a lawyer behaved aggressively, and that a Boy Scout grabbed the arm of an elderly woman crossing the street. Now imagine that a construction worker yelled at a sixteen-year-old girl, that an ex-con behaved aggressively, and that a skinhead grabbed the arm of an elderly woman crossing the street. Do very different images of these actions come to mind? This is a fundamental effect of stereotyping: Stereotypes of groups distort people's perceptions and interpretations of the behaviors of group members. This is especially likely when a target of a stereotype behaves in an ambiguous way; perceivers reduce the ambiguity by interpreting the behavior as consistent with the stereotype (Dunning & Sherman, 1997; Kunda et al., 1997). For example, in one study, black and white sixth-grade boys saw pictures and descriptions of ambiguously aggressive behaviors (such as one child bumping into another). Both the black and the white boys judged the behaviors as more mean and threatening if the behaviors were performed by black boys than white boys (Sagar & Schofield, 1980).

The effect of stereotypes on individuals' perceptions is a type of confirmation bias, which, as we saw in Chapter 4, involves people's tendencies to interpret, seek, and create information that seems to confirm their expectations. In a clever demonstration of this bias (specifically in the context of interpreting information), Jeff Stone and his colleagues (1997) had students listen to a college basketball game. Some were led to believe that a particular player was white; others thought he was black. After listening to the game, all of the students were asked to evaluate how the player had performed in the game. Consistent with racial stereotypes, those students who believed the player was black rated him as having played better and more athletically, whereas those who thought he was white rated him as having played with more intelligence and hustle (see Figure 5.2).

contrast effect The tendency to perceive stimuli that differ from expectations as being even more different than they really are.

FIGURE 5.2

"White Men Can't Jump"?

Students listened to a college basketball game and evaluated one particular player. Half of the students were led to believe the player was black; the other half, that he was white. Consistent with their stereotypes, the students perceived the player as having more physical ability if they thought he was black and as having more "court smarts" if they thought he was white. (Stone et al., 1997.)

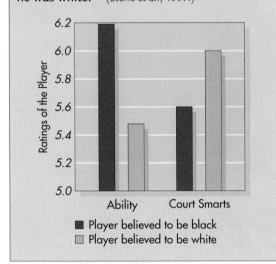

In addition to interpreting information in a biased manner, perceivers often seek information about stereotyped others in a way that prevents them from disconfirming the stereotype. For example, in a study by Yaacov Trope and Erik Thompson (1997), participants were requested to ask questions of another person in order to learn this person's attitudes. As it turns out, they asked fewer questions when led to believe that the other person was a member of a stereotyped group, and the questions they did ask were biased such that virtually all responses to them could be seen as consistent with the stereotype of that group.

Stereotypes are held not just by individuals but typically by many people within a culture, and they are often perpetuated through repeated communications. In a classic demonstration, Gordon Allport and Leo Postman (1947) showed participants a picture of a subway train filled with passengers. In the picture were a black man dressed in a suit and a white man holding a razor. One participant viewed the scene briefly and then described it to a second participant who had not seen it. The second participant communicated the description to a third participant and so on, through six rounds of communication. The result: In more than half the sessions, the final participant's report indicated that the black man, not the white man, held the razor.

In a more recent demonstration of a similar point, Anthony Lyons and Yoshihisa Kashima (2001) had Australian students read a story about an Australian Rules football player. The students were put in groups of four. One person read the story, and after a delay of a few minutes transmitted the story to the next student, and so on down the four-person chain. The students were supposed to relay the story as accurately as possible. Some of the information in the story was consistent with stereotypes about Australian Rules football players (e.g., "On the way, Gary and his mate drank several beers in the car"), and some of it was inconsistent with the stereotype (e.g., "He switched on some classical music"). Although the first student in the chain was likely to communicate both stereotype-consistent and stereotype-inconsistent information, as the story went from person to person the stereotype-inconsistent information was progressively screened out. By the time the fourth person told the story, the football player seemed much more clearly stereotypical than he had seemed in the original story.

Confirmation biases are bad enough. But even more disturbing are situations in which stereotyped group members themselves are led to behave in stereotype-confirming ways. In other words, stereotypes can create self-fulfilling prophecies. As noted in Chapter 4, a self-fulfilling prophecy occurs when a perceiver's false expectations about a person cause the person to behave in ways that confirm those expectations. Stereotypes can trigger such behavioral confirmation (Rosenthal, 2002). Consider a classic experiment by Carl Word and others (1974) involving a situation of great importance in people's lives: the job interview. White participants, without realizing it, sat farther away, made more speech errors, and held shorter interviews when interviewing black applicants than white applicants. This colder interpersonal style, in turn, caused the black applicants to behave in a nervous and awkward manner. In short, the whites' racial stereotypes and prejudice actually hurt the interview performance of the black candidates. Since the black candidates' interview performance tended to be objectively worse than that of the white candidates, it seemed to confirm the interviewers' negative stereotypes—but this poor performance was caused by the interviewers, not the interviewees.

In the aftermath of the Amadou Diallo killing, several questions persist: Did racial stereotypes bias the police officers' perception of Diallo's ambiguous behavior? Would the officers have been less likely to interpret his ducking into the apartment building and reaching for his wallet as suspicious and threatening if he were white? Did their suspicions of him cause Diallo to act in ways that seemed to confirm these suspicions? Whether racial stereotypes had precisely these effects may

"Not everybody's life is what they make it. Some people's life is what other people make it."

—Alice Walker

never be known, but the fact remains that their potential to shape perceptions and behavior is a clear and present danger.

Is Stereotyping Inevitable? Automatic Versus Intentional Processes

Stereotypes are defined as beliefs that associate a group of people with certain traits, but part of their power is that they can bias our perceptions and responses even if we don't personally agree with these beliefs. In other words, we don't have to believe a stereotype for it to trigger illusory correlations and self-fulfilling prophecies, or to bias how we think, feel, and behave toward group members. Sometimes just being aware of stereotypes in one's culture is enough to cause these effects. Moreover, stereotypes can be activated without our awareness. Indeed, they can operate at an unconscious, or "implicit," level (Blair, 2001).

These findings raise a provocative, and potentially depressing, question: Is stereotyping inevitable? When we encounter people from other groups, do our stereotypes of these groups always become activated in our minds? Can we do anything to prevent this from happening? Most people believe that they can resist stereotyping others, but recent research paints a far more complex picture.

Stereotypes as (Sometimes) Automatic Patricia Devine (1989) distinguished between automatic and controlled processes in stereotyping. She argued that people have become highly aware of the contents of many stereotypes through cultural influences, such as lessons learned from parents and images in the media. Because of this high awareness, people automatically activate stereotypes whenever they are exposed to members of groups for which popular stereotypes exist. Thus, just as many of us are automatically primed to think *eggs* after hearing *bacon,* we are also primed to think of concepts relevant to a stereotype when we think of a stereotyped group. To be sure, we can try to prevent this activated stereotype from influencing our judgments or behaviors. However, we are often unaware that a particular stereotype has been activated or how it can influence our perceptions and behaviors (Bargh, 1997). Thus, the stereotype can affect us in spite of our good intentions. In her study, Devine exposed white participants to **subliminal presentations** on a computer monitor. For one group, these presentations consisted of words relevant to stereotypes about black people, such as *Africa, ghetto, welfare,* and *basketball.* Subliminally presented information is presented so quickly that perceivers do not even realize that they have been exposed to it. Thus, these students were not consciously aware that they had seen these words. Those who were subliminally primed with many of these words seemed to activate the African American stereotype and see another person's behavior in a more negative, hostile light. These effects occurred *even among* participants *who did not consciously endorse the stereotypes in question.*

Devine's theory sparked an explosion of interest in these issues. Are we automatically biased by stereotypes, including those we disagree with? And are we inevitably prone to stereotyping after merely being exposed to stereotypes prevalent in our culture? Such questions are very complex, but within the past several years social psychologists have made great strides in addressing them. It is now clear that stereotype activation can be triggered implicitly and automatically, influencing subsequent thoughts, feelings, and behaviors even among perceivers who are relatively low in prejudice. But it also is clear that several factors can make such activation more or less likely to happen.

For example, some stereotypes are more likely than others to come to mind quickly and easily for any given person. How much exposure individuals have to a stereotype, and therefore how accessible the stereotype is in their mind, varies across time and cultures. People in Western Europe may be quicker to activate the "skinhead" stereotype than people in South America; students from El Paso, Texas, may be more prone to activate Mexican American stereotypes than students in Madison, Wisconsin. In the following sections, we explore several other sets of factors that help determine when stereotyping is and isn't inevitable. See Table 5.2 for a summary.

Very brief exposure to a member of a stereotyped group does not lead to biased judgments or responses, but longer exposure typically does. **False.**

subliminal presentation
A method of presenting stimuli so faintly or rapidly that people do not have any conscious awareness of having been exposed to them.

TABLE 5.2
Automatic Stereotype Activation: Important Factors

Based on very recent research, we can propose the following sets of factors as important in determining when people are more or less likely to activate stereotypes automatically—that is, without awareness or intention, whether or not they even endorse the stereotypes, upon exposure to minimal cues about a social group or group member. There are other factors that matter, and the effects of each of the factors below may depend on the presence or absence of the other factors, but these general conclusions can be offered at this time.

Factors That Make Automatic Activation More Likely	Factors That Make Automatic Activation Less Likely
Cognitive Factors	
• Accessible stereotype (e.g., recently activated or primed)	• Exposure to counter-stereotypic group members
• Depleted cognitive resources due to prior attempts at suppression, fatigue, age, intoxication	• Knowledge of personal information about the individual
Cultural Factors	
• Popular stereotype in culture	• Not common stereotype in culture
• Norms and values that accept stereotyping	• Norms and values that are opposed to stereotyping
Motivational Factors	
• Motivated to make inferences about the person quickly	• Motivated to avoid prejudice
• Motivated to feel superior to other person	• Motivated to be fair, egalitarian
Personal Factors	
• Endorse stereotypes, high in prejudice	• Disagree with stereotypes, low in prejudice

Motivation: Fueling Activation or Putting on the Brakes

There is a growing recognition of the role that motivational factors can play in stereotype activation (Blair, 2002; Bodenhausen et al., 2003; Gollwitzer & Schaal, 2001; Kunda & Spencer, 2003; Spencer et al., 2003). Whether or not we realize it, we often have particular goals when we encounter others, such as wanting to learn about them, impress them, get to our next task and not be interrupted by them, and so on. Some sets of goals make us more likely to activate stereotypes, and others have the opposite effect.

One important goal that can drive people's perceptions and behaviors is the desire to maintain, protect, and perhaps enhance their self-image and self-esteem. These goals can lead even people low in prejudice to activate negative stereotypes. For example, when their self-esteem is threatened, people may become motivated to stereotype others so that they will feel better about themselves (Fein & Spencer, 1997). Motivated in this way, they also become more likely to activate stereotypes automatically. To demonstrate these points, Steven Spencer and others (1998) conducted a series of experiments in which they threatened some participants' self-esteem by making them think that they had done poorly on an intelligence test. These participants became more likely to automatically activate negative stereotypes about African Americans or Asians when exposed briefly, even subliminally, to a drawing or videotape of a member of the stereotyped group.

Trying to protect one's self-image can not only promote activation of some stereotypes but can also inhibit activation of others. For example, imagine interacting with a black doctor. Two different stereotypes could come to mind about this person—about doctors and about Blacks. Lisa Sinclair and Ziva Kunda found that when white Canadian students in their study received praise from a black doctor, not only did they activate positive stereotypes about doctors but they also simultaneously *inhibited* activation of negative stereotypes about Blacks—a pattern presumably driven by the desire to see the person who praised them as especially smart and successful. If this is the effect that praise brings about, will criticism have the opposite effect? Sinclair and Kunda's (1999, 2000) research suggests that it can. They found that when a stereotyped group member criticizes or even simply disagrees with participants, the participants become more likely to activate negative stereotypes about the group (see Figure 5.3).

Another goal that people sometimes have when perceiving an individual is to form as accurate an impression as possible. At other times, people may be motivated

FIGURE 5.3

Motivated Stereotype Inhibition and Activation

Participants received either praise or criticism about their performance from either a black man or a white man who they were led to believe was a doctor. A computer task that measured how quickly the participants could respond to various stimuli was used to assess whether they activated stereotypes about Blacks. Compared to the reaction times of participants who received neither praise nor criticism ("no-feedback controls"), quicker reaction times indicate stereotype *activation*, whereas longer reaction times suggest stereotype *suppression*. Participants criticized by the black doctor strongly activated the black stereotypes, whereas participants praised by the black doctor inhibited black stereotypes.

(Sinclair & Kunda, 1999.)

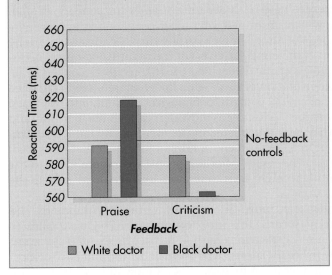

simply to get through the encounter as quickly and painlessly as possible. When social perceivers are highly motivated to form an accurate impression of someone (say, if they're dependent on this person or if they need to compete against the person), they often manage to set aside their pre-existing beliefs (Fiske, 2000).

In one intriguing set of experiments, Mary Wheeler and Susan Fiske (2005) manipulated the goals that perceivers had as they looked at black or white male faces. The European American and Asian American participants in these studies sometimes were instructed to perform a nonsocial visual search while looking at a face (*is there a dot present somewhere on the face?*), sometimes a social categorization task (*is the person over twenty-one years old?*), and sometimes a task designed to have them think of the person as an individual (*would he like a particular vegetable?*). In one experiment, the researchers used fMRI to monitor the participants' brain activity. The fMRI revealed that when the participants had a goal of categorization, they showed more activity in part of the amygdala when looking at black faces than when looking at white faces, suggesting that the black faces triggered more emotional, threat-related responses. In a second experiment, participants with this same goal showed more stereotype activation on a cognitive task in response to black faces than to white faces. When participants instead were given a nonsocial goal or the goal to perceive the person as an individual, these effects were eliminated.

Despite all that we've written so far about the pervasiveness of stereotypes and their effects, there is no question that an important goal for many people today is to *not* use stereotypes or be prejudiced (Brodish & Devine, 2005; Sommers & Norton, 2006). Interestingly, in some cases this goal can create an *opposite* bias. For example, Natalie Wyer (2004) found that participants very low in prejudice toward African Americans showed a bias toward stereotype *dis*confirmation when seeking information and making judgments about African Americans. Similarly, Samuel Sommers, Michael Norton, and others have found that white participants, particularly those low in prejudice, often process information and make judgments about black individuals more favorably than about white individuals in various contexts, such as in hypothetical judgments about college admissions or jury verdicts (Norton et al., 2006; Sommers, 2006).

In these last examples, perceivers *were* influenced by race, but in the direction that ran counter to the stereotypes. The question remains, though: Can people's motivation enable them to completely avoid stereotyping under conditions that typically lead to automatic stereotyping? This, of course, raises a related question: How can something automatic be controllable? Consider the process of driving a car. Especially if the route you're taking is familiar, much of what you do is automatic. Without stopping to think about it, you steer, check the mirrors, and know when and how hard to press your foot against the gas and brake pedals. Indeed, the process is so automatic that you would find it difficult to articulate to someone else exactly what you're doing and how you're doing it. Yet this automatic process can be interrupted—by an unexpected event, say, or a compelling emotion such as concern about making a mistake in front of a parent, blind date, or police officer. By the same token, the often-automatic route from exposure to a stereotyped group member to stereotype activation can be diverted under particular conditions.

You may wonder: What if I just try really hard to not think about a stereotype? Research in other contexts suggests that sometimes the harder you try to suppress an unwanted thought, the less likely you are to succeed. Try not to think about a white bear for the next thirty seconds, and that image will come to mind with remarkable frequency. Try not to worry about how long it's taking you to fall asleep, and you'll stay awake. Try not to think about an itch, or the chocolate cheesecake in the fridge, or a particular sexist thought—well, you get the idea (Wegner, 1997).

Research on the effectiveness of trying to suppress stereotyping is mixed. On the one hand, it can sometimes cause a post-suppression rebound: After a person spends energy suppressing a stereotype, the stereotype pops up even more, like a volleyball that's been held under water (e.g., Macrae et al., 1994). On the other hand, research suggests that when people are intrinsically motivated to suppress a stereotype that they truly don't believe in, they may be successful at avoiding rebound effects (Gordijn et al., 2004; Monteith et al., 1998; Wyer et al., 2000).

Exerting Control: The Need for Cognitive Resources Trying to suppress stereotyping takes mental effort, and using this effort can drain individuals of cognitive resources for some period of time (Gordijn et al., 2004; Richeson & Trawalter, 2005). This can lead to a stereotype rebound effect because individuals no longer have the cognitive resources left to continue the surprisingly difficult task of suppression. Also, some people are more likely than others to have the cognitive resources available to inhibit stereotyping. One factor is age. William von Hippel and others (2000) found that older people have a harder time suppressing stereotypes than younger people, which may explain in part why older people often appear more prejudiced than younger people. Also, being physically tired, or affected by strong emotion or arousal, can sap even young perceivers of the cognitive resources necessary to avoid stereotyping (Bless et al., 1996; Gilbert & Hixon, 1991; Lambert et al., 2003). In an intriguing demonstration of this, Galen Bodenhausen (1990) classified participants by their circadian arousal patterns, or biological rhythms, into two types: "morning people" (who describe themselves as most alert early in the morning) and "night people" (who say they peak much later, in the evening). By random assignment, participants took part in an experiment in human judgment that was scheduled at either 9 A.M. or 8 P.M. The result? Morning people were more likely to use stereotypes when tested at night; night owls were more likely to do so early in the morning.

Movie star Mel Gibson's mug shot, taken on the night of his anti-Semitic and sexist outburst directed at police after being stopped for driving under the influence of alcohol, July 28, 2006.

A well-known consequence of intoxication is its lowering of inhibitions, and therefore it should come as no surprise that intoxication impairs people's ability to control stereotype activation and application (Bartholow et al., 2006). After movie star Mel Gibson was stopped by police for appearing to drive under the influence of alcohol late one summer night in 2006, reports soon surfaced that he unleashed a torrent of hateful anti-Semitic and sexist remarks to police officers. Although Gibson later apologized for these remarks, many critics of Gibson interpreted this incident as evidence of Gibson's true beliefs coming to the surface because of the disinhibiting effects of the alcohol.

Automaticity Versus Control: Additional Factors Although the automatic nature of stereotyping can sometimes overwhelm personal attitudes and beliefs, individual differences in these attitudes and beliefs can play an important part in determining stereotyping. Individuals relatively low in prejudice, for example, are less likely than their high-prejudice counterparts to automatically activate stereotypes when exposed to only minimal information such as a category label like "African American" or "gay" (Kawakami et al., 1998; Lepore & Brown, 1997, 2002; Wittenbrink et al., 1997). Gordon Moskowitz and others (2004) have identified people who have a particularly strong goal of being fair, or egalitarian, and when this goal is activated, they are less likely to stereotype others. This research has also found that this egalitarian goal can be induced temporarily in individuals if they are made to feel that they have been biased and unfair. When people feel that they have violated their own, their group's, or their culture's standards of fairness and morality, they are less likely to activate negative stereotypes of others (Fein et al., 2003; Hing, Li, & Zanna, 2002; Monin & Miller, 2001; Monteith & Voils, 2001).

Rather than try to suppress thoughts about a stereotyped group, one of the best strategies for avoiding the influence of stereotypes is to try instead to activate thoughts about the *individual* who happens to be a member of that group. When we have specific, personal information about an individual, stereotypes and other preconceptions can lose relevance and have less impact on how we respond to that person (Hilton & Fein, 1989; Locksley et al., 1980; Yzerbyt et al., 1998). This point was illustrated in a provocative series of studies by Ziva Kunda and others (2003). When the white Canadian participants in this research were exposed to a member of a stereotyped group, such as a black or Asian individual, they tended to activate stereotypes of these groups immediately. But if they continued to be exposed to the individual for fifteen minutes and learned personal information about him or her, the participants no longer exhibited any stereotype activation. It is interesting to note, however, that if the person then said something the participants disagreed with, the participants once again showed activation of the stereotype. Perhaps in these instances the participants' emotions and motivations took over and overwhelmed the other personalized information they had learned.

Researchers today continue to explore ways to give people control over stereotyping. These techniques include receiving training and practice in resisting stereotype activation when confronted with information about a group; being primed to think in unusual, creative ways; being primed with counter-stereotypic examples (such as female business leaders and scientists, or well-loved members of outgroups); and taking the perspective of a member of the stereotyped group (Dasgupta & Asgari, 2004; Galinsky & Ku, 2004; Kawakami et al., 2000, 2007; Olson & Fazio, 2006).

"41 Shots" Revisited: Did Racial Stereotypes Make the Police More Likely to Shoot Amadou Diallo?

Despite the heated arguments made by people on both sides of the story, there is no way to know if the police would have refrained from shooting Amadou Diallo if he had been white instead of black. Even the police officers themselves couldn't know for sure whether race entered into their decision. The research reported thus far illustrates that stereotypes can be activated quickly and without awareness or intention.

Nevertheless, it is possible to apply social psychology research to answer related questions, such as whether, in general, a person who is black is more likely to be mistakenly seen as holding a gun rather than a wallet, and whether making such a mistake signals that a perceiver is prejudiced. Indeed, since the time of the Diallo shooting, several social psychology experiments have examined these very questions.

Keith Payne (2001) was the first to publish a study directly inspired by these questions. The participants in his study were undergraduate students, not police officers, but their task was to try to make the kind of decision the police had to make: very quickly identify an object as a weapon or not (such as a tool). Pictures of these objects were presented on a computer screen, but immediately preceding them was a quick presentation of a black or a white male face. The pictures were presented for fractions of a second. Payne found that the participants were more likely to mistake a harmless object for a weapon if it was preceded by a black face than a white face. This difference was less likely to emerge if the participants were given more time to make this judgment.

Joshua Correll and his colleagues (2002) also investigated this issue, but they made the situation even more like the one faced by the police. Rather than first present the race of a person and then present an object, these researchers designed a video game to present them together, and the participants had to decide whether to shoot or not shoot the person who appeared on their screen (see Figure 5.4). Some of these targets were white men, and others were black men. Some of them held guns, and others held harmless objects (such as a black cell phone or wallet). If the target held a gun, the participants were supposed to hit a "shoot" button as quickly as possible. If he held a harmless object, they were to hit a "don't shoot" button as quickly as they could. As in the Payne study, participants showed a bias consistent with racial stereotypes. If the target held a gun, they were quicker to press the "shoot" button if he was black than if he was white. If the target held a harmless object, they took longer to press the "don't shoot" button if he was black than if he was white. In addition, participants were more likely to mistakenly "shoot" an unarmed target if he was black than if he was white.

Since these first publications, several others have followed to examine the processes involved more closely (e.g., Greenwald et al., 2003; Govorun & Payne, 2006; Judd et al., 2004). For example, in one provocative experiment, Joshua Correll and others (2006) found additional evidence for this racial bias, but they also used physiological measures to determine that when participants exhibited this bias, they also tended to show brain activity that is associated with the perception of being threatened.

Although these studies have used somewhat different methods and been conducted in different locations, they provide converging evidence that when the decision must be made very quickly, a black man in the United States is more likely to be mistakenly perceived as holding a gun than is a white man. It is important to note, though, that the participants in the initial studies were not police officers; they were undergraduate students or individuals from a community sample. Police officers receive extensive training in these kinds of tasks. But as the quote by social psychologist Anthony Greenwald in the margin indicates, the police may not be trained to avoid activating racial stereotypes, and given the prevalence and power of these stereotypes in our society, there is no reason to be confident that they would be impervious to them in split-second decisions.

For this reason, social psychologists have begun to study actual police officers. Jennifer Eberhardt and others (2004) conducted an experiment in which 182 police officers viewed a series of pictures of faces presented on a screen. Some of the officers were shown white faces, and others were shown black faces. The results revealed that the officers were more likely to rate a black face as "criminal" than a white face. Moreover, black faces that other officers had rated as particularly "stereotypical" of Blacks were especially likely to be identified as looking like a criminal. Other researchers have also found evidence that perceivers are more likely to automatically activate negative evaluations in response to African American faces if the faces are more racially prototypic (Blair et al., 2002, 2004; Livingston & Brewer, 2002).

"Police receive training to make them more sensitive to weapons, but they don't get training to undo unconscious race stereotypes or biases."

—Anthony Greenwald

FIGURE 5.4

Shoot or Not?

These are examples of scenes from the video game that Joshua Correll and his colleagues (2002) created to investigate whether perceivers, playing the role of police officers, would be biased by the target's race when trying to determine very quickly whether they should shoot him because he is holding a weapon or refrain from shooting because he is holding a harmless object.

(Correll et al., 2002.)

The death of Amadou Diallo is remembered as people protest a new tragedy, in which police officers fired 50 shots at Sean Bell and his friends in New York in November 2006, killing the unarmed Bell just hours before his wedding.

More recently, two sets of studies have examined police officers' responses in the "shoot" or "don't shoot" simulations that most relate to the Diallo tragedy. In one set of experiments using over 200 police officers from fifteen U.S. states, Joshua Correll and others (2007) found that, in contrast to a civilian sample that did show the typical racial bias, trained police officers were *not* more likely to "shoot" an unarmed black target than an unarmed white target. Like the civilians, however, they did take longer to decide to not shoot an unarmed black target than an unarmed white target, and they were quicker to decide to shoot an armed black target than an armed white target. In other words, the police officers did not show evidence of racial bias in the mistakes they made, but they did have a harder time making decisions that went against the racial stereotype.

In a different experiment with 50 police officers, B. Michelle Peruche and E. Ashby Plant (2006) found that in initial trials the officers were more likely to erroneously decide to "shoot" an unarmed target if the target was black rather than white. With more and more trials, however, eventually this racial bias was reduced. This greater accuracy with practice is consistent with the encouraging results of another line of research by E. Ashby Plant and her colleagues (2005). In a series of studies using undergraduate students playing the role of police officers, the researchers replicated the finding of a racial bias in the decision to shoot or not, but they also found that training the participants, by exposing them to repeated trials in which the race of the target was unrelated to criminality, eliminated this bias, both immediately after the training and 24 hours later.

A second question we posed above was whether exhibiting this racial bias signals that a perceiver has racist attitudes and beliefs. The evidence thus far suggests that this may not be the case. For example, Correll et al. (2002) found that the magnitude of the bias was not related to participants' levels of racial prejudice, as measured by a series of questionnaires. In addition, these researchers also found that African American participants showed the same bias against black targets as did white participants, again suggesting that racial prejudice is not necessarily reflected in this bias. Consistent with much of the research we've reported in this chapter, *awareness* of the stereotype was a necessary factor, but endorsing it was not. More research is needed on this point, however, because the data on this question are not entirely clear (e.g., Correll et al., 2007; Peruche & Plant, 2006).

The Diallo shooting was by no means the first or last incident of its kind. Indeed, in November 2006, New York City police officers fired 50 shots at a small group of African American men, killing one of them—just hours before he was supposed to be getting married later that day. Although at least one of the officers thought that one of the men had a gun, no evidence that any of them was armed was found. Incidents like this illustrate that it is all the more important for social psychology research to continue to help identify and understand the factors that contribute to these tragedies, as well as the factors that, we hope, can help prevent them in the future.

Prejudice

Stereotypes have implications for not only the way we *think* about groups, but also for how we feel about the social groups we encounter. If you look back at Figure 5.1, you'll see that stereotypes and prejudice are related but distinct, each influencing the other while also having separate effects on discrimination. In this section, we trace the roots of prejudice—one's negative feelings toward people based on their membership in a group—and examine some of its causes and consequences.

 Intergroup Conflict

Clearly, some people are more prejudiced than others. The problem is so widespread, however, that nobody seems immune. Social psychologists have thus sought to identify the situational factors that give rise to prejudice. This section describes a classic study of intergroup conflict, a study that sets the stage for theories focusing on the role of social situations.

Robbers Cave: Setting the Stage The 2006–2007 season of the hit reality television show *Survivor* began with great controversy. Each season of *Survivor* features a number of individuals, placed in very remote locations around the world, competing against each other through often brutal challenges and harsh elements to win a huge cash prize. On this season, however, the producers introduced a new social experiment: They divided the contestants into four rival "tribes" based entirely on race. Many critics attacked this move as playing on, and perpetuating, racial stereotypes and prejudices. After only two episodes, the producers dropped the racial division and merged the tribes into two mixed-race groups.

Survivor's would-be experiment probably reminded more than a few social psychologists of a real study conducted more than a half century before that illustrated how quickly, and intensely, prejudice can be created between competing groups in the wilderness. It was an unlikely place for a social psychology study: Robbers Cave State Park, Oklahoma. In the summer of 1954, a small group of eleven-year-old boys—all white, middle-class youngsters, all strangers to one another—arrived at a 200-acre camp located in a densely wooded area of the park. The boys spent the first week or so hiking, swimming, boating, and camping out. After a while, they gave themselves a group name and printed it on their caps and T-shirts. At first, the boys thought they were the only ones at the camp. Soon, however, they discovered that there was a second group and that tournaments had been arranged between the two groups.

What these boys didn't know was that they were participants in an elaborate study conducted by Muzafer Sherif and his colleagues (1961). Parents had given permission for their sons to take part in an experiment for a study of competitiveness and cooperation. The two groups were brought in separately, and only after each had formed its own culture was the other's presence revealed. Now, the "Rattlers" and the "Eagles" were ready to meet. They did so under tense circumstances, competing against each other in football, a treasure hunt, a tug-of-war, and other events. For each event, the winning team was awarded points, and the tournament winner was promised a trophy, medals, and other prizes. Almost overnight, the groups turned into hostile antagonists; and their rivalry escalated into a full-scale war. Group flags were burned, cabins were ransacked, and a food fight that resembled a riot exploded in the mess hall. Keep in mind that the participants in this study were well-adjusted boys. Yet as Sherif (1966) noted, a naive observer would have thought the boys were "wicked, disturbed, and vicious" (p. 85).

Creating a monster through competition was easy. Restoring the peace, however, was not. First the experimenters tried saying nice things to the Rattlers about the Eagles and vice versa, but the propaganda campaign did not work. Then the two groups were brought together under noncompetitive circumstances, but that didn't help either. What did eventually work was the introduction of **superordinate goals**, mutual goals that could be achieved only through cooperation between the groups. For example, the experimenters arranged for the camp truck to break down, and both groups were needed to pull it up a steep hill. This strategy worked like a charm. By the end of camp, the two groups were so friendly that they insisted on traveling home on the same bus. In just three weeks, the Rattlers and Eagles experienced the kinds of changes that often take generations to unfold: They formed close-knit groups, went to war, and made peace.

superordinate goal A shared goal that can be achieved only through cooperation among individuals or groups.

American fans bask in the glory of their team's success at a World Cup soccer game.

The events of Robbers Cave mimicked the kinds of conflict that plague people all over the world. The simplest explanation for this conflict is competition. Assign strangers to groups, throw the groups into contention, stir the pot, and soon there's conflict. Similarly, the intergroup benefits of reducing the focus on competition by activating superordinate goals are also evident around the world. Consider, for example, the remarkable aftermath of the natural disasters that befell Greece and Turkey in 1999. Fraught with conflict and mistrust for generations, Greek-Turkish relations improved dramatically in the wake of earthquakes that rocked both countries. Television images of Turkish rescue workers pulling a Greek child from under a pile of rubble in Athens generated an outpouring of good will. Uniting against a shared threat, as the boys in Robbers Cave did when the camp truck broke down, the two nations began to bridge a significant gulf (Kinzer, 1999).

Realistic Conflict Theory   The view that direct competition for valuable but limited resources breeds hostility between groups is called **realistic conflict theory** (Levine & Campbell, 1972). As a simple matter of economics, one group may fare better in the struggle for land, jobs, or power than another group. The loser becomes frustrated and resentful, the winner feels threatened and protective—and before long, conflict heats to a rapid boil. Chances are, a good deal of prejudice in the world is driven by the realities of competition (Duckitt & Mphuthing, 1998; Stephan et al., 2005; Zárate et al., 2004).

But there is much more to prejudice than real competition. "Realistic" competition for resources may in fact be imagined—a perception in the mind of an individual who is not engaged in any real conflict. In addition, people may become resentful of other groups not because of their conviction that their own security or resources are threatened by these groups but because of their sense of **relative deprivation**, the belief that they fare poorly compared with others. What matters to the proverbial Smiths is not the size of their house per se but whether it is larger than the Jones's house next door (Walker & Smith, 2002).

Social Identity Theory

Why are people so sensitive about the status and integrity of their ingroups relative to rival outgroups, even when personal interests are not at stake? Could it be that personal interests really *are* at stake, but that these interests are more subtle and psychological than simply about competition for valuable resources? If so, could that explain why people all over the world believe that their own nation, culture, language, and religion are better and more deserving than others?

These questions were first raised in a study of high school boys in Bristol, England, conducted by Henri Tajfel and his colleagues (1971). The boys were shown a series of dotted slides, and their task was to estimate the number of dots on each. The slides were presented in rapid-fire succession, so the dots could not be counted. Later, the experimenter told the participants that some people are chronic "overestimators" and that others are "underestimators." As part of a second, entirely separate task, participants were supposedly divided for the sake of convenience into groups of overestimators and underestimators (in fact, they were divided randomly). Knowing

realistic conflict theory
The theory that hostility between groups is caused by direct competition for limited resources.
relative deprivation
Feelings of discontent aroused by the belief that one fares poorly compared with others.

FIGURE 5.5

Social Identity Theory

Tajfel and Turner claim that people strive to enhance self-esteem, which has two components: a personal identity and various social identities that derive from the groups to which we belong. Thus, people may boost their self-esteem by viewing their ingroups more favorably than outgroups.

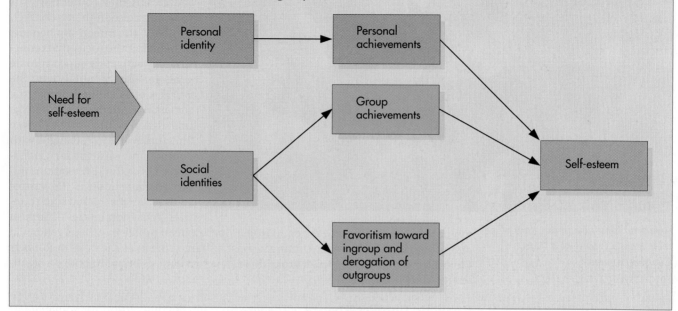

who was in their group, participants were told to allocate points to each other, points that could be cashed in for money.

This procedure was designed to create *minimal groups:* persons categorized on the basis of trivial, minimally important similarities. Tajfel's overestimators and under-estimators were not long-term rivals, did not have a history of antagonism, were not frustrated, did not compete for a limited resource, and were not even acquainted with each other. Still, participants consistently allocated more points to members of their own group than to members of the other group. This pattern of discrimination, called **ingroup favoritism**, has been found in studies performed in many countries and using a variety of different measures (Capozza & Brown, 2000). The preference for ingroups is so powerful that its effects can be elicited simply by the language we use. Charles Perdue and others (1990) found that subtly priming ingroup pronouns such as *we, us,* and *ours* triggered positive emotions in participants, while outgroup pronouns such as *they, them,* and *theirs* elicited negative emotions.

To explain ingroup favoritism, Tajfel (1982) and John Turner (1987) proposed **social identity theory**. According to this theory, each of us strives to enhance our self-esteem, which has two components: a *personal* identity and various collective or *social* identities that are based on the groups to which we belong. In other words, people can boost their self-esteem through their own personal achievements or through affiliation with successful groups. What's nice about the need for social identity is that it leads us to derive pride from our connections with others, even if we don't receive any direct benefits from these others (Gagnon & Bourhis, 1996). What's sad, however, is that we often feel the need to belittle "them" in order to feel secure about "us." Religious fervor, racial and ethnic conceit, and aggressive nationalism may all fulfill this more negative side of our social identity. Even gossiping can play this role; Jennifer Bosson and others (2006) found that when people shared negative attitudes about a third party, they felt closer to each other.

ingroup favoritism The tendency to discriminate in favor of ingroups over outgroups.

social identity theory The theory that people favor ingroups over outgroups in order to enhance their self-esteem.

Basic Predictions   Social identity theory is summarized in Figure 5.5. Two basic predictions arose from social identity theory: (1) Threats to one's self-esteem heighten the need for ingroup favoritism, and (2) expressions of ingroup favoritism enhance

FIGURE 5.6

Self-Esteem and Prejudice

Participants received positive or negative feedback and then evaluated a female job applicant believed to be Italian or Jewish. There were two key results: (1) participants whose self-esteem had been lowered by negative feedback evaluated the woman more negatively when she was Jewish than when she was Italian (left); and (2) negative-feedback participants given the opportunity to belittle the Jewish woman showed a post-experiment increase in self-esteem (right). (Fein & Spencer, 1997.)

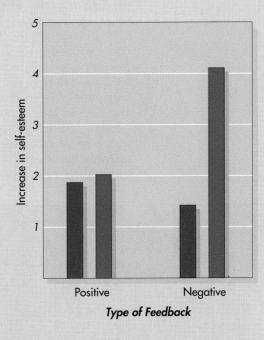

one's self-esteem. Research generally supports these predictions (Brewer & Brown, 1998; Hunter et al., 2005; Rubin & Hewstone, 1998; Smurda et al., 2006). In one study, Steven Fein and Steven Spencer (1997) gave participants positive or negative feedback about their performance on a test of social and verbal skills—feedback that temporarily raised or lowered their self-esteem. These participants then took part in what was supposed to be a second experiment in which they evaluated a job applicant. All participants received a photograph of a young woman, her résumé, and a videotape of a job interview. In half the cases, the woman was called Maria D'Agostino and depicted as Italian; in the other half, she was called Julie Goldberg and depicted as Jewish (on the campus where the study was held, there was a popular negative stereotype of the "Jewish American Princess," often targeting upper-middle-class Jewish women from New York).

As predicted by social identity theory, there were two important results (see Figure 5.6). First, among participants whose self-esteem had been lowered by negative feedback, Julie Goldberg was rated more negatively than Maria D'Agostino, even though their pictures and their credentials were the same. Second, negative-feedback participants given a chance to belittle the Jewish woman later exhibited a post-experiment increase in self-esteem. A blow to one's self-image evokes prejudice, and the expression of prejudice helps to restore that image.

According to Jamie Arndt and others (2002; Castano et al., 2002; See & Petty, 2006), when people feel threatened by thoughts of their own mortality, they tend to seek greater affiliation with their ingroups and exhibit greater prejudice against outgroups, in part to reaffirm their sense of place and purpose in the world. A case in point is the finding that Christian participants rated Christian targets more positively and Jewish targets more negatively when they were made to think about their own mortality (Greenberg et al., 1990). More recently, Pyszczynski and his colleagues (2002) applied this theory in predicting the wave of ingroup pride and outgroup

Being reminded of one's own mortality makes people put things into greater perspective, thereby tending to reduce ingroup-outgroup distinctions and hostilities. **False.**

hostilities that many Americans displayed in the days and weeks following the terrorist attacks of September 11, 2001.

Situational and Individual Differences Recent work has extended social identity theory by making more specific distinctions among various types of esteem-relevant threats (such as whether the threat is to the group's status or to the individual's role within the group), various types of groups (such as whether they have high or low status in a culture), and various ingroup members (such as whether they are strongly or weakly identified with their group) (Platow et al., 2005; Roccas, 2003; Scheepers & Ellemers, 2005; Schmitt et al., 2006; Wann & Grieve, 2005). Greater ingroup identification, for example, has been found across many studies to be associated with stronger social identity effects. In one of the early demonstrations of this point, Nyla Branscombe and Daniel Wann (1994) found that U.S. students who identified strongly with the group "Americans" were especially likely to derogate outgroups in response to a threat to America's status. More recently, Manfred Schmitt and Juergen Maes (2002) found that the more East Germans identified with East Germany, the more they showed increased ingroup bias when making comparisons with West Germany during the German unification process—an effect heightened by increased feelings of relative deprivation during unification. Identification with a superordinate group (such as Europeans), on the other hand, can reduce expressions of bias between particular subgroups (such as Greeks and Turks), particularly when the superordinate group is made salient (e.g., Klein et al., 2003; Lipponen et al., 2003).

Being part of a small, close-knit group can be an important, rewarding part of one's personal identity.

Although our membership in various social groups gives us an important part of our personal identity, not all of the groups to which we belong are equally likely to be important to our sense of self. According to Marilynn Brewer and Cynthia Pickett (1999; Brewer, 2003), one important consideration is the relative size and distinctiveness of one's ingroup. Noting that people want to belong to groups that are small enough for them to feel unique, Brewer and Pickett observed that ingroup loyalty and outgroup prejudice are more intense for groups that are in the minority than for members of large and inclusive majorities. Particularly in individualistic cultures, people often try to strike a delicate balance between their drive for belonging and loyalty to their ingroups with their drive for being distinct and independent (Hornsey & Jetten, 2005).

Another important factor in social identity processes is a person's status relative to others in the ingroup. Jeffrey Noel and his colleagues (1995) found that people are most motivated to derogate outsiders when their ingroup status is marginal—such as when they are pledges (under initiation) rather than active (fully initiated) members of fraternities and sororities, and when they are in the presence of fellow ingroup members. Wanting to prove themselves worthy members of the group, they publicly derogate outsiders in part to win the favor of fellow ingroup members. Group members who feel they have relatively low status in the group tend to present themselves as especially likely to conform to the will of the group (Jetten et al., 2006).

Culture and Social Identity Individuals' social identities are clearly important to people across cultures. Indeed, collectivists are more likely than individualists to value their connectedness and interdependence with the people and groups around them, and so their personal identities are tied closely with their social identities. However, according to a number of researchers, people from collectivist cultures are less likely than people from individualist cultures to show biases favoring their ingroups in order to boost their self-esteem (Heine, 2005; Lehman et al., 2004; Yuki, 2003). In one study, for instance, Japanese students exhibited less ingroup-enhancing bias than Japanese-Canadian students, who, in turn, exhibited less ingroup-enhancing bias than European-Canadian students (Heine & Lehman, 1997). In a more recent study, students at a football game either in the United States or Japan evaluated their own and their rival universities. Whereas the evaluations made by the American students showed a strong ingroup favoritism bias, this bias was not evident in the evaluations made by the Japanese students, who were just as strongly identified with their school as were the American students (Snibbe et al., 2003).

However, collectivists are not completely immune from being biased in favor of their ingroup (Capozza et al., 2000; Chen et al., 2002; Ruffle & Sosis, 2006). Collectivists may be less likely to overtly exaggerate the strengths of their ingroups, but some research indicates that they draw sharper distinctions between ingroup and outgroup members than individualists do (Gudykunst & Bond, 1997). Among a sample of sixth-graders in Korea, for example, children who were more collectivistic exhibited greater discrimination between ingroup and outgroup members than did more individualistic children (Han & Park, 1995).

Implicit Theories and Ideologies

Earlier in the chapter we discussed how stereotyping is influenced by individuals' implicit theories about their social worlds, such as whether they see groups more as fixed entities or as dynamic and malleable. These implicit theories also play an important role in prejudice in general, and in social identity in particular. Seeing groups as fixed entities promotes the exaggeration of intragroup similarity and intergroup differences, makes people more anxious about accepting outsiders into one's ingroup, and creates a greater tendency for ingroup favoritism (Corneille et al., 2001; Keller, 2005; Levy et al., 2006).

People also vary in their ideologies about intergroup relations in society, such as concerning equality and access to power and social mobility. For example, a growing body of research has examined the **social dominance orientation**: a desire to see one's ingroups as dominant over other groups and a willingness to adopt cultural values that facilitate oppression over other groups. Research in numerous countries throughout the world has found that ingroup identification and outgroup derogation can be especially strong among people with a social dominance orientation (Duckitt, 2006; Eibach & Keegan, 2006; Haley & Sidanius, 2006; Levin, 2004).

Social dominance orientations promote self-interest. But some ideologies support a social structure that may actually oppose one's self-interest, depending on the status of one's groups. John Jost and his colleagues (2004; Jost, 2008) have focused on what they call *system justification*: processes that endorse and legitimize existing social arrangements. System-justifying beliefs protect the status quo. Groups with power, of course, may promote the status quo to preserve their own advantaged position. But although disadvantaged groups may be better off challenging the current economic or political system, their group members may hold system-justifying beliefs. To the extent that they do, members of low-status groups may show *out*group favoritism—toward more powerful outgroups.

So far, we have traced the roots and examined some consequences of stereotypes and prejudice. We now concentrate more specifically on two forms of prejudice and discrimination: sexism and racism. There are many other forms of prejudice and discrimination, of course. For example, there is a growing interest in *ageism*: prejudice and discrimination against people because of their age. Researchers today are also studying prejudice and discrimination toward people based on their sexual orientation, physical appearance, and physical and mental challenges. Sexism and racism, however, have received by far the most attention in social psychology research.

social dominance orientation A desire to see one's ingroup as dominant over other groups and a willingness to adopt cultural values that facilitate oppression over other groups.

Sexism

When a baby is born, the first words uttered ring loud and clear: "It's a boy!" or "It's a girl!" In many hospitals, the newborn boy immediately is given a blue hat and the newborn girl a pink hat. The infant receives a gender-appropriate name and is showered with gender-appropriate gifts. Over the next few years, the typical boy is supplied with toy trucks, baseballs, pretend tools, guns, and chemistry sets; the typical girl is furnished with dolls, stuffed animals, pretend make-up kits, kitchen sets, and tea sets. As they enter school, many expect the boy to earn money by delivering newspapers and to enjoy math and computers, while they expect the girl to babysit and to enjoy crafts, music, and social activities. These distinctions persist in college, as more male students major in economics and the sciences and more female students in the arts, languages, and humanities. In the work force, more men become doctors, construction workers, auto mechanics, airplane pilots, investment bankers, and engineers. In contrast, more women become secretaries, schoolteachers, nurses, flight attendants, bank tellers, and housewives. Back on the home front, the life cycle begins again when a man and woman have their first baby and discover that "It's a girl!" or "It's a boy!"

The traditional pinks and blues are not as distinct today as they used to be. Many gender barriers of the past have broken down, and the colors have somewhat blended together. Nevertheless, **sexism**—prejudice and discrimination based on a person's gender—still exists. Indeed, it begins with the fact that sex is the most conspicuous social category we use to identify ourselves and others (Stangor et al., 1992).

 ## Gender Stereotypes: Blue for Boys, Pink for Girls

What do people say when asked to describe the typical man and woman? Males are said to be more adventurous, assertive, aggressive, independent, and task-oriented; females are thought to be more sensitive, gentle, dependent, emotional, and people-oriented. These images are so universal that they were reported by 2,800 college students from thirty different countries of North and South America, Europe, Africa, Asia, and Australia (Williams & Best, 1982). The images are also salient to young children, who distinguish men from women well before their first birthday, identify themselves and others as boys or girls by three years of age, form gender-stereotypic beliefs and preferences about stories, toys, and other objects soon after that, and then use their simplified stereotypes in judging others and favoring their own gender over the other in intergroup situations (Golombok & Hines, 2002; Knobloch et al., 2005; Leinbach & Fagot, 1993; Ruble & Martin, 1998). Children also begin quite early to distinguish between stereotypically masculine and feminine behaviors. One study, for instance, found that by their second birthday toddlers exhibited more surprise when adults performed behaviors inconsistent with gender roles (Serbin et al., 2002). In another study preschool-age boys and girls liked a new toy less if they were told that it was a toy that opposite-sex children liked (Martin et al., 1995).

Gerianne Alexander (2003), citing data concerning children exposed prenatally to atypical levels of sex hormones and data concerning sex differences in toy preferences among nonhuman primates, argues that children's sex-based toy preferences, while partly due to gender socialization, may also have neurobiological and evolutionary roots. For example, a fascinating study reported that vervet monkeys showed sex differences in toy preferences similar to those seen in human children (Alexander & Hines, 2002).

Although biological and evolutionary factors may play a role in some of these preferences, it is clear that children have ample opportunity to learn gender stereotypes and roles from their parents and other role models. A recent meta-analysis of more than forty studies showed a significant correlation between parents' gender stereotypes and their children's gender-related thinking (Tenenbaum & Leaper, 2002).

Beliefs about males and females are so deeply ingrained that they influence the

sexism Prejudice and discrimination based on a person's gender.

The Blues and the Pinks. Even a very quick look at a toy store illustrates dramatic differences in how boys and girls are socialized. For example, boys are encouraged to play active, loud, and violent games (top), while girls are encouraged to engage in quieter, nurturing role play (bottom).

social role theory The theory that small gender differences are magnified in perception by the contrasting social roles occupied by men and women.

behavior of adults literally the moment a baby is born. In a fascinating study, the first-time parents of fifteen girls and fifteen boys were interviewed within twenty-four hours of the babies' births. There were no differences between the male and female newborns in height, weight, or other aspects of physical appearance. Yet the parents of girls rated their babies as softer, smaller, and more finely featured. The fathers of boys saw their sons as stronger, larger, more alert, and better coordinated (Rubin et al., 1974). Could it be there really were differences that only the parents were able to discern? Doubtful. In another study, Emily Mondschein and others (2000) found that mothers of eleven-month-old girls underestimated their infants' crawling ability, whereas mothers of eleven-month-old boys overestimated it.

As they develop, boys and girls receive many divergent messages, in many different settings. Barbara Morrongiello and Tess Dawber (2000) conducted a study that was relevant to this point. They showed mothers videotapes of children engaging in somewhat risky activities on a playground and asked them to stop the tape and indicate whatever they would ordinarily say to their own child in the situation shown. Mothers of daughters intervened more frequently and more quickly than did mothers of sons. As shown in Table 5.3, mothers of daughters were more likely to caution the child about getting hurt, whereas mothers of sons were more likely to encourage the child's risky playing. Another study by Morrongiello and others (2000) revealed that although boys typically experience more injuries from risky playing than girls, all children by the age of six tend to think that girls are at greater risk of injury than boys.

Culture and Popular Media

As children develop, not only are they influenced by the explicit and implicit lessons their parents and important others provide for them, but they also begin to look around at the larger culture around them and see who occupies what roles in society, as well as how these roles are valued. According to Alice Eagly's (1987; Eagly et al., 2004) **social role theory**, although the perception of sex differences may be based on some real differences, it is magnified by the unequal social roles occupied by men and women. The process involves three steps. First, through a combination of biological and social factors, a division of labor between the sexes has emerged over time, both at home and in the work setting. Men are more likely to work in construction or business; women are more likely to care for children and to take lower-status jobs. Second, since people behave in ways that fit the roles they play, men are more likely than women to wield physical, social, and economic power.

TABLE 5.3
What Mothers Would Say

Mothers of young boys or girls watched a videotape of another child engaging in somewhat risky behavior on a playground. The mothers were instructed to stop the videotape whenever they would say something to the child if the child were theirs, and to indicate what they would say. Mothers of daughters stopped the tape much more often than mothers of sons to express caution ("Be careful!"), worry about injury ("You could fall!"), and directives to stop ("Stop that this instant!"). In contrast, mothers of sons were more likely to indicate encouragement ("Good job! Let me see you go higher!").

(Adapted from Morrongiello & Dawber, 2000.)

Context of Statement	Frequency of Statement by:	
	Mothers of Girls	Mothers of Boys
Caution	3.9	0.7
Worry about injury	9.2	0.2
Directive to stop	9.3	0.6
Encouragement	0.5	3.0

Third, these behavioral differences provide a continuing basis for social perception, leading us to perceive men as dominant "by nature" and women as domestic "by nature," when in fact the differences reflect the roles they play. In short, sex stereotypes are shaped by—and often confused with—the unequal distribution of men and women into different social roles (see Figure 5.7). According to this theory, perceived differences between men and women are based on real behavioral differences that are mistakenly assumed to arise from gender rather than from social roles.

More than ever, children, adolescents, and adults seem to be immersed in popular culture transmitted via the mass media. Watching TV shows on our iPods while on the stationary bike at the gym, checking out the latest viral video sweeping the Internet while taking a break at the office or coffee shop, seeing advertisements popping up like weeds, glancing at the tabloid cover shots of the latest starlet hounded by relentless paparazzi—there often seems no escape. Through the ever-present media, we are fed a steady diet of images of men and women. Depending on how men and women are presented, these images have the potential to perpetuate gender stereotypes and sexism.

Fortunately, gone are the days of the media almost exclusively portraying women in stereotypical, powerless roles. Still, research indicates that some gender stereotyping persists—for example, in TV commercials and programs in countries around the world (Bartsch et al., 2000; Coltraine & Messineo, 2000; Furnham et al., 2001), music videos (Gan et al., 1997; Ward et al., 2005), and even media guide photographs for collegiate sports teams (Buysse & Embser-Herbert, 2004).

More to the point is the fact that media depictions can influence viewers, often without their realizing it (Ward et al., 2005; Ward & Friedman, 2006). Think about TV commercials for beer or men's cologne. There's a good chance that the commercials that come to mind include images of women as sex objects whose primary purpose in the ads is to serve as "the implied 'reward' for product consumption" (Rudman & Borgida, 1995, p. 495). Can these commercials affect not only men's attitudes toward women but their immediate behavior as well? Yes, according to research by Laurie Rudman and Eugene Borgida (1995) in which male undergraduates watched a videotape containing either sexist TV commercials or TV commercials for similar products that contained no sexual imagery. After watching the commercials, each participant went to a room to meet and interview a woman, who actually was a confederate of the experimenter. Each student's interaction with the woman was se-

FIGURE 5.7
Eagly's Social Role Theory of Gender Stereotypes
According to social role theory, stereotypes of men as dominant and women as subordinate persist because men occupy higher-status positions in society. This division of labor, a product of many factors, leads men and women to behave in ways that fit their social roles. But rather than attribute the differences to these roles, people attribute the differences to gender.

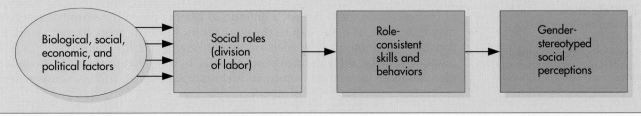

Although looking at images of attractive people is a pleasant experience for many people, these popular images may also produce negative consequences, perpetuating stereotypes and promoting dangerous behaviors among those who try to achieve what are often impossible, unhealthy standards of masculinity and femininity.

Even brief exposure to sexist television commercials can significantly influence the behaviors of men and women. **True.**

ambivalent sexism A form of sexism characterized by attitudes about women that reflect both negative, resentful beliefs and feelings and affectionate, chivalrous, but potentially patronizing beliefs and feelings.

cretly videotaped. Later, female judges watched these videotaped interactions and evaluated the male students' behavior toward the female confederate on several dimensions. The results revealed that the men who had seen sexist commercials were rated as behaving in a more sexualized, objectifying manner than the men who had seen the neutral ads. Having been primed with images of women as sex objects on TV, the men treated the woman in objectifying ways.

TV commercials influence not only men's but also women's attitudes and behavior. Studies have shown that female college students who had just watched a set of commercials in which the female characters were portrayed in stereotypic fashion tended to express lower self-confidence, less independence, and fewer career aspirations, and even performed more poorly on a math test, than did those who viewed stereotype-irrelevant or counter-stereotypical ads (Davies et al., 2002; Geis et al., 1984; Jennings et al., 1980).

Immersed in popular culture, people implicitly learn stereotypes about how men and women are supposed to look. Media images of impossibly thin or proportioned female models can have powerful effects on women's body images and esteem, and are implicated in the near-epidemic incidence of eating disorders and debilitating anxiety over physical appearance, particularly among young European American women (Henderson-King et al., 2001; Moradi et al., 2005; Ward & Friedman, 2006). The media's impact may be especially negative among individuals who already have concerns about their appearance or are particularly concerned with other people's opinions (Henderson-King & Henderson-King, 1997; Ricciardelli et al., 2000).

A more recent phenomenon is the growing number of teenage boys and men who are hurting themselves through their obsession with their bodies—trying to gain muscle mass while remaining extremely lean. Here, too, the media appear to play a critical role; indeed, graphic displays of images of muscular and lean male models have become increasingly prevalent of late. More and more cases come to light every year of boys and young men copying star athletes by taking steroids and other drugs that can make them look more like their role models but that can seriously threaten their health (Hanc, 2006; McCabe et al., 2002; Pope et al., 2000; Taylor, 2006).

Ambivalent Sexism

Overall, stereotypes of women tend to be more positive than stereotypes about men (Eagly et al., 1994); however, the positive traits associated with women are less valued in important domains such as business than the positive traits associated with men.

These contradictions are reflected in Peter Glick and Susan Fiske's (2001a) concept of **ambivalent sexism**. Ambivalent sexism consists of two elements: *hostile sexism,* characterized by negative, resentful feelings about women's abilities, value, and ability to challenge men's power; and *benevolent sexism,* characterized by affectionate, chivalrous feelings founded on the potentially patronizing belief that women need and deserve protection. Although hostile sexism is clearly more negative and many women feel favorably toward benevolent sexism (Kilianski & Rudman, 1998), the two forms of sexism are positively correlated. In a study of 15,000 men and women in nineteen nations across six continents, Glick, Fiske, and others

FIGURE 5.8

Hostile Sexism Across Countries

Respondents from nineteen countries completed measures of hostile and benevolent sexism. The average hostile sexism scores for male respondents from eleven of these countries are depicted here. The countries are listed from left to right in order of how unequal the sexes are in terms of political and economic power as defined by United Nations criteria. It is clear both from this figure and from the data more generally that hostile sexism is also positively correlated with gender inequality.

(Data from Glick, based on author correspondence.)

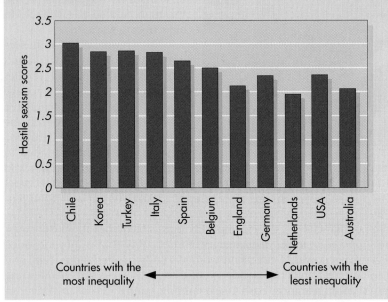

(2000) found evidence of prevalent ambivalent sexism around the world. Among their most intriguing findings is the fact that people from countries with the greatest degree of economic and political inequality between the sexes tend to exhibit the most hostile and benevolent sexism. Figure 5.8 depicts the average hostile sexism scores for each of several countries.

Sex Discrimination: Double Standards and Pervasive Stereotypes

Many years ago, Philip Goldberg (1968) asked students at a small women's college to evaluate the content and writing style of some articles. When the material was supposedly written by John McKay rather than Joan McKay, it received higher ratings, a result that led Goldberg to wonder if even women were prejudiced against women. Certain other studies showed that people often devalue the performance of women who take on tasks usually reserved for men (Lott, 1985) and attribute their achievements to luck rather than ability (Deaux & Emswiller, 1974; Nieva & Gutek, 1981). These studies generated a lot of attention, but it now appears that this kind of devaluation of women is not commonly found in similar studies. More than a hundred studies modeled after Goldberg's indicate that people are not generally biased by gender in the evaluation of performance (Swim and Sanna, 1989, 1996; Top, 1991).

This does not mean, however, that sex discrimination no longer exists all these years after the Goldberg study. Look at Tables 5.4 and 5.5, for instance, and you'll notice some striking sex differences in occupational choice. How many female airline pilots have you met lately? What about male secretaries? The question is, of course, what explains these differences? Decades of social science research point to sexist attitudes and discrimination as a key part of the equation. Sex discrimination during the early school years may pave the way for diverging career paths in adulthood. Then, when equally qualified men and women compete for a job, gender considerations enter in once again, as some research indicates that business professionals favor men for so-called masculine jobs (such as a manager for a machinery company) and women for so-called feminine jobs (such as a receptionist) (Eagly, 2004; Kmec, 2005). Even when women and men have comparable jobs, the odds are good that the women will be paid less than their male counterparts (Morgan & Arthur, 2005). They are also frequently confronted with a hostile, unfair work environment. Although American society is becoming less tolerant of sexual harassment, Ida Castro, chairwoman of the U.S. Equal Employment Opportunity Commission, reported that women on Wall Street frequently file complaints of "sexual jokes, derogatory comments, pornographic material, strippers at the office and company-sponsored trips to strip clubs and male-only golf and ski outings" (Knox, 2000, p. 1B).

Women vying for jobs and career advancement are often confronted with a virtually impossible dilemma: They are seen as more competent if they present themselves with stereotypically masculine rather than feminine traits; yet they are also perceived as less socially skilled and attractive—a perception that may ultimately cost them the job or career advancement they were seeking (Eagly, 2004; Fiske et al., 1991; Jackson et al., 2001; Rudman & Glick, 2001). Rebecca Holloway and Lucy Johnston (2007) found that men who had recently had an unsuccessful job interview gave

TABLE 5.4
Gender Differences in Specific Occupations in the United States

Recent labor statistics reveal that men and women occupy very different positions in the U.S. work force.

(Data from U.S. Bureau of Labor Statistics, 2000.)

Occupation	% Women	% Men	Occupation	% Women	% Men
Architect	16	84	Medicine and health manager	77	23
Athlete	28	72	Physician	24	76
Bartender	48	52	Physician's assistant	53	47
Child-care worker	97	3	Police, detective	14	86
Computer systems analyst	29	71	Psychologist	65	35
Construction worker	3	97	Sales (apparel)	78	22
Cook	44	56	Sales (motorized vehicles and boats)	11	89
Dental hygienist	99	1	Secretary	98	2
Dentist	16	84	Speech therapist	93	7
Dietician	84	16	Teacher (college)	42	58
Financial manager	51	49	Teacher (elementary school)	84	16
Firefighter	2	98	Truck driver	5	95
Lawyer, judge	29	71	Waitress/waiter	77	23
Licensed nurse	95	5			
Mechanical engineer	7	93			

Students protest Harvard University President Larry Summers, whose remarks about possible reasons for the lack of women in the sciences and engineering sparked controversy, eventually leading to his resignation in 2006.

lower ratings of the competence of the interviewer if the interviewer was a woman than if the interviewer was a man. Women did not show this bias in the ratings they gave after an unsuccessful job interview.

Women like Martha Stewart, Hilary Clinton, and Condoleeza Rice often are the targets of unusually harsh criticism for their alleged abrasiveness and controlling natures. They each have questioned whether a man with the exact same qualities would elicit a fraction of this contempt. Indeed, there is reason to believe that disconfirming gender stereotypes will often trigger a different response than disconfirming other stereotypes: Gender stereotypes are distinct from virtually all other stereotypes in that they often are *prescriptive* rather than merely *descriptive*. That is, they indicate what the many people in a given culture believe men and women *should* be. Few Americans, for example, think that gays should be artistic and sensitive or that old people should be forgetful and conservative; but many more think that women should be nurturing and that men should be unemotional. Even though ambition and drive are valued in our society, women who exhibit such traits may be viewed in especially harsh terms. These values put pressure on women and men to conform to gender stereotypes, and they increase perceivers' resistance against accepting stereotype-inconsistent evidence (Cuddy et al., 2004; DeWall et al., 2005; Prentice & Carranza, 2002; Rudman & Glick, 2001).

TABLE 5.5
Women in Work Settings Around the World

International labor statistics indicate that in most of the countries represented, women are especially likely to work in clerical occupations (e.g., as secretaries or bookkeepers), sales occupations (e.g., as salespeople, real estate agents, or insurance agents), and service occupations (e.g., as caretakers, cooks, hairdressers, or barbers), and especially unlikely to work in production/transport occupations (e.g., as woodworkers, miners, or shipping clerks).

(Data from International Labor Office, 1996.)

Percent of Workers Who Are Women

	Australia	Brazil	Canada	Costa Rica	Egypt	Israel	Italy	Japan	Mexico	Nether-lands	New Zealand	Niger	Spain	USA	UK
Total	42%	39%	45%	30%	20%	42%	35%	40%	32%	41%	44%	8%	34%	46%	45%
Professional/ technical	25	63	56	45	30	54	15	43	45	45	50	8	48	53	44
Administrative/ managerial	43	39	42	33	12	19	54	9	20	17	24	8	12	43	33
Clerical	47	41	80	49	35	71	34	60	55	59	77	30	51	79	76
Sales	10	86	45	37	14	38	50	38	51	47	48	—	45	50	64
Service	78	35	57	58	6	59	46	55	39	65	65	—	58	60	66
Production/ transport	29	25	14	19	4	13	22	28	19	10	16	2	12	18	15

Stereotypes and beliefs about innate, biological differences in ability for valued disciplines such as science and engineering may affect girls and women in powerful ways, as we will see in a later section of this chapter. These kinds of beliefs received international attention in response to remarks made by Larry Summers, the president of Harvard University, at a conference about diversifying the sciences and engineering in January 2005. Summers speculated that the relative lack of women in these fields may be due to "intrinsic differences of aptitude," along with the "lesser factors involving socialization and continuing discrimination." His speech triggered a great controversy, leading eventually to Summers being forced to resign as Harvard's president a little more than a year later. The intensity of the protests, as well as of those who criticized the protests as a political-correctness motivated attack against free speech, illustrate both how important the topic is to many people and how heated and emotional the discussions of it can be. In the meantime, girls and young women every day are taking their first steps on their career paths, trying not to be too discouraged or hurt by the din of these arguments that plays out around them.

Racism

Every four years the best soccer players in the world play for their home countries and compete in the World Cup tournament. The tournament provides a fun escape from the daily grind for millions of passionate fans around the world. It is not a complete escape, however, when some players, coaches, and fans at these or other major soccer matches find themselves the targets of racist taunts, and even violence, with increasing frequency. For example, Oguchi Onyewu, an African American who has played for teams in France and Belgium, said about a game in Europe, "I was going to throw the ball in, and some fans started doing monkey chants and I made a gesture like, 'Whatever.' And a guy reached over and punched me in the mouth" (Whiteside, 2006, p. 12C). France coach Raymond Domenech reported that his players were subjected to racist taunts by Spanish fans during the World Cup. The international soccer agency running the World Cup announced it would suspend national associations that did not impose new rules designed to reduce such racist behavior (BBC, July 31, 2006).

These ugly incidents reflect **racism**—prejudice and discrimination based on a person's racial background. None of us is completely immune from racism, whether as perpetrators or targets. But it is important to realize that racism exists at several different levels. At the individual level, any of us can be racist toward anyone else. And at the institutional and cultural levels, some people are privileged while others are discriminated against. When Kanye West criticized George Bush and the United States government in the aftermath of Hurricane Katrina, for example, he was implicating a broad, cultural level of discrimination that was much bigger in scope than the bigotry of mere individuals.

Going Under Cover: Modern and Implicit Racism

A close examination of legislation, opinion polls, sociological data, and social psychological research indicates that racial prejudice and discrimination have been lessening in the United States over the last several decades (Dovidio & Gaertner, 1998; Dovidio et al., 2002)—although they may once again be on the rise in Western Europe (Pettigrew, 1998b), as rioting in France in 2005 and the 2006 World Cup incidents may have illustrated. In a classic study of ethnic stereotypes published in 1933, Daniel Katz and Kenneth Braly found that white college students viewed the average white American as smart, industrious, and ambitious. Yet they saw the average African American as superstitious, ignorant, lazy, and happy-go-lucky. In multiple follow-up surveys with demographically similar samples of white students conducted from 1951 through 1993, these negative images of Blacks largely faded (Dovidio et al., 1996). Similarly, public opinion polls have indicated that racial prejudice in the United States has dropped sharply since World War II. Table 5.6 reports some of the changes in racial prejudice illustrated by these and other studies.

Although there certainly are exceptions, it is clear that blatant racism is increasingly less acceptable today than in the past. But racism can also be much more subtle, lurking beneath surfaces and behind corners. We may see its shadow and not be sure whether it is real or an apparition. Subtle, undercover forms of racism can be just as hurtful as more blatant forms, in part because their subtlety allows them to slip through people's defenses. In this section of the chapter, we consider some of the blatant and subtle forms and consequences of racism.

Modern Racism   One example is **modern racism**, a subtle form of prejudice that surfaces in direct ways whenever it is safe, socially acceptable, or easy to rationalize. According to theories of modern racism, many people are racially ambivalent. They want to see themselves as fair, but they still harbor feelings of anxiety and discomfort concerning other racial groups (Hass et al., 1992). There are several specific theories of modern racism, but they all emphasize contradictions and tensions that lead to subtle, often unconscious forms of prejudice and discrimination (Dovidio & Gaertner, 2004; Levy et al., 2006; Liu & Mills, 2006; Sears & Henry, 2005).

In modern racism, prejudice against minorities surfaces primarily under circumstances when the expression of prejudice is safe, socially acceptable, and easy to rationalize because of its ambiguity. For example, in a study by John Dovidio, Jennifer Smith, and others (1997), white participants read about a trial in which the defendant was found guilty of murdering a white police officer. Some were led to believe that the defendant was black; others, that he was white. High-prejudice participants were more likely to recommend the death penalty if the defendant was black than if he was white. Low-prejudice white participants, however, exhibited a more complex pattern of results, reflecting modern racism: They tended to be *less* likely to recommend death if the defendant was black than if he was white—unless they learned that a black juror advocated the death penalty, in which case they were more likely to recommend death if the defendant was black. In short, knowing that a black juror

racism Prejudice and discrimination based on a person's racial background.

modern racism A form of prejudice that surfaces in subtle ways when it is safe, socially acceptable, and easy to rationalize.

TABLE 5.6
Changes in Overt Racism

The results of many studies and surveys like these demonstrate that overt, negative stereotyping and racism have declined dramatically over the years. Although these results are encouraging, research on more subtle, modern racism reveals that the picture is much more complex than these self-reports suggest.

(Dovidio et al., 1996; Peterson, 1997.)

Percentage of White Participants Selecting a Trait to Describe Black Americans

Trait	1933	1967	1993
Superstitious	84%	13%	1%
Lazy	75	26	5
Happy-go-lucky	38	27	2
Ignorant	38	11	5
Musical	26	47	12
Very religious	24	8	17
Stupid	22	4	0

Percentage of White Participants Who Report Being Willing to Admit Blacks into Various Relationships with Them

	1949	1968	1992
Willing to Admit Blacks to:			
Employment in my occupation	78%	98%	99%
My club as personal friends	51	97	96
My street as neighbors	41	95	95
Close kinship by marriage	0	66	74

Percentage of Adult Participants Who Agree with the Statement "It's All Right for Blacks and Whites to Date Each Other."

1987	1997
48%	69%

had advocated the death penalty may have made them less worried about appearing racist themselves. The implication is that when circumstances allow Whites to excuse a negative response, they become more likely to discriminate against African Americans.

Many whites who consider themselves non-prejudiced admit that on some occasions they do not react toward Blacks, or other groups such as gay men, as they should—an insight that causes them to feel embarrassed, guilty, and ashamed (Monteith et al., 2002). Indeed, when they have reason to suspect that racism could bias their judgments, low-prejudice Whites may show an *opposite* bias on explicit, consciously controlled tasks, responding more favorably to Blacks than to Whites (Dovidio, Kawakami, et al., 1997; Fein et al., 1997; Norton et al., 2006; Wyer, 2004).

Just as with any other form of prejudice, individuals differ in the degree to which they exhibit underlying racist tendencies. But because of the covert nature of these tendencies, measuring the differences is difficult. Several questionnaires have been developed to ask individuals relatively subtle, indirect questions about their attitudes toward particular groups, including the Modern Racism Scale (McConahay, 1986) and scales designed to measure subtle forms of racism in Western Europe and modern forms of sexism (Pettigrew & Meertens, 1995; Swim et al., 1995; Tougas et al., 1995). Although these scales have been used successfully in many studies (e.g., Vescio et al., 2006; Wittenbrink et al., 1997), other research has demonstrated that people who are highly motivated to control their expressions of prejudice may score low on them even if they do harbor prejudiced attitudes (Dunton & Fazio, 1997; Plant & Devine, 1998). Part of the limitation of these scales is that they *explicitly* ask respondents about their attitudes toward various groups, when research today is showing more and more how *implicit* these attitudes can be (Blair, 2001; Castelli et al., 2005; Olson & Fazio, 2006; Son Hing et al., 2005).

Implicit Racism Just as stereotypes can be activated and applied without conscious awareness or intent, so, too, racism and other forms of prejudice and discrimination can operate unconsciously and unintentionally. Undetected by individuals who want to be fair and unbiased, implicit racism can skew their judgments, feelings, and behaviors—without inducing the guilt that more obvious, explicit forms of racism would trigger.

For example, consider the research showing that perceivers are more likely to exhibit negative stereotype activation and evaluations in response to African American faces if the faces are more racially prototypic (Blair et al., 2004; Maddox, 2004; Livingston & Brewer, 2002). This is not a bias that most people are aware of or, therefore, concerned about. Its effects, however, can be profound, as suggested by research by Jennifer Eberhardt and others (2006), which studied predictors of whether a criminal defendant was likely to be sentenced to death. Examining more than 600 death-penalty-eligible cases tried in Philadelphia, Pennsylvania, between 1979 and

1999, these researchers found that in cases involving a white victim, the more the defendant's physical appearance was stereotypically black (see Figure 5.9), the more likely he would be sentenced to death.

As with modern racism, the question of how to detect and measure implicit racism is a challenging one. Because of its implicit nature, covert measures that do not require individuals to answer questions about their attitudes typically are used. By far the most well-known such measure is the Implicit Association Test (IAT), first developed and tested by Anthony Greenwald and others (1998). The IAT measures the extent to which two concepts are associated. Implicit racism toward African Americans, for example, is detected to the extent that participants can associate African American cues, such as a black face, faster with negative concepts and slower with positive concepts, relative to how fast they can make the same kinds of associations with European American cues. Other IATs focus on associations concerning older versus younger people, men versus women, and so on. The IAT is discussed in more detail in Chapter 6, on Attitudes. It has sparked an explosion of research in the past few years concerning racism and other forms of prejudice and discrimination, and it has been so popular that between October 1998 and October 2006 more than 4.5 *million* IATs were completed by visitors to the IAT Web site (Nosek, 2006).

Additional measures of implicit biases are being added to researchers' toolboxes. One of the first successful measures of implicit racism was developed by Russell Fazio and others (1995), which measures the extent to which exposure to faces of different races primes individuals to evaluate subsequently presented positive or negative adjectives more or less quickly. Fazio and his colleagues found that their measure predicted white participants' nonverbal behaviors toward Blacks in an interaction much better than did these participants' scores on the Modern Racism Scale. More recently, Brian Nosek and Mahzarin Banaji (2001) created a variation of the IAT called the Go/No-Go Association Task (GNAT), which enables researchers to measure bias against a single group at a time rather than only in comparison to another. Denise Sekaquaptewa and her colleagues (2003) developed a very different implicit measure of racial stereotyping that focuses on how individuals respond to descriptions of behaviors that are either consistent or inconsistent with stereotypes. And Keith Payne and others (2005) introduced a measure of implicit racial and other attitudes based on how people made attributions for their own emotional reactions.

Regardless of the specific measure, social psychologists have found that individuals' degree of implicit racism sometimes predicts differences in their perceptions of and reactions to others as a function of race. For example, Kurt Hugenberg and Galen Bodenhausen (2003) found that individuals' levels of implicit racism predicted how biased they were in perceiving hostility in black faces. European American participants watched brief movies of facial expressions of white or black targets. In their first study, the facial expression began as displaying hostility and gradually became more neutral. In a second study, the expression began as neutral and gradually became more hostile. The participants' task was to indicate when the face no longer expressed the initial emotion—in other words, when did the emotion change from hostile to neutral in the first study, or from neutral to hostile in the second study? The researchers found that participants with relatively high levels of implicit bias, as measured by the IAT, saw the black faces as staying hostile longer in the first study, and becoming hostile quicker in the second study, relative to the white faces. Participants who showed relatively low racism on the IAT did not show this bias. In a later study (2004), these authors found that participants who showed a

FIGURE 5.9

Facial Features and the Death Penalty

In the study by Jennifer Eberhardt and others (2006), the face on the right would be considered more stereotypically black than the face on the left. Neither of these two people depicted had any criminal history, and their pictures here are for illustrative purposes only. However, if they were found guilty of a crime and were eligible for the death penalty, the man on the right would be more likely to be sentenced to death than the man on the left, according to Eberhardt et al.'s research.

(Eberhardt et al., 2006.)

strong race bias on the IAT were more likely to categorize a racially ambiguous face as African American if the face expressed hostility than if it expressed happiness.

Interracial Perceptions and Interactions

Among the ways in which racism differs from sexism, one of the most dramatic is the extent to which members of the ingroups and outgroups interact with each other, in terms of both frequency and intimacy. While women and men often live with each other, are in the same family, and often seek each other for love and support, the divides between racial and ethnic groups tend to be more vast and may promote stronger feelings of hostility, fear, and distrust. In addition, in contemporary society, the stigma of being perceived as racist typically is much worse than being perceived as sexist. These factors—less contact, stronger negative emotions, and anxiety about appearing racist—combine to make interracial perception and interaction particularly challenging and fraught with emotion and tension.

Indeed, just perceiving a member of a racial outgroup may trigger different, more emotional reactions than perceiving an ingroup member. This is a conclusion suggested by a study by Allen Hart and others (2000). They monitored the brain activity of European American and African American participants using an fMRI technique while they showed the participants pictures of individuals from their racial ingroup or outgroup. The fMRI revealed differential responses in the amygdala, a structure in the brain associated with emotion. Pictures of racial outgroup members tended to elicit stronger amygdala activation than did pictures of ingroup members. Elizabeth Phelps and others (2000) also found that European Americans showed greater amygdala activation in response to black than white faces. In addition, this greater activation was associated with higher levels of implicit prejudice. Since these initial studies, several other researchers have found further support for heightened amygdala activity in Whites in response to black faces (e.g., Cunningham et al., 2004; Wheeler & Fiske, 2005). One study has even reported this amygdala activation in response to black faces not only by white perceivers but also by black perceivers (Lieberman et al., 2005).

If perceptions of a member of a racial outgroup are associated with various biases and emotional reactions, interracial interactions are all the more complex and challenging. This is evident in a study by Wendy Mendes and others (2002), in which nonblack participants interacted with either a black or a white confederate on a series of tasks. Participants were more likely to exhibit cardiovascular reactions (such as changes in the amount of blood pumped by the heart per minute) associated with feelings of threat if the confederate was black than if the confederate was white. According to Jacquie Vorauer (2003), individuals engaging in intergroup interactions often activate *metastereotypes,* or thoughts about the outgroup's stereotypes about them, and worry about being seen as consistent with these stereotypes.

When engaging in interracial interactions, Whites may be concerned about a number of things, including not wanting to be, or appear to be, racist. They may therefore try to regulate their behaviors, become particularly vigilant for signs of distrust or dislike from their interaction partners, and so on. What should ideally be a smooth-flowing normal interaction can become awkward, and even exhausting. This, in turn, can affect their partner's perceptions of them, possibly leading to the ironic outcome of their appearing to be racist because they were trying not to be. A number of researchers have been examining such phenomena (e.g., Amodio et al., 2007; Devine et al., 2005; Dovidio et al., 2002). Jennifer Richeson, Nicole Shelton,

This illustration highlights (in red) areas of the brain that showed significantly greater activation in response to black faces than white faces among relatively prejudiced participants in a study by Jennifer Richeson and others (2003). This pattern of increased activation suggests that participants were trying to control their prejudiced reactions to black faces.

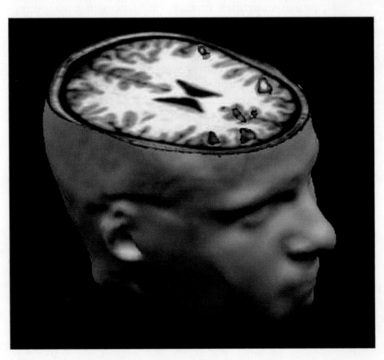

FIGURE 5.10

Colorblind?

When playing a face-matching game with a confederate, in which they had to ask questions of the confederate to guess which of a series of photographs the confederate had on a particular round, white participants were much less likely to ask about the race of the people in the photographs if they were interacting with a black confederate than a white confederate, even though this hurt their performance in the game.

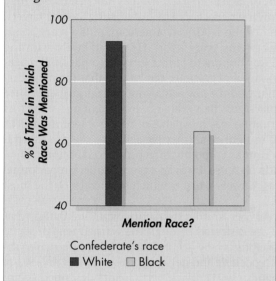

Confederate's race
■ White   □ Black

and their colleagues have found across a number of recent experiments that for white participants, particularly if they score relatively high on a measure of implicit racism, interacting with a black individual can be cognitively and emotionally exhausting because they are so worried about appearing racist. Indeed, in response to images of black faces, such participants are more likely than less prejudiced individuals to show activity in brain regions that are thought to involve self-regulation and control, and they are more likely to perform worse on a simple cognitive task after interacting with a black than a white confederate—evidence that the interaction was cognitively draining for them (Richeson et al., 2003; Shelton & Richeson, 2007; Shelton et al., 2005; Trawalter & Richeson, 2006).

It may not be surprising, then, that people may try to avoid interracial interaction for fear of appearing racist or being treated in a racist way, and this avoidant behavior can have the ironic effect of making things all the worse. Ashby Plant and David Butz (2006), for example, found that when nonblack participants with this avoidant concern interacted with a black confederate, they had shorter and less pleasant interactions. In a clever demonstration of this kind of anxiety, Michael Norton and others (2006) paired white participants with either a white or black confederate in a game in which the participants had to ask questions of the confederate in order to identify which of a series of photographs the confederate had been given. As can be seen in Figure 5.10, participants were significantly less likely to mention race when asking questions of the black confederate than the white confederate, even though this hurt their ability to win the game. It seemed that the white participants would rather lose the game than run the risk of appearing racist by paying any attention to the race of the people in the photographs.

Unfortunately, the vast majority of the work on interracial perceptions and interactions focuses on Whites' perceptions of and behaviors toward Blacks. There is an obvious need to expand this research to look at the more diverse and dynamic nature of interracial perception and interaction, and social psychologists are beginning to pursue this (e.g., Plant, 2004; Shelton, 2003). Michael Inzlicht and others (2006), for example, recently found evidence suggesting that the anxieties associated with interracial interactions can deplete the cognitive resources of those concerned with being the potential *targets,* rather than just the potential perpetrators, of prejudice. Social psychologists are also examining interactions across other social groups. Irene Blair and others (2003), for example, are studying anxiety experienced by straight individuals as they anticipate interacting with gays.

A Threat in the Air: Effects on the Targets of Stereotypes and Prejudice

We are all the targets of other people's stereotypes and prejudices. We are stereotyped and treated differently based on how we look, how we talk, and where we come from. People infer numerous things about us by whether we are "morning people" or "night owls," what sports teams we root for, and whether we prefer a Mac or a PC. None of us is immune from having our work evaluated in a biased way, our motives questioned, or our attempts at making new friends rejected because of stereotypes and prejudices.

But for the targets of some stereotypes and prejudices, these concerns are relentless and profound. For them, there seem to be few safe havens. Social psychologists often refer to these targets as *stigmatized*—"individuals who, by virtue of their membership in a particular social group, or by possession of particular characteristics, are targets of negative stereotypes, are vulnerable to being labeled as deviant, and are devalued in society" (Major & Crocker, 1993, p. 345). What are some of the effects of being stigmatized by stereotypes and prejudice? In this section we first examine some of the effects that perceiving discrimination can have on individuals; we then focus on the impact that the perceived threat of being stereotyped can have on academic achievement, particularly that of women and minorities.

Perceiving Discrimination

Members of different groups disagree dramatically about the prevalence and magnitude of discrimination that is directed at their groups. Many surveys have shown, for example, that white Americans and black Americans have very different impressions of the degree to which racism still exists (Dovidio et al., 2002; Eibach & Keegan, 2006). The more covert, subtle forms of racism characterized as modern racism may often be barely visible to observers, but their effects can be humiliating to their targets. In *Color-Blind,* writer Ellis Cose (1997), who is African American, tells a story about how he was treated in a job interview twenty years before. He was an award-winning newspaper reporter at the time and was hoping to land a job with a national magazine. The editor he met with was pleasant and gracious, but he said that the magazine didn't have many black readers. "All the editor saw was a young black guy, and since *Esquire* was not in need of a young black guy, they were not in need of me . . . he had been so busy focusing on my race that he was incapable of seeing me or my work" (p. 150). Then a few years later, and in light of affirmative action, Cose was asked if he was interested in a position in a firm as corporate director of equal opportunity. "I was stunned, for the question made no sense. I was an expert neither on personnel nor on equal employment law; I was, however, black, which seemed to be the most important qualification" (p. 156).

The targets of stigmatizing stereotypes wonder frequently whether and to what extent others' impressions of them are distorted through the warped lens of social categorization. Over time, such suspicions can be deeply frustrating. In particular situations, however, they can have both positive and negative consequences. In a study by Jennifer Crocker and her colleagues (1991), black participants described themselves on a questionnaire, supposedly to be evaluated by an unknown white student who sat in an adjacent room. Participants were told that they were either liked or disliked by this student on the basis of the questionnaire; then they took a self-esteem test. If the participants thought that the white student could not see them and did not know their race, their self-esteem scores predictably rose after positive feedback and declined after negative feedback. But when participants thought the evaluating student had seen them through a one-way mirror, negative feedback did not lower their self-esteem. In this situation, participants blamed the unfavorable evaluations on prejudice. However, there was a drawback: One-way-mirror participants who received positive feedback showed a *decrease* in self-esteem. The reason? Instead of internalizing the credit for success, these participants attributed the praise to patronizing, reverse discrimination.

Attributing negative feedback to discrimination can sometimes protect one's self-esteem, but it can have costs as well. First, such an attribution can sometimes be inaccurate, and the recipient of the feedback might miss an opportunity to learn information relevant for self-improvement. Consider the dilemma faced by a white teacher who wants to give negative feedback to black students regarding the term papers they have handed in. If the students dismiss this criticism as biased, they may fail to learn from their mistakes and the teacher's advice. But if the teacher sugarcoats the feedback in an attempt to avoid the appearance of racism, the students may

"*You look like this sketch of someone who is thinking about committing a crime*"

Research on stereotype threat illustrates some of the challenges that can undermine the effectiveness of a white teacher providing feedback and mentorship to a black student, as well as strategies to overcome these challenges.

likewise fail to learn. Studying this dilemma in a pair of experiments, Geoffrey Cohen and others (1999) came up with a twofold prescription for solving it. What they found was that black students responded most positively to negative feedback when the teacher both (a) made it clear that he or she had high standards and (b) assured the students that they had the capacity to achieve those standards. Without such wise mentoring, the attributional ambiguity in which some students often live can diminish their confidence in, and accuracy about, what they really do and do not know well (Aronson & Inzlicht, 2004).

Second, although attributing negative feedback to discrimination can protect one's overall self-esteem, it can also make people feel as if they have less personal control over their lives. Individuals from low-status groups may be threatened by this vulnerability to discrimination and thus feel worse about themselves when they perceive that they were discriminated against, especially if they have reason to think that the discrimination against them could persist over time (Schmitt et al., 2002). Such concerns can have tremendous costs: Perceiving persistent discrimination over time is associated with a number of physical and mental health problems and drug use (Gibbons et al., 2004; Williams et al., 2003).

Whether individuals are more or less likely to perceive discrimination, or to be affected negatively by such perceptions, depends in part on how and to what extent they identify with their stigmatized group (Major et al., 2002, 2004; Sellers & Shelton, 2003). For example, people who are highly identified with their group are more likely to perceive discrimination against them than are people who are less identified. In a study by Brenda Major and others (2003), for instance, female participants received negative feedback from a male confederate about their performance on a test of their creativity. The women also learned information about the man that either clearly indicated that he was sexist ("he never picks a girl to be a team leader"), indicated nothing about whether he was sexist, or offered ambiguous cues about his sexism ("he grades guys and girls differently"). Later, the women were asked to indicate the extent to which the feedback they received about their test performance was due to discrimination. The researchers found that the participants who exhibited strong gender identification (such as agreeing strongly with the statement "Being a woman is an important reflection of who I am") were no more likely than less identified women to attribute the feedback to discrimination if there were no cues about sexism or if the cues were very clear that the man was sexist. But gender identification did make a difference when the cues were *ambiguous:* Highly identified women were significantly more likely to attribute the negative feedback to sex discrimination than were less identified women.

Robert Sellers and Nicole Shelton (2003) specify several different dimensions of African Americans' racial identification, each of which has different implications for perceptions of racial discrimination. In their study of 267 African American first-year college students, the researchers found that the more the students endorsed a *nationalist* racial ideology, which stresses uniqueness due to their African heritage, the more racial discrimination they reported experiencing within the past year. On the other hand, the more they endorsed a *humanist* ideology, which stresses the common humanity of all people, the less racial discrimination they reported. In addition, particular ideologies were associated with more or less protection against the negative feelings associated with perceived discrimination.

 ## Stereotype Threat and Academic Achievement

Easily some of the most exciting developments in the field in the past decade have been the waves of research triggered by a theory introduced by Claude Steele. Steele proposed that in situations in which a negative stereotype can apply to certain groups, members of these groups can fear being seen "through the lens of diminishing stereotypes and low expectations" (1999, p. 44). Steele (1997) called this predicament *stereotype threat,* for it hangs like "a threat in the air" while the individual is in the stereotype-relevant situation. The predicament can be particularly threatening for individuals whose identity and self-esteem are invested in domains for which the stereotype is relevant. Steele argued that stereotype threat plays a crucial role in influencing the intellectual performance and identity of stereotyped group members. More recently, Steele and his colleagues (2002; Adams et al., 2006) have broadened the scope of their analysis to include *social identity threats* more generally, which are not necessarily tied to specific stereotypes but instead reflect a more general devaluing of a person's social group.

Threats to African Americans and Women   Steele cited disturbing statistics pointing to the underperformance of African Americans in school and of women in domains requiring advanced math skills. According to his theory, stereotype threat can hamper achievement in academic domains in two ways. First, reactions to the "threat in the air" can directly interfere with performance—for example, by increasing anxiety and triggering distracting thoughts. Second, if this stereotype threat is chronic in the academic domain, it can cause individuals to *disidentify* from that domain—to dismiss the domain as no longer relevant to their self-esteem and identity.

To illustrate, imagine a black student and a white student who enter high school equally qualified in academic performance. Imagine that while taking a particularly difficult test at the beginning of the school year, each student struggles on the first few problems. The white student may begin to worry about failing, but the black student may have a whole set of additional worries about appearing to confirm a negative stereotype. Even if the black student doesn't believe the stereotype at all, the threat of being reduced to a stereotype in the eyes of those around her can trigger anxiety and distraction, impairing her performance. And if she experiences this threat in school frequently—perhaps because she stands out as one of only a few black students in the school or because she is treated by others in a particular way—the situation may become too threatening to her self-esteem. To buffer herself against the threat, she may disidentify with school; if so, her academic performance will become less relevant to her identity and self-esteem. In its place, some other domain of life, such as social success or a particular nonacademic talent, will become a more important source of identity and pride.

Steele and others conducted a series of experiments in which they manipulated factors likely to increase or decrease stereotype threat as students took academic tests. For example, Steele and Joshua Aronson (1995) had black and white students from a highly selective university take a very difficult standardized verbal test. To some participants, it was introduced as a test of intellectual ability; to others, as a laboratory problem-solving task unrelated to ability. Steele and Aronson reasoned that because of the difficulty of the test, *all* the students would struggle with it. If the test was said to be related to intellectual ability, however, the black students would also feel the threat of a negative stereotype. In contrast, if the test was simply a laboratory task and not a real test of intelligence, then negative stereotypes would be less applicable, and the stereotype threat would be reduced. In that case, black students would be less impaired while taking the test. As shown in Figure 5.11, the results supported these predictions.

Thus, a seemingly minor change in the setting—a few words about the meaning of a test—had a powerful effect on the black students' performance. In a second study, the researchers used an even more subtle manipulation of stereotype threat: whether or not the students were asked to report their race just before taking the test (which was described as unrelated to ability). Making them think about race for a few seconds just before taking the test impaired the performance of black students but had no effect on white students.

Steele's theory predicts that because negative stereotypes concerning women's advanced math skills are prevalent, women may often experience stereotype threat

Sports Illustrated surveyed almost 2,000 students in U.S. middle schools and high schools and asked them to choose from a list of careers the ones they thought they could successfully pursue. Of all the careers listed, professional sports was the only one selected more often by black students than by white or Hispanic students.

—S. L. Price

FIGURE 5.11

Stereotype Threat and Academic Performance

Black and white students took a very difficult standardized verbal test. Before taking the test, some students were told that it was a test of their intellectual ability, but others were told that it was simply a laboratory task unrelated to intellectual ability. All students' scores on this test were adjusted based on their scores from standardized college entrance verbal examinations. Despite this adjustment, black students did significantly worse than white students on the test if it had been introduced as a test of intellectual ability (left). In contrast, among the students who had been told the test was unrelated to ability, black students and white students performed equally well (right).
(Steele & Aronson, 1995.)

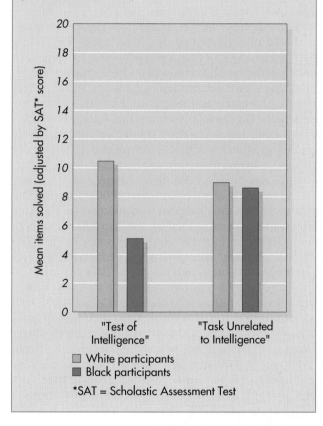

in settings relevant to these skills. Reducing stereotype threat in these settings, therefore, should reduce the underperformance that women tend to exhibit in these areas. To test this idea, Steven Spencer and others (1999) recruited male and female students who were good at math and felt that math was important to their identities. The researchers gave these students a very difficult standardized math test, one on which all of them would perform poorly. Before taking the test, some students were told that the test generally showed no gender differences—thereby implying that the negative stereotype of women's ability in math was *not* relevant to this particular test. Other students were told that the test *did* generally show gender differences. As Steele's theory predicted, women performed worse than men when they were told that the test typically produced gender differences, but they performed as well as men when told that the test typically did not produce gender differences.

This kind of stereotype threat effect on women in math and related fields has been replicated many times in various contexts since the original research. In one recent series of experiments, for example, women did worse on a logic test if they were exposed to a suggestion about the sexism of a male instructor (Adams et al., 2006). Emily Pronin and others (2004) found that stereotype threat can cause women to devalue aspects of their femininity, as if they had to choose between being feminine or being serious about math. Ilan Dar-Nimrod and Steven Heine (2006) found that women performed worse in math if they were exposed to explanations that gender differences in math are due to genetic differences than if they were exposed to explanations that focused on more temporary factors, such as teachers treating boys and girls differently when they were young.

An interesting experiment by Barbara Fredrickson and others (1998) also examined how the math performance of women can be affected by the context in which they are tested. Male and female participants in their study were asked to evaluate some consumer products, including an item of clothing that they tried on and wore for some amount of time. For some participants, the clothing was a one-piece swimsuit; for others, it was a crewneck sweater. While wearing the clothing alone in a room in front of a mirror, each participant took a math test. Fredrickson and her colleagues proposed that because women in our society are made to feel more shame and anxiety about their bodies than are men, they should feel more anxious when taking the test while wearing the swimsuit, whereas men should be relatively unaffected by the manipulation of clothing. As can be seen in Figure 5.12, the results supported their predictions. After adjusting the participants' test scores based on their past performance on standardized math tests, these researchers found that women did significantly worse when wearing a swimsuit than a sweater, whereas men's performance was unaffected by the clothing manipulation.

In a more recent creative experiment that also highlights how the experience of threat to a woman's body image can interfere with her academic performance, Amy Kiefer and others (2006) found that relative to women who saw an unaltered photograph of themselves, women who saw a digitally altered photograph of themselves that made them look 20 percent wider than they really were did worse on a reading comprehension test. It is worth noting that this effect occurred only if the women thought they were working with male students who saw this photograph; if they thought they were working in an all-female group, the manipulation of the photo had no effect on their test performance.

FIGURE 5.12

The Swimsuit Becomes You

While wearing either a sweater or a swimsuit in front of a mirror, male and female students took a challenging standardized math test. All students' scores on this test were adjusted based on their scores from standardized college entrance math examinations. The men's scores were unaffected by what clothes they were wearing (left). The women's scores were affected (right): Women did significantly worse on the test if they were wearing a swimsuit than if they were wearing a sweater. (Fredrickson et al., 1998.)

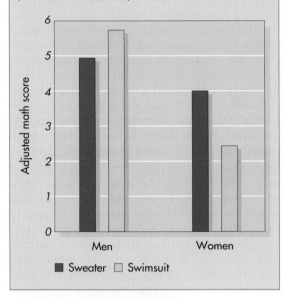

An African American student is likely to perform worse on an athletic task if the task is described as one reflecting sports intelligence than if it is described as reflecting natural athletic ability.
True.

Diversity of Threats   Stereotype threats can affect any group for which strong, well-known, negative stereotypes are relevant in particular settings. Social identity threats can be more general than that, affecting groups that may be devalued even in the absence of specific negative stereotypes about a particular domain. The examples of these threats run far and wide. For instance, many white athletes feel stereotype threat whenever they step onto a court or playing field where they constitute the minority. Will the white athlete feel the added weight of this threat while struggling against other athletes in a game? To address this question, Jeff Stone and others (1999) had black and white students play miniature golf. When the experimenters characterized the game as diagnostic of "natural athletic ability," the white students did worse. But when they characterized it as diagnostic of "sports intelligence," the black students did worse. In a subsequent series of experiments, Stone (2002) found that white students who were made to experience stereotype threat about their athletic ability practiced less than nonthreatened students before an athletic task. Thus they exhibited a form of self-handicapping, which, as discussed in Chapter 3, involves sabotaging one's own performance in order to provide an excuse for failure.

Because individuals are members of multiple groups, they can feel either threatened or emboldened by a stereotype—depending on which of their social identities has been activated. Consider, for example, a study by Margaret Shih and others (1999) in which Asian American women were examined. In the United States, there is a negative stereotype about women and math but a positive stereotype about Asians and math. The researchers found that these women performed worse on a math test when their gender identity was made salient (by means of questions they had to answer about their gender before taking the test), whereas they performed better on the test when their ethnic identity was made salient. In an interesting follow-up, though, Sapna Cheryan and Galen Bodenhausen (2000) reported that if the high expectations of Asian American women's math abilities are made particularly salient to them as they are about to take a math test, the concern about living up to these expectations can itself be distracting, leading to a "choking" effect and worse performance.

In general, members of a group (such as men) that has the relative advantage of being compared to an outgroup targeted by a negative stereotype (such as women in math) may benefit from what Gregory Walton and Geoffrey Cohen (2003) call *stereotype lift*. In a meta-analysis of forty-three relevant studies, members of non-stereotyped groups tended to perform better on tasks when the stereotype threat against the outgroup was relevant than when it was reduced. Reducing the threat, such as ensuring the targeted group that a particular test is not relevant to a negative stereotype, therefore not only improves the performance of the targeted group but also seems to remove some of the boost that the nonstereotyped group members get from being in the allegedly "superior" group.

Since Claude Steele introduced the concept of stereotype threat, the amount of research it has inspired is absolutely staggering. Stereotype threat effects have been demonstrated with a wide variety of groups: European American men on a math test when compared with Asians; women on a math test in a co-ed rather than all-female setting; low-socioeconomic-status French students on a verbal test when the test was said to be diagnostic of intellectual ability; Latina women on a test of math and spatial ability; white participants taking an IAT; individuals with a history of mental illness on a reasoning test when their illness was revealed; women or men on a negotiation task, depending on whether success on the task was said to be associated with masculine or feminine traits; students primed to think about their identity as athletes before taking a difficult math test; older adults on a memory test when it was presented as a memory test rather than an impression formation task; and women driving after being reminded of demeaning stereotypes about female drivers (Aronson et al., 1999; Ben-Zeev et al., 2005; Chasteen et al., 2005; Croizet & Claire, 1998; Frantz

Stereotype threat can undermine the performance of individuals from any group for which strong, well-known, negative stereotypes are relevant. White male basketball players, for example, may experience stereotype threat in the presence of an African American majority.

et al., 2004; Gonzales et al., 2002; Kray et al., 2002; Quinn et al., 2004; Sekaquaptewa & Thompson, 2003; von Hippel et al., 2005; Yopyk & Prentice, 2005). And the list goes on.

Stereotype Threat Effects: Causes and Solutions   How exactly does stereotype threat interfere with performance? And who within a target group is most vulnerable to these effects? These are among the questions currently being investigated. It is clear that one does not need to *believe in* a negative stereotype in order for it to have an effect. Just knowing about the stereotype seems to be enough, particularly if the individual identifies strongly with the group and cares about performing well. Recent work suggests that stereotype threat can trigger physiological arousal, which may interfere with people's ability to perform well on the task at hand (Ben-Zeev et al., 2005; Blascovich et al., 2001; O'Brien & Crandall, 2003). Stereotype threat may also cause threatened individuals to try to suppress thoughts about the stereotype, which can have the ironic effect of draining cognitive resources away from the task they are working on (Steele et al., 2002). Other factors that recent research suggests contribute to the effects of stereotype threat include impaired working memory, feelings of dejection, and negative thoughts (Croizet et al., 2004; Keller & Dauenheimer, 2003; Schmader & Johns, 2003).

But although stereotype threat effects are widespread, the growing body of research on this subject also gives us reason to hope. Social psychologists have been uncovering some ways in which people can be better protected against these threats. These include being reminded of things about themselves that make them feel good about themselves, even about things unrelated to the domain under threat; blurring boundaries between groups; coping with threat by using humor; attributing the arousal triggered by the threat to something nonthreatening; and thinking of examples of other group members who have been successful in the domain under threat (Ben-Zeev et al., 2005; Ford et al., 2004; McIntyre et al., 2003; Rosenthal & Crisp, 2006).

In one particularly ambitious line of research, Geoffrey Cohen and others (2006) conducted a pair of experiments with seventh-graders from lower-middle-class and middle-class families in a school in the United States. When they were first measured, the grades of the African American students tended to be significantly lower than those of the European American students. Half of the students were then given a writing task in which they wrote about values and aspects of their lives that they cared deeply about—a process that previous research has shown to reaffirm for individuals that they are good, valued people. The other half wrote about values and aspects of life that they did not care much about. African American students performed significantly better in the class if they had written about values they cared about, but the writing manipulation had no effect on the European American students. Cohen and his colleagues reported that this subtle, simple manipulation reduced the racial achievement gap among these students by 40 percent.

Perhaps most encouraging for readers of this section of the textbook: Simply learning about stereotype threat enabled women in one study to avoid succumbing to the underperformance on a math test that was exhibited by threatened women who were not educated about stereotype threat (Johns et al., 2005).

Part of the initial excitement when Claude Steele introduced this theory was that it spoke to a profound social problem but offered encouragement rather than pessimism. It illustrated that through changes in the situational factors that give rise to this phenomenon, the tremendous weight of negative stereotypes can be reduced, allowing the targets of stereotypes to perform to their potential. In fact, outside of the laboratory, Steele and his colleagues were quick to apply their theory by creating a model program informed by the theory in a real university setting: what Steele called a "wise" environment that fostered interracial contact and cooperation and reduced factors that contribute to stereotype threat. Researchers found that the black students in this program showed almost no underperformance in their grades and were much less likely than other black students to drop out of school (Steele, 1997).

Reducing Stereotypes, Prejudice, and Discrimination

The descriptions of the Kanye West remarks and the Amadou Diallo tragedy that open the chapter and the exciting research of Claude Steele and others that closed the last section illustrate some of the problems and prospects concerning stereotypes, prejudice, and discrimination. In this final section, we focus more specifically on some of the approaches that have been suggested for combating stereotypes, prejudice, and discrimination, and we point to directions we expect future research to follow on the road toward more progress.

 Intergroup Contact

One of the classic books written on prejudice is Gordon Allport's (1954) *The Nature of Prejudice*. The book was unprecedented in its scope and gave important insights into the social psychology of prejudice. One of the many enduring ideas that Allport advanced was the **contact hypothesis**, which states that under certain conditions, direct contact between members of rival groups will reduce stereotyping, prejudice, and discrimination.

"See that man over there?"

"Yes."

"Well, I hate him."

"But you don't know him."

"That's why I hate him."

—Gordon Allport

Around the time of the publication of this book, in the historic 1954 case of *Brown v. Board of Education of Topeka,* the U.S. Supreme Court ruled that racially separate schools were inherently unequal, in violation of the Constitution. In part, the decision was informed by empirical evidence supplied by thirty-two eminent social scientists on the harmful effects of segregation on the self-esteem and academic achievement of black students as well as on race relations (Allport et al., 1953). The Supreme Court's decision propelled the nation into a large-scale social experiment. What would be the effect?

Despite the Court's ruling, desegregation proceeded slowly. There were stalling tactics, lawsuits, and vocal opposition to busing. Many schools remained untouched until the early 1970s. Then, as the dust began to settle, research brought the grave realization that little had changed—that contact between black and white schoolchildren was not having the intended effect. Walter Stephan (1986) reviewed studies conducted during and after desegregation and found that although 13 percent reported a decrease in prejudice among Whites, 34 percent reported no change, and 53 percent reported an *increase*. These findings forced social psychologists to challenge the wisdom of their testimony to the Supreme Court and to re-examine the contact hypothesis that had guided that advice in the first place.

Groups with a history of prejudice toward each other tend to become much less prejudiced soon after they are made to interact with each other in a desegregated setting. **False.**

Is the original contact hypothesis wrong? No. Although desegregation did not immediately produce the desired changes, it's important to realize that the ideal conditions for successful intergroup contact did not exist in the public schools. Nobody ever said that deeply rooted prejudices could be erased just by throwing groups together. According to the contact hypothesis, four conditions must exist for contact to succeed (see Table 5.7). In a recent meta-analysis involving research conducted on approximately 90,000 subjects from twenty-five different nations, Thomas Pettigrew and Linda Tropp (2000) found that when intergroup contact satisfies the chief requirements of the contact hypothesis, it does indeed tend to be successful in reducing prejudice. Furthermore, their analysis suggests that these conditions do not all have to be present for contact to reduce prejudice, although their presence clearly does enhance the positive effects of contact. This conclusion was bolstered by the results of a more recent meta-analysis by Pettigrew and Tropp (2006) of 515 studies, which indicated not only that intergroup contact often is successful in reducing intergroup prejudice, but also that contact theory can apply to a greater variety of different groups than the racial and ethnic groups that originally were the focus of this theory. Although many problems have plagued school and other desegregation efforts, such findings offer cause for optimism.

One of the most successful demonstrations of desegregation took place on the baseball diamond. On April 15, 1947, Jackie Robinson played for baseball's Brooklyn

contact hypothesis The theory that direct contact between hostile groups will reduce prejudice under certain conditions.

Dodgers—and became the first black man to break the color barrier in American sports. Robinson's opportunity came through Dodgers owner Branch Rickey, who felt that integrating baseball was both moral and good for the game (Pratkanis & Turner, 1994). Rickey knew all about the contact hypothesis and was assured by a social scientist friend that a team could furnish the conditions needed for it to work: equal status among teammates, personal interactions, dedication to a common goal, and a positive climate from the owner, managers, and coaches. The rest is history. Rickey signed Robinson and tried to create the situation necessary for success. Although Robinson did face a great deal of racism, he endured, and baseball was integrated. At the end of his first year, Jackie Robinson was named rookie of the year; and in 1962, he was elected to the Baseball Hall of Fame. At his induction ceremony, Robinson asked three people to stand beside him: his mother, his wife, and his friend Branch Rickey.

Another potential cause for optimism, although coupled perhaps with reasons to feel regret, is the finding by Nicole Shelton and Jennifer Richeson (2005) that both Whites and Blacks would like to have more contact with each other but believe that the other group does not want to have contact with them! As with stereotype threat, this may be a case in which education about the problem can be an important tool in correcting it.

With more frequent and more meaningful contact across racial and ethnic divides, a variety of the kinds of barriers we've discussed in this chapter can be weakened.

(Left) Students at Central High School in Little Rock, Arkansas, in September 1957 shout insults at Elizabeth Eckford, sixteen, as she walks toward the school entrance. National Guardsmen blocked the entrance and would not let her enter. (Right) Jackie Robinson and Branch Rickey discuss Robinson's contract with the Brooklyn Dodgers. In 1947 Robinson became the first African American to cross "the color line" and play Major League Baseball, thereby beginning the integration of major American sports.

According to a longitudinal study by Shana Levin and others (2007) of dating in college, for example, white, Asian American, and Latino students who dated outside their group more during college showed less ingroup bias and intergroup anxiety at the end of college.

 ## The Jigsaw Classroom

As the third condition in Table 5.7 indicates, cooperation and shared goals are necessary for intergroup contact to be successful. Yet the typical classroom is filled with competition, exactly the wrong ingredient. Picture the scene. The teacher stands in front of the class and asks a question. Many children wave their hands, each straining to catch the teacher's eye. Then, as soon as one student is called on, the others groan in frustration. In the competition for the teacher's approval, they are losers—hardly a scenario suited to positive intergroup contact. To combat this problem in the classroom, Elliot Aronson and his colleagues (1978) developed a cooperative learning method called the **jigsaw classroom**. In newly desegregated public schools in Texas and California, they assigned fifth-graders to small racially and academically mixed groups. The material to be learned within each group was divided into subtopics, much the way a jigsaw puzzle is broken into pieces. Each student was responsible for learning one piece of the puzzle, after which all members took turns teaching their material to one another. In this system, everyone—regardless of race, ability, or self-confidence—needs everyone else if the group as a whole is to succeed.

The method produced impressive results (Aronson, 2004). Compared with children in traditional classes, those in jigsaw classrooms grew to like each other more, liked school more, were less prejudiced, and had higher self-esteem. What's more, academic test scores improved for minority students and remained the same for white students. Much like an interracial sports team, the jigsaw classroom offers a promising way to create a truly integrated educational experience. It also provides a model of how to use interpersonal contact to promote greater tolerance of diversity.

 ## Decategorization and Recategorization

One important consequence of the jigsaw classroom technique is that individuals became more likely to classify outgroup members as part of their own ingroup. Instead of seeing racial or ethnic "others" within the classroom, the students now see fellow classmates, all in the same boat together. A growing body of research has emerged in support of the idea that intergroup contact emphasizing shared goals and fates, and involving the cross-cutting of group memberships (such that an individual in one's outgroup in one context will be in his or her ingroup in another context), can be very successful at reducing prejudice and discrimination—specifically by changing how group members categorize each other (Bettencourt & Dorr, 1998; Brewer, 2000; Devon, 2004).

According to the Common Ingroup Identity Model developed by John Dovidio, Samuel Gaertner, and others (Gaertner & Dovidio, 2000, 2005), this change comes about through two separate processes: *de*categorization and *re*categorization. Decategorization leads people not only to pay less attention to categories and intergroup boundaries but also to perceive outgroup members as individuals. Recategorization, in turn, leads people to change their conception of groups, allowing them to develop a more inclusive sense of the diversity characterizing their own ingroup. By recognizing members of an outgroup as ingroup members, just as the Rattlers and Eagles did when they converted from competitors to collaborators in Robbers Cave, "they" become "we," and a common ingroup identity can be forged.

 ## Changing Cultures and Motivations

Earlier in the chapter we reported some of the research showing the role that culture can play in perpetuating stereotypes and prejudice. It is at the cultural level that

jigsaw classroom A cooperative learning method used to reduce racial prejudice through interaction in group efforts.

While on the set of their hit television show, Grey's Anatomy, *Isaiah Washington (far right) used a derogatory term about gays, apparently in reference to his co-star, T. R. Knight (standing next to him in this photo). Not too many years ago such a slur might have been laughed off or ignored, but norms have changed in recent years. The public criticism of Washington eventually led him to publicly apologize and announce that he would undergo psychological treatment.*

much potential for positive change can be found as well. Exposure to images that reflect the diversity within social groups, for example, can help weaken stereotypes and combat their automatic activation. These images might also change people's implicit theories away from seeing groups as relatively fixed entities and toward seeing them as dynamic and with less rigid borders.

Motivations, norms, and values can and often do change over time. Here again popular culture is one key player. People—especially younger people—look to images in popular culture, as well as to their peers and role models, for a sense of current fashions and interests, but also, typically without realizing it, for what attitudes and behaviors are cool or out of date. We also look to our peers to get a sense of the local norms around us, including norms about stereotypes and prejudice (e.g., Crandall & Eshleman, 2003; Fein et al., 2003; Stangor et al., 2001). In a particular high school, a senior might feel comfortable calling a friend a "fag" and mean little by it and think nothing of it, and yet several months later in college this student might realize how wrong that is and feel guilty for ever having done so. If this lesson is learned, it's more likely to have been learned by watching and interacting with one's peers than from having been lectured to about diversity and sensitivity by a campus speaker. Learning these norms can make us motivated to adopt them. Legislating against hate speech, unequal treatment, and hostile environments can also be an important weapon, of course. Although they can create resistance and backlashes, laws and policies requiring behavior change can—if done right, with no suggestion of compromise, and with important leaders clearly behind them—cause hearts and minds to follow (Aronson, 1992).

Social psychologists today recognize that more and more people are motivated to not be prejudiced. The motivation may begin as a concern with not appearing to others to be prejudiced, but for many it becomes internalized—a much more effective antidote (Devine et al., 2005; Monteith et al., 2002).

Much of the hope, therefore, rests with what is at the very core of social psychology: the social nature of the human animal. Some of our baser instincts, such as intergroup competition breeding intergroup biases, may always be present, but we also can learn from each other the thoughts, values, and goals that make us less vulnerable to perpetuating or being the targets of stereotypes, prejudice, and discrimination.

REVIEW

- Stereotypes are beliefs that associate groups of people with certain characteristics.
- Prejudice refers to negative feelings toward persons based on their membership in certain groups.

- Discrimination concerns negative behaviors directed against persons because of their membership in a particular group. It is influenced by both beliefs and feelings about social groups.

Stereotypes

How Stereotypes Form

- Our shared history and culture influence the types of explanations that we give for the associations that we see in the world, thereby giving rise to stereotypes.
- The tendency for people to group themselves and others into social categories is also a key factor in stereotype formation.
- Social categories can be energy-saving devices, allowing perceivers to make quick inferences about group members; but these categories can lead to inaccurate judgments.
- Cultural and motivational factors can influence social categorization.
- Social categorization spawns the outgroup homogeneity effect, a tendency to assume that there is more similarity among members of outgroups than ingroups.
- Cultures differ in how they make ingroup-outgroup distinctions.
- Entity theorists, who tend to see groups more in trait terms and expect more similarity and consistency within groups, are more likely to use stereotypes when judging group members than are incremental theorists, who tend to see groups as more dynamic and malleable.
- Judging the accuracy of stereotypes is challenging, in part because "accuracy" can have different meanings. Some stereotypes are more accurate than others, but, in general, stereotypes exaggerate intergroup differences and understate intergroup similarities.

How Stereotypes Survive and Self-Perpetuate

- People perceive illusory correlations between groups and traits when the traits are distinctive or when the correlations fit prior notions.
- People tend to make attributions about the causes of group members' behaviors in ways that help maintain their stereotypes.
- Group members who do not fit the mold are often subtyped, leaving the overall stereotype intact. They force a revision of beliefs only when they are otherwise typical members of the group.
- Behaviors that differ markedly from stereotypic expectations can be judged even more discrepant than they really are as the result of a contrast effect.
- In general, though, people tend to interpret and remember information in ways that confirm existing stereotypes.

- The stereotypes that people hold about group members can lead them to behave in biased ways toward those members, sometimes causing the latter to behave consistently with the stereotypes and, hence, producing a self-fulfilling prophecy.

Is Stereotyping Inevitable? Automatic Versus Intentional Processes

- Stereotypes are often activated without our awareness and operate at an unconscious, or "implicit," level.
- Stereotype activation occurs automatically under some conditions, but it can also be influenced by a number of factors, including the accessibility of various stereotypes in perceivers' minds.
- Some motivations make stereotype activation more likely to occur, and others make it less likely. For example, when perceivers are highly motivated to form an accurate impression of someone, they are less likely to rely on stereotypes.
- Simply trying to suppress stereotypes from being activated can sometimes backfire, although it can work for people who are intrinsically motivated and do not believe the stereotype.
- Trying to suppress stereotyping can be cognitively tiring. When age, fatigue, busyness, or other cognitive impairment reduces people's cognitive resources, they are less able to control their stereotypes.
- Individual differences in prejudice and in being motivated by egalitarian goals can also affect the likelihood of automatic stereotyping.
- Recent research suggests a variety of strategies—such as training, taking the perspective of others, and thinking of counter-stereotypic examples—that can help suppress automatic activation of stereotypes.

"41 Shots" Revisited: Did Racial Stereotypes Make the Police More Likely to Shoot Amadou Diallo?

- Several recent studies have found that perceivers tend to be biased toward seeing an unarmed man as holding a weapon and posing a threat if he is black rather than white.
- Training may be effective in reducing civilians' or police officers' tendency to exhibit this bias.
- This bias is evident even among perceivers who do not endorse negative stereotypes or prejudiced attitudes.

Prejudice

Intergroup Conflict

- In the Robbers Cave study, boys divided into rival groups quickly showed intergroup prejudice, which was reduced when they were brought together through tasks that required intergroup cooperation.
- Realistic conflict theory maintains that direct competition for resources gives rise to prejudice.
- Prejudice is aroused by perceived threats to an important ingroup.

Social Identity Theory

- Participants categorized into arbitrary minimal groups discriminate in favor of the ingroup.
- Social identity theory proposes that self-esteem is influenced by the fate of social groups with which we identify.
- Research shows that threats to the self cause derogation of outgroups, which in turn increases self-esteem.

- Ingroup favoritism is more intense among people whose identity and self-esteem are closely tied to their group, people in relatively small minority groups, and people who need to secure or elevate their ingroup status because of their tenuous position in the group.
- Cultural differences can influence social identity processes, with individualists more likely to show overt ingroup-enhancing biases but collectivists possibly drawing sharper distinctions between ingroups and outgroups.

Implicit Theories and Ideologies

- People with a social dominance orientation exhibit a desire to see their ingroups as dominant over other groups, and they tend to show stronger ingroup identification and outgroup derogation.
- People who tend to endorse and legitimize existing social arrangements can show signs of outgroup favoritism even when their group holds a relatively disadvantaged position in society.

Sexism

- Sexism is a form of prejudice and discrimination based on a person's gender.

Gender Stereotypes: Blue for Boys, Pink for Girls

- Across the world, men are described as assertive, independent, and task-oriented; women as sensitive, dependent, and people-oriented.
- Boys and girls tend to show gender-stereotypical preferences for things like toys at very early ages.
- Gender stereotypes are so deeply ingrained that they bias perceptions of males and females from the moment they are born.

Culture and Popular Media

- Perceived differences between men and women are magnified by the contrasting social roles they occupy.
- The mass media foster gender distinctions in portrayals of males and females.
- Stereotypic media images of women and men have been implicated in the increased incidence of eating disorders and anxiety about physical appearance, and these images can affect both men's and women's behavior.

Ambivalent Sexism

- Ambivalent sexism reflects both hostile sexism, characterized by negative, resentful feelings toward women,

and benevolent sexism, characterized by affectionate, chivalrous, but potentially patronizing feelings toward women.
- Individuals from countries with the greatest degree of economic and political inequality between men and women tend to exhibit high levels of both hostile and benevolent sexism.

Sex Discrimination: Double Standards and Pervasive Stereotypes

- There are some striking sex differences in occupational choices.
- Men and women are judged more favorably when they apply for jobs that are consistent with gender stereotypes.
- Women often face a difficult dilemma: If they behave consistently with gender stereotypes, they may be liked more but respected less.
- Unlike most other stereotypes, gender stereotypes are more than just descriptive: They also indicate what the majority of people in a society believe men and women should be.

Racism

- Racism is a form of prejudice and discrimination based on a person's racial background.
- Individual, institutional, and cultural factors fuel racism.

Going Under Cover: Modern and Implicit Racism

- Over the years, surveys have recorded a decline in negative views of black Americans.
- However, more subtle, modern racism surfaces in less direct ways when people can rationalize racist behavior.

- People's ambivalence concerning race can lead them to exhibit biases in favor of or against particular groups, depending on the context.
- Racism often works implicitly, as stereotypes and prejudice can fuel discrimination without conscious intent or awareness on the part of perceivers.
- Researchers use covert measures to detect and measure modern and implicit racism and other subtle forms of prejudice and discrimination.

- Consistent with the concept of implicit racism is the finding that in criminal cases involving a white victim, the more a defendant's physical appearance is stereotypically black, the more likely he is to be given the death penalty.
- Individual differences in implicit racism can predict differences in perceptions of and reactions to others based on their race. For example, white perceivers relatively high in implicit racism are more likely to perceive hostility in the facial expressions of a black person than in a white person.

Interracial Perceptions and Interactions

- Seeing a member of a racial outgroup is associated with increased activation in the amygdala, a brain structure associated with emotion.
- Interracial interactions can feel threatening, anxiety-provoking, and cognitively draining, particularly among people relatively high in implicit racism.
- Worried about appearing racist in these interactions, Whites in particular may try to avoid interracial interactions, or they may go out of their way to avoid any mention of race even when it is relevant.

A Threat in the Air: Effects on the Targets of Stereotypes and Prejudice

- Stigmatized groups are negatively stereotyped and devalued in society.

Perceiving Discrimination

- When members of stigmatized groups perceive others' reactions to them as discrimination, they experience both benefits and drawbacks to their self-esteem and feelings of control.
- The frequency, and effects, of such perceptions depend in part on how and to what extent the target identifies with his or her stigmatized group.

Stereotype Threat and Academic Achievement

- Situations that activate stereotype threat cause individuals to worry that others will see them in negative, stereotypic ways.
- Social identity threat is similar to stereotype threat but concerns the experience of a threat that is not tied to specific stereotypes but instead reflects a more general devaluing of a person's social group
- Stereotype threat can impair the intellectual performance and affect the identity of stereotyped or devalued group members.
- Stereotype threat can cause African American and female students to fail to perform to their potential in academic settings.
- Threats to women's body image can cause women to underperform on an intellectual task.

- Research has documented a huge and growing list of groups whose members show underperformance and performance-impairing behaviors when a negative stereotype about their abilities is made relevant.
- Some new evidence points to increased arousal, attempts at suppressing negative stereotypes, impaired working memory, and experiencing dejection emotions or negative thinking as mechanisms through which stereotype threat creates underperformance.
- New research is also pointing to ways that individuals can be protected against these negative effects, such as through thinking about values that are important to them, blurring boundaries between groups, coping with threat through humor; attributing the arousal triggered by the threat to something nonthreatening, and thinking of examples of other group members who have been successful under threat.
- A study of seventh-graders showed that the simple manipulation of having some students think about values that were important to them dramatically improved the performance of African American students.
- Learning about stereotype threat may protect one against its negative effects.
- Reducing stereotype threat through slight changes in a setting can dramatically improve the performance of stereotyped group members.

Reducing Stereotypes, Prejudice, and Discrimination

Intergroup Contact

- In its 1954 ruling in *Brown v. Board of Education,* the U.S. Supreme Court ordered public schools to desegregate.
- Although, according to the contact hypothesis, desegregation should reduce prejudice, it did not cure the problem in the absence of key conditions of intergroup contact: equal status, personal interactions, the need to achieve a common goal, and social norms. When these conditions are met, intergroup contact tends to be much more successful in reducing prejudice.

The Jigsaw Classroom

- Schools often fail to meet the conditions for reducing prejudice, often because competition is too high. A program that is designed to foster intergroup cooperation and

interdependence suggests that the right kinds of contact can improve attitudes and behaviors in a school setting.

Decategorization and Recategorization

- Recent research has demonstrated that changing how group members categorize each other can reduce prejudice and discrimination.

Changing Cultures and Motivations

- Changes in the kinds of information perpetuated in one's culture can alter how we perceive social groups.
- As the general culture, and local norms, change to promote values consistent with fairness and diversity and inconsistent with prejudice and discrimination, individuals' motives can change accordingly.

KEY TERMS

PUTTING COMMON SENSE TO THE TEST

Very brief exposure to a member of a stereotyped group does not lead to biased judgments or responses, but longer exposure typically does.

False. Even very brief exposure to a member of a stereotyped group can activate the stereotype about the group, and this activation can bias subsequent judgments and reactions. Learning more information about the individual, however, sometimes reduces the effects of the stereotype.

Being reminded of one's own mortality makes people put things into greater perspective, thereby tending to reduce ingroup-outgroup distinctions and hostilities.

False. Research has shown that when people feel threatened by thoughts of their own mortality, they tend to seek greater affiliation with their ingroups and exhibit greater prejudice against outgroups, in part to reaffirm their sense of place and purpose in the world.

Even brief exposure to sexist television commercials can significantly influence the behaviors of men and women.

True. Exposure to sexist commercials can make men behave in more sexist ways toward women and can make women engage in more stereotypical behaviors.

An African American student is likely to perform worse on an athletic task if the task is described as one reflecting sports intelligence than if it is described as reflecting natural athletic ability.

True. Research on stereotype threat suggests that African American students are likely to be concerned about being seen through the lens of negative stereotypes concerning their intelligence if the task is described as one that is diagnostic of their sports intelligence—a situation that could undermine their performance. White students tend to show the opposite effect: Their performance is worse if the task is described as reflecting natural athletic ability.

Groups with a history of prejudice toward each other tend to become much less prejudiced soon after they are made to interact with each other in a desegregated setting.

False. When the contact between groups involves unequal status between them, lacks personal interaction between individual group members, and does not involve cooperation to achieve shared goals, contact is not likely to reduce prejudice.

6

Attitudes

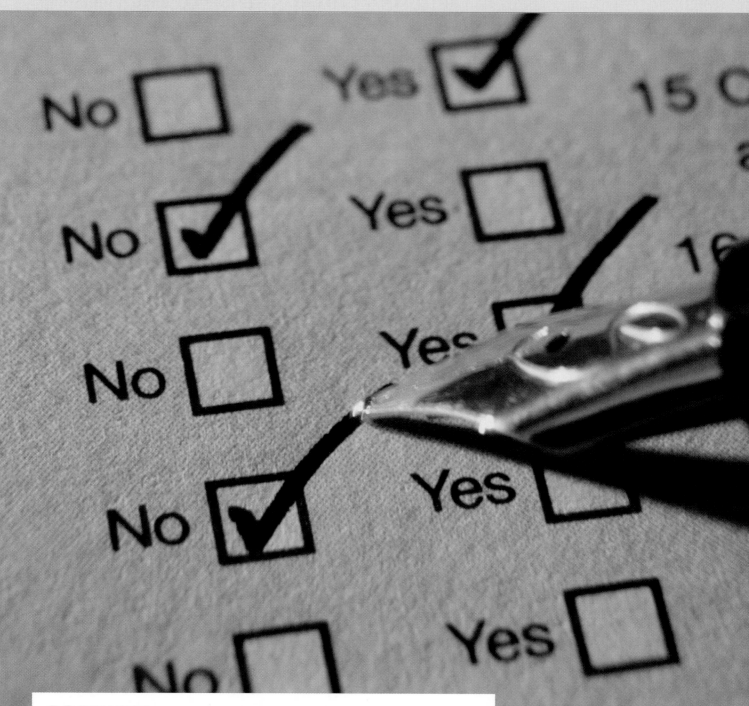

PREVIEW

This chapter examines social influences on *attitudes*. We define attitudes and then discuss how they are measured and when they are related to behavior. Then we consider two methods of changing attitudes. First, we look at source, message, and audience factors that win *persuasion through the media of communication*. Second, we consider theories and research showing that people often *change their attitudes* as a consequence of their own actions.

T/F

_____ Researchers can tell if someone has a positive or negative attitude by measuring physiological arousal.

_____ In reacting to persuasive communications, people are influenced more by superficial images than by logical arguments.

_____ People are most easily persuaded by commercial messages that are presented without their awareness.

_____ The more money you pay people to tell a lie, the more they will come to believe it.

_____ People often come to like what they suffer for.

Al Qaeda. Abortion rights. The death penalty. The stock market. Gay marriage. Illegal immigration. Gun control. War and peace. The SATs. Democrats and Republicans. Israelis and Palestinians. Anyone who has followed recent events in the United States—or anywhere else in the world, for that matter—knows how passionately people feel about the issues of the day. Attitudes and the mechanisms of attitude change, or persuasion, are a vital part of human social life. This chapter addresses three sets of questions: (1) What is an attitude, how can it be measured, and what is its link to behavior? (2) What kinds of persuasive communications lead people to change their attitudes? (3) Why do we often change our attitudes as a result of our own actions?

The Study of Attitudes

Do you favor or oppose a ban on assault weapons? Should smoking be prohibited in public places? Should the United States build a fence across its borders with Mexico? Would you rather listen to rock music or jazz, drink Coke or Pepsi, work on a PC or a Mac? Should terrorism be contained by war or conciliation? As these questions suggest, each of us has positive and negative reactions to various persons, objects, and ideas. These reactions are called **attitudes**. Skim the chapters in this book, and you'll see just how pervasive attitudes are. You'll see, for example, that self-esteem is an attitude we hold about ourselves, that attraction is a positive attitude toward another person, and that prejudice is a negative attitude often directed against certain groups. Indeed, the study of attitudes—what they are, where they come from, how they can be measured, what causes them to change, and how they interact with behavior—is central to the whole field of social psychology (Ajzen, 2001; Albarracín et al., 2005; Crano & Prislin, 2006; Perloff, 2003; Petty & Chaiken, 2004).

An attitude is a positive, negative, or mixed evaluation of an object, expressed at some level of intensity—nothing more, nothing less. *Like, love, dislike, hate, admire,* and *detest* are the kinds of words that people use to describe their attitudes.

It's important to realize that attitudes cannot simply be represented along a single continuum ranging from wholly positive to wholly negative—as you might expect if attitudes were like the balance knob on a stereo that directs sound to the left or right speaker or like the lever on a thermostat that raises or lowers temperature. Rather, as depicted in Figure 6.1, our attitudes can vary in strength along both positive and negative dimensions. In other words, we can react to something with positive affect,

attitude A positive, negative, or mixed reaction to a person, object, or idea.

FIGURE 6.1

Four Possible Reactions to Attitude Objects

As shown, people evaluate objects along both positive and negative dimensions. As a result, our attitudes can be positive, negative, ambivalent, or indifferent.

(Cacioppo et al., 1997.)

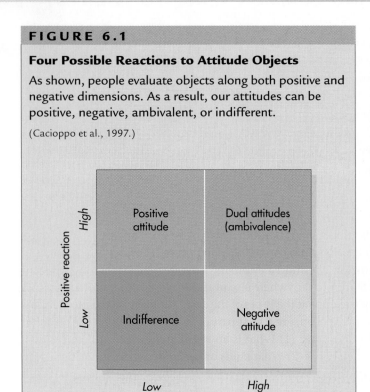

with negative affect, with ambivalence (strong but mixed emotions), or with apathy and indifference (Cacioppo et al., 1997). Some people more than others are troubled by this type of inconsistency (Newby-Clark et al., 2002). In fact, at times we can have both positive and negative reactions to the same attitude object without feeling conflict, as when we are conscious of one reaction but not the other. Someone who is openly positive toward racial minorities but unconsciously harbors prejudice is a case in point (Wilson et al., 2000).

Everyone routinely forms positive and/or negative evaluations of the people, places, objects, and ideas they encounter. This process is often immediate and automatic, like a reflex action (Bargh et al., 1996; Cunningham et al., 2003; Duckworth et al., 2002). It now appears, however, that individuals differ in the extent to which they tend to react to stimuli in strong positive and negative terms. What about you—do you form opinions easily? Do you have strong likes and dislikes? Or do you tend to react in more objective, nonevaluative ways? People who describe themselves as high rather than low in the *need for evaluation* are more likely to view their daily experiences in judgmental terms. They are also more opinionated on a whole range of social, moral, and political issues (Jarvis & Petty, 1996).

Before we examine the elusive science of measuring people's attitudes, let's stop for a moment and ponder this question: Why do human beings bother to have attitudes? Does forming a positive or negative judgment of people, objects, and ideas serve any useful purpose?

Over the years, researchers have found that attitudes serve important functions, such as enabling us to judge, quickly and without much thought, whether something we encounter is good or bad, helpful or hurtful, and to be sought or avoided (Maio & Olson, 2000). The problem is that having pre-existing attitudes about persons, objects, and ideas can lead us to become closed-minded, bias the way we interpret new information, and make us more resistant to change. For example, Russell Fazio and others (2000) found that people who were focused on their positive or negative attitudes toward computerized faces, compared to those who were not, were later slower to notice when the faces were "morphed" and no longer the same.

 ## How Attitudes Are Measured

In 1928, Louis Thurstone published an article entitled "Attitudes Can Be Measured." What Thurstone failed to anticipate, however, is that attitude measurement is tricky business. One review of research uncovered more than five hundred different methods of determining an individual's attitudes (Fishbein & Ajzen, 1972).

Self-Report Measures   The easiest way to assess a person's attitude about something is to ask. All over the world, public opinions are assessed on a range of issues—in politics, the economy, health care, foreign affairs, science and technology, sports, entertainment, religion, and lifestyles. Simply by asking, recent Harris polls have revealed that Americans prefer football to baseball as a favorite sport; prefer reading to watching TV; rate scientists, firefighters, doctors, and teachers as the most prestigious occupations; like California, Florida, Hawaii, and Colorado as states to live in other than their own; and are most eager to vacation in Australia, Italy, Great Britain, and France (http://www.harrisinteractive.com/).

Self-report measures are direct and straightforward. But attitudes are sometimes too

As seen in this Mexican American rally for immigration rights, which was part of a nationwide work boycott, people can be very passionate about the attitudes they hold.

complex to be measured by a single question. As you may recall from Chapter 2, one problem recognized by public opinion pollsters is that responses to attitude questions can be influenced by their wording, the order and context in which they are asked, and other extraneous factors (Schwarz, 1999; Tourangeau et al., 2000). Several years ago, for example, six hundred Americans were asked if the U.S. government spent too much money on "assistance to the poor," and only 23 percent agreed. Yet when the very same question was asked about "welfare," the agreement rate rose to 53 percent (*Time*, 1994).

Recognizing the shortcomings of single-question measures, researchers who study people's social and political opinions often use multiple-item questionnaires known as **attitude scales** (Robinson, Shaver, & Wrightsman, 1991, 1998). Attitude scales come in different forms, perhaps the most popular being the *Likert Scale*, named after its inventor, Rensis Likert (1932). In this technique, respondents are presented with a list of statements about an attitude object and are asked to indicate on a multiple-point scale how strongly they agree or disagree with each statement. Each respondent's total attitude score is derived by summing his or her responses to all the items. However, regardless of whether attitudes are measured by one question or by a full-blown scale, the results should be taken with caution. All self-report measures assume that people honestly express their true opinions. Sometimes this assumption is reasonable and correct, but often it is not. Wanting to make a good impression on others, people are often reluctant to admit to their failures, vices, weaknesses, unpopular opinions, and prejudices.

One approach to this problem is to increase the accuracy of self-report measures. To get respondents to answer attitude questions more truthfully, researchers sometimes use the **bogus pipeline**, an elaborate mechanical device that supposedly records our true feelings like a lie-detector test. Not wanting to get caught in a lie, and embarrassed, respondents tend to answer attitude questions with less social desirability bias when they think that deception would be detected by the bogus pipeline (Jones & Sigall, 1971; Roese & Jamieson, 1993). For example, Roger Tourangeau and others (1997) found that people were more likely to admit to drinking too much, using cocaine, having frequent oral sex, and not exercising enough when the bogus pipeline was used than when it was not.

Covert Measures   A second general approach to the self-report problem is to collect indirect, covert measures of attitudes that cannot be controlled. One possibility in this regard is to use observable behavior such as facial expressions, tone of voice, and body language. In one study, Gary Wells and Richard Petty (1980) secretly videotaped college students as they listened to a speech and noticed that when the speaker took a position that the students agreed with (that tuition costs should be lowered), most made vertical head movements. But when the speaker took a contrary position (that tuition costs should be raised), head movements were in a horizontal direction. Without realizing it, the students had signaled their attitudes by nodding and shaking their heads.

Although behavior provides clues, it is far from perfect as a measure of attitudes. Sometimes, we nod our heads because we agree; at other times, we nod to be polite. The problem is that people monitor their overt behavior just as they monitor self-reports.

attitude scale   A multiple-item questionnaire designed to measure a person's attitude toward some object.

bogus pipeline   A phony lie-detector device that is sometimes used to get respondents to give truthful answers to sensitive questions.

"No, I don't want to know what my approval rating is."

These days, it seems, attitude measurement is all around us.

Researchers can tell if someone has a positive or negative attitude by measuring physiological arousal. **False.**

facial electromyograph (EMG) An electronic instrument that records facial muscle activity associated with emotions and attitudes.

implicit attitude An attitude, such as prejudice, that one is not aware of having.

Implicit Association Test (IAT) A covert measure of unconscious attitudes derived from the speed at which people respond to pairings of concepts—such as *black* or *white* with *good* or *bad*.

But what about internal, physiological reactions that are difficult if not impossible to control? Does the body betray how we feel? In the past, researchers tried to divine attitudes from involuntary physical reactions such as perspiration, heart rate, and pupil dilation. The result, however, was always the same: Measures of arousal reveal the intensity of one's attitude toward an object but not whether that attitude itself is positive or negative. On the physiological record, love and hate look very much the same (Petty & Cacioppo, 1983).

Although physiological arousal measures cannot distinguish between positive and negative attitudes, some exciting alternatives have been discovered. One is the **facial electromyograph (EMG)**. As shown in Figure 6.2, certain muscles in the face contract when we are happy, and different facial muscles contract when we are sad. Some of the muscular changes cannot be seen with the naked eye, however, so the facial EMG is used. To determine whether the EMG can be used to measure the affect associated with attitudes, John Cacioppo and Richard Petty (1981) recorded facial muscle activity of college students as they listened to a message with which they agreed or disagreed. The agreeable message increased activity in the cheek muscles—the facial pattern that is characteristic of happiness. The disagreeable message sparked activity in the forehead and brow area—the facial patterns that are associated with sadness and distress. Outside observers who later watched the participants were unable to see these subtle changes. Apparently, the muscles in the human face reveal smiles, frowns, and other reactions to attitude objects that otherwise are hidden from view (Cacioppo et al., 1986; Tassinary & Cacioppo, 1992).

From a social neuroscience perspective, electrical activity in the brain may also assist in the measure of attitudes. In 1929, Hans Burger invented a machine that could detect, amplify, and record "waves" of electrical activity in the brain through electrodes pasted to the surface of the scalp. The instrument is called an *electroencephalograph*, or EEG, and the information it provides takes the form of line tracings called *brain waves*. Based on an earlier discovery, that certain patterns of electrical brain activity are triggered by exposure to stimuli that are novel or inconsistent, Cacioppo and others (1993) had participants list ten items they liked and ten they did not like within various object categories (fruits, sports, movies, universities, etc.). Later, these participants were brought into the laboratory, wired to an EEG, and presented with a list of category words that depicted objects they liked and disliked. The result: Brain-wave patterns normally triggered by inconsistency increased more when a disliked stimulus appeared after a string of positive items, or when a liked stimulus was shown after a string of negative items, than when either stimulus evoked the same attitude as the items that preceded it. In another study, researchers used fMRI to record brain activity in participants as they read names of famous figures, such as Adolph Hitler and Bill Cosby. When the names were read, they observed greater activity in the amygdala, a structure in the brain associated with emotion—regardless of whether or not participants evaluated the famous figures (Cunningham et al., 2003). This suggests that people react automatically to positive and negative attitude objects. Although more research is needed, it appears that attitudes may be measurable by electrical activity in the brain.

The Implicit Association Test (IAT) When it comes to covert measurement, one particularly interesting development is based on the notion that each of us has all sorts of **implicit attitudes** that we cannot self-report in questionnaires because we are not aware of having them (Fazio & Olson, 2003). To measure these unconscious attitudes, Anthony Greenwald, Mahzarin Banaji, Brian Nosek, and others have developed the **Implicit Association Test (IAT)**. As we saw in Chapter 5, the IAT measures the speed with which people associate pairs of concepts (Greenwald et al., 1998). To see how it works, try visiting the IAT Web site by typing "Implicit Association Test" in a search engine or www.yale.edu/implicit.

students were, the more consistent their environmental attitudes were with their behavior (Kallgren & Wood, 1986).

Second, the strength of an attitude is indicated not only by the *amount* of information on which it is based but also by *how* that information was acquired. Research shows that attitudes are more stable and more predictive of behavior when they are born of direct personal experience than when based on indirect, second-hand information. In a series of experiments, for example, Russell Fazio and Mark Zanna (1981) introduced two groups of participants to a set of puzzles. One group worked on sample puzzles; the other group merely watched someone else work on them. All participants were then asked to rate their interest in the puzzles (attitude) and were given an opportunity to spend time on them (behavior). As it turned out, attitudes and behaviors were more consistent among participants who had previously sampled the puzzles.

Third, an attitude can be strengthened, ironically, by an attack against it from a persuasive message. According to Zakary Tormala and Richard Petty (2002), people hold attitudes with varying degrees of certainty, and they become more confident after they successfully resist changing that attitude in response to a persuasive communication. In one study, researchers confronted university students with an unpopular proposal to add senior comprehensive exams as a graduation requirement. Each student read a pro-exam argument that was described as strong or weak, after which they were asked to write down counterarguments and indicate their attitude toward the policy. The result: Students who continued to oppose the policy despite reading what they thought to be a strong argument became even more certain of their opinion. Additional studies have shown that this effect depends on how satisfied people are with their own resistance. When people resist a strong message and believe that they have done so in a compelling way, they become more certain of their attitude and more likely to form a behavioral intention that is consistent with it. When people resist a persuasive message "by the skin of their teeth," however, and see their own counterarguments as weak, they become less certain of their initial attitude and more vulnerable to subsequent attack (Tormala et al., 2006).

A fourth key factor is that strong attitudes are highly accessible to awareness, which means they are quickly and easily brought to mind (Fazio, 1990). To return to our earlier examples, computer jocks think often about their computer preferences, and political activists think often about their party allegiances. It turns out that many attitudes—not just those we feel strongly about—easily pop to mind by the mere sight or even just the mention of an attitude object (Bargh et al., 1992). When this happens, the attitude can trigger behavior in a quick, spontaneous way or by leading us to think carefully about how we feel and how to respond (Fazio & Towles-Schwen, 1999).

To summarize, research on the link between attitudes and behavior leads to an important conclusion. Our evaluations of an object do not always determine our actions because other factors must be taken into account. However, when attitudes are strong and specific to a behavior, the effects are beyond dispute. Under these conditions, voting is influenced by political opinions, consumer purchasing is affected by product attitudes, and racial discrimination is rooted in feelings of prejudice. Attitudes are important determinants of behavior. The question now is, How can attitudes be changed?

Persuasion by Communication

Television provides a major outlet for commercial persuasion. The average American watches 30 hours of TV per week and views roughly 37,822 commercials per year.

On a day-to-day basis, we are all involved in the process of changing attitudes. Advertisers flood consumers with ad campaigns designed to sell cars, soft drinks, MP3 players, sneakers, and Internet services. Likewise, politicians make speeches, run TV commercials, pass out bumper stickers, and kiss babies to win votes. Attitude change is sought whenever parents socialize their children, scientists advance theories, religious groups seek converts, financial analysts recommend stocks, or trial lawyers argue cases to a jury. Some appeals work; others do not. Some are soft and subtle; others are hard and blatant. Some serve the public interest, whereas others serve personal interests. The point is, there is nothing inherently evil or

In U.S. presidential politics, candidates try to win votes by addressing the issues, as in debates and speeches delivered from a podium (the central route), or through the use of banners, balloons, music, and other theatrics (the peripheral route).

virtuous about changing attitudes, a process known as **persuasion**. We do it all the time.

If you wanted to change someone's attitude on an issue, you'd probably try by making a persuasive *communication*. Appeals made in person and through the mass media rely on the spoken word, the written word, and the image that is worth a thousand words. What determines whether an appeal succeeds or fails? To understand why certain approaches are effective while others are not, social psychologists have, for many years, sought to understand *how* and *why* persuasive communications work. For that, we need a road map of the persuasion process.

Two Routes to Persuasion

It's a familiar scene in American politics: Every four years, two or more presidential candidates launch extensive campaigns for office. In a way, if you've seen one election, you've seen them all. The names and dates may change; but over and over again, opposing candidates accuse each other of ducking the issues and turning the election into a flag-waving popularity contest. True or not, these accusations show that politicians are keenly aware that they can win votes through two different methods. They can stick to the issues, or they can base their appeals on other grounds.

To account for these alternative approaches, Richard Petty and John Cacioppo (1986) proposed a dual-process model of persuasion. This model assumes that we do not always process communications the same way. When people think critically about the contents of a message, they are said to take a **central route to persuasion** and are influenced by the strength and quality of the arguments. When people do not think critically about the contents of a message but focus instead on other cues, they take a **peripheral route to persuasion**. As we'll see, the route taken depends on whether one is willing and able to scrutinize the information contained in the message itself. Over the years, this model has provided an important framework for understanding the factors that elicit persuasion (Petty & Wegener, 1999).

The Central Route In the first systematic attempt to study persuasion, Carl Hovland and colleagues (1949, 1953) started the Yale Communication and Attitude Change Program. They proposed that for a persuasive message to have influence, the recipients of that message must learn its contents and be motivated to accept it. According to this view, people can be persuaded only by an argument they attend to, comprehend, and retain in memory for later use. Regardless of whether the message takes the form of a live personal appeal, a newspaper editorial, a Sunday sermon, a TV commercial, or a popup window on a Web site, these basic requirements remain the same.

A few years later, William McGuire (1969) reiterated the information-processing steps necessary for persuasion and, like the Yale group before him, distinguished between the learning, or *reception,* of a message, a necessary first step, and its later *acceptance.* In fact, McGuire (1968) used this distinction to explain the surprising finding

persuasion The process by which attitudes are changed.

central route to persuasion The process by which a person thinks carefully about a communication and is influenced by the strength of its arguments.

peripheral route to persuasion The process by which a person does not think carefully about a communication and is influenced instead by superficial cues.

that a recipient's self-esteem and intelligence are unrelated to persuasion. In McGuire's analysis, these characteristics have opposite effects on reception and acceptance. People who are smart or high in self-esteem are better able to learn a message but are less likely to accept its call for a change in attitude. People who are less smart or low in self-esteem are more willing to accept the message but they may have trouble learning its contents. Overall, then, neither group is generally more vulnerable to persuasion than the other—a prediction that is supported by a good deal of research (Rhodes & Wood, 1992).

Anthony Greenwald (1968) and others then argued that persuasion requires a third, intermediate step: **elaboration**. To illustrate, imagine you are offered a job and your prospective employer tries to convince you over lunch to accept. You listen closely, learn the terms of the offer, and understand what it means. But if it's an important interview, your head will spin with questions as you weigh all the pros and cons and contemplate the implications: What would it cost to move? Is there potential for advancement? Am I better off staying where I am? When confronted with personally significant messages, we don't just listen for the sake of collecting information—we think about that information. The message is then effective to the extent that it leads us to focus on favorable rather than unfavorable thoughts.

These theories of attitude change all share the assumption that the recipients of persuasive appeals are attentive, active, critical, and thoughtful of every word spoken. This assumption is correct—some of the time. When it is, and when people consider a message carefully, their reaction to it depends on the strength of its contents. In these instances, messages have greater impact when they are easily learned rather than difficult, when they are memorable rather than forgettable, and when they stimulate favorable rather than unfavorable elaboration. Ultimately, strong arguments are persuasive, and weak arguments are not.

On the central route to persuasion, the process is eminently rational. It's important to note, however, that thinking carefully about a persuasive message does not guarantee that the process is objective or that it necessarily promotes truth-seeking. At times, each of us prefers to hold a particular attitude, thus becoming biased in the way we process information (Petty & Wegener, 1999). Among college students who were politically conservative or liberal, the tendency to agree with a social welfare policy was influenced more by whether it was said to have the support of Democrats or Republicans than by the substantive merits of the policy itself (Cohen, 2003). Similarly, college students were less likely to be persuaded by a proposed tuition hike to fund campus improvements when the increase would take effect in one year, thus raising the personal stakes, than after eight years (Darke & Chaiken, 2005). To further complicate matters, people who want to hold the right attitudes may fear that they are biased or overly influenced by nonrelevant factors and try to correct for that bias, sometimes with an ironic result: overcorrection. In one study, for example, audience members who were forewarned that people are prone to agree with speakers they like later exhibited more attitude change in response to a speaker who was clearly not likable (Petty et al., 1998).

The Peripheral Route "The receptive ability of the masses is very limited, their understanding small; on the other hand, they have a great power of forgetting." The author of this statement was Adolf Hitler (1933, p. 77). Believing that human beings are incompetent processors of information, Hitler relied heavily in his propaganda on the use of slogans, uniforms, marching bands, flags, and other symbols. For Hitler, "Meetings were not just occasions to make speeches; they were carefully planned theatrical productions in which settings, lighting, background music, and the timing of entrances were devised to maximize the emotional fervor of an audience" (Qualter, 1962, p. 112). Do these ploys work? Can the masses be handily manipulated into persuasion? History shows that they can. Audiences are not always thoughtful. Sometimes people do not follow the central route to persuasion but instead take a short cut through the peripheral route. Rather than try to learn about a message and think through the issues, they respond with little effort on the basis of superficial, peripheral cues.

On the peripheral route to persuasion, people will often evaluate a communication by using simple-minded heuristics, or rules of thumb (Chaiken, 1987; Chen

Getting the audience's attention is a first step to persuasion that cannot be taken for granted. According to a Harris poll, 7 out of 10 Americans said they often lower the volume or switch channels to avoid TV commercials.

elaboration The process of thinking about and scrutinizing the arguments contained in a persuasive communication.

& Chaiken, 1999). If a communicator has a good reputation, speaks fluently, or writes well, we tend to assume that his or her message must be correct. And when a speaker has a reputation for being honest, people think less critically about the specific contents of his or her communication (Priester & Petty, 1995). Likewise, we assume that a message must be correct if it contains a long litany of arguments, or statistics, or an impressive list of supporting experts; if it's familiar; if it elicits cheers from an audience; or if the speaker seems to be arguing against his or her own interests. In some cases, simply knowing that an argument has majority support will get people to change their attitudes (Giner-Sorolla & Chaiken, 1997).

On the mindless peripheral route, people are also influenced by a host of attitude-irrelevant factors, such as cues from their own body movements. In one study, participants were coaxed into nodding their heads up and down (as if saying "yes") or shaking them from side to side (as if saying "no") while listening via headphones to an editorial, presumably to test whether the headphones could endure the physical activity. Those coaxed into nodding later agreed more with the arguments than those coaxed into shaking their heads (Wells & Petty, 1980). In other studies, participants viewed and rated graphic symbols or word-like stimuli (*surtel*, *primet*) while using an exercise bar to either stretch their arms out (which mimics what we do to push something away) or flex their arms in (which we do to bring something closer). These stimuli were later judged to be more pleasant when associated with the flexing of the arm than with the stretching-out motion (Cacioppo et al., 1993; Priester et al., 1996).

Route Selection Thanks to Petty and Cacioppo's (1986) two-track distinction between the central and peripheral routes, we can better understand why the persuasion process seems so logical on some occasions yet so illogical on others—why voters may select candidates according to issues or images, why juries may base their verdicts on evidence or a defendant's appearance, and why consumers may base their purchases on marketing reports or product images. The process that is engaged depends on whether the recipients of a persuasive message have the *ability* and the *motivation* to take the central route or whether they rely on peripheral cues instead.

To understand the conditions that lead people to take one route or the other, it's helpful to view persuasive communication as the outcome of three factors: a *source* (who), a *message* (says what and in what context), and an *audience* (to whom). Each of these factors steers a recipient's approach to a persuasive communication. If a source speaks clearly, if the message is important, if there is a bright, captive, and involved audience that cares deeply about the issue and has time to absorb the information, then audience members will be willing and able to take the effortful central route. But if the source speaks at a rate too fast to comprehend, if the message is trivial or too complex to process, or if audience members are distracted, pressed for time, or uninterested, then the less strenuous peripheral route is taken.

Figure 6.5 presents a road map of persuasive communication. In the next three sections, we will follow this map from the input factors (source, message, and audience), through the central or peripheral route processing strategies, to the final destination: persuasion.

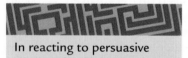

In reacting to persuasive communications, people are influenced more by superficial images than by logical arguments. **False.**

The Source

Golfer Tiger Woods is a living legend, one of the most gifted athletes of our time. He has also been paid more millions of dollars per year than just about anyone else—to endorse *Nike*, American Express, and other products. Why is Woods considered an effective spokesman? What makes some communicators, in general, more effective than others? As we'll see, there are two key attributes: credibility and likability.

Credibility Imagine you are waiting in line in a supermarket, and you catch a glimpse of a swollen headline: "Doctors Discover Cure for AIDS!" As your eye wanders across the front page, you discover that you are reading a supermarket tabloid. What would you think? Next, imagine that you are reading through scientific periodicals in a university library, and you come across a similar article, but this time it appears in the *New England Journal of Medicine*. Now what would you think?

FIGURE 6.5

Two Routes to Persuasion

Based on characteristics of the source, message, and audience, recipients of a communication take either a central or peripheral route to persuasion. On the central route, people are influenced by strong arguments and evidence. On the peripheral route, persuasion is based more on heuristics and other superficial cues. This two-process model helps explain how persuasion can seem logical on some occasions and illogical on others.

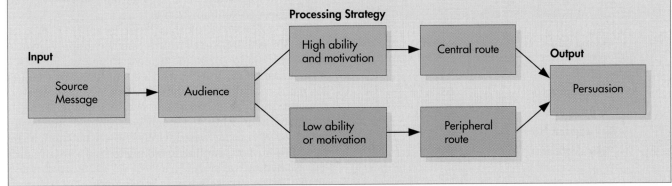

Chances are, you'd react with more excitement to the medical journal than to the tabloid, even though both sources report the same news item. In a study conducted during the cold war era of the 1950s, participants read a speech that advocated for the development of nuclear submarines. The speech elicited more agreement when it was attributed to an eminent American physicist than when the source was said to be the Soviet government newspaper *Pravda* (Hovland & Weiss, 1951). Likewise, when participants read a lecture favoring more lenient treatment of juvenile offenders, they changed their attitudes more when they thought the speaker was a judge rather than a convicted drug dealer (Kelman & Hovland, 1953). Now, after more than fifty years of research, it is clear that high-credibility sources are generally more persuasive than low-credibility sources (Pornpitakpan, 2004).

Why are some sources more believable than others? Why were the medical journal, the physicist, and the judge more credible than the tabloid, *Pravda*, and the drug dealer? For communicators to be seen as credible, they must have two characteristics: (1) competence, or expertise, and (2) trustworthiness. *Competence* refers to a speaker's ability. People who are knowledgeable, smart, or well spoken or who have impressive credentials are persuasive by virtue of their expertise (Hass, 1981). Experts can have a disarming effect on us. We assume they know what they're talking about. So when they speak, we listen. And when they take a position, even one that is extreme, we often yield. Unless an expert contradicts us on issues that are personally important, we tend to accept what he or she says without too much scrutiny (Maddux & Rogers, 1980), even when the message itself is ambiguous (Chaiken & Maheswaran, 1994).

Still, each of us is confronted by plenty of experts in life whose opinions do not sway us. The reason is that expertise alone is not enough. To have credibility, sources must also be *trustworthy;* that is, they must be seen as willing to report what they know truthfully and without compromise. What determines whether we trust a communicator? To some extent, we make these judgments on the basis of stereotypes. For example, the Gallup Organization asked a thousand Americans to rate how honest people were in various occupational categories. As shown in Table 6.1, nurses topped the list as the most trusted occupational group. Car salesmen were the least trusted.

In judging the credibility of a source, common sense arms us with a simple rule of caution: Beware of those who have something to gain from successful persuasion. If a speaker has been paid off, has an ax to grind, or is simply telling us what we want to hear, we suspect some degree of bias. This rule sheds light on a classic dilemma in advertising concerning the value of celebrity spokespersons: The more products a celebrity endorses, the less trustworthy he or she appears to consumers (Tripp et al., 1994). In the courtroom, the same rule of caution can be used to evaluate witnesses. In one study, research participants served as jurors in a mock trial in

TABLE 6.1
Whom Do You Trust?

In 2003, a CNN/USA Today Gallup poll was conducted to determine the level of honesty attributed to people from various occupational groups. Indicated below are the percentages of respondents who rated each group as "high" or "very high" in honesty.

Occupation	Honest? (%)
Nurses	83
Medical doctors	68
Pharmacists	68
College teachers	59
Police officers	59
Clergy	56
Bankers	35
Journalists	25
Business executives	18
Lawyers	16
Stockbrokers	15
Insurance salesmen	12
Car salesmen	7

which a man claimed that his exposure to an industrial chemical at work had caused him to contract cancer. Testifying in support of this claim was a biochemist who was paid either $4,800 or $75 for his expert testimony. You might think that jurors would be more impressed by the scientist who commanded the higher fee. Yet, while highly paid, the expert was perceived to be a "hired gun"—and was, as a result, less believable and less persuasive (Cooper & Neuhaus, 2000).

The self-interest rule has other interesting implications. One is that people are impressed by others who take unpopular stands or argue against their own interests. When research participants read a political speech accusing a large corporation of polluting a local river, those who thought that the speechmaker was a pro-environment candidate addressing a staunch environmentalist group perceived him to be biased, while those who thought he was a pro-business candidate talking to company supporters assumed he was sincere (Eagly et al., 1978). Trust is also established by speakers who are not purposely trying to change our views. Thus, people are influenced more when they think that they are accidentally overhearing a communication than when they receive a sales pitch clearly intended for their ears (Walster & Festinger, 1962). That's why advertisers sometimes use the "overheard communicator" trick, in which the source tells a buddy about a new product that really works. As if eavesdropping on a personal conversation, viewers assume that what one friend says to another can be trusted.

Likability   More than anything else, the celebrity power of Tiger Woods is based on his athletic dominance, his popularity, his youthful charm, and his winning smile. But do these qualities enhance someone's impact as a communicator? Yes. As Dale Carnegie (1936) implied in the title of his classic bestseller, *How to Win Friends and Influence People*, being liked and being persuasive go hand in hand. The question is, What makes a communicator likable? As we'll see in Chapter 9, two factors that spark attraction are *similarity* and *physical attractiveness*.

A study by Diane Mackie and others (1990) illustrates the persuasive power of similarity. Students enrolled at the University of California at Santa Barbara read a strong or a weak speech that argued against continued use of the SATs in college admissions. Half the participants were led to believe that the speech was written by a fellow UCSB student; the other half thought the author was a student from the University of New Hampshire. Very few participants were persuaded by the weak arguments. In contrast, many of those who read the strong message did change their attitudes, but only when they believed it was given by a fellow UCSB student.

Just as source similarity can spark persuasion, dissimilarity can have the opposite inhibiting effect. In a study of people's taste in music, Clayton Hilmert and others (2006) introduced participants to a confederate who seemed to like the same or different kinds of music, such as rock, pop, country, or classical. Others did not meet a confederate. When later asked to rate a particular song, participants were positively influenced by the similar confederate's opinion and negatively influenced by the dissimilar confederate's opinion. In fact, although the effect is more potent when the points of similarity seem relevant to the attitude in question (Berscheid, 1966), the participants in this study were also more or less persuaded by a confederate whose similarities or differences were wholly unrelated to music—for example, when the confederate had similar or different interests in shopping, world politics, museums, trying new foods, or surfing the Internet.

The effect of source similarity on persuasion has obvious implications for those who wish to exert influence. We're all similar to one another in some respects. We might agree in politics, share a common friend, have similar tastes in food, or enjoy spending summers on the same beach. If aware of the social benefits of similarity and the

Just out of high school, basketball star LeBron James (left) signed a multimillion dollar contract with Nike. Even more recently, Russian tennis star Maria Sharapova (right) was signed by a number of companies to promote cameras, tennis rackets, cell phones, cars, and watches. Can celebrities sell products? Targeting the peripheral route to persuasion, the advertising industry seems to think so.

social costs of dissimilarity, the astute communicator can use common bonds to enhance his or her impact on an audience.

When it comes to physical attractiveness, advertising practices presuppose that beauty is also persuasive. After all, billboards, magazine ads, and TV commercials routinely feature young and glamorous "supermodels" who are tall and slender (for women) or muscular (for men) and who have glowing complexions and radiant smiles. Sure, these models can turn heads, you may think, but can they change minds?

In a study that addressed this question, Shelly Chaiken (1979) had male and female college students approach others on campus. They introduced themselves as members of an organization that wanted the university to stop serving meat during breakfast and lunch. In each case, these student assistants gave reasons for the position and then asked respondents to sign a petition. The result: Attractive communicators were able to get 41 percent of respondents to sign the petition, whereas those who were less attractive succeeded only 32 percent of the time. Additional research has shown that attractive male and female salespersons elicit more positive attitudes and purchasing intentions from customers even when they are up front about their desire to make a sale (Reinhard et al., 2006).

When What You Say Is More Important Than Who You Are To this point, it must seem as if the source of a persuasive communication is more important than the communication itself. Is this true? Advertisers have long debated the value of high-priced celebrity endorsements. David Ogilvy (1985), often referred to as "the king of advertising," used to say that celebrities are not effective because viewers know they've been bought and paid for. Ogilvy was not alone in his skepticism. Still, many advertisers scramble furiously to sign up high-priced entertainers and athletes. From Tiger Woods to Derek Jeter, LeBron James, Peyton Manning, Maria Sharapova, and Teri Hatcher, TV commercials regularly feature a parade of stars. The bigger the star, they say, the more valuable the endorsement.

Compared with the contents of a message, does the source really make the big difference that advertisers pay for? Are we so impressed by the expert, and so drawn to the charming face, that we embrace whatever they have to say? And are we so scornful of ordinary or unattractive people that their presentations fall on deaf ears?

Advertisers are so convinced that beauty sells products that they pay millions of dollars for supermodels to appear in their ads. Here, top models Esther Canadas, from Spain, and Mark Vanderloo, her Dutch husband, launched the ad campaign for a DKNY fragrance for women.

In light of what is known about the central and peripheral routes to persuasion, the answer to these questions is "it depends."

First, a recipient's level of involvement plays an important role. When a message has personal relevance to your life, you pay attention to the source and think critically about the message, the arguments, and the implications. When a message does not have personal relevance, however, you may take the source at face value and spend little time scrutinizing the information. In a classic study, Richard Petty and others (1981) had students listen to a speaker who proposed that all seniors should be required to take comprehensive exams in order to graduate. Three aspects of the communication situation were varied. First, participants were led to believe that the speaker was either an education professor at Princeton University or a high school student. Second, participants heard either well-reasoned arguments and hard evidence or a weak message based only on anecdotes and personal opinion. And third, participants were told either that the proposed exams might be used the following year (Uh oh, that means me!) or that they would not take effect for another ten years (Who cares, I'll be long gone by then!).

As predicted, personal involvement determined the relative impact of source expertise and speech quality. Among participants who would not be affected by the proposed change, attitudes were based largely on the speaker's credibility: The professor was persuasive, the high school student was not. Among participants who thought that the proposed change would affect them directly, attitudes were based on the quality of the speaker's proposal: Strong arguments were persuasive, weak arguments were not. As depicted in Figure 6.6, people followed the source rather than the message under low levels of involvement, illustrating the peripheral route to persuasion. But message factors outweighed the source under high levels of involvement, when participants cared enough to take the central route to persuasion. Likewise, research has shown that the tilt toward likable and attractive communicators is reduced when recipients take the central route (Chaiken, 1980).

There is a second limit to source effects. It is often said that time heals all wounds. Well, time may also heal the effects of a bad reputation. Hovland and Weiss (1951) varied communicator credibility (for example, the physicist versus *Pravda*) and found that the change had a large and immediate effect on persuasion. But when they remeasured attitudes four weeks later, the effect had vanished. Over time, the attitude change produced by the high-credibility source decreased, and the change caused by the low-credibility source increased. This latter finding of a delayed persuasive impact of a low-credibility communicator is called the **sleeper effect**.

To explain this unforeseen result, the Hovland research group proposed the *discounting cue hypothesis*. According to this hypothesis, people immediately discount the arguments made by noncredible communicators; but over time, they dissociate what was said from who said it. In other words, we tend to remember the message but forget the source (Pratkanis et al., 1988). To examine the role of memory in this process, Kelman and Hovland (1953) reminded a group of participants of the source's identity before reassessing their attitudes. If the sleeper effect was caused by forgetting, they reasoned, then it could be eliminated through reinstatement of the link between the source and the message. As shown in Figure 6.7 (see p. 198), they were right. When attitudes were measured after three weeks, participants who were not reminded of the source showed the usual sleeper effect. Yet those who did receive a source reminder did not. For these latter participants, the effects of high and low credibility endured. Recent studies by cognitive psychologists have confirmed that, over time, people "forget" the connection between information and its source (Underwood & Pezdek, 1998).

The sleeper effect generated a good deal of controversy. There was never a doubt that credible communicators lose some impact over time. But researchers had a harder time finding evidence for delayed persuasion by noncredible sources. Exasperated at one point by their own failures to obtain this result, Paulette Gillig and

sleeper effect A delayed increase in the persuasive impact of a noncredible source.

FIGURE 6.6

Source Versus Message: The Role of Audience Involvement

People who were high or low in their personal involvement heard a strong or weak message from an expert or nonexpert. For high-involvement participants (left), persuasion was based on the strength of arguments, not on source expertise. For low-involvement participants (right), persuasion was based more on the source than on the arguments. Source characteristics have more impact on those who don't care enough to take the central route.

(Petty et al., 1981.)

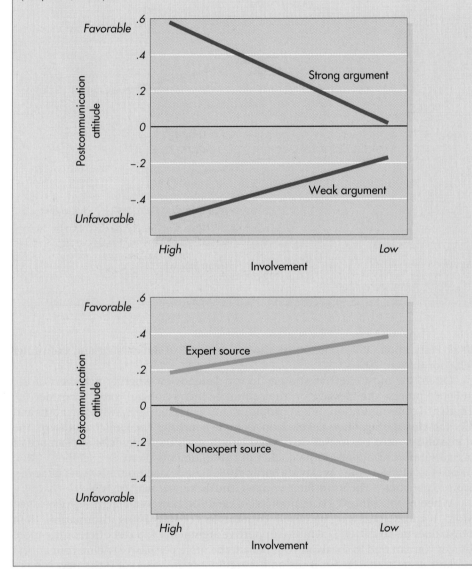

Anthony Greenwald (1974) wondered, "Is it time to lay the sleeper effect to rest?" As it turned out, the answer was no. More recent research showed that the sleeper effect is reliable provided that participants do not learn who the source is until *after* they have received the original message (Greenwald et al., 1986; Kumkale & Albarracín, 2004).

To appreciate the importance of timing, imagine that you're surfing the Internet and you come across what appears to be a review of a new CD. Before you begin reading, however, you notice in the fine print that this so-called review is really an advertisement. Aware that you can't always trust what you read, you skim the ad and reject it. Now imagine the same situation, except that you read the entire ad before realizing what it is. Again, you reject it. But notice the difference. This time, you have read the message with an open mind. You may then have rejected it; but after a few weeks, the information will have sunk in to influence your evaluation of the music. This experience illustrates the sleeper effect.

The Message

Obviously, not all sources are created equal; some are more credible or likable than others. On the peripheral route to persuasion, audiences are influenced heavily, maybe too heavily, by these and other source characteristics. But when people care about an issue, the strength of a message determines its impact. On the central route to persuasion, what matters most is whether a scientist's

> *"The truth is always the strongest argument."*
>
> —Sophocles

theory is supported by the data or whether a company has a sound product. Keep in mind, however, that the target of a persuasive appeal comes to know a message only through the medium of communication: *what* a person has to say and *how* that person says it.

Informational Strategies   Communicators often struggle over how to present an argument to maximize its impact. Should a message be long and crammed with facts or short and to the point? Is it better to present a highly partisan, one-sided message or take a more balanced, two-sided approach? And how should the various arguments be ordered—from strongest to weakest or the other way around? These are the kinds of questions often studied by persuasion researchers (Crano & Prislin,

FIGURE 6.7

The Sleeper Effect

In Experiment 1, participants changed their immediate attitudes more in response to a message from a high-credibility source than from a low-credibility source. When attitudes were remeasured after three weeks, the high-credibility source lost impact, and the low-credibility source gained impact—the sleeper effect. In Experiment 2, the sleeper effect disappeared when participants were reminded of the source.

(Kelman & Hovland, 1953.)

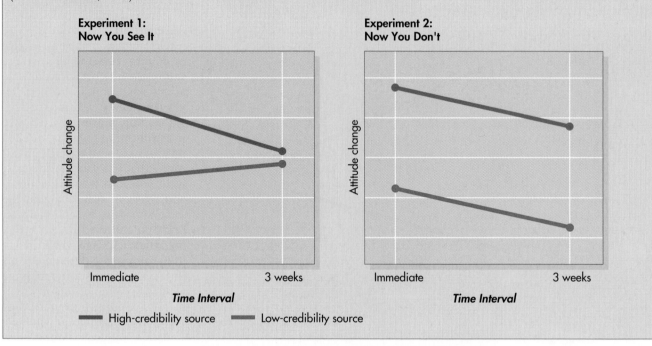

2006; Petty et al., 1997), including those interested in advertising and consumer behavior (Loken, 2006).

Often, the most effective strategy to use depends on whether members of the audience process the message on the central or the peripheral route. Consider the length of a communication. When people process a message lazily, with their eyes and ears half-closed, they often fall back on a simple heuristic: The longer a message, the more valid it must be. In this case, word length gives the superficial appearance of factual support regardless of the quality of the arguments (Petty & Cacioppo, 1984; Wood et al., 1985). Thus, as David Ogilvy (1985) concluded from his years of advertising experience, "The more facts you tell, the more you sell" (p. 88).

When people process a communication carefully, however, length is a two-edged sword. If a message is long because it contains lots of supporting information, then longer does mean better. The more supportive arguments you can offer, or the more sources you can find to speak on your behalf, the more persuasive will be your appeal (Harkins & Petty, 1981). But if the added arguments are weak, or if the new sources are redundant, then an alert audience will not be fooled by length alone. When adding to the length of a message dilutes its quality, an appeal might well *lose* impact (Friedrich et al., 1996; Harkins & Petty, 1987).

When two opposing sides try to persuade the same audience, presentation order becomes a relevant factor as well. During the summer of 2004, before the November presidential election, the Democrats held their national convention about a month before the incumbent Republicans held theirs. These events were watched on television by millions of voters. Do you think the order in which they were scheduled put one party at an advantage? If you believe that information presented first has more impact, you'd predict a *primacy effect* (advantage to the Democrats). If you believe that the information presented last has the edge, you'd predict a *recency effect* (advantage to the Republicans).

"It is a superb vision of America, all right, but I can't remember which candidate projected it."

Research on the sleeper effect shows that people often remember the message but forget the source.

There are good reasons for both predictions. On the one hand, first impressions are important. On the other hand, memory fades over time, and people often recall only the last argument they hear before making a decision. In light of these contrasting predictions, Norman Miller and Donald Campbell (1959) searched for the "missing link" that would determine the relative effects of primacy and recency. They discovered that the missing link is *time*. In a jury simulation study, they had people (1) read a summary of the plaintiff's case, (2) read a summary of the defendant's case, and (3) make a decision. The researchers varied how much time separated the two messages and then how much time elapsed between the second message and the decisions. When participants read the second message right after the first and then waited a whole week before reporting their opinion, a primacy effect prevailed, and the side that came first was favored. Both messages faded equally from memory, so only the greater impact of first impressions was left. Yet when participants made a decision immediately after the second message but a full week after the first, there was a recency effect. The second argument was fresher in memory, thus favoring the side that went last. Using these results as a guideline, let's return to our original question: What is the impact on election day of how the national conventions are scheduled? Think for a moment about the placement and timing of these events. The answer appears in Table 6.2.

Message Discrepancy Persuasion is a process of changing attitudes. But just how much change should be sought? Before addressing an audience, speakers confront what is perhaps the most critical strategic question: How extreme a position should they take? How *discrepant* should a message be from the audience's existing position in order to have the greatest impact? Common sense suggests two opposite answers. One approach is to take an extreme position in the hope that the more change you advocate, the more you get. Another approach is to exercise caution and not push for too much change so that the audience will not reject the message outright. Which approach seems more effective? Imagine trying to convert your politically conservative friends into liberals, or the other way around. Would you stake out a radical position in order to move them toward the center, or would you preach moderation so as not to be cast aside?

Research shows that communicators should adopt the second, more cautious approach. To be sure, some discrepancy is needed to produce a change in attitude. But the relationship to persuasion can be pictured as an upside-down U with the most change being produced at moderate amounts of discrepancy (Bochner & Insko, 1966). A study by Kari Edwards and Edward Smith (1996) helps to explain why taking a more extreme position is counterproductive. These investigators first measured people's attitudes on a number of hot social issues—for example, whether lesbian and gay couples should adopt children, whether employers should give preference in hiring to minorities, and whether the death penalty should be abolished. Several weeks later, they asked the same people to read, think about, and rate arguments that were either consistent or inconsistent with their own prior attitudes. The result: When given arguments to read that preached attitudes that were discrepant from their own, the participants

TABLE 6.2
Effects of Presentation Order and Timing on Persuasion

A study by Miller and Campbell (1959) demonstrated the effect of presentation order and the timing of opposing arguments on persuasion. As applied to our example, the Democratic and Republican conventions resemble the fourth row of this table. From these results, it seems that the scheduling of such events is fair, promoting neither primacy nor recency.

		Conditions				Results
1. **Message 1**	**Message 2**	One week	Decision			**Primacy**
2. **Message 1**	One week	**Message 2**	Decision			**Recency**
3. **Message 1**	**Message 2**	Decision				**None**
4. **Message 1**	One week	**Message 2**	One week	Decision		**None**

Public health organizations often use fear, or scare tactics, to change health-related attitudes and behavior.

Since the Ad Council initiated its "Friends don't let friends drive drunk" campaign, 79 percent of Americans say that they have personally stopped someone who had been drinking from taking the wheel of a car.

If you're interested in public service advertising, visit the Ad Council (www.adcouncil .org), an organization that created such highly effective public service characters as Smokey the Bear ("Only you can prevent forest fires") and the Crash Test Dummies ("Don't be a dummy— buckle up").

spent more time scrutinizing the material and judged the arguments to be weak. Apparently, people are quick to refute and reject persuasive messages they don't agree with. In fact, the more personally important an issue is to us, the more stubborn and resistant to change we become (Zuwerink & Devine, 1996).

Fear Appeals To win cases, many trial lawyers say that they have to appeal to jurors through the heart rather than through the mind. The evidence is important, they admit; but it also matters whether the jury reacts to their client with anger, disgust, sympathy, or sadness. Of course, very few messages are entirely based on rational argument or on emotion.

Fear is a particularly primitive and powerful emotion, serving as an early warning system that signals danger. Neuroscience research shows that fear is aroused instantly in response to pain, noxious stimulation, or threat, enabling us to respond in a rapid-fire manner without having to stop to think about it (LeDoux, 1996). Not surprisingly, the use of fear appeals to change attitudes is common. Certain religious cults use scare tactics to indoctrinate new members. So do public health organizations that graphically portray the victims of cigarette smoking, drugs, overeating, and unsafe sex.

Political campaigns are notorious for exploiting fear through negative advertising. The most hard-hitting and controversial ever was a TV commercial that aired just once, on September 7, 1964. In an ad to reelect Democratic president Lyndon Johnson, running against Republican Barry Goldwater, a young girl pictured in a field counted to ten as she picked the petals off a daisy. As she reached nine, an adult voice broke in to count down from ten to zero, followed by a blinding nuclear explosion and this message: "Vote for President Johnson on November 3. The stakes are too high for you to stay home."

The effects of fear arousal in politics are still evident today. Guided by Terror Management Theory (Greenberg et al., 1997; Pyszczynski et al., 2003; see Chapter 3) and the prediction that a deeply rooted fear of death motivates people to rally around their leaders as a way to ward off anxiety, Mark Landau and his colleagues (2004) found that college students expressed more support for President George W. Bush and his policies if they were reminded of their own mortality or subliminally exposed to images of 9/11 than if they were not. This result is not limited to the laboratory. Analyzing patterns of government-issued terror warnings and Gallup polls, Robb Willer (2004) found that increased terror alerts were predictably followed by increases in presidential approval ratings.

Is fear similarly effective for commercial and other purposes? If so, is it better to arouse a little nervousness or to trigger a full-blown anxiety attack? To answer these questions, social psychologists over the years have compared communications that vary in their fearfulness. In the first such study, Irving Janis and Seymour Feshbach (1953) found that high levels of fear did not generate increased agreement with a persuasive communication. Since then, however, research has shown that high fear often does motivate change—in part, by increasing our incentive to think carefully about the arguments contained in the message (Baron et al., 1994).

Fear arousal increases the incentive to change for those who do not actively resist it, but its ultimate impact depends on the strength of the arguments and on whether the message also contains reassuring advice on how to avoid the threatened danger (Keller, 1999; Leventhal, 1970; Rogers, 1983). This last point is important. Without specific instructions on how to cope, people feel helpless, panic, and tune out. In one study, for example, participants with a chronic fear of cancer were less likely than others to detect the logical errors in a message that called for regular cancer checkups (Jepson & Chaiken, 1990). When clear instructions are included, however, high dosages of fear can be effective. Antismoking films that tell smokers how to quit thus elicit more negative attitudes about cigarettes when they show gory lung-cancer operations than charts filled with dry statistics (Leventhal et al., 1967). Driving-safety films are more effective when they show broken bones and bloody accident

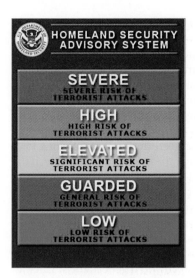

HOMELAND SECURITY
ADVISORY SYSTEM

SEVERE
SEVERE RISK OF
TERRORIST ATTACKS

HIGH
HIGH RISK OF
TERRORIST ATTACKS

ELEVATED
SIGNIFICANT RISK OF
TERRORIST ATTACKS

GUARDED
GENERAL RISK OF
TERRORIST ATTACKS

LOW
LOW RISK OF
TERRORIST ATTACKS

Suggesting that a fear of death leads people to rally around their leaders, public opinion polls have shown that as terror threat levels increase, so do presidential approval ratings.

victims than controlled collisions involving plastic crash dummies (Rogers & Mewborn, 1976). As for changing not only attitudes but also health-related behaviors, research shows that the more personally vulnerable people feel about a threatened outcome, the more attentive they are and the more likely they are to follow the recommendations contained within the fear appeal (Das et al., 2003; de Hoog et al., 2005).

Positive Emotions   It's interesting that just as fear helps to induce a change in attitude, so do positive emotions. In one study, people were more likely to agree with a series of controversial arguments when they snacked on peanuts and soda than when they did not eat (Janis et al., 1965). In another study, participants liked a television commercial more when it was embedded in a program that was upbeat rather than sad (Mathur & Chattopadhyay, 1991). Research shows that people are "soft touches" when they are in a good mood. Depending on the situation, food, drinks, a soft reclining chair, tender memories, a success experience, breathtaking scenery, and pleasant music can lull us into a positive emotional state ripe for persuasion (Schwarz et al., 1991).

According to Alice Isen (1984), people see the world through rose-colored glasses when they are feeling good. Filled with high spirits, we become more sociable, more generous, and generally more positive in our outlook. We also make decisions more quickly and with relatively little thought. The result: Positive feelings activate the peripheral route to persuasion, facilitating change and allowing superficial cues to take on added importance (Petty et al., 1993; Worth & Mackie, 1987).

What is it about feeling good that leads us to take short cuts rather than the more effortful central route to persuasion? There are three possible explanations. One is that a positive emotional state is cognitively distracting, causing the mind to wander and impairing our ability to think critically about the persuasive arguments (Mackie & Worth, 1989; Mackie et al., 1992). A second explanation is that when people are in a good mood, they assume that all is well, let down their guard, and become somewhat lazy processors of information (Schwarz, 1990). A third explanation is that when people are happy, they become motivated to savor the moment and maintain their happy mood, not spoil it by thinking critically about new information (Wegener & Petty, 1994).

This last notion raises an interesting question: What if happy people are presented with a positive and uplifting persuasive message? Would they still appear cognitively distracted, or lazy, or would they pay close attention in order to prolong the rosy glow? To find out, Duane Wegener and others (1995) showed some college students a funny segment from the TV show *Late Night with David Letterman*. Others, less fortunate, watched a somber scene from an HBO movie, *You Don't Have to Die*. All students were then asked to read and evaluate either an uplifting, pro-attitudinal article about a new plan to cut tuition or a distressing, counter-attitudinal article about a new plan to raise tuition. In half the cases, the article they read contained strong arguments; in the others, the arguments were weak. Did the students read the material carefully enough to distinguish between the strong and weak arguments? Those in the somber condition clearly did. Among those in the happy condition, however, the response depended on whether they expected the message to be one they wanted to hear. When the happy students read about a tuition increase, they tuned out and were equally persuaded by the strong and weak arguments. When they read about the proposal to cut tuition, however, they were persuaded more when the arguments were strong than when they were weak. Being in a good mood, and receiving a pro-attitudinal message that would not spoil it, these happy students took the effortful central route to persuasion.

Subliminal Messages   In a bizarre twist during the 2000 U.S. presidential election, the Bush campaign ran a TV ad attacking Gore's health-care proposal. The printed message for all to see was simple: "The Gore Prescription Plan: Bureaucrats Decide." Yet for just a fraction of a second, the noxious word "RATS," was also flashed across the screen in large capital letters. If you paid close attention, you'd notice the word. If not, you'd see it but not realize it. Linking Gore to rats was presumed to have an effect through *subliminal persuasion*, influence without awareness (www.ABCNews.com, September 12, 2000).

In 1957, Vance Packard published *The Hidden Persuaders*, an exposé of Madison

PEOPLE HAVE BEEN TRYING TO FIND THE BREASTS IN THESE ICE CUBES SINCE 1957.

The advertising industry is sometimes charged with sneaking seductive little pictures into ads.

Supposedly, these pictures can get you to buy a product without your even seeing them.

Consider the photograph above. According to some people, there's a pair of female breasts hidden in the patterns of light refracted by the ice cubes.

Well, if you really searched you probably *could* see the breasts. For that matter, you could also see Millard Fillmore, a stuffed pork chop and a 1946 Dodge.

The point is that so-called "subliminal advertising" simply doesn't exist. Overactive imaginations, however, most certainly do.

So if anyone claims to see breasts in that drink up there, they aren't in the ice cubes.

They're in the eye of the beholder.

ADVERTISING
ANOTHER WORD FOR FREEDOM OF CHOICE.
American Association of Advertising Agencies

For years, advertisers have defended against the charge that they embed suggestive and sexual images in print ads. This piece by the American Association of Advertising Agencies addresses the claim.

People are most easily persuaded by commercial messages that are presented without their awareness.
False.

Avenue. As the book climbed the best-seller list, it awakened in the public a fear of being manipulated by forces they could not see or hear. What had Packard uncovered? In the 1950s, amid growing fears of communism and the birth of rock 'n' roll, a number of advertisers were said to have used *subliminal advertising*, the presentation of commercial messages outside of conscious awareness. It all started in a drive-in movie theater in New Jersey, where the words "Drink Coke" and "Eat popcorn" were secretly flashed on the screen during intermissions for a third of a millisecond. Although the audience never noticed the message, Coke sales were said to have increased 18 percent and popcorn sales 58 percent over a six-week period (Brean, 1958).

This incident was followed by several others. A Seattle radio station presented sub-audible anti-TV messages during its programs ("TV is a bore"), and department stores played music tapes over public address systems that contained sub-audible anti-theft warnings ("If you steal, you'll get caught"). Later, in books entitled *Subliminal Seduction* (1973) and *The Age of Manipulation* (1989), William Bryan Key charged that advertisers routinely sneak faint sexual images in visual ads to heighten the appeal of their products. Several years ago, concerns were also raised about subliminal messages in rock music. In one case, the families of two boys who committed suicide blamed the British rock group Judas Priest for subliminal lyrics ("Do it") that promoted satanism and suicide (*National Law Journal*, 1990). Although the families lost their case, it's clear that many people believe in the power of hidden persuaders.

At the time of the New Jersey theater scandal, research on the topic was so sketchy, and the public so outraged by the sinister implications, that the matter was quickly dropped. But today there is renewed interest in subliminal influences, as well as new research developments. In one recent field study, for example, researchers played traditional German or French music, on alternating days for two weeks, at a supermarket display of wines. Keeping track of sales they found that, of the total number of wines bought, 83 percent were German on German-music days and 65 percent were French on French-music days. Yet when asked the reasons for their choices, customers did not cite the music as a factor, suggesting that they were not aware of the effect it had on them (North et al., 1999).

Current uses of subliminal influence are varied. In what is a multimillion-dollar industry, companies today sell self-help videos, tapes, and CDs that play New Age music or nature sounds and also contain fleeting messages that promise to help you relax, lose weight, stop smoking, make friends, raise self-esteem, and even improve your sex life. Can subliminal messages reflexively trigger behavior without our awareness? In 1982, Timothy Moore reviewed the existing research and concluded that "what you see is what you get"—nothing, "complete scams." Moore was right. The original Coke-and-popcorn incident was later exposed as a publicity stunt, a hoax (Pratkanis, 1992). And controlled experiments on subliminal self-help tapes to raise self-esteem, improve memory, or lose weight show that they offer no therapeutic benefits (Greenwald et al., 1991; Merikle & Skanes, 1992).

If there is no solid evidence of subliminal influence, why, you may wonder, does research demonstrate perception without awareness in studies of priming, described elsewhere in this book, but not in studies of subliminal persuasion? If you think about it, the two sets of claims are different. In the laboratory, subliminal exposures have a short-term effect on simple judgments and actions. But in claims of subliminal persuasion, the exposure is presumed to have long-term effects on eating, drinking, consumer purchases, voter sentiment, or even the most profound of violent acts, suicide. Psychologists agree that people can process information at an unconscious level, but they're quick to caution that this processing is "analytically limited" (Greenwald, 1992).

Erin Strahan and others (2002) suggest that although people *perceive* subliminal cues, those cues will not *persuade* them to take action unless they are already motivated to do so. To test this hypothesis, they brought thirsty college students into the lab for

FIGURE 6.8

Subliminal Influence

Thirsty and non-thirsty research participants were subliminally exposed to neutral or thirst-related words. Afterward they participated in a beverage taste test in which the amount they drank was measured. You can see that the subliminal thirst cues had little impact on non-thirsty participants but they did increase consumption among those who were thirsty. Apparently, subliminal cues can influence our behavior when we are otherwise predisposed.

(Strahan et al., 2002.)

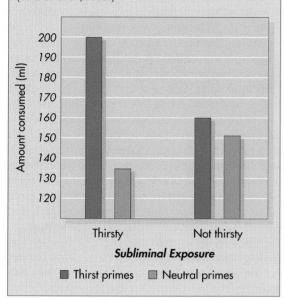

a marketing study and provided drinking water to some but not to others. Then, as part of a test administered by computer, they subliminally exposed these students to neutral words (*pirate, won*) or thirst-related words (*thirst, dry*). Did the subliminal "thirsty" message later lead the students, like automatons, to drink more in a taste test of the Kool-Aid beverages? Yes and no. Figure 6.8 shows that the subliminal thirst primes had little impact on students whose thirst had just been quenched, but they quite clearly increased consumption among those who were water-deprived and thirsty. For a subliminal message to influence behavior, it has to strike "while the iron is hot."

The Audience

Although source and message factors are important, the astute communicator must also take his or her audience into account. Presentation strategies that succeed with some people fail with others. Audiences on the central route to persuasion, for example, bear little resemblance to those found strolling along the peripheral route. In this section, we'll see that the impact of a message is influenced by two additional factors: the recipient's personality and his or her expectations.

Right from the start, social psychologists tried to identify types of people who were more or less vulnerable to persuasion. But it turned out that very few individuals are *consistently* easy or difficult to persuade. Based on this insight, the search for individual and group differences is now guided by an interactionist perspective. Assuming that each of us can be persuaded more in some settings than in others, researchers look for an appropriate "match" between characteristics of the message and the audience. Thus we ask, what kinds of messages turn you on?

The Need for Cognition Earlier, we saw that people tend to process information more carefully when they are highly involved. Involvement can be determined by the importance and self-relevance of a message. According to Cacioppo and Petty (1982), however, there are also individual differences in the extent to which people become involved and take the central route to persuasion. Specifically, they have found that individuals differ in the extent to which they enjoy and participate in effortful cognitive activities, or, as they call it, the **need for cognition (NC)**. People who are high rather than low in their need for cognition like to work on hard problems, search for clues, make fine distinctions, and analyze situations. These differences can be identified by the items contained in the Need for Cognition Scale, some of which appear in Table 6.3.

The need for cognition has interesting implications for changing attitudes. If people are prone to approach or avoid effortful cognitive activities, then the prepared communicator could design messages unique to a particular audience. In theory, the high-NC audience should receive information-oriented appeals, and the low-NC audience should be treated to appeals that rely on the use of peripheral cues. The theory is fine, but does it work? Can a message be customized to fit the information-processing style of its recipients? In one test of this hypothesis, participants read an editorial that consisted of either a strong or a weak set of arguments. As predicted, the higher their NC scores were, the more the participants thought about the material, the better they later recalled it, and the more persuaded they were by the strength of its arguments (Cacioppo et al., 1983). In contrast, people who are low in the need for cognition are persuaded by cues found along the peripheral route—such as a speaker's reputation and physical appearance, the overt reactions of others in the audience, and a positive mood state (Cacioppo et al., 1996). At times, they are mindlessly influenced by a reputable source even when his or her arguments are weak (Kaufman et al., 1999).

need for cognition (NC)
A personality variable that distinguishes people on the basis of how much they enjoy effortful cognitive activities.

Self-Monitoring Just as people high in the need for cognition crave information, other personality traits are associated with an attraction to other kinds

TABLE 6.3
Need for Cognition Scale: Sample Items

Are you high or low in the need for cognition? These statements are taken from the NC Scale. If you agree with items 1, 3, and 5 and disagree with items 2, 4, and 6, you would probably be regarded as high in NC.

(Cacioppo & Petty, 1982.)

1. I really enjoy a task that involves coming up with new solutions to problems.
2. Thinking is not my idea of fun.
3. The notion of thinking abstractly is appealing to me.
4. I like tasks that require little thought once I've learned them.
5. I usually end up deliberating about issues even when they do not affect me personally.
6. It's enough for me that something gets the job done; I don't care how or why it works.

FIGURE 6.9
Informational and Image-Oriented Ads: The Role of Self-Monitoring

High and low self-monitors estimated how much they would pay for products presented in image-oriented or informational magazine ads. As shown, high image-oriented self-monitors preferred products depicted in image-oriented ads (left), while low self-monitors preferred those depicted in informational ads (right).

(Snyder & DeBono, 1985.)

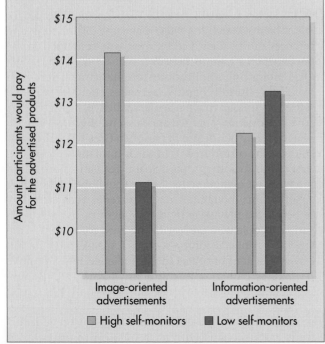

of messages. Consider the trait of *self-monitoring*. As described in Chapter 3, high self-monitors regulate their behavior from one situation to another out of concern for public self-presentation. Low self-monitors are less image conscious and behave instead according to their own beliefs, values, and preferences. In the context of persuasion, high self-monitors may be particularly responsive to messages that promise desirable social images. Whether the product is beer, soda, blue jeans, or cars, this technique is common in advertising, where often the image is the message.

To test the self-monitoring hypothesis, Mark Snyder and Kenneth DeBono (1985) showed image- or information-oriented print ads to high and low self-monitors. In an ad for Irish Mocha Mint coffee, for example, a man and woman were depicted as relaxing in a candlelit room over a steamy cup of coffee. The image-oriented version promised to "Make a chilly night become a cozy evening," while the informational version offered "A delicious blend of three great flavors—coffee, chocolate, and mint." As predicted, high self-monitors were willing to pay more for products after reading imagery ads, while low self-monitors were influenced more by the information-oriented appeals (see Figure 6.9). Imagery can even influence the way that high self-monitors evaluate a product, independent of its quality. DeBono and his colleagues (2003) presented people with one of two perfume samples packaged in more or less attractive bottles. Whereas low self-monitors preferred the more pleasant-scented fragrance, high self-monitors preferred whatever scent came from the more attractive bottles.

Forewarning and Resistance When our attitudes or values come under attack, we can succumb to the challenge and change the attitude, or we can resist it and maintain the attitude. There are different means of resistance. In a series of studies, Julia Jacks and Kimberly Cameron (2003) asked people to describe and rate the ways in which they manage to resist persuasion in their attitudes on abortion or the death penalty. They identified seven strategies, the most common being attitude bolstering ("I think about all the reasons I believe the way I do") and the least common being source derogation ("I look for faults in the person who challenges my belief"). These means of resistance are listed in Table 6.4.

What leads people to invoke these mechanisms of resistance? Does it help to be forewarned that your attitude is about to come under attack? Perhaps the toughest audience to persuade is the one that knows you're coming. When people are aware that someone is trying to change their attitude, they become more likely to resist. All they need is some time to collect their thoughts and come up with a good defense. Jonathan Freedman and David Sears (1965) first discovered this when they told high school seniors to expect a speech on why teenagers should not be allowed to drive (an unpopular position, as you can imagine). The students were warned either two or ten minutes before the talk began or not at all. Those who were the victims of a sneak attack were the most likely to succumb to the speaker's position. Those who had a full ten minutes' warning were the least likely to agree. To be forewarned is to be forearmed. But why?

TABLE 6.4
Strategies for Resisting Persuasion

Strategy	Example
Attitude bolstering	"I reassure myself of facts that support the validity of my belief."
Counterarguing	"I would talk to myself and play devil's advocate."
Social validation	"I also rely on others with the same opinion to be there for me."
Negative affect	"I tend to get angry when someone tries to change my beliefs."
Assertions of confidence	"I doubt anybody could change my viewpoint."
Selective exposure	"Most of the time I just ignore them."
Source derogation	"I look for faults in the person presenting the challenging belief."

"To do just the opposite is also a form of imitation."

—Lichtenberg

inoculation hypothesis
The idea that exposure to weak versions of a persuasive argument increases later resistance to that argument.

psychological reactance
The theory that people react against threats to their freedom by asserting themselves and perceiving the threatened freedom as more attractive.

At least two processes are at work here. To understand them, let's take a closer look at what forewarning does. Participants in the Freedman and Sears (1965) study were put on notice in two ways: (1) They were informed of the position the speaker would take, and (2) they were told that the speaker intended to change their attitudes. Psychologically, these two aspects of forewarning have different effects.

The first effect is purely cognitive. Knowing in advance what position a speaker will take enables us to come up with counterarguments and, as a result, to become more resistant to change. To explain this effect, William McGuire (1964) drew an analogy: Protecting a person's attitudes from persuasion, he said, is like inoculating the human body against disease. In medicine, injecting a small dose of infection into a patient stimulates the body to build up a resistance to it. According to this **inoculation hypothesis**, an attitude can be immunized the same way. As with flu shots and other vaccines, our defenses can be reinforced by exposure to weak doses of the opposing position before we actually encounter the full presentation. Studies of negative political ads show that inoculation can be used to combat the kinds of attack messages that sometimes win elections (Pfau et al., 1990).

Simply knowing that someone is trying to persuade us also elicits a motivational reaction as we brace ourselves to resist the attempt regardless of what position is taken. As a TV viewer, you have no doubt heard the phrase "And now, we pause for a message from our sponsor." What does this warning tell us? Not knowing yet who the sponsor is, even the grouchiest among us is in no position to object. Yet imagine how you would feel if an experimenter said to you, "In just a few minutes, you will hear a message prepared according to well-established principles of persuasion and designed to induce you to change your attitudes." If you are like the participants who actually heard this forewarning, you might be tempted to reply, "Oh yeah? Try me!" Indeed, subjects rejected that message without counterargument and without much advance notice (Hass & Grady, 1975).

When people think that someone is trying to change their attitude or otherwise manipulate them, a red flag goes up. That red flag is called **psychological reactance**. According to Jack Brehm's theory of psychological reactance, all of us want the freedom to think, feel, and act as we (not others) choose. When we sense that a cherished freedom is being threatened, we become motivated to maintain it. And when we sense that a freedom is slipping away, we try to restore it (Brehm & Brehm, 1981). One possible result is that when a communicator comes on too strong, we may react with *negative attitude change*, by moving in the direction opposite the one advocated—even, ironically, when the speaker's position agrees with our own (Heller et al., 1973). Sometimes, the motive to protect our freedom to think as we choose trumps our desire to hold a specific opinion.

Forewarning does not always increase resistance to persuasion, however, because the effects are not that simple. Based on a meta-analysis of forty-eight experiments, Wendy Wood and Jeffrey Quinn (2003) found that when people are forewarned about an impending persuasive appeal on a topic that is personally not that important, they start to agree before they even receive the message in order to keep from appearing vulnerable to influence. Yet when people are forewarned about a persuasive appeal on a topic that is of personal importance, they feel threatened and think up counterarguments to bolster their attitude. This cognitive response strengthens their resistance to change once that appeal is delivered.

In a series of print ads, Apple Computer featured Thomas Edison and other creative geniuses who dared to "think different." In a marketing campaign that paid tribute to individualism, Apple saluted "the crazy ones. The misfits. The rebels. The troublemakers. The round pegs in the square holes. The ones who see things differently."

Culture and Persuasion

A communication is persuasive to the extent that the source is favorable and the message, however it is presented, meets the psychological needs of its audience. In this regard, cultural factors also play a subtle but important role.

In earlier chapters, we saw that cultures differ in the extent to which people are oriented toward individualism or collectivism. In light of these differences, Sang-Pil Han and Sharon Shavitt (1994) compared the contents of magazine advertisements in the United States, an individualistic country, and Korea, a country with a collectivistic orientation. They found that while American advertising campaigns were focused more on personal benefits, individuality, competition, and self-improvement ("She's got a style all her own," "Make your way through the crowd"), Korean ads appealed more to the integrity, achievement, and well-being of one's ingroups ("An exhilarating way to provide for your family," "Celebrating a half-century of partnership"). Clearly, there are different ways to appeal to the members of these two cultures. In a second study, Han and Shavitt created two sets of ads for various products. One set portrayed individuals ("Treat yourself to a breath-freshening experience"), and the other set featured groups ("Share this breath-freshening experience"). Both sets were presented to American and Korean participants. The result: Americans were persuaded more by individualistic ads, and Koreans preferred collectivistic ads. Similar differences are found in the way celebrity endorsements are used in the two cultures. In the United States, celebrities tend to portray themselves using or talking directly about a product; in Korean commercials that appeal to belongingness, family, and traditional values, they are more likely to play the role of someone else, without being singled out (Choi et al., 2005).

As people from all over the world come into contact with each other through travel, satellite television, international trade agreements, and the Internet, cultural values are not set in stone. Just as humans develop as they get older, cultures sometimes change over time from one generation to the next. Recent and substantial modernization efforts in China—home to 21 out of every 100 people on the planet—illustrate the point. There is so much recent change that Zhang and Shavitt (2003) sought to compare the contents of television commercials, primarily directed at the traditional mass market, with new magazine advertisements that specifically target eighteen- to thirty-five-year-old, educated, high-income citizens who constitute China's "X-generation." Based on their analysis of 463 ads, they found that while traditional and collectivist values predominated on mainstream TV, magazine ads were characterized by more modern and individualistic impulses. To be persuasive, a message should appeal to the culturally shared values of its audience.

Persuasion by Our Own Actions

Anyone who has ever acted on stage knows how easy it is to become so absorbed in a role that the experience seems real. Feigned laughter can make an actor feel happy, and crocodile tears can turn into sadness. Even in real life, the effect can be dramatic. In 1974, Patty Hearst, a sheltered college student from a wealthy family, was kidnapped. By the time she was arrested months later, she was a gun-toting revolutionary who called herself Tania. How could someone be so totally converted? In Hearst's own words, "I had thought I was humoring [my captors] by parroting their clichés and buzzwords without believing in them. . . . In trying to convince them I convinced myself."

Role Playing: All the World's a Stage

The Patty Hearst case illustrates the powerful effects of *role playing*. Of course, you don't have to be kidnapped or terrorized to know how it feels to be coaxed into behavior that is at odds with your inner convictions. People frequently engage in attitude-

Posing as a revolutionary named Tania, Patty Hearst was converted by the role her captors forced her to play. "In trying to convince them I convinced myself," she said.

discrepant behavior as part of a job, for example, or to please others. As commonplace as this seems, it raises a profound question. When we play along, saying and doing things that are privately discrepant from our own attitudes, do we begin to change those attitudes as a result? How we feel can determine the way we act. Is it also possible that the way we act can determine how we feel?

According to Irving Janis (1968), attitude change persists more when it is inspired by our own behavior than when it stems from passive exposure to a persuasive communication. Janis conducted a study in which one group of participants listened to a speech that challenged their positions on a topic and others were handed an outline and asked to give the speech themselves. As predicted, participants changed their attitudes more after giving the speech than after listening to it (Janis & King, 1954). According to Janis, role playing works because it forces people to learn the message. Hence, people tend to remember arguments they come up with on their own better than they remember arguments provided by others (Slamecka & Graff, 1978). In fact, attitude change is more enduring even when people who read a persuasive message merely *expect* that they will later have to communicate it to others (Boninger et al., 1990).

But there's more to role playing than improved memory. The effects of enacting a role can be staggering, in part because it is so easy to confuse what we do, or what we say, with how we really feel. Think about the times you've dished out compliments you didn't mean, or smiled at someone you didn't like, or nodded your head in response to a statement you disagreed with. We often shade what we say just to please a particular listener. What's fascinating is not that we make adjustments to suit others but that this role playing has such powerful effects on our own private attitudes. For example, participants in one study read about a man and then described him to someone else, who supposedly liked or disliked him. As you might expect, participants described the man in more positive terms when their listener was favorably disposed. In the process, however, they also convinced themselves. At least to some extent, "saying is believing" (Higgins & Rholes, 1978).

Consider the implications. We know that attitudes influence behavior, as when people help those whom they like and hurt those whom they dislike. But research on role playing emphasizes the flip side of the coin—that behavior can change attitudes. Perhaps we come to like people because we have helped them and blame people whom we have hurt. To change people's inner feelings, then, maybe we should begin by focusing on their behavior. Why do people experience changes of attitude in response to changes in their own behavior? One answer to this question is provided by the theory of cognitive dissonance.

Cognitive Dissonance Theory: The Classic Version

Many social psychologists believe that people are strongly motivated by a desire for cognitive consistency—a state of mind in which one's beliefs, attitudes, and behaviors are all compatible with each other (Abelson et al., 1968). Cognitive consistency theories seem to presuppose that people are generally logical. However, Leon Festinger (1957) turned this assumption on its head. Struck by the irrationalities of human behavior, Festinger proposed **cognitive dissonance theory**, which states that a powerful motive to maintain cognitive consistency can give rise to irrational and sometimes maladaptive behavior.

According to Festinger, all of us hold many cognitions about ourselves and the world around us. These cognitions include everything we know about our own beliefs, attitudes, and behavior. Although generally our cognitions coexist peacefully,

cognitive dissonance theory The theory that holding inconsistent cognitions arouses psychological tension that people become motivated to reduce.

TABLE 6.5

Ways to Reduce Dissonance

"I need to be on a diet, yet I just dived head first into a chocolate mousse." If this were you, how would you reduce dissonance aroused by the discrepancy between your attitude and your behavior?

Techniques	Examples
Change your attitude.	"I don't really need to be on a diet."
Change your perception of the behavior.	"I hardly ate any chocolate mousse."
Add consonant cognitions.	"Chocolate mousse is very nutritious."
Minimize the importance of the conflict.	"I don't care if I'm overweight—life is short!"
Reduce perceived choice.	"I had no choice; the mousse was prepared for this special occasion."

"Man is the only animal that learns by being hypocritical. He pretends to be polite and then, eventually, he becomes polite."

—Jean Kerr

at times they clash. Consider some examples. You say you're on a diet, yet you just dove head first into a chocolate mousse. Or you waited in line for hours to get into a concert, and then the band was disappointing. Or you baked for hours under the hot summer sun, even though you knew of the health risks. Each of these scenarios harbors inconsistency and conflict. You have already committed yourself to one course of action, yet you realize that what you did is inconsistent with your attitude.

Under certain conditions, discrepancies such as these can evoke an unpleasant state of tension known as cognitive dissonance. But discrepancy doesn't always produce dissonance. If you broke a diet for a Thanksgiving dinner with family, your indiscretion would not lead you to experience dissonance. Or if you mistakenly thought the mousse you ate was low in calories, only later to find out the truth, then, again, you would not experience much dissonance. As we'll see, what really hurts is the knowledge that you committed yourself to an attitude-discrepant behavior freely and with some knowledge of the consequences. When that happens, dissonance is aroused, and you become motivated to reduce it. As shown in Table 6.5, there are many possible ways to reduce dissonance, such as by rationalizing that everyone else is also a hypocrite (McKimmie et al., 2003) or denying personal responsibility for the behavior (Gosling et al., 2006). Often the easiest way to reduce dissonance is to change your attitude to bring it in line with your behavior.

Right from the start, cognitive dissonance theory captured the imagination. Festinger's basic proposition is simple, yet its implications are far-reaching. In this section, we examine three research areas that demonstrate the breadth of what dissonance theory has to say about attitude change.

Justifying Attitude-Discrepant Behavior: When Doing Is Believing

Imagine for a moment that you are a participant in a classic study by Leon Festinger and J. Merrill Carlsmith (1959). As soon as you arrive, you are greeted by an experimenter who says that he is interested in various measures of performance. Wondering what that means, you all too quickly find out. The experimenter hands you a wooden board containing forty-eight square pegs in square holes and asks you to turn each peg a quarter turn to the left, then a quarter turn back to the right, then back to the left, then back again to the right. The routine seems endless. After thirty minutes, the experimenter comes to your rescue. Or does he? Just when you think things are looking up, he hands you another board, another assignment. For the next half-hour, you are to take twelve spools of thread off the board, put them back, take them off, and put them back again. By now, you're just about ready to tear your hair out. As you think back over better times, even the first task begins to look good.

Finally, you're done. After one of the longest hours of your life, the experimenter lets you in on a secret: There's more to this experiment than meets the eye. You were in the control group. To test the effects of motivation on performance, other participants are being told that the experiment will be fun and exciting. You don't realize it, but you are now being set up for the critical part of the study. Would you be willing to tell the next participant that the experiment is enjoyable? As you hem and haw, the experimenter offers to pay for your services. Some participants are offered one dollar; others are offered twenty dollars. In either case, you agree to help out. Before you know it, you find yourself in the waiting room trying to dupe an unsuspecting fellow student (who is really a confederate).

"It's a crazy idea, but it just might work."

One way to reduce dissonance is to minimize the importance of the conflict.

By means of this elaborate, staged presentation, participants were goaded into an attitude-discrepant behavior, an action that was inconsistent with their private attitudes. They knew how dull the experiment really was, yet they raved about it. Did this conflict arouse cognitive dissonance? It depends on how much the participants were paid. Suppose you were one of the lucky ones offered twenty dollars for your assistance. By today's standards, that payment would be worth eighty dollars—surely a sufficient justification for telling a little white lie, right? Feeling well compensated, these participants experienced little if any dissonance. But wait. Suppose you were paid only one dollar. Surely your integrity is worth more than that, don't you think? In this instance, you have **insufficient justification** for going along, so you need a way to cope. According to Festinger (1957), unless you can deny your actions (which is not usually possible), you'll feel pressured to change your attitude about the task. If you can convince yourself that the experiment wasn't that bad, then saying it was interesting is all right.

The results were just as Festinger and Carlsmith had predicted. When the experiment was presumably over, participants were asked how they felt about the peg-board tasks. Those in the control group who did not mislead a confederate openly admitted that the tasks were boring. So did those in the twenty-dollar condition, who had ample justification for what they did. However, participants who were paid only one dollar rated the experiment as somewhat enjoyable. Having engaged in an attitude-discrepant act without sufficient justification, these participants reduced cognitive dissonance by changing their attitude. The results can be seen in Figure 6.10.

Two aspects of this classic study are noteworthy. First, it showed the phenomenon of self-persuasion: When people behave in ways that contradict their attitudes, they sometimes go on to change those attitudes without any exposure to a persuasive communication. Demonstrating the power of this phenomenon, Michael Leippe and Donna Eisenstadt (1994) found that white college students who were coaxed into writing essays in favor of new scholarship funds only for black students later reported more favorable attitudes in general toward African Americans. The second major contribution of Festinger and Carlsmith's results is that they contradicted the time-honored belief that big rewards produce greater change. In fact, the more money participants were offered for their inconsistent behavior, the more justified they felt and the less likely they were to change their attitudes.

Just as a small reward provides insufficient justification for attitude-discrepant behavior, mild punishment is **insufficient deterrence** for attitude-discrepant nonbehavior. Think about it. What happens when people refrain from doing something they really want to do? Do they devalue the activity and convince themselves that they never really wanted to do it in the first place? In one study, children were prohibited from playing with an attractive toy by being threatened with a mild or a severe punishment. All participants refrained. As cognitive dissonance theory predicts, however, only those faced with the mild punishment—an insufficient deterrent—later showed disdain for the forbidden toy. Those who confronted the threat of severe punishment did not (Aronson & Carlsmith, 1963). Once again, cognitive dissonance theory turned common sense on its head: The less severe the threatened punishment, the greater the attitude change produced.

Justifying Effort: Coming to Like What We Suffer For

Have you ever spent tons of money or tried really hard to achieve something, only to discover later that it wasn't worth all the effort? This kind of inconsistency between effort and outcome can arouse cognitive dissonance and motivate a change of heart toward the unsatisfying outcome. The hypothesis is simple but profound: We alter our attitudes to justify our suffering.

In a classic test of this hypothesis, Elliot Aronson and Judson Mills (1959) invited female students to take part in a series of group discussions about sex. But there was

The more money you pay people to tell a lie, the more they will come to believe it. **False.**

insufficient justification
A condition in which people freely perform an attitude-discrepant behavior without receiving a large reward.

insufficient deterrence
A condition in which people refrain from engaging in a desirable activity, even when only mild punishment is threatened.

FIGURE 6.10

The Dissonance Classic

Participants in a boring experiment (attitude) were asked to say that it was enjoyable (behavior) to a fellow student. Those in one group were paid a dollar to lie; those in a second group were offered twenty dollars. Members of a third group, who did not have to lie, admitted that the task was boring. So did the participants paid twenty dollars—ample justification for what they did. Participants paid only one dollar, however, rated the task as more enjoyable. Behaving in an attitude-discrepant manner without justification, the one-dollar participants reduced dissonance by changing their attitude.

(Festinger & Carlsmith, 1959.)

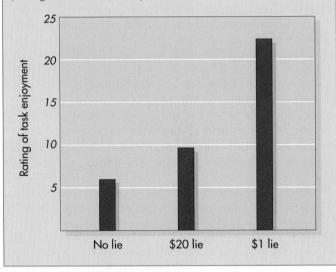

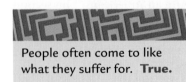

People often come to like what they suffer for. **True.**

a hitch. Because sex is a sensitive topic, participants were told that they would have to pass an "embarrassment test" before joining the group. The test consisted of reading sexual material aloud in front of a male experimenter. One group of participants experienced what amounted to a *severe* initiation in which they had to recite obscene words and lurid passages taken from paperback novels. A second group underwent a *mild* initiation in which they read a list of more ordinary words pertaining to sex. A third group was admitted to the discussions without an initiation test.

Moments later, all participants were given headphones and permitted to eavesdrop on the group they would soon be joining. Actually, what they heard was a tape-recorded discussion about "secondary sex behavior in the lower animals." It was dreadfully boring. When it was over, participants were asked to rate how much they liked the group members and their discussion. Keep in mind what dissonance theory predicts: The more time or money or effort you choose to invest in something, the more anxious you will feel if the outcome proves disappointing. One way to cope with this inconsistency is to alter your attitudes. That's exactly what happened. Participants who had endured a severe initiation rated the discussion group more favorably than did those who had endured little or no initiation.

It's important to note that social embarrassment is not the only kind of "effort" we feel the need to justify to ourselves. As a general rule, the more you pay for something—whether you pay in physical exertion, pain, time, or money—the more you will come to like it. This principle has provocative implications for hazing practices in fraternities and sororities, on sports teams, and in the military. Research even suggests that the harder psychotherapy patients have to work at their own treatment, the more likely they are to feel better when that treatment is over (Axsom, 1989; Axsom & Cooper, 1985).

Justifying Difficult Decisions: When Good Choices Get Even Better

Whenever we make difficult decisions—whether to marry, what school to attend, or what job to accept—we feel dissonance. By definition, a decision is difficult when the alternative courses of action are about equally desirable. Marriage offers comfort and stability; staying single enables us to seek out exciting new relationships. One job might pay more money; the other might involve more interesting work. Once people make tough decisions like these, they are at risk, as negative aspects of the chosen alternatives and positive aspects of the unchosen alternatives are at odds with their decisions. According to dissonance theory, people rationalize whatever they decide by exaggerating the positive features of the chosen alternative and the negative features of the unchosen alternative.

In an early test of this hypothesis, Jack Brehm (1956) asked female participants to evaluate various consumer products, presumably as part of a marketing research project. After rating a toaster, a coffee pot, a radio, a stopwatch, and other products, participants were told that they could take one home as a gift. In the high-dissonance condition, they were offered a difficult choice between two items they found equally attractive. In the low-dissonance group, they were offered an easier choice between a desirable and an undesirable item. After receiving the gift, participants read a few research reports and then re-evaluated all the products. The results provided strong support for dissonance theory. In the low-dissonance group, the participants' post-decision ratings were about the same as their pre-decision ratings. But in the high-dissonance condition, ratings increased for the chosen item and decreased for the nonchosen item. Participants torn between two equivalent alternatives coped by reassuring themselves that they had made the right choice.

This phenomenon appears in a wide range of settings. For example, Robert Knox and James Inskter (1968) took dissonance theory to the racetrack and found that bettors who had already placed two-dollar bets on a horse were more optimistic about winning than were those still standing in line. This type of optimism may even begin to set in once a thoughtful decision is made, even before the bet is placed (Brownstein et al., 2004). Similarly, Dennis Regan and Martin Kilduff (1988) visited several polling stations on election day and found that voters were more likely to think that their candidates would win when interviewed after submitting their ballots than before. Since bets and votes cannot be taken back, people who had committed themselves to a decision were motivated to reduce post-decision dissonance. So they convinced themselves that the decision they made was right.

Cognitive Dissonance Theory: A New Look

Following in Festinger's bold footsteps, generations of social psychologists have studied and refined the basic theory (Harmon-Jones & Mills, 1999). Nobody disputes the fact that when people are gently coaxed into performing an attitude-discrepant behavior, they often go on to change their attitudes. In fact, people will feel discomfort and change their attitudes when they disagree with others in a group (Matz & Wood, 2005) or even when they see inconsistent behavior from someone else with whom they identify—a process of *vicarious* dissonance (Norton et al., 2003). Through systematic research, however, it became evident early on that Festinger's (1957) original theory was not to be the last word. People do change their attitudes to justify attitude-discrepant behavior, effort, and difficult decisions. But for dissonance to be aroused, certain specific conditions must be present. As first summarized by Joel Cooper and Russell Fazio's (1984) "new look" at dissonance theory, we now have a pretty good idea of what those conditions are.

According to Cooper and Fazio, four steps are necessary for both the arousal and reduction of dissonance. First, the attitude-discrepant behavior must produce unwanted *negative consequences*. Recall the initial Festinger and Carlsmith (1959) study. Not only did participants say something they knew to be false, but they also deceived a fellow student into taking part in a painfully boring experiment. Had these participants lied without causing hardship, they would *not* have changed their attitudes to justify the action (Cooper et al., 1974). To borrow an expression from schoolyard basketball, "no harm, no foul." In fact, negative consequences can arouse dissonance even when people's actions are consistent with their attitudes, as when college students who wrote against fee hikes were led to believe that their essays had backfired, prompting a university committee to favor an increase (Scher & Cooper, 1989).

Suggesting that people need to justify difficult irrevocable decisions to quell the dissonance they arouse, researchers found that gamblers who had already bet on a horse rated themselves as more certain of winning than those who were still waiting to place a bet.

The second necessary step in the process is a feeling of *personal responsibility* for the unpleasant outcomes of behavior. Personal responsibility consists of two factors. The first is the freedom of *choice*. When people believe they had no choice but to act as they did, there is no dissonance and no attitude change (Linder et al., 1967). Had Festinger and Carlsmith coerced participants into raving about the boring experiment, the participants would not have felt the need to further justify what they did by changing their attitudes. But the experimental situation led participants to think that their actions were voluntary and that the choice was theirs. Pressured without realizing it, participants believed that they did not have to comply with the experimenter's request.

For people to feel personally responsible, they must also believe that the potential negative consequences of their actions were *foreseeable* at the time (Goethals et al., 1979). When the outcome could not realistically have been anticipated, then there's no dissonance and no attitude change. Had Festinger and Carlsmith's participants lied in private, only later to find out that their statements had been tape-recorded for subsequent use, then, again, they would not have felt the need to further justify their behavior.

The third necessary step in the process is physiological *arousal*. Right from the start, Festinger viewed cognitive dissonance as a state of discomfort and tension that people seek to reduce—much like hunger, thirst, and other basic drives. Research has shown that this emphasis was well placed. In a study by Robert Croyle and Joel Cooper (1983), participants wrote essays that supported or contradicted their own attitudes. Some were ordered to do so, but others were led to believe that the choice was theirs. During the session, electrodes were attached to each participant's fingertips to record levels of physiological arousal. As predicted by cognitive dissonance theory, those who freely wrote attitude-discrepant essays were the most aroused, an observation made by other researchers as well (Elkin & Leippe, 1986). In fact, participants who write attitude-discrepant essays in a "free-choice" situation report feeling high levels of discomfort—which subside once they change their attitudes (Elliot & Devine, 1994).

The fourth step in the dissonance process is closely related to the third. It isn't enough to feel generally aroused. A person must also make an *attribution* for that arousal to his or her own behavior. Suppose you just lied to a friend, or studied for an exam that was canceled, or made a tough decision that you might soon regret. Suppose further that although you are upset, you believe that your discomfort is caused by some external factor, not by your dissonance-producing behavior. Under these circumstances, will you exhibit attitude change as a symptom of cognitive dissonance? Probably not. When participants were led to attribute their dissonance-related arousal to a drug they had supposedly taken (Zanna & Cooper, 1974), to the anticipation of painful electric shocks (Pittman, 1975), or to a pair of prism goggles that they had to wear (Losch & Cacioppo, 1990), attitude change did not occur. Figure 6.11 summarizes these four steps in the production and reduction of dissonance.

To this day, social psychologists continue to debate the "classic" and "new look" theories of cognitive dissonance. On the one hand, research has shown that attitude-discrepant actions do not always produce dissonance, in part because not everyone cares about being cognitively consistent (Cialdini et al., 1995) and in part because a change in attitude often seems to require the production of negative consequences (R. W. Johnson et al., 1995). On the other hand, some researchers have found that inconsistency alone can trigger cognitive dissonance, even without the negative consequences. For example, Eddie Harmon-Jones and others (1996) had people drink a Kool-Aid beverage that was mixed with sugar or vinegar. The researchers either told participants (no choice) or asked them (high choice) to state in writing that they liked the beverage and then toss these notes, which were not really needed, into the

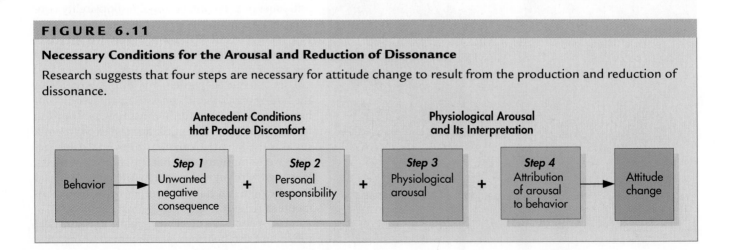

FIGURE 6.11

Necessary Conditions for the Arousal and Reduction of Dissonance

Research suggests that four steps are necessary for attitude change to result from the production and reduction of dissonance.

wastebasket. Afterward, they rated how much they really liked the drink. You may have noticed that this experiment parallels the Festinger and Carlsmith study, with one key exception: For participants in the high-choice situation who consumed vinegar and said they liked it, the lie—although it contradicted their true attitudes— did not cause harm to anyone. Did they experience dissonance that they would have to reduce by overrating the vinegar Kool-Aid? Yes. Compared with participants who lied about the vinegar in the no-choice situation, those in the high-choice situation rated its taste as more pleasant. The lie was harmless, but the feeling of inconsistency still forced a change in attitude.

Alternative Routes to Self-Persuasion

It is important to distinguish between the empirical facts uncovered by dissonance researchers and the theory that is used to explain them. The facts themselves are clear: Under certain conditions, people who behave in attitude-discrepant ways go on to change their attitudes. Whether this phenomenon reflects a human need to reduce dissonance, however, is a matter of some controversy. Over the years, three other explanations have been proposed.

Self-Perception Theory Daryl Bem's (1965) *self-perception theory*, as described in Chapter 3, posed the first serious challenge to dissonance theory. Noting that we don't always have firsthand knowledge of our own attitudes, Bem proposed that we infer how we feel by observing ourselves and the circumstances of our own behavior. This sort of self-persuasion is not fueled by the need to reduce tension or justify our actions. Instead, it is a cool, calm, and rational process in which people interpret ambiguous feelings by observing their own behavior. But can Bem's theory replace dissonance theory as an explanation of self-persuasion?

Bem confronted this question head-on. What if neutral observers who are not motivated by the need to reduce dissonance were to read a step-by-step description of a dissonance study and predict the results? This approach to the problem was ingenious. Bem reasoned that observers can have the same behavioral information as the participants themselves but not experience the same personal conflict. If observers generate the same results as real participants, it shows that dissonance arousal is not necessary for the resulting changes in attitudes.

To test his hypothesis, Bem (1967) described the Festinger and Carlsmith study to observers and had them guess participants' attitudes. Some were told about the one-dollar condition, some were told about the twenty-dollar condition, and others read about the control group procedure. The results closely paralleled the original study. As observers saw it, participants who said the task was interesting for twenty dollars didn't mean it; they just went along for the money. But those who made the claim for only one dollar must have been sincere. Why else would they have gone along? As far as Bem was concerned, participants themselves reason the same way. No conflict, no arousal—just inference by observation.

So should we conclude that self-perception, not dissonance, is what's necessary to bring about attitude change? That's a tough question. It's not easy to come up with a critical experiment to distinguish between the two theories. Both predict the same results, but for different reasons. And both offer unique support for their own points of view. On the one hand, Bem's observer studies show that dissonance-like results can be obtained without arousal. On the other hand, the participants of dissonance studies *do* experience arousal, which seems necessary for attitude change to take place. Can we say that one theory is right and the other wrong?

Fazio and his colleagues (1977) concluded that both theories are right but in different situations. When people behave in ways that are strikingly at odds with their attitudes, they feel the unnerving effects of dissonance and change their attitudes to rationalize their actions. When people behave in ways that are not terribly discrepant from how they feel, however, they experience relatively little tension and form their attitudes as a matter of inference. In short, highly discrepant behavior produces attitude change through dissonance, whereas slightly discrepant behavior produces change through self-perception.

Impression-Management Theory Another alternative to a dissonance view of self-persuasion is *impression-management theory*, which says that what matters is not a motive to be consistent but a motive to *appear* consistent. Nobody wants to be called fickle or be seen by others as a hypocrite. So we calibrate our attitudes and behaviors publicly just to present ourselves to others in a particular light (Baumeister, 1982; Tedeschi et al., 1971). Or perhaps we are motivated not by a desire to appear consistent but by a desire to avoid being held responsible for the unpleasant consequences of our actions (Schlenker, 1982). Either way, this theory places the emphasis on our concern for self-presentation. According to this view, participants in the Festinger and Carlsmith study mostly did not want the experimenter to think they had sold out for a paltry sum of money.

If the impression-management approach is correct, then cognitive dissonance does not produce attitude change at all—only reported change. In other words, if research participants were to state their attitudes anonymously, or if they were to think that the experimenter could determine their true feelings through covert measures, then dissonance-like effects should vanish. Sometimes, the effects do vanish; but other times, they do not. In general, studies have shown that although self-persuasion can be motivated by impression management, it can also occur in situations that do not clearly arouse self-presentation concerns (Baumeister & Tice, 1984).

Self-Esteem Theories A third competing explanation relates self-persuasion to the self. According to Elliot Aronson, acts that arouse dissonance do so because they threaten the self-concept, making the person feel guilty, dishonest, or hypocritical, and motivating a change in attitude or future behavior (Aronson, 1999; Stone et al., 1997). This being the case, perhaps Festinger and Carlsmith's participants needed to change their attitudes toward the boring task in order to repair damage to the self, not to resolve cognitive inconsistency.

If cognitive dissonance is aroused only by behavior that lowers self-esteem, then people with already low expectations of themselves should not be affected: "If a person conceives of himself as a 'schnook,' he will expect to behave like a schnook" (Aronson, 1969, p. 24). In fact, Jeff Stone (2003) found that when college students were coaxed into writing an essay in favor of a tuition increase (a position that contradicted their attitude) and into thinking about their own standards of behavior, those who had high self-esteem changed their attitude to meet their behavior, as dissonance theory would predict, more than those who had low self-esteem. Claude Steele (1988) takes this notion two steps further. First, he suggests that a dissonance-producing situation—engaging in attitude-discrepant behavior, exerting wasted effort, or making a difficult decision—sets in motion a process of *self-affirmation* that serves to revalidate the integrity of the self-concept. Second, this revalidation can be achieved in many ways, not just by resolving dissonance. Self-affirmation theory makes a unique prediction: If the active ingredient in dissonance situations is a threat to the self, then people who have an opportunity to affirm the self in other ways will not suffer from the effects of dissonance. Give Festinger and Carlsmith's one-dollar participants a chance to donate money, help a victim in distress, or solve a problem, and their self-concepts should bounce back without further need to justify their actions.

Research provides support for this hypothesis. For example, Steele and others (1993) gave people positive or negative feedback about a personality test they had taken. Next, they asked them to rate ten popular music CDs and then offered them a choice of keeping either their fifth- or sixth-ranked CD. Soon after making the decision, the participants were asked to re-rate the CDs. As predicted by dissonance theory, most inflated their ratings of the chosen CD relative to the unchosen one. The key word, however, is *most*. Among positive-feedback participants, the ratings did not change. Why not? According to Steele, they had just enjoyed a self-affirming experience, enough to overcome the need to reduce dissonance.

Steele's research suggests that there are many possible ways for people to repair a dissonance-damaged self. But if these efforts at indirect self-affirmation fail, would cognitive dissonance return and pressure a change in attitude? Yes. In one study, college students were asked (high-choice) or told (low-choice) to deliver an attitude-

FIGURE 6.12

When Self-Affirmation Fails

Students gave a dissonant speech advocating a ban on a popular campus tradition. Compared to those in a low-choice situation, students in a high-choice group changed their attitude more to favor the ban. As self-affirmation theory predicts, those given a chance to express their values afterward did not then favor the ban—unless their values were poorly received. Self-affirmation can repair the dissonance-damaged self. When it fails, however, cognitive dissonance returns to pressure the change in attitude.

(Galinsky et al., 2000.)

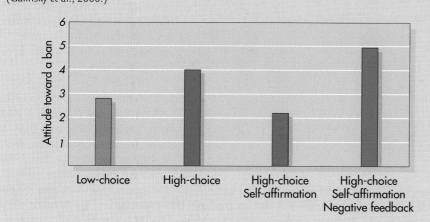

discrepant speech advocating that a popular campus tradition (running nude on the evening of the first snowfall) be banned. For those in the high-choice condition, cognitive dissonance was aroused, pressuring a change in attitude favoring the ban. Students in a third group who were subsequently given an opportunity to self-affirm by expressing some cherished values felt less discomfort and exhibited less attitude change. For them, self-affirmation provided the necessary relief. However, among students in a fourth group—who self-affirmed but then received negative feedback about the values they expressed—cognitive dissonance returned, pressuring a change in attitude toward the ban. In essence, cognitive dissonance and its impact on attitudes re-emerged from the failed attempt at self-affirmation (Galinsky et al., 2000; see Figure 6.12).

To summarize, dissonance theory maintains that people change their attitudes to justify their attitude-discrepant behaviors, efforts, and decisions. Self-perception theory argues that the change occurs because people infer how they feel by observing their own behavior. Impression-management theory claims that the attitude change is spurred by self-presentation concerns. And self-affirmation theory says that the change is motivated by threats to the self (see Figure 6.13).

FIGURE 6.13

Theories of Self-Persuasion: Critical Comparisons

Here we compare the major theories of self-persuasion. Each alternative challenges a different aspect of dissonance theory. Self-perception theory assumes that attitude change is a matter of inference, not motivation. Impression-management theory maintains that the change is more apparent than real, reported for the sake of public self-presentation. Self-affirmation theory contends that the motivating force is a concern for the self and that attitude change will not occur when the self-concept is affirmed in other ways.

	Theories			
	Cognitive Dissonance	Self-Perception	Impression Management	Self-Affirmation
Is the attitude change motivated by a desire to reduce discomfort?	Yes	No	Yes	Yes
Does a person's private attitude really change?	Yes	Yes	No	Yes
Must the change be directly related to the attitude-discrepant behavior?	Yes	Yes	Yes	No

FIGURE 6.14

Cognitive Dissonance as Both Universal and Culturally Dependent

Researchers compared Canadian and Japanese research participants in a post-decision dissonance study in which they rank-ordered items on a menu, chose their top dishes, then re-ranked the list. Half made the choices for themselves; the others were asked to imagine a close friend. When deciding for themselves, only the Canadians exhibited a significant justification effect; when deciding for a friend, however, Japanese exhibited the stronger effect.

(Hoshino-Browne et al., 2005.)

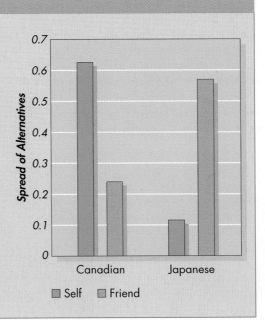

Cultural Influences on Cognitive Dissonance

Over the years, social psychologists have presumed that the cognitive dissonance effects uncovered in fifty years of research and described in this chapter are universal and characteristic of human nature. More and more, however, it appears that cultural context may influence both the arousal and reduction of cognitive dissonance.

In Western cultures, individuals are expected to make decisions that are consistent with their personal attitudes and to make those decisions free from outside influences. In East Asian cultures, however, individuals are also expected to make decisions that benefit their ingroup members and to take the well-being of others into account in making those decisions. In light of these differences, Etsuko Hoshino-Browne and colleagues (2005) compared the reactions of European-Canadian and Japanese research participants in a post-decision dissonance experiment in which they rank-ordered items on a menu, chose their top ten dishes, then re-ranked the list. Half made the choices for themselves; the others were asked to imagine a close friend whose tastes they knew and to choose on behalf of that friend. Did participants show the classic post-decisional justification effect, becoming more positive in their ratings of the chosen items relative to nonchosen items? Yes and no. When making the decisions for themselves, only the Canadian participants exhibited a significant justification effect. When making the decisions for a friend, however, Japanese participants exhibited the stronger effect (see Figure 6.14). Similar results have been found in other studies (Kitayama et al., 2004).

To sum up: Cognitive dissonance is both universal and culture-dependent. At times everyone feels and tries to reduce dissonance, but cultures influence the conditions under which these processes occur.

Changing Attitudes

Attitudes and attitude change are an important part of social life. In this chapter, we have seen that persuasion can be achieved in different ways. The most common approach is through communication from *others*. Faced with newspaper editorials, junk mail, books, TV commercials, Internet ads, and other messages, we take one of two routes to persuasion. On the central route, attitude change is based on the merits of the source and his or her communication. On the peripheral route, it is based on superficial cues. Either way, the change in attitude often precipitates a change in behavior. A second, less obvious means of persuasion originates within *ourselves*. When people behave in ways that run afoul of their true convictions, they often go on to change their attitudes. Once again, there is not one route to change, but many. Cognitive dissonance, self-perception, impression management, and self-esteem concerns are among the possible avenues. From attitudes to behavior and back again, the processes of persuasion are complex and interwoven.

REVIEW

The Study of Attitudes

- An attitude is an affective, evaluative reaction toward a person, place, issue, or object.

How Attitudes Are Measured

- The most common way to measure attitudes is through self-reports, such as attitude scales.

- To get respondents to answer questions honestly, the bogus pipeline may be used.

- Covert measures may also be used. Such measures include nonverbal behavior, the facial electromyograph (EMG), brain-wave patterns, and the Implicit Association Test (IAT).

How Attitudes Are Formed

- Twin studies suggest that people may be genetically predisposed to hold certain attitudes.

- However, research shows that attitudes are formed by experience and learning, as when people develop strong attitudes toward neutral objects because of their association with positive and negative stimuli.

The Link Between Attitudes and Behavior

- Attitudes do not necessarily correlate with behavior; but under certain conditions, there is a high correlation.

- Attitudes predict behavior best when they're specific rather than general and strong rather than weak.

- Attitudes compete with other influences on behavior.

Persuasion by Communication

- The most common approach to changing attitudes is through a persuasive communication.

Two Routes to Persuasion

- When people think critically about a message, they take the central route to persuasion and are influenced by the strength of the arguments.

- When people do not think carefully about a message, they take the peripheral route to persuasion and are influenced by peripheral cues.

- The route taken depends on whether people have the ability and the motivation to fully process the communication.

The Source

- Attitude change is greater for messages delivered by a source that is credible (competent and trustworthy).

- Attitude change is also greater when the source is likable (similar and attractive).

- When an audience has a high level of personal involvement, source factors are less important than message quality.

- The sleeper effect shows that people often forget the source but not the message, so the effects of source credibility dissipate over time.

The Message

- On the peripheral route, lengthy messages are persuasive. On the central route, length works only if the added information does not dilute the message.

- Whether it is best to present an argument first or second depends on how much time elapses—both between the two arguments and between the second argument and the final decision.

- Messages that are moderately discrepant from an audience's attitudes will inspire change, but highly discrepant messages will be scrutinized and rejected.

- High-fear messages motivate attitude change when they contain strong arguments and instructions on how to avoid the threatened danger.

- Positive emotion also facilitates attitude change because people are easier to persuade when they're in a good mood.

- Research shows that subliminal messages do not produce meaningful or lasting changes in attitudes.

The Audience

- People are not consistently difficult or easy to persuade. Rather, different kinds of messages influence different kinds of people.

- People who are high in the need for cognition are persuaded more by the strength of the arguments.

- People who are high in self-monitoring are influenced more by appeals to social images.

- To be persuasive, a message should also appeal to the cultural values of its audience.

- Forewarning increases resistance to persuasive influence. It inoculates the audience by providing the opportunity to generate counterarguments, and it arouses psychological reactance.

Culture and Persuasion

- Communications are successful to the extent that they appeal to the cultural values of an audience.

- Research shows that North Americans are persuaded more by individualistic ads, whereas East Asians prefer collectivistic ads.

Persuasion by Our Own Actions

Role Playing: All the World's a Stage
- The way people act can influence how they feel, as behavior can determine attitudes.

Cognitive Dissonance Theory: The Classic Version
- Under certain conditions, inconsistency between attitudes and behavior produces an unpleasant psychological state called cognitive dissonance.
- Motivated to reduce the tension, people often change their attitudes to justify (1) attitude-discrepant behavior, (2) wasted effort, and (3) difficult decisions.

Cognitive Dissonance Theory: A New Look
- According to the "new look" version of cognitive dissonance theory, four conditions must be met for dissonance to be aroused: (1) an act with unwanted consequences, (2) a feeling of personal responsibility, (3) arousal or discomfort, and (4) attribution of the arousal to the attitude-discrepant act.
- Social psychologists continue to debate whether dissonance can be aroused by cognitive inconsistency when no unwanted consequences are produced.

Alternative Routes to Self-Persuasion
- Alternative explanations of dissonance-related attitude change have been proposed.
- Self-perception theory states that people logically infer their attitudes by observing their own behavior.
- Impression-management theory says that people are motivated only to appear consistent to others.
- Self-esteem theories state that dissonance is triggered by threats to the self and can be reduced indirectly, without a change in attitude, through self-affirming experiences.

Cultural Influences on Cognitive Dissonance
- Recently, social psychologists have wondered whether cognitive dissonance effects are universal or specific to Western cultures.
- Research suggests that people all over the world will try to reduce dissonance when it arises but that the conditions that arouse it are influenced by cultural context.

Changing Attitudes

- Through persuasive communications and the mechanisms of self-persuasion, the processes of changing attitudes and behavior are complex and interwoven.

KEY TERMS

PUTTING COMMON SENSE TO THE TEST

Researchers can tell if someone has a positive or negative attitude by measuring physiological arousal.

False. Measures of arousal can reveal how intensely someone feels, but not whether the person's attitude is positive or negative.

In reacting to persuasive communications, people are influenced more by superficial images than by logical arguments.

False. As indicated by the dual-process model of persuasion, people can be influenced by images or arguments, depending on their ability and motivation to think critically about the information.

People are most easily persuaded by commercial messages that are presented without their awareness.

False. There is no research evidence to support the presumed effects of subliminal ads.

The more money you pay people to tell a lie, the more they will come to believe it.

False. Cognitive dissonance studies show that people believe the lies they are underpaid to tell as a way to justify their own actions.

People often come to like what they suffer for.

True. Studies show that the more people work or suffer for something, the more they come to like it as a way to justify their effort.

7

Conformity

PREVIEW

This chapter examines ways in which *social influences are "automatic."*
We then look at three processes. First, we consider the reasons why
people exhibit *conformity* to group norms. Second, we describe the
strategies used to elicit *compliance* with direct requests. Third, we analyze
the causes and effects of *obedience* to the commands of authority. The
chapter concludes with a discussion of the *continuum of social influence.*

*"We are discreet sheep;
we wait to see how the
drove is going and then go
with the drove."*

—Mark Twain

T/F

____ When all members of a group give an incorrect response to an easy question, most people most of the time conform to that response.

____ An effective way to get someone to do you a favor is to make a first request that is so large the person is sure to reject it.

____ In experiments on obedience, most participants who were ordered to administer severe shocks to an innocent person refused to do so.

____ As the number of people in a group increases, so does their impact on an individual.

____ Conformity rates vary across different cultures and from one generation to the next.

On July 24, 2003, two hundred people, strangers to one another, gathered in New York's Central Park, perched themselves near the Museum of Natural History, made bird sounds, and dispersed. One month later, another crowd gathered at Times Square, entered a Toys "R" Us, looked up at a giant roaring dinosaur, and fell to their knees, moaning and cowering at its feet. In both cases, participants had received instructions over the Internet, gathered voluntarily at a set time and place, performed a silly but harmless action, and dispersed. Illustrating the power of the Internet to serve as a vehicle for social influence, other "flash mobs" were then formed in London, Rome, Paris, Amsterdam, Berlin, Oslo, Melbourne, Budapest, Boston, Chicago, Los Angeles, Denver, Houston, and other cities.

Sometimes the social influences that move us are not entertaining and funny but potentially hazardous to our health. Consider the unusual events that occurred in a Tennessee high school. It started when a teacher noticed a gas-like smell in her classroom and then came down with a headache, nausea, shortness of breath, and dizziness. Word spread. Others soon reported the same symptoms and the school was evacuated, with eighty students and nineteen staff members taken to a local emergency room. Nothing showed up in blood tests, urine tests, or other medical procedures, nor were gases, pesticides, or other toxins detected. What the investigation did turn up was that students who reported feeling ill that day were more likely than others to have seen someone with symptoms, heard about someone with symptoms, or known a classmate who was ill. Reporting these findings in the *New England Journal of Medicine*, researchers concluded that the problems were the product of "mass psychogenic illness"—a profound, almost contagious form of social influence (Jones et al., 2000; Wang, 2006).

Flash mobs and the Tennessee school illness reveal the awesome power of social influence. The effects that people have on each other can also be seen in mundane human events. Thus, sports fans spread the "wave" around massive stadiums or chant "de-fense" in a spectacular show of unison. TV producers insert canned laughter into sitcoms to increase viewer responsiveness. Politicians trumpet the inflated results of their own favorable public opinion polls to attract voters. And bartenders, waiters, and waitresses stuff dollar bills into their tip jars as a way to get customers to follow suit. As they say, "Monkey see, monkey do."

You don't need to be a social psychologist to know that people have an impact on each other's behavior. The trickier question is, How, and with what effect? The term *social influence* refers to the ways in which people are affected by the real and imagined pressures of others (Cialdini & Goldstein, 2004; Kiesler & Kiesler, 1969). The kinds of influences brought to bear on an individual come in different shapes and

221

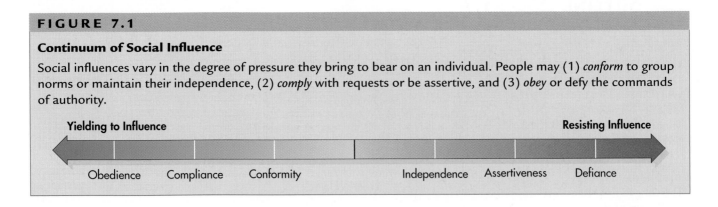

FIGURE 7.1

Continuum of Social Influence

Social influences vary in the degree of pressure they bring to bear on an individual. People may (1) *conform* to group norms or maintain their independence, (2) *comply* with requests or be assertive, and (3) *obey* or defy the commands of authority.

Yielding to Influence   Resisting Influence

Obedience   Compliance   Conformity   Independence   Assertiveness   Defiance

sizes. In this chapter, we look at social influences that are mindless and *automatic*; then we consider three forms of influence that vary in the degree of pressure exerted on an individual—*conformity, compliance,* and *obedience.* As depicted in Figure 7.1, conformity, compliance, and obedience are not distinct, qualitatively different "types" of influence. In all three cases, the influence may emanate from a person, a group, or an institution. And in all instances, the behavior in question may be constructive (helping oneself or others), or destructive (hurting oneself or others), or neutral. It is useful to note, once again, that social influence varies, as points along a continuum, according to the degree of pressure exerted on the individual. It is also useful to note that we do not always succumb under pressure. People may conform or maintain their independence from others; they may comply with direct requests or react with assertiveness; they may obey the commands of authority or oppose powerful others in an act of defiance. In this chapter, we examine the factors that lead human beings to yield to or resist social influence.

Social Influence as "Automatic"

Before we consider the explicit forms of social influence depicted in Figure 7.1, whereby individuals choose whether or not to "go along," it's important to note that, as social animals, humans are vulnerable to a host of subtle, almost reflex-like influences. Without realizing it, we often crack open a yawn when we see others yawning, laugh aloud when we hear others laughing, and grimace when we see others in pain. In an early demonstration, Stanley Milgram and others (1969) had research confederates stop on a busy street in New York City, look up, and gawk at the sixth-floor window of a nearby building. Films shot from behind the window indicated that about 80 percent of passers-by stopped and gazed up when they saw the confederates.

Rudimentary forms of imitation have been observed in various animal species, such as pigeons, monkeys, hamsters, and fish (Heyes & Galef, 1996; Zentall, 2003). There is even evidence to suggest that "cultures" are transmitted through imitation in groups of whales, as when humpback whales off the coast of Maine use "lobtail feeding," a technique in which they slam their tail flukes onto the water, then dive and exhale, forming clouds of bubbles that envelop schools of prey fish. This complex behavior was first observed in 1981. By 1989 it was measurably adopted by 50 percent of the whale population in that area (Rendell & Whitehead, 2001).

Do we really imitate one another automatically, without thought, effort, or conflict? It appears that we do. In recent years, controlled studies of human infants have shown that within seventy-two hours of birth, babies not only look at faces but—to the delight of parents all over the world—often mimic gestures such as moving the head, pursing the lips, and sticking out the tongue (Bremner, 2002; Gopnik et al., 1999).

You may not realize it, but human adults unwittingly mimic each other all the time. To demonstrate, Tanya Chartrand and John Bargh (1999) set up participants to work on a task with a partner, a confederate who exhibited the habit of rubbing his face or shaking his foot. Hidden cameras recording the interaction revealed that, with-

Among humpback whales off the coast of Maine, "lobtail feeding" (a complex behavior that traps prey fish) was first observed in 1981. Through imitation, it soon spread across the entire whale population in the region.

out realizing it, participants mimicked these motor behaviors, rubbing their face or shaking a foot to match their partner's behavior. Chartrand and Bargh dubbed this phenomenon the "chameleon effect," after the lizard that changes colors according to its physical environment (see Figure 7.2).

There are two possible reasons for this nonconscious form of imitation. Chartrand and Bargh speculated that such mimicry serves an important *social* function, that being "in synch" in their pace, posture, mannerisms, facial expressions, tone of voice, accents, speech patterns, and other behaviors enables people to interact more smoothly with one another. Accordingly, Chartrand and Bargh (1999) turned the tables in a second study in which they instructed their confederate to match in subtle ways the mannerisms of some participants but not others. Sure enough, participants who had been mimicked liked the confederate more than those who had not. Further demonstrating the social aspect of mimicry, research shows that people mimic others more when they are motivated to affiliate than when they are not (Lakin & Chartrand, 2003). Moreover, people who are mimicked, even if they do not realize it, become more helpful and more generous, not only to the mimicker but to others as well (van Baaren et al., 2004).

Social mimicry is so powerful that it can influence us even when the mimicker is not a real person. In a study entitled "digital chameleons," Jeremy Bailenson and Nick Yee (2005) immersed college students, one at a time, in a virtual reality environment in which they found themselves seated at a table across from a humanlike person that looked something like a three-dimensional cartoon character. This character proceeded to argue that students should be required to carry identification cards at all times for security purposes. In half the sessions, this virtual speaker's back-and-forth head movements perfectly mimicked the participant's head movements at a four-second delay. In the other half, the speaker repeated the head movements of an earlier recorded participant. Very few of the students who were mimicked were aware of it. Yet when later asked about the experience, they rated the virtual character as more likable and were persuaded by its speech more if it imitated their own head movements than if it imitated the previous participant.

The human impulse to mimic others may have adaptive social value, but these types of effects can also be found in *nonsocial* situations. In one study, Roland Neumann and Fritz Strack (2000) had people listen to an abstract philosophical speech that was recited on tape in a happy, sad, or neutral voice. Afterward, participants rated their own mood as more positive when they heard the happy voice and as more negative when they heard the sad voice. Even though the speakers and participants never interacted, the speaker's emotional state was infectious—an automatic effect that can be described as a form of "mood contagion."

It is also important to realize that mimicry is a dynamic process, as when two people who are walking together, or dancing, become more and more coordinated over time. To demonstrate, Michael Richardson and others (2005) sat pairs of college students side by side to work on visual problems while swinging a hand-held pendulum

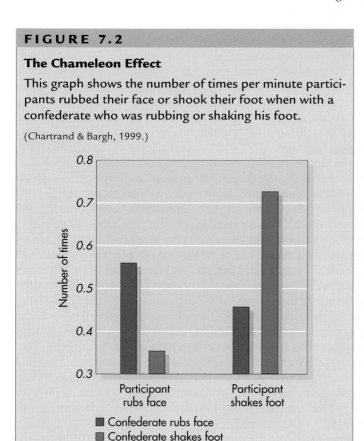

"I don't know why. I just suddenly felt like calling."

Often we are not aware of the influence other people have on our behavior.

FIGURE 7.2

The Chameleon Effect

This graph shows the number of times per minute participants rubbed their face or shook their foot when with a confederate who was rubbing or shaking his foot.

(Chartrand & Bargh, 1999.)

as "a distraction task." The students did not need to be synchronized in their swinging tempo in order to get along or solve the problems. Yet when each could see the other's pendulum, and even without speaking, their tempos gradually converged over time—like two hearts beating as one.

Conformity

It is hard to find behaviors that are not in some way affected by exposure to the actions of others. When social psychologists talk of **conformity**, they specifically refer to the tendency of people to change their perceptions, opinions, and behavior in ways that are consistent with group norms. With this definition in mind, would you call yourself a conformist or a nonconformist? How often do you feel inclined to follow what others are saying or doing? At first, you may deny the tendency to conform and, instead, declare your individuality. But think about it. When was the last time you appeared at a formal wedding dressed in blue jeans or remained seated during the national anthem at a sports event? People find it difficult to breach social norms. In an interesting demonstration of this point, social psychology research assistants were supposed to ask subway passengers to give up their seats—a conspicuous violation of the norm of acceptable conduct. Many of the assistants could not carry out their assignment. In fact, some of those who tried it became so anxious that they pretended to be ill just to make their request appear justified (Milgram & Sabini, 1978).

With conformity being so widespread, it is interesting and ironic that research participants (at least in North America) who are coaxed into following a group norm will often not admit to being influenced. Instead, they try to reinterpret the task and rationalize their own behavior as a way to see themselves as independent (Hornsey & Jetten, 2004). This resistance to the conformity label is particularly characteristic of individuals who have high status and seniority within a group (Jetten et al., 2006). People understandably have mixed feelings about the subject. After all, some degree of conformity is essential if individuals are to form communities and coexist peacefully, as when people assume their rightful place in a waiting line. Yet at other times, conformity can have harmful consequences, as when people drink too heavily at parties or tell offensive ethnic jokes because others are doing the same. For the social psychologist, the goal is to understand the conditions that promote conformity or independence and the reasons for these behaviors.

The Early Classics

In 1936, Muzafer Sherif published a classic laboratory study of how norms develop in small groups. His method was ingenious. Male students, who believed they were participating in a visual perception experiment, sat in a totally darkened room. Fifteen feet in front of them, a small dot of light appeared for two seconds, after which participants were asked to estimate how far it had moved. This procedure was repeated several times. Although participants didn't realize it, the dot of light always remained motionless. The movement they thought they saw was merely an optical illusion known as the *autokinetic effect*: In darkness, a stationary point of light appears to move, sometimes erratically, in various directions.

At first, participants sat alone and reported their judgments to the experimenter. After several trials, Sherif found that they settled in on their own stable perceptions of movement, with most estimates ranging from one to ten inches (although one participant gave an estimate of eighty feet!). Over the next three days, people returned to participate in three-person groups. As before, lights were flashed, and the participants, one by one, announced their estimates. As shown in Figure 7.3, initial estimates varied considerably, but participants later converged on a common perception. Eventually, each group established its own set of norms.

Some fifteen years after Sherif's demonstration, Solomon Asch (1951) constructed a very different task for testing how people's beliefs affect the beliefs of others. To ap-

conformity The tendency to change our perceptions, opinions, or behavior in ways that are consistent with group norms.

FIGURE 7.3

A Classic Case of Suggestibility

This graph, taken from Sherif's study, shows how three participants' estimates of the apparent movement of light gradually converged. Before they came together, their perceptions varied considerably. Once in groups, however, participants conformed to the norm that had developed.

(Sherif, 1936.)

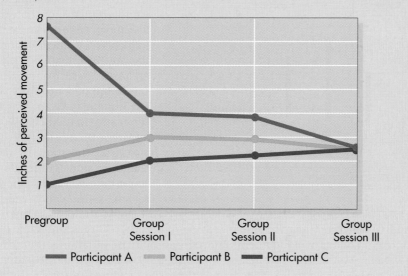

Participant A   Participant B   Participant C

After two uneventful rounds in Asch's study, the participant (seated second from the right) faces a dilemma. The answer he wants to give in the third test of visual discrimination differs from that of the first five confederates, who are all in agreement. Should he give his own answers, or conform to theirs?

preciate what Asch did, imagine yourself in the following situation. You sign up for a psychology experiment; and when you arrive, you find six other students waiting around a table. Soon after you take an empty seat, the experimenter explains that he is interested in the ability to make visual discriminations. As an example, he asks you and the others to indicate which of three comparison lines is identical in length to a standard line.

That seems easy enough. The experimenter then says that after each set of lines is shown, you and the others should take turns announcing your judgments out loud in the order of your seating position. Beginning on his left, the experimenter asks the first person for his judgment. Seeing that you are in the next-to-last position, you patiently await your turn. The opening moments pass uneventfully. The discriminations are clear, and everyone agrees on the answers. On the third set of lines, however, the first participant selects what is quite clearly the wrong line. Huh? What happened? Did he suddenly lose his mind, his eyesight, or both? Before you have the chance to figure this one out, the next four participants choose the same wrong line. Now what? Feeling as if you have entered the Twilight Zone, you wonder if you misunderstood the task. And you wonder what the others will think if you have the nerve to disagree. It's your turn now. You rub your eyes and take another look. What do you see? More to the point, what do you do?

Figure 7.4 gives you a sense of the bind in which Asch's participants found themselves—caught between the need to be right and the desire to be liked (Insko et al., 1982; Ross et al., 1976). As you may suspect by now, the other "participants" were actually confederates—and had been trained to make incorrect judgments on twelve out of eighteen presentations. There seems little doubt that the real participants knew the correct answers. In a control group, where they made judgments in isolation, they made almost no errors. Yet Asch's participants went along with the incorrect majority 37 percent of the time—far more often than most of us would ever predict. Not everyone conformed, of course. About 25 percent refused to agree on any of the incorrect group judgments. Yet 50 percent went along on at least half of the critical presentations, with the remaining participants conforming on an occasional basis. Similarly high levels

FIGURE 7.4

Line Judgment Task Used in Asch's Conformity Studies

Which comparison line—A, B, or C—is the same in length as the standard line? What would you say if you found yourself in the presence of a unanimous majority that answered A or C? The participants in Asch's experiments conformed to the majority about a third of the time.

(Asch, 1955.)

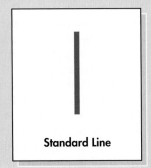 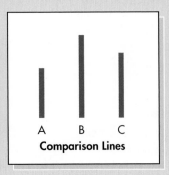

Standard Line

Comparison Lines

When all members of a group give an incorrect response to an easy question, most people most of the time conform to that response. **False.**

informational influence
Influence that produces conformity when a person believes others are correct in their judgments.

of conformity were observed when Asch's study was repeated thirty years later and in recent studies involving other cognitive tasks (Larsen, 1990; Schneider & Watkins, 1996).

Looking at Sherif's and Asch's research, let's compare these classic studies of social influence. Obviously, both demonstrate that our visual perceptions can be heavily influenced by others. But how similar are they, really? Did Sherif's and Asch's participants exhibit the same kind of conformity, and for the same reasons, or was the resemblance in their behavior more apparent than real?

From the start, it was clear that these studies differed in some important ways. In Sherif's research, participants were quite literally "in the dark," so they naturally turned to others for guidance. When physical reality is ambiguous and we are uncertain of our own judgments, as in the autokinetic situation, others can serve as a valuable source of information (Festinger, 1954). Asch's participants found themselves in a much more awkward position. Their task was relatively simple, and they could see with their own eyes what answers were correct. Still, they often followed the incorrect majority. In interviews, many of Asch's participants reported afterward that they went along with the group even though they were not convinced. Many who did not conform said they felt "conspicuous" and "crazy," like a "misfit" (Asch, 1956, p. 31).

Currently, more than 1 billion people worldwide, accounting for 16 percent of the planet's population, have access to communication over the Internet. This being the case, you may wonder: Do the social forces that influence people in the face-to-face encounters studied by Sherif and Asch also operate in virtual groups whose members are nameless, faceless, and anonymous? The answer is yes. McKenna and Bargh (1998) observed behavior in a number of Internet newsgroups, or blogs, in which people with common interests posted and responded to messages on a whole range of topics, from obesity and sexual orientation to money and the stock market. The social nature of the medium in this virtual situation was "remote." Still, these researchers found that in newsgroups that brought together people with "hidden identities" (such as gays and lesbians who had concealed their sexuality), members were highly responsive to social feedback. Those who posted messages that were met with approval rather than disapproval later became more active participants of the newsgroup. When it comes to social support and rejection, even remote virtual groups have the power to shape our behavior (Bargh & McKenna, 2004; Williams et al., 2000).

Why Do People Conform?

The Sherif and Asch studies demonstrate that people conform for two very different reasons: one informational, the other normative (Crutchfield, 1955; Deutsch & Gerard, 1955). Through **informational influence**, people conform because they want to make correct judgments and they assume that when others agree on something, they must be right. In Sherif's autokinetic task, as in other difficult or ambiguous tasks, it's natural to assume that four eyes are better than two. Hence, research shows that eyewitnesses trying to recall a crime or some other event will alter their recollections—and even create false memories—in response to what they hear other witnesses report (Gabbert et al., 2003). In a state of uncertainty, following the collective wisdom of

Nonconformists pay a price for dissent. At the start of the controversial U.S.-led war in Iraq, Dixie Chick Natalie Maines told a London audience, "We're ashamed the President of the United States is from Texas." At a time when most Americans supported the war, country music fans greeted this remark with scorn and boycotted the Dixie Chicks. Three years later, and without regret, the band revealed in a new Grammy award-winning CD that they are still being ostracized for their dissent.

others may prove to be an effective strategy. In the recent TV game show *Who Wants to Be a Millionaire?* contestants stumped on a question could invoke one of two human forms of assistance: (1) calling a friend or relative for help on the answer, a designated "expert," or (2) polling the studio audience, which would cast votes by computer for instant feedback. Overall, the "experts" were useful, offering the right answer 65 percent of the time. Illustrating the wisdom of crowds, however, the studio audiences picked the right answer 91 percent of the time (Surowiecki, 2005).

In contrast to the informational value of conformity, **normative influence** leads people to conform because they fear the consequences of appearing deviant. It's easy to see why. Early on, research showed that individuals who stray from a group's norm are often disliked, rejected, and ridiculed (Schachter, 1951). These negative social reactions can be hard to take. In a series of controlled studies, people who were socially *ostracized*—by being neglected, ignored, and excluded in a live or Internet chatroom conversation—reacted by feeling hurt, angry, alone, and lacking in self-esteem (Williams et al., 2002). "RU there?" Even being left out of a three-way text-messaging conversation on a cell phone can have this effect on us (Smith & Williams, 2004). Kipling Williams (2007) notes that the research on this point is clear: Some people become so distressed when they are rejected or excluded from a group that they become passive, numb, and lethargic—as though they had been hit with a stun gun.

Why does being ostracized hurt so much? Increasingly, social psychologists are coming to appreciate the extent to which human beings, over the course of evolution, have needed each other in order to survive and flourish. According to Geoff MacDonald and Mark Leary (2005), this need is so primitive that rejection inflicts a social pain that feels just like physical pain. You can sense the connection in the way people describe their emotional reactions to social loss using such words as "hurt," "brokenhearted," and "crushed." Recent brain-imaging research also lends provocative support to this linkage. In one brain-imaging study, for example, young people who were left out by other players in a three-person Internet game called "Cyberball" exhibited elevated neural activity in a part of the brain that is normally associated with physical pain (Eisenberger et al., 2003).

In group settings, both informational and normative influences are typically at work. Consider the Asch experiment. Even though many of his participants said they had conformed just to avoid being different, others said that they came to agree with their group's erroneous judgments. Is that possible? At the time, Asch had to rely on what his participants reported in interviews. Thanks to recent developments in social neuroscience, however, researchers can now peer into the socially active brain. In an ingenious medical school study that illustrates the point, Gregory Berns and others (2005) put thirty-two adults into a visual-spatial perception experiment in which they were asked to "mentally rotate" two geometric objects to determine if they were the same or different (see Figure 7.5). As in the original Asch study, the participants were accompanied by four confederates who unanimously made incorrect judgments on certain trials. Unlike in the original study, however, participants were placed in an fMRI scanner during the task. There were two noteworthy results. First, the participants conformed to 41 percent of the group's incorrect judgments. Second, these conforming judgments were accompanied by heightened activity in a part of the brain that controls spatial awareness—not in areas associated with conscious decision making. These results suggest that the group altered perceptions, not just behavior.

The distinction between the two types of influence—informational and normative—is important, not just for understanding why people conform but because the two sources of influence produce different types of conformity: private and public (Allen, 1965; Kelman, 1961). Like beauty, conformity may be skin deep, or it may

normative influence
Influence that produces conformity when a person fears the negative social consequences of appearing deviant.

FIGURE 7.5

Conformity Effects on Perception

In this study, participants tried to determine if pairs of geometric objects were the same or different after observing the responses of four unanimous confederates. Participants followed the incorrect group 41 percent of the time. Suggesting that the group had altered perceptions, not just behavior, fMRI results showed that these conforming judgments were accompanied by increased activity in a part of the brain that controls spatial awareness.

(Berns et al., 2005.)

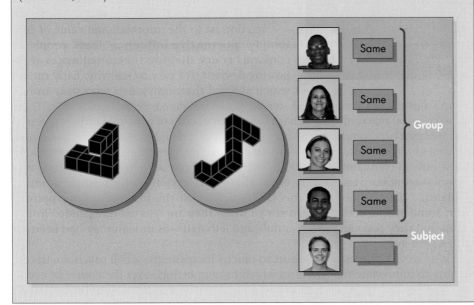

penetrate beneath the surface. **Private conformity**, also called true acceptance or conversion, describes instances in which others cause us to change not only our overt behavior but our minds as well. To conform at this level is to be truly persuaded that others in a group are correct. In contrast, **public conformity** (sometimes called *compliance,* a term used later in this chapter to describe a different form of influence) refers to a more superficial change in behavior. People often respond to normative pressures by pretending to agree even when privately they do not. This often happens when we want to curry favor with others. The politician who tells constituents whatever they want to hear is a case in point.

How, you might be wondering, can social psychologists ever tell the difference between the private and public conformist? After all, both exhibit the same change in their observable behavior. The difference is that compared with someone who merely acquiesces in public, the individual who is truly persuaded maintains that change long after the group is out of the picture. When this distinction is applied to Sherif's and Asch's research, the results come out as expected. At the end of his study, Sherif (1936) retested participants alone and found that their estimates continued to reflect the norm previously established in their group—even among those who were retested a full year after the experiment (Rohrer et al., 1954). In contrast, when Asch (1956) had participants write their answers privately, their level of conformity dropped sharply (Deutsch & Gerard, 1955; Mouton et al., 1956).

In a study that demonstrates both processes, Robert S. Baron and others (1996) had people in groups of three (one participant and two confederates) act as eyewitnesses: First they would see a picture of a person, then they would try to pick that person out of a line-up. In some groups, the task was difficult, like Sherif's, since participants saw each picture only once, for half a second. For other groups, the task was easier, like Asch's, in that they saw each picture twice for a total of ten seconds. How often did participants conform when the confederates made the wrong identification? It depended on how motivated they were. When the experimenter downplayed the task as only a "pilot study," the conformity rates were 35 percent when the task was difficult and 33 percent when it was easy. But when participants were offered a financial incentive to do well, conformity went up to 51 percent when the task was difficult—and down to 16 percent when it was easy (see Figure 7.6). With pride and money on the line, the Sherif-like participants conformed more, and the Asch-like participants conformed less.

Table 7.1 summarizes the comparison of Sherif's and Asch's studies and the depths of social influence that they demonstrate. Looking at this table, you can see that the difficulty of the task is crucial. When reality cannot easily be validated by physical evidence, as in the autokinetic situation, people turn to others for information and conform because they are truly persuaded by that information. When reality is clear, however, the cost of dissent becomes the major issue. As Asch found, it

private conformity The change of beliefs that occurs when a person privately accepts the position taken by others.

public conformity A superficial change in overt behavior, without a corresponding change of opinion, produced by real or imagined group pressure.

FIGURE 7.6

Distinguishing Types of Conformity

People made judgments under conditions in which they had a high or low level of motivation. Regardless of whether the judgment task was difficult or easy, there were moderate levels of conformity when participants had low motivation (left). But when they were highly motivated (right), participants conformed more when the task was difficult—as in Sherif's study, and less when it was easy—as in Asch's study.

(Baron et al., 1996.)

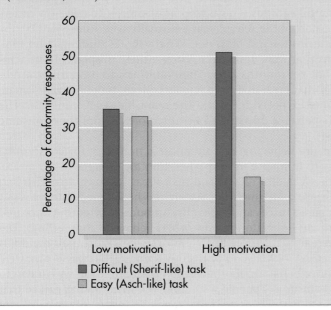

can be difficult to depart too much from others even when you know that they—not you—are wrong. So you play along. Privately, you don't change your mind. But you nod your head in agreement anyway.

Majority Influence

Realizing that people often succumb to peer pressure is only the first step in understanding the process of social influence. The next step is to identify the situational and personal factors that make us more or less likely to conform. We know that people tend to conform when the social pressure is intense and they are insecure about how to behave. But what creates these feelings of pressure and insecurity? Here, we look at four factors: the size of the group, a focus on norms, the presence of an ally, and gender.

Group Size: The Power in Numbers   Common sense would suggest that as the number of other people in a majority increases, so should their impact. Actually, it is not that simple. Asch (1956) varied the size of groups, using one, two, three, four, eight, or fifteen confederates, and he found that conformity increased with group size—but only up to a point. Once there were three or four confederates, the amount of *additional* influence exerted by the rest was negligible. Other researchers have obtained similar results (Gerard et al., 1968).

Beyond the presence of three or four others, additions to a group are subject to the law of "diminishing returns" (Knowles, 1983; Mullen, 1983). As we will see later, Bibb Latané (1981) likens the influence of people on an individual to the way light bulbs illuminate a surface. When a second bulb is added to a room, the effect is dramatic. When the tenth bulb is added, however, its impact is barely felt, if at all. Economists say the same about the perception of money. An additional dollar seems greater to the person who has only three dollars than to the person who has three hundred.

Another possible explanation is that as more and more people express the same opinion, an individual is likely to suspect that they are acting either in "collusion" or as "spineless sheep." According to David Wilder (1977), what matters is not the actual number of others in a group but one's perception of how many distinct others, thinking independently, there are. Indeed, Wilder found that people were more influenced by two groups of two than by one four-person group and by two groups of three than by one six-person group. Conformity increased even further when people were exposed

TABLE 7.1

Two Types of Conformity

A comparison of Sherif's and Asch's studies suggests different kinds of conformity for different reasons. Sherif used an ambiguous task, so others provided a source of information and influenced the participants' true opinions. Asch used a task that required simple judgments of a clear stimulus, so most participants exhibited occasional public conformity in response to normative pressure but privately did not accept the group's judgments.

Experimental Task	Primary Effect of Group	Depth of Conformity Produced
Sherif's ambiguous autokinetic effect	Informational influence	Private acceptance
Asch's simple line judgments	Normative influence	Public conformity

to three two-person groups. When faced with a majority opinion, we do more than just count the number of warm bodies—we try to assess the number of independent minds.

A Focus on Norms   The size of a majority may influence the amount of pressure that is felt, but social norms give rise to conformity only when we know and focus on those norms. This may sound like an obvious point, yet we often misperceive what is normative—particularly when others are too afraid or embarrassed to publicly present their true thoughts, feelings, and behaviors.

One common example of this "pluralistic ignorance" concerns perceptions of alcohol usage. In a number of college-wide surveys, Deborah Prentice and Dale Miller (1996) found that most students overestimated how comfortable their peers were with the level of drinking on campus. Those who most overestimated how others felt about drinking at the start of the school year eventually conformed to this misperception in their own attitudes and behavior. What's more, students who took part in discussion sessions that were designed to correct these misperceptions actually consumed less alcohol six months later. These findings are important. Additional research has shown that both male and female college students overestimate how frequently their same-sex peers drink and the quantities they consume. The more normative students perceive drinking to be, the more alcohol they consume (Lewis & Neighbors, 2004).

Knowing how others are behaving in a situation is necessary for conformity, but these norms are likely to influence us only when they are brought to our awareness, or "activated." Robert Cialdini (2003) and his colleagues have demonstrated this point in studies on littering. In one study, researchers had confederates pass out handbills to amusement park visitors and varied the amount of litter that appeared in one section of the park (an indication of how others behave in that setting). The result: The more litter there was, the more likely visitors were to toss their handbills to the ground (Cialdini et al., 1990). A second study showed that passers-by were most influenced by the prior behavior of others when their attention was drawn to the existing norm. In this instance, people were observed in a parking garage that was either clean or cluttered with cigarette butts, candy wrappers, paper cups, and trash. In half of the cases, the norm that was already in place—clean or cluttered— was brought to participants' attention by a confederate who threw paper to the ground as he walked by. In the other half, the confederate passed by without incident. As participants reached their cars, they found a "Please Drive Safely" handbill tucked under the windshield wiper. Did they toss the paper to the ground or take it with them? The results showed that people were most likely to conform (by littering more when the garage was cluttered than when it was clean) when the confederate had littered—an act that drew attention to the norm (Cialdini et al., 1991).

In sports stadiums, restaurants, and other settings, social norms influence us when they are brought to awareness by the current or past behavior of others.

An Ally in Dissent: Getting By with a Little Help In Asch's initial experiment, unwitting participants found themselves pitted against unanimous majorities. But what if they had an ally, a partner in dissent? Asch investigated this issue and found that the presence of a single confederate who agreed with the participant reduced conformity by almost 80 percent. This finding, however, does not tell us why the presence of an ally was so effective. Was it because he or she *agreed* with the participant or because he or she *disagreed* with the majority? In other words, were the views of the participants strengthened because a dissenting confederate offered validating information or because dissent per se reduced *normative* pressures?

A series of experiments explored these two possibilities. In one, Vernon Allen and John Levine (1969) led participants to believe that they were working together with four confederates. Three of these others consistently agreed on the wrong judgment. The fourth then followed the majority, agreed with the participant, or made a third judgment, which was also incorrect. This last variation was the most interesting: Even when the confederate did not validate their own judgment, participants conformed less often to the majority. In another study, Allen and Levine (1971) varied the competence of the ally. Some participants received support from an average person. In contrast, others found themselves supported by someone who wore very thick glasses and complained that he could not see the visual displays. Not a very reassuring ally, right? Wrong. Even though participants derived less comfort from this supporter than from one who seemed more competent at the task, his presence still reduced their level of conformity.

Two important conclusions follow from this research. First, it is substantially more difficult for people to stand alone for their convictions than to be part of even a tiny minority. Second, *any* dissent—whether it validates an individual's opinion or not—can break the spell cast by a unanimous majority and reduce the normative pressures to conform. In an interesting possible illustration of how uncommon it is for individuals to single-handedly oppose a majority, researchers examined voting patterns on the United States Supreme Court from 1953 to 2001. Table 7.2 shows that out of 4,178 decisions in which all nine justices voted, the 8 to 1 split was the least frequent, occurring in only 10 percent of all decisions (Granberg & Bartels, 2005).

Gender Differences Are there gender differences in conformity? Based on Asch's initial studies, social psychologists used to think that women, once considered the "weaker" sex, conform more than men. In light of all the research, however, it appears that two additional factors have to be considered. First, sex differences depend on how comfortable people are with the experimental task. Frank Sistrunk and John McDavid (1971) had male and female participants answer questions on stereotypically masculine, feminine, and gender-neutral topics. Along with each question, participants were told the percentage of others who agreed or disagreed. Although females conformed to the contrived majority more on the masculine items, males conformed more on the feminine items (there were no sex differences on the neutral questions). This finding suggests that one's familiarity with the issue at hand, not gender, is what affects conformity. Ask about football or video war games, and most women acquiesce more than most men. Ask about family planning and fashion design, and the pattern is reversed (Eagly & Carli, 1981).

A second factor is the type of social pressure people face. As a general rule, sex differences are weak and unreliable. But there is an important exception: In face-to-face encounters, where people must openly disagree with each other, small differences do emerge. In fact, when participants think they are being observed, women conform more

TABLE 7.2

On Being a Lone Dissenter: Voting Patterns on the U.S. Supreme Court

Out of 4,178 U.S. Supreme Court decisions from 1953 to 2001, the 8 to 1 breakdown involving a lone dissenter was the least common type of vote. This historical observation is consistent with conformity research showing the power of the majority over an individual who lacks an ally (Granberg & Bartels, 2005). Can you think of another explanation for this pattern?

Vote Breakdowns	Frequency
9-0	35%
8-1	10%
7-2	14%
6-3	20%
5-4	21%

and men conform less than they do in a more private situation. Why does being "in public" create such a divergence in behavior? Alice Eagly (1987) argues that in front of others, people worry about how they come across and feel pressured to behave in ways that are viewed as acceptable according to traditional gender-role constraints. At least in public, men behave with fierce independence and autonomy, while women play a gentler, more docile role. From an evolutionary perspective, Vladas Griskevicius and others (2006) add that people are most likely to behave in gender-stereotyped ways when motivated to attract someone of the opposite sex. Consistent with research showing that women tend to like men who are independent, whereas men prefer women who are agreeable, their research shows that women conform more—and that men conform less—when primed to think about themselves in a romantic situation.

Minority Influence

In a book entitled *Dissent in Dangerous Times*, Austin Sarat (2005) notes that while the freedom to dissent is highly valued within the American national psyche, individual dissenters are often vilified for their beliefs—especially in today's post-9/11 war on terror. The fact is, it has never been easy for individuals to express unpopular views and enlist support for these views from others. Philosopher Bertrand Russell once said, "Conventional people are roused to frenzy by departure from convention, largely because they regard such departure as criticism of themselves." He may have been right. Although people who stand up for their beliefs against the majority are generally seen as competent and honest, they are also disliked and roundly rejected (Bassili & Provencal, 1988; Levine, 1989). It's no wonder that people think twice before expressing unpopular positions. In a series of survey studies of what he called the "minority slowness effect," John Bassili (2003) asked people about their attitudes on social policy issues such as affirmative action or about their likes and dislikes for various celebrities, sports, foods, places, and activities. Consistently, and regardless of the topic, respondents who held minority opinions were slower to answer the questions than those in the majority.

Resisting the pressure to conform and maintaining one's independence may be socially difficult, but it is not impossible. History's famous heroes, villains, and creative minds are living proof: Joan of Arc, Jesus Christ, Charles Darwin, and Mahatma Gandhi, to name just a few, were dissenters of their time who continue to capture the imagination. Then there's human behavior in the laboratory. Social psychologists have been so intrigued by Asch's initial finding that participants conformed 37 percent of the time that textbooks such as this one routinely refer to "Asch's conformity study." Yet the overlooked flip side of the coin is that Asch's participants refused to acquiesce 63 percent of the time—thus also indicating the power of independence, truth telling, and a concern for social harmony (Friend et al., 1990; Hodges & Geyer, 2006).

Twelve Angry Men, a classic film starring Henry Fonda, illustrates how a lone dissenter can resist the pressure to conform and convince others to follow. Almost as soon as the jury room door closes, the jury in this film takes a show-of-hands vote. The result is an eleven-to-one majority in favor of conviction, with Fonda the lone holdout. Through ninety minutes of heated deliberation, Fonda works relentlessly to plant a seed of doubt in the minds of his trigger-happy peers. In the end, the jury reaches a unanimous verdict: *not* guilty.

Sometimes art imitates life; sometimes it does not. In this instance, Henry Fonda's heroics are highly atypical. When it comes to jury decision making, we'll see in Chapter 12 that the majority usually wins. Yet in trial juries, as in other small groups, there are occasional exceptions. Thanks to Serge Moscovici, Edwin Hollander, and others, we now know quite a bit about **minority influence** and the strategies that astute nonconformists use to act as agents of social change (De Dreu & De Vries, 2001; Hollander, 1985; Maass & Clark, 1984; Moscovici et al., 1985; Mugny & Perez, 1991).

minority influence The process by which dissenters produce change within a group.

The Power of Style   According to Moscovici, majorities are powerful by virtue of their sheer *numbers,* while nonconformists derive power from the *style* of their behavior. It is not just what nonconformists say that matters, but how they say it. To exert influence, says Moscovici, those in the minority must be forceful, persistent, and unwavering in support of their position. Yet at the same time, they must appear flexible and open-minded. Confronted with a consistent but evenhanded dissenter, members of the majority will sit up, take notice, and rethink their own positions.

Why should a consistent behavioral style prove effective? One possible reason is that unwavering repetition draws attention from those in the mainstream, which is a necessary first step to social influence. Another possibility is that consistency signals that the dissenter is unlikely to yield, which leads those in the majority to feel pressured to seek compromise. A third possible reason is that when confronted with someone who has the self-confidence and dedication to take an unpopular stand without backing down, people assume that he or she must have a point. Unless a dissenter is perceived in negative terms—as biased, obstinate, or just plain crazy—this situation stimulates others to re-examine their own views (Moskowitz, 1996). Of course, it helps to be seen as part of "us" rather than "them." Research shows that dissenters have more influence when people identify with them and perceive them to be similar in ways that are relevant and desirable (Turner, 1991; Wood et al., 1996).

Based on a meta-analysis of ninety-seven experiments investigating minority influence, Wendy Wood and her colleagues (1994) concluded that there is strong support for the consistency hypothesis. In one classic study, for example, Moscovici and others (1969) turned Asch's procedure on its head by confronting people with a *minority* of confederates who made incorrect judgments. In groups of six, participants took part in what was supposed to be a study of color perception. They viewed a series of slides—all blue, but varying in intensity. For each slide, the participants took turns naming the color. The task was simple, but two confederates announced that the slides were green. When the confederates were *consistent*—that is, when both made incorrect green judgments for all slides—they had a surprising degree of influence. About a third of all participants incorrectly reported seeing at least one green slide, and 8 percent of all responses were incorrect. Subsequent research confirmed that the perception of consistency increases minority influence (Clark, 2001; Crano, 2000).

Based on the fact that dissent often breeds hostility, Edwin Hollander (1958) recommended a different approach. Hollander warned that people who seek positions of leadership or challenge a group without first becoming accepted full-fledged members of that group run the risk that their opinions will fall on deaf ears. As an alternative to Moscovici's consistency strategy, Hollander suggested that to influence a majority, people should first conform in order to establish their credentials as competent insiders. By becoming members of the mainstream, they accumulate **idiosyncrasy credits**, or "brownie points." Then, as soon as they have accumulated enough good will within the group, a certain amount of their deviance will be tolerated. Several studies have shown that this "first conform, then dissent" strategy, like the "consistent dissent" approach, can be effective (Bray et al., 1982; Lortie-Lussier, 1987).

A Chip Off the Old Block?   Regardless of which strategy is used, minority influence is a force to be reckoned with. But does it work just like the process of conformity, or is there something different about the way that minorities and majorities effect change? Some theorists believe that a *single process* accounts for both directions of social influence—that minority influence is like a "chip off the old block" (Latané & Wolf, 1981; Tanford & Penrod, 1984). Others have taken a *dual-process* approach (Moscovici, 1980; Nemeth, 1986). In this second view, majorities and minorities exert influence in very different ways and for different reasons. Majorities, because they have power and control, elicit *public* conformity by bringing stressful normative pressures to bear on the individual. But minorities, because they are seen as seriously committed to their views, produce a deeper and more lasting form of *private* conformity, or *conversion*, by leading others to rethink their original positions.

idiosyncrasy credits
Interpersonal "credits" that a person earns by following group norms.

To evaluate these single- and dual-process theories, researchers have compared the effects of majority and minority viewpoints on participants who are otherwise neutral on an issue in dispute. On the basis of this research, two conclusions can be drawn. First, the relative impact of majorities and minorities depends on whether the judgment that is being made is objective or subjective, a matter of fact or opinion. In a study conducted in Italy, Ann Maass and others (1996) found that majorities have greater influence on factual questions, for which only one answer is correct ("What percentage of its raw oil does Italy import from Venezuela?"), but that minorities exert equal impact on opinion questions, for which there is a range of acceptable responses ("What percentage of its raw oil *should* Italy import from Venezuela?"). People feel freer to stray from the mainstream on matters of opinion—when there is no right or wrong answer.

The second conclusion is that the relative effects of majority and minority points of view depend on how conformity is measured. To be sure, majorities have a decisive upper hand on direct or public measures of conformity. After all, people are reluctant to stray conspicuously from the group norm. But on more indirect or private measures of conformity—when participants can respond without a fear of appearing deviant—minorities exert a strong impact (Clark & Maass, 1990; Moscovici & Personnaz, 1991; Wood et al., 1996). As Moscovici cogently argued, each of us is changed in a meaningful but subtle way by minority opinion. Because of social pressures, we may not openly admit to the influence; but the change is unmistakable (Wood et al., 1994).

According to Charlan Nemeth (1986), dissenters serve another valuable purpose regardless of whether their views are correct. Simply by their willingness to stay firmly independent, minorities can force other group members to think more carefully, more openly, and more creatively about a problem, enhancing the quality of a group's decision making. In one study, participants exposed to a minority viewpoint on how to solve anagram problems later found more novel solutions themselves (Nemeth & Kwan, 1987). In a second study, those exposed to a consistent minority viewpoint on how to recall information later recalled more words from a list they were trying to memorize (Nemeth et al., 1990). In a third study, interacting groups that contained one dissenting confederate produced more original analyses of complex business problems (Van Dyne & Saavedra, 1996). Interestingly, Nemeth and others (2001) have found that in order to have influence on a group, lone individuals must exhibit "authentic dissent," not merely play "devil's advocate"—a tactic that bolsters a majority's position.

 ## Culture, Conformity, and Independence

We humans are a heterogeneous and diverse lot. As a matter of *geography*, some of us live in large, heavily populated cities, while others live in small towns, affluent suburbs, rural farming or fishing communities, hot and humid jungles, expansive deserts, high-altitude mountains, tropical islands, and icy arctic plains. Excluding dialects, more than 6,800 different *languages* are spoken. There are also hundreds of *religions* that people identify with—the most common being Christianity (33 percent), Islam (22 percent), Hinduism (15 percent), and Buddhism (6 percent), with Judaism (0.4 percent) and others claiming fewer adherents. Roughly 15 to 20 percent of the world's population is not affiliated with a religion.

Linked together by historical time and geographical space, each culture has its own ideology, music, fashions, foods, laws, customs, and manners of expression. As many tourists and exchange students traveling abroad have come to learn, sometimes the hard way, the social norms that influence human conduct can vary in significant ways from one part of the world to another.

In *Do's and Taboos Around the World*, R. E. Axtell (1993) warns world travelers about some of these differences. Dine in an Indian home, he notes, and you should leave food on the plate to show the host that the portions were generous and you had enough to eat. Yet as a dinner guest in Bolivia, you would show your appreciation by cleaning your plate. Shop in an outdoor market in Iraq, and you should expect to negotiate the price of everything you buy. Plan an appointment in Brazil,

Cultures differ in their unique, often colorful norms. In Ecuador, many men wear handwoven "Panama hats" (top left). In India, brightly colored powders are sold for the Hindu religious festival of Holi, which marks the beginning of spring (top right). In Spain, revelers in Pamplona hold up their bandanas before the start of the San Fermín Festival, where six fighting bulls run through crowded streets in the center of town (above).

and the person you're scheduled to meet is likely to be late. It's nothing personal. In North America, it is common to sit casually opposite someone with your legs outstretched. Yet in Nepal, it is an insult to point the bottoms of your feet at someone. Even the way we space ourselves from each other is culturally determined. Americans, Canadians, British, and northern Europeans keep a polite distance between themselves and others and feel "crowded" by the touchier, nose-to-nose style of the French, Greeks, Arabs, Mexicans, and people of South America. In the affairs of day-to-day living, each culture operates by its own rules of conduct.

Just as cultures differ in their social norms, so too they differ in the extent to which people are expected to adhere to those norms. As we saw in Chapter 3, there are different cultural orientations toward persons and their relationships to groups. Some cultures primarily value **individualism** and the virtues of independence, autonomy, and self-reliance, while others value **collectivism** and the virtues of *inter*dependence, cooperation, and social harmony. Under the banner of individualism, personal goals take priority over group allegiances. Yet in collectivistic cultures, the person is first and foremost a loyal member of a family, team, company, church, and state.

What determines whether a culture becomes individualistic or collectivistic? Speculating on the origins of these orientations, Harry Triandis (1995) suggests that there are three key factors. The first is the *complexity* of a society. As people come to live in more complex industrialized societies (compared, for example, with a simpler life of food gathering among desert nomads), there are more groups to identify with, which means less loyalty to any one group and a greater focus on personal rather than collective goals. Second is the *affluence* of a society. As people prosper, they gain financial independence from each other, a condition that promotes social independence as well as mobility and a focus on personal rather than collective goals. The third factor is *heterogeneity*. Societies that are homogeneous or "tight" (where members share the same language, religion, and social customs) tend to be rigid and intolerant of those who veer from the norm. Societies that are culturally diverse or "loose" (where two or more cultures coexist) tend to be more permissive of dissent—thus allowing for more individual expression. According to Edward Sampson (2000), cultural orientations may also be rooted in religious ideologies—as in the link between Christianity and individualism.

Across nations, early research showed that autonomy and independence are most highly valued in the United States, Australia, Great Britain, Canada, and the Netherlands, in that order. In contrast, other cultures value social harmony and "fitting in" for the sake of community, the most collectivist people being from Venezuela, Colombia, Pakistan, Peru, Taiwan, and China (Hofstede, 1980). Although it now appears that cultures differ in other more complicated ways and that individuals differ even within cultures (Oyserman et al., 2002), it is clear that nations on average vary in their orientations on the dimension of individualism (Schimmack et al., 2005).

individualism A cultural orientation in which independence, autonomy, and self-reliance take priority over group allegiances.

collectivism A cultural orientation in which interdependence, cooperation, and social harmony take priority over personal goals.

These photographs were taken of "average-income" families posing in front of their homes and material possessions. Representing the individualistic orientation common among affluent societies is the Skeen family of Pearland, Texas (left). Representing the collectivist orientation found in more impoverished societies is the Natoma family of Kouakourou, Mali (right).

Do cultural orientations influence conformity? Among the Bantu of Zimbabwe, an African people in which deviance is scorned, 51 percent of participants who were placed in an Asch-like study conformed—more than the number typically seen in the United States (Whittaker & Meade, 1967). In fact, when John Berry (1979) compared participants from seventeen cultures, he found that conformity rates ranged from a low of 18 percent among Inuit hunters of Baffin Island to a high of 60 percent among village-living Temne farmers of West Africa. More recent analyses have shown that conformity rates are generally higher in cultures that are collectivistic rather than individualistic in their orientation (Bond & Smith, 1996). Hence, many anthropologists—interested in culture and its influence over individuals—study the processes of conformity and independence (Spradley & McCurdy, 2006).

Compliance

In conformity situations, people follow implicit or explicit group norms. But another common form of social influence occurs when others make *direct requests* of us in the hope that we will comply. Situations calling for **compliance** take many forms. These include a friend's plea for help, sheepishly prefaced by the question "Can you do me a favor?" They also include the pop-up ad on the Internet designed to lure you into clicking onto a commercial site and the salesperson's pitch for business prefaced by the dangerous words "Have I got a deal for you!" Sometimes, the request itself is up front and direct; what you see is what you get. At other times, it is part of a subtle and more elaborate manipulation.

How do people get others to comply with self-serving requests? How do police interrogators get crime suspects to confess? How do political parties draw millions of dollars in contributions from voters? How do *you* exert influence over others? Do you use threats, promises, politeness, deceit, or reason? Do you hint, coax, sulk, negotiate, throw tantrums, or pull rank whenever you can? To a large extent, the compliance strategies we use depend on how well we know the person we target, our status within a relationship, our personality, culture, and the nature of the request.

By observing the masters of influence—advertisers, fund raisers, politicians, and business leaders—social psychologists have learned a great deal about the subtle but effective strategies that are commonly used. What we see is that people often get others to comply with their requests by setting traps. Once caught in these traps, the unwary victim often finds it difficult to escape.

compliance Changes in behavior that are elicited by direct requests.

Con artists prosper from the tendency for people to respond mindlessly to requests that sound reasonable but offer no real basis for compliance.

The Language of Request

Sometimes people can be disarmed by the simple phrasing of a request, regardless of its merit. Consider, for example, requests that sound reasonable but offer no real basis for compliance. Ellen Langer and her colleagues (1978) have found that words alone can sometimes trick us into submission. In their research, an experimenter approached people who were using a library copying machine and asked to cut in. Three different versions of the request were used. In one, participants were simply asked, "Excuse me. I have five pages. May I use the Xerox machine?" In a second version, the request was justified by the added phrase "because I'm in a rush." As you would expect, more participants stepped aside when the request was justified (94 percent) than when it was not (60 percent). A third version of the request, however, suggests that the reason offered had little to do with the increase in compliance. In this case, participants heard the following: "Excuse me. I have five pages. May I use the Xerox machine because I have to make some copies?" If you read this request closely, you'll see that it really offered no reason at all. Yet 93 percent in this condition complied! It was as if the appearance of a reason, triggered by the word *because*, was all that was necessary. Indeed, Langer (1989) finds that the mind is often on "automatic pilot," as we respond *mindlessly* to words without fully processing the information they are supposed to convey. At least for requests that are small, "sweet little nothings" may be enough to win compliance.

It is interesting that although a state of mindlessness can make us vulnerable to compliance, it can also have the opposite effect. For example, many city dwellers will automatically walk past panhandlers on the street looking for a handout. Perhaps the way to increase compliance in such situations is to disrupt this mindless refusal response by making a request that is so unusual that it piques the target person's interest. To test this hypothesis, researchers had a confederate approach people on the street and make a request that was either typical ("Can you spare a quarter?") or atypical ("Can you spare 17 cents?"). The result: Atypical pleas elicited more comments and questions from those who were targeted—and produced a 60 percent increase in the number of people who gave money (Santos et al., 1994). In another study, researchers who went door to door selling holiday cards gained more compliance when they disrupted the mindless process and reframed the sales pitch. They sold more cards when they said the price was "three hundred pennies—that's three dollars, it's a bargain" than when they simply asked for three dollars (Davis & Knowles, 1999).

The Norm of Reciprocity

A simple, unstated, but powerful rule of social behavior known as the *norm of reciprocity* dictates that we treat others as they have treated us (Gouldner, 1960). On the negative side, this norm can be used to sanction retaliation against those who cause us harm: "an eye for an eye." On the positive side, it leads us to feel obligated to repay others for acts of kindness. Thus, whenever we receive gifts, invitations, and free samples, we usually go out of our way to return the favor.

The norm of reciprocity contributes to the predictability and fairness of social interaction. However, it can also be used to exploit us. Dennis Regan (1971) examined this possibility in the following laboratory study. Individuals were brought together with a confederate—who was trained to act in a likable or unlikable manner—for an experiment on "aesthetics." In one condition, the confederate did the participant an unsolicited favor. He left during a break and returned with two bottles of Coca-Cola, one for himself and the other for the participant. In a second condition, he returned from the break empty-handed. In a third condition, participants were treated to a Coke—but by the experimenter, not the confederate. The confederate then told participants in all conditions that he was selling raffle tickets at twenty-five cents apiece and asked if they would be willing to buy any. On the average, participants bought more raffle tickets when the confederate had earlier brought them a soft drink than when he had not. The norm of reciprocity was so strong that they returned the favor even when the confederate was not otherwise a likable character. In fact, participants in this condition spent an average of forty-three cents on raffle tickets. At a time when soft drinks cost less than a quarter, the confederate made a handsome quick profit on his investment!

It's clear that the norm of reciprocity can be used to trap us, unwittingly, into acts of compliance. For example, research conducted in restaurants shows that waiters and waitresses can increase their tip percentages by writing, "Thank you" on the back of the customer's check, by drawing a happy face on it, or by placing candy on the check tray (Rind & Strohmetz, 2001; Strohmetz et al., 2002). But does receiving a favor make us feel indebted forever, or is there a time limit to the social obligation that is so quietly unleashed? In an experiment designed to answer this question, Jerry Burger and others (1997) used Regan's soft drink favor and had the confederate try to "cash in" with a request either immediately or one week later. The result: Compliance levels increased in the immediate condition but not after a full week had passed. People may feel compelled to reciprocate, but that feeling—at least for small acts of kindness—is relatively short-lived.

Some people are more likely than others to trigger and exploit the reciprocity norm. According to Martin Greenberg and David Westcott (1983), individuals who use reciprocity to elicit compliance are called "creditors" because they always try to keep others in their debt so they can cash in when necessary. On a questionnaire that measures *reciprocation ideology*, people are identified as creditors if they endorse such statements as "If someone does you a favor, it's good to repay that person with a greater favor." On the receiving end, some people more than others try not to accept favors that might later set them up to be exploited. On a scale that measures *reciprocation wariness*, people are said to be wary if they express the suspicion, for example, that "asking for another's help gives them power over your life" (Eisenberger et al., 1987).

Setting Traps: Sequential Request Strategies

People who raise money or sell for a living know that it often takes more than a single plea to win over a potential donor or customer. Social psychologists share this knowledge and have studied several compliance techniques that are based on making two or more related requests. *Click!* The first request sets the trap. *Snap!* The second captures the prey. In a fascinating book entitled *Influence: The Psychology of Persuasion*, Robert Cialdini (2007) describes a number of sequential request tactics in vivid detail. These methods are presented in the following pages.

The Foot in the Door Folk wisdom has it that one way to get a person to comply with a sizable request is to start small. First devised by traveling salespeople peddling vacuum cleaners, hair brushes, cosmetics, magazine subscriptions, and encyclopedias, the trick is to somehow get your "foot in the door." The expression need not be taken literally, of course. The point of the **foot-in-the-door technique** is to break the ice with a small initial request that the customer can't easily refuse. Once that first commitment is elicited, the chances are increased that another, larger request will succeed.

Jonathan Freedman and Scott Fraser (1966) tested the impact of this technique in a series of field experiments. In one, an experimenter pretending to be employed by a consumer organization telephoned a large number of female homemakers in Palo Alto, California, and asked if they would be willing to answer some questions about household products. Those who consented were then asked a few quick and innocuous questions and thanked for their assistance. Three days later, the experimenter called back and made a considerable, almost outrageous, request. He asked the women if they would allow a handful of men into their homes for two hours to rummage through their drawers and cupboards so they could take an inventory of their household products.

The foot-in-the-door technique proved to be very effective. When the participants were confronted with only the very intrusive request, 22 percent consented.

foot-in-the-door technique A two-step compliance technique in which an influencer sets the stage for the real request by first getting a person to comply with a much smaller request.

Yet among those surveyed earlier, the rate of agreement more than doubled, to 53 percent. This basic result has now been repeated over and over again. People are more likely to donate time, money, food, blood, the use of their home, and other resources once they have been induced to go along with a small initial request. Although the effect is not always as dramatic as that obtained by Freedman and Fraser, it does appear in a wide variety of circumstances—and increases compliance rates, on average, by about 13 percent (Burger, 1999).

The practical implications of the foot-in-the-door technique are obvious. But why does it work? Over the years, several explanations have been suggested. One that seems plausible is based on self-perception theory—that people infer their attitudes by observing their own behavior. This explanation suggests that a two-step process is at work. First, by observing your own behavior in the initial situation, you come to see yourself as the kind of person who is generally cooperative when approached with a request. Second, when confronted with the more burdensome request, you seek to respond in ways that maintain this new self-image. By this logic, the foot-in-the-door technique should succeed only when you attribute an initial act of compliance to your own personal characteristics.

Based on a review of dozens of studies, Jerry Burger (1999) concludes that the research generally supports the self-perception account. Thus, if the first request is too trivial or if participants are paid for the first act of compliance, they won't later come to view themselves as inherently cooperative. Under these conditions, the technique *does not* work. Likewise, the effect occurs only when people are motivated to be consistent with their self-images. If participants are unhappy with what the initial behavior implies about them, if they are too young to appreciate the implications, or if they don't care about behaving in ways that are personally consistent, then again the technique does not work. Other processes may be at work, but it appears that the foot opens the door by altering self-perceptions, leading people who agree to the small initial request, without compensation, to see themselves as helpful (Burger & Caldwell, 2003). In fact, this process can still occur even when a person tries to comply with the initial small request but fails. In a series of studies, Dariusz Dolinski (2000) found that when people were asked if they could find directions to a nonexistent street address or decipher an unreadable message—small favors they could not satisfy—they, too, become more compliant with the next request.

Knowing that a foot in the door increases compliance rates is both exciting and troubling—exciting for the owner of the foot, troubling for the owner of the door. As Cialdini (2007) put it, "You can use small commitments to manipulate a person's self-image; you can use them to turn citizens into 'public servants,' prospects into 'customers,' prisoners into 'collaborators.' And once you've got a man's self-image where you want it, he should comply *naturally* with a whole range of your requests that are consistent with this view of himself" (p. 74).

Low-Balling   Another two-step trap, arguably the most unscrupulous of all compliance techniques, is also based on the "start small" idea. Imagine yourself in the following situation. You're at a local automobile dealership. After some negotiation, the salesperson offers a great price on the car of your choice. You cast aside other considerations and shake hands on the deal; and as the salesperson goes off to "write it up," you begin to feel the thrill of owning the car of your dreams. Absorbed in fantasy, you are suddenly interrupted by the return of the salesperson. "I'm sorry," he says. "The manager would not approve the sale. We have to raise the price by another $450. I'm afraid that's the best we can do." As the victim of an all-too-common trick known as **low-balling**, you are now faced with a tough decision. On the one hand, you're wild about the car. You've already enjoyed the pleasure of thinking it's yours; and the more you think about it, the better it looks. On the other hand, you don't want to pay more than you bargained for, and you have an uneasy feeling in the pit of your stomach that you're being duped. What do you do?

Salespeople who use this tactic are betting that you'll go ahead with the purchase despite the added cost. If the way research participants behave is any indication, they are often right. In one study, experimenters phoned introductory psychology students and asked if they would be willing to participate in a study for extra credit. Some were told up front that the session would begin at the uncivilized hour of 7 A.M. Knowing

low-balling A two-step compliance technique in which the influencer secures agreement with a request but then increases the size of that request by revealing hidden costs.

Low-balling is a common technique used in selling cars. For consumer advice on how to buy a car without falling into this and other compliance traps often set by dealers, visit the Edmunds Automobile Buyer's Guide (www.Edmunds.com).

that, only 31 percent volunteered. But other participants were low-balled. Only *after* they agreed to participate did the experimenter inform them of the 7 A.M. starting time. Would that be okay? Whether or not it was, the procedure achieved its objective—the sign-up rate rose to 56 percent (Cialdini et al., 1978).

Disturbing as it may be, low-balling is an interesting technique. Surely, once the low ball has been thrown, many recipients suspect that they were misled. Yet they go along. Why? The reason appears to be based on the psychology of commitment (Kiesler, 1971). Once people make a particular decision, they justify it to themselves by thinking of all its positive aspects. As they get increasingly committed to a course of action, they grow more resistant to changing their mind, even if the initial reasons for the action have been changed or withdrawn entirely. In the automobile dealership scenario, you might very well have decided to purchase the car because of the price. But then you would have thought about its sleek new appearance, the scent of the leather interior, and the brand new satellite radio. By the time you learned that the price would be more than you'd bargained for, it was too late—you were already hooked.

Low-balling also produces another form of commitment. When people do not suspect duplicity, they feel a nagging sense of unfulfilled obligation to the person with whom they negotiated. Thus, even though the salesperson was unable to complete the original deal, you might feel obligated to buy anyway, having already agreed to make the purchase. This commitment to the other person may account for why low-balling works better when the second request is made by the same person than by someone else (Burger & Petty, 1981). It may also explain why people are most vulnerable to the low-ball when they make their commitment in public rather than in private (Burger & Cornelius, 2003).

The Door in the Face   Although shifting from an initial small request to a larger one can be effective, as in the foot-in-the-door and low-ball techniques, oddly enough the opposite is also true. Cialdini (2007) describes the time he was approached by a Boy Scout and asked to buy two five-dollar tickets to an upcoming circus. Having better things to do with his time and money, he declined. Then the boy asked if he would be interested in buying chocolate bars at a dollar apiece. Even though he does not particularly like chocolate, Cialdini—an expert on social influence—bought two of them. After a moment's reflection, he realized what had happened. Whether the Boy Scout planned it that way or not, Cialdini had fallen for what is known as the **door-in-the-face technique**.

The technique is as simple as it sounds. An individual makes an initial request that is so large it is sure to be rejected and then comes back with a second, more reasonable request. Will the second request fare better after the first one has been declined? Plagued by the sight of uneaten chocolate bars, Cialdini and others (1975) tested the effectiveness of the door-in-the-face technique. They stopped college students on campus and asked if they would volunteer to work without pay at a counseling center for juvenile delinquents. The time commitment would be forbidding: roughly two hours a week for the next two years! Not surprisingly, everyone who was approached politely slammed the proverbial door in the experimenter's face. But then the experimenter followed up with a more modest proposal, asking the students if they would be willing to take a group of delinquents on a two-hour trip to the zoo. The strategy worked like a charm. Only 17 percent of the students confronted with only the second request agreed. But of those who initially declined the first request, 50 percent said yes to the zoo trip. You should note that the door-in-the-face technique does not elicit only empty promises. Most research participants who comply subsequently do what they've agreed to do (Cialdini & Ascani, 1976).

door-in-the-face technique
A two-step compliance technique in which an influencer prefaces the real request with one that is so large that it is rejected.

Why is the door-in-the-face technique such an effective trap? One possibility involves the principle of *perceptual contrast*: To the person exposed to a very large initial request, the second request "seems smaller." Two dollars' worth of candy bars is not bad compared with ten dollars for circus tickets. Likewise, taking a group of kids to the zoo seems trivial compared with two years of volunteer work. As intuitively sensible as this explanation seems, Cialdini and others (1975) concluded that perceptual contrast is only partly responsible for the effect. When participants heard the large request without actually having to reject it, their rate of compliance with the second request (25 percent) was only slightly larger than the 17 percent rate of compliance exhibited by those who heard only the small request.

A second, more compelling explanation for the effect involves the notion of *reciprocal concessions*. A close cousin of the reciprocity norm, this refers to the pressure to respond to changes in a bargaining position. When an individual backs down from a large request to a smaller one, we view that move as a concession that we should match by our own compliance. Thus, the door-in-the-face technique does not work if the second request is made by a different person (Cialdini et al., 1975). Nor does it work if the first request is so extreme that it comes across as an insincere "first offer" (Schwarzwald et al., 1979). On an emotional level, refusing to help on one request may also trigger feelings of guilt—which we can reduce by complying with the second, smaller request (O'Keefe & Figge, 1997; Millar, 2002).

That's Not All, Folks!   If the notion of reciprocal concessions is correct, then a person shouldn't actually have to refuse the initial offer in order for the shift to a smaller request to work. Indeed, another familiar sales strategy manages to use concession without first eliciting refusal. In this strategy, a product is offered at a particular price; but then, before the buyer has a chance to respond, the seller adds, "And that's not all!" At that point, either the original price is reduced, or a bonus is offered to sweeten the pot. The seller, of course, intends all along to make the so-called concession.

This ploy, called the **that's-not-all technique**, seems awfully transparent, right? Surely, no one falls for it, right? Jerry Burger (1986) was not so sure. He predicted that people are more likely to make a purchase when a deal seems to have improved than when the same deal is offered right from the start. To test this hypothesis, Burger set up a booth at a campus fair and sold cupcakes. Some customers who approached the table were told that the cupcakes cost 75 cents each. Others were told that they cost a dollar; but then, before they could respond, the price was reduced to 75 cents. Rationally speaking, Burger's manipulation did not affect the ultimate price, so it should not have affected sales. But it did. When customers were led to believe that the final price represented a reduction, sales increased from 44 to 73 percent.

At this point, let's step back and look at the various compliance techniques described in this section. All of them are based on a two-step process that involves a shift from a request of one size to another. What differs is whether the small or large request comes first and how the transition between steps is made (see Table 7.3). Moreover, all these strategies work in subtle ways by manipulating the target person's self-image, commitment to the product, feelings of obligation to the seller, or perceptions of the real request. It is even possible to increase compliance by first asking "How are you feeling?" (Howard, 1990) or by claiming some coincidental similarity, like having the same first name or birthday (Burger et al., 2004). When you consider these various traps, you have to wonder whether it's ever possible to escape.

Assertiveness: When People Say No

Cialdini (2007) opens his book with a confession: "I can admit it freely now. All my life I've been a patsy" (p. xi). As a past victim of compliance traps, he is not alone. Many people find it difficult to assert themselves in interpersonal situations. Faced with an unreasonable request from a friend, spouse, or stranger, they become anxious at the mere thought of putting a foot down and refusing to comply. Indeed, there are times when it is uncomfortable for anyone to say no. However, just as we can maintain

An effective way to get someone to do you a favor is to make a first request that is so large the person is sure to reject it. **True.**

that's-not-all technique
A two-step compliance technique in which the influencer begins with an inflated request, then decreases its apparent size by offering a discount or bonus.

TABLE 7.3
Sequential Request Strategies

Various compliance techniques are based on a sequence of two related requests. *Click!* The first request sets the trap. *Snap!* The second captures the prey. Research has shown that the four sequential request strategies summarized in this table are all effective.

Request Shifts	Technique	Description
From small to large	Foot in the door	Begin with a very small request; secure agreement; then make a separate, larger request.
	Low-balling	Secure agreement with a request, and then increase the size of that request by revealing hidden costs.
From large to small	Door in the face	Begin with a very large request that will be rejected; then follow that up with a more modest request.
	That's not all	Begin with a somewhat inflated request; than immediately decrease the apparent size of that request by offering a discount or bonus.

"Knowledge is power, and if you know when a clever technique is being used on you, then it becomes easier to ignore."

—Burke Leon

our autonomy in the face of conformity pressures, we can also refuse direct requests—even clever ones. The trap may be set, but you don't have to get caught.

According to Cialdini, being able to resist the pressure of compliance rests, first and foremost, on being vigilant. If a stranger hands you a gift and then launches into a sales pitch, you should recognize the tactic for what it is and not feel indebted by the norm of reciprocity. And if you strike a deal with a salesperson who later reneges on the terms, you should be aware that you're being thrown a low ball. Indeed, that is exactly what happened to one of the authors of this book. After a full Saturday afternoon of careful negotiation at a local car dealer, he and his wife finally came to terms on a price. Minutes later, however, the salesman returned with the news that the manager would not approve the deal. The cost of a power moonroof, which was to be included, would have to be added on. Familiar with the research, the author turned to his wife and exclaimed, "It's a trick; they're low-balling us!" Realizing what was happening, she became furious, went straight to the manager, and made such a scene in front of other customers that he backed down and honored the original deal.

What happened in this instance? Why did recognizing the attempted manipulation produce such anger and resistance? As this story illustrates, compliance techniques work smoothly only if they are hidden from view. The problem is, not only are they attempts to influence us, but they are also deceptive. Flattery, gifts, and other ploys often elicit compliance, but not if they are perceived as insincere (Jones, 1964) or if the target has a high level of reciprocity wariness (Eisenberger et al., 1987). Likewise, the sequential request traps are powerful only to the extent that they are subtle and cannot be seen for what they are (Schwarzwald et al., 1979). People don't like to be hustled. In fact, feeling manipulated typically leads us to react with anger, psychological reactance, and stubborn noncompliance . . . unless the request is a command and the requester is a figure of authority.

Obedience

Allen Funt, the creator and producer of the original TV program *Candid Camera* (a forerunner of the show *Punk'd*), spent as much time observing human behavior in the real world as most psychologists do. When asked what he learned from all his people-watching, Funt replied, "The worst thing, and I see it over and over, is how easily people can be led by any kind of authority figure, or even the most minimal signs of authority." He went on to cite the time he put up a road sign that read "Delaware Closed Today." The reaction? "Motorists didn't question it. Instead they asked, 'Is Jersey open?'" (Zimbardo, 1985, p. 47).

Funt was right about the way we react to authority. Taught from birth that it's important to respect legitimate forms of leadership, people think twice before defying parents, teachers, employers, coaches, and government officials. The problem is that mere symbols of authority—titles, uniforms, badges, or the trappings of success, even without the necessary credentials—can sometimes turn ordinary people into docile servants. Leonard Bickman (1974) demonstrated this phenomenon in a series of studies in which a male research assistant stopped passers-by on the streets of Brooklyn and ordered them to do something unusual. Sometimes, he pointed to a paper bag on the ground and said, "Pick up this bag for me!" At other times, he pointed to an individual standing beside a parked car and said, "This fellow is over-parked at the meter but doesn't have any change. Give him a dime!" Would anyone really take this guy seriously? When he was dressed in street clothes, only a third of the people stopped followed his orders. But when he wore a security guard's uniform, nearly nine out of every ten people obeyed! Even when the uniformed assistant turned the corner and walked away after issuing his command, the vast majority of passers-by followed his orders. Clearly, uniforms signify the power of authority (Bushman, 1988).

Blind **obedience** may seem funny; but if people are willing to take orders from a total stranger, how far will they go when it really matters? As the pages of history attest, the implications are sobering. In World War II, Nazi officials participated in the deaths of millions of Jews, as well as Poles, Russians, Gypsies, and homosexuals. Yet when tried for these crimes, their defense was always the same: "I was following orders."

Surely, you may be thinking, the Holocaust was a historical anomaly that says more about the Nazis as prejudiced and pathologically frustrated individuals than about the situations that lead people in general to commit acts of destructive obedience. In *Hitler's Willing Executioners*, historian Daniel Goldhagen (1996) argues on the basis of past records that many German citizens were willing anti-Semitic participants in the Holocaust—not mere ordinary people forced to follow orders. But two lines of evidence suggest that attaching responsibility to the German people is too simple as an explanation of what happened. First, interviews with Nazi war criminals and doctors who worked in concentration camps have suggested the provocative and disturbing conclusion that these people were "utterly ordinary" (Arendt, 1963; Lifton, 1986; Von Lang & Sibyll, 1983). Second, the monstrous events of World War II

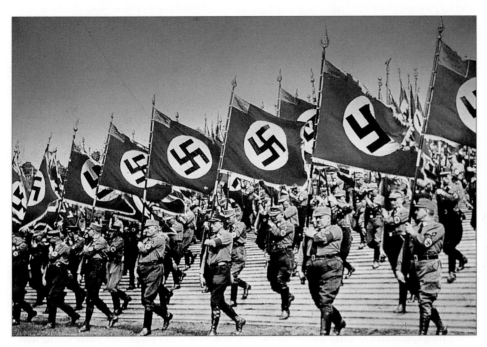

Taken to the extreme, blind obedience can have devastating results. Nazi officials killed millions during World War II, and many said they did it "because I was just following orders."

"Far more, and far more hideous, crimes have been committed in the name of obedience than have ever been committed in the name of rebellion."

—C. P. Snow

obedience Behavior change produced by the commands of authority.

do not stand alone in modern history. Even today, crimes of obedience—including suicide bombing and torture—are being committed in ruthless regimes, militaries, and terrorist organizations throughout the world (Kelman & Hamilton, 1989; Haritos-Fatouros, 2002). As seen in the recent Enron scandal, crimes of obedience are also found in the corporate world, where leaders and their subordinates "morally disengage" from bad actions by denying responsibility, minimizing consequences, and dehumanizing victims (Beu & Buckley, 2004). On extraordinary rare occasions, obedience is carried to its limit. In 1978, nine hundred members of the People's Temple cult obeyed an order from the Reverend Jim Jones to kill themselves. In 1997, in California, Marshall Applewhite and thirty-eight followers of the Heaven's Gate cult did the same. Fanatic cult members had committed mass suicide before, and they will likely do so again (Galanter, 1999).

Milgram's Research: Forces of Destructive Obedience

During the time that Adolf Eichmann was being tried for his Nazi war crimes, Stanley Milgram (1963) began a dramatic series of experiments that culminated in his 1974 book *Obedience to Authority*. For many years, the ethics of this research has been the focus of much debate. Those who say it was not ethical point to the potential psychological harm to which the participants were exposed. In contrast, those who believe that Milgram's research met appropriate ethical standards emphasize the contribution it makes to our understanding of an important social problem. They conclude that, on balance, the extreme danger that destructive obedience poses for all humankind justified Milgram's unorthodox methods. Consider both sides of the debate, which were summarized in Chapter 2, and make your own judgment. Now, however, take a more personal look. Imagine yourself as one of the approximately one thousand participants who found themselves in the following situation.

The experience begins when you arrive at a Yale University laboratory and meet two men. One is the experimenter, a stern young man dressed in a gray lab coat and carrying a clipboard. The other is a middle-aged gentleman named Mr. Wallace, an accountant who is slightly overweight and average in appearance. You exchange quick introductions, and then the experimenter explains that you and your co-participant will take part in a study on the effects of punishment on learning. After lots have been drawn, it is determined that you will serve as the teacher and that Mr. Wallace will be the learner. So far so good.

Soon, however, the situation takes on a more ominous tone. You find out that your job is to test the learner's memory and administer electric shocks of increasing intensity whenever he makes a mistake. You are then escorted into another room, where the experimenter straps Mr. Wallace into a chair, rolls up his sleeves, attaches electrodes to his arms, and applies "electrode paste" to prevent blisters and burns. As if that isn't bad enough, you may overhear Mr. Wallace telling the experimenter that he

This is the shock generator Milgram used (left). It still exists—and can be found in the Archives of the History of American Psychology at the University of Akron. Participants in Milgram's studies believed they were shocking Mr. Wallace, the man being strapped into his chair (right).

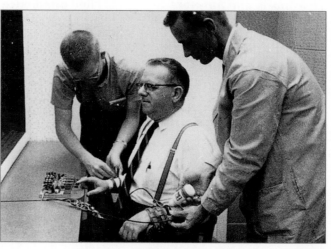

TABLE 7.4
The Learner's Protests in the Milgram Experiment

As participants administered progressively more intense shocks, they heard the learner moan, groan, protest, and complain. All participants heard the same programmed set of responses. Eventually, the learner fell silent and ceased to respond.

(Milgram, 1974.)

75 volts	Ugh!
90 volts	Ugh!
105 volts	Ugh! *(louder)*
120 volts	Ugh! Hey this really hurts.
135 volts	Ugh!!
150 volts	Ugh!!! Experimenter! That's all. Get me out of here. I told you I had heart trouble. My heart's starting to bother me now. Get me out of here, please. My heart's starting to bother me. I refuse to go on. Let me out.
165 volts	Ugh! Let me out! *(shouting)*
180 volts	Ugh! I can't stand the pain. Let me out of here! *(shouting)*
195 volts	Ugh! Let me out of here. Let me out of here. My heart's bothering me. Let me out of here! You have no right to keep me here! Let me out! Let me out of here! Let me out! Let me out of here! My heart's bothering me. Let me out! Let me out!
210 volts	Ugh!! Experimenter! Get me out of here. I've had enough. I won't be in the experiment any more.
225 volts	Ugh!
240 volts	Ugh!
255 volts	Ugh! Get me out of here.
270 volts	*(Agonized scream.)* Let me out of here. Let me out of here. Let me out of here. Let me out. Do you hear? Let me out of here.
285 volts	*(Agonized scream.)*
300 volts	*(Agonized scream.)* I absolutely refuse to answer any more. Get me out of here. You can't hold me here. Get me out. Get me out of here.
315 volts	*(Intensely agonized scream.)* I told you I refuse to answer. I'm no longer part of this experiment.
330 volts	*(Intense and prolonged agonized scream.)* Let me out of here. Let me out of here. My heart's bothering me. Let me out, I tell you. *(Hysterically)* Let me out of here. Let me out of here. You have no right to hold me here. Let me out! Let me out! Let me out! Let me out of here! Let me out! Let me out!

has a heart problem. The experimenter responds by conceding that the shocks will be painful but reassures Mr. Wallace that the procedure will not cause "permanent tissue damage." In the meantime, you can personally vouch for how painful the shocks are because the experimenter stings you with one that is supposed to be mild. From there, the experimenter takes you back to the main room, where you are seated in front of a "shock generator," a machine with thirty switches that range from 15 volts, labeled "slight shock," to 450 volts, labeled "XXX."

Your role in this experiment is straightforward. First you read a list of word pairs to Mr. Wallace through a microphone. Then you test his memory with a series of multiple-choice questions. The learner answers each question by pressing one of four switches that light up signals on the shock generator. If his answer is correct, you move on to the next question. If it is incorrect, you announce the correct answer and shock him. When you press the appropriate shock switch, a red light flashes above it, relay switches click inside the machine, and you hear a loud buzzing sound go off in the learner's room. After each wrong answer, you're told, the intensity of the shock should be increased by 15 volts.

You aren't aware, of course, that the experiment is rigged and that Mr. Wallace—who is actually a confederate—is never really shocked. As far as you know, he gets zapped each time you press one of the switches. As the session proceeds, the learner makes more and more errors, leading you to work your way up the shock scale. As you reach 75, 90, and 105 volts, you hear the learner grunt in pain. At 120 volts, he begins to shout. If you're still in it at 150 volts, you hear the learner cry out, "Experimenter! That's all. Get me out of here. My heart's starting to bother me now. I refuse to go on!" Screams of agony and protest continue. At 300 volts, he says he absolutely refuses to continue. By the time you surpass 330 volts, the learner falls silent and fails to respond—not to be heard from again. Table 7.4 lists his responses in grim detail.

Somewhere along the line, you turn to the experimenter for guidance. "What should I do? Don't you think I should stop? Shouldn't we at least check on him?" You might even confront the experimenter head-on and refuse to continue. Yet in answer to your inquiries, the experimenter—firm in his tone and seemingly unaffected by the learner's distress—prods you along as follows:

TABLE 7.5
Milgram's Baseline Results

In Milgram's original experiment, participants exhibited a troubling inclination to obey blindly. This table shows the number and percentage of male participants who delivered shocks of varying maximum intensity in response to the experimenter's commands.

(Milgram, 1974.)

Shock Level (Volts)	Participants Who Stopped at This Level	
	Number	Percent
300	5	12.5
315	4	10.0
330	2	5.0
345	1	2.5
360	1	2.5
375	1	2.5
450	26	65.0

- Please continue (or please go on).
- The experiment requires that you continue.
- It is absolutely essential that you continue.
- You have no other choice; you must go on.

What do you do? In a situation that begins to feel more and more like a bad dream, do you follow your own conscience or obey the experimenter?

Milgram described this procedure to psychiatrists, college students, and middle-class adults, and he asked them to predict how they would behave. On average, these groups estimated that they would call it quits at the 135-volt level. Not a single person thought he or she would go all the way to 450 volts. When asked to predict the percentage of *other* people who would deliver the maximum shock, those interviewed gave similar estimates. The psychiatrists estimated that only one out of a thousand people would exhibit that kind of extreme obedience. They were wrong. In Milgram's initial study, involving forty men from the surrounding New Haven community, participants exhibited an alarming degree of obedience, administering an average of twenty-seven out of thirty possible shocks. In fact, twenty-six of the forty participants—that's *65 percent*—delivered the ultimate punishment of 450 volts. The results are shown in Table 7.5.

The Obedient Participant   At first glance, you may see these results as a lesson in the psychology of cruelty and conclude that Milgram's participants were seriously disturbed. But research does not support such a simple explanation. To begin with, those in a control group who were not prodded along by an experimenter refused to continue early into the shock sequence. What's more, Milgram found that virtually all participants, including those who had administered severe shocks, were tormented by the experience. Many of them pleaded with the experimenter to let them stop. When he refused, they went on. But in the process, they trembled, stuttered, groaned, perspired, bit their lips, and dug their fingernails into their flesh. Some burst into fits of nervous laughter. On one occasion, said Milgram, "we observed a [participant's] seizure so violently convulsive that it was necessary to call a halt to the experiment" (1963, p. 375).

Was Milgram's 65 percent baseline level of obedience attributable to his unique sample of male participants? Not at all. Forty women who participated in a later study exhibited precisely the same level of obedience: 65 percent threw the 450-volt switch. Before you jump to the conclusion that something was amiss in New Haven, consider the fact that Milgram's basic finding has been obtained in several different countries and with children as well as college students and older adults (Shanab & Yahya, 1977, 1978). Obedience in the Milgram situation is so universal that it led one author to ask, "Are we all Nazis?" (Askenasy, 1978).

The answer, of course, is no. An individual's character can make a difference; and some people, depending on the situation, are far more obedient than others. In the aftermath of World War II, a group of social scientists, searching for the root causes of prejudice, sought to identify individuals with an *authoritarian personality* and developed a questionnaire known as the F-Scale to measure it (Adorno et al., 1950; Stone et al., 1993). What they found is that people who get high scores on the F-Scale (F stands for "Fascist") are rigid, dogmatic, sexually repressed, ethnocentric, intolerant of dissent, and punitive. They are submissive toward figures of authority but aggressive toward subordinates. Indeed, people with high F scores are also more willing than low scorers to administer high-intensity shocks in Milgram's obedience situation (Elms & Milgram, 1966).

Although personality characteristics may make someone vulnerable or resistant to destructive obedience, what seems to matter most is the situation in which people find

FIGURE 7.7

Factors That Influence Obedience

Milgram varied many factors in his research program. Without commands from an experimenter, fewer than 3 percent of the participants exhibited full obedience. Yet in the standard baseline condition, 65 percent of male and female participants followed the orders. To identify factors that might reduce this level, Milgram varied the location of the experiment, the status of the authority, the participant's proximity to the victim, and the presence of confederates who rebel. The effects of these variations are illustrated here.

(Milgram, 1974.)

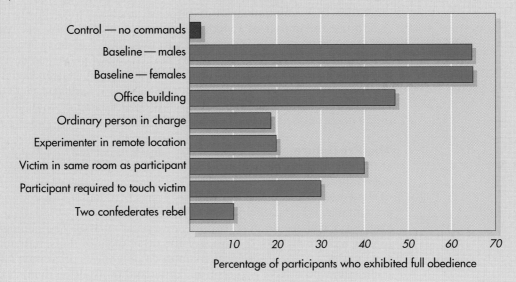

Percentage of participants who exhibited full obedience

themselves. By carefully altering particular aspects of his basic scenario, in more than twenty variations of the basic experiment, Milgram was able to identify factors that increase and decrease the 65 percent baseline rate of obedience (see Figure 7.7). Three factors in particular are important: the authority figure, the proximity of the victim, and the experimental procedure (Blass, 1992; Miller, 1986).

The Authority   What is perhaps most remarkable about Milgram's findings is that a lab-coated experimenter is *not* a powerful figure of authority. Unlike a military superior, employer, coach, or teacher, the experimenter in Milgram's research could not ultimately enforce his commands. Still, his physical presence and his apparent legitimacy played major roles in drawing obedience. When Milgram diminished the experimenter's status by moving his lab from the distinguished surroundings of Yale University to a rundown urban office building in nearby Bridgeport, Connecticut, the rate of total obedience dropped to 48 percent. When the experimenter was replaced by an ordinary person—supposedly another participant—there was a sharp reduction to 20 percent. Similarly, Milgram found that when the experimenter was in charge but issued his commands by telephone, only 21 percent fully obeyed. (In fact, when the experimenter was not watching, many participants in this condition feigned obedience by pressing the 15-volt switch.) One conclusion, then, is clear. At least in the Milgram setting, destructive obedience requires the physical presence of a prestigious authority figure.

If an experimenter can exert such control over research participants, imagine the control wielded by truly powerful authority figures—present or not. An intriguing field study examined the extent to which hospital nurses would obey unreasonable orders from a doctor. Using a fictitious name, a male physician called several female nurses on the phone and told them to administer a drug to a specific patient. His order violated hospital regulations: The drug was uncommon, the dosage was too large, and the effects could have been harmful. Yet out of the twenty-two nurses who were contacted, twenty-one had to be stopped as they prepared to obey the doctor's orders (Hofling et al., 1966).

The Victim   Situational characteristics of the victim are also important factors in destructive obedience. Milgram noted that Nazi war criminal Adolf Eichmann felt sick when he toured concentration camps but only had to shuffle papers from behind a desk to play his part in the Holocaust. Similarly, the B-29 pilot who dropped the atom bomb on Hiroshima in World War II said of his mission, "I had no thoughts, except what I'm supposed to do" (Miller, 1986, p. 228). These events suggest that because Milgram's participants were physically separated from the learner, they were able to distance themselves emotionally from the consequences of their actions.

To test the impact of a victim's proximity on destructive obedience, Milgram seated the learner in one of his studies in the same room as the participant. Under these conditions, only 40 percent fully obeyed. When participants were required to physically grasp the victim's hand and force it onto a metal shock plate, full obedience dropped to 30 percent. These findings represent significant reductions from the 65 percent baseline. Still, three out of ten participants were willing to use brute force in the name of obedience.

The Procedure   Finally, there is the situation created by Milgram. A close look at the dilemma his participants faced reveals two important aspects of the experimental procedure. First, participants were led to feel relieved of any personal sense of *responsibility* for the victim's welfare. The experimenter said up front that he was accountable. When participants were led to believe that they were responsible, their levels of obedience dropped considerably (Tilker, 1970). The ramifications of this finding are immense. In the military and other organizations, individuals often occupy positions in a hierarchical chain of command. Eichmann was a middle-level bureaucrat who received orders from Hitler and transmitted them to others for implementation. Caught between individuals who make policy and those who carry it out, how personally responsible do those in the middle feel? Wesley Kilham and Leon Mann (1974) examined this issue in an obedience study that cast participants in one of two roles: the *transmitter* (who took orders from the experimenter and passed them on) and the *executant* (who actually pressed the shock levers). As they predicted, transmitters were more obedient (54 percent) than executants (28 percent).

The second feature of Milgram's scenario that promoted obedience is gradual escalation. Participants began the session by delivering mild shocks and then, only gradually, escalated to voltage levels of high intensity. After all, what's another 15 volts compared with the current level? By the time participants realized the frightening implications of what they were doing, it had become more difficult for them to escape (Gilbert, 1981). This sequence is much like the foot-in-the-door technique. In Milgram's words, people become "integrated into a situation that carries its own momentum. The subject's problem . . . is how to become disengaged from a situation which is moving in an altogether ugly direction" (1974, p. 73). We should point out that obedience by momentum is not unique to Milgram's research paradigm. As reported by Amnesty International, many countries today torture political prisoners—and those who are recruited for the dirty work are trained, in part, through an escalating series of commitments (Haritos-Fatouros, 2002).

 Milgram in the Twenty-First Century

When Stanley Milgram published the results of his first experiment in 1963, at the age of twenty-eight, a *New York Times* headline read: "Sixty-Five Percent in Test Blindly Obey Order to Inflict Pain." Milgram had pierced the public consciousness and was poised to become one of the most important and controversial figures in psychology—and beyond. In a fascinating biography, *The Man Who Shocked the World*, Thomas Blass (2004) tells of how Milgram became interested in obedience and the impact his studies have had on social scientists, legal scholars, the U.S. military, and popular culture around the world (Milgram's obedience book has been translated into eleven languages).

Today, with the air we breathe filled with threats of global conflict, fanaticism, terrorism, and new forms of lethal weaponry, obedience to authority is an issue of such massive importance that social psychologists all over the world continue to ponder its ramifications (Blass, 2000).

Would Milgram's results be repeated today, in a different but analogous situation? To answer this question, Dutch researchers Wim Meeus and Quinten Raaijmakers (1995) constructed a moral dilemma like Milgram's. Rather than command participants to inflict physical pain, however, they arranged for them to cause psychological harm. When participants arrived at a university laboratory, they met a confederate supposedly there to take a test as part of a job interview. If the confederate passed the test, he'd get the job; if he failed, he would not. As part of a study of performance under stress, the experimenter told participants to distract the test-taking applicant by making an escalating series of harassing remarks. On cue, the applicant pleaded with participants to stop, became angry, faltered, and eventually fell into a state of despair and failed. As in Milgram's research, the question was straightforward: How many participants would obey orders through the entire set of fifteen stress remarks, despite the apparent harm caused to a real-life job applicant? In a control group that lacked a prodding experimenter, no one persisted. But when the experimenter ordered them to go on, 92 percent exhibited complete obedience despite seeing the task as unfair and distasteful. It appears that obedience is a powerful aspect of human nature brought about by the docile manner in which people relate to figures of authority—even today.

Before leaving the Milgram studies, consider an awkward but important moral question: By providing a situational explanation for the evils of Nazi Germany or of modern-day terrorism, are social psychologists unwittingly excusing the perpetrators? Does blaming what they did on the situation let them off the responsibility hook? In a series of studies, Arthur Miller and others (1999) found that after people were asked to come up with explanations for acts of wrongdoing, they tended to be more forgiving of the individuals who committed those acts—and were seen as more forgiving by others. This appearance of forgiveness was certainly not Milgram's intent, nor is it the intent of other researchers today who seek to understand cruelty, even while continuing to condemn it. Miller and his colleagues are thus quick to caution, "To explain is not to forgive" (p. 265).

Defiance: When People Rebel

"A little rebellion now and then is a good thing."

—Thomas Jefferson

It is easy to despair in light of the impressive array of forces that compel people toward blind obedience. But there's also good news. Just as social influence processes can breed subservience to authority, they can also breed rebellion and defiance. Few people realize it, but this phenomenon, too, was seen during World War II. In *Resistance of the Heart*, historian Nathan Stoltzfus (1996) describes a civil protest in Berlin in which the non-Jewish wives of two thousand newly captured Jews congregated outside the prison. The women were there, initially, seeking information about their husbands. Soon they were filling the streets chanting and refusing to leave. After eight straight days of protest, the defiant women prevailed. Fearing the negative impact on public opinion, the Nazis backed down and released the men.

Are the actions of a group harder to control than the behavior of a single individual? Consider the following study. Pretending to be part of a marketing research firm, William Gamson and others (1982) recruited people to participate in a supposed discussion of "community standards." Scheduled in groups of nine, participants were told that their discussions would be videotaped for a large oil company that was suing the manager of a local service station who had spoken out against higher gas prices. After receiving a summary of the case, most participants sided with the station manager. But there was a hitch. The oil company wanted evidence to win its case, said the experimenter posing as the discussion coordinator. He told each of the group members to get in front of the camera and express the company's viewpoint. Then he told them to sign an affidavit giving the company permission to edit the tapes for use in court.

You can see how the obedience script was supposed to unfold. Actually, only one of thirty-three groups even came close to following the script. In all others, people became incensed by the coordinator's behavior and refused to continue. Some groups were so outraged that they planned to take action. One group even threatened to blow the whistle on the firm by calling the local newspapers. Faced with one emotionally charged mutiny after another, the researchers had to discontinue the experiment.

Why did this study produce such active, often passionate revolt when Milgram's revealed such utterly passive obedience? Could it reflect a change in values from the 1960s, when Milgram's studies were run? Many college students believe that people would conform less today than in the past, but an analysis of obedience studies has revealed that there is no correlation between the year a study was conducted and the level of obedience that it produced (Blass, 1999). So what accounts for the contrasting results? One key difference is that people in Milgram's studies took part alone and those in Gamson's were in groups. Perhaps Michael Walzer was right: "Disobedience, when it is not criminally but morally, religiously, or politically motivated, is always a *collective act*" (cited in R. Brown, 1986, p. 17).

Our earlier discussion of conformity indicated that the mere presence of one ally in an otherwise unanimous majority gives individuals the courage to dissent. The same may hold true for obedience. Notably, Milgram never had more than one participant present in the same session. But in one experiment, he did use two confederates who posed as co-teachers along with the real participant. In these sessions, one confederate refused to continue at 150 volts, and the second refused at 210 volts. These models of disobedience had a profound influence on participants' willingness to defy the experimenter: In their presence, only 10 percent delivered the maximum level of shock (see Figure 7.7).

We should add that the presence of a group is not a guaranteed safeguard against destructive obedience. Groups can trigger aggression, as we'll see in Chapter 11. For example, the followers of Jim Jones were together when they collectively followed his command to die. And lynch mobs are just that—groups, not individuals. Clearly, there is power in sheer numbers. That power can be destructive, but it can also be used for constructive purposes. Indeed, the presence and support of others often provide the extra ounce of courage that people need to resist orders they find offensive.

The Continuum of Social Influence

As we have seen, social influence on behavior ranges from the implicit pressure of group norms, to the traps set by direct requests, to the powerful commands of authority. In each case, people choose whether to react with conformity or independence, compliance or assertiveness, obedience or defiance. From all the research, it is tempting to conclude that the more pressure brought to bear on people, the greater the influence. Is it possible, however, that more produces less? In a series of conformity studies, Lucian Conway and Mark Schaller (2005) cast participants into a corporate decision-making task in which they were asked to choose between two business options after watching others make the same decision. Consistently, the participants followed the group more when its members had formed their opinions freely than when they were compelled by a leader. It appears that strong-arm tactics that force people to change their behavior may backfire when it comes to changing opinions.

At this point, let's step back and ask two important questions. First, although different kinds of pressure influence us for different reasons, is it possible to predict all effects with a single, overarching principle? Second, what does the theory and research on social influence say about human nature?

social impact theory The theory that social influence depends on the strength, immediacy, and number of source persons relative to target persons.

Social Impact Theory

In 1981, Bibb Latané proposed that a common bond among the different processes involved in social influence leads people toward or away from such influence. Specifically, Latané proposed **social impact theory**, which states that social influence

"I invited a few friends over who think you should see a psychiatrist."

According to social impact theory, this "intervention" should prove persuasive.

of any kind—the total impact of others on a target person—is a function of the others' strength, immediacy, and number. According to Latané, social forces act on individuals in the same way that physical forces act on objects. Consider, for example, how overhead lights illuminate a surface. The total amount of light cast on a surface depends on the strength of the bulbs, their distance from the surface, and their number. As illustrated in the left portion of Figure 7.8, the same factors apply to social impact.

The *strength* of a source is determined by his or her status, ability, or relationship to a target. The stronger the source, the greater the influence. When people view the other members of a group as competent, they are more likely to conform in their judgments. When it comes to compliance, sources enhance their strength by making targets feel obligated to reciprocate a small favor. And to elicit obedience, authority figures gain strength by wearing uniforms or flaunting their prestigious affiliations.

Immediacy refers to a source's proximity in time and space to the target. The closer the source, the greater its impact. Milgram's research offers the best example. Obedience rates were higher when the experimenter issued commands in person rather than from a remote location; and when the victim suffered in close proximity to the participant, he acted as a contrary source of influence and obedience levels dropped. Consistent with this hypothesis, Latané and others (1995) asked individuals to name up to seven people in their lives and to indicate how far away those people lived and how many memorable interactions they'd had with them. In three studies, the correlation was the same: The closer others are, geographically, the more impact they have on us.

Finally, the theory predicts that as the *number* of sources increases, so does their influence—at least up to a point. You may recall that when Asch (1956) increased the number of live confederates in his line-judgment studies from one to four, conformity levels rose; yet further increases had only a negligible additional effect.

FIGURE 7.8

Social Impact: Source Factors and Target Factors

According to social impact theory, the total influence of other people on a target individual depends on three factors related to the source persons: their strength (size of source circles), immediacy (distance to the target), and number (number of the source circles). Similarly, the total influence is diffused, or reduced, by the strength (size of target circles), immediacy (distance from source circle), and number of target persons.

(Latané, 1981.)

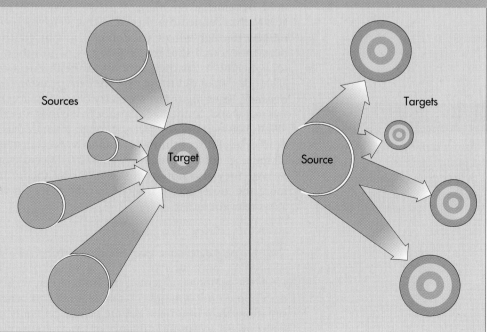

Sources

Target

Targets

Source

According to social impact theory, a Marine sergeant will exert influence to the extent that he is strong (in a position of power), immediate (physically close), and numerous (backed by others in the institution) relative to his trainees.

As the number of people in a group increases, so does their impact on an individual. **False.**

Social impact theory also predicts that people sometimes resist social pressure. According to Latané, this resistance is most likely to occur when social impact is *divided* among many strong and distant *targets*, as seen in the right part of Figure 7.8. There should be less impact on a target who is strong and far from the source than on one who is weak and close to the source; and there should be less impact on a target who is accompanied by other target persons than on one who stands alone. Thus, we have seen that conformity is reduced by the presence of an ally and that obedience rates drop when people are in the company of rebellious peers.

Over the years, social impact theory has been challenged, defended, and refined on various grounds (Jackson, 1986; Mullen, 1985; Sedikides & Jackson, 1990). On the one hand, critics say that it does not enable us to *explain* the processes that give rise to social influence or answer *why* questions. On the other hand, the theory enables us to predict the emergence of social influence and determine *when* it will occur. Whether the topic is conformity, compliance, or obedience, this theory has set the stage for interesting new research in the years to come.

A number of social psychologists have recently argued that social impact is a fluid, dynamic, ever-changing process (Vallacher et al., 2002). Latané and L'Herrou (1996) thus refined the theory in that vein. By having large groups of participants interact through e-mail, for example, and by controlling their lines of communication, they found that the individuals within the network formed "clusters." Over time, neighbors (participants who were in direct contact) became more similar to each other than did those who were more distant (not in direct contact) within the network. Referring to the geometry of social space, Latané and L'Herrou note that in the real world, immediacy cannot be defined strictly in terms of physical distance. "Walls between houses, rivers through towns, open spaces between cities, these and other spatial discontinuities all tend to prevent the equal flow of influence among all members of a population" (p. 1229). Speculating on the role of computer technology, they also note that social impact theory has to account for the fact that, more and more, people interact in cyberspace—perhaps making physical proximity a less relevant factor.

 Perspectives on Human Nature

From the material presented in this chapter, what general conclusions might you draw about human nature? Granted, social influence is more likely to occur in some situations than in others. But are people generally malleable or unyielding? Is there a tilt toward accepting influence or toward putting up resistance?

There is no single, universal answer to these questions. As we saw earlier, some cultures value autonomy and independence, while others place more emphasis on conformity to one's group. Even within a given culture, values may change over time. To demonstrate the point, ask yourself: If you were a parent, what traits would you like your child to have? When this question was put to American mothers in 1924, they chose "obedience" and "loyalty," key characteristics of conformity. Yet when mothers were asked the same question in 1978, they cited "independence" and "tolerance of others," key characteristics of autonomy. Similar trends were found in surveys conducted not only in the United States but also in West Germany, Italy, England, and Japan (Alwin, 1990; Remley, 1988)—and in laboratory experiments, where conformity rates are somewhat lower today than in the past (Bond & Smith, 1996).

Is it possible that today's children—tomorrow's adults—will exhibit greater resistance to the various forms of social influence? If so, what effects will this trend have on society as a whole? Cast in a positive light, conformity, compliance, and obedience are good and necessary human responses. They promote group solidarity and agreement—qualities that keep groups from being torn apart by dissension. Cast in a negative light, a lack of independence, assertiveness, and defiance are undesirable behaviors that lend themselves to narrow-mindedness, cowardice, and destructive obedience—often with terrible costs. For each of us, and for society as a whole, the trick is to strike a balance.

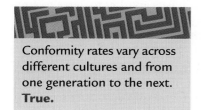

Conformity rates vary across different cultures and from one generation to the next. **True.**

REVIEW

- Conformity, compliance, and obedience are three kinds of social influence, varying in the degree of pressure brought to bear on an individual.

Social Influence as "Automatic"

- Sometimes we are influenced by other people without our awareness.

- Studies show that people mimic each other's behaviors and moods, perhaps as a way of smoothing social interactions.

Conformity

- Conformity is the tendency for people to change their behavior to be consistent with group norms.

The Early Classics

- Two classic experiments illustrate contrasting types of conformity.
- Sherif presented groups of participants with an ambiguous task and found that their judgments gradually converged.
- Using a simpler line-judgment task, Asch had confederates make incorrect responses and found that participants went along about a third of the time.

Why Do People Conform?

- Sherif found that people exhibit private conformity, using others for information in an ambiguous situation.
- Asch's studies indicated that people conform in their public behavior to avoid appearing deviant.

Majority Influence

- As the size of an incorrect unanimous majority increases, so does conformity—up to a point.
- People conform to perceived social norms when these norms are brought to mind.

- The presence of one dissenter reduces conformity, even when he or she disagrees with the participant and lacks competence at the task.
- Women conform more than men on "masculine" tasks and in face-to-face settings, but not on "feminine" or gender-neutral tasks or in private settings.

Minority Influence

- Sometimes minorities resist pressures to conform and are able to influence majorities.
- In general, minority influence is greater when the source is an ingroup member.
- According to Moscovici, minorities can exert influence by taking a consistent and unwavering position.
- Hollander claims that to exert influence, a person should first conform, then dissent.
- Majority influence is greater on direct and public measures of conformity, but minorities show their impact in indirect or private measures of conformity.
- By forcing other group members to think more openly about a problem, minorities enhance the quality of a group's decision making.

- People gain courage to resist conformity pressures after watching others do the same.

Culture, Conformity, and Independence

- Just as cultures differ in their social norms, so too they differ in the extent to which people are expected to adhere to those norms.

- Research shows that people from collectivist cultures conform more than people from individualistic cultures.

Compliance

- A common form of social influence occurs when we respond to direct requests.

The Language of Request

- People are more likely to comply when they are taken by surprise and when the request sounds reasonable.

The Norm of Reciprocity

- We often comply when we feel indebted to a requester who has done us a favor.
- People differ in the extent to which they use reciprocity for personal gain and are wary of falling prey to this strategy.

Setting Traps: Sequential Request Strategies

- Four compliance techniques are based on a two-step request: The first step sets a trap, and the second elicits compliance.

- Using the foot-in-the-door technique, a person sets the stage for the "real" request by first getting someone to comply with a smaller request.
- In low-balling, one person gets another to agree to a request but then increases the size of it by revealing hidden costs. Despite the increase, people often follow through on their agreement.
- With the door-in-the-face technique, the real request is preceded by a large one that is rejected. People then comply with the second request because they see it as a concession to be reciprocated.
- The that's-not-all technique begins with a large request. Then the apparent size of the request is reduced by the offer of a discount or bonus.

Assertiveness: When People Say No

- Many people find it hard to be assertive. Doing so requires that we be vigilant and recognize the traps.

Obedience

- When the request is a command and the requester is a figure of authority, the resulting influence is called obedience.

Milgram's Research: Forces of Destructive Obedience

- In a series of experiments, participants were ordered by an experimenter to administer increasingly painful shocks to a confederate.
- Sixty-five percent obeyed completely but felt tormented by the experience.
- Obedience levels are influenced by various situational factors, including a participant's physical proximity to both the authority figure and the victim.
- Two other aspects of Milgram's procedure also contributed to the high levels of obedience: (1) Participants did not feel personally responsible, and (2) the orders escalated gradually.

- In more recent studies, people exhibited high rates of obedience when told to inflict psychological harm on another person.

Milgram in the Twenty-First Century

- Milgram's studies have remained relevant and controversial into the twenty-first century.
- Researchers note that a situational explanation for acts of destructive obedience does not forgive them.

Defiance: When People Rebel

- Just as processes of social influence breed obedience, they can also support acts of defiance, since groups are more difficult to control than individuals.
- Provision of a situational explanation for cruel behavior does not excuse that behavior.

The Continuum of Social Influence

Social Impact Theory

- Social impact theory predicts that social influence depends on the strength, immediacy, and number of sources who exert pressure relative to target persons who absorb that pressure.

Perspectives on Human Nature

- There is no single answer to the question of whether people are conformists or nonconformists.
- There are cross-cultural differences in social influence, and values change over time even within specific cultures.

KEY TERMS

collectivism (235)
compliance (236)
conformity (224)
door-in-the-face
technique (240)
foot-in-the-door
technique (238)
idiosyncrasy credits (233)
individualism (235)
informational influence (226)
low-balling (239)
minority influence (232)
normative influence (227)
obedience (243)
private conformity (228)
public conformity (228)
social impact theory (250)
that's-not-all technique (241)

PUTTING COMMON SENSE TO THE TEST

When all members of a group give an incorrect response to an easy question, most people most of the time conform to that response.

False. In Asch's classic conformity experiments, respondents conformed only about a third of the time.

An effective way to get someone to do you a favor is to make a first request that is so large the person is sure to reject it.

True. This approach, known as the door-in-the-face technique, increases compliance by making the person feel bound to make a concession.

In experiments on obedience, most participants who were ordered to administer severe shocks to an innocent person refused to do so.

False. In Milgram's classic research, 65 percent of all participants obeyed the experimenter and administered the maximum possible shock.

As the number of people in a group increases, so does their impact on an individual.

False. Increasing group size boosts the impact on an individual only up to a point, beyond which further increases have very little added effect.

Conformity rates vary across different cultures and from one generation to the next.

True. Research shows that conformity rates are higher in cultures that are collectivistic rather than individualistic in orientation, and that values change over time even within cultures.

8

Group Processes

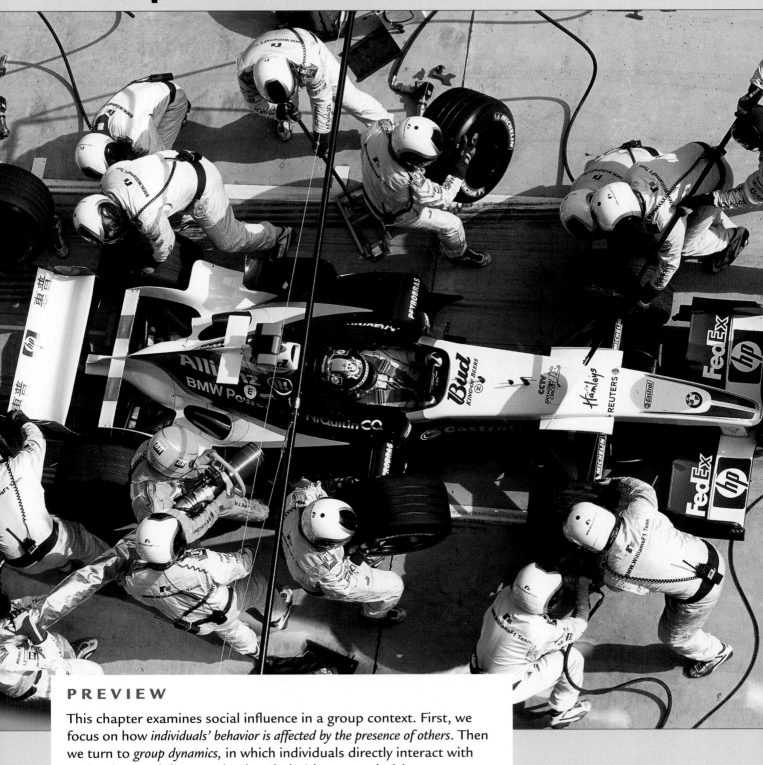

PREVIEW

This chapter examines social influence in a group context. First, we focus on how *individuals' behavior is affected by the presence of others*. Then we turn to *group dynamics,* in which individuals directly interact with each other, and discuss why the whole (the group decision or performance) is different from the sum of its parts (the attitudes and abilities of the group members). In the final section, on *cooperation, competition,* and *conflict,* we examine how groups intensify or reconcile their differences.

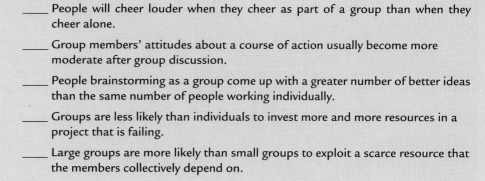

T/F

_____ People will cheer louder when they cheer as part of a group than when they cheer alone.

_____ Group members' attitudes about a course of action usually become more moderate after group discussion.

_____ People brainstorming as a group come up with a greater number of better ideas than the same number of people working individually.

_____ Groups are less likely than individuals to invest more and more resources in a project that is failing.

_____ Large groups are more likely than small groups to exploit a scarce resource that the members collectively depend on.

t was a spectacular kind of fireworks display when the space shuttle *Discovery* blasted off into space on July 4, 2006, the first time a shuttle had been launched on America's Independence Day. *Discovery* traveled 5.3 million miles during its twelve-and-a-half-day journey. To put this achievement in perspective, consider the fact that it was barely a hundred years earlier that humans had first taken flight for twelve *seconds* in a machine-powered plane. On December 17, 1903, as Orville and Wilbur Wright's plane flew precariously through the cold, windy air near Kitty Hawk, North Carolina, fantasy as old as human history finally, remarkably, became reality. Many had tried and failed to accomplish what the Wright brothers finally achieved, and so it wouldn't have been surprising if progress in aviation would continue to move at a painstakingly slow rate after 1903. But looking back now, the speed of this progress seems as close to miraculous as anything humans have achieved. After its long history as an earthbound species, within a few decades of Orville's first brief flight, people would fly across vast lands and oceans. Within one person's lifetime, humans would go from celebrating a dozen seconds of staying above Earth to celebrating men walking on the moon.

Fans of aviation celebrated the one-hundredth anniversary of the Wright brothers' incredible achievement in December 2003. But in the world of aviation, 2003 was a year of mourning as well as celebration. Just as the anniversary of the Wright brothers' ascent was a great leap for humanity, the descent of the space shuttle *Columbia* back toward Earth on February 1, 2003, was a tragic fall. Sixteen days after its launch into space, *Columbia* was only minutes away from its scheduled landing when it disintegrated during re-entry into the atmosphere, killing all seven crew members on board.

The fact that humans could achieve so much in one century, from learning how to fly several feet above the ground to launching probes to the ends of the solar system, is a testament to what can be accomplished when people work together. The Wright brothers could not have achieved their great feat without each other and without the help, expertise, and fresh perspectives that several others offered. And certainly the numerous, stunning achievements since then were possible only through people collaborating in groups. But as we will see in this chapter, the tragedy of the *Columbia* also reveals a cautionary lesson about groups and about how group processes can lead to bad, even catastrophic, decision making.

For example, several days before *Columbia* exploded, a team of engineers at the U.S. National Aeronautics and Space Administration (NASA) reviewed a video of foam breaking off the *Columbia* during launch and hitting the area near the left wing, and they speculated about whether the impact could have damaged the heat-shielding tiles there. One engineer, Rodney Rocha, made more than a half dozen requests of NASA managers to go outside the agency and seek images from spy satellite photos

Photos of the seven astronauts killed in the space shuttle Columbia *tragedy on February 1, 2003, adorn a table at a memorial service in remembrance of the crew.*

The Space Shuttle Discovery *streaks across the sky over Daytona Beach, Florida, after a rare nighttime liftoff on December 9, 2006. The* Columbia *disaster and the* Discovery *success together illustrate how people working together in groups can achieve great things but can also make terrible mistakes.*

or powerful telescopes that could provide a better look at the possible damage to the *Columbia* while it was in space. These requests were ignored or rejected. One manager said that he refused to be a "Chicken Little." The flight director e-mailed his rejection of the engineer's request: "I consider it to be a dead issue" (Glanz & Schwartz, 2003).

As investigators concluded months later, aspects of the "culture" at NASA were to blame for the failure to adequately consider concerns like these. In the end, the investigators pointed to the group dynamics at NASA as much as to the physical problems in explaining what led the *Columbia* and its crew to disaster.

And one of the most disturbing revelations was this: Although the physical causes in this incident were very different from those implicated in the previous NASA tragedy, when the space shuttle *Challenger* exploded during its ascent seventeen years before, the flawed group dynamics were shockingly similar. Several engineers at the Morton Thiokol Corporation, which had made the *Challenger's* solid rocket boosters, warned that launching in cold temperatures could cause the O-ring seals in the rocket boosters to fail, which would cause a catastrophic explosion. Some wanted to ban a liftoff if the temperature was below 50 degrees. On the morning of January 28, 1986, the temperature at the launch pad was below freezing. But high-level officials at Morton Thiokol and NASA were motivated not to delay the launch. NASA had heavily promoted the mission because it marked the first time that "an ordinary citizen," a New Hampshire high school teacher named Christa McAuliffe, would travel into space along with the astronauts. The decision was made to launch. Seventy-three seconds after liftoff, the *Challenger* exploded, killing all seven people on board. Apparently, the O-ring seals had indeed failed.

In both cases, group members recognized the very problems that would cause the catastrophes and tried to warn people higher up in the chain of command, but aspects of the culture and structure of their organization created obstacles that prevented these warnings from being heeded. Observers around the world held their breaths again on July 4, 2006, when once *again* questions about foam that had broken off from the shuttle caused many, including NASA's head of safety and a chief engineer, to want *Discovery's* launch to be postponed, and once again NASA decided that launching was worth the risk. Fortunately, this time everything went well.

On a much more mundane, earthbound scale, we all work in groups, and we are all affected by them. And the same kinds of group processes that contributed to both the accomplishments and tragedies of the first century of flight affect our own lives in countless ways. Most of us won't learn "rocket science," but we can and should learn about group processes. The more we learn how to harness the good that groups can bring, and avoid their pitfalls, the better our lives will be.

People are often at their best—and their worst—in groups. It is through groups that individuals form communities, pool resources, and share successes. But it is also through groups that stereotypes turn into oppression, frustrations turn into mob violence, and conflicts into wars.

Clearly, it is important that we understand how groups work and how individuals influence, and are influenced by, groups. The research reported in this chapter reveals a fascinating fact: *Groups can be quite different from the sum of their parts.* When you think about that statement, it suggests something almost mystical or magical about groups, like quantum physics (or the enduring careers of any of several untalented actors or pop stars!). How can a group be better, or worse, than the individuals that constitute it? The math may not seem to add up, but the theory and research discussed in this chapter will help answer this question. We examine groups on several levels: At the individual level, we explore how individuals are influenced by groups; at the group level, we explore how groups perform; and at the intergroup level, we explore how groups interact with each other in cooperation and competition.

Individuals in Groups: The Presence of Others

"You think because you understand 'one,' you must understand 'two,' because one and one make two. But you must also understand 'and.'"

—ancient Sufi saying

In Chapter 5, we focused on how individuals perceive groups and group members. In that context, we characterized a group as a set of individuals with at least one of the following characteristics: (1) direct interactions with each other over a period of time; (2) joint membership in a social category based on sex, race, or other attributes; (3) a shared, common fate, identity, or set of goals. The current chapter focuses on groups themselves rather than others' perceptions of groups and group members. In this context, we emphasize the first and third criteria: direct interactions among group members over a period of time and a shared, common fate, identity, or set of goals.

Also in Chapter 5, we discussed how groups may vary in the extent to which they are seen as distinct entities, often with rigid boundaries that make them distinct from other groups. In other words, some groups seem more "groupy" than others (Brewer et al., 2004; Ip et al., 2006). On the very low end of the dimensions of entity or social integration would be people attending a concert or working out near each other in a gym. These are not real groups. Such assemblages are sometimes called **collectives**—people engaging in a common activity but having little direct interaction with each other (Milgram & Toch, 1969). We begin our discussion by examining some basic effects that the presence of others has on individuals, whether those others are part of an actual group, a looser collective of people, or sometimes just others who happen to be around.

Social Facilitation: When Others Arouse Us

Social psychologists have long been fascinated by how the presence of others affects behavior. In Chapter 1, we reported that one of the founders of social psychology was Norman Triplett, whose article "The Dynamogenic Factors in Pacemaking and Competition" (1897–1898) is often cited as the earliest publication in the field. Triplett began his research by studying the official bicycle records from the Racing Board of the League of American Wheelmen for the 1897 season. He noticed that cyclists who competed against others performed better than those who cycled alone against the clock. After dismissing various theories of the day (our favorite is "brain worry"), he proposed his own hypothesis: The presence of another rider releases the competitive instinct, which increases nervous energy and enhances performance. To test this proposition, Triplett got forty children to wind up fishing reels, alternating between performing alone and working in parallel. On the average, winding time was faster when the children worked side by side than when they worked alone.

Later research following Triplett's studies proved disappointing. Sometimes the presence of others (side by side or with an audience out front) enhanced performance; at other times, performance declined. It seemed that Triplett's promising lead had turned into a blind alley, and social psychologists had largely abandoned this research by World War II. But years later, Robert Zajonc (1965, 1980) saw a way to reconcile the contradictory results by integrating research from experimental psychology with social psychological research. Zajonc offered an elegant solution: The presence of

collective People engaged in common activities but having minimal direct interaction.

others increases arousal, which can affect performance in different ways, depending on the task at hand. Let's see how this works.

The Zajonc Solution   According to Zajonc, the road from presence to performance requires three steps.

1. The presence of others creates general physiological *arousal,* which energizes behavior. Based on experimental psychology research and principles of evolution, Zajonc argued that all animals, including humans, tend to become aroused when in the presence of *conspecifics*—that is, members of their own species.

2. Increased arousal enhances an individual's tendency to perform the *dominant response.* The dominant response is the reaction elicited most quickly and easily by a given stimulus. Here again, Zajonc drew from experimental psychology research, particularly research concerning learning.

3. The quality of an individual's performance varies according to the type of *task.* On an easy task (one that is simple or well learned), the dominant response is usually correct or successful. But on a difficult task (one that is complex or unfamiliar), the dominant response is often incorrect or unsuccessful.

Putting these three steps together (see Figure 8.1) yields the following scenarios. Suppose you are playing the violin. If you're an excellent player and are performing a well-learned, familiar arrangement, having other people around should enhance your performance; the presence of others will increase your arousal, which will enhance your dominant response. Because this arrangement is so well learned, your dominant response will be to perform it well. However, if you are just learning to play the violin and you are unfamiliar with this arrangement, the presence of others is the last thing you'll want. The increase in arousal should enhance the dominant response, which in this case would be *unsuccessful* violin playing.

When you think about it, this makes intuitive sense. If you are just learning how to perform some complicated task, such as playing the violin or riding a bike, it helps if you are not aroused. In contrast, if you are already good at the task, you may need the extra "juice" that comes from performing in front of others to help you rise to new heights and perform even better than you would if performing alone. Sports fans may be able to think of many instances in which the best athletes, such as baseball player Derek Jeter or tennis player Serena Williams, seem to rise to the occasion when the pressure is on, while lesser athletes "choke" under the same kind of pressure. And physical performances are not the only ones influenced; the effects also hold for social judgment or cognitive tasks, such as forming impressions of

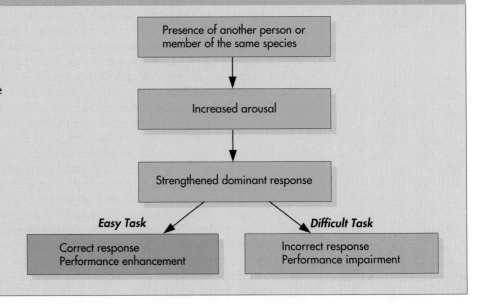

FIGURE 8.1

Social Facilitation: The Zajonc Solution

According to Zajonc, the presence of others increases arousal, which strengthens the dominant response to a stimulus. On an easy task, the dominant response is usually correct, and thus the presence of others enhances performance. On a difficult task, the dominant response is often incorrect, and thus the presence of others impairs performance.

Through social facilitation, seasoned performers like world-class gymnast Zhang Nan of China benefit from the presence of an audience when performing well-learned routines. On the other hand, when first learning a difficult—and dangerous—exercise like this, a performer would be advised not to try it in front of an arousing crowd!

others or applying stereotypes (Lambert et al., 2003; Thomas et al., 2002).

Taken as a package, these two effects of the presence of others—helping performance on easy tasks but hurting performance on difficult tasks—are known as **social facilitation**. Unfortunately, this term has been a prime source of confusion for countless students. The trick is to remember that the presence of others facilitates the dominant response, not necessarily the task itself. This facilitation of the dominant response does, in effect, facilitate easy tasks, but it makes difficult tasks even more difficult.

Zajonc says that social facilitation is universal, occurring not only in human activities but also among other animals, even insects. Consider, for instance, cockroaches. How fast will they run? In a study by Zajonc and his colleagues (1969), participating insects were placed in a brightly lit start box connected to a darkened goal box. When the track was a simple one, with a straight runway between the start box and the goal box, cockroaches running in pairs ran more quickly toward the goal box than did those running alone. But in a more complex maze, with a right turn required to reach the goal box, solitary cockroaches outraced pairs. In a particularly creative follow-up experiment, Zajonc and his colleagues found that cockroaches completed the easy maze faster, and the difficult maze slower, if they raced in front of a crowd of spectator cockroaches than if they raced with no audience. You may wonder, How did the researchers get cockroaches to participate as spectators? The researchers placed cockroaches in plexiglass "audience boxes" along either side of the maze, and this "audience" produced social facilitation.

Zajonc's formulation revived interest in the issues raised by Triplett's early research, and suddenly the inconsistent findings that had been reported began to make sense. The results of a meta-analysis of 241 studies were consistent with much of Zajonc's account (Bond & Titus, 1983). Moreover, Jim Blascovich and others (1999) have recently found physiological evidence supporting and extending Zajonc's theory: The presence of others triggered arousal in individuals performing a task, and the specific pattern of cardiovascular responses associated with this arousal was consistent with social facilitation theory.

It is because of the effects of social facilitation that firefighters, police officers, military personnel, and others must train so much to be ready to make split-second decisions under highly arousing situations. They may seem to practice scenarios to the point of overtraining, but it is only through such repetition that their dominant response can be assured to typically be the correct one. When in the midst of a raging fire or military firefight, careful deliberation is often impossible, and arousal will tend to elicit their dominant responses (e.g., Gladwell, 2005).

Social facilitation effects have been replicated across many domains, but not all of Zajonc's theory has received universal support. Zajonc proposed that the **mere presence** of others is sufficient to produce social facilitation. Some have argued, however, that the presence of others will produce social facilitation only under certain conditions. These issues have produced various alternative explanations of social facilitation, and we turn now to two of the major variations on Zajonc's theme.

Evaluation Apprehension   The first and most thoroughly researched alternative, **evaluation apprehension theory**, proposes that performance will be enhanced or impaired only in the presence of others who are in a position to evaluate that performance (Geen, 1991; Henchy & Glass, 1968). In other words, it's not simply because others are around that I'm so aroused and therefore inept as I try to learn to snowboard on a crowded mountain. Rather, it's because I worry that the others are watching and probably laughing at me. I imagine them telling stories about me at dinner, or perhaps uploading a video of my performance to *youtube* or some other Internet site, to be laughed at by millions. These concerns increase my dominant response, which, unfortunately, is falling.

social facilitation   A process whereby the presence of others enhances performance on easy tasks but impairs performance on difficult tasks.

mere presence theory   The proposition that the mere presence of others is sufficient to produce social facilitation effects.

evaluation apprehension theory   A theory holding that the presence of others will produce social facilitation effects only when those others are seen as potential evaluators.

Usually, presence and potential evaluation go hand in hand. To pry them apart, researchers have come up with some rather unusual procedures. In one study, for example, participants worked on a task alone, in the presence of two other supposed participants (actually confederates), or in the presence of two blindfolded confederates supposedly preparing for a perception study. Compared with participants working alone, those working in the presence of seeing confederates were more likely to come up with dominant responses. In the presence of the blindfolded confederates, however, dominant responses were no more frequent than among participants working alone (Cottrell et al., 1968).

People may experience evaluation apprehension when they are targets of negative stereotypes about their group's ability to perform in a particular domain. As discussed in Chapter 5, women taking a math test, for instance, may fail to perform to their potential because of concerns about negative stereotypes of women's ability in math—a condition called stereotype threat. Talia Ben-Zeev and her colleagues (2005) predicted that women who thought they were going to take a difficult math test under conditions associated with stereotype threat would be aroused by the threat, and this in turn would lead to social facilitation effects on their performance on an unrelated task. Supporting this prediction, women under stereotype threat did worse than women not under threat on a difficult unrelated task (writing their names backward repeatedly), but they did better on a very easy one (writing their names forward repeatedly). In both conditions—under stereotype threat versus not—the women performed these tasks in the presence of other people, but it was only under threat that evaluation apprehension was likely to be most pronounced.

Distraction   Another approach to social facilitation, **distraction-conflict theory**, points out that being distracted while we're working on a task creates attentional conflict (Baron, 1986; Sanders, 1981). We're torn between focusing on the task and inspecting the distracting stimulus. Conflicted about where to pay attention, our arousal increases. Surprisingly, the distraction caused by the presence of others can actually enhance individuals' performance on some tasks, especially when such distraction is countered by a narrowing of attention (Muller et al., 2004). In one study, Pascal Huguet and his colleagues (1999) found that this "tunnel vision" response helped people's performance on a task in which focused attention was beneficial, but it hurt their performance on a task in which peak performance required the use of a broader, more complex array of information.

Distraction-conflict theory maintains that there's nothing uniquely social about "social" facilitation. People, of course, can be distracting; but so can crashing objects, blaring music, and glittering lights. The effect of mere presence has also been called into question. People are not always distracting; a familiar presence that we take for granted will likely leave our performance untouched.

Integration?   Consider again the three theories of social facilitation we have described. Is one of them right and the others wrong? Probably not. For example, the mere presence account can explain social facilitation among cockroaches better than the evaluation apprehension account can, but evaluation apprehension is better than mere presence at explaining why blindfolded others have less impact than others who are not blindfolded. Comprehensive reviews of the research evidence have drawn different conclusions about which theory has the best track record (Bond & Titus, 1983; Guerin, 2003). It seems likely that all three of the basic elements described by these theories (mere presence, evaluation, and attention) contribute to the impact others have on our own performance. But as we are about to see in the next section, there is even more to the story of how individuals are affected by the presence of others.

distraction-conflict theory
A theory holding that the presence of others will produce social facilitation effects only when those others distract from the task and create attentional conflict.

🔵 Social Loafing: When Others Relax Us

The tasks employed in research on social facilitation produce individually identifiable results. That is, behavior can be identified and evaluated. But on some tasks, efforts are pooled so that the specific performance of any one individual cannot be determined.

FIGURE 8.2

Social Loafing: When Many Produce Less

Social loafing is a group-produced reduction in individual output on simple tasks. In this study, college students were told to cheer or clap as loudly as they could. The sound pressure produced by each of them decreased as the size of the group increased.

(Latané et al., 1979.)

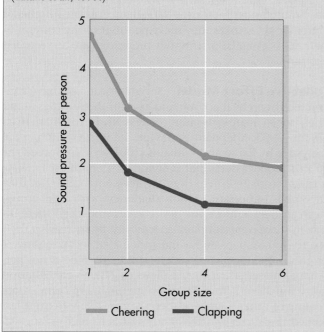

That other founder of social psychology, French agricultural engineer Max Ringelmann, investigated group performance on these kinds of collective endeavors. In research conducted during the 1880s, Ringelmann discovered that, compared with what people produced when they worked on their own, individual output declined when they worked together on simple tasks like pulling a rope or pushing a cart (Kravitz & Martin, 1986; Ringelmann, 1913).

Why did individual output decline? One explanation is that the individuals exerted less effort when they acted collectively, but another explanation is that the individuals simply demonstrated poor coordination when working together—some pulled while others relaxed and vice versa. How can you distinguish lack of effort from poor coordination in a task like this? Nearly a hundred years after Ringelmann's research, Alan Ingham and his colleagues (1974) answered this question by using a rope-pulling machine and blindfolding participants. In one condition, participants were led to *think* that they were pulling with a bunch of other participants; and in another condition, the participants were informed that they were pulling alone (which, in fact, they were). The researchers told the participants to pull as hard as they could. Ingham and colleagues were able to measure exactly how hard each individual participant pulled, and they observed that the participants pulled almost 20 percent harder when they thought they were pulling alone than when they thought they were pulling with others. Naoki Kugihara (1999) found a similar decline in rope-pulling among Japanese men (but not women) in a collective setting.

Bibb Latané and his colleagues (1979) found that group-produced reductions in individual output, which they called **social loafing**, are common in other types of tasks as well. For example, imagine being asked as part of a psychology experiment to cheer or clap as loudly as you can. Common sense might lead you to think that you would cheer and clap louder when doing this together with others in a group than when performing alone because you would be less embarrassed and inhibited if others were doing the same thing as you. But Latané and his colleagues found that when performing collectively, individual students loafed—they exerted less effort. The sound pressure generated by each individual decreased as the size of the group increased (see Figure 8.2). This social loafing occurred even among cheerleaders, who are supposed to be experts at cheering and clapping with others! And social loafing is not restricted to simple motor tasks. Sharing responsibility with others reduces the amount of effort that people put into more complex motor tasks, such as swimming in a relay race; cognitive tasks, such as trying to remember information or working on math or verbal tests; and important, enduring real-world behaviors, such as working collaboratively on collective farms or on classroom or workgroup projects (Latané et al., 1979; Liden et al., 2004; Miles & Greenberg, 1993; Plaks & Higgins, 2000; Weldon et al., 2000). When others are there to pick up the slack, people slack off.

Steven Karau and Kipling Williams (1993) conducted a meta-analysis of seventy-eight studies and found social loafing to be a reliable phenomenon, displayed across numerous tasks and in countries around the world. But social loafing is not inevitable; a number of factors can reduce it. Social loafing is less likely to occur when one of the following conditions is present:

People will cheer louder when they cheer as part of a group than when they cheer alone. **False.**

social loafing A group-produced reduction in individual output on easy tasks where contributions are pooled.

- People believe that their own performance can be identified and thus evaluated, by themselves or others.

- The task is important or meaningful to those performing it.

- People believe that their own efforts are necessary for a successful outcome.

"We just haven't been flapping them hard enough."

Individuals often don't try as hard in groups as they do alone. If they can be convinced that their efforts will pay off, however, their output can soar.

- The group expects to be punished for poor performance.

- The group is small.

- The group is cohesive; that is, membership in the group is valuable and important to the members, and the individuals like each other.

Businesses have taken note of social loafing and have applied these research findings to try to reduce it in the workplace. One result is that workers' actions on the job are coming under increasing surveillance, as the number of computer key strokes they make per hour or the content of their calls, e-mails, or Internet browsing can be recorded electronically.

Collective Effort Model Several researchers have constructed theoretical accounts to explain the findings about when social loafing is more or less likely to occur (e.g., Guerin, 2003; Shepperd & Taylor, 1999). One influential analysis is by Karau and Williams (2001), who proposed the collective effort model. This model asserts that individuals try hard on a collective task when they think their efforts will help them achieve outcomes that they personally value. If the outcome is important to individual members of the group, and if they believe that they can help achieve the desired outcome, then these individuals are likely to engage in *social compensation*—specifically, by increasing their efforts on collective tasks to try to compensate for the anticipated social loafing or poor performance of other group members. Conversely, if the outcome is not personally important to individual members, if they believe that their contribution won't affect the outcome very much, or if they feel they are unable to compensate for the anticipated social loafing of other members, then they are likely to exert less effort. This is sometimes called the *sucker effect:* Nobody wants to be the "sucker" who does all the work while everyone else goofs off, so everyone withholds effort, and the result is very poor group performance (Houldsworth & Mathews, 2000; Kerr, 1983; Shepperd, 1993a). The next time you work on a group project, such as a paper that you and several other students are supposed to write together, consider the factors that increase and decrease social loafing. You might want to try to change aspects of the situation so that all group members are motivated to do their share of the work.

Culture and Social Loafing Although men and women in a wide variety of populations and cultures exhibit social loafing, it is less prevalent among women than among men and less prevalent among people from eastern, collectivist cultures (such as China, Japan, and Taiwan) than among people from western, individualist cultures (such as Canada and the United States). Women and people engaging in primarily collectivistic cultural contexts tend to be relatively more interdependent and connected to others than men and people in individualistic contexts. With a more interdependent self, people tend to be more aware of their connections and mutual reliance on others, and therefore may be more concerned about the possible negative impact of social loafing on others.

Groups in collectivistic cultures may be more likely to have group norms promoting productive teamwork and discouraging social loafing. Within a culture, though, such norms vary from group to group. When norms encourage productivity, personal involvement, and social support, social loafing is less likely to occur (Hoigaard et al., 2006).

Individual differences matter as well. For example, Brian Smith and others (2001) reported that individuals with a relatively high need for cognition (that is, people who enjoy effortful cognitive activities) did not socially loaf on a cognitively engaging task, whereas those lower in need for cognition did. Jason Hart and others (2004) found that people low in achievement motivation engaged in social loafing on

collective effort model
The theory that individuals will exert effort on a collective task to the degree that they think their individual efforts will be important, relevant, and meaningful for achieving outcomes that they value.

Here, Chinese farmers cooperate on a task in which individual contributions cannot be identified. Social loafing on such tasks occurs less often in eastern cultures than in western ones.

a collective task when they expected their co-workers would work hard, but those high in achievement motivation resisted social loafing, regardless of their expectations about their co-workers.

Facilitation and Loafing: Unifying the Paradigms

Social facilitation and social loafing represent two separate research traditions, but the connection between them—the fact that both arise in the presence of others—has prompted some investigators to attempt a unified approach that highlights the arousal associated with possible performance evaluation (Guerin, 2003; Harkins & Szymanski, 1987; Sanna, 1992).

- When individual contributions can be identified (social facilitation), the presence of others *increases* arousal and the possibility of being evaluated: The individual is in the spotlight.

- When individual contributions are pooled (social loafing), the presence of others *decreases* arousal and the possibility of being evaluated: Each person's performance is swallowed up in the group product, and the individual can relax and be lost in the crowd.

Now, how do arousal and possible evaluation affect performance? It depends on the difficulty of the task to be performed. Four predictions can be made.

- When the presence of others increases the possibility of evaluation of an individual's work: (1) Performance on easy tasks is enhanced because the individual is more motivated. That's social facilitation, part one. (2) Performance on difficult tasks is impaired because the pressure gets to the individual. That's social facilitation, part two.

- When the presence of others decreases the possibility of evaluation of an individual's work: (3) Performance on easy tasks is impaired because the individual is uninspired. That's social loafing. (4) Performance on difficult tasks is enhanced because being lost in the crowd frees the individual from anxiety. There's no official name for this effect, but we're inclined to call it "social security."

These predictions have been confirmed in several studies using different methods and measures (Jackson & Williams, 1985; Sanna, 1992). The typical pattern of results is diagrammed in Figure 8.3. A unified view of social facilitation and social loafing has important practical implications for maximizing performance when individuals are working together. In team sports, for example, coaches would be well advised to evaluate each player's performance against a weak opponent but to stress team spirit and overall group effort during a tough game. Unification is also historically satisfying: the two founders of social psychology, Triplett and Ringelmann, together at last.

FIGURE 8.3

Unifying the Paradigms: Presence and Evaluation

The relationship between the presence of others and the potential for evaluation is the key to a unified paradigm of social facilitation and social loafing. When individual performance can be evaluated, the presence of others enhances performance on easy tasks but impairs performance on difficult endeavors. When contributions are pooled across individuals, the pattern reverses, as performance declines on easy tasks but improves on difficult ones.

(Adapted from Jackson & Williams, 1985; Sanna, 1992.)

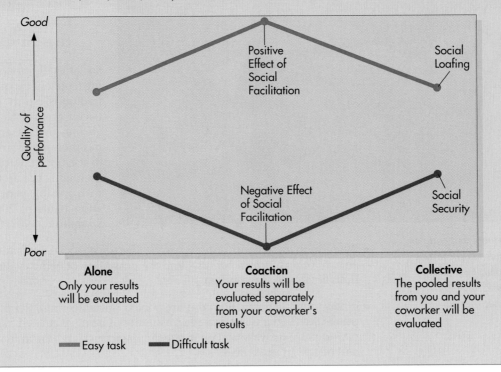

Deindividuation

Some pioneers in social psychology regarded the presence of others as considerably more profound and more troubling. Based on their research in France, Gabriel Tarde (1890) and Gustave Le Bon (1895) thought of collective influence as virtually mesmerizing. They maintained that, under the sway of the crowd, people turn into copycat automatons or, worse still, uncontrollable mobs.

The destructive capacity of collectives has left a bloody trail through human history; the examples are too many to name here, and the list continues to grow. What turns an unruly crowd into a violent mob? No doubt many of the factors described in Chapter 11 on Aggression contribute to violence by groups as well as by individuals. These include imitation of aggressive models, intense frustration, high temperatures, alcohol consumption, and the presence of weapons that trigger aggressive thoughts and actions. But there's also **deindividuation**, the loss of a person's sense of individuality and the reduction of normal constraints against deviant behavior. Most investigators believe that deindividuation is a collective phenomenon that occurs only in the presence of others (Diener et al., 1976; Festinger et al., 1952). Philip Zimbardo (1969) observed that arousal, anonymity, and reduced feelings of individual responsibility together contribute to deindividuation.

deindividuation The loss of a person's sense of individuality and the reduction of normal constraints against deviant behavior.

Environmental Cues In order to understand deindividuation, we must examine the physical and social environment in which it takes place. According to Steven Prentice-Dunn and Ronald Rogers (1982, 1983), two types of environmental cues—accountability cues and attentional cues—increase deviant behavior.

It has become fairly commonplace in recent years for celebrations by groups of fans after their team's victory in a championship to escalate from joy to mayhem and destruction, as in this post-Super Bowl rioting. In the midst of a crowd like this, people may feel deindividuated, which can lead to deviant behavior.

Accountability cues affect the individual's cost-reward calculations. When accountability is low, those who commit deviant acts are less likely to be caught and punished, and people may deliberately choose to engage in gratifying but usually inhibited behaviors. Consider, for instance, features of the environment that create anonymity (such as being in a large crowd or wearing a mask or hood). What would *you* do if you could be totally anonymous—indeed, invisible—for twenty-four hours? Among college students asked this question, their most frequent responses involved criminal acts; the single most common response was "rob a bank" (Dodd, 1985). Andrew Silke (2003) observed that of the 500 violent interpersonal attacks he studied in Northern Ireland, the offenders in almost half of the incidents wore disguises to mask their identities, and those attacks tended to be the most violent.

One place where many people spend a great deal of time anonymously is online. If you have ever been part of an online community where people can post comments anonymously, there is a good chance that you've witnessed some of the nasty effects of deindividuation. Many well-intentioned sites or discussions soon devolve into a torrent of crude, hostile, and prejudiced venting and taunting that would never happen without the cloak of anonymity (Klein et al., 2003; Postmes et al., 2002).

Attentional cues, the second type of environmental characteristic that increases deviant behavior, focus a person's attention away from the self. When a person's self-awareness declines, a change in consciousness takes place. In this "deindividuated state," the individual attends less to internal standards of conduct, reacts more to the immediate situation, and is less sensitive to long-term consequences of behavior (Diener, 1980). Behavior slips out from the bonds of cognitive control, and people act on impulse.

Have you ever been at a party with flashing strobe lights and music so loud that you could feel the room vibrate? If so, did it seem that you were somehow merging with the pulsating crowd and that your individual identity was slipping away? Intense stimulation from the environment is probably the most common attentional cue reducing self-awareness. In laboratory research, groups of participants placed in a highly stimulating environment (loud music, colorful video games) were more uninhibited, extreme, and aggressive in their actions (Diener, 1979; Spivey & Prentice-Dunn, 1990).

One particularly creative set of field experiments by Edward Diener and Arthur Beaman and their colleagues (Beaman et al., 1979; Diener et al., 1976) demonstrated how accountability cues and attentional cues can affect behavior on a night when many otherwise well-behaved individuals act in antisocial ways: Halloween. When you think about it, Halloween can be a perfect time to study deindividuation; children often wear costumes with masks, travel in large groups at night, and are highly aroused. In one study, the researchers unobtrusively observed more than 1,300 children who came trick-or-treating to twenty-seven homes spread around Seattle. At each of these homes, a researcher met and greeted the children, who were either alone or in groups. In one condition, the researcher asked the children their names and where they lived; in another condition, the researcher did not ask them any questions about their identities. When asked to identify themselves, the children should have become more self-aware and more accountable for their actions. Children who were not asked to reveal their identities should have felt relatively deindividuated, safe and anonymous in their costumes.

The children were then invited to take *one* item from a bowl full of candy and were left alone with the bowl. Hidden observers watched to see how many pieces of candy each child took. What did the observers see? The children took the most candy when they were the most deindividuated: when they were in a group and had not been asked to identify themselves. In another experiment, the researchers placed a mirror behind the candy bowl in some conditions. As noted in Chapter 3, the presence of a mirror tends to increase people's self-awareness. Children who had been asked their names, especially older children, were much less likely to steal candy if there was a mirror present than if there wasn't. Older children are more likely to have internal standards against stealing, and making these children self-aware made them more likely to act according to those standards.

Being in a large crowd can decrease both accountability and self-awareness. Perhaps because of this double impact, larger groups are associated with greater violence (Mullen, 1986). And Leon Mann (1981) found that when a crowd gathers to watch someone who is threatening to commit suicide by jumping from a building or other tall structure, those in the crowd are more likely to jeer and taunt the person if the crowd is large rather than small—especially at night, when the people in the crowd can feel more anonymous.

Moving from Personal to Social Identity   Despite the association between crowds and violence, the loss of personal identity does not always produce antisocial behavior. In a study conducted by Robert Johnson and Leslie Downing (1979), female undergraduates donned garments resembling either robes worn by Ku Klux Klan members or nurses' uniforms. Half of the participants were individually identified throughout the study; the others were not. All of the participants were then given the opportunity to increase or decrease the intensity of electric shocks delivered to a supposed other participant (actually, an experimental confederate) who had previously behaved in an obnoxious manner. Participants wearing Ku Klux Klan costumes increased shock levels in both the identified and anonymous conditions. However, among those in nurse's apparel, anonymous participants *decreased* shock intensity four times more frequently than did identified participants!

These findings (displayed in Figure 8.4) make a telling point: Sometimes becoming less accountable, or less self-aware, allows us to be more responsive to the needs of others. According to the *social identity model of deindividuation effects (SIDE)*, whether deindividuation affects people for better or for worse seems to reflect the characteristics and norms of the group immediately surrounding the individual (Cronin & Reicher, 2006; Douglas & McGarty, 2002; Postmes & Spears, 2002; Reicher, 2001). As personal identity and internal controls are submerged, social identity emerges and conformity to the group increases. If a group defines itself ("us") in terms of prejudice and hatred against another group ("them"), deindividuation can ignite an explosion of violence. The occasional stories of horrendous violation of the human rights of prisoners of war may illustrate this, as the intergroup hostilities the fighting has fueled, along with the numerous ways in which the military depersonalizes its members, create a social identity that can overwhelm personal values of right and wrong. In contrast, if a group defines itself in terms of concern for the welfare of others, deindividuation can spark an expansion of goodness. The consequences of losing your personal identity depend on what you lose it to.

FIGURE 8.4

Deindividuation and Social Identity

Regardless of whether they were individually identified or anonymous, female participants wearing KKK robes increased the intensity of shocks they administered to an experimental confederate. Among those wearing nurses' uniforms, however, anonymous participants *decreased* shock intensity more than did individually identified participants.

(Data from Johnson & Downing, 1979.)

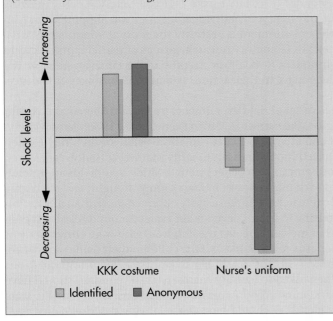

Group Dynamics: Interacting with Others

Social facilitation, social loafing, and deindividuation can all affect individuals, whether they are working in real groups or are merely part of a collective or crowd. In this section, we examine social influence and other processes specific to groups, where interaction among members is more direct and meaningful.

 Joining a Group

Groups come in all shapes and sizes: large and small, highly organized and quite informal, short term and long lasting. Sometimes group membership is involuntary. You didn't choose your family, for example, or your social class. But membership in many groups is voluntary. You decide to join an existing group or get together with others to create a brand-new one. Why do people join groups? How do groups develop over time? We address these questions next.

Why Join a Group?   There are several reasons for joining groups. One obvious reason is that people need to join groups in order to accomplish things that they cannot accomplish as individuals. Neither symphonies nor football games can be played by one person alone, and many types of work require team effort. At a more fundamental level, people may have an innate need to belong to groups, stemming from evolutionary pressures that increased people's chances of survival and reproduction when in groups rather than in isolation (Baumeister & Twenge, 2003; Kurzban & Leary, 2001). This need may also be driven by the desire to feel protected against threat and uncertainty in everyday life or to gain a greater sense of personal and social identity (Aharpour & Brown, 2002; Schmitt et al., 2003; Taubman-Ben-Ari et al., 2002). According to social identity theory, which was discussed in Chapter 5 on Stereotypes, Prejudice, and Discrimination, an important part of people's feelings of self-worth comes from their identification with particular groups. As social beings, we come to understand ourselves and our place in the world with reference to the groups that comprise our identities. On the other side of the coin, being rejected by a group is one of life's most painful experiences (Leary et al., 2003; Vandevelde & Miyahara, 2005; Williams et al., 2005).

People join a group for any of several reasons, such as to affiliate with others, to obtain social status, and to interact with individual group members.

Group Development   Once an individual has joined a group, a process of adjustment takes place. The individual assimilates into the group, making whatever changes are necessary to fit in. At the same time, the group accommodates to the newcomer, making whatever changes are necessary to include that individual. Socialization of a new member into a group often relies heavily on the relationship between newcomers and established members. Newcomers model their behavior on what the old-timers do; old-timers may hold explicit training sessions for newcomers or serve as mentors, developing personal relationships with newcomers to help them be successful in the group (Arrow & Burns, 2004; Holmes, 2005; Levine et al., 2004).

The socialization of group members is one way in which groups develop and maintain themselves. Group development may proceed through several stages. Group members first investigate and evaluate each other and the group as a whole. To the extent that the members accept each other and the group at large, their commitment to the group increases. Eventually, however, individuals may begin to diverge from the group, and the group may try to resocialize them. If the resocialization is unsuccessful, these individuals may exit the group, or the group may dissolve (Levine et al., 2004; Levine & Moreland, 2004).

Bruce Tuckman (1965; Tuckman & Jensen, 1977) proposed a particularly memorable set of stages through which groups often develop: forming, storming, norming, performing, and adjourning. These stages are described in Table 8.1. According to this model, groups gradually progress from a period of initial orientation through stages of conflict, compromise, and action, followed by a period of withdrawal if the group no longer satisfies members' needs. Although many groups do seem to pass through these stages, not all groups do. Contemporary theory on group development offers more complex models of group development, including the recognition that groups often develop in ways that are not linear and that different groups may develop in different ways (e.g., Chang et al., 2003; Chidambaram & Bostrom, 1997). For example, Connie Gersick (1988, 1994) observed that groups often do not proceed gradually through a uniform series of stages but instead operate in starts and stops, going through periods of relative inactivity until triggered by awareness of time and deadlines. According to Gersick, many groups adopt a problem-solving strategy very quickly—much quicker than Tuckman's theory suggests— but then they procrastinate until they have wasted about half the time they have allotted for the task, after which point they spring into action. Think about the work groups that *you've* been a part of: Do the stages described in Table 8.1 seem to apply, or do the groups described by Gersick seem more familiar to you?

TABLE 8.1
Stages of Group Development

- **Forming:** Members try to orient themselves to the group. They often act in polite, exploratory ways with each other.

- **Storming:** Members try to influence the group so that it best fits their own needs. They become more assertive about the group's direction and what roles they would like to play in the group. A great deal of conflict and hostility may arise, along with feelings of excitement about what might be achieved.

- **Norming:** Members try to reconcile the conflicts that emerged during storming and develop a common sense of purpose and perspective. They establish norms and roles and begin to feel more commitment to the group.

- **Performing:** Members try to perform their tasks and maximize the group's performance. They operate within their roles in the group and try to solve problems to allow them to achieve their shared goals.

- **Adjourning:** Members disengage from the group, distancing themselves from the other members and reducing their activities within the group. This may occur if members believe that the benefits of staying in the group no longer outweigh the costs.

(Based on Tuckman, 1965; Tuckman & Jensen, 1977.)

Roles, Norms, and Cohesiveness

Despite their variation in specific characteristics, all groups can be described in terms of three essential components: roles, norms, and cohesiveness (Forsyth, 1999; Levine & Moreland, 1990). We consider each of these in the following sections.

Roles People's *roles* in a group, their set of expected behaviors, can be formal or informal. Formal roles are designated by titles: teacher or student in a class, vice president or account executive in a corporation. Informal roles are less obvious but still powerful. For example, Robert Bales (1958) proposed that regardless of people's titles, enduring groups give rise to two fundamental types of roles: an *instrumental* role to help the group achieve its tasks and an *expressive* role to provide emotional support and maintain morale. The same person can fill both roles, but often they are assumed by different individuals, and which of these roles is emphasized in groups may fluctuate over time depending on the needs of the group.

"I've had to be both hunter and gatherer."

When roles in a group are not distributed properly, group performance suffers.

Having a set of clear roles is beneficial to a group. A meta-analysis of studies involving more than 11,000 individuals found a significant negative correlation between role ambiguity and job performance—the more role ambiguity, the worse one's job performance (Tubre & Collins, 2000). Teams often strive to organize themselves and to distribute task roles based on group members' particular skills and preferences. The better a team does in assigning roles that match the individual's characteristics, the better the individual will function in the group. However, when a person's role in the group is ambiguous, conflicts with other roles the person has (as when a group member needs to be demanding but also is the person who typically provides emotional support to others), or changes over time, stress and loss of productivity are likely to result (Bettencourt & Sheldon, 2001; Hechanova et al., 2003; Jackson & Schuler, 1985; Stempfle et al., 2001).

Organizations can sometimes lock individuals into particular roles, keeping them from maximizing the contributions they might otherwise be able to make. At NASA, for example, both for the 2003 *Columbia* and the 1986 *Challenger* missions, some of the engineers felt constrained in their roles and were not given access to the managers who were making the final, fateful decisions. And when a vice president for engineering voiced his objection to the *Challenger* being launched on schedule, a manager pressured him to change his vote by telling him to "take off your engineer hat and put on your management hat." Pressured to abandon one role and adopt the other, he changed his vote, and the tragic fate of the *Challenger* and its crew may have been sealed at that moment.

Norms   In addition to roles for its members, groups also establish *norms,* rules of conduct for members. Like roles, norms may be either formal or informal. Fraternities and sororities, for example, usually have written rules for the behavior expected from their members. Informal norms are more subtle. What do I wear? How hard can I push for what I want? Who pays for this or that? At a more general level, these norms provide individuals with a sense of what it means to be a good group member. Figuring out the unwritten rules of the group can take time and cause anxiety.

Researchers have investigated the development and consequences of a huge array of group norms, involving things as varied as binge drinking, smoking, exercising, sexual behavior, prejudice, and even the use of language and symbols in Internet chat groups (Crandall & Eshleman, 2003; Johnston & White, 2003; Latimer & Ginis, 2005; Sassenberg, 2002; Schofield et al., 2003; Selvan et al., 2001). Brendan McAuliffe and others (2003) found that even a group norm of individualism can be established, resulting in members conforming to the norm of not conforming! Similarly, Matthew Hornsey and others (2006) manipulated collectivistic or individualistic norms in a group and found that, with an individualistic norm, group members were more likely to tolerate and even like group members who disagreed with the rest of the group on some issue. You probably know of groups that vary in this way, with some fostering individuality and others emphasizing solidarity. These norms can play a role in group cohesiveness, which we discuss next.

On the Internet, you can find dozens of sites containing information about work teams, case studies of organizations and businesses, tips for meetings and leadership, and so forth. To get started, try the following site: www.teambuildersplus.com.

Cohesiveness   The third characteristic of groups, *cohesiveness,* refers to the forces exerted on a group that push its members closer together (Cartwright & Zander, 1960; Festinger, 1950). Members of cohesive groups tend to feel commitment to the group task, like the other group members, feel group pride, and engage in many—and often intense—interactions in the group (Carless & De-Paola, 2000; Cota et al., 1995; Dion, 2000). Various factors can affect cohesiveness, including the type of leadership style a group leader has, the kinds of tasks the group is working on, and even

An ineffective leader can hurt the cohesiveness of a group, as is evident in the amusingly inept boss (played by Steve Carell) and his disgruntled employees in the TV comedy, The Office.

factors such as the design of the workspace or the use of humor by leaders or members (Greatbatch & Clark, 2003; Lee & Brand, 2005; Man & Lam, 2003; Pillai & Williams, 2004). Outside forces, too, affect cohesiveness. Groups in dangerous or unusual environments and groups threatened by other groups often become more cohesive, especially if the group members think that they can cope with these forces effectively as a group (Depret & Fiske, 1999; Dion, 1979; Harrison & Connors, 1984; Lanzetta, 1955). However, threats from within the group, such as envy between group members, can tear apart group cohesion (Duffy & Shaw, 2000).

Cohesiveness and group performance are causally related, but the relationship is not a simple one. When a group is cohesive, group performance improves, and when a group performs well, it becomes more cohesive. In their meta-analysis of the research on cohesiveness and group performance, Brian Mullen and Carolyn Copper (1994) found more evidence for an effect of performance on cohesiveness than for an effect of cohesiveness on performance. They also found that the positive relationship between cohesiveness and group performance may depend on the size of the group: The relationship tended to be stronger in small groups than in large ones.

A separate meta-analysis conducted by Stanley Gully and others (1995) indicates that the positive relationship between cohesiveness and performance is much stronger for tasks that require interdependence among group members than for tasks that do not require interdependence. Interdependent tasks are those in which group members must interact, communicate, cooperate, and observe each other (as in a military operation or a game of football). Possibly because women tend to be more interdependent than men, a recent meta-analysis of forty-six studies of cohesiveness in sports teams found not only a generally positive correlation between cohesiveness and team performance, but also that the relationship was particularly strong for female sports teams (Carron et al., 2002). Cohesiveness should help performance on interdependent tasks, but it can hurt performance in situations where creative, innovative ideas and behaviors are needed (as when designing a new advertising campaign for a product that is not selling well).

In addition, when groups find themselves worrying about their cohesiveness, their ability to focus on other goals, such as performing optimally on some task, may be compromised. Indeed, on some tasks, groups perform worse if group members are more concerned with trying to minimize disagreements and avoid hurting one another's feelings than with trying to reach the best group decision. This is what Roger Nibler and Karen Harris (2003) found in their cross-cultural research. They studied five-person groups of strangers and friends in China and the United States. The groups' task was to rank fifteen items to be taken aboard a lifeboat from a ship that was about to sink. This task tends to trigger a fair amount of initial disagreement among group members until a consensus can be reached. With the Chinese groups and the groups of American strangers, these kinds of disagreements tended to be perceived as troubling and interfered with group performance. To the groups of American friends, in contrast, these disagreements were more likely to be seen as simply part of a freewheeling debate, and the sense of freedom to exchange opinions and disagree with one another tended to improve performance on this task.

Finally, the effect of cohesiveness on group performance depends on the norms that have been established in the group. If the norms are positive and consistent with an organization's goals, then high cohesiveness should improve group performance. If, however, a group has established negative, counterproductive norms, then high cohesiveness should lead to *poor* group performance. For example, a group of workers might establish a relatively low work standard as a norm. If this group is

Two officers for the U.S. Army Corps of Engineers, Bunnatine Greenhouse and Christy Watts, testify before a Senate committee in September 2005. These women had reported corruption in the awarding of government contracts, and after raising their concerns, they both lost their jobs. Blowing the whistle on corruption in one's group can be a terrifying—and heroic—act.

cohesive, its members may threaten or socially reject any group member who deviates from the others by working harder than the norm; so cohesiveness promotes poor performance. In contrast, other groups set very ambitious goals for each other and establish positive norms; the more cohesive these groups are, the more likely they are to push each other to succeed (Langfred, 1998; Prapavessis & Carron, 1997; Stogdill, 1972).

Sometimes, breaking a norm in a cohesive group can be very difficult and even traumatic for a group member. Coworkers are especially reluctant to report the unethical behavior of others on their work teams, fearing the social consequences of reporting on a member of the group. Consultants involved in employee relations frequently observe the dilemma that workers in cohesive teams face when they witness unethical conduct. As one consultant noted, "[Team workers] have a fear they'll be seen as divisive. We're social animals, and we so very much want to belong" (Armour, 1998, p. 6B).

As a testament to how difficult this is, *Time* magazine named its 2002 *Person of the Year* "The Whistleblowers"—three women who in separate instances stood up against enormous group pressures to try to correct, and eventually unveil, the immoral, illegal, or irresponsible practices at their organizations. Sherron Watkins and Cynthia Cooper both revealed the fraud and corruption at their respective corporations, Enron and WorldCom. These corrupt practices led to what at the time were the biggest bankruptcies in corporate history, costing the economy billions of dollars and wiping out the savings and retirement funds of a large number of innocent people. Coleen Rowley was a United States Federal Bureau of Investigations (FBI) attorney who repeatedly sent pleas from her field office in Minnesota in the days before 9/11 to investigate one of the men who later would be implicated as a conspirator in the September 11, 2001, terrorist attacks. Her requests were brushed off by her superiors in the bureau. The women risked their careers and reputations—Watkins was almost fired, Cooper was screamed at, Rowley was called "disloyal"—but each felt compelled to tell the truth about what was going on in their organizations (Kelly, 2002/2003).

More recently, a number of individuals working in or with the U.S. government and military received similar treatment when they publicly criticized high-ranking officials concerning their actions and decisions in the buildup to and execution of the war in Iraq, as well as when they revealed secret policies of torture or humiliation of prisoners held by the military. Each of the people who came forward did so with the understanding that his or her career and reputation could be threatened and possibly destroyed.

 ## Group Polarization

Once a group has formed—with roles, norms, and some degree of cohesiveness—it begins to make decisions and take actions. The issues faced by groups range from the trivial ("Where do we party?") to the profound ("Should we make war or peace?"). Whatever the issue, the attitudes of group members affect what they do. How does being in a group influence people's opinions?

The key to answering this question is to realize that most groups consist of individuals who hold roughly similar views. People are attracted to groups that share their attitudes, and those who disagree with the group usually leave by their own choice or are ejected by the others. But similar does not mean identical. Although the range of opinion is relatively restricted, there are still differences.

"A committee is a cul-de-sac down which ideas are lured and then quietly strangled."

—Barnett Cocks

What do you think should be the result of a group discussion of these differing points of view? For example, imagine that a group is discussing whether someone should behave in a risky or a cautious manner, such as whether an entrepreneur should risk trying to expand his or her business or whether an employee in a stable but boring job should quit and take a more creative job in a new but unproven Internet company. Are groups more likely to advocate risky or cautious decisions about issues like these?

Common sense suggests two alternative predictions. Perhaps the most reasonable prediction is that after the group members discuss their differing points of view, the group decision will represent an overall compromise as everyone moves toward the group average. But common sense also suggests another prediction. Many people familiar with committees agree that forming a committee is a good way *not* to get something done. The idea is that individuals are willing to take risks and implement new ideas, whereas groups tend to be cautious and slow moving. Wary of leading the group toward a risky decision, people become more cautious in their views as they discuss them with the other group members.

So, which prediction is the correct one: movement toward the average attitude or movement toward caution? James Stoner (1961) tested this question by comparing decisions made by individuals with decisions made by groups, and he found that *neither* prediction was correct: Group decisions tended to be riskier than individuals' decisions. Was this a fluke? Several subsequent studies found similar results, and the tendency for groups to become riskier than the average of the individuals became known as the *risky shift* (Cartwright, 1971).

But the story doesn't end there. Later studies seemed to contradict the idea of the risky shift, finding that for some choices groups tended to become more *cautious* (Knox & Safford, 1976). How can we make sense of these contradictory findings?

Researchers concluded that group discussion tends to enhance or exaggerate the initial leanings of the group. Thus, if most group members initially lean toward a risky position on a particular issue, the group's position becomes even riskier after the discussion; but if group members in general initially lean toward a cautious position, the group discussion leads to greater caution. This effect is called **group polarization**: the exaggeration through group discussion of initial tendencies in the thinking of group members (Moscovici & Zavalloni, 1969; Myers & Lamm, 1976).

Group polarization is not restricted to decisions involving risk versus caution. Any group decision can be influenced by group polarization, from serious decisions such as how to allocate scarce medical resources, to more mundane decisions such as a sorority's decision about what theme to use at its next party (Chandrashekaran et al., 1996; Furnham et al., 2000). Consider, for example, racial prejudice. In one study, high school students responded to an initial questionnaire and were classified as high, medium, or low on racial prejudice. Groups of like-minded students then met for a discussion of racial issues, with their individual attitudes on these issues assessed before and after their interaction. Group polarization was dramatic. Students low in prejudice to begin with were even less prejudiced after the group discussion; students moderate or high in prejudice became even more prejudiced (Myers & Bishop, 1970).

What creates group polarization? Three processes are usually emphasized:

1. According to *persuasive arguments theory*, the greater the number and persuasiveness of the arguments to which group members are exposed, the more extreme their attitudes become (Vinokur & Burnstein, 1974). Some arguments provide new information to group members hearing them for the first time. If most group members favor a cautious decision, for example, most of the arguments discussed will favor caution, giving the members more and more reason to want to be cautious. In addition, realizing that others favor caution, members may focus on pro-caution arguments when talking to each other and fail to bring up pro-risk arguments that may also be important to consider (Pavitt, 1994). Simply hearing others repeat our arguments (without offering any new ones) can validate our own reasoning, giving us more confidence in what may originally have been only a slight leaning (Baron, Hoppe, et al., 1996; Brauer et al., 1995).

Group members' attitudes about a course of action usually become more moderate after group discussion. **False.**

group polarization The exaggeration through group discussion of initial tendencies in the thinking of group members.

2. Group polarization is also created as group members simply discover other people's opinions, even if no arguments are presented (Sanders & Baron, 1977). Here, *social comparison* is at work. As described in Chapter 3, individuals develop their view of social reality by comparing themselves with others. The construction of social reality in like-minded groups is a two-step process. First, people discover more support for their own opinion than they had originally anticipated. Second, this discovery sets up a new, more extreme norm and motivates group members to go beyond that norm. If believing X is good, then believing double X is even better. Through social comparison, group members learn the group members' values. By adopting a more extreme attitudinal position consistent with these values, people can distinguish themselves in the group in a manner approved by the group (Lamm & Myers, 1978).

3. In addition, group polarization is influenced by a concept you may recall from Chapter 5: *social categorization,* the tendency for people to categorize themselves and others in terms of social groups. The social categorization approach compares how individuals react to information from ingroups (to which they belong or want to belong) and outgroups (to which they don't belong and don't want to). Ingroup members may want to distinguish their group from other groups, and so they overestimate the extremity of their group's position and distance themselves from the position of an outgroup (Hogg et al., 1990; McGarty et al., 1992).

Now that you know about group polarization, you should be able to see evidence of it often as you observe the groups around you. At a broad level, it seems that political groups today have become more and more polarized, moving to extremes rather than toward moderation and compromise. Resolving international conflict is so much more difficult because of the group polarization that heightens these conflicts. On a less global level, observe how the culture of a team may evolve over the course of a season, or follow the attitudes of a group as they prepare for a debate, and you're likely to see group polarization develop through the processes we've just described.

 ## Groupthink

The processes involved in group polarization may set the stage for an even greater, and perhaps more dangerous, bias in group decision making. Recall the discussion at the opening of this chapter about the NASA catastrophes in 1986 and 2003. These were not the only cases in which high-level groups associated with the U.S. government made decisions that in hindsight seem remarkably ill-conceived. For instance, toward the end of 1941, U.S. intelligence leaders dismissed numerous signs of an imminent attack by the Japanese on Pearl Harbor, leaving the base unprepared and vulnerable. The attack proved disastrous for the United States, costing almost 4,000 lives and a significant portion of the nation's arsenal of ships and planes. Sixty years later, American intelligence leaders again missed and dismissed signs of an imminent attack—the September 11, 2001, terrorist attacks in New York and Washington— such as when they rejected Coleen Rowley's pleas to the FBI to investigate a suspected terrorist who subsequently played a critical role in the attacks.

Or consider one of the greatest fiascoes in U.S. history: the decision to invade Cuba in 1961. When John Kennedy became president of the United States in 1961, he assembled one of the most impressive groups of advisers in the history of American government. These individuals—highly intelligent, educated at the best universities, led by a new president brimming with ambition, charisma, and optimism—were called "the best and the brightest" (Halberstam, 1972). But the Kennedy administration had inherited a plan from the previous administration to invade Cuba at the Bay of Pigs in order to spark a people's revolt that would overthrow Fidel Castro's government. Kennedy and his advisers, after much deliberation, eventually approved an invasion plan that, in hindsight, was hopelessly flawed. For example, once the invaders landed at the Bay of Pigs, they were to be supported by anti-Castro guerrillas camped in the mountains nearby. But had Kennedy and his advisers consulted a

" 'It is always best on these occasions to do what the mob do.' 'But suppose there are two mobs?' suggested Mr. Snodgrass. 'Shout with the largest,' replied Mr. Pickwick."

—Charles Dickens

FIGURE 8.5

Charting the Course of Groupthink

Irving Janis depicted groupthink as a kind of social disease, complete with antecedents and symptoms, that increased the chance of making a bad decision.

(Based on Janis, 1982.)

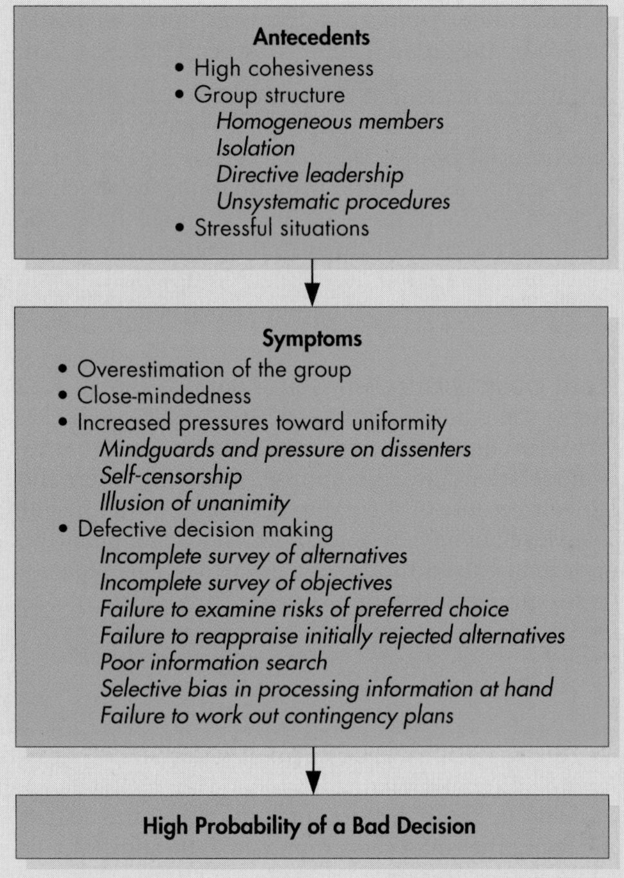

Antecedents
- High cohesiveness
- Group structure
  Homogeneous members
  Isolation
  Directive leadership
  Unsystematic procedures
- Stressful situations

Symptoms
- Overestimation of the group
- Close-mindedness
- Increased pressures toward uniformity
  Mindguards and pressure on dissenters
  Self-censorship
  Illusion of unanimity
- Defective decision making
  Incomplete survey of alternatives
  Incomplete survey of objectives
  Failure to examine risks of preferred choice
  Failure to reappraise initially rejected alternatives
  Poor information search
  Selective bias in processing information at hand
  Failure to work out contingency plans

High Probability of a Bad Decision

groupthink A group decision-making style characterized by an excessive tendency among group members to seek concurrence.

map, they might have noticed that the invaders were to land eighty miles away from these mountains and were separated from them by a huge swamp. Ultimately, the invasion failed miserably. The invaders were quickly killed or captured, the world was outraged at the United States, and Cuba allied itself more closely with the Soviet Union—exactly the opposite of what Kennedy had intended. The United States was humiliated. After the fiasco, Kennedy himself wondered, "How could we have been so stupid?" (Janis, 1982).

According to Irving Janis (1982), the answer to this question, and similar questions that could be posed of any of the other fiascoes we've described, lies in a particular kind of flawed group dynamic, which he called **groupthink**, an excessive tendency to seek concurrence among group members. Groupthink emerges when the need for agreement takes priority over the motivation to obtain accurate information and make appropriate decisions. Figure 8.5 outlines the factors that contribute to groupthink, along with its symptoms and consequences.

Janis believed that three characteristics contribute to the development of groupthink:

1. Since *highly cohesive groups* are more likely to reject members with deviant opinions, Janis thought they would be more susceptible to groupthink.

2. *Group structure* is also important. Groups that are composed of people from similar backgrounds, isolated from other people, directed by a strong leader, and lacking in systematic procedures for making and reviewing decisions should be particularly likely to fall prey to groupthink.

3. Finally, Janis emphasized that *stressful situations* can provoke groupthink. Under stress, urgency can overrule accuracy, and the reassuring support of other group members becomes highly desirable.

In Janis's formulation, groupthink is a kind of social disease, and infected groups display the behavioral symptoms indicated in the middle of Figure 8.5. For example, Kennedy and his advisers exhibited *overestimation of the group*, assuming that as "the best and the brightest," they could pull off a little invasion, even if some of the details were worrisome. And NASA's refusal to ask for outside help in obtaining images of the *Columbia* in space clearly illustrated the symptom of *closed-mindedness*. Another symptom, *pressures toward uniformity*, was evident in all these examples. In groupthink, group members may censor their own thoughts or act as "mindguards" to discourage deviant thoughts by other group members. During the planning of the Bay of Pigs invasion, the president's brother, Robert Kennedy, served as a mindguard and warned dissenting members to keep quiet. And, as we indicated earlier, when a vice president for engineering argued to delay launching the *Challenger*, he was told by a manager to take off his "engineering hat" and put on his "management hat." He switched hats, and his vote. In the end, this helped foster an illusion of unanimity because top-level managers at NASA never knew of all the dissent voiced by the engineers that morning.

More recently, some scholars have proposed that the group dynamics behind the decision to invade Iraq in 2003 by primarily American and British forces reflected groupthink, particularly in the decision makers' serious failures in information gathering and analysis and in the underestimation of risks (Rodrigues et al., 2005).

When alternatives are not considered, the behavioral symptoms of groupthink can result in the defective decision making outlined in Figure 8.5. In turn, a defec-

"On second thought, don't correct me if I'm wrong."

A controlling leader who discourages disagreement can promote group-think, leading to bad decisions.

tive decision-making process increases the likelihood that a group will make bad decisions.

Research on Groupthink   Groupthink is a rather distinctive theory in social psychology. On the one hand, its impact has been unusually broad: It is discussed in a variety of disciplines outside psychology, including business, political science, and communication, and it has spawned numerous workshops as well as a best-selling management training video. Yet, on the other hand, there is not a great deal of empirical support for the model, certainly not in proportion to its fame. This may be partly due to the difficulty of experimentally testing such a broad set of variables in high-pressure group settings. However, research has been conducted on various aspects of Janis's model, typically through case studies and historical analyses of groups and organizational settings around the world, and some experimental research has been done as well (Baron, 2005; Eaton, 2001; Esser, 1998).

Some researchers disagree with Janis about the specific conditions that make groups vulnerable to groupthink (Choi & Kim, 1999; Henningsen et al., 2006; Kramer, 1998; t'Hart et al., 1995; Tetlock, 1998; Whyte, 1998). But when multiple antecedents of groupthink are evident simultaneously, such as high cohesiveness, a strong and controlling leader, and a great deal of stress, groups are particularly vulnerable to the kinds of faulty decision making that Janis described (Esser, 1998; Mullen et al., 1994).

One important trend in the business world is the increased use of self-directed, autonomous teams (Molleman & Slomp, 2006). Such teams typically comprise four to twelve individuals who work together closely and are responsible, as groups, for completing whole projects. Gregory Moorhead and others (1998) predicted that most U.S. employees in the twenty-first century will work in self-managed work teams. These teams can be productive and efficient, generating a sense of commitment, even enjoyment, among their members. However, Moorhead and his colleagues also proposed that work teams are particularly susceptible to groupthink because they tend to be homogeneous, highly cohesive, insulated from others, confronted by pressure and time constraints, and headed up by controlling leaders. Clearly, then, further research on groupthink will be important in the years to come.

Preventing Groupthink   To guard against groupthink, Janis urged groups to make an active effort to process information more carefully and accurately. He recommended that decision-making groups use the following strategies:

- To avoid isolation, groups should consult widely with outsiders.

- To reduce conformity pressures, leaders should explicitly encourage criticism and not take a strong stand early in the group discussion.

- To establish a strong norm of critical review, subgroups should separately discuss the same issue, a member should be assigned to play devil's advocate and question all decisions and ideas, and a "second chance" meeting should be held to reconsider the group decision before taking action.

Indeed, President Kennedy himself appeared to arrive at similar conclusions after the Bay of Pigs disaster. In the following year, 1962, the United States and the Soviet Union appeared to be at the brink of war after U.S. military intelligence discovered that Soviet missiles in Cuba were aimed at the United States. During this crisis, Kennedy stayed away from initial meetings about how to respond to the situation; he consulted with experts outside his inner circle of advisers; and he told his brother Robert to play the devil's advocate and challenge all ideas—in sharp contrast to Robert's role of "mindguard" during the Bay of Pigs planning. Unlike the Bay of Pigs invasion, the Cuban missile crisis ended exactly as Kennedy had hoped: The Soviet Union withdrew its missiles from Cuba, and a war was avoided.

TABLE 8.2
How Computerized Group Support Systems Help Groups Avoid Groupthink

1. Allow group members to raise their concerns anonymously through the computer interface, enabling them to risk challenging group consensus without fear of direct attacks

2. Reduce the directive role of the leader

3. Enable group members to provide input simultaneously, so they don't have to wait for a chance to raise their ideas

4. Allow the least assertive group members to state their ideas as easily as the most dominating

5. Provide a systematic agenda of information gathering and decision making

6. Keep the focus in the group meetings on the ideas themselves rather than on the people and relationships within the group

(Based on Miranda, 1994.)

More recent research has shown empirical support for the effectiveness of some strategies in curtailing groupthink tendencies. These include inserting someone in the group to play the role of a "reminder" who is responsible for informing the group about the dangers of biased decision making; making individual group members believe that they will be held personally responsible for the outcome of their group's decisions; increasing the diversity of group members; and creating a group norm encouraging critical thinking and discouraging the search for concurrence (Kroon et al., 1991; Postmes et al., 2001; Schultz et al., 1995; t'Hart, 1998). And computer-based technology can be used during meetings to help avoid groupthink (Miranda, 1994). Table 8.2 lists some of the ways in which computerized *group support systems,* in which groups use specialized, interactive computer programs to guide their meetings, can enhance group decision making.

In recent research, Laura Kray and Adam Galinsky (2003; Liljenquist et al., 2004) point to the effectiveness of encouraging groups to engage in counterfactual thinking, which, as discussed in Chapter 4, involves imagining alternative events or outcomes that might have occurred but did not. In a set of clever experiments, Kray and Galinsky had groups of students discuss and make decisions about a problem that was modeled after the space shuttle *Challenger* disaster. To prevent participants from realizing what the case was really about, details were changed so that the problem was whether or not a race car team should go ahead with a race despite cold weather, which could affect car engines. Prior to making decisions about this scenario, however, groups were exposed to a different, unrelated scenario, which for some groups was designed so that the groups would easily imagine a desired, counterfactual alternative outcome. Kray and Galinsky found that the groups primed to think of counterfactuals were much more likely than the other groups to seek disconfirmatory information when discussing whether to go ahead with the race, and as a result their decisions were much more accurate. Two-thirds of the groups primed with counterfactual thinking made the correct decision to pull out of the race, whereas fewer than a quarter of the groups not primed did so.

Group Performance: Are More Heads Better Than One?

Group polarization and groupthink are examples of how groups can go wrong, ending up with attitudes that are too extreme and decisions that are seriously flawed. But aren't two, or more, heads generally better than one? How does the performance of a group compare with the performance of the same number of people working individually? Researchers investigating this question have uncovered a number of important factors that affect group performance, as we will see in the sections that follow.

Types of Tasks and Process Loss According to Ivan Steiner (1972), how a group's performance compares to the potential of its individuals depends on the type of task. For instance, on an *additive* task, the group product is the *sum* of all the members' contributions. Donating to a charity is an additive task, and so is making noise at a pep rally. As we have seen, people often indulge in social loafing during additive tasks. Even so, groups usually outperform a single individual. Each

Just as the strength of a chain depends on its weakest link, the group product of a conjunctive task is determined by the individual with the poorest performance. In mountain climbing, for example, if one person slips or falls, the whole team is endangered.

member's contribution may be less than it would be if that person worked alone, but the group total is still greater than what could be provided by one person.

On a *conjunctive* task, the group product is determined by the individual with the *poorest* performance. Mountain-climbing teams are engaged in such a task; the "weakest link" will determine their success or failure. Because of this vulnerability to the poor performance of a single group member, group performance on conjunctive tasks tends to be worse than the performance of a single, average individual.

On a *disjunctive* task, the group product is (or can be) determined by the performance of the individual with the *best* performance. Trying to solve a problem or develop a strategy is a disjunctive task: What the group needs is a single successful idea or answer, regardless of the number of failures. In principle, groups have an edge on individuals in the performance of disjunctive tasks: The more people involved, the more likely it is that someone will make a breakthrough. In practice, however, group processes can interfere with coming up with ideas and getting them accepted—a phenomenon that Steiner called **process loss**.

Process loss is not restricted to disjunctive tasks. It can result from lack of motivation, as in social loafing on additive tasks. Lack of coordination can also cause process loss, as when the group is slowed down by weaker members on conjunctive tasks. On disjunctive tasks, groups may not realize which group members have the best ideas or are most expert. Unless the best solution for a particular problem is easily identifiable once it has been suggested, the group may fail to implement it; as a result, the group performs worse than its best members (Gigone & Hastie, 1997; Laughlin & Ellis, 1986; Stasser et al., 1995; Stasson & Bradshaw, 1995). Have you ever had the experience of *knowing* you had the right idea but being unable to convince others in your group until it was too late? If so, then you have experienced first-hand the problem of process loss on a disjunctive task. Fortunately, as groups gain experience with each other, they can become better at recognizing and utilizing the expertise of their members, particularly when group members vary greatly in their expertise (Baumann & Bonner, 2004; Bonner, 2004; Bonner et al., 2002).

On some kinds of tasks, groups can even show *process gain,* in which they outperform even the best members. Of course, the expectation of process gain is one of the key reasons to work in groups in the first place, but as we have seen, there are many obstacles in the way. On tasks that may be divided into subtasks and assigned to group members, groups may perform better than the best individuals (Steiner, 1966). Patrick Laughlin and his colleagues (2002, 2006) found that groups performed better than the best individuals on tasks in which the correct answer was clearly evident to everyone in the group once it was presented and in which the work could be divided up so that various subgroups worked on different aspects of the task. This effect seems to operate for groups of at least three to five members but not for groups of only two people, indicating that true group dynamics are necessary to produce this process gain.

Setting Goals   Groups, like individuals, tend to perform better on a task when they have specific, challenging, and reachable goals, particularly if the group members are committed to the goals and believe they have the ability to achieve them. Such goals are generally more effective than "do your best" goals or no goals at all (Locke & Latham, 2002; Wegge, 2000; Wegge & Haslam, 2005). You've probably worked in many groups in which the goal was simply to "do your best." Despite the popularity of such goals, the research clearly shows that they are not as effective as specific goals. As Edwin Locke and Gary Latham (2002) concluded from their review of thirty-five years' worth of studies, "When people are asked to do their best, they do not do so" (p. 706). People are indeed capable of better than their vaguely defined "best."

process loss   The reduction in group performance due to obstacles created by group processes, such as problems of coordination and motivation.

TABLE 8.3
Brainstorming in Groups: Problems and Solutions

Factors That Reduce the Effectiveness of Group Brainstorming

- **Production blocking:** When people have to wait for their turn to speak, they may forget their ideas, may be too busy trying to remember their ideas to listen to others or to generate new ones, or may simply lose interest.

- **Free riding:** As others contribute ideas, individuals may feel less motivated to work hard themselves. They see their own contributions as less necessary or less likely to have much impact.

- **Evaluation apprehension:** In the presence of others, people may be hesitant to suggest wild, off-the-wall ideas for fear of looking foolish and being criticized. Even if they are willing to suggest such ideas, they may spend time preparing to justify them—time that they otherwise could have spent coming up with more ideas.

- **Performance matching:** Group members work only as hard as they see others work. Once the other three factors have reduced the performance of a brainstorming group, performance matching can help maintain this relatively inferior performance.

Why Electronic Brainstorming Is Effective

- Production blocking is reduced because members can type in ideas whenever they come to mind.

- Free riding can be reduced by having the computer keep track of each member's input.

- Evaluation apprehension is reduced because group members contribute their ideas anonymously.

- Performance matching is reduced because group members spend less time focusing on the performance of others as they type in their own ideas. In addition, performance matching is less of a problem because the initial performance of groups brainstorming electronically is likely to be high.

- Group members can benefit by seeing the ideas of others, which can inspire new ideas that they might not otherwise have considered.

Brainstorming: Coming Up with Ideas During the 1950s, advertising executive Alex Osborn developed a technique called **brainstorming**, designed to enhance the creativity and productivity of problem-solving groups. The ground rules for brainstorming call for a free-wheeling, creative approach:

- Express *all* ideas that come to mind, even if they sound crazy.

- The more ideas, the better.

- Don't worry whether the ideas are good or bad, and don't criticize anyone's ideas; they can be evaluated later.

- All ideas belong to the group, so members should feel free to build on each other's work.

Osborn (1953) claimed that by using these procedures, groups could generate more and better ideas than could individuals working alone. The gimmick caught on. Brainstorming was soon a popular exercise in business, government, and education; and it remains so today. But when the research caught up with the hype, it turned out that Osborn's faith in the group process was unfounded. In fact, "nominal groups" (several individuals working alone) produce a greater number of better ideas than do real groups in which members interact with each other. Brainstorming can indeed be effective, but people brainstorming individually produce more and higher-quality ideas than the same number of people brainstorming together. One meta-analysis concluded that brainstorming groups are only about half as productive as an equal number of individuals working alone (Mullen et al., 1991). Rather than being inspired by each other and building on each other's ideas, people brainstorming in a group underperform (Diehl & Stroebe, 1987; Nijstad et al., 2003, 2006; Paulus & Brown, 2003).

The top half of Table 8.3 presents several possible explanations that have been proposed for why brainstorming is ineffective. It's particularly ironic, then, that people who engage in group brainstorming typically think that it works wonderfully. Despite the research evidence, brainstorming is still a popular device in many organizations. People who participate in interactive brainstorming groups evaluate their own performance more favorably than do individuals in nominal groups. They also enjoy themselves more. And those who have not participated in an interactive brainstorming group believe that such groups are highly productive. Both the experienced and the inexperienced cling to the illusion that group brainstorming is much better than individual brainstorming (Nijstad et al., 2003; Paulus & Brown, 2003).

Group brainstorming may indeed benefit the group in indirect ways—for example, it can be a fun experience that promotes good will and cohesion—but, as

People brainstorming as a group come up with a greater number of better ideas than the same number of people working individually. **False.**

brainstorming A technique that attempts to increase the production of creative ideas by encouraging group members to speak freely without criticizing their own or others' contributions.

we have seen, its effect on idea generation is much poorer than most group members realize. One strategy to improve productivity while also promoting the enjoyment that group brainstorming can produce is to alternate brainstorming sessions, having members brainstorm together and then individually (Paulus & Brown, 2003). Another strategy is to use a facilitator trained to understand the factors that impair group brainstorming. The facilitator can cut people off who stray from the task, discourage evaluation, call on individuals to prevent them from free riding, and keep motivating them to do more ("Come on, a few more ideas and we break fifty!") (Oxley et al., 1996; Paulus et al., 2006).

Computers offer a relatively new and promising way to improve group brainstorming. Electronic brainstorming combines the freedom of working alone at a computer with the stimulation of receiving the ideas of others on a screen. The bottom half of Table 8.3 presents some of the factors that make this type of brainstorming effective. The research on electronic brainstorming is encouraging, suggesting that interactive groups often perform about as well as nominal groups, and—in some situations, such as when the group is relatively large—may even perform better than nominal groups (Dennis & Williams, 2003; Michinov & Primois, 2005; Valacich et al., 1994). Brainstorming may have found its true home in a technology that Osborn could have only dreamed about a half century before.

Biased Sampling and Communication: Getting Ideas on the Table

Brainstorming stresses the need for creativity. On some tasks, however, simply sharing information is crucial for good performance. Unfortunately, as Garold Stasser (1992; Stasser & Birchmeier, 2003) points out, not all the information available to individual members will necessarily be brought before the group. Rather, information that is known to many group members is more likely to enter the group discussion than information known to only one or a few group members. Imagine, for example, that your group is discussing which of several candidates should be supported for an election. You have read some potentially damaging personal information about one of the candidates, and you assume that the others are also aware of it. If you observe during group discussion that nobody else mentions this information, you may further assume that the others don't think the information is relevant or credible; so you may not mention it yourself. Stasser calls this process *biased sampling*. Because of biased sampling, a group may fail to consider important information that is not common knowledge in the group. Inadequately informed, the group may make a bad decision.

Recent research has discovered several conditions in which biased sampling is less likely to occur. For example, leaders who encourage a lot of group participation are more likely to elicit unshared (as well as shared) information during group discussions than are more directive leaders (Larson et al., 1998). As groups gain more experience, they often become better at sharing information (Greitemeyer et al., 2006).

As with so many aspects of group dynamics, the norms that develop in a group can play a crucial role in determining its effectiveness. Norms often exist about how and what the group communicates, such as whether the group members tend to reinforce or challenge the dominant ideas that have been expressed. Tom Postmes and others (2001) conducted an experiment in which they manipulated the establishment of group norms that promoted either consensus or critical thinking. They did this by having some groups work on creating a collage—a collective, creative task in which collaboration (consensus) was essential. Other groups worked on assessing a controversial campus policy to which the group members would be strongly opposed—a task that encouraged critical thinking. Although the group members would quickly agree on their opposition to this policy, the task fostered independent, critical analysis because each group member could contribute numerous arguments attacking this policy. The researchers presumed that working on these different types of tasks would create two different types of group norms, which would then carry over and influence a group's performance on a subsequent task.

For both types of groups, the subsequent task was evaluating a set of three candidates for a teaching position at the university. Within each group, each member received information about the candidates that all the other group members had,

"A committee should consist of three men, two of whom are absent."

—Herbert Beerbolm Tree

but each member also had information that the other members did not have. Previous studies using this task had shown that groups tend to discuss the shared but not the unshared information. But only if individuals brought the unshared information to the table could the group have enough information to realize that one candidate was clearly the best one for the job. If they relied only on shared information, they typically would reach an incorrect judgment.

As can be seen in Figure 8.6, when group members first received their information but had not discussed it with each other, they were very unlikely to make a correct decision. Only through a discussion of the unshared information could groups recognize the best candidate. But if groups focused only on shared information during their discussion, their chances of making the correct decision would not improve. This is what happened for the groups that had engaged first in the consensus-norm task. These groups did not discuss the unshared information much, so their post-discussion decisions were not significantly better than their pre-discussion decisions. But the groups that had engaged first in the task that promoted critical thinking were much more likely to make the correct decision after the discussion, because they discussed unshared information.

Sometimes, biased sampling can have tragic consequences. The commission formed to investigate the explosion of the space shuttle *Challenger* concluded that inadequate sharing of information contributed to the disaster. As we discussed earlier, some engineers had information indicating that it would be unsafe to launch the shuttle that morning because of the low temperature, but this information was not shared with everyone. The people who ultimately made the decision to launch therefore were not aware of all the information that was relevant for their decision. The commission concluded, "If the decision-makers had known all the facts, it is highly unlikely that they would have decided to launch" (*Report of the Presidential Commission,* 1986, p. 82). Lessons learned after that tragedy appear to have been forgotten seventeen years later because inadequate sharing of vital information also appeared to have contributed to the *Columbia* disaster in 2003.

Part of the problem in the NASA disasters was that the *communication network,* which defines who can speak with whom based on a group's structure, made it difficult for information to be distributed to all of the decision makers. In many organizations, information is passed up a chain of command through layers of middle management, and only some of this information makes it all the way up to the executives who make the final decisions. This was the case at NASA. The engineers who were most familiar with the physical details of the shuttle could not communicate directly with the NASA officials at the top of the chain of command. According to Rodney Rocha, one of the engineers who most emphatically warned about the possible damage to the *Columbia,* "Engineers were often told not to send messages much higher than their own rung in the ladder" (Glanz & Schwartz, 2003). Those who occupied positions in the middle of the chain felt pressure from both sides—they were pressured by some engineers below them to delay the launch of the *Challenger* or to solicit more information about the *Columbia* before its return to Earth, but they were pressured by administrators above them to act against these recommendations. The high-level engineer who was told the morning of the *Challenger* launch to take off his "engineering hat"

FIGURE 8.6

Sharing Information in a Group: The Role of Group Norms

Groups that had been induced to establish a group norm of either consensus or critical thinking worked on a task in which they were to decide which of three candidates was best suited for a job. Each group member had some information about the candidates that everyone else also knew, but each also had unique information. Only by discussing the unshared as well as shared information would the group be likely to make a correct decision. Before getting the chance to have any discussion of the information, groups rarely chose the best qualified candidate. But would their performance improve after they had a discussion? Relative to the consensus-norm groups, the critical-norm groups were much more likely to make the right decision after discussion because they were much more likely to bring the unshared information into their discussions.

(Postmes et al., 2001.)

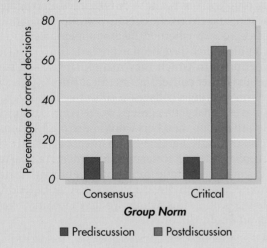

The magnitude of the Boston construction project known as the "Big Dig" is evident in this photo. Construction took more than a decade longer and cost billions of dollars more than planned, and even after the final ramp opened in 2006, significant problems remained. Groups that have spent a great deal of time, effort, or money on a project such as this one often feel entrapped, and rather than consider changing their decision they escalate their commitment to it to try to justify what they have already invested.

Groups are less likely than individuals to invest more and more resources in a project that is failing. **False.**

"Nor is the people's judgment always true: The most may err as grossly as the few."

—John Dryden

escalation effect The condition in which commitments to a failing course of action are increased to justify investments already made.

and put on his "management hat" illustrates this position. Because warnings were suppressed as the flow of information moved up the chain of command, the people at the top did not know the extent of the concerns of those lower in the chain.

Escalation effects A trap that can be very costly to organizations and businesses is known as the **escalation effect** (and is sometimes referred to as *entrapment*). Escalation effects occur when commitment to a failing course of action is increased to justify investments already made (Karlsson et al., 2005; Staw, 1997; Tan & Yates, 2002; Wong et al., 2006). Laboratory experiments show that groups are more likely to escalate commitment to a failing project, and are likely to do so in more extreme ways, than are individuals (Dietz-Uhler, 1996; Whyte, 1993). In numerous instances, groups, businesses, and governments have incurred huge costs because they kept throwing more money, time, and other resources into a project that should have been terminated long before (Ross & Staw, 1986). We will revisit this concept again in Chapter 13, in discussing how businesses and individuals can fall into a "sunk cost" trap as they spend more and more money trying to justify an already bad investment of time and money.

A recent example is the construction project in Boston known as the "Big Dig," designed to turn a congested stretch of highway into a high-speed tunnel. Originally budgeted in 1983 for about $2.6 billion, it was expected to be completed by 1995. More than ten years after it should have been completed, it was still not finished, and the final price tag was estimated to be around $15 billion. These 7.5 miles of road were costing millions of dollars a day, but with so much money already spent, no one could conceive of terminating the project. As U.S. representative Barney Frank wryly suggested, it would have been cheaper to raise the city than to dig the tunnel (Roane, 2000).

Outrage over the Big Dig was renewed in July 2006 when twelve tons of concrete collapsed from the ceiling in a Big Dig tunnel, killing a woman who was driving through the tunnel with her husband. In the aftermath of this tragedy, reports indicated that despite the billions of dollars and numerous years in escalating commitment to this project, decision makers may have sacrificed safety in order to save money, such as by ordering only half the number of bolts designers indicated were needed to hold up the heavy concrete ceiling in the tunnel. It was the failure of these bolts that caused the fatal collapse of the tunnel ceiling (Allen & Murphy, 2006).

Information Processing Once a group has all the available information, group members must process that information and use it to make judgments or perform tasks. How well do groups process information, compared with individuals? In general, groups are susceptible to the same information-processing biases as individuals—only more so. In reviewing the research on group information processing, Verlin Hinsz and others (1997) concluded, "If some bias, error, or tendency predisposes individuals to process information in a particular way, then groups exaggerate this tendency. However, if this bias, error, or tendency is unlikely among individuals processing the information (e.g., less than half the sample), then groups are even less likely to process information in this fashion" (pp. 49–50).

One advantage of groups is that they can divide a large body of information into smaller portions and delegate different members to remember these more manageable portions, ideally by matching information to individuals based on their expertise and interest. This shared process is known as **transactive memory**, which helps groups remember more information more efficiently than individuals (Austin, 2003; Lewis et al., 2005; Wegner et al., 1991). But process loss can occur in this domain as well. Social loafing may occur, as group members don't do their share of the work while expecting others to pick up the slack, or groups may not distribute the information among group members in a rational or efficient manner. As groups gain more experience and learn to match tasks well to the abilities of particular group members, their transactive memory may improve significantly (Brandon & Hollingshead, 2004; Palazzolo et al., 2006).

Computer Technology and Group Support Systems   Some of the obstacles that get in the way of good group discussion and decision making can be reduced through the use of interactive computer-mediated programs. Recently there has been an explosion of research on the use of such programs. Often referred to as *group support systems (GSSs)* or *group decision support systems (GDSSs)*, these programs help remove communication barriers and provide structure and incentives for group discussions and decisions. You may recall our earlier reference to the benefits of computer-mediated brainstorming (see Table 8.3). Many of the same benefits apply to information processing and discussion in groups. Multiple people can "speak" at the same time; they can read and be inspired by each other's ideas; and they can remain anonymous and yet still be held accountable for their individual input. Compared to groups employing more conventional face-to-face modes of discussion, groups that use these systems often do a better job of sampling information, communicating, and arriving at good decisions (Campbell & Stasser, 2006; Fjermestad, 2004; Rains, 2005).

Diversity   As we move forward in the twenty-first century, groups around the world, whether in schools, organizations, businesses, sports, arts, or governments, are becoming increasingly diverse, most obviously in terms of sex, race, ethnicity, and cultural background. How does diversity affect group performance? How can a group best use diversity to its advantage? The answers to such questions—and even the meaning of *diversity*—are likely to change as society changes in terms of its demographics and attitudes. In addition, diversity is not restricted to demographic differences among group members but can also mean differences in attitudes, personalities, skill levels, and so on. Thus, the issues surrounding diversity are particularly challenging. In the meantime, though, because of their increasing importance in today's world, a great deal of new research is addressing these issues, and some tentative conclusions can be offered.

The evidence from empirical research concerning the effects of diversity on group performance is decidedly mixed (Levine & Moreland, 2004). Diversity often is associated with negative group dynamics (Levine & Moreland, 1998; Maznevski, 1994). Miscommunications and misunderstandings are more likely to arise among heterogeneous group members, causing frustration and resentment and damaging group performance by weakening coordination, morale, and commitment to the group. Cliques often form in diverse groups, causing some group members to feel alienated (Jackson et al., 1995; Maznevski, 1994). And even if diversity doesn't appear to hurt a group in any objective way, group members may *think* that it does. For example, S. Gayle Baugh and George Graen (1997) compared how diverse and homogeneous project teams rated their own effectiveness. Project teams that were diverse in terms of gender and race rated themselves as less effective—even though external evaluators judged the diverse teams to be no less effective than the homogeneous teams.

Research has also demonstrated positive effects of diversity. Recent research on the effects of diversity in educational settings, for example, provides support for the benefits of diversity, such as on college students' patterns of socialization, classroom dynamics, and complexity of group discussions (Antonio et al., 2004; Gurin et al., 2002; Juvonen et al., 2006). Other recent research suggests that racially diverse juries may exchange a wider range of information, cite more case facts, and make

transactive memory
A shared system for remembering information that enables multiple people to remember information together more efficiently than they could alone.

As groups have become increasingly diverse in many settings today, it is more important than ever that groups learn how to utilize the great benefits and minimize the costs of diversity in group processes.

fewer errors in their deliberations than racially homogenous juries, at least when the defendant is black (Sommers, 2006). Diversity can give a group flexibility, creativity, and the ability to succeed on tasks that require innovative approaches (Levine & Moreland, 1998; Nemeth & Nemeth-Brown, 2003; Paulus, 2000). As more and more organizations try to attract customers and investors from diverse cultures, diversity in personnel should offer more and more advantages. In one study, for example, ethnically diverse groups and all-white groups brainstormed to come up with ideas to get more tourists to visit the United States, a topic that the researchers chose for its relevance to diversity. The ideas produced by the ethnically diverse groups were judged to be more effective and feasible than the ideas produced by the all-white groups (McLeod et al., 1996).

In reviewing the literature on diversity and group performance, Martha Maznevski (1994) concluded that diversity can enhance a group's performance if the group is truly integrated. Heterogeneity is not as likely to help a group if there are many cliques, if there is little communication or equal-status interaction among the diverse group members, and if there is a lack of shared identity.

William Swann and his colleagues (2003, 2004) note that people often think that for diversity in groups to work, group members must de-emphasize their individuality and instead emphasize their commonality as group members. Although there is some value to this idea, it also clashes with one of the fundamental reasons to encourage diversity in the first place! According to Swann and his colleagues, diversity in small groups is much more likely to succeed when individuals feel that their personal identity is verified and accepted by the other group members.

Fears about the negative effect of increased diversity on group cohesion can influence important policy decisions. When Bill Clinton became president of the United States in 1992, one of his first acts was to try to change military policy in the direction of allowing gays to serve openly in the armed forces. High-level military officials fought Clinton's attempts, claiming that this new policy would compromise the cohesiveness of groups whose members sometimes have to depend on each other for survival. Clinton knew about some of the meta-analytic research that, for example, Brian Mullen and others (1991) had been working on. One of their findings, based in part on studies conducted with military teams, was that when groups are committed to their tasks, they tend to perform well even if the members do not like or feel comfortable with each other. In the process of arguing why the integration of gays into the military should not hurt group performance, Clinton cited evidence from Mullen's work, ultimately persuading his opponents to reach a compromise on this position.

Cooperation, Competition, and Conflict

The importance of group performance is crystal clear for some of the crucial issues confronting our world today. What determines whether people will act responsibly to protect the environment? What factors contribute to the escalation of conflict? Are there ways to reduce conflict once it has started? For answers to these questions, both individual characteristics and group processes must be considered. In Chapter 13, we examine the effectiveness of specific kinds of leadership in specific organizational circumstances. Here, we describe individual and group influences on cooperation, competition, and conflict. When there are differences between us, how do we respond?

Mixed Motives and Social Dilemmas

Imagine that you have to choose between cooperating with others in your group and pursuing your own self-interests, which can hurt the others. Examples of these mixed-motive situations are everywhere. An actor in a play may be motivated to try to "steal" a scene, a basketball player may be inclined to hog the ball, an executive may want to keep more of the company's profits, a family member may want to eat more than her fair share of the leftover birthday cake, and a citizen of the Earth may want to use more than his fair share of finite, valuable resources. In each case, the individual can gain something by pursuing his or her self-interests; but if everyone in the group pursues self-interests, all of the group members will ultimately be worse off than if they had cooperated with each other. Each option, therefore, has possible benefits along with potential costs. When you are in a situation like this, you may feel torn between wanting to cooperate and wanting to compete, and these mixed motives create a difficult dilemma. What do you do?

The notion that the pursuit of self-interest can sometimes be self-destructive forms the basis for what is called a **social dilemma**. In a social dilemma, what is good for one is bad for all. If everyone makes the most self-rewarding choice, everyone suffers the greatest loss. This section examines how people resolve the tension between their cooperative and competitive inclinations in social dilemmas.

The Prisoner's Dilemma
We begin with a detective story. Two partners in crime are picked up by the police for questioning. Although the police believe they have committed a major offense, there is only enough evidence to convict them on a minor charge. In order to sustain a conviction for the more serious crime, the police will have to convince one of them to testify against the other. Separated during questioning, the criminals weigh their alternatives (see Figure 8.7). If neither confesses, they will both get light sentences on the minor charge. If both confess and plead guilty, they will both receive moderate sentences. But if one confesses and the other stays silent, the confessing criminal will secure immunity from prosecution while the silent criminal will pay the maximum penalty.

This story forms the basis for the research paradigm known as the **prisoner's dilemma**. In the two-person prisoner's dilemma, participants are given a series of choices in which they have the option of cooperating or competing with each other, but either option has potential costs. Consider an example: Imagine that you're Prisoner A in Figure 8.7. It appears that no matter what Prisoner B does, you're better off if you compete with B and confess. If B doesn't confess to the police (in other words, if he cooperates with you), you get a lighter sentence if you do confess (you'd get no jail time) than if you don't confess (you'd get one year in jail). If B does confess, you still get a lighter sentence if you confess than if you don't—five versus ten years. So, clearly, you should confess, right? But here's the dilemma: If you *both* confess, each of you gets five years. If *neither* of you confesses, each of you gets only one year. It's really a perplexing situation. What do you think you would do?

FIGURE 8.7

The Prisoner's Dilemma

In the original prisoner's dilemma, from which the game took its name, each of two criminals is offered immunity from prosecution in exchange for a confession. If both stay silent, both get off with a light sentence on a minor charge (upper left). If both confess, both receive a moderate sentence (lower right). But if one turns state's evidence while the other stays mum, the confessing criminal goes free and the silent one spends a long time in jail.

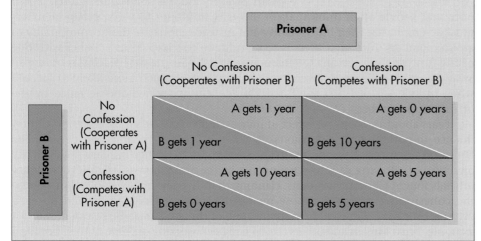

	Prisoner A	
	No Confession (Cooperates with Prisoner B)	**Confession** (Competes with Prisoner B)
No Confession (Cooperates with Prisoner A)	A gets 1 year / B gets 1 year	A gets 0 years / B gets 10 years
Confession (Competes with Prisoner A)	A gets 10 years / B gets 0 years	A gets 5 years / B gets 5 years

(Prisoner B labels the rows)

---

social dilemma A situation in which a self-interested choice by everyone creates the worst outcome for everyone.

prisoner's dilemma A type of dilemma in which one party must make either cooperative or competitive moves in relation to another party; typically designed in such a way that competitive moves are more beneficial to either side, but if both sides make competitive moves, they are both worse off than if they both cooperated.

This kind of social dilemma is not limited to situations involving only two individuals at a time. Imagine, for example, being in a burning building or a sinking ship. Everyone might want to race for the exit or the lifeboats as quickly as possible and push others out of the way; but if everyone does that, more people will die in the panic. More lives will be saved if people leave in an orderly fashion. Soldiers engaged in combat may be better off individually if they take no chances and duck for cover, but if their comrades did the same thing, they all would be slaughtered by the enemy. Nations face such dilemmas as well. Two countries locked in an arms race would be better off if they stopped spending money and resources on weapons of mass destruction, but neither country wants to risk falling behind the other (Dawes, 1980).

By now, tens of thousands of participants in research on the prisoner's dilemma have confronted various versions of this mixed-motive problem. One strategy that many people eventually adopt over the course of multiple trials is known as *tit-for-tat*—a reciprocal strategy in which cooperation by one elicits cooperation by the other, while competition by one provokes competition by the other. This strategy tends to result in relatively positive joint outcomes for the people involved in the dilemma, eliciting higher levels of cooperation than most other strategies (Au & Komorita, 2002; Axelrod, 1984; Nowack et al., 2004; Pruitt, 1998). But cooperation and competitiveness are not equally powerful. Competitiveness is a very strong determinant of reciprocity. Once one party makes a competitive move, the other party is highly likely to follow suit (Kelley & Stahelski, 1970). In contrast, a cooperative move may not elicit cooperation: People who are consistently and unconditionally cooperative can be exploited and taken advantage of (Komorita et al., 1993). A case in point is when British Prime Minister Neville Chamberlain tried to prevent war in the 1930s by cooperating with Hitler; this behavior only gave Hitler the opportunity to become more aggressive.

An alternative to simple reciprocity that is often successful is *win-stay, lose-shift*—a strategy consistent with basic learning principles and conditioning. Using this strategy, individuals continue to compete or cooperate as long as the payoff they receive is high, but they shift to the opposite action whenever the payoff is low (Kraines & Kraines, 1995; Nowak & Sigmund, 1993).

Resource Dilemmas   The prisoner's dilemma sets up a trap for those who play it: Attempts to gain an advantage will backfire if the other party also makes the competitive choice. This conflict of motives also forms the basis for another category of social dilemmas: **resource dilemmas**, which concern how two or more people share a limited resource. Resource dilemmas come in two basic types: (1) commons dilemmas and (2) public goods dilemmas.

The *commons dilemma* is a situation in which, if people take as much as they want of a limited resource that does not replenish itself, nothing will be left for anyone. Robyn Dawes (1980) called this situation the *take-some dilemma,* one popular version of which is known as the "tragedy of the commons" (Hardin, 1968). In earlier times, people would let their animals graze on the town's lush, grassy commons. But if all the animals grazed to their hearts' content, and to their owners' benefit, the commons would be stripped, the animals' food supply diminished, and the owners' welfare threatened. Today, the tragedy of the commons is a clear and present danger on a global scale. Deforestation, air pollution, carbon emission, ocean dumping, massive irrigation, overfishing, commercial development of wilderness areas, a rapidly increasing population in some developing countries, and an over-consuming population in the richest nations—all pit individual self-interest against the common good. Selfish responses to commons dilemmas are social sins of commission; people take too much.

In *public goods dilemmas,* all of the individuals are supposed to contribute resources to a common pool. Examples of these public goods include the blood supply, public broadcasting, schools, libraries, roads, and parks. If no one gives, the service can't continue (Olson, 1965). If club members don't pay their dues or contribute their time, the club will fail. Again, private gain conflicts with the public good.

Solving Social Dilemmas: Groups and Individuals   When does individual desire prevail in social dilemmas? When, in contrast, do people see beyond

Would you like to try participating in a prisoner's dilemma game online? Some Web sites offer a chance for you to do this. To find them, search for "Prisoner's Dilemma" in a search engine.

"If a free society cannot help the many who are poor, it cannot save the few who are rich."

—John F. Kennedy

resource dilemmas   Social dilemmas concerning how two or more people share a limited resource.

TABLE 8.4
Solving Social Dilemmas

Behavior in a social dilemma is influenced by both psychological factors and structural arrangements. The characteristics listed here contribute to the successful solution of social dilemmas.

Psychological Factors

- Individual and cultural differences

  Having a prosocial, cooperative orientation

  Trusting others

  Being a member of a collectivistic culture

- Situational factors

  Being in a good mood

  Having had successful experience managing resources and working cooperatively

  Seeing unselfish models

  Having reason to expect others to cooperate

- Group dynamics

  Acting as an individual rather than in a group

  Being in a small group rather than in a large group

  Sharing a social identity or superordinate goals

Structural Arrangements

- Creating a payoff structure that rewards cooperative behavior and/or punishes selfish behavior

- Removing resources from the public domain and handing them over to private ownership

- Establishing an authority to control the resources

their own immediate potential for gain and consider the long-term benefits of cooperation? Social dilemmas pose a serious threat to the quality of life and even to life itself. How do people try to solve them? What factors make them more or less cooperative when faced with these dilemmas? There is a huge body of research on these questions. Table 8.4 summarizes some of the factors that extensive research has identified as facilitating the best solutions to social dilemmas.

Groups tend to be more competitive in mixed-motive situations than individuals. The competitiveness of groups has its roots in fear and greed—the fear that the other group will exploit one's own group and the greedy desire to maximize the outcomes achieved by one's own group at the other group's expense. Individuals, too, can be driven by fear and greed, but competition between groups intensifies such motives. In order for groups to have any real chance of cooperating voluntarily, it is especially important that trust be established (Insko et al., 2005; Stouten et al., 2006). Establishing trust is one reason why communication between and within groups is a key ingredient in helping solve social dilemmas (Hopthrow & Hulbert, 2005; Kerr & Kaufman-Gilliland, 1994; Tazelaar et al., 2004).

Another reason why groups are more competitive than individuals is that group members feel less identifiable by members of the other group. The greater anonymity that a group offers frees individual group members to act in a self-interested, aggressive manner (Wildschut et al., 2003). This is one reason why large groups are more likely to exploit scarce resources than are small ones (Pruitt, 1998; Seijts & Latham, 2000).

The fact remains that social dilemmas often do involve very large groups—a city, a state, a nation, the whole world. In these circumstances, the structural arrangements listed in Table 8.4 may be most appropriate. Resolving social dilemmas well is crucial for maintaining the quality of our lives, both immediately and even more so for the future. Understanding the psychological and structural factors that affect groups' behaviors when confronted with these dilemmas is therefore one of the most vital contributions that social psychological research can make.

Solving Social Dilemmas: Culture and Individual Difference Although people around the world are susceptible to exploiting each other in social dilemmas, there are cultural and individual differences that predict whether one is more or less likely to resolve social dilemmas in cooperative ways.

Some studies have suggested that collectivists are more likely to cooperate in social dilemmas than individualists, but there is not yet enough research pointing to a reliable general difference. More specifically, however, it may be that collectivists tend to cooperate more when dealing with friends or ingroup members than with

FIGURE 8.8

Culture and the Prisoner's Dilemma

Students from Hong Kong who were very familiar with both Chinese and American cultures played the prisoner's dilemma game with a friend or a stranger. Before playing, they were exposed to pictures of Chinese, American, or neutral images. When playing with a friend, students primed with Chinese or neutral pictures cooperated more than did students primed with American pictures. When playing with a stranger, there was no significant difference in cooperativeness as a function of which culture was primed.

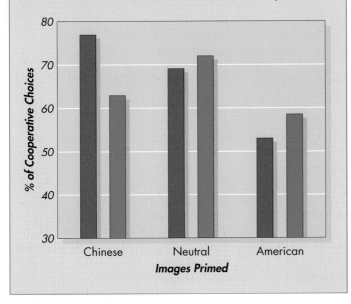

Large groups are more likely than small groups to exploit a scarce resource that the members collectively depend on. **True.**

strangers or outgroup members; this difference tends not to be as strong among individualists (Oyserman et al., 2002). This point was supported recently in an interesting experiment by Rosana Yin-mei Wong and Ying-yi Hong (2005). Participants in this experiment were Hong Kong Chinese college students who could be considered bicultural; that is, they were exposed extensively throughout their lives to both Chinese and American cultures. These students played a prisoner's dilemma game with either friends or strangers. Before playing, the students were exposed to one of three sets of pictures: pictures associated with Chinese culture (such as a Chinese dragon or a person performing kung fu); pictures associated with American culture (such as the American flag or an American football game); or culturally neutral pictures (geometric figures). Would seeing the Chinese or American images prime one or the other culture and cause the students to respond in the prisoner's dilemma game differently?

The results revealed that the pictures did make a difference (see Figure 8.8). When playing the prisoner's dilemma game with a friend, students exposed to the Chinese or the neutral symbols cooperated much more than did students exposed to the American symbols. When playing with a stranger, on the other hand, there was no significant difference in cooperativeness as a function of which culture was primed. These results suggest that exposure to the Chinese prime led the students to respond in ways consistent with collectivistic norms: a lot of cooperation with friends and less cooperation with strangers. Exposure to the American prime led to less cooperation in general, but not a bias for friends and against strangers.

Within a culture, people differ in their own tendencies toward cooperation and competition. A growing body of research has examined individual differences in social value orientations. People with a *prosocial, cooperative* orientation seek to maximize joint gains or achieve equal outcomes, those with an *individualist* orientation seek to maximize their own gain, and those with a *competitive* orientation seek to maximize their own gain relative to that of others. People with a cooperative orientation are less likely to behave in a competitive, resource-consuming fashion than are people with individualistic or competitive orientations (De Cremer & Van Lange, 2001; de Kwaadsteniet et al., 2006; Eek & Gärling, 2006; Parks et al., 2003).

 ## Conflict Escalation

Social dilemmas can create important conflicts between groups, and how groups resolve these dilemmas can make the difference between war and peace. There are, of course, many other sources of conflict between groups. The very fact that groups differ from each other on any of a number of dimensions—religious, ethnic, racial, cultural, political—can spark conflict. Again and again, throughout human history, differences between groups explode in hatred and bloodshed. What fans the flames of an escalating conflict? And what can extinguish these flames? We address these questions in the remaining sections of the chapter.

Conflicts between groups are caused by many factors, including competition for scarce resources, stereotypes and prejudice, and competing ideologies. But once a conflict is in place, it can feed on itself. Indeed, *conflict spirals* are frequent, as one party annoys the other party, who retaliates, prompting a more extreme reaction from the first party, and so on (Brett et al., 1998; Rubin et al., 1994). Table 8.5 lists several factors that contribute to conflict escalation. The first three concern group processes

> ### TABLE 8.5
> #### Factors That Promote and Sustain the Escalation of Between-Group Conflict
>
> - The group polarization process, which increases the extremity of group members' attitudes and opinions
> - Pressures for conformity, such as group cohesiveness and groupthink, which make it difficult for individuals to oppose the group's increasingly aggressive position
> - Escalation of commitment, which seeks to justify past investments through the commitment of additional resources
> - Premature use of threat capacity, which triggers aggressive retaliation
> - Negative perceptions of "the other," which promote acceptance of aggressive behavior and enhance cohesiveness of the ingroup "us" against the outgroup "them"

discussed earlier in the chapter. The fourth one, concerning the capacity to use threat, may seem more surprising. We discuss this, and a fifth factor (perceptions of the other), in the next sections.

Threat Capacity   It seems obvious that the ability to punish someone who engages in a prohibited behavior can act as a deterrent to conflict escalation. You're less likely to mess with someone who can mess right back with you. If both parties hold their fire, a balance of terror can work. But having the capacity to attack can present an irresistible temptation to do so.

A classic study conducted by Morton Deutsch and Robert Krauss (1960) makes the point. These investigators had pairs of female participants engage in a simulated work environment in which each was in charge of a trucking company carrying merchandise over a road to a specific destination. Because they had to share parts of the road, they had to coordinate their efforts. However, in one condition of the study, one of the women in each pair had the capacity to take control of the road and block the other's progress, which would increase her own profit and reduce the other participant's profit. In another condition, both participants in each pair had this capacity. What was the result?

In general, when a participant had the ability to block the other, she did—and both participants suffered. Overall, participants earned more money if neither could block the other than if one of them could, and when *both* members of the pair could block the other, the participants earned least of all. These results suggest that once coercive means are available, people tend to use them, even when doing so damages their own outcomes.

Perceptions of the Other   The fifth factor listed in Table 8.5 calls to mind our earlier discussion of stereotypes and prejudice, including the favoring of ingroups over outgroups (see Chapter 5). During conflict, the opposing group and its members are often perceived as "the other"—strange, foreign, alien. They are characterized in simplistic, exaggerated ways. Held at a psychological distance, the other becomes a screen on which it is possible to project one's worst fears. Indeed, groups often see each other as *mirror images:* They see in their enemies what their enemies see in them. As Urie Bronfenbrenner (1961) discovered when he visited the former Soviet Union during the cold war, the Soviets saw Americans as aggressive, exploitative, and untrustworthy—just as the Americans saw them. The same is true of Israelis and Palestinians today.

Taken to extremes, negative views of the other can result in *dehumanization,* the perception that people lack human qualities or are "subhuman." Jeroen Vaes, Jacques-Philippe Leyens, and others call this *infrahumanization* and propose that it

Group conflict is tragically hard to stop, as in the ongoing struggles between Israelis and Palestinians. In the midst of the fighting depicted here, a boy is shot in the stomach.

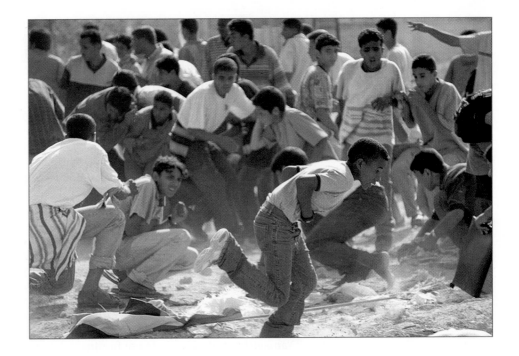

plays an important role in intergroup prejudice and conflict (Leyens et al., 2003; Vaes et al., 2003). Based on malicious stereotypes about outgroups, dehumanization is both a consequence of hostility between groups and a trigger of more intergroup conflict. Aggression *by* an outgroup can cause the ingroup to see them in a dehumanizing way, and also an ingroup's aggression *toward* an outgroup can make the ingroup dehumanize the outgroup. When an ingroup aggresses against the outgroup, for example, the ingroup may justify this aggression by dehumanization, which is used to excuse even more aggression, which requires more dehumanization to justify, and so on (Castano & Giner-Sorolla, 2006; McAlister et al., 2006). As the Nazis began the Holocaust, they released propaganda that characterized Jews as less than human—as rats that spread disease and needed to be exterminated. During World War II, the United States portrayed the Japanese people as cold, identical robots. At the same time, the Japanese media portrayed Americans as bloodthirsty animals, as in cartoons depicting eagles flying off with bloodied Japanese citizens in their talons.

Dehumanization is the ultimate version of "us" versus "them," removing all religious and ethical constraints against the taking of human life. As George Orwell (1942) discovered during the Spanish Civil War, the cure for dehumanization is to restore the human connection. Sighting an enemy soldier holding up his trousers with both hands while running beside a nearby trench, Orwell was unable to take the easy shot: "I had come here to shoot at 'Fascists'; but a man who is holding up his trousers isn't a 'Fascist,' he is visibly a fellow creature, similar to yourself, and you don't feel like shooting at him" (p. 254).

Reducing Conflict Through GRIT

With all the forces pressing it forward (see Table 8.5 for a summary), conflict escalation is hardly surprising. In this and the next section, we examine the kind of sustained effort that peacemaking requires.

Every once in a while, individual leaders try to break the gridlock of intergroup conflict by taking a unilateral step toward peace. U.S. president John Kennedy banned atmospheric nuclear tests without a pledge from the Soviets to do likewise; Egyptian President Anwar Sadat flew to Jerusalem uncertain of the reception he would receive; Soviet general secretary Mikhail Gorbachev withdrew Soviet forces from Afghanistan before meeting with U.S. president Ronald Reagan in Moscow.

The notion that unilateral concessions can reverse an escalating conflict is central to a peacemaking strategy developed by Charles Osgood (1962): **graduated and reciprocated initiatives in tension-reduction (GRIT)**.

To see how GRIT works, imagine that two groups, A and B, are in conflict. (1) The members of group A state their intention to reduce conflict, announce a few tension-reducing initiatives, and invite the other side to reciprocate. (2) Group A carries out these initiatives, putting public pressure on group B to respond cooperatively. (3) If group B makes a cooperative move, group A quickly reciprocates with a move that risks at least as much as—and, if possible, more than—group B's cooperative behavior. (4) Group A maintains a retaliatory capability in order to deter exploitation by group B. If group B attacks, group A retaliates at precisely the same level. Once it has retaliated, it resumes its unilateral tension-reducing efforts.

Reciprocal, tit-for-tat strategies like GRIT are maximally responsive: Cooperation is met with cooperation, attack with attack. Because the other party is given a greater sense of control over the interaction, the perceived risk of being cooperative is reduced. GRIT also prevents exploitation by allowing for retaliation if it is necessary and avoids conflict escalation by keeping retaliatory actions within the level established by the other party. But GRIT is not simply reactive. It patiently, persistently, and proactively seeks peace. Research on GRIT is encouraging; even people with a competitive orientation tend to respond cooperatively to this strategy, and the positive effects of GRIT can be enduring (Lindskold & Han, 1988; Yamagishi et al., 2005). These findings also suggest that it is not necessary to like an opponent to cooperate on various ventures. Instead, the essential elements are establishing at least a minimal level of trust and recognizing that one's own interests will benefit.

Negotiation

Unilateral concessions are useful for beginning the peace process, but extended negotiations are usually required to reach a final agreement. Negotiations on complex issues such as nuclear arms control and international environmental protection, as well as efforts to make peace in volatile regions such as the Middle East, often go on for years or even decades.

But negotiations are not restricted to the international scene. Unions and management engage in collective bargaining to establish employee contracts. Divorcing couples negotiate the terms of their divorce, by themselves or through their lawyers. Dating couples negotiate about which movie to attend. Families negotiate about who does which annoying household chores. Indeed, negotiations occur whenever there is a conflict that the parties wish to resolve without getting into an open fight or relying on an imposed legal settlement. There is an immense amount of research on negotiation and bargaining (Bazerman, 2005; De Dreu & Carnevale, 2003; Thompson, 2006). Here, we focus on those findings most relevant to conflict reduction.

Keys to Successful Negotiating Conflicts can be reduced through successful negotiation. But what constitutes success in this context? Perhaps the most common successful outcome is a 50-50 compromise. Here, the negotiators start at extreme positions and gradually work toward a mutually acceptable midpoint. Some negotiators, however, achieve an even higher level of success. Most negotiations are not simply fixed-sum situations in which each side must give up something until a middle point is reached. Instead, there often exist ways in which both sides can benefit (Bazerman & Neale, 1992). When an **integrative agreement** is reached, both parties obtain outcomes that are superior to a 50-50 split.

Take, for instance, the tale of the orange and the two sisters (Follett, 1942). One sister wanted the juice to drink; the other wanted the peel for a cake. So they sliced the orange in half and each one took her portion. These sisters suffered from an advanced case of the "*fixed-pie*" syndrome. They assumed that whatever one of them won, the other lost. In fact, however, each of them could have had the whole thing: all of the juice for one, all of the peel for the other. An integrative agreement was well within their grasp, but they failed to see it. Unfortunately, research indicates

---

Negotiating with car dealers is a form of negotiation in which many of us engage from time to time. Want some tips? Try Edmund's Web site at www.edmunds.com.

graduated and reciprocated initiatives in tension-reduction (GRIT)
A strategy for unilateral, persistent efforts to establish trust and cooperation between opposing parties.

integrative agreement
A negotiated resolution to a conflict in which all parties obtain outcomes that are superior to what they would have obtained from an equal division of the contested resources.

Chief negotiators from the United States and several Central American countries meet in Nicaragua in September 2003 to negotiate a free trade agreement. Such negotiations are both important and complex, involving nations with different resources, needs, relationships, and cultures. They highlight the usefulness of social psychological research, which has specified a number of factors that can make negotiations more or less likely to succeed.

that this happens all too often. Leigh Thompson and Dennis Hrebec (1996) conducted a meta-analysis of thirty-two experiments and found that in over 20 percent of negotiations that could have resulted in integrative agreements, the participants agreed to settlements that were worse for both sides. The ability to achieve integrative agreements is an acquired skill: Experienced negotiators obtain them more often than do inexperienced ones (Druckman, 1994; Thompson, 1990).

What are the characteristics of experienced negotiators? Negotiators who can appear both flexible and strong are particularly successful (McGillicuddy et al., 1984; Nemeth & Brilmayer, 1987). Two other key elements are communicating and trying to understand the point of view of the other person (De Drue et al., 2006). It is always difficult for participants in a dispute to listen carefully to each other and to reach some reasonable understanding of each other's perspective. But communication in which both sides disclose their goals and needs is critically important in allowing each side to see opportunities for joint benefits. This may seem obvious, and yet people in negotiations very often fail to communicate their goals and needs. For one thing, negotiators tend to think that their goals and objectives are clearer to the other party than they actually are (Vorauer & Claude, 1998). Furthermore, in conflict negotiations each party is likely to distrust and fear the other. Neither wants to reveal too much for fear of losing power at the bargaining table. Again, this is part of the fixed-pie syndrome. But if one party does disclose information, the disclosure can have dramatic effects. If one side discloses, the other party becomes much more likely to do so, enhancing the likelihood of integrative agreement (Thompson, 1991).

In addition to disclosure of information, several other factors can improve negotiations and increase the chances that both sides will benefit. These factors include training negotiators in conflict-resolution techniques and using computerized negotiation support systems (Davis & Hall, 2003; Shakun, 1999; Thompson et al., 2000). Being aware of the group processes we have covered in this chapter puts you in a good position to help reduce conflicts.

During particularly difficult or significant negotiations, outside assistance may be sought. Some negotiations rely on an *arbitrator,* who has the power to impose a settlement. But it is more common for conflicting parties to request the participation of a *mediator,* who works with them to try to reach a voluntary agreement. Traditionally, mediators have been employed in labor-management negotiations and international conflicts. But increasingly, mediators help resolve a wide range of other disputes, such as those involving tenants and landlords, divorcing couples, and feuding neighbors. Trained in negotiation and conflict management, mediators can often increase the likelihood of reaching a cooperative solution (Bercovitch & Houston, 2000; Bowling & Hoffman, 2000; Carnevale, 2002; Wilkenfeld et al., 2003).

Culture and Negotiation As the world becomes smaller because of advances in technology, the globalization of business and the economy, and global threats concerning the environment and terrorism, the ability to negotiate effectively across cultures becomes increasingly important. Table 8.6 lists some common assumptions made by negotiators from western, individualistic cultures that are not always shared by representatives from other cultures (Brett & Gelfand, 2006; Gelfand et al., 2007; Kimmel, 1994, 2000).

Consider, for example, our statement that good communication is a key ingredient in successful negotiation. Communication across cultures can present special challenges. Whereas an individualistic perspective emphasizes direct communication and confrontation, a collectivistic perspective emphasizes more indirect information sharing and a desire to avoid direct conflict. Individualistic negotiators may emphasize rationality and a lack of emotion in negotiation, whereas a greater tolerance of contradiction and emotionality is characteristic of a collectivistic style—although emotionality should not be confrontational. Individualists tend to prefer to make compromises and concessions toward the end of a negotiation, whereas collectivists may prefer to begin with generous concessions and gradually reduce their concessions later. Even something that may seem as basic as *time* is perceived and valued differently as a function of culture (see bottom of Table 8.6).

If negotiators are not aware of these kinds of cross-cultural differences, or if they cannot respond effectively to them, the inevitable misunderstandings may prevent them from achieving a successful outcome. Wendi Adair and Jeanne Brett (2005) de-

TABLE 8.6
Cultural Assumptions About Negotiating

People from different cultures make different assumptions about the negotiation process. This table summarizes some assumptions commonly made by U.S. and other western negotiators. It also presents some alternative assumptions that may be held by negotiators from other cultures. As you can see, such different assumptions could make it very difficult to reach a successful agreement.

(Based on Brett & Gelfand, 2006; Kimmel, 1994, 2000.)

Assumptions Made by Negotiators from the U.S. and Other Western Countries	Alternatives
Negotiation is a business, not a social activity.	The first step in negotiating is to develop a trusting relationship between the individual negotiators.
Points should be made with rational, analytical arguments, without contradiction.	Arguments may be more holistic, and emotionality and contradiction tolerated.
Communication is direct and verbal.	Some of the most important communications are nonverbal or indirect.
Written contracts are binding; oral commitments are not.	Written contracts are less meaningful than oral communications because the nonverbal context clarifies people's intentions.
Current information and ideas are more valid than historical or traditional opinions and information.	History and tradition are more valid than current information and ideas. Information must be understood in its greater context.
Time is very important; punctuality is expected; deadlines should be set and adhered to.	Building a relationship takes time and is more important than punctuality; setting deadlines is an effort to humiliate the other party.

Although they are competitors on the field, these soccer players from England and Germany (along with officials) found common ground and shared a superordinate goal—combating racism—before their match in Germany in October 2006.

scribe negotiation as a kind of dance, as the partners move with each other according to various rhythms, and the dance will work only if they can synchronize their movements and work together. Negotiations across cultures can be challenging because the participants have different ways of performing these dances. As Adair and Brett put it, "Just as it will take time for a Cuban, who is accustomed to the rapid, staircase movements of Latin social dancing, and an American—accustomed to smooth walking dances like the waltz—to get in sync, it will take time for cross-cultural negotiators to synchronize their movements" (p. 46). It is in their best interests, therefore, to learn each other's perspectives so they can work together more effectively and fluently without stepping on each other's toes.

Finding Common Ground   Every conflict is unique, as is every attempt at conflict resolution. Still, all efforts to find a constructive solution to conflict require some common ground to build upon. Recognition of a *superordinate identity* is one way to establish common ground between groups in conflict. When group members perceive that they have a shared identity—a sense of belonging to something larger than and encompassing their own groups—the attractiveness of outgroup members increases, and interactions between the groups often become more peaceful.

Superordinate goals have another valuable characteristic: They can produce a superordinate identity. The experience of intergroup cooperation increases the sense of belonging to a single superordinate group. Even the mere expectation of a cooperative interaction increases empathy, which, in turn, enhances helpfulness and reduces aggression. Indeed, empathic connections between various members of each group can lay the foundation for an inclusive, rather than exclusive, social identity (Dovidio et al., 2005; Kane et al., 2005).

On the road to peace, both kinds of common ground are needed. Cooperation to meet shared goals makes similarities more visible, and a sense of a shared identity makes cooperation more likely. Those who would make peace, not war, realize that it is in their own self-interest to do so and understand that the cloak of humanity is large enough to cover a multitude of lesser differences.

REVIEW

Individuals in Groups: The Presence of Others

- Individuals in groups have direct interactions with each other over a period of time and share a common fate, identity, or set of goals.

- In collectives, people engage in common activities but have minimal direct interaction.

Social Facilitation: When Others Arouse Us

- In an early experiment, Triplett found that children performed faster when they worked side by side rather than alone.

- Social facilitation refers to two effects that occur when individual contributions are identifiable: The presence of others enhances performance on easy tasks but impairs performance on difficult tasks.

- The theories of mere presence, evaluation apprehension, and distraction-conflict give different answers to questions concerning (1) whether social facilitation is necessarily social and (2) whether the mere presence of others is sufficient to affect performance.

Social Loafing: When Others Relax Us

- In early research on easy tasks involving pooled contributions, Ringelmann found that individual output declined when people worked with others.

- But social loafing is reduced or eliminated when people think their individual efforts will be important, relevant, and meaningful. In such cases, individuals may engage in social compensation in an effort to offset the anticipated social loafing of others.

- Groups in collectivistic cultures may be more likely to have group norms promoting productive teamwork and discouraging social loafing.

Facilitation and Loafing: Unifying the Paradigms

- A unified paradigm integrates social facilitation, social loafing, and what we've called "social security": when the presence of others enhances performance on difficult tasks involving pooled contributions.

Deindividuation

- Deindividuation diminishes a person's sense of individuality and reduces constraints against deviant behavior.

- Two types of environmental cues can increase deviant behavior: (1) Accountability cues, such as anonymity, signal that individuals will not be held responsible for their actions; and (2) attentional cues, such as intense environmental stimulation, produce a deindividuated state in which the individual acts impulsively.

- Large crowds can both increase anonymity and decrease self-awareness, which together can increase violent or other deviant behavior.

- The effects of deindividuation depend on the characteristics of the immediate group. In the context of an antagonistic social identity, antisocial behavior increases; in the context of a benevolent social identity, prosocial behavior increases.

Group Dynamics: Interacting with Others

Joining a Group

- People join a group for a variety of reasons, including to perform tasks that can't be accomplished alone, to enhance self-esteem and social identity, to gain a sense of identity, and to interact with group members.

- The socialization of newcomers into a group relies on the relationships they form with old-timers, who act as models, trainers, and mentors.

- Groups often proceed through several stages of development, from initial orientation through periods of conflict, compromise, and action.

- Some groups pass through periods of inactivity followed by sudden action in response to time pressures.

Roles, Norms, and Cohesiveness

- Interacting groups have three major features: an expected set of behaviors for members (roles), rules of conduct for members (norms), and forces that push members together (cohesiveness).

- Establishing clear roles can help a group; but when members' roles are ambiguous, conflict with other roles, or change, stress and poor performance can result.

- The relationship between cohesiveness and group performance is complex, depending on factors such as the size of the group, the kind of task that the group is performing, and the kinds of norms that have been established.

Group Polarization

- When individuals who have similar, though not identical, opinions participate in a group discussion, their opinions become more extreme.

- Explanations for group polarization emphasize the number and persuasiveness of arguments heard, social comparison with a perceived group norm, and the influence of one's own ingroup.

Groupthink

- Groupthink refers to an excessive tendency to seek concurrence among group members.

- The symptoms of groupthink produce defective decision making, which can lead to a bad decision.

- A highly cohesive group is more likely to experience groupthink if other contributors to groupthink are present, such as a controlling leader and a stressful situation.

- Self-managed work teams, though increasingly popular, may be particularly susceptible to groupthink.

- Strategies that have been successful in helping groups avoid groupthink include consulting with outsiders, having the leader play a less controlling role, encouraging criticism and a thorough information search, and having a group member play the devil's advocate and challenge the consensus.

- Computer-based technology can help groups avoid groupthink by guiding them to follow systematic agendas and focus on ideas.

- Encouraging counterfactual thinking can also be effective.

Group Performance: Are More Heads Better Than One?

- Group performance is influenced by the type of task (additive, conjunctive, or disjunctive).

- Because of process loss, a group may perform worse than it would if every individual performed up to his or her potential.

- Among the factors that create process loss are social loafing, poor coordination, and failure to recognize the expertise of particular group members.

- Groups can do better than even the best members of the group on tasks that can be divided among subgroups and in which the correct answer is clearly demonstrable to the rest of the group members.

- Setting specific, ambitious goals can improve group performance.

- Contrary to illusions about the effectiveness of interactive brainstorming, groups in which members interact face-to-face produce fewer creative ideas than the same number of people working alone.

- Computer-based technology can improve group brainstorming.

- Biased sampling refers to the tendency for groups to pay more attention to shared information than to unshared information.

- Information may not be communicated adequately in a group because of problems in the group's communication network, such as suppression of relevant information at some point in the decision-making chain.

- Group norms that foster critical thinking can prevent biased sampling.

- Groups are susceptible to an escalation effect, which occurs when commitment to a failing course of action is increased to justify investments already made. Instead of cutting their losses, they essentially throw good money and time after bad.

- Groups are also susceptible to the same information-processing biases as individuals—only more so.

- Groups can remember more information than individuals through transactive memory, a shared process in which the information can be divided among the group members.

- Many groups and businesses today use interactive computer-mediated systems that are designed to improve how groups process and communicate information, leading to better decisions.

- The effects of diversity on group performance depend on the nature of the task, how well integrated the group is, and whether group members feel their individual identities are verified by the others.

Cooperation, Competition, and Conflict

Mixed Motives and Social Dilemmas

- In mixed-motive situations, such as the prisoner's dilemma, there are incentives for both competition and cooperation.

- In a social dilemma, personal benefit conflicts with the overall good.

- Resource dilemmas involve sharing limited resources. In the commons dilemma, a group of people can take resources from a common pool; whereas in the public goods dilemma, the maintenance of a common resource requires the contributions of a group of people.

- Behavior in a social dilemma is influenced by psychological factors—including situational factors, group dynamics, and structural arrangements.

- Some studies have suggested that collectivists are more likely to cooperate in social dilemmas than are individualists.

- Participants in one experiment who were primed with Chinese symbols cooperated more when playing a prisoner's dilemma with a friend than did participants who were primed with American symbols. Participants primed with Chinese symbols cooperated less when playing with a stranger than with a friend, but those primed with American symbols did not behave differently toward strangers than they did toward friends.

Conflict Escalation

- Conflicts can escalate for many reasons, including conflict spirals and escalation of commitment.

- The premature use of the capacity to punish can elicit retaliation and escalate conflict.

- Perceptions of the other that contribute to conflict escalation include unfavorable mirror images and dehumanization.

Reducing Conflict Through GRIT

- GRIT—an explicit strategy for the unilateral, persistent pursuit of trust and cooperation between opposing parties—is a useful strategy for beginning the peace process.

Negotiation

- Many negotiations have the potential to result in integrative agreements, in which outcomes exceed a 50-50 split; but negotiators often fail to achieve such outcomes.

- Flexibility, communication, and an understanding of the other party's perspective are key ingredients of successful negotiation.

- Mediators can often be helpful in achieving success in negotiations.

- People from different cultures may have very different assumptions and styles concerning negotiations, such as whether direct or indirect communication is preferred, how important context is, and whether direct conflict should be avoided.

- Superordinate goals and a superordinate identity increase the likelihood of a peaceful resolution of differences.

KEY TERMS

PUTTING COMMON SENSE TO THE TEST

People will cheer louder when they cheer as part of a group than when they cheer alone.

False. People tend to put less effort into collective tasks, such as group cheering, than into tasks when their individual performance can be identified and evaluated.

Group members' attitudes about a course of action usually become more moderate after group discussion.

False. Group discussion often causes attitudes to become more extreme as the initial tendencies of the group are exaggerated.

People brainstorming as a group come up with a greater number of better ideas than the same number of people working individually.

False. Groups in which members interact face-to-face produce fewer creative ideas when brainstorming than the same number of people brainstorming alone.

Groups are less likely than individuals to invest more and more resources in a project that is failing.

False. Although individuals often feel entrapped by previous commitments and make things worse by throwing good money (and other resources) after bad, groups are even more prone to having this problem.

Large groups are more likely than small groups to exploit a scarce resource that the members collectively depend on.

True. Large groups are more likely to behave selfishly when faced with resource dilemmas, in part because people in large groups feel less identifiable and more anonymous.

9

Attraction and Close Relationships

PREVIEW

This chapter examines how people form relationships with each other. First, we describe the fundamental human need for *being with others,* why people affiliate, and the problem of loneliness. Then we consider various personal and situational factors that influence our *initial attraction* to specific others. Third, we examine different types of *close relationships*—what makes them rewarding, how they differ, the types of love they arouse, and the factors that keep them together or break them apart.

PUTTING COMMON SENSE TO THE TEST

T/F

_____ People seek out the company of others, even strangers, in times of stress.

_____ Infants do not discriminate between faces considered attractive and unattractive in their culture.

_____ People who are physically attractive are happier and have higher self-esteem than those who are unattractive.

_____ When it comes to romantic relationships, opposites attract.

_____ Men are more likely than women to interpret friendly gestures by the opposite sex in sexual terms.

_____ After the honeymoon period, there is an overall decline in levels of marital satisfaction.

No topic fascinates the people of this planet more than interpersonal attraction. Needing to belong, we humans are obsessed about friendships, romantic relationships, dating, love, sex, reproduction, sexual orientation, marriage, and divorce. Playwrights, poets, and musicians write with eloquence and emotion about loves desired, won, and lost. Television is filled with relationship-centered reality TV shows like *The Bachelor, The Bachelorette, Are You Hot?, Wife Swap,* and *Newlyweds*. More and more, people are meeting romantic partners online rather than in bars, in Facebook.com, chatrooms, Internet bulletin boards such as Craigslist, and dating services such as Match.com. Both in our hearts and in our minds, the relationships we seek and enjoy with other people are more important than anything else.

At one time or another, each of us has been startled by our reaction to someone we have met. In general, why are human beings drawn to each other? Why are we so attracted to some people and yet indifferent to or repelled by others? What determines how our intimate relationships evolve? What does it mean to love someone, and what problems are likely to arise along the way? As these questions reveal, attraction among people—from the first spark through the flames of an intimate connection—often seems like a kind of wild card in the deck of human behavior. This chapter unravels some of the mysteries.

Being with Others: A Fundamental Human Motive

Although born helpless, human infants are equipped with reflexes that orient them toward people. They are uniquely responsive to human faces, they turn their head toward voices, and they are able to mimic certain facial gestures on cue. Then, a few weeks later, comes a baby's first smile, surely the warmest sign of all. Much to the delight of parents all over the world, the newborn seems an inherently social animal. But wait. If you reflect on the amount of time that you spend talking to, being with, flirting with, confiding in, pining for, or worrying about other people, you'll realize that we are all social animals. It seems that people need people.

According to Roy Baumeister and Mark Leary (1995), the need to belong is a basic human motive, "a pervasive drive to form and maintain at least a minimum quantity of lasting, positive, and significant interpersonal relationships" (p. 497). This general proposition is supported by everyday observation and a great deal of research. All over the world, people feel joy when they form new social attachments and react with anxiety and grief when these bonds are broken—as when separated from a loved one by distance, divorce, or death. The need to belong runs deep, which is why people are distressed when they are neglected by others, rejected, excluded, stigmatized, or ostracized, all forms of "social death" (Leary, 2001; Williams et al., 2002).

We care deeply about what others think of us, which is why we spend so much time and money to make ourselves presentable and attractive. In fact, some people are so worried about how they appear to others that they suffer from *social anxiety disorders* characterized by intense feelings of discomfort in situations that invite public scrutiny (Leary & Kowalski, 1995). One very familiar example is public-speaking anxiety, or "stage fright"—a performer's worst nightmare. If you've ever had to make a presentation, only to feel weak in the knees and hear your voice quiver, you will have endured a hint of this disorder. When sufferers are asked what there is to fear, the most common responses are: shaking and showing other signs of anxiety, going blank, saying something foolish, and being unable to continue (Stein et al., 1996). For people with high levels of social anxiety, the problem is also evoked by other social situations, such as eating at a public lunch counter, signing a check in front of a store clerk, and, for males, urinating in a crowded men's room. In extreme cases, the reaction can become so debilitating that the person just stays at home (Beidel & Turner, 1998; Crozier & Alden, 2005).

Our need to belong is a fundamental human motive. We'll see in Chapter 14 that people who have a network of close social ties—in the form of lovers, friends, family members, and co-workers—tend to be happier and more satisfied with life than those who are more isolated (Diener et al., 1999). In fact, people who are socially connected are also physically healthier and less likely to die a premature death (Cohen et al., 2000; House et al., 1988; Uchino et al., 1996; Uchino, 2006).

The Thrill of Affiliation

People are motivated to establish and maintain an optimum level of social contact.

"At this point, my privacy needs are interfering with my intimacy goals."

As social beings, humans are drawn to each other like magnets to metal. We work together, play together, live together, and often make lifetime commitments to grow old together. This social motivation begins with the **need for affiliation**, defined as a desire to establish social contact with others (McAdams, 1989). Individuals differ in the strength of their need for affiliation, but it seems that people are highly motivated to establish and maintain an *optimum* balance of social contact—sometimes craving the company of others, sometimes wanting to be alone—the way the body maintains a certain level of caloric intake. In an interesting study, Bibb Latané and Carol Werner (1978) found that laboratory rats were more likely to approach others of their species after a period of isolation and were less likely to approach others after prolonged contact. These researchers suggested that rats, like many other animals, have a built-in "sociostat" (social thermostat) to regulate their affiliative tendencies.

Is there evidence of a similar mechanism in humans? Shawn O'Connor and Lorne Rosenblood (1996) recruited college students to carry portable beepers for four days. Whenever the beepers went off (on average, every hour), the students wrote down whether at the time they were *actually* alone or in the company of other people and whether they *wanted* to be alone or with others. The results showed that students were in the state they desired two-thirds of the time—and that the situation they desired on one occasion predicted their actual situation the next time they were signaled. Whether it was solitude or social contact that the students sought, they successfully managed to regulate their own personal needs for affiliation.

need for affiliation The desire to establish and maintain many rewarding interpersonal relationships.

When Italy won the World Cup Soccer Championship in the summer of 2006, the people of Rome and other cities across the country spilled into the streets, piazzas, and fountains in order to be with one another for the occasion.

People may well differ in the strength of their affiliative needs, but there are times when we all want to be with other people. Recall the scenes in Chicago, St. Louis, Dallas, Pittsburgh, Miami, Los Angeles, and other recent championship sports cities, whenever the home team won the final championship game. From one city to the next, jubilant fans stayed long after the game had ended, milling about and exchanging high-fives, slaps on the back, and hugs and kisses. In each of these cities, it's clear that people wanted to celebrate together rather than alone.

Affiliating can satisfy us for other reasons as well, as others provide energy, attention, stimulation, information, and emotional support (Hill, 1987). One condition that strongly arouses our need for affiliation is stress. Have you ever noticed the way neighbors who never stop to say hello come together in snowstorms, hurricanes, power failures, and other major crises? Many years ago, Stanley Schachter (1959) theorized that external threat triggers fear and motivates us to affiliate, particularly with others who face a similar threat. In a laboratory experiment that demonstrated the point, Schachter found that people who were expecting to receive painful electric shocks chose to wait with other nervous participants rather than alone. So far, so good. But when Irving Sarnoff and Philip Zimbardo (1961) led college students to expect that they would be engaging in an embarrassing behavior—sucking on large nipples and pacifiers—their desire to be with others fell off. It seemed puzzling. Why do people in fearful misery love company, while those in embarrassed misery seek solitude?

Yacov Rofé (1984) proposed a simple answer: utility. Rofé argued that stress increases the desire to affiliate only when being with others is seen as useful in reducing the negative impact of the stressful situation. Schachter's participants had good reason to believe that affiliation would be useful. They would have the opportunity to compare their emotional reactions with those of others to determine whether they really needed to be fearful. For those in the Sarnoff and Zimbardo study, however, affiliation had little to offer. Facing embarrassment, being with others is more likely to increase the stress than reduce it.

Returning to Schachter's initial study, what specific benefit do people get from being in the presence of others in times of stress? Research suggests that people facing an imminent threat seek each other out in order to gain *cognitive clarity* about the danger they are in. In one study, James Kulik and Heike Mahler (1989) found that hospital patients waiting for open-heart surgery preferred to have as roommates other patients who were post-operative rather than pre-operative, presumably because they were in a position to provide information about the experience. Patients in a second study who had been assigned post-operative rather than pre-operative roommates became less anxious about the experience and were later quicker to recover from the surgery (Kulik et al., 1996).

Even within a laboratory setting, Kulik and others (1994) found that people anticipating the painful task of soaking a hand in ice-cold water (compared with those told that the task would not be painful) preferred to wait with someone who had already completed the task than with someone who had not. They also asked more questions of these experienced peers. Under stress, we adaptively become motivated to affiliate with others who can help us cope with an impending threat. Summarizing his own work, Schachter (1959) had noted that misery loves miserable company. Based on their more recent studies, Gump and Kulik (1997) further amended this assertion: "Misery loves the company of those in the same miserable situation" (p. 317).

People seek out the company of others, even strangers, in times of stress. **True.**

The Agony of Loneliness

People need other people—to celebrate with, share news with, commiserate with, talk to, and learn from. But some people are painfully shy, socially awkward, inhibited, and reluctant to approach others (Bruch et al., 1989). Shyness is a pervasive problem. Roughly 49 percent of all Americans describe themselves as shy, as do 31 percent in Israel, 40 percent in Germany, 55 percent in Taiwan, and 57 percent in Japan (Henderson & Zimbardo, 1998). People who are shy find it difficult to approach strangers, make small talk, telephone someone for a date, participate in small groups, or mingle at parties. What's worse, they often reject others, perhaps because they fear being rejected themselves. The sad result is a pattern of risk avoidance that sets them up for unpleasant and unrewarding interactions (Crozier, 2001).

Shyness can arise from different sources. In some cases, it may be an inborn personality trait. Jerome Kagan (1994) and others have found that some infants are highly sensitive to stimulation, inhibited, and cautious shortly after birth. In other cases, shyness develops as a learned reaction to failed interactions with others. Thus, interpersonal problems of the past can ignite social anxieties about the future (Leary & Kowalski, 1995). Not all infants grow up to become inhibited adults. But longitudinal research indicates that there is some continuity, that this aspect of our personalities may be predictable from our temperament and behavior as young children. Thus, toddlers observed to be inhibited, shy, and fearful at age three were more likely than toddlers who were more outgoing to be socially isolated and depressed at age twenty-one (Caspi, 2000).

Whatever the source, shyness is a real problem, and it has painful consequences. Studies show that shy people evaluate themselves negatively, expect to fail in their social encounters, and blame themselves when they do. As a result, many shy people go into self-imposed isolation, which makes them feel lonely (Cheek & Melchior, 1990; Jackson et al., 2002). In part, the problem stems from a paralyzing fear of rejection, which inhibits people from making friendly or romantic overtures to those they are interested in. If you ever wanted to approach someone you liked, only to stop yourself, you know that this situation often triggers an approach-avoidance conflict, pulling you between the desire for contact and a fear of being rejected. What's worse, research shows that people who fear rejection think that their friendly or romantic interest is transparent to others, which leads them to back off (Vorauer et al., 2003).

Loneliness is a sad and heart-wrenching emotional state. To be lonely is to feel deprived of social relations. Some researchers maintain that loneliness is triggered by a discrepancy between the level of social contact that a person has and the level he or she wants (Peplau & Perlman, 1982). Others find, more simply, that the less social contact people have, the lonelier they feel (Archibald et al., 1995). Unfortunately, people in some parts of the world are lonelier today than ever before. In *Bowling Alone,* Harvard Professor of Public Policy Robert Putnam (2001) argued that Americans are more disconnected from their families, neighbors, co-workers, and communities than in the past. Not too long ago, he wrote, thousands of people belonged to bowling leagues. Today they are more likely to bowl alone. Lamenting the adverse effects, Putnam (2006) preaches: "You gotta have friends."

Who is lonely, and when? Loneliness is most likely to occur during times of transition or disruption—as in the first year at college, after a romantic breakup, or when a loved one moves far away. Surveys show that people who are unattached are lonelier than those who have romantic partners, but that those who are widowed, divorced, and separated are lonelier than people who have never been married. Despite the stereotypic image of the lonely old man passing time on a park bench, the loneliest groups in American society are adolescents and young adults eighteen to thirty years old. In fact, loneliness seems to decline over the course of adulthood—at least until health problems in old age limit social activities (Peplau & Perlman, 1982).

How do people cope with this distressing state? When college students were asked what behavioral strategies they use to combat loneliness, 96 percent said they sometimes or often tried harder to be friendly to other people, 94 percent took their

loneliness A feeling of deprivation about existing social relations.

mind off the problem by reading or watching TV, and 93 percent tried extra hard to succeed at another aspect of life. Others said that they distracted themselves by running, shopping, washing the car, or staying busy at other activities. Still others sought new ways to meet people, tried to improve their appearance, or talked to a friend, relative, or therapist about the problem. Though fewer in number, some are so desperate that they use alcohol or drugs to wash away feelings of loneliness (Rook & Peplau, 1982). We will see in Chapter 14 that as people age, loneliness becomes a risk factor for a broad range of physical and mental health problems, including depression (Cacioppo et al., 2003, 2006).

The Initial Attraction

Affiliation is a necessary first step in the formation of a social relationship. But each of us is drawn to some people more than to others. If you've ever had a crush on someone, felt the tingly excitement of a first encounter, or enjoyed the first few moments of a new friendship, then you know the meaning of the term *attraction*. When you meet someone for the first time, what do *you* look for? Does familiarity breed fondness or contempt? Do birds of a feather flock together, or do opposites attract? Is beauty the object of your desire, or do you believe that outward appearances are deceiving? And what is it about a situation, or the circumstances of an initial meeting, that draws you in for more?

According to one classic perspective, people are attracted to others with whom they can have a relationship that is rewarding (Byrne & Clore, 1970; Lott & Lott, 1974). The rewards may be direct, as when people provide us with attention, support, money, status, information, and other valuable commodities. Or the rewards may be indirect, as when it feels good to be with someone who is beautiful, smart, or funny, or who happens to be in our presence when times are good. A second perspective on attraction has also emerged in recent years—that of evolutionary psychology, the subdiscipline that uses principles of evolution to understand human social behavior. According to this view, human beings all over the world exhibit patterns of attraction and mate selection that favor the conception, birth, and survival of their offspring. This approach has a great deal to say about differences in this regard between men and women (Buss, 2004; Schaller et al., 2006; Simpson & Kenrick, 1997).

Internet dating services enable strangers to meet online, using e-mails, pictures, and chatroom conversations. Interested in first encounters of this nature, researchers try to determine what factors draw people to each other. Here, aboard the Ocean Princess, *one hundred singles meet for the first time in Match.com's "world's largest floating blind date."*

Recognizing the role of rewards and the call of our evolutionary past provides broad perspectives for understanding human attraction. But there's more to the story. Much more. Over the years, social psychologists have identified many determinants of attraction and the development of intimate relationships (Berscheid & Regan, 2004; Fletcher, 2002; Miller et al., 2006). It's important to note that most of the research has focused on heterosexuals, so we often do not know how well specific findings apply to the homosexual population. At the same time, it is important to realize that many of the basic processes described in this chapter affect the development of all close relationships, regardless of whether the individuals involved are gay, lesbian, or straight (Herek, 2006; Kurdek, 2000; Peplau & Fingerhut, 2007).

Familiarity: Being There

It seems so obvious that people tend to overlook it: We are most likely to become attracted to someone whom we have seen and become familiar with. So let's begin with two basic and necessary factors in the attraction process: proximity and exposure.

The Proximity Effect   The single best predictor of whether two people will get together is physical proximity, or nearness. Sure, we interact at remote distances with the help of telephones, e-mail, online chatrooms, and message boards. These days it's common for people to find friends, lovers, and sexual partners from a distance. Yet some of the most important social interactions still occur among people who find themselves in the same place at the same time (Latané et al., 1995).

To begin with, where we live influences the friends we make. Many years ago, Leon Festinger and his colleagues (1950) studied friendship patterns in married-student college housing and found that people were more likely to become friends with residents of nearby apartments than with those who lived farther away. More recent research has also shown that college students—who live in off-campus apartments, dormitories, or fraternity and sorority houses—tend to date those who live either nearby (Hays, 1985) or in the same type of housing as they do (Whitbeck & Hoyt, 1994).

The Mere Exposure Effect   Proximity does not necessarily spark attraction, but to the extent that it increases frequency of contact, it's a good first step. Folk wisdom often suggests a dim view of familiarity, which is said to "breed contempt." But in a series of experiments, Robert Zajonc (1968) found that the more often people saw a novel stimulus—whether it was a foreign word, a geometric form, or a human face—the more they came to like it. This phenomenon, which Zajonc called the **mere exposure effect**, has since been observed in more than two hundred experiments (Bornstein, 1989).

People do not even have to be aware of their prior exposures for this effect to occur. In a typical study, participants are shown pictures of several stimuli, each for one to five milliseconds, which is too quick to register in awareness and too quick for anyone to realize that some stimuli are presented more often than others. After the presentation, participants are shown each of the stimuli and asked two questions: Do you like it, and have you ever seen it before? Perhaps you can predict the result. The more frequently the stimulus is presented, the more people like it. Yet when asked if they've ever seen the liked stimulus before, they say no. These results demonstrate that the mere exposure effect can influence us without our awareness (Kuntz-Wilson & Zajonc, 1980). In fact, the effect is stronger under these conditions (Bornstein & D'Agostino, 1992; Zajonc, 2001).

To appreciate the implications in a naturalistic situation, imagine yourself in a psychology class that is held in a large lecture hall. Three times a week, you trudge over to class, shake the cobwebs out of your head, and try your best to be alert. The room holds several hundred students. You come in and look down the tiered seats to the front where your instructor stands. During the semester, you're vaguely aware of another student who sits up front, but you never talk to her, and you probably would not recognize her if you saw her somewhere else. Then, at the end of the semester, you attend a special session where you are shown photographs of four women and asked some questions about them. Only then do you learn that you have participated in a study of the mere exposure effect.

Now view the same events from the perspective of Richard Moreland and Scott Beach (1992). These researchers selected four women who looked like typical students to be confederates in this study. One had a very easy job: She had her picture taken. But the other three also attended the class—five, ten, or fifteen times. Did the frequency of exposure spark attraction among the real students in this situation? Yes. In questionnaires they completed after viewing pictures of all four women, students rated each woman on various traits (such as popularity, honesty, intelligence, and physical attractiveness) and recorded their beliefs about how much they would like

mere exposure effect   The phenomenon whereby the more often people are exposed to a stimulus, the more positively they evaluate that stimulus.

her, enjoy spending time with her, and want to work with her on a mutual project. The results lined up like ducks in a row: The more classes a woman attended, the more attracted the students were to her.

Familiarity can even influence our self-evaluations. Imagine that you had a portrait photograph of yourself developed into two pictures: one that depicted your actual appearance and the other a mirror-image copy. Which image would you prefer? Which would a friend prefer? Theodore Mita and others (1977) tried this interesting experiment with female college students and found that most preferred their own mirror images, while their friends liked the actual photos. In both cases, the preference was for the view of the face that was most familiar.

Physical Attractiveness: Getting Drawn In

"Beauty is a greater recommendation than any letter of introduction."

—Aristotle

What do you look for in a friend or romantic partner: intelligence? kindness? a sense of humor? How important, really, is a person's looks? As children, we were told that "beauty is only skin deep" and that we should not "judge a book by its cover." Yet as adults, we react more favorably to others who are physically attractive than to those who are not. Over the years, studies have shown that in the affairs of our social world, beauty is a force to be reckoned with (Armstrong, 2004; Langlois et al., 2000; Patzer, 2006).

The bias for beauty is pervasive. In one study, fifth-grade teachers were given background information about a boy or girl, accompanied by a photograph. All teachers received identical information, yet those who saw an attractive child saw that child as being smarter and more likely to do well in school (Clifford & Walster, 1973). In a second study, male and female experimenters approached students on a college campus and tried to get them to sign a petition. The more attractive the experimenters were, the more signatures they were able to get (Chaiken, 1979). In a third study, Texas judges set lower bail and imposed smaller fines on suspects who were rated as attractive rather than unattractive on the basis of photographs (Downs & Lyons, 1991). In a fourth study conducted in the United States and Canada, economists discovered that within numerous occupational groups, physically attractive men and women earn more money than others who are comparable except for being less attractive (Hamermesh & Biddle, 1994). There is no doubt about it: Across a range of settings, people fare better if they are attractive than if they are not (Hosoda et al., 2003).

It all seems so shallow, so superficial. But before we go on to accept the notion that people prefer others who are physically attractive, let's stop for a moment and consider a fundamental question: What constitutes physical beauty? Is it an objective and measurable human characteristic like height, weight, or hair color? Or is beauty a subjective quality, existing in the eye of the beholder? There are advocates on both sides.

What Is Beauty? No one would argue that there is a "gold standard" for beauty. However, some researchers do believe that certain faces are inherently more attractive than others. There are three sources of evidence for this proposition.

First, when people are asked to rate faces on a 10-point scale, there is typically a high level of agreement among children and adults, men and women, and people from the same or different cultures (Langlois et al., 2000). For example, Michael Cunningham and others (1995) asked Asian and Latino students, along with black and white American students, to rate the appearance of women from all these groups. Overall, some faces were rated more attractive than others, leading these investigators to argue that people everywhere share an image of what is beautiful.

People also tend to agree about what constitutes an attractive body. For example, men tend to be drawn to the "hourglass" figure seen in women of average weight whose waists are a third narrower than their hips, a shape that is thought to be associated with reproductive fertility. In contrast, women like men with a waist-to-hip ratio that forms a tapering V-shaped physique, signaling more muscle than fat (Singh, 1993, 1995). If marriage statistics are any indication, women also seem to have a

Perceptions of facial beauty are largely consistent across cultures. Those regarded as good-looking in one culture also tend to be judged as attractive by people from other cultures. From left to right, the individuals pictured here are from Venezuela, Kenya, Japan, and the United States (the American was the actress Marilyn Monroe).

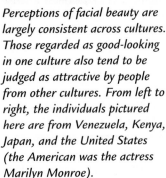

Infants do not discriminate between faces considered attractive and unattractive in their culture. **False.**

preference for height. Comparisons made in Europe indicate that married men are a full inch taller, on average, than unmarried men (Pawlowski et al., 2000).

Second, a number of researchers have identified physical features of the human face that are reliably associated with ratings of attractiveness, such as smooth skin, a pleasant expression, and youthfulness (Rhodes, 2006). Particularly intriguing are studies showing that people like faces in which the eyes, nose, lips, and other features are not too different from the average. Judith Langlois and Lori Roggman (1990) showed college students both actual yearbook photos and computerized facial composites that "averaged" features from four, eight, sixteen, or thirty-two of the photos. Time and again, they found that the students preferred the averaged composites to the individual faces—and that the more faces used to form the composite, the more highly it was rated. Other studies have since confirmed this result (Langlois et al., 1994; Rhodes et al., 1999).

It seems odd that "averaged" faces are judged attractive when, after all, the faces we find the most beautiful are anything but average. What accounts for these findings? Langlois and others (1994) believe that people like averaged faces because they are more prototypically face-like and have features that are less distinctive, and so they seem more familiar to us. Consistent with this notion, research shows that just as people are more attracted to averaged faces than to individual faces, they also prefer averaged dogs, birds, fish, wristwatches, and cars (Halberstadt & Rhodes, 2000, 2003).

Computerized averaging studies also show that people are drawn to faces that are symmetrical, in which the paired features of the right and left sides line up and mirror each other (Grammer & Thornhill, 1994; Mealey et al., 1999). Why do people prefer symmetrical faces? Although the research support is mixed, evolutionary psychologists have speculated that our pursuit of symmetry is adaptive because symmetry is naturally associated with biological health, fitness, and fertility, qualities that are highly desirable in a mate (Rhodes et al., 2001; Shackelford & Larsen, 1999; Thornhill & Gangestad, 1993). Perhaps for that reason, people throughout the world try to enhance their appeal by wearing or painting symmetrical designs on their faces and bodies—designs that others find attractive (Cárdenas & Harris, 2006).

A third source of evidence for the view that beauty is an objective quality is that babies who are far too young to have learned the culture's standards of beauty exhibit a nonverbal preference for faces considered attractive by adults. Picture the scene in an infant laboratory: A baby, lying on its back in a crib, is shown a series of faces previously rated by college students. The first face appears and a clock starts ticking as the baby looks at it. As soon as the baby looks away, the clock stops and the next face is presented. The result: young infants spend more time tracking and looking at attractive faces than at unattractive ones, regardless of whether the faces are young or old, male or female, or black or white (Game et al., 2003; Langlois et al., 1991). "These kids don't read *Vogue* or watch TV," notes Langlois, "yet they make the same judgments as adults" (Cowley, 1996, p. 66).

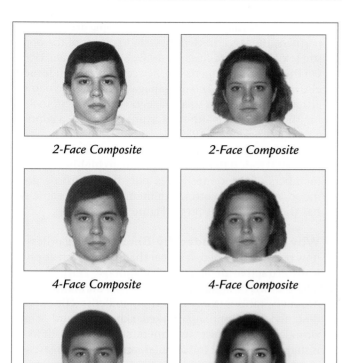

2-Face Composite   *2-Face Composite*

4-Face Composite   *4-Face Composite*

32-Face Composite   *32-Face Composite*

Computer-generated images that average the features of different faces are seen as more attractive than the individual faces on which they were based. In fact, up to a point, the more faces represented in a composite, the more attractive it is. Shown here are sets of male and female composites that combine 2, 4, and 32 faces. Which do you prefer? (Langlois & Roggman, 1990.)

"There is no known culture in which people do not paint, pierce, tattoo, reshape or simply adorn their bodies."

—Enid Schildkrout, anthropologist

In contrast to this objective perspective, other researchers argue that physical attractiveness is subjective, and they point for evidence to the influences of culture, time, and the circumstances of our perception. When Johannes Hönekopp (2006) had large numbers of people rate the same faces, he found that although some faces were seen as more attractive than others, individuals differed a great deal in their private preferences. To some extent, beauty really is in the eye of the beholder.

One source of evidence for our variability in taste, first noted by Charles Darwin (1872), is that people from different cultures enhance their beauty in very different ways through face painting, makeup, plastic surgery, scarring, tattoos, hairstyling, the molding of bones, the filing of teeth, braces, and the piercing of ears and other body parts—all contributing to the "enigma of beauty" (Newman, 2000). In dramatic ways, what people find attractive in one part of the world may be seen as repulsive in another part of the world (Landau, 1989).

Ideals also vary when it comes to bodies. Looking at preferences for female body size in fifty-four cultures, Judith Anderson and others (1992) found that heavy women are judged more attractive than slender women in places where food is frequently in short supply. In one study, for example, Douglas Yu and Glenn Shepard (1998) found that Matsigenka men living in the Andes Mountains of southeastern Peru see female forms with "tubular" shapes—as opposed to hourglass shapes—as healthier, more attractive, and more desirable in a mate.

Differences in preference have also been found among racial groups within a given culture. Michelle Hebl and Todd Heatherton (1998) asked black and white female college students from the United States to rate thin, average, and overweight women from a set of magazine photographs. The result: The white students saw the heavy women as the least attractive, but the black students did not similarly discriminate. A follow-up study showed the same difference in perceptions of black and white men (Hebl & Turchin, 2005). Why the difference? Based on the fact that white Americans are, on average, thinner than black Americans, one possible explanation is that they simply prefer a body type that is more typical of their group. Another possibility is that white Americans identify more with the "mainstream" weight-obsessed culture as portrayed in TV shows, magazine ads, and other media.

Standards of beauty also change over time, from one generation to the next. Brett Silverstein and others (1986) examined the measurements of female models appearing in women's magazines from the years 1901 to 1981, and they found that "curvaceousness" (as measured by the bust-to-waist ratio) varied over time, with a boyish, slender look becoming particularly desirable in recent years. More recently, researchers took body measurements from all *Playboy* centerfolds, beginning with the first issue, in 1953, which featured Marilyn Monroe, through the last issue of 2001, with Eva Herzigova. The result: Over time, models became thinner and had lower bust-to-waist ratios—away from the ample "hourglass" to a more slender, athletic, stick-like shape (Voracek & Fisher, 2002).

Still other evidence for the subjective nature of beauty comes from many research laboratories. Time and again, social psychologists have found that our perceptions of someone's beauty can be inflated or deflated by various circumstances. Research shows, for example, that people often see others as more physically attractive if they have non-physical qualities that make them likable (Kniffin & Wilson, 2004). This connection is illustrated in the student evaluations posted on www.ratemyprofessor.com, a popular Web site. An analysis of ratings revealed that both male and female professors who were rated highly for their teaching were also more likely to be described as "hot" (Riniolo et al., 2006). Particularly interesting in

How Does It Feel to See a Perfect 10?

When people viewed facial photos of same-sex individuals, those who saw highly attractive people felt worse than those who saw average people. However, when viewing photos of opposite-sex individuals, those who saw highly attractive people felt better.

(Data from Kenrick et al., 1993.)

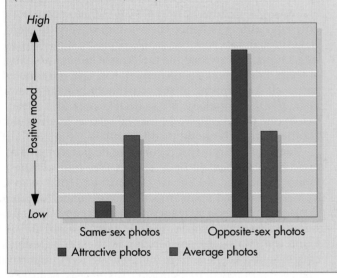

"Love looks not with the eyes, but with the mind; And therefore is wing'd Cupid painted blind."

—William Shakespeare,
A Midsummer Night's Dream

"Cyberdating works because the courting process is reversed; people get to know each other from the inside out."

—Trish McDermott, Match.com

what-is-beautiful-is-good stereotype The belief that physically attractive individuals also possess desirable personality characteristics.

this regard is that the more in love people are with their partners, the less attracted they are to others of the opposite sex (Johnson & Rusbult, 1989; Simpson et al., 1990). On the other hand, men who viewed ravishing nude models in *Playboy* and *Penthouse* magazines later gave lower attractiveness ratings to average-looking women, including their own wives—the unfortunate result of a contrast effect (Kenrick et al., 1989). Even our self-evaluations are malleable in this regard. Hence, Douglas Kenrick and others (1993) found that while exposure to highly attractive members of the opposite sex puts people into a good mood, exposure to attractive members of the same sex has the opposite effect (see Figure 9.1).

Why Are We Blinded by Beauty?   Regardless of how beauty is defined, it's clear that people seen as physically attractive are at a social advantage. Perhaps that's why billions of dollars a year are spent on makeup, hair products, tattoos, body piercings, and cosmetic surgery designed to plump up sunken skin, peel and scrape wrinkles from the face, vacuum out fat deposits, lift faces, reshape noses, tuck in tummies, and enlarge breasts.

What creates the bias for beauty, and why are we drawn like magnets to people who are physically attractive? One possibility is that it is inherently rewarding to be in the company of people who are aesthetically appealing—that we derive pleasure from beautiful men and women the same way that we enjoy a breathtaking landscape or a magnificent work of art. In an fMRI study of men, for example, researchers found that areas of the brain known to respond to rewards such as food, money, and drugs like cocaine are also activated by facial beauty (Aharon et al., 2001). Or perhaps the rewards are more extrinsic. Perhaps, for example, we expect the glitter of another's beauty to rub off on us. When average-looking men and women are seen alongside someone else of the same sex, they are rated as more attractive when the other person is good-looking and as less attractive when he or she is plain-looking (Geiselman et al., 1984).

A second possible reason for the bias for beauty is that people tend to associate physical attractiveness with other desirable qualities, an assumption known as the **what-is-beautiful-is-good stereotype** (Dion et al., 1972). Think about children's fairy tales, where Snow White and Cinderella are portrayed as beautiful *and* kind, while the witch and stepsisters are said to be both ugly *and* cruel. This link between beauty and goodness can even be seen in Hollywood movies. Stephen Smith and others (1999) asked people to watch and rate the main characters who appeared in the one hundred top-grossing movies between 1940 and 1990. They found that the more attractive the characters were, the more frequently they were portrayed as virtuous, romantically active, and successful. In a second study, these investigators showed college students a film that depicted either a strong or a weak link between the beauty and goodness of the characters. Then, in a supposedly unrelated experiment, these students were asked to evaluate two graduate school applicants whose credentials were equivalent but whose photographs differed in terms of physical attractiveness. The result was both interesting and disturbing: Students who had watched a film depicting the beautiful-is-good stereotype were more likely than those who had watched a nonstereotypic film to favor the physically attractive applicant in their evaluations (see Figure 9.2). It appears that the entertainment industry unwittingly helps to foster and perpetuate our tendency to judge people by their physical appearance.

Studies have shown that good-looking people are judged to be smart, successful, happy, well-adjusted, socially skilled, confident, and assertive—though also vain (Eagly et al., 1991). So, is this physical attractiveness stereotype accurate? Only to a limited extent. Research shows that good-looking people do have more friends, better

FIGURE 9.2

Media Influences on the Bias for Beauty

In this study, participants evaluated graduate school applicants who differed in their physical attractiveness. Indicating the power of the media to influence us, those who had first watched a stereotypic film in which beauty was associated with goodness were more likely to favor the attractive applicant than those who had first seen a nonstereotypic film.

(Smith et al., 1999.)

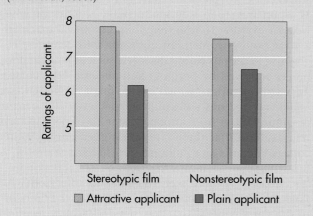

This painting depicts a Greek myth in which Pygmalion, the king of Cyprus, sculpted his ideal woman in an ivory statue he called Galatea. Illustrating the power of a self-fulfilling prophecy, Pygmalion fell in love with his creation, caressed it, adorned it with jewelry, and eventually brought it to life.

social skills, and a more active sex life—and they are more successful at attracting a mate (Rhodes et al., 2005). Yet beauty is *not* related to objective measures of intelligence, personality, adjustment, or self-esteem. In these domains, our popular perceptions appear to exaggerate the reality (Feingold, 1992b). It also seems that the specific nature of the stereotype depends on cultural conceptions of what is "good." When Ladd Wheeler and Youngmee Kim (1997) asked people in Korea to rate photos of various men and women, they found that people seen as physically attractive were also assumed to have "integrity" and "a concern for others"—traits that are highly valued in this collectivist culture. In contrast to what is considered desirable in more individualistic cultures, attractive people in Korea were not assumed to be dominant or assertive. What is beautiful is good; but what is good is, in part, culturally defined.

If the physical attractiveness stereotype is true only in part, why does it endure? One possibility is that each of us creates support for the bias via the type of *self-fulfilling prophecy* model described in Chapter 4. In a classic study of interpersonal attraction, Mark Snyder and others (1977) brought together unacquainted pairs of male and female college students. All the students were given biographical sketches of their partners. Each man also received a photograph of a physically attractive or unattractive woman, supposedly his partner. At that point, the students rated each other on several dimensions and had a phone-like conversation over headphones. The results were provocative. Men who thought they were interacting with a woman who was attractive (1) formed more positive impressions of her personality and (2) were friendlier in their conversational behavior. And now for the clincher: (3) the female students whose partners had seen the attractive picture were later rated by listeners to the conversation as warmer, more confident, and more animated. Fulfilling the prophecies of their own expectations, men who expected an attractive partner actually created one. These findings call to mind the Greek myth of Pygmalion, who fell in love with a statue he had carved and brought it to life.

The Benefits and Costs of Beauty   No doubt about it, good-looking people have a significant edge. As a result, they are more popular, more sexually experienced, more socially skilled, and more likely to attract a mate. In light of these advantages, it's interesting that physical attractiveness is not a sure ticket to health, happiness, or high self-esteem (Diener et al., 1995; Feingold, 1992b; Langlois et al., 2000). The life of Marilyn Monroe is a case in point. Monroe was considered one of the most ravishing women of her time and one of the hottest actresses in Hollywood. Yet she was terribly vulnerable and insecure. Why?

One problem is that highly attractive people can't always tell if the attention and praise they receive from others are due to their talent or just their good looks. A study by Brenda Major and others (1984) illustrates the point. Male and female participants who saw themselves as attractive or unattractive wrote essays that were later positively evaluated by an unknown member of the opposite sex. Half the participants were told that their evaluator would be watching them through a one-way mirror as they wrote the essay; the other half were led to believe that they could not be seen. In actuality, there was no evaluator, and all participants received identical, very positive evaluations of their work. Participants were then asked why their essay had been so favorably reviewed. The result: Those who saw themselves as unattractive felt better about the quality of their work after getting a glowing evaluation from someone who had seen them. Yet those who saw themselves as attractive and thought they had been seen attributed the glowing feedback to their looks, not to the quality of their

FIGURE 9.3

When Being Seen Leads to Disbelief

People who believed they were physically unattractive were more likely to cite the quality of their work as the reason for receiving a positive evaluation when they thought they were seen by the evaluator. However, people who believed they were attractive were less likely to credit the quality of their work when they thought they were seen.

(Major et al., 1984.)

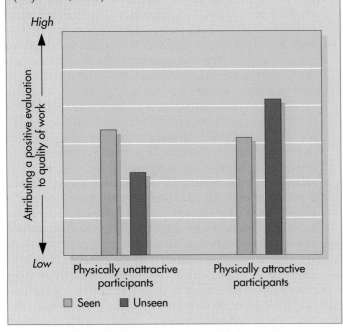

People who are physically attractive are happier and have higher self-esteem than those who are unattractive.
False.

work. For people who are highly attractive, positive feedback is sometimes hard to interpret (see Figure 9.3). This distrust may be well founded. In one study, many men and women openly admitted that if a prospective date was highly attractive, they would lie to present themselves well (Rowatt et al., 1999).

Another cost of having physical attractiveness as a social asset is the pressure to maintain one's appearance. In today's American society, such pressure is particularly strong when it comes to the body. This focus on the human form can produce a healthy emphasis on nutrition and exercise. But it can also have unhealthy consequences, as when men pop steroids to build muscles or when women overdiet to lose weight and inches. Particularly among young women, an obsession with thinness can give rise to serious eating disorders such as *bulimia* (food binges followed by purging) and *anorexia nervosa* (self-imposed starvation, which can be fatal). Although estimates vary, recent studies indicate that less than 1 percent of women suffer from anorexia, that 2 to 3 percent have bulimia, and that these rates are higher among female college students than among nonstudents (Fairburn & Brownell, 2002; Thompson, 2003).

Women are more likely than men to suffer from what Janet Polivy and others (1986) once called the "modern mania for slenderness." This slender ideal is regularly projected in the mass media. Studies have shown that young women who see magazine ads or TV commercials that feature ultra-thin models become more dissatisfied with their own bodies than those who view neutral materials (Posavac et al., 1998). Trying to measure up to the multi-million-dollar supermodels can only prove frustrating to most. What's worse, the cultural ideal for thinness may be set early in childhood. Several years ago, Kevin Norton and his colleagues (1996) projected the life-size dimensions of the original Ken and Barbie dolls that are popular all over the world. They found that both were unnaturally thin compared with the average young adult. In fact, the estimated odds that any young woman would have Barbie's shape are approximately 1 in 100,000.

In sum, being beautiful may be a mixed blessing. There are some real benefits that cannot be denied, but there may be some costs as well. This tradeoff makes you wonder about the long-term effects. Some years ago, Ellen Berscheid and others (1972) compared the physical attractiveness levels of college students (based on yearbook pictures) to their adjustment when they reached middle age. There was little relationship between their appearance in youth and their later happiness. Those who were especially good-looking in college were more likely to be married, but they were not more satisfied with marriage or more content with life. Beauty may confer advantage, but it is not destiny.

First Encounters: Getting Acquainted

Proximity increases the odds that we will meet someone, familiarity puts us at ease, and beauty draws us in like magnets to a first encounter. But what determines whether sparks will fly in the early getting-acquainted stages of a relationship? In this section, we consider three characteristics of others that can influence our attraction: similarity, liking, and being hard to get.

Liking Others Who Are Similar The problem with proverbial wisdom is that it often contradicts itself. Common sense tells us that "birds of a feather flock together." Yet we also hear that "opposites attract." So which is it? Before answering this question, imagine sitting at a computer, meeting someone in an online chatroom, and striking up a conversation about school, sports, restaurants, movies, where you live, where you've traveled, or your favorite band—only to realize that the two of you have a lot in common. Now imagine the opposite experience of chatting with someone who is very different in his or her background, interests, values, and outlook on life. Which of the two strangers would you want to meet, the one who is similar or the one who is different?

Over the years, research has consistently shown that people tend to associate with others who are similar to themselves. The vast array of Internet dating sites illustrate the point. In addition to generic services such as Match.com, eHarmony, and HookUp.Com, there are several specialty services designed to bring together people of like minds—hence, ConservativeMatch.com, LiberalHearts.com, Jdate.com, Christian Cafe.com, and HappyBuddhist.com.

There are four types of similarity that are most relevant. The first is demographic. On a whole range of demographic variables—such as age, education, race, religion, height, level of intelligence, and socioeconomic status—people who go together as friends, dates, lovers, or partners in marriage tend to resemble each other more than randomly paired couples (Warren, 1966). These correlations cannot be used to prove that similarity causes attraction. A more compelling case could be made, however, by first measuring people's demographic characteristics and then determining whether these people, when they met others, liked those who were similar to them more than those who were dissimilar. This is what Theodore Newcomb (1961) did. In an elaborate study, Newcomb set up an experimental college dormitory and found that students who were similar in their backgrounds grew to like each other more than did those who were dissimilar. Is demographic similarity still a factor even today, with all the choices we have in our diverse and multicultural society? Yes. Commenting on the persistently magnetic appeal of similarity, sociologist John Macionis (2003) notes that "Cupid's arrow is aimed by society more than we like to think." One unfortunate result, as we saw in Chapter 5, is that by associating only with similar others, people form social niches that are homogeneous and divided along the lines of race, ethnic background, age, religion, level of education, and occupation (McPherson et al., 2001).

People can also be similar in other ways, as when they share the same opinions, interests, and values. For example, what about the role of *attitude* similarity in attraction? Here, the time course is slower, because people have to get to know each other first. In Newcomb's study, the link between actual similarity and liking increased gradually over the school year. Laboratory experiments have confirmed the point. For example, Donn Byrne (1971) had people give their opinions on a whole range of issues and then presented them with an attitude survey supposedly filled out by another person (the responses were rigged). In study after study, he found that participants liked this other person better when they perceived his or her attitudes as being more similar to theirs (Byrne, 1997).

The link between attitudes and attraction is evident among newly married couples. In a comprehensive study, Shanhong Luo and Eva Klohnen (2005) tested 291 newlywed couples and found that people tended to marry others who shared their political attitudes, religiosity, and values but who did not necessarily have similar personalities (for example, both being introverted or extroverted). Yet once in the relationship, similarities in personality became relevant: The more similar they were, the happier was the marriage. Clearly, birds of a feather both flock together and stay together. But wait. Does this necessarily mean that similarity breeds attraction, or might attraction breed similarity? In all likelihood, both mechanisms are at work. Luo and Klohnen compared couples who had been together for varying lengths of time before marriage and found

"I can't wait to see what you're like online."

FIGURE 9.4

A Two-Stage Model of the Attraction Process

Proposed by Byrne and his colleagues (1986), the two-stage model of attraction holds that first we avoid dissimilar others; then we approach similar others.

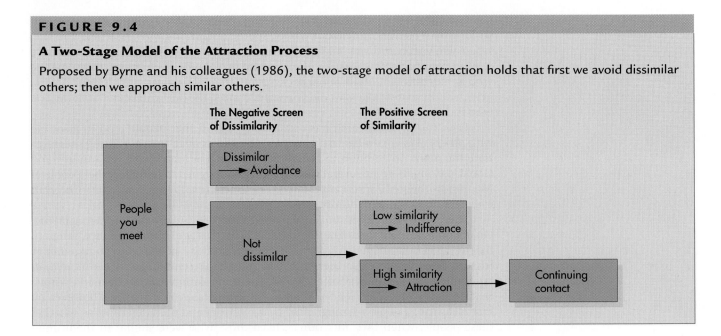

that similarity was unrelated to the length of the relationship. Yet another study of dating couples showed that when partners who are close discover that they disagree on important moral issues, they bring their views on these issues into alignment and become more similar from that point on (Davis & Rusbult, 2001).

According to Milton Rosenbaum (1986), attraction researchers have overplayed the role of attitudinal similarity. Similarity does not spark attraction, he says; rather, *dis*similarity triggers repulsion: the desire to avoid someone. Rosenbaum maintains that people expect most others to be similar, which is why others who are different grab our attention. Taking this hypothesis one step further, David Lykken and Auke Tellegen (1993) argue that in mate selection, *all* forms of interpersonal similarity are irrelevant. After a person discards the 50 percent of the population who are least similar, they claim, a random selection process takes over.

So which is it: Are we turned on by others who are similar in their attitudes, or are we turned off by those who are different? As depicted in Figure 9.4, Donn Byrne and his colleagues proposed a two-step model that takes both reactions into account. First, they claim, we avoid associating with others who are dissimilar; then, among those who remain, we are drawn to those who are most similar (Byrne et al., 1986; Smeaton et al., 1989). Our reactions may also be influenced by expectations. People expect similarity from ingroup members, like fellow Democrats or Republicans, or fellow straights or gays. In a series of studies, Fang Chen and Douglas Kenrick (2002) found that research participants were particularly attracted to outgroup members who expressed similar attitudes, and they were most repulsed by ingroup members who expressed dissimilar attitudes.

In addition to demographics and attitudes, there is a third source of similarity and difference also at work, at least in romantic relationships. Have you ever noticed the way people react to couples in which one partner is gorgeous and the other plain? Typically, we are startled by "mismatches" of this sort, as if expecting people to pair off with others who are similarly attractive—not more, not less. This reaction has a basis in reality. Early on, laboratory studies showed that both men and women yearn for partners who are highly attractive. Thus, when incoming first-year students at the University of Minnesota were randomly coupled for a dance, their desire for a second date was influenced more by their partner's physical attractiveness than by any other variable (Walster et al., 1966). In real-life situations, however, where one can be accepted or rejected by a prospective partner, people shy away from romantic encounters with others who are "out of their league" (Berscheid et al., 1971). Correlational studies of couples who are dating, engaged, living together, or married thus support a **"matching hypothesis"**: the idea that people tend to

matching hypothesis The proposition that people are attracted to others who are similar in physical attractiveness.

become involved romantically with others who are equivalent in their physical attractiveness (Feingold, 1988).

There is a fourth type of similarity that can trigger attraction among strangers: a similarity in subjective experience. Imagine that a professor says something in class that strikes you as funny. You glance at the student next to you, who glances back, and the two of you burst out laughing, as if bonded by a private joke. Whenever two people who are at a common event laugh, cry, jump to their feet, cheer, shake their heads, or roll their eyes at the same time, they feel as if they have shared a subjective experience. Elizabeth Pinel and others (2006) called this experience "I-sharing" and theorized that people who I-share, even if they are otherwise dissimilar would feel a profound sense of connection to one another—like "kindred spirits." In a series of experiments, participants were asked to imagine themselves with a similar or dissimilar stranger with whom they did or did not react in the same way to an external event. Consistently, the participants liked the I-sharers more than everyone else, even when they had different backgrounds. The implications are intriguing. As Pinel and her colleagues (2006) put it, "A fundamentalist Christian and an atheist can find themselves enjoying the same sunset; a staunch Republican and an equally staunch Democrat can share a laugh. When two objectively different people I-share in these and other ways, their disliking for one another might lessen, if only for a moment" (p. 245).

Before concluding that similarity is the key to attraction, though, what about the common-sense notion that opposites attract? Many years ago, sociologists proposed the *complementarity* hypothesis, which holds that people seek others whose needs "oppose" their own—that people who need to dominate, for example, are drawn to those who are submissive (Winch et al., 1954). Is there any support for this view? Surprisingly, the answer is no. Of course, most human beings are romantically attracted to others of the opposite sex. But when it comes to fitting mutual needs and personality traits the way keys fit locks, research shows that complementarity does not influence attraction (Luo & Klohnen, 2005; O'Leary & Smith, 1991).

Liking Others Who Like Us   Many years ago, Fritz Heider (1958) theorized that people prefer relationships that are psychologically "balanced" and that a state of imbalance causes distress. In groups of three or more individuals, a balanced social constellation exists when we like someone whose relationships with others parallel our own. Thus, we want to like the friends of our friends and the enemies of our enemies (Aronson & Cope, 1968). If you've ever had a good friend who dated someone you detested, then you know just how awkward and unpleasant an *un*balanced relationship can be. The fact is, we don't expect our friends and enemies to get along (Chapdelaine et al., 1994).

Between two people, a state of balance exists when the relationship is characterized by **reciprocity**: a mutual exchange between what we give and what we receive. Liking is mutual, which is why we tend to like others who indicate that they like us. In one experiment, Rebecca Curtis and Kim Miller (1986) brought pairs of students into the laboratory, arranged for them to talk, and then "revealed" to one member in each pair that he or she was liked by the partner or disliked. When the students were later reunited for conversation, those who thought that they were liked were, in turn, warmer, more agreeable, and more self-disclosing. Feeling liked is important. When groups of men and women were asked to reflect on how they fell in love or developed friendships with specific people, many spontaneously said they had been turned on initially by the realization that they were liked (Aron et al., 1989).

But wait. Does reciprocity mean, simply, that the more people like us, the more we will like them back? Many years ago, Elliot Aronson and Darwyn Linder (1965) conducted an interesting study in which female college students met in pairs several times to discuss various topics. In each pair, one student was a research participant, and her partner was a confederate. After each meeting, the participant overheard a follow-up conversation between the experimenter and the confederate in which she was discussed and evaluated. Over time, the confederate's evaluation of the participant either was consistently positive or negative or underwent a change, either from negative to positive (gain) or from positive to negative (loss). Put yourself in the participant's shoes. All else being equal, in which condition would you like your

When it comes to romantic relationships, opposites attract. **False.**

reciprocity   A mutual exchange between what we give and receive (for example, liking those who like us).

Consistent with reactance theory, studies conducted in bars like this have shown that men and women who are not in committed relationships see each other as more attractive as the night wears on.

"Love ceases to be a pleasure when it ceases to be a secret."

—Aphra Behn

hard-to-get effect The tendency to prefer people who are highly selective in their social choices over those who are more readily available.

partner most? In this study, participants liked the partner more when her evaluation changed from negative to positive than when it was positive all along. As long as the "conversion" is gradual and believable, people like others more when their affection takes time to earn than when it comes easily.

Pursuing Those Who Are Hard to Get The Aronson and Linder (1965) finding suggests that we like others who are socially selective. This seems to support the popular notion that you can spark romantic interest by playing hard to get. A few years ago, Ellen Fein and Sherri Schneider (1996) wrote a paperback book for women seductively titled *The Rules: Time-Tested Secrets for Capturing the Heart of Mr. Right*. What were the rules? Here's one: "Don't call him and rarely return his calls." Here's another: "Let him take the lead." In all cases, the theme was that men are charmed by women who are hard to get. It's an interesting hypothesis. Yet researchers have found that the **hard-to-get effect** is harder to get than originally anticipated (Walster et al., 1973). One problem is that we tend to prefer people who are moderately selective compared with those who are nonselective (they have poor taste, or low standards) or too selective (they are snobs). Another problem is that we are turned *off* by those who reject us because they are committed to someone else or have no interest in us (Wright & Contrada, 1986).

But now suppose that someone you are interested in is hard to get for external reasons. What if a desired relationship is opposed or forbidden by parents, as in the story of Romeo and Juliet? What about a relationship threatened by catastrophe, as in the love story portrayed in the movie *Titanic*? What about distance, a lack of time, or renewed interest from a partner's old flame? As you may recall from Chapter 6, the theory of psychological reactance states that people are highly motivated to protect their freedom to choose and behave as they please. When a valued freedom is threatened, people reassert themselves, often by over-wanting the endangered behavior—like the proverbial forbidden fruit (Brehm & Brehm, 1981).

Consider what happens when you think that your chance to get a date for the evening is slipping away. Is it true, to quote country-and-western musician Mickey Gilley, that "the girls all get prettier at closing time"? To find out, researchers entered some bars in Texas and asked patrons three times during the night to rate the physical attractiveness of other patrons of the same and opposite sex. As Gilley's lyrics suggested, people of the opposite sex were seen as more attractive as the night wore on (Pennebaker et al., 1979). The study is cute, but the correlation between time and attraction can be interpreted in other ways (perhaps attractiveness ratings rise with blood-alcohol levels!). More recently, however, Scott Madey and his colleagues (1996) also had patrons in a bar make attractiveness ratings throughout the night. They found that these ratings increased as the night wore on only among patrons who were not committed to a relationship. As reactance theory would predict, closing time posed a threat—which sparked desire—only to those on the lookout for a late-night date.

Another possible instance of passion fueled by reactance can be seen in "the allure of secret relationships." In a clever experiment, Daniel Wegner and others (1994) paired up male and female college students to play bridge. Within each foursome, one couple was instructed in writing to play footsie under the table, either secretly or in the open. Got the picture? After a few minutes, the game was stopped, and the players were asked to indicate privately how attracted they were to their own partner and to the opposite-sex member of the other team. The result: Students who played footsie in secret were more attracted to each other than those who played in the open or not at all. This finding is certainly consistent with reactance theory. But there may be more to it. As we'll see later, the thrill of engaging in a forbidden act, or the sheer excitement of having to keep a secret, may help fan the flames of attraction.

"Gee, but I miss the heightened eroticism of those five and a half years of conjugal visits."

Finally, it's important to realize that sometimes reactance reduces interpersonal attraction. Have you ever tried to play the matchmaker by insisting that two of your unattached single friends get together? Be forewarned: Setting people up can backfire. Determined to preserve the freedom to make their own romantic choices, your friends may become *less* attracted to each other than they would have been without your encouragement (Wright et al., 1992).

Mate Selection: The Evolution of Desire

Before moving on to the topic of close relationships, let's stop and consider this question: When it comes to the search for a short-term or long-term mate, are men and women similarly motivated? If not, what are the differences? Later in this chapter, we'll see that most men appear more sex-driven than most women—desiring more frequent and more casual sex, more partners, and more variety, all of which leads researchers in the area to conclude that "men desire sex more than women" (Baumeister et al., 2001, p. 270).

The Evolutionary Perspective   Why do these differences exist, and what do they mean? In *The Evolution of Desire*, David Buss (2003) argues that the answer can be derived from evolutionary psychology. According to this perspective, human beings all over the world exhibit mate-selection patterns that favor the conception, birth, and survival of their offspring—and women and men, by necessity, employ different strategies to achieve that common goal (Buss & Schmitt, 1993; Gangestad & Simpson, 2000; Trivers, 1972).

According to Buss, women must be highly selective because they are biologically limited in the number of children they can bear and raise in a lifetime. A woman must, therefore, protect those she has and so searches for a mate who possesses (or has the potential to possess) economic resources and is willing to commit those resources to support her offspring. The result is that women should be attracted to men who are older and financially secure or who have ambition, intelligence, stability, and other traits predictive of future success.

In contrast, men can father an unlimited number of children and ensure their reproductive success by inseminating many women. Men are restricted, however, by their ability to attract fertile partners and by their lack of certainty as to whether the babies born are actually their own. With these motives springing from their evolutionary past, men seek out women who are young and physically attractive (having smooth skin, full lips, lustrous hair, good muscle tone, and other youthful features)—attributes that signal health and reproductive fertility. To minimize their paternal uncertainty, men should also favor chastity, pursuing women they think will be sexually faithful rather than promiscuous.

To test this theory, Buss (1989) and a team of researchers surveyed 10,047 men and women in thirty-seven cultures in North and South America, Asia, Africa, Eastern and Western Europe, and the Pacific. All respondents were asked to rank-order and rate the importance of various attributes in choosing a mate. The results were consistent with predictions. Both men and women gave equally high ratings to certain attributes, such as "having a pleasant disposition." But in the vast majority of countries, "good looks" and "no previous experience in sexual intercourse" were valued more by men, whereas "good financial prospect" and "ambitious and industrious" were more important to women. Analyses of personal ads appearing in magazines and newspapers have also revealed that in the dating marketplace the "deal" is that

This young man spies through his sunglasses at women on the beach. From an evolutionary perspective, his attraction is biologically, though not consciously, driven by the search for a fertile reproductive partner.

women offer beauty, while men offer wealth (Feingold, 1992a; Rajecki et al., 1991; Sprecher et al., 1994). In the words of one investigator, the search for a heterosexual mate seems to feature "men as success objects and women as sex objects" (Davis, 1990).

Some researchers have suggested that these gendered preferences are not mere luxuries, but necessities in the mating marketplace. In Buss's (1989) study, men were more likely to prefer good looks, and women were more likely to prefer good financial prospects, but both sexes saw other characteristics—such as funny, dependable, and kind—as more important. But what happens in real life, where mate seekers who can't have it all must prioritize their desires? Studying "the necessities and luxuries in mate preferences," Norman Li and others (2002) asked research participants to design their ideal marriage partner by purchasing different characteristics using "mate dollars." In some cases, they were granted a large budget to work with; in other cases, the budget was limited. In the large-budget condition, men spent somewhat more play money on physical attractiveness and women spent somewhat more on social status, but both were just as interested in a partner who was kind, lively, and creative. In the low-budget condition, however, men spent even more of their play money on physical attractiveness and women spent even more on social status. When mate seekers can't have it all and must therefore focus on what's most important, they prioritize their choices in the ways predicted by evolutionary theory (see Figure 9.5).

Also consistent with the evolutionary perspective is a universal tendency for men to seek younger women (who are most likely to be fertile) and for women to desire older men (who are most likely to have financial resources). Buss (1989) found this age-preference discrepancy in all the cultures he studied, with men on average wanting to marry women who were 2.7 years younger and women wanting men who were 3.4 years older. Based on their analysis of personal ads, Douglas Kenrick and Richard Keefe (1992) found that men in their twenties are equally interested in younger women and slightly older women still of fertile age. But men in their thirties seek out women who are five years younger, while men in their fifties prefer women ten to twenty years younger. In contrast, girls and women of all ages are attracted to men who are older than they are. These patterns can also be seen in marriage statistics taken from different cultures and generations. There is one interesting

"Men seek to propagate widely, whereas women seek to propagate wisely."
—Robert Hindle

FIGURE 9.5

Sex Differences in Mate Preference: Evolutionary Necessities?

In this study, participants built an ideal mate by purchasing characteristics. Given a large budget, men spent a somewhat higher percentage of money on physical attractiveness and women spent somewhat more on social status—relative to other characteristics. On a low budget, however, men spent even more on physical attractiveness and women spent even more on social status.

(Li et al., 2002.)

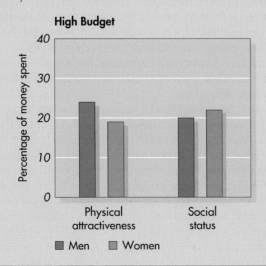

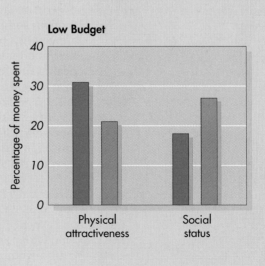

exception: Teenage boys say they are most attracted to women who are slightly *older* than they are, women in their fertile twenties (Kenrick et al., 1996).

Also supportive of evolutionary theory is research on *jealousy,* "the dangerous passion"—a negative emotional state that arises from a perceived threat to one's relationship. Although jealousy is a common and normal human reaction, men and women may well be aroused by different triggering events. According to the theory, a man should be most upset by *sexual* infidelity because a wife's extramarital affair increases the risk that the children he supports are not his own. In contrast, a woman should feel threatened more by *emotional* infidelity because a husband who falls in love with another woman might leave and withdraw his financial support (Buss, 2000).

A number of studies support this hypothesis. In one, male and female college students were asked whether they would be more upset if their romantic partner were to form a deep emotional attachment or have sexual intercourse with another person. Think for a moment about this choice. Which situation would *you* find more distressing? The results revealed a striking sex difference: 60 percent of the men said they would be more upset by a partner's sexual infidelity, but 83 percent of the women felt that emotional infidelity was worse (Buss et al., 1992).

In a second study, newly married husbands and wives were interviewed about how they would react if they suspected their partner of cheating. Interestingly, the men said they would use more "mate-retention" tactics (concealing or threatening the wife or taking action against the male rival) when their wives were young and attractive. In contrast, women said they would use more mate-retention tactics (being watchful or enhancing their appearance) when married to men who strived for status and made more money (Buss & Shackelford, 1997). In a third study, male and female students were asked to imagine their girlfriend or boyfriend flirting at a party with a person of the opposite sex—someone depicted as attractive or unattractive, and as socially dominant or submissive. The result: Men said they would be most jealous when their imagined male rival was dominant, while women were most jealous when their female rival was physically attractive (Dijkstra & Buunk, 1998).

Sociocultural Perspectives   Although the gender differences are intriguing, critics of the evolutionary approach are quick to argue that some of the results can be interpreted in terms that are "psychological" rather than "evolutionary." One common argument is that women trade youth and beauty for money not for reproductive purposes but, rather, because they often lack *direct* access to economic power. With this hypothesis in mind, Steven Gangestad (1993) examined women's access to wealth in each of the countries in Buss's cross-cultural study. He found that the more economic power women had, the more important male physical attractiveness was to them. This result suggests that it may be the generally low social and economic status of women relative to men that leads them to care less about the physical attributes of a potential mate.

Another argument concerns the finding that men are more fearful of a mate's sexual infidelity (which threatens paternal certainty), while women worry more about emotional infidelity (which threatens future support). The difference is consistent, but what does it mean? There are two criticisms. First, in contrast to the explanation provided by evolutionary theory, some researchers have found that men become more upset over sexual infidelity not because of uncertain paternity but because they reasonably assume that a married woman who has a sexual affair is also likely to have intimate feelings for her extramarital partner. In other words, the man's concern, like the woman's, may be over the threat to the relationship, not fatherhood issues (DeSteno & Salovey, 1996; Harris & Christenfeld, 1996). Second, although men and women react differently when asked to imagine a partner's sexual or emotional infidelity, they are equally more upset by emotional infidelity when asked to recall actual experiences from a past relationship (Harris, 2002). At present, then, researchers continue to debate the meaning of observed sex differences in romantic jealousy and the evolutionary model that is used to explain them (Harris, 2005; Sagarin, 2005).

A third argument is that the differences typically found between the sexes are small compared to the similarities. This is an important point. In Buss's original cross-cultural study, both men and women gave their highest ratings to such attributes as kindness, dependability, a good sense of humor, and a pleasant disposition (physical attractiveness and financial prospects did not top the lists). In fact, research shows that women desire physical attractiveness as much as men do when asked about what they want in a short-term casual sex partner (Li & Kenrick, 2006; Regan & Berscheid, 1997).

Finally, the sex differences often observed are neither predictable nor universal. Human societies are remarkably flexible in terms of the ways people adapt to their environments, and there are revealing exceptions to the rules that are supposed to govern human play on the evolutionary field. For example, David Geary (2000) points out that while human fathers spend less time at child care than mothers do, they are unique among mammals—including baboons and chimpanzees, our evolutionary cousins—in the amount of care they give to their offspring. Geary speculates that human men care for their children in part because they enjoy more paternal certainty than do other male primates. Consider, too, the puzzling observation that most women of the Bari tribe in Venezuela are highly promiscuous. From an evolutionary standpoint, this behavior does not seem adaptive since women who "sleep around" may scare off potential mates fearful of wasting their resources on children who are not their own. So why is female promiscuity the norm in this culture? In *Cultures of Multiple Fathers,* anthropologists Stephen Beckerman, Paul Valentine, and others note that the Bari and some other aboriginal people in lowland South America believe that a baby can have multiple fathers and that all men who have sex with a pregnant woman make a biological contribution to the unborn child (some groups assume that more than one father, or at least more than one insemination, are *required* to form a fetus). Thus, by taking many lovers a woman increases the number of men who provide for her child. It appears that this strategy works. A multi-fathered Bari child is 16 percent more likely than a single-fathered child to survive to the age of fifteen (Beckerman & Valentine, 2002).

The Bari tribeswomen of Venezuela are sexually promiscuous. The Bari believe that a baby can have multiple fathers, so being promiscuous enables a woman to secure child support from many men. This exception to the evolutionary norm illustrates that human behavior is flexible and that people can develop mating strategies to suit their cultural environment.

Summing Up The evolutionary perspective offers social psychologists an interesting but controversial perspective on relationships. The approach continues to draw criticism that the results are weak, limited, or explainable by nonevolutionary means (Harris, 2003; Hazan & Diamond, 2000; Pedersen et al., 2002). However, it also continues to generate new ideas. At present, scientists in this area are studying a range of issues, such as the possible links between facial appearance and health and fertility (Geary, 2005; Grammer et al., 2005; Weeden & Sabini, 2005); the flexibility or "plasticity" of sexual orientation in men and women (Baumeister, 2000; Lippa, 2006); the potentially deadly link between sexual jealousy and violence (Buss, 2000); the reason that some men refuse to make child support payments (Shackelford et al., 2005); and mate poachers who seek sex partners from already committed relationships (Schmitt, 2004). Interested in the cognitive mechanisms that underlie mate selection behavior, one researcher found that after college-age men are visually exposed to highly attractive young women, they begin to report more favorable attitudes toward wealth and more ambition—precisely the attributes said to be desired by women. This result suggests that people know what others consider attractive and then try to present themselves accordingly when primed to do so (Roney, 2003).

Close Relationships

Being attracted to people can be exhilarating or frustrating depending on how the initial encounters develop. How important is a good relationship to you? Researchers asked three hundred students to weigh the importance of having a satisfying romantic relationship against the importance of other life goals (such as getting a good education, having a successful career, contributing to a better society) and found that 73 percent said they would sacrifice most other goals before giving up a good relationship (Hammersla & Frease-McMahan, 1990).

People have many significant relationships in their lives, but social psychologists have concentrated on friends, dating partners, lovers, and married couples (Berscheid & Regan, 2004; Fletcher, 2002; Hendrick & Hendrick, 2000; Miller et al., 2006). These **intimate relationships** often involve three basic components: (1) feelings of attachment, affection, and love; (2) the fulfillment of psychological needs; and (3) interdependence between partners, each of whom has a meaningful influence on the other.

Not all intimate relationships contain all these ingredients. A summer romance is emotionally intense; but in the fall, both partners resume their separate lives. An "empty shell" marriage revolves around coordinated daily activities; but emotional attachment is weak, and psychological needs go unmet. Clearly, relationships come in different shapes and sizes. Some are sexual; others are not. Some involve partners of the same sex; others, partners of the opposite sex. Some partners commit to a future together; others drop by for a brief stay. Feelings run the gamut from joyful to painful and from loving to hateful, with emotional intensity ranging all the way from mild to megawatt.

How do we advance from our first encounters to the intimate relationships that warm our lives? Do we proceed gradually over time, in stages, step by step, or by leaps and bounds? According to one perspective, relationships progress in order through a series of stages. For example, Bernard Murstein's (1986) *stimulus-value-role (SVR) theory* says there are three: (1) the stimulus stage, in which attraction is sparked by external attributes such as physical appearance; (2) the value stage, in which attachment is based on similarity of values and beliefs; and (3) the role stage, in which commitment is based on the performance of such roles as husband and wife. All three factors are important throughout a relationship, but each one is said to be first and foremost during only one stage.

In evaluating any stage theory, the critical issue is *sequence*. Does the value stage always precede the role stage, or might a couple work out roles before exploring whether their values are compatible? Most researchers do not believe that intimate relationships progress through a fixed sequence of stages. What, then, does account for how they change? Every relationship has a developmental history with ups, downs, stalls, and accelerations. What pushes a relationship up, pulls it down, or keeps it steady? One common answer is *rewards*. Love, like attraction, depends on the experience of positive emotions in the presence of a partner. Step by step, as the rewards pile up, love develops. Or, as rewards diminish, love erodes. In reward theories of love, quantity counts. But some would disagree. Think about your own relationships. Are your feelings toward someone you love simply a more intense version of your feelings toward someone you like? Is the love of a close friend the same as the love of a romantic partner? If not, then you can appreciate that there are qualitative differences among relationships. Both views have something to offer. Progress on the road from attraction to love depends on the quantity of fuel in the tank *and* on the kind of engine providing the power. The next section examines the reward-based approach to building a relationship. Then we consider differences among the various types of relationships.

intimate relationship
A close relationship between two adults involving emotional attachment, fulfillment of psychological needs, or interdependence.

The Intimate Marketplace: Tracking the Gains and Losses

Earlier, we saw that people are initially attracted to others who provide them with direct or indirect rewards. But is "What's in it for me?" still important in a relationship that has blossomed and grown? Can an economic approach be used to predict the future of a close relationship?

Social Exchange Theory Social exchange theory is an economic model of human behavior according to which people are motivated by a desire to maximize profit and minimize loss in their social relationships just as they are in business (Homans, 1961; Thibaut & Kelley, 1959). The basic premise of social exchange theory is simple: Relationships that provide more rewards and fewer costs will be more satisfying and endure longer. Between intimates, the rewards include love, companionship, consolation in times of distress, and sexual gratification if the relationship is of this nature. The costs include the work it takes to maintain a relationship, conflict, compromise, and the sacrifice of opportunities elsewhere.

The development of an intimate relationship is very clearly associated with the overall level of rewards and costs. Research has shown that dating couples who

© The New Yorker Collection 2000 William Hamilton from cartoonbank.com. All Rights Reserved.

"I've done the numbers, and I will marry you."

experience greater increases in rewards as their relationship progresses are more likely to stay together than are those who experience small increases or declines (Berg & McQuinn, 1986). People do not worry about costs during the honeymoon phase of a relationship (Hays, 1985). After a few months, however, both rewards and costs start to contribute to levels of satisfaction, both in married couples (Margolin & Wampold, 1981) and in gay and lesbian couples who are living together (Kurdek, 1991a).

Rewards and costs do not arise in a psychological vacuum. People bring to their relationships certain expectations about the balance sheet to which they are entitled. John Thibaut and Harold Kelley (1959) coined the term *comparison level (CL)* to refer to this average expected outcome in relationships. A person with a high CL expects his or her relationships to be rewarding; someone with a low CL does not. Situations that meet or exceed a person's expectations are more satisfying than those that fall short. Even a bad relationship can look pretty good to someone who has a low CL.

According to Thibaut and Kelley, a second kind of expectation is also important. They coined the term *comparison level for alternatives (CLalt)* to refer to people's expectations about what they would receive in an alternative situation. If the rewards available elsewhere are believed to be high, a person will be less committed to staying in the present relationship (Drigotas & Rusbult, 1992). If people perceive few acceptable alternatives (a low CLalt), they will tend to remain, even in an unsatisfying relationship that fails to meet expectations (CL). Of course, just as these alternatives can influence our commitment, commitment can influence our perceptions of the alternatives. If you have ever been in love, you probably were not cold, calculating, and altogether objective in your perceptions of the alternatives. In close and intimate relationships, we tend to act like lovers, not scientists, and harbor positive illusions. Research shows that people who are in love tend to see other prospective partners as less appealing (Johnson & Rusbult, 1989; Simpson et al., 1990). They also tend to see their own partners and relationships through rose-colored glasses (Collins & Feeney, 2000; Gagne & Lydon, 2001; Sanderson & Evans, 2001). Fully aware of the bias that love brings, people expect to be judged in this way by their partners (Boyes & Fletcher, in press). Having a generally positive perspective on one's partner is thus conducive to a happy and stable relationship (Murray et al., 1996; Murray & Holmes, 1999), except when people are in denial about their partners and incorrect in their perceptions of their partners' specific characteristics (Neff & Karney, 2005).

social exchange theory
A perspective that views people as motivated to maximize benefits and minimize costs in their relationships with others.

FIGURE 9.6

Relational Building Blocks

The building blocks of social exchange are rewards, costs, comparison level for alternatives, and investments. These factors are strongly associated with the satisfaction and commitment partners experience in their relationship.

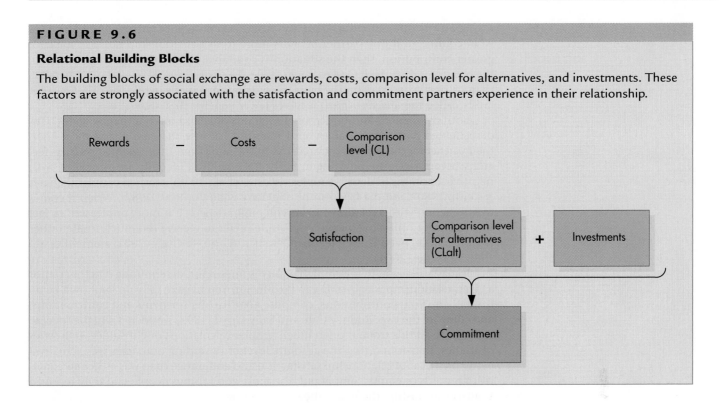

A third element in the social exchange is investment. An *investment* is something a person puts into a relationship that he or she cannot recover if the relationship ends. If you don't like the way an intimate relationship is working out, you can pack your clothes, grab your laptop or CD player, and drive away. But what about all the time you put into trying to make it last? What about all the romantic and career opportunities you sacrificed along the way? As you might expect, investments increase commitment. Because of those things we can't take with us, we're more likely to stay (Rusbult & Buunk, 1993).

Over the years, research has shown that the building blocks of the social exchange framework—as depicted in Figure 9.6 and as incorporated into Caryl Rusbult et al.'s (1998) Investment Model—can be used to determine the level of commitment that partners bring to a relationship (Le & Agnew, 2003). This model is important because commitment levels predict how long relationships will last. In studies of dating and married couples, research shows that the best-adjusted ones are those in which each partner is committed and sees the other as mutually committed (Drigotas et al., 1999). Particularly important for the durability of a relationship, people who are committed are more likely to forgive and forget when their partners betray a spoken or unspoken relationship norm by flirting, lying, forgetting an anniversary, revealing an embarrassing story in public, or having an affair (Finkel et al., 2002). Unfortunately, there are times when commitment can be a trap. A recent study of battered women showed that the investment model can be used to predict whether battered women will remain in an abusive relationship (Rhatigan & Axsom, 2006).

Equity Theory **Equity theory** provides a special version of how social exchange operates in interpersonal interactions (Adams, 1965; Messick & Cook, 1983; Walster et al., 1978). According to this theory, people are most content with a relationship when the ratio between what they get out of it (benefits) and what they put into it (contributions) is similar for both partners. Thus, the basic equity formula is:

equity theory The theory that people are most satisfied with a relationship when the ratio between benefits and contributions is similar for both partners.

$$\frac{\text{Your Benefits}}{\text{Your Contributions}} = \frac{\text{Your Partner's Benefits}}{\text{Your Partner's Contributions}}$$

Equity is different from equality. According to equity theory, the balance is what counts. So if one partner benefits more from a relationship but also makes a greater contribution, then the situation is equitable. In an *in*equitable relationship, the balance is disturbed: One partner (called the *overbenefited*) receives more benefits than he or she deserves on the basis of contributions made, while the other partner (aptly called the *underbenefited*) receives fewer benefits than deserved.

Both overbenefit and underbenefit are unstable and often unhappy states. Underbenefited partners feel angry and resentful because they are giving more than their partner for the benefits they receive. At the same time, overbenefited partners feel guilty because they are profiting unfairly. Both kinds of inequity are associated with negative emotions in dating couples (Walster et al., 1978), married couples (Schafer & Keith, 1980), and the friendships of elderly widows (Rook, 1987). When it comes to satisfaction with a relationship, as you might expect, it is more unpleasant to feel underbenefited than overbenefited. People prefer to receive too much in life rather than too little, even if they feel bad about it (Grote & Clark, 2001; Hatfield et al., 1982; Sprecher, 2001).

It may strike you that although equity is important, determining whether or not a given relationship is equitable can be difficult. You have to tally up your own benefits, tally up your contributions, compute your partner's benefits and contributions, and compare the two. Rodney Cate and Sally Lloyd (1992) wondered whether people really go to all this trouble when much simpler calculations might suffice. In a series of studies, they found that the absolute level of rewarding outcomes was actually a better predictor of relationship satisfaction and endurance than was either an equality of rewards or equity. Simply put, the more good things people said they received from a relationship, the better they felt about it.

Types of Relationships

Social exchange models focus on quantity: The more (rewards, equity), the better (satisfaction, endurance). But is reward always necessary? And what about the qualitative differences in our relationships? Does more reward turn casual acquaintances into friends, and friends into lovers, or are these types of relationships different from each other in other ways?

Exchange and Communal Relationships   According to Margaret Clark and her colleagues, people operate by a reward-based model when they are in **exchange relationships**, which are characterized by an immediate tit-for-tat repayment of benefits. In these situations, people want costs to be quickly offset by compensation, leaving the balance at zero. But not all relationships fit this mold. Clark maintains that in **communal relationships**, partners respond to each other's needs and well-being over time, without regard for whether they have given or received a benefit (Clark, 1984; Clark & Mills, 1979).

Exchange relationships typically exist between strangers and casual acquaintances and in certain long-term arrangements such as business partnerships. In contrast, strong communal relationships are usually limited to close friends, romantic partners, and family members (Clark & Mills, 1993). Based on fieldwork in West Africa, Alan Fiske (1992) is convinced that this distinction applies to human interactions all over the world. But the cynics among us wonder: Are communal relationships truly free of social exchange considerations? Can people really give without any desire to receive, or do partners in a communal relationship follow a more subtle version of social exchange, assuming that the benefits will balance out in the long run? Clark and Judson Mills (1993) believe that true communal relationships do exist—that once a communal norm has been adopted in a relationship, regardless of how it started, the motivation to respond to the other's needs becomes automatic.

Secure and Insecure Attachment Styles   Another interesting approach to understanding relationships is provided by Phillip Shaver, Cindy Hazan, and their

exchange relationship
A relationship in which the participants expect and desire strict reciprocity in their interactions.

communal relationship
A relationship in which the participants expect and desire mutual responsiveness to each other's needs.

colleagues, who have theorized that just as infants display different kinds of attachment toward their parents, so do adults exhibit specific **attachment styles** in their romantic relationships (Cassidy & Shaver, 1999; Rholes & Simpson, 2004).

For many years, child development psychologists had noticed that infants form intense, exclusive bonds with their primary caretakers. This first relationship is highly charged with emotion, and it emerges with regularity from one culture to the next. By observing the way babies react to both separations from and reunions with the primary caretaker, usually the mother, researchers also noticed that babies have different attachment styles. Those with *secure* attachments cry in distress when the mother leaves and then beam with sheer delight when she returns. Those with *insecure* attachments show one of two patterns. Some babies, described as anxious, cling and cry when the mother leaves but then greet her with anger or apathy upon her return. Others are generally more detached and *avoidant,* not reacting much on either occasion (Ainsworth et al., 1978).

How important is this first attachment? Does a secure and trusting bond in the first year of life set a foundation for close relationships later in life? John Bowlby (1988), a psychiatrist and influential theorist, argues that there is a link—that infants form "internal working models" of attachment figures, and that these models guide their relationships later in life. Research shows that infants classified as securely attached are later more positive in their outlook toward others (Cassidy et al., 1996). Looking back, adults with a secure attachment style described having positive family relationships, while avoidant and anxious adults recalled having problems with one or both parents (Feeney & Noller, 1990; Hazan & Shaver, 1987).

Whether or not adult attachment styles are rooted in the first year of life, the distinction made among adults has proved to be a useful one. Read the descriptions of three attachment types in Table 9.1. Which fits you best? Hazan and Shaver (1987) presented this task initially in a "love quiz" that appeared in a Denver newspaper and then in a study of college students. As shown in Table 9.1, the distribution of responses was similar in the two samples, and it proved similar again in a later nationwide sample of eight thousand adults (Mickelson et al., 1997). In addition, the researchers found that people who have a secure attachment style report having satisfying relationships that are happy, friendly, based on mutual trust, and enduring. Cognitively, they see people as good-hearted; and they believe in romantic love. In contrast, avoidant lovers fear intimacy and believe that romantic love is doomed to fade; and anxious lovers report a love life full of emotional highs and lows, obsessive preoccupation, a greater willingness than others to make long-term commitments, and extreme sexual attraction and jealousy.

To some extent, our attachment styles can be seen in our everyday behavior. For example, Jeffrey Simpson and others (1996) videotaped dating couples as they tried

TABLE 9.1
Attachment Styles (Hazan & Shaver, 1987.)

Question: Which of the following best describes your feelings?

Answers and Percentages	Newspaper Sample	University Sample
Secure I find it relatively easy to get close to others and am comfortable depending on them and having them depend on me. I don't often worry about being abandoned or about someone getting too close to me.	56%	56%
Avoidant I am somewhat uncomfortable being close to others; I find it difficult to trust them completely, difficult to allow myself to depend on them. I am nervous when anyone gets too close, and often, love partners want me to be more intimate than I feel comfortable being.	25%	23%
Anxious I find that others are reluctant to get as close as I would like. I often worry that my partner doesn't really love me or won't want to stay with me. I want to merge completely with another person, and this desire sometimes scares people away.	19%	21%

attachment style The way a person typically interacts with significant others.

to resolve various conflicts and then showed the tapes to outside observers. They found that men classified from a questionnaire as having an insecure-avoidant attachment style were the least warm and supportive and that women with an insecure-anxious style were the most upset and negative in their behavior. There is also reason to believe that people's attachment styles influence their physiological reactions to relationship conflict. In one study, Sally Powers and her colleagues (2006) brought 124 college-age dating couples into the laboratory to discuss a heated conflict they'd been having. Before and after this "conflict negotiation task," the researchers took saliva samples from all participants to measure levels of cortisol, a stress hormone. The results showed that boyfriends and girlfriends who were insecurely attached exhibited more physiological stress in response to the conflict task than did those who were securely attached.

What about the future? Does the attachment style you endorse today foretell relational outcomes tomorrow? On this question, the evidence is mixed. People who are secure do tend to have more lasting relationships. But the prognosis for those classified as insecure is harder to predict, with the results less consistent. What's important to realize is that although styles of attachment are modestly stable over time—perhaps as holdovers from infancy and childhood—they are not fixed, or set in stone. To illustrate this point, Lee Kirkpatrick and Cindy Hazan (1994) tracked down participants from an earlier study and found, four years later, that 30 percent had different attachment styles. In keeping with the central theme of social psychology—that we are profoundly shaped by the situations we are in—research suggests that people may continuously revise their own attachment styles in response to relationship experiences (Baldwin & Fehr, 1995; Keelan et al., 1994; Scharfe & Bartholomew, 1994).

 ## How Do I Love Thee? Counting the Ways

The poet Elizabeth Barrett Browning asked, "How do I love thee?" and then went on to "count the ways"—of which there are many. When college students were asked to list all the kinds of love that came to mind, they produced 216 items, such as friendship, parental, brotherly, sisterly, romantic, sexual, spiritual, obsessive, possessive, and puppy love (Fehr & Russell, 1991).

Over the years, various schemes for classifying different types of love have been proposed (Sternberg & Weis, 2006). On the basis of ancient writings, sociologist John Alan Lee (1988) identified three primary love styles: *eros* (erotic love), *ludus* (game-playing, uncommitted love), and *storge* (friendship love). As with primary colors, Lee theorized, these three styles can be blended together to form new secondary types of love, such as *mania* (demanding and possessive love), *pragma* (pragmatic love), and *agape* (other-oriented, altruistic love). On a scale designed to measure these "colors of love," men tend to score higher than women on *ludus*, while women score higher on *storge, mania,* and *pragma* (Hendrick & Hendrick, 1995).

Another popular taxonomy is derived from Robert Sternberg's (1986) **triangular theory of love**. According to Sternberg, there are eight basic subtypes of love (seven different forms of love and an eighth combination that results in non-love)—and all can be derived from the presence or absence of three components. The combination can thus be viewed as the vertices of a triangle (see Figure 9.7). These three components—and sample items used to measure each one—are described below:

Intimacy: The emotional component, which involves liking and feelings of closeness. ("I have a comfortable relationship with _____.")

Passion: The motivational component, which contains drives that trigger attraction, romance, and sexual desire. ("Just seeing _____ is exciting for me.")

Commitment: The cognitive component, which reflects the decision to make a long-term commitment to a loved partner. ("I will always feel a strong responsibility for _____.")

"I have studied love because it is my life's difficult problem. Although I have made much progress, the 'impossible dream' of a truly fulfilling mutual love remains a goal I have yet to achieve."

—John Alan Lee

triangular theory of love A theory proposing that love has three basic components—intimacy, passion, and commitment—which can be combined to produce eight subtypes.

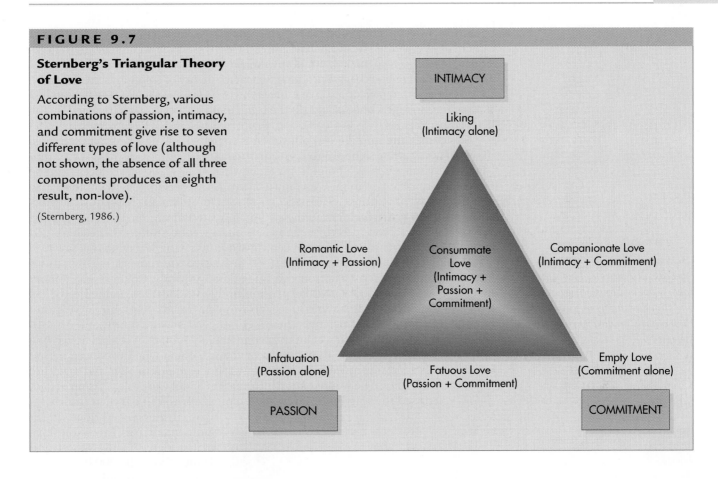

FIGURE 9.7

Sternberg's Triangular Theory of Love

According to Sternberg, various combinations of passion, intimacy, and commitment give rise to seven different types of love (although not shown, the absence of all three components produces an eighth result, non-love).

(Sternberg, 1986.)

Research provides pretty good support for this tri-component model of love (Sternberg, 1999). In one study, Arthur Aron and Lori Westbay (1996) asked people to rate sixty-eight prototypical features of love and found that all the various features fell into three categories: passion *(gazing at the other, euphoria, butterflies in the stomach)*, intimacy *(feeling free to talk about anything, supportive, understanding)*, and commitment *(devotion, putting the other first, long-lasting)*. In a second study, Sternberg (1997) asked people to state what they see as important in different kinds of relationships and found that the results were consistent with the theory. For example, "ideal lover" scored high on all three components, "friend" scored high on intimacy and commitment but low on passion, and "sibling" scored high on commitment but low on intimacy and passion.

In light of infant attachments, colors, triangles, and other love classification schemes that have been proposed over the years, one wonders: How many types of love are there, really? It's hard to tell. But there are two basic types that are built into all models: *liking,* the type of feeling you would have for a platonic friend, and *loving,* the kind of feeling you would have for a romantic partner. According to Zick Rubin (1973), liking and loving are two distinct reactions to an intimate relationship. There is some question, however, about how sharp the difference is. Kenneth and Karen Dion (1976) questioned casual daters, exclusive daters, engaged couples, and married couples. Although casual daters reported more liking than loving, liking and loving did not differ among those in the more committed dating relationships. More pointed is the two-pronged distinction made by Elaine Hatfield (1988) and her colleagues (Hatfield & Rapson, 1993) between passionate love and companionate love. According to Hatfield, **passionate love** is an emotionally intense and *often erotic state* of absorption in another person, whereas **companionate love** is a secure, trusting, and stable partnership, similar to what Rubin called liking.

Passionate Love: The Thrill of It   Passionate love is an intense emotional, heart-thumping state of absorption in another person. From ecstatic highs to agonizing lows, it is the bittersweet stuff of romance paperbacks, popular music, poems, and soap

passionate love Romantic love characterized by high arousal, intense attraction, and fear of rejection.

companionate love A secure, trusting, stable partnership.

operas. What is passionate love, and where does it come from? According to Ellen Berscheid and Elaine Walster (later Hatfield) (1974), the key to understanding passionate love is to recognize that it is an emotion and can be analyzed like any other emotion. Drawing on Schachter's (1964) two-factor theory of emotion (see Chapter 3), they theorized that passionate love is fueled by two key ingredients: (1) a heightened state of physiological *arousal* and (2) the *belief* that this arousal was triggered by the beloved person.

Sometimes, the arousal-love connection is obvious, as when a person feels a surge of sexual desire at the sight of a romantic partner. At other times, however, the symptoms of arousal—such as a pounding heart, sweaty palms, and weak knees—can be hard to interpret. When in the company of an attractive person, these symptoms may be attributed or "misattributed" to passionate love. Dolf Zillmann (1984) calls the process **excitation transfer**. According to Zillmann, arousal triggered by one stimulus can be transferred or added to the arousal from a second stimulus. The combined arousal is then perceived as having been caused only by the second stimulus.

Donald Dutton and Arthur Aron (1974) first tested this provocative hypothesis in a field study that took place on two bridges above British Columbia's Capilano River. One was a narrow, wobbly suspension bridge (450 feet long and 5 feet wide, with a low handrail) that sways 230 feet above rocky rapids—a nightmare for anyone the least bit afraid of heights. The other bridge was wide, sturdy, and only 10 feet from the ground. Whenever an unaccompanied young man walked across one of these bridges, he was met by an attractive young woman who introduced herself as a research assistant, asked him to fill out a brief questionnaire, and gave her phone number in case he wanted more information about the project. As predicted, men who crossed the scary bridge were later more likely to call her than those who crossed the stable bridge. In an amusement park study of "love at first fright," Cindy Meston and Penny Frohlich (2003) similarly found that men and women who were not with a romantic partner rated a pictured person of the opposite sex as more attractive just after they rode on a roller coaster than before they began the ride. Perhaps terror can fan the hot flames of romance.

Or maybe not. Maybe it's just a relief to be with someone when we're in distress. To rule out the possibility that it's relief rather than arousal that fuels attraction, Gregory White and his colleagues (1981) had to create arousal without distress. How? A little exercise can do it. Male participants ran in place for either two minutes or fifteen seconds and then saw a videotape of a woman they expected to meet. The woman had been made up to look physically attractive or unattractive. After watching the video, participants rated her appearance. The result: Those who exercised for two minutes as opposed to only fifteen seconds saw the physically attractive woman as even more attractive and the unattractive woman as less attractive. This study, and others like it (Allen et al., 1989), showed that arousal—even without distress—intensifies emotional reactions, positive or negative.

The implication of this research—that our passions are at the mercy of bridges, roller coasters, exercise, and anything else that causes the heart to race—is intriguing. It is certainly consistent with the common observation that people are vulnerable to falling in love when their lives are turbulent. But does the effect occur, as theorized, because people *mis*attribute their arousal to a person they have just met?

According to excitation transfer theory, bodily arousal triggered by one stimulus can be misattributed to another stimulus. This theory suggests that the energy that springs from dancing may intensify a person's feelings for his or her partner, fanning the flames of passion.

excitation transfer The process whereby arousal caused by one stimulus is added to arousal from a second stimulus and the combined arousal is attributed to the second stimulus.

Yes and no. Based on their review of thirty-three experiments, Craig Foster and others (1998) confirmed that the arousal-attraction effect does exist. They also found, however, that the effect occurs even when people know the actual source of their arousal—in other words, even without misattribution. According to these investigators, just being aroused, even if we know why, facilitates whatever is the most natural response. If the person we meet is good-looking and of the right sex, we become more attracted. If the person is not good-looking or is of the wrong sex, we become less attracted. No thought is required. The response is automatic.

It is now clear that passionate love is highly sexualized. In a book entitled *Lust: What We Know About Human Sexual Desire,* Pamela Regan and Ellen Berscheid (1999) present compelling evidence for the proposition that intense sexual desire and excitement are a vital part of passionate love. In this regard, they are quick to note that "to love" is different from "being in love." To illustrate, Berscheid and Meyers (1996) asked college men and women to make three lists: people they loved, people they were in love with, and people they were sexually attracted to. As it turned out, only 2 percent of those in the "love" category also appeared in the sex list. Yet among those in the "in love" category, the overlap with sex was 85 percent. And when Regan and her colleagues (1998) asked people to list the characteristics of romantic love, two-thirds cited sexual desire—more than the number who put happiness, loyalty, communication, sharing, or commitment on the list.

Romantic ideals notwithstanding, it is also clear that people have doubts about the staying power of passionate love. Does the fire within a relationship burn hot and bright over time, or is it just a passing fancy? Comparisons of couples at different stages of their relationships and longitudinal studies that measure changes in the same couples over time suggest that passionate love does diminish somewhat over time (Acker & Davis, 1992; Tucker & Aron, 1993).

"True love never grows old."

—proverb

Companionate Love: The Self-Disclosure in It In contrast to the intense, emotional, and erotic nature of passionate love, companionate love is a form of affection found between close friends as well as lovers. Companionate relationships rest more on a foundation of mutual trust, caring, respect, friendship, and long-term commitment—characteristics that John Harvey and Julie Omarzu (2000) see as necessary for "minding the close relationship."

Compared with the passionate form of love, companionate love is less intense but in some respects deeper and more enduring. Susan Sprecher and Pamela Regan (1998) administered passionate and companionate love scales to heterosexual couples who had been together for varying amounts of time and found that passionate love scores of both men and women initially rose over time but then peaked and declined somewhat during marriage. Companionate love scores, however, did not similarly decline. In fact, in couples that stay together, partners are likely to report that "I love you more today than yesterday" (Sprecher, 1999). Like the sturdy, steady tortoise in Aesop's fable, companionate love may seem outpaced by the flashier start of passionate love, but it can still cross the finish line well ahead.

"As soon as you cannot keep anything from a woman, you love her."

—Paul Geraldy

Companionate love is characterized by high levels of **self-disclosure**, a willingness to open up and share intimate facts and feelings. In a way, self-disclosure is to companionate love what arousal is to passionate love. Think for a moment about your most embarrassing moment, your most cherished ambitions, or your sex life. Would you bare your soul on these private matters to a complete stranger? What about a casual acquaintance, date, friend, or lover? Whether or not to self-disclose—what, when, how much, and to whom—is a decision that each of us makes based on a consideration of what we stand to gain and lose in a relationship (Omarzu, 2000).

Still, it is the willingness to disclose intimate facts and feelings that lies at the heart of our closest and most intimate relationships (Derlega et al., 1993). Research shows that the more emotionally involved people are in a close relationship, the more they self-disclose to each other. Nancy Collins and Lynn Miller (1994) note three possible reasons for this correlation: (1) We disclose to people we like, (2) we like people who disclose to us, and (3) we like people to whom we have disclosed. Thus, among pairs of college students brought together in a laboratory for brief getting-acquainted conversations, the more they self-disclosed, the better they felt about each other afterward (Vittengl & Holt, 2000). In a recent longitudinal study of adult

self-disclosure Revelations about the self that a person makes to others.

FIGURE 9.8

From a Sliver to a Wedge

According to the theory of social penetration, as a relationship becomes closer, partners increase both the breadth (covering a wider range of topics) and depth (revealing more intimate information) of their exchanges.

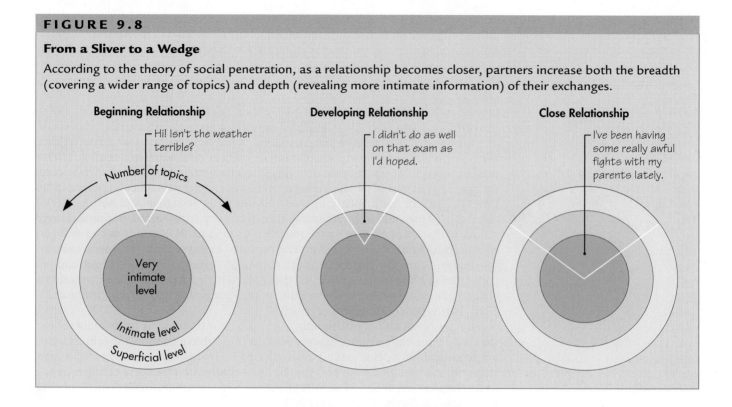

dating couples, partners who reported higher levels of self-disclosure also expressed more satisfaction, commitment, and love (Sprecher & Hendrick, 2004).

Over the years, researchers have made three major observations about self-disclosure patterns in relationships. One is that partners reveal more to each other as their relationship grows over time. According to Irving Altman and Dalmas Taylor (1973), self-disclosure is a basic form of social exchange that unfolds as relationships develop. Their *social penetration theory* holds that relationships progress from superficial exchanges to more intimate ones. At first, people give relatively little of themselves to each other and receive little in return. If the initial encounters prove rewarding, however, the exchanges become both *broader* (covering more areas of their lives) and *deeper* (involving more sensitive areas). As shown in Figure 9.8, social interaction grows from a narrow, shallow sliver to a wider, more penetrating wedge.

This increase in self-disclosure can be seen in the fact that the more intimate people are in a relationship, the less likely they are to lie to each other. In a naturalistic study of this point, Bella DePaulo and Deborah Kashy (1998) asked people to keep a one-week diary of all social encounters and record every instance in which they tried to mislead someone, regardless of how self-serving or well-meaning the intent (some lies are told to advance the liar's self-interest, and others are told for the other person's benefit). As it turned out, the rate of lying among participants decreased according to the closeness of their relationships. On average, they lied most to strangers, followed by casual acquaintances, then family members and friends. Also consistent with the presumed patterns of self-disclosure is that unmarried participants lied three times more often to their romantic partners than married participants did to their spouses. These results are presented in Figure 9.9.

A second observation is that patterns of self-disclosure change according to the state of a relationship. During a first encounter, and in the budding stages of a new relationship, people tend to reciprocate another's self-disclosure with their own—at a comparable level of intimacy. If a new acquaintance opens up, it is polite to match that self-disclosure by revealing more of ourselves. Once a relationship is well established, however, strict reciprocity occurs less frequently (Altman, 1973; Derlega et al., 1976). Among couples in distress, two different self-disclosure patterns have been observed. For some, both breadth and depth decrease as partners withdraw

FIGURE 9.9

To Whom Do People Lie?

For one week, people recorded every instance in which they tried to mislead someone. As you can see, they lied most to strangers, followed by acquaintances, family members, and friends (left). Also shown is that people lied more often to their unmarried romantic partners than to their spouses (right). These results suggest that the closer two people are, the less likely they are to lie to each other.

(Data from DePaulo & Kashy, 1998.)

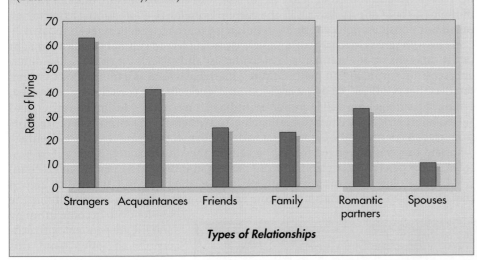

from each other and cease to communicate (Baxter, 1987). For others, the breadth of self-disclosure declines, but depth increases as the partners hurl cruel and angry statements at each other (Tolstedt & Stokes, 1984). In this case, the social *de*penetration process resembles neither the sliver of a superficial affiliation nor the wedge of a close relationship—but, rather, a long, thin dagger of discontent.

A third common observation is that individuals differ in the tendency to share private, intimate thoughts with others. For example, Kathryn Dindia and Mike Allen (1992) conducted a meta-analysis of 205 studies involving 23,702 white North Americans and found, on average, that women are more open than men—and that people in general are more self-disclosing to women than to men. This being the case, it comes as no surprise that women rate their same-sex friendships more highly than men rate theirs. At least in North America, male friends seem to bond more by taking part in common activities, while female friends engage more in a sharing of feelings (Duck & Wright, 1993). As Paul Wright (1982) put it, women tend to interact "face-to-face"; men go "side-by-side."

 ## Cultural Influences on Attraction and Close Relationships

In looking at attraction, desire, relationships, and love, one wonders: Are people all over the world similar or different? To what extent are these processes universal or different from one culture to another? In recent years, a number of social psychologists have raised these kinds of questions (Hatfield et al., 2007).

In his original cross-cultural study of mate selection, for example, Buss (1989) found that physical attractiveness is more important to men all over the world and that financial resources are more important to women—gender differences that appeared to be universal. Yet even Buss was struck by the powerful impact that culture had on mate preferences. In China, India, Indonesia, Iran, Taiwan, and the Palestinian territories of Israel, for example, people valued chastity in a mate. Yet in Finland, France, Norway, Sweden, the Netherlands, and West Germany, chastity was either unimportant or negatively valued.

When it comes to close relationships, research has shown that passionate love is a widespread and universal emotion. In surveys conducted throughout the world, William Jankowiak and Edward Fischer (1992) detected indications of passionate love in 147 out of 166 cultures as varied as Indonesia, China, Turkey, Nigeria, Trinidad, Morocco, Australia, and Micronesia. Drawing on this universality, some researchers have begun to explore the underlying neuroscience. For example, anthropologist Helen Fisher (2004) believes that romantic love is hard-wired in the neurochemistry of the brain. In particular, Fisher argues that the neurotransmitter dopamine, which drives animals to seek rewards such as food and sex, is essential to the pleasure that is felt when these drives are satisfied. Hence, she argues, dopamine levels are associated with both the highs of romantic passion and the lows of rejection. Citing evidence from

"To an American in love, his/her emotions tend to overshadow everything else . . . to a Chinese in love, his/her love occupies a place among other considerations"

—Hsu

studies of humans and other animals, she also points to neurochemical parallels between romantic love and substance addiction.

Although most people in the world agree that sexual desire is what injects the passion into passionate love, not everyone sees it as necessary for marriage. Think about this question: If a man or woman had all other qualities you desired, would you marry this person if you were *not* in love? When American students were surveyed in 1967, 35 percent of men and 76 percent of women said yes. Twenty years later, only 14 percent of men and 20 percent of women said they would marry someone with whom they were not in love (Simpson et al., 1986). The shift among women may reflect the pragmatic point that marrying for love is an economic luxury that few women of the past could afford. As seen in the current popularity of prenuptial agreements, pragmatic considerations continue to influence marriage practices, even today.

The willingness to marry without love is also subject to cultural variation. In light of the different values that pervade individualist and collectivist cultures, the differences are not surprising. In many cultures, marriage is seen as a transaction between families that is influenced by social, economic, and religious considerations. Indeed, arranged marriages are still common in India, China, many Muslim countries, and sub-Saharan Africa. So, when Robert Levine and others (1995) asked college students from eleven countries about marrying without love, they found that the percentage who said they would ranged from 4 percent in the United States, 5 percent in Australia, and 8 percent in England up to 49 percent in India and 51 percent in Pakistan.

Culture's influence on love is interesting. On the one hand, it could be argued that the rugged individualism found in many western cultures would inhibit the tendency to become intimate and interdependent with others. On the other hand, this same orientation leads people to give priority in making marital decisions to their own feelings rather than to family concerns, social obligations, religious constraints, income, and the like (Dion & Dion, 1996). In an illustration of this point, Fred Rothbaum and Bill Yuk-Piu Tsang (1998) compared popular love songs in the United States and China. They found that the American lyrics focused more on the two lovers as isolated entities, independent of social context ("There is nobody here, it's just you and me, the way I want it to be").

Tushar Agarwal and his bride Richa are married in a wedding ceremony in Bombay. Fulfilling a tradition that seems strange to most Americans, for whom being in love is essential, this Indian marriage was arranged.

Relationship Issues: The Male-Female "Connection"

Browse the shelves of any real or online bookstore, and you'll see one paperback title after another on the general topic of gender. There are books for men and books for women, books that preach the masculine ideal and books that tell us how to be more feminine, books that portray men and women as similar and books that accentuate the differences, the so-called gender gap. Is it true, to borrow John Gray's (1997) provocative book title, that *Men Are from Mars, Women Are from Venus*? And if so, what are the implications when it comes to male-female relationships?

Sexuality One hundred years ago, Sigmund Freud shocked the scientific community by proposing psychoanalytic theory, which placed great emphasis on sex as a driving force in human behavior. At the time, Freud's closest associates rejected this

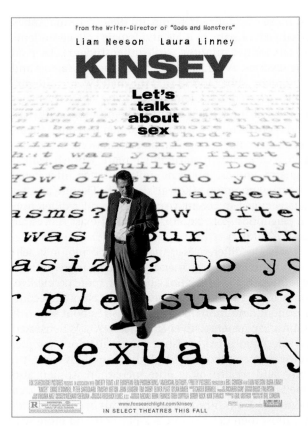

In the movie Kinsey, *Liam Neeson plays biologist Alfred Kinsey, the first scientist to study sexual practices in the United States.*

Men are more likely than women to interpret friendly gestures by the opposite sex in sexual terms. **True.**

focus on sexual motivation. But was he wrong? Sexual images and themes pop up, quite literally, in our dreams, in the jokes we tell, in the TV shows we watch, in the novels we read, in the music we hear, and in the sex scandals that swirl around public figures in the news. It's no wonder that advertisers use sex to sell everything from blue jeans to perfumes, soft drinks, and cars.

With sex the most private aspect of human relations, it is difficult to study systematically. If you saw the 2004 movie *Kinsey,* starring Liam Neeson, you'd know that during the 1940s biologist Alfred Kinsey and colleagues (1948, 1953) conducted the first large-scale survey of sexual practices in the United States. Based on confidential interviews of more than 17,000 men and women, these researchers sought for the first time to describe what nobody would openly talk about: sexual activity. Many of his results were shocking, with reported sexual activity more frequent and more varied than anyone had expected. His books were instant bestsellers. Certain aspects of his methodology were flawed, however. For example, participants were mostly young, white, urban, and middle class—hardly a representative sample. He also asked leading questions to enable respondents to report on sexual activities— or make up stories (Jones, 1997). Kinsey died in 1954, but his Institute for Sex Research at Indiana University remains a major center for the study of human sexuality (Bancroft, 1997).

Since Kinsey's groundbreaking study, many sex surveys have been conducted, and they form part of the research history chronicled in *Kiss and Tell: Surveying Sex in the Twentieth Century* (Ericksen & Steffen, 1999). The limits of self-reports—regardless of whether they are taken in face-to-face interviews, telephone surveys, or the Internet—is that we can never know for sure how accurate the results are. Part of the problem is that respondents may not be honest in their disclosures. Also problematic is that people differ in their interpretations of survey questions. Consider this deceptively simple question: What does it mean to say you had sex? In an article published in the *Journal of the American Medical Association,* Stephanie Sanders and June Reinisch (1999) asked college students from twenty-nine states, "Would you say you *had sex* with someone if the most intimate behavior you engaged in was . . . ?" The results showed that most students agreed that vaginal and anal intercourse constitute having sex and that deep kissing, oral contact with breasts, and manual contact with genitals do not. Yet there was little consensus about oral-genital contact. At the time this study was published, former President Clinton, mired in a sex scandal, claimed he did not have "sexual relations" with intern Monica Lewinsky despite oral-genital contact. This finding suggests that there is some ambiguity in this regard (see Table 9.2).

In recent years, researchers have used an array of methods to measure sexual attitudes and behavior. Studies of everyday interactions reveal that men view the world

TABLE 9.2
What Constitutes "Having Sex"?

In this study, male and female college students were asked, "Would you say you had sex with someone if the most intimate behavior you engaged in was _____?" As you can see, there was consensus for some behaviors but disagreement for others.

(Sanders & Reinisch, 1999.)

Contact	% Who Said Yes	Contact	% Who Said Yes
Deep kissing	2%	Oral contact with genitals	40%
Oral contact with breasts	3%	Anal intercourse	81%
Touching genitals	14%	Vaginal intercourse	99%

"Sex brought us together, but gender drove us apart."

In an ABC Primetime survey of 1,501 American adults, a number of gender differences were found (Langer et al., 2004):

	Men	Women
Think about sex every day	70%	34%
Have visited a sex Web site	34%	10%
Have fantasized about a threesome	33%	9%

sexual orientation A person's preference for members of the same sex (homosexuality), opposite sex (heterosexuality), or both sexes (bisexuality).

in more "sexualized" terms. In 1982, Antonia Abbey arranged for pairs of male and female college students to talk for five minutes, while other students observed the sessions. When she later questioned the actors and observers, Abbey found that the males were more sexually attracted to the females than vice versa. The males also rated the female actors as being more seductive and more flirtatious than the women had rated themselves as being. Among men more than women, eye contact, a compliment, a friendly remark, a brush against the arm, and an innocent smile are often interpreted as sexual come-ons (Kowalski, 1993). Despite all that has changed in recent years, these gender differences in perceptions of sexual interest still exist (Levesque et al., 2006).

Gender differences are particularly common in self-report surveys, where men report being more promiscuous, more likely to think about sex, more permissive, more likely to enjoy casual sex without emotional commitment, and more likely to fantasize about sex with multiple partners (Oliver & Hyde, 1993). When asked to select ten private wishes from a list, for example, most men and women similarly wanted love, health, peace on earth, unlimited ability, and wealth. But more men than women also wanted "to have sex with anyone I choose" (Ehrlichman & Eichenstein, 1992). In a large-scale study of 16,000 respondents from fifty-two countries all over the world, David Schmitt (2003) found that most men desire more sex partners and more sexual variety than most women do, regardless of their relationship status or sexual orientation. Based on this research, Roy Baumeister and others (2001) concluded that "men desire sex more than women" (p. 270).

Sexual Orientation At a time when policy makers, judges, religious leaders, scholars, and laypeople openly debate the topic of gay marriage, no discussion of human sexuality is complete without a consideration of differences in **sexual orientation**—defined as one's sexual preference for members of the same sex (homosexuality), opposite sex (heterosexuality), or both sexes (bisexuality).

How common is homosexuality, and where does it come from? Throughout history, and in all cultures, a vast majority of people have been heterosexual in their orientation. But how vast a majority is a subject of some debate. A 1970 survey funded by the Kinsey Institute revealed that 3.3 percent of American men sampled said that they had frequent or occasional homosexual sex (Fay et al., 1989). Between 1989 and 1992, the National Opinion Research Center reported that 2.8 percent of American men and 2.5 percent of women had exclusive homosexual activity. Together, large-scale surveys in the United States, Europe, Asia, and the Pacific suggest that the exclusively homosexual population in the world is 3 or 4 percent among men and about half that number among women (Diamond, 1993).

Although an exclusive homosexual orientation is relatively rare among humans and other animals, homosexual *behaviors* are more common. In *Biological Exuberance,* Bruce Bagemihl (1999) reports that sexual encounters among male-male and female-female pairs have been observed in more than 450 species, including giraffes, goats, birds, chimpanzees, and lizards. Among humans, the incidence of homosexual behavior varies from one generation and culture to the next, depending on prevailing attitudes. In *Same Sex, Different Cultures,* Gilbert Herdt (1998) notes that in parts of the world, stretching from Sumatra to Melanesia, it's common for adolescent males to engage in homosexual activities before being of age for marriage, even though homosexuality as a permanent trait is rare. It's important, then, to realize that sexual orientation cannot be viewed in black-or-white terms but along a continuum. In the center of that continuum, 1 percent of people describe themselves as actively *bi*sexual.

To explain the roots of homosexuality, various theories have been proposed. The Greek philosopher Aristotle believed that it was inborn but strengthened by habit;

post-Freud psychoanalysts argue that it stems from family dynamics—specifically, a child's overattachment to a parent of the same or opposite sex; social learning theorists point to rewarding sexual experiences with same-sex peers in childhood. Yet there is little hard evidence to support these claims. In a particularly comprehensive study, Alan Bell and others (1981) interviewed 1,500 homosexual and heterosexual adults about their lives. There were no differences in past family backgrounds, absence of a male or female parent, relationship with parents, sex abuse, age of onset of puberty, or high school dating patterns. Except for the fact that homosexual adults described themselves as less conforming as children, the two groups could not be distinguished by past experiences. Both groups strongly felt that their sexual orientation was set long before it was "official."

Increasingly, there is scientific evidence of a biological disposition. In a highly publicized study, neurobiologist Simon LeVay (1991) autopsied the brains of nineteen homosexual men who had died of AIDS, sixteen heterosexual men (some of whom had died of AIDS), and six heterosexual women. LeVay examined a tiny nucleus in the hypothalamus known to be involved in regulating sexual behavior and known to be larger in heterosexual men than in women. The specimens were numerically coded, so LeVay did not know whether the donor he was examining was male or female, straight or gay. The result: In the male homosexual brains he studied, the nucleus was half the size as in male heterosexual brains—and comparable to those found in female heterosexual brains. This research is fully described in LeVay's (1993) book *The Sexual Brain*.

It's important to recognize that this study revealed only a correlation between sexual orientation and the brain and cannot be used to draw conclusions about cause and effect. More convincing support for the biological roots of sexual orientation comes from twin studies suggesting that there is a genetic predisposition. Michael Bailey and Richard Pillard (1991) surveyed 167 gay men and their twins and adopted brothers. Overall, 52 percent of the identical twins were gay, compared to only 22 percent of fraternal twins and 11 percent of adoptive brothers. Two years later, Bailey and others (1993) conducted a companion study of lesbians with similar results.

The origins of sexual orientation are complex for two reasons. First, it's not clear that sexual orientation for men and women are similarly rooted. In Australia, Bailey and others (2000) had hundreds of pairs of twins rate their own sexuality on a seven-point continuum that ranged from "exclusively heterosexual" to "exclusively homosexual." Overall, 92 percent of both men and women saw themselves as exclusively heterosexual. Among the others, however, more women said that they had bisexual tendencies and more men said they were exclusively homosexual. In another study, a longitudinal investigation of eighteen- to twenty-five-year-old women, Lisa Diamond (2003) found that more than a quarter of those who had initially identified themselves as lesbian or bisexual changed their orientation over the next five years—far more change than is ever reported among men.

Recent experiments in which people are brought into the laboratory reinforce the point. In one study, Meredith Chivers and others (2004) recruited men and women who had identified themselves as heterosexual or homosexual in their orientation. In a private, dimly lit room, these participants watched a series of brief sex clips—some involving male couples, others of female couples. While watching, the participants rated their subjective feelings of sexual attraction on a scale. At the same time, genital arousal was measured using devices that recorded penile erection (for males) and vaginal pulse (for females). The results showed that the women were genitally aroused by both male *and* female sex clips, regardless of whether they identified themselves as straight or lesbian in their orientation. Yet male participants exhibited more genital arousal in response to men *or* women, depending on their sexual orientation. In fact, although self-identified bisexual men reported an attraction to both sexes, most were genitally aroused by men or by women—but not both (Rieger et al., 2005). These findings, and others (Lippa, 2006), compel the conclusion that women are sexually more flexible than men, having more *erotic plasticity*. Simply put, women are more open and more likely to change sexual preferences over the course of a lifetime (Baumeister, 2000; Peplau, 2003).

A second complicating factor is that although there is evidence for a biological disposition, this does not mean that there's a "gay gene" (Hamer et al., 1999). Daryl

Bem (1996, 2000) sees the development of sexual orientation as a *psycho*biological process. According to Bem, genes influence a person's temperament at birth, leading some infants and young children to be naturally more active, energetic, and aggressive than others. These differences in temperament draw some children toward male play-mates and "masculine" activities and others toward female playmates and "feminine" activities. Bem refers to children who prefer same-sex playmates as gender-conformists and to those who prefer opposite-sex playmates as gender-nonconformists ("sissies" and "tomboys").

Activity preferences in childhood may be biologically rooted, but what happens next is the psychological part. According to Bem, gender-conforming children come to see members of the opposite sex as different, unfamiliar, and arousing, even "ex-otic." Gender-nonconforming children, in contrast, come to see same-sex peers as different, unfamiliar, arousing, and exotic. Later, at puberty, as children become phys-ically and sexually mature, they find that they are attracted to members of the same or opposite sex—depending on which is the more exotic. Bem describes his proposed chain of events as the "exotic becomes erotic" theory of sexual orientation.

At present, there is only sketchy support for this theory. It is true that genetic makeup can influence temperament and predispose a child to favor certain kinds of activities over others (Kagan, 1994). It is also true that gay men are more likely to have been "sissies" and that lesbians are more likely to have been "tomboys" as chil-dren (Bailey & Zucker, 1995; Bell et al., 1981). It may even be true that people are genetically hardwired to become sissies and tomboys as children (Bailey et al., 2000). But do peer preferences in childhood alter adult sexual orientation, as Bem suggests, because exotic becomes erotic? Or, is there a "gay gene" that fosters gender non-conformity in childhood as well as homosexuality in adolescence and adulthood? And can a single theory explain homosexuality in both men and women, or are sep-arate theories needed, as some have suggested (Peplau et al., 1998)? At present, more research is needed to answer these questions and tease apart the biological and psy-chological influences. Either way, one point looms large: People, especially men, do not seem to willfully choose their sexual orientation, nor can they easily change it.

Is there any reason to believe that the attraction process and the formation of intimate relationships are any different for same-sex couples? Not really. According to the U.S. Census, an estimated 600,000 same-sex couples were living together in the United States in 2000. Recent research shows that gays and lesbians meet people in the same ways as straights, seeking out others who are attractive and similar in their attitudes; that their satisfaction and commitment levels are similarly affected by social exchange and equity concerns; and that they report com-parable levels of liking and loving in their intimate relationships. There are two ways in which same-sex couples differ from straight couples: They are more likely to retain friendships with former sex partners after break-ing up, and they tend to divide chores more equally within a household (Kurdek, 2005; Peplau & Fingerhut, 2007). In light of the striking similar-ities, Gregory Herek (2006) argues that same-sex couples should be entitled to the psychological, social, and health benefits of marriage.

The Marital Trajectory Because we are social beings, having close relationships is important to us all—for our happiness and emotional well-being and even for our physical health and longevity. As noted at the start of this chapter, 73 percent of American college students surveyed said they would sacrifice most other life goals rather than give up a satis-fying relationship (Hammersla & Frease-McMahan, 1990). Yet sadly, these students live in a society where 40 to 50 percent of first marriages are likely to end in divorce. With at least one previously divorced partner, the odds of divorce are even greater (Gottman, 1998). This discrepancy between the stability most people want and the disruption they may have to con-front is dramatic. Couples argue, break up, separate, and divorce. How do marriages evolve over time, and why do some last while others dissolve?

Ellen Berscheid and Harry Reis (1998) say that for social psychologists who study intimate relationships, this is the most frequently asked and vex-

On July 1, 2000, Vermont became the first state ever to grant the legal benefits of "civil unions" to same-sex couples. Shown here, Carolyn Conrad and Kathleen Peterson leave the Brattleboro Town Hall just after midnight on July 1, when they became the first couple to benefit from that new law.

FIGURE 9.10

Marital Satisfaction over Time

In a longitudinal study that spanned ten years, married couples rated the quality of their marriages. On average, these ratings were high, but they declined among both husbands and wives. As you can see, there were two steep drops, occurring during the first and eighth years of marriage.

(Kurdek, 1999.)

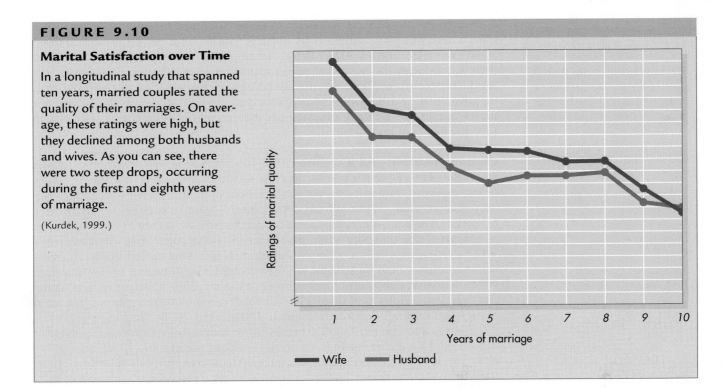

ing question. Is there a typical developmental pattern? No and yes. No, it's clear that all marriages are different and cannot be squeezed into a single mold. But yes, certain patterns do emerge when survey results are combined from large numbers of married couples that are studied over long periods of time. Lawrence Kurdek (1999) reported on a longitudinal study of married couples in which he measured each spouse's satisfaction every year for ten years (out of 522 couples he started with, 93 completed the study). Figure 9.10 shows that there was an overall decline in ratings of marital quality and that the ratings given by husbands and wives were very similar. There are two particularly sharp periods of decline. The first occurs during the first year of marriage. Newlyweds tend to idealize each other and to enjoy an initial state of marital bliss (Murray et al., 1996). However, this "honeymoon" is soon followed by a decline in satisfaction (Bradbury, 1998). After some stabilization, a second decline is then observed at about the eighth year of marriage—a finding that is consistent with the popular belief in a "seven-year itch" (Kovacs, 1983).

Are there specific factors that predict future outcomes? To address this question, Benjamin Karney and Thomas Bradbury (1995) reviewed 115 longitudinal studies of more than 45,000 married couples and found only that certain positively valued variables (education, employment, constructive behaviors, similarity in attitudes) are somewhat predictive of positive outcomes. They did find, however, that the steeper the initial decline in satisfaction, the more likely couples are to break up later. This decline is, in part, related to the stress of having and raising children, a stress that is common among newly married couples.

Is there anything a couple can do to keep the honeymoon alive? Perhaps there is. Arthur Aron and his colleagues (2000) have theorized that after the exhilaration of a new relationship wears off, partners can combat boredom by engaging together in new and arousing activities. By means of questionnaires and a door-to-door survey, these researchers found that the more new experiences spouses said they'd had together, the more satisfied they were with their marriages. To test this hypothesis in a controlled experiment, they brought randomly selected couples into the laboratory, spread gymnasium mats across the floor, tied the partners together at a wrist and ankle, and had them crawl on their hands and knees, over a barrier, from one end of the room to the other—all while carrying a pillow between their bodies. Other couples

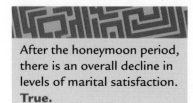

After the honeymoon period, there is an overall decline in levels of marital satisfaction. **True.**

were given the more mundane task of rolling a ball across the mat, one partner at a time. A third group received no assignment. Afterward, all participants were surveyed about their relationships. As predicted, the couples that had struggled and laughed their way through the novel and arousing activity reported more satisfaction with the quality of their relationships than did those in the mundane and no-task groups. It's possible that the benefit of shared participation in this study was short-lived. But maybe, just maybe, a steady and changing diet of exciting new experiences can help keep the flames of love burning.

Communication and Conflict Disagreements about sex, children, in-laws, and other matters can stir conflict in close relationships. Research shows that economic pressures, in particular, put an enormous amount of strain on marital relations (Conger et al., 1999). Whatever the cause, all couples experience some degree of friction. The issue is not whether it occurs but how we respond to it. One source of conflict is the difficulty some people have talking about their disagreements. When relationships break up, communication problems are indeed among the most common causes cited by straight and gay couples alike (Kurdek, 1991b; Sprecher, 1994). But what constitutes "bad communication"? Comparisons between happy and distressed couples have revealed a number of communication patterns that often occur in troubled relationships (Fincham, 2003).

One common pattern is called *negative affect reciprocity*—a tit-for-tat exchange of expressions of negative feelings. Generally speaking, expressions of negative affect within a couple trigger more in-kind responses than do expressions of positive affect. But negative affect reciprocity, especially in nonverbal behavior, is greater in couples that are unhappy, distressed, and locked into a duel. For couples in distress, smiles pass by unnoticed, but every glare, every disgusted look, provokes a sharp reflex-like response. The result, as observed in unhappy couples around the world, is an inability to break the vicious cycle and terminate unpleasant interactions (Gottman, 1998).

Men and women react differently to conflict. Women usually report more intense emotions and are more expressive (Grossman & Wood, 1993). She tells him to "warm up"; he urges her to "calm down." Thus, unhappy marriages also tend to be characterized by a *demand/withdraw interaction pattern,* in which the wife demands to discuss the relationship problems, only to become frustrated when her husband withdraws from such discussions (Christensen & Heavey, 1993). This configuration is not unique to married couples. When dating partners were asked about how they typically deal with problems, the same female-demand/male-withdraw pattern was found (Vogel et al., 1999). Married or not, then, it's clear that couples caught in this bind often find themselves echoing the title of Deborah Tannen's (1990) once popular book on gender and communication, *You Just Don't Understand.* According to John Gottman (1994), there is nothing wrong with either approach to dealing with conflict. The problem, he says, lies in the discrepancy—that healthy relationships are most likely when both partners have similar styles of dealing with conflict.

Whatever one's style, there are two basic approaches to reducing the negative effects of conflict. The first is so obvious that it is often overlooked: Increase rewarding behavior in other aspects of the relationship. According to Gottman and Levenson (1992), marital stability rests on a "fairly high balance of positive to negative behaviors" (p. 230). If there's conflict over one issue, partners can and should search for other ways to reward each other. As the balance of positives to negatives improves, so should overall levels of satisfaction, which can reduce conflict (Huston & Vangelisti, 1991). A second approach is to try to understand the other's point of view. Being sensitive to what the partner thinks and how he or she feels enhances the quality of the relationship (Honeycutt et al., 1993; Long & Andrews, 1990). What motivates individuals in the heat of battle to make that effort to understand? For starters, it helps if they agree that there is a communication problem.

The attributions that partners make for each other's behaviors and the willingness to forgive are correlated with the quality of their relationship (Bradbury & Fincham, 1992; Fincham et al., 2004; Harvey & Manusov, 2001). As you might expect, happy couples make *relationship-enhancing attributions:* They see the partner's undesirable behaviors as caused by factors that are situational ("a bad day"), temporary ("It'll pass"), and limited in scope ("That's just a sore spot"). Yet they see desirable behaviors as

FIGURE 9.11

Changes in Life Satisfaction Before and After Divorce

In this study, 817 men and women who were divorced at some point rated how satisfied they were with life on a scale of 0 to 10 every year for eighteen years. Overall, divorcees were less satisfied than their married counterparts—a common result. On the question of whether time heals the wound, you can see that satisfaction levels dipped before divorce, rebounded afterward, but did not return to original levels. It appears that people adapt but do not fully recover from this experience.

(Lucas, 2005.)

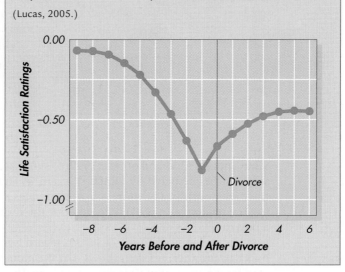

caused by factors that are inherent in the partner, permanent, and generalizable to other aspects of the relationship. In contrast, unhappy couples flip the attributional coin on its tail by making the opposite *distress-maintaining attributions*. Thus, while happy couples minimize the bad and maximize the good, distressed couples don't give an inch. In light of these differing attributional patterns, it would seem, over time, that happy couples would get happier and miserable couples more miserable. Do they? Yes. By tracking married couples in multi-year longitudinal studies, researchers have found that husbands and wives who made distress-maintaining causal attributions early in marriage reported less satisfaction at a later point in time (Fincham et al., 2000; Karney & Bradbury, 2000). The link between causal attributions and marital bliss or distress may be reciprocal, with each influencing the other.

Breaking Up   When an intimate relationship ends, the effect can be traumatic (Kitson & Morgan, 1990). As part of a longitudinal study of adults in Germany, Richard Lucas (2005) zeroed in on 817 men and women who at some point were divorced. Every year for eighteen years, these participants were interviewed and asked to rate how satisfied they were with their lives on a scale of 0 to 10. On average, the divorcees were more than a half point less satisfied than their married counterparts. But does time heal the wound? Figure 9.11 shows three interesting patterns: Participants had become less and less satisfied even before divorce, satisfaction levels rebounded somewhat immediately afterward, and satisfaction levels never did return to original baseline levels. In short, people adapt but do not fully recover from the experience.

How do people cope with divorce? The answer is, it depends on the nature of the loss. One vital factor is the closeness of a relationship, or the extent to which the line between self and other becomes so blurred that mine and yours are one and the

FIGURE 9.12

How Close Is Your Relationship?

The Inclusion of Other in the Self (IOS) Scale is a one-item, pictorial measure of relationship closeness. Choosing a picture with less overlap between the circles indicates less closeness; choosing one with more overlap indicates more closeness.

(Aron et al., 1992.)

Circle the picture below which best describes your relationship

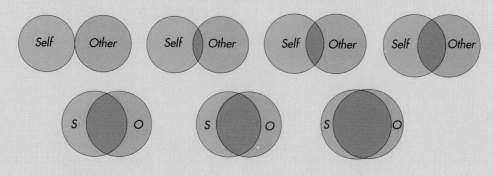

same. Indeed, Aron and others (1992) found that the longevity of a romantic relationship can be predicted by which diagram in Figure 9.12 people choose to describe their relationship. The more one incorporates a partner into the self, the more lasting the relationship is likely to be—but the more distress one anticipates if there is a breakup.

Another important factor in this regard is interdependence, the social glue that bonds us together. Research shows that the more interdependent couples are (as measured by the amount of time they spend together, the variety of shared activities, and the degree of influence each partner has over the other) and the more invested they are in the relationship, the longer it will likely last (Berscheid et al., 1989; Rusbult & Buunk, 1993)—and the more devastated they will become when it ends (Fine & Sacher, 1997; Simpson, 1987). In trying to explain how people regulate the risks of forming close romantic relationships, Sandra Murray and others (2006) note that an ironic theme runs through much of the research: "The relationships that have the most potential to satisfy adult needs for interpersonal connection are the very relationships that activate the most anxiety about rejection" (p. 661). We are, to put it mildly, darned if we do and darned if we don't. Those factors that contribute to the endurance of a relationship (closeness, interdependence) turn out to be the same factors that intensify fear of rejection and make coping more difficult after a relationship ends. So, how do you balance making the psychological investment necessary for a lasting relationship against holding back enough for self-protection?

In the United States and other western countries, various demographic markers indicate how problematic traditional forms of commitment have become: a high divorce rate, more single-parent families, more couples living together, and more never-married individuals. Yet the desire for long-term intimate relationships has never wavered or disappeared. To the contrary, gays and lesbians actively seek legal recognition of same-sex marriages, the vast majority of divorced individuals remarry, and stepfamilies forge a new sense of what it means to be a "family." It seems that we are in the midst of a great and compelling search, as millions of men and women try to find ways to affiliate with, attract, get closer to, love, and commit themselves with permanence to others.

REVIEW

Being with Others: A Fundamental Human Motive

- The need to belong is a basic human motive, a pervasive drive to form and maintain lasting relationships.

The Thrill of Affiliation

- This social motivation begins with the need for affiliation, a desire to establish social contact with others.
- People differ in the strength of their affiliative needs.
- Stressful situations in particular motivate us to affiliate with others who face a similar threat.

The Agony of Loneliness

- Shyness is a pervasive problem that sets people up to have unrewarding interactions with others.
- People who are painfully shy are at risk for loneliness, a feeling of isolation and social deprivation.

The Initial Attraction

- According to one perspective, people are attracted to others with whom the relationship is rewarding; rewards can be direct or indirect.
- Evolutionary psychologists argue that human beings exhibit patterns of attraction and mate selection that favor the passing on of their own genes.

Familiarity: Being There

- Proximity sets the stage for social interaction, which is why friendships are most likely to form between people who live near each other.
- Supporting the mere exposure effect, studies show that the more often people see a stimulus, the more they come to like it.
- We do not have to be aware of our prior exposures for the increase in liking to occur.

Physical Attractiveness: Getting Drawn In

- In a wide range of social settings, people respond more favorably to men and women who are physically attractive.
- Some researchers believe that certain faces (averaged and symmetrical) are inherently attractive—across cultures and to infants as well as adults.
- Others argue that beauty is in the eye of the beholder and point to the influences of culture, time, and context.
- One reason for the bias for beauty is that it's rewarding to be in the company of others who are attractive.
- A second reason is that people associate beauty with other positive qualities, a belief known as the what-is-beautiful-is-good stereotype.
- People seen as physically attractive are more popular, more sexually experienced, and more socially skilled; however, they are not happier or higher in self-esteem.
- One reason for the latter is that people who see themselves as attractive often discount the praise they get for nonsocial endeavors.

- Another problem with having beauty as a social asset is that people, notably women, feel pressured to keep up their appearance and are often dissatisfied with how they look.

First Encounters: Getting Acquainted

- People tend to associate with, befriend, and marry others who are similar in their demographic backgrounds, attitudes, and interests.
- People first avoid others who are dissimilar and then are drawn to those remaining who are most similar.
- Supporting the matching hypothesis, people tend to become romantically involved with others who are equivalent in physical attractiveness.
- Contrary to popular belief, complementarity in needs or personality does not spark attraction.
- Indicating the effects of reciprocity, we tend to like others who indicate that they like us.
- But indiscriminate likers can be taken for granted and not liked as much.
- Research on the hard-to-get effect shows that people like others best who are moderately selective in their social choices.

Mate Selection: The Evolution of Desire

- Evolutionary psychologists say that women seek men with financial security or traits predictive of future success in order to ensure the survival of their offspring.
- In contrast, men seek women who are young and attractive (physical attributes that signal health and fertility) and not promiscuous (an attribute that diminishes certainty of paternity).
- Cross-cultural studies tend to support these predicted sex differences, but critics note that many results are not that strong and can be viewed in terms that are more psychological than evolutionary.

Close Relationships

- Intimate relationships include at least one of three components: feelings of attachment, fulfillment of psychological needs, and interdependence.
- Stage theories propose that close relationships go through specific stages, but evidence for a fixed sequence is weak.
- Two other views emphasize either a gradual accumulation of rewards or a sharp distinction between types of relationships.

The Intimate Marketplace: Tracking the Gains and Losses

- According to social exchange theory, people seek to maximize gains and minimize costs in their relationships.
- Higher rewards, lower costs, and an outcome that meets or exceeds a partner's comparison level (CL) predict high levels of satisfaction.
- Lower expectations about alternatives (CLalt) and more investment in the relationship are associated with higher levels of commitment.
- Equity theory holds that satisfaction is greatest when the ratio between benefits and contributions is similar for both partners.
- Both overbenefit and underbenefit elicit negative emotions, but the underbenefited are usually less satisfied.

Types of Relationships

- In exchange relationships, people are oriented toward reward and immediate reciprocity; in communal relationships, partners are responsive to each other's needs.
- People with secure attachment styles have more satisfying romantic relationships than do those with insecure (anxious or avoidant) styles.

How Do I Love Thee? Counting the Ways

- According to the triangular theory of love, there are eight subtypes of love produced by the combinations of intimacy, passion, and commitment.
- Inherent in all classifications of love are two types: passionate and companionate.
- Passionate love is an intense, emotional, often erotic state of positive absorption in another person.
- In one theory, passionate love is sparked by physiological arousal and the belief that the arousal was caused by the loved person.
- Consistent with excitation transfer, arousal can increase or decrease attraction, depending on the initial attractiveness of the person whom one is with.
- Compared with passionate love, companionate love is less intense but in some respects deeper and more enduring.

- Companionate love rests on mutual trust, caring, friendship, commitment, and willingness to share intimate facts and feelings.
- Self-disclosure between partners often becomes broader and deeper over time, though self-disclosure varies with the state of the relationship.

Cultural Influences on Attraction and Close Relationships

- Although Buss identified universal gender differences in mate preference, he also found some striking cultural differences, as in the preference for chastity.
- The universality of passionate love has led some researchers to explore the neuroscientific bases for this experience.
- Cultures differ in the extent to which romantic love is seen as necessary for marriage.

Relationship Issues: The Male-Female "Connection"

- People vary in how they define what it means to "have sex."
- On average, men report being sexually more active than women and see opposite-sex interactions in more sexualized terms.
- An estimated 3 or 4 percent of men and 2 percent of women are exclusively homosexual in orientation.
- Both biological and environmental theories are used to explain the origins of homosexuality.
- When relationships break up, communication problems are among the most common causes.
- Unhappy couples often engage in negative affect reciprocity and exhibit a demand/withdraw interaction pattern.
- During conflict, women are more likely to be demanding; men are more likely to withdraw.
- Partners can reduce conflict by behaving in rewarding ways in other areas and by trying to understand each other's point of view.
- Happy couples make relationship-enhancing attributions, while unhappy couples make distress-maintaining attributions.
- On average, marital satisfaction starts high, declines during the first year, stabilizes, and then declines again at about the eighth year.
- Partners who are close and interdependent and for whom relationships are important to the self-concept (characteristics that normally promote stability) suffer more after breaking up.

KEY TERMS

PUTTING COMMON SENSE TO THE TEST

People seek out the company of others, even strangers, in times of stress.

True. Research has shown that external threat causes stress and leads people to affiliate with others who are facing or have faced a similar threat.

Infants do not discriminate between faces considered attractive and unattractive in their culture.

False. Two-month-old infants spend more time gazing at attractive than unattractive faces, indicating that they do make the distinction.

People who are physically attractive are happier and have higher self-esteem than those who are unattractive.

False. Attractive people are at an advantage in their social lives, but they are not happier, better adjusted, or higher in self-esteem.

When it comes to romantic relationships, opposites attract.

False. Consistently, people are attracted to others who are similar—not opposite or complementary—on a whole range of dimensions.

Men are more likely than women to interpret friendly gestures by the opposite sex in sexual terms.

True. Experiments have shown that men are more likely than women to interpret friendly opposite-sex interactions as sexual come-ons.

After the honeymoon period, there is an overall decline in levels of marital satisfaction.

True. High marital satisfaction levels among newlyweds are often followed by a measurable decline during the first year and then, after a period of stabilization, by another decline at the eighth year—a pattern found among parents and non-parents alike.

10

Helping Others

PREVIEW

This chapter describes the social psychology of giving and receiving help. First, we examine the *evolutionary, motivational, situational, personal,* and *interpersonal* factors that predict whether a potential helper will provide assistance to a person in need. Then, we consider people's *reactions to receiving help.* In the concluding section, we discuss the *helping connection,* the role of social ties in promoting helpfulness to others.

PUTTING COMMON SENSE TO THE TEST

T/F

_____ People are more likely to help someone in an emergency if the potential rewards seem high and the potential costs seem low.

_____ In an emergency, a person who needs help has a much better chance of getting it if three other people are present than if only one other person is present.

_____ People are much more likely to help someone when they're in a good mood.

_____ People are much less likely to help someone when they're in a bad mood.

_____ Attractive people have a better chance than unattractive people of getting help when they need it.

_____ In any situation, people are more likely to help a friend succeed than a stranger.

_____ Women seek help more often than men do.

It was their bravery that compelled them to risk their lives, but it was their compassion that ultimately saved them. Six firefighters from New York City's Ladder Company Six were among the numerous firefighters, police officers, and other rescue workers who courageously climbed up the stairs of the World Trade Center on September 11, 2001. The jets that had flown into each of the Twin Towers of the skyscraper were hemorrhaging fuel, causing an inferno of unprecedented proportion. A massive stream of people trying to flee raced down the narrow stairs, passing the firefighters who were going up. Awed by their courage and resolve, people yelled encouragement and blessings to the firefighters as they passed them. Under the burden of more than 100 pounds of equipment, the men of Company Six reached the 27th floor of the North Tower when they heard the horrifying sound of the South Tower collapsing. Their captain ordered them to turn back, realizing that if the other tower could collapse, so could theirs.

On their way down, around the 14th or 15th floor, they encountered a frail woman named Josephine Harris. She had walked down almost 60 flights already, and she was exhausted. The firefighters helped her walk, but she was slowing them down dangerously. Their captain, John Jonas, was growing more anxious: "I could hear the clock ticking in the back of my head. I'm thinking, 'C'mon, c'mon. We've got to keep moving.'" But none of the six men considered leaving her behind, so they slowly walked down together. Josephine didn't think she could go on, but one of the firefighters asked her about her family and told her that her children and grandchildren wanted to see her again. She continued, but finally collapsed as they got near the 4th floor. On the 4th floor they tried to find a chair to carry her in. And then, the 110-story skyscraper collapsed.

Other rescue workers who had passed this slow-moving group on the stairs were killed on the floors below them. Virtually everyone who was still above them was killed. And yet somehow this group survived, trapped in an inexplicable pocket of safety amidst the unimaginable wreckage, along with two other firefighters, a Fire Department chief, and a Port Authority police officer. After a harrowing search for a way out, eventually they found a small ray of light—a literal ray of hope—and followed it to safety.

The firefighters later called Josephine Harris their guardian angel and thanked _her_ for saving _their_ lives. They realized that had they not encountered her, they would have gone down the stairs faster, and had she not kept walking despite exhaustion, they would have been a few floors above—either way, they would have been killed. But Josephine Harris knew that she owed her life to these brave men, who risked not seeing their own children again so that she could see hers.

Displaying bravery that seems to defy instinct, firefighter Mike Kehoe climbs the stairs of one of the towers of the World Trade Center to assist with the rescue efforts during the terrorist attacks on the morning of September 11, 2001. This photograph became a famous symbol of the heroism exhibited by so many people on that horrific day. Kehoe was one of the fortunate ones who survived.

Residents wait on a rooftop to be rescued from the flood waters of Hurricane Katrina in New Orleans, September 2005.

There were many other heroes that day, including ordinary citizens whose acts of self-sacrifice to help others were not part of their job descriptions. Some of the help was dramatically heroic, like that of the passengers aboard highjacked United Airlines Flight 93. They decided to fight the terrorists on their flight and sacrifice their own lives in order to try to prevent the terrorists from killing many more people on the ground. And much of the help was behind the scenes, as in the cases of people volunteering endless hours doing the grueling work of cleaning up the disaster area, helping the injured and the grieving, and donating money, clothes, and other resources.

When people read stories such as these, it is natural for them to wonder what they would have done: Would they have risked their lives to help others? What makes some people, at some times, act to help others? The wonderful acts of helping during the chaos of 9/11 are inspiring, to be sure. But there were also many stories that day of people who turned their backs on others, even on people who had just helped them.

Every day there are numerous unheralded acts of helping others and of failing to help others. A volunteer works tirelessly in an AIDS clinic, a college student tutors a child, a congregation raises money for a religious cause, an older sister lets her little brother win at checkers. And yet every day someone ignores the screams outside his or her window, drives past motorists stranded on the side of a road, or tries to avoid making eye contact with a homeless person on the street. Every few months we see a story like that of Wesley Autrey, who saw a young man collapse onto a subway track in New York City as a train approached in January 2007. Autrey jumped onto the track and rolled with the man into a drainage trough. As the train operator hit the emergency brakes, some of the train's cars passed over Autrey and the other man with inches to spare. "If I let him lay there by himself, he's going to be dismembered," Autrey reported thinking as he saw the train coming (Hajela, 2007). And every few months we also learn of a story like Omar Wellington's, a seventeen-year-old who was stripped to his underwear by a group of young people and beaten for an hour in July 2006 in a densely populated housing complex in Toronto. He was later found dead with multiple stab wounds to the neck. Parents who saw the attack took their young children away from the scene, and dozens of neighbors watched from their backyards. Not only did no one intervene during the attack, but no one even called the police. The boy's mother asked later, "How could people stand by and watch as my son was tortured for more than an hour?" (Huffman, 2006, p. B1).

There is no simple answer to the question of why some people help and others don't or why some situations lead to quick assistance and others to shocking displays of inaction. The determinants of helping behavior are complex and multifaceted. But social psychologists have learned a great deal about these determinants—and, therefore, about human nature—over the last several decades; and as you will see in the pages to come, some of their findings are quite surprising.

In this chapter, we examine several questions about helping: *Why* do people help? *When* do they help? *Who* is likely to help? *Whom* do they help? We then explore the other side of helping: how people react to the help they receive. The concluding section concentrates on a major, recurring theme—social connection—that underlies much of the theory and research on helping.

Evolutionary and Motivational Factors: Why Do People Help?

Although few individuals reach the heights of heroic helping, virtually everyone helps somebody sometime. People give their friends a ride to the airport; donate money, food, and clothing for disaster relief; baby-sit for a relative; work as a volunteer for charitable activities; pick up the mail for a neighbor who's out of town. The list of **prosocial behaviors**—actions intended to benefit others—is endless. But *why* do people help? Several factors have an impact.

Evolutionary Factors in Helping

According to a report by the Giving USA Foundation, about 70 to 80 percent of Americans contribute to at least one charity, and Americans gave $249 billion to charitable causes in 2004. The results of the Canadian Survey of Giving, Volunteering, and Participating show that Canadians donated almost $9 billion in 2004, with 85 percent of adults giving at least one donation.

We begin with evolution. Evolutionary scientists use principles of evolution to understand human social behavior. Can evolutionary principles help explain why people help? At first glance, some may think it unlikely. From an evolutionary perspective, what possible function can there be in helping others, especially at the risk of one's own life? Doesn't risking one's life for others fly in the face of evolutionary principles like "survival of the fittest"?

The "Selfish Gene"   In fact, evolutionary perspectives emphasize not the survival of the fittest individuals but the survival of the individuals' genes (Dawkins, 1989; Hamilton, 1964). From the perspective of evolution, human social behavior should be analyzed in terms of its contribution to reproductive success in ancestral environments: the conception, birth, and survival of offspring over the course of many generations. If a specific social behavior enhances reproductive success, the genetic underpinnings of that behavior are more likely to be passed on to subsequent generations. In this way, the behavior can eventually become part of the common inheritance of the species.

Of course, in order to reproduce, the individual must survive long enough to do so. Being helped *by* others should increase the chances of survival. But what about being helpful *to* others? Since helping others can be costly in terms of time and effort, and is sometimes dangerous to the helper, being helpful would seem to decrease one's chances of survival. Shouldn't any genetically based propensities for helping have dropped out of the gene pool long ago?

Not necessarily. There is an alternative to individual survival. You can also preserve your genes by promoting the survival of those who share your genetic make-up, even if you perish in the effort to help them. By means of this indirect route to genetic survival, the tendency to help genetic relatives, called **kin selection**, could become an innate characteristic—that is, a characteristic that is not contingent on learning for its development, although it can be influenced by learning, culture, and other factors. Kin selection is evident in the behavior of many organisms. Just as humans often risk their lives to save close relatives, squirrels emit an alarm to nearby relatives to warn them of a predator—which helps their relatives but makes the squirrel who sounds the alarm more vulnerable to attack (Hauber & Sherman, 1998; McCowan & Hooper, 2002). In what might seem to defy evolutionary principles, in some species individuals delay breeding in order to stay close to home and assist their parents in raising little siblings. Why would they delay reproducing their own genes to help raise genetically related, but not identical, kin? In the conditions in which this *cooperative breeding* typically occurs, this strategy actually is advantageous, helping these individuals perpetuate their own genes at a time and place in which they would be unable to rear their own offspring (Doerr & Doerr , 2006; Fitzpatrick et al., 2006).

prosocial behaviors
Actions intended to benefit others.

kin selection   Preferential helping of genetic relatives, which results in the greater likelihood that genes held in common will survive.

Because kin selection serves the function of genetic survival, preferential helping of genetic relatives should be strongest when the biological stakes are particularly high. This appears to be the case. Eugene Burnstein and others (1994) conducted a series of studies testing several predictions based on evolutionary theory. These researchers asked students in the United States and Japan to report how they would respond to a variety of situations in which someone needed help. Consistent with predictions based on kin selection, participants indicated they were more likely to help a person who was closely related (for example, a sibling or parent) than a person who was more distantly related (for example, an uncle or grandmother), especially in life-and-death situations as opposed to more everyday situations. In addition, intentions to help kin in life-threatening situations were influenced by reproductive-related factors; for example, participants reported they would help youthful relatives more than older adults, and healthy relatives more than those in poor health. In a more recent study, Josephine Korchmaros and others (2006) also found support for the role of kinship in individuals' intentions to perform a risky rescue behavior. These researchers proposed that the willingness to help kin operates through the greater emotional closeness that people feel with those most genetically related to them. Do these intentions to help translate to actual behaviors? According to Yossi Shavit and others (1994), they can. These researchers asked residents of metropolitan Haifa, Israel, to report from whom they received support during the missile attacks in the 1991 Gulf War. Although residents reported receiving comfort and advice from friends as well as kin, more immediate and direct aid was much more likely to come from kin.

Reciprocal Altruism   Kin selection provides only a partial explanation for helping. Relatives are not always helpful to each other. And even though relatives may get preferential treatment, most people help out non-kin as well. What's the reproductive advantage of helping someone who isn't related to you? The most common answer is reciprocity. Through *reciprocal altruism,* helping someone else can be in your best interests because it increases the likelihood that you will be helped in return (Krebs, 1987; Trivers, 1985). If Chris helps Sandy and Sandy helps Chris, both Chris and Sandy increase their chances of survival and reproductive success. Over the course of evolution, therefore, individuals who engage in reciprocal altruism should survive and reproduce more than individuals who do not, thus enabling this kind of altruism to flourish.

Robert Trivers (1971) cites several examples of reciprocal altruism in animals. Many animals groom each other; for instance, monkeys groom other monkeys and cats groom other cats. Large fish (such as groupers) allow small fish (such as wrasses) to swim in their mouths without eating them; the small fish get food for themselves and at the same time remove parasites from the larger fish. And chimps who share with other chimps at one feeding are repaid by the other chimps at another feeding;

"Scratch my back and I'll scratch yours."

—proverb

Many animals groom each other, whether they be chimpanzees in Tanzania or young girls in the United States. According to evolutionary psychologists, such behavior often reflects reciprocal altruism.

those who are selfish are rebuffed, sometimes violently, at a later feeding (de Waal, 1996, 2006). An additional illustration is provided by Robert Seyfarth and Dorothy Cheney (1984). In a creative field experiment, these researchers audiotaped female vervet monkeys calling out for help and then played the recorded vocalizations near other female monkeys. Half of these other monkeys heard a female who had recently groomed them; the other half heard a female who had not recently done so. Consistent with the idea of reciprocal altruism, they were significantly more likely to respond attentively to the request for help if the solicitor had just groomed them than if she had not. Interestingly, if the solicitor was genetically related to the monkeys who heard the tape, the monkeys' response was equally strong whether or not she had groomed them.

Franz de Waal (2003) observed a group of chimpanzees engaged in nearly 7,000 interactions and recorded their grooming and food-sharing behaviors. He noted striking evidence of reciprocal altruism among these chimps. If Chimp A groomed Chimp B, for instance, B was much more likely to then share his or her food with A than if A had not groomed B first, or than B would with some other chimp. Moreover, Chimp A would be relatively unlikely to share his or her own food with Chimp B before B had reciprocated; after all, A had already groomed B, and now it was B's turn to help A! It's interesting that these chimps were able to negotiate this kind of reciprocity across acts: in grooming and food sharing. It was as if they were operating under a norm of "You scratch my back, I'll scratch yours—or maybe I'll give you some of my apples." In another study, de Waal and Michelle Berger (2000) observed same-sex pairs of capuchin monkeys working cooperatively in a test chamber to obtain a tray of food. The two monkeys were separated from each other by a mesh partition. One monkey by itself could not pull the tray, but the two monkeys could accomplish the task cooperatively. When successful, the monkey that wound up with the food consistently shared it with its helper. When rewarded in this way, the monkeys became even more likely to help each other subsequently.

In some human environments, reciprocal altruism is essential for survival even today. Burnstein and his colleagues (1994) cite the !Kung of Africa as an example. The !Kung have been pushed by other groups into barren lands where food and water are scarce. As a result, the !Kung share all resources within the band. An individual who gets food will share with the others and will expect the same in return. "The idea of eating alone is shocking to the !Kung. It makes them shriek with an uneasy laughter. Lions could do that, they say, not men" (Marshall, 1979, p. 357).

Reciprocal altruism is not restricted to basic needs such as food acquisition. Think of file sharing instead of food sharing. The swapping of music and videos online through file-sharing services may be considered a form of reciprocal altruism, since an individual makes his or her own files available to others so that he or she can have access to theirs. (Of course, the record labels and movie studios have other terms for these activities, such as *criminal* and *unethical*.) Strong norms often develop in these peer-to-peer networks. An individual who downloads songs or videos from others' computers but doesn't make his or her own files available is likely to be chastised quickly and emphatically. Indeed, the development of norms and the punishment of individuals who deviate from the norm are key factors in maintaining reciprocal altruism, especially in groups of non-kin. Even though in some situations individuals risk personal costs in order to punish violators, they do so anyway to preserve a norm that tends to benefit everyone in the group (Gintis et al., 2003; O'Gorman et al., 2005). Indeed, in one recent study, Dominique de Quervain and others (2004) found that when individuals punished such violators, even at some cost to themselves, they showed increased activity in the dorsal striatum, an area in the brain associated with experiencing personally rewarding actions.

Other Evolutionary Approaches   Kin selection and reciprocal altruism emphasize helping specific others based on genetic relatedness or the probability of being helped in return. But much helping goes beyond these limits. For example, injured or sick animals are often aided by others in their group, even if they are unrelated and there is little chance that the recipients will return the favor (de Waal, 1996). Can altruism operate at a broader level than specific genes or specific reciprocal relationships between individuals?

> *"When you give to someone else, you get so much more."*
>
> —former U.S. secretary of state Colin Powell

Cooperation within the group, as is evident in this communal barn building, is an essential feature of the Amish way of life. Some evolutionary theorists believe that helping other members of one's social group may be an evolved tendency.

Some scholars recently have examined indirect reciprocity, which Martin Nowak and Karl Sigmund (2005) describe as "I help you and somebody else helps me." This kind of more complex system of altruism may play a role in *group selection*. The idea behind group selection is that groups with altruistic members may be less likely to become extinct than groups with only self-ish individuals (Caporael, 2004; Henrich, 2004; Sober & Wilson, 1998). According to this perspective, cooperation and helpful-ness among members of a social group (es-pecially when the group faces an external threat) could be an evolved tendency. Franz de Waal (1996) reports remarkable instances of within-group helping among animals—for example, a Japanese monkey born without hands and feet who was fully accepted and helped by the other monkeys in its group and a retarded rhesus mon-key given special care by the other monkeys in its group. Barry Sinervo and others (2006) recently reported cooperative partnerships among nonrelated lizards to protect their territories. Many evolutionary scientists are skeptical of the concept of group selection, however, and so it remains to be seen how this idea itself will evolve in the years to come.

Particularly when examining the behavior of humans, some scholars have focused less on kin selection and more on the evolution of parental caregiving (Bell, 2001). Many mammals, and especially humans, display impulses to care for offspring. Parental caregiving will, of course, tend to help kin survive, but these behaviors can sometimes generalize to helping offspring who are not kin. Daniel Batson and others (2005) propose that this nurturing impulse can cause people to feel empathy for others in need, even if the others are not related or even very similar to them. College students in one of their studies, for example, felt greater empathy for the suffering (from a se-verely broken leg) of a young child or of a dog than they did for a fellow student from their university. Batson and his colleagues believe that the greater empathy for the small child or dog reflects a parental instinct in humans that is more generalized than what might be predicted simply from a kin selection perspective. Stories of pets helping small children in emergencies may reflect a similar impulse.

Rewards of Helping: Helping Others to Help Oneself

People are more likely to help someone in an emergency if the potential rewards seem high and the potential costs seem low. **True.**

arousal: cost-reward model The proposition that people react to emergency situations by acting in the most cost-effective way to reduce the arousal of shock and alarm.

Whether or not it can be traced to evolutionary factors, one important reason why people help others is because it often is rewarding, even if the rewards are psy-chological rather than material. We all like the idea of being the hero, lifted onto the shoulders of our peers for coming to the rescue of someone in distress. Helping helps the helper.

The empirical evidence on this point is clear: People are much more likely to help when the potential rewards of helping seem high relative to the potential costs. This effect does not appear to be limited to the very individualistic cultures of the United States, Canada, and Western Europe; evidence has been found also in Sudan and in Japan, for example (Hedge & Yousif, 1992; Imai, 1991). The research of Jane Piliavin, John Dovidio, and their colleagues suggests that potential helpers conduct a cost-ben-efit analysis not only when making deliberate decisions to behave prosocially, as when donating blood, but also in more impulsive, sudden decisions to intervene in an emergency (e.g., Dovidio et al., 2006). Indeed, the **arousal: cost-reward model** of helping stipulates that both emotional and cognitive factors determine whether by-standers to an emergency will intervene. Emotionally, bystanders experience the shock and alarm of personal distress; this unpleasant state of arousal motivates them to do something to reduce it. What they do, however, depends on the "bystander calculus," their computation of the costs and rewards associated with helping. When potential rewards (to self and victim) outweigh potential costs (to self and victim), bystanders will help. But raise those costs and lower those rewards, and victims stand a good chance of having to do without (Fritzsche et al., 2000; Piliavin et al., 1981).

Feeling Good   Helping often simply *feels* good (Smith et al., 1989; Williamson & Clark, 1992). A growing body of recent research has pointed to a strong relationship between giving help and feeling better, including on measures of mental *and* physical health (Brown et al., 2003; Dulin & Hill, 2003; Piliavin, 2003; Post, 2005; Schwartz et al., 2003). One recent example is a study by Heidi Wayment (2004). Wayment found that women who engaged in any of a variety of helping behaviors in the aftermath of the September 11, 2001, terrorist attacks in the United States showed greater reduction in their distress over time than women who did not engage in these acts of helping.

In a provocative set of studies using brain-imaging techniques, James Rilling and others (2002) examined the brain activity of women playing a Prisoner's Dilemma game, which, as was discussed in Chapter 8, is a game in which individuals compete or cooperate with each other for individual and joint payoffs. The researchers found that when the women were engaged in mutual cooperation during the game, activation was observed in areas of the brain that are linked to processing rewards. Despite the fact that these individuals could earn more money by competing with their partner after their partner had cooperated, their brain activity suggested that cooperation was intrinsically rewarding, and this feeling could reinforce altruism and inhibit selfishness.

Even when helping doesn't feel good immediately, it can pay off in the long run. When parents reluctantly sacrifice relaxing with a good book or DVD at the end of a hard day in order to help their child finish some homework, they might not feel immediate joy from giving help; but in the long run, they will reap the benefits of their behavior (Salovey et al., 1991).

Children learn that helping others can be rewarding (Grusec, 1991). Younger children focus on the rewards they get from parents and others; but as they develop into adolescence, they begin to reward themselves for helping, taking pride in their actions. Their helpful behavior can then be internally motivated, leading them to help even without the promise of immediate material or social rewards (Cialdini et al., 1981; Piliavin & Callero, 1991).

The process of helping others to feel good about oneself is often not conscious, but it can be. For example, participants in one study rated the relative importance of a number of considerations in deciding whether to help someone else. Two of the three considerations that the participants rated as most important concerned the rewards ("It would make me feel good about myself") and costs ("I might get hurt") of helping. The other consideration was "It's the right thing to do" (Smitherman, 1992). People's awareness that helping feels good is evident in the words offered by no less an authority than the venerable "Dear Abby," the world's most famous syndicated advice columnist. She recently offered this advice to her readers: "The surest way to forget your own troubles is to do something nice for those less fortunate. The adrenaline rush you'll get is more powerful than speed, and the 'high' is perfectly legal" ("Dear Abby," 2003).

Being, or Appearing to Be, Good   In addition to the rewards of helping, the consideration that "It's the right thing to do" reflects, at least in

A Peace Corps worker teaches English in Honduras. Volunteering one's time, energy, and skills to help others can make one feel good about oneself. Even if not financial, the rewards can be tremendous.

part, a sense of moral obligation or duty. Being motivated to behave in ways consistent with moral principles may drive people to help each other, and affirming one's morality in this way can make one feel good about oneself. Conversely, inhibiting or disengaging oneself from such moral concerns may be the critical factor in enabling humans to act inhumanely toward one another, through violence, terrorism, discrimination, and other acts of destruction (Bandura, 2004; McAlister et al., 2006; Staub, 2004).

Another motive for helping has the appearance of morality but reflects a more selfish desire to reap the social rewards of helping. The reference here is to *moral hypocrisy,* whereby people try to convince themselves and others that they are driven to help others by moral principles when in actuality they are motivated to benefit themselves by *appearing* to be moral. For example, imagine that you and a friend meet a musician you both admire and she gives you a back-stage pass for her next concert. There's just the one pass, and it's in your hands. Do you keep it, or do you flip a coin for it? Furthermore, what if you know that if you flip the coin, you can increase the likelihood that you're going to win? If you are motivated by moral hypocrisy, you might make a big, noble show of your willingness to flip the coin— as long as you know that you're probably going to win. Truly moral motivation, on the other hand, would compel you to ask a disinterested third person to flip the coin under perfectly fair conditions, even though you might suffer a cost. Using experimental scenarios that mimicked dilemmas similar to this one, Daniel Batson and others (1997, 2003) have demonstrated the prevalence of moral hypocrisy in their research. They found that participants were likely to act morally when their action benefited themselves; but when it did not benefit them, and if the situation permitted them to behave in a self-interested way without appearing selfish, they were much less likely to take the moral action.

A particularly disturbing version of moral hypocrisy can be seen when individuals deliberately hurt or endanger others so that they can swoop in and apparently try to save the day. A case in point was Kristen Gilbert, a nurse and mother of two, who was sentenced to life in prison in 2001 for killing four patients at a Veterans Affairs hospital in Massachusetts. She killed the patients by injecting them with epinephrine, a stimulant that caused their hearts to beat out of control. Why did she do it? According to her lawyers, "Her aim was to cause a medical emergency so she could become a hero" (Bayles, 2001).

Another kind of hypocrisy involves *overhelping.* Picture the following: A child who feels threatened by the attention given to a younger sibling proceeds to "help" the toddler right off his or her feet and onto the floor with a crash. "Oops," says the older child. "I was only trying to help." Adults can be more subtle in their approach, but they may have a similar motivation: to appear to help another only to hurt him or her. According to Daniel Gilbert and David Silvera (1996), people sometimes offer help to another who doesn't really need it, or they offer more help than the recipient needs, in order to raise suspicions about the recipient's successful performance. Thus the adult version of the previous situation might play out like this: Ryan knows that Christina doesn't need any help on a project she's completing, but he makes a public display of assistance, hoping that she'll get less of the credit than she deserves. He hopes others will say, "Sure, Christina did a great job on the project, but I wonder if she could have done it without Ryan."

Cost of Helping, or of Not Helping Clearly, helping has its rewards; but it has its costs as well. The firefighters in Ladder Company Six who risked their lives to help Josephine Harris as the World Trade Center was about to collapse on September 11, 2001, were among the lucky ones. Many people were killed while helping others that day, such as Abraham Zelmanowitz, a computer programmer who refused to leave his quadriplegic friend who could not descend the stairs. And beyond 9/11, we often are struck by stories of the costs paid by those who offer help, such as Elizabeth Ottomeyer, a thirty-six-year-old nurse from St. Louis, Missouri, who ran across a highway to help motorists who had been in an accident and was killed by a hit-and-run driver—who, it turned out, was a doctor (Bell, 2003). Another example is Rudy Tomjanovich, a longtime coach of the Houston Rockets basketball team, whose professional playing career was cut short when he intervened to break up a fight on the court and was punched so hard that numerous bones in his face shattered.

Other helpers have done more sustained and deliberate helping, such as the people who helped hide runaway slaves in the nineteenth-century American South, or the people who helped hide Jews during the Holocaust. Sharon Shepela and others (1999) call this type of thoughtful helping in the face of potentially enormous costs *courageous resistance*. And although giving help is often associated with positive affect and health, when the help involves constant and exhausting demands, which is often the case when taking long-term care of a very ill person, the effects on the helper's physical and mental health can be quite negative (Schwartz et al., 2003).

To shift the balance between the costs and benefits of helping more toward the benefits, some legislatures have created "Good Samaritan" laws that require people to provide or summon aid in an emergency—so long as they do not endanger themselves in the process. Such laws are not uncommon in Europe. In fact, several photographers were initially accused by French authorities of breaking France's Good Samaritan laws following the automobile crash that killed Princess Diana, her companion, and their driver in Paris in 1997. Reportedly, these photographers arrived early at the crash scene and took pictures rather than attempting to help the victims. Good Samaritan laws were recently under consideration in western Australia (*The Daily Telegraph,* 2006). In the United States, Good Samaritan laws are relatively rare, although such a law was passed in California following an incident in which a University of California student failed to intervene, or even to notify the police, when he witnessed a friend rape and murder a seven-year-old girl in a bathroom (Gledhill & Lucas, 2000). (A Good Samaritan law also played an important role in the final episode of the popular TV series *Seinfeld,* as the four main characters were arrested and sentenced to a year in prison for callously failing to help someone in need.) Other states, instead of raising the cost of not helping by adopting Good Samaritan laws, have attempted to lower the cost of helping by enacting laws that protect Good Samaritans against lawsuits. These states encourage bystanders to intervene in emergencies by offering them legal protection, particularly doctors who volunteer medical care when they happen upon emergencies (Brown, 1999; Corrigan, 2006).

Altruism or Egoism: The Great Debate

At the end of 1996, *People* magazine honored Binti Jua as one of the twenty-five "most intriguing people" of the year; and *Newsweek* named her "hero of the year." On August 16, while caring for her own seventeen-month-old daughter, Binti came across a three-year-old boy who had fallen about twenty feet onto a cement floor and been knocked unconscious. She picked up the boy and gently held him, rocking him softly, and then turned him over to paramedics. What was most "intriguing" about Binti? The fact that she was a gorilla.

When the boy climbed over a fence and fell into the primate exhibit at the Brookfield Zoo, near Chicago, witnesses feared the worst. One paramedic said, "I didn't know if she was going to treat him like a doll or a toy." With her own daughter clinging to her back the entire time, Binti "protected the toddler as if he were her own," keeping other gorillas at bay and eventually placing him gently at the entrance where zookeepers and paramedics could get to him. "I could not believe how gentle she was," observed a zoo director (O'Neill et al., 1996, p. 72).

It was, of course, a terrific story; and it soon sparked national debate about whether or not Binti's act was a heartwarming example of altruism, motivated by kindness and compassion. At the Democratic National Convention, held in Chicago a few weeks after the incident, Hillary Clinton referred to the gorilla as "a typical Chicagoan. Tough on the outside but with a heart of gold underneath" (Rubenstein, 1996, p. A17). Others countered that Binti had been trained to pick up and fetch things that fell into her cage and had simply acted as she had been trained to act—with no kindness or compassion involved.

altruistic Motivated by the desire to improve another's welfare.

egoistic Motivated by the desire to increase one's own welfare.

The same debate exists about human behavior. Are humans ever truly **altruistic**—motivated by the desire to increase another's welfare? Or are our helpful behaviors always **egoistic**—motivated by selfish concerns or simple conformity

Binti Jua, a gorilla in the Brook-field Zoo, near Chicago, gently rocks a three-year-old boy who had fallen eighteen feet into the primate exhibit. The gorilla was acclaimed a hero for her role in saving the boy. Did Binti Jua act out of kindness and empathy? Or did she simply do what she was taught—fetch objects that fall into her cage? This episode brings the altruism debate to life, even in the animal world.

to socialized norms? Although most psychological theories assume an egoistic, self-interested bottom line, not everyone is content with this account of the motives of human behavior. Consider, for example, the many college students who participate in volunteer activities: tutoring refugees and disadvantaged youngsters, serving meals at food kitchens, signing up potential bone-marrow donors, working in community service agencies—the list goes on and on. Are they all just looking out for number one?

Daniel Batson (2002) thinks not. He believes that the motivation behind some helpful actions is at least in part truly altruistic. Batson defines *altruistic* as we defined it above: motivated by the desire to increase another's welfare. This definition is narrower than those that characterize any helpful action in the absence of a clear external reward as altruistic. At the same time, it is broader than those that restrict altruism to helpful actions requiring personal sacrifice by the helper. According to this perspective, it's the nature of the helper's motive that counts, not whether the helper receives benefits or suffers costs for helping.

Batson's model of altruism is based on his view of the consequences of empathy, which has long been viewed as a basic factor in promoting positive behavior toward others. Although the definition of *empathy* has been much debated, most researchers regard empathy as a complex phenomenon with both cognitive and emotional components (Davis et al., 2004; Eisenberg et al., 2006; Preston & de Waal, 2002). The major cognitive component of empathy is *perspective taking:* using the power of imagination to try to see the world through someone else's eyes. A key emotional component of empathy is *empathic concern,* which involves other-oriented feelings, such as sympathy, compassion, and tenderness. In contrast to empathic concern is *personal distress,* which involves self-oriented reactions to a person in need, such as feeling alarmed, troubled, or upset.

A fascinating recent study suggests that even infants and possibly even young chimpanzees are capable of at least a rudimentary degree of perspective taking and ensuing helping behavior. Felix Warneken and Michael Tomasello (2006) placed eighteen-month-old human infants with an adult experimenter. At various points in time, the experimenter appeared to have trouble reaching a goal. For example, he accidentally dropped a marker on the floor and tried unsuccessfully to reach it, or he couldn't put some magazines into a cabinet because the doors were closed. Twenty-two of the twenty-four infants tested helped the experimenter in at least one of the tasks, and many infants helped on several tasks. In doing so, the infants apparently understood that the experimenter needed help—that is, that he was having trouble completing a task by himself. There are two additional details worth noting about the study. First, the experimenter never requested help from the infants, nor did he praise or reward the infants when they did help. Second, for every task in which he needed help, the experimenter created a similar situation but one in which he did not seem to have a problem. For example, rather than accidentally drop the marker on the floor and try to reach it, at other times the experimenter intentionally threw the marker on the floor and did not try to retrieve it. In these situations, the infants were not likely to take action such as pick up the marker. This suggested that when they did "help" the experimenter, the infants did so because they understood he was trying to achieve some goal.

The researchers also tested three young chimpanzees (between three and five years old) using a similar procedure. The chimpanzees also helped the human experimenter in response to seeing that he appeared to need help reaching his goal, although not across as many tasks or as reliably as the human infants did. The authors

FIGURE 10.1

The Empathy-Altruism Hypothesis

According to the empathy-altruism hypothesis, taking the perspective of a person in need creates feelings of empathic concern, which produce the altruistic motive to reduce the other person's distress. When people do *not* take the other's perspective, they experience feelings of personal distress, which produce the egoistic motive to reduce their own discomfort.

(Based on Batson, 1991.)

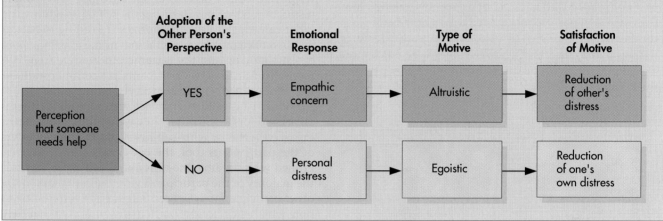

reported that this was the first experimental evidence of helping of this kind (helping others who are struggling to achieve some goal without any benefit to the self) by nonhuman primates.

The Empathy-Altruism Hypothesis   Although the human infants and young chimpanzees in Warneken and Tomasello's study appeared to take the perspective of someone else enough to realize that the person was struggling to achieve some goal, it is of course not clear if they were actually *feeling* empathic concern for the person in need. According to Batson, perspective taking is but the first step toward altruism. If you perceive someone in need and imagine how *that person* feels, you are likely to experience other-oriented feelings of empathic concern, which in turn produce the altruistic motive to reduce the other person's distress.

There are, however, instances in which people perceive someone in need and focus on their *own* feelings about this person or on how *they* would feel in that person's situation. Although many people may think of this as "empathy," Batson contrasts this with instances in which people's concern is with how the *other person* is feeling (Batson, Early, & Salvarini, 1997; Stotland, 1969). It's when your focus is on the other person that true altruism is possible. The basic features of Batson's **empathy-altruism hypothesis** are outlined in Figure 10.1.

Now comes the hard part. How can we tell the difference between egoistic and altruistic motives? In both cases, people help someone else, but the helpers' reasons are different. Confronted with this puzzle, Batson came up with an elegant solution. It depends, he says, on whether one can obtain the relevant self-benefits without relieving the other's need. For example, when a person's motive is egoistic, helping should decline if it's easy for the individual to escape from the situation, and therefore escape from his or her own feelings of distress. When a person's motive is altruistic, however, help will be given regardless of the ease of escape.

Batson and others have conducted numerous experiments that have found support for the empathy-altruism hypothesis. For example, participants in one study (Batson et al., 2003) were given the opportunity to assign themselves and another participant of the same sex to an experimental task. One of the tasks was clearly more desirable than the other, and the participants had to decide whether to choose the desirable task for themselves or give it to the other person. The experimenter explained that they might consider flipping a coin if they wished, or make the decision however they wanted to. What would *you* do?

empathy-altruism hypothesis The proposition that empathic concern for a person in need produces an altruistic motive for helping.

FIGURE 10.2

Perspective Taking

Participants had to decide which of two tasks to assign to themselves and which to assign to another participant. One of the tasks was much less desirable than the other. If primed to think about how they *themselves* would feel if *they* were in the other person's situation ("imagine self"), or if not primed with any kind of perspective taking ("no perspective"), participants tended to keep the better task for themselves. If primed to think about the *other* person's feelings ("imagine other"), however, they were much more likely to do the altruistic thing and give the other person the better task.

(Based on Batson et al., 2003.)

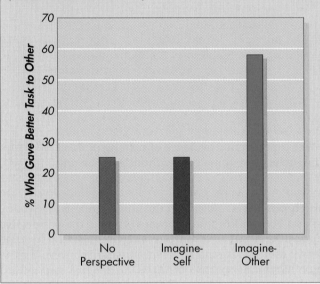

Before making their decision, some of the participants were assigned to a condition in which they were primed to imagine *themselves* in the other participant's situation. These participants were asked, for example, to imagine "how you will feel when told which task you are to do." Other participants were primed instead to imagine how the *other* person would feel. They were asked, for example, to imagine "how the other participant will likely feel when told which task he or she is to do." This simple distinction between imagining the self or imagining the other can trigger different motives, according to Batson and his colleagues: the imagine-self prime triggers a more egoistic motive, and the imagine-other prime triggers a more altruistic motive. Participants in a control condition were not primed with any perspective.

Which task did the participants choose for themselves and for the other? If they were primed with nothing or with the imagine-self instructions, three-quarters of the participants took the better task for themselves. Primed with the imagine-other perspective, in contrast, the majority of the participants gave the better task to the other participant (see Figure 10.2). It is also interesting to note whether or not the participants indicated that they flipped a coin to make their decision. Most of the participants in the imagine-other condition did not; rather, they tended simply to give the other person the better task. In contrast, most of the participants in the imagine-self condition *did* say they flipped a coin. In a display of either moral hypocrisy or incredible luck, two-thirds of the participants in the imagine-self condition who said they flipped a coin wound up giving themselves the better task! By having at least the illusion of fairness, these participants may have relieved some of their egoistic feelings of distress (for example, after losing the first coin flip, they may have decided, "Well, what's really fair is two out of three . . ."), without actually helping the other person. Primed to think more altruistically, however, the imagine-other participants tended to act to help the other, at a personal cost to themselves.

In a subsequent experiment using a somewhat different procedure, Batson and his colleagues found that the imagine-self instructions did lead to increased helping, relative to no perspective taking at all. Based on these findings, the researchers concluded that this kind of perspective can lead to helping in some situations, but it is more limited than a perspective that emphasizes the other rather than the self.

Egoistic Alternatives Can we conclude, then, that altruism really does exist? Batson and his colleagues believe so and have amassed a growing body of research consistent with this conclusion. Others are not so sure and offer egoistic alternatives.

One alternative is that empathy encourages helping not because of concern for the other but because of concern about the costs to the *self* of not helping. People may learn that they will feel guilty after experiencing empathy for others in need but failing to help them. Having learned to anticipate such guilt, these people may help others simply to avoid it. Batson and his colleagues counter, however, that guilt cannot account for the helpful inclinations associated with empathic concern found in their work (Batson & Weeks, 1996).

A second alternative is that empathy highlights the potential *rewards* for helping others. As we noted earlier in this chapter, helping makes people feel good. In their **negative state relief model**, Robert Cialdini and his colleagues (1987) propose that because of this positive effect of helping, people who are feeling bad may be inclined to help others in order to improve their mood. Thus, perhaps empathy promotes helping in the following way: Empathic concern for a person in need in-

negative state relief model The proposition that people help others in order to counteract their own feelings of sadness.

According to the empathy-altruism hypothesis, taking the perspective of someone in need is the first step toward altruism. When Sarah DeCristoforo returned to school after receiving chemotherapy for leukemia, her teacher and two friends actually put themselves in her place in one highly visible respect—they shaved their heads. Here, Sarah, wearing a scarf, is surrounded by her supporters.

According to a poll published in 1998 in USA Today, adults say they volunteer for the following reasons: to help people (87 percent), to make the community a better place (72 percent), to be with the people they enjoy (56 percent), to be with people with the same ideals (51 percent), to learn about the issue/problem (41 percent), and to fulfill a civic duty (39 percent).

creases feelings of sadness, which in turn increase the need for mood enhancement, which in turn brings about helping behavior. This egoistic account has generated a flurry of studies—some that support it and others that do not (Dovidio et al., 2006).

Another egoistic alternative involving empathy-specific rewards emphasizes positive well-being rather than negative relief. Kyle Smith and his colleagues (1989) maintain that empathic concern enhances the helper's sensitivity to the good feelings experienced by the person receiving help, causing the helper to experience *empathic joy*. Thus, we help those with whom we empathize because helping them makes us feel especially good.

Altruism Versus Egoism: Limits and Convergence Despite the egoistic alternatives that have been proposed, the evidence for the empathy-altruism hypothesis is strong. Nevertheless, it has its limits. First of all, Batson has never claimed that *all* helping is altruistically motivated. No doubt, there are multiple motives for helping, and many helpful acts are best explained in terms of the processes we consider elsewhere in this chapter. And any single helpful action can be the result of a mixture of egoistic and altruistic motives. Mark Snyder (1993) suggests, for example, that the most effective way to increase helping is to encourage people to recognize and feel comfortable with the convergence of self-oriented and other-oriented concerns.

Another limit is created by the fact that motives do not guarantee behavior. Empathy leads to altruistic motivations, but not necessarily to helpful behaviors. For example, someone with empathic concern for another might not help this person if he or she fears that the potential cost of offering the help is very high (Batson et al., 1983).

A possible third limitation cuts even closer to the fundamental nature of altruism. Distinguishing between egoistic and altruistic motives requires the assumption that there is a clear divide between the self and the other. But what if there isn't? What if, as Daniel Wegner (1980, p. 133) suggests, empathy reflects "a basic confusion between ourselves and others"? What if, as Arthur and Elaine Aron (2001) propose, those in close relationships incorporate the other into the self? When one and one equals "oneness" or "we-ness," helping this close other person may be seen as helping oneself, or at least helping an important part of oneself (Maner et al., 2002; Piliavin et al., 1981). Perhaps the egoistic account and the altruistic account actually merge on this point. In relationships in which the self-other distinction is virtually eliminated and you feel someone else's needs as deeply as you feel your own, the distinction between an egoistic motive and an altruistic one may be eliminated as well.

 Distinguishing Among the Motivations to Help: Why Does It Matter?

On the surface, the debate between altruistic and egoistic accounts of helping may seem to be irrelevant quibbling about semantics or philosophy. After all, if someone pulls you out of a burning car, you don't care if your rescuer did it to increase the chances that your similar genes will be passed down to future generations, to be lauded as a hero as the action news team approaches with its cameras, or simply because he or she was concerned for your safety. You just are thankful that the person helped, no matter what the motivation. So why does it matter whether we attribute the motivation of the helper to altruism or egoism?

Perhaps the most important reason to consider people's motivations is that they help us determine whether or not the helping will occur in the first place. Imagine again needing to be saved from a burning car, but this time imagine that one or two individuals have observed your accident. If these witnesses are motivated by egoistic

TABLE 10.1
Motivations to Volunteer to Help People with AIDS

Allen Omoto and Mark Snyder identified five categories of motivations underlying people's initial decisions to become volunteers to help people with AIDS. Within each category, three examples of specific statements representative of the general motive are presented.

(Omoto & Snyder, 1995.)

Values

Because of my humanitarian obligation to help others

Because I enjoy helping other people

Because I consider myself a loving and caring person

Understanding

To learn more about how to prevent AIDS

To learn how to help people with AIDS

To deal with my personal fears and anxiety about AIDS

Personal Development

To get to know people who are similar to myself

To meet new people and make new friends

To gain experience dealing with emotionally difficult topics

Community Concern

Because of my sense of obligation to the gay community

Because I consider myself an advocate for gay-related issues

Because of my concern and worry about the gay community

Esteem Enhancement

To feel better about myself

To escape other pressures and stress in my life

To feel less lonely

Interested in volunteering? One place to look for information about volunteering, and for finding matches between people who want to volunteer and those who need volunteers, is Volunteermatch.org.

concern, then they are likely to help only if they expect to benefit from doing so—such as with the hope of some material or psychological reward, or to reduce their own feelings of guilt and distress. They might fail to help if there is an easy way for them to escape the situation and avoid experiencing personal distress. If they are motivated by altruism, they may try to help you despite the potential costs.

Motivational factors also play important roles in more long-term helping behavior, such as volunteerism. Research has found a number of important motivations underlying why people volunteer. Some of these motives are associated with empathy, such as perspective taking and empathic concern, whereas other motives are more egoistic, such as wanting to enhance one's resume, relieve negative emotions, or conform to prosocial norms (Hur, 2006; Omoto & Snyder, 2002; Penner et al., 2005; Piferi et al., 2006; Reeder et al., 2001; Snyder & Clary, 2004).

Table 10.1 lists five categories of motives that Allen Omoto and Mark Snyder (1995) determined were behind volunteers' decisions to help people with AIDS. AIDS volunteers who had initially endorsed self-oriented motives, such as gaining understanding and developing personal skills, remained active volunteers longer than did those who had initially emphasized other-oriented motives, such as humanitarian values and community concern. Why were the more egoistic goals associated with longer service? As Mark Snyder notes, "The good, and perhaps romanticized, intentions related to humanitarian concern simply may not be strong enough to sustain volunteers faced with the tough realities and personal costs of working with [persons with AIDS]" (Snyder, 1993, p. 258). When helping demands more of us, self-interest may keep us going.

Self-interest as a motive for helping, therefore, is not necessarily a bad thing. Indeed, the fact that many people find helping others to be so personally rewarding is a positive aspect of human nature. One's feelings of empathic concern for others are usually limited to a few other people at a time and perhaps to relatively brief periods. Those people who derive a great deal of personal satisfaction from helping others, however, may be motivated much more frequently and consistently to engage in helping behaviors. Indeed, commitment to prosocial actions can become an important part of one's identity (Piliavin et al., 2002).

Situational Influences: When Do People Help?

Thus far, we have focused on *why* people help others. We now turn to the question of *when* people help. We begin by discussing a remarkably creative and provocative set of research findings that make a surprising point: If you need help in an emergency, you may be better off if there is only one witness to your plight than if there are several. We then focus on a wide range of other situational factors on helping, including where we live, whether we are experiencing time pressure, what kind of mood we're in, and whether we've been exposed to particular role models or social norms.

 ## The Unhelpful Crowd

At about 3:20 on the morning of March 13, 1964, twenty-eight-year-old Kitty Genovese was returning home from her job as a bar manager. Suddenly, a man attacked her with a knife. She was stalked, stabbed, and sexually assaulted just thirty-five yards from her own apartment building in the New York City borough of Queens. Lights went on and windows went up as she screamed, "Oh my God! He stabbed me! Please help me!" She broke free from her attacker twice, but only briefly. Thirty-eight of her neighbors witnessed her ordeal, but not one intervened. Finally, after nearly forty-five minutes of terror, one man called the police; but by then, Genovese was dead.

The murder of Kitty Genovese shocked the nation. Were her neighbors to blame? It seemed unlikely that all thirty-eight of them could have been moral monsters. Most of the media attention focused on the decline of morals and values in contemporary society and on the anonymity and apathy seen in large American cities such as New York. A few days after the incident, John Darley and Bibb Latané discussed over dinner the events and the explanations being offered for it. They were not convinced that these explanations were sufficient to account for why Kitty Genovese didn't get the help she needed; and they wondered if other, social psychological processes might have been at work. They speculated that because each witness to the attack could see that many other witnesses had turned on their lights and were looking out their windows, each witness may have assumed that others would, or should, take responsibility and call the police. To test their ideas, Darley and Latané (1968) set out to see if they could produce unresponsive bystanders under laboratory conditions. Let's take a look at one of their studies.

When a participant arrived, he or she was taken to one of a series of small rooms located along a corridor. Speaking over an intercom, the experimenter explained that he wanted participants to discuss personal problems often faced by college students. Participants were told that, to protect confidentiality, the group discussion would take place over the intercom system, and the experimenter would not be listening. They were required to speak one at a time, taking turns. Some participants were assigned to talk with one other person; others joined larger groups of three or six people.

Although one participant did mention in passing that he suffered from a seizure disorder that was sometimes triggered by study pressures, the opening moments of the conversation were uneventful. But soon, an unexpected problem developed. When the time came for this person to speak again, he stuttered badly, had a hard time speaking clearly, and sounded as if he were in very serious trouble:

> I could really-er-use some help so if somebody would-er-give me a little h-help-uh-er-er-er-er c-could somebody-er-er-help-er-uh-uh-uh [choking sounds]. . . . I'm gonna die-er-er-I'm . . . gonna die-er-help-er-er-seizure-er [chokes, then quiet].

Confronted with this situation, what would *you* do? Would you interrupt the experiment, dash out of your cubicle, and try to find the experimenter? Or would you sit there—concerned, but unsure how to react?

The murder of Kitty Genovese, pictured here, shocked the nation in 1964. How could thirty-eight witnesses stand by and do nothing? Research conducted in the aftermath of this tragedy suggests that if there had been only one witness rather than almost forty, Kitty Genovese might have had a better chance of receiving help, and she might be alive today.

FIGURE 10.3

The Five Steps to Helping in an Emergency

On the basis of their analysis of the decision-making process in emergency interventions, Latané and Darley (1970) outline five steps that lead to providing assistance. But there are obstacles that can interfere; and if a step is missed, the victim won't be helped.

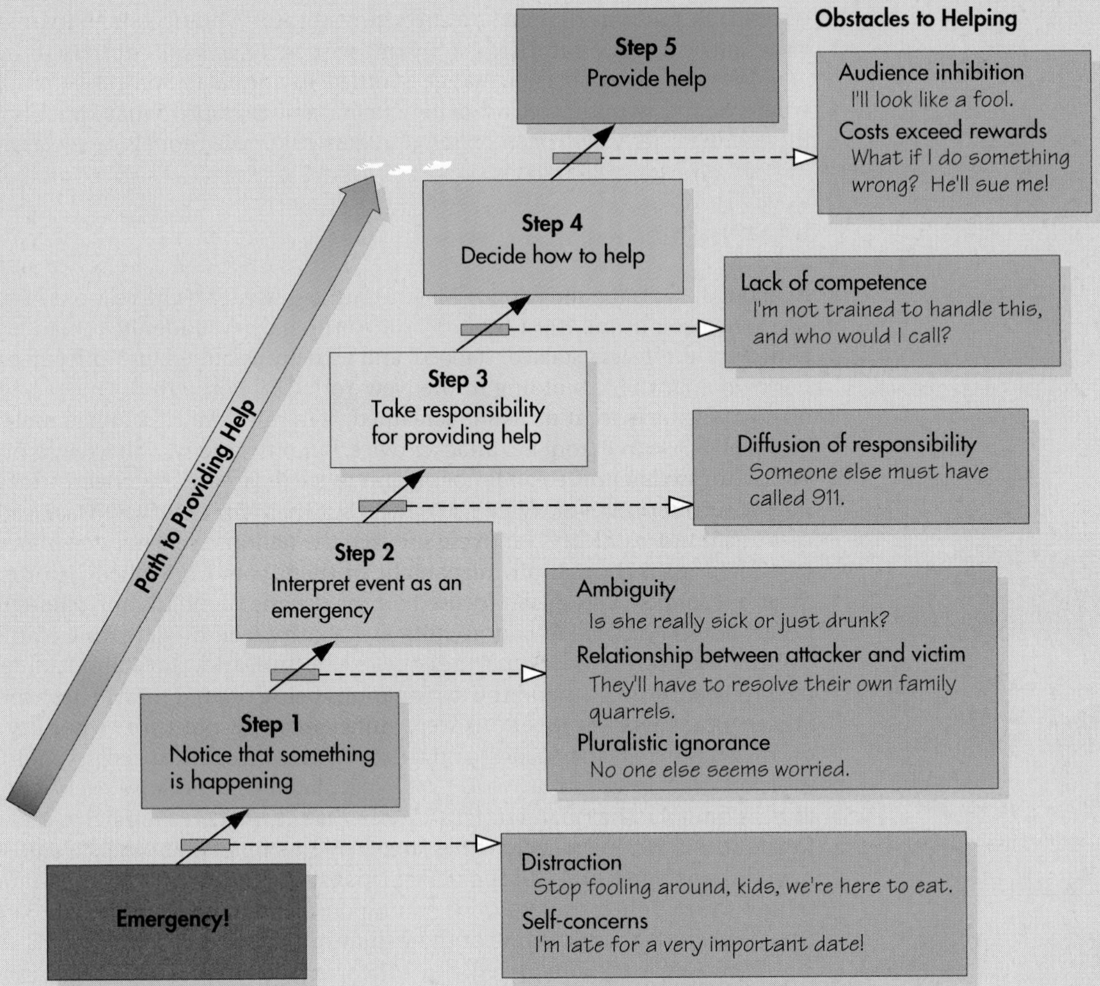

Obstacles to Helping

Step 5
Provide help

Audience inhibition
I'll look like a fool.

Costs exceed rewards
What if I do something wrong? He'll sue me!

Step 4
Decide how to help

Lack of competence
I'm not trained to handle this, and who would I call?

Step 3
Take responsibility for providing help

Diffusion of responsibility
Someone else must have called 911.

Step 2
Interpret event as an emergency

Ambiguity
Is she really sick or just drunk?

Relationship between attacker and victim
They'll have to resolve their own family quarrels.

Pluralistic ignorance
No one else seems worried.

Step 1
Notice that something is happening

Distraction
Stop fooling around, kids, we're here to eat.

Self-concerns
I'm late for a very important date!

Emergency!

Path to Providing Help

As it turns out, participants' responses to this emergency were strongly influenced by the size of their group. Actually, all participants were participating alone, but tape-recorded material led them to believe that others were present. All the participants who thought that only they knew about the emergency left the room quickly to try to get help. In the larger groups, however, participants were less likely and slower to intervene. Indeed, 38 percent of the participants in the six-person groups never left the room at all! This research led Latané and Darley to a chilling conclusion: The more bystanders, the *less* likely the victim will be helped. This is the **bystander effect**, whereby the presence of others inhibits helping.

Before the pioneering work of Latané and Darley, most people would have assumed just the opposite. Isn't there safety in numbers? Don't we feel more secure rushing in to help when others are around to lend their support? Latané and Darley overturned this common-sense assumption and provided a careful, step-by-step analysis of the decision-making process involved in emergency interventions. In the following sections, we examine each of five steps in this process: noticing something unusual, interpreting it as an emergency, taking responsibility for getting help, decid-

bystander effect The effect whereby the presence of others inhibits helping.

In an emergency, a person who needs help has a much better chance of getting it if three other people are present than if only one other person is present. **False.**

ing how to help, and providing assistance. We also consider the reasons why people sometimes fail to take one of these steps and, therefore, do not help. These steps, and the obstacles along the way, are summarized in Figure 10.3.

Noticing   The first step toward being a helpful bystander is to notice that someone needs help or, at least, that something out of the ordinary is happening. Participants in the seizure study could not help but notice the emergency. In many situations, however, the problem isn't always perceived. The presence of others can be distracting and can divert attention away from indications of a victim's plight. In addition, people may fail to notice that someone needs help because they are caught up in their own self-concerns. People who live in big cities and noisy environments may become so used to seeing people lying on sidewalks or hearing screams that they begin to tune them out, becoming susceptible to what Stanley Milgram (1970) called *stimulus overload*.

Interpreting   Noticing the victim is a necessary first step toward helping, but it is not enough. People must interpret the meaning of what they notice. Cries of pain can be mistaken for shrieks of laughter; heart-attack victims can appear to be drunk. So observers wonder: Does that person really need help? In general, the more ambiguous the situation, the less likely it is that bystanders will intervene (Clark & Word, 1972).

Interpretations of the relationship between a victim and an attacker also affect whether help will be provided. Consider, for example, how people react when they see a woman attacked by a man. Research by Lance Shotland and Margaret Straw (1976) indicates that many observers of such an incident believe that the attacker and the victim have a close relationship as dates, lovers, or spouses—even when no information about the relationship is actually available. This inference can have very serious implications, since, as Shotland and Straw documented, intervening in domestic violence is perceived to be more dangerous to the helper and less desired by the victim than is intervening in an attack by a stranger. Given such beliefs, the response to a scene staged by Shotland and Straw was predictable: In the scene, a woman was supposedly being assaulted either by a stranger or by her husband. More than three times as many observers tried to stop the assault by the stranger.

It's not only women who are in danger if they are perceived as having a close relationship with their attacker: Children also suffer. The 1993 murder of two-year-old James Bulger by two ten-year-old boys was the British equivalent of the Kitty Genovese slaying. James was dragged, kicking and screaming, for two and a half miles

The first step toward providing help is to notice that someone needs assistance. Distracted by their own concerns or by the overwhelming stimuli of a big, bustling city, these people walking in midtown Manhattan may not even notice the homeless couple begging for spare change.

from a shopping mall to a railroad track, where he was battered to death. Sixty-one people admitted that they had seen the boys. Most did nothing. One asked a few questions but didn't intervene. The reason? As one witness put it, he thought the boys were "older brothers taking a little one home." When people think "family," they think "It's OK, it's safe." But sometimes it isn't.

Perhaps the most powerful information available during an emergency is the behavior of other people. Startled by a sudden, unexpected, possibly dangerous event, each person looks quickly to see what others are doing. As everyone looks at everyone else for clues about how to behave, the entire group is paralyzed by indecision. When this happens, the person needing help is a victim of **pluralistic ignorance**. In this state of ignorance, each individual believes that his or her own thoughts and feelings are different from those of other people, even though everyone's behavior is the same. Each bystander thinks that other people aren't acting because somehow they know there isn't an emergency. Actually, everyone is confused and hesitant; but, imputing wisdom to others, each observer concludes that help is not required.

Latané and Darley (1968) put this phenomenon to the test in an experiment in which participants completed a questionnaire in a room in which they were either (a) alone, (b) with two confederates who remained passive and took no action, or (c) with two other naïve participants just like them. A few minutes after participants had started to fill out the questionnaire, smoke began to seep into the room through a vent. Was this an emergency? How do you think you would respond? Within four minutes, half of the participants who were working alone took some action, such as leaving the room to report the smoke to someone. Within six minutes—the maximum time allotted before the researchers terminated the experiment—three-quarters of these participants took action. Clearly, they interpreted the smoke as a potential emergency. But what about the participants working in groups of three? Common sense suggests that the chances that somebody will take action should be greater when more people are present. But only one of the twenty-four participants in this condition took action within four minutes, and only three did so before the end of the study—even though, at that point, the smoke was so thick they had to fan it away from their faces to see the questionnaire! The rate of action was even lower when participants were in a room with two passive confederates; in this condition, only one in ten participants reported the smoke. If the participants in either of the two group conditions had interpreted the smoke as a potential emergency, they would have acted, because their own lives would have been at stake. But instead, they quickly, coolly looked at the reactions of the others in the room, saw that nobody else seemed too concerned, and so became convinced that nothing could be wrong.

Pluralistic ignorance is not restricted to emergency situations (Miller & McFarland, 1987; Miller et al., 2000; Monin & Norton, 2003; Suls & Green, 2003). Have you ever sat through a class feeling totally lost? You want to ask a question, but you're too embarrassed. No one else is saying anything, so you assume they all find the material a snap. Finally, you dare to ask a question. And suddenly, hands shoot up in the air all over the classroom. No one understood the material, yet everyone assumed that everyone else was breezing along. Pluralistic ignorance in the classroom interferes with learning. In an emergency situation, it can lead to disaster unless someone breaks out of the pack and dares to help. Then others are likely to follow.

Taking Responsibility Noticing a victim and recognizing an emergency are crucial steps; but by themselves, they don't ensure that a bystander will come to the rescue. The issue of responsibility remains. When help is needed, who is responsible for providing it? If a person knows that others are around, it's all too easy to place the responsibility on *them*. People often fail to help because of the **diffusion of responsibility**: the belief that others will or should intervene. Presumably, each of those thirty-eight people who watched and listened to Kitty Genovese's murder thought someone else would do something to stop the attack. But remember those helpful participants in the seizure study who thought that they alone heard the other person's cry for help? Diffusion of responsibility cannot occur if an individual believes that only he or she is aware of the victim's need.

An interesting recent set of experiments by Stephen Garcia and others (2002) found that the presence of others can promote diffusion of responsibility even when they are present only in one's mind! Garcia and his colleagues (including John Darley) had participants simply *imagine* being in a crowd or being alone, and soon after, these participants were given an opportunity to help someone. The results indicated that participants who had just thought of being with many other people were less likely to help than were the participants who had imagined themselves alone. In one study, for example, some students were asked to imagine themselves at dinner with ten friends, others were asked to imagine themselves at dinner with one friend, and others were asked a nonsocial question. Soon after, the students were asked if they would be willing to volunteer to help with an experiment in another room.

pluralistic ignorance The state in which people mistakenly believe that their own thoughts and feelings are different from those of others, even when everyone's behavior is the same.

diffusion of responsibility The belief that others will or should take the responsibility for providing assistance to a person in need.

Figure 10.4 depicts the average number of minutes the students in each condition volunteered to spend on this other experiment. As can be seen, those students who had imagined going out to dinner with a big group of friends tended to volunteer less of their time to help out with the subsequent experiment than did students who had imagined being out with only one friend, or who had not imagined being out with friends at all. In another experiment, these researchers found that having students think about being in a crowd made concepts like *unaccountable* and *exempt* more accessible in the students' minds, suggesting that merely thinking about the presence of others can promote diffusion of responsibility relatively automatically.

Diffusion of responsibility usually takes place under conditions of anonymity. Bystanders who do not know the victim personally are more likely to see others as responsible for providing help. Accordingly, if the psychological distance between a bystander and the victim is reduced, there will be less diffusion of responsibility and more help. Reducing the psychological distance among bystanders can also counteract the diffusion of responsibility. Established groups in which the members know each other are usually more helpful than groups of strangers (Rutkowski et al., 1983).

In addition, the diffusion of responsibility can be defeated by a person's role. A group leader, even if only recently assigned to that position, is more likely than other group members to act in an emergency (Baumeister et al., 1988). And some occupational roles increase the likelihood of intervention. Registered nurses, for example, do not diffuse responsibility when confronted by a possible physical injury (Cramer et al., 1988). Even when there's no direct relationship between one's occupation and the type of assistance that's needed, job requirements can still influence helping behavior. In 1994, Jack Santos, a YMCA security guard, ran across two highways, passed a dozen passive observers, and put out the fire from the burning clothes of Jack Ordner, who had been thrown from his gasoline tanker when it overturned and burst into flames. Santos was neither a professional fire-fighter nor a medical specialist, but he was used to taking charge during an emergency. Wesley Autrey's daring rescue of a man who had collapsed onto subway tracks in New York City in January 2007 was described at the beginning of the chapter. Autrey, a fifty-year-old construction worker when he saved the man's life, was a veteran of the U.S. Navy.

Deciding How to Help Having assumed the responsibility to help, the person must now decide how to help. Bystanders are more likely to offer direct help when they feel competent to perform the actions required. For instance, individuals who have received Red Cross training in first-aid techniques are more likely to provide direct assistance to a bleeding victim than are those without training (Shotland & Heinold, 1985).

But people who do not possess the skills that would make them feel competent to intervene directly often do have an option available. They can decide to help indirectly by calling for assistance from others. In many situations, indirect helping is by far the wiser course of action. Physical injuries are best treated by medical personnel; dangerous situations such as domestic violence are best handled by police officers; and that friendly-looking individual standing by the side of a stalled car on a lonely road is best picked up by the highway patrol. Even people trained in CPR are now advised to call 911 before starting CPR on an adult victim. Calling others in to help is safe, simple, and effective. A prompt phone call can be a lifeline. Such a call might have saved Kitty Genovese's life.

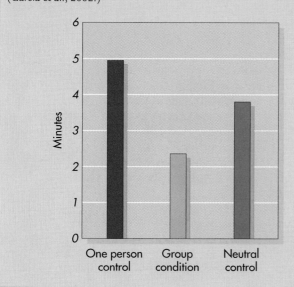

FIGURE 10.4

The Implicit Bystander Effect

Students in this study imagined having dinner with either one person or with a large group of friends, or they were not asked to imagine a social situation (neutral control group). Later they were asked if they would be willing to volunteer some of their time to help in a different experiment. The students who had imagined a large group volunteered the least amount of time. This result was consistent with the idea that even imagining being in a crowd can prompt thoughts of a lack of responsibility and create a bystander effect.

(Garcia et al., 2002.)

Providing Help   The final step in the intervention process is to take action. Here, too, the presence of others can have an impact. Latané and Darley point out that people sometimes feel too socially awkward and embarrassed to act helpfully in a public setting. When observers do not act in an emergency because they fear making a bad impression on other observers, they are under the influence of **audience inhibition**. Worrying about how others will view us does not, however, always reduce helping. When people think they will be scorned by others for failing to help, the presence of an audience *increases* their helpful actions (Schwartz & Gottlieb, 1980).

The Legacy of the Bystander Effect Research   As you can see in Figure 10.3, providing help in an emergency is a challenging process. At each step along the way, barriers and diversions can prevent a potential helper from becoming an actual one. Most of these obstacles are social in nature, demonstrating Latané and Darley's point that an individual is less likely to intervene in an emergency when others are present than when he or she is alone with the victim.

The power and relevance of Latané and Darley's analysis are evident in the fact that newspapers around the world often cite their work when reporting the latest shocking incident of bystander nonintervention. In 1995, for example, Deletha Word was involved in a traffic accident with Martell Welch, Jr., on a traffic-clogged bridge over the Detroit River. Welch, who was over six feet tall and about 270 pounds, dragged Word, who was under five feet tall and weighed about 115 pounds, out of her car, ripped off some of her clothes, and hit her repeatedly while yelling threats at her in an outburst that lasted at least ten minutes. The attack itself was shocking; but perhaps more shocking was that about forty people witnessed it, and not one of them attempted to come to the woman's aid. Finally, as Welch approached Word, allegedly while holding his car jack, she climbed over the bridge rail and jumped into the river. Within moments, she disappeared into the water, and her body was found hours later. Soon after this incident, *Dateline NBC* interviewed John Darley about this case and his research on the bystander effect, and they simulated some of the experiments he had done with Latané.

Two incidents in the Toronto area brought the bystander effect research back into discussion in Canadian newspapers in the summer of 2006. One incident was described earlier in the chapter concerning the fatal beating of a teenager in the presence of numerous witnesses who did nothing to assist the boy. A second incident involved Mike Cuevas and Isabelita Malenjana, who were found dead in Cuevas's garage, each shot multiple times in the head. About twenty people had heard gun-

Dortha Word, second from the left, and friends pray on the bridge from which Dortha's daughter, Deletha, jumped to her death three days earlier, trying to escape a man who had been attacking her. About forty people witnessed the attack but did not intervene. Their failure to help her daughter stunned Dortha: "I can't believe all those people stood around and watched."

audience inhibition
Reluctance to help for fear of making a bad impression on observers.

shots that summer evening in the quiet North Toronto neighborhood, but none of them called the police. "When it came down to it, everyone else thought someone else called. No one took the initiative," said Detective Wayne Fowler. The same kind of diffusion of responsibility that led to tragic inaction of the witnesses to Kitty Genovese's murder was apparently present here. Along with diffusion of responsibility, the inaction of the witnesses to the fatal beating of the teenager apparently can be attributed also to the perceived costs of helping and to norms associated with not helping. One nineteen-year-old mother of a small boy reported, "When you're used to living in the area, you don't call 911. Snitching is not acceptable. If you mind your business and stay out of trouble, you won't have trouble" (Huffman, 2006, p. B1).

The bystander effect apparently made it into the world of cyberspace, as news spread in February 2003 of the death of twenty-one-year-old Brandon Vedas. Vedas overdosed on drugs and lay dying in front of a crowded room full of people, many of whom egged him on to take even more drugs. The modern-day twist was that this room was virtual; it was a chatroom, and the bystanders watched Vedas, who used the name "Ripper" online, poison himself to death via the webcam in his Phoenix, Arizona, bedroom. "That's not much," said a teenager from rural Oklahoma whose alias was "Smoke2K." "Eat more. I wanna see if you survive or if you just black out." Another wrote in, "Ripper—you should try to pass out in front of the cam." Not everyone was so callous. Some wrote in warning Ripper to be careful; one wrote, "Don't OD on us, Ripper." One person did begin to call the police, but, astonishingly, others talked her out of it. Vedas posted his cell number with the instructions "Call if I look dead." The last coherent words Vedas wrote were "I told u I was hardcore" (Kennedy, 2003, p. 5).

This incident was different from the Kitty Genovese one in several ways, including the fact that it was not clear if the onlookers could have done anything about this. Without knowing Ripper's real name or address, the police probably would not have been able to find him in time even had someone called promptly. But several processes central to Darley and Latané's research clearly were evident. (Indeed, in 2005 Carrie Blair and others found clear evidence for the diffusion of responsibility effect in an experiment conducted entirely online, with "virtual" witnesses to someone requesting assistance.) Several witnesses suggested that "somebody" call poison control or the police but did not do so themselves. Some questioned whether Ripper was really dying or had just passed out. One person told another *not* to call the police because that could get Ripper arrested. Together, these Internet bystanders were struggling on the decision tree, spreading doubt and diffusion of responsibility. And newspapers throughout the world were soon referring to Kitty Genovese once again, for a fourth decade.

Many of us who teach social psychology have stories of former students who witnessed an emergency and jumped in to help while consciously thinking of the lessons they'd learned in their social psychology classes about Darley and Latané's bystander intervention research. Indeed, one of the authors of this book remembers being at a lecture in a room filled with social psychologists when a loud crash suddenly emanated from an adjacent room. After a few seconds of delay, dozens of social psychologists burst out of their chairs, almost trampling each other as they rushed to see if there was an emergency. And the only ones who were not explicitly thinking "Darley & Latané" while doing so were the ones thinking "Latané & Darley."

Getting Help in a Crowd: What Should You Do?   But what do all these stories and experiments teach you about what to do if you need help in the presence of many people? Is there anything you can do to enhance the chances that someone will come to your aid? Try to counteract the ambiguity of the situation by making it very clear that you do need help, and try to reduce diffusion of responsibility by singling out particular individuals for help, such as with eye contact, pointing, or direct requests (Moriarty, 1975; Shotland & Stebbins, 1980). Consistent with this advice, and with Latané and Darley's research, are the results of a study by P. M. Markey (2000) involving people in Internet chatrooms: As the number of people present in each chatroom group grew larger, individuals took increasingly more time to respond to someone's plea for help; however, this effect was eliminated when the person asking for help specified a particular individual's name (see Figure 10.5). In light

FIGURE 10.5

Cyberhelping

In a study that extends Latané and Darley's research on the bystander effect by bringing it into cyberspace, individuals participating in an online chatroom saw a plea for help from another person in the chatroom. Consistent with Latané and Darley's findings, individuals responded more slowly if they thought that many other people were in the chatroom than if they thought that there were few others present. However, if an individual's name was specified in the request for help, then that person responded quickly regardless of how many other people were in the chatroom.

(Source: Markey, 2000.)

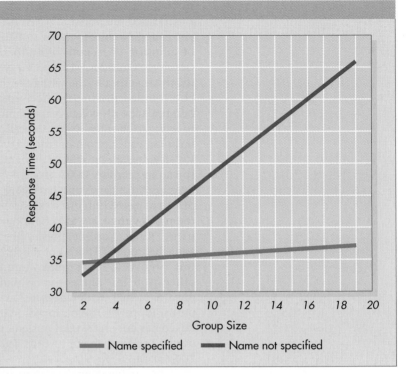

Time Pressure

The presence of others can create obstacles at each step on the way toward helping in an emergency. Other factors, too, can affect multiple steps in this process. Our good intentions to help those in need can sometimes conflict with other motivations. One such source of conflict is time pressure. When we are in a hurry or have a lot on our minds, we may be so preoccupied that we fail to notice others who need help, we may become less likely to accept responsibility for helping someone, or we may decide that the costs of helping are too high because of the precious time that will be lost. When we have other demands on us that seem very important, getting involved in someone else's problems may seem like a luxury we can't afford (Batson et al., 1978; Moore, 2005). John Darley and Daniel Batson (1973) examined the role of time pressure in an experiment that produced what may be the most ironic finding in the history of social psychology.

Their study was based on the parable of the Good Samaritan, from the Gospel of Luke. This parable tells the story of three different people—a priest, a Levite, and a Samaritan—each traveling on the road from Jerusalem to Jericho. Each encounters a man lying half-dead by the roadside. The priest and the Levite—both considered busy, important, and relatively holy people—pass by the man without stopping. The only one who helps is the Samaritan, a social and religious outcast of that time. A moral of the tale is that people with low status are sometimes more virtuous than those enjoying high status and prestige. Why? Perhaps in part because high-status individuals tend to be busy people, preoccupied with their own concerns and rushing around to various engagements. Such characteristics may prevent them from noticing or deciding to help a victim in need of assistance.

Darley and Batson brought this ancient story to life. They asked seminary students to think about what they wanted to say in an upcoming talk. Half of them were told that the talk was to be based on the parable of the Good Samaritan; the other half expected to discuss the jobs that seminary students like best. All participants were then instructed to walk over to a nearby building where the speech would be recorded. At this point, participants were told that they were running ahead of schedule, that they were right on time, or that they were already a few minutes behind schedule. On the way to the other building, all participants passed a research confederate slumped in a doorway, coughing and groaning. Which of these future ministers stopped to lend a helping hand?

Perhaps surprisingly, the topic of the upcoming speech had little effect on helping. The pressure of time, however, made a real difference. Of those who thought they were ahead of schedule, 63 percent offered help—compared with 45 percent of those who believed they were on time and only 10 percent of those who had been told they were late. In describing the events that took place in their study, Darley and Batson noted that "on several occasions a seminary student going to give his talk on the parable of the Good Samaritan literally stepped over the victim as he hurried on his way!" These seminary students unwittingly demonstrated the very point that the parable they would be discussing warns against.

Location and Culture

If the presence of others often inhibits helping, do individuals have a worse chance of being helped in an emergency in a big city than in a small town? In the midst of the hectic pace and large crowds of a big city, are pleas for help more likely to go unanswered?

Although place of residence does not seem to affect how much those in close relationships help each other (Franck, 1980; Korte, 1980), a large city does have a number of characteristics that might reduce help to strangers. For example, as we discussed earlier in the context of "noticing" an emergency, Stanley Milgram (1970) proposed that cities produce stimulus overload among their inhabitants. Bombarded by sights and sounds, city residents may wear a coat of unresponsive armor to protect themselves from being overwhelmed by stimulation (Korte et al., 1975). Claude Fischer (1976) noted that the residents of large urban areas are a heterogeneous group—composed of diverse nationalities, races, and ethnic backgrounds. Such diversity could diminish the sense of similarity with others, reduce empathic concern, and result in less helping. Also, people may feel more anonymous and less accountable for their actions in large cities than in smaller communities in which people are more likely to know their neighbors.

Whatever the exact causes, people are less likely to help in urban areas than in rural ones. This relationship has been found in several countries, including Canada, Israel, Great Britain, and the Sudan (Hedge & Yousif, 1992; Steblay, 1987). For example, Paul Amato (1983) studied fifty-five Australian communities, and he found that spontaneous, informal help to strangers was greater where the population was smaller. In a similar vein, Robert Levine and his colleagues (1994) examined six kinds of helping in thirty-six U.S. cities As you can see in Table 10.2, Rochester, New York, wins the title of "Most Helpful City." Greater population density (population per square mile) was associated with less helping. As we will see a bit later in this section, however,

TABLE 10.2
Helping in the U.S.A.

Several types of helping, including acts such as helping someone cross the street and making contributions to a charity, were studied in 36 U.S. cities. The top 6 and bottom 6 cities are listed in this table. Although there was a great deal of variability from one helping measure to the next, some overall patterns emerged, including the findings that higher density (population per square mile) and higher cost of living were strongly associated with less helping.

(Based on data from Levine et al., 1994.)

Top Six Cities for Helping		Bottom Six Cities for Helping	
Overall Rank	Region	Overall Rank	Region
1. Rochester, NY	Northeast	31. Shreveport, LA	South
2. Houston, TX	South	32. Philadelphia, PA	Northeast
3. Nashville, TN	South	33. Fresno, CA	West
4. Memphis, TN	South	34. Los Angeles, CA	West
5. Knoxville, TN	South	35. New York, NY	Northeast
6. Louisville, KY	South	36. Patterson, NJ	Northeast

the picture of helping in the United States is different if one focuses specifically on charitable giving or volunteering.

Around the world as well, some cities seem to have more helpful citizens than others. Robert Levine and others (2001) conducted field experiments in a major city in each of twenty-three large countries around the world. In each city, experimenters would position themselves near a passer-by and drop a pen, drop a pile of magazines (while limping with an apparently injured leg), or play the role of a blind person needing help crossing a street. Would pedestrians help? Table 10.3 reports how the cities ranked in their propensity to help, with pedestrians in Rio de Janeiro, Brazil, exhibiting the highest rates of helping and pedestrians in Kuala Lampur, Malaysia, the lowest rates. Levine and his colleagues examined a number of measures of each city to try to determine what factors predicted these differences in helping, such as how hectic the pace of life seemed to be (as determined by pedestrians' walking speed) or how individualistic or collectivistic the culture was. Only two measures correlated with helping rates. One was a measure of economic well-being—cities from countries with the greatest levels of economic well-being tended to exhibit the least helping, although this relationship was not very strong.

The other variable that predicted helping concerned the notion of what is called *simpatia* in Spanish or *simpatico* in Portuguese. Some researchers report that this is an important element of Spanish and Latin American cultures and involves a concern with the social well-being of others (Markus & Lin, 1999; Sanchez-Burks et al., 2000). The five *simpatia* cultures in Levine et al.'s study did tend to show higher rates of helping than the non-*simpatia* cultures.

You may find it surprising that collectivism was not a predictor of helping, but the research on the relationship between individualism-collectivism and prosocial behavior is quite mixed at this time. This inconsistency may stem in part from differences in the kinds of helping studied. Relative to individualists, collectivists may be more likely to help ingroup members, but they are less likely to help outgroup members (Conway et al., 2001; Schwartz, 1990). Lucian Conway and others (2001) studied differences in people's levels of individualism and collectivism within the United States. They found that collectivism was positively associated with the kind of direct, spontaneous, non-serious help assessed in the Levine et al. (2001) cross-cultural study described above, such as picking up a dropped pen for a stranger. However, for helping that is less spontaneous and more deliberate, such as mailing a sealed and stamped letter that someone (unseen) had apparently dropped or making contributions to a particular charity, collectivism was associated with *less* helping. These

TABLE 10.3
Helping Around the World

Three types of spontaneous helping—helping someone who dropped a pen, who dropped a pile of magazines, or who needed help crossing the street—were examined in field experiments in a major city in each of 23 different countries around the world. The top 6 and bottom 6 cities are listed below, along with their respective ranks on a measure of economic prosperity, relative to the 22 cities for which there were available data. Cities with asterisks are considered to have *simpatia* cultural values, which are characterized by a concern with the social well-being of others.

(Based on Levine et al., 2001.)

Top Six Cities for Helping

City	Helping Rank	Economic Rank
*Rio de Janeiro, Brazil	1	16
*San Jose, Costa Rica	2	15
Lilongwe, Malawi	3	22
Calcutta, India	4	21
Vienna, Austria	5	4
*Madrid, Spain	6	9

Bottom Six Cities for Helping

City	Helping Rank	Economic Rank
Taipei, Taiwan	18	[data unavailable]
Sofia, Bulgaria	19	17
Amsterdam, Netherlands	20	6
Singapore, Singapore	21	2
New York, United States	22	1
Kuala Lampur, Malaysia	23	10

correlations did not seem to be due to differences in economic variables. Conway et al. speculated that a possible explanation for these results is that collectivists are more responsive to the immediate needs of a person near them but less responsive in the more abstract situations, as in the found letter situation or making charitable contributions.

Conway et al.'s speculation received support in a recent investigation of charitable giving and volunteerism in the United States. Using data from random samples drawn from forty of the fifty states in the United States, Markus Kemmelmeier and others (2006) examined the relationship between the degree of individualism associated with each state and the amount of helping the individuals from within those states offered to strangers in the form of donations and volunteering. The states' degree of individualism was determined in a previous study by Vandello and Cohen (1999) using a number of variables, such as the percentage of people living alone, the percentage of people with no religious affiliation, and the percentage of people self-employed. In general, states in the Mountain West and Great Plains were the most individualistic, followed by the Northeast and Midwest. The least individualistic states tended to be in the South and Southwest.

Kemmelmeier and colleagues found that people from the more individualistic states tended to exhibit greater charitable giving and volunteering than people from the more collectivistic states, particularly for donations and volunteering that were not specific to one's ingroup affiliations. The authors propose that when helping involves this more abstract kind of giving—as opposed to, for example, helping someone from within one's ingroup—individualism may be associated with greater helping.

Moods and Helping

Helping someone can put people in a better mood, but can being in a good mood increase people's likelihood of helping someone? Are we less likely to help if we're in a bad mood? What's your prediction?

Good Moods and Doing Good   Sunshine in Minneapolis and pleasant odors in Albany give us some clues about the relationship between good mood and helping. Over the course of a year, pedestrians in Minneapolis were stopped and asked to participate in a survey of social opinions. When Michael Cunningham (1979) tabulated their responses according to the weather conditions, he discovered that people answered more questions on sunny days than on cloudy ones. Moving his investigation indoors, Cunningham found that sunshine is truly golden: The more the sun was shining, the more generous were the tips left by restaurant customers. Sunshine and helping seem to go together, but what's the connection? Probably it's the mood we're in, as a sunny day cheers us up and a cloudy day damps us down.

When the sun is not shining, many people head for the mall. One of the more powerful sensations you can count on experiencing while strolling through the mall comes when you pass a bakery or coffee shop, the pleasant aroma of freshly baked chocolate chip cookies or freshly brewed French roast stopping you in your tracks. Robert Baron (1997) believed that these pleasant scents put people in a good mood, and he wondered if this good mood would make them more likely to help someone in need. He tested this with passers-by in a large shopping mall in Albany, New York. Each selected passer-by was approached by a member of the research team and asked for change for a dollar. This interaction took place in a location containing either strong, pleasant odors (such as near a bakery or a coffee-roasting cafe) or no discernible odor (such as near a clothing store). As can be seen in Figure 10.6, people approached in a pleasant-smelling location were much more likely to help than people approached in a neutral-smelling location. Baron also found that people were in a better mood when they were in the pleasant-smelling environments. This effect on their mood appears to have caused their greater tendency to help.

Of course, sunshine and sweet scents are not the only enhancers of mood and helping. In fact, helping is increased by all kinds of pleasant, mood-lifting experiences, such as being successful on a task, reading pleasant positive statements, being

People are much more likely to help someone when they're in a good mood. **True.**

FIGURE 10.6

Scents and Sensibilities

People walking in a mall were approached by someone who asked them for change. This encounter took place in areas of the mall with either pleasant ambient odors or no clear odors. The stranger also gave the individuals a questionnaire that measured their mood on a 5-point scale, ranging from 1 (very bad) to 5 (very good). As shown on the left, the people approached in a pleasant-smelling area were in a better mood than those approached in neutral-smelling locations. In addition (right), people were more likely to help the stranger by giving him change if they were in a pleasant-smelling area than if they were in a neutral-smelling area.

(Data from Baron, 1997.)

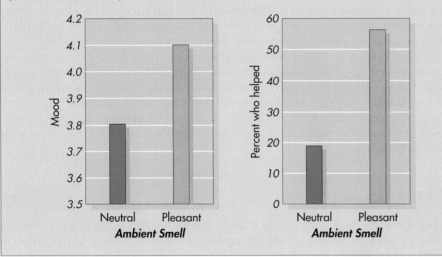

offered a cookie, imagining a Hawaiian vacation, and listening to uplifting music (Aderman, 1972; Isen & Levin, 1972; North et al., 2004). On the job, being in a good mood seems to be the major determinant of a wide range of behaviors (such as helping co-workers, making constructive suggestions, and spreading good will) that improve workplace quality and increase organizational effectiveness (George & Brief, 1992). When we're happy, we're helpful—a state of affairs known as the **good mood effect**.

Why do good moods increase helping? There seem to be several factors at work. Table 10.4 summarizes some of the reasons why feeling good often leads to doing good, and it also describes some of the forks in this road that can lead away from helping. Whatever its exact cause, the good mood effect kicks in quite early in life. It occurs among people of all ages, and even young children help more when they feel happy and cheerful (Moore et al., 1973).

Bad Moods and Doing Good   Since a good mood increases helping, does a bad mood decrease it? Not necessarily. Under many circumstances, negative feelings can elicit positive behavior toward others (Carlson & Miller, 1987). One such circumstance is when people feel guilt. We feel guilty when we believe that we have violated our own personal standards or fear that others may perceive such a violation. Have you ever felt guilty about getting too worked up during a trivial disagreement with a friend? Did you gratefully seize the next available opportunity to help that individual? In such cases, being helpful restores an existing relationship that we value (Estrada-Hollenbeck & Heatherton, 1998). But the impact of guilt on helping can be much more widespread.

Imagine yourself in the following situation. A stranger approaches you on the street and asks you to use his camera to take his picture for a school project. You get ready, aim, and . . . nothing. The camera doesn't work. Looking concerned, the stranger says the camera is rather delicate, asks you if you touched any of the dials, and informs you that it will have to be fixed. You continue on your way down the street. As you pass a young woman, she drops a file folder containing some papers. Now, here's the question: Are you more likely to help the woman pick up her papers because you think you broke the other person's camera?

Probably. In an experiment that used this setup, 80 percent of participants who had been led to believe that they had broken the man's camera helped the woman pick up her papers; only 40 percent of participants who had had no broken-camera experience stopped to help (Cunningham et al., 1980). Thus, participants who unintentionally harmed one individual were more helpful to the next person. According to Roy Baumeister and others (1994), such spillover effects provide an especially vivid demonstration of the interpersonal nature of guilt and its function of enhancing, maintaining, and repairing relationships. Feeling guilty, they contend, motivates us to strengthen whatever social relations are at hand.

good mood effect   The effect whereby a good mood increases helping behavior.

TABLE 10.4
Good Moods Lead to Helping: Reasons and Limitations

Research shows that people in positive moods are more likely to help someone in need than are people in neutral moods. There are several explanations for this effect, as well as some limiting conditions that can weaken or reverse the help-promoting effects of good moods.

Why Feeling Good Leads to Doing Good

- *Desire to maintain one's good mood.* When we are in a good mood, we are motivated to maintain that mood. Helping others makes us feel good, and so it can help maintain a positive mood.

- *Positive expectations about helping.* If we have more positive expectations about the rewards of helping, we are more likely to help.

- *Positive thoughts.* Positive moods trigger positive thoughts, and if we have positive thoughts about others, we should like them more, which makes us more likely to help them.

- *Positive thoughts and expectations about social activities.* Positive moods trigger positive thoughts and expectations about interacting with others and engaging in social activities. These positive thoughts and expectations can promote interacting with others in prosocial ways, including helping them.

When Feeling Good Might Not Lead to Doing Good

- *Costs of helping are high.* If the anticipated costs of helping in a particular situation seem high, helping would put our good mood at risk. In this case, if we can avoid getting involved and thus maintain our good mood (for example, if we can justify our failure to help), we are less likely to help.

- *Positive thoughts about other social activities that conflict with helping.* If our good mood makes us want to go out and party with our friends, our motivation to engage in this social activity may prevent us from taking the time to notice or take responsibility for helping someone in need.

People are much less likely to help someone when they're in a bad mood. **False.**

More generally, negative moods often promote helping. Why might this be? As noted earlier, people know that helping makes them feel good. Recall that in our discussion of the motivations that promote helping, we described the negative state relief model, which holds that people who are feeling bad are motivated to repair their mood and they realize that one way to do it is by helping others. This model seems reasonable, but the evidence is mixed, leading to a vigorous debate on the pros and cons of the negative state relief model (Cialdini & Fultz, 1990; Miller & Carlson, 1990).

An interesting aspect of the negative state relief model involves children. Although young children are more helpful when they are happy, they do not help more when they are sad. Robert Cialdini and his colleagues (1981) propose that helping is not as rewarding to young children as it is to older children and adults. As they develop, children become not only more empathic but also more aware of the potential benefits of helping, which may in turn make them more likely to try to help others to make themselves feel better (Shorr & McClelland, 1998).

In sum, the relationship between good moods and helping is a strong and consistent one. The relationship between negative moods and helping is more complex. Although feeling bad often leads to helping behavior, there are several limits to this effect (see Table 10.5). One important variable is whether people accept responsibility for their bad feelings (Rogers et al., 1982). Negative moods are less likely to promote helping if we blame others for them (such as when we're angry at another person) than if we take personal responsibility (such as when we regret a poor decision we just made). In addition, negative moods are less likely to increase helping if they cause us to become very self-focused (such as when we experience intense grief or depression or when we dwell on our own problems and concerns) than if they direct our focus outward (such as when we feel sad after watching a public service advertisement about child abuse) (Bagozzi & Moore, 1994; Tangney et al., 1996; Wood et al., 1990).

TABLE 10.5
Bad Moods and Helping: When Does Feeling Bad Lead to Doing Good, and When Doesn't It?

Research shows that people in negative moods are often more likely to help someone in need than are people in neutral moods. However, there are several limitations to this effect. This table summarizes some of the factors that make it more or less likely for people to do good when they feel bad.

When Negative Moods Make Us More Likely to Help Others

• If we take responsibility for what caused our bad mood ("I feel guilty for what I did")

• If we focus on other people ("Wow, those people have suffered so much")

• If we are made to think about our personal values that promote helping
  ("I really shouldn't act like such a jerk next time; I have to be nicer")

When Negative Moods Make Us Less Likely to Help Others

• If we blame others for our bad mood ("I feel so angry at that jerk who put me in this situation")

• If we become very self-focused ("I am so depressed")

• If we are made to think about our personal values that do not promote helping ("I have to wise up and start thinking about my own needs more")

 ## Role Models and Social Norms: A Helpful Standard

We mentioned earlier that children become more aware as they get older of the potential benefits of helping. How, in general, do children learn about helping? One important way is through role models. Seeing important people in their lives behave prosocially, or antisocially, encourages children to follow suit. Role models can be real people in children's lives or characters they see on television (Moriarty & McCabe, 1977; Rushton, 1981a; Sprafkin et al., 1975). Indeed, although politicians, educators, researchers, and parents pay a great deal of attention to the negative effects of TV on children (discussed in Chapter 11 on Aggression), TV can also have positive effects on children through the modeling of prosocial behavior. After reviewing an extensive research literature, Susan Hearold (1986) concluded that the effect of prosocial TV on prosocial behavior was about twice as large as the effect of TV violence on aggressive behavior. She argued that rather than advocating primarily to "eliminate the negative" by removing shows with sex and violence, the public should focus more on "accentuating the positive" by encouraging the creation of more shows with prosocial themes and positive role models (p. 116). More recently, a meta-analysis of thirty-four studies involving more than five thousand children found a reliable positive effect of prosocial television on children's prosocial behavior, especially when specific acts of altruism were modeled on TV (Mares & Woodard, 2005).

Helpful models are important not only for children but for all of us. Observing helpful models increases helping in a variety of situations (Bryan & Test, 1967; Ng & van Dyne, 2005; Sarason et al., 1991; Siu et al., 2006). Why do models of other people helping inspire us to help? Three reasons stand out. First, they provide an example of behavior for us to imitate directly. Second, when they are rewarded for their helpful behavior, models teach us that helping is valued and rewarding, which strengthens our own inclination to be helpful. Third, the behavior of models makes us think about and become more aware of the standards of conduct in our society.

General rules of conduct established by society are called **social norms**. These norms embody standards of socially approved and disapproved behavior. Two sets of social norms bear directly on when people are likely to help. The first consists of norms based on fairness. As we mentioned in Chapter 7, the *norm of reciprocity* establishes quid-pro-quo transactions as a socially approved standard: People who give to you should be paid back (Schopler, 1970). Accordingly, people usually help those who have helped them, especially when the initial assistance was given voluntarily (Gross & Latané, 1974; Whatley et al., 1999). Equity is the basis of another norm calling for fairness in our treatment of others. The *norm of equity* prescribes that when people are in a situation

social norm A general rule of conduct reflecting standards of social approval and disapproval.

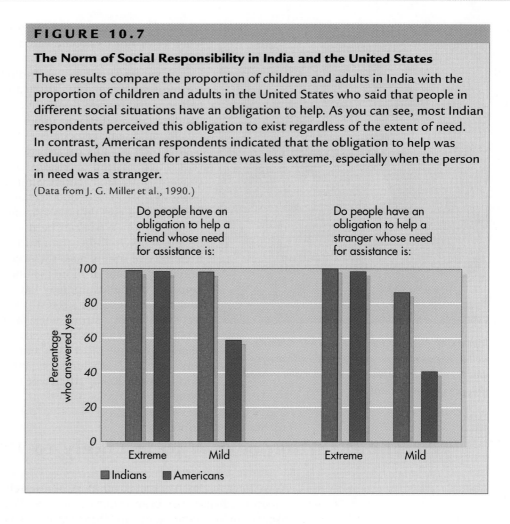

FIGURE 10.7

The Norm of Social Responsibility in India and the United States

These results compare the proportion of children and adults in India with the proportion of children and adults in the United States who said that people in different social situations have an obligation to help. As you can see, most Indian respondents perceived this obligation to exist regardless of the extent of need. In contrast, American respondents indicated that the obligation to help was reduced when the need for assistance was less extreme, especially when the person in need was a stranger.
(Data from J. G. Miller et al., 1990.)

Do people have an obligation to help a friend whose need for assistance is:

Do people have an obligation to help a stranger whose need for assistance is:

Percentage who answered yes

Extreme   Mild   Extreme   Mild

■ Indians ■ Americans

**norm of social
responsibility**   A moral
standard emphasizing that
people should help those who
need assistance.

in which they feel overbenefited (receiving more benefits than earned), they should help those who are underbenefited (receiving fewer benefits than earned). Such help restores an equitable balance (Walster, Walster, & Berscheid, 1978).

Other help-relevant social norms go beyond an immediate sense of fairness to a larger sense of what is right. The **norm of social responsibility** dictates that people should help those who need assistance. This norm creates a sense of duty and obligation, to which people respond by giving more help to those in greater need of it (Berkowitz, 1972; Bornstein, 1994). When people are more motivated by concerns about *justice or fairness,* however, their intentions to help someone will be driven more by their belief that this person *deserves* their assistance than by their belief that he or she simply needs it (Lerner, 1998).

Concerns with reciprocity, equity, social responsibility, and justice can have powerful effects. Yet sometimes they fail to produce the helpful behavior they prescribe. Why? One problem with social norms is their generality. They are so general, so abstract, that it is not clear when they apply. When you encounter two people fighting, should you follow the norm prescribing "Help those in need" or the one instructing you to "Mind your own business"? (Darley & Latané, 1970).

Social norms can vary dramatically across cultures. For instance, Joan Miller and her colleagues (1990) found that children and adults in the United States are less likely than children and adults in India to believe that people have an obligation to provide assistance to friends or strangers whose need for help is not extreme (see Figure 10.7). It appears that the Hindu Indians who participated in this study regard social responsibilities as an absolute moral obligation, while Americans apply the norm of social responsibility more selectively. Jonathan Baron and Joan Miller (2000) also found that Indian students were more likely than U.S. students to view donating bone marrow to save someone's life as morally required. U.S.

Movie star Angelina Jolie has used her celebrity, as well as her own time and energy, to raise awareness and resources for impoverished and malnourished children around the world.

students were much more likely than Indian students to say that whether or not to donate was a personal choice for the potential donor to make.

As we discussed earlier, inhibiting or disengaging from one's concerns with morality can be a critical step away from prosocial behavior and toward destructive and violent transgressions. Albert Bandura (1999, 2004) documents a variety of factors that facilitate this moral disengagement. For example, the use of euphemistic labeling, such as "surgical strikes" instead of "bombing missions" or "casualties" instead of "deaths" in war, may reduce people's moral concerns with such actions. Similarly, through stereotypes and prejudice, people may exclude certain other groups from their moral concerns and end up rationalizing inhumane actions against them (Staub, 1996). What can be done to increase the likelihood that people will help rather than hurt outgroups? Whereas ignoring the humanity of others makes it easier to hurt them, emphasizing the humanity of one or more members of the group, such as through empathy or friendship, may have the opposite effect. Indeed, a recent wave of research suggests that individuals who are induced to feel empathy or a strong sense of connection with a particular outgroup member or to simply take the perspective of an outgroup member, become more likely to help members of the outgroup (Batson et al., 2002; Dovidio et al., 2004; Galinsky & Ku, 2004; Galinsky & Moskowitz, 2000; Pettigrew & Tropp, 2000; Stephan & Finlay, 1999; Wright et al., 1997).

Personal Influences: Who Is Likely to Help?

As we have just seen, social psychological research addressing the question "When do people help?" has been quite productive. What about the question "Who is likely to help?" When we think about extreme acts of helping, or of failing to help, or when we think about long-term, well-planned acts of helping such as volunteering at a clinic or shelter or serving as a Big Brother or Big Sister, we tend to wonder not about the situational influences but about the nature of the people involved. In this section, we consider some of the individual differences between people that address the question "Who is likely to help?" Researchers interested in this question have tried to identify *an altruistic personality* that distinguishes people who help from those who don't. Some of their research has focused on whether certain people tend to be more helpful across situations than others and whether and to what extent these differences might be genetically based. Other research has sought to identify what general personality characteristics and traits constitute the altruistic personality. In this section, we review both of these lines of research.

Are Some People More Helpful Than Others?

> *"The purpose of human life is to serve and to show compassion and the will to help others."*
>
> —Albert Schweitzer

Although situational factors clearly can overwhelm individual differences in influencing helping behaviors in many contexts (Latané & Darley, 1970), researchers have demonstrated some evidence of individual differences in helping tendencies that endure across at least some situations. People who are more helpful than others in one situation are likely to be more helpful in other situations as well (Hampson, 1984; Rushton, 1981b). In addition, longitudinal research by Nancy Eisenberg and others (1999, 2002) suggests that this individual difference may be relatively stable over time. They found, for example, that the degree to which preschool children exhibited spontaneous helping behavior predicted how helpful they would be in later childhood and early adulthood.

According to J. Philippe Rushton and his colleagues (1984), this individual difference in helpfulness is in part genetically based. Studies of twins offer some support

Rock star Bruce Springsteen may not seem to have a lot in common with Dikembe Mutombo and Mother Teresa and other people mentioned on this page as models of altruism, but like them, he donates a tremendous amount of time and money to helping others. At every stop on his concert tours in recent years, Springsteen has raised money for local causes, such as food banks, youth centers, and shelters.

Someone relatively low in empathic concern for another.

"It's always poor you, isn't it, Albert?"

for Rushton's argument. Genetically identical (monozygotic) twins are more similar to each other in their helpful behavioral tendencies and their helping-related emotions and reactions, such as empathy, than are fraternal (dizygotic) twins, who share only a portion of their genetic make-up (Knafo & Plomin, 2006; Scourfield et al., 2004). These findings suggest that there may be a heritable component to helpfulness.

What Is the Altruistic Personality?

Even if we identify some people who help others a lot and other people who don't, we have not addressed the question of what distinguishes people who help from those who don't—other than their helpfulness, of course. What are the various components of the altruistic personality? Can we predict who is likely to be altruistic by looking at people's overall personalities?

Consider some examples of people who have acted very altruistically. Do they seem to have very similar personality traits and characteristics? Take, for example, Oskar Schindler, the wealthy German businessman during the Nazi regime who became the hero of the book and movie, *Schindler's List.* Schindler was a shady operator, cheating in business and marriage, partying with sadistic German military officers. From his overall personality, could anyone have predicted his altruistic actions of risking his own life to save over four thousand Jews during the Holocaust? It is doubtful.

What about more contemporary models of altruism? Consider these people: Bill Gates, a computer geek who co-founded Microsoft and became the richest man in the world; Bono, the extraverted Irishman rock star; Ted Turner, an eccentric American from the South who started the first 24-hour news cable station (CNN); Dikembe Mutombo, a 7-foot, 2-inch professional basketball player originally from the Congo; Mother Teresa, a Roman Catholic nun from Macedonia. These well-known figures seem *quite* different from each other in overall personality—except for their concern with helping others. Gates and his wife Melinda have pledged *billions* of dollars to charity, much of it to target health issues around the world. Bono has worked tirelessly to raise money and awareness about the plight of poor African nations. Turner pledged a personal donation of $1 billion to the United Nations. Mutombo has raised millions of dollars for and overseen the construction of hospitals in the Congo. Mother Teresa devoted her life to the poor in India.

The quest to discover the altruistic personality has not been an easy one. Much of the research conducted over the years has failed to find consistent, reliable personality characteristics that predict helping behavior across situations. The situational variables that we've already discussed in this chapter have predicted people's behaviors much better than personality variables (Piliavin et al., 1981). Some researchers have changed the nature of the quest, however, focusing on personality variables that predict helping in some specific situations rather than across all situations; and their studies have been more successful in identifying traits that predict such behavior (Carlo et al., 2005; Penner, 2004; Reynolds & Karraker, 2003). George Knight and his colleagues (1994) suggested that an interacting "conglomerate" of numerous dispositional traits influences prosocial behavior and that the traits differ depending on

Microsoft's Bill Gates, his wife Melinda, and rock star Bono are pictured on the cover of Time magazine, December 26, 2005, which honored "The Good Samaritans" as its Persons of the Year in 2005.

"True kindness presupposes the faculty of imagining as one's own the suffering and joy of others."

—André Gide

the situation. For example, in dangerous emergencies, people who are high in self-confidence and independence are more likely to help than other people, but they are no more likely to help in response to a request to donate money to a charity (Wilson, 1976).

Two qualities that the research thus far suggests are most essential for an altruistic personality are empathy and advanced moral reasoning (e.g., Hoffman, 2000). We have already discussed empathy in this chapter, such as in the context of Batson's empathy-altruism hypothesis. Being able to take the perspective of others and experience empathy is associated positively with helping and other prosocial behaviors in children and adults (Batson, 1998; Davis et al., 1999; Eisenberg et al., 2004, 2006; Li et al., 2005).

The second characteristic associated with helping is moral reasoning. Children and adults who exhibit internalized and advanced levels of moral reasoning behave more altruistically than others. Such moral reasoning involves adhering to moral standards independent of external social controls, and taking into account the needs of others when making decisions about courses of action. In contrast, people whose reasoning is focused on their own needs or on the concrete personal consequences that their actions are likely to have tend not to engage in many helping behaviors (Carlo et al., 1996; Krebs & Rosenwald, 1994; Midlarsky et al., 1999; Schonert-Reichl, 1999).

The combination of empathy and advanced moral reasoning may be an especially strong predictor of helping tendencies. Paul Miller and his colleagues (1996) propose that "cold" cognitive moral principles may not be enough to trigger self-sacrificing prosocial action; when these principles are activated together with the experience of "hot" empathic or sympathetic emotional responses to another's suffering, however, helping is much more likely.

Recently Elizabeth Midlarsky and others (2005) conducted a fascinating study of "non-Jewish heroes of the Holocaust"—people who risked their lives to help Jews despite having no expectation of any extrinsic rewards. The researchers found that these rescuers did indeed tend to differ from bystanders who did not help on a combination of several variables associated with prosocial behavior, including empathic concern and moral reasoning. These qualities are both reflected in the quote of one woman who sheltered thirty Jews in her home in Poland: "Helping to give shelter was the natural thing to do, the human thing. When I looked into those eyes, how could I not care? Of course I was afraid—always afraid—but there was no choice but to do the only decent thing" (p. 908).

Interpersonal Influences: Whom Do People Help?

However influential they might be, personal factors alone do not a helper make. The characteristics of the person in need are important as well. Are some people more likely than others to receive help? Are some helpers particularly responsive to certain kinds of individuals who need assistance? Here, we explore some of the interpersonal aspects of helping.

 ### Perceived Characteristics of the Person in Need

Although many characteristics of a person in need might affect whether that individual is helped, researchers have paid special attention to two: the personal attractiveness of the person in need and whether or not the person seems responsible for being in the position of needing assistance.

Attractiveness   In Chapter 9, we described the social advantages enjoyed by physically attractive individuals. The bias for beauty also affects helping, as Peter Benson and his colleagues (1976) observed in a large metropolitan airport. Darting into a phone booth to make a call, each of 604 travelers discovered some materials supposedly left behind accidentally by the previous caller (but actually planted by the experimenters): a completed graduate school application form, a photograph of the applicant, and a stamped, addressed envelope. In some packets, the photo depicted a physically attractive individual; in others, the person was relatively unattractive. What was a busy traveler to do? When the researchers checked their mail, they found that people were more likely to send in the materials of the good-looking applicants than those of the less attractive applicants.

Physical appearance, of course, is only one aspect of attractiveness. Friendly individuals also receive a more generous response (Lynn & Mynier, 1993). In one rather original field experiment conducted in France (Guéguen & Fischer-Lokou, 2005), where hitchhiking is legal and relatively common, male and female confederates of "average attractiveness" hitchhiked along a road, signaling to a total of 800 motorists. The confederates varied whether or not they smiled. Smiling worked, at least for the female confederates. Drivers were much more likely to stop for smiling women than women not smiling. Smiling did not, however, improve the male confederates' chances of getting picked up.

Sometimes the charisma of one person can determine how much help other people receive. On November 7, 1991, basketball superstar Earvin "Magic" Johnson announced to a stunned public that he had contracted HIV, the virus that causes AIDS. By coincidence, Louis Penner and Barbara Fritzsche (1993) had just completed a study in which college undergraduates were given the opportunity to assist a graduate student who was described as having AIDS. These investigators decided to repeat

FIGURE 10.8

Magic's Influence on Helping Others

Soon after basketball superstar Magic Johnson announced that he was infected with HIV, there was an increase in the amount of time volunteered by college undergraduates to assist a graduate student who had AIDS. However, by four and one-half months after the announcement, the amount of time volunteered had returned to the pre-announcement level.

(Penner & Fritzsche, 1993.)

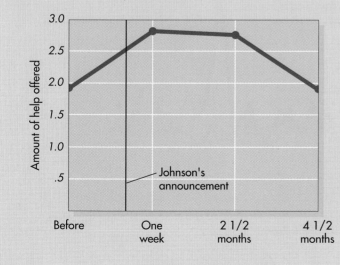

their study three more times after Magic's announcement. As you can see in Figure 10.8, the amount of time participants were willing to volunteer increased after the announcement but then declined back to the pre-announcement baseline. It appears that for a while, the immense attractiveness of Magic Johnson spread like a protective cloak over others who were HIV-positive and increased the help they received. Unfortunately, once the shock wore off, so did the help.

The shock of the terrorist attacks of September 11, 2001, in the United States also inspired a huge, but short-lived, spike in helping behavior, as can be seen in Figure 10.9. Louis Penner and his colleagues (2005) found that 3,826 people went to the Web site run by Volunteermatch.org and offered to volunteer during the week of September 17, 2000. That same week a year later, soon after the horror of 9/11, that number jumped to 13,227. However, the increase lasted for only about three weeks.

Attributions of Responsibility At some time or another, most students have had the experience of being asked to lend their class notes to a classmate. Has this ever happened to you? If so, you can compare your reactions with those of the students in a study conducted by Richard Barnes and his colleagues (1979). In this research, students received a call from an experimental confederate posing as another student, who asked to borrow their class notes to prepare for an upcoming exam. The reason for this request varied. To some students, the caller said, "I just don't seem to have the ability to take good notes. I really try to take good notes, but sometimes I just can't do it." Other students were told that "I just don't seem to have the motivation to take good notes. I really can take good notes, but sometimes I just don't try." You probably won't be surprised to learn that the caller received much more help from those who were informed he had tried yet failed than from those who were told he hadn't tried at all.

Attractive people have a better chance than unattractive people of getting help when they need it. **True.**

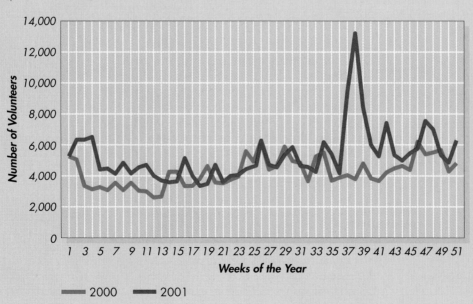

FIGURE 10.9

Volunteering Before and After 9/11

The shock of the terrorist attacks of September 11, 2001 (during the 37th week of 2001), triggered a huge increase in the number of people going to Volunteermatch.org and offering to volunteer. A few weeks after 9/11, however, rates of volunteering went back down to close to the previous year's (blue line) levels.

(Penner et al., 2005.)

Bluntly stating that you didn't even try to help yourself may seem like an obvious way to ensure that others won't help you out. But even when the circumstances are more complex and the causes more subtle, people's beliefs about the needy individual's responsibility influence helping. For example, participants in an experiment by Pamela Dooley (1995) read scenarios about someone who had just been diagnosed with AIDS. If the participants read that the person had contracted the disease through a blood transfusion rather than through sexual activity or drug use, they considered the situation less controllable, and they felt more pity for the person. In addition, those who felt pity indicated a greater desire to engage in helping behaviors. Similarly, Nadine Mackay and Christine Barrowclough (2005) report that the medical and nursing staff at an emergency room felt more negatively and were less helpful toward patients whose injuries they felt were more controllable and avoidable.

The Fit Between Giver and Receiver

Some potential helpers are particularly responsive to some kinds of potential recipients. In this section, we look at a variety of ways in which helping depends on the fit between a giver and a receiver.

Similarity: Helping Those Just like Us   We are more likely to help others who are similar to us. All kinds of similarity—from dress to attitudes to nationality—increase our willingness to help, and signs of dissimilarity decrease it (Dovidio, 1984). People are much more likely to help fellow ingroup members than they are to help members of an outgroup (Bernhard et al., 2006; Levine et al., 2005; Stürmer et al., 2006).

Why are we more likely to help those who seem similar to us? There are probably several reasons. For one thing, as seen in Chapter 9, we are more likely to be attracted to and develop relationships with people who are similar to ourselves. In addition, it may be easier to empathize with similar others. The influence of similarity could even be a form of kin selection, as people may use similarity in appearance as a signal of potential kinship (Segal, 1993). We might help similar, though biologically unrelated, individuals because we overgeneralize, assuming that what looks alike must genetically be alike (Krebs, 1987).

The effects of similarity on helping suggest that members of the same race should help each other more than members of different races. However, research on black-white helping in the United States indicates that the effects of racial similarity are highly inconsistent. In a recent meta-analysis of more than thirty studies, Donald Saucier and others (2005) found no consistent overall relationship between racial similarity and helping. What accounts for these inconsistencies? First, although helping can be a compassionate response to another, it can also be seen as a sign of superiority over the person who needs help (Ames et al., 2004). Thus, cross-racial helping isn't always a sign of egalitarian attitudes. Second, public displays of racial prejudice risk social disapproval, and prejudiced individuals may bend over backward, in public at least, to avoid revealing their attitudes. As discussed in Chapter 5, however, modern racism relies on more subtle forms of discrimination. Consistent with predictions from theories of modern racism, Saucier et al.'s meta-analysis found that when the situation provides people with excuses or justifications for not helping, racial discrimination in helping is more likely.

Intergroup biases in helping can be reduced significantly, however, if the members of the different groups can perceive themselves as members of a common group. Through fostering perceptions of shared identities, encouraging meaningful contact that defies group boundaries, and highlighting similarities on other dimensions unrelated to group distinctions, an ingroup and an outgroup can begin to see each other as more similar than different, thereby promoting helping and other positive behaviors (Gaertner & Dovidio, 2005; Levy et al., 2002).

FIGURE 10.10

Not Giving Much Help to Our Friends

People usually help their friends more than they help strangers, but not always. In this study, people who thought they had performed poorly on a task gave clues on the same task to a friend and to a stranger. When the task was not important for participants' self-esteem, they gave more helpful clues to the friend than to the stranger. When the task was highly ego-relevant, they gave slightly less helpful clues to the friend than to the stranger.

(Data from Tesser & Smith, 1980.)

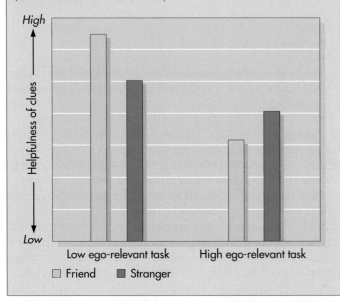

Friend □   Stranger ■

In any situation, people are more likely to help a friend succeed than a stranger.
False.

Closeness: A Little Help for Our Friends As we would expect, people are usually more helpful toward those they know and care about than toward strangers or superficial acquaintances (Bell et al., 1995; Clark & Mills, 1993). People in a *communal* relationship, such as close friends or romantic partners, feel mutual responsibility for each other's needs. People in an *exchange* relationship, such as acquaintances or business associates, give help with the expectation of receiving comparable benefits in return—"If I help you move your furniture, you'd better give me a ride to the airport." When people are, or desire to be, in a communal relationship with each other, they attend more to each other's needs, are more likely to help, and are less likely to be concerned with keeping track of rewards and costs. People in a communal relationship also feel better about having helped the other, and they feel worse if they were unable to help (Williamson et al., 1996).

So, common sense seems correct here: People help their friends more than strangers or acquaintances. But there may be an exception to this general rule: What if a person's ego is threatened? According to the *self-evaluation maintenance model* (Erber & Tesser, 1994), we can respond in two very different ways to superior performance by a significant other. If the achievement occurs in an area not relevant to our own ego, we can indulge in the delight of BIRGing—basking in reflected glory, as described in Chapter 3. If the area is relevant to our own ego, however, we may experience envy and resentment.

To apply this perspective to helping behavior, suppose you have just finished working on a task and are told that you performed "a little below average." Then two other people take their turns at the same task; one of them is a stranger, and the other a close friend. You are asked to give some clues to each individual. The available clues differ in their level of difficulty. Some are easy and will boost the person's performance; others are so difficult that they will interfere with a good performance. Will you give your friend easier, more helpful clues than you give to the stranger?

As the self-evaluation maintenance model would predict, it depends on the task. When participants found themselves in the situation we've just described, those who believed that the task was a trivial game helped their friend more than they helped the stranger (Tesser & Smith, 1980). But when the task was important and relevant to their own self-esteem, participants were slightly less helpful to their friend than to the stranger (see Figure 10.10). In a conflict between our own egos and the welfare of a friend, the need to protect our self-esteem can sometimes overcome our helpful inclinations. The self-evaluation maintenance model applies even to very close relationships, such as married couples (Beach et al., 1996). Note, however, that superior performance by a close other on an important task is not always threatening. Indeed, Hart Blanton and others (2000) found that when an ingroup member's superior performance challenged negative stereotypes about that group's abilities, other members of his or her group felt better rather than worse about themselves.

Gender and Helping

Here's a quick, one-question quiz: Who helps more, men or women? Before you answer, consider the following situations:

A. Two strangers pass on the street. Suddenly, one of them needs help that might be dangerous to give. Other people are watching. The person in need is female.

"Are you telling me you won't even ask the computerized navigational system for directions?"

Men are less likely to seek help than women, possibly because it is more threatening to their self-esteem.

Women seek help more often than men do. **True.**

B. Two individuals have a close relationship. Every so often, one of them needs assistance that takes time and energy to provide but is not physically dangerous. No one else is around to notice whether help is given. The person who needs help is either male or female.

Is your answer the same for both situations? It shouldn't be. Situation A is a classic male-helper scenario. Here, the helper is a "knight in shining armor"—physically brave and chivalrous, rescuing a lady in distress. Because social psychologists have tended to focus on these kinds of emergency situations, their research has found that, on the average, men are more helpful than women and women receive more help than do men (Eagly & Crowley, 1986).

Situation B is the classic female-helper scenario. Every day, millions of women—mothers, sisters, wives, and female friends—provide support for their friends and loved ones, and they are more likely to provide this kind of help than are men (George et al., 1998; McGuire, 1994). Though it lacks the high drama of an emergency intervention, this type of helping, called "social support," plays a crucial role in the quality of our lives. Chapter 14 reports evidence indicating that social support is associated with better physical and psychological health.

Many of the stories from September 11, 2001, fit these two classic senses of helping. Most of the dramatic rescue stories were of men engaged in dangerous acts of helping, such as the account of the firefighters featured in the opening to this chapter. And many women worked behind the scenes in the more unheralded acts of helping, such as tending to the wounded, raising money for the families of the victims, and helping with the cleanup of the disaster sites at the World Trade Center and Pentagon. But, as with most gender differences, there were many exceptions. Many men worked along with women to lend support in the aftermath, and several women risked, and lost, their lives while trying to help others in the World Trade Center that morning. Indeed, Susan Hagen and Mary Carouba, outraged at the lack of coverage of women's sacrifices on 9/11, wrote a book in 2002 to correct this oversight, *Women at Ground Zero: Stories of Courage and Compassion.*

Gender is related not only to differences in helping behavior but also to differences in the willingness to *seek* help. Have you ever had the experience of getting lost while driving with a member of the opposite sex? Who wanted to stop early on and ask for directions? Who kept insisting that help wasn't necessary? In this case, the male stereotype is true: For relatively minor problems, at least, men ask for help less frequently than do women (McMullen & Gross, 1983). Less socially acceptable for men, help-seeking is more threatening to their self-esteem (Wills & De-Paulo, 1991).

As we will see in the following section, reactions to receiving help are more complex than one might think.

Reactions to Receiving Help

Thus far, we've described factors that influence whether helping will occur. Now, we turn to what happens after it takes place. The last time someone helped you, how did you feel? Grateful, relieved, comforted—anything else? Embarrassed, obligated, inferior? Receiving help is often a positive experience, but sometimes it has drawbacks for the recipient. There are costs in providing help, and there can be costs in receiving it.

According to Daniel Ames and others (2004), how recipients of help perceive the motives behind the helper's actions can vary dramatically, and the recipients' reactions to the help will depend on these perceptions. Jeffrey Fisher, Arie Nadler, and their collaborators also have extensively examined people's reactions to receiving help (Ames et al., 2004; Fisher et al., 1982; Nadler & Fisher, 1986). According to their **threat-to-self-esteem model**, receiving help is experienced as *self-supportive* when the recipient feels appreciated and cared for, but as *self-threatening* when the recipient feels inferior and overly dependent. If recipients feel supported by the help they receive, they respond positively: feeling good, accepting the help, and being grateful to the donor. If, however, recipients feel threatened, they have a negative emotional reaction and evaluate both the help and the helper unfavorably.

There are three conditions under which receiving help is most likely to be perceived as threatening. First, individuals with high self-esteem tend to react more negatively to receiving help than do those with low self-esteem. Presumably, people who regard themselves as highly competent are especially sensitive to the implication that they are unable to take care of themselves. Second, being helped by a similar other highlights the contrast between the recipient's need for assistance and the competence of the provider. This one difference between people alike in other ways may imply that the recipient is inferior. The third condition under which receiving help can be threatening involves the type of relationship the recipient has with the provider and the area in which help has been received. As would be expected from the self-evaluation maintenance model, receiving help from a significant other on an ego-relevant task can be threatening to an individual's self-esteem.

Usually, however, help from those who are close to us will be seen as supportive. High self-esteem does not appear to prompt negative reactions to assistance by a sibling (Searcy & Eisenberg, 1992). And the negative effects of similarity probably do not apply to close relationships, in which similarity is expected and desired (Wills, 1992). Even ego-relevant help may elicit positive, rather than negative, reactions from partners in an interdependent relationship (Clark, 1983; Cook & Pelfrey, 1985). In such relationships, feelings of inferiority are less likely to arise, as each person sometimes helps, sometimes receives help. Mutuality makes receiving help less threatening. So does a very young age. Because dependency is more acceptable for children than for adolescents and adults, children less often react negatively to being helped (Shell & Eisenberg, 1992).

People who are stigmatized by being the targets of negative stereotypes and feeling devalued in the larger society often face a difficult attributional dilemma when they receive help from members of nonstigmatized groups: Is the helping sincere and unassuming, is it well intentioned but patronizing, or is it controlling and designed to keep the recipient dependent? These are questions that members of nonstigmatized groups aren't as likely to consider when they receive help from another. Members of stigmatized groups may feel worse about themselves after receiving help from an outgroup member, particularly if the help was unsolicited (Blaine et al., 1995; Schneider et al., 1996).

The Helping Connection

Although whether or not people help others can be quite variable, there is a consistent theme that appears repeatedly in this chapter: a sense of connection. Throughout the chapter, this connection has taken various forms—genetic relatedness, empathic concern, sense of responsibility for someone, perceived similarity, shared group membership, and so on.

The importance of a sense of connection is vividly demonstrated by a cross-cultural comparison. First, consider one of the great social tragedies of our time: homelessness. In the United States, one of the richest countries on earth, thousands of men, women, and children are without a home. Many sleep on the street, carry their belongings in grocery carts, and rummage through piles of garbage to find food. Now, compare American homelessness with an anthropologist's account of life among the Moose (pronounced "MOH-say") in West Africa:

Moose welcome anyone who wishes to join the community and move into the village. New arrivals have only to say where they wish to build their homes, and the user of the land in question gives it up for the newcomer's

threat-to-self-esteem model The theory that reactions to receiving assistance depend on whether help is perceived as supportive or threatening.

The heroic firefighters from New York City's Ladder Company Six are reunited with Josephine Harris, the woman they risked their lives to save in the World Trade Center on September, 11, 2001. The men presented Josephine with a jacket honoring her as their "Guardian Angel"—a reminder of how their selfless act of helping her may have in turn saved their own lives as the 110-story skyscraper collapsed around them.

residence. . . . Each of the two years that I lived there, the well ran dry and villagers had to walk miles to get water for themselves and their stock from other villages, carrying it home on their heads. Each of these other villages shared their water until their wells were nearly dry, without expecting any reciprocation for the water. Even in these circumstances, any stranger who comes into the village may ask for a drink, and any visitor is offered water. (Fiske, 1991, pp. 190–191)

Among some of the poorest people on earth, no one goes without shelter or remains thirsty as long as anyone has water to drink.

How can we account for the extraordinary difference between American homelessness and Moose hospitality? Homelessness is, of course, a complex phenomenon affected by many specific economic and political factors. But it may also be a symptom of a profound loss of social connection in American society (Wuthnow, 1991). Among the Moose, no such loss has occurred. Their sense of being intimately connected to others binds them to those who live in their village and to strangers who arrive in their midst.

Consider, however, the outpouring of helping by Americans after tragedies such as 9/11 or Hurricane Katrina. After Katrina, for example, families throughout the country took in those who lost their homes, schools and colleges offered displaced students the chance to continue their education, countless college students resisted the hedonistic temptations of Spring Break to volunteer their time helping to rebuild New Orleans, young children helped raise money and food, and on and on. A tragedy like Katrina can remind people of their common humanity, highlighting their social connection while, temporarily at least, rendering their differences insignificant.

The relationship between helping and interpersonal connection runs like a bright red thread through much of the research on helping. For example:

- Evolutionary perspectives emphasize the genetic connection of reciprocal, kin, and within-group helping.

- Two kinds of connections lie at the heart of the empathy-altruism hypothesis: the cognitive connection of perspective taking and the emotional connection of empathic concern.

- In an emergency, bystanders who know the victim or know each other are more likely to intervene.

- People who respond empathically to another's suffering and consider the plight of others in their own moral reasoning are more likely to help than are others.

- Perceived similarity increases helping.

- In a close relationship, it's easier to give and more comfortable to receive.

Taken as a whole, these theories and research findings suggest that helping requires the recognition of individual human beings with whom we can have a meaningful connection. Which brings us back to Ladder Company Six, and the so many others who risked, and even lost, their lives that day. Most of the people didn't know the others they were helping. But suddenly, horribly, fate had thrown them together, and suddenly their lives deeply mattered to each other. They felt responsible for each other. Many of those who helped in the face of grave danger may never have read the words that English poet John Donne wrote almost four hundred years ago. But they would have understood them:

No man is an island, entire of itself. Every man is a piece of the continent, a part of the main. If a clod be washed away by the sea, Europe is the less, as well as if a promontory were, as well as if a manor of thy friends or of thine own were. Any man's death diminishes me, because I am involved in mankind. And therefore never send to know for whom the bell tolls; it tolls for thee.

REVIEW

Evolutionary and Motivational Factors: Why Do People Help?

Evolutionary Factors in Helping

- Evolutionary perspectives emphasize two ways in which helping could become an innate, universal behavioral tendency: kin selection, in which individuals protect their own genes by helping close relatives; and reciprocal altruism, in which those who give also receive.

- Other evolutionary approaches include the idea of group selection, in which members of a social group help each other survive.

- Some scholars believe that humans, along with many mammals, exhibit impulses of parental caregiving.

Rewards of Helping: Helping Others to Help Oneself

- People are much more likely to help when the potential rewards of helping seem high relative to the potential costs.

- Helping others often makes the helper feel good, it can relieve negative feelings such as guilt, and it is associated with better health.

- People sometimes help in order to appear to be moral, or to take credit away from someone else, rather than because of more sincere motivations.

- Emphasizing the costs of helping, or the costs of not helping, can affect people's decisions about whether to offer help.

Altruism or Egoism: The Great Debate

- A recent study demonstrated that infants and even chimpanzees could take the perspective of an adult male enough to recognize when he needed help reaching a goal, and they often helped him.

- According to the empathy-altruism hypothesis, taking the perspective of a person perceived to be in need creates the other-oriented emotion of empathic concern, which in turn produces the altruistic motive to reduce the other's distress.

- The self-oriented emotion of personal distress produces the egoistic motive to reduce one's own distress.

- When people are altruistically motivated, they will help even when escaping from the helping situation is easy.

- Thinking about the other person's feelings is more likely to trigger helping behavior than is thinking about one's own feelings about the person's situation.

- Alternatives to the empathy-altruism hypothesis include empathy-specific punishments for not helping and empathy-specific rewards for helping, such as negative state relief and empathic joy.

- In relationships in which the self-other distinction is eliminated and one person feels the other's needs as deeply as his or her own, the difference between altruistic and egoistic motivations may disappear.

Distinguishing Among the Motivations to Help: Why Does It Matter?

- People's motivations influence whether or not they are likely to help someone in a particular situation.

- People who help someone for egoistic reasons will feel good or bad about their actions to the extent that they are rewarded for the actions, whereas people who help someone for altruistic reasons will feel good or bad as a function of the other person's fate.

- Longer-term acts of helping, such as volunteerism, reflect both altruistic and egoistic motivations. Self-interested goals in this context can be a good thing in that they promote a commitment to helping behavior to the extent that such goals are met.

Situational Influences: When Do People Help?

The Unhelpful Crowd

- Research on the bystander effect, in which the presence of others inhibits helping in an emergency, indicates why the five steps necessary for helping—noticing, interpreting, taking responsibility, deciding how to help, and providing help—may not be taken.
- The distractions of others and our own self-concerns may impair our ability to notice that someone needs help.
- Under ambiguous circumstances, some interpretations—such as the belief that an attacker and a victim have a close relationship or the mistaken inferences drawn from pluralistic ignorance—reduce bystander intervention.
- People may fail to take responsibility because they assume that others will—a phenomenon called diffusion of responsibility.
- Bystanders are less likely to offer direct aid when they do not feel competent to do so. They can, however, call for assistance from others.
- Even if people want to help, they may not do so if they fear that behaving in a helpful fashion will make them look foolish.

Time Pressure

- When people are in a hurry, they are less likely to notice or choose to help others in need.

Location and Culture

- Residents of densely populated areas are less likely to provide spontaneous, informal help to strangers than are residents of smaller or less densely populated communities.
- Cross-cultural research has found variation in the helping rates of people in cities around the world. According to one study, people in cities with relatively low levels of economic well-being were somewhat more likely to help strangers, and people from *simpatia* cultures were more likely to help strangers than people from non-*simpatia* cultures.
- Research concerning the relationship between individualism-collectivism and helping has yielded rather mixed results. According to some analyses, collectivists may be more responsive than individualists to the immediate needs of a particular person but less helpful in more abstract situations.

Moods and Helping

- A good mood increases helpfulness.
- People in a good mood may help in order to maintain their positive mood or because they have more positive thoughts and expectations about helpful behavior, the person in need, or social activities in general.
- A bad mood can often increase helpfulness, such as when people feel guilty about something.
- People in a bad mood may be motivated to help others in order to improve their mood.
- A bad mood is less likely to increase helpfulness if the bad mood is attributed to the fault of others, or if it causes the person to become very self-focused.

Role Models and Social Norms: A Helpful Standard

- Observing a helpful model increases helping.
- Social norms that promote helping are based on a sense of fairness or on standards about what is right.
- Cultural differences exist in how people interpret and apply social norms.
- De-emphasizing the humanity of outgroup members can facilitate destructive actions against them, whereas recognizing their humanity can facilitate positive attitudes and behaviors toward them.

Personal Influences: Who Is Likely to Help?

Are Some People More Helpful Than Others?

- There is some evidence of relatively stable individual differences in helping tendencies.

What Is the Altruistic Personality?

- Some personality traits are associated with helpful behavioral tendencies in some situations, but no one set of traits appears to define the altruistic personality.
- Two qualities that do predict helping behaviors are empathy and advanced moral reasoning.

Interpersonal Influences: Whom Do People Help?

Perceived Characteristics of the Person in Need

- Attractive individuals are more likely to receive help than are those who are less attractive.

- People are more willing to help when they attribute a person's need for assistance to uncontrollable causes rather than to events under the person's control.

The Fit Between Giver and Receiver

- In general, perceived similarity to a person in need increases willingness to help. But research on racial similarity has yielded inconsistent results.

- People usually help significant others more than strangers, except when helping threatens their own egos.

Gender and Helping

- Men help female strangers in potentially dangerous situations more than women do; women help friends and relations in everyday situations more than men do.

- Compared to women, men are more hesitant to seek help, especially for relatively minor problems.

Reactions to Receiving Help

- The threat-to-self-esteem model distinguishes between help perceived as supportive, which produces positive reactions, and help perceived as threatening, which creates negative reactions.

- Help is most likely to be perceived as threatening by a recipient with high self-esteem who receives help from a similar provider or from a significant other on an ego-relevant task.

- In close, interdependent relationships, receiving help is usually a positive experience.

- Members of stigmatized groups sometimes feel threatened and depressed after receiving unsolicited help from members of nonstigmatized groups.

The Helping Connection

- Theory and research seem to indicate that helping requires the recognition of meaningful connections among individuals.

KEY TERMS

altruistic (353)

arousal: cost-reward model (350)

audience inhibition (364)

bystander effect (360)

diffusion of responsibility (362)

egoistic (353)

empathy-altruism hypothesis (355)

good mood effect (370)

kin selection (347)

negative state relief model (356)

norm of social responsibility (373)

pluralistic ignorance (362)

prosocial behaviors (347)

social norm (372)

threat-to-self-esteem model (382)

PUTTING COMMON SENSE TO THE TEST

People are more likely to help someone in an emergency if the potential rewards seem high and the potential costs seem low.

True. For both emergency situations and more long-term, well-planned helping, people's helping behaviors are determined in part by a cost-benefit analysis.

In an emergency, a person who needs help has a much better chance of getting it if three other people are present than if only one other person is present.

False. In several ways, the presence of others inhibits helping.

People are much more likely to help someone when they're in a good mood.

True. Compared to neutral moods, good moods tend to elicit more helping and other prosocial behaviors.

People are much less likely to help someone when they're in a bad mood.

False. Compared to neutral moods, negative moods often elicit more helping and prosocial behaviors. This effect depends on a number of factors, including whether people take responsibility for their bad mood or blame it on others; but in many circumstances, feeling bad leads to doing good.

Attractive people have a better chance than unattractive people of getting help when they need it.

True. People are more likely to help those who are attractive. This attractiveness can be based on physical appearance or friendliness.

In any situation, people are more likely to help a friend succeed than a stranger.

False. Although we tend to help those closest to us more than we help others, this tendency is often eliminated or even reversed if the task is very important to our own self-esteem and if our friend's success is threatening to our ego.

Women seek help more often than men do.

True. At least for relatively minor problems, men ask for help less frequently than women do.

11

Aggression

PREVIEW

In this chapter, we examine a disturbing aspect of human behavior: aggression. First, we ask, *"What is aggression?"* and consider its definition. After describing how aggression may vary across *culture, gender,* and *individual differences,* we examine various theories concerning the *origins of aggression.* We then explore a variety of situational factors that influence when people are likely to behave aggressively. Next, we focus on two critically important issues in our society. One issue concerns the *media effects* on aggression, including the consequences of exposure to media violence and pornography. The other issue is the *intimate violence* that can occur in close relationships. We conclude by discussing ways of *reducing violence.*

PUTTING COMMON SENSE TO THE TEST

T/F

_____ In virtually every culture, males are more violent than females.

_____ For virtually any category of aggression, males are more aggressive than females.

_____ Children who are spanked or otherwise physically disciplined (but not abused) for behaving aggressively tend to become less aggressive.

_____ Blowing off steam by engaging in safe but aggressive activities (such as sports) makes people less likely to aggress later.

_____ Exposure to TV violence in childhood is related to aggression later in life.

_____ Men are much more likely than women to aggress against their spouses or partners.

_____ Adults who as children were abused by their parents are less likely to inflict abuse on their own children than are other adults.

Around lunchtime on September 13, 2006, Kimveer Gill, a twenty-five-year-old man who lived in his parents' basement, drove up to Dawson College, in Montreal, and pulled three guns from the trunk of his car. Wearing black combat boots and a black, *Matrix*-style trench coat, he pointed one of the guns at a group of boys but didn't fire. The boys didn't think the gun was real. He walked past the Dawson daycare center, with almost fifty toddlers inside. He approached a main entrance to the college and came upon several students smoking outside. He shot two of them. He then went inside to the atrium, where many people were milling about and eating lunch, and began shooting. One of the people he shot was Anastasia De Sousa, an eighteen-year-old business student. "Today is the day she's going to die," Gill said to a young man who was trying to drag De Sousa to safety. Gill shot her several more times, killing her. In total, Gill shot twenty people. His final act of violence, after being shot in the arm by a police officer, was suicide, as he put his gun under his chin and shot himself (Wong, 2006).

Gill had no apparent connection or dispute with Dawson College or its students. Rather, it seemed, he had a tremendous amount of hostility toward the world in general. He had written numerous postings on the Internet about his loathing for humanity and about his fascination with guns, death, and violent video games. On a Web site popular with Goth culture, he had posted entries about his fantasies of killing people, much of which foreshadowed the events of September 13. "Life is a video game. You've got to die sometime," he wrote in one blog (Struck, 2006, p. A12). These are the same words another young killer had used after killing police officers in Alabama in 2003, in a scene similar to one depicted in the killer's favorite violent video game ("Lawsuit Claims," *The Herald (Glasgow)*, 2005).

The sudden, horrific, seemingly random rampage in Montreal was, of course, shocking. And yet it was neither the first nor the last school shooting during the 2006–2007 school year in Canada and the United States. In fact, there were six by early October, and the year ended with the most lethal of them all, with 33 people killed at Virginia Tech University in April, 2007.

There may be nothing more important to society than to protect and educate its children, and so when violence invades a school, the horror is felt deeply. The terrifying image of teenagers Dylan Klebold and Eric Harris roaming the halls of Columbine High School in Littleton, Colorado, on April 20, 1999, armed with a semi-automatic rifle, a semi-automatic handgun, two sawed-off shotguns, and more than thirty homemade bombs, has served as a chilling icon of this sickening kind of aggression. These boys first shot and killed two students in the school parking lot. Then they entered the cafeteria, where they threw pipe bombs and opened fire, filling

Snapshots of terror. On the top left is one of the pictures that Kimveer Gill posted of himself on a website, along with his fantasies about killing people, before shooting 20 people at Dawson College in September 2006. Eric Harris and Dylan Klebold are seen in the photo on the top right as they walk through Columbine High School on the day of their murderous rampage in April 1999. Below that is an image of Seung-Hui Cho, which he sent to NBC News on the day he killed 32 people plus himself at Virginia Tech University in April 2007.

the room with bullets. From there, the boys went upstairs, shot a school police officer, then shot and killed a teacher, ten other students, and themselves.

Personal accounts of what happened that day were chilling. One of the young killers asked a student if she believed in God. When she said yes, he replied, "There is no God," and shot her in the head. When teacher David Sanders heard the commotion, he raced to the cafeteria to get students out of harm's way and was shot twice in the back. As the teacher lay dying, a student pulled pictures of his daughters from his wallet to show him while other students propped up his head and tried to keep him alive.

Profound questions are raised by these tragedies. What triggered the Columbine massacre? Was it the fact that the two adolescent gunmen, members of the so-called "trench coat" mafia, were social outcasts in school? Was it the fact that they idolized Hitler, spent hours playing vicious video games, and had ready access to an arsenal of weapons? And why did the news of this incident seem to trigger threats, pranks, and, in some cases, actual violence in other schools around the country? Did Kimveer Gill's experience playing a video game based on the Columbine shootings, or Seung-Hui Cho's admiration of the Columbine killers' fame, play a role in their rampages at Dawson College and Virginia Tech? Did their fascination with guns, or experience of being bullied and socially rejected, play a role? These are some of the issues that social psychologists study, and these kinds of questions are a focus of this chapter.

There are few safe havens from aggression. Take a drive, and you might be another victim of "road rage," as aggressive drivers cut each other off and exchange heated words, gestures, and even gunshots. Go to work and you may experience or observe "desk rage," as work-related stress drives people to tears, hostility, and violence. Read a college newspaper and learn about the violent hazing endured by fraternity pledges or military academy students. Watch sports on TV and see clips of the latest fight between a player and another player, coach, or fan—or perhaps between a coach or parent and an umpire at a Little League game.

As the twenty-first century began, the world hoped for a more peaceful century than the previous one, with its world wars, genocide, and so-called ethnic cleansing.

But with new wars, terrorism, and the constant fear of weapons of mass destruction, biological and chemical warfare, and suicide bombings, it is clear that the human animal is as aggressive as ever (see Table 11.1, p. 392). What can account for this aggression? This chapter examines the origins and immediate triggers of aggression, as well as factors that reduce aggression. It focuses primarily on aggression by individuals; aggression by groups, such as rampaging mobs and warring nations, was discussed in Chapter 8.

What Is Aggression?

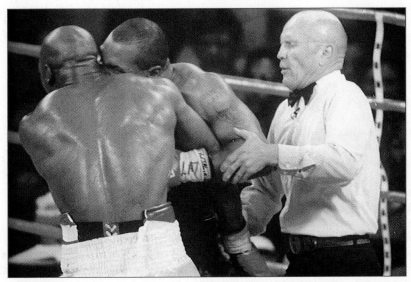

During their heavyweight boxing championship fight in June 1997, former champion Mike Tyson viciously bites champion Evander Holyfield's ear. After chewing off pieces of both of Holyfield's ears, Tyson was disqualified, and a near riot ensued in the ring. Was Tyson's attack an instance of instrumental aggression, in which he bit Holyfield's ears in order to stop a fight he felt he could not win, or emotional aggression, in which he lost his composure and snapped because of the frustration and pain he was experiencing?

aggression Behavior intended to harm another individual.

instrumental aggression Inflicting harm in order to obtain something of value.

emotional aggression Inflicting harm for its own sake.

The word is a familiar one, part of our everyday vocabulary, but the concept of "aggression" can be surprisingly hard to pin down. According to one analysis, there were more than 250 different definitions of aggression in the psychological literature (Harré & Lamb, 1983). Most definitions used today share a number of common features, however. Putting them together, we can define **aggression** as behavior that is intended to harm another individual.

Of course, any definition that relies on an individual's intentions has a serious drawback. We can't see another person's intentions, so how do we know what they are? And whose view do we accept if people disagree about someone's intentions? When defined in terms of intent, aggression lies ultimately in the eye of the beholder. The consequences of a harmful act may be obvious to everyone, but its characterization as aggressive is a matter of subjective judgment.

Aggressive behaviors come in many forms. Words as well as deeds can be aggressive. Quarreling couples who intend their spiteful remarks to hurt are behaving aggressively. Spreading a vicious rumor about someone is another form of aggression. Even failure to act can be aggressive, if that failure is intended to hurt someone, such as by not helping someone avoid what you know will be a humiliating outcome.

To distinguish them from less harmful behaviors, extreme acts of aggression are called *violence*. Some other terms in the language of aggression refer to emotions and attitudes. *Anger* consists of strong feelings of displeasure in response to a perceived injury; the exact nature of these feelings (for example, outrage, hate, or irritation) depends on the specific situation. *Hostility* is a negative, antagonistic attitude toward another person or group. Anger and hostility are often closely connected to aggression, but not always. People can be angry at others and regard them with great hostility without ever trying to harm them. And aggression can occur without a trace of anger or hostility, as when a contract killer murders a perfect stranger in order to "make a killing" financially.

The aggression of a hired gun is an example of **instrumental aggression**, in which harm is inflicted as a means to a desired end. Aggression aimed at harming someone for personal gain, attention, or even self-defense fits this definition. If the aggressor believes that there is an easier way to obtain the goal, aggression will not occur.

In **emotional aggression**, the means and the end coincide. Harm is inflicted for its own sake. Emotional aggression is often impulsive, carried out in the heat of the moment. The jealous lover strikes out in rage; fans of rival soccer teams go at each other with fists and clubs. Emotional aggression, however, can also be calm, cool, and calculating. Revenge, so the saying goes, is a dish best served cold.

Of course, sometimes it is hard to distinguish between instrumental and emotional aggression. Why did Mike Tyson viciously bite Evander Holyfield's ear during their 1997 championship boxing match? Why did Virginia Tech's star quarterback Marcus Vick stomp on the left calf of a star defender who lay prone on the field in their football bowl game in 2006? Were these deliberate, sneaky attempts to gain an advantage over their frustrating opponents, or did these athletes simply lose control and lash out unthinkingly in frustration? Perhaps no one, not even Tyson or Vick themselves, can answer this question, in part because it is difficult to know where to draw the line between the two types of aggression and motives. Indeed, some scholars believe that all aggression is fundamentally instrumental, serving some need, and still others suggest that instrumental and emotional aggression are not distinct categories but endpoints on a continuum (Anderson & Huesmann, 2003; Tedeschi & Bond, 2001).

Culture, Gender, and Individual Differences

Just as not all types of aggression are alike, not all groups of people are alike in their attitudes and propensities toward aggression. Before we discuss the sources of aggression and what can be done about it, we need to consider how aggression is similar and how it differs across cultures, gender, and individuals.

Culture and Aggression

Cultures vary dramatically in how, and how much, their members aggress against each other. We can see this variation across societies and across specific groups, or subcultures, within a society.

Comparisons Across Societies The United States has enjoyed recent decreases in its rates of violent crimes, but it continues to be an exceptionally violent country. Its murder rate is one of the highest among industrialized nations, far worse than the rates for Canada, Australia, New Zealand, and much of Western Europe. However, several countries in Eastern Europe, Africa, Asia, and the Americas have worse rates than the United States. Figure 11.1 illustrates some of the variation in homicide rates around the world.

Based on data from INTERPOL, the world's largest police organization, Nigel Barber (2006) reports that rates of violent crimes are higher in the Americas than in many other regions in the world. According to these data, the rates of murder, rape, and assault among eleven countries in the Americas (including Argentina, the Bahamas, Chile, Costa Rica, and the United States) were about double the world averages. Barber proposes that a key factor that may explain this difference is the relatively high rate of single parenthood in the Americas, which correlates with violent crime.

The forms violence typically takes, and people's attitudes toward various kinds of aggression, also differ internationally. Relative to most of the world, the United States has a tremendous amount of gun-related violence. The prevalence of handguns in the United States is exceptionally high, and even when compared to countries with which it shares much culturally, such as England and Australia, attitudes about guns tend to be much more permissive and positive in the United States, especially among males (Cooke, 2004). More than 70 percent of the murders in the United States in 2005 were committed with guns. The violence in this country also tends to involve individuals rather than groups of people. Groups attacking other groups in political, ethnic, tribal, or other institutionalized conflict are seen throughout the world but are particularly associated with the Middle East, Africa, Eastern Europe, and parts of South America. And violent mobs of European football (what Americans call "soccer") fans are not uncommon in England and other parts of

TABLE 11.1
The Violent Crime Clock

Although the rates of violent crimes in the United States have declined in recent years, they are still distressingly high, as these averaged statistics illustrate, and are much higher than they were several decades ago.

(Based on Federal Bureau of Investigation statistics.)

In the United States in 2002, there was, on average:	
One MURDER	every 32 minutes
One FORCIBLE RAPE	every 6 minutes
One AGGRAVATED ASSAULT	every 35 seconds
One VIOLENT CRIME	every 22 seconds

FIGURE 11.1

Violence Around the World

These figures indicate the number of recorded intentional homicides per 100,000 people in each of several countries in 2004, according to United Nations statistics published in 2006 (the U.S. data come from the U.S. Department of Justice data). Interpret the numbers with caution because there are wide differences in reporting and recording practices in the various countries, but the basic point is clear: There is wide variation in the frequency of murder around the world.

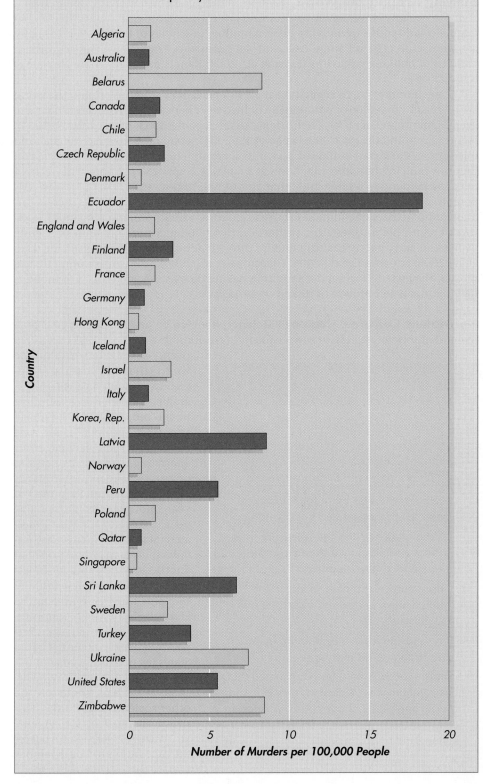

Europe—behavior rarely seen at American sports events.

Cultures also differ in their attitudes about aggression. In a study involving students at thirty-six universities in nineteen different countries around the world, there was considerable variation in how acceptable the students found different actions, such as a husband slapping a wife or vice versa (Douglas & Straus, 2006). For example, almost 80 percent of the respondents from a university in India did not strongly disapprove of a husband slapping a wife, compared to only about 24 percent at a university in the United States. In general, samples from Europe were more approving of a husband slapping a wife than were samples from Australia and New Zealand, which in turn tended to be somewhat more approving than samples from North America. In contrast, these trends were reversed for the question of whether respondents had ever injured a dating partner, with North American rates tending to be highest.

What is considered to be aggression and unacceptable in relation to children also can differ across cultures. For example, in Japan, it is not uncommon for Japanese adult businessmen to grope schoolgirls on public transportation, a practice that would be considered aggressive and unacceptable in many other cultures, including the far more violent United States. Indeed, the problem has become so bad that some train companies in Tokyo have introduced female-only cars to protect women and girls against this practice, such as on one train line that was considered "a gropers' paradise" because of long gaps between stops and many schoolgirl passengers (Joyce, 2005, p. A6). Exploiting this behavior, three clubs opened in the Kabukicho district with reconstructed train cars and short-skirted young women dressed as schoolgirls for the men to grope (Radar Online, 2006).

Another example concerns female genital mutilation—any of

several procedures in which, according to some estimates, approximately 6,000 girls a day have their genitals cut in several countries around the world, particularly in parts of Africa and Asia. One recent analysis estimates that more than 100 million females worldwide have undergone this procedure, mostly in childhood and often without anesthesia or sterile techniques. The cultures that practice this consider it an important, sacred ritual; but the cultures that condemn it consider it an inhumane and dangerous act of violence and have vigorously called for a worldwide ban (Leye et al., 2006; Rosenthal, 2006).

Bullying Around the World   One form of aggression involving children that seems to be fairly consistent across cultures is bullying. Although some differences in frequency and forms of bullying exist, a number of studies of bullying across many countries, especially in Europe, Asia, and North America, have shown fairly consistent patterns of bullying behaviors (Eslea et al., 2003; Kanetsuna et al., 2006; Nesdale & Naito, 2005).

Some recent research suggests that 5 to 15 percent of students around the world are physically, sexually, or emotionally bullied by other students; other estimates are even higher than that (Dao et al., 2006; Juvonen et al., 2003; Olweus, 2003, 2004). Wendy Craig and others (2000; Pepler et al., 2004) set up hidden video cameras and microphones to get an unfiltered peek into aggression in schoolyards in Canada, and they saw bullying in midsized schools at a rate of 4.5 episodes per hour. This team of researchers found in a later study that almost half of boys in eighth grade and girls in ninth grade reported having recently bullied others (Pepler et al., 2006). These seemingly ordinary rites of childhood can lead to extraordinary suffering, including feelings of panic, nervousness, and distraction in school; recurring memories of abuse; depression and anxiety that can endure through adulthood; and even suicide (Dao et al., 2006; Friedman et al., 2006; Gladstone et al., 2006). It is worth noting that in most of the instances of school shootings during the past several years, the shooters had reportedly felt bullied or picked on by peers.

Nonviolent Cultures   Although violence seems to be just about everywhere, a handful of societies stand out as nonviolent exceptions. Bruce Bonta (1997) described twenty-five societies around the world that are almost completely without violence. For example, the Chewong, who live in the mountains of the Malay Peninsula, do not even have words in their language for quarreling, fighting, aggression, or warfare. The most serious act of aggression noted during a year among the Ifaluk, who live on a small atoll in the Federated States of Micronesia, involved a man who "touched another on the shoulder in anger, an offense which resulted in a stiff fine." The Amish, the Hutterites, and the Mennonites are all societies that reside in the relatively violent United States (as well as in Canada) but remain remarkably nonviolent. Table 11.2 lists some of the other societies that Bonta identified as nonviolent. What makes all of these societies so peaceful? According to Bonta, all but two of these twenty-five socie-

TABLE 11.2
Nonviolent Societies

In addition to those discussed in the text, this table lists a few of the other societies that Bruce Bonta (1997) identified as nonviolent.

Society	Comments
Balinese (Indonesian island of Bali)	A researcher who was there for four years never even witnessed two boys fighting.
Glwi (Central Kalahari Desert of southern Africa)	They abhor violence and take pleasure from fortunate events only if they are in the company of group members.
Inuit (Arctic regions, including those in Siberia, Alaska, Canada, and Greenland)	They use strategies to control anger and prevent violence; they have a strong fear of aggression.
Ladakhis (Tibetan Buddhist society in northern India)	Villagers indicate that they have no memory of any fighting in the village.
Zapotec (Native American society in southern Mexico)	"Several researchers have been fascinated that one community is particularly peaceful, with very strong values that oppose violence, in contrast to other communities nearby where fighting and machismo are comparable with the rest of Mexico" (p. 320).

ties strongly oppose competition and endorse cooperation in all aspects of their lives. This raises the possibility that cooperation and lack of competition may promote nonviolence.

The peace of one of these nonviolent communities was shattered, however, on the morning of October 2, 2006. A thirty-two-year-old milk truck driver named Charles Roberts, a father of three, burst into a one-room Amish schoolhouse in Pennsylvania, carrying three firearms, two knives, and up to six hundred rounds of ammunition, along with other materials to carry out a horrific attack. He let the boys and a few adults leave, and then lined up the girls—ages six to thirteen—against the blackboard, tied them up, and shot them one by one. After police burst in, Roberts shot and killed himself. Five of the girls were killed, and five more were critically injured.

The details of the massacre were truly nightmarish. At least two of the girls who were shot had asked the killer to shoot them first, in the hopes of sparing some of the younger girls. And yet, in a remarkable display of this community's commitment to its principles of peace and forgiveness, families of the slain and injured children offered prayers for the killer and his family. According to some reports, the very night of the killings some Amish "stood in the kitchen of the murderer's family, their arms around his sobbing father, and said, 'We will forgive Charlie.'" One member of the community suggested that the forgiveness displayed by the Amish in this incident could be "a gift to the world. . . . Maybe there's something to learn about how nations might treat other nations" (Dueck, 2006, p. A25).

Subcultures Within a Country There are important variations in aggression within particular societies as a function of age, class, race, and region. For example, teenagers and young adults, aged fourteen through twenty-four, have a much greater rate of involvement in violent crime—as both offenders and victims—than any other age group. The fact that the American population has been aging in recent years is one of the reasons cited for the drop in violent crime rates. (Other factors that are noted frequently include longer jail sentences for criminals, more visible and community-oriented policing, a decline in the market for crack cocaine, tougher gun-control laws, and a strong economy.)

What about race? Despite the stories that get the most attention on the news, the large majority of murders are intra-racial rather than inter-racial. Among incidents when the killer's race was identified in the United States in 2005, 93 percent of black murder victims were killed by black offenders, and 85 percent of white murder victims were slain by white offenders. Nevertheless, African Americans live in a much more violent America than do Whites. FBI analyses in 1999 projected that 1 in 40 black males, and 1 in 199 black females, are likely to be murdered in their lifetime, compared to 1 in 280 white males and 1 in 794 white females.

Regional differences are also striking. In the United States, the murder rate is consistently highest in the South, followed by the West. Some scholars have attributed the greater violence in the South and West to a "culture of honor" that is prevalent among white males in these regions. The culture of honor encourages violent responses to perceived threats against one's status as an honorable, powerful man (Cohen et al., 1998; Hayes & Lee, 2005; Vandello & Cohen, 2004). We will focus more on the culture of honor later in the chapter.

Gender and Aggression

Despite all the variation across cultures, one thing is universal: Men are more violent than women. This has been found in virtually all cultures studied around the world. According to U.S. Department of Justice data, 90 percent of murderers in 2005 were male, and 79 percent of murder victims were male. Despite the significant variation in total violence from one country to another, the gender difference remains remarkably stable over time and place: Men commit the very large majority of homicides, and men constitute the very large majority of murder victims (Buss, 2004; Daly & Wilson, 1989). And in the spate of school shootings discussed earlier in this chapter, all of the perpetrators were males.

In virtually every culture, males are more violent than females. **True.**

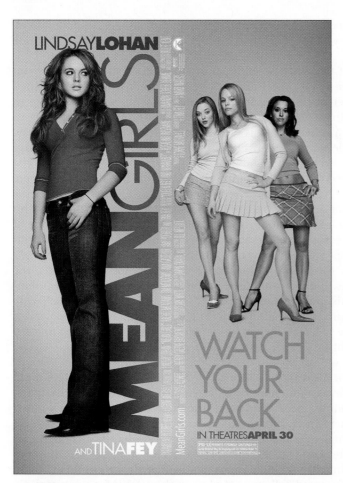

The movie Mean Girls, *starring Linsday Lohan and Rachel McAdams, depicted high school girls engaged in an escalating battle of indirect, relational aggression.*

For virtually any category of aggression, males are more aggressive than females.
False.

What about aggression in general, as opposed to violence? In a recent series of meta-analyses involving hundreds of samples from numerous countries, John Archer and others (Archer, 2004; Archer & Mehdikhani, 2003) found that males are consistently more physically aggressive than females. This was true across all ages and cultures sampled. Females were as likely to feel anger as males, but they were much less likely to act on their anger in aggressive ways. Even among children between one and six years old, boys show higher rates of physical aggression than girls.

So, does all this mean that the stereotype of males as more aggressive than females is correct? Not necessarily. Most of the research has focused on the aggression typical of males: physical aggression. But think back to our definition of aggression: It concerns intent to harm. There are many ways to harm someone other than through physical means. Recent research has recognized this, and the results challenge the notion that males are more aggressive than females. The findings emerging can be summarized by a child's remark noted by Britt Galen and Marion Underwood (1997) in their research on aggression among adolescent girls and boys: "Boys may use their fists to fight, but at least it's over with quickly; girls use their tongues, and it goes on forever" (p. 589).

This research reveals that although boys tend to be more *overtly* aggressive than girls, girls often are more *indirectly*, or *relationally*, aggressive than boys. Indirect forms of aggression include acts such as telling lies to get someone in trouble or shutting them out of desired activities. Relational aggression can be one kind of indirect aggression, particularly targeting a person's relationships and social status, such as by threatening to end a friendship, engaging in gossip and backbiting, and trying to get others to dislike the target. Why are girls more likely to use relational aggression than boys? Researchers believe that one reason is because females typically care more about relationships and intimacy than males do and so may see injuring someone socially as particularly effective.

A growing body of studies conducted in many countries around the world has found that females tend to engage in indirect aggression more often than males, although a few studies have found no significant gender differences (Archer, 2004; Björkqvist et al., 1992; Coyne et al., 2006; Crick et al., 1997; Galen & Underwood, 1997; Owens et al., 2000). For example, Katy Tapper and Michael Boulton (2004, 2005) used wireless microphones and hidden cameras to observe physical, verbal, and indirect aggression among children ages seven to eleven in two British primary schools. The average rates per hour of acts of physical, direct verbal, and indirect aggression among the ten- and eleven-year-olds are presented in Figure 11.2. Consistent with many recent studies, boys exhibited more physical aggression than girls, but girls engaged in more indirect aggression than boys. As is often the case, the rates of verbal aggression were fairly similar in both genders.

Girls as young as preschool age have been found to be more relationally aggressive than their male peers. The gender difference tends to be clear through the school years, particularly from about age eleven. The difference begins to decline as the girls and boys become young adults, primarily because boys show a marked decrease in physical aggression from the age of fifteen to eighteen and a corresponding increase in their use of verbal and indirect aggression. Recent research also suggests that adult women use relational aggression more often than adult men, who, in turn, aggress verbally more often than they aggress relationally (Crick & Rose, 2000; Geen, 1998; Huesmann et al., 2003).

In addition to gender differences, there may be differences in the types of aggression exhibited by people as a function of sexual orientation. Mark Sergeant and others (2006), for example, found that gay men reported significantly lower levels of physical aggression than straight men did, but there was no difference between the two groups on self-reported rates of indirect aggression.

FIGURE 11.2

Gender and Types of Aggression

Reseachers used hidden cameras and wireless microphones to observe the frequency of various types of aggression among schoolchildren during morning and lunch breaks at two British primary schools. Depicted here are the rates per hour of acts of physical, verbal, and indirect aggression among ten- and eleven-year-old girls (orange) and boys (green). Boys engaged in acts of physical aggression more than girls did, but girls used indirect aggression more than boys did.

(Based on Tapper & Boulton, 2004.)

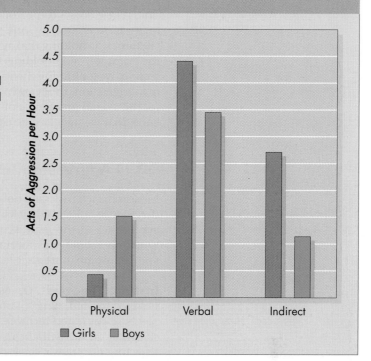

Individual Differences

Although it is clear that aggression can vary across cultures and gender, a different question is whether there is consistency in aggression within specific individuals. In other words, do some people simply tend to be more aggressive than others, across ages and situations? The evidence on this point is fairly clear: Although situational variables, as we will see later in this chapter, certainly do influence whether and how someone will aggress, there are some stable individual differences in aggressiveness. Aggression in childhood does predict aggression in adolescence and adulthood, along with adult criminality, alcohol abuse, and other antisocial behaviors (Harachi et al., 2006; Vierikko et al., 2006).

What types of personalities tend to be associated with aggressiveness? Ann Bettencourt and others (2006) recently conducted a meta-analysis of sixty-three studies to answer this question. People who tend to hold hostile cognitions, express anger, and exhibit irritability tend to behave more aggressively. Other traits associated with aggression, however, tend to predict aggression reliably only under conditions of provocation—that is, situations that are perceived to be aversive or stressful. Among these traits are *emotional susceptibility* (tendency to feel distressed, inadequate, and vulnerable to perceived threats), *narcissism* (tendency to have an inflated sense of self-worth and self-love, but without a strong set of beliefs to support these feelings, thereby leaving the person's self-esteem unstable and sensitive to criticism), *Type A personality* (tendency to be driven by feelings of inadequacy to try to prove oneself through personal accomplishments), and *impulsivity* (being relatively unable to control one's thoughts and behaviors). When not provoked, individuals with these traits are not much more likely than others to behave aggressively. Provocation, however, can light the relatively short fuses of these individuals, leading to the potential explosion of aggression.

Origins of Aggression

Regardless of these various cultural, gender, and individual differences, aggression has been a prevalent part of human interaction throughout human history and around the world. It is not surprising that many have speculated about the origins of aggression. Where does it come from? Are we *born* aggressive, or are we *taught* to be aggressive? Many have argued for one side or the other of the "nature-nurture" debate—the "nature" side holding that aggression is an innate characteristic of human beings and the "nurture" side holding that aggression is learned through experience. In this section, we look at the theory and research most relevant to tracing the origins of human aggression. In reviewing each perspective, we examine how well it can account for the overall prevalence of aggression, as well as for the cultural and gender differences that we have discussed.

Is Aggression Innate?

Innate characteristics are not contingent on learning for their development, although they can be influenced by learning, culture, and other factors. Here, we examine three approaches to the issue of whether aggression is innate: instinct theories; evolutionary psychological accounts; and biological factors, including genes, hormones, and neurotransmitters.

Instinct Theories   On November 11, 1918, a human catastrophe finally ended. Covered in mud, lungs blasted by gas, millions of soldiers had died to gain bits and pieces of contested territory. For an Austrian physician named Sigmund Freud, the slaughter on the battlefields of Europe during World War I marked a turning point. Rejecting his prewar version of psychoanalysis, Freud (1920) proposed a grim new concept: the *death instinct*—a profound, unconscious desire to escape the tensions of living by becoming still, inanimate, dead. This impulse toward self-destruction does not, according to Freud, exist unchallenged. There is also a life instinct, which motivates human beings to preserve and reproduce themselves. Paradoxically, Freud considered aggression toward others to be a momentary victory for the life instinct. In aggression, the force of the death instinct is deflected outward at others rather than aimed inward toward the original target, the self.

Like Freud, Konrad Lorenz (1966) regarded aggression as an innate, instinctual motivation. Unlike Freud, who believed that the life and death instincts are antagonistic, Lorenz saw the will to live and the will to aggress as entirely compatible. Based on his observations of animals in their natural habitat, Lorenz argued that aggression secures an advantage in the struggle to survive. The individual who successfully aggresses against others gains access to valuable resources such as food, territory, and desirable mates. Because only those who survive are able to reproduce, natural selection would produce an aggressive instinct in humans as well as in other animals.

Despite the widespread attention that these theories received at the time they were formulated, they no longer have much influence on scientific research. The primary reason for their fall from favor is their reliance on circular reasoning. Why do people aggress? Because they have an aggressive instinct. How do we know that aggression is instinctive? Because people aggress. Case closed. But shut off from the exploration of testable alternatives, circular reasoning is a logical and scientific dead end. In addition, instinct theories cannot account adequately for the cultural and gender differences in aggression—except through more circular reasoning.

Evolutionary Psychology   There are clear similarities between Lorenz's instinct theory and evolutionary psychology, which uses principles of evolution to understand human social behavior. For example, John Tooby and Leda Cosmides (1988) share Lorenz's belief that human warfare originated in attempts to obtain valuable resources. These investigators, however, maintain that the earliest battles between men were fought over women rather than over food or land. To be well fed and have a safe territory can prolong life and indirectly enhance reproductive success—but having a mate is essential.

In contrast to Lorenz, evolutionary accounts emphasize genetic survival rather than survival of the individual. Because at least some of a person's genes can be transmitted through the reproductive success of genetic relatives, evolution should have favored the inhibition of aggression against those who are genetically related to us.

"It's a guy thing."

For example, according to Martin Daly and Margo Wilson (1988, 1996, 2005), birth parents are much less likely to abuse or murder their own offspring than stepparents are to harm stepchildren. In two samples studied, preschool children living with a stepparent or foster parent were 70 to 100 times more likely to be fatally abused than were children living with both biological parents.

What can account for the gender differences in aggression? From a strictly evolutionary perspective, for males to best ensure the survival of their genes, they should mate with attractive, healthy females and invest their time and resources only in offspring who are genetically related to them. Males are competitive with each other because females select high-status males for mating, and aggression is a means by which males traditionally have been able to achieve and maintain status. In addition, because human men, unlike women, cannot be sure that they are the genetic parents of their children, men are predisposed to sexual jealousy. Behaviors triggered by sexual jealousy, including aggression and the threat of aggression, may be designed to enhance the male's confidence in his paternity of offspring. Consistent with evolutionary reasoning, crime statistics indicate that male-to-male violence is most likely to occur when one is perceived as challenging the other's status or social power, such as by attempting to humiliate him or to challenge his sexual relationships. Male-to-female violence is predominantly triggered by sexual jealousy (Buss, 2005; Shackelford et al., 2005; Wilson & Daly, 1996).

Of course, as noted earlier, women also aggress. From an evolutionary perspective, reproductive success is dependent on the survival of one's offspring. Because women are much more limited than men in terms of the number of children they can have, evolution presumably favored those women who were committed to protecting their children. Indeed, much research on aggression by females has focused on maternal aggression, whereby females aggress to defend their offspring against threats by others. For example, females in a variety of species attack male strangers who come too close to their offspring (Ferreira et al., 2000; Gammie et al., 2000). In a similar vein, Anne Campbell (1999) proposes that females tend to place a higher value on protecting their own lives—again, so as to protect their offspring. This hypothesis may explain not only why human males engage more often in risky, potentially self-destructive behaviors, but also why human females, when they do aggress, are more likely to use less obvious, and thus less dangerous, means—such as indirect or relational aggression rather than overt, physical aggression.

Evolutionary accounts have been challenged for a variety of reasons, including the historical and cultural diversity of human aggression (Buller, 2005; Ruback & Weiner, 1995). Within any society, the amount of aggression varies across time; and between societies, as illustrated in Figure 11.1, there are large differences in rates of violence. If aggression is innate and universal, how could people differ so much in when and where they display it?

Responding to these challenges, evolutionary psychologists argue that the presence of cultural and historical variation is not inconsistent with evolution-based theories. Rather, evolutionary and social factors should be seen as compatible and complementary. Evolved psychological mechanisms operate in response to specific environmental contexts. David Buss (1995) points out, for example, that few doubt that our ability to develop calluses on our skin is an evolved physical reaction to environmental influences. Just because some people have lots of calluses and others don't does not invalidate the argument that evolutionary factors played a role in causing humans to evolve mechanisms that produce calluses to protect their skin. Similarly, the argument goes, one should not deny the role of evolution in human aggression just because some cultures are more violent than others. In addition, cultural differences themselves may be products of evolution, traced to different environmental pressures that required dissimilar adaptive responses (Buss & Malamuth, 1996).

Behavior Genetics   Evolutionary psychology involves tying together evolution, genetic transmission, and behavior. Behavior genetics focuses on the latter two. As we said earlier, aggressiveness is a relatively stable personality characteristic; children relatively high in aggressiveness are more likely to be aggressive later in life. Can this aggressive personality type be due to genes?

To trace a line of genetic transmission (heritability), scientists examine differences between individuals or groups. Two types of studies are typically employed in research on humans. In twin studies, monozygotic twins (who are identical in their genetic make-up) are compared with dizygotic twins (who share only part of their genes). On any heritable trait, monozygotic twins will be more similar than dizygotic twins. Adoptee studies are also used in behavior genetics research. On any inherited trait, adopted children will resemble their biological parents more than they resemble their adoptive parents. The results of twin and adoptee studies have produced somewhat inconsistent results, although some recent research has produced evidence supporting the heritability of human aggressive behavior (Hines & Saudino, 2002; Miles & Carey, 1997; Vierikko et al., 2006). One interesting recent finding from a study of twins in the Montreal area was that there was much stronger evidence for the role of genes in physical aggression than in more indirect, relational aggression (Brendgen et al., 2005).

The Role of Testosterone   In addition to the question of heritability, researchers have long been interested in determining what specific biological factors influence aggression (Renfrew, 1997). Because of the persistent sex differences in physical aggression found among humans and other animals, many researchers have wondered if testosterone plays a role. Although men and women both have this "male sex hormone," men usually have higher levels than do women. Research conducted on a variety of animals has found a strong correlation between testosterone levels and aggression. The relationship is far weaker among humans, however. Even so, a number of studies have documented an association between testosterone and aggression. Using diverse samples of people, such as young boys, prison inmates, college students, and elderly men with dementias such as Alzheimer's disease, these studies tend to show a positive correlation between testosterone levels and physical aggression or violence (Archer, 2006; Book et al., 2001; Dabbs & Dabbs, 2000; van Bokhoven et al., 2006). For example, one study found that college fraternities whose members tended to have higher testosterone levels were more rambunctious and exhibited more crude behavior than other fraternities; fraternities with lower testosterone levels tended to be more academically successful and socially responsible, and their members smiled more (Dabbs et al., 1996). The relationship between testosterone and aggression is not limited to males. Studies have also shown a positive relationship between testosterone and aggression and related behaviors (such as competitiveness) in women (Cashdan, 2003; Dabbs & Dabbs, 2000; von der Pahlen et al., 2002).

Look at your index and ring fingers. Which is longer? Believe it or not, your answer may be a clue to how aggressive you are likely to be! Well, that may be overstating it a bit, but research has shown some intriguing correlations among finger length ratio, testosterone, and aggression. Men tend to have relatively longer ring fingers than index fingers; larger ratios (especially on the right hand) are considered more "masculine." (The author who just typed that sentence is feeling rather macho as he looks at his very masculine ratio right now.) Larger ratios are thought to be associated with exposure to higher prenatal testosterone levels. Allison Bailey and Peter Hurd (2005) found in a sample of Canadian college students that men with larger, more masculine finger length ratios had higher trait physical aggression scores. This correlation did not emerge among women (see Figure 11.3).

Intriguing as they are, such correlational findings cannot prove that testosterone causes aggression. There are alternative explanations. For example, aggression itself can cause temporary increases in testosterone—if the aggression is successful (Gladue et al., 1989; Mazur et al., 1992). Stress may also be involved in the correlation between testosterone and aggression: Higher levels of stress are associated with higher levels

FIGURE 11.3

Fingers, Testosterone, and Aggression

According to some research, the longer one's right ring finger is relative to one's right index finger, the more "masculine" one's finger ratio is said to be, as these ratios are thought to be associated with exposure to higher prenatal testosterone levels. This figure presents the partial correlations found in one study (with some other factors statistically controlled for) found in one study between students' finger ratios and how much physical and verbal aggression they exhibited. Among men, more masculine finger ratios were associated with more physical, but not verbal, aggression. This correlation did not emerge among women.

(Based on Bailey & Hurd, 2005.)

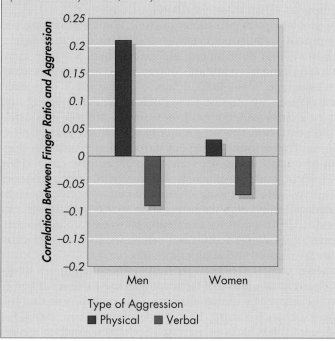

of testosterone (Thompson et al., 1990). Stress may simultaneously elevate both testosterone and aggression, resulting in a correlation that may reflect the effects of stress rather than the effects of testosterone.

For ethical reasons, researchers do not manipulate people's levels of testosterone to measure its effects on aggression and other behaviors. But Stephanie Van Goozen and others (1995; Cohen-Ketteinis & Van Goozen, 1997) have studied individuals who were voluntarily manipulating their sex hormones—transsexuals undergoing sex reassignment treatments. The researchers administered tests of aggression to thirty-five female-to-male transsexuals and fifteen male-to-female transsexuals shortly before and three months after the start of cross-sex hormone treatment in a Dutch hospital. With their increase in male hormones, the female-to-male transsexuals exhibited increased aggression-proneness. In contrast, the deprivation of these hormones in the male-to-female group was associated with a decrease in aggression-proneness. It is important to note, however, that these changes in aggressiveness may have been caused not by the hormone treatment per se but, rather, by indirect factors such as the transsexuals' expectations or other people's reactions to them.

The Role of Serotonin   Testosterone is not the only biological factor linked to human aggression. There has been an explosion of interest recently in the role of the neurotransmitter serotonin (Beitchman et al., 2006; Cleare & Bond, 2000; Holmes et al., 2003; Suarez & Krishnan, 2006). Neurotransmitters such as serotonin act as chemical messengers in the nervous system, transmitting information. Serotonin appears to work like a braking mechanism to restrain impulsive acts of aggression. Low levels of serotonin in the nervous systems of humans and many animals are associated with high levels of aggression. Drugs that boost serotonin's activity can dampen aggressiveness, along with a range of other impulsive and socially deviant behaviors. Such drugs have even been used to treat "road rage"—people's impulsive acts of aggression and violence while driving.

Is the lack of serotonin, then, an innate cause of aggression? Like testosterone, serotonin appears to be both a cause and a consequence of behaviors relevant to social status and dominance. In their work with vervet monkeys, for example, Gary Brammer and his colleagues (1994) found that individual monkeys' social status influenced their levels of serotonin at least as much as their serotonin levels influenced their social status. Here again, biological and social factors interact with each other.

Is Aggression Learned?

Regardless of the precise contribution of genetic and biological factors, it is clear that aggressive behavior is strongly affected by learning (Bandura, 1973). Rewards obtained by aggression today increase its use tomorrow. Such rewards come in two flavors: *positive reinforcement,* when aggression produces desired outcomes, and *negative reinforcement,* when aggression prevents or stops undesirable outcomes. The child who gets a toy by hitting the toy's owner is likely to hit again. So, too, the child who can stop other children from teasing by shoving them away has learned the fateful lesson that aggression pays. Children who see aggression producing more good outcomes, and fewer bad ones, are more aggressive than other children (Boldizar et al., 1989).

Rewards are one part of the learning equation, but what about punishment? Punishment is often promoted as a way to reduce aggressive behavior. Can people learn not to act aggressively through punishment? Some politicians and police officials in New York City believe that the dramatic reduction in crime in the city in recent years (from 2,245 murders in 1990 to 539 in 2005—a drop of more than 400 percent!) is due in large part to swift, more effective punishment of all kinds of crimes, even relatively minor crimes such as vandalism, which sends the message that crime will lead to punishment. Jennifer Hall and others (1998) found among a sample of children from relatively poor economic backgrounds that those children who most expected to be punished for bad behavior scored lower on self-reported aggression. Punishment is most likely to decrease aggression when it (1) immediately follows the aggressive behavior, (2) is strong enough to deter the aggressor, and (3) is consistently applied and perceived as fair and legitimate by the aggressor. However, such stringent conditions are seldom met, and when they are not met, punishment can backfire. When courts are overburdened and prisons are overcrowded, which is often the case, the relationship between crime and punishment can seem more like a lottery than a rational system in which the punishment fits the crime. In short, the *certainty* of punishment is more important than its *severity* (Berkowitz, 1998).

There are some other problems with punishment as well. Punishment perceived as unfair or arbitrary can provoke retaliation, creating an escalating cycle of aggression. Perhaps most troubling is that punishment, especially when delivered in an angry or hostile manner, offers a model to imitate. Murray Straus and his colleagues (Donnelly & Straus, 2005; Douglas & Straus, 2007; Straus, 2000) have been outspoken critics of the use of *corporal punishment*: physical force (such as spanking, hitting, and pinching) intended to cause a child pain, but not injury, for the purpose of controlling or correcting the child's behavior. The large majority of children in the United States experience spanking and other forms of corporal punishment. Numerous studies, however, report a positive relationship between corporal punishment and the likelihood of aggression: More corporal punishment is associated with more aggression. Elizabeth Gershoff (2002) investigated this issue with a meta-analysis of eighty-eight studies conducted over six decades and involving more than 36,000 participants. Her analysis revealed strong evidence for a positive correlation between corporal punishment and several categories of subsequent antisocial behaviors, such as aggression later as a child, aggression as an adult, and adult criminal behavior.

The relationship between parental corporal punishment and children's subsequent aggression is influenced by a number of factors, including the overall family environment, the emotions displayed by the parents during the punishment, and cultural and ethnic differences (Benjet & Kazdin, 2003; Pinderhughes et al., 2000). For example, corporal punishment is less likely to increase aggressiveness when it is administered in the context of an overall warm and supportive parent-child relationship (Baumrind, 1997; Deater-Deckard et al., 1998).

Social Learning Theory   One of the authors of this book remembers many a late, cold afternoon during his middle school and high school years playing informal but competitive games of football and hockey with friends. Both games were played without protective equipment and were quite rough, but the way he and his friends played them, football was the more physically brutal of the two. Yet despite the fact that virtually every play culminated in a pile of boys jumping on the flattened body of an opponent, it was very rare that an actual fight would break out. When this same group of friends played hockey, on the other hand, virtually every single game they played featured at least one fight. Why? Although he was years away from his first social psychology class, this future social psychologist was quite sure that he and his friends were basing their behavior on role models. Rarely had they seen professional football players stop and fight on the field. But rarely had they seen a professional hockey game in which that *didn't* happen.

The power of models to modify behavior is a crucial tenet of Albert Bandura's (1977) **social learning theory**. Social learning theory emphasizes that we learn from the example of others as well as from direct experience with rewards and punishments. Models influence the prosocial, helpful behavior described in Chapter 10. They also affect antisocial, aggressive behavior. In a classic study, Bandura and

Children who are spanked or otherwise physically disciplined (but not abused) for behaving aggressively tend to become less aggressive. **False.**

social learning theory   The theory that behavior is learned through the observation of others as well as through the direct experience of rewards and punishments.

Iraqi boys in Baghdad play with toy guns in January 2004, imitating the adult behavior they have observed in their war-torn country.

his associates (1961) observed the behavior of mildly frustrated children. Those who had previously watched an adult throw around, punch, and kick an inflatable doll were more aggressive when they later played with the doll than were those who had watched a quiet, subdued adult. These children followed the adult model's lead not only in degree of aggression but also in the kinds of aggression they exhibited. Subsequent research has amply demonstrated that a wide range of aggressive models can elicit a wide range of aggressive imitations. Furthermore, these models do not have to be present; people on TV—and even cartoon characters—can serve as powerful models of aggression (Bandura, 1983; Baron & Richardson, 1994; Berkowitz, 1993).

Models who obtain desired goals through the use of aggression and are not punished for their behavior are the most likely to increase aggression among observers. But even those who are punished can have an effect. Postwar increases in homicide rates have been documented not only in rewarded, victorious countries that watched their soldiers prevail, but also in punished, defeated nations that saw their soldiers overwhelmed (Archer & Gartner, 1984).

People learn more than specific aggressive behaviors from aggressive models. They also develop more positive attitudes and beliefs about aggression in general, and they construct aggressive "scripts" that serve as guides for how to behave and solve social problems. These scripts can be activated automatically in various situations, leading to quick, often unthinking aggressive responses that follow the scripts they have learned (Bennett et al., 2005; Huesmann, 1998).

Fortunately, changing the model can change the consequences: Nonaggressive models decrease aggressive behavior. Observing a nonaggressive response to a provoking situation teaches a peaceful alternative and strengthens existing restraints against aggression. In addition, observing someone who is calm and reasonable may help an angry person settle down rather than strike out. Aggression can spread like wildfire. But nonviolence and prosocial behavior, too, can be contagious (Donnerstein & Donnerstein, 1976; Gibbons & Ebbeck, 1997).

Bandura's social learning theory has been one of the most important social psychological approaches to the study of human aggression since his classic early experiments in the early 1960s. Its simplicity should not obscure the fact that it can help explain a great amount of human behavior. Daniel Batson and Adam Powell (2003) recently wrote that social learning theory "has probably come closer to [the goal of accounting for the most facts with the fewest principles] than has any other theory in the history of social psychology" (p. 466).

Socialization and Gender Differences: "Boys Will Be Boys" To account for gender differences in aggression, learning approaches emphasize that males and females are taught different lessons about aggression; they are rewarded and punished differently for aggression and are presented with different models. Whether or not gender differences in aggressive behavior originated from innate biological factors, today they are maintained and perpetuated through lessons that are passed on from one generation to the next about the acceptability of various kinds and degrees of aggression.

Most researchers agree that social roles have a strong influence on gender differences in physical aggression. As described in Chapter 5, males and females are socialized to fill different roles in society. Overt aggression tends to be more socially acceptable in stereotypically male roles than in female roles. Indeed, highly aggressive boys are sometimes among the most popular and socially connected children in elementary school (Rodkin et al., 2000; Vaillancourt & Hymel, 2006). Boys who use their fists to deal with conflict are much more likely to be rewarded with increased social status than are girls, who might suffer scorn and ridicule for fighting. On the other hand, a girl who successfully uses relational aggression, such as through social manipulation, can reap social benefits more easily than a boy (Crick & Rose, 2000).

Socialization and Cultural Differences: Cultures of Honor   Socialization of aggression also varies from culture to culture. For example, in a study of students at a high school near Detroit, Michigan, Violet Souweidane and Rowell Huesmann (1999) found that those born in the United States were more accepting of aggression than those who had immigrated from the Middle East, especially if they did so after the age of eleven. Likewise, in a sample of Hispanic schoolchildren in Chicago, those who had been in the United States longer showed greater approval of aggression (Guerra et al., 1993). Giovanna Tomada and Barry Schneider (1997) report that adolescent boys in traditional villages in Italy are encouraged to aggress as an indication of their sexual prowess and preparation for their dominant role in the household. These authors believe that this is why schoolyard bullying among elementary school boys is significantly higher in central and southern Italy than it is in Norway, England, Spain, or Japan. Similarly, some researchers believe that *machismo*—which in its most stereotyped characterization prescribes that challenges, abuse, and even differences of opinion "must be met with fists or other weapons" (Ingoldsby, 1991, p. 57)—contributes to the fact that rates of violence are higher among Latin American men than European American men (Harris, 1995).

Machismo may represent one form of what anthropologists call a *culture of honor*, which emphasizes honor and social status, particularly for males, and the role of aggression in protecting that honor. Even minor conflicts or disputes are often seen as challenges to social status and reputation and can therefore trigger aggressive responses. Several such subcultures exist around the world (and *Star Trek* fans might recognize the Klingon empire as an intergalactic example of a culture of honor). In an extensive series of studies, Dov Cohen and Richard Nisbett examined the culture of honor among white men in the American South. Nisbett and Cohen (1996) report that rates of violence are consistently higher in the South than in all other regions. Data from surveys, field experiments, and laboratory experiments suggest that the culture of honor persists today and that this culture promotes violent behavior. Southerners are more likely than northerners to agree that "a man has the right to kill" in order to defend his family and house, and they are more accepting of using violence to protect one's honor than are people from other parts of the country. (Note, however, that southerners are *not* more likely than other Americans to accept violence unrelated to the protection of honor.)

In one series of experiments Cohen and others (1996) investigated how white male students who had grown up either in the North or in the South responded to insults. The experiments, conducted on a large midwestern campus, involved an encounter that took place as the participant and the confederate were passing each other in a narrow hallway. The confederate did not give way to the participant, bumped into him,

U.S. Marine paratroopers earn a pair of gold pins upon completion of ten training jumps. In February 1997 it was revealed, as captured on videotape, that this achievement is sometimes marked by "blood pinning"—a brutal hazing in which veteran Marines punch, pound, and grind the pins into the chests of the new initiates, who scream and writhe in pain. As military leaders try to crack down on this violent "rite of passage," others defend it as an important part of the "macho," honor-bound culture of the Marines.

and hurled the insult. Compared with northerners, southerners were more likely to think that their masculine reputations had been threatened; exhibited greater physiological signs of being upset; appeared more physiologically primed for aggression (their testosterone levels rose); and engaged in more aggressive and dominant subsequent behavior, such as giving firmer handshakes and being more unwilling to yield to a subsequent confederate as they walked toward each other in a very narrow hallway (see Figure 11.4).

Institutions support norms about the acceptability of honor-based violence. Cohen and Nisbett (1997) sent letters to employers all over the United States from a fictitious job applicant who admitted having been convicted of a felony. To half the employers, the applicant reported that he had impulsively killed a man who had been having an affair with his fiancée and then taunted him about it in a crowded bar. To the other half, the applicant reported that he had stolen a car because he needed the money to pay off debts. Employers from the South and the West (which has a culture of honor similar to the South's) were more likely than their northern counterparts to respond in an understanding and cooperative way to the letter from the convicted killer—but not from the auto thief.

In Chapter 2 we discussed more recent work on cultures of honor and aggression by Joseph Vandello and Dov Cohen (2003). Brazil, rather than the U.S. South, was the culture of honor examined in this research. Vandello and Cohen found that a wife's infidelity harmed a man's reputation more in the eyes of Brazilian students than in the eyes of students from the northern United States. These researchers propose that because the reputations of men from cultures of honor are so important to them and are perceived to be more vulnerable, men from these cultures may be more likely than men from other cultures to react to their wives' and girlfriends' honor-threatening behaviors with violence, both as a way to prevent infidelity and to restore their own honor.

FIGURE 11.4

Insult, Aggression, and the Southern Culture of Honor

White male participants from either North or South regions of the United States either were bumped and insulted by a male confederate, or they passed the confederate without incident (control condition). As you can see, the incident had a greater effect on southern participants. Specifically, they thought that they would be seen as less masculine (left); their testosterone levels increased more (center); and they were slower to yield to a confederate who later approached them in a narrow corridor (right).

(Cohen et al., 1996.)

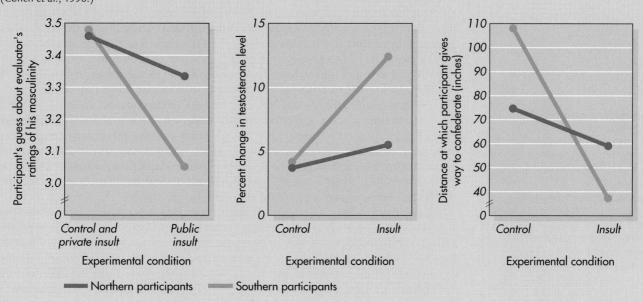

Nature Versus Nurture: A False Debate?

The origins of aggression are a source not only of scientific disagreement but also of political controversy. Heated debates about funding research and treatment programs frequently occur among politicians who disagree strongly on whether aggression is, to any significant extent, attributable to genetic inheritance or stable biological characteristics present at birth. However important it may be, this contentious issue should not obscure the considerable agreement that exists on other points. The effects of learning are not disputed; aggression is, at least to some extent, "made" by experience. Nor is there any doubt that in aggression, as in all human behavior, biology and environment interact. Evolutionary accounts emphasize genetic predispositions as well as adaptations to immediate environmental contexts. Biological factors affect, and are affected by, social interactions. Social and cultural norms may have their roots in evolutionary and biological phenomena, but they exert direct influences on individuals today largely independent of their contemporary adaptive or biological significance. The debate between nature and nurture may rage on politically, but scientifically it is clear that the origins of human aggression represent a profound interaction of evolved mechanisms and environmental and social factors.

Situational Influences on Aggression

Whatever the ultimate causes of aggression, it is clear that specific, immediate situational factors can promote or inhibit aggressive thoughts and actions. In this section, we take a close look at several of these factors: frustration, negative affect, arousal, and factors that influence people's thoughts and information processing.

 ### Frustration: Aggression as a Drive

In 1939, the year that World War II began, John Dollard and his colleagues published *Frustration and Aggression,* one of the most influential books on aggression ever written. This book set forth two major propositions, which taken together were called the **frustration-aggression hypothesis**: (1) Frustration—which is produced by interrupting a person's progress toward an expected goal—will always elicit the motive to aggress. (2) All aggression is caused by frustration.

Dollard and his colleagues claimed that the motive to aggress is a psychological drive that resembles physiological drives like hunger. According to this theory, just as food deprivation elicits a hunger drive, so frustration elicits an aggressive drive. Just as the hunger drive prompts the search for food, so the aggressive drive prompts the attempt to inflict injury. But what if we're unable to aggress against the source of our frustration? After all, we can't hit the boss; nor can we strike out against abstractions such as health problems or financial setbacks. Dollard and his colleagues believed that in such instances the aggressive drive can seep out in the form of **displacement**. Here, the inclination to aggress is deflected from the real target only to land on a substitute. After a bad day at work or at school, do you sometimes come home and yell at the first available target—be it man, woman, or beast? If so, what is the effect on you? Does yelling at an innocent bystander reduce your inclination to take revenge on the person who gave you a hard time?

Drawing from the ancient idea of **catharsis**, Dollard and his colleagues believed that displacing aggression in these safer ways can be effective. Just as hunger can be satisfied by hamburgers as well as by caviar, so any aggressive act should reduce the motive to engage in any other aggressive behavior. Since the Dollard group defined aggression quite broadly—to include making hostile jokes, telling violent stories, cursing, and observing the aggression of others, real or fictional—they held out the hope that engaging in some relatively harmless pursuit could drain away energy from more violent tendencies.

frustration-aggression hypothesis The idea that (1) frustration always elicits the motive to aggress and (2) all aggression is caused by frustration.

displacement Aggressing against a substitute target because aggressive acts against the source of the frustration are inhibited by fear or lack of access.

catharsis A reduction of the motive to aggress that is said to result from any imagined, observed, or actual act of aggression.

Aggressive behavior while driving—what has been labeled "Road Rage"—can be a dangerous, and not uncommon, problem on the road. A large majority of these acts of aggression stem from frustration—such as frustration about being stuck in traffic or cut off by another driver.

The Frustration-Aggression Hypothesis: Does the Evidence Support It? Obviously, there is a connection between frustration and aggression. Break into a line of shoppers at the supermarket or interrupt a student cramming for an exam, and you can see it for yourself. On a more extreme level, it was clear that Dylan Klebold and Eric Harris in the Columbine killing, and Kimveer Gill in the Dawson College shootings, had been feeling extremely frustrated, such as from their exclusion from popular cliques. Indeed, in thirteen of the fifteen school shootings between 1995 and 2001 that Mark Leary and others (2003) examined, the shooters had apparently been frustrated by social rejection. Social rejection has been cited as the most significant risk factor for adolescent violence (Leary et al., 2006).

Soon after the frustration-aggression theory was proposed, however, critics pointed out that the Dollard group had overstated their case. Early on, Neal Miller (1941), one of the originators of the hypothesis, acknowledged that frustration does not always produce aggressive inclinations. The other absolute, that all aggression is caused by frustration, was soon overturned as well. In the following pages, we will consider many other causes of aggression.

The concept of displacement was also subjected to close scrutiny. In 1940, Carl Hovland and Robert Sears proposed that aggression by Whites against Blacks reflected the displacement of aggressive tendencies actually caused by economic frustration. Reviewing information on fourteen southern states from 1882 to 1930, these investigators found a strong negative correlation between economic indicators and the number of lynchings of African American men. When the southern economy declined, more lynchings occurred. However, subsequent analyses, using more sophisticated statistical techniques to examine both the original data and the relationship between economic conditions and recent hate crimes, have failed to find a reliable association (Green et al., 1998).

Ervin Staub (1996, 2004) has proposed that genocide and mass killing, such as during the Holocaust, the "ethnic cleansing" in the former Yugoslavia, and recent acts of terrorism, may typically have their roots in societal frustrations arising from economic and social difficulties. These frustrations give rise to *scapegoating*—or blaming a particular minority group or groups for the problems the overall society is facing. In contrast, when the economy and social conditions are improving, aggression may decrease.

However, these correlational findings do not prove the validity of the concept of displacement. Indeed, acceptance of displacement's role in channeling aggressive behavior quickly diminished within the field after scholars pointed to theoretical weaknesses and inconclusive empirical evidence (Marcus-Newhall et al., 2000; Zillmann, 1979). Yet recent work by Norman Miller and others (2003; Vasquez et al., 2005) may revive interest in it. A meta-analysis of forty-nine published articles has found reliable evidence for displaced aggression in response to provocation (Marcus-Newhall et al., 2000). In one pair of experiments, for example, a relatively trivial frustration caused by one person triggered displaced aggression by participants who had earlier been provoked by a different person (Pedersen et al., 2000). In a recent study of workers from a variety of industries, Jenny Hoobler and Daniel Brass (2006) found support for the old idea that when workers feel abused by their supervisors at work, their families at home—rather than their bosses at work—are likely to feel the brunt of their frustration-driven aggression.

The concept of catharsis also received a great deal of attention, perhaps because it seemed to offer a way to control aggression. Dollard and his colleagues described catharsis as a two-step sequence. First, aggression reduces the level of physiological arousal. Second, because arousal is reduced, people are less angry and less likely to aggress further. It sounds logical, and many people believe it. For example, Gordon Russell and his colleagues (1995) reported that more than two-thirds of Canadian respondents in their research agreed with statements reflecting a belief in the effectiveness of catharsis (such as the statement that participating in aggressive sports is a good way to get rid of aggressive urges). Catharsis has also been used by school administrators and others to justify aggressive sports (Bennett, 1991).

But, put to the test, catharsis has not lived up to its advertisement. Most researchers have concluded that the catharsis idea is a myth. It is more counterproductive than effective in reducing subsequent aggression (Bushman, 2002; Geen & Quanty, 1977). Here's why:

- Imagined aggression or the observation of aggressive models is more likely to increase arousal and aggression than to reduce them. Indeed, this is a central point of social learning theory.

- Actual aggression can lower arousal levels. However, if aggressive intent remains, "cold-blooded" aggression can still occur. Furthermore, if aggression-produced reduction of arousal feels good to the aggressor, this reward makes it more likely that aggression will occur again—another important point from social learning theory.

- Blowing off steam by hitting a punching bag or screaming may feel good to people who intuitively believe in catharsis. Yet their feelings of hostility and anger may persist—and possibly even increase.

- Even relatively low levels of aggression can chip away at restraints against more violent behavior.

Aggressive behavior may sometimes reduce the likelihood of further immediate aggression, but so can just letting the frustration simply dissipate over time. For that matter, a response incompatible with aggression, such as distracting oneself with laughter, can be more effective. In the long run, successful aggression sets the stage for more aggression later. In sum, relying on catharsis is dangerous medicine—more likely to inflame aggression than to put it out.

Frustration-Aggression Theory Revised   After bearing so much criticism, the frustration-aggression hypothesis seemed torn and tattered. But Leonard Berkowitz's (1989) reformulation put the hypothesis in a new perspective. According to Berkowitz, frustration is but one of many unpleasant experiences that can lead to aggression by creating negative, uncomfortable feelings. It is these negative feelings, not the frustration itself, that can trigger aggression. And as we'll see, negative feelings play a major role in influencing aggression.

Negative Affect

In addition to frustrating experiences, a wide variety of noxious stimuli and bad feelings can create negative feelings and increase aggression: noise, crowding, physical pain, threatened self-esteem, feelings of jealousy, social rejection, bad odors, and having your home team lose a professional football playoff game (Baumeister et al., 2000; Berkowitz, 1998; De Steno et al., 2006; Leary et al., 2006; Panee & Ballard, 2002; Verona et al., 2002; Warburton et al., 2006). Most aggressive incidents can be directly linked to some type of provocation, and the negative affect caused by the provocation plays a critically important role in triggering aggression. Reactions to a very common unpleasant condition, hot weather, are especially intriguing. Many people assume that temperature and tempers rise together, while others think it's just a myth. Who is right?

Heat and Aggression: Losing Your Cool   Craig Anderson and others have conducted extensive research on the question of whether heat leads to aggression; and data across time, cultures, and methodologies strongly support the notion that people lose their cool in hot temperatures and behave more aggressively (Anderson

Blowing off steam by engaging in safe but aggressive activities (such as sports) makes people less likely to aggress later. **False.**

"By far, the worst thing about the firehouse was the heat. It got really, really hot inside there the last few weeks of shooting. We had no air conditioning and the hotter it got, the angrier we got."

—Jason, one of the people living in the firehouse on MTV's *The Real World: Boston*

FIGURE 11.5

The Link Between Heat and Violence

Worldwide weather records and crime statistics reveal that more violent crimes are committed during the summer than in the other seasons.

(Anderson, 1989.)

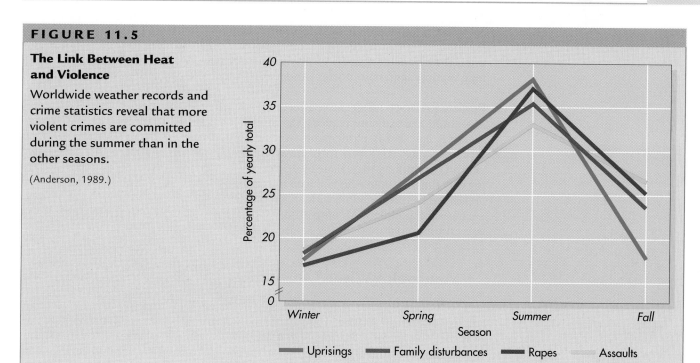

et al., 2000; Bushman et al., 2004). More violent crimes occur in the summer than in the winter, during hot years than in cooler years, and in hot cities than in cooler cities at any given time of year. The numbers of political uprisings, riots, homicides, assaults, rapes, and reports of violence all peak in the summer months (see Figure 11.5). Indirect acts of aggression also increase in excessive heat. As temperatures rise to uncomfortable levels, laboratory participants become more likely to interpret ambiguous events in hostile terms (Rule et al., 1987), and drivers in cars without air-conditioning honk their horns longer at motorists whose cars are stalled in front of them (Kenrick & MacFarlane, 1986). Alan Reifman and others (1991) found that as the temperature rises, Major League Baseball pitchers are more likely to hit batters with a pitch; the pitchers aren't wilder in general (such as in their number of walks or wild pitches)—just more likely to hit batters (see Figure 11.6).

Given the earlier discussion of the culture of honor and the high incidence of violence in the American South, you may wonder whether it is culture or heat that

FIGURE 11.6

Temper and Temperature in Baseball

This figure shows the average number of players hit by pitches (HBPs) per game during the 1986 through 1988 Major League Baseball seasons. As the temperature increased, so did the likelihood that pitchers would hit batters (with balls often thrown around 90 miles per hour and often thrown at a batter's head). Players' general wildness or fatigue, as measured by walks, wild pitches, passed balls, and errors, did not increase with temperature, suggesting that the heat-HBP correlation may be due to hotter temperatures leading to hotter tempers.

(Reifman et al., 1991.)

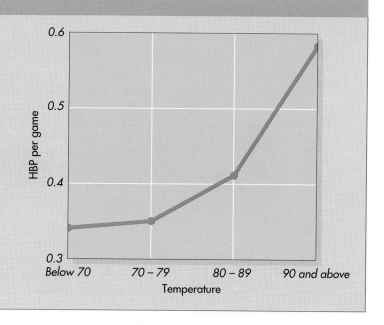

contributes to the violence. At this point, evidence points to both influences as important. Each probably has independent effects on aggression. In addition, they may interact with each other; for example, the relatively high temperatures of the region may support aggressive norms (Anderson et al., 2000; Nisbett & Cohen, 1996).

Positive Affect   If negative affect increases the likelihood of aggressing, can positive emotional reactions reduce it? Some evidence suggests that they can. In one study (Baron & Ball, 1974), participants were first provoked and angered by an experimental confederate. They were then shown funny cartoons or neutral pictures. Presented with an opportunity to retaliate by delivering electric shocks as part of a supposed learning experiment, those who had seen the cartoons delivered fewer shocks. Feeling good appears to be incompatible with anger and aggression. Feeling concerned about others has similar effects. An empathic response to another person reduces aggression against that individual (Miller & Eisenberg, 1988; Sergeant et al., 2006).

Arousal: "Wired" for Action

Research on affect clearly indicates that the type of emotion (positive or negative) influences aggression. The intensity of arousal is important as well. In Chapter 9, we described the process of *excitation transfer,* in which the arousal created by one stimulus can intensify an individual's emotional response to another stimulus. For example, men who engaged in vigorous exercise were later more attracted to an attractive female than were those who had barely moved (White et al., 1981). Physical exercise is a highly arousing but emotionally neutral experience. Can it increase aggression as well as attraction? The research of Dolf Zillmann (1983, 2003) suggests that it can. The scope of excitation transfer is not limited to physical exercise. Noise, violent motion pictures, arousing music—all have been shown to increase aggression. Heat has an interesting effect on arousal: Although people believe that heat lowers arousal, it actually increases it. This misperception makes heat a prime candidate for excitation transfer, as people are likely to misattribute arousal caused by heat to something else, such as anger, which can then lead to aggression (Anderson et al., 1996). Later in this chapter, we describe the effects of another arousing stimulus—pornography—on the inclination to aggress.

Thus far, we have treated the type of emotion and the intensity of physiological arousal as separate territories. But they can be unified. Focusing primarily on retaliatory aggression, the **arousal-affect model** (Sapolsky, 1984; Zillmann & Bryant, 1984) provides a systematic integration that summarizes a number of the findings we've discussed. As you can see in Figure 11.7, experiences that create negative emotions increase aggression; add high arousal, and the combination could be lethal. Experiences that are emotionally neutral have little impact on aggression, *unless* they are highly arousing. Experiences that create positive emotions and low arousal decrease aggression. Now comes the hard part: experiences that produce positive emotions and high arousal. Will aggression decrease because a positive emotional experience is incompatible with unpleasant angry feelings? Or will aggression increase because there's a lot of arousal available for transfer? It's a tough call and could go either way—depending on the individual, the situation, and the thoughts that come to mind. What is more clear, however, is that

FIGURE 11.7

The Arousal-Affect Model

According to this model, aggression is influenced by both the intensity of physiological arousal and the type of emotion produced by a stimulus.

Intensity of Physiological Arousal

Type of Emotion	Low	High
Negative	Aggression increases	Aggression greatly increases
Neutral	No effect	Aggression increases
Positive	Aggression decreases	Aggression increases or Aggression decreases

arousal-affect model   The proposition that aggression is influenced by both the intensity of arousal and the type of emotion produced by a stimulus.

reducing arousal can reduce aggression. Using physiological models, Paul Tyson (1998) has proposed that relaxation techniques may be particularly effective in reducing aggressive responses to anger and arousal. Indeed, Christopher Lopata (2003) found that progressive muscle relaxation reduced the aggressiveness of elementary school children who had been classified as having emotional disabilities.

Thought: Automatic and Deliberate

Step by step, we have been making our way toward a comprehensive theory of social and situational influences on aggression, particularly emotional aggression. We've examined several kinds of unpleasant experiences (frustration, noxious stimuli, and provocation) that create negative affect. We've considered how changes in negative affect (decreasing it by positive emotions, intensifying it by high arousal) produce corresponding changes in aggression. The next step is to add cognition. People don't just feel; they also think. What is the role of thought in aggressive behavior?

According to Leonard Berkowitz's **cognitive neoassociation analysis**, it has a star part. This theory proposes that feelings and thoughts interact. Negative affect automatically stimulates various thoughts, memories, and other reactions that are relevant to two basic tendencies: fight and flight. These automatic thoughts and reactions give rise to basic emotional experiences of anger and fear. How individuals ultimately respond to these automatic thoughts and emotions is influenced by subsequent higher-order cognitive processing. People interpret the situation they are in (Was that an insult or a joke?), think about how they feel (How angry am I?), make causal attributions for what led them to feel this way (I'm angry because of that remark), and weigh the consequences of acting on their feelings (What would be the risk of retaliation?). These thoughts produce more clearly differentiated feelings of anger or fear, as well as intentions to act (Berkowitz, 1993).

Let's take a closer look at two major influences on cognition: situational cues, which trigger automatic thoughts, and cognitive mediators, which influence more deliberate, higher-order thinking.

Automatic Cognition: Situational Cues   The deadliest aggression in the United States comes from the barrel of a gun. The statistics are staggering. No other stable, industrialized country in the world comes even close to the United States in terms of the prevalence of guns used in violent crime. In fact, the large majority of murders in this country are committed with guns. According to one report, every day over 100,000 children carry guns to school, and gun-related violence kills an American child every three hours (Geen & Donnerstein, 1998). The school shootings discussed earlier in the chapter are vivid illustrations of these numbers.

Faced with such gruesome statistics, the National Rifle Association (NRA) responds that guns should not be blamed. People, the NRA says, pull the trigger. Guns are the instrument, not the cause. But are guns entirely neutral? Or does the presence of a weapon act as a situational cue that automatically triggers aggressive thoughts and feelings, thereby increasing the likelihood of aggression? In a classic study designed to address these questions, male participants who had been provoked by an experimental confederate delivered more shocks to him when a revolver and rifle were present (allegedly for use in a different study) than when badminton racquets and shuttlecocks were scattered about (Berkowitz & LePage, 1967). This tendency for the presence of guns to increase aggression is called the **weapons effect**. As Berkowitz put it: "The finger pulls the trigger, but the trigger may also be pulling the finger" (1968, p. 22).

More recent studies by Craig Anderson and others (1998) have provided data in support of the weapons effect. In these studies, participants exposed to pictures of guns automatically activated aggression-related thoughts. They were more likely to have words like *assault, butcher, punch,* and *torture* accessible in their minds than were participants exposed to neutral pictures.

Individuals may differ in what associations they have with various weapons. Bruce Bartholow and others (2005) found that hunters were less likely than nonhunters to associate hunting guns with aggression. Hunters had more positive associations with hunting guns; for example, they linked guns with sport and the pleasurable

Forty-two percent of respondents to an April 2000 Gallup Poll in the United States reported that they had a gun in their home.

cognitive neoassociation analysis   The view that unpleasant experiences create negative affect, which in turn stimulates associations connected with anger and fear. Emotional and behavioral outcomes then depend, at least in part, on higher-order cognitive processing.

weapons effect   The tendency of weapons to increase the likelihood of aggression by their mere presence.

experiences they had had hunting with friends and family. Nonhunters not only had more negative, aggressive thoughts after exposure to hunting guns than did hunters, but they also behaved more aggressively while doing a subsequent task. However, exposure to assault guns had a very different effect: Hunters had more negative, aggressive associations with assault guns than did nonhunters, and they behaved more aggressively than nonhunters after exposure to them. Hunters cognitively differentiated hunting from assault guns more than nonhunters did, and so these two types of weapons triggered very different effects.

A recent experiment by Jennifer Klinesmith and others (2006) found an effect of weapons on men's testosterone levels, as well as on their aggression. Male college students in this experiment handled either a handgun or a children's game for 15 minutes. Relative to the students who interacted with the game, the students who interacted with the gun showed increased testosterone levels and exhibited greater aggression against another person (by adding a lot of "Frank's Red Hot Sauce" to a cup of water they thought another subject would have to drink!) (Figure 11.8). The greater the increase in testosterone in response to the gun, the more hot sauce the students added to the other person's drink.

In general, any object or external characteristic that is associated with (1) successful aggression or (2) the negative affect of pain or unpleasantness can serve as an aggression-enhancing situational cue (Berkowitz, 1993, 1998). Such cues can have very strong effects, increasing people's hostility and likelihood of aggressing. In addition, stimuli that would not serve as aggression-enhancing cues for some people can be aggression cues for others. People who tend to be aggressive associate significantly more cues with aggression and hostility than do people who are not as chronically aggressive; thus, they are particularly prone to automatically activating aggression-related thoughts (Bushman, 1996, 1998).

Higher-Order Cognition: Cognitive Control Situational cues affect a network of automatic associations. More complex information about one's situation, however, influences the deliberate, thoughtful consideration that we call higher-order cognitive processing. For example, an angry person might refrain from acting aggressively if the potential costs of fighting seem too high. In this case, the person might choose to

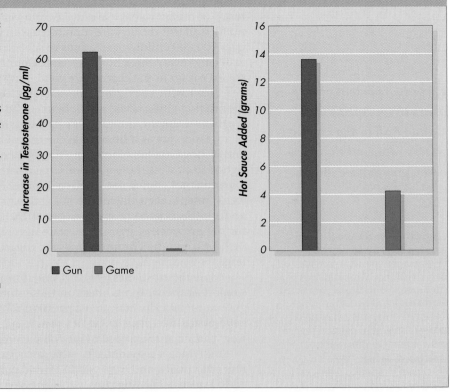

FIGURE 11.8

Guns, Testosterone, and Hot Sauce: Evidence for the Weapons Effect

Male college students handled either a gun (actually just a pellet gun, but identical in size, shape, and feel to a real automatic handgun) or a children's game for 15 minutes. The bars on the left show the increase in testosterone measured in the students after interacting with the gun (purple) or game (teal). The bars on the right illustrate a measure of aggressive behavior: how much hot sauce the students secretly put in a drink they thought the confederate would have to swallow. Consistent with the weapons effect research, students who handled the gun showed a much greater increase in testosterone, as well as significantly more aggressive behavior, relative to students who handled the game.

(Based on Klinesmith et al., 2006.)

flee rather than fight. In addition, people who believe that aggression is inappropriate in a particular situation, or whose moral values and principles mandate nonviolent behavior, may realize that better alternatives to aggression exist (Huesmann & Guerra, 1997). The behavior of other people in the immediate situation can also influence an individual's considerations. If one or more others in a group are reacting aggressively to the situation, aggression can be contagious (Levy & Nail, 1993).

People's thoughts about the intentions of other people can determine whether they are likely to respond aggressively. Some individuals exhibit a **hostile attribution bias** in that they tend to perceive hostile intent in others. For example, socially maladjusted children who are chronically aggressive and have been rejected by their peers see hostile intent where others don't (Crick & Dodge, 1994). Such perceptions then increase their aggression, and their peers respond by rejecting them further, locking these children into an ever-escalating vicious cycle. Chronically aggressive adults, too, tend to expect and perceive hostility in others' motives and behaviors (Dill et al., 1997).

Another cognitive factor that can affect how aggressively individuals are likely to react is whether they perceive a provocation to be intentional or not. **Mitigating information** indicating that an individual should not be held responsible for aggressive acts should diminish perceived intent to harm, particularly if the other person is aware of the mitigating information before being provoked. Sometimes, however, mitigating information is "too little, too late" (Dill & Anderson, 1995; Zillmann, 1996).

Perhaps because it reduces the perception of intent, apologizing for having hurt someone reduces the victim's tendency to retaliate (Eaton & Struthers, 2006; Ohbuchi et al., 1989). Indeed, one strategy suggested to curb "road rage" is to encourage drivers to offer nonverbal apologies to other drivers whom they may have angered. A company in Scotland marketed a road rage-reducing electronic device that mounted inside a car's rear window and flashed friendly messages such as "Thanks" and "Sorry" to other motorists (Johnson, 2000).

Alcohol   Some conditions make it more difficult to engage in the higher-order cognition that can inhibit aggressive impulses. High arousal, for example, impairs the cognitive control of aggression (Zillmann et al., 1975). So does alcohol. Alcohol is implicated in the majority of violent crimes, suicides, and automobile fatalities. The evidence is quite clear about this point: Alcohol consumption often increases aggressive behavior (Bushman & Cooper, 1990; Exum, 2006; Graham et al., 2006; Leonard et al., 2003). Even among individuals who are usually not aggressive, those who drink more, aggress more (Bailey & Taylor, 1991; Pihl et al., 1997).

But *how* does alcohol increase aggression? A meta-analysis of forty-nine studies indicates that alcohol reduces anxiety, which in turn lowers people's inhibitions against aggressing (Ito et al., 1996). In addition, drinking disrupts the way we process information (Leonard, 1989). For example, according to Claude Steele and Robert Josephs (1990), intoxication causes *alcohol myopia*. That is, it narrows people's focus of attention. Intoxicated people respond to initial, salient information about the situation but often miss later, more subtle indicators. Alcohol myopia is related to other potentially destructive behaviors well, such as intentions to engage in risky sexual behavior (MacDonald et al., 2000). In combination with the reduced inhibitions that alcohol can produce, this behavior can be lethal.

In addition to its pharmacological effects, alcohol can also affect aggressiveness because of people's *expectations* about alcohol's effects. The more people expect alcohol to affect them and make them more aggressive, the more likely it will have that effect (Barnwell et al., 2006; Bushman & Cooper, 1990; Quigley & Leonard, 2006). And alcohol, even if not consumed, can serve as an aggression cue for some people, priming aggressive thoughts and hostile perceptions through their associations of alcohol with aggression (Bartholow & Heinz, 2006).

hostile attribution bias The tendency to perceive hostile intent in others.

mitigating information Information about a person's situation indicating that he or she should not be held fully responsible for aggressive actions.

FIGURE 11.9

A Model of Situational Influences on Emotional Aggression

Unpleasant experiences and situational cues can trigger negative affect, high arousal, and aggression-related thoughts. Due to individual differences, some people are more likely than others to experience these feelings and thoughts. Higher-order thinking then shapes these feelings and thoughts into more well-defined emotions and behavioral intentions. Depending on the outcome of this thinking (which can occur beneath the individual's conscious awareness and can be affected by factors such as alcohol or stress), the individual may choose to aggress.

(Based on Anderson et al., 1996.)

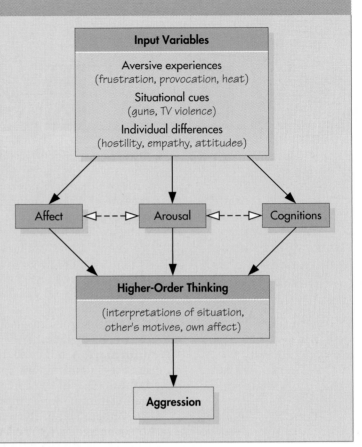

Situational Influences: Putting It All Together

We have seen that negative affect, arousal, and aggression-related thoughts can lead to aggression. And a number of factors influence whether one is likely to experience negative affect, arousal, and aggressive thoughts, such as aversive experiences (frustration, crowding, heat, provocation), situational cues (guns, violent movies), and individual and cultural differences (chronic hostility, cultures of honor). Figure 11.9 diagrams how these various factors interact to lead to emotional aggression.

Media Effects: Scenes of Violence

Having looked at origins and specific factors that contribute to aggression, we now focus on a special topic that has been a major concern of politicians, families, and social scientists alike for many years: violence in television, film, video games, and other media. We explore two types of mass media presentations—nonsexual violence and pornography—in which the display of aggression may elicit more of it.

Violence in TV, Movies, Music Lyrics, and Video Games

According to one report, when Danny Ledonne heard about the shootings at Dawson College in Montreal, he threw up. Ledonne, living in Colorado, had no connection to Kimveer Gill or his victims, but Ledonne heard that the killer was a big fan of the extremely violent video game he had posted on the Internet, called *Super Columbine Massacre*. The game was based on the massacre at Columbine High School, and Gill was fascinated by the shootings, both the real event and the video game version. "When

Can playing violent video games cause children and young adults to become more aggressive and violent? A growing body of research suggests that it can.

"People asked me, 'Gosh. How do you feel to have blood on your hands?'"

—Danny Ledonne, after learning that the school shooter at Dawson College in 2006 was a fan of the video game he had posted on the Internet

I heard about the Dawson shootings," Ledonne said, "people asked me 'Gosh. How do you feel to have blood on your hands?'" (Gerson, 2006, p. A12).

Despite what Ledonne's physical reaction to the Dawson College news might suggest, Ledonne asserts that he doesn't believe his game promotes real violence. But Gill, like the killers in Columbine and many other school shootings, was an avid fan of several extremely violent, vicious video games. The question is, then: Do these games, and violence depicted in other popular media, cause real-world aggression and violence?

Violence depicted in the media has been a target of attack and counterattack for decades. But the amount, intensity, and graphic nature of the violence have continued to escalate. Testifying before a U.S. Senate subcommittee, social psychologist Leonard Eron estimated that by the end of elementary school a typical American child would have seen 8,000 murders and more than 100,000 other acts of violence (DeAngelis, 1993). And the numbers seem to only rise. A 2003 study by the Parents Television Council, for example, counted 534 separate episodes of prime-time violence on the six major American television networks during the first two weeks of November 2002, compared to 292 from the year before.

The most violent TV shows ironically enough are targeted to children directly—namely, cartoons and other children's programming (*National Television Violence Study,* 1998). At the same time, children and adolescents are heavily exposed to violent depictions in movies, video games, and virtual reality games. Particularly popular among young males is "professional" wrestling, which in recent years has become increasingly violent and graphic. Young men and women are also heavy consumers of music that includes violent imagery in its lyrics and accompanying videos. A more recent phenomenon is the abundance of videos that individuals upload to various Web sites, often depicting very aggressive, extreme behavior, including fist fights, beatings, and violent pranks. The people seen in these videos are usually of the same age and backgrounds of the people watching them, and so their influence may be especially strong in inducing copycat behavior.

If consumers didn't enjoy violence in their steady diet of TV, film, music, videos, and video games, these media would not be featuring it. So can it really be harmful? We explore this question in the sections that follow.

Linking Media Violence to Real-World Violence   Does life imitate art? It often seems that way. Brad Bushman, whose work is cited in several places in this chapter, first became interested in research on media violence when a store owner he knew was the victim of a heinous crime: Two armed men came into the store and forced the owner and customers into the basement, forced them to drink Drano (a highly corrosive, toxic fluid used to clean plumbing pipes), and put duct tape over their mouths—the day after these men had allegedly watched (three times) the Clint Eastwood movie *Magnum Force,* which features a scene depicting this very act of brutality (Leland, 1995). People who have lost family members to violence that seemed to be copied directly from such games have recently sued the makers and distributors of violent video games such as *Manhunt* and *Grand Theft Auto.* Dylan Klebold and Eric Harris were big fans of the violent video game *Doom* when they went on their 1999 shooting spree at Columbine High School, and reports indicate that they based their plans for their massacre on the game. As we have already discussed, many of the boys involved in the recent waves of school shootings had consumed a steady diet of violent video games. Each shooting, moreover, was soon followed by additional threats and violent acts. According to one analysis, there were four hundred copycat incidents in the United States and Canada in the month after the Columbine shooting, most of which were not fatal (Tobin, 2006). Table 11.3 lists just a few of the many violent incidents that may have been inspired by exposure to violence depicted in popular media. Yet no one can ever prove that a specific fictional depiction was the primary cause of a specific act of violence. There are always other possibilities.

If you ask people whether exposure to media violence causes real aggression, most would probably say that they doubt that it does, or that there has never been

TABLE 11.3
Copycat Violence?

Although it's impossible to prove that any specific media depiction caused a specific violent action, there have been some close connections.

Violent Fiction	Subsequent Violent Fact
The Matrix (a trilogy of films starring Keanu Reeves)	Numerous killers have cited the influence of these movies in their violent outbursts; many of them believed they were in a real-life version of the matrix.
The Sopranos (TV series about a Mob family)	Two brothers strangled their mother and chopped off her head and hands to hide her identity; they later told investigators that they had seen this done on *The Sopranos*.
Money Train (movie starring Wesley Snipes and Woody Harrelson)	In several incidents in New York City, people doused subway token collectors with flammable liquids and burned them, just as had been depicted in the movie.
Natural Born Killers (movie starring Woody Harrelson and Juliette Lewis)	At least eight murders have been cited as having been inspired by this violent film, such as a student who decapitated a classmate because he "wanted to be famous, like the natural born killers" (Brooks, 2002, p. 10).
**** the *Police* (song by gangsta rap group, N.W.A.)	Rifles used in the shooting of a police officer in North Carolina were emblazoned with the letters N.W.A.
Scream (movie starring Neve Campbell, Courtney Cox, and Drew Barrymore)	Several brutal attacks apparently copied elements of the movie, including the costume worn and the scare tactics used by the fictional killer. For example, a Belgian man put on a *Scream* costume before killing a fifteen-year-old girl with two kitchen knives.
American Psycho (novel by Bret Ellis, about a vicious serial killer who rapes and tortures various young women; made into a movie starring Christian Bale)	A copy of the book was found at the bedside of a man who was convicted for the torture killings of two schoolgirls from Ontario, Canada.
Professional wrestling	Mimicking a dangerous wrestling move he had seen on TV, a seven-year-old boy accidentally killed his three-year-old brother in Dallas.
The Life and Death of Lord Erroll (a controversial book)	The author's son was killed in an act very similar to the murder that had been described in her book; the author later said, "In some terrible way, I think I pressed the trigger" (Alderson, 2001, p. 6).
Grand Theft Auto (video game)	Two teenagers in Tennessee fired shotgun blasts at passing cars on a highway, leaving one dead and another wounded. They claimed they didn't mean to kill anyone but simply wanted to emulate *Grand Theft Auto*, their favorite video game.

"I see television's violent content as therapeutic for the population."

—Jib Fowles, author of *The Case for Television Violence*

"There's an audience of people who love this genre who are not violent. In fact, they sort of use it to vent their violent nature so they don't have to act it out in real life."

—actress Jamie Lee Curtis, defending horror movie blood and gore, as in her "Halloween" movies

"The pervasiveness of false beliefs about catharsis makes them potentially harmful."

—social psychologists Brad Bushman and Roy Baumeister

clear evidence one way or another on this question. When this issue is discussed on the news or in the media in general, the reports tend to conclude that the relevant scientific evidence is weak and mixed, at best. Defenders of the entertainment industry consistently argue that there is no evidence that viewing media violence causes real-world aggression. Social psychologists and others who study this issue are often confronted by people who assert, "I've played lots of violent video games and I never killed anyone."

But what does the social psychological research *really* say on this matter? Here, we do not need to qualify the answer with "It depends." Although media violence is neither a necessary nor a sufficient cause of real-world aggression and violence (that is, exposure to media violence does not necessarily cause one to aggress, nor is it ever the only cause of an act of aggression or violence), the evidence is impressive and clear: Media violence contributes to real aggression and violence. In one review, Brad Bushman and Rowell Huesmann (2001) asked and answered this question emphatically: "Does TV violence have any effect on aggressive and violent behavior of children? The answer is yes! The scientific evidence . . . is overwhelming on this point. The relation between TV violence and aggression is about as strong as the relation between smoking and cancer" (p. 223). Not everyone who smokes gets lung cancer, and not everyone who gets lung cancer smoked. But it is clear that smoking is an important cause of lung cancer, and research suggests that the same is true of media violence and real-world aggression. Figure 11.10 illustrates the relative magnitude of the correlation between TV violence and aggression.

What is the evidence behind these numbers and conclusions? The best way to investigate the issue of media violence is to use multiple methods, each of which has different sets of strengths and weaknesses. This is exactly what researchers in this area have done. What has been particularly impressive about this research is that the results have been strikingly consistent across methods. Longitudinal research, which examines individuals' exposure to violent media early in life and then examines their real-world aggression years later, has found, for example, that the extent to which eight-year-olds watched violent TV predicts their aggressiveness and criminality as adults, even when statistically controlling for other factors such as socioeconomic status and parenting practices (Huesmann et al., 2003) (Figure 11.11). In experimental research, individuals are randomly assigned to watch or play with violent or nonviolent media, and their aggressive thoughts, feelings, and behaviors are measured immediately after the exposure. Craig Anderson and Christine Murphy (2003), for example, found that female college students who had just played a violent video

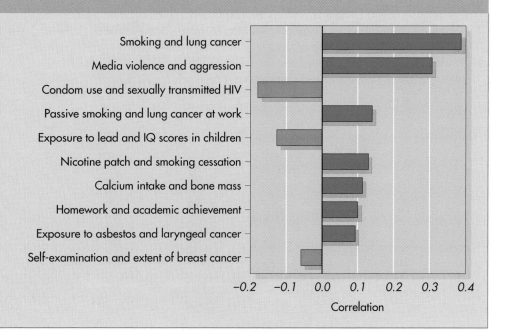

FIGURE 11.10

How Strong Is the Relationship Between Media Violence and Real-World Aggression?

The correlation between exposure to violence in the media and aggressive behavior is compared here to the correlations of several other well-established relationships. This comparison illustrates the relative magnitude of the link between media violence and aggressive behavior.

(Bushman & Huesmann, 2001.)

FIGURE 11.11

Violent TV Viewing and Aggression Fifteen Years Later

A longitudinal study tracked individuals over a fifteen-year period. Based on how much TV violence they viewed as eight-year-olds, individuals were categorized into low (lower 20 percent), medium (middle 60 percent), or high (upper 20 percent) in TV violence viewing. Their aggressiveness as adults was measured fifteen years later. For both females and males, those who tended to watch the most violent TV as children tended to be the most aggressive as adults.

(Based on Huesmann et al., 2003.)

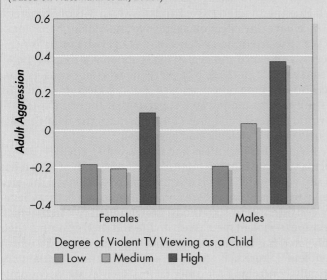

Degree of Violent TV Viewing as a Child
☐ Low   ☐ Medium   ■ High

FIGURE 11.12

Media Violence Effects Across Types of Studies

This figure depicts the correlation between exposure to media violence and real aggression in laboratory experiments, field experiments, cross-sectional surveys, and longitudinal studies. Despite the very different methods used in these types of studies, the effect sizes are quite consistent—pointing to a positive association between media violence and real aggression.

(Anderson & Bushman, 2002a.)

game behaved more aggressively (delivering very loud, aversive blasts of noise against an opponent during a competitive reaction time task) than did women who had played a nonviolent video game. Another example of a recent experiment was conducted by a team of researchers in Madrid, who found that eight- to twelve-year-old children, particularly boys, were more aggressive after viewing televised bullfights (Graña et al., 2004).

In one extensive review, researchers examined the relationship between exposure to media violence and real aggression in 46 longitudinal studies, 86 cross-sectional surveys (which look, at one point in time, at the relation between individuals' exposure to violent media and their aggressive behavior), 28 field experiments, and 124 laboratory experiments—totaling more than 50,000 participants. As can be seen in Figure 11.12, the magnitude of the positive relationship between exposure to media violence and real aggressive behavior was consistent across all four types of studies, with the laboratory experiments tending to show the strongest effects and the other three types of studies showing only slightly weaker relationships (Anderson & Bushman, 2002a; Anderson et al., 2004).

Violent video games have not been around as long as violent television, but there has been enough research on these games within the past several years now that researchers have found reliable effects. A recent meta-analysis of video-game studies, consisting of both experimental and correlational methods, reports that exposure to violent video games is significantly linked to increases in aggressive behavior, aggressive cognitions, aggressive affect, and physiological arousal and to decreases in helping behavior (Anderson et al., 2004).

Based on the accumulated research, six major professional societies in the United States—the American Psychological Association, the American Academy of Pediatrics, the American Academy of Child and Adolescent Psychiatry, the American Medical Association, the American Academy of Family Physicians, and the American Psychiatric Association—together concluded that the research "reveals unequivocal evidence that media violence increases the likelihood of aggressive and violent behavior in both immediate and long-term contexts" (Anderson, Berkowitz, et al., 2003, p. 81). The general public may not be aware of this, but the scientific community is more convinced than ever.

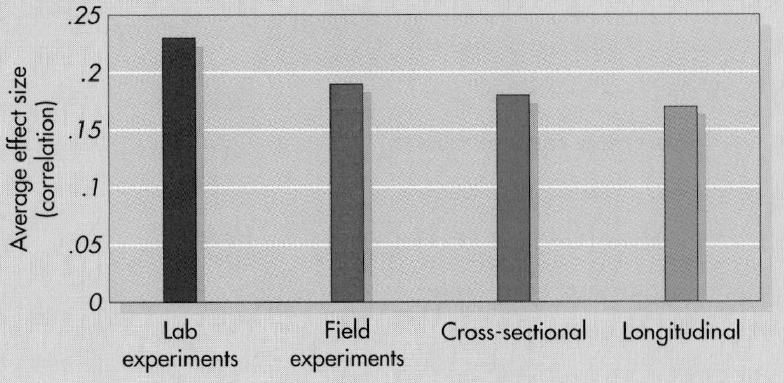

Of course, the media do not operate in a vacuum. People are influenced by their families, peers, social values, and opportunities for education and employment. Nor are all individuals the same; differences in personality can heat up or tone down the impact of exposure to aggressive displays. Media effects tend to be especially

A high school student screams at seeing the scene of the shootings in her school in Paducah, Kentucky, after a fourteen-year-old student shot eight classmates—killing three of them—on December 1, 1997. The student's rampage may have been influenced by seeing the movie, The Basketball Diaries. *This incident, in turn, may have influenced subsequent high school shootings.*

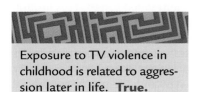

Exposure to TV violence in childhood is related to aggression later in life. **True.**

strong among people who are high in trait aggressiveness, irritability, or hostility as well as among those who lack empathy (Anderson & Bushman, 2002b; Arriaga et al., 2006; Bushman & Huesmann, 2001).

Physical violence is not the only kind of aggression portrayed in the media. Sarah Coyne and John Archer (2004) found examples of indirect aggression in 92 percent of programs on British television shows that are popular with adolescents, a rate much higher than physical aggression. Compared to physical aggressors, the indirect aggressors portrayed tended to be more rewarded for their aggression, and they were more likely to be female and attractive. In a later experiment, Coyne and her colleagues (2004) found that television exposure to indirect aggression had immediate effects on adolescents' own behavior, such as leading to less helping behavior, more negative evaluations of others, and greater endorsement of using indirect aggression in response to an ambiguous situation.

How Does Media Violence Cause These Effects? The evidence from hundreds of studies is clear that media violence—whether from TV, movies, music lyrics or videos, video games, and so on—can have both immediate and long-term effects. Another question, though, is *how* it can have these effects.

Social psychologists have found several paths through which media violence travels to produce real-world aggression. Media violence can trigger aggressive and hostile thoughts, which in turn can lead individuals to interpret others' actions in hostile ways and promote aggression. Playing violent video games, for example, has been found to cause increases in aggressive cognitions and affect, in addition to aggressive behavior (Anderson, 2004).

In one series of experiments, Peter Fischer and Tobias Greitemeyer (2006) found that male participants who had just listened to misogynous song lyrics recalled more negative attributes about women, reported more feelings of vengeance, and behaved more aggressively toward a female confederate than did male participants who had listened to neutral music. Listening to men-hating lyrics had a similar effect on female participants' aggressive-related responses toward men. Because of the sexual and sexist overtones of many video games, they may promote not only aggression but sexist attitudes and behaviors (Dietz, 1998). Steven Fein and Emily Eustis (2001) found that among male college students with higher-than-average levels of hostility, the attitudes they expressed were more sexist following their participation in a video game that featured sexist behavior.

Rap star 50 Cent has achieved a great deal of popularity and acclaim over the past several years, while at the same time sparking controversy because of the violent nature of many of his songs, which his critics claim promote violence and sexism.

Another effect of media violence is to desensitize individuals to violence. **Desensitization** to violence refers to a reduction in emotion-related physiological reactivity to real violence. Desensitization is one form of *habituation*. A novel stimulus gets our attention and, if it's sufficiently interesting or exciting, elicits physiological arousal. But when we get used to something, our reactions diminish. Familiarity with violence reduces physiological arousal to new incidents of violence (Geen, 1981). Desensitized to violence, we may become more accepting of it.

Desensitization to violence from media exposure can have both immediate and long-term effects. Nicholas Carnagey and others (2007) demonstrated some immediate effects in a pair of experiments in which they had college students play either a violent video game (such as *Duke Nukem* or *Mortal Kombat*) or a nonviolent video game (such as *Glider Pro* or *3D Pinball*) for twenty minutes. In one experiment, the participants then watched a ten-minute videotape depicting several scenes of real violence, such as shootings and prison fights. Consistent with the idea that violent video games desensitize players to real violence, participants had lower heart rates and galvanic skin response (which is one measure of emotional arousal) while watching the real violence if they had earlier played a violent rather than nonviolent video game. In a second experiment, after playing the video game, participants overheard a (staged) fight between two people that ended with one of the fighters leaving and the other groaning on the floor, apparently injured. Participants who had played a violent video game were less likely to come to the aid of the injured person than participants who had played a nonviolent game. Those who had played the violent game also rated the fight as sounding less severe than did the participants who had played the nonviolent video game.

These researchers also found in the second experiment that those participants who had a history of playing a lot of violent video games were less helpful than were participants who had not been habitual players of violent video games. This finding suggests that playing these violent games can lead to a more long-term desensitization to violence.

Media violence can also produce long-term effects by influencing people's values and attitudes toward aggression, making it seem more legitimate and even necessary for social interaction and resolution of social conflicts. Through the processes of social learning, children may learn that aggression and violence are common, normal ways of dealing with threats or problems and may even be rewarding. Frequent exposure to such imagery fuels the aggression scripts that children and adolescents develop, which they subsequently use to guide their behavior (Anderson & Huesmann, 2003).

Media violence can affect people also through what George Gerbner and his colleagues (1986) call **cultivation**. Cultivation refers to the capacity of the mass media to construct a social reality that people perceive as true, even if it isn't. The media tend to depict the world as much more violent than it actually is. This can make people become more fearful, more distrustful, more likely to arm themselves, and more likely to behave aggressively in what they perceive as a threatening situation (Nabi & Sullivan, 2001).

Pornography

Just as citizens, scientists, and politicians have been concerned about the consequences of mass media presentations of violence, they have also been troubled by mass media displays of sexual material. Such displays are highly visible and widely available. Books, magazines, videos, and Internet sites cater to a wide range of sexual interests. Heavy metal, electronica, and rap groups often rely on obscenities to get their fans' attention. Porn Web sites and phone services rake in millions of dollars. Opposition to pornography is equally prominent. Parents, religious leaders, consumer groups, and feminist activists lobby legislators and go to court to obtain greater restraints on the availability of sexually explicit materials.

desensitization Reduction in emotion-related physiological reactivity in response to a stimulus.

cultivation The process by which the mass media (particularly television) construct a version of social reality for the public.

The question of whether exposure to erotic or pornographic images can influence aggression toward women has triggered a good deal of social psychological research over the years. The importance of understanding the impact of such material is underscored by the prevalence of such images in our society, as is evident in this picture: The huge billboard of porn star Jenna Jameson is hard to miss for the endless stream of adults and children on one of the busiest streets in the world, in New York's Times Square.

In a meta-analysis of forty-six published studies, Elizabeth Oddone-Paolucci and others (2000) found that men were significantly more likely to report sexually aggressive behaviors and attitudes if they also reported exposure to pornography. Of course, this correlational evidence does not prove that pornography caused these behaviors and attitudes; indeed, such evidence must be supported by experimental research, which we review below. But it is important to recognize the challenges of conducting research on such a controversial and sensitive issue. Even defining the variables is rarely straightforward. Attempts to ban specific works, such as James Joyce's novel *Ulysses* and Robert Mapplethorpe's photos, indicate that the definitions of such terms as *obscenity, erotica,* and *pornography* are often a matter of personal opinion. One person's smut is another person's masterpiece. Because of the subjectivity in such definitions, the term **pornography** is used here to refer to explicit sexual material, regardless of its moral or aesthetic qualities. It is crucial, however, to distinguish between nonviolent and violent pornography in discussing the relationship between pornographic displays and aggression.

Nonviolent Pornography   Earlier in this chapter, we described the arousal-affect model, which proposes that both the type of emotion and the intensity of arousal produced by a stimulus influence aggression. The results of research on nonviolent pornography confirm the importance of these factors (Donnerstein et al., 1987). For many people, viewing attractive nudes elicits a pleasant emotional response and low levels of sexual arousal. Such materials usually reduce retaliatory aggression against a same-sex confederate. However, most people are more disturbed by crude displays of sexual activities. Their emotional response is negative, and their arousal is heightened by alarm, sexual feelings, or both. These kinds of pornographic materials usually increase aggression toward a same-sex confederate.

But what about aggression toward the opposite sex? Since the vast majority of pornography is designed to appeal to heterosexual males, investigators have been especially interested in whether pornographic material has a specific effect on men's aggression against women. It does, but only when restraints that ordinarily inhibit male-to-female aggression are reduced, such as when there are repeated opportunities to aggress (Donnerstein & Hallam, 1978).

In general, though, according to Michael Seto and colleagues (2001), there is little support for a direct causal link between pornography use and sexual aggression. These researchers do note, however, that men who are already predisposed to sexually offend are the most likely to be affected by pornography exposure. This latter point is also consistent with a conclusion reached by Neil Malamuth and others (2000). They propose that relatively aggressive men may interpret and react to the same images differently than less aggressive men, making them more likely to be affected by them in negative ways.

Violent Pornography   Adding violence to pornography greatly increases the possibility of harmful effects. Violent pornography is a triple threat: It brings together high arousal; negative emotional reactions such as shock, alarm, and disgust; and aggressive thoughts. Numerous internet sites—including many that are free and can be viewed easily by minors—focus specifically on images of sexual violence against women, and they use the many depictions of women's pain as a selling point (Gossett & Byrne, 2002).

According to a meta-analysis of 217 studies on the relationship between TV violence and aggression, violent pornography had a stronger effect than any other type of program (Paik & Comstock, 1994). And there is substantial evidence that this

pornography   Explicit sexual material.

effect is gender-specific. Male-to-male aggression is no greater after exposure to violent pornography than after exposure to highly arousing but nonviolent pornography. Male-to-female aggression, however, is markedly increased (Donnerstein & Malamuth, 1997; Linz et al., 1987; Malamuth & Donnerstein, 1982).

Like most experiences that intensify arousal (such as physical exercise), nonviolent pornography increases aggression only among individuals who have been provoked. But, like guns and alcohol, some violent pornography can increase aggression even in the absence of provocation. The prime ingredient in such materials is the portrayal of women as willing participants who "enjoy" their own victimization. In one study (Donnerstein & Berkowitz, 1981), violent pornography that emphasized the victim's suffering increased aggression only among men who had been provoked. But films that depicted female sexual arousal in response to acts of sexual violence increased aggression among both provoked and unprovoked male participants (see Figure 11.13).

Not everyone is affected by violent pornography in the same way. Neil Malamuth has developed what he calls the "rapist's profile." Men fit the profile if they have relatively high levels of sexual arousal in response to violent pornography and also express attitudes and opinions indicating acceptance of violence toward women (see Table 11.4). These individuals report more sexually coercive behavior in the past and more sexually aggressive intentions for the future. Among male college students given an opportunity to retaliate against a female confederate who had angered them, those who fit the rapist's profile were more aggressive (Malamuth, 1983, 1986). In another study illustrating the volatile mix of negative attitudes and violent pornography, Dano Demaré and his colleagues (1993) found that male college students' negative attitudes toward women and their frequent consumption of violent pornography both predicted the students' self-reported sexually aggressive intentions; the best prediction, however, was obtained when both pornography *and* attitudes were included in the equation.

The potential dangers of mixing violence and sexual arousal are not limited to the pornography industry. Many popular movies, video games, and music videos also mix the two frequently and strategically. This has been true in the movie industry since the time of silent movies, in which the hero saves the damsel in distress, who is perhaps tied to the train tracks; and it continues a century later as action movies try to top each other with increasingly arousing, graphic scenes of fighting and sex.

FIGURE 11.13

When Provocation Isn't Necessary

Arousing stimuli usually increase aggression only when someone is angry because of a previous provocation. Accordingly, violent pornography depicting a suffering female victim significantly increased aggression only among provoked male participants in this study. As you can see, however, violent pornographic films depicting a sexually aroused female victim increased aggression even among unprovoked men.

(Data from Donnerstein & Berkowitz, 1981; figure adapted from Donnerstein et al., 1987.)

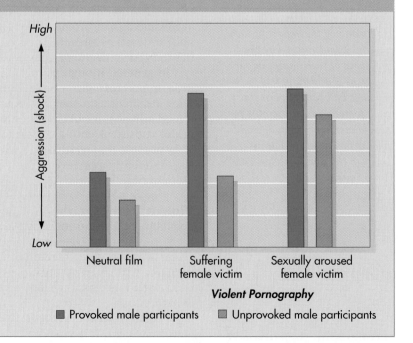

Provoked male participants   Unprovoked male participants

TABLE 11.4
Attitudes About Sex and Aggression

Widely used in research on pornography, these two scales assess attitudes about violence toward women and beliefs about the nature of rape. A few items from each scale are shown here.

(Based on Burt, 1980.)

Acceptance of Interpersonal Violence (Toward Women): AIV Scale

1. Being roughed up is sexually stimulating to many women.

2. Many times a woman will pretend she doesn't want to have intercourse because she doesn't want to seem loose, but she's really hoping the man will force her.

3. A man is never justified in hitting his wife.

Scoring: Persons scoring high in acceptance of violence toward women agree with items 1 and 2 but disagree with item 3.

Rape Myth Acceptance: RMA Scale

1. If a woman engages in necking or petting and she lets things get out of hand, it is her own fault if her partner forces sex on her.

2. Any female can get raped.

3. Many women have an unconscious wish to be raped, and may then unconsciously set up a situation in which they are likely to be attacked.

4. In the majority of rapes, the victim is promiscuous or has a bad reputation.

Scoring: Persons scoring high in acceptance of rape myths agree with items 1, 3, and 4 but disagree with item 2.

Many violent video games mix intense violence with pornographic, gratuitous images of women. These games offer what seems to be an especially dangerous combination of ingredients: a tremendous amount of violence; degradation of and violence against women that are rewarded; and very arousing action and music. In at least one popular video game, players not only get to have their character kill numerous people and animals in numerous inventive ways, but they also can urinate on a woman before killing her. Meanwhile, professional wrestling organizations have become notorious for their accelerating use of violence and sexual imagery targeted to young males. Defenders claim that viewing such material is harmless at worst—and at best offers a cathartic release for viewers, thereby reducing real-world violence. Opponents cite evidence pointing strongly against catharsis (Bushman, 2002; Forbes et al., 2006).

Intimate Violence: Trust Betrayed

All violence is shocking, but aggression between intimates is especially disturbing. We want to feel safe with those we know and love; and yet far too often, that sense of security is destroyed by violence. Among the homicides committed in the United States in 2005, almost half of the victims knew their murderer. According to a U.S. Department of Justice report released in 2000, nearly 25 percent of surveyed women and 7.6 percent of surveyed men reported that they had been raped and/or physically assaulted by their spouse, date, or other intimate partner. The victims of intimate violence are children as well as adults, and the assault that takes place is often sexual as well as physical. In this section, we examine three major types of intimate violence: sexual aggression among college students, physical aggression between partners, and child abuse.

 ### Sexual Aggression Among College Students

Acquaintance rape (often called "date rape") is a serious problem among college students. According to one recent report (Cole, 2006), the incidence of rape among female college students in the United States is estimated to be 35 per 1,000 female students. This study also estimates that 90 percent of college women who are raped know their assailants, and most rapes occur in social situations, such as at a party. Other research estimates that the incidence is even higher, approximately 15 to 20 percent of female college students (Carr & VanDeusen, 2004). When all types of unwanted sexual interactions are included, a majority of college women and about a

FIGURE 11.14

Alcohol and Perception of Sexual Aggression

Male college students listened to an audiotape of what was designed to sound like a date rape. Before listening to the tape, some of the men consumed alcohol and others did not. The experimenter recorded how long it took each participant to determine that the man on the tape should stop attempting further sexual contact with the woman. Students who consumed alcohol took significantly longer to determine that the man should refrain from attempting further sexual contact.

(Marx et al., 1999.)

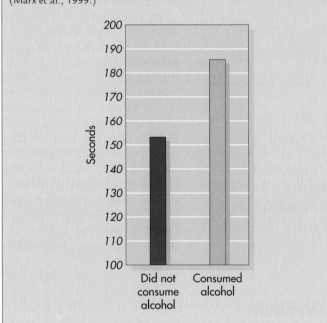

third of college men say they have experienced coercive sexual contact (Cate & Lloyd, 1992; Struckman-Johnson & Struckman-Johnson, 1994). Rates of sexual coercion among Canadian college students appear to be similar (DeKeseredy et al., 1993).

A number of factors are associated with sexual aggression among college students. Two of the most important are gender and alcohol. First, both men and women report that men are more likely to engage in coercive behavior—psychological as well as physical—in order to obtain sex (Poppen & Segal, 1988). Second, alcohol consumption is involved in a majority of sexually aggressive incidents between college students (Carr & VanDeusen, 2004; Cate & Lloyd, 1992; Cole, 2006). Not only does actual consumption increase aggressive behavior, but the mere *belief* that one has consumed alcohol (even if one hasn't) heightens sexual arousal and sexual interest (Baron & Richardson, 1994). The cognitive effects of intoxication, in which salient cues are noticed but subtle ones are missed, may disrupt interpersonal communication; and the anxiety-reducing effects of intoxication may weaken inhibitions against aggressive behavior. These conclusions are consistent with the results of an experiment by Brian Marx and others (1999) in which male college students listened to an audiotape of a simulated date rape. As illustrated in Figure 11.14, those participants who had consumed alcohol took significantly longer to determine that the man should refrain from attempting further sexual contact with the woman. A recent particularly disturbing development has been the growing use of so-called date-rape drugs, such as Rohypnol (sometimes called "Roofies") or Gamma Hydroxy Butyrate (GHB, sometimes called "Liquid Ecstasy"), to render a person, often a date, helpless. Numerous stories around the world have documented its use in acquaintance rape, such as by secretly putting the drug in a target's drink at a club or party.

A third important factor concerns attitudes toward rape and toward women. As we indicated earlier, men who fit Malamuth's concept of the rapist's profile—relatively high sexual arousal in response to violent pornography and attitudes indicating acceptance of violence toward women (again, see Table 11.4)—report using more sexually coercive behavior (Malamuth, 1996). In light of these findings, it is encouraging that rape-awareness workshops appear to reduce acceptance of rape myths and increase sympathy for female rape victims (Hong, 2000; Proto-Campise et al., 1998). Education has a crucial role to play in reducing sexual aggression.

Physical Aggression Between Partners

In the United States, approximately one-third to one-half of female homicide victims are murdered by a husband or a boyfriend. Of course, partner abuse is not limited to the United States; it is a worldwide phenomenon. Neither is it a new development; it has occurred throughout history. Indeed, evolutionary psychologists point to a number of factors that predict such behavior, including males' concerns about paternity (in particular, uncertainty over whether they are the biological fathers of their children). These concerns are known to fuel intense sexual jealousy and distrust, both of which have been implicated in a large percentage of spousal homicides and acts of physical aggression (Buss & Duntley, 2005; Shackelford, 2001; Shackelford & Goetz, 2005).

One of the most surprising results of national surveys in 1975 and 1985 was the high level of wife-to-husband violence, which in terms of severe violence (such as

Despite their fame and wealth, the relationship of actress Pamela Anderson and Tommy Lee has elements shared by many couples who have been scarred by spousal abuse. The early days of their marriage were passionate and intense, but within a few years Pamela revealed that Tommy had been violent toward her, including in front of the children. In 1998 Tommy was sentenced to six months in prison for felony spousal abuse. Even after the arrest, divorce, and Pamela's brief marriage to another man, they have maintained an on-and-off-again relationship.

kicking, hitting, beating, threatening with a weapon, and using a weapon) was consistently higher than the level of husband-to-wife abuse. Research on aggression during the early years of marriage has also found somewhat higher rates of wife-to-husband aggression (Frye & Karney, 2006; O'Leary et al., 1989). These statistics were initially met with doubt, but they have since received support from the results of research by Murray Straus and his colleagues (Douglas & Straus, 2006; Straus, 1999; Straus, 2006) and from a series of meta-analyses conducted by John Archer (2000, 2002), involving more than eighty published articles, books, and other sources of data concerning aggression between heterosexual partners in several countries. Across these many studies, the rates of female-to-male aggression in intimate relationships are either higher or similar to the rates of male-to-female aggression.

These statistics tell only part of the story. Although women aggress against men in intimate relationships as much or somewhat more than vice versa, the consequences of aggression between partners tend to be much more damaging to women, who are more often killed, seriously injured, or sexually assaulted during domestic disputes than are men (Archer, 2000, 2002; Straus & Ramirez, 2005). As Barbara Morse (1995) put it, "Women were more often the victims of severe partner assault and injury not because men strike more often, but because men strike harder" (p. 251).

Like most aggressive actions, violence between partners is caused by multiple factors. Among the factors associated with increased partner aggression are personal characteristics (such as age, attitudes toward violence, drug and alcohol abuse, and personality), socioeconomic status (which includes income and education), interpersonal conflict, stress, social isolation, and the experience of growing up in a violent family (Herzberger, 1996; Tjaden & Thoennes, 2000).

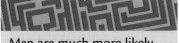

Men are much more likely than women to aggress against their spouses or partners. **False.**

 Child Abuse

Children who grow up in a violent family not only witness aggression; they often bear the brunt of it. More than 3 million American children between the ages of three and seventeen years witness domestic violence every year (U.S. Department of Justice, 1998). It has been estimated that almost half of those children are also abused themselves (Hornor, 2005; Kohl et al., 2005). Tragically, child abuse is not a rare occurrence. Hundreds of thousands of children are abused each year by a parent or close relative. And many other children each year are abused by a caregiver or other trusted person.

Like partner aggression, child abuse is multiply determined. Among the factors associated with increased child abuse are personal characteristics of the abusing parent (such as personality and substance abuse) and of the child (younger children are more often abused by family members); the family's socioeconomic status; stressful experiences; social isolation; marital conflict; and the abusing parent's having been abused as a child (Belsky, 1993; Davies & Cummings, 1994; Herzberger, 1996).

Adults who as children were abused by their parents are less likely to inflict abuse on their own children than are other adults. **False.**

The Cycle of Violence At this point, you should begin to see a pattern emerging: the connection between violence in childhood and violence as an adult. This connection is called the **cycle of violence**. Children who witness parental violence or who are themselves abused are more likely as adults to inflict abuse on intimate partners or their children, or, perhaps, to be victims of intimate violence (Brems & Namyniuk, 2002; Fagan, 2005; Heyman & Slep, 2002; Murrell et al., 2005). This intergenerational transmission of domestic violence is by no means inevitable, however. Most people who witness or experience abuse in their families of origin are not abusive or abused in their families of procreation. The cycle of violence refers to a greater tendency, not an absolute certainty.

Reducing Violence

 ## Multiple Causes, Multiple Cures

A variety of factors contribute to aggression—and, as we have seen, the impact of any one factor often involves other factors simultaneously. Hot temperatures, for instance, influence arousal and aggressive thoughts as well as affect. The effects of watching violence in the media may depend on the chronic level of hostility that a viewer has. Thus we cannot hope for a single, simple cure. The most effective strategies for reducing aggression recognize this complexity and work on multiple levels. Indeed, one of the most successful treatment programs for violent juvenile delinquents is called *multisystemic therapy*. This approach addresses individuals' problems at several different levels, including the needs of the adolescents and the many contexts in which they are embedded, such as family, peer group, school, and neighborhood (Borduin et al., 2003; Huey et al., 2000; Saldana & Henggeler, 2006; Timmons-Mitchell & Bender, 2006).

Situational and Sociocultural Factors What about steps to reduce aggression more generally? Given that negative affect and thinking contribute to aggression, reducing stressors such as frustration, discomfort, and provocation should reduce aggression. Toward this end, an improved economy, healthier living conditions, and social support are extremely important. The prevalence of weapons has also been associated with aggressive thoughts and emotions. Reducing the number of guns may reduce not only access to the weapons but also the incidence of such thoughts and emotions. At the same time, teaching and modeling nonviolent responses to frustrations and social problems—and encouraging thoughtful responses incompatible with anger, such as humor and relaxation—are among the most effective things we can do for our society's children, and for each other.

Having observed the relative nonviolence of cultures that emphasize cooperation over competitiveness, social psychologists have concluded that cooperation and shared goals across groups are effective methods for reducing intergroup hostilities and aggression. In addition, because communities beset by broken windows and petty crime reveal a loss of control and support—thus possibly signaling to those who live there that aggression and antisocial behavior are left unpunished—police departments in numerous cities have begun to crack down on relatively minor acts of vandalism and aggression in the hope that doing so will prevent more serious acts of violence (Taylor, 2000). Finally, changing the cost-reward payoffs associated with aggression can have profound effects on the aggressive tendencies exhibited within a culture. Socialization practices that reward prosocial rather than antisocial behavior therefore have the potential to greatly reduce the tendency among boys, in particular, to engage in bullying, fighting, and other aggressive behaviors. Conversely, when violence is legitimized, we are all at risk.

Media Effects The media, of course, play an important role in legitimizing—even glorifying—violence. What, then, can we do about it? Government censorship is one answer; but it is not a very popular one, for a number of reasons. Another alternative is to use public pressure to increase media self-censorship. Of course, the most

cycle of violence The transmission of domestic violence across generations.

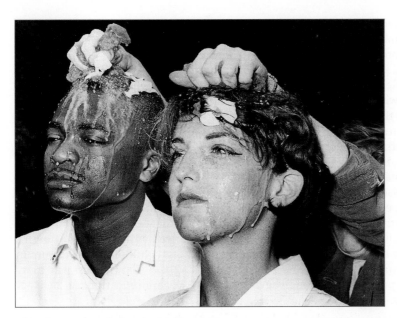

This photo, taken during the 1960s, shows civil rights demonstrators being trained to remain nonviolent despite the abusive and aggressive behavior they would encounter.

powerful kind of public pressure would be a commercial boycott. If violence did not sell, the media would not produce it. Unfortunately, however, violence continues to be a moneymaker.

At this point, education may well be the most effective approach. For example, treatment programs have been developed to curb children's undesirable reactions to TV. These programs recommend that parents select shows that provide compelling, vivid prosocial models for their children. Research on the effects of prosocial television are encouraging in this regard (Hearold, 1986; Mares & Woodard, 2005). As discussed in Chapter 10, this research suggests that prosocial TV programs produce stronger effects on behavior than do antisocial TV programs. Parents have also been advised to watch television with their children and to teach them how TV differs from real life, how imitating TV characters can produce undesirable outcomes, and how children might be harmed by watching TV. This kind of ongoing parental tutorial takes significant time and effort. But given the extent of media depictions of violence in our society, strengthening children's critical viewing skills is a wise investment.

Several of the social psychologists whose work is described in this chapter, such as Craig Anderson, Rowell Huesmann, and Brad Bushman, have spoken with countless government officials, media outlets, and citizen groups to educate them about the scientific facts regarding the effects of media violence. Slowly but surely they seem to be chipping away at some of the myths that policy makers and laypeople have about these issues. Educating parents about the ratings systems used on video games is one relatively simple example of a change that can make a difference. In a survey done by Craig Anderson and Douglas Gentile (2007), fewer than half of 657 fourth-through twelfth-grade students said that their parents understood these ratings, and only one in four said that a parent *ever* stopped them from getting a video game because of its rating. On this particular front, unfortunately, it seems that the old Will Smith song may be right: Parents just don't understand. Education about the social psychology findings presented in this chapter can be an important antidote to this lack of awareness.

The question of what to do about the potentially harmful effects of pornography leads to the same options described for depictions of nonsexual violence. Should pornography be banned? Should consumers be educated? Banning pornography raises a number of philosophical, political, and practical concerns. In addition, banning explicit sexual material would not prevent dehumanizing portrayals of women as sex objects or titillating but fully clothed scenes of rape and sexual assault.

According to Daniel Linz and others (1992), the real villains are violence, sexual or not, and the demeaning and degrading messages about women contained in pornographic depictions, violent or not. These researchers encourage educational efforts to increase viewers' critical skills in evaluating media depictions of violence and sex. A model for such efforts can be found in the debriefing provided to research participants exposed to violent pornography in experiments (Donnerstein et al., 1987). This debriefing emphasizes that rape myths are inaccurate and that violent pornography is unrealistic. Among individuals presented with this information, there are long-term reductions in acceptance of rape myths.

Intimate Violence   Sex-education programs that emphasize the desirability of being respectful and considerate toward one's sexual partner, in addition to rape-awareness programs that debunk various rape myths and increase sensitivity can be important tools in the effort to reduce sexual aggression. Many college campuses experience persistent problems with alcohol abuse, which can be a key factor in many rapes and other forms of sexual aggression. Preventing and treating alcohol abuse, therefore, can make for healthier, safer campuses.

Family violence, too, is a matter of grave societal concern; and, because it is caused by multiple factors, it must be addressed by a variety of approaches. Laws and programs that protect victims of abuse and reduce the likelihood of continued violence by abusers are vitally important. But family violence takes place in a larger context. For example, Peter Sidebothom and Jon Heron (2006) concluded recently, "The association between poverty and child maltreatment is one of the most consistent observations in the published research" (p. 499). Thus, protecting families from violence also requires providing family members with educational and employment opportunities. Furthermore, because abuse of alcohol and other drugs so often leads to family violence, better education about the effects of such substances, as well as support for individuals who need help dealing with them, would be a worthy investment not only for these individuals but also for the people around them.

Ultimately, effective communication is the key to reducing intimate violence. Jealousy and distrust contribute to much of the violence that occurs between intimate partners. Insensitivities to others' needs and fears, as well as acceptance of myths about rape, play important roles in sexual aggression. And children who grow up in abusive homes may learn aggressive scripts that teach them that the best way to respond to social problems is through aggression. Better communication can help address all of these problems.

Conclusions

We conclude where we began, by discussing the recent waves of school shootings in the United States and Canada. A review of this chapter will reveal social psychological research in each section that is relevant to various aspects of the lives of the children and young men involved in these shootings. Some of the perpetrators grew up in a "culture of honor" that may have glorified violence in response to perceived threats to their status and manhood. Many experienced great frustrations in their lives, felt isolated and lonely, had easy access to weapons and hate-filled propaganda, and

---

TABLE 11.5
Some Steps to Reduce Aggression and Violence

Although there may be other reasons to endorse or reject these ideas, social psychological research on aggression suggests that each has the potential to reduce aggression.

- Enlarge opportunities to achieve the goals valued by society (such as social approval, status, financial success) through nonviolent means.
- Reward nonaggressive behavior.
- Provide attractive models of peaceful behavior.
- Reduce all forms of aggression in our society, including physical punishment of children, capital punishment of criminals, and war.
- Reduce frustration by improving the quality of life in housing, health care, employment, and child care.
- Provide fans and air-conditioned shelters when it's hot.
- Reduce access to and display of weapons.
- Apologize when you've angered someone, and regard apologies as a sign of strength—not weakness. Encourage others to do likewise.
- Stop and think when you feel your temper rising. Control it instead of letting it control you.
- Discourage excessive drinking of alcohol and support efforts to provide treatment for alcohol abuse.
- Develop good communication skills in families and relationships, thereby helping to avoid misperceptions, jealousy, and distrust.
- Pay attention and respond to warning signs of trouble in adolescents, including social isolation, talk of violence, and consumption of violence-filled literature and other media.

were consumers of brutal violence in TV shows, movies, and especially video games. Some were exposed to abuse within their families.

The problem of violence in schools grew to such proportions that the U.S. Secret Service, whose mission is to protect the president, became involved, launching an intensive study. The initial findings indicated that the best way to predict those most likely to aggress was to listen to what the students themselves had to say, as many of them revealed, in one way or another, their aggressive thoughts and hostile attitudes. This conclusion parallels the crucial point we have already stated: Communication and social support are critically important factors in reducing violence.

Table 11.5 lists some of the possible steps suggested by the research we've reviewed. Personally, you may not agree that all of these actions are desirable, and you may prefer others that are not mentioned. What's important is to realize that each of us can do something to reduce aggression. There are many paths to take toward this common goal. And because aggression is caused by multiple factors, it is only through multiple paths that we can reach this goal.

"Since war begins in the minds of men, it is in the minds of men that the defenses of peace must be constructed."

—Constitution of UNESCO

REVIEW

What Is Aggression?

- Aggression is behavior intended to harm another individual.
- Anger is an emotional response to perceived injury; hostility is an antagonistic attitude.

- Instrumental aggression is a means to obtain a desired outcome.
- In emotional aggression, harm is inflicted for its own sake.

Culture, Gender, and Individual Differences

Culture and Aggression

- The rates of violence and the forms violence takes vary dramatically from one society to another.
- According to one analysis, the relatively high rates of violent crime in the Americas may be due to the greater incidence of single parenthood.
- Attitudes about whether various practices should be considered aggression sometimes vary across cultures.
- Bullying is a persistent and widespread problem that affects a large number of young people in the world.
- Within a society, different subcultures exhibit different norms concerning aggression.
- Teenagers and young adults, African Americans, and people in the South are the groups most prone to violence in the United States.

Gender and Aggression

- Men are more violent than women in virtually every culture and time period that has been studied.
- Males tend to be more overtly, physically aggressive than females.
- Females are often more indirectly, or relationally, aggressive than males.

Individual Differences

- There is some stability in aggression: Aggression in childhood predicts aggression in adulthood.
- People who tend to hold hostile cognitions, express anger, and exhibit irritability tend to behave more aggressively.
- Some other personality traits are associated with aggression only after provocation. These include emotional susceptibility, narcissism, Type A personality, and impulsivity.

Origins of Aggression

Is Aggression Innate?

- Both Freud and Lorenz regarded aggression as an innate instinct, but the circular reasoning of such instinct theories is unscientific.
- Evolutionary psychology views aggression as a universal, innate characteristic that has evolved from natural and sexual selection pressures.
- Evolutionary accounts propose that gender differences in aggression can be traced to competition for status (and the most desirable mates) and sexual jealousy.
- Some research suggests that individual differences in aggression are produced by genetic inheritance.
- The sex hormone testosterone and the neurotransmitter serotonin appear to play roles in human aggression.
- Biological factors interact with social factors in producing or regulating aggression.

Is Aggression Learned?

- Aggression is increased by rewards.
- Aggression is decreased by punishment only under specific conditions that are often not met in the real world.
- Physical punishment of children is associated with increases in their subsequent aggressive behavior.

- Social learning theory emphasizes the influence of models on the behavior of observers.
- Models who obtain desired goals through the use of aggression and are not punished for their behavior are the most likely to be imitated. But even punished models may encourage aggression by observers.
- Aggressive models teach not only specific behaviors but also more general attitudes and ideas about aggression.
- Peaceful models can decrease aggressive responses by observers.
- Gender and cultural differences in human aggression may be due in part to differences in socialization practices—lessons taught, reinforcements and punishments given, models offered, and roles and norms emphasized.
- A culture of honor promotes status-protecting aggression among white males in the American South and West, as well as among men in other parts of the world, such as in Brazil.

Nature Versus Nurture: A False Debate?

- Human aggression clearly is affected by learning and experience.
- In aggression, as in all human behavior, biological and environmental influences interact.

Situational Influences on Aggression

Frustration: Aggression as a Drive

- The frustration-aggression hypothesis proposes that frustration produces the motive to aggress and that aggression is caused by frustration.

- But, in fact, frustration produces many motives, and aggression is caused by many factors.

- According to the frustration-aggression hypothesis, displacement occurs if aggression against the source of frustration is inhibited.

- The frustration-aggression hypothesis holds that engaging in any aggressive action reduces the motive to engage in further aggression, a process called catharsis.

- In the long run, however, aggression now is likely to increase aggression later.

- Frustration is only one of a number of unpleasant experiences that produce negative affect and increase aggression.

- Some studies support the idea of displacement of aggression; however, most research does not support the idea of catharsis as an effective means to reduce aggression.

Negative Affect

- A wide variety of noxious stimuli can create negative feelings and increase aggression.

- The negative affect due to provocation is a key factor behind much aggression.

- Hot temperatures are associated with increased aggression and violence.

- Positive emotional responses are incompatible with negative affect and reduce retaliatory aggression.

Arousal: "Wired" for Action

- Highly arousing stimuli, neutral as well as negative, increase retaliatory aggression.

- The arousal-affect model proposes that both the type of emotion and the intensity of arousal influence aggression, which is greatest in response to experiences that combine negative affect and high arousal.

Thought: Automatic and Deliberate

- Berkowitz's cognitive-neoassociation analysis of aggression proposes that unpleasant experiences create negative affect, which in turn stimulates automatic associations connected with anger and fear. Behavioral and emotional outcomes then depend, at least in part, on higher-order cognitive processing.

- Situational cues associated with aggression, such as the presence of a gun, can automatically activate aggression-related thoughts and increase aggressive behavior.

- Individuals differ in what associations they have with different kinds of weapons. One study found that hunters associate hunting guns less with aggression, and are less affected by exposure to them, than are nonhunters. But hunters associate assault guns more with aggression, and are more affected by exposure to them, than are nonhunters.

- In one study, interacting with a weapon led to raised testosterone levels in men, which in turn were associated with their behaving more aggressively toward another person.

- More deliberate thoughts that affect aggression include the perception of intent, which is reduced by mitigating information indicating that a person was not fully responsible for harmful acts.

- Individual differences, such as in chronic aggressiveness, influence how individuals interpret the aggression-related motives of others and how they react to mitigating information.

- High arousal impairs the cognitive control of aggression, as does alcohol.

Situational Influences: Putting It All Together

- Aggression is influenced by separate and interactive influences of affect, arousal, and cognitions.

Media Effects: Scenes of Violence

Violence in TV, Movies, Music Lyrics, and Video Games

- There is a tremendous amount of violence depicted in the media, and much of it is targeted to children and adolescents.

- A large number of studies, using a variety of different methods, have by now shown a significant positive relationship between exposure to media violence and real-world aggressive cognitions and behaviors.

- Exposure to TV violence in childhood is related to aggression later in life.

- In laboratory and field experiments, exposure to aggressive models increases aggressive behavior among adults and children.

- Exposure to indirect aggression on TV can promote subsequent real-world indirect aggression.

- Observing violence in the media can trigger aggressive cognitions and hostility.

- Because we habituate to familiar stimuli, repeated observation of violence desensitizes people to violence, reducing physiological arousal to new incidents. This desensitization can increase aggressive behavior and decrease helping behavior.

- Habitual viewing of media violence can suggest that aggression is rewarded, encourage imitation, and promote aggressive scripts, which can guide subsequent behavior.

- Through cultivation of a social reality, the mass media can intensify fear of aggression and encourage aggressive behavior.

Pornography

- Nonviolent pornography that is only mildly arousing reduces retaliatory aggression against someone of the same sex.

- When normative restraints against male-to-female aggression are reduced, nonviolent but arousing pornography increases male-to-female aggression more than male-to-male aggression.

- In general, the evidence pointing to a causal link between viewing nonviolent pornography and aggressive behavior is weak, but the effect is stronger among individuals who are already predisposed to sexual aggression.

- Violent pornography increases male-to-female aggression more than male-to-male aggression.

- When a female is portrayed as enjoying violent sex, even unprovoked men become more aggressive and more accepting of violence against women.

- The combination of interest in violent pornography and negative attitudes toward women is a strong predictor of self-reported sexual aggression in the past and sexually aggressive intentions for the future.

Intimate Violence: Trust Betrayed

Sexual Aggression Among College Students

- Men are more likely than women to engage in sexually coercive behavior.

- Alcohol consumption is involved in a majority of sexually aggressive incidents.

- Attitudes toward rape and toward women are associated with coercive sexual behavior.

Physical Aggression Between Partners

- Sexual jealousy and distrust fuel a great deal of violence between intimate partners.

- National surveys reveal that relative to men, women engage in as much or more aggressive behavior against a partner; but women are more likely to be killed, seriously injured, or sexually abused by a partner.

Child Abuse

- A shockingly high number of children are victimized, often by parents and caretakers.

- Children who witness parental violence or are themselves abused are more likely as adults to abuse their partners and their own children. But most people escape from this cycle of violence.

Reducing Violence

Multiple Causes, Multiple Cures

- Recognizing that aggression has multiple levels of causes, multisystemic therapy has been effective in reducing aggressive behaviors among violent adolescents.

- Situational and sociocultural factors that can help reduce violence include avoidance of negative affect, aggressive thinking, the presence of weapons, competitiveness, minor acts of aggression and vandalism, and social rewards for aggressive behavior. Also useful is the modeling of nonviolent responses to social problems.

- Educational efforts emphasizing the unrealistic nature of violent pornography have proved effective in reducing acceptance of rape myths.

- Sex-education and rape-awareness programs can be effective in helping prevent sexual aggression.

- Because of the role of alcohol in rape and other forms of sexual aggression, it is all the more important for college campuses to develop more effective prevention and treatments of alcohol abuse.

- Protecting the victims of family violence and preventing its recurrence require a wide range of interventions.

Conclusions

- Communication and social support are critically important factors in reducing violence.

KEY TERMS

PUTTING COMMON SENSE TO THE TEST

In virtually every culture, males are more violent than females.

True. In almost all cultures and time periods that have been studied, men commit the large majority of violent crimes.

For virtually any category of aggression, males are more aggressive than females.

False. Girls are often more indirectly, or relationally, aggressive than boys; and women often exhibit levels of aggression similar to men's when they have been provoked or when they feel relatively anonymous and deindividuated.

Children who are spanked or otherwise physically disciplined (but not abused) for behaving aggressively tend to become less aggressive.

False. Evidence indicates that the use of even a little physical punishment to discipline children is associated with increases in subsequent aggressive and anti-social behavior by the children, even years later, although this relationship may depend on a variety of other factors.

Blowing off steam by engaging in safe but aggressive activities (such as sports) makes people less likely to aggress later.

False. Although people may be less likely to aggress immediately after such activities, initial aggression makes future aggression more, not less, likely.

Exposure to TV violence in childhood is related to aggression later in life.

True. Laboratory experiments, field experiments, and correlational research all suggest a link between exposure to violence on TV and subsequent aggressive behavior.

Men are much more likely than women to aggress against their spouses or partners.

False. Evidence suggests that women engage in as much or more acts of serious aggression against their partners than men do; but men are much more likely to injure, sexually abuse, or kill their partners.

Adults who as children were abused by their parents are less likely to inflict abuse on their own children than are other adults.

False. Although most people who have experienced such abuse do break the cycle of violence, on average they are more likely to abuse their own children than are people who never experienced parental abuse.

12

Law

PREVIEW

This chapter examines applications of social psychology to the law. First, we consider three stages in the life of a jury trial: *jury selection,* an often controversial process; the *courtroom drama* in which confessions, eyewitness identifications, and other types of evidence are presented; and *jury deliberation,* where the jury reaches a group decision. Next, we consider *posttrial* factors such as sentencing and prison, the possible result of a guilty verdict. Finally, we discuss *perceptions of justice* both inside and outside the courtroom.

*If you're interested in
following current trials in
the news, you can do so by
visiting Court TV's Web
site at www.courttv.com.*

T/F

_____ Contrary to popular opinion, women are harsher as criminal trial jurors than men are.

_____ Without being beaten or threatened, innocent people sometimes confess to crimes they did not commit.

_____ A person can fool a lie-detector test by suppressing arousal when questions about the crime are asked.

_____ Eyewitnesses find it relatively difficult to recognize members of a race other than their own.

_____ The more confident an eyewitness is about an identification, the more accurate he or she is likely to be.

_____ One can usually predict a jury's final verdict by knowing where the individual jurors stand the first time they vote.

It seems there is always a high-profile trial in the news that spotlights a crime of sex, violence, money, passion, or celebrity and that captures our interest. The twenty-first century is still young, and yet we have already witnessed the very public trials of former Enron executives Kenneth Lay and Jeffrey Skilling, both convicted by a Houston jury of conspiracy and fraud; Andrea Yates, the depressed mother found not guilty by reason of insanity despite drowning her three children in a bathtub; and the bizarre federal trial of Zacarias Moussaoui, the so-called twentieth hijacker who was found guilty of conspiring to kill Americans as part of the 9/11 terrorist attacks. As this chapter is being written, charges have been dropped against three Duke University lacrosse players accused of raping a local exotic dancer. Overseas, Iraqi ex-president Saddam Hussein, defeated in war and captured by American forces, was tried in Baghdad, convicted, and hung for crimes committed against the people of Iraq.

Regardless of how you feel about these cases and their outcomes, they illustrate the profound importance of social psychology at work in the legal system. There are many questions raised, at least in the American cases: What kinds of people do lawyers select as jurors, and why? Can partisans set aside their biases in decision making? How reliable are confessions, eyewitnesses, and other types of evidence presented in court? Are the decision makers contaminated by pretrial publicity and other information not in evidence? How do juries reach unanimous verdicts after days, weeks, or months of presentations, often followed by exhausting deliberation? In this chapter, we take social psychology into the courtroom to answer these questions. But first, let's place the trial process in a broader context.

In the American criminal justice system, trials are just the tip of an iceberg. Once a crime is committed, it must be detected and reported if it is to receive further attention. Through investigation, the police must then find a suspect and decide whether to make an arrest. If they do, the suspect is jailed or bail is set, and a judge or grand jury decides if there is sufficient evidence for a formal accusation. If there is, then the prosecuting and defense lawyers begin a lengthy process known as "discovery," during which they gather evidence. At this point, many defendants plead guilty as part of a deal negotiated by the lawyers. In cases that do go to trial, the ordeal does not then end with a verdict. After conviction, the judge imposes a sentence, and the defendant decides whether to appeal to a higher court. For those in prison, decisions concerning their release are made by parole boards.

As Figure 12.1 illustrates, the criminal justice apparatus is complex and the actors behind the scenes are numerous. Yet through it all, the trial—a relatively infrequent event—is the heart and soul of the system. The threat of trial motivates parties to gather evidence and, later, to negotiate a deal. And when it's over, the trial

Americans are fascinated by trials, particularly when they involve celebrities and horrific crimes. In recent years, high-profile trials have involved former Enron CEO Kenneth Lay, convicted of conspiracy and fraud (left); Andrea Yates, found not guilty by reason of insanity despite drowning her three children in a bathtub (center); and Zacarias Moussaoui, found guilty of conspiring to murder for the 9/11 terrorist attacks (right).

by judge or jury forms the basis for sentencing and appeals decisions. Social psychologists have a lot to say about trials and other aspects of the legal system as well (Brewer & Williams, 2005; Costanzo, 2004; Greene et al., 2006; Gabbert et al., 2003; Wrightsman & Fulero, 2004). At present, for example, researchers are looking at whether police can tell when someone is lying and how they can make these judgments more accurately (Granhag & Strömwall, 2004; Hartwig et al., 2005; Vrij, 2000); at how juries make decisions on how much money to award plaintiffs in lawsuits involving large sums of money (Greene & Bornstein, 2003; Sunstein et al., 2002); at how the legal system can make juries more competent through various procedural innovations (Diamond et al., 2003; ForsterLee et al., 2005; Horowitz & ForsterLee, 2001); at how people are affected by laws that govern behavior in the workplace (Kovera, 2004); at how people evaluate claims of sexual harassment within different legal frameworks (Wiener et al., 2002); and at how the U.S. Supreme Court makes decisions (Wrightsman, 2006). Importantly, much of what social psychologists have discovered in the legal arena

FIGURE 12.1

Overview of the American Criminal Justice System

This flow chart presents the movement of cases through different branches of the criminal justice system. As illustrated here, the trial is just one aspect of the criminal justice system.

(Adapted from the President's Commission on Law Enforcement and Administration of Justice, 1967.)

Crime committed → No arrest

Arrest → Charges dropped or taken to juvenile court

Formal accusation → Case dismissed

Trial → Not guilty verdict

Plea-bargain

Sentencing

- Fine
- Probation
- Other alternatives

Prison

is not already known by judges, lawyers, and laypeople as a matter of common sense (Borgida & Fiske, 2007). In the coming pages, we divide the trial process into three basic stages: jury selection, the presentation of evidence, and the jury's deliberations.

Jury Selection

If you're ever accused of a crime in the United States, or involved in a lawsuit, you have a constitutional right to a trial by an impartial jury from your community. This right is considered essential to doing justice within a democracy. Yet it often seems that whenever a controversial verdict is reached in a high-profile case, people, right or wrong, blame the twelve individuals who constituted the jury. That's why it is important to know how juries are selected.

Jury selection is a three-stage process. First, the court uses voter registration lists, telephone directories, and other sources to compile a master list of eligible citizens who live in the community. Second, so that a representative sample can be obtained, a certain number of people from the list are randomly drawn and summoned for duty.

"I see jury selection has begun."

If you've ever been called, you know what happens next. Before people who appear in court are placed on a jury, they are subject to what is known as the **voir dire**, a pretrial interview in which the judge and lawyers question the prospective jurors for signs of bias. If someone knows one of the parties, has an interest in the outcome of the case, or has already formed an opinion, the judge will excuse that person "for cause." In fact, if it can be proven that an entire community is biased, perhaps because of pretrial publicity, then the trial might be postponed or moved to another location.

Although the procedure seems straightforward, there is more to the story. In addition to de-selecting individuals who are clearly biased, the lawyers are permitted to exercise **peremptory challenges**. That is, they can reject a certain limited number of prospective jurors even if they seem fair and open-minded, and they can do so without having to state reasons or win the judge's approval. Why would a lawyer challenge someone who appears to be impartial? What guides the decision to accept some jurors and reject others? These questions make the process of voir dire particularly interesting to social psychologists (Hans & Vidmar, 1986; Hastie, 1993; Kassin & Wrightsman, 1988).

Trial Lawyers as Intuitive Psychologists

Rumor has it that trial lawyers have used some unconventional methods to select juries. Under pressure to make choices quickly and without much information, lawyers rely on implicit personality theories and stereotypes. As described in Chapter 4, an implicit personality theory is a set of assumptions that people make about how certain attributes are related to each other and to behavior. When we believe that all members of a group share the same attributes, these implicit theories are called stereotypes.

As far as trial practice is concerned, how-to books claim that the astute lawyer can predict a juror's verdict by his or her gender, race, occupation, ethnic heritage, and other simple demographics. It has been suggested, for example, that athletes lack sympathy for fragile and injured victims, that engineers are unemotional, that men with beards resist authority, and that cabinetmakers are so meticulous in their work that they will never be completely satisfied with the evidence. Clarence Darrow, one of the most prominent trial attorneys of the twentieth century, advised that jurors of southern European descent favored the defense whereas those from Scandinavia favored the prosecution. Other lawyers have theorized that women are more skeptical as jurors

voir dire The pretrial examination of prospective jurors by the judge or opposing lawyers to uncover signs of bias.

peremptory challenge A means by which lawyers can exclude a limited number of prospective jurors without the judge's approval.

Contrary to popular opinion, women are harsher as criminal trial jurors than men are. **False.**

than men, particularly in response to attractive female witnesses. Still others offer selection advice based on faces, facial expressions, body language, and clothing. Perhaps the most interesting rule of thumb is also the simplest: "If you don't like a juror's face, chances are he doesn't like yours either!" (Wishman, 1986, pp. 72–73).

If assumptions based on surface appearances were correct, it would be easy to predict how jurors would vote. But the folk wisdom of trial lawyers is not supported by research, most of which shows that a juror's demographic factors such as gender, age, race, income, education, marital status, and occupation do not predict juror verdicts in simple or consistent ways (Hastie et al., 1983). Still, individuals may generally be prone to favor the prosecution or the defense—dispositions that can be measured using items from the Juror Bias Scale presented in Table 12.1 (De La Fuente et al., 2003; Kassin & Wrightsman, 1983; Lecci & Myers, 2002). Thus, when Andrea Chapdelaine and Sean Griffin (1997) administered this scale along with an attitude survey on the infamous O. J. Simpson case, they found that respondents with higher prosecution-bias scores were more likely to judge Simpson as guilty. Research has also shown that jurors who have an authoritarian personality—which leads them to identify with figures of authority, while being punitive and intolerant of others who are nonconventional—are also generally prone to convict (Narby et al., 1993).

Clearly, the intuitive approach to jury selection is flawed. Thus, although some experienced trial attorneys take pride in their jury-selection skills, researchers have found that most lawyers cannot effectively predict how jurors will vote, either on the basis of their intuitive rules of thumb (Olczak et al., 1991) or by how prospective jurors answer questions during the voir dire (Kerr et al., 1991; Zeisel & Diamond, 1978). Apparently, whether a juror characteristic predicts verdicts depends on the specifics of each and every case. Hence the birth of a new, controversial service industry: scientific jury selection.

TABLE 12.1
Some Items Used to Measure Juror Bias

Taken from the Juror Bias Scale, these statements can be used to measure the extent to which people are predisposed to favor the criminal prosecution or the defense. Agreement with items 1, 2, and 5 indicates a bias for the prosecution, while agreement with items 3, 4, and 6 indicates a bias for the defense.

(Kassin & Wrightsman, 1983.)

1. Too often jurors hesitate to convict someone who is guilty out of pure sympathy.
2. In most cases where the accused presents a strong defense, it is only because of a good lawyer.
3. The death penalty is cruel and inhumane.
4. Too many innocent people are wrongfully imprisoned.
5. Generally, the police make an arrest only when they are sure who committed the crime.
6. Circumstantial evidence is too weak to use in court.

Scientific Jury Selection

In John Grisham's *Runaway Jury*, a ruthless jury consultant named Rankin Fitch, played by Gene Hackman, helps lawyers select jurors through the use of intrusive high-tech surveillance work. Burrowing deep into the lives of prospective jurors, Fitch trails them, investigates them, and even resorts at times to bribery, blackmail, and intimidation. Determined to stack the jury in order to defend gun company defendants against a multimillion-dollar wrongful death lawsuit, Fitch declares, "A trial is too important to be left up to juries."

Grisham's depiction of jury consulting is a work of fiction, not fact. But it is based on a kernel of truth. Rather than rely on their hunches, successful stock market investors, baseball managers, and gamblers play the odds whenever they can. Now, many trial lawyers do too. In recent years, the "art" of jury selection has been transformed into a "science" (Lieberman & Sales, 2006).

This use of jury consultants began during the Vietnam War era, when the federal government prosecuted a group of antiwar activists known as the Harrisburg Seven. The case against the defendants was strong, and the trial was to be held in the conservative city of Harrisburg, Pennsylvania. To help the defense select a jury, sociologist Jay Schulman and his colleagues (1973) surveyed the local community by interview-

In John Grisham's The Runaway Jury, *Gene Hackman played a feared jury consultant, Rankin Fitch. In a film that blurred fact and fiction, Fitch not only researched prospective jurors for jury selection purposes but also engaged in jury tampering, blackmail, and other illegal tactics in a desperate but failed effort to win the verdict.*

ing 840 residents. Two kinds of information were taken from each resident: demographic (for example, sex, race, age, and education) and attitudes relevant to the trial (for example, attitudes toward the government, the war, and political dissent). By correlating these variables, Schulman's team came up with a profile of the ideal defense juror: "a female Democrat with no religious preference and a white-collar job or a skilled blue-collar job" (p. 40). Guided by this result, the defense went on to select its jury. The rest is history. Against all odds, the trial ended in a hung jury, split 10 to 2 in favor of acquittal.

Twenty-five years later, in the criminal trial against O. J. Simpson, the defense team hired a jury consultant to help in the selection process. Based on pretrial surveys, this consultant predicted that African American women would prove to be Simpson's strongest defenders. Public opinion polls and other research later confirmed the more general point that race may have played a role in this particular case (Murray et al., 1997). Prosecutor Marcia Clark also had the help of a jury consultant who found exactly the same result. However, Clark rejected his advice in favor of her intuitive belief that black women would be enraged by Simpson's history of domestic violence. Again, the rest is history. After four hours of deliberation, the criminal jury found Simpson not guilty of all charges (Toobin, 1996).

Today, the technique known as **scientific jury selection** is used often, especially in high-profile criminal trials and civil trials in which large sums of money are at stake. Research shows, for example, that jurors are differently predisposed when confronted with cases that pit lone individuals against large corporations, with some people favoring big business and others harboring anti-business prejudice (Hans, 2000). How is scientific jury selection carried out? What are the methods used? The procedure is simple. Because lawyers are often not allowed to ask jurors intrusive and personal questions, they try to determine jurors' attitudes and verdict tendencies from information that is known about their backgrounds. The relevance of this information can be determined through focus groups, mock juries, or community-wide surveys, in which statistical relationships are sought between general demographic factors and attitudes relevant to a particular case. Then, during the voir dire, lawyers ask prospective jurors about their backgrounds and use peremptory challenges to exclude those whose profiles are associated with unfavorable attitudes.

As you might expect, scientific jury selection is a controversial enterprise. By law, consultants are not permitted to communicate with or approach the prospective jurors themselves—despite the tactics portrayed in *Runaway Jury*. But how effective are the techniques that are employed? It's hard to say. On the one hand, trial lawyers who have used scientific jury selection boast an impressive winning percentage. On the other hand, it is impossible to know the extent to which these victories are attributable to the jury-selection surveys (Strier, 1999). So, does scientific jury selection work? Although extensive data are lacking, it appears that attitudes can influence verdicts in some cases and that pretrial research can help lawyers identify these attitudes (Seltzer, 2006). As we'll see, the linkage between attitudes and verdicts is particularly strong in cases that involve capital punishment.

Before concluding our review of scientific jury selection, let's stop to consider an ethical question: Is justice enhanced or impaired by the intervention of professional jury consultants? Is the real goal for lawyers to eliminate jurors who are biased or to create juries slanted in their favor? Those who practice scientific jury selection argue that picking juries according to survey results is simply a more refined version of what lawyers are permitted to do by intuition. If there's a problem, they say, it is not in the *science* but in the *law* that permits trial attorneys to use peremptory challenges to exclude jurors who are not obviously biased. In response, critics argue that scientific jury selection tips the scales of justice in favor of wealthy clients who can afford the service, an outcome that further widens the socioeconomic gap that exists within the courts. Hence, Neil and Dorit Kressel (2002), authors of *Stack and Sway: The New Science*

scientific jury selection
A method of selecting juries through surveys that yield correlations between demographics and trial-relevant attitudes.

of Jury Consulting, argue that peremptory challenges, which enable lawyers and their consultants to strike jurors who are not overtly biased, should be abolished.

 ## Juries in Black and White: Does Race Matter?

The year was 1995; the scene was a Los Angeles courthouse. All eyes were focused on the so-called trial of the century. O. J. Simpson was charged with the murders of his ex-wife Nicole Brown and her friend Ronald Goldman. The trial was packed with drama: Simpson was a Hall of Fame football hero, sportscaster, and actor; the crime was violent, and the defense lawyers claimed that Simpson was framed by racist police. To many Americans who followed the case, the evidence against Simpson seemed overwhelming. So when he was found not guilty by a twelve-person jury that included eight African Americans, the verdict was seen as a symptom of the racial divide in America. More recently as well, when Duke University lacrosse students, who are white, stood accused of raping a local prostitute, who is black, speculation about the biasing effects of race was rampant.

To what extent does a juror's race color his or her decision making? Research suggests that there is no simple answer. In one study, Norbert Kerr and others (1995) tested the most intuitive hypothesis of all, that jurors favor defendants who are similar to themselves. They presented mixed-race groups with a strong or weak case involving a black or white defendant. They found that when the evidence was weak, the participants were more lenient in their verdicts toward the defendant of the same race. Yet when the evidence was strong, they were harsher against that similar defendant, as if distancing themselves from his or her wrongdoing.

In a second study, Samuel Sommers and Phoebe Ellsworth (2001) tested the popular notion that jurors will show preference for others of their racial group when a crime involves race, as when it is a motivated hate crime or when attorneys "play the race card" in arguments to the jury. Yet they found the opposite pattern. When race was not an issue that is "on the radar," white jurors predictably treated the defendant more favorably when he was white than when he was black. Yet when race was made a prominent issue at trial, white jurors bent over backward *not* to appear prejudiced and did not discriminate. Other research as well has shown that jurors may, at times, be motivated to watch for racist tendencies in themselves, leading them to process

FIGURE 12.2

Effects of Racial Diversity on the Jury

Six person mock juries watched the trial of an African American defendant in groups that were homogeneous (all white) or diverse (four white, two black). In some cases, the issue of race was raised during the voir dire; in others, it was not. Either way, the white jurors in homogeneous groups were more likely to vote guilty than white jurors in diverse groups who, in turn, were more likely to vote guilty than black jurors in diverse groups. It seems that individual jurors are influenced in their decisions by the racial composition of their groups.

(Sommers, 2006.)

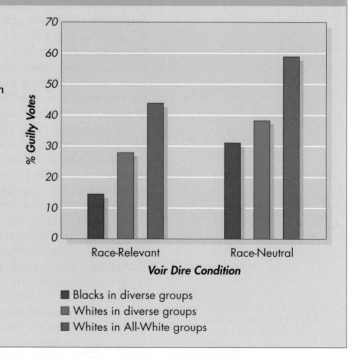

Juries most often decide whether to sentence a convicted murderer to death—in this case, in a gas chamber.

Worldwide, the most common methods of execution are by hanging, shooting, and beheading. In the United States, the most commonly used methods are electrocution, poisonous gas, and lethal injection. For more information on the death penalty, including up-to-date lists of death-row inmates, visit www.deathpenaltyinfo .org/index.html.

death qualification A jury-selection procedure used in capital cases that permits judges to exclude prospective jurors who say they would not vote for the death penalty.

trial information even more carefully when a defendant is black than when he or she is white (Sargent & Bradfield, 2004).

The biasing potential of race on individual jurors may also depend on the composition of the jury with whom they expect to deliberate. In a courthouse located in Ann Arbor, Michigan, Sommers (2006) showed a *Court TV* summary of a sexual assault trial in which the defendant was African American. A total of two hundred locals participated in 29 six-person mock juries after a voir dire that either did or did not make race an issue. Ultimately, the juries that were formed were either all white in composition or heterogeneous, consisting of four Whites and two Blacks. After the videotaped trial summary but before the groups deliberated, each juror was asked to indicate his or her verdict preference. Look at Figure 12.2, and you'll see that jurors were influenced by the racial composition of their groups as a whole. In diverse groups, 34 percent of white jurors voted guilty compared to 23 percent of black jurors—a small difference. In the all-white groups, however, 51 percent of jurors voted guilty, which represented a significant jump compared to both Blacks and Whites in the more diverse groups.

Death Qualification

It was February 3, 1998, when a thirty-eight-year-old convicted ax murderer named Karla Faye Tucker died by lethal injection in Huntsville, Texas. At 6:45 P.M., eight minutes after fatal chemicals were pumped into her arms, Tucker moaned, then moved her lips as in prayer, gasped twice, and died with her eyes open. Outside the prison walls, one group of protesters lit candles and sang songs, while another crowd cheered and waved signs that read "God bless the death penalty." Because Tucker was a woman and a born-again Christian, her execution drew worldwide attention. Pope John Paul II wrote a letter on her behalf, as did the European Parliament and the United Nations. On the question of her punishment, people were divided.

If you had to sentence someone to die, could you do it? Not everyone answers this question in the same way. Yet your answer could mean the difference between life and death for a defendant convicted of murder. Today, a majority of American states permit capital punishment. Among those that do, the jury decides not only the verdict but the sentence as well. In these cases, it is not surprising that sentencing decisions are influenced not only by the facts of a specific case but also by jurors' general attitudes toward the death penalty. Indeed, Kevin O'Neil and his colleagues (2004) have found that these attitudes are composed of various beliefs, such as beliefs in the legitimacy of retribution and revenge ("There are some murderers whose death would give me a sense of personal satisfaction"), deterrence ("The death penalty makes criminals think twice before committing murder"), and cost ("Executing a murderer is less expensive than keeping him in jail for the rest of his life").

In cases involving crimes punishable by death, and in which the jury makes both decisions, a special jury-selection practice known as **death qualification** is typically used. Through death qualification, judges may exclude all prospective jurors who say that they would refuse to vote for the death penalty. These jurors are excluded for the entire trial. To ensure that *sentencing* decisions are unbiased, it makes sense to exclude those who admit they are close-minded. But does this same selection practice tip the balance toward the prosecution when it comes to the *verdict?* In other words, are death-qualified juries prone to convict?

Through a series of studies, Phoebe Ellsworth, Craig Haney, and others have examined this question. Their results have shown that when compared with people who oppose the death penalty, those who support it are more prosecution-minded on a host of issues. For example, they are more concerned about crime, more trustful of police, more cynical about defense lawyers, and less tolerant of procedures that are designed to protect the accused (Fitzgerald & Ellsworth, 1984; Haney et al., 1994). When it comes to trial verdicts, the difference can be substantial. In one study, 288 people

"Ask the judge whether we can find the defendant not guilty and still execute him."

Cartoonbank.com

watched a videotaped murder trial and then participated in mock juries. The results showed that jurors who said they were willing to impose the death penalty were more likely to vote guilty, both before and after deliberating, than were those who would have been excluded for their refusal to impose a death sentence (Cowan et al., 1984). Similar results have also been found in studies of real jurors (Moran & Comfort, 1986). In fact, Haney (1984) found that death-qualification voir dire questions themselves are biasing because they presume the defendant's guilt and communicate to prospective jurors that the courts consider death a desirable form of punishment. In his studies, even randomly selected mock jurors were more likely to vote for conviction—and for the death penalty—when exposed to such questions during the voir dire than when they were not.

As the research evidence mounted, American courts had to face a sobering prospect. Had hundreds of prisoners on death row been tried by juries that were biased against them? In the case of *Lockhart v. McCree* (1986), the U.S. Supreme Court considered the issue. To inform the Court of recent research, the American Psychological Association submitted an exhaustive review of the literature (Bersoff & Ogden, 1987)—but to no avail. In an opinion that disappointed many social psychologists, the Court rejected the research and ruled that death qualification does not violate a defendant's right to a fair trial.

Should the Supreme Court have been persuaded more by the evidence? Some say yes (Ellsworth, 1991); others say no (Elliott, 1991). Either way, it may now be important to devise alternative, non-prejudicial methods that can be used to select capital juries. For example, research shows that many people who would be excluded because of a *general* opposition to capital punishment also admit that they would consider the death penalty for *specific* defendants found guilty of committing atrocious acts of violence—suggesting that perhaps these individuals should not be removed from the jury (Cox & Tanford, 1989). This issue continues to spark interest and concern among social psychologists (Costanzo, 1997). It is especially relevant these days, in light of sobering revelations brought about by DNA tests showing that many prisoners, including many on death row, have been innocent of the crimes for which they were convicted.

The Courtroom Drama

Once a jury is selected, the trial officially begins, and much of the evidence previously gathered comes to life. The evidence produced in the courtroom can range far and wide, from confessions to autopsy results, medical tests, bloodstains, hair samples, handwriting samples, diaries, fingerprints, photographs, and business documents. The trial itself is a well-orchestrated event. Lawyers for both sides make opening statements. Witnesses then answer questions under oath. Lawyers make closing arguments. The judge instructs the jury. Yet there are many problems in this all-too-human enterprise: The evidence may not be accurate or reliable, jurors may be biased by extraneous factors, and judges' instructions may fall on deaf ears. In this section, we identify some of the problems and possible solutions.

Confession Evidence

Every now and then, an extraordinary event comes along that shakes the way you think. The Central Park jogger case was one of these events. In 1989, five boys, fourteen to sixteen years old, were found guilty of a monstrous assault and rape of a female jogger in New York's Central Park after they confessed, four of them on videotape, in vivid detail. Thirteen years later, a serial rapist named Matias Reyes stepped forward from prison to say that he alone, not the boys, had committed the crime. As part of a thorough investigation of Reyes's claim, the district attorney DNA-tested the

In 1989, sixteen-year-old Kharey Wise (left) and four other teenagers confessed to raping a jogger in New York's Central Park. Based solely on his confession, Wise was convicted and sent to prison. Thirteen years later, Matias Reyes (right) admitted that he alone, not the boys, had committed the crime. DNA tests confirmed that Reyes was the rapist. The boys, despite their confessions, were innocent.

semen from the crime scene and found that it was a match: Reyes was the rapist. The five boys, now men, were innocent. Their confessions were false and the convictions were vacated (Kassin, 2002; Saulny, 2002).

Police Interrogations: Social Influence Under Pressure   As these events unfolded, questions mounted: Why would five boys, or anyone else for that matter, confess to a crime they did not commit? In general, what social influences are brought to bear on suspects interrogated by police? Many years ago, police detectives would use bright lights, brute force, the rubber hose, and physical intimidation to get confessions. Today, however, the police are required to warn suspects of their *Miranda* rights to silence and to an attorney, and the "third degree" tactics they use are more psychological in nature. In *Criminal Interrogation and Confessions*, the most popular how-to manual written for the police, Fred Inbau and others (2001) advise interrogators to put suspects alone into a small, bare, soundproof room—a physical environment designed to arouse feelings of social isolation, helplessness, and discomfort. Next, they present a vivid nine-step procedure designed to get suspects to confess (see Table 12.2).

Once a suspect is isolated, there are two approaches contained within this method of interrogation. One approach is to pressure the suspect into submission by expressing certainty of his or her guilt and even, at times, claiming to have damaging evidence such as fingerprints or an eyewitness. In this way, the accused is led to believe that it is futile to mount a defense. A second approach is to befriend the suspect, offer sympathy and friendly advice, and "minimize" the offense by offering face-saving excuses or blaming the victim. Lulled into a false sense of security, and led to expect leniency, the suspect caves in. These tactics may sound as if they come from a *Law and Order* TV script, but in real life they are frequently used (Gudjonsson, 2003; Kassin, 1997, 2005; Kassin & Gudjonsson, 2004; Lassiter, 2004; Zimbardo, 1967).

In an observational study of 182 live and videotaped interrogations, Richard Leo (1996) found that detectives used an average of five to six tactics per suspect. In a survey of 631 police investigators, Kassin and others (2007) found that the most common reported tactics were to physically isolate suspects, identify contradictions in their accounts, establish rapport, confront suspects with evidence of their guilt, appeal to self-interests, and offer sympathy and moral justification. In the wake of 9/11, one wonders what additional methods of persuasion are used to interrogate suspected terrorists—and with what effect (Bowden, 2003).

The Risk of False Confessions   It could be argued that the use of trickery and deception does not pose a

TABLE 12.2

The Nine Steps of Interrogation

(Inbau et al., 2001.)

1. Confront the suspect with assertions of his or her guilt.
2. Develop "themes" that appear to justify or excuse the crime.
3. Interrupt all statements of innocence and denial.
4. Overcome all of the suspect's objections to the charges.
5. Keep the increasingly passive suspect from tuning out.
6. Show sympathy and understanding, and urge the suspect to tell all.
7. Offer the suspect a face-saving explanation for his or her guilty action.
8. Get the suspect to recount the details of the crime.
9. Convert that statement into a full written confession.

serious problem because innocent people never confess to crimes they did not commit. This assumption, however, is incorrect. As hard as it is to believe, there are a number of chilling cases on record. In fact, among prisoners who were convicted and later proved innocent by DNA evidence, more than 20 percent had given false confessions to police (Scheck et al., 2000; www.innocenceproject.org/), and this sample represents the mere tip of an iceberg (Drizin & Leo, 2004).

Sometimes innocent suspects confess as an act of *compliance*, merely to escape a bad situation. In the Central Park jogger case, the boys were in custody and interrogated by several detectives for some fourteen to thirty hours before giving their videotaped confessions (most interrogations last an hour or two). Very long periods of time bring fatigue, despair, and a deprivation of sleep and other need states. The jogger detectives and suspects disagree about what transpired during these unrecorded hours, so it is impossible to know for sure. The defendants claimed that they were threatened, that promises were made in exchange for cooperation, and that the crime details that appeared in their confessions were suggested to them. Put simply, they said they cooperated thinking they would go home.

There are other instances in which interrogation causes innocent suspects to believe that they might be guilty of the crime, illustrating an even stronger form of social influence known as *internalization*. This process was evident in the story of Paul Ingram, a man charged with rape and a host of satanic ritual cult crimes. For a period of six months, Ingram was hypnotized, informed of graphic crime details, told by a police psychologist that sex offenders typically repress their offenses, and urged by the minister of his church to confess. Eventually he "recalled" crime scenes to specification, pleaded guilty, and was sentenced to prison. In fact, there was no physical evidence that the alleged events had even occurred, and an expert who reviewed the case concluded that Ingram had been "brainwashed." At one point, this expert accused Ingram of a phony crime. Ingram denied the charge at first, but eventually he confessed and embellished the story in the process (Ofshe & Watters, 1994).

Is it really possible to get people to confess to an act they did not commit? Based on the events of actual cases, Kassin and Kiechel (1996) theorized that two factors can increase this risk: (1) a suspect who lacks a clear memory of the event in question and (2) the presentation of false evidence. To test this hypothesis, they recruited pairs of college students to work on a fast- or slow-paced computer task. At one point, the computer crashed, and students were accused of having caused the damage by pressing a key they had been specifically instructed to avoid. All students were truly innocent and denied the charge. In half the sessions, however, the second student (who was really a confederate) said that she had seen the student hit the forbidden key.

Demonstrating the process of compliance, many students confronted by this false witness agreed to sign a confession handwritten by the experimenter. Further demonstrating the process of internalization, some students later "admitted" guilt to a stranger (also a confederate) after the study was supposedly over and the two were alone. In short, innocent people who are vulnerable to suggestion can be induced to confess and to internalize guilt by the presentation of false evidence—an interrogation tactic sometimes used by the police (see Table 12.3).

In another laboratory study, innocent students were led to confess to cheating, a possible violation of their university honor code. In this situation, Melissa Russano and others (2005) asked participants to solve a series of problems, sometimes alone and sometimes with a fellow participant—a role played by a confederate. In the alone trials, participants were instructed not to seek or provide assistance. In a guilty condition, the confederate asked for help, inducing most participants to break the rule. In an innocent condition, no such request was made. Moments later, the experimenter returned and interrogated everyone as to whether they had cheated. As part of this interrogation, the experimenter offered leniency for cooperation to

TABLE 12.3
Factors That Promote False Confessions

As participants worked on a fast- or slow-paced task, the computer crashed, and they were accused of causing the damage. A confederate then said that she had or had not seen the participants hit the forbidden key. As shown, many participants signed a confession (compliance), and some even "admitted" their guilt in private to another confederate (internalization). Despite their innocence, many participants in the fast-false witness condition confessed on both measures.

(Kassin & Kiechel, 1996.)

	Control		False Witness	
	Slow	Fast	Slow	Fast
Compliance	35%	65%	89%	100%
Internalization	0%	12%	44%	65%

TABLE 12.4
More Factors that Promote False Confessions

Condition	Guilty	Innocent
Control	46%	6%
Promise	72%	14%
Minimization	81%	18%
Both	87%	43%

(Russano, et al., 2005.)

Participants were asked to solve a series of problems, sometimes alone and sometimes with a confederate. In a guilty condition, the confederate asked for help during an alone trial, inducing participants to break the rule. In an innocent condition, no such request was made. The experimenter later interrogated everyone by promising leniency, minimizing the seriousness of the violation, using both tactics, or using no tactics at all. As shown by confession rates, both promises and minimization increased true confessions to cheating by students who broke the rule—but they also increased false confessions in students who did nothing wrong.

some participants, minimized the seriousness of the violation to others, used both tactics, or used no tactics at all. Would students sign a confession to cheating? Yes. Table 12.4 shows that both promises and minimization increased the number of true confessions among students who broke the rule. But these same tactics also increased the rate of false confessions among students who did nothing wrong.

Confessions and the Jury: An Attributional Dilemma   How does the legal system treat confessions brought out by various methods of interrogation? The procedure is straightforward. Whenever a suspect confesses but then withdraws the statement, pleads not guilty, and goes to trial, the judge must determine whether the statement was voluntary or coerced. If the confession was clearly coerced—as when a suspect is isolated for long periods of time, deprived of food or sleep, threatened, or abused—it is excluded. If not, it is admitted into evidence for the jury to evaluate. Juries are thus confronted with a classic attribution dilemma: A suspect's statement may indicate guilt (personal attribution), or it may simply be a way to avoid the aversive consequences of silence (situational attribution). According to attribution theory, jurors should reject all confessions made in response to external pressure. But wait. Remember the fundamental attribution error? In Chapter 4, we saw that people tend to overattribute behavior to persons and overlook the influence of situational forces. Is it similarly possible, as in the Central Park jogger case, that jurors view suspects who confess as guilty even if they were highly pressured to confess during interrogation?

To examine this question, Kassin and Holly Sukel (1997) had mock jurors read one of three versions of a double murder trial. In a control version that did not contain a confession, only 19 percent voted guilty. In a low-pressure version in which the defendant was said to have confessed immediately upon questioning, the conviction rate rose considerably, to 62 percent. But there was a third, high-pressure condition in which participants were told that the defendant had confessed out of fear and with his hands cuffed painfully behind his back. How did jurors in this situation react? Reasonably, they judged the confession to be coerced, and they said it did not influence their verdicts. Yet the conviction rate in this situation significantly increased, this time to 50 percent. Apparently, people are powerfully influenced by evidence of a confession, even when they concede that it was coerced.

The jury's reaction to confession evidence may also depend on how that evidence is presented. Today, many police departments videotape confessions for presentation in court. But could you tell the difference between a true confession and a false confession? Maybe not. In a recent study, Kassin, Meissner, and Norwick (2005) videotaped male prison inmates giving full confessions to the crimes for which they were incarcerated and concocting false confessions to offenses suggested by the researchers that they did not commit. College students and police investigators then watched and judged ten different inmates, each giving a true or false confession to one of five crimes: aggravated assault, armed robbery, burglary, breaking and entering, and automobile theft. The results showed that although the police were generally confident in their performance, neither group exhibited high levels of accuracy.

In light of recently discovered false confessions, a number of states and cities are beginning to require that the full interrogations be videotaped. In this way, judges and juries can see for themselves the process by which the confessions came about and the extent to which the suspect was coerced. But how are these events staged for the camera? As

"Before we begin, may I ask which of you is the good cop, and which is the bad?"

Without being beaten or threatened, innocent people sometimes confess to crimes they did not commit. **True.**

described in Chapter 4, research has shown that observers who watch two people engage in a conversation overemphasize the impact on that interaction of the person who is visually salient. Similarly, in a series of important experiments, Daniel Lassiter and his colleagues (2001) taped mock confessions from three different camera angles so that either the suspect or the interrogator or both were visible. All participants heard the same exchanges of words, but those who watched the suspects saw the situations as less coercive overall than did those who focused on the interrogators. The practical policy implications are striking. When the camera directs all eyes at the accused, jurors are likely to underestimate the amount of pressure exerted by the "hidden" interrogator.

 ## The Lie-Detector Test

Often, people confess after being told that they have failed the **polygraph**, or lie-detector, test. A polygraph is an electronic instrument that simultaneously records multiple channels of physiological arousal. The signals are picked up by sensors attached to different parts of the body. For example, rubber tubes are strapped around a suspect's torso to measure breathing; blood pressure cuffs are wrapped around the upper arm to measure pulse rate; and electrodes are placed on the fingertips to record sweat-gland activity, or perspiration. These signals are then boosted by amplifiers and converted into a visual display.

The polygraph is used to detect deception on the assumption that when people lie, they become anxious and aroused in ways that can be measured. Here's how the test is conducted. After convincing a suspect that the polygraph works and establishing his or her baseline level of arousal, the examiner asks a series of yes-no questions and compares how the suspect reacts to emotionally arousing *crime-relevant questions* ("Did you steal the money?") and *control questions* that are arousing but not relevant to the crime ("Did you take anything that did not belong to you when you were younger?"). In theory, suspects who are innocent—whose denials are truthful—should be more aroused by the control questions, while guilty suspects—whose denials are false—should be more aroused by the crime-relevant questions.

Does the lie-detector test really work? Many laypeople think it is foolproof, but scientific opinion is split (Iacono & Lykken, 1997). Some researchers report accuracy rates of up to 80 to 90 percent (Honts, 1996; Raskin, 1986). Others say that such claims are exaggerated and misleading (Lykken, 1998). One well-documented problem is that truthful persons too often fail the test. A second problem is that people who understand the test can fake the results. Studies show that you can beat the polygraph by tensing your muscles, squeezing your toes, or using other physical countermeasures while answering the *control* questions. By artificially inflating the responses to "innocent" questions, one can mask the stress that is aroused by lying on the crime-relevant questions (Honts et al., 1994).

What, then, are we to conclude? Careful reviews of the research suggest that there is no simple answer (Honts et al., 2002; National Research Council, 2003). Under certain conditions—for example, when the suspect is naive and the examiner is competent—it is possible for the polygraph to detect truth and deception at fairly high levels of accuracy. Still, the problems are hard to overcome, which is why the U.S. Supreme Court recently ruled, in the context of a military court martial, that judges may refuse to admit polygraph test results into evidence (*United States v. Scheffer*, 1998). As an alternative, researchers are now trying to develop tests that distinguish between truth and deception through the measurement of involuntary electrical activity in the brain (Bashore & Rapp, 1993); pupil dilation when the person being tested is asked to lie, which requires more cognitive effort than telling the truth (Dionisio et al., 2001); involuntary muscle movements in the face that betray grimaces and other expressions that are too subtle to detect with the naked eye (Bartlett et al., 1999); and the use of fMRI to measure blood oxygen levels in areas of the brain associated with deception (Kozel et al., 2004). Research suggests it may even be possible to judge truth and deception by measuring how long it takes people to react to crime-relevant information, with guilty suspects taking longer to react than innocent ones (Seymour et al., 2000).

A person can fool a lie-detector test by suppressing arousal when questions about the crime are asked. **False.**

polygraph A mechanical instrument that records physiological arousal from multiple channels; it is often used as a lie-detector test.

Eyewitness Testimony

"I'll never forget that face!" When these words are uttered, police officers, judges, and juries all take notice. Often, however, eyewitnesses make mistakes. Consider the story of Jennifer Thompson and Ronald Cotton. One night in 1984, in North Carolina, a man broke into Thompson's apartment, cut the phone wires, and raped her. She described him to the police, helped construct a composite sketch, and then positively identified Ronald Cotton as her assailant. Cotton had alibis for his whereabouts that night, but based on the eyewitness identification, he was found guilty and sentenced to life in prison. Ten years later, DNA tests of semen stains revealed that Cotton was innocent and that Bobby Poole, a known offender, was the real assailant. In 1995, after ten years in prison, Cotton was released and offered $5,000 in compensation. He is now trying to put the pieces of his life back together. Thompson, upon realizing that she had identified an innocent man, said, "I remember feeling sick, but also I remember feeling just an overwhelming sense of just guilt. . . . I cried and cried and I wept and I was angry at me and I beat myself up for it for a long time."

An estimated 77,000 people a year are charged with crimes solely on the basis of eyewitness evidence (Goldstein et al., 1989). Many of these eyewitness accounts are accurate, but many are not—which is why psychologists have been interested in the topic for one hundred years (Doyle, 2005). Recently, the National Institute of Justice reported on twenty-eight wrongful convictions in which convicted felons were proved innocent by DNA evidence after varying numbers of years in prison. Remarkably, as in Ronald Cotton's case, every one of these convictions involved a mistaken identification (Connors et al., 1996). The number of DNA innocence cases soon climbed to sixty-two—fifty-two of which contained positive but false identifications (Scheck et al., 2000). Then, in 1999, the U.S. Department of Justice took a bold step in response to this problem, assembling a group of police, prosecutors, defense attorneys, and research psychologists to devise a set of "how-to" guidelines. Led by Gary Wells, this Technical Working Group went on to publish *Eyewitness Evidence: A Guide for Law Enforcement* (U.S. Department of Justice, 1999; Wells et al., 2000).

As eyewitnesses, people can be called upon to remember just about anything—perhaps a face, an accident, or a conversation. Over the years, hundreds of tightly controlled studies have been conducted. Based on this research, three conclusions can be drawn: (1) Eyewitnesses are imperfect, (2) certain personal and situational factors can systematically influence their performance, and (3) judges, juries, and lawyers are not adequately informed about these factors (Cutler & Penrod, 1995; Sporer et al., 1996; Thompson et al., 1998; Wells & Olson, 2003).

People tend to think that human memory is like a videotape camera: If you turn on the power and focus the lens, all events will be recorded for subsequent playback. Unfortunately, it's not that simple. Over the years, researchers have found it useful to view memory as a three-stage process involving the *acquisition, storage,* and *retrieval* of information. The first of these stages, acquisition, refers to a witness's perceptions

Jennifer Thompson was traumatized twice: the first time when she was raped, the second when she learned that she had identified a man proved to be innocent by DNA tests ten years later. Here you can see Thompson, the victim, talking to Ronald Cotton, the innocent man she picked from a lineup. Notice the resemblance between Cotton and Bobby Poole, her actual assailant. For pictures, tapes, interviews, and other information about this case, which was the subject of PBS Frontline's "What Jennifer Saw," you can log on to the Web site, www.pbs.org/wgbh/pages/frontline/shows/dna.

Poole

Cotton

After the tragic assassination of President John F. Kennedy, dozens of eyewitnesses came forward to describe what they saw. Some reported one gunman in the sixth-floor window of a nearby building; others reported two or three gunmen in the building; and still others thought the shots were fired from the ground. Such are the pitfalls of eyewitness testimony.

at the time of the event in question. Second, the witness stores that information in memory to avoid forgetting. Third, the witness retrieves the information from storage when needed. This model suggests that errors can occur at three different points.

Acquisition Some kinds of persons and events are more difficult to perceive than others. Common sense tells us that brief exposure time, poor lighting, long distance, physical disguise, and distraction can all limit a witness's perceptions. Research has uncovered other, less obvious factors as well.

Consider the effects of a witness's emotional state. Often people are asked to recall a bloody shooting, a car wreck, or an assault—emotional events that trigger high levels of stress. Arousal has a complex effect on memory. Realizing the importance of what they are seeing, highly aroused witnesses zoom in on the central features of an event such as the culprit, the victim, or a weapon. As a direct result of this narrowed field of attention, however, arousal impairs a witness's memory for other less central details (Brown, 2003; Christianson, 1992). Alcohol, a drug often involved in crime, also causes problems. When participants in one study witnessed a live staged crime, those who had earlier consumed fruit juice were more accurate in their recollections than were those who had been served an alcoholic beverage (Yuille & Tollestrup, 1990). Under the influence of alcohol, people can recognize the perpetrator in a lineup, but they too often make false identifications when the actual perpetrator is absent (Dysart et al., 2002).

The **weapon-focus effect** is also an important factor. Across a wide range of settings, research shows that when a criminal pulls out a gun, a razor blade, or a knife, witnesses are less able to identify that culprit than if no weapon is present (Pickel, 1999; Steblay, 1992). There are two reasons for this effect. First, people are agitated by the sight of a menacing stimulus, as when participants in one study were approached by an experimenter holding a syringe or threatening to administer an injection (Maass & Kohnken, 1989). Second, even in a harmless situation, a witness's eyes lock in on a weapon like magnets, drawing attention away from the face. To demonstrate, Elizabeth Loftus and others (1987) showed people slides of a customer who walked up to a bank teller and pulled out either a pistol or a checkbook. By tracking eye movements, these researchers found that people spent more time looking at the gun than at the checkbook. The net result was an impairment in their ability to identify the criminal in a lineup.

There is still another important consideration. By varying the racial make-up of participants and target persons in laboratory and real-life interactions, researchers discovered that people find it relatively difficult to recognize members of a race other than their own—an effect known as the **cross-race identification bias** (Malpass & Kravitz, 1969). In one field study, for example, eighty-six convenience store clerks in El Paso, Texas, were asked to identify three customers—one white, one black, and one Mexican American—all experimental confederates who had stopped in and made a purchase earlier that day. It turned out that the white, black, and Mexican American clerks were all most likely to accurately identify customers belonging to their own racial or ethnic group (Platz & Hosch, 1988). The finding that "they all look alike" (referring to members of other groups) is found reliably and in many different racial and ethnic groups. Indeed, Christian Meissner and John Brigham (2001) statistically combined the results of thirty-nine studies involving a total of five thousand mock witnesses. They found that the witnesses were consistently less accurate and more

weapon-focus effect The tendency for the presence of a weapon to draw attention and impair a witness's ability to identify the culprit.

cross-race identification bias The tendency for people to have difficulty identifying members of a race other than their own.

Eyewitnesses find it relatively difficult to recognize members of a race other than their own. **True.**

prone to making false identifications when they tried to recognize target persons from racial and ethnic groups other than their own.

Storage   Can remembrances of the remote past be trusted? As you might expect, memory for faces and events tends to decline with the passage of time. Longer intervals between an event and its retrieval are generally associated with increased forgetting (Shapiro & Penrod, 1986). But not all recollections fade, and time alone does not cause memory slippage. Consider the plight of bystanders who witness firsthand such incidents as terrorist bombings, shootings, plane crashes, or fatal car accidents. Afterward, they may talk about what they saw, read about it, hear what other bystanders have to say, and answer questions from investigators and reporters. By the time witnesses to these events are officially questioned, they are likely to have been exposed to so much postevent information that one wonders if their original memory is still "pure."

According to Elizabeth Loftus (1996), it probably is not. Many years ago, based on her own studies of eyewitness testimony, Loftus proposed a theory of reconstructive memory. After people observe an event, she said, later information about that event—whether it's true or not—becomes integrated into the fabric of their memory. A classic experiment by Loftus and John Palmer (1974) illustrates the point. Participants viewed a film of a traffic accident and then answered questions, including: "About how fast were the cars going when they *hit* each other?" Other participants answered the same question, except that the verb *hit* was replaced by *smashed, collided, bumped,* or *contacted.* All participants saw the same accident, yet the wording of the question affected their reports. Figure 12.3 shows that participants given the "smashed" question estimated the highest average speed and those responding to the "contacted" question estimated the lowest. But there's more. One week later, participants were called back for more probing. Had the wording of the questions caused them to reconstruct their memories of the accident? Yes. When asked whether they had seen broken glass at the accident (none was actually present), 32 percent of the "smashed" participants said they had. As Loftus had predicted, what these participants

FIGURE 12.3

Biasing Eyewitness Reports with Loaded Questions

Participants viewed a film of a traffic accident and then answered this question: "About how fast were these cars going when they (hit, smashed, or contacted) each other?" As shown, the wording of the question influenced speed estimates (top). One week later, it also caused participants to reconstruct their memory of other aspects of the accident (bottom).

(Loftus & Palmer, 1974.)

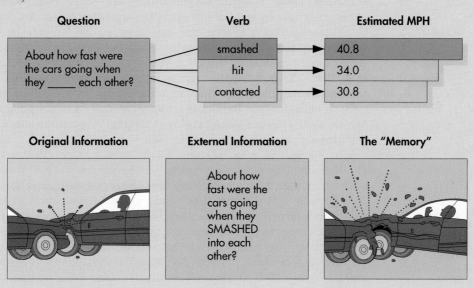

remembered of the accident was based on two sources: the event itself and post-event information.

This **misinformation effect** has aroused a great deal of controversy. It's clear that eyewitnesses can be compromised when exposed to postevent information—as when they are told, for example, what other witnesses had reported seeing (Shaw et al., 1997). But does postevent information actually alter a witness's real memory, so that it can never be retrieved again? Or do participants merely follow the experimenter's suggestion, leaving their true memory intact for retrieval under other conditions? Either way, whether memory is truly altered or not, eyewitness *reports* are hopelessly biased by postevent information. This effect can be hard to erase (Johnson & Seifert, 1998). It can also be dramatic. In one laboratory study, people were led through a process of imagination to create false memories of having performed some bizarre behaviors two weeks earlier—like balancing a spoon on the nose, sitting on dice, and rubbing lotion on a chair (Thomas & Loftus, 2002).

This phenomenon raises an additional, potentially troubling question. If adults can be misled by postevent information, what about young children? On August 2, 1988, Margaret Kelly Michaels, a twenty-six-year-old preschool teacher, was found guilty of 115 counts of sex abuse committed at the Wee Care Nursery School in New Jersey. The charges against her were shocking. For a period of over seven months, the jury was told, she danced nude in the classroom, stripped the children, licked peanut butter off their genitals, and raped them with knives, forks, spoons, and Lego blocks.

Were the children's stories accurate? On the one hand, there were some striking consistencies in the testimonies of nineteen child witnesses. On the other hand, the social workers and investigators who conducted the interviews often prompted the children with suggestive leading questions, told them that Michaels was a bad person, urged them to describe acts they had initially denied, offered bribes for disclosures, and pressured those who claimed ignorance. Except for this testimony, there was no physical evidence of abuse and no other witnesses even though the acts were supposed to have occurred during school hours in an open classroom. Michaels was found guilty and sentenced to forty-seven years in prison. After serving five of those years, she was released when the state appeals court overturned the conviction on the ground that the children's testimony could not be trusted. "One day you're getting ready for work and making coffee, minding your business," said Michaels, "and the next minute you are an accused child molester."

Can suggestive interview procedures cause young children to confuse appearance and reality? Over the years, thousands of sex abuse charges have been filed against babysitters, preschool teachers, and family members. In some of these cases, the suspects were falsely accused of performing ritual abuse as part of satanic cults (Bottoms & Davis, 1997). In light of these events, judges struggle to decide: Are preschoolers competent to take the witness stand, or are they too suggestible, too prone to confuse reality and fantasy? To provide guidance to the courts, researchers have studied the factors that influence children's eyewitness memory (Bruck & Ceci, 1999).

This research has evolved through several stages. At first, simple laboratory experiments showed that preschoolers were more likely than older children and adults to incorporate misleading "trick" questions into their memories for simple stories (Ceci et al., 1987). Other studies showed that interviewers could get young children to change their memories, or at least their answers, simply by repeating a question over and over—a behavior that implies that the answer given is not good enough (Poole & White, 1991). But are young children similarly suggestible about stressful real-life experiences?

In one study, Michelle Leichtman and Stephen Ceci (1995) told nursery school children about a clumsy man named Sam Stone who always broke things. A month later, a man visited the school, spent time in the classroom, and left. The next day, the children were shown a ripped book and a soiled teddy bear and asked what happened. Reasonably, no one said that they saw Stone cause the damage. But then, over the next ten weeks, they were asked suggestive questions ("I wonder if Sam Stone was wearing long pants or short pants when he ripped the book?"). The result: When a new interviewer asked the children in the class to tell what happened, 72 percent of the three- and four-year-olds blamed Stone for the damage, and 45 percent said they saw him do it. One child "recalled" that Stone took a paintbrush and painted melted chocolate on the bear. Others "saw" him spill coffee, throw toys in the air, rip the book in

misinformation effect
The tendency for false postevent misinformation to become integrated into people's memory of an event.

"Do you swear to tell your version of the truth as you perceive it, clouded perhaps by the passage of time and preconceived notions?"

anger, and soak the book in warm water until it fell apart. It's important to realize that false memories in children are not necessarily a byproduct of bad questioning procedures. Even when interviews are fair and neutral, false reports can stem from young children's exposure to misinformation from such outside sources as television (Principe et al., 2000), parents (Poole & Lindsay, 2001), and classmates (Principe & Ceci, 2002).

To summarize, research shows that repetition, misinformation, and leading questions can bias a child's memory report and that preschoolers are particularly vulnerable in this regard. The effects can be dramatic. In dozens of studies, these kinds of procedures have led children to falsely report that they were touched, hit, kissed, and hugged; that a thief came into their classroom; that something "yukky" was put into their mouth; and even that a doctor had cut a bone from their nose to stop it from bleeding. Somehow, the courts must distinguish between true and false claims—and do so on a case-by-case basis. To assist in this endeavor, researchers have proposed that clear interviewing guidelines be set so that future child witnesses will be questioned in an objective, nonbiasing manner (Poole & Lamb, 1998).

Retrieval   For eyewitnesses, testifying is only the last in a series of efforts to retrieve what they saw from memory. Before witnesses reach the courtroom, they are questioned by police and lawyers, view a lineup or mugshots, and even assist in the construction of a facial composite or an artist's sketch of the perpetrator. Yet each of these experiences increases the risk of error and distortion.

Imagine trying to reconstruct a culprit's face by selecting a set of eyes, a nose, a mouth, a hairstyle, and so on, from vast collections of features, and then combining them into a composite of the face. Research shows that this process seldom produces a face that resembles the actual culprit (Kovera et al., 1997). To further complicate matters, the face construction process itself may confuse witnesses, making it more difficult for them later to identify the culprit. In one study, for example, participants were asked to select from six pictures a person's face they had seen two days earlier. Sixty percent accurately identified the target. When they first tried to reconstruct the face using a computerized facial composite program, however, their identification accuracy dropped to 18 percent (Wells et al., 2005).

When there are multiple eyewitnesses to a crime, it is common for descriptions of the culprit to vary from one witness to the next. But what if the various descriptions could somehow be averaged into a single face? Is a collection of witnesses better than one? To answer this question, Lisa Hasel and Gary Wells (2007) had participants view a series of target faces and construct a sketch for each one, resulting in four sketches per face. Then for each target they used morphing software to create one composite image that combined the four sketches. To see if these morphs resembled the actual faces better than the average of the individual sketches, a new sample of participants rated the similarity of each set of sketches and morphed composite image to the original target. The results were encouraging: On average, the morphs were rated as more similar to the targets than were the individual sketches on which they were based (see Figure 12.4).

Nothing an eyewitness does has greater impact than making an identification from a photographic or live lineup. Once police have made an arrest, they often call on their witnesses to view a lineup that includes the suspect and five to seven other individuals. This procedure may take place within days of a crime or months later. Either way, the lineup often results in tragic cases of mistaken identity. Through the application of eyewitness research findings, as we'll see, this risk can be reduced (Wells et al., 1998).

Basically, four factors affect identification performance. The first is the lineup *construction*. To be fair, a lineup should contain four to eight innocent persons, or "foils," who match the witness's general description of the culprit. If the witness describes seeing a white male in his twenties with curly hair, for example, foils should not be included that are old, nonwhite, and bald. Also, anything that makes a suspect distinctive, compared with the others, increases his or her chance of being selected

FIGURE 12.4

Morphing Composite Faces to Catch a Thief

Students from Iowa State University volunteered to use software to answer the question: If there are multiple eyewitnesses to a crime, would it help to average their sketches of the perpetrator's face? In this study, participants constructed sketches of target faces of student volunteers they had viewed. Using the morphing software, a single image that combined four sketches was created for each target. Other participants then rated the similarity of each set of sketches and morphed image to the original target. Overall, the morphs were more similar to targets than were the individual sketches on which they were based.

(Hasel & Wells, 2007.)

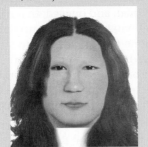
Sketch 1

Sketch 2

Sketch 3

Sketch 4

Morphed Composite

Target Face

(Buckhout, 1974). This is what happened to Steve Titus, a man mistakenly accused of rape when the police showed the victim his photograph alongside those of five other men. Although the foils resembled Titus in appearance, his picture stood out like a sore thumb. It was smaller than the others and was the only one without a border. Titus was also the only man in the group with a smile on his face (Loftus & Ketcham, 1991). Indeed, an author of this book once served as an expert for a case in which the witness—who had described an armed robber as a dark-skinned African American male—was shown a picture of a suspect that was visibly darker than all the surrounding pictures (*United States v. Hines*, 1999).

Second, lineup *instructions* to the witness are very important. In a study by Roy Malpass and Patricia Devine (1981), students saw a staged act of vandalism, after which they attended a lineup. Half of the students received "biased" instructions: They were led to believe that the culprit was in the lineup. The others were told that he might or might not be present. Lineups were then presented either with or without the culprit. When the students received biased instructions, they felt compelled to identify *someone* and often picked an innocent person (see Table 12.5). Additional studies have both confirmed and qualified this basic result: When the criminal is present in the lineup, biased instructions are not problematic; when the criminal is not in the lineup, however—which occurs when the police suspect is innocent—biased instructions substantially increase the rate of mistaken identifications (Clarke, 2005; Steblay, 1997). Again, the story of Steve Titus is a case in point. The police told the victim to pick her assailant from a group of six. After studying the pictures for several minutes and shaking her head in confusion, she was urged to concentrate and make a choice. "This one is the closest," she said. "It has to be this one" (Loftus & Ketcham, 1991, p. 38).

Third, the *format* of a lineup also influences whether a witness feels compelled to make a selection. When witnesses are presented with a spread of photographs, they tend

TABLE 12.5

Effects of Lineup and Instructions on False Identifications

After witnessing a crime, participants were told either that the culprit was in the lineup (biased instruction) or that he might or might not be present (unbiased instruction). Participants then viewed a lineup in which the real culprit was present or absent. Notice the percentage of participants in each group who identified an innocent person. Those who received the biased instruction were more likely to make a false identification, picking an innocent person rather than no one at all—especially when the real culprit was not in the lineup.

(Malpass & Devine, 1981.)

	Percentage of False Identifications	
	Unbiased Instructions	Biased Instructions
Culprit present	0	25
Culprit absent	33	78

to make relative, multiple-choice-like judgments, comparing the different alternatives and picking the one who looks most like the criminal. This strategy increases the tendency to make a false identification. The solution: When the same photos are shown sequentially, one at a time, witnesses tend to make absolute judgments by comparing each target person with their memory of the criminal. This situation diminishes the risk of a forced and often false identification of an innocent suspect (Lindsay & Bellinger, 1999; Lindsay et al., 1991; Lindsay & Wells, 1985). Currently, some researchers are concerned that the benefit of the sequential format will depend on how it is implemented and that it may also reduce correct identifications when the actual perpetrator is in the lineup (McQuiston-Surrett et al., 2006).

The fourth factor is perhaps the most subtle, as it pertains to *familiarity-induced* biases. Research shows that people often remember a face but forget the circumstances in which they saw that face. In one study, for example, participants witnessed a staged crime and then looked through mugshots. A few days later, they were asked to view a lineup. The result was startling: Participants were just as likely to identify an innocent person whose photograph was in the mugshots as they were to pick the actual criminal! (Brown et al., 1977). Many different studies have shown that witnesses will often identify from a lineup someone they had seen in another context, including innocent bystanders who also happened to be at the crime scene (Deffenbacher et al., 2006).

Courtroom Testimony   Eyewitnesses can be inaccurate, but that's only part of the problem. The other part is that their testimony in court is persuasive and not easy to evaluate. To examine how juries view eyewitness testimony, Gary Wells, Rod Lindsay, and others conducted a series of experiments in which they staged the theft of a calculator in the presence of unsuspecting research participants, who were later cross-examined after trying to pick the culprit from a photo spread. Other participants, who served as mock jurors, observed the questioning and judged the witnesses. The results were sobering: Jurors overestimated how accurate the eyewitnesses were and could not distinguish between witnesses whose identifications were correct and those whose identifications were incorrect (Lindsay et al., 1981; Wells et al., 1979).

There appear to be two problems. First, people generally do not know about these aspects of human perception and memory through common sense. Brian Cutler and others (1988) found that mock jurors were not sensitive enough to the effects of lineup instructions, weapon focus, and other aspects of an eyewitnessing situation, such as cross-race bias in evaluating the testimony of an eyewitness (Abshire & Bernstein, 2003). This lack of knowledge is not limited to trial juries. Wise and Safer (2004) surveyed 160 judges for their beliefs about eyewitness testimony and found that although they were aware of some issues, they were naïve about others. Yet a witness's behavior may provide clues to his or her accuracy. One possible way to distinguish between accurate and inaccurate identifications is by asking witnesses to describe the decision-making process. David Dunning and Lisa Beth Stern (1994) staged a crime and found that witnesses who made a correct identification from photographs described the judgment as quick, effortless, and automatic ("His face just popped out at me"). Those who were inaccurate described a more careful and deliberate process-of-elimination strategy ("I compared the photos to each other to narrow the choices"). The witness who recognizes the culprit's face is most likely to do so instantly, without much thought (Sporer, 1993). In fact, Dunning and Perretta (2002) discovered that there is a 10- to 12-second rule. In a series of studies, they found that witnesses making identifications faster than 10 to 12 seconds were nearly 90 percent accurate, while those who took longer were only 50 percent accurate.

The second problem is that people tend to base their judgments largely on how *confident* the witness was, a factor that only modestly predicts accuracy. This statement may seem surprising, but studies have shown that the witness who declares "I am absolutely certain" is often not more likely to be right than the one who appears unsure (Penrod & Cutler, 1995; Sporer et al., 1995; Wells & Murray, 1984). Why are eyewitness confidence and accuracy not highly related? The reason is that confidence levels can be raised and lowered by factors that do not have an impact on identification accuracy.

To demonstrate, Elizabeth Lüüs and Wells (1994) staged a theft in front of pairs of participants and then had each separately identify the culprit from a photographic lineup. After the participants made their identifications, the experimenters led them to believe that their partner, a co-witness, either had picked the same person, a similar-looking different person, or a dissimilar-looking different person, or had said that the thief was not in the lineup. Participants were then questioned by a police officer who asked, "On a scale from 1 to 10, how confident are you in your identification?" The result: Participants became more confident when told that a co-witness picked the same person or a dissimilar alternative and less confident when told that the co-witness picked a similar alternative or none at all. Other research confirms how important such post-identification feedback can be. In fact, John Shaw (1996) found that witnesses who are repeatedly questioned about their observations become increasingly confident over time but not more accurate.

Wells and Amy Bradfield (1998) then found that eyewitnesses who received positive feedback about their false identifications went on to reconstruct other aspects of their eyewitnessing experience. In a series of studies, they showed participants a security camera videotape of a man who shoots a guard followed by a set of photographs that did not contain the actual gunman (in other words, all identifications made were false). The experimenter then said to some witnesses, but not to others, "Oh good. You identified the actual murder suspect." When witnesses were later asked about the whole experience, those given the confirming feedback recalled that they had paid more attention to the event, had a better view of the culprit, and found it easier to make the identification (see Figure 12.5). Apparently, an eyewitness's confidence

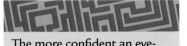

The more confident an eyewitness is about an identification, the more accurate he or she is likely to be. **False.**

FIGURE 12.5

Biasing Effects of Post-identification Feedback

Participants saw a gunman on videotape and then tried to make an identification from a set of photographs in which he was absent. Afterward, the experimenter gave some witnesses but not others confirming feedback about their selection. As shown, those given the confirming feedback later recalled that they had paid more *attention* to the event, had a better *view* of it, could make out *details* of the culprit's face, and found it *easier* to make the identification. They were also more willing to testify in court.

(Wells & Bradfield, 1998.)

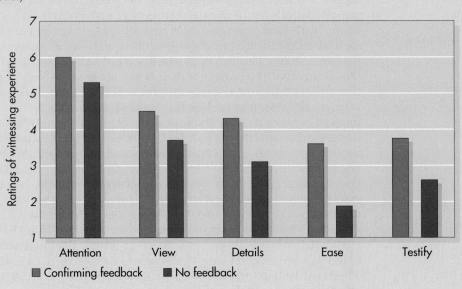

TABLE 12.6
What Eyewitness Experts Say in Court

Presented with a list of eyewitness factors, 64 experts were asked what research findings were strong enough to present in court. In order of how much support they elicited, the following are among the most highly regarded topics of expert testimony.

(Kassin et al., 2001.)

Eyewitness Factor	Statement
Wording of questions	An eyewitness's testimony about an event can be affected by how the questions put to the witness are worded.
Lineup instructions	Police instructions can affect an eyewitness's willingness to make an identification.
Mugshot-induced bias	Exposure to mugshots of a suspect increases the likelihood that the witness will later choose that suspect in a lineup.
Confidence malleability	An eyewitness's confidence can be influenced by factors that are unrelated to identification accuracy.
Postevent information	Eyewitness testimony about an event often reflects not only what they actually saw but information they obtained later on.
Child suggestibility	Young children are more vulnerable than adults to interviewer suggestion, peer pressures, and other social influences.
Alcoholic intoxication	Alcoholic intoxication impairs an eyewitness's later ability to recall persons and events.
Cross-race bias	Eyewitnesses are more accurate when identifying members of their own race than members of other races.
Weapon focus	The presence of a weapon impairs an eyewitness's ability to accurately identify the perpetrator's face.
Accuracy-confidence	An eyewitness's confidence is not a good predictor of his or her identification accuracy.

about the entire experience can be raised or lowered by social feedback—and this makes confidence even less predictive of accuracy (Bradfield et al., 2002).

The Eyewitness Expert
Having described the problems with information obtained from eyewitnesses, social psychologists are in a position to put their knowledge to use by educating juries so they can better evaluate the evidence. But can this goal be achieved? Just like medical doctors who testify about a patient's physical condition, economists who testify on monopolies and other antitrust matters, and architectural engineers who testify on the structural integrity of buildings, psychologists are often called by one party or the other to tell the jury about relevant aspects of human perception, memory, and behavior (Leippe, 1995). What, specifically, do these experts say to the jury? What findings do they present in court? Recently, researchers surveyed sixty-four eyewitness experts, many of whose studies are described in this chapter. The principles listed in Table 12.6 were seen by the vast majority as highly reliable and worthy of expert testimony (Kassin et al., 2001).

Does the jury need to be informed? In some cases, yes. Researchers have found that there's a great deal about eyewitnesses that the average person does not know as a matter of common sense (Devenport et al., 1997). In fact, judges and lawyers themselves are not aware of many of the factors that influence eyewitnesses. Veronica Stinson and others (1996, 1997) presented large groups of Florida judges and defense lawyers with hypothetical cases that included a lineup identification that varied in important ways. In general, the judges and lawyers were able to reasonably distinguish between lineups and instructions that were fair as opposed to suggestive. But they did not understand that witnesses are more likely to pick someone from photographs—even someone innocent—when the pictures are shown all at once (which leads people to make relative judgments) than when they are shown sequentially, one at a time (which leads people to make absolute judgments). Getting it backward, the judges and lawyers criticized the sequential format for not allowing witnesses to compare photographs, which is precisely what should not be done.

 Nonevidentiary Influences

A trial is a well-orchestrated event that follows strict rules of evidence and procedure. The goal is to ensure that juries base their verdicts solely on the evidence and testimony presented in court—not on rumors, newspaper stories, a defendant's attire, and other information. The question is: To what extent is this goal achieved, and to what extent are jury verdicts tainted by nonevidentiary influences?

Pretrial Publicity   As in the high-profile trials involving the Enron executives, Andrea Yates, and Zacarias Moussaoui, many cases find their way into newspapers and other mass media long before they appear in court. In each instance, the legal system struggles with this dilemma: Does exposure to pretrial news stories corrupt the prospective jurors? Public opinion surveys consistently show that the more people know about a case, the more likely they are to presume the defendant guilty, even when they claim to be impartial (Kovera, 2002; Moran & Cutler, 1991). There is nothing mysterious about this result. The information in news reports usually comes from the police or district attorney's office, so it often reveals facts unfavorable to the defense. The question is whether these reports have an impact on juries that go on to hear evidence in court and deliberate to a verdict.

To examine the effects of pretrial publicity, Geoffrey Kramer and his colleagues (1990) played a videotaped re-enactment of an armed robbery trial to hundreds of people participating in 108 mock juries. Before watching the tape, participants were exposed to news clippings about the case. Some read news material that was neutral. Others read information that was incriminating—revealing, for example, that the defendant had a prior record or implicating him in a hit-and-run accident in which a child was killed. Even though participants were instructed to base their decisions solely on the evidence, pretrial publicity had a marked effect. Among those exposed to neutral material, 33 percent voted guilty after deliberating in a jury. Among those exposed to the prejudicial material, that figure increased to 48 percent. What's worse, neither judges nor defense lawyers could identify in a simulated voir dire which jurors were biased by the publicity. As shown in Figure 12.6, 48 percent of jurors who were questioned and perceived to be impartial—those who said they were unaffected—went on to vote guilty (Kerr et al., 1991). The impact of pretrial publicity is even more powerful when the news is seen on television rather than in print (Ogloff & Vidmar, 1994).

Pretrial publicity is potentially dangerous in two respects. First, it often divulges information that is not later allowed into the trial record. Second is the matter of timing. Because many news stories precede the actual trial, jurors learn certain facts even before they enter the courtroom. From what is known about the power of first impressions, the implications are clear. If jurors receive prejudicial news information about a defendant *before* trial, that information will distort the way they interpret the facts of the case—an effect that has been found in recent research (Hope et al., 2004). So, is there a solution? Since the biasing effects persist despite the practices of jury selection, the presentation of hard evidence, cautionary words from the judge, and

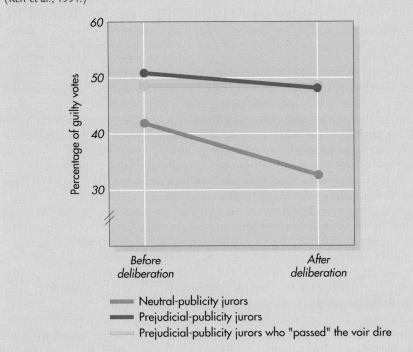

FIGURE 12.6

Contaminating Effects of Pretrial Publicity

In this study, participants were exposed to prejudicial or neutral news reports about a defendant, watched a videotaped trial, and voted before and after participating in a mock jury deliberation. As shown, pretrial publicity increased the conviction rate both before and after deliberation—even among participants perceived to be impartial by judges and lawyers.

(Kerr et al., 1991.)

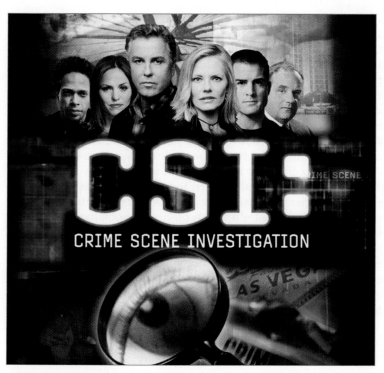

CSI, *which stands for* Crime Scene Investigation, *is a popular TV show about police investigators who collect and analyze forensic evidence. Does this show lead jurors to set unrealistic high expectations for evidence, causing them to acquit criminals? At least for now, there is no evidence to support this "CSI effect" hypothesis.*

open jury deliberations, justice may demand that highly publicized cases be postponed or moved to other, less informed communities (Steblay et al., 1999; Studebaker & Penrod, 1997).

Is it possible that juries are influenced by pre-trial publicity of a more general nature, unrelated to their specific case? Perhaps you have watched the popular television drama *CSI*, which stands for *Crime Scene Investigation* and focuses on the process by which police investigators collect and analyze fingerprints, bodily fluids, and other types of forensic evidence (the original is set in Las Vegas; spinoffs now include *CSI: Miami* and *CSI: New York*). Many legal commentators are speculating that the public's exposure to this show is influencing jury verdicts. Called the "CSI effect," the fear is that it leads jurors to hold unrealistically high expectations that cause them to vote cautiously for acquittal because they find the actual evidence insufficient to support a guilty verdict. If true, then the CSI effect would represent a special type of pretrial publicity, potentially influencing an entire population of juries. Tom Tyler (2006a) is quick to note, however, that although the hypothesis is plausible, there is at present no hard evidence to support it.

Inadmissible Testimony   Just as jurors are biased by news stories, so they occasionally receive extralegal information within the trial itself. In the 1995 trial of O. J. Simpson, who was acquitted of murder, Simpson's lawyers repeatedly referred to witnesses who would not later testify. With each passing reference, the prosecutor objected. Eventually, the judge issued a warning to Simpson's lawyers and ordered the jury to disregard the information. Then, just a few weeks later, the judge had to warn prosecutors, and again instruct the jury to disregard that information.

If something seems wrong with this series of events, you should know that it is a scene often replayed in the courtroom. But can people really strike information from their minds the way court reporters can strike it from the record? Can people on a jury resist the forbidden fruit of inadmissible testimony? Although common sense suggests they cannot, the research is mixed. In one study, a group of mock jurors read about a murder case based on evidence so weak that not a single juror voted guilty. A second group read the same case, except that the prosecution introduced an illegally obtained tape recording of a phone call made by the defendant: "I finally got the money to pay you off. . . . When you read the papers tomorrow, you'll know what I mean." The defense argued that the illegal tape should not be admissible but the judge disagreed. At this point, the conviction rate increased to 26 percent. In a third group, as in the second, the tape was brought in and the defense objected. Yet this time, the judge sustained the objection and told jurors to disregard the tape. The result: 35 percent voted for conviction (Sue et al., 1973). Other studies as well have revealed that jurors are often not deterred by "limiting instructions" (Steblay et al., 2006).

Why do people not follow a judge's order to disregard inadmissible evidence? There are a number of possible explanations (Lieberman & Arndt, 2000). Imagine yourself in the jury box, and three reasons will become apparent. First, the added instruction draws attention to the information in controversy. It's like being told not to think about white bears. As we saw in Chapter 3, trying to suppress a specific thought increases its tendency to intrude upon our consciousness (Wegner, 1994). A second reason is that a judge's instruction to disregard, much like censorship, restricts a juror's decision-making freedom. Accordingly, it can backfire by arousing reactance. Thus, when a judge emphasizes the ruling by *forbidding* jurors from using the information ("You have no choice but to disregard it"), they become even *more* likely to use it (Wolf & Montgomery, 1977). The third reason is the easiest to understand. Jurors want to reach the right decision. If they stumble onto relevant information, they want to use it whether it satisfies the law's technical rules or not. In other words, jurors find it hard to ignore information that seems relevant to a case (Wissler & Saks, 1985).

To test this third hypothesis, Kassin and Samuel Sommers (1997) had mock jurors read a transcript of a double-murder trial that was based on weak evidence, leading only 24 percent to vote guilty. Three other groups read the same case except that the state's evidence included a wiretapped phone conversation in which the defendant confessed to a friend. In all cases, the defense lawyer objected to the disclosure. When the judge ruled to admit the tape into evidence, the conviction rate increased considerably, to 79 percent. But when the judge excluded the tape and instructed jurors to disregard it, their reaction depended on the reason for the tape's being excluded. When told to disregard the tape because it was barely audible and could not be trusted, participants mentally erased the information, as they should, and delivered the same 24 percent conviction rate as in the no-tape control group. But when told to disregard the item because it had been illegally obtained, 55 percent voted guilty. Despite the judge's warning, these latter participants were unwilling to ignore testimony they saw as highly relevant merely because of a legal "technicality." Additional studies indicate that jurors in this situation may comply with a judge's instruction to disregard when the technicality involves a *serious* violation of the defendant's rights (Fleming et al., 1999)—and that the process of deliberation increases compliance, which minimizes the bias (London & Nunez, 2000).

The Judge's Instructions

One of the most important rituals in any trial is the judge's instructions to the jury. It is through these instructions that juries are educated about relevant legal concepts, informed of the verdict options, admonished to disregard extralegal factors, and advised on how to conduct their deliberations. To make verdicts adhere to the law, juries are supposed to comply with these instructions. The task seems simple enough, but there are problems.

To begin with, the jury's intellectual competence has been called into question. For years, the courts have doubted whether jurors understood their instructions. One skeptical judge put it bluntly when he said that "these words may as well be spoken in a foreign language" (Frank, 1949, p. 181). He may well have been right. When actual instructions are tested with community mock jurors, the results reveal high levels of misunderstanding—a serious problem in light of the fact that jurors seem to have many preconceptions about crimes and the requirements of the law. Comprehensibility is even problematic when it comes to the death penalty instructions that are required in capital cases (Wiener et al., 1995) and for college students as well as ordinary jurors from the community (Rose & Ogloff, 2001). There is, however, reason for hope. Research has shown that when conventional instructions—which are poorly structured, esoteric, and filled with complex legal terms—are rewritten in plain English, comprehension rates increase markedly (Elwork et al., 1982; English & Sales, 1997). Also effective is to supplement a judge's instructions with flow charts, computer animations, and other audiovisual aids (Brewer et al., 2004).

A lack of comprehension is one reason that a judge's instruction may have little impact. But there's a second reason: Sometimes juries disagree with the law, thus raising the controversial issue of **jury nullification**. You may not realize it, but juries, because they deliberate in private, can choose to disregard, or "nullify," the judge's instructions. The pages of history are filled with poignant examples. Consider the case of someone tried for euthanasia, or "mercy killing." By law, it is murder. But to the defendant, it might be a noble act on behalf of a loved one. Faced with this kind of conflict—an explosive moral issue on which public opinion is sharply divided—juries often evaluate the issue in human terms, use their own notions of common-sense justice, and vote despite the law for acquittal (Finkel, 1995; Horowitz & Willging, 1991; Niedermeier et al., 1999). This nullification tendency is particularly likely to occur when jurors who disagree with the law are informed of their right to nullify it (Meissner et al., 2003).

Jury nullification is what happened in cases pertaining to physician-assisted suicide, as was practiced by Jack Kevorkian, a retired pathologist. During the 1990s, Kevorkian presided over 130 deaths. For three of these incidents, he was tried for

jury nullification The jury's power to disregard, or "nullify," the law when it conflicts with personal conceptions of justice.

In this Detroit Courtroom, Dr. Jack Kevorkian was tried for an assisted suicide. Although physician-assisted suicide is illegal in Michigan, the jury in this case "nullified" the law in favor of its own conceptions of justice and voted not guilty. However, Kevorkian was eventually convicted and sent to prison.

murder and the juries, sympathetic to his plight, practiced nullification and acquitted him. Then he injected a terminally ill man with a lethal dose of drugs, videotaped the death, gave the tape to CBS-TV news, and again challenged authorities to take him to court. They did, and in 1999, after having defied the law in the boldest of ways, Kevorkian was found guilty. He was Prisoner #284797 in a Michigan state prison until he was released on parole in June 2007.

Jury Deliberation

Anyone who has seen the original *Twelve Angry Men* can appreciate how colorful and passionate a jury's deliberation can be. This film classic opens with a jury eager to convict a young man of murder—no ifs, ands, or buts. The group selects a foreperson and takes a show-of-hands vote. The result is an 11-to-1 majority, with actor Henry

In the classic movie Twelve Angry Men, *Henry Fonda plays a lone juror who single-handedly converts his eleven guilty-voting peers to vote for acquittal. Sometimes life imitates art; in this case, it does not. Research shows that majorities on the first jury vote usually prevail in the final verdict.*

Fonda the lone dissenter. After many tense moments, Fonda manages to convert his peers, and the jury votes unanimously for acquittal.

It is often said that the unique power of the jury stems from the wisdom that emerges when individuals come together privately as one *group*. Is this assumption justified? *Twelve Angry Men* is a work of fiction, but does it realistically portray what transpires in the jury room? And in what ways does the legal system influence the group dynamics? By interviewing jurors after trials, and by recruiting people to participate on mock juries and then recording their deliberations, researchers have learned a great deal about how juries make their decisions.

Leadership in the Jury Room

In theory, all jurors are created equal. In practice, however, dominance hierarchies tend to develop. As in other decision-making groups, a handful of individuals lead the discussion, while others join in at a lower rate or watch from the sidelines, speaking only to cast their votes (Hastie et al., 1983). It's almost as if there is a jury within the jury. The question is, what kinds of people emerge as leaders?

It is often assumed that the foreperson is the leader. The foreperson, after all, calls for votes, acts as a liaison between the judge and jury, and announces the verdict in court. It seems like a position of importance, yet the selection process is very quick and casual. It's interesting that foreperson selection outcomes do follow a predictable pattern (Stasser et al., 1982). People of higher occupational status or with prior experience on a jury are frequently chosen. Interestingly too, the first person who speaks is often chosen to be the foreperson (Strodtbeck et al., 1957). And when jurors deliberate around a rectangular table, those who sit at the heads of the table are more likely to be chosen than are those seated in the middle (Bray et al., 1978; Strodtbeck & Hook, 1961).

If you find such inequalities bothersome, fear not: Forepersons may act as nominal leaders, but they do *not* exert more than their fair share of influence over the group. In fact, although they spend more time than other jurors talking about procedural matters, they spend less time expressing opinions on the verdict (Hastie et al., 1983). Thus, it may be most accurate to think of the foreperson not as the jury's leader but as its moderator. In *Twelve Angry Men*, actor Martin Balsam—not Henry Fonda—was the foreperson. He was also among the least influential members of the jury.

The Dynamics of Deliberation

If the walls of the jury room could talk, they would tell us that the decision-making process typically passes through three stages (Hastie et al., 1983; Stasser et al., 1982). Like other problem-solving groups, juries begin in a relaxed *orientation* period during which they set an agenda, talk in open-ended terms, raise questions, and explore the facts. Then, once differences of opinion are revealed—usually after the first vote is taken—factions develop, and the group shifts abruptly into a period of *open conflict*. With the battle lines sharply drawn, discussion takes on a more focused, argumentative tone. Together, jurors scrutinize the evidence, construct stories to account for that evidence, and discuss the judge's instructions (Pennington & Hastie, 1992). If all jurors agree, they return a verdict. If not, the

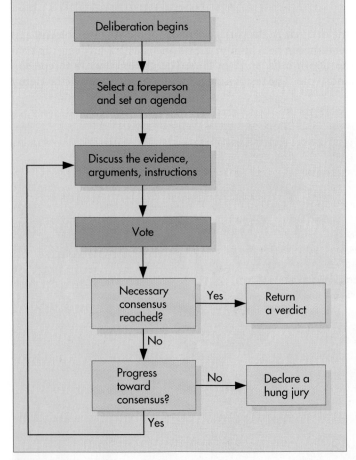

FIGURE 12.7

Jury Deliberations: The Process

Juries move through various tasks en route to a verdict. They begin by setting and reviewing the case. If all jurors agree, they return a verdict. If not, they continue to discuss the case until they reach a consensus. If the holdouts refuse to vote with the majority, the jury becomes deadlocked.

TABLE 12.7
The Road to Agreement: From Individual Votes to a Group Verdict

Research has shown how verdicts are reached by mock juries that begin with different combinations of initial votes. You can see that the results support the majority-wins rule. But also note the evidence for a leniency bias: When the initial vote is split, juries gravitate toward acquittal.

(Kerr, 1981, as cited in Stasser et al., 1982.)

Initial Votes (Guilty–Not Guilty)	Final Jury Verdicts (percent)		
	Conviction	Acquittal	Hung
6–0	100	0	0
5–1	78	7	16
4–2	44	26	30
3–3	9	51	40
2–4	4	79	17
1–5	0	93	7
0–6	0	100	0

One can usually predict a jury's final verdict by knowing where the individual jurors stand the first time they vote. **True.**

leniency bias The tendency for jury deliberation to produce a tilt toward acquittal.

majority tries to achieve a consensus by converting the holdouts through information and social pressure. If unanimity is achieved, the group enters a period of *reconciliation,* during which it smoothes over the conflicts and affirms its satisfaction with the outcome. If the holdouts continue to disagree, the jury declares itself hung. This process is diagrammed in Figure 12.7.

When it comes to decision-making *outcomes,* deliberations follow a predictable course first discovered by Harry Kalven and Hans Zeisel (1966). By interviewing the members of 225 juries, they were able to reconstruct how these juries split on their very first vote. Out of 215 juries that opened with an initial majority, 209 reached a final verdict consistent with that first vote. This finding—later bolstered by the results of mock jury studies (Kerr, 1981; Stasser & Davis, 1981; see Table 12.7)—led Kalven and Zeisel to conclude that "the deliberation process might well be likened to what the developer does for an exposed film; it brings out the picture, but the outcome is predetermined" (1966, p. 489). Henry Fonda's *Twelve Angry Men* heroics notwithstanding, one can usually predict the final verdict by knowing where the individual jurors stand the first time they vote. Juries are not generally more or less subject to bias than the individuals who constitute the groups (Kerr et al., 1999). Hence, "majority rules" seems to describe what happens not only in juries but in most other small decision-making groups (Hastie & Kameda, 2005).

There is one exception to this majority-wins rule in the jury room. It is that in criminal trials, deliberation tends to produce a **leniency bias** favoring the defendant. All other factors being equal, individual jurors are more likely to vote guilty on their own than in a group; they are also more prone to convict before deliberations than after (MacCoun & Kerr, 1988). Look again at Table 12.7, and you'll see that juries that are equally divided in their initial vote are ultimately likely to return not-guilty verdicts. Perhaps it is easier to raise a "reasonable doubt" in other people's minds than to erase all doubt. In this regard, it is interesting to note that in their classic study entitled *The American Jury* (1966), Kalven and Zeisel surveyed 555 judges who reported how they would have voted in some 3,500 jury trials. Judges agreed with their juries 78 percent of the time. When they disagreed, it was usually because the jury acquitted a defendant thought to be guilty by the judge. Perhaps these disagreements are due, in part, to the fact that juries decide as groups, and judges, as individuals.

Knowing that the majority tends to prevail doesn't tell us how juries manage to resolve disagreements en route to a verdict. From the conformity studies discussed in Chapter 7, we know that there are two possibilities. Sometimes, people conform because, through a process of *informational influence,* they are genuinely persuaded by what others say. At other times, people yield to the pressures of *normative influence* by changing their overt behavior in the majority's direction even though they disagree in private. When it comes to the decision making of juries, justice demands that they reach a consensus through a vigorous exchange of views and information, not by heavy-handed social pressure. But is that how it works? Research shows that juries achieve unanimity not by one process or the other but by a combination of both (Kaplan & Schersching, 1981). Research also shows that certain factors can upset the delicate balance between informational and normative influence. Social pressure is increased, for example, in juries that vote by a public roll call or show of hands (Davis et al., 1989) and in deadlocked juries that are called back into the courtroom and urged by the judge to resolve their differences (Smith & Kassin, 1993).

Over the years, the U.S. Supreme Court has in two ways addressed the decision-making dynamics of the jury. In the following pages, we look at these important issues and what they mean.

Jury Size: How Small Is Too Small?

How many people does it take to form a jury? In keeping with British tradition, twelve has been the magic number. Then, in the case of *Williams v. Florida* (1970), the defendant was convicted of armed robbery by a six-person jury. He appealed the verdict to the U.S. Supreme Court but lost. As a result of this precedent, American courts are now permitted to cut trial costs by using six-person juries in cases that do not involve the death penalty. Juries consisting of fewer than six are not permitted (*Ballew v. Georgia,* 1978).

What is the impact of moving from twelve to six? The Supreme Court approached this question as a social psychologist would. It sought to determine whether the change would affect the decision-making process. Unfortunately, the Court misinterpreted the available research so badly that Michael Saks concluded it "would not win a passing grade in a high school psychology class" (1974, p. 18). Consider whether a reduction in size affects the ability of those in the voting minority to resist normative pressures. The Supreme Court did not think it would. Citing Asch's (1956) conformity studies, the Court argued that an individual juror's resistance depends on the *proportional* size of the majority. But is that true? Is the lone dissenter caught in a 5-to-1 bind as well insulated from the group norm as the minority in a 10-to-2 split? The Court argued that these 83-to-17 percent divisions are psychologically identical. But wait. Asch's research showed exactly the opposite—that the mere presence of a single ally enables dissenters to keep their independence better than anything else. Research has shown that the size of a jury has other effects too. Michael Saks and Molli Marti (1997) conducted a meta-analysis of studies involving fifteen thousand mock jurors who deliberated in over two thousand six-person or twelve-person juries. Overall, they found that the smaller juries were less likely to represent minority segments of the population. They were also more likely to reach a unanimous verdict and to do so despite deliberating for shorter periods of time. Even in civil trials, in which juries have to make complex decisions on how much money to award the plaintiff, six-person groups spend less time discussing the case (Davis et al., 1997).

Less-Than-Unanimous Verdicts

The jury's size is not all that has changed. In 1972, the Supreme Court considered whether states may accept jury verdicts that are not unanimous. In one opinion, two defendants had been convicted by non-unanimous juries—one by a vote of 11 to 1, the other by 10 to 2 (*Apodaca v. Oregon,* 1972). In a second opinion, a guilty verdict was determined by a 9-to-3 margin (*Johnson v. Louisiana,* 1972). In both decisions, the Supreme Court upheld the convictions.

The Court was divided in its view of these cases. Five justices argued that a non-unanimous decision rule would not adversely affect the jury; four justices believed that it would reduce the intensity of deliberations and undermine the potential for minority influence. Table 12.8 presents these dueling points of view. Which do you find more convincing? Imagine yourself on a jury that needs only a 9-to-3 majority to return a verdict. You begin by polling the group and find that you already have the nine votes needed. What next? According to one script, the group continues to argue vigorously and with open minds. According to the alternative scenario, the group begins to deliberate, but the dissenters are quickly cast aside because their votes are not needed. Again, which scenario seems more realistic?

To answer that question, Reid Hastie and others (1983) recruited more than eight hundred people from the Boston area to take part in sixty-nine mock juries. After watching a reenactment of a murder trial, the groups were instructed to reach a verdict by a 12-to-0, a 10-to-2, or an 8-to-4 margin. The differences were striking. Compared with juries needing unanimous decisions, the others spent less time discussing the case and more time voting. After reaching the required number of votes, they often rejected the holdouts, terminated discussion, and returned a verdict. Afterward, participants in the non-unanimous juries rated their peers as more close-minded and themselves as less informed and less confident about the verdict. What's worse, Hastie's

TABLE 12.8
Johnson v. Louisiana (1972): Contrasting Views

Notice the contrasting views in the U.S. Supreme Court's decision to permit non-unanimous jury verdicts. Justice White wrote the majority opinion, and Justice Douglas wrote the dissent. The decision was reached by a vote of 5 to 4.

Mr. Justice White, for the Majority:

We have no grounds for believing that majority jurors, aware of their responsibility and power over the liberty of the defendant, would simply refuse to listen to arguments presented to them in favor of acquittal, terminate discussion, and render a verdict. On the contrary, it is far more likely that a juror presenting reasoned argument in favor of acquittal could either have his arguments answered or would carry enough other jurors with him to prevent conviction. A majority will cease discussion and outvote a minority only after reasoned discussion has ceased to have persuasive effect or to serve any other purpose—when a minority, that is, continues to insist upon acquittal without having persuasive reasons in support of its position.

Mr. Justice Douglas, for the Minority:

Non-unanimous juries need not debate and deliberate as fully as most unanimous juries. As soon as the requisite majority is attained, further consideration is not required either by Oregon or by Louisiana even though the dissident jurors might, if given the chance, be able to convince the majority. . . . The collective effort to piece together the puzzle of historical truth . . . is cut short as soon as the requisite majority is reached in Oregon and Louisiana. . . . It is said that there is no evidence that majority jurors will refuse to listen to dissenters whose votes are unneeded for conviction. Yet human experience teaches us that polite and academic conversation is no substitute for the earnest and robust argument necessary to reach unanimity.

team saw in tapes of the deliberations that majority-rule juries often adopted "a more forceful, bullying, persuasive style" (1983, p. 112). After being permitted to videotape fifty non-unanimous civil juries in Arizona, Shari Diamond and colleagues (2006) similarly observed that thoughtful minorities were sometimes "marginalized" by majorities that had the power to ignore them.

Today, only two states permit less-than-unanimous verdicts in criminal trials. A substantial number do so for civil cases. Yet research has shown that this procedure weakens jurors who are in the voting minority, breeds close-mindedness, short-circuits the discussion, and leaves many jurors uncertain about the decision. Henry Fonda, step aside. The jury has reached its verdict.

Posttrial: To Prison and Beyond

After conspiring in a series of cold-blooded killings, most at gas stations and convenience stores, D.C. snipers Muhammad, forty-two, and Malvo, eighteen, were caught and tried by Virginia juries. Their crimes were identical. Yet while Muhammad's jury sentenced him to death in November of 2003, Malvo's jury sentenced him to life in prison one month later. Both supporters and opponents of the death penalty complained of the disparity. But did the different sentences reflect on the capricious nature of jury decision making (some had suggested that Malvo benefited from a jury's charitable spirit the week of Christmas), or were the differences rationally and morally based on the fact that Muhammad was older and more in control—the "mastermind," not the "puppet"?

Based on current rates, an estimated 5 percent of all Americans (9 percent of men, 1 percent of women) will serve prison time in the course of their lives.

 **The Sentencing Process**

For defendants convicted of crimes, the jury's verdict is followed by a sentence. Sentencing decisions are usually made by judges, not juries, and they are often controversial. One reason for the controversy is that many people see judges as being too lenient (Stalans & Diamond, 1990). Another is that people disagree on the goals served by imprisonment. For many judges, the goal of a prison sentence is a practical one:

to incapacitate offenders and deter them from committing future crimes. For many citizens, however, there is a more powerful motive at work: to exact retribution, or revenge, against the offender for his or her misdeeds. Research shows that people are driven by this "just deserts" motive, recommending sentences of increasing harshness for crimes of increasing severity—regardless of whether the offender is seen as likely to strike again and regardless of whether such sentences deter crime or serve other useful purposes (Carlsmith et al., 2002; Carlsmith, 2006; Darley et al., 2000; Darley & Pittman, 2003).

Judges also disagree about issues related to sentencing. Thus, a recurring public complaint is that there is too much **sentencing disparity**—that punishments for crime are inconsistent from one judge to the next. To document the problem, Anthony Partridge and William Eldridge (1974) compiled identical sets of files from twenty actual cases, sent them to fifty federal judges, and found major disparities in the sentences they said they would impose. In one case, for example, judges had read about a man who was convicted of extortion and tax evasion. One judge recommended a three-year prison sentence, while another recommended twenty years in prison and a fine of $65,000. It's hard to believe these two judges read the same case. But other studies have uncovered similar differences.

Some judges are unusually "creative" in their sentencing of convicted felons. For example, a judge in Houston ordered a piano teacher who molested two students to donate his piano to a local school, a South Dakota judge sentenced cattle rustlers to shovel manure for a week, and a Florida judge ordered drunk drivers to display a bumper sticker on their cars that said "Convicted DUI" (Greene et al., 2006). In recent years, the federal government and many state governments have created sentencing guidelines to minimize the disparities and bring greater consistency to the process (Ruback & Wroblewski, 2001).

Still, sentencing decisions can be influenced by irrelevant factors. For example, Birte Englich and others (2006) theorized that judges would be influenced by the well-known "anchoring effect"—the tendency to use one stimulus as an "anchor," or reference point, in judging a second stimulus (Tversky & Kahneman, 1974). In a series of studies conducted in Germany, these researchers presented legal professionals—mostly judges—with materials about a criminal case. All participants received the same file except that some files suggested a low sentencing number (one year) and others suggested a high number (three years). Regardless of whether the number was presented as a prosecutor's recommendation, a question from a journalist, or a random roll of the dice, those first exposed to the high anchor point assigned harsher sentences than those exposed to the lower anchor point.

Some influences on this very human decision-making process are even more disturbing. By combing through U.S. death penalty statistics, researchers long ago discovered that sentencing decisions are consistently biased by race: All else being equal, convicted murderers are more likely to be sentenced to death if they are black or if the victim is white (Baldus et al., 1990). Informed by the racial stereotyping studies we saw in Chapter 5, Jennifer Eberhardt and her colleagues (2006) revisited a number of capital cases involving black defendants, this time looking for an even more subtle effect. For each case, they obtained a photograph of the defendant and had college students rate the degree to which he had a stereotypically black appearance—for example, a broad nose, thick lips, and dark skin. Using these ratings, they found that when the victim was black, the defendant's appearance was unrelated to sentencing. When the victim was white, however, the death penalty odds were predictable by the blackness of the defendant's appearance (24 percent among the least stereotypical; 58 percent among the most stereotypical). It seems that there are shades of black that influence whether judges and juries perceive defendants to be "deathworthy."

The Prison Experience

It is no secret that many prisons are overcrowded and that the situation has worsened as a result of recently toughened sentencing guidelines. It is also no secret that prison life can be cruel, violent, and degrading. The setting is highly oppressive and regimented, many prison guards are abusive, and many inmates fall into a state of

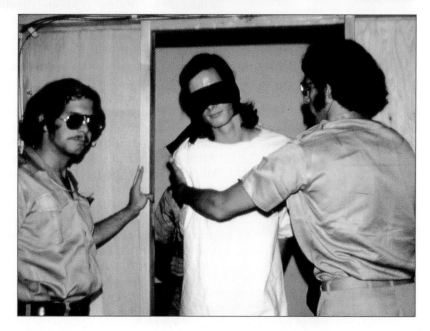

In this simulation study of prison behavior, subjects were arbitrarily assigned to be prisoners or guards. Local police officers arrested the prisoner, who was brought to a jail constructed at Stanford University. After several days, the guards took on cruel, authoritarian roles that demoralized the prisoners to such an extent that the experiment was terminated.

despair (Paulus, 1988). Indeed, many are psychologically disturbed and in need of treatment they do not receive (Kupers, 1999). Thus, it is natural for social psychologists to wonder: Is there something in the situation that leads guards and prisoners to behave as they do? Would the rest of us react in the same way?

For ethical reasons, one obviously cannot place research participants inside a real prison. So, many years ago, a team of researchers from Stanford University did the next best thing. They constructed their own prison in the basement of the psychology department building (Haney et al., 1973; Haney & Zimbardo, 1998; Zimbardo et al., 1973). Complete with iron-barred cells, a solitary-confinement closet, and a recreation area for guards, the facility housed twenty-one participants—all healthy and stable men between the ages of seventeen and thirty who had answered a newspaper ad promising fifteen dollars a day for a two-week study of prison life. By the flip of a coin, half the participants were designated as guards; the other half became prisoners. Neither group was told specifically how to fulfill its role.

On the first day, each of the participant prisoners was unexpectedly "arrested" at his home, booked, fingerprinted, and driven to the simulated prison by officers of the local police department. These prisoners were then stripped, searched, and dressed in loose-fitting smocks with an identification number, a nylon stocking to cover their hair, rubber sandals, and a chain bolted to the ankle. The guards were dressed in khaki uniforms and supplied with nightsticks, handcuffs, reflector sunglasses, keys, and whistles. The rules specified that prisoners were to be called by number, routinely lined up to be counted, fed three bland meals, and permitted three supervised toilet visits per day. The stage was set. It remained to be seen just how seriously the participants would take their roles and react to one another in this novel setting.

The events of the next few days were startling. Filled with a sense of power and authority, a few guards became progressively more abusive. They harassed the inmates, forced them into crowded cells, woke them during the night, and subjected them to hard labor and solitary confinement. These guards were particularly cruel when they thought they were alone with a prisoner. The prisoners themselves were rebellious at first, but their efforts were met with retaliation. Soon they all became passive and demoralized. After thirty-six hours, the experimenters had to release their first prisoner, who was suffering from acute depression. On subsequent days, other prisoners had to be released. By the sixth day, those who remained were so shaken by the experience that the study was terminated. It is reassuring, if not remarkable, that after a series of debriefing sessions, participants seemed to show no signs of lasting distress.

This study has been criticized on both methodological and ethical grounds (Banuazizi & Movahedi, 1975; Savin, 1973). Still, the results are impressive. Within a brief period of time, under relatively mild conditions, and with a group of men not prone to violence, the Stanford study recreated some of the prisoner and guard behaviors actually found behind prison walls. But would this occur today, in the twenty-first century? To find out, social psychologists Alex Haslam and Steve Reicher worked in the spring of 2002 with the British Broadcasting Corporation, or BBC, to create a survivor-like reality TV special called "The Experiment," modeled after Zimbardo's study. Shown in four episodes, they brought together fifteen men, all carefully screened, forewarned that they would be exposed to hardships, and randomly assigned to prisoner and guard roles. Determined to set limits, monitor events closely, and adhere to ethical guidelines for research with human subjects, Haslam and Reicher did not fully recreate the conditions of the original study and did not observe the same kinds of brutality from the guards. In their view, these findings challenge the conclusion that normal people could so easily be dehumanized by institutional roles (for more information, visit the BBC Web site at www.bbc.co.uk/science/theexperiment/). Yet Zimbardo is quick to note the striking parallels between behavior in his simulated prison and the disturbing abuses of prisoners perpetrated in 2004 by military guards at the Abu Ghraib Prison in Iraq (for this perspective, visit www.prisonexp.org; also see Zimbardo, 2007).

Perceptions of Justice

People tend to measure the success of a legal system by its ability to produce fair and accurate results. But is that all there is to justice? Let's step back for a moment from the specifics and ask if it is possible to define justice in a way that is unrelated to outcomes.

Justice as a Matter of Procedure

In a book entitled *Procedural Justice* (1975), John Thibaut and Laurens Walker proposed that our satisfaction with the way legal and other disputes are resolved depends not only on outcomes but also on the procedures used to achieve those outcomes. Two aspects of procedure are important in this regard: One is *decision control*—whether a procedure affords the involved parties the power to accept, reject, or otherwise influence the final decision. The other is *process control*—whether it offers the parties an opportunity to present their case to a third-party decision maker. In the courtroom, of course, the disputants are limited in their decision control. Thus, their satisfaction must depend on whether they feel that they had a chance to express their views.

There are two ways to look at the effects of process control on perceptions of justice. Originally, it was thought that people want an opportunity to express their opinions only because having a voice in the process improves the odds of achieving a favorable ruling. In this view, process control is satisfying only because it increases decision control (Thibaut & Walker, 1978). Recent research, however, suggests that people value the chance to present their side of a story to an impartial decision maker even when they do not prevail in the ultimate outcome. In other words, process control is more than just an instrumental means to an end. When people believe that they had a voice in the proceedings, were treated with respect, and were judged by an impartial decision maker, process control can be an end in itself (Lind et al., 1990).

This aspect of the legal system is very important. It means, for example, that regardless of whether people agree or disagree with how a case turns out, they can find solace in the fact that both sides had their "day in court"—at least when the decision maker is seen as impartial. Yet certain members of the legal community are openly critical of that so-called day in court. As law professor Alan Dershowitz once put it, "Nobody really wants justice. Winning is the only thing to most participants in the criminal justice system, just as it is to professional athletes" (1982, p. xvi). Dershowitz's skepticism is centered on something that many of us take for granted: the **adversarial model** of justice. In the adversarial system (as practiced in North America, Great Britain, and a handful of other countries) the prosecution and defense oppose each other, each presenting one side of the story in an effort to win a favorable verdict. In contrast, most other countries use an **inquisitorial model**, in which a neutral investigator gathers the evidence from both sides and presents the findings in court. With two such different methods of doing justice, social psychologists could not resist the temptation to make comparisons. Which system, they ask, do people prefer?

To find out, Laurens Walker and others (1974) constructed a business simulation in which two companies competed for a cash prize. Assigned to the role of president of a company, participants learned that someone on their staff was accused of spying on the competition. To resolve the dispute, a "trial" was held. In some cases, the trial followed an adversarial procedure in which the two sides were presented by law students who were chosen by participants and whose payment was contingent on winning. Other cases followed an inquisitorial model in which a single law student who was appointed by the experimenter and paid regardless of the outcome presented both sides. Regardless of whether they had won or lost the verdict, participants who took part in an adversarial trial were more satisfied than those involved in an inquisitorial trial. Even impartial observers preferred the adversarial proceedings.

Other researchers found similar results, not only in the United States and Great Britain, where citizens are accustomed to the adversarial system, but in France and West Germany as well (Lind et al., 1978). This perception of procedural justice is not limited to adversarial methods of resolving legal disputes. Rather, it seems that any method that offers participants a *voice* in the proceedings, including methods that are nonadversarial, is seen as most fair and just—not only in law, but also in business, politics, school settings, and intimate relationships (Folger & Greenberg, 1985; Sheppard, 1985). Also important in this regard is for people to perceive that they were granted as much "voice" as others were (Van Prooijen et al., 2006) and that the decision maker was open-minded and not acting out of self-interest (De Cremer, 2004). In matters of justice, people all over the world are motivated not only by the desire for personal gain but by their need to be recognized, respected, and treated fairly by others who are impartial. Research thus shows that for people to accept the rule of law and comply with outcomes they do not like, they must see the decision-making procedures as fair (Tyler, 2006b).

 ## Culture, Law, and Justice

When it comes to the basics of human behavior, much of the research in this chapter can be universally applied. In police interrogations, suspects all over the world, including some who are innocent, are more likely to confess when they are isolated and intensely pressured than when they are not. In eyewitness testimony, the problems and limitations of human memory—as seen in our ability to accurately perceive, store, and retrieve certain types of information—are universal. In courtrooms wherever juries are used, their decision making will invariably reflect the joint influences of their personal dispositions, the information they receive in court, and the

adversarial model
A dispute-resolution system in which the prosecution and defense present opposing sides of the story.

inquisitorial model
A dispute-resolution system in which a neutral investigator gathers evidence from both sides and presents the findings in court.

conformity dynamics that seize hold of small groups. Finally, recurring stories of prison abuses have shown that prison is a social setting that tends to bring out the worst in guards and their prisoners—wherever they are.

Although the similarities are clear, they should not mask important cross-cultural differences. Because cultures have different norms, customs, and values, they also create different laws to regulate their citizens' behavior. To be sure, certain universal values have evolved among humans and are passed from one generation to the next—such as the prohibitions against physical violence, the taking of someone's property without consent, and deception in important transactions. In other ways, however, the world's cultural and religious groups differ markedly in the behaviors that they scorn and seek to regulate. In some countries but not in others, it is against the law to have sex outside of marriage, take more than one husband or wife, assist in a suicide, gamble, eat meat, or drink alcohol. Based on the belief in an afterlife, some religions prohibit autopsies. Others impose strict dress codes, particularly for women.

In diverse populations such as the United States, these cultural practices can put governments and cultures into conflict with one another. In one highly publicized case, a Japanese woman living in California was prosecuted for drowning her two children in the Pacific Ocean before being rescued trying to drown herself. At trial, she testified that she had tried to commit 'oyaku-shinju, a Japanese custom of parent-child suicide, after learning that her husband was having an affair. Her motive, she said, was to save her children from the shame that their father had brought to the family. In a second case, a Navajo defendant was prosecuted for using the hallucinogen peyote, an illegal substance in the United States. He argued that the substance is used to achieve spiritual exaltation and should be protected by the freedom of religion (immigrants from Yemen, Kenya, and Somalia have similarly been arrested for chewing native Khat leaves in social gatherings, the way Americans chew tobacco, even though the effect is comparable to drinking three espressos). In a third case, two Cambodian immigrants were prosecuted for trying to eat a four-month-old puppy, an acceptable practice in their homeland but not in the United States. As these examples illustrate, judges and juries are sometimes asked to consider *cultural defenses* in their decision making (Renteln, 2004).

Just as nations differ in the crime laws that are set, the study of *comparative law* shows that they also differ in the processes used to enforce these laws. In Great Britain, the United States, Canada, and Australia, the accused has a right to be tried by a jury composed of fellow citizens. In France, Russia, and Brazil, that right is reserved for only the most serious crimes. In India and throughout Asia, all defendants are tried by professional judges, not juries. Yet China recently introduced mixed panels consisting of one judge and two lay jurors. Beginning in 2009, Japan will also start using a quasi-jury system, called *saiban-in*, in which three law-trained judges and six lay citizens chosen by lottery will come together to render verdicts and sentencing decisions by a majority vote. Ever since juries were abolished during World War II, all Japanese defendants have been tried by three-judge panels; almost all have been convicted, typically after confessing to save face and minimize embarrassment to the family.

For people judged guilty of serious crimes, the consequences may also vary from one country to another. The most notable difference concerns the death penalty. When Iraq's ex-president Saddam Hussein was executed by hanging in December of 2006, many world leaders, including many of Hussein's enemies, took the opportunity to condemn the execution and, more generally, capital punishment. According to Amnesty International, there are substantial differences of opinion and practice across the world regarding the death penalty (http://www.amnesty.org/). Currently, eighty-six countries prohibit the death penalty for all crimes (Australia, Austria, Belgium, Canada, Colombia, Denmark, England, France, Germany, Greece, Ireland, Italy, Mexico, the Netherlands, Norway, Portugal, Spain, Sweden, Switzerland, Turkey, and Venezuela are prominent examples); eleven ban the death penalty as a general rule but permit it for exceptional crimes, like espionage, or crimes committed in exceptional circumstances (Brazil, Chile, Israel, and Peru are some examples); twenty-six countries allow for the death penalty in law but do not execute people as a matter of practice (Algeria, Kenya, Morocco, and Russia are some examples); and seventy-three countries permit and use the death penalty (in addition to the United States, they include China, Cuba, Egypt, Iran, Iraq, India, Japan, Pakistan, Saudi Arabia, and Thailand). On matters of crime and punishment, it is clear that cultural influences are substantial.

Closing Statement

This chapter focuses on the trial process, the events that precede it, and the events that follow from it. Yet we've only scratched the surface. In recent years, more and more judges, lawyers, and policy makers have come to recognize that social psychology can make important contributions to the legal system. Thus, with increasing frequency, social psychologists are called on for expert advice in and out of court and are cited in the opinions written by judges. Clearly, the collection, presentation, and evaluation of evidence are imperfect human enterprises and subject to bias. Through an understanding of social psychology, however, we can now identify some of the problems—and perhaps even the solutions.

REVIEW

- Embedded in a large criminal justice system, relatively few cases come to trial.

- Yet the trial is the heart and soul of the system.

Jury Selection

- Once called for service, prospective jurors are questioned by the judge or lawyers in a process known as voir dire.

- Those who exhibit a clear bias are excluded. Lawyers may also strike a limited number through the use of peremptory challenges.

Trial Lawyers as Intuitive Psychologists

- Pressured to make juror selections quickly, lawyers rely on implicit personality theories and stereotypes.

- But general demographic factors do not reliably predict how jurors will vote.

Scientific Jury Selection

- Lawyers sometimes hire psychologists to conduct surveys that identify correlations between demographics and trial-relevant attitudes.

- Scientific jury selection raises ethical issues concerning its effects on justice.

Juries in Black and White: Does Race Matter?

- On the question of whether race influences a juror's decision making, research suggests that there is no simple answer.

- Whether jurors are biased by race may depend on the strength of the evidence, the extent to which attention is drawn to race, and the diversity of the jury as a whole.

Death Qualification

- In capital cases, prospective jurors who say they would not vote for the death penalty are excluded in a process known as death qualification.

- Jurors who favor the death penalty are more likely to find defendants guilty than are jurors who oppose the death penalty.

The Courtroom Drama

- Once the jury is selected, evidence previously gathered is presented in court.

Confession Evidence

- The police employ various methods of interrogation.

- One method is to befriend the suspect and "minimize" the offense; a second is to scare the suspect into believing that it is futile to deny the charges.

- Under pressure, people sometimes confess to crimes they did not commit.

- Although juries are supposed to reject coerced confessions, their verdicts are still influenced by such evidence.

The Lie-Detector Test

- By recording physiological arousal, the polygraph can be used as a lie-detector.

- Polygraphers report high rates of accuracy; but truthful persons are too often judged guilty, and the test can be fooled.

Eyewitness Testimony

- Eyewitness memory is a three-stage process involving acquisition, storage, and retrieval.

- During acquisition, witnesses who are highly aroused zoom in on the central features of an event but lose memory for peripheral details.

- The presence of a weapon hinders a witness's ability to identify the perpetrator.

- Witnesses have trouble recognizing members of a race other than their own.

- During storage, misleading postevent information biases eyewitness memory.

- Young children are particularly suggestible in this regard.
- Lineups are biased when a suspect is distinctive, when the police imply that the criminal is in the lineup, when witnesses make relative judgments, and when the suspect is familiar for other reasons.
- In court, jurors overestimate eyewitnesses' accuracy and cannot distinguish between accurate and inaccurate witnesses.
- People are too readily persuaded by a witness's confidence—a factor that does not reliably predict identification accuracy.
- Psychologists are sometimes called to testify as experts on eyewitness evidence.

Nonevidentiary Influences

- The more pretrial knowledge people have about a case, the more likely they are to presume the defendant guilty.

- Research shows that pretrial publicity can bias jury verdicts.
- Once inadmissible testimony leaks out in court, the jury is contaminated by it.
- A judge's cautionary instruction may worsen the situation by drawing attention to the forbidden testimony, arousing reactance, or leading jurors to see the information as relevant.

The Judge's Instructions

- The judge's instructions often have little impact, in part because they are often incomprehensible.
- The instructions are usually delivered after the evidence, after many jurors have formed an opinion.
- Jurors may not follow instructions that conflict with their own conceptions of justice, a phenomenon known as jury nullification.

Jury Deliberation

Leadership in the Jury Room

- Dominance hierarchies develop in the jury room.
- Certain people are more likely than others to be elected foreperson, but the foreperson tends to play the role of moderator rather than group leader.

The Dynamics of Deliberation

- Jury deliberations pass through three stages: orientation, open conflict, and reconciliation.
- The period of open conflict is filled with informational and normative pressures.
- When it comes to outcomes, the initial majority typically wins, although deliberation tends to produce a leniency bias.

Jury Size: How Small Is Too Small?

- The U.S. Supreme Court has ruled that the use of six-person juries is acceptable.
- But these smaller groups do not deliberate for as long as twelve-person juries and contain less minority representation.

Less-Than-Unanimous Verdicts

- In some states, juries are permitted to reach verdicts by a less-than-unanimous majority.
- But research shows that once a required majority is reached, these juries reject the holdouts, terminate discussion, and return a verdict.

Posttrial: To Prison and Beyond

The Sentencing Process

- Many people believe that judges are too lenient and that punishments for the same offense are often inconsistent from one case to another.
- Part of the problem is that people have different views of the goals of sentencing and punishment.

The Prison Experience

- Stanford researchers built a simulated prison and recruited male adults to act as guards and prisoners.
- Some guards were abusive, prisoners became passive, and the study had to be terminated.

Perceptions of Justice

Justice as a Matter of Procedure

- Satisfaction with justice depends not only on winning and losing but also on the procedures used to achieve the outcome.
- People of all cultures prefer models of justice that offer participants a voice in the proceedings and the opportunity to be judged by an impartial decision maker.

Culture, Law, and Justice

- Reflecting cultural and religious values, countries set different laws in an effort to regulate behavior.
- In diverse populations, differing cultural practices sometimes put governments into conflict with segments of their population.
- Cultures also differ in the processes used to enforce laws and the consequences for those who are convicted.

Closing Statement

- Increasingly, social psychologists have become involved in studying the legal system—identifying the problems and seeking solutions.

KEY TERMS

adversarial model (467)

cross-race identification bias (448)

death qualification (441)

inquisitorial model (467)

jury nullification (458)

leniency bias (461)

misinformation effect (450)

peremptory challenge (437)

polygraph (446)

scientific jury selection (439)

sentencing disparity (464)

voir dire (437)

weapon-focus effect (448)

PUTTING COMMON SENSE TO THE TEST

Contrary to popular opinion, women are harsher as criminal trial jurors than men are.

False. Demographic factors such as gender do not consistently predict juror verdicts; men may be harsher in some cases, women in others.

Without being beaten or threatened, innocent people sometimes confess to crimes they did not commit.

True. Innocent suspects sometimes confess, either to escape an unpleasant situation or because they are led to believe they committed a crime they cannot recall.

A person can fool a lie-detector test by suppressing arousal when questions about the crime are asked.

False. It is possible to beat a lie-detector test, but by elevating arousal when "innocent" questions are asked, not by trying to suppress arousal in response to "guilty" questions.

Eyewitnesses find it relatively difficult to recognize members of a race other than their own.

True. Researchers have observed this cross-race identification bias in both laboratory and field settings.

The more confident an eyewitness is about an identification, the more accurate he or she is likely to be.

False. Studies have shown that eyewitness confidence does not reliably predict accuracy, in part because confidence is influenced by post-identification factors.

One can usually predict a jury's final verdict by knowing where the individual jurors stand the first time they vote.

True. As a result of both informational and normative group influences, the preference of the initial voting majority usually prevails.

13

Business

PREVIEW

This chapter examines the social side of business—specifically, the role of social factors in the workplace and their influence on economic decisions. First, we look at social influences on *personnel selection* and *performance appraisals* made within organizations. Then, we examine the roles of *leadership* and *worker motivation*. Finally, we explore *economic decision making* in the stock market and other business settings.

PUTTING COMMON SENSE TO THE TEST

T/F

_____ Although flawed, job interviews consistently make for better hiring decisions.

_____ A problem with having workers evaluate their own job performance is that self-ratings are overly positive.

_____ The most effective type of leader is one who knows how to win support through the use of reward.

_____ People who feel "overpaid" work harder on the job than those who see their pay as appropriate.

_____ People losing money on an investment tend to cut their losses rather than hang tough.

Every year, around Labor Day, the Harris poll asks Americans to estimate how much time they spend working. Since 1973, there has been a steady increase—from 41 hours per week up to about 50 hours per week. The International Labor Organization reports that Americans in a year work 137 hours more than the Japanese, 260 hours more than the British, and 499 hours more than the French (Greenhause, 2001).

W henever two adults meet for the first time, the opening line of their conversation is predictable: "So, what do you do?" "Oh, I'm a (social psychologist). And you?" For many people, work is an integral part of their personal identity. Sure, most of us would rather spend next Monday morning lying on a warm and breezy beach, reading a novel, and sipping a tropical fruit drink, but most people spend more time working than playing. In large part, we work to make money. Yet jobs also provide us with activity, a sense of purpose, and a social community. Thus, people who lose their jobs are psychologically devastated, even when they are not to blame and even when they have enough money to see them through the period of unemployment. Imagine that you had won $10 million in a lottery. Would you continue to work? In a 2005 Gallup poll of hundreds of Americans, 41 percent said they would stop working, but 59 percent said they would continue either at their current jobs or elsewhere. Thus, it is important to identify the social influences on this significant human experience.

This chapter considers applications of social psychology to business. First, we'll look at **industrial/organizational (I/O) psychology**, the study of human behavior in the workplace. This subdiscipline of psychology is broad and includes in its ranks both social and nonsocial psychologists who conduct research, teach in business schools or universities, and work in private industry. Whatever the setting, I/O psychology raises important practical questions about job interviewing, evaluations and promotions, leadership, motivation, and other aspects of life on the job. Next, we'll examine some social influences on economic decision making in the stock market and elsewhere in the business world.

The impact of social psychological factors in the workplace was first recognized many years ago—thanks, oddly enough, to a study of industrial lighting. The year was 1927. Calvin Coolidge was president, Babe Ruth hit sixty home runs, Charles Lindbergh flew across the Atlantic for the first time, and the U.S. economy seemed sound, though it would soon become depressed. Just outside Chicago, the Hawthorne plant of the Western Electric Company employed thirty thousand men and women in the manufacture of telephones and central office equipment. As in other companies, management wanted to boost productivity. The bottom line was important.

industrial/organizational (I/O) psychology The study of human behavior in business and other organizational settings.

473

These women were among the assembly plant workers who took part in the classic Hawthorne studies of productivity in the workplace.

At first, managers thought that they could make workers at the plant more productive by altering the illumination levels in the factory. Proceeding logically, they increased the lighting for one group of workers in a special test room, kept the same lighting in a control room, and compared the effects. Much to their surprise, productivity rates increased in both rooms. At that point, a team of psychologists was brought in to vary other conditions in the factory. Over the next five years, groups of employees from various departments were selected to do their work in a test room where, at different times, they were given more rest periods, coffee breaks, a free mid-morning lunch, shorter work days, shorter weeks, a new location, overtime, financial incentives, dimmer lights, or just a different method of payment. At one point, the researchers even went back and reinstated the original pre-study conditions inside the test room. Yet no matter what changes were made, productivity levels always increased.

The Hawthorne project, described in a classic book entitled *Management and the Worker* (Roethlisberger & Dickson, 1939), has had a great impact on the study of behavior in the workplace. At first, the researchers were both puzzled and discouraged. With positive effects observed among all test-room workers (even when the original pretest conditions were in place), it seemed that the project had failed. Ponder the results, however, and you'll see why these studies are important. With striking consistency, workers became more productive—not because of the specific changes made but because they had been singled out for special assignment. Many researchers have criticized the methods used in this study and the interpretation of the results (Adair, 1984; Parsons, 1974). Still, the phenomenon that has become known as the **Hawthorne effect** laid a foundation for I/O psychology.

The Hawthorne plant no longer exists, but the study conducted there helped psychologists to understand the profound impact of social influences in the workplace. Interested in the conditions that affect satisfaction, motivation, and performance, today's researchers study all aspects of life in the workplace—including the practice of observing workers by monitoring their activity on the computer (Alge, 2001), perceptions of sexual harassment (Pryor & McKinney, 1995), illicit drug use in the workplace (Frone, 2006), the motivations underlying overtime work (Brett & Stroh, 2003), and antisocial work behaviors such as theft, incivility, bullying, and various manifestations of "desk rage" (Fox & Spector, 2004).

The three of us who wrote this textbook all work on college campuses amidst students, professors, and administrators. We spend most of our time in classrooms, offices, laboratories, and libraries. For women and men in other occupations—store clerks, taxicab drivers, carpenters, doctors, Internet companies, farmers, teachers, accountants, firefighters, and airline pilots—the workplace is very different. Yet despite the diversity of roles and settings, certain common concerns arise: How are applicants selected for jobs? How is performance then evaluated? What makes for an effective leader who can influence others and mobilize their support? What motivates people to work hard and feel satisfied with this aspect of their lives? And what factors influence the kinds of economic decisions that people make? Let's enter the workplace and address these important questions.

"And the dim fluorescent lighting is meant to emphasize the general absence of hope."

Cartoonbank.com

Hawthorne effect The finding that workers who were given special attention increased their productivity regardless of what actual changes were made in the work setting.

Personnel Selection

For all kinds of organizations, the secret to success begins with the recruitment and development of a competent work staff. For that reason, personnel selection is the first important step (Evers et al., 2005; Guion & Highhouse, 2006).

Traditional Employment Interviews

Anyone who has ever applied for a desirable job knows that sometimes you have to climb hurdles and jump through hoops to land a job that matches your desires. The routine is a familiar one: You submit a résumé or post one on the Internet, fill out an application, and perhaps bring in samples of your work or take a standardized test of your abilities, personality traits, or honesty. You may even be placed on the "hot seat" in a live face-to-face interview. In a traditional interview, a representative of the organization and an applicant meet in person to discuss the job. Interviews thus provide a two-way opportunity for the applicant and employer to evaluate each other. What a social perception dilemma these opportunities present! As an applicant, you have only a half-hour or so to make a favorable impression. As an interviewer, you have the same brief period of time to penetrate the applicant's self-presentation while, at the same time, presenting the company in a favorable light.

"Even the most elaborate hiring methodologies eventually boil down to one of the dreaded rituals of business life: the job interview" (Hotjobs.com).

Very few employers would consider hiring a complete stranger for a responsible position without an interview. Would you? Like most of us, you probably trust your own ability to size people up. But should you? Do interviews promote sound hiring, or do they produce decisions that are biased by job-irrelevant personal characteristics? Civil rights laws explicitly forbid employers to discriminate on the basis of sex, race, age, religion, national origin, or disability. Does the interview process itself intensify or diminish these possible sources of bias? And are interviews valid and predictive of performance?

Research suggests that interviewing has mixed effects. On the positive side, live interviews may actually diminish the tendency to make simple stereotyped judgments. Studies on gender have shown that when prospective employers rate job applicants from résumés and other written materials, they often evaluate men more highly than they do comparable women, although this bias is reduced as employers get more information about each applicant's credentials (Tosi & Einbender, 1985). So, what happens in a live interview? Does gender then become more salient, or do job-relevant attributes take over? To answer this question, Laura Graves and Gary Powell (1988) studied 483 interviewers who visited various college campuses to recruit seniors for entry-level corporate jobs. Each interviewer rated one student and answered this question: "What are the chances that this applicant will receive a job offer from your company?" Of the applicants sampled, 53 percent were male, 47 percent female. More to the point, there was no sex discrimination, with men and women being equally likely to get hired.

Monster.com founder Jeff Taylor (left) talks to employees about the company. Today, many job seekers and companies meet online through websites like Monster.com.

Other researchers have reported somewhat good news when it comes to race. By statistically combining the results of thirty-one studies involving more than eleven thousand job applicants, Allen Huffcutt and Philip Roth (1998) found that black and Hispanic applicants receive interview ratings only slightly lower on average than those obtained by their

FIGURE 13.1

The Bias for Beauty in Hiring

In this study, managers rank-ordered four job applicants: two men and two women—one of each attractive, the other plain. As shown, a majority selected an attractive male or female applicant as their top choice.

(Marlowe et al., 1996.)

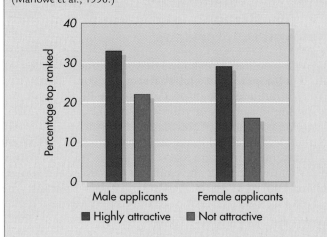

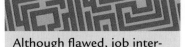

Although flawed, job interviews consistently make for better hiring decisions. **False.**

white counterparts. Perhaps the face-to-face interactions provided by interviews humanize applicants, bringing to life their interest in the job, social skills, and other relevant attributes that do not show up on paper. This relative lack of bias also seems to characterize subjective evaluations of job performance—where supervisor (and peer) ratings of black, white, and Hispanic workers are more similar to one another, not less so, than "objective" measures of performance (Roth et al., 2003).

Although most employers have learned to guard against discriminatory hiring practices, there is one possible source of bias that is difficult to regulate: physical attractiveness. Except for certain types of work (such as modeling), beauty is not relevant to performance on the job. Yet as we saw in Chapter 9, people tend to favor others who are good-looking. Does this bias operate in hiring situations? To answer this question, Cynthia Marlowe and others (1996) presented a set of job application folders—including résumés, data sheets, and photographs—to 112 male and female managers of a financial institution. Believing they were evaluating actual prospective employees, each manager rank-ordered four equivalent and qualified applicants: two men and two women, one of each of whom was highly attractive. Who was selected? Look at Figure 13.1, and you'll see that there was a slight tendency to favor male applicants, but physical appearance had a greater impact, as 62 percent of all managers selected an attractive applicant as their top choice. Other research has since confirmed that human resource professionals exhibit a hiring preference for male and female applicants who are attractive (Jawahar & Mattsson, 2005). On a positive note, Marlowe et al.'s results showed that managers who had the most experience did not exhibit the bias for beauty.

Although interviews often result in the right selection of new employees, they sometimes lack predictive validity (Eder & Harris, 1999). Part of the problem may be that job applicants present themselves in a positive light, as you'd expect, and that those who engage in the most self-promotion (not necessarily those best qualified) are the most likely to get hired (Stevens & Kristof, 1995). Some college seniors who enter the job market are also more confident in their interviewing skills than others—and confidence predicts success months later (Tay et al., 2006). Another problem is that an employer's preconceptions about an applicant can distort the whole interview process. When participants in an interview experiment were led to believe that the applicant they would meet was not suitable for a particular job, they prepared questions that sought negative rather than positive information (Binning et al., 1988).

In a field study illustrating the problem, Amanda Phillips and Robert Dipboye (1989) surveyed 34 managers from different branch offices of a large corporation and 164 job applicants whom these managers had interviewed. They found that the managers' pre-interview expectations, which were based on written application materials, influenced the kinds of interviews they conducted as well as the outcomes: The higher their expectations, the more time they spent "recruiting" rather than evaluating and the more likely they were to make a favorable hiring decision. Similarly, Thomas Dougherty and others (1994) found that interviewers with positive rather than negative expectations sounded warmer, more outgoing, and more cheerful. They also gave more information and spent more time promoting the company. It seems that job interviews can become part of a vicious cycle, or self-fulfilling prophecy. Without realizing it, employers use the opportunity to create realities that bolster their pre-existing beliefs (see Figure 13.2).

 ### "Scientific" Alternatives to Traditional Interviews

Face-to-face interviews bring to life both job-relevant and irrelevant personal characteristics. Given that the process is so variable, should interviews be eliminated?

FIGURE 13.2

Job Interviews: A Self-Fulfilling Prophecy?

One study indicates that interviewers' expectations influence the kinds of interviews conducted and applicants' performance. The higher the expectations, the more the interviewer tries to impress rather than evaluate the applicant and make a favorable hiring decision. Without realizing it, employers may use job interviews to create a reality that supports their prior beliefs.

(Phillips & Dipboye, 1989.)

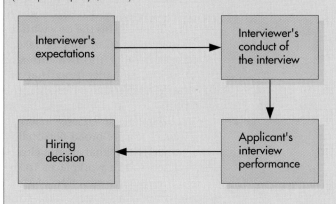

Should they, perhaps, be computerized, leaving applicants to interact with companies via a programmed sequence of questions and answers administered by computer? Online interviews may offer a forum for an initial screening of applicants. Chances are, however, not too many people would feel comfortable making important life decisions in such an impersonal manner. Is it possible, then, to preserve the human touch of an interview while eliminating the bias and error?

Some organizations use the *polygraph,* or lie-detector test, as a screening device. As described in Chapter 12, the polygraph is an instrument that records physiological arousal in different parts of the body. Based on the assumption that lying creates stress, a polygraph examiner conducts an interview and compares the interviewee's level of arousal in response to various questions. Those who administer lie-detector tests argue that it enhances their ability to identify prospective employees who are honest. But opponents argue that the test invades an individual's privacy, that it is too easily misused, and that its results are not sufficiently accurate. For these reasons, the U.S. government in 1988 passed a law that prohibits the use of lie-detector tests except in matters of public safety and national security, such as for screening scientists who work at nuclear testing facilities (Beardsley, 1999).

Standardized Tests   Today, many companies use standardized written tests in the selection process. Three general types of tests are used for this purpose. Tests of intelligence are designed to measure intellectual and cognitive abilities, job-specific knowledge and skills, or "street smarts" and common sense, all of which may contribute to success on the job. When it comes to measures of general intelligence, the use of cognitive ability tests in the workplace is a matter of serious debate. Based on extensive research, some psychologists believe that cognitive ability tests are useful because they are predictive of job success (Gottfredson, 2002; Schmidt, 2002); others caution that general intelligence is only one relevant factor and that this focus discriminates against individuals with other abilities who don't happen to score well on these tests (Sternberg & Hedlund, 2002). As a group, I/O psychologists are ambivalent about intelligence testing for personnel selection. When Kevin Murphy and others (2003) surveyed more than seven hundred professionals in the area, they found that most agreed that intelligence is not fully captured by standardized tests, that different jobs require different cognitive abilities, and that both cognitive and non-cognitive selection measures should be used.

Currently, it is estimated that 2,500 U.S. companies also use personality testing to measure traits that are predictive of such work-related outcomes as leadership potential, helpfulness, lateness, absenteeism, and theft (Cha, 2005). For example, people who score high rather than low in the trait of conscientiousness—which tends to make them more achievement oriented, dependable, orderly, and cautious—are more likely in general to perform well on the job (Dudley et al., 2006). Another example: People who score as extroverted rather than introverted are especially likely to succeed as business managers and salespersons (Hurtz & Donovan, 2000; Salgado, 1997). Research shows that children and young adults who have high self-esteem, self-confidence, and a sense of control tend to seek out more challenging lines of work and, as a result, are more satisfied with their jobs later in life (Judge et al., 2000). Research also shows that high self-monitors—people who closely regulate their behavior to be socially appropriate—are more likely to get promoted and become leaders within an organization (Day et al., 2002).

Third, many companies have recently begun to administer **integrity tests**— questionnaires designed specifically to assess an applicant's honesty and character by asking direct questions concerning illicit drug use, shoplifting, petty theft, and other transgressions. The responses are scored by computer. Narrative profiles are provided, and arbitrary cutoff scores are often used to determine if an applicant

integrity tests   Paper-and-pencil questionnaires designed to test a job applicant's honesty and character.

FIGURE 13.3

Can Integrity Tests Be Faked?

Alliger and others (1996) gave college students overt and covert integrity tests. Some just took the test; others were told to "fake good"; others were coached. On the overt test, scores increased for subjects who faked good or were coached (left). On the covert test, scores were unaffected by these interventions (right).

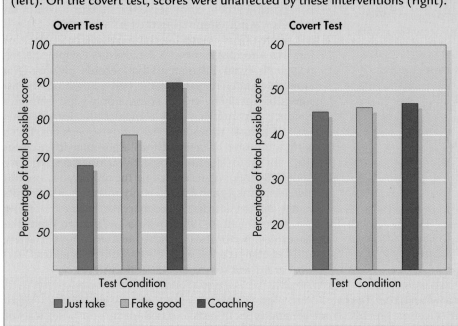

has passed or failed (Camara & Schneider, 1994).

A major concern about integrity tests and personality tests too, for that matter, is that applicants may be able to fake the tests on their own or with the help of coaching. The concern is that applicants will use the tests to present themselves in overly positive ways, perhaps as highly stable, conscientious, agreeable, or extroverted (Schmitt & Oswald, 2006). But is this the case with integrity tests? Can they be faked? Let's consider the two different types of integrity tests that are used: (1) *overt tests,* in which the purpose is obvious to the test-taker, and (2) *covert tests,* in which items measure broad personality characteristics that are not clearly related to the workplace. To examine the susceptibility of these tests to faking, George Alliger and others (1996) gave both overt and covert tests to college students. Some were told to just take the tests, others were instructed to "fake good," and still others were coached and given specific strategies for how to beat the tests. Figure 13.3 shows how well the students did. On the overt test, the scores increased for those instructed to fake good and then increased again among those who were specifically coached. Yet on the covert personality test, scores were unaffected by these interventions. Other studies, too, demonstrate the point: When it comes to faking, the covert tests, quite literally, pass the test (Alliger & Dwight, 2000).

But are such instruments sufficiently valid to be used for personnel selection? Although there is reason for skepticism, the research suggests that both types of tests do predict various work-related behaviors (Goldberg et al., 1991; Sackett et al., 1989). In an experiment using overt integrity tests, Michael Cunningham and others (1994) found that actual job applicants scored higher on these tests than did non-motivated research participants and that their scores matched those obtained from participants specifically instructed to fake good. So, does this self-presentation bias compromise a test's validity? Not necessarily. In a second experiment, these same investigators overpaid participants by $5 and found that those with high rather than low test scores were also more likely to return the extra cash. Other researchers have arrived at similar findings (Barrick & Mount, 1996). Indeed, when Deniz Ones and others (1993) conducted a meta-analysis of tests taken by thousands of workers, they found that the test scores were highly predictive of both job performance and counterproductive behaviors such as theft, absenteeism, lateness, and disciplinary problems.

Structured Interviews Another way to improve selection judgments is through the use of **structured interviews**. A structured interview is much like a standardized test in that the same information is obtained in the same situation from all applicants, who are then compared on a common, relevant set of dimensions (Campion et al., 1988). By asking exactly the same set of questions or using the same set of tasks, employers can prevent themselves from unwittingly conducting biased interviews that merely confirm their pre-existing conceptions. Over the years, studies have shown that structured interviews are better than conventional interviews in the selection of insurance agents, sales clerks, and other workers (Wiesner & Cronshaw, 1988)—and that they are more predictive than paper-and-pencil personality tests (Huffcutt

structured interview
An interview in which each job applicant is asked a standard set of questions and evaluated on the same criteria.

et al., 2001), perhaps because they are more difficult to fake (Van Iddekinge et al., 2005). In fact, structured interviews can be conducted over the telephone and later scored from a taped transcript of what was said. Even in this way, the information received can be used to predict a future worker's attendance rate, productivity, and tenure on the job (Schmidt & Rader, 1999).

To create a more structured, multidimensional setting for selection and evaluation purposes, many organizations use **assessment centers**, in which several applicants take part in a group of activities—written tests, situational tests, role-playing exercises, and so on—that are monitored by a group of different evaluators. Instead of one method (an interview) and one evaluator (an interviewer), multiple methods and evaluators are used. Assessment centers are widely assumed to be more effective than traditional interviews at identifying applicants who will succeed in a particular position (Thornton & Rupp, 2006). When companies struggle to cut hiring costs, assessments are sometimes streamlined to involve fewer evaluators, fewer exercises, briefer exercises, and other types of shortcuts (Borman et al., 1997). Still, research shows that an assessment center's multidimensional approach is a good way to make hiring decisions that are ultimately more predictive of job performance (Arthur et al., 2003; Bowler & Woehr, 2006).

Personnel Selection as a Two-Way Street   For many years, researchers focused on the ways in which different personnel selection procedures serve employers. As we noted earlier, however, the hiring process is an interpersonal two-way street in which organizations and applicants size each other up. So how do job seekers feel about the methods just described? What is *your* reaction to these methods? Research shows that people generally see concrete, job-specific tests and interview situations as the most fair and they dislike being evaluated by general, standardized tests of intelligence, personality, and honesty (Rosse et al., 1994; Rynes & Connerly, 1993). For employers on the lookout for strong recruits, the perceived fairness of the selection process that is used may well influence whether top applicants accept the offers that are made (Bauer et al., 1998).

Even the format of an interview can leave a lasting impression. Flawed as it may be, how does the face-to-face interview compare with computer-mediated interviews? In today's highly global economy, interviewers and job applicants are often geographically separated, which necessitates either costly travel or the use of technology for computer-mediated interviews, telephone interviews, and videoconferencing. If you've ever communicated in these ways, you know how "different" the interaction can be. But how effective are these media for job interviews—not just for the employer, but also for the applicant? At a campus recruitment center of a large Canadian university, 970 students who submitted résumés to jobs that were posted on the Internet interviewed with 346 organizations. These were actual interviews. Most were held in person, but some were conducted by telephone or videoconferencing. When questioned about the experience afterward, the students in the in-person interviews saw the process as fairer, saw the outcome as more favorable, and were more likely to accept the job if offered. It may be difficult to replace the connection and caring that are signaled by in-person contact (Chapman et al., 2003).

 ## Affirmative Action

Affirmative action is a policy whereby special consideration in recruitment, hiring, admissions, and promotion is given to women and underrepresented minority groups. This policy is among the most emotional and explosive social issues of our time. On one side of the debate is the argument that preferential treatment is necessary as a way both to overcome historical inequities and to bring the benefits of diversity to the workplace. On the other side is the claim that the policy results in unfair reverse discrimination. Surveys show that Americans are sharply divided on the issue—with women more supportive than men, and African Americans more supportive than Whites (Crosby et al., 2006; Kravitz & Platania, 1993; Parker et al., 1997).

Differences of opinion were apparent during the summer of 2003, just after the United States Supreme Court ruled on a pair of historic affirmative action lawsuits

assessment center
A structured setting in which job applicants are exhaustively tested and judged by multiple evaluators.

Representing both sides of the debate, Americans demonstrated outside the U.S Supreme Court, passionate in their opinions on affirmative action. On June 23, 2003, the Court—by a 5 to 4 margin—upheld a university's right to consider race in admissions in order to create a diverse student body.

filed by students rejected from the University of Michigan. Upholding the law school's policy but not the undergraduate policy, the Court ruled by a 5 to 4 margin that it is proper for a university to take race into account as a way to bring diversity to the campus so long as a specific quota or point system is not used. That day, in a Gallup poll of 1,385 Americans, 59 percent favored affirmative action for women; 49 percent favored affirmative action for racial minorities. In both cases, women and minorities were more favorable toward the policy (see Figure 13.4).

Proponents of affirmative action often accuse opponents of harboring conscious or unconscious prejudice. In contrast, the opponents argue that they merely support a meritocracy, a form of justice in which everyone receives an equal opportunity and then rewards are matched to contributions. In support of this reasoning, Ramona Bobocel and others (1998) studied affirmative action attitudes and found that opposition to it was associated with a strong belief in the principle of merit, not with measures of racial prejudice. So, would these opponents favor preferential selection procedures to rectify the injustice of a workplace contaminated by discrimination? It appears that many would. When affirmative action opponents were led to see women and minorities as the targets of discrimination in a particular workplace, which itself undermines the principle of merit, they became more favorable toward a system of preferential treatment (Son Hing et al., 2002).

As political debate rages, many questions are being raised. According to Rupert Nacoste (1996), affirmative action affects those whom the policy is designed to help, those who feel excluded by it, the organizations that implement it, and the interactions among these three interested groups. In addition, Nacoste argues that people react not to the abstract concept of affirmative action but to the procedures that are used to implement the concept and that these reactions can set off "procedural re-

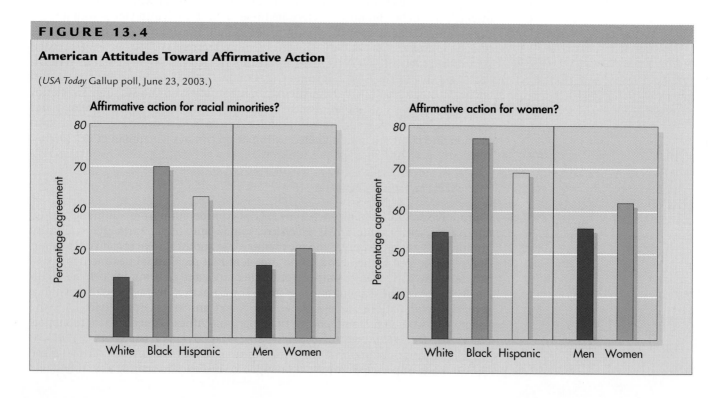

FIGURE 13.4

American Attitudes Toward Affirmative Action

(*USA Today* Gallup poll, June 23, 2003.)

verberations" within the system. For example, people will be dissatisfied and the system will reverberate to the extent that the policy is set secretly rather than in the open, to the extent that interested parties have no opportunity to express their personal views, and to the extent that group membership considerations are seen as more important than the individual contributions of each applicant. Nacoste's notion of procedural interdependence is diagrammed in Figure 13.5.

After years of research on attitudes toward affirmative action, it is now clear that although there are sharp differences of opinion, people's reactions depend—and can be changed by—how the policy is implemented. There is no single approach. Faye Crosby and her colleagues (2006) note that policies range from "soft" forms of affirmative action, such as outreach programs designed to identify, recruit, or specially train applicants from underrepresented groups, to "hard" forms of affirmative action that give preference in hiring to applicants from targeted groups who are equally or less qualified than others. Based on a meta-analysis of 126 studies involving 29,000 respondents, David Harrison and others (2006) found that people are most favorable toward the softer forms of affirmative action and least favorable toward quotas and other hard policies that favor some applicants over others independent of their qualifications.

As you might expect, people who do not personally benefit from affirmative action react negatively to the policy and to those who benefit from it (Heilman et al., 1996). But what about the recipients of this policy themselves? Does affirmative action psychologically undermine those whom it is intended to help? In an early series of provocative studies, Madeline Heilman and others (1987) selected male and female college students to serve as leaders of a two-person task. These students were then led to think that they had been chosen for the leadership role either by a preferential-selection process based on gender or by a merit-selection process based solely on qualifications. The result: The women (but not the men) who believed they were chosen because of their gender later devalued their own performance, even after receiving positive feedback.

There are three explanations as to why preferential selection policies may have a range of negative effects. First, people perceive a procedure as unjust to the extent that it excludes those who are qualified simply because of their non-membership in a group (Barnes Nacoste, 1994; Heilman et al., 1996). Second, the recipients become less able to attribute success on the job to their own abilities and efforts, leading them and co-workers to harbor doubts about their competence (Heilman et al., 1992; Major et al., 1994). Third, preferential selection is seen as a form of assistance, a situation that can lead recipients to feel stigmatized by the assumed negative perceptions of others (Heilman & Alcott, 2001).

Are the recipients of affirmative action doomed to feel stigmatized, like second-class citizens? Not necessarily. The way people react to a preferential selection procedure may well depend on how it is structured and implemented (Kravitz et al., 1997). A good deal of research shows that people draw negative inferences about

FIGURE 13.5

Affirmative Action: Effects on Individuals, Groups, and Organizations

Affirmative action affects target group members whom the policy is designed to help, nontarget group members who feel excluded by it, organizations that implement it, and the interactions among these groups. According to Nacoste, people's reactions to affirmation action procedures can set off "procedural reverberations" (P) within the system.

(Nacoste, 1996.)

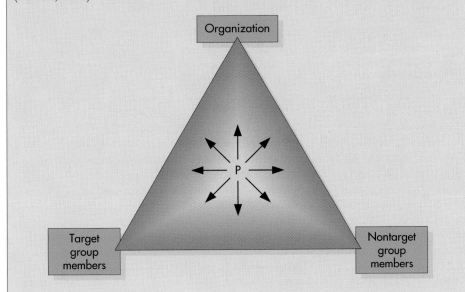

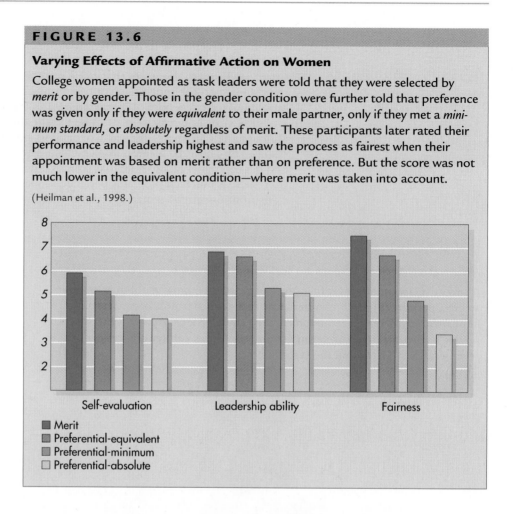

FIGURE 13.6

Varying Effects of Affirmative Action on Women

College women appointed as task leaders were told that they were selected by *merit* or by gender. Those in the gender condition were further told that preference was given only if they were *equivalent* to their male partner, only if they met a *minimum standard*, or *absolutely* regardless of merit. These participants later rated their performance and leadership highest and saw the process as fairest when their appointment was based on merit rather than on preference. But the score was not much lower in the equivalent condition—where merit was taken into account.

(Heilman et al., 1998.)

Self-evaluation   Leadership ability   Fairness

■ Merit
■ Preferential-equivalent
■ Preferential-minimum
□ Preferential-absolute

themselves and others when employment selections are made *solely* on the basis of sex, skin color, or ethnic background. But would they react more favorably to a preferential selection process if it is clear that merit-based factors also play a role and that the person chosen is competent and qualified for the position?

To find out, Heilman and her colleagues (1998) again brought together male and female participants to take part in a joint two-person task that required a leader and a follower. As in prior experiments, the researchers administered a bogus qualifications test and then assigned each female to the leadership role. Some participants were told that the appointment was based strictly on *merit* (that the person with the higher test score had been selected as the leader). Others were told that the process favored the woman in a way that was *preferential-equivalent* (that she was chosen only when her score was similar to that of her male counterpart), *preferential-minimum standard* (that she was chosen only if minimally qualified), or *preferential-absolute* (that she was chosen regardless of merit). The result: The appointed female leaders later rated their own performance and leadership abilities most favorably and saw the process as fairest when their appointment was based on merit, not gender (see Figure 13.6). Importantly, they also did not devalue their performance or see the selection process as unfair in the preferential-equivalent condition, where merit was clearly taken into account. Similarly, neither male co-participants nor observers were troubled by this type of preferential selection process. In light of these findings, Table 13.1 offers guidelines for managing affirmative action programs in a way that minimizes criticism from all concerned.

 Culture and Organizational Diversity

For many years, the study of organizational behavior was "culture blind and culture bound" (Gelfand et al., 2007; Triandis, 1994). In light of two dramatic historical

TABLE 13.1
Managing Affirmative Action

Preferential selection practices are often seen as unjust, and they often lead recipients to doubt their own competence. Pratkanis and Turner (1996) recommend that the steps listed here be taken to minimize these negative effects.

1. Set and communicate clear and explicit qualifications criteria (background, knowledge, skills, etc.) to be used in selection decisions.
2. Be certain that selection procedures are perceived as fair by targeted applicants and their co-workers.
3. Provide the target applicant and co-workers with specific feedback concerning the target's job qualifications.
4. Develop socialization strategies that keep target applicants from making negative self-attributions.
5. Emphasize the target applicant's unique contributions to the organization.
6. Point out that affirmative action does not imply hiring by quotas, since other job-relevant attributes are considered as well.
7. Recognize that affirmative action is not a panacea and that it cannot be expected to solve all the problems faced by the targeted groups.

The globalization of business is a fact of life. More than 63,000 multinational corporations and 821,000 foreign subsidiaries now employ 90 million people around the world (Gabel & Brunner, 2003).

changes, researchers now look at the workplace through a broader lens. The first change has resulted from affirmative action programs, which forced an increase in the number of women and minorities who populate most organizations. The second is the worldwide trend toward globalization, which has brought more and more people from disparate cultures into daily contact with each other, often as co-workers. Georgia Chao and Henry Moon (2005) note that every individual worker has a multidimensional identity that can be characterized within a *cultural mosaic* consisting of the various "tiles" of his or her demographic groups (such as age, gender, race, and ethnic heritage), geographical background (such as country of origin, region, climate, and population density), and personal associations (such as with religion, profession, and political affiliation). In some ways, everyone is similar; in other ways, no two people are alike. For researchers who study organizational behavior, the challenge is to represent the full complexity that comes with a diverse workplace.

As diversity has become a fact of life, researchers have sought to understand what effect this change will have on motivation, morale, and performance in the workplace. On the one hand, a pessimist would predict that diversity would breed division and conflict, making worker teams less effective. In Chapter 5, on Stereotypes, Prejudice, and Discrimination, we saw that people categorize one another into ingroups and outgroups based on gender, age, race, and other visible characteristics and show a marked preference for "us" over "them." We also saw in Chapter 9, on Attraction and Close Relationships, that people prefer the company of others who are similar rather than dissimilar in their attitudes and values. To the extent that people dislike each other, they will not work well together. On the other hand, an optimist would predict that diversity increases the range of perspectives and skills that are brought to bear on a problem, enhancing productivity and creative problem solving by providing a group with a larger pool of resources to draw from. So, what is the net impact of diversity on group performance? There is a hint of evidence for both effects. Hence, researchers at present agree that there is no single or simple answer because the effect is likely to depend on the nature of the diversity, whether similarities or differences are accentuated, the proportion of majority to minority members, whether there is a culture of smooth integration within the organization, the type of work to be completed, the group's ability and motivation, and other factors (Mannix & Neale, 2005; van Knippenberg & Schippers, 2007; Williams & O'Reilly, 1998).

Performance Appraisals

Even after a person is hired, the evaluation process continues. Nobody enjoys being scrutinized by a boss or anyone else, for that matter. Still, **performance appraisal**—the process of evaluating an employee's work and communicating the results to that person—is an inevitable fact of life in the workplace. Performance appraisals provide a basis for placement decisions, transfers, promotions, raises and cuts in salary, bonuses, and layoffs. They also give feedback to employees about the quality of their work and status within the organization. It's no wonder that I/O psychologists have studied this process in great detail.

It would be easy if a worker's performance could be measured by purely *objective* and quantifiable criteria, as when typists are judged by the number of words they type in a minute, automobile dealers by the number of cars they sell, and sales agents by the number of customers they service. These kinds of quantitative measures are often not available, however, and they do not take into account the quality of work. By necessity, then, performance appraisals are usually based on more *subjective* measures such as perceptions of employees by supervisors, co-workers, and sometimes even themselves (Landy & Farr, 1983).

 ### Supervisor Ratings

Based on the assumption that supervisors keep themselves informed about the performance of their subordinates, they are most often called on to make evaluations. But are these ratings accurate? And is the process fair? The process has both benefits and drawbacks. On the one hand, research shows that supervisors are influenced more by a worker's job knowledge, ability, technical proficiency, and dependability than by less relevant factors such as friendliness (Borman et al., 1995). On the other hand, as we'll see, evaluators predictably fall prey to many of the social perception biases described elsewhere in this book.

Over the years, a number of appraisal-related problems have been identified. One is the *halo effect,* a failure to discriminate among different and distinct aspects of a worker's performance (Cooper, 1981). In Chapter 4, we saw that people's impressions of one another are guided by implicit personality theories—that is, by the preconceptions they have about the relationships among different traits. Believing that someone is warm, we assume that he or she is also generous and good-natured. In a similar manner, supervisors who believe that a worker is unproductive may also rate that worker negatively on teamwork, independence, creativity, and other distinct dimensions. Halo effects are most pronounced when evaluators rate someone they do not know well or when a time delay has caused their memory of performance to fade (Kozlowski et al., 1986; Murphy & Balzer, 1986). Lacking concrete details in these situations, they fall back on their past impressions and implicit theories and assume that one aspect of performance implies other aspects as well.

Second, it's difficult for supervisors to make repeated evaluations of the same worker, each time through fresh eyes. In a series of experiments, participants were asked to watch a teacher present three videotaped lectures and then evaluate his or her speaking ability, clarity, preparation, rapport, and so on (Murphy et al., 1985; Smither et al., 1988). For some, the first two lectures were low in quality; for others, they were high in quality. On the third tape, all participants watched the same average performance. The result: Even though participants rated each lecture independently, their final evaluations showed signs of a *contrast effect:* Those who had first observed negative performances judged the average lecture more favorably than did those who had seen the positive performances. Practically speaking, this finding suggests that supervisors who do multiple performance appraisals may judge an employee's work in light of all previous observations. One performance sets a standard for another. It's no wonder that entertainers worry about taking the stage right after a "tough act to follow."

performance appraisal
The process of evaluating an employee's work within the organization.

A third problem is that evaluators differ in the average numerical ratings they give to others. Because of what is known as the *restriction of range problem,* some people provide uniformly high, lenient ratings; others are inclined to give stingy, low ratings; and still others gravitate toward the center of the numerical scale. In all cases, people who use a restricted range fail to make adequate distinctions. Sometimes the differences among raters are considerable, as seen in a study of managers employed in numerous organizations (Scullen et al., 2000). Other researchers have observed that performance evaluations are influenced by the rater's personality. Individuals who have agreeable personalities, for example, tend to be lenient in their ratings of others, while those who are highly conscientious tend to be harsher (Bernardin et al., 2000). In a meta-analysis of twenty-five studies—some conducted in the workplace, others in a laboratory—John Georgesen and Monica Harris (1998) found that people who are in power, compared to those who are not in power, consistently give lower performance ratings to others who are in subordinate positions.

 ## Self-Evaluations

Although performance appraisals are typically made by supervisors, input is often sought from co-workers, subordinates, clients, customers, and others whose opinions are relevant. You may not realize it, but by filling out course-evaluation surveys in college, you may have had an influence on tenure and promotion decisions involving your own professors. As when workers are asked to evaluate their managers, these evaluations provide valuable "upward feedback."

One particularly interesting source of information comes from self-evaluations. If you've ever had to describe yourself in a job application, you know that a self-evaluation is not exactly a lesson in modesty. As discussed in Chapter 3, most people see themselves in overly flattering terms, taking credit for success, denying the blame for failure, having an inflated sense of control, and exhibiting unrealistic optimism about the future. Add the fact that people like to present themselves favorably to others, and it comes as no surprise that self-evaluations in the workplace are consistently more positive than the ratings made by supervisors (Campbell & Lee, 1988) and less predictive of job success (Shore et al., 1992). To illustrate, studies have shown that workers tend to underestimate the number of times they had been absent compared with co-workers (Harrison & Shaffer, 1994; Johns, 1994).

Another reason why self-evaluations should be taken with a grain of salt is that individuals differ in the extent to which they tend to present themselves in a positive light. Research shows that the more power people have in an organization, the higher are their self-evaluations (Georgesen & Harris, 1998). Similarly, men are more boastful in general than women and more likely to overestimate their own performance (Beyer, 1990). Insofar as work appraisals are based on self-evaluations, then, these differences put both subordinates and female employees at a disadvantage.

A problem with having workers evaluate their own job performance is that self-ratings are overly positive. **True.**

 ## New and Improved Methods of Appraisal

Performance appraisals cannot always be trusted. When more objective measures of work output are not available, however, organizations have no choice but to rely on the imperfect and sometimes prejudiced human judge. For researchers, the challenge is to find ways to boost the accuracy of the evaluations that are made.

One solution concerns the timing of evaluations in relation to the observation of performance. Evaluations are less prone to error when made right after performance than when there's a delay of days, weeks, or months. Alternatively, evaluators should take notes and keep clear records of their observations, perhaps using behavioral checklists. Part of the problem is that once memory for details begins to fade, evaluators fall back on stereotypes and other biases (Murphy & Balzer, 1986; Sanchez & De La Torre, 1996).

A second possible solution is to teach raters some of the skills necessary for making accurate appraisals. Over the years, various training programs have been developed, and research suggests that accuracy can be boosted by alerting evaluators to the biases of social perception, focusing their attention on job-relevant behaviors, sharpening their memory skills, informing them of performance norms that serve as a frame of reference within the organization, and providing them with practice and feedback in the use of rating scales (Day & Sulsky, 1995; Hedge & Kavanagh, 1988). No system will ever be perfect, but much improvement is possible, particularly when people are motivated to be accurate (Salvemini et al., 1993).

Third, and now common in most organizations, is to collect and combine a full circle of ratings from multiple evaluators in a process that is referred to as a 360-degree performance appraisal. As in assessment centers, a multiple-rater system in which a final evaluation represents the average of ratings made by independent sources with different perspectives is more complete than the conventional single-rater approach (Conway & Huffcutt, 1997; Sackett & Wilson, 1982). In a typical 360-degree assessment, an employee's performance is rated by superiors, peers, subordinates, the employees themselves, and even outside stakeholders such as customers, clients, students, and patients. In this way, whatever idiosyncratic bias a single individual might bring to his or her ratings can be offset by others. Although there is debate over how to combine, compare, and contrast different sources, research shows that this approach is generally an improvement over single-rater methods (Craig & Hannum, 2006; Morgeson et al., 2005).

Due Process Considerations

In the all-too-human enterprise of performance appraisal, accuracy is not the only concern. There's also another problem: perceptions of fairness. Precisely because they influence personnel decisions, performance ratings may be biased, and sometimes even deliberately distorted, by those motivated by political and self-serving agendas within the workplace. Particularly at the executive level, office politics is an organizational fact of life (Gioia & Longnecker, 1994).

To enhance perceptions of fairness, Robert Folger and his colleagues (1992) proposed a "due process" model of performance appraisal. In general, this model is designed to guard the rights of employees in the same way that the criminal justice system seeks to protect the accused. The model consists of three principles. The first is that there should be *adequate notice*—that is, clear performance standards that employees can understand and ask questions about. The second is that employees should receive a *fair hearing* in which they are evaluated by a supervisor who knows their work, and in which they receive timely feedback as well as an opportunity to present their own case. The third principle is that appraisals should be based on *evidence* of job performance, not on prejudice, corruption, or other external considerations. As indicated by research on how people react to pay raises, pay cuts, and the implementation of affirmative action policies, procedural fairness (*how* decisions are made) can be just as important to people as a favorable outcome (*what* decisions are made). Thus, workers who are dissatisfied with their pay are more likely to retaliate (for example, by calling in sick, stealing or wasting the company's supplies, or damaging equipment) when they see the procedures used to determine pay as unfair and when they were not consulted about the decision (Skarlicki & Folger, 1997).

Leadership

Regardless of where you're employed, the work experience depends in large part on the quality of the leadership in the organization. A leader is someone who can move a group of people toward a common goal. He or she may be a head of state, the president of a college or university, the principal investigator of a research team, the executive officer of a corporation, or the manager or head coach of a sports team. Across a wide range of settings, researchers have long wondered: What personal and situational factors make for effective leadership? There is no single formula. Some leaders succeed by winning supporters; others lead by mending fences, uniting rivals, negotiating deals, building coalitions, solving problems, or stirring emotions (see Table 13.2).

TABLE 13.2
Quotable Conceptions of Leadership

The purpose of all rulers is the well-being of those they rule.
—Saint Augustine

The most important quality in a leader is that of being acknowledged as such.
—Andre Maurois

I am a leader by default, only because nature does not allow a vacuum.
—Bishop Desmond Tutu

If one is lucky, a solitary fantasy can totally transform one million realities.
—Maya Angelou

When the effective leader is finished with his work, the people say it happened naturally.
—Lao Tse

Never tell people how to do things. Tell them what to do and they will surprise you with their ingenuity.
—General George Patton

We must become the change we want to see.
—Mahatma Gandhi

The final test of a leader is that he leaves behind him in other men the conviction and will to carry on.
—Walter J. Lippmann

Leadership should be born out of the understanding of the needs of those who would be affected by it.
—Marian Anderson

No man will make a great leader who wants to do it all himself, or to get all the credit for doing it.
—Andrew Carnegie

The task of the leader is to get his people from where they are to where they have not been.
—Henry Kissinger

Whatever the strategy, there is one common denominator: Good leadership is about social influence (Goethals et al., 2004).

 ## The Classic Trait Approach

One approach to the study of leadership is to identify the traits that characterize "natural-born" leaders, those who have the "right stuff." According to the Great Person Theory of history, exceptional individuals rise up to determine the course of human events. This approach has had some support over the years, since certain traits—such as ambition, intelligence, a need for power, self-confidence, a high energy level, and an ability to be flexible and adapt to change—are characteristic of people who go on to become leaders (Hogan et al., 1994; Kenny & Zaccaro, 1983). Even physical height may play a role. In this regard, it is striking that across the entire twentieth century, the tallest candidate for United States president won an astonishing twenty-three out of twenty-five elections—for a 92 percent winning record (1972 and 1976 were the only exceptions).

On the basis of past research, Shelley Kirkpatrick and Edwin Locke (1991) argue that certain personality characteristics are associated with successful leadership among business executives. In particular, they point to the central importance of *cognitive ability* (intelligence, an ability to quickly process large amounts of information), *inner drive* (a need for achievement, ambition, and a high energy level), *leadership motivation* (a desire to influence others in order to reach a common goal), *expertise* (specific knowledge of technical issues relevant to the organization), *creativity* (an ability to generate

"If you could fire your current boss, would you?" In a survey of American workers, 24 percent said yes.

original ideas), *self-confidence* (faith in one's own abilities and ideas), *integrity* (openness of communication, reliability, and honesty), and *flexibility* (an ability to adapt to the needs of followers and to changes in the situation). "Regardless of whether leaders are born or made," they say, "it is unequivocally clear that leaders are not like other people" (p. 58). Locke (2000) picks up on this theme in *The Prime Movers,* a book in which he describes the traits that "great wealth creators"—self-made multimillionaires and billionaires—seem to have in common. Zaccaro (2007) adds that leadership can best be predicted, not by single traits, but by unique combinations of attributes.

In contrast to this approach, more situationally oriented theories were introduced based on the notion that the emergence of a given leader depends on time, place, and circumstances—that different situations call for different types of leaders (Vroom & Jago, 2007). Thus, as the needs, expectations, and resources of a group change, so too will the person best suited to lead it. This need for a match was evident in New York City, the day of the terrorist attacks on the World Trade Center, when then Mayor Rudolph Giuliani stepped up to address the crisis, offer a visible presence, calm the city, and mobilize rescue, recovery, cleanup, and rebuilding efforts. Studies of presidential leadership also illustrate the point about situations and leadership (Goethals, 2005). For example, David Winter (1987) found that presidential candidates are more likely to be elected and reelected when their primary motive in life—whether it is for achievement, power, or affiliation—matches what Americans want most at that time. An alternative to the trait perspective, then, is a view that leadership is the product of a unique interaction between the person and the surrounding situation.

Situations may well dictate the success of a particular leadership style. During the emergence of the dot-com era, for example, the traditional image of a leader who presides from the top down over a hierarchical command structure gave way to a corporate culture in which a leader should be accessible, fluid, lateral, and relationship oriented. But is this situational doctrine necessarily incompatible with the classic trait approach to leadership? Maybe not. In *Primal Leadership,* Daniel Goleman, Richard Boyatzis, and Annie McKee (2002) argue that the primal job of leadership is emotional—and that great leaders are endowed with *emotional intelligence,* an ability to know how people are feeling and how to use that information to guide their own actions. Great leaders are men and women who exude interest, enthusiasm, and other positive emotions and whose energy is contagious. Precisely because demands change from one time, situation, and organization to the next, however, leaders with emotional intelligence are by nature flexible in their style, serving as visionaries, coaches, pacesetters, and so on, as needed.

Contingency Models of Leadership

Illustrative of this interactional perspective is Fred Fiedler's (1967) **contingency model of leadership**. Fiedler argues that a key difference among leaders is whether they are *primarily task oriented* (single-mindedly focused on the job) or *relations oriented* (concerned about the feelings of employees). The amount of control that a leader has determines which type of leadership is more effective. Leaders enjoy *high situational control* when they have good relations with their staff, a position of power, and a clearly structured task. In contrast, leaders exhibit *low situational control* when they have poor relations with their staff, limited power, and a task that is not clearly defined.

Combining these personal and situational components, studies of various work groups suggest that task-oriented leaders are the most effective in clear-cut situations that are either low or high in control and that relations-oriented leaders perform better in situations that afford a moderate degree of control. In low-control situations, groups need guidance, which task-oriented leaders provide by staying focused on the job. In high-control situations, where conditions are already favorable, these same leaders maintain a relaxed, low profile. Relations-oriented leaders are different. They offer too little guidance in low-control situations, and they meddle too much in high-control situations. In ambiguous situations, however, relations-oriented leaders—precisely because of their open, participative, social style—motivate workers to solve problems in creative ways.

contingency model of leadership   The theory that leadership effectiveness is determined both by the personal characteristics of leaders and by the control afforded by the situation.

Studies of military units, sports teams, schools, hospitals, and other organizations generally support Fiedler's model. While this support is far from unanimous, the main point is well taken: Good leadership requires a match between an individual's personal style and the demands of a specific situation (Fiedler & Chemers, 1984). A mismatch—that is, the wrong type of person for the situation—can have negative consequences for both the leader and his or her organization. For example, Martin Chemers and others (1985) surveyed college administrators to determine both their leadership style and their situational control. They found that mismatches were associated with increased job stress, stress-related illness, and absence from work, symptoms that diminish a leader's productivity and competence (Fiedler & Garcia, 1987; Fiedler et al., 1992).

Shown at his famous "I have a dream" speech in Washington, D.C., in August 1963, Martin Luther King, Jr., was a transformational leader who inspired massive change by making supporters believe that anything was possible.

One of the most important tasks for any leader is to make decisions. In the two-way street between leaders and followers, however, it is often important to solicit the opinions of others. How much participation should leaders invite? According to the **normative model of leadership** proposed by Victor Vroom and Philip Yetton (1973), leaders vary widely in this regard. Some are highly autocratic and directive (they invite no feedback from workers), while others are highly participative (they frequently seek and use suggestions from workers). For effective long-term leadership, the key is to invite just the right amount of worker participation—not too much (which is often not efficient) and not too little (which can lower morale). As to what constitutes the right amount, Vroom and Yetton argued that it depends on various factors such as the clarity of the problem, the information available to the leader and followers, and whether it's more important that the decision be right or that one have support.

Although the ideal leader is one who adjusts his or her style to meet the situation, people generally prefer leaders who involve them in important decisions. Research shows that participative decision making boosts worker morale, motivation, and productivity—and reduces turnover and absenteeism rates. Benefits such as these have been found especially in situations where employees want to have input (Vroom & Jago, 1988) and when they are involved in decision making directly rather than through elected representatives (Rubenowitz et al., 1983).

 Transactional Leadership

Although contingency models take both the person and situation into account, Edwin Hollander (1985) criticizes these "top-down" views of leadership in which the workers are portrayed as inert, passive, faceless creatures to be soothed or aroused at the management's discretion. Instead, leadership is seen as a two-way social exchange in which there is mutual and reciprocal influence between a leader and his or her followers. According to Hollander, a good **transactional leader** is one who gains compliance and support from followers by setting clear goals for them, by offering tangible rewards, by providing assistance, and by fulfilling psychological needs in exchange for an expected level of job performance. Transactional leadership thus rests on the leader's willingness and ability to reward subordinates who keep up their end of the bargain—and to correct those who do not.

normative model of leadership The theory that leadership effectiveness is determined by the amount of feedback and participation that leaders invite from workers.

transactional leader A leader who gains compliance and support from followers primarily through goal setting and the use of rewards.

Pioneers of the technology revolution that started in the 1970s, Bill Gates, co-founder of Microsoft (left), and Steven Jobs, co-founder of Apple (right), are two of the most forward-looking business leaders of our time.

Transformational Leadership

Think about some of the greatest leaders of the past century, those who were able to transform the status quo by making supporters believe that anything is possible. Martin Luther King, Jr., was that kind of leader. So were Franklin D. Roosevelt, Mahatma Gandhi, John F. Kennedy, Ronald Reagan, and Nelson Mandela. In their classic book *In Search of Excellence,* Thomas Peters and Robert Waterman (1982) studied sixty-two of America's best businesses and found that their success was due largely to the ability of the leaders to elicit extraordinary efforts from ordinary human beings.

Today, two prominent models of such leadership are Bill Gates and Steven Jobs— co-founders of two of the most important technology companies in the world. In 1975, Gates dropped out of Harvard and co-founded what was then a small company by the name of Microsoft. Long before it seemed possible, he envisioned a day when there would be a PC in every home and office. Then as it was becoming clear that the future resided in cyberspace, he shocked the business world by refocusing Microsoft around the Internet. He is now one of the richest and most philanthropic people in the world. In 1973, Steven Jobs, like Gates, also dropped out of college. He soon co-founded Apple and helped popularize and innovate the "Mac," bringing to it the mouse, a sleek design, and other creative elements. His most recent innovations are the iPod portable music player and the all-in-one gadget, iPhone. In an industry that demands an ability to anticipate the future, adapt quickly to change, take great risks, and enlist support from others, both Gates and Jobs have been leaders.

What's special about Gates, Jobs, and other successful leaders? Based on the work of political scientist James MacGregor Burns (1978, 2003), Bernard Bass (1998; Bass & Riggio, 2006) calls them **transformational leaders**. Transformational leaders motivate others to transcend their personal needs in the interest of a common cause—particularly in times of growth, change, and crisis. Through consciousness raising and raw emotional inspiration, they articulate a clear vision for the future and

transformational leader
A leader who inspires followers to transcend their own needs in the interest of a common cause.

then mobilize others to join in that vision. Over the years, Bass and his colleagues have asked people who work for various business managers and executives, military officers, school principals, government bureaucrats, fire chiefs, and store owners to describe the most outstanding leaders they know (Bass & Avolio, 1990; Hater & Bass, 1988). As shown in Table 13.3, the descriptions they gave revealed four sets of attributes: charisma, inspirational motivation, intellectual stimulation, and an individualized consideration of others. Other studies have shown that transformational leaders are also more extroverted than the average person (Bono & Judge, 2004).

To measure the extent to which individuals possess the attributes of transactional and transformational leadership styles, Bass (1985) devised the Multifactor Leader Questionnaire, or MLQ. Using this instrument, researchers have studied leadership in different cultures and in different types of organizations—including automakers, express-mail companies, multinational corporations, banks, government agencies, and military groups. Others have varied the use of the different leadership styles in controlled laboratory settings. Indicating that inspiration is universally a more power-ful motivator than reward, the results have shown that transformational leaders are more effective than transactional leaders (Bass, 1998; Lowe et al., 1996) and exert in-fluence by getting others to identify personally with them and the social group they represent (Kark et al., 2003). In light of their ability to exert influence, it is not surpris-ing that in a study of 39 managers and 130 employees in six companies, those who emerged as transformational leaders on the MLQ were also more socially networked within their organizations (Bono & Anderson, 2005).

People are drawn like magnets to transformational leaders who have what it takes. But wait. Does this mean that Adolf Hitler, Saddam Hussein, and other author-itarian heads of state were leaders of the same stripe as Mahatma Gandhi, Franklin D. Roosevelt, and Nelson Mandela? One would hope not. To separate human evil from virtue, Bass and Steidlmeier (1999) sought to distinguish between what they call *pseudo*-transformational leaders who appeal to emotions rather than to reason and manipulate ignorant followers to further their own personal interests and *authentic* transformational leaders, who morally uplift followers and help them to transform their collective visions into realities.

The most effective type of leader is one who knows how to win support through the use of reward. **False.**

TABLE 13.3
Characteristics of Transformational Leaders

When people are asked to describe the best leaders they know, four characteristics are most often cited: charisma, an ability to inspire others, intellectual stimulation, and individualized consideration. These attributes are evident in the self-descriptions given here.

(Based on Bass & Avolio, 1990.)

Characteristic	Description	Sample Items
Charisma	Has a vision; gains respect, trust, and confidence; promotes a strong identification of followers.	I have a sense of mission which I communicate to them. They are proud to be associated with me.
Inspiration	Gives pep talks, increases optimism and enthusiasm, and arouses emotion in communications.	I present a vision to spur them on. I use symbols and images to focus their efforts.
Intellectual Stimulation	Actively encourages a re-examination of existing values and assumptions; fosters creativity and the use of intelligence.	I enable them to think about old problems in new ways. I place strong emphasis on careful problem solving before taking action.
Individualized Consideration	Gives personal attention to all members, acts as adviser and gives feedback in ways that are easy to accept, understand, and use for personal development.	I coach individuals who need it. I express my appreciation when they do a good job.

Leadership Among Women and Minorities

Look at the leaders of America's Fortune 500 companies at the start of 2007, and you'll find that only 5 percent of the CEOs are women—a percentage that is not much higher in the health-care industry, government, or educational institutions. Now look at the percentage of African Americans, Hispanics, and Asians in the top ranks of the same organizations, and you'll find that they don't fare any better. Even today, in the twenty-first century, there are proportionally few U.S. senators who are female or Major League Baseball managers who are black. Despite progress that has been made in entry- and middle-level positions, working women and minorities who seek positions of leadership have still not fully broken through the "glass ceiling"—a barrier so subtle that it is transparent yet so strong that it keeps them from reaching the top of the hierarchy (Morrison & Von Glinow, 1990). Indeed, women may also encounter "glass walls" that keep them from moving laterally within an organization—for example, from positions in public relations to those in core areas such as production, marketing, and sales (Lopez, 1992).

Many women are highly qualified for positions of power. Research shows that male and female managers have very similar aspirations, abilities, values, and job-related skills. Indeed, Alice Eagly and Blair Johnson (1990) meta-analyzed the results of 150 studies of sex differences in leadership and found that female leaders in the workplace are as task oriented as their male counterparts. Similarly, Eagly and others (1995) found that male and female leaders are equally effective. The only difference seems to be that men are more controlling and women more democratic in their approaches. As a result, men may be more effective as leaders in positions that require a more directive style (for example, in the military), whereas women may be more effective in managerial settings that require openness and cooperation. When college students in one study were assigned to participate in long-term work groups, centralized leadership structures emerged over time in all-male groups, while more balanced

Meg Whitman is the successful president and CEO of the online marketplace, eBay. She is one of the very few female CEOs of a Fortune 500 Company and is determined to internationalize eBay in what has become a highly competitive market.

and decentralized leadership structures emerged in all-female groups (Berdahl & Anderson, 2005).

This portrayal of women leaders is consistent with Judy Rosener's (1995) observation that today's leading women draw effectively on qualities traditionally seen as feminine. It is also consistent with Sally Helgesen's (1995) observation that female managers interact more with subordinates, invite them to participate in the decision-making process, share information and power, and spin more extensive networks, or "webs of inclusion"—a leadership style she sees as a feminine advantage. Research shows that men and women differ in their style, not in the capacity for leadership. A recent meta-analysis of forty-five comparative studies suggests that female leaders may even be slightly more transactional and transformational than men (Eagly et al., 2003). Other researchers are quick to caution that all claims of a gender advantage in favor of men or women are based on stereotypes and overstated (Vecchio, 2002).

If women are competent to serve as leaders, why have so relatively few managed to reach the top? For women, the path to power—from their entry into the labor market, to recruitment in an organization, and up the promotion ladder—is something of an obstacle course (Ragins & Sundstrom, 1989). One problem is that many women are deeply conflicted about having to juggle a career and family responsibilities (Crosby, 1991). As a result, women even in the executive ranks take more leaves of absence and are somewhat less mobile (Lyness & Thompson, 1997). A second reason is that some women shy away from competitive, hierarchical positions that offer the potential for leadership in favor of professions that involve helping people (Pratto et al., 1997). A third problem is societal. Lingering stereotypes portray women as followers, not as leaders, so some people are uneasy about women in leadership roles—particularly women who have a task-oriented and directive style or who occupy "masculine" positions, as in business (Eagly & Karau, 2002). Thus, in a survey of one hundred male and female corporate executives, Karen Lyness and Donna Thompson (2000) found that while the men and women were equally successful, the women had overcome more barriers to get where they were going. Among the barriers cited were being excluded from informal social networks, being passed over for jobs that required relocating, and not fitting into the corporate culture—perhaps because they lacked role models and mentors, felt like outsiders, or had to meet higher standards of performance.

Statistics show that minorities also fight an uphill battle for leadership positions in business. In interviews, 84 percent of African American MBA graduates from five prestigious business schools said they believed that race had a negative impact on their salaries, performance appraisals, and promotions (Jones, 1986). Research is mixed on the question of whether employee evaluations are biased by race (Roth et al., 2003; Sackett & DuBois, 1991; Stauffer & Buckley, 2005; Waldman & Avolio, 1991). Still, in light of what social psychologists now know about the subtleties of modern racism, as described in Chapter 5, business leaders should beware of the indirect ways in which minorities are handicapped in the pursuit of leadership. In a study of African Americans in the banking industry, for example, many said they felt excluded socially from informal work groups, were not "networked," and lacked the sponsors, role

Attitudes about gender and leadership have changed. In public opinion polls, the number of Americans who say they'd vote for a woman as president rose from 33 percent in 1937 up to 92 percent in 2006.

Born in 1951, Kenneth Irvine Chenault has been chief executive officer of American Express since 2001. He is one of the very few African Americans ever to serve as CEO of a Fortune 500 company. Several years ago, Ebony listed him alongside Rosa Parks, Michael Jordan, Bill Cosby, and Colin Powell as one of fifty "living pioneers" in the African American community.

models, and mentors needed for advancing within an organization (Irons & Moore, 1985). Similarly, a study of business school graduates revealed that African American and Hispanic men were less likely than others to have mentoring relationships with the influential white men in their respective companies (Dreher & Cox, 1996).

Overcoming the obstacles, some minorities do manage to break through the racial divide into positions of leadership. U.S. Secretary of State Condoleezza Rice is one prominent exception. Others include Barack Obama, the Democratic U.S. senator from Illinois, and Kenneth Chenault, chairman and CEO of American Express. How did these individuals, and others who have risen to executive ranks, do it? In *Breaking Through*, David Thomas and John Gabarro (1999) studied the career trajectories and experiences of fifty-four managers and executives in three large companies. Referring to the corporate career ladder as a tournament, they discovered that the successful African-, Asian-, and Hispanic-American executives they studied climbed slowly at first to positions of middle management but were then fast-tracked relative to their white peers into the executive suite. Minority managers have to build a solid foundation early, they suggested, "because they are promoted only after proving themselves again and again." At every step of this developmental process, they found that mentors played a vital role—by opening doors, offering challenging assignments, and sponsoring them for recruitment into important, high-profile positions. In *Leading in Black and White*, Ancella Livers and Keith Caver (2003) further suggested, based on surveys and interviews of black professionals, that success involved some common ingredients such as having a distinct identity and a heightened focus on race, office politics, networking, and again, the need for mentors. People need other people, and the corporate world is no exception.

Motivation

In January 2007, based on surveys of 105,000 employees from 446 companies, Fortune *named Google the best company to work for in America. Located in Mountain View, California, Google provides its staff with free gourmet meals, onsite doctors, daycare, a spa, massages, a laundry service, and time to spend on independent projects. It's no wonder that Google's employees are so motivated—and that the company gets 1,300 résumés a day.*

What motivates individuals to work hard, and to work well? What determines your on-the-job performance? Are you driven by strictly economic concerns, or do you have other personal needs to fulfill? There is no single answer. At work, as in the rest of life, our behavior often stems from the convergence of many different motives.

Economic Reward Models

Out of necessity, people work to make a living. Yet in strictly economic terms, payment is more complicated than it may appear. To begin with, an employee's overall satisfaction with his or her compensation depends not only on salary (gross income, take-home pay) but also on raises (upward or downward changes in pay, how these changes are determined), method of distribution (number of checks received, salary differences within the company), and benefits (stock options, tuition credits, on-site gym facilities, vacation time, sick leave, health insurance, pensions, and other services). Each of these factors constitutes part of a formula for satisfaction (Heneman & Schwab, 1985; Judge & Welbourne, 1994). In fact, many rewards are not monetary but symbolic—such as titles, office size, location, carpeting, furnishings, windows, and the ability to regulate access by others (Becker, 1981; Sundstrom, 1986).

Perhaps the most popular theory of worker motivation is Victor Vroom's

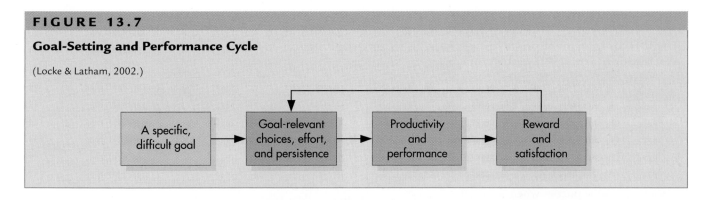

FIGURE 13.7

Goal-Setting and Performance Cycle

(Locke & Latham, 2002.)

(1964) **expectancy theory**. According to Vroom, people are rational decision makers who analyze the benefits and costs of the possible courses of action. Accordingly, he says, workers become motivated and exert effort when they believe that: (1) their effort will result in an improved performance, (2) their performance will be recognized and rewarded, and (3) the monetary and symbolic rewards that are offered are valuable and desirable. Over the years, this theory has been used with some success to predict worker attendance, productivity, and other job-related behaviors (Mitchell, 1974; Van Eerde & Thierry, 1996).

Goal setting is particularly important for motivation. Research shows that people perform better at work and are more productive when they are given specific goals and clear standards for success and failure than when they're simply told to "do your best" (Locke & Latham, 1990). Financial incentives, in particular, can effectively boost worker productivity without compromising the quality of the work (Jenkins et al., 1998). Based on past research, Edwin Locke and Gary Latham (2002) offer a practically useful theory of goal setting. The key, they maintain, is for people to set specific and difficult goals for themselves or others. This practice increases goal-related choice, effort, and persistence, increases productivity and other aspects of performance, brings reward and satisfaction, and triggers a willingness to take on new challenges and set new goals, thus setting into motion a self-perpetuating cycle of high performance (see Figure 13.7).

Bonuses, Bribes, and Intrinsic Motivation

People may strive for reward, but there's more to money than just economics and more to motivation than the size of a paycheck. Social psychological factors must also be considered. Under certain conditions, reward systems that increase *extrinsic motivation* may undermine *intrinsic motivation*. As we saw in Chapter 3, people are thought to be extrinsically motivated when they engage in an activity for money, recognition, or other tangible rewards. In contrast, people are said to be intrinsically motivated when they perform for the sake of interest, challenge, or sheer enjoyment. Business leaders want employees to feel intrinsically motivated and committed to their work. So where do expectancy theory and incentive programs fit in? Is tangible reward the bottom line or not?

Research shows that when people start getting paid for a task they already enjoy, they sometimes lose interest in it. In the first demonstration of this effect, Edward Deci (1971) recruited college students to work for three one-hour sessions on block-building puzzles they found interesting. During the first and third sessions, all participants were treated in the same manner. In the second session, however, half were paid one dollar for each puzzle they completed. To measure intrinsic motivation, Deci left participants alone during a break in the first and third sessions and recorded the amount of time they spent on the puzzles rather than on other available activities. Compared with participants in the unrewarded group, those who had been paid in the second session later showed less interest in the puzzles when the money was no longer available (see Figure 13.8).

This paradoxical finding that rewards undermine intrinsic motivation has been observed in many laboratory and field studies (Deci & Ryan, 1985; Lepper & Greene, 1978; Tang & Hall, 1995). By making people feel controlled rather than autonomous, various extrinsic factors commonly found in the workplace—deadlines, punishment,

expectancy theory
The theory that workers become motivated when they believe that their efforts will produce valued outcomes.

FIGURE 13.8

The Effect of Payment on Intrinsic Motivation: Turning Play into Work

In this study, participants worked three times on puzzles they found interesting. After each session, the amount of free time spent on the puzzles served as a record of intrinsic motivation. During the second session, half of the participants were paid for puzzles they completed, and half were not. Those paid in the second session later showed less interest in the puzzles when the money was no longer available.

(Deci, 1971.)

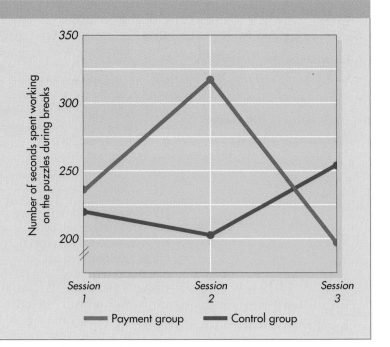

close supervision, evaluation, and competition—also have adverse effects on motivation and performance. Thus, Teresa Amabile (1996) found that people who were paid for artistic activities, compared with others who were not paid, produced work that was later judged to be less creative by independent raters. To be maximally productive, people should feel internally driven, not compelled by outside forces.

But wait. If money undermines intrinsic motivation, should employers *not* use monetary incentives? Are the pay-for-performance programs often used in the workplace doomed to fail, as some have suggested? (Kohn, 1993). Not at all. To answer these questions, it's important to realize that any given reward can be interpreted in two ways, depending on how it is presented. On the one hand, being offered payment can make a person feel bribed, bought off, and controlled, which can result in the detrimental effects just described. On the other hand, rewards often provide people with positive feedback about the quality of their performance, as when people earn bonuses, scholarships, and verbal praise from others they respect. Research now shows that although controlling rewards tend to lower intrinsic motivation, informational rewards have the opposite positive effect both on motivation (Eisenberger & Cameron, 1996) and on creativity (Eisenberger & Rhoades, 2001).

Equity Considerations

A second aspect of payment that influences motivation is the perception that it is fair. According to *equity theory*, presented in Chapter 9, people want rewards to be equitable. In other words, the ratio between inputs and outcomes should be the same for the self as it is for others. Relative to co-workers, then, the more effort you exert and the more you contribute, the more money you should earn. If you feel overpaid or underpaid, however, you will experience distress and try to relieve it by (1) restoring actual equity, say, by working less or getting a raise, or (2) convincing yourself that equity already exists (Cropanzano, 1993).

"We are prepared to offer you a compensation package that includes a significant portion of the Western Hemisphere."

Equity theory has some fascinating implications for behavior in the workplace. Consider Jerald Greenberg's (1988) study of employees in a large insurance firm. To allow for refurbishing, nearly two hundred workers had to be moved temporarily from one office to another. Randomly, the workers were assigned to offices that usually belonged to others who were higher, lower, or equal in rank. Predictably, those with the higher rank had a more spacious office, fewer occupants, and a larger desk. Would the random assignments influence job performance? By keeping track of the number of insurance cases processed, and by rating the complexity of the cases and the quality of the decisions made, Greenberg was able to derive a measure of job performance for each worker before, during, and after the office switch. To restore equity, he reasoned, workers assigned to higher-status offices would feel overcompensated and improve at their job performance, and those sent to lower-status offices would feel undercompensated and slow their performance. That is exactly what happened. Figure 13.9 shows that the results offered sound support for equity theory.

Satisfaction depends not only on equity outcomes but also on the belief that the means used to determine those outcomes were fair and clearly communicated (Brockner & Wiesenfeld, 1996; Folger, 1986). For example, Greenberg (1990) studied workers in three manufacturing plants owned by the same parent company. Business was slow, so the company reduced its payroll through temporary pay cuts. Would the cuts make workers feel underpaid? If so, how would the workers restore equity? Concerned that the policy might trigger employee theft, Greenberg randomly varied the conditions in the three plants. In one, the employees were told, without an explanation, that they would receive a 15 percent pay cut for ten weeks. In the second plant, the same pay cut was accompanied by an explanation and expressions of regret. In the third plant, salaries were not cut. By keeping track of inventories for the ten weeks

FIGURE 13.9

Equity in the Workplace

Insurance company workers were moved temporarily to offices that were higher, lower, or equal in status to their own rank. Supporting equity theory, those assigned to higher-status offices increased their job performance, and those sent to lower-status offices showed a decrease. When workers were reassigned to original offices, productivity levels returned to normal.

(Greenberg, 1988.)

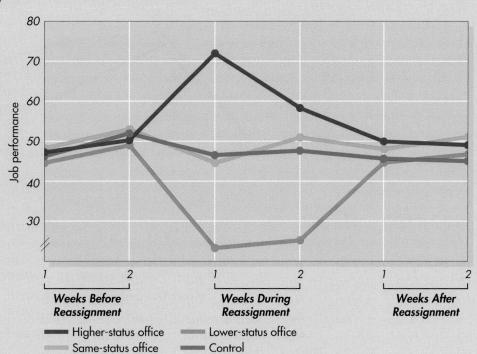

before, during, and after the pay cuts, Greenberg was able to estimate the employee theft rate. The result: Workers whose pay had been cut stole more from the company, presumably to restore equity, but only when not provided with an adequate explanation for their loss. When it comes to getting paid, praised, and treated with respect, people are most dedicated to their jobs when they believe they are being treated fairly (Folger & Cropanzano, 1998).

People are so sensitive to unfairness, underpayment, and maltreatment that these feelings can cause stress and compromise their health. In a survey of more than 3,500 workers, Bennett Tepper (2001) discovered that those who felt victimized by injustice in the workplace also reported the most exhaustion, anxiety, and depression. Particularly stressful is the combination of feeling underpaid and unfairly treated. Theorizing that people will lose sleep over these concerns, Greenberg (2006) studied 467 nurses at four private hospitals, two of which cut nurses' salaries by 10 percent. In one hospital from each group, he taught nursing supervisors how to promote feelings of organizational justice. Across a six-month period, participants periodically reported on their nighttime sleep patterns. The results showed two interesting patterns: (1) Underpaid nurses reported more symptoms of insomnia than those whose salaries were unchanged, and (2) this problem was reduced among underpaid nurses whose supervisors had been trained to treat them fairly (see Figure 13.10).

Equity in the workplace is important, perhaps more so for men than for women. In studies of reward allocation, people are led to believe that they and a

FIGURE 13.10

Losing Sleep over Underpayment and Organizational Injustice

Nurses were studied at four hospitals—two that cut their salaries, two that did not. In one hospital of each group, supervisors were trained to promote feelings of organizational justice. For six months, participating nurses reported on their nighttime sleep patterns. As shown, those whose salaries had been cut reported more sleep loss than the others, but the problem was reduced among nurses whose supervisors had been trained to treat them fairly.

(Greenberg, 2006.)

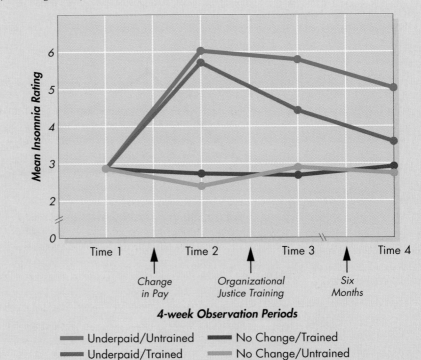

"Productivity is up nine percent since I made everyone a vice-president."

partner are working at a task for which they will be paid. They work separately, receive false feedback on their performance, and then are told that they must decide how to divide a joint reward. In this situation, women typically pay themselves less than men do and react less strongly when they are underpaid by others (Major & Deaux, 1982). Studies of outcomes outside the laboratory reinforce the point. A study of male and female graduates of an Ivy League business school showed that the men were more likely than the women to negotiate starting salaries that were higher than those initially offered (Gerhart & Rynes, 1991). Other studies have confirmed this result: Men negotiate more aggressively than women do (Babcock & Laschever, 2003; Stuhlmacher & Walters, 1999).

The gender wage gap has been narrowing in recent years, but it has not been fully closed. In 1980, American women earned only 60 cents for every dollar that men were paid. By 1990, the figure was up slightly, to 72 cents. By 2006, it had climbed to 87 cents. There are many possible explanations for this gender wage gap. One is that women expect less pay than men do, even when they are equally qualified—an expectation that stems, perhaps, from a long history of discrimination (Major & Konar, 1984). Second, women sometimes care less about money and more about interpersonal relationships (Crosby, 1982). Third, women may be satisfied with less money because they compare themselves with other women instead of their more highly paid male counterparts (Bylsma et al., 1995; Chesler & Goodman, 1976). Fourth, women on average tend to rate themselves less favorably than do men; so even when they work harder and perform better, they feel less entitled (Major et al., 1984). Whatever the explanation, it is clear that the gender gap in wages is deeply rooted in history (Goldin, 1990). However, it appears equally clear that today's working women are not content to remain underpaid relative to men. The gender wage gap should thus vanish as successive generations of women become more established in high-paying careers.

People who feel "overpaid" work harder on the job than those who see their pay as appropriate. **True.**

Economic Decision Making

"Money is power, freedom, a cushion, the root of all evil, the sum of blessings."
—Carl Sandburg

People are intensely focused on money—anxious to have more of it and fearful to be without it. In powerful ways, money arouses emotion, activates thought, and motivates action. We ran a Google search on the word *money* at the start of 2007 and found that there were 92.6 million entries, exceeding the 82.8 million entries generated by the word *happiness* (being social psychologists, we were interested to find that *love* conquered all at 1.47 *b*illion entries).

Although actor and comedian W. C. Fields once said that a rich man is nothing but a poor man with money, common sense—and now recent research—suggest that money can change people. In a series of laboratory studies, Kathleen Vohs and her colleagues (2006) found that when college students were primed to think about money, they became more self-sufficient, more autonomous, and less social in relation to others. In each experiment, the researchers primed money in some participants but not others in subtle ways—for example, by having them read an essay that mentioned money, by presenting them with scrambled sentences that relate to money, by having them count a large stack of Monopoly money, or by seating them at a computer with a screensaver that featured floating bills. Across the board, those exposed to money cues later became more independent. Put into a social situation, they preferred working alone rather than on a team, put more distance between themselves and a fellow participant, sought less help on a puzzle they could not solve, and gave less help to someone who needed it. Discussing these findings, Vohs speculates that "money changes people at a core, basic level," that "having money makes people feel less connected and more independent, whereas having little money makes you feel more interdependent with others" (Carpenter, 2005, p. 27).

In recent years, social psychologists have become interested in how people make economic decisions, as when they invest in the stock market. The stock market can be remarkably volatile, as it has been over the past decade—surging up, plummeting down, and inching its way back up, in ways that resemble a roller coaster. Why does the market fluctuate so much? Are the companies we invest in unpredictable from day to day, or are social psychological factors at work? To what extent are the day-to-day price movements determined by rational economic indicators such as the gross domestic product, interest rates, budget surpluses and deficits, inflation, employment statistics, company earnings, political uncertainty, consumer confidence, and stock prices that are too high or too low and in need of correction? To what extent, for that matter, is the stock market influenced by fear, greed, false beliefs, financial experts like CNBC's Jim Cramer who appear on business shows, rumors that spread over the Internet, conformity pressures, and other social influences, all compounded by the speed with which people can now trade stocks online?

 ## Social Influences in the Stock Market

The odds of making money are far better in the stock market than in the slot machines found in gambling casinos. Most of the time, most investors come out ahead. In many ways, however, choosing stocks is like gambling. In *A Random Walk down Wall Street,* first published in 1981, economist Burton Malkiel (2007) reported that over the long haul, mutual fund portfolios compiled by experts perform no better than randomly selected groups of stocks. Thus, when *Consumer Reports* evaluated the advice given by professional brokers, it concluded that "a monkey throwing darts at the stock pages . . . could probably do as well in overall investment performance, perhaps even better" (Shefrin & Statman, 1986, p. 52).

But don't some professionals turn a greater profit than others? And if stock prices rise and fall in reaction to market conditions and the success of a company in relation to its competitors, can't the astute investor, or short-term day trader, take advantage of these relationships? The answer to both questions is "not necessarily." It is certainly true that some brokers perform better than others do for a period of time, perhaps even for a few years. But individuals are no more likely to succeed after a string of wins than after a string of losses. Since many investors and traders have access to the same information and since stock prices can change at a moment's notice, short-term price movements in the market cannot be predicted with precision or reliability. The only way to guarantee profit is to use confidential inside information, which is illegal. Yet studies show that the average person has great faith in professional investors, overestimating their success relative to actual performance (Törngren & Montgomery, 2004).

If stock market decisions are not made on strictly economic grounds, then on what are they based? As described in *Greed and Fear,* Hersh Shefrin's (2006) book on the behavioral finance and the psychology of investing, predictions of the future on Wall Street are heavily influenced by social psychological factors. In October of 1987, for example, the U.S. stock market crashed, resulting in an estimated loss of $500 billion. Shortly afterward, economist Robert Shiller sent questionnaires to a large group of active traders to try to determine what caused the crisis. For the one thousand or so investors who responded, the key event was news concerning the market itself—including a sharp decline

"I don't buy stocks simply because others are buying them. I buy them because many, many others are buying them."

Today's stock market investors are bombarded by social influences on TV business shows, such as CNBC's hit show Mad Money, *with Jim Cramer.*

Roughly 50 percent of American adults have money invested in the stock market.

that occurred on the morning of the crash. In other words, price movements in the stock market were triggered not by objective economic information but by other price movements in the market. Does this phenomenon ring a bell? Studies on the processes of social comparison and conformity have shown that when people feel they cannot clearly and concretely measure their own opinion, they turn to others for guidance. Perhaps that is why investors are more influenced by news and stock market tips during periods of rising or falling prices than during periods of relative stability (Schachter et al., 1985).

With respect to coin flips and other chance events, gamblers too often assume that hot streaks are due to turn cold, and vice versa. Yet when it comes to games of skill, such as basketball, people often make the opposite assumption that a hot streak forecasts continued success, while a cold spell predicts failure. Both assumptions are incorrect. One event does not imply another. But what about the ups and downs of a stock market? Do either of these beliefs color the decisions made by investors?

To explore this question, Stanley Schachter and his colleagues (1987) presented college students with recent price histories of stocks that had increased, decreased, or remained stable over a three-week period. The conventional wisdom on Wall Street, of course, is that investors should "buy low and sell high." Yet most participants decided to buy stocks that had risen and sell those that had fallen. In a follow-up study, very similar decisions were made by more sophisticated students attending the business school at Columbia University.

Do people always go with the flow of the marketplace, or do they sometimes buck the trend to buy low and sell high? Paul Andreasson (1987) argued that the answer depends on attributions. According to Andreasson, investors may follow conventional wisdom. But, he asked, what about price changes for which they have a ready explanation? What if a rise in a stock's price is attributed to certain company or world events? As far as the stock market is concerned, attributions such as these can produce self-fulfilling prophecies by leading investors to believe that the changes will persist—that rising prices will continue to climb or that declining prices will continue to fall. To test his hypothesis, Andreasson simulated a stock market on the computer and found that without news stories to explain the fluctuations, research participants assumed that prices would gravitate to previous levels. The result: They bought stocks when the price was low and sold when the price was high. However, those who also received *Wall Street Journal* explanations for the changes pursued the less profitable strategy, buying stocks that were climbing (based on the assumption that they would continue to do so) and selling those that were on the decline (based on the same assumption of continuity).

Even unpublished rumors can have this effect. Nicholas DiFonzo and Prashant Bordia (1997) conducted a stock market simulation in which unconfirmed company rumors were leaked to some participants but not others. Interestingly, the participants said that the rumors were not credible and did not sway their decisions. Yet they traded on these rumors as if they were hard facts. It doesn't stretch the imagination to see how all these findings might relate to actual behavior in the stock market. Faced with upward and downward movements, the financial news media often seize upon current events for a quick explanation. In some cases, the rumors spread like fire through the business community. Whether the news is true or false is irrelevant. Either way, it can turn an initial rise into a bull rally and an initial dip into a steep dive. At present, researchers are using laboratory simulations to mimic the decision making that causes stock market bubbles, crashes, and other phenomena (Porter & Smith, 2003).

Sometimes emotional factors can lead us astray. Contradicting rational theories of economic decision making, research shows that people often fall prey to the **endowment effect**, a tendency to inflate the value of objects they already own (Thaler, 1980). In a study that demonstrates this point, people demanded a higher price for a coffee mug that had been given to them than for a comparable mug they did not yet own (Kahneman et al., 1990). In a second study, researchers observed the orders placed by Australian stock market investors and found that sellers valued their own shares higher than buyers did, regardless of the current market price (Furche & Johnstone, 2006).

Commitment, Entrapment, and Escalation

Stock market behavior, like all other business decisions that individuals and organizations make, is complicated by another social factor. Shefrin and Meir Statman (1985) argued that many investors lack the self-control necessary for sound investment decisions. When people own shares of a stock that is climbing, they sometimes sell too early so they can enjoy the quick pleasure of making a profit. This tendency is easy to understand. But when people own stock that is falling, they often wait too long before selling in the hope that they might avoid a financial loss. Why do people often continue to hang on in a failing situation—a decision-making disease that Shefrin (2006) calls "Get-Evenitis"? When the handwriting is on the wall, why compound the problem by throwing good money after bad?

In *Too Much Invested to Quit,* Alan Teger (1980) described a dollar-auction game that illustrates part of the dilemma. Imagine yourself in this situation: The auctioneer tells you and other participants that a one-dollar bill is about to be sold. As in a typical auction, the highest bidder will receive the dollar in exchange for the amount bid. Yet contrary to convention, the second highest bidder must also pay the amount bid and will receive nothing in return. You and the other participants are asked not to communicate, and the minimum opening bid is set at five cents. Then before you know it, the bidding begins. In laboratory experiments, two participants compete in the auction. They are supplied with a small amount of money that is theirs to keep, and they are free to quit the experiment at any time. What happens next can be startling. Some pairs reasonably choose to take the money and run without making a single bid. Other pairs, however, get involved in escalating bidding wars. According to Teger, bidding for the dollar frequently climbs into the five-dollar range—more than the amount allocated for play by the experimenter. On one occasion, the auctioneer had to terminate the game after the two participants had bid $24.95 and $25.00!

The dollar auction helps us to understand how we can become financially overcommitted in real life. In Chapter 8, we saw that individuals and groups can become *entrapped* by their own initial commitments as they try to justify or salvage investments already made. In business, the economic conditions in which an investment is made sometimes justify continued commitment. When there is a reasonable likelihood of success, and when potential earnings are high relative to the additional necessary costs, it may pay to persist. With certain long-term investments, sizable up-

endowment effect The tendency for people to inflate the value of objects, goods, or services they already own.

front costs have to be endured before the delayed benefits are likely to materialize. As in the dollar auction, however, entrapment may also occur when economic conditions do not provide a basis for optimism.

Why do investors, business executives, and others losing money on a failing investment so often "hang tough," only to sink deeper and deeper? Why do supervisors who recommend that a worker be hired later overrate that worker's job performance compared with others in the company who were not involved in the hiring? (Schoorman, 1988). Why do NBA basketball teams continue to start players who were selected as top draft picks but have not performed well? (Staw & Hoang, 1995). One explanation for these *escalation effects* is that while people ordinarily avoid taking large financial risks to gain money, they are often willing to take risks to keep from losing money. When offered a hypothetical choice between a certain gain of $1,000 and a fifty-fifty shot at a gain of $2,500, most people choose the smaller guaranteed alternative. Yet when offered a choice between a certain loss of $1,000 and a fifty-fifty shot at a loss of $2,500, most people roll the dice (Kahneman & Tversky, 1979).

Our aversion to loss accounts for part of the problem, but it's clear that social psychological factors also contribute heavily to the escalation effect. Research has shown that those individuals who make the decisions that lead to loss are more likely than others to persist, or even to invest further, when they feel personally responsible. Why? There are two reasons, both valid (Moon, 2001). One is that people are trained to finish what they have started—a desire for completion that can lead people to throw good money or time after bad (Garland & Conlon, 1998). The second, according to Barry Staw, Joel Brockner, and others, is that people often remain committed to a failing course of action in order to justify their prior decisions, protect their self-esteem, or save face in front of others. Thus, Staw and his colleagues (1997) found that banks were less likely to cut their losses on bad business and real estate loans when the executives who had funded those loans were still with the bank than when they were not. Zhang and Baumeister (2006) found that participants whose self-esteem was threatened were more likely to become entrapped in a failing laboratory game, losing more money as a result.

In organizations, escalation effects can be minimized by removing the individuals who made the initial losing investment from the decision making later on. Fortunately, individual investors can also learn to use various de-escalation strategies designed to make them more responsive to available evidence and keep them from throwing good money after bad (Simonson & Staw, 1992). In one study, for example, Richard Larrick and others (1990) found that people often violate the **sunk cost principle** of economics, which states that only future costs and benefits, not past commitments, or "sunk costs," should be considered in making a decision. To appreciate the practical implications, imagine that you've bought a forty-dollar ticket to a basketball game weeks in advance. Now, on the day of the game, you don't feel well, it's snowing, and your favorite player is injured. Do you still go to the game to make sure you use the ticket? Not wanting to "waste" the money, many of us would go even though the money is already sunk, and even though we would have to bear the added costs of getting sick, driving in bad weather, and sitting through a boring game. To see if there is a more rational economic choice, ask yourself this question: Would you go to the game if someone called on game day and offered you a free ticket? If you said that you would go if you'd paid for the ticket but not if it were free, then—like investors who don't know when to cut their losses—you fell into the sunk cost trap and should have stayed home.

Over and over again, studies have shown that human adults fall prey to the sunk cost effect, allowing their economic decisions to be biased by past investments of time, money, and effort, a maladaptive tendency that, curiously, is *not* exhibited by children or laboratory animals (Arkes & Ayton, 1999). Thankfully, we are trainable. In a study of University of Michigan professors, Larrick and others (1990) found that the economists among them were more likely than their counterparts in other disciplines to use the sunk cost principle—not only in hypothetical problems but also in personal decisions. More important, they found that others can be taught to apply the rule as well. Indeed, a full month after exposure to a brief training session, college students were more likely to report using the rule in their own lives. Sometimes a little knowledge can go a long way.

People losing money on an investment tend to cut their losses rather than hang tough. **False.**

sunk cost principle The economic rule of thumb that only future costs and benefits, not past commitments, should be considered in making a decision.

REVIEW

- The classic Hawthorne studies showed that worker productivity was increased by the attention paid to the workers.

- In the workplace and other business settings, behavior is heavily influenced by social psychological factors.

Personnel Selection

- Recruiting a competent staff is the first important step in the development of a successful organization.

Traditional Employment Interviews

- Employment interviews may actually diminish the tendency to make simple stereotyped judgments.

- But interviews often give rise to poor selection decisions, in part because of applicant self-presentations and interviewer expectations that bias the interview.

"Scientific" Alternatives to Traditional Interviews

- Many companies use standardized tests of cognitive ability, personality, and integrity as part of the selection process.

- Although overt integrity tests are easy to fake, covert tests are not, and the results are somewhat predictive of job performance.

- A more effective selection method is the structured interview, in which all applicants are evaluated in a standardized manner.

- Many organizations use assessment centers, in which multiple applicants take part in multiple activities monitored by a group of evaluators.

Affirmative Action

- Affirmative action affects those whom it is designed to help, those who feel excluded by it, organizations that implement it, and interactions among these three groups.

- Research shows that women devalue their own performance when they think they have been preferentially selected.

- But reactions are more favorable when procedures are seen as fair, when merit-based factors are thought to play a role.

Culture and Organizational Diversity

- Affirmative action and the globalization of business have combined to increase diversity in the workplace.

- One prediction is that diversity will breed division and conflict, making worker teams less effective.

- A more optimistic prediction is that diversity will increase the range of perspectives brought to bear on a problem, enhancing group performance.

- At present, research provides a hint of support for both predictions, suggesting that there is no single or simple effect.

Performance Appraisals

- Performance appraisals involve the evaluation of an employee and communication of the results to that person.

- Sometimes objective measures of performance are available, but usually evaluations are based on subjective judgments.

Supervisor Ratings

- Research shows that supervisor ratings are based largely on job-relevant characteristics.

- These ratings may be biased by halo effects, contrast effects, and individual differences in the tendency to give high, low, or neutral ratings on a numeric scale.

Self-Evaluations

- Self-evaluations also figure into performance appraisals, but they tend to be self-serving and inflated.

- Self-evaluations are higher among those who have power in an organization; they are also higher among men than among women.

New and Improved Methods of Appraisal

- Performance appraisals can be improved by making ratings shortly after observation, taking careful notes, using multiple raters, and training raters in the necessary skills.

Due Process Considerations

- Procedural fairness (not just outcomes) is an important factor in the way people react to evaluations of their performance.

Leadership

- Everyone agrees that leadership requires social influence.

The Classic Trait Approach

- One approach is to identify the traits that characterize people who appear to have leadership qualities.
- Situational theories are based on the notion that different situations call for different types of leaders.

Contingency Models of Leadership

- In Fiedler's contingency model, task-oriented leaders excel in high- and low-control situations, whereas relations-oriented leaders are effective in moderate-control situations.
- According to the normative model, leaders range from autocratic to participative; the key to good leadership is to invite the right amount of worker participation.

Transactional Leadership

- Transactional leaders reward followers who keep up their end of the bargain and correct those who do not.

Transformational Leadership

- Transformational leaders motivate followers through their charisma, inspiration, intellectual stimulation, and personal concern for others.
- Studies show that transformational leaders are more effective than transactional leaders.

Leadership Among Women and Minorities

- Despite recent gains, working women and minorities are underrepresented in positions of leadership.
- Many women are qualified, but they encounter obstacles at home and at work, where people hold stereotypes about women in leadership roles.
- Part of the problem for minorities is that they are excluded from social networks and influential mentors in the workplace.

Motivation

- Both economic and social factors influence motivation in the workplace.

Economic Reward Models

- On the economic side, Vroom's expectancy theory states that workers behave in ways designed to produce the most desirable outcome.
- Various incentive programs are thus used to motivate by reward.

Bonuses, Bribes, and Intrinsic Motivation

- When people perceive a reward as a bribe and a means of controlling their behavior, they lose interest in the work itself.
- But when a reward is presented as a bonus, giving positive information about the quality of work, it can enhance intrinsic motivation.

Equity Considerations

- Equity theory says that the ratio between inputs and outcomes should be the same for all workers.
- Thus, research shows that workers do adjust their productivity levels upward when they feel overpaid and downward when they feel underpaid.
- For various reasons, women accept as equitable a lower level of pay than men do.

Economic Decision Making

- Research shows that money makes people feel more independent, more self-sufficient, and less in need of others.
- Economic decisions are often influenced by social psychological factors.

Social Influences in the Stock Market

- Sharp changes in the stock market can be triggered by news of what other investors are doing.
- The goal in the stock market is to buy low and sell high, yet various factors can lead investors to follow less profitable strategies.
- Stock market simulations have shown that investors can be influenced by news stories and unconfirmed rumors, which can set in motion a self-fulfilling prophecy.

Commitment, Entrapment, and Escalation

- People often become entrapped by their initial commitments and so stick to failing courses of action and throw good money after bad.
- At an organizational level, escalation can be minimized by removing those who made the initial losing investment from later decision making.
- Individually, people can be taught de-escalation strategies, such as the rule that only future costs and benefits, not sunk costs, are relevant to economic decisions.

KEY TERMS

assessment center (479)

contingency model of leadership (488)

endowment effect (502)

expectancy theory (495)

Hawthorne effect (474)

industrial/organizational (I/O) psychology (473)

integrity tests (477)

normative model of leadership (489)

performance appraisal (484)

structured interview (478)

sunk cost principle (503)

transactional leader (489)

transformational leader (490)

PUTTING COMMON SENSE TO THE TEST

Although flawed, job interviews consistently make for better hiring decisions.

False. Although interviews may lessen the tendency among employers to make simple stereotyped judgments, they often lack predictive validity.

A problem with having workers evaluate their own job performance is that self-ratings are overly positive.

True. Self-evaluations of job performance are not only more positive than ratings made by others but also less predictive of success.

The most effective type of leader is one who knows how to win support through the use of reward.

False. Great leaders articulate a vision and then inspire others to join in that vision and work for a common cause.

People who feel "overpaid" work harder on the job than those who see their pay as appropriate.

True. People who feel overpaid work harder to restore their sense of equity.

People losing money on an investment tend to cut their losses rather than hang tough.

False. People often remain committed to a failing course of action in order to justify the initial decision to themselves and others.

14

Health

PREVIEW

This chapter explores the social psychology of physical and mental health. We focus first on the links between *stress and health*. Four questions are asked in this regard: *What causes stress, how does it affect the body, how do we appraise* potentially stressful situations, and what are some *ways of coping with stress*? Next we discuss some of the social influences on *treatment and prevention*. We then conclude on a positive note, looking at the *roots of happiness*.

PUTTING COMMON SENSE TO THE TEST

T/F

_____ The accumulation of daily hassles does more to make people sick than catastrophes or major life changes.

_____ Like humans, zebras get ulcers.

_____ Stress can weaken the heart, but it cannot affect the immune system.

_____ When it comes to physical health, research does not support popular beliefs about the power of positive thinking.

_____ People who have lots of friends are healthier and live longer than those who live more isolated lives.

_____ As role models, celebrities have great influence over public health-care decisions.

W hen Laurence Sterne, an eighteenth-century English novelist, weighed the value of good health, he concluded that it was "above all gold and treasure." Most would agree. Because health matters so much, health care is always near the top of the list of priorities in every country. The long and complex debate about health care in the United States and elsewhere clearly illustrates the intensity of feelings on this issue. Everyone cares about health and its care, including social psychologists.

The reasons that social psychologists study *mental health* and such disorders as anxiety and depression are obvious. We humans are inherently social creatures, and our psychological well-being can be both damaged and repaired by our relationships with other people. But social psychologists are also intensely interested in *physical health,* a domain normally associated with medicine. Working in universities, medical schools, hospitals, and government agencies, many social psychologists are deeply involved in an emerging area of **health psychology**—the application of psychology to the promotion of physical health and the prevention and treatment of illness (Friedman & Silver, 2006; Suls & Wallston, 2003; Taylor, 2006a). You may wonder: What does social psychology have to do with catching a cold, having a heart attack, or being afflicted by cancer? If you could turn the clock back a few years and ask your family doctor, his or her reply would be "nothing." In the past, physical illness was considered a purely biological event. But this strict medical perspective has now given way to a broader model, which holds that health is a joint product of biological, psychological, and social factors.

Part of the reason for this expanded view is that illness patterns over the years have changed in significant ways. In the year 1900, the principal causes of death in the United States were contagious diseases such as polio, smallpox, tuberculosis, typhoid fever, malaria, influenza, and pneumonia. Today, none of these infectious illnesses is a leading killer. Instead, Americans are most likely to die, in order of risk, from heart disease, cancers, strokes, respiratory diseases, and accidents (AIDS is twentieth on the list in the United States but fourth worldwide)—problems that are sometimes preventable through changes in lifestyle, outlook, and behavior. In light of the useful research that has been conducted in recent years, this chapter focuses first on stress: what causes it, what it does to the body, and how we appraise stressful situations in an effort to cope. Next, we look at some social influences on the treatment and prevention of illness. Finally, we consider the pursuit of happiness itself.

health psychology The study of physical health and illness by psychologists from various areas of specialization.

According to the World Health Organization, the average life expectancy ranges from a low of thirty-three years in Swaziland up to eighty-three in Andorra (the average life expectancy is seventy-eight years in the United States, eighty in Canada).

For up-to-date health statistics, you can visit online the World Health Organization (www.who.org) and the National Center for Health Statistics (www.cdc.gov/nchs).

FIGURE 14.1

The Stress-and-Coping Process

This process involves a potentially stressful event, the appraisal of that event, and attempts to cope. Played out against a variety of background factors unique to each individual, the stress-and-coping process influences health outcomes.

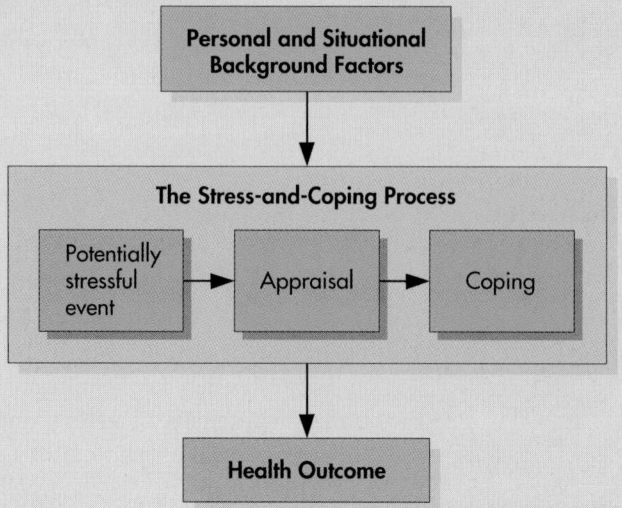

Stress and Health

Anthony Robbins offers a simple two-step formula for handling stress: (1) Don't sweat the small stuff, and (2) remember that it's all small stuff.

stress An unpleasant state of arousal in which people perceive the demands of an event as taxing or exceeding their ability to satisfy or alter those demands.

appraisal The process by which people make judgments about the demands of potentially stressful events and their ability to meet those demands.

coping Efforts to reduce stress.

Stress is an unpleasant state of arousal that arises when we perceive that the demands of a situation threaten our ability to cope effectively. Nobody knows the precise extent of the problem, but stress is a potent killer. Regardless of who you are, when you were born, or where you live, you have no doubt experienced stress. Sitting in rush-hour traffic, packing your belongings to move, getting married or divorced, losing hours of work to a computer crash, getting into an argument with a close friend, worrying about an unwanted pregnancy or the health of your child, living in a high-crime neighborhood, struggling to make financial ends meet, and caring for a loved one who is sick are the kinds of stresses and strains we all must live with. Whether the stress is short term or long term, serious or mild, no one is immune, and there is no escape. But there are ways to cope.

According to Richard Lazarus and Susan Folkman (1984), the stress-and-coping process is an ongoing transaction between a person and his or her environment. Faced with an event that may prove threatening, our subjective **appraisal** of the situation determines how we will experience the stress and what **coping** strategies we will use—in other words, what thoughts, feelings, and behaviors we will employ to try to reduce the stress. At times, people also take proactive steps to keep a potentially stressful event from occurring in the first place. As we'll see, effective coping helps to maintain good health; ineffective coping can cause harm (Snyder, 2001).

In the next two sections, we examine two questions of relevance to health and well-being: (1) What causes stress? (2) How does stress "get into" the body? Then we look at appraisal and coping, processes that account for why an event that flattens one person can prove harmless to another. As all the pieces come together, we'll see that the answers to these questions provide a broad and useful model of the stress-and-coping process (see Figure 14.1).

What Causes Stress?

There are many different sources of stress, or **stressors**, and these can be defined and measured in different ways (Cohen et al., 1995). What events do *you* find stressful? Try jotting down some of the stressors in your own life, and you'll probably find that the items on your list can be sorted into three major categories: catastrophes, major life events, and daily hassles.

Crises and Catastrophes

"We are running from the wave, and we can see the water right behind us. We run toward the other side of the island. When we get about halfway across, we meet people running and screaming from the other direction. Then we see the water in front of us too. The waves meet, and we are under water" (Dittmann, 2005, p. 36).

On December 26, 2004, one of the worst natural disasters in history spread over Southeast Asia, India, Indonesia, and Africa. It started when a powerful earthquake struck deep under the Indian Ocean, triggering massive tsunamis that obliterated cities, seaside communities, and holiday resorts. Approximately 320,000 people in a dozen countries were killed; thousands of survivors were injured and traumatized in the process.

Eight months later, in August of 2005, Hurricane Katrina stampeded through the Gulf Coast of the United States with winds of up to 175 miles per hour, devastating areas in Florida, Mississippi, Alabama, and Louisiana and killing nearly two thousand people. In New Orleans, the surge breached the levees, ultimately flooding 80 percent of the city and many neighboring parishes. Causing an estimated $81 billion in damage, Hurricane Katrina was the costliest natural disaster in U.S. history.

The intense stress that natural catastrophes impose on a population can also be caused by human beings. The terrorist assault on the World Trade Center and the Pentagon on September 11, 2001, was a different kind of tragedy that no one old enough to witness will ever forget. Americans all over the world took the attack personally and were touched by it, whether they were present or not. In a nationwide telephone survey of 560 adults conducted later that week, 90 percent said they were experiencing some symptoms of stress—and 44 percent reported "substantial" symptoms such as recurring thoughts, dreams, and memories; difficulty falling or staying asleep; difficulty concentrating on work; and unprovoked outbursts of anger (Schuster et al., 2001). These problems were far more common among New Yorkers than among people living in other areas (Schlenger et al., 2002). Even within Manhattan, researchers found that the closer residents lived to Ground Zero, the more traumatized and depressed they were from the experience (Galea et al., 2002). Most profoundly affected were those at work in the towers or nearby, those with friends and family in the vicinity, and rescue workers called to the scene.

Other events that can have similarly traumatic effects include war, motor vehicle accidents, plane crashes, violent crimes, physical or sexual abuse, the death of a loved one, and other natural disasters such as fires, tornadoes, and earthquakes (Kubany et al., 2000). The harmful effects of catastrophic stressors on health are well documented. Paul and Gerald Adams (1984) examined the public records in Othello, Washington, before and after the 1980 eruption of the Mount Saint Helens volcano, which spewed thick layers of ash all over the area. They observed post-eruption increases in calls made to a mental health crisis line, police reports of domestic violence, referrals to a local alcohol treatment center, and visits to the emergency room. Then there was an earthquake that shook San Francisco in 1989. Houses collapsed, highways buckled, overpasses fell apart, water mains burst, and fires raged out of control, leaving thousands of people homeless. By coincidence, Susan Nolen-Hoeksema and Jannay Morrow (1991) had administered some trauma-relevant measures to a

stressor Anything that causes stress.

Natural disasters can devastate entire populations. In December of 2004, the tsunami that destroyed parts of South Asia traumatized survivors on Phi Phi Island, a beautiful vacation resort in Thailand (left). Months later, in August of 2005, Hurricane Katrina stormed through the U.S. Gulf Coast. In New Orleans, where 80 percent of the city was flooded, residents waiting for help hugged the rooftops of flooded buildings (right).

group of Stanford University students two weeks before the earthquake. Follow-up assessments ten days later, and again after six weeks, provided these investigators with a before-and-after examination of coping. They found that people who had initially been more distressed and those who had encountered more danger during the quake experienced the most psychological distress afterward.

The scarring effects of large-scale disasters are without dispute. Based on their review of fifty-two studies, Anthony Rubonis and Leonard Bickman (1991) found that high rates of psychological disorders—such as anxiety, phobias, depression, alcohol abuse, and somatic complaints—are common among residents of areas that have been hit by these catastrophic events. In a more recent study of disasters involving 377 counties, a team of researchers found that, compared with the years preceding each disaster, the suicide rate increased by 14 percent after floods, by 31 percent after hurricanes, and by 63 percent after earthquakes (Krug et al., 1998).

War in particular leaves deep, permanent psychological scars. Soldiers in combat believe that they have to kill or be killed. They suffer intense anxiety and see horrifying injuries, death, and destruction, all of which leaves them with images and emotions that do not fade. Given this level of stress, it's not surprising that when a war is over, some veterans suffer greatly. In World War I, the problem was called "shell shock." In World War II, it was called "combat fatigue." It is now referred to as **posttraumatic stress disorder (PTSD)** and is identified by such enduring symptoms as recurring anxiety, sleeplessness, nightmares, flashbacks, intrusive thoughts, attention problems, and social withdrawal. A survey of veterans who served in the Persian Gulf War revealed that 16 to 19 percent reported various PTSD symptoms four to ten months after coming home (Sutker et al., 1993). It's no wonder that families are often shattered when a loved one returns from war and seems different, as if still trapped in combat (McCarty-Gould, 2000).

War can traumatize non-combat civilian populations as well. In Israel, 16 percent of adults had personally been exposed to a terrorist attack; 37 percent had a close friend or family member who had been exposed (Bleich et al., 2003). As to the mental health consequences of such exposure, a study of 905 Jewish and Palestinian citizens revealed that exposure to terrorism was associated with PTSD symptoms in both groups—more so among the Palestinian citizens, members of an ethnic minority who have fewer coping resources to turn to when in distress (Hobfoll et al., 2006).

Over the years, clinical psychologists have studied PTSD and the life experiences that precipitate its onset. Based on a nationwide survey of six thousand Americans,

posttraumatic stress disorder (PTSD) A condition in which a person experiences enduring physical and psychological symptoms after an extremely stressful event.

These soldiers, like thousands of other troops and civilians, experienced the recent war in Lebanon firsthand. It has long been recognized that combat leaves psychological scars and increases the risk of posttraumatic stress disorder.

from fifteen to fifty-four years old, Ronald Kessler and others (1995) estimated that 8 percent of the population (5 percent of men, 10 percent of women) suffer posttraumatic stress disorder in the course of a lifetime and that the symptoms often persist for many years. Among the experiences that produced these traumas were the witnessing of a murder or injury, the death of a loved one, life-threatening accidents, serious illness, war, fires and natural disasters, physical and sexual assaults, and prison. From a meta-analysis of 290 studies involving thousands of participants, it is clear that PTSD is more prevalent among women than among men, even though men are more likely to experience potentially traumatic events (Tolin & Foa, 2006). Situations over which we have no control are particularly toxic. For example, people involved in serious car accidents exhibited more PTSD symptoms and suffered for a longer period of time when the other driver was responsible for what happened than when they were to blame (Delahanty et al., 1997).

 ## Major Life Events

Some people are lucky enough to avoid major catastrophes. But nobody can completely avoid stress. Indeed, change itself may cause stress by forcing us to adapt to new circumstances. This hypothesis was first proposed by Thomas Holmes and Richard Rahe (1967), who interviewed hospital patients and found that their illnesses had often been preceded by major changes in some aspect of their lives. Some of the changes were negative (getting hurt, divorced, or fired), but others were positive (getting married or promoted or having a baby). To measure life stress, Holmes and Rahe then devised the Social Readjustment Rating Scale (SRRS), a checklist of forty-three major life events each assigned a numerical value based on the amount of readjustment it requires. Among the events sampled (and the numerical values they were assigned) were the death of a spouse (100), divorce (73), imprisonment (63), marriage (50), job loss (47), pregnancy (40), school transfer (20), and even vacations (13).

The simple notion that change is inherently stressful has an intuitive ring about it. But is change per se, positive or negative, necessarily harmful? There are two problems with this notion. First, although there is a statistical link between negative events and illness, research does not similarly support the claim that positive "stressors" such as taking a vacation, graduating, winning a lottery, starting a new career, or getting married, are similarly harmful (Stewart et al., 1986). Happiness is not the absence of distress, nor is distress the absence of happiness. A person can simultaneously experience both emotions (Carver & Scheier, 1990), and the health consequences are different (Taylor, 1991). The second complicating factor is that the impact of any change depends on who the person is and how the change is interpreted. Moving to a new country, for example, is less stressful to immigrants who can speak the new language (Berry et al., 1992); a diagnosis of infertility is less devastating to married couples who want children when they confront the issue, emotionally, than when they avoid it (Berghuis & Stanton, 2002). Victims of physical assault who engage in counterfactual "what if?" thinking take longer to recover emotionally than those who do not (El Leithy et al., 2006). The amount of change in a person's life may provide crude estimates of stress and future health, but the predictive equation is not that simple.

 ## Microstressors: The Hassles of Everyday Life

Think again about the sources of stress in your life, and catastrophes and other exceptional events spring to mind. Yet the most common source of stress arises from

Waiting in line at Chicago's O'Hare Airport, a common occurrence in these days of heightened security, is the kind of microstressor that plagues air travelers on a daily basis.

the hassles that irritate us every day. Environmental factors such as population density, loud noise, extreme heat or cold, and cigarette smoke are all sources of stress. Car problems, waiting in lines, losing keys, bad work days, money troubles, and other "microstressors" also place a constant strain on us. Unfortunately, there is nothing "micro" about the impact of these stressors on health and well-being. Studies suggest that the accumulation of daily hassles contributes more to illness than do major life events (Kohn et al., 1991), with interpersonal conflicts being the most upsetting of our daily stressors and having a longer-lasting impact than most others (Bolger et al., 1989).

Some daily aggravations are architecturally induced. Consider two common types of college dormitories: those with long corridors and those divided into suites (see Figure 14.2). When Andrew Baum and Stuart Valins (1979) compared first-year college students living in these two types of dorms, they found that corridor residents experienced more stress than those in suites. Why? The answer lies in the way these spatial arrangements affect social control. Because corridor residents have to share more space with more people (such as in the bathroom and lounge areas), it is more difficult for them to avoid unwanted social contacts. Research on prison overcrowding reveals a similar pattern, as the number of inmates sharing a space has a greater effect on stress than does the total amount of space available (Paulus, 1988).

One problem that plagues many people in the workplace is occupational stress (Barling et al., 2005). One type of reaction is *burnout*—a prolonged response to job stress that is characterized by emotional exhaustion, cynicism, disengagement, and a lack of personal accomplishment. Teachers, doctors, nurses, police officers, social work-

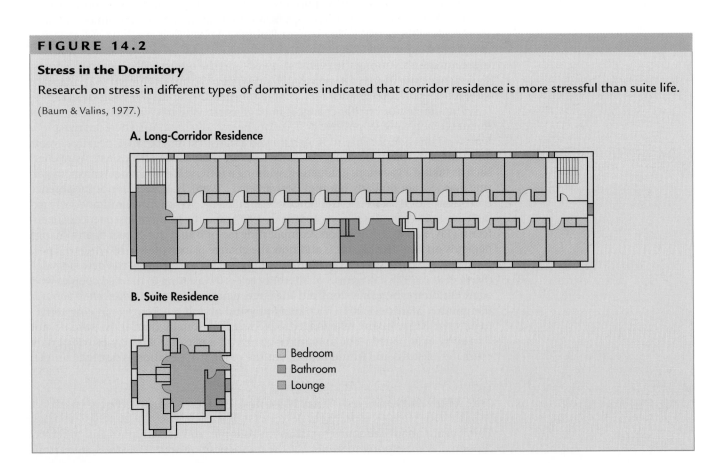

FIGURE 14.2

Stress in the Dormitory

Research on stress in different types of dormitories indicated that corridor residence is more stressful than suite life.

(Baum & Valins, 1977.)

A. Long-Corridor Residence

B. Suite Residence

☐ Bedroom
■ Bathroom
☐ Lounge

ers, and others in human-service professions are especially at risk. Under relentless job pressures, those who are burned out describe themselves as feeling drained, frustrated, hardened, apathetic, and lacking in energy and motivation (Maslach, 1982; Maslach et al., 2001). People are most likely to have this experience when there are not enough resources at work—like support from supervisors and friendly relations with coworkers—to meet the demands of the job (Lee & Ashforth, 1996; Viswesvaran et al., 1999). To make matters worse, research shows that people who experience burnout at work are more at risk for cardiovascular disease (Melamed et al., 2006).

Another form of daily stress comes from commuting. At present, an estimated 100 million Americans commute to work each weekday—and for longer periods of time than ever before. Research has shown that driving to work can increase stress (Koslowsky et al., 1995). It now appears that commuting by train can have the same effect. In a study of railroad commuters who traveled regularly from their homes in suburban New Jersey to work in Manhattan, Gary Evans and Richard Wener (2006) found that the longer their commute was, the more stress they reported feeling, the sloppier they were at a simple proofreading task, and the higher was their level of cortisol—a stress hormone that they measured by taking saliva samples after the morning trips.

On the home front, economic pressure is another common source of stress. In a three-year study of over four hundred married couples, researchers found that those who are strained by a tight budget and have difficulty paying the bills experience more distress and conflict in their marriages (Conger et al., 1999). A follow-up study of African American families further showed that economic hardship spells emotional distress for parents and adjustment problems for their children (Conger et al., 2002).

The accumulation of daily hassles does more to make people sick than catastrophes or major life changes. **True.**

How Does Stress Affect the Body?

The term *stress* was first popularized by Hans Selye (1936), an endocrinologist. As a young medical student, Selye noticed that patients who were hospitalized for many different illnesses often had similar symptoms, such as muscle weakness, a loss of weight and appetite, and a lack of ambition. Maybe these symptoms were part of a generalized response to an attack on the body, he thought. In the 1930s, Selye tested this hypothesis by exposing laboratory rats to various stressors, including heat, cold, heavy exercise, toxic substances, food deprivation, and electric shock. As anticipated, the different stressors all produced a similar physiological response: enlarged adrenal glands, shrunken lymph nodes, and bleeding stomach ulcers. Borrowing a term from engineering, Selye called the reaction *stress*—a word that quickly became part of everyday language.

 ## The General Adaptation Syndrome

According to Selye, the body naturally responds to stress in a three-staged process that he called the **general adaptation syndrome** (see Figure 14.3). Sparked by the recognition of a threat—such as a predator, enemy soldier, speeding car, or virus—the body has an initial *alarm* reaction. To meet the challenge, adrenaline and other hormones are poured into the bloodstream, creating physiological arousal. Heart rate, blood pressure, and breathing rates increase, while slower, long-term functions such as growth, digestion, and the operation of the immune system are inhibited. At this stage, the body mobilizes all of its resources to ward off the threat. Next comes a *resistance* stage, during which the body remains aroused and on the alert. There is continued release of stress hormones, and local defenses are activated. But if the stress persists for a prolonged period of time, the body will fall into an *exhaustion* stage. According to Selye, our anti-stress resources are limited. In fact, however, research has shown that exhaustion occurs not because our stress-fighting resources are limited but because their overuse causes other systems in the body to break down, which puts us at risk for illness and even death. Selye's basic model thus makes an important point: Stress may be an adaptive

general adaptation syndrome A three-stage process (alarm, resistance, and exhaustion) by which the body responds to stress.

FIGURE 14.3

The General Adaptation Syndrome

According to Selye, the human body responds to threat in three phases: alarm, resistance, and exhaustion.

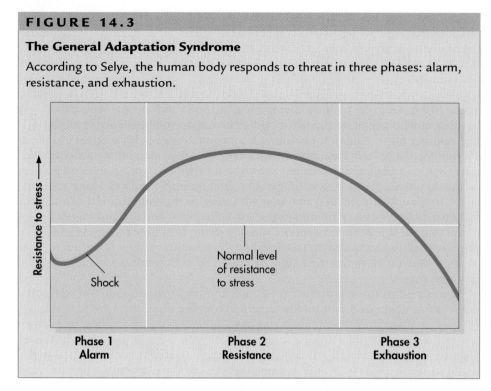

Resistance to stress

Shock

Normal level
of resistance
to stress

Phase 1
Alarm

Phase 2
Resistance

Phase 3
Exhaustion

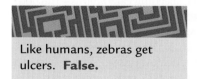

Like humans, zebras get ulcers. **False.**

short-term reaction to threat, but over time it compromises our health and well-being.

A stress response is found in all mammals. So why, asks neuroscientist Robert Sapolsky (2004), don't zebras get ulcers? Sapolsky notes that the physiological stress response is superbly designed through evolution to help animals mobilize to fight or escape in acute emergencies. For the zebra, this occurs when a hungry lion leaps out from a bush and sprints at top speed across the savanna. For humans, it occurs in combat or in competitive sports and perhaps even on first dates and in job interviews. But think about the list of situations you find stressful, and you'll see that people become anxious over things that would make no sense to a zebra. "We humans live well enough and long enough, and are smart enough, to generate all sorts of stressful events purely in our heads," says Sapolsky. From the perspective of the evolution of the animal kingdom, he notes, psychological stress is a "recent invention" (p. 5). The reason that stress causes ulcers and other illnesses, then, is that the response is designed for acute physical emergencies, yet we turn it on often and for prolonged periods of time as we worry about taxes, mortgages, oral presentations, job interviews, marital problems, and the inevitability of death.

All humans respond bodily to stress, which is what enables us to mount a defense. Physiologically, the sympathetic nervous system is activated and more adrenaline is secreted, which increases the heart rate and heightens arousal. Then all at once the liver pours extra sugar into the bloodstream for energy, the pupils dilate to let in more light, breathing speeds up for more oxygen, perspiration increases to cool down the body, blood clots faster to heal wounds, saliva flow is inhibited, and digestion slows down to divert blood to the brain and skeletal muscles. Faced with threat, the body readies itself for action. But what, behaviorally, is the nature of the defense?

Many years ago, Walter Cannon (1932) described the body as prepared for "fight or flight." To be sure, men often lash out aggressively when under siege. But do women respond similarly? In her book, *The Tending Instinct,* Shelley Taylor (2002) argues that while men frequently exhibit the classic fight-or-flight reaction to stress, women are more likely to exhibit a "tend-and-befriend" response. Prepared by evolution, and necessary to enhance the survival of their offspring, she argues, women adapt to hardship by caring for their children and seeking out others who might help. Consistent with this argument, studies have shown that, under stress, women become more nurturing than men—and more affiliative. Interestingly, animal and human studies show that when females are isolated, unsupported, and in social distress, they exhibit elevated levels of the hormone oxytocin, which, in turn, increases their tendency to seek out social contact (Taylor, 2006b).

 What Stress Does to the Heart

Coronary heart disease (CHD) is a narrowing of the blood vessels that carry oxygen and nutrients to the heart muscle. It is currently the leading cause of death in the United States. An estimated 69 million Americans suffer from CHD. For many, the

For more information on heart disease, you can visit the American Heart Association's Web site (www.americanheart.org).

result is a heart attack, which occurs when the blood supply to the heart is blocked. This causes an uncomfortable feeling of pressure, fullness, squeezing, or pain in the center of the chest—and sometimes sweating, dizziness, nausea, fainting, and shortness of breath. Every year, 1.5 million Americans have heart attacks. One-third do not survive.

Several factors are known to increase the risk of CHD. The three most important are hypertension, or high blood pressure; cigarette smoking; and high cholesterol (others include a family history of CHD, a high-fat diet, obesity, and a lack of exercise). People with one of these three major risk factors are twice as likely to develop CHD, those with two risk factors are three and a half times as likely, and those with all three are six times as likely. These statistics are compelling and should not be taken lightly. Combined, however, these variables account for fewer than half the known cases of CHD. What's missing from the equation is the fourth major risk factor: psychological stress—from work, from marital troubles, and from the negative life events that plague people who lack resources because of low socioeconomic status (Gallo & Matthews, 2003; Matthews, 2005).

In 1956, cardiologists Meyer Friedman and Ray Rosenman were studying the relationship between cholesterol and coronary heart disease. After noticing that husbands were more likely than their wives to have CHD, they speculated that work-related stress might be the reason (at the time, most women did not work outside the home). To test this hypothesis, Friedman and Rosenman interviewed three thousand healthy, middle-aged men. Those who seemed to be the most hard-driving, competitive, impatient, time-conscious, and quick to anger were classified as having a **Type A behavior pattern**. Roughly an equal number of men who were easygoing, relaxed, and laid back were classified as having a Type B pattern of behavior. Interestingly, out of 258 men who went on to have heart attacks over the following nine years, 69 percent had been classified as Type A's and only 31 percent as Type B's (Rosenman et al., 1975).

The Type A behavior pattern is made up of a cluster of traits, including competitive drive, a sense of time urgency, and a dangerous mix of anger, cynicism, and hostility (Friedman & Booth-Kewley, 1987; Matthews, 1988). In interviews and written questionnaires, Type A's report that they walk fast, talk fast, work late, interrupt speakers in mid-sentence, detest waiting in lines, race through yellow lights when they drive, lash out at others in frustration, strive to win at all costs, and save time by doing many things at once. In contrast, "there are those who breeze through the day as pleased as park rangers—despite having deadlines and kids and a broken down car and charity work and scowling Aunt Agnes living in the spare bedroom" (Carey, 1997, p. 75).

By the early 1980s, the influence of the Type A behavior pattern on CHD was widely accepted. A panel of distinguished scientists convened by the National Heart, Lung and Blood Institute concluded that the Type A pattern was a risk factor for CHD, comparable to more traditional risks such as high blood pressure, smoking, high blood cholesterol, and obesity. But science, like time, moves on. Later studies of Type A and CHD obtained weaker results that varied depending on how Type A was measured and the kind of population that was studied (Matthews, 1988). Certainty about the bad effects of "hurry sickness" and "workaholism" began to crumble.

One issue that arose concerned measurement. Specifically, it turns out that the strength of the link between Type A behavior and coronary heart disease depends on how people are diagnosed. In the original study, Friedman and Rosenman classified men by means of a structured interview in which they could observe their verbal and nonverbal behavior. Afterward, however, many psychologists—in their haste to pursue this vital line of research—tried to identify Type A people using quick, easy-to-take questionnaires instead of time-consuming interviews. The questionnaires were not nearly as predictive. Apparently, the Type A pattern is more evident from a person's interview *behavior* (whether he or she constantly checks the time, speaks quickly, interrupts the interviewer, and makes restless fidgety movements) than from *self-reports*. When interviews are used to make the diagnosis, 70 percent of men who have CHD also have a Type A behavior pattern—compared with only 46 percent of those who are healthy (Miller et al., 1991).

Type A behavior pattern
A pattern of behavior characterized by extremes of competitive striving for achievement, a sense of time urgency, hostility, and aggression.

TABLE 14.1

How "Hostile" Is Your Pattern of Behavior?

(Williams, 1993.)

- When in the express checkout line at the supermarket, do you often count the items in the baskets of the people ahead of you to be sure they aren't over the limit?
- When an elevator doesn't come as quickly as it should, do your thoughts quickly focus on the inconsiderate behavior of the person on another floor who's holding it up?
- When someone criticizes you, do you quickly begin to feel annoyed?
- Do you frequently find yourself muttering at the television during a news broadcast?
- When you are held up in a slow line in traffic, do you quickly sense your heart pounding and your breath quickening?

The Type A behavior pattern was also refined conceptually, and a new line of inquiry sprang up. This research showed the main toxic ingredient in CHD is *hostility*—as seen in people who are constantly angry, resentful, cynical, suspicious, and mistrustful of others (see Table 14.1). Apparently, people who are always in a negative emotional state, and are quick to explode, are besieged by stress. Because the heart is a dumb pump and the blood vessels mere hoses, the health result is predictable: "The cardiovascular stress-response basically consists of making them work harder for a while, and if you do that on a regular basis, they will wear out, just like any pump or hoses you could buy at Sears" (Sapolsky, 1994, p. 42). In the long run, chronic hostility and anger can be lethal (Miller et al., 1996; Siegman & Smith, 1994). In fact, people who have lots of anger and suppress it are as likely to develop high blood pressure as those with anger who express it. It's the emotion that is toxic, not whether you hold it in or let it out (Everson et al., 1998).

What else explains the connection between hostility and coronary heart disease? One possibility is that hostile people are less health-conscious—that they tend to smoke more, consume more caffeine and alcohol, exercise less, sleep less, and eat less healthy foods and are also less likely to comply with advice from doctors (Leiker & Hailey, 1988; Siegler, 1994). A second explanation is that hostile people are physiologically reactive, so in tense social situations they exhibit greater increases in blood pressure, pulse rate, and adrenaline—a hormone that accelerates the build-up of fatty plaques on the artery walls, causing hardening of the arteries (Krantz & McCeney, 2002). In fact, research shows that people who are hostile exhibit more intense cardiovascular reactions not only during the event that makes them angry—say, being involved in a heated argument (Davis et al., 2000)—but long afterward as well, when asked to relive the event (Frederickson et al., 2000).

What Stress Does to the Immune System

Increasingly, it has become clear that psychological stress produces a wide range of effects on the body, including increases in the risk of chronic back pain, diabetes, appendicitis, upper respiratory infections, arthritis, herpes, gum disease, common colds, and some forms of cancer. How can stress have so broad a range of disabling effects? Answer: by compromising the body's immune system, the first line of defense against illness (Ader, 2007).

The **immune system** is a complex surveillance system that fights bacteria, viruses, parasites, fungi, and other "nonself" substances that invade the body. The system contains more than a trillion specialized white blood cells called *lymphocytes* that circulate throughout the bloodstream and secrete chemical antibodies. These sharklike search-and-destroy cells protect us twenty-four hours a day by patrolling the body and attacking trespassers. The immune system is also equipped with large scavenger cells that zero in on viruses and cancerous tumors. Serving as a "sixth sense" for foreign invaders, the immune system continually renews itself. During the few seconds it takes to read this sentence, your body will have produced 10 million new lymphocytes.

Today, many health psychologists specializing in **psychoneuroimmunology, or PNI** (*psycho* for mind, *neuro* for nervous system, *immunology* for the immune system)

immune system A biological surveillance system that detects and destroys "nonself" substances that invade the body.

psychoneuroimmunology (PNI) A subfield of psychology that examines the links among psychological factors, the brain and nervous system, and the immune system.

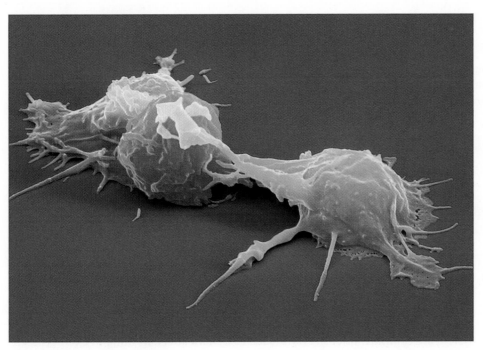

This color-enhanced microscopic image shows two "natural killer" immune cells (in yellow) engulfing and destroying a leukemia cell (in red). The human immune system contains more than a trillion specialized white blood cells.

study the connections among the brain, behavior, the immune system, health, and illness. Before we get into some of the fascinating results, let's pause for a moment and consider three of the methods that these researchers use to spy on the operations of the immune system. One method is to take blood samples from animal or human participants exposed to varying degrees of stress and simply count the numbers of lymphocytes and other white blood cells circulating in the bloodstream. A second is to extract blood, add cancerous tumor cells to the mix, and measure the extent to which the natural killer cells destroy the tumors. A third method is to "challenge" the living organism by injecting a foreign agent into the skin and measuring the amount of swelling that arises at the site of the injection. The more swelling there is, the more potent the immune reaction is assumed to be (Ader, 2007).

It is now clear that stress can affect the immune system, at least temporarily. The medical community used to reject the idea, but no longer. What changed? First, animal experiments showed that rats exposed to noise, overcrowding, or inescapable shocks, and primates separated from their social companions, exhibit a drop in immune cell activity compared with nonexposed animals (Coe, 1993; Moynihan & Ader, 1996). A link was also observed in humans. Intrigued by the fact that people often become sick and die shortly after they are widowed, R. W. Barthrop and others (1977) took blood samples from twenty-six men and women whose spouses had recently died. Compared with nonwidowed controls, these grief-stricken spouses exhibited a weakened immune response. This demonstration was the first of its kind.

Additional studies soon revealed weakened immune responses in NASA astronauts after their reentry into the atmosphere and splashdown, in people deprived of sleep for a prolonged period of time, in students in the midst of final exams, in men and women recently divorced or separated, in people caring for a family member with Alzheimer's disease, in snake phobics being exposed to a live snake, and in workers who have just lost their jobs. Even in the laboratory, people who are given complex arithmetic problems to solve or painful stimuli to tolerate exhibit changes in immune cell activity that last for one or more hours after the stress has subsided (Cohen & Herbert, 1996).

In an intriguing study, Arthur Stone and others (1994) paid forty-eight adult volunteers to take a harmless but novel protein pill every day for twelve weeks—a substance that would lead the immune system to respond by producing an antibody. Every day, the participants completed a diary in which they reported on their moods and on experiences at work, at home, in financial matters, in leisure activities, and in social relationships with their friends, spouses, and children. The participants also gave daily saliva samples that were later used to measure the amount of antibody produced. The results were striking, as are their implications: The more positive events participants experienced in a given day, the more antibody was produced. The more negative events they experienced, the less antibody was produced. In many ways, it is now clear that negative experiences and the emotions they elicit can weaken our immune system's ability to protect us from injuries, infections, and a wide range of illnesses (Kiecolt-Glaser et al., 2002). On the question of whether positive psychological interventions can be used to reinvigorate immune responses, however, more research is needed (Miller & Cohen, 2001).

FIGURE 14.4

Pathways from Stress to Illness

Hostility, stress, and other negative emotional states may cause illness in two ways: (1) by promoting unhealthful behaviors (more alcohol, less sleep, and so on) and (2) by triggering the release of hormones that weaken the immune system.

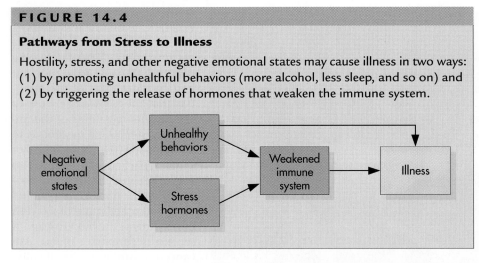

It appears that psychological states "get into" the immune system. As illustrated in Figure 14.4, there are two possible ways this can happen. First, people who are under intense stress tend to smoke more, ingest more alcohol and drugs, sleep less, exercise less, and have poorer diets, behaviors that tend to compromise the immune system. For example, one study showed that when healthy male adults were kept awake between 3:00 and 7:00 A.M., immune cell activity diminished and returned to normal only after a full night of uninterrupted sleep (Irwin et al., 1994). Second, stress triggers the release of adrenaline and other stress hormones into the bloodstream, and these hormones tend to suppress immune cell activity. The result is a temporary lowering of the body's resistance (Cohen & Williamson, 1991). Either way, hundreds of studies now show that the effects of stress on the immune system are complex. Brief stressors (such as a shark attack or difficult exam) can enhance the immune response in ways that are adaptive in the short term, but chronic life stressors (such as a high-pressure job or distressed marriage) can suppress the immune response over time, putting the organism at risk (Segerstrom & Miller, 2004).

 ### The Links Between Stress and Illness

If chronic stress can weaken the immune system, are people who are stressed in life more likely to become sick? Sheldon Cohen and his colleagues (1993) conducted a fascinating and elaborate study to help answer this question. They paid 420 volunteers to spend nine days in a medical experiment and risk exposure to a common cold virus. In the first two days, participants filled out several questionnaires, including one that measured recent stressful experiences in their lives. They were also given a physical examination, including a blood test. Then, to simulate the person-to-person transmission of a virus, the researchers dropped a clear liquid solution into each participant's nose. Those randomly assigned to the control group received a placebo saline solution. Others, less fortunate, received a cold virus in doses that tend to produce illness rates of 20 to 60 percent.

For the next week, participants were quarantined in large apartments, where they were examined daily by a nurse who took their temperatures, extracted mucus samples, and looked for signs of colds, such as sneezing, watery eyes, stuffy nose, and sore throat (participants did not realize it, but the nurse also kept track of the number of tissues they used). All participants were healthy at the start of the project, and not a single one in the saline control group developed a cold. Yet among those exposed to a virus, 82 percent became infected, and 46 percent of those who were infected caught a cold, symptoms and all. A virus is a virus, and there is no escape. Most interesting, however, is that life stress made a difference. Among those who became infected, high-stress participants were more likely to catch a cold than were low-stress participants—53 percent compared with 40 percent. In short, people whose lives are filled with stress are particularly vulnerable to illness.

In a follow-up of this experiment, Cohen and others (1998) interviewed 276 volunteers about recent life stressors, infected them with a cold virus, and then measured whether or not they developed a cold. They found that some types of stress were more toxic than others. Specifically, people who had endured *chronic* stressors that lasted for more than a month (such as ongoing marital problems or unemployment) were more likely to catch a cold than those who had experienced *acute* short-term stress (such as a fight with a spouse or a reprimand at work). Figure 14.5 shows that the longer a stressor had lasted, the more likely a person was to catch a cold. Over time, stress breaks down the body's immune system. In another

FIGURE 14.5

Stress Duration and Illness

Two hundred seventy-six volunteers were interviewed about recent life stress, then infected with a cold virus. As shown above, the longer a stressor had lasted, in months, the more likely a person was to catch the cold. Over time, stress breaks down the body's immune system.

(Cohen et al., 1998.)

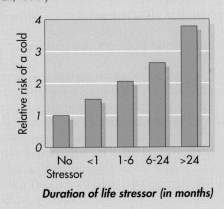

Duration of life stressor (in months)

Stress can weaken the heart, but it cannot affect the immune system. **False.**

follow-up, Cohen and his colleagues (2006) found that the more sociable people were in life, the more resistant they were to developing the lab-induced cold.

These common-cold studies are important because they demonstrate not only that stress can weaken the immune system but also that it can leave us vulnerable to illness as a result. Does stress have similar effects on more serious illnesses? Can it, for example, hasten the spread of cancer? In an early test of this hypothesis, Madeline Visintainer and others (1982) implanted tumorous cancer cells into laboratory rats, some of which were then exposed repeatedly to shocks they could not escape. After one month, 50 percent of the animals not shocked died of cancer. Yet relative to that baseline, the death rate climbed to 73 percent among those subjected to the inescapable shock. This study was among the first to show that psychological states such as a feeling of helplessness can influence the spread of cancer.

The growth of tumors in helpless white laboratory rats is interesting, but does the same principle apply to people? For obvious ethical reasons, researchers cannot fill humans with despair or inject lethal tumors into their bodies to test the cause-and-effect chain directly. But they can examine the medical records of people whose lives have been struck by tragedy. Investigations of this sort have revealed that cancer appears more often than normal in people prone to being in a negative emotional state (Sklar & Anisman, 1981). In one large-scale study, investigators looked up two thousand male employees of the Western Electric Company in Chicago whose personalities had been assessed in 1958. At the time, test scores had shown that some of the men were low in self-esteem, unhappy, and depressed. The outcome: Some twenty years later, these men were more likely than their coworkers to have died of cancer (Persky et al., 1987). Let's be clear about what these results mean. Nobody disputes that cancer is caused by exposure to toxic substances and other biological factors. But individuals who are clinically depressed or under great stress have weakened immune systems which, in some cases, may result in a higher death rate from cancer and other diseases (Herbert & Cohen, 1993; Robles et al., 2005).

Processes of Appraisal

Some 2,500 years ago, an anonymous author wrote an extraordinary poem about human suffering: the Book of Job. A pious and prosperous man as the poem opens, Job is soon beset by great calamities. He loses his property, his children, and his health. Job and his friends try to understand how these terrible things could happen. His friends argue that Job's plight must be a punishment sent by God and tell Job to repent. Because he believes that his sufferings far exceed any wrongdoing on his part, Job cannot accept this explanation. In despair, he doubts his capacity to withstand continued hardship and longs for death. But eventually Job finds strength and peace through trusting in God's will. From the perspective of the stress-and-coping model shown in Figure 14.1, Job and his friends were engaged in the process of appraisal. They considered possible explanations for Job's suffering and formed expectations about his ability to cope with his situation. These same themes are found in research on stress and coping.

Attributions and Explanatory Styles

Depression is a mood disorder characterized by feelings of sadness, low self-esteem, pessimism, apathy, and slowed thought processes. Other symptoms include disturbances in sleeping and eating patterns, and reduced sexual interest. Per year, 3 percent

FIGURE 14.6

Using Attributional Styles to Predict Depression

In this study, researchers measured the explanatory styles of first-year college students. As juniors two years later, those with a negative rather than positive style in their first year were more likely to suffer from a major or minor depressive disorder.

(Alloy et al., 2006.)

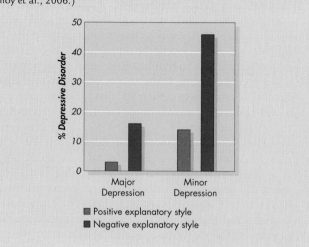

- Positive explanatory style
- Negative explanatory style

of the U.S. population experiences a major depression. Many more suffer from brief, mild bouts with the blues. The problem is so widespread that it has been called the "common cold" of psychological disorders.

About twice as many women as men seek treatment for being depressed. During the course of a lifetime, an estimated 12 percent of American men and 21 percent of women will suffer from a major depression (Kessler et al., 1994). This sex difference first begins to appear in adolescence, although the disparity is a bit smaller in less developed nations (Culbertson, 1997). While depression has many causes, some researchers have focused on the attributions people make for the positive and negative events of their lives.

In 1975, Martin Seligman argued that depression results from a feeling of **learned helplessness**, the acquired expectation that one cannot control important outcomes. In a classic series of experiments, Seligman had found that dogs strapped into a harness and exposed to painful electric shocks soon became passive and gave up trying to escape, even in new situations where escape was possible. In contrast, dogs that had not received uncontrollable shocks quickly learned the escape routine. As applied to humans, this finding suggested that prolonged exposure to uncontrollable events might similarly cause apathy, inactivity, a loss of motivation, and pessimism. In human research participants, those exposed to inescapable bursts of noise thus failed to protect themselves in a later situation where the noise could be easily avoided. Seligman was quick to note that people who are exposed to uncontrollable events become, in many ways, like depressed individuals: discouraged, pessimistic about the future, and lacking in initiative. Thus, he saw depression as a form of learned helplessness.

Lynn Abramson and her colleagues (1989) later proposed that depression is a state of *hopelessness* brought on by the negative self-attributions people make for failure. In fact, some people have a **depressive explanatory style**—a tendency to attribute bad events to factors that are internal rather than external ("It's my fault"), stable rather than unstable ("It will not change"), and global rather than specific ("It spreads to all parts of my life"). Research supports this proposition. Whether people are trying to explain social rejection, a sports defeat, low grades, or their inability to solve an experimenter's puzzle, those who are depressed are more likely than others to blame factors that are within the self, unlikely to change, and broad enough to impair other aspects of life. The result: hopelessness and despair (Abramson et al., 1989; Metalsky et al., 1993). This way of thinking may even signal a vulnerability to future depression. Indeed, when Lauren Alloy and her colleagues (2006) measured the explanatory styles of nondepressed newly entered college students and then followed up on these students in their junior year, they found that those with a negative explanatory style in their first year—compared to classmates with a more positive style—were far more likely to have suffered from a major or minor depressive disorder (see Figure 14.6).

The Human Capacity for Resilience

Stress affects people differently, an observation that led Suzanne Kobasa and her colleagues (1982) to wonder why some of us are more resilient than others in the face of stress. Kobasa studied some two hundred business executives who were under stress. Many said they were frequently sick, affirming the link between stress and illness; others had managed to stay healthy. The two groups were similar in terms of age, education, job status, income, and ethnic and religious background. But it was clear from various tests that they differed in their attitudes toward themselves, their

learned helplessness
A phenomenon in which experience with an uncontrollable event creates passive behavior toward a subsequent threat to well-being.

depressive explanatory style   A habitual tendency to attribute negative events to causes that are stable, global, and internal.

jobs, and the people in their lives. Based on these differences, Kobasa identified a personality style that she called *hardiness* and concluded that hardy people have three characteristics: (1) commitment, a sense of purpose with regard to one's work, family, and other domains; (2) challenge, an openness to new experiences and a desire to embrace change; and (3) control, the belief that one has the power to influence important future outcomes.

Research supports the general point that resilience, or hardiness, serves as a buffer against stress (Funk, 1992). As you might expect, most people are exposed to at least one highly traumatic event during the course of a lifetime. Yet while many react with PTSD, others maintain their equilibrium and mental health: "Roughly 50 percent to 60 percent of the U.S. population is exposed to traumatic stress but only 5 percent to 10 percent develop PTSD" (Ozer et al., 2003, p. 54). Thus, Ann Masten (2001) and George Bonanno (2004) both argue that most human beings are highly resilient, exhibiting a remarkable capacity to thrive in the wake of highly aversive events. In fact, Vicki Helgeson and her colleagues (2006) note that many people who confront heart attacks, cancer, divorce, war, family illness, and other traumas find ways to accept, benefit, and grow from the experience. So, what are the characteristics of hardiness, resilience, and the ability to find benefit in loss?

"Amazing, three failed marriages, scores of disastrous relationships, many financial reversals, and countless physical ailments, but through it all I've always had good luck parking."

People often have feelings of self-efficacy in some life domains but not others.

Self-Efficacy When Kobasa et al. (1982) first identified hardiness as an adaptive trait, they—and others—were quick to notice that the perception of control is an important ingredient (Florian et al., 1995). Early on, research showed that the harmful effects of crowding, noise, heat, and other stressors are reduced when people think they can exert control over these aspects of their environment (Glass & Singer, 1972). The perception of control is especially meaningful for people whose lives are regulated to a large extent by others. For example, elderly residents of nursing homes who were given more control over daily routines became happier and more active (Langer & Rodin, 1976; Schulz, 1976). Other studies showed that patients with heart disease, cancer, and AIDS were better adjusted, emotionally, when they felt that they could influence the course of their illness (Helgeson, 1992; Rodin, 1986; Thompson et al., 1993).

The perception of control refers to the expectation that our behaviors can produce satisfying outcomes. But people also differ in the extent to which they believe that they can perform these behaviors in the first place. These concepts seem related; but in fact they refer to different beliefs, both of which are necessary for us to feel that we control important outcomes in our lives (Skinner, 1996). According to Albert Bandura (1997), these latter expectations are based on feelings of competence, or **self-efficacy**. Some individuals may be generally more confident than others, says Bandura, but self-efficacy is a state of mind that varies from one specific task and situation to another. In other words, you may have high self-efficacy about meeting new people, but not about raising your grades. Or you may have high self-efficacy about solving a math problem but not about writing a paper.

Research on self-efficacy has shown that the more of it you have at a particular task, the more likely you are to take on that task, try hard, persist in the face of failure, and succeed. The implications for mental and physical health are particularly striking. For example, individuals with high self-efficacy on health-related matters are more likely, if they want, to stay physically fit, abstain from alcohol, and tolerate the pain of arthritis, childbirth, and migraine headaches (Bandura, 1999a; Maddux, 1995)—and even to stop smoking (Baldwin et al., 2006) or lose weight (Linde et al., 2006). People who have a high rather than low level of self-efficacy about their

self-efficacy A person's belief that he or she is capable of the specific behavior required to produce a desired outcome in a given situation.

ability to cope with stress also exhibit an enhanced functioning of the immune system (Wiedenfeld et al., 1990).

Dispositional Optimism The reason it's important to understand our attributions for past outcomes and our perceptions of control in present situations is that both have implications for our outlook on the future. In *Learned Optimism,* Seligman (1991) argues that a generalized tendency to expect positive outcomes is characterized by a non-depressive explanatory style. According to Seligman, optimists tend to blame failure on factors that are external, temporary, and specific, and to credit success to factors that are internal, permanent, and global. Thankfully, in light of the advantages that optimism brings, Suzanne Segerstrom (2006a), like Seligman, notes that even pessimists can retrain themselves to think in optimistic ways.

Consider your own view of the future. Are you the eternal optimist who looks on the bright side and generally expects good things to happen, or do you tend to believe in Murphy's Law, that if something can go wrong it will? By asking questions such as these, Michael Scheier and Charles Carver (1985) categorized college students along this dimension and found that dispositional optimists reported fewer illness symptoms during the semester than did pessimists. Correlations between optimism and health are common. Studies have shown that optimists are more likely to take an active problem-focused approach in coping with stress (Nes & Segerstrom, 2006). As a result, they are more likely to complete a rehabilitation program for alcoholics; make a quicker, fuller recovery from coronary artery bypass surgery; and, among gay men concerned about AIDS, take a more active approach to the threat (Scheier & Carver, 1992). In a study of 1,306 healthy adult men from the Boston area, those reporting high levels of optimism rather than pessimism were half as likely to have coronary heart disease ten years later (Kubzansky et al., 2001). In a study of 5,000 municipal workers in Finland, those who were high rather than low in optimism were healthier and missed fewer days from work if they were struck by a death or serious illness in the family over the next five years (Kivimäki et al., 2005)

In the course of a lifetime, everyone has setbacks. But an optimistic disposition helps us to weather the storms better. There may even be long-term health implications. In one study, researchers collected personal essays written in the 1940s by ninety-nine men who had just graduated from Harvard and then analyzed these materials to determine what each man's explanatory style had been in his youth. Thirty-five years later, those who in their youth had an optimistic outlook were healthier than their more pessimistic peers (Peterson et al., 1988).

How can these results be explained? There are two possibilities: one biological, the other behavioral. In research that supports a biological explanation, investigators analyzing blood samples have found that optimists exhibit a stronger immune response to stress than pessimists do (Kamen-Siegel et al., 1991; Segerstrom et al., 1998). In research that supports a behavioral explanation, Christopher Peterson and others (1988) scored the explanatory styles of 1,528 healthy young adults from questionnaires they had filled out between 1936 and 1940. After fifty years, the optimists (spe-

"The optimist proclaims we live in the best of all possible worlds; and the pessimist fears this is true."

—James Campbell

FIGURE 14.7

Hopelessness and the Risk of Death

Among middle-aged men in Finland, those who were initially high rather than low in hopelessness were more likely to die within six years—overall, from cancer, and from cardiovascular disease. Those who were moderate in hopelessness fell between the two extremes.

(Everson et al., 1996.)

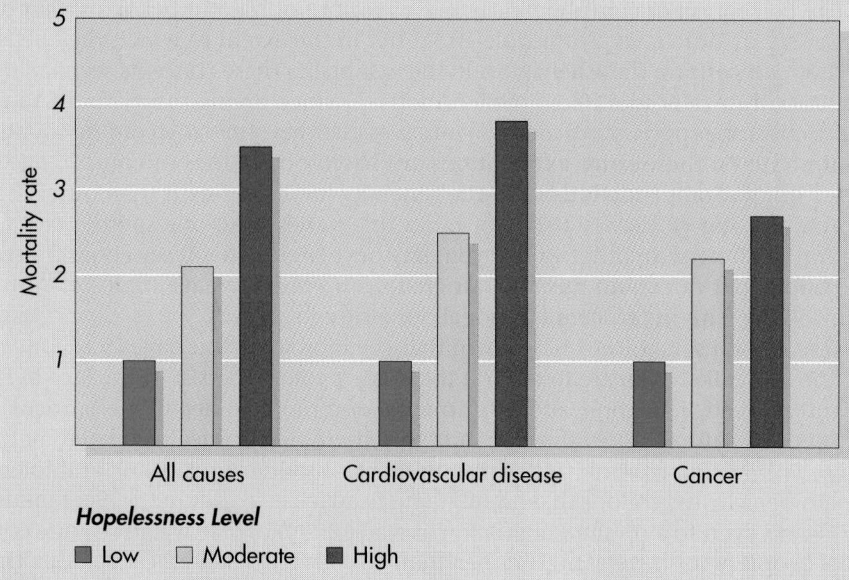

cifically, those who had made global rather than specific attributions for good events) were less likely to have died an accidental, reckless, or violent death.

There's an old saying, "Where there's life, there's hope." Perhaps the opposite is also true: "Where there's hope, there's life." In a stunning illustration of this possibility, Susan Everson and others (1996) studied 2,428 middle-aged men in Finland. Based on the extent to which they agreed with two simple statements ("I feel that it is impossible to reach the goals I would like to strive for" and "The future seems hopeless, and I can't believe that things are changing for the better"), the men were initially classified as having a high, medium, or low sense of hopelessness. When the investigators checked the death records roughly six years later, they found that the more hopeless the men were at the start, the more likely they were to have died of various causes—even when the men were otherwise equated for their age and prior health status. Compared with those who were low in hopelessness, the highs were more than twice as likely to die from cancer and four times more likely to die of cardiovascular disease (see Figure 14.7). These results bring to life what Norman Cousins (1989) described as "the biology of hope," reminding us that "positive expectations can be self-fulfilling" (Peterson, 2000).

Pollyanna's Health

Pollyanna is the upbeat heroine created by American writer Eleanor Porter. Although she used to get bad press for her boundless belief that even the most ominous cloud has a bright silver lining, the research in this section suggests that Pollyanna should be an extraordinarily healthy person.

Let's be clear about what the research means. The mind is a powerful tool that can be used to hurt, heal, and protect the body (Ray, 2004). Still, no credible scientist believes that our attributions, perceptions of control, optimism, or other sources of resilience are the sole determinants of a long life. A positive outlook cannot guarantee future good health. So although we should appreciate the powers of the mind to influence the body, it would be a cruel mistake to blame victims of illness for having a bad outlook on life. As Howard Friedman (1991) put it, in *The Self-Healing Personality,* "We must walk a fine line between blaming patients on the one hand and absolving them of any role in their health on the other" (p. 96).

It's also important to recognize that there may be drawbacks to positive thinking, especially if it leads us to see ourselves and the events around us in ways that are grossly unrealistic. As we saw in Chapter 3, people with overly positive views of themselves are sometimes disliked by their friends and seen as boastful, inconsiderate, and oversensitive to criticism (Colvin et al., 1995; Heatherton & Vohs, 2000). It may also be detrimental for people to believe that they have control over events when they do not. In a study of patients suffering from a loss of kidney function, those who felt that they had control over their health became more depressed, not less, after having a transplant that failed (Christensen et al., 1991). In a study of first-year law students, optimists exhibited a stronger immune response than did pessimists when their transition to law school was easy but a weaker immune response when the transition was difficult (Segerstrom, 2006b). Faced with some setbacks, a sense of control can help us bounce back. But setting control expectations too high can do more harm than good in the wake of negative outcomes.

Which brings us back to Job. At the end of this biblical account, Job recovers his health, his property, and his family prosperity. He does not, however, regain the sense of personal control and optimism that he enjoyed prior to being struck by calamity. Instead, Job's hard-won serenity is based on his belief that life has meaning and purpose. Pollyanna has her charm, but Job is a hero of the human condition.

Ways of Coping with Stress

Leaving home. Taking final exams. Breaking up with a boyfriend or girlfriend. Working long nights. Waiting on long security lines at an airport. Looking for work in a tight job market. Having children. Raising children. Struggling to meet the deadline

---

"The most important thing in illness is never to lose heart."

—Nikolai Lenin

When it comes to physical health, research does not support popular beliefs about the power of positive thinking. **False.**

TABLE 14.2
Ways of Coping with Stress

These statements describe some coping strategies that people say they use. The strategies are listed in order from those that are relatively common to those that are less common.

(Carver et al., 1989.)

Planning/Active Coping
- I try to come up with a strategy about what to do.
- I take additional action to try to get rid of the problem.

Positive Reinterpretation
- I look for something good in what is happening.
- I try to make it seem more positive.

Acceptance
- I learn to live with it.
- I accept that this has happened and can't be changed.

Seeking Social Support
- I talk to someone about how I feel.
- I ask people who had similar experiences what they did.

Restraint Coping
- I force myself to wait for the right time to do something.
- I make sure not to make matters worse by acting too soon.

Focusing on/Venting Emotions
- I get upset and let my emotions out.
- I let my feelings out.

Suppression of Competing Activities
- I put aside other activities to concentrate on this.
- . . . if necessary let other things slide a little

Mental Disengagement
- I turn to work . . . to take my mind off things.
- I go to the movies or watch TV, to think about it less.

Turning to Religion
- I seek God's help.
- I try to find comfort in my religion.

Behavioral Disengagement
- I give up the attempt to get what I want.
- I admit to myself that I can't deal with it.

Denial
- I refuse to believe that it has happened.
- I pretend that it hasn't really happened.

Alcohol and Drugs
- I drink alcohol or take drugs to think about it less.

problem-focused coping
Cognitive and behavioral efforts to alter a stressful situation.

emotion-focused coping
Cognitive and behavioral efforts to reduce the distress produced by a stressful situation.

to complete a textbook. Stress is inevitable. No one can prevent it. The best we can do is to minimize its harmful effects on our health. Depending on the person and stressor, people can cope by trying to solve the problem, talking to friends, inviting distractions, sleeping or drinking too much to escape, praying, brooding, venting, lashing out, laughing it off, getting outside help, pretending that all is well—or freaking out. Combining all psychological theories and research, it appears that there are about four hundred specific ways to cope with stress (Skinner et al., 2003).

By grouping specific strategies that are similar, researchers are able to study different general types of coping. Based on the self-reports of large numbers of people, Charles Carver and others (1989) constructed a multidimensional questionnaire they called COPE that measures twelve distinct methods of coping (see Table 14.2). While acknowledging that people can use different coping strategies, Richard Lazarus and Susan Folkman (1984) distinguished two general types. The first is **problem-focused coping**, cognitive and behavioral efforts to reduce stress by overcoming the source of the problem. Difficulties in school? Study harder, hire a tutor, or reduce your workload. Marriage on the rocks? Talk it out or see a counselor. Problems at work? Consult with your boss or look for another job. As indicated in several of the items in Table 14.2, the goal is to attack the source of stress. A second approach is **emotion-focused coping**, which consists of efforts to manage our emotional reactions to stressors rather than trying to change them. If you struggle at school, at work, or in a romantic relationship, you can keep a stiff upper lip, accept what is happening, tune out, or vent your emotions. According to Lazarus and Folkman, we tend to take an active, problem-focused approach when we think we can overcome a stressor but fall back on an emotion-focused approach when we perceive the problem to be out of our control. Lisa Aspinwall and Shelley Taylor (1997) note that there is a third alternative: **proactive coping**, which consists of up-front efforts to ward off or modify the onset of a stressful event. As we'll see, coping is an ongoing process by which we try to prevent—not just react to—life's bumps and bruises.

Problem-Focused Coping

Problem-focused coping seems like the prime candidate for a starring role in the war against stress. Surely our most active and assertive efforts are associated with better health (Aspinwall & Taylor, 1992). And clearly we often benefit from confronting a stressor head-on rather than avoiding it. Consider something we all are guilty of on occasion: procrastination, a purposive delay in the beginning or completing of a task, often accompanied by feelings of discomfort (Ferrari et al., 1995). In a longitudinal study of college students enrolled in a health psychology class, Dianne Tice and Roy Baumeister (1997) administered at the start of the semester a questionnaire that assesses the extent to which people tend to procrastinate. True to their word, those students who were classified from their test scores as procrastinators turned in their term papers later than did their classmates and also received lower grades. More interesting was the relationship to daily reports of stress and physical health. Early on, while procrastinators were in the "putting it off" stage of their projects, they were relatively stress-free compared with others. Later in the semester, however, as the deadline neared and passed, procrastinators were under greater stress and reported having more symptoms of illness. In the end, the short-term benefits of avoidance were outweighed by the long-term costs.

In dealing with essential tasks, it is better to confront and control than to avoid. But is this always the more beneficial approach? There are two reasons why sometimes it is not. First, to exert control a person must stay vigilant, alert, and actively engaged, which is physiologically taxing (Light & Obrist, 1980). Second, a controlling orientation can cause problems if it leads us to develop an over-controlling, stress-inducing, Type A pattern of behavior—whether that means always having the last word in an argument, "driving" from the back seat of a car, or planning every last detail of a leisurely vacation. Not all events are within our control or important enough to worry about. There are times when it's better to just let go (Friedland et al., 1992; Wright et al., 1990).

When we use the word *control*, we usually have in mind active efforts to manage something: win an argument, work out a marital problem, change a job requirement. But control comes in many guises. Knowledge, for instance, is a form of control. Knowing why something happens increases your chance of making sure it goes your way—if not now, then the next time. Sometimes, we can cope effectively with tragedies such as technological disasters, terrorist acts, and spousal abuse, by blaming the perpetrators for their actions. In these situations, holding others responsible can force a helpful response, such as financial compensation or police protection.

But what about self-blame? Is it ever adaptive to cope with a bad situation by blaming oneself? According to Ronnie Janoff-Bulman (1979), it depends on whether you blame your behavior or yourself as a person. People can change their own behavior, she notes, so behavioral self-blame paves the way for control in an effort to reduce current stresses or avoid future ones. But it is not similarly adaptive, she warns, to blame your own enduring personal characteristics, which are hard to change. Janoff-Bulman (1992) later amended this hypothesis, noting that it may take time to realize the mental health benefits of behavioral self-blame. This prediction was tested in studies of how female rape victims adjust to the trauma. Consistently, the results showed that both behavioral and characterological self-blame are associated with an increase in distress. Contrary to prediction, rape victims who blame their own behavior for what happened do *not* cope better than those who blame their character (Frazier & Schauben, 1994; Hall et al., 2003).

In light of past research, Patricia Frazier (2003) offers a somewhat more complex perspective on blame, control, and coping. Clearly, she notes, it can be adaptive for the victims of rape and other traumas to own a sense of future control (Carver et al., 2000; Frazier et al., 2004). But noting that behavioral self-blame for a past trauma

proactive coping Up-front efforts to ward off or modify the onset of a stressful event.

does not guarantee the prevention of future trauma, she distinguishes past, present, and future control—and what each implies about the dreaded possibility of a future recurrence. In a longitudinal study of female rape victims appearing in an emergency room, she assessed attributions of blame and responsibility, perceptions of control, and feelings of distress periodically from two weeks up to a year later. Overall, women blamed the rapist more than they blamed themselves, a tendency that strengthened over time. As in other studies, however, those who assigned more blame to the rapist or to themselves were more distressed. Apparently, the problem with behavioral self-blame, once thought to be adaptive, is that it did not engender feelings of future safety. In this regard, the most useful sense of control was over the *present:* women who believed that they could help themselves get better and facilitate their own recovery were more optimistic about the future and the least distressed.

Emotion-Focused Coping

Stress is by definition an unpleasant and arousing experience that fills us with negative and unhealthy emotions. Following the terrorist attacks of 9/11, large numbers of Americans reported in public opinion polls that they cried and felt sad, angry, fearful, anxious, and disgusted. Under circumstances so tragic, you would not also expect people to experience positive emotions, but positive and negative emotions can coexist—as when people find consolation in loss, or a silver lining in the dense gray clouds (Folkman & Moskowitz, 2000).

In laboratory studies, Barbara Frederickson and others (2000) have found that positive emotions help people cope with adversity by providing a welcome distraction from the anger, fear, and other negative states that increase blood pressure and other aspects of autonomic arousal and that narrow the focusing of attention. People who cope well and are resilient tend to experience positive emotions in the face of stress—a common capacity that Masten (2001) termed "ordinary magic." To test the hypothesis that positive emotions are adaptive in this way, Frederickson and her colleagues (2003) contacted forty-six college students days after September 11, 2001, who had previously taken part in a study on stress and coping. Across the board, the students felt angry, sad, fearful, and scornful about the attack. But many also expressed positive feelings of gratitude (to be alive), love (a renewed appreciation for loved ones), and interest (in unfolding world events). In fact, those who scored as most resilient before the crisis were later the most likely to have these positive emotions and least likely to suffer depression after the crisis. It's important not to overintellectualize the coping process and underestimate the value of emotion-focused coping.

Look back at Table 14.2, and you will see many instances of emotion-focused coping, such as acceptance, denial, a focusing on or venting of emotions, mental and behavioral disengagement, or a turning to religion. By and large, there are two general ways to cope with the emotional aspects of stress: shutting down and opening up. This section examines the health effects of each of these strategies.

Shutting Down: Suppressing Unwanted Thoughts   Often we react to stress by shutting down and trying to deny or suppress the unpleasant thoughts and feelings. One specific form of avoidance coping is distraction. Consider what happens when terrorists or street criminals take innocent victims hostage. Police surround the airplane or building, and negotiations begin. Are certain ways of coping with this frightening situation particularly effective? To help answer this question, fifty-seven airline employees voluntarily participated in a remarkable training exercise conducted by the Special Operations and Research Staff of the FBI Academy (Auerbach et al., 1994; Strentz & Auerbach, 1988). Some volunteers were trained in problem-focused coping techniques such as helping each other, interacting with their captors, and gathering intelligence. Others were trained in emotion-focused techniques designed to decrease anxiety—such as distraction, deep breathing, and muscle relaxation. Volunteers in a control condition did not receive any specific instruction.

After the training session, the volunteers were "abducted" by FBI agents acting as terrorists. Automatic weapons were fired (with blanks), and bloody injuries were simulated. The volunteers were then "held captive" in one room and isolated by having

In a daring rescue, French commandos stormed an Air France jetliner, killed four Algerian terrorists who had hijacked the plane and murdered two passengers, and freed 173 passengers and crew. Simulation research conducted by the FBI examined what techniques would help people cope effectively when they were held hostage.

pillowcases placed over their heads. A few cooperative "hostages" were released. Four days later, other FBI agents "stormed" the building and "rescued" the remaining hostages. The exercise was conducted in a realistic manner, and the volunteers found it exceedingly stressful. Those who had been instructed in anxiety-management techniques coped better than those given problem-solving training or no training at all. In this kind of situation, where individuals have little actual control over events, distraction and other emotion-focused techniques were more effective in reducing distress than were problem-focused efforts to exert control.

Although potentially effective, the suppression of unwanted thoughts from awareness can also have a peculiar, paradoxical effect. As described in Chapter 3, Daniel Wegner (1994, 1997) conducted a series of studies in which he told people not to think of a white bear and found that they could not then keep the image from popping to mind. What's more, he found that among participants who were permitted later to think about the bear, those who had earlier tried to suppress the image were unusually preoccupied with it, providing evidence of a rebound effect. Sometimes, the harder you try not to think about something, the less likely you are to succeed (Wegner et al., 1998). The solution: focused distraction. When participants were told to imagine a tiny red Volkswagen every time the forbidden bear intruded into consciousness, the rebound effect vanished (Wenzlaff & Wegner, 2000).

What do white bears and red cars have to do with coping? Lots. When people try to block stressful thoughts from awareness, the problem may worsen. That's where focused distraction comes in. In a study of pain tolerance, Delia Cioffi and James Holloway (1993) had people put a hand into a bucket of ice-cold water and keep it there until they could no longer bear the pain. One group was instructed to avoid thinking about the sensation. A second group was told to form a mental picture of their home. Afterward, those who had coped through suppression were slower to recover from the pain than were those who had used focused self-distraction. To manage stress—whether it's caused by physical pain, a strained romance, final exams, or problems at work—distraction ("think about lying on the beach") is a better coping strategy than mere suppression ("don't think about the pain").

Keeping secrets and holding in strong emotions may also be physically taxing. In the laboratory, James Gross and Robert Levenson (1997) showed female students funny, sad, and neutral films. Half the time, they told the students to not let their feelings show. From a hidden camera, videotapes confirmed that when asked to conceal their feelings, the students were less expressive. But physiological recordings revealed that as they watched the funny and sad films, the students exhibited a greater cardiovascular response when they tried to inhibit their feelings than when they did not. Physiologically, the effort to suppress the display of emotion backfired. A study by Steve Cole and others (1996) pushes this point a suggestive but profound step further. These investigators identified eighty gay men in the Los Angeles area who were newly infected with the HIV virus but had no symptoms, administered various psychological tests, and monitored their progress every six months for nine years. They found that in men who were partly "in the closet"—compared with those who were completely open about their homosexuality—the infection spread more rapidly, causing them to die sooner. This provocative correlation does not prove that "coming out" is healthier than "staying in." In a controlled laboratory experiment, however, participants who were instructed to suppress rather than express turbulent emotional thoughts exhibited a temporary decrease in the activity of certain immune cells (Petrie et al., 1998). It appears that actively concealing your innermost thoughts and feelings can be hazardous to your health.

Opening Up: Confronting One's Demons The research just described suggests that just as shutting down can, at times, have benefits, so too can the opposite form of coping: opening up. There are two aspects to this emotional means of coping with stress. The first is to acknowledge and understand our emotional reactions to important events; the second is to express these inner feelings to ourselves and others (Stanton et al., 2000).

According to James Pennebaker (1997), psychotherapy, self-help groups, and various religious rituals have something in common: All offer a chance for people to confide in someone, spill their guts, confess, and talk freely about their troubles— maybe for the first time. To test for the healing power of opening up, Pennebaker conducted a series of controlled studies in which he brought college students into a laboratory and asked them to talk into a tape recorder or write for twenty minutes either about past traumas or about trivial daily events. While speaking or writing, the students were upset and physiologically aroused. Many tearfully recounted accidents, failures, instances of physical or sexual abuse, loneliness, the death or divorce of their parents, shattered relationships, and their fears about the future. Soon, however, these students felt better than ever. Pennebaker found that when they opened up, their systolic blood pressure levels rose during the disclosures but then later dipped below their pre-experiment levels. The students even exhibited a decline in their number of visits to the campus health center over the next six months. Other studies, too, have shown that keeping personal secrets can be stressful and that "letting it out" and "getting it off your chest" can have true therapeutic effects on mental and physical health. These effects are especially strong when participants are comfortable with disclosure, when the disclosures are made across multiple sessions, and when the events being described are recent and traumatic (Frattaroli, 2006; Lepore & Smyth, 2002).

It appears that confession may be good for the body as well as the soul. But why does it help to open up? Why do *you* sometimes feel the need to talk out your problems? One possibility, recognized a full century ago by Sigmund Freud, is that the experience provides a much-needed *catharsis,* a discharge of tension—like taking the lid off a boiling pot of water to slow the boiling. People who experience trauma—whether it's a bout with cancer, death, accident, a natural disaster, or exposure to violence— are often haunted by intrusive images of their stressor, images that pop to mind and cannot be stopped. In these cases, disclosure may bring closure. Research shows, for example, that women who had an abortion and who talked about it to an experimenter, compared to others who were not asked to open up, were later less distressed by intrusive thoughts about the traumatic experience (Major & Gramzow, 1999).

Another explanation for the benefits of opening up, one favored by Pennebaker, is that talking about a problem can help you to sort out your thoughts, understand the problem better, and gain *insight,* in cognitive terms. Whatever the reason, it's clear that opening up, perhaps to someone else, can be therapeutic—provided that the listener can be trusted. This last point is critical: Despite the potential for gain, opening up can also cause great distress when the people we confide in react with rejection or unwanted advice or, worse, betray what was said to others (Kelly & McKillop, 1996).

Indicating the importance of the "to whom" part of opening up, Stephen Lepore and colleagues (2000) exposed college students to disturbing Nazi Holocaust images. Afterward, the students were randomly divided into groups and asked to talk about their reactions to themselves while alone in a room, to a validating confederate who smiled and agreed, or to an invalidating confederate who avoided eye contact and disagreed. An additional group was given no opportunity to talk. As reported two days later, students who talked alone or to a validating confederate—compared to those who did not talk—said they had fewer intrusive Holocaust thoughts in the intervening period and were less stressed when re-exposed to the original images. However, for students who talked to an invalidating confederate the benefits of opening up were muted. This finding supports our earlier conclusion: It is better to discuss one's demons than to conceal them—but the extent of the benefit depends on whether the people we talk to are supportive. It's no wonder, then, that people are more likely to join mutual support groups, both live and online, when they suffer from stigmatizing disorders such as AIDS, alcoholism, breast cancer, and prostate cancer than when they have less embarrassing but equally toxic illnesses such as heart disease and diabetes (Davison et al., 2000).

Self-Focus: Getting Trapped Versus Getting Out   In Chapter 3, we saw that people spend little time actually thinking about the self—and when they do, they wish they were doing something else (Csikszentmihalyi & Figurski, 1982). According to self-awareness theory, self-focus brings out our personal shortcomings the way staring in a mirror draws our attention to every blemish on the face. It comes as no surprise, then, that self-focus seems to intensify some of the most undesirable consequences of emotion-focused coping. Here's the script.

The state of self-awareness can be induced in us by external stimuli such as mirrors, cameras, and audiences. Mood, too, plays a role. Peter Salovey (1992) found that, compared with a neutral mood state, both positive and negative moods increase awareness of the self. Thus, when a stressful event occurs, the negative feelings that arise magnify self-focus. What happens next depends on a person's self-esteem, as people with a negative self-concept experience more negative moods when self-focused than do those with a positive self-concept (Sedikides, 1992). The end result is a self-perpetuating feedback loop: Being in a bad mood triggers self-focus, which in people with low self-esteem further worsens the mood. This vicious circle forms the basis for a self-focusing model of depression according to which coping with stress by attending to your own feelings only makes things worse (Pyszczynski & Greenberg, 1992).

Women and men differ in the likelihood of getting trapped in a self-focused state in response to negative emotions. Over the years, and in a range of different cultures, research has shown that women are more likely to ruminate, confront negative feelings, and seek treatment for being depressed, while men tend to resort to alcohol and other drugs, physical activity, antisocial behavior, and other means of distraction (Culbertson, 1997; Cyranowski et al., 2000; Nolen-Hoeksema & Girgus, 1994). Thus, women brood, while men act out. Both suffer.

Thankfully, there are healthier alternatives. To redirect attention away from the self, it helps to become absorbed in an activity such as aerobic exercise, gardening, writing, or reading a book. Whatever the activity, it should be difficult, demanding, and fully engaging. Ralph Erber and Abraham Tesser (1992) found that people who were in a bad mood felt better after performing a difficult task than a simple task or none at all. Difficult tasks, it appears, can "absorb" a bad mood. Meditation can have beneficial effects for the same reason. Referring to his own techniques of focused relaxation, cardiologist Herbert Benson recommended that people sit comfortably, close their eyes, relax the muscles, breathe deeply, and silently utter some word over and over again. Says Benson (1993), "By practicing two basic steps—the repetition of a sound, word, phrase, prayer, or muscular activity; and a passive return to the repetition whenever distracting thoughts recur—you can trigger a series of physiological changes that offer protection against stress" (p. 256).

Healthy distractions like exercise are a good way to break out of the trap of self-focused depression. Unhealthy distractions, like an alcohol binge, reduce self-focus at a self-destructive cost.

Proactive Coping

According to Lisa Aspinwall and Shelley Taylor (1997), people often benefit from *proactive coping,* which consists of up-front efforts to ward off or modify the onset of a stressful event. As illustrated in Figure 14.8, coping can be seen as an ongoing process by which we try to prevent as well as react to the bumps and bruises of daily life. Also as shown, the first line of defense consists of the accumulation of resources—personal, financial, social, and otherwise—that can later, if needed, serve as a buffer against stress. In this section, we look at two possible "resources": social support and religion.

Social Support If the world is crashing down around you, what do you do? Do you try to stop it? Do you try to manage your emotions? Or do you try to get help from others? Throughout this book, we have seen that no man or woman is an island, that human beings are social animals, that people need people, and that to get by you need a little help from your friends. But does our social nature, and do our connections to others, have anything to do with health? Do close family ties, lovers, buddies, community or online support groups, and relationships at work serve as a buffer against stress? The answer is yes. An overwhelming amount of evidence shows that **social support** has therapeutic effects on both our psychological and physical well-being (Cohen et al., 2000; Uchino et al., 1996; Wills, 1990).

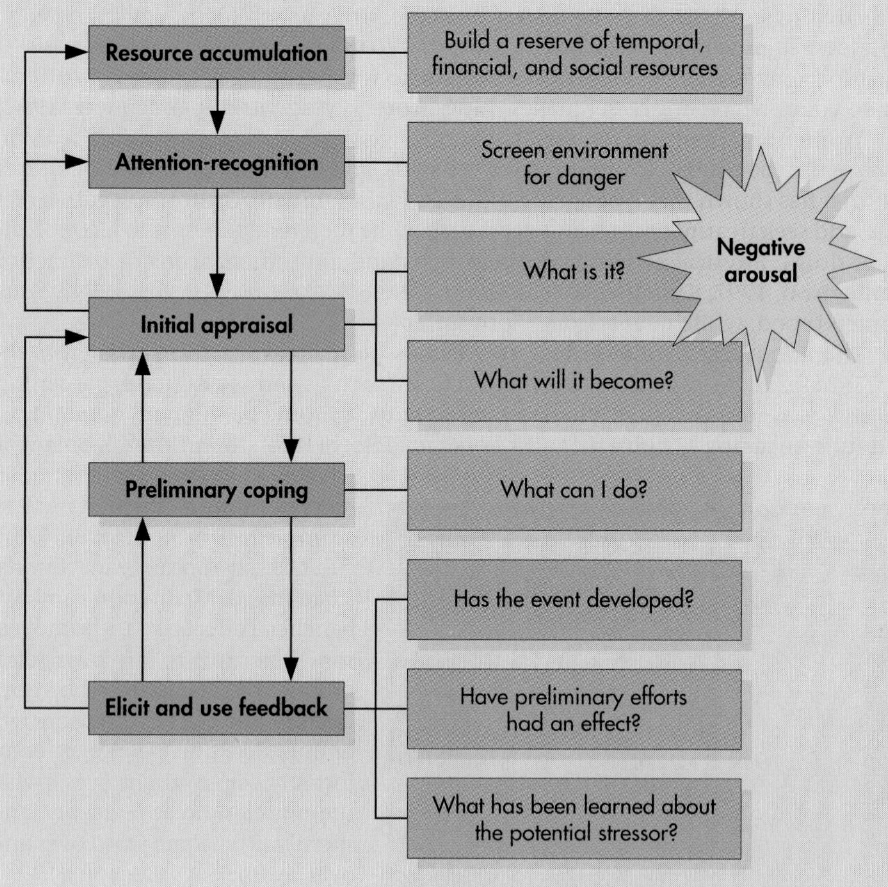

David Spiegel, of Stanford University's School of Medicine, came to appreciate the value of social connections many years ago when he organized support groups for women with advanced breast cancer. The groups met weekly in ninety-minute sessions to laugh, cry, share stories, and discuss ways of coping. Spiegel had fully expected the women to benefit, emotionally, from the experience. But he found something else he did not expect: These women lived an average of eighteen months longer than did similar others who did not attend the groups. According to Spiegel (1993), "The added survival time was longer than any medication or other known medical treatment could be expected to provide for women with breast cancer so far advanced" (pp. 331–332).

Similar discoveries were then made by other researchers. In one study, Lisa Berkman and Leonard Syme (1979) surveyed seven thousand residents of Alameda County, California; conducted a nine-year follow-up of mortality rates; and found that the more social contacts people had, the longer they lived. This was true of men

FIGURE 14.8

Aspinwall and Taylor's Model of Proactive Coping

Coping can be seen as an ongoing, multistep process by which people try to prevent, not just react to, life's daily stressors.

(Aspinwall & Taylor, 1997.)

Resource accumulation → Build a reserve of temporal, financial, and social resources

Attention-recognition → Screen environment for danger

Initial appraisal → What is it? / What will it become? → Negative arousal

Preliminary coping → What can I do?

Elicit and use feedback → Has the event developed? / Have preliminary efforts had an effect? / What has been learned about the potential stressor?

social support The helpful coping resources provided by friends and other people.

FIGURE 14.9

Does Being Popular Always Promote Health?

Young adults were asked about recent stressful events and about their social lives—and then kept a health diary for three months. As you can see, social contact made no difference for people under low stress. For people under high stress, however, those with active social lives were *more* likely to get sick. Social contact increases exposure to infectious agents—and can bring illness for those whose resistance is compromised by stress.

(Hamrick et al., 2002.)

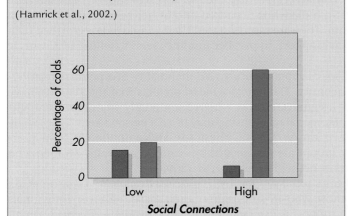

and women, young and old, rich and poor, and people from all racial and ethnic backgrounds. James House and others (1988) studied 2,754 adults interviewed during visits to their doctors. He found that the most socially active men were two to three times less likely to die within nine to twelve years than others of similar age who were more isolated. According to House, social isolation was, statistically, just as predictive of an early death as smoking or high cholesterol.

Research findings like these are now common. For example, married people are more likely than those who are single, divorced, or widowed to survive cancer for five years (Taylor, 1990), gay men infected with HIV are less likely to contemplate suicide if they have close ties than if they do not (Schneider et al., 1991), people who have a heart attack are less likely to have a second one if they live with someone than if they live alone (Case et al., 1992), and perceptions of racism among black college women are associated with less physiological stress in those who tend to seek social support (Clark, 2006). Based on a review of eighty-one studies, Bert Uchino and others (1996) concluded that in times of stress, having social support lowers blood pressure, lessens the secretion of stress hormones, and strengthens immune responses. On the flip side of the coin, people who are lonely exhibit greater age-related increases in blood pressure and more difficulty sleeping at night (Cacioppo et al., 2002; Hawkley et al., 2003). In fact, a study of first-year college students showed that feelings of loneliness during the semester were associated with elevated levels of the stress hormone cortisol and a weakened immune response to a flu shot they had received at the university health clinic (Pressman et al., 2005). There's no doubt about it: Being isolated from other people can be hazardous to your health.

There is, however, a vital exception to this rule. Of all the social networks that support us, romantic partnerships, as in marriage, are the most powerful. But while men and women who are happily married live longer than those who are single or divorced, marital conflict breeds stress, elevated blood pressure, ulcers, depression, alcohol and drug abuse, changes in immune function, and other unhealthy effects—especially for women (Kiecolt-Glaser & Newton, 2001).

Our social connections are therapeutic for many reasons. Friends may encourage us to get out, eat well, exercise, and take care of ourselves. They also provide sympathy, reassurance, someone to talk to, advice, and a second opinion. The value of social support is so basic that people who support us don't need to be physically present. In one study, for example, the physiological responses of research participants were measured as they played a competitive fire-fighting simulation on computer. Via closed-circuit monitor, some participants thought they were being watched, spoken to, and comforted by a friendly person of the same sex, while others were left alone. The result: Social support delivered over a monitor, even from a confederate who was not physically present, had a calming influence on participants. It lowered their heart rate, reduced the level of cortisol (a stress hormone) in their saliva, and led them to see the task as easier (Thorsteinsson et al., 1998).

The health benefits of social support show just how important it is to connect with others. Are there any drawbacks to an active social life? Is it possible, for example, that the more people we see within a day—such as family, friends, classmates, teammates, co-workers, and neighbors—the more exposed we are to catch colds or the flu? Natalie Hamrick and others (2002) asked eighteen- to thirty-year-old adults about recent stressful events and about their social lives, then had them keep a health diary for three months. Based on past research, they expected that participants who were under high stress would get sick more than those under low stress. But what about people with high versus low levels of social contact? What do you think? Would their social connections make them vulnerable to illness or protect them? It depends. Look at Figure 14.9 and you'll see that for people under low stress, social connections did not matter. For people under high stress, however, those with high levels of social contact were *more* likely to catch a cold or flu. It's healthy to be popular except, perhaps, during flu season.

Precisely because researchers agree that social support is vital to health, they have struggled mightily to come up with ways to measure it (Cohen et al., 2000). In some studies, social support is defined by the sheer *number of social contacts* a person has. This measure can be useful, but a simple social contact model has some limitations. One is that it glosses over the fact that people who are stuck in bad social relationships are sometimes more distressed, not less (Rook, 1984). Another problem is that having too many contacts can actually reduce levels of support. Consider the plight of the urban poor in India who are packed into overcrowded residences of up to eleven people per room. They are more stressed than people in less crowded conditions and have *less* social support, in part because they tend to withdraw (Evans & Lepore, 1993).

A second model of social support focuses on the quality of a person's relationships rather than their quantity. The *intimacy model* predicts that the key is to have a close relationship with a significant other who is emotionally on call for late-night conversations. Having one special relationship may be all a person needs. Thus, while many women with breast cancer benefit physically and emotionally from peer-discussion groups, these groups are not needed by—and do not help—women who have supportive partners at home (Helgeson et al., 2000).

A third approach defines social support by its *perceived availability* (Sarason et al., 1983). Compared with those who are uncertain of their social resources, individuals who believe that ample support is available as needed cope more effectively. In almost any demanding situation that you can imagine, perceived support is associated with better adjustment—even when these perceptions are not entirely accurate (Lakey & Cassady, 1990). Why are beliefs so important? According to Irwin Sarason and others (1994), people who perceive that they have others to turn to are "social optimists" who enjoy a strong sense of self-efficacy, high self-esteem, good social skills, and a positive outlook about future interactions.

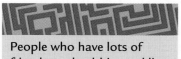

People who have lots of friends are healthier and live longer than those who live more isolated lives. **True.**

The Religious Connection Finally, it is clear that religion provides a deeply important source of social and emotional support for many people. There are more than 6 billion people in the world that belong to hundreds of religions—the most populated, in order, being Christianity, Islam, Hinduism, and Buddhism (Judaism and others have much fewer adherents). Only about 15 to 20 percent of the world's population is unaffiliated with a religious group. In the United States, 67 percent of adults describe religion as a "very important" part of their lives. Is there a link between religiosity and health?

This is an interesting but controversial question. On the one hand, population surveys suggest that people who regularly attend religious services live longer than those who do not (McCullough et al., 2000). When you think about it, this correlation makes some intuitive sense. Religious faith may fill people with hope and optimism rather than despair, offer the physiological benefits of relaxation in prayer, provide a community lifeline of social support to prevent isolation, and promote a safe and healthy way of life by discouraging such toxic habits as drinking and smoking. After analyzing thirty years of health data from 2,600 California adults, for example, William Strawbridge and others (2001) found that men and women who regularly attend

Religion provides an important source of support for many people. Here, people meditate in New York's Central Park during "Change Your Mind Day," which consists of yoga, meditation, music, and various spiritual practices from Buddhist traditions.

religious services drink less, smoke less, and exercise more. On the other hand, some researchers caution that the correlations between religiosity and longevity are modest and can be interpreted in other ways. For example, it's possible that nonsmokers, teetotalers, and others who regularly abstain from unhealthful behaviors are more likely to adopt religion as part of their lives than smokers, drinkers, and risk-takers—that their survival comes from who they are, not from their attendance at religious services (Sloan et al., 1999). At this point, the research is suggestive but not conclusive: A religious way of life is associated with physiological benefits, health, and longevity, but the basis for these correlations—and the ultimate question of whether becoming religious will increase one's health—remain to be determined (Miller & Thoresen, 2003; Powell et al., 2003; Seeman et al., 2003).

 ## Cultural Influences on Coping

Everyone in the world feels stress during the course of a lifetime. Whether the result of a natural disaster, the death of a loved one, the breakup of a relationship, war, serious illness, an accident, or the chronic microstressors of studying, working, and trying to make ends meet, stress is universal to the human experience. But do people in all cultures solve problems and cope in the same ways?

Most of the research on coping is conducted with people from Western cultures, in which individualism and independence are highly valued. Do people from collectivist cultures that value interdependence use the same coping mechanisms that are listed in Table 14.2? The answer may not be as obvious as it seems. In view of the differences between Eastern and Western cultures, for example, one might predict that Asians are more likely than Americans to cope with stress by turning to others for support. Yet Taylor and her colleagues (2004) found that when they asked college students to describe what they do to relieve stress, 57 percent of Americans—but only 39 percent of South Koreans—cited social support seeking. Additional probing shed light on this surprising difference. In individualistic cultures, people often use others to service their personal goals. In collectivist cultures, however, where social groups take precedence over the self, people are more reluctant to strain their relationships by calling on others for support.

To better understand the "collectivist coping style," Paul Heppner and others (2006) administered extensive questionnaires to more than three thousand Asian college students in Taiwan, many of whom had endured the kinds of traumatic events described in this chapter (the three most frequent were breakups, academic pressure, and the death or illness of a loved one). Table 14.3 shows five ways of coping that were identified. In order of how often they are used, these strategies are (1) acceptance, reframing, and striving, (2) avoidance and detachment, (3) family support, (4) religion and spirituality, and (5) private emotional outlets. Of the five strategies, participants rated acceptance as the most helpful. Do these results describe how Taiwanese adults cope with stress? What about Asians from Korea, Japan, mainland China, and elsewhere? Stay tuned. Interest is growing in these questions and, more generally, in the intersections of social psychology, culture, and health (Gurung, 2006).

TABLE 14.3
Collectivist Coping Styles

The following sample statements describe five common types of coping styles, in order of frequency of usage, to emerge from studies in Taiwan.

(Heppner et al., 2006.)

Acceptance, Reframing, and Striving   **91%**
- Tried to accept the trauma for what it offered me
- Believed I would grow from surviving the traumatic event
- Realized that the trauma served an important purpose in my life

Avoidance and Detachment   **71%**
- Saved face by not telling anyone
- Pretended to be okay
- Kept my feelings within myself in order not to worry my parents

Family Support   **66%**
- Shared my feelings with my family
- Knew that I could ask assistance from my family
- Followed the guidance of my elders

Religion and Spirituality   **40%**
- Found comfort in my religion or spirituality
- Found guidance from my religion
- Found comfort through prayer or other religious rituals

Private Emotional Outlets   **30%**
- Saved face by seeking advice from a professional I did not know
- Chatted with people about the trauma on the Internet
- Ate in excess

Treatment and Prevention

Understanding what social support is and how it operates is important in the study of health because so many of life's problems and prospects occur in a social context and so many of our efforts to cope with stress involve other people. Indeed, as we'll see in this section, health psychologists are actively trying to find ways in which social influences can be used to improve the development of treatment and prevention programs.

 ## Treatment: The "Social" Ingredients

Often, what ails us can be treated through medical intervention. The treatments vary widely—from a simple change in diet to vitamin supplements, aspirins, antibiotics, surgery, and the like. There's no doubt about it. Medicine is vital to health. In addition, however, treatment has a social component—what the family doctor used to call "bedside manner." What are the active social ingredients? To begin to answer this question, let's consider research on the benefits of psychotherapy. Over the years, studies have shown that although there are vastly different schools of thought and techniques for doing psychotherapy, all approaches are effective and, surprisingly, all are generally equivalent (Smith et al., 1980; Wampold et al., 1997). Apparently, despite the surface differences, all psychotherapies have a great deal in common at a deeper level and these common factors, more than the specific techniques used, provide the active ingredients necessary for change. The question is: What are some of these factors?

First, all healers—regardless of whether they are medical doctors, psychologists, or others—provide *social support,* a close human relationship characterized by warmth, expressions of concern, a shoulder to cry on, and someone to talk to. Earlier, we discussed the benefits to health and longevity of having social contacts. In psychological therapy, studies have shown that the better the "working alliance" is between a therapist and client, the more favorable the outcome is likely to be (Horvath & Luborsky, 1993). As psychotherapist Hans Strupp (1996) put it, "The simple and incontrovertible truth is that if you are anxious or depressed, or if you are experiencing difficulties with significant people in your life, chances are that you feel better if you talk to someone you can trust" (p. 1017).

Second, all therapies offer a ray of *hope* to people who are sick, demoralized, unhappy, or in pain. In all aspects of life, people are motivated by positive expectations. Although some of us are generally more optimistic than others, optimism is a specific expectation that can be increased or decreased in certain situations (Armor & Taylor, 1998). Indeed, a common aspect of all treatments is that they communicate and instill positive expectations. It has been suggested that high expectations can spark change even when they are not justified (Prioleau et al., 1983). This suggestion is consistent with the well-known placebo effect in medicine, whereby patients improve after being given an inactive drug or treatment. Believing can help make it so, which is how faith healers, shamans, and witch doctors all over the world have managed to perform "miracle cures" with empty rituals. Even modern medicine exploits the power of hope. As Walter Brown (1998) puts it, "The symbols and rituals of healing—the doctor's office, the stethoscope, the physical examination—offer reassurance" (p. 91).

A third important ingredient is *choice.* Allowing patients to make meaningful choices, such as deciding on a type of treatment, increases the effectiveness of treatments for alcoholism (Miller, 1985) and obesity (Mendonca & Brehm, 1983). The choice to undergo an effortful or costly treatment is particularly beneficial in this regard. The person who voluntarily pays in time, money, or discomfort needs to self-justify that investment—a predicament sure to arouse cognitive dissonance (see Chapter 6). One way to reduce dissonance is to become ultra-motivated to succeed: "Why have I chosen to do this? Because I really want to get better." Perhaps

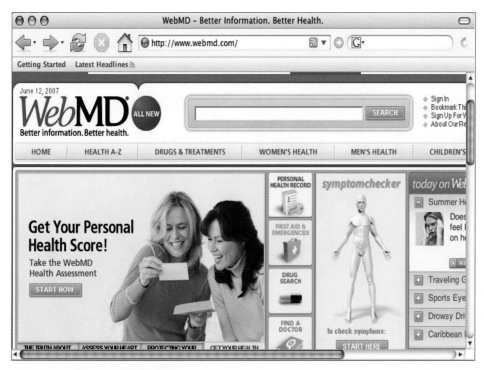

Today, people can find all sorts of information and advice on health-related issues on WebMD and other Internet sites.

because highly motivated individuals are more careful and conscientious about carrying out the prescribed treatment, they tend to improve more.

Danny Axsom (1989) tested this specific proposition in a study of snake phobias. Participants, all highly snake-phobic, were or were not given an explicit choice about undertaking a treatment that was described as either requiring "extreme exertion" or being "easy." Among the four experimental conditions, participants given an explicit choice about continuing an effortful treatment reported the greatest motivation to change their phobic behavior and came closest to the five-foot-long New Jersey corn snake used to measure approach behavior.

Prevention: Getting the Message Across

We live in what could aptly be described as the era of prevention in that many serious health threats are preventable. Just watch TV, leaf through a magazine, or surf the Internet: There are programs for AIDS prevention, campaigns to persuade smokers to break the habit, sunscreens that protect the skin from harmful rays, and laws that mandate the use of seat belts. To a large extent, we know what to do and what not to do to promote good health and to avoid disease and injury. But just how do we convince ourselves and others to translate that knowledge into action?

Nowhere is this problem more acute than among people who suffer from AIDS. Earlier in the chapter, we noted that heart attacks, cancer, strokes, and accidents are now more common causes of death than infectious diseases. But AIDS, the first truly global epidemic, has spread at an alarming rate. AIDS has been described as a microbiological time bomb (Mann, 1992). In 1981, five homosexual men in North America were diagnosed with AIDS and were among only 189 cases reported that year. By 1996, the number of cases in North America had skyrocketed to three-quarters of a million and included heterosexual men, women, and children. At the close of 2006, the World Health Organization estimated that 39 million people worldwide were infected with HIV; 3 million died in that year alone. The number of new infections will climb even higher in Latin America, sub-Saharan Africa, North Africa, the Middle East, Eastern Europe, and most of Asia (see Figure 14.10).

The AIDS virus is transmitted from one person to another in infected blood, semen, and vaginal secretions. People who are HIV-positive may have no symptoms for several years and may not even realize they are infected. Eventually, however, the virus will ravage the immune system by destroying lymphocytes that help ward off disease. What's frightening about AIDS is that it appears fatal, that it is increasing at a rate of one new case every few seconds, and that there is no vaccine that can prevent its occurrence (Stine, 2007). At present, the most effective way to control the spread of AIDS is to alter people's beliefs, motivations, and risk-taking behaviors (Fisher et al., 1994; Gerrard et al., 1996; Kalichman, 1998)—and that's where social psychology comes in. Across a range of perspectives, several basic steps emerge (see Figure 14.11).

The first step toward good health depends on the relative pleasure to be derived from healthy versus unhealthy behaviors. If a healthy behavior is more enjoyable than an unhealthy one, then presumably all we need to do is try it out and we'll be

FIGURE 14.10

The Spread of AIDS Across the Globe

This map shows the estimated number of adults and children around the world who were living with AIDS at the start of 2000.

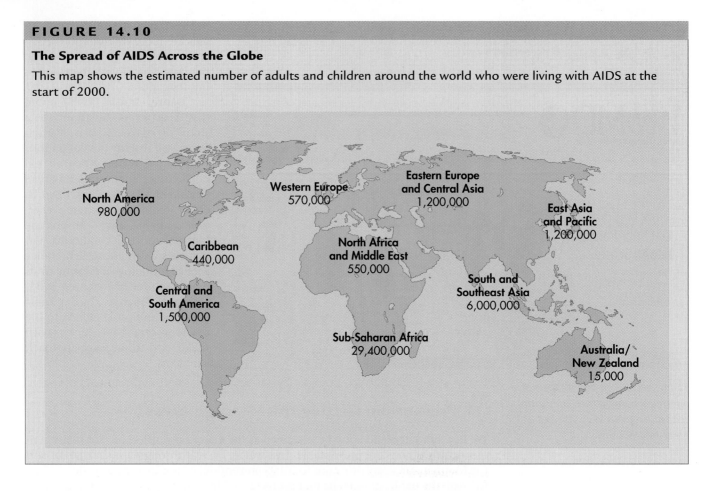

convinced. Usually, however, it's not this easy. Many unhealthy habits are sinfully enjoyable, and many healthy behaviors require self-control. To be convinced to switch, people have to recognize that their health is at risk. As described in Chapter 6, graphic fear appeals are a popular method of persuasion in public service advertisements: the gruesome lung-cancer operation to scare smokers into quitting, the bloody accident victim to get people to use seat belts. Fear appeals can increase the incentive to change attitudes and behavior. Other persuasion techniques developed in research laboratories can also be used (Devos-Comby & Salovey, 2002).

The next two steps toward good health involve other people. When those around us behave in healthful ways, they serve as role models that help to set healthy norms. Direct modeling can be especially useful. Celebrities in particular have a great deal of influence over public health issues. In the most poignant moment of the 1996 Olympics, former heavyweight boxing champion Muhammad Ali—who, like actor Michael J. Fox, suffers from Parkinson's disease, a motor disorder—stood upright with his arm trembling and his face frozen as he lit the ceremonial flame. The National Parkinson's Foundation, which went on to adopt a torch as its symbol, was flooded with donations (Nattinger et al., 1998). Unfortunately, the sword of influence cuts both ways, which is why it is so troubling to see role models of *un*healthy behavior among high-profile athletes, entertainers, and other celebrities who occupy center stage.

Besides eliciting direct imitation, spokespersons contribute to the development of subjective norms, beliefs we hold about how people expect us to behave. According to the theories of reasoned action (Fishbein, 1980) and planned behavior (Ajzen, 1991) presented in Chapter 6, both attitudes and subjective norms affect our intentions to take action. Indeed, both positive attitudes toward safe sex and felt pressure from significant others increase intentions to practice safe sex (Chan & Fishbein, 1993; Cochran et al., 1992). As to who the most effective spokespersons might be, a recent meta-analysis of 354 HIV intervention programs spanning seventeen years revealed that health professionals promote greater behavioral change than peers and other community sources (Durantini et al., 2006).

Intervention strategies that make use of social pressure can be very effective. In

FIGURE 14.11

Aiming for Good Health

Several major factors help convince people to engage in healthy practices. Recognition that a threat to health exists is a necessary first step. Positive models and healthy subjective norms encourage people to adopt health-protective behaviors. A sense of self-efficacy about being able to carry out healthy behaviors and the belief that such behaviors will be effective increase the likelihood of active efforts.

| The recognition that a threat to health exists | Imitating the healthy behaviors of others | Conforming to a subjective norm favoring healthy behaviors | A sense of self-efficacy about one's ability to perform healthy behaviors | Accurate beliefs that healthy behaviors will have the desired effect | → | **Healthy Behavior** |

a series of studies, Jeffrey Kelly and others (1991) found that self-reports by gay men of high-risk sexual behavior diminished after opinion leaders in the gay community had been trained to advocate safe-sex practices to their peers. Unfortunately, subjective norms often sustain unhealthy behaviors. There are two reasons why this occurs. First, people who smoke or drink excessively overestimate the prevalence of such practices among their peers. Second, these inflated estimates serve to support and increase unhealthy practices at a later time. For example, Deborah Prentice and Dale Miller (1996) found that college students who overestimate the level of alcohol use on campus at the start of a school year are eventually more likely to conform to this misperception in their own attitudes and behavior. For those trapped within this closed circle, the best way to cut through it is to provide accurate information about *who* does *what*. Prentice and Miller found that students who took part in a program designed to correct their misperceptions of campus norms actually consumed less alcohol six months later.

The fourth step to health emphasizes a person's confidence in his or her ability to succeed. Self-efficacy—the belief that we can do what needs to be done—enhances the adoption of various healthy behaviors, including safe-sex practices, nonsmoking, and abstinence from alcohol (Bandura, 1999; Maddux, 1995). If people don't know how to perform the necessary corrective behaviors, then they should be taught. For example, smoking-prevention programs often teach children techniques for resisting peer pressures and refusing the offer of a cigarette (Baum, 1984; Evans et al., 1984).

Finally, people need reliable and accurate information about the effectiveness of the healthy behaviors they are urged to adopt (Weinstein, 1989). If people believe that something works, they will be more likely to try it out. Beware, however, of someone who is too easily convinced. In one study, participants who had been reassured that a proposed prevention program would be successful were positive in their evaluation of the program regardless of the quality of the arguments that supported it. Those given a lower expectation of success were more discerning and based their evaluations on the quality of the arguments presented (Gleicher & Petty, 1992). In the short run, people can be tricked by false promises. In the long run, accurate information will prevail.

For social psychologists, the challenge in addressing the HIV crisis is to convert the science into a practice that works. In an excellent illustration, Jeffrey Fisher and his colleagues (2002) theorized that HIV prevention in city schools, which is essential for controlling the number of newly infected teens, requires a three-pronged attack. In their model, students must be provided with accurate *information* about HIV transmission and how to prevent it, with a personal and social *motivation* to engage in HIV-preventative behaviors, and with the *behavioral skills* necessary to follow through—notably, by using condoms. Armed with this model, these investigators set up HIV prevention programs in four urban high schools, devised a control group that lacked these "active ingredients," and found that the program, when administered by the classroom teachers,

As role models, celebrities have great influence over public health-care decisions.
True.

changed HIV-prevention behavior, increasing condom use up to a year later—all for an estimated cost of $2.22 per student. Other social psychologically oriented efforts have been developed as well, also with good success (Albarracín et al., 2005).

The Pursuit of Happiness

Long before the emergence of social psychology, philosophers regarded happiness to be the ultimate state of being. In the U.S. Declaration of Independence, Thomas Jefferson thus cited life, liberty, and "the pursuit of happiness" as the most cherished of human rights. But what is happiness, and how is it achieved? Aristotle said it was the reward of an active life. Freud linked it with both work and love. Others have variously suggested that happiness requires money and power, health and fitness, religion, beauty, the satisfaction of basic needs, and an ability to derive pleasure from the events of everyday life. In recent years, social psychologists have applied their theories and methods to study this most basic human motive: the pursuit of happiness (Diener et al., 2006; Gilbert, 2006; Haidt, 2006).

To study happiness—or **subjective well-being**, as social psychologists like to call it—one must be able to measure it. How do researchers know whether someone is happy? Simple: They ask. Better yet, they use questionnaires such as the Satisfaction with Life Scale, in which people respond to statements such as "If I could live my life over, I would change almost nothing" (Diener et al., 1984; Pavot & Diener, 1993). As Marcus Aurelius said, "No man is happy who does not think himself so."

Using self-reports, surveys show that 75 percent of American adults describe themselves as happy and that in 86 percent of all nations sampled, the ratings are, on average, more often positive than neutral (Diener, 2000). In general, people who are happy also have cheerful moods, high self-esteem, physical health, a sense of personal control, more memories for positive as opposed to negative events, and optimism about the future (Myers & Diener, 1995). It's no secret that our outlook on life becomes rosy right after we win a game, fall in love, land a great job, or make money—and that the world seems gloomy right after we lose, fall out of love, or suffer a personal tragedy or financial setback. Predictably, the events of everyday life trigger fluctuations in mood. For example, people are most happy on Fridays and Saturdays and least happy on Mondays and Tuesdays (Larsen & Kasimatis, 1990). Even during the day, happiness levels fluctuate like clockwork. For example, David Watson and others (1999) asked college students to rate their mood states once a day for forty-five days, always at a different hour. They found, on average, that the students felt best during the middle of the day (noon to 6 P.M.) and worst in the early morning and late evening hours.

But what determines our long-term satisfaction, and why are some of us happier in general than others? Seeking the roots of happiness, Ed Diener and his colleagues (1999) reviewed many years of research and found that subjective well-being is not meaningfully related to demographic factors such as age, sex, race, ethnic background, IQ, education level, or physical attractiveness. Contrary to popular belief, people are not less happy during the so-called crisis years of midlife or in old age than during their youth and "peak" young-adult years. Men and women do not differ on this measure, and, in the United States, African and Hispanic Americans are as happy as white Americans.

Overall, there are three key predictors of happiness: *social relationships* (people with an active social life, close friends, and a happy marriage are more satisfied than those who lack these intimate connections), *employment status* (regardless of income, employed people are happier than those who are out of work), and *physical and mental health* (people who are healthy are happier than those who are not). Reflecting the impact of these factors, worldwide surveys of more than 100,000 respondents in fifty-five countries have shown that happiness levels vary from one culture to the next (Diener & Suh, 2000). National happiness ratings are the highest in Iceland, Sweden, and Australia; they are the lowest in the Dominican Republic, Cameroon, and China. Canada ranked fifth in the world, and the United States ranked seventh (Diener et al., 1995; Veenhoven, 1993).

Perhaps the most interesting statistical relationship is between income and subjective well-being. We all know the saying that "money can't buy happiness"—though

subjective well-being One's happiness, or life satisfaction, as measured by self-report.

This image probably arouses positive feelings. But can money buy happiness? Recent research shows that there is no simple answer.

some people (particularly those who are financially strapped) do not believe it. But is wealth truly a key to happiness? To some extent, yes, but the evidence is complex. Ed Diener and Martin Seligman (2004) note that multimillionaires from the Forbes list of the four hundred richest Americans report high levels of life satisfaction (5.8 on a 7-point scale), but so do the Masai, a herding people in East Africa with no electricity or running water who live in huts made with dung (5.7 on the same 7-point scale).

Cross-national studies reveal a strong positive association between a nation's wealth and the subjective well-being of its people. There are some exceptions. But as a general rule, the more money a country has, the happier its citizens are, at least up to a point. Within any given country, however, the differences between wealthy and middle-income people are modest. In one survey, for example, a group of the wealthiest Americans said they were happy 77 percent of the time, which was only moderately higher than the 62 percent figure reported by those of average income. And when comparisons within a single culture are made over time, there is no relationship between affluence and happiness. Americans on average are two to three times richer now than fifty years ago—before we had computers, flat-screen TVs, cell phones, iPods, and digital cameras that fit into the palm of your hand. Yet the number of respondents who said they were "very happy" was 35 percent in 1957 and only 32 percent in 1998 (see Figure 14.12). So what are we to conclude? At this point, it appears that having shelter, food, safety, and security is essential for subjective well-being. But once these basic needs are met, particularly in an already prosperous society, additional increases in wealth do not appreciably raise levels of happiness.

Why doesn't money contribute more to subjective well-being? One reason is that our perceptions of wealth are not absolute but, instead, relative to certain personally set standards (Parducci, 1995). These standards are derived from two sources: other people and our own past.

According to *social comparison theory*, as described in Chapter 3, people tend to naturally compare themselves to others and feel contented or deprived depending on how they fare in this comparison. To demonstrate, Ladd Wheeler and Kunitate Miyake (1992) had college students for two weeks keep a written record of every time they mentally compared their own grades, appearance, abilities, possessions, or personality traits to someone else's. Consistently, these diaries revealed that making "upward comparisons" (to others who were better off) sparked negative feelings, while making "downward comparisons" (to others who were worse off) triggered positive feelings. That is why the middle-class worker whose neighbors can't pay their bills feels fortunate but the upper-class social climber who rubs elbows with the rich and famous feels deprived. This relativity may also help to explain why there are only modest relationships between actual income, perceptions of financial status, and happiness (Johnson & Krueger, 2006).

It is also natural for people to use their own recent past as a basis of comparison. According to *adaptation-level theory*, our

FIGURE 14.12

Wealth and Subjective Well-Being

Over a period of more than forty years, Americans became twice as wealthy, as measured by adjusted per person income—but they were no happier, as measured in public opinion polls.

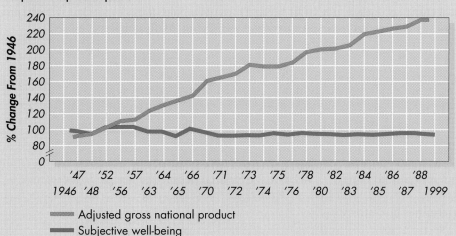

Adjusted gross national product
Subjective well-being

"Remember how I said I was happiest when I had nothing?"

satisfaction with the present depends on the level of success to which we are accustomed. Get married, buy a new house, or make a killing in the stock market, and you will surely enjoy a wave of euphoria. Before long, however, the glitter will wear off, and you'll adapt to your better situation and raise your standard of comparison. Indeed, when Philip Brickman and others (1978) interviewed twenty-two people who had won between $50,000 and $1 million in a lottery, they found that these people did not rate themselves as happier than in the past. Compared to others from similar backgrounds, the winners said that they now derived less pleasure from routine activities like shopping, reading, and talking to a friend. Perhaps the more money you have, the more you need to stay happy. The results of a Chicago public opinion poll suggest that this is the case: Whereas people who earned less than $30,000 a year said that $50,000 would fulfill their dreams, those who earned more than $100,000 said it would take $250,000 to make them happy (Csikszentmihalyi, 1999). Highlighting a dark side to the "American dream," research shows that the more materialistic people are, the less satisfied they seem to be (Nickerson et al., 2003). Economists are thus coming to appreciate that, to some extent, our sense of well-being stems from the gap between income and material aspirations (Stutzer, 2004).

There's one other possible and intriguing explanation for why money, per se, is not more predictive of happiness: Perhaps each of us, as a result of both biological and environmental factors, has a set baseline level of happiness, a "set point" toward which we gravitate. This notion is supported by three recent findings. One is that ratings of happiness are higher among pairs of identical twins than among fraternal twins—leading David Lykken (2000) to suggest that there may be a genetic basis for having a certain set level of contentment. A second finding is that the fluctuations in mood that accompany positive and negative life events tend to wear off over time. For example, in a study spanning two years, Eunkook Suh and others (1996) studied participants for two years and found that only experiences occurring in the last three months correlated with reports of subjective well-being. Getting engaged or married, breaking up, starting a new job, and being hospitalized are the kinds of high-impact experiences that people assume to have lasting if not permanent effects on happiness levels (Gilbert et al., 1998); but, in fact, the impacts are temporary. A third finding is that happiness levels, like personality traits, are relatively stable over time and place, which leads to the conclusion that some people are, in general, happier than others (DeNeve & Cooper, 1998).

The pursuit of happiness is a powerful human motivation that is not very well understood. Although people may be predisposed toward a particular set point, it is clear that happiness is not set in stone. Thus, researchers are now seeking ways to produce sustainable increases in subjective well-being (Lyubomirsky et al., 2005).

REVIEW

Stress and Health

- Stress is an unpleasant state that arises when we perceive that the demands of an event strain our ability to cope effectively.

- A person's appraisal of a situation determines how stress is experienced and how he or she copes.

- Coping responses consist of the thoughts, feelings, and behaviors by which people attempt to reduce stress.

What Causes Stress?

- There are many different causes of stress, or stressors.

Crises and Catastrophes

- Natural disasters and other catastrophic events can have harmful, long-term effects on mental and physical health.
- People with posttraumatic stress disorder suffer from psychological and physical symptoms long after the event is over.
- Soldiers exposed to combat often suffer from posttraumatic stress.

Major Life Events

- Early research suggested that all change is stressful.
- However, more recent studies suggest that only negative events are harmful.

Microstressors: The Hassles of Everyday Life

- The most common sources of stress are minor everyday hassles.
- Constant noise, job pressures, and living in shared space are all stressful in this regard.

How Does Stress Affect the Body?

- Selye coined the term *stress* upon observing that different stressors produce similar physiological effects on the body.

The General Adaptation Syndrome

- The body responds to stress in three stages: alarm, resistance, and exhaustion.
- The stress response is designed for acute emergencies, not for the constant long-term stress that humans often experience.

What Stress Does to the Heart

- Stress is a major risk factor in coronary heart disease (CHD).
- Early research suggested that the hard-driving Type A behavior pattern is associated with CHD.
- This link was found when the Type A pattern was assessed in structured interviews but not when it was measured by questionnaire.
- Hostility is now known to be the "toxic" element in the Type A behavior pattern.

What Stress Does to the Immune System

- The immune system contains specialized white blood cells called lymphocytes that detect and destroy foreign substances in the body.
- Laboratory and field research shows that stress affects the activity of these cells, sometimes resulting in a weakened immune response.
- Stress can "get into" the immune system by causing people to behave in unhealthy ways or by triggering the release of stress hormones that suppress immune cell activity.

The Links Between Stress and Illness

- Stress weakens the immune system, so people under stress are more likely to catch a cold when exposed to a virus.
- There may also be a link between negative emotional states and serious diseases such as cancer, but the evidence is less strong.

Processes of Appraisal

Attributions and Explanatory Styles

- According to the learned helplessness model of depression, exposure to an uncontrollable event sparks passive, apathetic, depression-like symptoms.
- Research shows that the attributions people make for their lack of control are of central importance.
- The depressive explanatory style is a tendency to make stable, global, internal attributions for bad events; it is associated with depression and perhaps physical illness.

The Human Capacity for Resilience

- Some individuals are more resilient than others in the face of stress, a trait called hardiness.

- The key ingredient of hardiness is the belief that one has the power to control future outcomes through one's own behavior.
- Depending on the situation, people may have a high or low self-efficacy, the belief that they can perform the behaviors needed to produce positive outcomes.
- Some individuals are characteristically more optimistic than others, and optimism at one point in time is predictive of later positive health outcomes.

Pollyanna's Health

- Positive thinking is associated with good health, but the causal relationship is unclear.
- Unrealistic positive illusions may have undesirable interpersonal and health consequences.

Ways of Coping with Stress

Problem-Focused Coping

- In problem-focused coping, people try to reduce stress by overcoming the source of the problem.

- Problem-focused coping is often effective, but at times there are drawbacks.
- For example, exerting control is physiologically taxing and can increase stress rather than reducing it.

- Also, both behavioral and characterological self-blame are associated with increased distress.

Emotion-Focused Coping

- In emotion-focused coping, people try to manage the emotional turmoil produced by a stressful situation.
- In situations that one cannot control, mental distraction and avoidance can reduce stress.
- But the suppression from awareness of unwanted thoughts and feelings can backfire, causing us to become preoccupied with them.
- Research shows that opening up and confronting one's feelings about upsetting events improves mental and physical health.
- Among people with low self-esteem, self-focus worsens their mood and heightens their distress.
- In contrast, it is helpful to become absorbed in demanding external activities such as reading, exercise, and gardening.

Proactive Coping

- As a first line of defense, people can ward off stress through proactive coping efforts such as the accumulation of resources.

Treatment and Prevention

Treatment: The "Social" Ingredients

- Medical treatment includes an important social component.
- Doctors, therapists, and other health-care workers provide patients with social support and a ray of hope.
- Choice of treatment is also an important factor—particularly when patients choose an effortful treatment, which increases commitment.

Prevention: Getting the Message Across

- Many causes of death are preventable through changes in lifestyle and behavior—which is where social psychology comes in.

- Having many different roles and identities serves as a buffer against stressors in any one domain of life.
- Friendships and other sources of social support have strong beneficial effects on physical health and psychological well-being.
- All researchers agree that social support is healthy, but they measure it in different ways, focusing on such factors as the number of social contacts a person has, the presence of special close relationships, or the perceived availability of social support.
- Social psychologists are also studying the role of religion in reducing stress.

Cultural Influences on Coping

- Stress is universal, but do people from different cultures cope in the same ways?
- Suprisingly, people from collectivist cultures appear to rely less often on social support as a means of coping compared to people from individualist cultures.
- Recent research on collectivist coping styles has identified, in order, uses of acceptance, avoidance, family support, religion, and private emotional outlets.

- First, people have to recognize that a threat to their health exists.
- Others serve as important role models and spokespersons for healthy or unhealthy behavior.
- Subjective norms can also encourage healthy or unhealthy behaviors.
- A sense of self-efficacy enhances the adoption and maintenance of healthy behaviors.
- Accurate information is needed to sustain people's commitment to healthy behaviors.

The Pursuit of Happiness

- Most people report being relatively happy, but there are individual differences.
- Three important factors are social relationships, employment, and health.
- Evidence that money can buy happiness is mixed. More affluent nations have happier citizens, but intra-nation correlations are modest.

- One reason for the limited association between wealth and happiness is that our perceptions of wealth are relative—not only to what others have but also to what we have become accustomed to.
- Research suggests that each of us possesses a baseline level of happiness toward which we gravitate over time.

KEY TERMS

appraisal (510)
coping (510)
depressive explanatory
style (522)
emotion-focused coping (526)
general adaptation
syndrome (515)
health psychology (509)
immune system (518)
learned helplessness (522)
posttraumatic stress disorder
(PTSD) (512)
proactive coping (527)
problem-focused coping (526)
psychoneuroimmunology
(PNI) (518)
self-efficacy (523)
social support (532)
stress (510)
stressor (511)
subjective well-being (540)
Type A behavior pattern (517)

PUTTING COMMON SENSE TO THE TEST

The accumulation of daily hassles does more to make people sick than catastrophes or major life changes.

True. Car problems, arguments with friends, and other "microstressors" contribute more to our levels of stress than larger but less frequent stressors.

Like humans, zebras get ulcers.

False. Stress causes ulcers in humans, not zebras. That's because the stress response is designed for acute emergencies; but in people, it is activated often and for long periods of time.

Stress can weaken the heart, but it cannot affect the immune system.

False. Recent research has shown that stress and other psychological states can alter the activity of white blood cells in the immune system and affect our resistance to illness.

When it comes to physical health, research does not support popular beliefs about the power of positive thinking.

False. Consistently, people who are optimistic—and situations that promote optimism—are associated with better health outcomes.

People who have lots of friends are healthier and live longer than those who live more isolated lives.

True. Across a range of studies, researchers have found that social support is strongly associated with positive health outcomes.

As role models, celebrities have great influence over public health-care decisions.

True. As a result of all the media attention given to celebrities, the health-care decisions they make exert a great deal of influence on others.

GLOSSARY

actor-observer effect The tendency to attribute our own behavior to situational causes and the behavior of others to personal factors. *(p. 110)*

adversarial model A dispute-resolution system in which the prosecution and defense present opposing sides of the story. *(p. 467)*

affective forecasting The process of predicting how one would feel in response to future emotional events. *(p. 57)*

aggression Behavior intended to harm another individual. *(p. 391)*

altruistic Motivated by the desire to improve another's welfare. *(p. 353)*

ambivalent sexism A form of sexism characterized by attitudes about women that reflect both negative, resentful beliefs and feelings and affectionate, chivalrous, but potentially patronizing beliefs and feelings. *(p. 157)*

applied research Research whose goals are to enlarge the understanding of naturally occurring events and to find solutions to practical problems. *(p. 27)*

appraisal The process by which people make judgments about the demands of potentially stressful events and their ability to meet those demands. *(p. 510)*

arousal-affect model The proposition that aggression is influenced by both the intensity of arousal and the type of emotion produced by a stimulus. *(p. 410)*

arousal: cost-reward model The proposition that people react to emergency situations by acting in the most cost-effective way to reduce the arousal of shock and alarm. *(p. 350)*

assessment center A structured setting in which job applicants are exhaustively tested and judged by multiple evaluators. *(p. 479)*

attachment style The way a person typically interacts with significant others. *(p. 325)*

attitude A positive, negative, or mixed reaction to a person, object, or idea. *(p. 181)*

attitude scale A multiple-item questionnaire designed to measure a person's attitude toward some object. *(p. 183)*

attribution theory A group of theories that describe how people explain the causes of behavior. *(p. 103)*

audience inhibition Reluctance to help for fear of making a bad impression on observers. *(p. 364)*

availability heuristic The tendency to estimate the likelihood that an event will occur by how easily instances of it come to mind. *(p. 105)*

base-rate fallacy The finding that people are relatively insensitive to consensus information presented in the form of numerical base rates. *(p. 106)*

basic research Research whose goal is to increase the understanding of human behavior, often by testing hypotheses based on a theory. *(p. 27)*

bask in reflected glory (BIRG) To increase self-esteem by associating with others who are successful. *(p. 78)*

behavioral genetics A subfield of psychology that examines the role of genetic factors in behavior. *(p. 16)*

belief in a just world The belief that individuals get what they deserve in life, an orientation that leads people to disparage victims. *(p. 113)*

belief perseverance The tendency to maintain beliefs even after they have been discredited. *(p. 121)*

bogus pipeline A phony lie-detector device that is sometimes used to get respondents to give truthful answers to sensitive questions. *(p. 183)*

brainstorming A technique that attempts to increase the production of creative ideas by encouraging group members to speak freely without criticizing their own or others' contributions. *(p. 280)*

bystander effect The effect whereby the presence of others inhibits helping. *(p. 360)*

catharsis A reduction of the motive to aggress that is said to result from any imagined, observed, or actual act of aggression. *(p. 406)*

central route to persuasion The process by which a person thinks carefully about a communication and is influenced by the strength of its arguments. *(p. 190)*

central traits Traits that exert a powerful influence on overall impressions. *(p. 118)*

cognitive dissonance theory The theory that holding inconsistent cognitions arouses psychological tension that people become motivated to reduce. *(p. 207)*

cognitive neoassociation analysis The view that unpleasant experiences create negative affect, which in turn stimulates associations connected with anger and fear. Emotional and behavioral outcomes then depend, at least in part, on higher-order cognitive processing. *(p. 411)*

collective People engaged in common activities but having minimal direct interaction. *(p. 259)*

collective effort model The theory that individuals will exert effort on a collective task to the degree that they think their individual efforts will be important, relevant, and meaningful for achieving outcomes that they value. *(p. 264)*

collectivism A cultural orientation in which interdependence, cooperation, and social harmony take priority over personal goals. *(p. 235)*

communal relationship A relationship in which the participants expect and desire mutual responsiveness to each other's needs. *(p. 324)*

companionate love A secure, trusting, stable partnership. *(p. 327)*

compliance Changes in behavior that are elicited by direct requests. *(p. 236)*

confederate Accomplice of an experimenter who, in dealing with the real participants in an experiment, acts as if he or she is also a participant. *(p. 44)*

confirmation bias The tendency to seek, interpret, and create information that verifies existing beliefs. *(p. 120)*

conformity The tendency to change our perceptions, opinions, or behavior in ways that are consistent with group norms. *(p. 224)*

construct validity The extent to which the measures used in a study measure the variables they were designed to measure and the manipulations in an experiment manipulate the variables they were designed to manipulate. *(p. 28)*

contact hypothesis The theory that direct contact between hostile groups will reduce prejudice under certain conditions. *(p. 172)*

contingency model of leadership The theory that leadership effectiveness is determined both by the personal characteristics of leaders and by the control afforded by the situation. *(p. 488)*

contrast effect The tendency to perceive stimuli that differ from expectations as being even more different than they really are. *(p. 139)*

coping Efforts to reduce stress. *(p. 510)*

correlational research Research designed to measure the association between variables that are not manipulated by the researcher. *(p. 34)*

correlation coefficient A statistical measure of the strength and direction of the association between two variables. *(p. 35)*

counterfactual thinking The tendency to imagine alternative events or outcomes that might have occurred but did not. *(p. 106)*

covariation principle A principle of attribution theory holding that people attribute behavior to factors that are present when a behavior occurs and absent when it does not. *(p. 104)*

cross-cultural research Research designed to compare and contrast people of different cultures. *(p. 17)*

cross-race identification bias The tendency for people to have difficulty identifying members of a race other than their own. *(p. 448)*

cultivation The process by which the mass media (particularly television) construct a version of social reality for the public. *(p. 420)*

culture A system of enduring meanings, beliefs, values, assumptions, institutions, and practices shared by a large group of people and transmitted from one generation to the next. *(p. 17)*

cycle of violence The transmission of domestic violence across generations. *(p. 426)*

death qualification A jury-selection procedure used in capital cases that permits judges to exclude prospective jurors who say they would not vote for the death penalty. *(p. 441)*

debriefing A disclosure, made to participants after research procedures are completed, in which the researcher explains the purpose of the research, attempts to resolve any negative feelings, and emphasizes the scientific contribution made by the participants' involvement. *(p. 47)*

deception In the context of research, a method that provides false information to participants. *(p. 44)*

deindividuation The loss of a person's sense of individuality and the reduction of normal constraints against deviant behavior. *(p. 266)*

dependent variable In an experiment, a factor that experimenters measure to see if it is affected by the independent variable. *(p. 39)*

depressive explanatory style A habitual tendency to attribute negative events to causes that are stable, global, and internal. *(p. 522)*

desensitization Reduction in emotion-related physiological reactivity in response to a stimulus. *(p. 420)*

diffusion of responsibility The belief that others will or should take the responsibility for providing assistance to a person in need. *(p. 362)*

discrimination Behavior directed against persons because of their membership in a particular group. *(p. 133)*

displacement Aggressing against a substitute target because aggressive acts against the source of the frustration are inhibited by fear or lack of access. *(p. 406)*

distraction-conflict theory A theory holding that the presence of others will produce social facilitation effects only when those others distract from the task and create attentional conflict. *(p. 262)*

door-in-the-face technique A two-step compliance technique in which an influencer prefaces the real request with one that is so large that it is rejected. *(p. 240)*

downward social comparison The defensive tendency to compare ourselves with others who are worse off than we are. *(p. 79)*

egoistic Motivated by the desire to increase one's own welfare. *(p. 353)*

elaboration The process of thinking about and scrutinizing the arguments contained in a persuasive communication. *(p. 191)*

emotional aggression Inflicting harm for its own sake. *(p. 391)*

emotion-focused coping Cognitive and behavioral efforts to reduce the distress produced by a stressful situation. *(p. 526)*

empathy-altruism hypothesis The proposition that empathic concern for a person in need produces an altruistic motive for helping. *(p. 355)*

endowment effect The tendency for people to inflate the value of objects, goods, or services they already own. *(p. 502)*

entity theorists People who tend to see social groups as relatively fixed, static entities and the borders between groups as relatively clear and rigid. *(p. 136)*

equity theory The theory that people are most satisfied with a relationship when the ratio between benefits and contributions is similar for both partners. *(p. 323)*

escalation effect The condition in which commitments to a failing course of action are increased to justify investments already made. *(p. 283)*

evaluation apprehension theory A theory holding that the presence of others will produce social facilitation effects only when those others are seen as potential evaluators. *(p. 261)*

evolutionary psychology A subfield of psychology that uses the principles of evolution to understand human social behavior. *(p. 17)*

exchange relationship A relationship in which the participants expect and desire strict reciprocity in their interactions. *(p. 324)*

excitation transfer The process whereby arousal caused by one stimulus is added to arousal from a second stimulus and the combined arousal is attributed to the second stimulus. *(p. 328)*

expectancy theory The theory that workers become motivated when they believe that their efforts will produce valued outcomes. *(p. 495)*

experiment A form of research that can demonstrate causal relationships because (1) the experimenter has control over the events that occur and (2) participants are randomly assigned to conditions. *(p. 37)*

experimental realism The degree to which experimental procedures are involving to participants and lead them to behave naturally and spontaneously. *(p. 43)*

experimenter expectancy effects The effects produced when an experimenter's expectations about the results of an experiment affect his or her behavior toward a participant and thereby influence the participant's responses. *(p. 42)*

external validity The degree to which there can be reasonable confidence that the results of a study would be obtained for other people and in other situations. *(p. 43)*

facial electromyograph (EMG) An electronic instrument that records facial muscle activity associated with emotions and attitudes. *(p. 184)*

facial feedback hypothesis The hypothesis that changes in facial expression can lead to corresponding changes in emotion. *(p. 58)*

false-consensus effect The tendency for people to overestimate the extent to which others share their opinions, attributes, and behaviors. *(p. 106)*

foot-in-the-door technique   A two-step compliance technique in which an influencer sets the stage for the real request by first getting a person to comply with a much smaller request. *(p. 238)*

frustration-aggression hypothesis   The idea that (1) frustration always elicits the motive to aggress and (2) all aggression is caused by frustration. *(p. 406)*

fundamental attribution error   The tendency to focus on the role of personal causes and underestimate the impact of situations on other people's behavior. *(p. 107)*

general adaptation syndrome   A three-stage process (alarm, resistance, and exhaustion) by which the body responds to stress. *(p. 515)*

good mood effect   The effect whereby a good mood increases helping behavior. *(p. 370)*

graduated and reciprocated initiatives in tension-reduction (GRIT)   A strategy for unilateral, persistent efforts to establish trust and cooperation between opposing parties. *(p. 292)*

group   Two or more persons perceived as related because of their interactions, membership in the same social category, or common fate. *(p. 133)*

group polarization   The exaggeration through group discussion of initial tendencies in the thinking of group members. *(p. 274)*

groupthink   A group decision-making style characterized by an excessive tendency among group members to seek concurrence. *(p. 276)*

hard-to-get effect   The tendency to prefer people who are highly selective in their social choices over those who are more readily available. *(p. 316)*

Hawthorne effect   The finding that workers who were given special attention increased their productivity regardless of what actual changes were made in the work setting. *(p. 474)*

health psychology   The study of physical health and illness by psychologists from various areas of specialization. *(p. 509)*

hostile attribution bias   The tendency to perceive hostile intent in others. *(p. 413)*

hypothesis   A testable prediction about the conditions under which an event will occur. *(p. 26)*

idiosyncrasy credits   Interpersonal "credits" that a person earns by following group norms. *(p. 233)*

illusory correlation   An overestimate of the association between variables that are only slightly or not at all correlated. *(p. 138)*

immune system   A biological surveillance system that detects and destroys "nonself" substances that invade the body. *(p. 518)*

implicit association test (IAT)   A covert measure of unconscious attitudes derived from the speed at which people respond to pairings of concepts—such as *black* or *white* with *good* or *bad*. *(p. 184)*

implicit attitude   An attitude, such as prejudice, that one is not aware of having. *(p. 184)*

implicit egotism   A nonconscious form of self-enhancement. *(p. 75)*

implicit personality theory   A network of assumptions people make about the relationships among traits and behaviors. *(p. 118)*

impression formation   The process of integrating information about a person to form a coherent impression. *(p. 114)*

incremental theorists   People who tend to see social groups as relatively dynamic and changeable, with less consistency within groups and more malleability between groups. *(p. 137)*

independent variable   In an experiment, a factor that experimenters manipulate to see if it affects the dependent variable. *(p. 38)*

individualism   A cultural orientation in which independence, autonomy, and self-reliance take priority over group allegiances. *(p. 235)*

industrial organizational (I/O) psychology   The study of human behavior in business and other organizational settings. *(p. 473)*

informational influence   Influence that produces conformity when a person believes others are correct in their judgments. *(p. 226)*

information integration theory   The theory that impressions are based on (1) perceiver dispositions and (2) a weighted average of a target person's traits. *(p. 115)*

informed consent   An individual's deliberate, voluntary decision to participate in research, based on the researcher's description of what will be required during such participation. *(p. 46)*

ingroup favoritism   The tendency to discriminate in favor of ingroups over outgroups. *(p. 150)*

ingroups   Groups with which an individual feels a sense of membership, belonging, and identity. *(p. 135)*

inoculation hypothesis   The idea that exposure to weak versions of a persuasive argument increases later resistance to that argument. *(p. 205)*

inquisitorial model   A dispute-resolution system in which a neutral investigator gathers evidence from both sides and presents the findings in court. *(p. 467)*

instrumental aggression   Inflicting harm in order to obtain something of value. *(p. 391)*

insufficient deterrence   A condition in which people refrain from engaging in a desirable activity, even when only mild punishment is threatened. *(p. 209)*

insufficient justification   A condition in which people freely perform an attitude-discrepant behavior without receiving a large reward. *(p. 209)*

integrative agreement   A negotiated resolution to a conflict in which all parties obtain outcomes that are superior to what they would have obtained from an equal division of the contested resources. *(p. 292)*

integrity tests   Paper-and-pencil questionnaires designed to test a job applicant's honesty and character. *(p. 477)*

interaction   A statistical term indicating the change in the effect of each independent variable as a function of other independent variables. *(p. 39)*

interactionist perspective   An emphasis on how both an individual's personality and environmental characteristics influence behavior. *(p. 13)*

internal validity   The degree to which there can be reasonable certainty that the independent variables in an experiment caused the effects obtained on the dependent variables. *(p. 42)*

interrater reliability   The degree to which different observers agree on their observations. *(p. 30)*

intimate relationship   A close relationship between two adults involving emotional attachment, fulfillment of psychological needs, or interdependence. *(p. 321)*

jigsaw classroom   A cooperative learning method used to reduce racial prejudice through interaction in group efforts. *(p. 174)*

jury nullification   The jury's power to disregard, or "nullify," the law when it conflicts with personal conceptions of justice. *(p. 458)*

kin selection   Preferential helping of genetic relatives, which results in the greater likelihood that genes held in common will survive. *(p. 347)*

learned helplessness A phenomenon in which experience with an uncontrollable event creates passive behavior toward a subsequent threat to well-being. *(p. 522)*

leniency bias The tendency for jury deliberation to produce a tilt toward acquittal. *(p. 461)*

loneliness A feeling of deprivation about existing social relations. *(p. 304)*

low-balling A two-step compliance technique in which the influencer secures agreement with a request but then increases the size of that request by revealing hidden costs. *(p. 239)*

main effect A statistical term indicating the overall effect that an independent variable has on the dependent variable, ignoring all other independent variables. *(p. 39)*

matching hypothesis The proposition that people are attracted to others who are similar in physical attractiveness. *(p. 314)*

mere exposure effect The phenomenon whereby the more often people are exposed to a stimulus, the more positively they evaluate that stimulus. *(p. 306)*

mere presence theory The proposition that the mere presence of others is sufficient to produce social facilitation effects. *(p. 261)*

meta-analysis A set of statistical procedures used to review a body of evidence by combining the results of individual studies to measure the overall reliability and strength of particular effects. *(p. 44)*

minority influence The process by which dissenters produce change within a group. *(p. 232)*

misinformation effect The tendency for false postevent misinformation to become integrated into people's memory of an event. *(p. 450)*

mitigating information Information about a person's situation indicating that he or she should not be held fully responsible for aggressive actions. *(p. 413)*

modern racism A form of prejudice that surfaces in subtle ways when it is safe, socially acceptable, and easy to rationalize. *(p. 161)*

multicultural research Research designed to examine racial and ethnic groups within cultures. *(p. 17)*

mundane realism The degree to which the experimental situation resembles places and events in the real world. *(p. 43)*

need for affiliation The desire to establish and maintain many rewarding interpersonal relationships. *(p. 302)*

need for closure The desire to reduce cognitive uncertainty, which heightens the importance of first impressions. *(p. 119)*

need for cognition (NC) A personality variable that distinguishes people on the basis of how much they enjoy effortful cognitive activities. *(p. 203)*

negative state relief model The proposition that people help others in order to counteract their own feelings of sadness. *(p. 356)*

nonverbal behavior Behavior that reveals a person's feelings without words—through facial expressions, body language, and vocal cues. *(p. 98)*

normative influence Influence that produces conformity when a person fears the negative social consequences of appearing deviant. *(p. 227)*

normative model of leadership The theory that leadership effectiveness is determined by the amount of feedback and participation that leaders invite from workers. *(p. 489)*

norm of social responsibility A moral standard emphasizing that people should help those who need assistance. *(p. 373)*

obedience Behavior change produced by the commands of authority. *(p. 243)*

operational definition The specific procedures for manipulating or measuring a conceptual variable. *(p. 28)*

outgroup homogeneity effect The tendency to assume that there is greater similarity among members of outgroups than among members of ingroups. *(p. 135)*

outgroups Groups with which an individual does not feel a sense of membership, belonging, or identity. *(p. 135)*

overjustification effect The tendency for intrinsic motivation to diminish for activities that have become associated with reward or other extrinsic factors. *(p. 59)*

passionate love Romantic love characterized by high arousal, intense attraction, and fear of rejection. *(p. 327)*

peremptory challenge A means by which lawyers can exclude a limited number of prospective jurors without the judge's approval. *(p. 437)*

performance appraisal The process of evaluating an employee's work within the organization. *(p. 484)*

peripheral route to persuasion The process by which a person does not think carefully about a communication and is influenced instead by superficial cues. *(p. 190)*

personal attribution Attribution to internal characteristics of an actor, such as ability, personality, mood, or effort. *(p. 103)*

persuasion The process by which attitudes are changed. *(p. 190)*

pluralistic ignorance The state in which people mistakenly believe that their own thoughts and feelings are different from those of others, even when everyone's behavior is the same. *(p. 362)*

polygraph A mechanical instrument that records physiological arousal from multiple channels; it is often used as a lie-detector test. *(p. 446)*

pornography Explicit sexual material. *(p. 421)*

posttraumatic stress disorder (PTSD) A condition in which a person experiences enduring physical and psychological symptoms after an extremely stressful event. *(p. 512)*

prejudice Negative feelings toward persons based on their membership in certain groups. *(p. 133)*

primacy effect The tendency for information presented early in a sequence to have more impact on impressions than information presented later. *(p. 118)*

priming The tendency for recently used or perceived words or ideas to come to mind easily and influence the interpretation of new information. *(p. 116)*

prisoner's dilemma A type of dilemma in which one party must make either cooperative or competitive moves in relation to another party; typically designed in such a way that competitive moves are more beneficial to either side, but if both sides make competitive moves, they are both worse off than if they both cooperated. *(p. 286)*

private conformity The change of beliefs that occurs when a person privately accepts the position taken by others. *(p. 228)*

private self-consciousness A personality characteristic of individuals who are introspective, often attending to their own inner states. *(p. 72)*

proactive coping Up-front efforts to ward off or modify the onset of a stressful event. *(p. 527)*

problem-focused coping Cognitive and behavioral efforts to alter a stressful situation. *(p. 526)*

process loss The reduction in group performance due to obstacles created by group processes, such as problems of coordination and motivation. *(p. 279)*

prosocial behaviors Actions intended to benefit others. *(p. 347)*

psychological reactance The theory that people react against threats to their freedom by asserting themselves and perceiving the threatened freedom as more attractive. *(p. 205)*

psychoneuroimmunology (PNI) A subfield of psychology that examines the links among psychological factors, the brain and nervous system, and the immune system. *(p. 518)*

public conformity A superficial change in overt behavior, without a corresponding change of opinion, produced by real or imagined group pressure. *(p. 228)*

public self-consciousness A personality characteristic of individuals who focus on themselves as social objects, as seen by others. *(p. 72)*

racism Prejudice and discrimination based on a person's racial background. *(p. 161)*

random assignment A method of assigning participants to the various conditions of an experiment so that each participant in the experiment has an equal chance of being in any of the conditions. *(p. 37)*

random sampling A method of selecting participants for a study so that everyone in a population has an equal chance of being in the study. *(p. 34)*

realistic conflict theory The theory that hostility between groups is caused by direct competition for limited resources. *(p. 149)*

reciprocity A mutual exchange between what we give and receive—for example, liking those who like us. *(p. 315)*

relative deprivation Feelings of discontent aroused by the belief that one fares poorly compared with others. *(p. 149)*

resource dilemmas Social dilemmas concerning how two or more people share a limited resource. *(p. 287)*

scientific jury selection A method of selecting juries through surveys that yield correlations between demographics and trial-relevant attitudes. *(p. 439)*

self-awareness theory The theory that self-focused attention leads people to notice self-discrepancies, thereby motivating either an escape from self-awareness or a change in behavior. *(p. 70)*

self-concept The sum total of an individual's beliefs about his or her own personal attributes. *(p. 54)*

self-disclosure Revelations about the self that a person makes to others. *(p. 329)*

self-efficacy A person's belief that he or she is capable of the specific behavior required to produce a desired outcome in a given situation. *(p. 523)*

self-esteem An affective component of the self, consisting of a person's positive and negative self-evaluations. *(p. 67)*

self-fulfilling prophecy The process by which one's expectations about a person eventually lead that person to behave in ways that confirm those expectations. *(p. 122)*

self-handicapping Behaviors designed to sabotage one's own performance in order to provide a subsequent excuse for failure. *(p. 77)*

self-monitoring The tendency to change behavior in response to the self-presentation concerns of the situation. *(p. 85)*

self-perception theory The theory that when internal cues are difficult to interpret, people gain self-insight by observing their own behavior. *(p. 57)*

self-presentation Strategies people use to shape what others think of them. *(p. 83)*

self-schema A belief people hold about themselves that guides the processing of self-relevant information. *(p. 54)*

sentencing disparity Inconsistency of sentences for the same offense from one judge to another. *(p. 464)*

sexism Prejudice and discrimination based on a person's gender. *(p. 154)*

sexual orientation A person's preference for members of the same sex (homosexuality), opposite sex (heterosexuality), or both sexes (bisexuality). *(p. 334)*

situational attribution Attribution to factors external to an actor, such as the task, other people, or luck. *(p. 103)*

sleeper effect A delayed increase in the persuasive impact of a noncredible source. *(p. 196)*

social categorization The classification of persons into groups on the basis of common attributes. *(p. 134)*

social cognition The study of how people perceive, remember, and interpret information about themselves and others. *(p. 15)*

social comparison theory The theory that people evaluate their own abilities and opinions by comparing themselves to others. *(p. 61)*

social dilemma A situation in which a self-interested choice by everyone creates the worst outcome for everyone. *(p. 286)*

social dominance orientation A desire to see one's in-groups as dominant over other groups and a willingness to adopt cultural values that facilitate oppression over other groups. *(p. 153)*

social exchange theory A perspective that views people as motivated to maximize benefits and minimize costs in their relationships with others. *(p. 322)*

social facilitation A process whereby the presence of others enhances performance on easy tasks but impairs performance on difficult tasks. *(p. 261)*

social identity theory The theory that people favor in-groups over outgroups in order to enhance their self-esteem. *(p. 150)*

social impact theory The theory that social influence depends on the strength, immediacy, and number of source persons relative to target persons. *(p. 250)*

social learning theory The theory that behavior is learned through the observation of others as well as through the direct experience of rewards and punishments. *(p. 402)*

social loafing A group-produced reduction in individual output on easy tasks where contributions are pooled. *(p. 263)*

social neuroscience The study of the relationship between neural and social processes. *(p. 16)*

social norm A general rule of conduct reflecting standards of social approval and disapproval. *(p. 372)*

social perception A general term for the processes by which people come to understand one another. *(p. 93)*

social psychology The scientific study of how individuals think, feel, and behave in a social context. *(p. 5)*

social role theory The theory that small gender differences are magnified in perception by the contrasting social roles occupied by men and women. *(p. 155)*

social support The helpful coping resources provided by friends and other people. *(p. 532)*

stereotype A belief that associates a group of people with certain traits. *(p. 133)*

stress An unpleasant state of arousal in which people perceive the demands of an event as taxing or exceeding their ability to satisfy or alter those demands. *(p. 510)*

stressor Anything that causes stress. *(p. 511)*

structured interview An interview in which each job applicant is asked a standard set of questions and evaluated on the same criteria. *(p. 478)*

subjective well-being One's happiness, or life satisfaction, as measured by self-report. *(p. 540)*

subject variable A variable that characterizes pre-existing differences among the participants in a study. *(p. 39)*

subliminal presentation A method of presenting stimuli so faintly or rapidly that people do not have any conscious awareness of having been exposed to them. *(p. 141)*

sunk cost principle The economic rule of thumb that only future costs and benefits, not past commitments, should be considered in making a decision. *(p. 503)*

superordinate goal A shared goal that can be achieved only through cooperation among individuals or groups. *(p. 148)*

terror management theory   The theory that humans cope with the fear of their own death by constructing worldviews that help to preserve their self-esteem. *(p. 67)*

that's-not-all technique   A two-step compliance technique in which the influencer begins with an inflated request, then decreases its apparent size by offering a discount or bonus. *(p. 241)*

theory   An organized set of principles used to explain observed phenomena. *(p. 26)*

theory of planned behavior   The theory that attitudes toward a specific behavior combine with subjective norms and perceived control to influence a person's actions. *(p. 187)*

threat-to-self-esteem model   The theory that reactions to receiving assistance depend on whether help is perceived as supportive or threatening. *(p. 382)*

transactional leader   A leader who gains compliance and support from followers primarily through goal setting and the use of rewards. *(p. 489)*

transactive memory   A shared system for remembering information that enables multiple people to remember information together more efficiently than they could alone. *(p. 284)*

transformational leader   A leader who inspires followers to transcend their own needs in the interest of a common cause. *(p. 490)*

triangular theory of love   A theory proposing that love has three basic components—intimacy, passion, and commitment—which can be combined to produce eight subtypes. *(p. 326)*

two-factor theory of emotion   The theory that the experience of emotion is based on two factors: physiological arousal and a cognitive interpretation of that arousal. *(p. 62)*

Type A behavior pattern   A pattern of behavior characterized by extremes of competitive striving for achievement, a sense of time urgency, hostility, and aggression. *(p. 517)*

voir dire   The pretrial examination of prospective jurors by the judge or opposing lawyers to uncover signs of bias. *(p. 437)*

weapon-focus effect   The tendency for the presence of a weapon to draw attention and impair a witness's ability to identify the culprit. *(p. 448)*

weapons effect   The tendency of weapons to increase the likelihood of aggression by their mere presence. *(p. 411)*

what-is-beautiful-is-good stereotype   The belief that physically attractive individuals also possess desirable personality characteristics. *(p. 310)*

REFERENCES

Abbey, A. (1982). Sex differences in attributions for friendly behavior: Do males misperceive females' friendliness? *Journal of Personality and Social Psychology, 42,* 830–838.

ABCNews.com (September 12, 2000). Democrats smell a rat.

Abelson, R. P. (1981). Psychological status of the script concept. *American Psychologist, 36,* 715–729.

Abelson, R. P., Aronson, E., McGuire, W. J., Newcomb, T. M., Rosenberg, M. J., & Tannenbaum, P. H. (1968). *Theories of cognitive consistency: A sourcebook.* Chicago: Rand McNally.

Aberson, C. L., & Howanski, L. M. (2002). Effects of self-esteem, status, and identification on two forms of ingroup bias. *Current Research in Social Psychology, 7,* 225–243.

Aberson, C. L., Healy, M., & Romero, V. (2000). Ingroup bias and self-esteem: A meta-analysis. *Personality and Social Psychology Review, 4,* 157–173.

Abramson, L. Y., Metalsky, G. I., & Alloy, L. B. (1989). Hopelessness depression: A theory-based subtype of depression. *Psychological Review, 96,* 358–372.

Abshire, J., & Bernstein, B. H. (2003). Juror sensitivity to the cross-race effect. *Law and Human Behavior, 27,* 471–480.

Acker, M., & Davis, M. H. (1992). Intimacy, passion, and commitment in adult romantic relationships: A test of the triangular theory of love. *Journal of Social and Personal Relationships, 9,* 21–50.

Adair, J. G. (1984). The Hawthorne effect: A reconsideration of the methodological artifact. *Journal of Applied Psychology, 69,* 334–345.

Adair, W. L., & Brett, J. M. (2005). The negotiation dance: Time, culture, and behavioral sequences in negotiation. *Organization Science, 16,* 33–51.

Adams, G., Garcia, D. M., Purdie-Vaughns, V., & Steele, C. M. (2006). The detrimental effects of a suggestion of sexism in an instruction situation. *Journal of Experimental Social Psychology, 42,* 602–615.

Adams, J. S. (1965). Equity in social exchange. *Advances in Experimental Social Psychology, 2,* 267–299.

Adams, P. R., & Adams, G. R. (1984). Mount Saint Helens's ash-fall: Evidence for a disaster stress reaction. *American Psychologist, 39,* 252–260.

Ader, R. (Ed.). (2007). *Psychoneuroimmunology* (4th ed.). Burlington, MA: Elsevier.

Aderman, D. (1972). Elation, depression, and helping behavior. *Journal of Personality and Social Psychology, 24,* 91–101.

Adorno, T., Frenkel-Brunswik, E., Levinson, D., & Sanford, R. N. (1950). *The authoritarian personality.* New York: Harper.

Aharon, I., Etcoff, N., Ariely, D., Chabris, C. F., O'Connor, E., & Breiter, H. C. (2001). Beautiful faces have variable reward value: fMRI and behavioral evidence. *Neuron, 32,* 537–551.

Aharpour, S., & Brown, R. (2002). Functions of group identification: An exploratory analysis. *Revue Internationale de Psychologie Sociale, 15,* 157–186.

Ahlfinger, N. R., & Esser, J. K. (2001). Testing the groupthink model: Effects of promotional leadership and conformity predisposition. *Social Behavior and Personality, 29,* 31–41.

Aiello, J. R., & Douthitt, E. A. (2001). Social facilitation from Triplett to electronic performance monitoring. *Group Dynamics, 5,* 163–180.

Ainsworth, M., Blehar, M. C., Waters, E., & Wall, S. (1978). *Patterns of attachment: A psychological study of the strange situation.* Hillsdale, NJ: Erlbaum.

Ajzen, I. (1991). The theory of planned behavior. *Organizational Behavior and Human Decision Processes, 50,* 179–211.

Ajzen, I. (2001). Nature and operation of attitudes. *Annual Review of Psychology, 52,* 27–58.

Ajzen, I., & Fishbein, M. (1977). Attitude-behavior relations: A theoretical analysis and review of empirical research. *Psychological Bulletin, 84,* 888–918.

Ajzen, I., & Fishbein, M. (2005). The influence of attitudes on behavior. In D. Albarracín, B. T. Johnson, & M. P. Zanna (Eds.), *The handbook of attitudes* (pp. 173–221). Hillsdale, NJ: Erlbaum.

Akimoto, S. A., & Sanbonmatsu, D. M. (1999). Differences in self-effacing behavior between European and Japanese Americans: Effect on competence evaluations. *Journal of Cross-Cultural Psychology, 30,* 159–177.

Albarracín, D., Gillette, J. C., Earl, A. N., Glasman, L. R., Durantini, M. R., & Ho, M-H. (2005). A test of major assumptions about behavior change: A comprehensive look at the effects of passive and active HIV-prevention interventions since the beginning of the epidemic. *Psychological Bulletin, 131,* 856–897.

Albarracín, D., Johnson, B. T., & Zanna, M. P. (Eds.). (2005). *The handbook of attitudes.* Hillsdale, NJ: Erlbaum.

Albarracín, D., Johnson, B. T., Fishbein, M., & Muellerleile, P. A. (2001). Theories of reasoned action and planned behavior as models of condom use: A meta-analysis. *Psychological Bulletin, 127,* 142–161.

Alexander, G. M. (2003). An evolutionary perspective of sex-typed toy preferences: Pink, blue, and the brain. *Archives of Sexual Behavior, 32,* 7–14.

Alexander, G. M. (2003). An evolutionary perspective of sex-typed toy preferences: Pink, blue, and the brain. *Archives of Sexual Behavior, 32,* 7–14.

Alexander, G. M., & Hines, M. (2002). Sex differences in response to children's toys in nonhuman primates (*Cercopithecus aethiops sabaeus*). *Evolution and Human Behavior, 23,* 467–479.

Alexander, M. G., & Fisher, T. D. (2003). Truth and consequences: Using the bogus pipeline to examine sex differences in self-reported sexuality. *Journal of Sex Research, 40,* 27–35.

Alge, B. J. (2001). Effects of computer surveillance on perceptions of privacy and procedural justice. *Journal of Applied Psychology, 86,* 797–804.

Alicke, M. D., & Largo, E. (1995). The role of the self in the false consensus effect. *Journal of Experimental Social Psychology, 31,* 28–47.

Allen, B. (1995). Gender stereotypes are not accurate: A replication of Martin (1987) using diagnostic vs. self-report and behavioral criteria. *Sex Roles, 32,* 583–600.

Allen, J. B., Kenrick, D. T., Linder, D. E., & McCall, M. A. (1989). Arousal and attribution: A response-facilitation alternative to misattribution and negative-reinforcement models. *Journal of Personality and Social Psychology, 57,* 261–270.

Allen, S., & Murphy, S. P. (2006, September 17). Designer proposed more bolts in Big Dig; managers cut numbers in half. *Boston Globe,* p. A1.

Allen, V. L. (1965). Situational factors in conformity. In L. Berkowitz (Ed.), *Advances in Experimental Social Psychology, 2,* 133–175.

Allen, V. L., & Levine, J. M. (1969). Consensus and conformity. *Journal of Experimental Social Psychology, 5,* 389–399.

Allen, V. L., & Levine, J. M. (1971). Social support and conformity: The role of independent assessment of reality. *Journal of Experimental Social Psychology, 7*, 48–58.

Alliger, G. M., & Dwight, S. A. (2000). A meta-analytic investigation of the susceptibility of integrity tests to faking and coaching. *Educational and Psychological Measurement, 60*, 59–72.

Alliger, G. M., Lilienfeld, S. O., & Mitchell, K. E. (1996). The susceptibility of overt and covert integrity tests to coaching and faking. *Psychological Science, 7*, 32–39.

Alloy, L. B., Abramson, L.Y., Whitehouse, W. G., Hogan, M. E., Panzarella, C., & Rose, D. T. (2006). Prospective incidence of first onsets and recurrences of depression in individuals at high and low cognitive risk for depression. *Journal of Abnormal Psychology, 115*, 145–156.

Allport, F. H. (1924). *Social psychology*. Boston: Houghton Mifflin.

Allport, F. H., et al. (1953). The effects of segregation and the consequences of desegregation: A social science statement. *Minneapolis Law Review, 37*, 429–440.

Allport, G. W. (1954). *The nature of prejudice*. Reading, MA: Addison-Wesley.

Allport, G. W. (1985). The historical background of social psychology. In G. Lindzey & E. Aronson (Eds.), *Handbook of social psychology* (3rd ed., Vol. I, pp. 1–46). New York: Random House.

Allport, G. W., & Postman, L. J. (1947). *The psychology of rumor*. New York: Holt.

Altman, I. (1973). Reciprocity of interpersonal exchange. *Journal for Theory of Social Behavior, 3*, 249–261.

Altman, I., & Taylor, D. A. (1973). *Social penetration: The development of interpersonal relationships*. New York: Holt, Rinehart and Winston.

Alvidrez, A., & Weinstein, R. S. (1999). Early teacher perceptions and later student academic achievement. *Journal of Educational Psychology, 91*, 731–746.

Alwin, D. F. (1990). Cohort replacement and changes in parental socialization values. *Journal of Marriage and the Family, 52*, 347–360.

Amabile, T. M. (1996). *Creativity in context*. New York: Westview.

Amabile, T. M., Hill, K. G., Hennessey, B. A., & Tighe, E. M. (1994). The work preference inventory: Assessing intrinsic and extrinsic motivation orientations. *Journal of Personality and Social Psychology, 66*, 950–967.

Amato, P. R. (1983). Helping behavior in urban and rural environments: Field studies based on a taxonomic organization of helping episodes. *Journal of Personality and Social Psychology, 45*, 571–586.

Ambady, N., & Rosenthal, R. (1993). Half a minute: Predicting teacher evaluations from thin slices of nonverbal behavior and physical attractiveness. *Journal of Personality and Social Psychology, 64*, 431–441.

American Psychological Association (1992). Ethical principles of psychologists and code of conduct. *American Psychologist, 47*, 1597–1611.

Ames, D. R., Flynn, F. J., & Weber, E. U. (2004). It's the thought that counts: On perceiving how helpers decide to lend a hand. *Personality and Social Psychology Bulletin, 30*, 461–474.

Amnesty International, http:www.amnesty.org/.

Amodio, D. M., Kubota, J. T., Harmon-Jones, E., & Devine, P. G. (2007). Alternative mechanisms for regulating racial responses according to internal vs. external cues. *Social Cognitive and Affective Neuroscience*, in press.

Andersen, S. M., & Chen, S. (2002). The relational self: An interpersonal social-cognitive theory. *Psychological Review, 109*, 619–645.

Anderson, C. A. (1989). Temperature and aggression: Ubiquitous effects of heat on occurrence of human violence. *Psychological Bulletin, 106*, 74–96.

Anderson, C. A. (2002). Aggression. In E. Borgatta (Ed.), *The encyclopedia of sociology* (rev. ed., pp. 68–78). New York: Macmillan.

Anderson, C. A. (2004). An update on the effects of playing violent video games. *Journal of Adolescence, 27*, 113–122.

Anderson, C. A., & Bushman, B. J. (2002a). The effects of media violence on society. *Science, 295*, 2377–2379.

Anderson, C. A., & Bushman, B. J. (2002b). The general aggression model: An integrated social-cognitive model of human aggression. *Annual Review of Psychology, 53*, 27–51.

Anderson, C. A., & Gentile, D. A. (2007). Media violence, aggression, and public policy. In E. Borgida & S. Fiske (Eds.), *Psychological science in court: Beyond common knowledge*. Oxford, UK: Blackwell.

Anderson, C. A., & Murphy, C. R. (2003). Violent video games and aggressive behavior in young women. *Aggressive Behavior, 29*, 423–429.

Anderson, C. A., & Sechler, E. S. (1986). Effects of explanation and counterexplanation on the development and use of social theories. *Journal of Personality and Social Psychology, 50*, 24–34.

Anderson, C. A., Anderson, K. B., & Deuser, W. E. (1996). Examining an affective framework: Weapon and temperature effects on aggressive thoughts, affect, and attitudes. *Personality and Social Psychology Bulletin, 22*, 366–376.

Anderson, C. A., Anderson, K. B., Dorr, N., DeNeve, K. M., & Flanagan, M. (2000). Temperature and aggression. In M. P. Zanna (Ed.), *Advances in experimental social psychology* (Vol. 32, pp. 63–133). San Diego, CA: Academic Press.

Anderson, C. A., Benjamin, A. J., Jr., & Bartholow, B. D. (1998). Does the gun pull the trigger? Automatic priming effects of weapon pictures and weapon names. *Psychological Science, 9*, 308–314.

Anderson, C. A., Berkowitz, L., Donnerstein, E., Huesmann, L. R., Johnson, J., Linz, D., Malamuth, N., & Wartella, E. (2001). The influence of media violence on youth. *Psychological Science in the Public Interest, 4*, 81–110.

Anderson, C. A., Berkowitz, L., Donnerstein, E., Huesmann, L. R., Johnson, J. D., Linz, D., Malamuth, N. M., & Wartella, E. (2003). The influence of media violence on youth. *Psychological Science in the Public Interest, 4*, 81–110.

Anderson, C. A., Carnagey, N. L., & Eubanks, J. (2003). Exposure to violent media: The effects of songs with violent lyrics on aggressive thoughts and feelings. *Journal of Personality and Social Psychology, 84*, 960–971.

Anderson, C. A., Carnagey, N. L., Flanagan, M., Benjamin, A. J., Eubanks, J., & Valentine, J. C. (2004). Violent video games: Specific effects of violent content on aggressive thoughts and behavior. *Advances in Experimental Social Psychology, 36*, 199–249.

Anderson, C. A., Gentile, D. A., & Buckley, K. E. (2007). *Violent video game effects on children and adolescents: Theory, research, and public policy*. Oxford, UK: Oxford University Press.

Anderson, C. A., Lepper, M. R., & Ross, L. (1980). Perseverance of social theories: The role of explanation in the persistence of discredited information. *Journal of Personality and Social Psychology, 39*, 1037–1049.

Anderson, C. A., Lindsay, J. J., & Bushman, B. J. (1999). Research in the psychological laboratory: Truth or triviality? *Current Directions in Psychological Science, 8*, 3–9.

Anderson, J. L., Crawford, C. B., Nadeau, J., & Lindberg, T. (1992). Was the Duchess of Windsor right? A cross-cultural review of the socioecology of ideals of female body shape. *Ethology and Sociobiology, 13*, 197–227.

Anderson, N. H. (1965). Averaging versus adding as a stimulus combination rule in impression formation. *Journal of Experimental Social Psychology, 70*, 394–400.

Anderson, N. H. (1968). Likableness ratings of 555 personality-trait words. *Journal of Personality and Social Psychology, 9,* 272–279.

Anderson, N. H. (1981). *Foundations of information integration theory.* New York: Academic Press.

Anderson, N. H., & Hubert, S. (1963). Effects of concomitant verbal recall on order effects in personality impression formation. *Journal of Verbal Learning and Verbal Behavior, 2,* 379–391.

Andreasson, P. B. (1987). On the social psychology of the stock market: Aggregate attributional effects and the regressiveness of prediction. *Journal of Personality and Social Psychology, 53,* 490–496.

Antonio, A. L., Chang, M. J., Hakuta, K., Kenny, D. A., Levin, S., & Milem, J. F. (2004). Effects of racial diversity on complex thinking in college students. *Psychological Science, 15,* 507–510.

Apodaca v. Oregon, 406 U.S. 404 (1972).

Archer, D., & Gartner, R. (1984). *Violence and crime in cross-national perspective.* New Haven, CT: Yale University Press.

Archer, J. (2000). Sex differences in aggression between heterosexual partners: A meta-analytic review. *Psychological Bulletin, 126,* 651–680.

Archer, J. (2002). Sex differences in physically aggressive acts between heterosexual partners: A meta-analytic review. *Aggression and Violent Behavior: A Review Journal, 7,* 313–351.

Archer, J. (2004). Sex differences in aggression in real-world settings: A meta-analytic review. *Review of General Psychology, 8,* 291–322.

Archer, J. (2006). Testosterone and human aggression: An evaluation of the challenge hypothesis. *Neuroscience and Biobehavioral Reviews, 30,* 319–345.

Archer, J., & Mehdikhani, M. (2003). Variability among males in sexually selected attributes. *Review of General Psychology, 7,* 219–236.

Archibald, F. S., Bartholomew, K., & Marx, R. (1995). Loneliness in early adolescence: A test of the cognitive discrepancy model of loneliness. *Personality and Social Psychology Bulletin, 21,* 296–301.

Arendt, H. (1963). *Eichmann in Jerusalem: A report on the banality of evil.* New York: Viking.

Arkes, H. R., & Ayton, P. (1999). The sunk cost and Concorde effects: Are humans less rational than lower animals? *Psychological Bulletin, 125,* 591–600.

Arkin, R. M. (1981). Self-presentation styles. In J. T. Tedeschi (Ed.), *Impression management theory and social psychological research* (pp. 311–333). New York: Academic Press.

Armor, D. A., & Taylor, S. E. (1998). Situated optimism: Specific outcome expectancies and self-regulation. *Advances in Experimental Social Psychology, 30,* 309–379.

Armour, S. (1998, February 17). Office ethics: Teams make it hard to tattle. *USA Today,* p. 6B.

Armstrong, J. (2004). *The secret power of beauty: Why happiness is in the eye of the beholder.* London: Allen Lane.

Arndt, J., Greenberg, J., Schimel, J., Pyszczynski, T., & Solomon, S. (2002). To belong or not to belong, that is the question: Terror management and identification with gender and ethnicity. *Journal of Personality and Social Psychology, 83,* 26–43.

Aron, A., & Aron, E. N. (2001). The self-expansion model: Motivation and including other in the self. In W. Ickes & S. Duck (Eds.), *The social psychology of personal relationships.* Chichester, England: Wiley.

Aron, A., & Westbay, L. (1996). Dimensions of the prototype of love. *Journal of Personality and Social Psychology, 70,* 535–551.

Aron, A., Aron, E. N., & Smollan, D. (1992). Inclusion of Other in the Self Scale and the structure of interpersonal closeness. *Journal of Personality and Social Psychology, 63,* 596–612.

Aron, A., Aron, E. N., Tudor, M., & Nelson, G. (1991). Close relationships as including other in the self. *Journal of Personality and Social Psychology, 60,* 241–253.

Aron, A., Dutton, D. G., Aron, E. N., & Iverson, A. (1989). Experiences of falling in love. *Journal of Social and Personal Relationships, 6,* 243–257.

Aron, A., Norman, C. C., Aron, E. N., McKenna, C., & Heyman, R. E. (2000). Couples' shared participation in novel and arousing activities and experienced relationship quality. *Journal of Personality and Social Psychology, 78,* 273–284.

Aronoff, J., Barclay, A. M., & Stevenson, L. A. (1988). The recognition of threatening facial stimuli. *Journal of Personality and Social Psychology, 54,* 647–655.

Aronoff, J., Woike, B. A., & Hyman, L. M. (1992). Which are the stimuli in facial displays of anger and happiness? *Journal of Personality and Social Psychology, 62,* 1050–1066.

Aronson, E. (1969). The theory of cognitive dissonance: A current perspective. *Advances in Experimental Social Psychology, 4,* 1–34.

Aronson, E. (1992). Stateways can change folkways. In R. M. Baird & S. E. Rosenbaum (Eds.), *Bigotry, prejudice, and hatred: Definitions, causes, and solutions* (pp. 185–201). Buffalo, NY: Prometheus.

Aronson, E. (1999). Dissonance, hypocrisy, and the self-concept. In E. Harmon-Jones & J. Mills (Eds.), *Cognitive dissonance: Progress on a pivotal theory in social psychology* (pp. 103–126). Washington, DC: American Psychological Association.

Aronson, E. (2004). Reducing hostility and building compassion: Lessons from the jigsaw classroom. In A. G. Miller (Ed.), *The social psychology of good and evil* (pp. 469–488). New York: Guilford.

Aronson, E., & Carlsmith, J. M. (1963). Effect of severity of threat on the devaluation of forbidden behavior. *Journal of Abnormal and Social Psychology, 66,* 584–588.

Aronson, E., & Carlsmith, J. M. (1968). Experimentation in social psychology. In G. Lindzey & E. Aronson (Eds.), *Handbook of social psychology* (2nd ed., Vol. 2, pp. 1–79). Reading, MA: Addison-Wesley.

Aronson, E., & Cope, V. (1968). My enemy's enemy is my friend. *Journal of Personality and Social Psychology, 8,* 8–12.

Aronson, E., & Linder, D. (1965). Gain and loss of esteem as determinants of interpersonal attractiveness. *Journal of Experimental Social Psychology, 1,* 156–172.

Aronson, E., & Mills, J. (1959). The effect of severity of initiation on liking for a group. *Journal of Abnormal and Social Psychology, 59,* 177–181.

Aronson, E., Blaney, N., Stephan, C., Sikes, J., & Snapp, M. (1978). *The jigsaw classroom.* Beverly Hills, CA: Sage.

Aronson, J., & Inzlicht, M. (2004). The ups and downs of attributional ambiguity: Stereotype vulnerability and the academic self-knowledge of African American college students. *Psychological Science, 15,* 829–836.

Aronson, J., Lustina, M. J., Good, C., Keough, K., Steele, C. M., & Brown, J. (1999). When white men can't do math: Necessary and sufficient factors in stereotype threat. *Journal of Experimental Social Psychology, 35,* 29–46.

Arriaga, P., Esteves, F., Carneiro, P., & Monteiro, M. B. (2006). Violent computer games and their effects on state hostility and physiological arousal. *Aggressive Behavior, 32,* 358–371.

Arrow, H., & Burns, K. L. (2004). Self-organizing culture: How norms emerge in small groups. In M. Schaller & C. S. Crandall (Eds.), *The psychological foundations of culture* (pp. 171–199). Mahwah, NJ: Erlbaum.

Arthur, W., Day, E. D., McNelly, T. L., & Edens, P. S. (2003). A meta-analysis of the criterion-related validity of assessment center dimensions. *Personnel Psychology, 56,* 125–154.

Asch, S. E. (1946). Forming impressions of personality. *Journal of Abnormal and Social Psychology, 41,* 258–290.

Asch, S. E. (1951). Effects of group pressure upon the modification and distortion of judgments. In H. Guetzkow (Ed.), *Groups, leadership, and men.* Pittsburgh, PA: Carnegie Press.

Asch, S. E. (1955, November). Opinions and social pressure. *Scientific American,* pp. 31–35.

Asch, S. E. (1956). Studies of independence and conformity: A minority of one against a unanimous majority. *Psychological Monographs, 70,* 416.

Asch, S. E., & Zukier, H. (1984). Thinking about persons. *Journal of Personality and Social Psychology, 46,* 1230–1240.

Askenasy, H. (1978). *Are we all Nazis?* Secaucus, NJ: Lyle Stuart.

Aspinwall, L. G., & Taylor, S. E. (1992). Modeling cognitive adaptation: A longitudinal investigation of the impact of individual differences and coping on college adjustment and performance. *Journal of Personality and Social Psychology, 63,* 989–1003.

Aspinwall, L. G., & Taylor, S. E. (1993). The effects of social comparison direction, threat, and self-esteem on affect, self-evaluation, and expected success. *Journal of Personality and Social Psychology, 64,* 708–722.

Aspinwall, L. G., & Taylor, S. E. (1997). A stitch in time: Self-regulation and proactive coping. *Psychological Bulletin, 121,* 417–436.

Associated Press. (1988, October 10). Skirting the issue? *The National Law Journal,* p. 43.

Au, W. T., & Komorita, S. S. (2002). Effects of initial choices in the prisoner's dilemma. *Journal of Behavioral Decision Making, 15,* 343–359.

Auerbach, S. M., Kiesler, D. J., Strentz, T., Schmidt, J. A., & Serio, C. D. (1994). Interpersonal impacts and adjunctment to the stress of simulated captivity: An empirical test of the Stockholm Syndrome. *Journal of Social and Clinical Psychology, 13,* 207–221.

Austin, J. R. (2003). Transactive memory in organizational groups: The effects of content, consensus, specialization, and accuracy on group performance. *Journal of Applied Psychology, 88,* 866–878.

Axelrod, R. (1984). *The evolution of cooperation.* New York: Basic Books.

Axsom, D. (1989). Cognitive dissonance and behavior change in psychotherapy. *Journal of Experimental Social Psychology, 25,* 234–252.

Axsom, D., & Cooper, J. (1985). Cognitive dissonance and psychotherapy: The role of effort justification in inducing weight loss. *Journal of Experimental Social Psychology, 21,* 149–160.

Axtell, R. E. (1993). *Do's and taboos around the world* (3rd ed.). New York: John Wiley.

Babcock, L., & Laschever, S. (2003). *Women don't ask: Negotiation and the gender divide.* Princeton, NJ: Princeton University Press.

Bagemihl, B. (1999). *Biological exuberance: Animal homosexuality and natural diversity.* New York: St. Martin's Press.

Bagozzi, R. P., & Moore, D. J. (1994). Public service advertisements: Emotions and empathy guide prosocial behavior. *Journal of Marketing, 58,* 56–70.

Bahrick, H. P., Hall, L. K., & Berger, S. A. (1996). Accuracy and distortion in memory for high school grades. *Psychological Science, 7,* 265–271.

Bailenson, J. N., & Yee, N. (2005). Digital chameleons: Automatic assimilation of nonverbal gestures in immersive virtual environments. *Psychological Science, 16,* 814–819.

Bailenson, J. N., Beall, A. C., Loomis, J., Blascovich, J., & Turk, M. (2005). Transformed social interaction, augmented gaze, and social influence in immersive virtual environments. *Human Communication Research, 31,* 511–537.

Bailey, A. A., & Hurd, P. L. (2005). Finger length ratio (2D:4D) correlates with physical aggression in men but not in women. *Biological Psychology, 68,* 215–222.

Bailey, D. S., & Taylor, S. P. (1991). Effects of alcohol and aggressive disposition on human physical aggression. *Journal of Research in Personality, 25,* 334–342.

Bailey, J. M., & Pillard, R. C. (1991). A genetic study of male sexual orientation. *Archives of General Psychiatry, 48,* 1089–1096.

Bailey, J. M., & Zucker, K. J. (1995). Childhood sex-typed behavior and sexual orientation: A conceptual analysis and quantitative review. *Developmental Psychology, 31,* 43–55.

Bailey, J. M., Dunne, M. P., & Martin, N. G. (2000). Genetic and environmental influences on sexual orientation and its correlates in an Australian twin sample. *Journal of Personality and Social Psychology 78,* 524–536.

Bailey, J. M., Pillard, R. C., Neale, M. C., & Agyei, Y. (1993). Heritable factors influence sexual orientation in women. *Archives of General Psychiatry, 50,* 217–223.

Baldus, D. C., Woodworth, G., & Pulaski, C. A. (1990). *Equal justice and the death penalty: A legal and empirical analysis.* Boston: Northeastern University Press.

Baldwin, A. S., Rothman, A. J., Hertel, A. W., Linde, J. A., Jeffery, R. W., Finch, E. A., & Lando, H. A. (2006). Specifying the determinants of the initiation and maintenance of behavior change: An examination of self-efficacy, satisfaction, and smoking cessation. *Health Psychology, 25,* 626–634.

Baldwin, M. W., & Sinclair, L. (1996). Self-esteem and "if . . . then" contingencies of interpersonal acceptance. *Journal of Personality and Social Psychology, 71,* 1130–1141.

Baldwin, M., & Fehr, B. (1995). On the instability of attachment style ratings. *Personal Relationships, 2,* 247–261.

Bales, R. F. (1958). Task roles and social roles in problem-solving groups. In E. E. Maccoby, T. M. Newcomb, & E. L. Hartley (Eds.), *Readings in social psychology* (3rd ed., pp. 437–447). New York: Holt.

Ballew v. Georgia, 435 U.S. 223 (1978).

Banaji, M. R., & Hardin, C. D. (1996). Automatic gender stereotyping. *Psychological Science, 7,* 136–141.

Banaji, M. R., & Steele, C. M. (1989). Alcohol and self-evaluation: Is a social cognition approach beneficial? *Social Cognition, 7,* 137–151.

Banaji, M. R., Hardin, C., & Rothman, A. J. (1993). Implicit stereotyping in person judgment. *Journal of Personality and Social Psychology, 65,* 272–281.

Bancroft, J. (Ed.) (1997). *Researching sexual behavior: Methodological issues.* Bloomington: Indiana University Press.

Bandura, A. (1973). *Aggression: A social learning analysis.* Englewood Cliffs, NJ: Prentice-Hall.

Bandura, A. (1977). *Social learning theory.* Englewood Cliffs, NJ: Prentice-Hall.

Bandura, A. (1983). Psychological mechanisms of aggression. In R. G. Geen & E. I. Donnerstein (Eds.), *Aggression: Theoretical and empirical reviews: Vol. l. Theoretical and methodological issues* (pp. 1–40). New York: Academic Press.

Bandura, A. (1997). *Self-efficacy: The exercise of control.* New York: W. H. Freeman.

Bandura, A. (1999a). Moral disengagement in the perpetration of inhumanities. *Personality and Social Psychology Review, 3,* 193–209.

Bandura, A. (1999b). A sociocognitive analysis of substance abuse: An agentic perspective. *Psychological Science, 10,* 214–218.

Bandura, A. (2004). The role of selective moral disengagement in terrorism and counterterrorism. In F. M. Moghaddam & A. J. Marsella (Eds.), *Understanding terrorism: Psychosocial roots, consequences, and interventions* (pp. 121–150). Washington, DC: American Psychological Association.

Bandura, A. (2004). The role of selective moral disengagement in terrorism and counterterrorism. In F. M. Moghaddam & A. J. Marsella (Eds.), *Understanding terrorism: Psychosocial roots, consequences, and interventions* (pp. 121–150). Washington, DC: American Psychological Association.

Bandura, A., Ross, R., & Ross, S. (1961). Transmission of aggression through imitation of aggressive models. *Journal of Abnormal and Social Psychology, 63,* 575–582.

Banuazizi, A., & Movahedi, S. (1975). Interpersonal dynamics in a simulated prison: A methodological analysis. *American Psychologist, 30,* 152–160.

Barber, N. (2006). Why is violent crime so common in the Americas? *Aggressive Behavior, 32*, 442–450.

Bargh, J. A. (1997). The automaticity of everyday life. In R. S. Wyer (Ed.), *The automaticity of everyday life: Advances in social cognition* (Vol. 10, pp. 1–61). Mahwah, NJ: Erlbaum.

Bargh, J. A., & Chartrand, T. L. (1999). The unbearable automaticity of being. *American Psychologist, 54*, 462–479.

Bargh, J. A., & Chartrand, T. L. (2000). The mind in the middle: A practical guide for priming and automaticity research. In H. T. Reis and C. M. Judd (Eds.), *Handbook of research methods in social and personality psychology* (pp. 253–285). New York: Cambridge University Press.

Bargh, J. A., & McKenna, K. Y. A. (2004). The internet and social life. *Annual Review of Psychology, 55*, 20.1–20.18.

Bargh, J. A., & Pietromonaco, P. (1982). Automatic information processing and social perception: The influence of trait information presented outside of conscious awareness on impression formation. *Journal of Personality and Social Psychology, 43*, 437–449.

Bargh, J. A., & Williams, E. L. (2006). The automaticity of social life. *Current Directions in Psychological Science, 15*, 1-4.

Bargh, J. A., Chaiken, S., Govender, R., & Pratto, F. (1992). The generality of the automatic attitude activation effect. *Journal of Personality and Social Psychology, 62*, 893–912.

Bargh, J. A., Chaiken, S., Raymond, P., & Hymes, C. (1996). The automatic evaluation effect: Unconditional automatic attitude activation with a pronunciation task. *Journal of Experimental Social Psychology, 31*, 104–128.

Bargh, J. A., Chen, M., & Burrows, L. (1996). Automaticity of social behavior: Direct effects of trait construct and stereotype activation on action. *Journal of Personality and Social Psychology, 71*, 230–244.

Bargh, J. A., Fitzsimons, G. M., & McKenna, K. Y. A. (2003). The self, online. In S. J. Spencer, S. Fein, M. P. Zanna, & J. P. Olson (Eds.), *Motivated social perception: The Ontario symposium* (Vol. 9, pp. 195–213). Mahwah, NJ: Erlbaum.

Bargh, J. A., Lombardi, W. J., & Higgins, E. T. (1988). Automaticity of chronically accessible constructs in person x situation effects on person perception: It's just a matter of time. *Journal of Personality and Social Psychology, 55*, 599–605.

Barling, J., Kelloway, K., & Frone, M. (2005). *Handbook of occupational stress*. Los Angeles: Sage.

Barnes Nacoste, R. (1994). If empowerment is the goal . . . : Affirmative action and social interaction. *Basic and Applied Social Psychology, 15*, 87–112.

Barnes, R. D., Ickes, W., & Kidd, R. F. (1979). Effects of the perceived intentionality and stability of another's dependency on helping behavior. *Personality and Social Psychology Bulletin, 5*, 367–372.

Barnwell, S. S., Borders, A., & Earleywine, M. (2006). Alcohol-aggression expectancies and dispositional aggression moderate the relationship between alcohol consumption and alcohol-related violence. *Aggressive Behavior, 32*, 517–527.

Baron, J., & Miller, J. G. (2000). Limiting the scope of moral obligations to help: A cross-cultural investigation. *Journal of Cross Cultural Psychology, 31*, 703–725.

Baron, R. A. (1997). The sweet smell of helping: Effects of pleasant ambient fragrance on prosocial behavior in shopping malls. *Journal of Personality and Social Psychology, 23* (5), 498–503.

Baron, R. A., & Ball, R. L. (1974). The aggression-inhibiting influence of nonhostile behavior. *Journal of Experimental Social Psychology, 10*, 23–33.

Baron, R. A., & Richardson, D. R. (1994). *Human aggression* (2nd ed.). New York: Plenum.

Baron, R. S. (1986). Distraction-conflict theory: Progress and problems. In L. Berkowitz (Ed.), *Advances in experimental social psychology* (Vol. 19, pp. 1–40). Orlando, FL: Academic Press.

Baron, R. S. (2005). So right it's wrong: Groupthink and the ubiquitous nature of polarized group decision making. In M. P. Zanna (Ed.), *Advances in experimental social psychology* (pp. 219–253). San Diego: Elsevier Academic Press.

Baron, R. S., Hoppe, S. I., Kao, C. F., Brunsman, B., Linneweh, B., & Rogers, D. (1996). Social corroboration and opinion extremity. *Journal of Experimental Social Psychology, 32*, 537–560.

Baron, R. S., Vandello, J. A., & Brunsman, B. (1996). The forgotten variable in conformity research: Impact of task importance on social influence. *Journal of Personality and Social Psychology, 71*, 915–927.

Baron, R., Logan, H., Lilly, J., Inman, M., & Brennan, M. (1994). Negative emotion and message processing. *Journal of Experimental Social Psychology, 30*, 181–201.

Barrett, H. C., Todd, P. M., Miller, G. F., & Blythe, P. W. (2005). Accurate judgments of intention from motion cues alone: A cross-cultural study. *Evolution and Human Behavior, 26*, 313–331.

Barrick, M. R., & Mount, M. K. (1996). Effects of impression management and self-deception on the predictive validity of personality constructs. *Journal of Applied Psychology, 81*, 261–272.

Bar-Tal, D. (1996). Development of social categories and stereotypes in early childhood: The case of "the Arab" concept formation, stereotype and attitudes by Jewish children in Israel. *International Journal of Intercultural Relations, 20*, 341–370.

Bartholow, B. D., & Heinz, A. (2006). Alcohol and aggression without consumption: Alcohol cues, aggressive thoughts, and hostile perception bias. *Psychological Science, 17*, 30–37.

Bartholow, B. D., Anderson, C. A., Carnagey, N. L., & Benjamin, A. J., Jr. (2005). Interactive effects of life experience and situational cues on aggression: The weapons priming effect in hunters and nonhunters. *Journal of Experimental Social Psychology, 41*, 48–60.

Bartholow, B. D., Dickter, C. L., & Sestir, M. A. (2006). Stereotype activation and control of race bias: Cognitive control of inhibition and its impairment by alcohol. *Journal of Personality and Social Psychology, 90*, 272–287.

Barthrop, R. W., Lazarus, L., Luckhurst, E., Kiloh, L. G., & Penny, R. (1977). Depressed lymphocyte function after bereavement. *Lancet, 1*, 834–839.

Bartlett, M. S., Hagar, J. C., Ekman, P., & Sejnowski, T. J. (1999). Measuring facial expressions by computer image analysis. *Psychophysiology, 36*, 253–263.

Bartsch, R. A., Burnett, T., Diller, T. R., & Rankin-Williams, E. E. (2000). Gender representation in television commercials: Updating an update. *Sex Roles, 43*, 735–743.

Bartsch, R. A., Judd, C. M., Louw, D. A., Park, B., & Ryan, C. S. (1997). Cross-national outgroup homogeneity: United States and South African stereotypes. *South African Journal of Psychology, 27*, 166–170.

Bashore, T. R., & Rapp, P. E. (1993). Are there alternatives to traditional polygraph procedures? *Psychological Bulletin, 113*, 3–22.

Bass, B. M. (1985). *Leadership and performance beyond expectations*. New York: Free Press.

Bass, B. M. (1997). Does the transactional-transformational leadership paradigm transcend organizational and national boundaries? *American Psychologist, 52*, 130–139.

Bass, B. M. (1998). *Transformational leadership: Industry, military, and educational impact*. Mahwah, NJ: Erlbaum.

Bass, B. M., & Avolio, B. J. (1990). *Manual: The multifactor leadership questionnaire*. Palo Alto, CA: Consulting Psychologists Press.

Bass, B. M., & Riggio, R. E. (2006). *Transformational leadership* (2nd ed.). Mahwah, NJ: Erlbaum.

Bass, B. M., & Steidlmeier, P. (1999). Ethics, character, and the authentic transformational leadership behavior. *Leadership Quarterly, 10*, 181–217.

Bassili, J. N. (2003). The minority slowness effect: Subtle inhibitions in the expression of views not shared by others. *Journal of Personality and Social Psychology, 84,* 261–276.

Bassili, J. N., & Provencal, A. (1988). Perceiving minorities: A factor-analytic approach. *Personality and Social Psychology Bulletin, 14,* 5–15.

Bateson, M., Nettle, D., & Roberts, G. (2006). Cues of being watched enhance cooperation in a real-world setting. *Biology Letters, 2,* 412–414.

Batson, C. D. (1991). *The altruism question.* Hillsdale, NJ: Erlbaum.

Batson, C. D. (1998). Altruism and prosocial behavior. In D. T. Gilbert, S. T. Fiske, & G. Lindzey (Eds.), *The handbook of social psychology* (4th ed., Vol. 2, pp. 282–316). New York: McGraw-Hill.

Batson, C. D. (2002). Addressing the altruism question experimentally. In S. G. Post & L. G. Underwood (Eds.), *Altruism and altruistic love: Science, philosophy, and religion in dialogue* (pp. 89–105). London: Oxford University Press.

Batson, C. D., & Powell, A. A. (2003). Altruism and prosocial behavior. In T. Millon & M. J. Lerner (Eds.), *Handbook of psychology: Personality and social psychology* (Vol. 5, pp. 463–484). New York: Wiley.

Batson, C. D., & Weeks, J. L. (1996). Mood effects of unsuccessful helping: Another test of the empathy-altruism hypothesis. *Personality and Social Psychology Bulletin, 22,* 148–157.

Batson, C. D., Chang, J., Orr, R., & Rowland, J. (2001). Empathy, attitudes, and action: Can feeling for a member of a stigmatized group motivate one to help the group? *Personality and Social Psychology Bulletin, 28,* 1656–1666.

Batson, C. D., Cochran, P. J., Biederman, M. F., Blosser, J. L., Ryan, M. J., & Vogt, B. (1978). Failure to help when in a hurry: Callousness or conflict? *Personality and Social Psychology Bulletin, 4,* 97–101.

Batson, C. D., Early, S., & Salvarani, G. (1997). Perspective taking: Imagining how another feels versus imagining how you would feel. *Personality and Social Psychology Bulletin, 23,* 751–758.

Batson, C. D., Kobrynowicz, D., Dinnerstein, J. L., & Kampf, H. C. (1997). In a very different voice: Unmasking moral hypocrisy. *Journal of Personality and Social Psychology, 72,* 1335–1348.

Batson, C. D., Lishner, D. A., Carpenter, A., Dulin, L., Harjusola-Webb, S., Stocks, E. L., Gale, S., Hassan, O., & Sampat, B. (2003). "As you would have them do unto you": Does imagining yourself in the other's place stimulate moral action? *Personality and Social Psychology Bulletin, 29,* 1190–1201.

Batson, C. D., Lishner, D. A., Cook, J., & Sawyer, S. (2005). Similarity and nurturance: Two possible sources of empathy for strangers. *Basic and Applied Social Psychology, 27,* 15–25.

Batson, C. D., O'Quin, K., Fultz, J., Vanderplas, M., & Isen, A. M. (1983). Influence of self-reported distress and empathy on egoistic versus altruistic motivation to help. *Journal of Personality and Social Psychology, 45,* 706–718.

Batson, C. D., Polycarpou, M. P., Harmon-Jones, E., Imhoff, H. J., Mitchener, E. C., Bednar, L. L., Klein, T. R., & Highberger, L. (1997). Empathy and attitudes: Can feeling for a member of a stigmatized group improve feelings toward the group? *Journal of Personality and Social Psychology, 72,* 105–118.

Batson, C. D., Sager, K., Garst, E., Kang, M., Rubchinsky, K., & Dawson, K. (1997). Is empathy-induced helping due to self-other merging? *Journal of Personality and Social Psychology, 73,* 495–509.

Batson, C. D., Thompson, E. R., & Chen, H. (2002). Moral hypocrisy: Addressing some alternatives. *Journal of Personality and Social Psychology, 83,* 330–339.

Bauer, T. N., Maertz, C. P., Dolen, M. R., & Campion, M. A. (1998). Longitudinal assessment of applicant reactions to employment testing and test outcome feedback. *Journal of Applied Psychology, 83,* 892–903.

Baugh, S. G., & Graen, G. B. (1997). Effects of team gender and racial composition on perceptions of team performance in cross-functional teams. *Group and Organization Management, 22,* 366–383.

Baum, A. (Ed.). (1984). Social psychology and cigarette smoking [Special issue]. *Journal of Applied Social Psychology, 14*(3).

Baum, A., & Valins, S. (1977). *Architecture and social behavior: Psychological studies of social density.* Hillsdale, NJ: Erlbaum.

Baum, A., & Valins, S. (1979). Architectural mediation of residential density and control: Crowding and the regulation of social contact. In L. Berkowitz (Ed.), *Advances in experimental social psychology* (Vol. 12, pp. 131–175). New York: Academic Press.

Baumann, M. R., & Bonner, B. L. (2004). Expertise in collective decision-making: Variability, expectations, and utilization. *Organizational Behavior and Human Decision Processes, 93,* 89–101.

Baumeister, R. F. (1982). A self-presentational view of social phenomena. *Psychological Bulletin, 91,* 3–26.

Baumeister, R. F. (1984). Choking under pressure: Self-consciousness and paradoxical effects of incentives on skillful performance. *Journal of Personality and Social Psychology, 46,* 610–620.

Baumeister, R. F. (1991). *Escaping the self.* New York: Basic Books.

Baumeister, R. F. (2000). Gender differences in erotic plasticity: The female sex drive as socially flexible and responsive. *Psychological Bulletin, 126,* 347–374.

Baumeister, R. F., & Leary, M. R. (1995). The need to belong: Desire for interpersonal attachments as a fundamental human motivation. *Psychological Bulletin, 117,* 497–529.

Baumeister, R. F., & Scher, S. J. (1988). Self-defeating behavior patterns among normal individuals: Review and analysis of common self-destructive tendencies. *Psychological Bulletin, 104,* 3–22.

Baumeister, R. F., & Tice, D. M. (1984). Role of self-presentation and choice in cognitive dissonance under forced compliance: Necessary or sufficient causes? *Journal of Personality and Social Psychology, 46,* 5–13.

Baumeister, R. F., & Twenge, J. M. (2003). The social self. In T. Millon & M. J. Lerner (Eds.), *Handbook of psychology: Personality and social psychology* (Vol. 5, pp. 327–352). New York: Wiley.

Baumeister, R. F., & Vohs, K. D. (Eds.). (2004). *Handbook of self-regulation: Research, theory, and applications.* New York: Guilford.

Baumeister, R. F., Bratslavsky, E., Finkenauer, C., & Vohs, K. D. (2001). Bad is stronger than good. *Review of General Psychology, 5,* 323–370.

Baumeister, R. F., Bushman, B. J., & Campbell, W. K. (2000). Self-esteem, narcissism, and aggression: Does violence result from low self-esteem or from threatened egotism? *Current Directions in Psychological Science, 9,* 26–29.

Baumeister, R. F., Catanese, K. R., & Vohs, K. D. (2001). Is there a gender difference in the strength of sex drive? Theoretical views, conceptual distinctions, and a review of relevant evidence. *Personality and Social Psychology Review, 5,* 242–273.

Baumeister, R. F., Chesner, S. P., Sanders, P. S., & Tice, D. M. (1988). Who's in charge here? Group leaders do lend help in emergencies. *Personality and Social Psychology Bulletin, 14,* 17–22.

Baumeister, R., Stillwell, A. M., & Hetherington, T. F. (1994). Guilt: An interpersonal approach. *Psychological Bulletin, 115,* 243–267.

Baumeister, R. F., Campbell, J. D., Krueger, J. I., & Vohs, K. D. (2003). Does high self-esteem cause better performance, interpersonal success, happiness, or healthier lifestyles? *Psychological Science in the Public Interest, 4,* 1–44.

Baumrind, D. (1997). Necessary distinctions. *Psychological Inquiry, 8,* 176–229.

Baxter, L. A. (1987). Self-disclosure and disengagement. In V. J. Derleg & J. H. Berg (Eds.), *Self-disclosure: Theory, research, and therapy* (pp. 155–174). New York: Plenum.

Bayles, F. (2001, March 27). Nurse gets life in prison for killing 4 veterans. Experts explore motives of medical murderers. *USA Today*, p. 6A.

Bazerman, M. H. (Ed.). (2005). *Negotiation, decision making and conflict management* (Vols. 1–3). Northampton, MA: Edward Elgar Publishing.

Bazerman, M. H., & Neale, M. A. (1992). *Negotiating rationally.* New York: Free Press.

BBC (2006, July 31). UEFA issues new anti-racism rules. http://news.bbc.co.uk/sport2/hi/football/europe/5232208.stm

Beach, S. R. H., Tesser, A., Mendolia, M., Anderson, P., et al. (1996). Self-evaluation maintenance in marriage: Toward a performance ecology of the marital relationship. *Journal of Family Psychology, 10*, 379–396.

Beaman, A. L., Klentz, B., Diener, E., & Svanum, S. (1979). Objective self-awareness and transgression in children: A field study. *Journal of Personality and Social Psychology, 37*, 1835–1846.

Beardsley, T. (1999, October). Truth or consequences. *Scientific American*, pp. 21, 24.

Becker, F. D. (1981). *Workspace.* New York: Praeger.

Beckerman, S., & Valentine, P. (Eds.). (2002). *Cultures of multiple fathers: The theory and practice of partible paternity in lowland South America.* Gainesville: University Press of Florida.

Beidel, D. C., & Turner, S. M. (1998). *Shy children, phobic adults: Nature and treatment of social phobia.* Washington, DC: American Psychological Association.

Beilock, S. L., & Carr, T. H. (2001). On the fragility of skilled performance: What governs choking under pressure? *Journal of Experimental Psychology: General, 130*, 701–725.

Beitchman, J. H., Baldassarra, L., Mik, H., De Luca, V., King, N., Bender, D., Ehtesham, S., & Kennedy, J. L. (2006). Serotonin transporter polymorphisms and persistent, persuasive childhood aggression. *American Journal of Psychiatry, 163*, 1103–1105.

Bell, A. P., Weinberg, M. S., & Hammersmith, S. K. (1981). *Sexual preference: Its development in men and women.* Bloomington: Indiana University Press.

Bell, D. C. (2001). Evolution of parental caregiving. *Personality and Social Psychology Review, 5*, 216–229.

Bell, J., Grekul, J., Lamba, N., Minas, C., & Harrell, W. A. (1995). The impact of cost on student helping behavior. *Journal of Social Psychology, 135*, 49–56.

Bell, K. (2003, June 14). Des Peres doctor charged in hit-and-run that killed nurse. *St. Louis Post-Dispatch*, p. 13.

Belmore, S. M. (1987). Determinants of attention during impression formation. *Journal of Experimental Psychology: Learning, Memory, and Cognition, 13*, 480–489.

Belsky, J. (1993). Etiology of child maltreatment: A developmental-ecological analysis. *Psychological Bulletin, 114*, 413–434.

Bem, D. J. (1965). An experimental analysis of self-persuasion. *Journal of Experimental Social Psychology, 1*, 199–218.

Bem, D. J. (1967). Self-perception: An alternative interpretation of cognitive dissonance phenomena. *Psychological Review, 74*, 183–200.

Bem, D. J. (1972). Self-perception theory. In L. Berkowitz (Ed.), *Advances in experimental social psychology* (Vol. 6, pp. 1–62). New York: Academic Press.

Bem, D. J. (1996). Exotic becomes erotic: A developmental theory of sexual orientation. *Psychological Review, 103*, 320–335.

Bem, D. J. (2000). Exotic becomes erotic: Interpreting the biological correlates of sexual orientation. *Archives of Sexual Behavior, 29*, 531–548.

Bem, S. L. (1981). Gender schema theory: A cognitive account of sex typing. *Psychological Review, 88*, 354–364.

Benjet, C., & Kazdin, A. E. (2003). Spanking children: The controversies, findings and new directions. *Clinical Psychology Review, 23*, 197–224.

Bennett, D. A., Schneider, J. A., Tang, Y., Arnold, S. E., & Wilson, R. S. (2006). The effect of social networks on the relation between Alzheimer's disease pathology and level of cognitive function in old people: A longitudinal cohort study. *Lancet Neurology, 5*, 406–412.

Bennett, J. C. (1991). The irrationality of the catharsis theory of aggression as justification for educators' support of interscholastic football. *Perceptual and Motor Skills, 72*, 415–418.

Bennett, S., Farrington, D. P., & Huesmann, L. R. (2005). Explaining gender differences in crime and violence: The importance of social cognitive skills. *Aggression and Violent Behavior, 10*, 263–288.

Benson, H. (1993). The relaxation response. In D. Goleman & J. Gurin (Eds.), *Mind body medicine: How to use your mind for better health* (pp. 233–257). Yonkers, NY: Consumer Reports Books.

Benson, P. L., Karabenick, S. A., & Lerner, R. M. (1976). Pretty pleases: The effects of physical attractiveness, race, and sex on receiving help. *Journal of Experimental Social Psychology, 12*, 409–415.

Ben-Zeev, T., Fein, S., & Inzlicht, M. (2005). Arousal and stereotype threat. *Journal of Experimental Social Psychology, 41*, 174–181.

Bercovitch, J., & Houston, A. (2000). Why do they do it like this? An analysis of the factors influencing mediation behavior in international conflicts. *Journal of Conflict Resolution, 44*, 170–202.

Berdahl, J. L., & Anderson, C. (2005). Men, women, and leadership centralization in groups over time. *Group Dynamics: Theory, Research, and Practice, 9*, 45–57.

Berg, J. H., & McQuinn, R. D. (1986). Attraction and exchange in continuing and noncontinuing dating relationships. *Journal of Personality and Social Psychology, 50*, 942–952.

Berghuis, J. P., & Stanton, A. L. (2002). Adjustment to a dyadic stressor: A longitudinal study of coping and depressive symptoms in infertile couples over an insemination attempt. *Journal of Consulting and Clinical Psychology, 70*, 433–438.

Berglas, S., & Jones, E. E. (1978). Drug choice as a self-handicapping strategy in response to noncontingent success. *Journal of Personality and Social Psychology, 36*, 405–417.

Bergstrom, B. (2003, October 8). Blacks outraged at board game. Associated Press.

Berkman, L., & Syme, S. L. (1979). Social networks, host resistance, and mortality: A nine-year follow-up study of Alameda County residents. *American Journal of Epidemiology, 109*, 186–204.

Berkowitz, L. (1965). Some aspects of observed aggression. *Journal of Personality and Social Psychology, 2*, 359–369.

Berkowitz, L. (1968). Impulse, aggression, and the gun. *Psychology Today, 2*(4), 18–22.

Berkowitz, L. (1972). Social norms, feelings, and other factors affecting helping and altruism. In L. Berkowitz (Ed.), *Advances in experimental social psychology* (Vol. 6, pp. 63–108). New York: Academic Press.

Berkowitz, L. (1989). Frustration-aggression hypothesis: Examination and reformulation. *Psychological Bulletin, 106*, 59–73.

Berkowitz, L. (1993). *Aggression: Its causes, consequences, and control.* New York: McGraw-Hill.

Berkowitz, L. (1998). Affective aggression: The role of stress, pain, and negative affect. In R. G. Geen & E. Donnerstein (Eds.), *Human aggression: Theories, research, and implications for social policy* (pp. 49–72). San Diego: Academic Press.

Berkowitz, L., & Donnerstein, E. (1982). External validity is more than skin deep: Some answers to criticisms of laboratory experiments. *American Psychologist, 37*, 245–257.

Berkowitz, L., & LePage, A. (1967). Weapons as aggression-eliciting stimuli. *Journal of Personality and Social Psychology, 7*, 202–207.

Bernardin, H. J., Cooke, D. K., & Villanova, P. (2000). Conscientiousness and agreeableness as predictors of rating leniency. *Journal of Applied Psychology, 85*, 232–236.

Berndsen, M., Spears, R., Pligt, J., & McGarty, C. (2002). Illusory correlation and stereotype formation: Making sense of group differences and cognitive biases. In C. McGarty, V. Y. Yzerbyt, & R. Spears (Eds.), *Stereotypes as explanations: The formation of meaningful beliefs about social groups* (pp. 90–110). Cambridge, UK: Cambridge University Press.

Bernhard, H., Fischbacher, U., & Fehr, E. (2006). Parochial altruism in humans. *Nature, 442,* 912–915.

Bernhardt, P. C., Dabbs, J. M., Fielden, J. A., & Lutter, C. D. (1998). Testosterone changes during vicarious experiences of winning and losing among fans at sporting events. *Physiology and Behavior, 65,* 59–62.

Berns, G. S., Chappelow, J., Zink, C. F., Pagnoni, G., Martin-Skurski, M. E., & Richards, J. (2005). Neurobiological correlates of social conformity and independence during mental rotation. *Biological Psychiatry, 58,* 245–253.

Berry, D. S., & Finch Wero, J. L. (1993). Accuracy in face perception: A view from ecological psychology. *Journal of Personality, 61,* 497–520.

Berry, D. S., & Zebrowitz-McArthur, L. (1986). Perceiving character in faces: The impact of age-related craniofacial changes in social perception. *Psychological Bulletin, 100,* 3–18.

Berry, J. W. (1979). A cultural ecology of social behavior. *Advances in Experimental Social Psychology, 12,* 177–206.

Berry, J. W., Poortinga, Y. H., Segall, M. H., & Dasen, P. R. (1992). *Cross-cultural psychology: Research and application.* Cambridge, UK: Cambridge University Press.

Berscheid, E. (1966). Opinion change and communicator-communicatee similarity and dissimilarity. *Journal of Personality and Social Psychology, 4,* 670–680.

Berscheid, E., & Meyers, S. A. (1996). A social categorical approach to a question about love. *Personal Relationships, 3,* 19–43.

Berscheid, E., & Regan, P. (2004). *The psychology of interpersonal relationships.* Upper Saddle River, NJ: Prentice-Hall.

Berscheid, E., & Reis, H. T. (1998). Attraction and close relationships. In D. Gilbert, S. Fiske, & G. Lindzey (Eds.), *Handbook of social psychology* (4th ed.). New York: McGraw-Hill.

Berscheid, E., & Walster, E. (1974). A little bit about love. In T. Huston (Ed.), *Foundations of interpersonal attraction* (pp. 355–381). New York: Academic Press.

Berscheid, E., Dion, K., Walster, E., & Walster, G. W. (1971). Physical attractiveness and dating choice: A test of the matching hypothesis. *Journal of Experimental Social Psychology, 7,* 173–189.

Berscheid, E., Snyder, M., & Omoto, A. M. (1989). The relationship closeness inventory: Assessing the closeness of interpersonal relationships. *Journal of Personality and Social Psychology, 57,* 792–807.

Berscheid, E., Walster, E., & Campbell, R. (1972). *Grow old along with me.* Unpublished manuscript, Department of Psychology, University of Minnesota.

Bersoff, D. N. (Ed.). (2003). *Ethical conflicts in psychology* (3rd ed.). Washington, DC: American Psychological Association.

Bersoff, D. N., & Ogden, D. W. (1987). In the Supreme Court of the United States: *Lockhart v. McCree. American Psychologist, 42,* 59–68.

Bessenoff, G. R. (2006). Can the media affect us? Social comparison, self-discrepancy, and the thin ideal. *Psychology of Women Quarterly, 30,* 239–251.

Bettencourt, B. A., & Dorr, N. (1998). Cooperative interaction and intergroup bias: Effects of numerical representation and cross-cut role assignment. *Personality and Social Psychology Bulletin, 24,* 1276–1293.

Bettencourt, B. A., & Sheldon, K. (2001). Social roles as mechanism for psychological need satisfaction within social groups. *Journal of Personality and Social Psychology, 81,* 1131–1143.

Bettencourt, B. A., Talley, A., Benjamin, A. J., & Valentine, J. (2006). Personality and aggressive behavior under provoking and neutral conditions: A meta-analytic review. *Psychological Bulletin, 132,* 751–777.

Beu, D. S., & Buckley, M. R. (2004). This is war: How the politically astute achieve crimes of obedience through the use of moral disengagement. *Leadership Quarterly, 15,* 551–568.

Beyer, S. (1990). Gender differences in the accuracy of self-evaluations of performance. *Journal of Personality and Social Psychology, 59,* 960–970.

Bickman, L. (1974). The social power of a uniform. *Journal of Applied Social Psychology, 4,* 47–61.

Binning, J. F., Goldstein, M. A., Garcia, M. F., & Scatteregia, J. H. (1988). Effects of preinterview impressions on questioning strategies in same- and opposite-sex employment interviews. *Journal of Applied Psychology, 73,* 30–37.

Björkqvist, K., Österman, K., & Kaukiainen, A. (1992). The development of direct and indirect aggressive strategies in males and females. In K. Björkqvist & P. Niemelä (Eds.), *Of mice and women: Aspects of female aggression* (pp. 51–64). San Diego: Academic Press.

Blaine, B., Crocker, J., & Major, B. (1995). The unintended negative consequences of sympathy for the stigmatized. *Journal of Applied Social Psychology, 25,* 889–905.

Blair, C. A., Thompson, L. F., & Wuensch, K. L. (2005). Electronic helping behavior: The virtual presence of others makes a difference. *Basic and Applied Social Psychology, 27,* 171–178.

Blair, I. V. (2001). Implicit stereotypes and prejudice. In G. B. Moskowitz (Ed.), *Cognitive social psychology: On the future of social cognition* (pp. 359–374). Mahwah, NJ: Erlbaum.

Blair, I. V. (2002). The malleability of automatic stereotypes and prejudice. *Personality and Social Psychology Review, 6,* 242–261.

Blair, I. V., Judd, C. M., & Fallman, J. L. (2004). The automaticity of race and Afrocentric facial features in social judgments. *Journal of Personality and Social Psychology, 87,* 763–778.

Blair, I. V., Judd, C. M., Sadler, M. S., & Jenkins, C. (2002). The role of Afrocentric features in person perception: Judging by features and categories. *Journal of Personality and Social Psychology, 83,* 5–25.

Blair, I. V., Ma, J. E., & Lenton, A. P. (2001). Imagining stereotypes away: The moderation of implicit stereotypes through mental imagery. *Journal of Personality and Social Psychology, 81,* 828–841.

Blair, I. V., Park, B., & Bachelor, J. (2003). Understanding intergroup anxiety: Are some people more anxious than others? *Group Processes and Intergroup Relations, 6,* 151–169.

Blanton, H., Crocker, J., & Miller, Dale T. (2000). The effects of in-group versus out-group social comparison on self-esteem in the context of a negative stereotype. *Journal of Experimental Social Psychology, 36,* 519–530.

Blanton, H., Jaccard, J., Gonzales, P. M., & Christie, C. (2006). Decoding the implicit association test: Implications for criterion prediction. *Journal of Experimental Social Psychology, 42,* 192–212.

Blascovich, J., Mendes, W. B., Hunter, S. B., & Salomon, K. (1999). Social "facilitation" as challenge and threat. *Journal of Personality and Social Psychology, 77,* 68–77.

Blascovich, J., Seery, M. D., Mugridge, C. A., Norris, R. K., & Weisbuch, M. (2004). Predicting athletic performance from cardiovascular indexes of challenge and threat. *Journal of Experimental Social Psychology, 40,* 683–688.

Blascovich, J., Spencer, S. J., Quinn, D., & Steele, C. (2001). African Americans and high blood pressure: The role of stereotype threat. *Psychological Science, 12,* 225–229.

Blass, T. (1991). Understanding behavior in the Milgram obedience experiment: The role of personality, situations, and their interactions. *Journal of Personality and Social Psychology, 60,* 398–413.

Blass, T. (1992). The social psychology of Stanley Milgram. *Advances in Experimental Social Psychology, 25,* 227–329.

Blass, T. (1999). The Milgram paradigm after 35 years: Some things we now know about obedience to authority. *Journal of Applied Social Psychology, 25,* 955–978.

Blass, T. (2004). *The man who shocked the world.* New York: Basic Books.

Blass, T. (Ed.) (2000). *Obedience to authority: Current perspectives on the Milgram paradigm.* Mahwah, NJ: Erlbaum.

Bleich, A., Gelkopf, M., & Solomon, Z. (2003). Exposure to terrorism, stress-related mental health symptoms, and coping behaviors among a nationally representative sample in Israel. *Journal of the American Medical Association, 290,* 612–620.

Bless, H., Schwarz, N., & Wieland, R. (1996). Mood and stereotyping: The impact of category membership and individuating information. *European Journal of Social Psychology, 26,* 935–959.

Bloom, A. (1981). *The linguistic shaping of thought.* Hillsdale, NJ: Erlbaum.

Bobocel, D. R., Son Hing, L. S., Davey, L. M., Stanley, D. J., & Zanna, M. P. (1998). Justice-based opposition to social policies: Is it genuine? *Journal of Personality and Social Psychology, 75,* 653–669.

Bochner, S. (1994). Cross-cultural differences in the self-concept: A test of Hofstede's individualism/collectivism distinction. *Journal of Cross Cultural Psychology, 25,* 273–283.

Bochner, S., & Insko, C. A. (1966). Communicator discrepancy, source credibility, and opinion change. *Journal of Personality and Social Psychology, 4,* 614–621.

Bodenhausen, G. V. (1990). Stereotypes as judgmental heuristics: Evidence of circadian variations in discrimination. *Psychological Science, 1,* 319–322.

Bodenhausen, G. V., & Macrae, C. N. (1998). Stereotype activation and inhibition. In R. S. Wyer, Jr. (Ed.), *Stereotype activation and inhibition: Advances in social cognition* (Vol. 11, pp. 1–52). Mahwah, NJ: Erlbaum.

Bodenhausen, G. V., Macrae, C. N., & Hugenberg, K. (2003). Social cognition. In T. Millon & M. J. Lerner (Eds.), *Handbook of psychology: Personality and social psychology* (Vol. 5., pp. 257–282). New York: Wiley.

Bogart, L. M., & Helgeson, V. S. (2000). Social comparisons among women with breast cancer: A longitudinal investigation. *Journal of Applied Social Psychology, 30,* 547–575.

Boldero, J., & Francis, J. (2000). The relation between self-discrepancies and emotion: The moderating roles of self-guide importance, location relevance, and social self-domain centrality. *Journal of Personality and Social Psychology, 78,* 38–52.

Boldizar, J. P., Perry, D. G., & Perry, L. (1989). Outcome values and aggression. *Child Development, 60,* 571–579.

Bolger, N., DeLongis, A., Kessler, R. C., & Schilling, E. A. (1989). Effects of daily stress and negative mood. *Journal of Personality and Social Psychology, 57,* 808–818.

Bonanno, G. A. (2004). Loss, trauma, and human resilience: Have we underestimated the human capacity to thrive after extremely aversive events? *American Psychologist, 59,* 20–28.

Bond, C. F., Jr., & Titus, L. T. (1983). Social facilitation: A meta-analysis of 241 studies. *Psychological Bulletin, 94,* 265–292.

Bond, C., & DePaulo, B. (2006). Accuracy of deception judgments. *Personality and Social Psychology Review, 10,* 214–234.

Bond, R., & Smith, P. B. (1996). Culture and conformity: A meta-analysis of studies using Asch's (1952b, 1956) line judgment task. *Psychological Bulletin, 119,* 111–137.

Boninger, D. S., Brock, T. C., Cook, T. D., Gruder, C. L., & Romer, D. (1990). Discovery of reliable attitude change persistence resulting from a transmitter tuning set. *Psychological Science, 1,* 268–271.

Boninger, D. S., Krosnick, J. A., & Berent, M. K. (1995). Origins of attitude importance: Self-interest, social identification, and value relevance. *Journal of Personality and Social Psychology, 68,* 61–80.

Bonner, B. L. (2004). Expertise in group problem-solving: Recognition, social combination, and performance. *Group Dynamics: Theory, Research, and Practice, 8,* 277–290.

Bonner, B. L., Baumann, M. R., & Dalal, R. S. (2002). The effects of member expertise on group decision-making and performance. *Organizational Behavior and Human Decision Processes, 88,* 719–736.

Bonnie, K. E., & de Waal, F. B. M. (2004). Primate social reciprocity and the origin of gratitude. In R. A. Emmons & M. E. McCullough (Eds.), *The psychology of gratitude.* Oxford: Oxford University Press.

Bono, J. E., & Anderson, M. H. (2005). The advice and influence networks of transformational leaders. *Journal of Applied Psychology, 90,* 1306–1314.

Bono, J. E., & Judge, T. A. (2004). Personality and transformational and transactional leadership: A meta-analysis. *Journal of Applied Psychology, 89,* 901–910.

Bonta, B. D. (1997). Cooperation and competition in peaceful societies. *Psychological Bulletin, 121,* 299–320.

Book, A. S., Starzyk, K. B., & Qunisey, V. L. (2001). The relationship between testosterone and aggression: A meta-analysis. *Aggression and Violent Behavior, 6,* 579–599.

Borduin, C. M., Schaeffer, C. M., & Ronis, S. T. (2003). Multisystemic treatment of serious antisocial behavior in adolescents. In C. A. Essau (Ed.), *Conduct and oppositional defiant disorders: Epidemiology, risk factors, and treatment* (pp. 299–318). Mahwah, NJ: Erlbaum.

Borges, B., Gigerenzer, G., & Goldstein, D. (1999). Can ignorance beat the stock market? In G. Gigerenzer, P. Todd, & the ABC Research Group (Eds.), *Simple heuristics that make us smart.* New York: Oxford University Press.

Borgida, E., & Fiske, S. T. (Eds.). (2007). *Psychological science in court: Beyond common knowledge.* Oxford, England: Blackwell.

Borkenau, P., Mauer, N., Riemann, R., Spinath, F. M., & Angleitner, A. (2004). Thin slices of behavior as cues of personality and intelligence. *Journal of Personality and Social Psychology, 86,* 599–614.

Borman, W. C., Hanson, M. A., & Hedge, J. W. (1997). Personnel selection. *Annual Review of Psychology, 48,* 299–337.

Borman, W. C., White, L. A., & Dorsey, D. W. (1995). Effects of ratee task performance and interpersonal factors on supervisor and peer performance ratings. *Journal of Applied Psychology, 80,* 168–177.

Bornstein, R. F. (1989). Exposure and affect: Overview and meta-analysis of research, 1968–1987. *Psychological Bulletin, 106,* 265–289.

Bornstein, R. F. (1994). Dependency as a social cue: A meta-analytic review of research on the dependency—helping relationship. *Journal of Research in Personality, 28,* 182–213.

Bornstein, R. F., & D'Agostino, P. R. (1992). Stimulus recognition and the mere exposure effect. *Journal of Personality and Social Psychology, 63,* 545–552.

Bosson, J. K., Johnson, A. B., Niederhoffer, K., & Swann, W. B., Jr. (2006). Interpersonal chemistry through negativity: Bonding by sharing negative attitudes about others. *Personal Relationships, 13,* 135–150.

Bottoms, B. L., & Davis, S. L. (1997). The creation of satanic ritual abuse. *Journal of Social and Clinical Psychology, 16,* 112–132.

Bowden, M. (2003, October 29). The persuaders. *The Observer,* pp. 28–40.

Bowlby, J. (1988). *A secure base.* New York: Basic Books.

Bowler, M. C., & Woehr, D. J. (2006). A meta-analytic evaluation of the impact of dimension and exercise factors on assessment center ratings. *Journal of Applied Psychology, 91,* 1114–1124.

Bowling, D., & Hoffman, D. (2000). Bringing peace into the room: The personal qualities of the mediator and their impact on the mediation. *Negotiation Journal, 16,* 5–28.

Boyes, A. D., & Fletcher, G. J. O. (2006). Meta-perceptions of bias in intimate relationships. *Journal of Personality and Social Psychology, 55,* 387-395.

Boysen, S. T., & Himes, G. T. (1999). Current issues and emerging theories in animal cognition. *Annual Review of Psychology, 50,* 683–705.

Bradbury, T. N. (Ed.). (1998). *The developmental course of marital dysfunction*. New York: Cambridge University Press.

Bradbury, T. N., & Fincham, F. D. (1992). Attributions and behavior in marital interaction. *Journal of Personality and Social Psychology, 63,* 613–628.

Bradfield, A. L., Wells, G. L., & Olson, E. A. (2002). The damaging effect of confirming feedback on the relation between eyewitness certainty and identification accuracy. *Journal of Applied Psychology, 87,* 112–120.

Brammer, G. L., Raleigh, M. J., & McGuire, M. T. (1994). Neurotransmitters and social status. In L. Ellis (Ed.), *Social stratification and socioeconomic inequality, Vol. 2: Reproductive and interpersonal aspects of dominance and status* (pp. 75–91). Westport, CT: Praeger/Greenwood.

Brandon, D. P., & Hollingshead, A. B. (2004). Transactive memory systems in organizations: Matching tasks, expertise, and people. *Organization Science, 15,* 633–644.

Branscombe, N. R., & Wann, D. L. (1994). Collective self-esteem consequences of outgroup derogation when a valued social identity is on trial. *European Journal of Social Psychology, 24,* 641–657.

Branscombe, N. R., Wann, D. L., Noel, J. G., & Coleman, J. (1993). In-group or out-group extremity: Importance of the threatened social identity. *Personality and Social Psychology Bulletin, 19,* 381–388.

Brauer, M., Judd, C. M., & Gliner, M. D. (1995). The effects of repeated expressions on attitude polarization during group discussions. *Journal of Personality and Social Psychology, 68,* 1014–1029.

Bray, R. M., Johnson, D., & Chilstrom, J. T., Jr. (1982). Social influence by group members with minority opinions: A comparison of Hollander & Moscovici. *Journal of Personality and Social Psychology, 43,* 78–88.

Bray, R. M., Struckman-Johnson, C., Osborne, M., McFarlane, J., & Scott, J. (1978). The effects of defendant status on decisions of student and community juries. *Social Psychology, 41,* 256–260.

Brean, H. (1958, March 31). What hidden sell is all about. *Life,* pp. 104–114.

Brehm, J. W. (1956). Post-decision changes in desirability of alternatives. *Journal of Abnormal and Social Psychology, 52,* 384–389.

Brehm, S. S., & Brehm, J. W. (1981). *Psychological reactance: A theory of freedom and control.* New York: Academic Press.

Bremner, J. G. (2002). The nature of imitation by infants. *Infant Behavior and Development, 25,* 65–67.

Brems, C., & Namyniuk, L. (2002). The relationship of childhood abuse history and substance use in an Alaska sample. *Substance Use and Misuse, 37,* 473–494.

Brendgen, M., Dionne, G., Girard, A., Boivin, M., Vitaro, F., & Pérusse, D. (2005). Examining genetic and environmental effects on social aggression: A study of 6-year-old twins. *Child Development, 76,* 930–946.

Bressan, P., & Martello, M. F. D. (2002). Talis Pater, Talis Filius: Perceived resemblance and the belief in genetic relatedness. *Psychological Science, 13,* 213–218.

Brett, J. M., & Gelfand, M. (2006). A cultural analysis of the underlying assumptions of negotiation theory. In L. L. Thompson (Ed.), *Negotiation theory and research* (pp. 173–201). Madison, CT: Psychological Press.

Brett, J. M., & Stroh, L. K. (2003). Working 61 plus hours a week: Why do managers do it? *Journal of Applied Psychology, 88,* 67–78.

Brett, J. M., Shapiro, D. L., & Lytle, A. L. (1998). Breaking the bonds of reciprocity in negotiations. *Academy of Management Journal, 41,* 410–424.

Brewer, M. B. (1988). A dual process model of impression formation. In T. K. Srull & R. S. Wyer, Jr. (Eds.), *A dual process model of impression formation. Advances in social cognition* (Vol. 1, pp. 1–36). Hillsdale, NJ: Erlbaum.

Brewer, M. B. (2000). Reducing prejudice through cross-categorization: Effects of multiple social identities. In S. Oskamp (Ed.), *Reducing prejudice and discrimination* (pp. 165–183). Mahwah, NJ: Erlbaum.

Brewer, M. B. (2003). Optimal distinctiveness, social identity, and the self. In M. R. Leary & J. P. Tangney (Eds.), *Handbook of self and identity* (pp. 480–491). New York: Guilford.

Brewer, M. B., & Brown, R. J. (1998). Intergroup relations. In D. T. Gilbert, S. T. Fiske, & G. Lindzey (Eds.), *The handbook of social psychology* (4th ed., Vol. 2, pp. 554–594). New York: McGraw-Hill.

Brewer, M. B., & Pickett, C. L. (1999). Distinctiveness motives as a source of the social self. In T. R. Tyler & R. M. Kramer (Eds.), *The psychology of the social self: Applied social research* (pp. 71–87). Mahwah, NJ: Erlbaum.

Brewer, M. B., Hong, Y., & Li, Q. (2004). Dynamic entitivity: Perceiving groups as actors. In C. Judd, V. Yzerbyt, & O. Corneille (Eds.), *The psychology of group perception: Contributions to the study of homogeneity, entitivity, and essentialism* (pp. 25–38). Philadelphia, PA: Psychology Press.

Brewer, N., & Williams, K. D. (Eds.). (2005). *Psychology and law: An empirical perspective.* New York: Guilford.

Brewer, N., Harvey, S., & Semmler, C. (2004). Improving comprehension of jury instructions with audio-visual presentation. *Applied Cognitive Psychology, 18,* 765–776.

Brickman, P., Coates, D., & Janoff-Bulman, R. J. (1978). Lottery winners and accident victims: Is happiness relative? *Journal of Personality and Social Psychology, 36,* 917–927.

Brockner, J. (1983). Low self-esteem and behavioral plasticity: Some implications. In L. Wheeler & P. Shaver (Eds.), *Review of personality and social psychology* (Vol. 4, pp. 237–271). Beverly Hills, CA: Sage.

Brockner, J., & Wiesenfeld, B. M. (1996). An integrative framework for explaining reactions to decisions: Interactive effects of outcomes and procedures. *Psychological Bulletin, 120,* 189–208.

Brodish, A. B., & Devine, P. G. (2005). The dynamics of prejudice, stereotyping, and intergroup relations: Intrapersonal and interpersonal processes. *Social Psychological Review, 7,* 54–70.

Brodkey, H. (1993, July 5). The central face. *The New Yorker,* p. 31.

Bronfenbrenner, U. (1961). The mirror-image in Soviet-American relations. *Journal of Social Issues, 17,* 45–56.

Brooks, P. (2000). *Troubling confessions.* Chicago: University of Chicago Press.

Brooks, R., & Meltzoff, A.N. (2002). The importance of eyes: How infants interpret adult looking behavior. *Developmental Psychology, 38,* 958–966.

Brooks, X. (2002, December 20). Natural Born Copycats: Eight murders have been blamed on Oliver Stone's evil 1995 film. *The Guardian (London),* p. 10.

Brown, E., Deffenbacher, K., & Sturgill, W. (1977). Memory for faces and the circumstances of encounter. *Journal of Applied Psychology, 62,* 311–318.

Brown, J. D. (2003). The self-enhancement motive in collectivistic cultures: The rumors of my death have been greatly exaggerated. *Journal of Cross-Cultural Psychology, 34,* 603–605.

Brown, J. D., & Dutton, K. A. (1995). The thrill of victory, the complexity of defeat: Self-esteem and people's emotional reactions to success and failure. *Journal of Personality and Social Psychology, 68,* 712–722.

Brown, J. D., & Smart, S. A. (1991). The self and social conduct: Linking self-representations to prosocial behavior. *Journal of Personality and Social Psychology, 60,* 368–375.

Brown, J. M. (2003). Eyewitness memory for arousing events: Putting things into context. *Applied Cognitive Psychology, 17,* 93–106.

Brown, R. (1986). *Social psychology* (2nd ed.). New York: Free Press.

Brown, R., & Kulik, J. (1977). Flashbulb memories. *Cognition, 5,* 73–99.

Brown, S. L., Nesse, R. M., Vinokur, A. D., & Smith, D. M. (2003). Providing social support may be more beneficial than receiving it: Results from a prospective study of mortality. *Psychological Science, 14,* 320–327.

Brown, S. M. (1999). Good Samaritan laws: Protection and limits. *RN, 62,* 65.

Brown, W. A. (1998, January). The placebo effect. *Scientific American,* pp. 90–95.

Brownstein, A., Read, S. J., & Simon, D. (2004). Bias at the racetrack: Effects of individual expertise and task importance on predecision reevaluation of alternatives. *Personality and Social Psychology Bulletin, 30,* 891–904.

Bruch, M. A., Gorsky, J. M., Collins, T. M., & Berger, P. A. (1989). Shyness and sociability examined: A multicomponent analysis. *Journal of Personality and Social Psychology, 57,* 904–915.

Bruck, M., & Ceci, S. J. (1999). The suggestibility of children's memory. *Annual Review of Psychology, 50,* 419–439.

Bruner, J. S., & Potter, M. C. (1964). Interference in visual recognition. *Science, 144,* 424–425.

Bruner, J. S., & Tagiuri, R. (1954). Person perception. In G. Lindzey (Ed.), *Handbook of social psychology* (Vol. 2, pp. 634–654). Reading, MA: Addison-Wesley.

Bryan, J. H., & Test, M. A. (1967). Models and helping: Naturalistic studies in aiding behavior. *Journal of Personality and Social Psychology, 6,* 400–407.

Buckhout, R. (1974, December). Eyewitness testimony. *Scientific American,* pp. 23–31.

Buhs, E. S., Ladd, G. W., & Herald, S. L. (2006). Peer exclusion and victimization: Processes that mediate the relation between peer group rejection and children's classroom engagement and achievement. *Journal of Educational Psychology, 98,* 1–13.

Buller, D. J. (2005). Evolutionary psychology: The emperor's new paradigm. *Trends in Cognitive Sciences, 9,* 277–283.

Burger, J. M. (1986). Increasing compliance by improving the deal: The that's-not-all technique. *Journal of Personality and Social Psychology, 51,* 277–283.

Burger, J. M. (1999). The foot-in-the-door compliance procedure: A multiple-process analysis and review. *Personality and Social Psychology Review, 3,* 303–325.

Burger, J. M., & Caldwell, D. F. (2003). The effects of monetary incentives and labeling on the foot-in-the-door effect: Evidence for a self-perception process. *Basic and Applied Social Psychology, 25,* 235–241.

Burger, J. M., & Cornelius, T. (2003). Raising the price of agreement: Public commitment and the low-ball compliance procedure. *Journal of Applied Social Psychology, 33,* 923–934.

Burger, J. M., & Petty, R. E. (1981). The low-ball compliance technique: Task or person commitment? *Journal of Personality and Social Psychology, 40,* 492–500.

Burger, J. M., Horita, M., Kinoshita, L., Roberts, K., & Vera, C. (1997). Effects of time on the norm of reciprocity. *Basic and Applied Social Psychology, 19,* 91–100.

Burger, J. M., Messian, N., Patel, S., del Prado, A., & Anderson, C. (2004). What a coincidence! The effects of incidental similarity on compliance. *Personality and Social Psychology Bulletin, 30,* 35–43.

Burman, B., & Margolin, G. (1992). An analysis of the association between marital relationships and health problems: An interactional perspective. *Psychological Bulletin, 112,* 39–63.

Burns, J. M. (1978). *Leadership.* New York: Harper & Row.

Burns, J. M. (2003). *Transformational leadership.* New York: Atlantic Monthly Press.

Burnstein, E., & Schul, Y. (1982). The informational basis of social judgments: The operations in forming an impression of another person. *Journal of Experimental Social Psychology, 18,* 217–234.

Burnstein, E., Crandall, C., & Kitayama, S. (1994). Some neo-Darwinian decision rules for altruism: Weighing cues for inclusive fitness as a function of the biological importance of the decision. *Journal of Personality and Social Psychology, 67,* 773–789.

Burt, M. C. (1980). Cultural myths and supports for rape. *Journal of Personality and Social Psychology, 38,* 217–230.

Bushman, B. J. (1988). The effects of apparel on compliance: A field experiment with a female authority figure. *Personality and Social Psychology Bulletin, 14,* 459–467.

Bushman, B. J. (1996). Individual differences in the extent and development of aggressive cognitive-associative networks. *Personality and Social Psychology Bulletin, 22,* 811–819.

Bushman, B. J. (1998). Priming effects of violent media on the accessibility of aggressive constructs in memory. *Personality and Social Psychology Bulletin, 24,* 537–545.

Bushman, B. J. (2002). Does venting anger feed or extinguish the flame? Catharsis, rumination, distraction, anger, and aggressive responding. *Personality and Social Psychology Bulletin, 28,* 724–731.

Bushman, B. J., & Cooper, H. M. (1990). Effects of alcohol on human aggression: An integrative research review. *Psychological Bulletin, 107,* 341–354.

Bushman, B. J., & Huesmann, L. R. (2001). Effects of televised violence on aggression. In D. G. Singer & J. L. Singer (Eds.), *Handbook of children and the media* (pp. 223–254). Thousand Oaks, CA: Sage.

Bushman, B. J., Wang, M. C., & Anderson, C. A. (2005). Is the curve relating temperature to aggression linear or curvilinear? Assaults and temperature in Minneapolis reexamined. *Journal of Personality and Social Psychology, 89,* 62–66.

Bushman, B. J., Wang, M. C., & Anderson, C. A. (2005). Reanalysis and perspective in the heat-aggression debate. *Journal of Personality and Social Psychology, 89,* 71–73.

Buss, A. H. (1980). *Self-consciousness and social anxiety.* San Francisco: Freeman.

Buss, D. M. (1989). Sex differences in human mate preferences: Evolutionary hypotheses tested in 37 cultures. *Behavioral and Brain Sciences, 12,* 1–14.

Buss, D. M. (1995). Evolutionary psychology: A new paradigm for psychological science. *Psychological Inquiry, 6,* 1–30.

Buss, D. M. (2000). *The dangerous passion: Why jealousy is as necessary as love and sex.* New York: Free Press.

Buss, D. M. (2003). *The evolution of desire: Strategies of human mating* (rev. ed.). New York: Basic Books.

Buss, D. M. (2004). *Evolutionary psychology: The new science of the mind* (2nd ed.). Boston: Allyn & Bacon.

Buss, D. M. (2005). *The murderer next door: Why the mind is designed to kill.* New York: Penguin.

Buss, D. M. (2007). The evolution of human mating strategies: Consequences for conflict and cooperation. In S. W. Gangestad & J. A. Simpson (Eds.), *The evolution of mind: Fundamental questions and controversies.* New York: Guilford.

Buss, D. M., & Duntley, J. D. (2005). The evolution of gender differences in aggression. In S. Fein, G. R. Goethals, & M. J. Sandstrom (Eds.), *Gender and aggression: Interdisciplinary perspectives.* Mahwah, NJ: Erlbaum.

Buss, D. M., & Malamuth, N. M. (Eds.). (1996). *Sex, power, conflict: Evolutionary and feminist perspectives.* New York: Oxford University.

Buss, D. M., & Schmitt, D. P. (1993). Sexual strategies theory: An evolutionary perspective on human mating. *Psychological Review, 100,* 204–232.

Buss, D. M., & Shackelford, T. K. (1997). From vigilance to violence: Mate retention tactics in married couples. *Journal of Personality and Social Psychology, 72,* 346–361.

Buss, D. M., Larsen, R. J., Westen, D., & Semmelroth, J. (1992). Sex differences in jealousy: Evolution, physiology, and psychology. *Psychological Science, 3,* 251–255.

Buysse, J. A. M., & Embser-Herbert, M. S. (2004). Constructions of gender in sport: An analysis of intercollegiate media guide cover photographs. *Gender and Society, 18,* 66–81.

Bylsma, W. H., Major, B., & Cozzarelli, C. (1995). The influence of legitimacy appraisals on the determinants of entitlement beliefs. *Basic and Applied Social Psychology, 17,* 223–237.

Byrne, D. (1971). *The attraction paradigm.* New York: Academic Press.

Byrne, D. (1997). An overview (and underview) of research and theory within the attraction paradigm. *Journal of Social and Personal Relationships, 14,* 417–431.

Byrne, D., & Clore, G. L. (1970). A reinforcement model of evaluative processes. *Personality: An International Journal, 1,* 103–128.

Byrne, D., Clore, G. L., & Smeaton, G. (1986). The attraction hypothesis: Do similar attitudes affect anything? *Journal of Personality and Social Psychology, 51,* 1167–1170.

Byrne, R. M. J., & McEleney, A. (2000). Counterfactual thinking about actions and failures to act. *Journal of Experimental Psychology: Learning, Memory, and Cognition, 26,* 1318–1331.

Cacioppo, J. T., & Petty, R. E. (1981). Electromyograms as measures of extent and affectivity of information processing. *American Psychologist, 36,* 441–456.

Cacioppo, J. T., & Petty, R. E. (1982). The need for cognition. *Journal of Personality and Social Psychology, 42,* 116–131.

Cacioppo, J. T., Crites, S. L., Berntson, G. G., & Coles, M. G. H. (1993). If attitudes affect how stimuli are processed, should they not affect the event-related brain potential? *Psychological Science, 4,* 108–112.

Cacioppo, J. T., Gardner, W. L., & Bernston, G. G. (1997). Beyond bipolar conceptualizations and measures: The case of attitudes and evaluative space. *Personality and Social Psychology Review, 1,* 3–25.

Cacioppo, J. T., Hawkley, L. C., & Bernston, G. G. (2003). The anatomy of loneliness. *Current Directions in Psychological Science, 12,* 71–74.

Cacioppo, J. T., Hawkley, L. C., Berntson, G. G., Ernst, J. M., Gibbs, A. C., Stickgold, R., & Hobson, J. A. (2002). Lonely days invade the nights: Social modulation of sleep efficiency. *Psychological Science, 13,* 385–388.

Cacioppo, J. T., Hughes, M. E., Waite, L. J., Hawkley, L. C., & Thisted, R. A. (2006). Loneliness as a specific risk factor for depressive symptoms: Cross-sectional and longitudinal analyses. *Psychology and Aging, 21,* 140–151.

Cacioppo, J. T., Petty, R. E., & Morris, K. (1983). Effects of need for cognition on message evaluation, recall, and persuasion. *Journal of Personality and Social Psychology, 45,* 805–818.

Cacioppo, J. T., Petty, R. E., Feinstein, J. A., & Jarvis, W. B. G. (1996). Dispositional differences in cognitive motivation: The life and times of individuals varying in need for cognition. *Psychological Bulletin, 119,* 197–253.

Cacioppo, J. T., Petty, R. E., Losch, M. E., & Kim, H. S. (1986). Electromyographic activity over facial muscle regions can differentiate the valence and intensity of affective reactions. *Journal of Personality and Social Psychology, 50,* 260–268.

Cacioppo, J. T., Priester, J. R., & Bernston, G. G. (1993). Rudimentary determinants of attitudes. II. Arm flexion and extension have differential effects on attitudes. *Journal of Personality and Social Psychology, 65,* 5–17.

Callaway, M. R., Marriott, R. G., & Esser, J. K. (1985). Effects of dominance on group decision making: Toward a stress-reduction explanation of groupthink. *Journal of Personality and Social Psychology, 49,* 949–952.

Camara, W. J., & Schneider, D. L. (1994). Integrity tests: Facts and unresolved issues. *American Psychologist, 49,* 112–119.

Cameron, J., & Pierce, W. D. (1994). Reinforcement, reward, and intrinsic motivation: A meta-analysis. *Review of Educational Research, 64,* 363–423.

Campbell, A. (1999). Staying alive: Evolution, culture, and women's intrasexual aggression. *Behavioral and Brain Sciences, 22,* 203–252.

Campbell, D. J., & Lee, C. (1988). Self-appraisal in performance evaluation: Development versus evaluation. *Academy Management Review, 13,* 302–313.

Campbell, J., & Stasser, G. (2006). The influence of time and task demonstrability on decision-making in computer-mediated and face-to-face groups. *Small Group Research, 37,* 271–294.

Campion, M. A., Pursell, E. D., & Brown, B. K. (1988). Structured interviewing: Raising the psychometric properties of the employment interview. *Personnel Psychology, 41,* 25–42.

Cannon, W. B. (1932). *The wisdom of the body.* New York: Norton.

Caporael, L. (2004). Bones and stones: Selection for sociality. *Journal of Cultural and Evolutionary Psychology, 2,* 195–211.

Capozza, D., & Brown, R. (2000). *Social identity processes: Trends in theory and research.* London: Sage.

Capozza, D., Voci, A., & Licciardello, O. (2000). Individualism, collectivism, and social identity theory. In D. Capozza & R. Brown (Eds.), *Social identity processes: Trends in theory and research.* London: Sage.

Cárdenas, R. A., & Harris, L. J. (2006). Symmetrical decorations enhance the attractiveness of faces and abstract designs. *Evolution and Human Behavior, 27,* 1–18.

Carey, B. (1997, April). Don't face stress alone. *Health,* pp. 74–76, 78.

Carless, S. A., & De-Paola, C. (2000). The measurement of cohesion in work teams. *Small Group Research, 31,* 71–88.

Carlo, G., Koller, S. H., Eisenberg, N., Da Silva, M. S., & Frohlich, C. B. (1996). A cross-national study on the relations among prosocial moral reasoning, gender role orientations, and prosocial behaviors. *Developmental Psychology, 32,* 231–240.

Carlo, G., Okun, M. A., Knight, G. P., & de Guzman, M. R. T. (2005). The interplay of traits and motives on volunteering: Agreeableness, extraversion and prosocial value motivation. *Personality and Individual Differences, 38,* 1293–1305.

Carlsmith, K. M. (2006). The roles of retribution and utility in determining punishment. *Journal of Experimental Social Psychology, 42,* 437–451.

Carlsmith, K. M., Darley, J. M., & Robinson, P. H. (2002). Why do we punish? Deterrence and just deserts as motives for punishment. *Journal of Personality and Social Psychology, 83,* 284–299.

Carlson, M., & Miller, N. (1987). Explanation of the relation between negative mood and helping. *Psychological Bulletin, 102,* 91–108.

Carnagey, N. L., Bushman, B. J., & Anderson, C. A. (2007). The effect of video game violence on physiological desensitization and helping behavior. *Journal of Experimental Social Psychology,* in press.

Carnegie, D. (1936). *How to win friends and influence people.* New York: Pocket Books. (Reprinted in 1972)

Carnevale, P. J. (2002). Mediating from strength. In J. Bercovitch (Ed.), *Studies in international mediation: Essays in honor of Jeffrey Z. Rubin* (pp. 25–40). London: Palgrave-MacMillan.

Carpenter, S. (2005). The rich science of economic choice. *APS Observer, 18,* No. 4, 21–27.

Carr, J. L., & VanDeusen, K. M. (2004). Risk factors for male sexual aggression on college campuses. *Journal of Family Violence, 19,* 279–289.

Carr, S. C., & MacLachlan, M. (1998). Psychology in developing countries: Reassessing its impact. *Psychology and Development Societies, 10,* 1–20.

Carron, A. V., Colman, M. M., Wheeler, J., & Stevens, D. (2002). Cohesion and performance in sport: A meta analysis. *Journal of Sport and Exercise Psychology, 24,* 168–188.

Carter, S. L. (1991). *Reflections of an affirmative action baby.* New York: Basic Books.

Cartwright, D. (1971). Risk taking by individuals and groups: An assessment of research employing choice dilemmas. *Journal of Personality and Social Psychology, 20,* 245–261.

Cartwright, D. (1979). Contemporary social psychology in historical perspective. *Social Psychology Quarterly, 42,* 82–93.

Cartwright, D., & Zander, A. (1960). Group cohesiveness: Introduction. In D. Cartwright & A. Zander (Eds.), *Group dynamics: Research and theory* (2nd ed., pp. 69–94). Evanston, IL: Row, Peterson.

Carver, C. S., & Scheier, M. F. (1981). *Attention and self-regulation: A control-theory approach to human behavior.* New York: Springer-Verlag.

Carver, C. S., & Scheier, M. F. (1990). Origins and functions of positive and negative affect: A control-process view. *Psychological Review, 97,* 19–35.

Carver, C. S., & Scheier, M. F. (1998). *On the self-regulation of behavior.* New York: Cambridge University Press.

Carver, C. S., Harris, S. D., Lehman, J. M., Durel, L. A., Antoni, M. H., Spencer, S. M., & Pozo-Kaderman, C. (2000). How important is the perception of personal control? Studies of early stage breast cancer patients. *Personality and Social Psychology Bulletin, 26,* 139–149.

Carver, C. S., Scheier, M. F., & Weintraub, J. K. (1989). Assessing coping strategies: A theoretically based approach. *Journal of Personality and Social Psychology, 56,* 267–283.

Case, R. B., Moss, A. J., Case, N., McDermott, M., & Eberly, S. (1992). Living alone after myocardial infarction: Impact on prognosis. *Journal of the American Medical Association, 267,* 515–519.

Cashdan, E. (2003). Hormones and competitive aggression in women. *Aggressive Behavior, 29,* 107–115.

Caspi, A. (2000). The child is the father of man: Personality continuities from childhood to adulthood. *Journal of Personality and Social Psychology, 78,* 158–172.

Cassidy, J., & Shaver, P. R. (Eds.). (1999). *Handbook of attachment: Theory, research, and clinical applications.* New York: Guilford Press.

Cassidy, J., Kirsh, S. J., Scolton, K. L., & Parke, R. D. (1996). Attachment and representations of peer relationships. *Developmental Psychology, 32,* 892–904.

Castano, E., & Giner-Sorolla, R. (2006). Not quite human: Infrahumanization in response to collective responsibility for intergroup killing. *Journal of Personality and Social Psychology, 90,* 804–818.

Castano, E., Sacchi, S., & Gries, P. H. (2003). The perception of the other in international relations: Evidence for the polarizing effect of entitativity. *Political Psychology, 24,* 449–468.

Castano, E., Yzerbyt, V. Y., Bourguignon, D., & Seron, E. (2002). Who may enter? The impact of in-group identification on ingroup/out-group categorization. *Journal of Experimental Social Psychology, 38,* 315–322.

Castano, E., Yzerbyt, V. Y., Paladino, M. P., & Sacchi, S. (2002). I belong, therefore, I exist: Ingroup identification, ingroup entitativity, and ingroup bias. *Personality and Social Psychology Bulletin, 28,* 135–143.

Castelli, L., Arcuri, L., & Zogmaister, C. (2003). Perceiving ingroup members who use stereotypes: Implicit conformity and similarity. *European Journal of Social Psychology, 33,* 163–175.

Castelli, L., Zecchini, A., Deamicis, L., & Sherman, S. J. (2005). The impact of implicit prejudice about the elderly on the reaction to stereotype confirmation and disconfirmation. *Current Psychology: Developmental, Learning, Personality, Social, 24,* 134–146.

Cate, R. M., & Lloyd, S. A. (1988). Courtship. In S. Duck (Ed.), *Handbook of personal relationships: Theory, research, and interventions* (pp. 409–427). New York: Wiley.

Cate, R. M., & Lloyd, S. A. (1992). *Courtship.* Newbury Park, CA: Sage.

Cavaliere, F. (1995, August). Parents killing kids: A nation's shame. *APA Monitor,* p. 34.

Ceci, S. J., Ross, D. F., & Toglia, M. P. (1987). Suggestibility of children's memory: Psycholegal implications. *Journal of Experimental Psychology, 116,* 38–49.

Cesario, J., Plaks, J. E., & Higgins, E. T. (2006). Automatic social behavior as motivated preparation to interact. *Journal of Personality and Social Psychology, 90,* 893–910.

Cha, A. E. (2005, March 27). Employers relying on personality tests to screen applicants. *Washington Post,* p. A01.

Chaiken, S. (1979). Communicator physical attractiveness and persuasion. *Journal of Personality and Social Psychology, 37,* 1387–1397.

Chaiken, S. (1980). Heuristic versus systematic information processing and the use of source versus message cues in persuasion. *Journal of Personality and Social Psychology, 39,* 752–766.

Chaiken, S. (1987). The heuristic model of persuasion. In M. P. Zanna, J. M. Olson, & C. P. Herman (Eds.), *Social influence: The Ontario symposium* (Vol. 5, pp. 3–39). Hillsdale, NJ: Erlbaum.

Chaiken, S., & Baldwin, M. W. (1981). Affective-cognitive consistency and the effect of salient behavioral information on the self-perception of attitudes. *Journal of Personality and Social Psychology, 41,* 1–12.

Chaiken, S., & Maheswaran, D. (1994). Heuristic processing can bias systematic processing: Effects of source credibility, argument ambiguity, and task importance on attitude judgment. *Journal of Personality and Social Psychology, 66,* 460–473.

Chan, D. K., & Fishbein, M. (1993). Determinants of college women's intentions to tell their partners to use condoms. *Journal of Applied Social Psychology, 23,* 1455–1470.

Chandrashekaran, M., Walker, B. A., Ward, J. C., & Reingen, P. H. (1996). Modeling individual preference evolution and choice in a dynamic group setting. *Journal of Marketing Research, 33,* 211–223.

Chang, A., Bordia, P., & Duck, J. (2003). Punctuated equilibrium and linear progression: Toward a new understanding of group development. *Academy of Management Journal, 46,* 106–117.

Chao, G. T., & Moon, H. (2005). The cultural mosaic: A metatheory for understanding the complexity of culture. *Journal of Applied Psychology, 90,* 1128–1140.

Chapdelaine, A., & Griffin, S. F. (1997). Beliefs of guilt and recommended sentence as a function of juror bias in the O. J. Simpson trial. *Journal of Social Issues, 53,* 477–485.

Chapdelaine, A., Kenny, D. A., & LaFontana, K. M. (1994). Matchmaker, matchmaker, can you make me a match? Predicting liking between two unacquainted persons. *Journal of Personality and Social Psychology, 67,* 83–91.

Chapman, D. S., Uggerslev, K. L., & Webster, J. (2003). Applicant reactions to face-to-face and technology-mediated interviews: A field investigation. *Journal of Applied Psychology, 88,* 944–953.

Chapman, L. J. (1967). Illusory correlation in observational report. *Journal of Verbal Learning and Verbal Behavior, 6,* 151–155.

Chartrand, T. L., & Bargh, J. A. (1999). The chameleon effect: The perception-behavior link and social interaction. *Journal of Personality and Social Psychology, 76,* 893–910.

Chasteen, A. L., Bhattacharyya, S., Horhota, M., Tam, R., & Hasher, L. (2005). How feelings of stereotype threat influence older adults' memory performance. *Experimental Aging Research, 31,* 235–260.

Chatman, C. M., & von Hippel, W. (2001). Attributional mediation of in-group bias. *Journal of Experimental Social Psychology, 37,* 267–272.

Cheek, J. M., & Melchior, L. A. (1990). Shyness, self-esteem, and self-consciousness. In H. Leitenberg (Ed.), *Handbook of social and evaluation anxiety.* New York: Plenum.

Chemers, M. M., Hays, R. B., Rhodewalt, F., & Wysocki, J. (1985). A person-environment analysis of job stress: A contingency model explanation. *Journal of Personality and Social Psychology, 49,* 628–635.

Chen, F. F., & Kenrick, D. T. (2002). Repulsion or attraction: Group membership and assumed attitude similarity. *Journal of Personality and Social Psychology, 83,* 111–125.

Chen, M., & Bargh, J. A. (1997). Nonconscious behavioral confirmation processes: The self-fulfilling consequences of automatic stereotype activation. *Journal of Experimental Social Psychology, 33,* 541–560.

Chen, S., & Chaiken, S. (1999). The heuristic-systematic model in its broader context. In S. Chaiken & Y. Trope (Eds.), *Dual-process theories in social psychology* (pp. 73–96). New York: Guilford.

Chen, S., Chen, K. Y., & Shaw, L. (2004). Self-verification motives at the collective level of self-definition. *Journal of Personality and Social Psychology, 86,* 77–94.

Chen, Y.-R., Brockner, J., & Chen, X.-P. (2002). Individual-collective primacy and ingroup favoritism: Enhancement and protection effects. *Journal of Experimental Social Psychology, 38,* 482–491.

Cheng, C. M., & Chartrand, T. L. (2003). Self-monitoring without awareness: Using mimicry as a nonconscious affiliation strategy. *Journal of Personality and Social Psychology, 85,* 1170–1179.

Cheng, P. W., & Novick, L. R. (1990). A probabilistic contrast model of causal induction. *Journal of Personality and Social Psychology, 58,* 545–567.

Cherry, E. C. (1953). Some experiments on the recognition of speech, with one and with two ears. *Journal of the Acoustical Society of America, 25,* 975–979.

Cheryan, S., & Bodenhausen, G. V. (2000). When positive stereotypes threaten intellectual performance: The psychological hazards of "model minority" status. *Psychological Science, 11,* 399–402.

Chesler, P., & Goodman, E. J. (1976). *Women, money, and power.* New York: Morrow.

Chidambaram, L., & Bostrom, R. P. (1997). Group development (I): A review and synthesis of development models. *Group Decision and Negotiation, 6,* 159–187.

Chiu, C., Morris, M. W., Hong, Y., & Menon, T. (2000). Motivated cultural cognition: The impact of implicit cultural theories on dispositional attribution varies as a function of need for closure. *Journal of Personality and Social Psychology, 78,* 247–259.

Chivers, M. L., Rieger, G., Latty, E., & Bailey, J. M. (2004). A sex difference in the specificity of sexual arousal. *Psychological Science, 15,* 736–744.

Choi, I., Nisbett, R. E., & Norenzayan, A. (1999). Causal attribution across cultures: Variation and universality. *Psychological Bulletin, 125,* 47–63.

Choi, J. N., & Kim, M. U. (1999). The organizational application of groupthink and its limitations in organizations. *Journal of Applied Psychology, 84,* 297–306.

Choi, S. M., Lee, W-N., & Kim, H-J. (2005). Lessons from the rich and famous: A cross-cultural comparison of celebrity endorsement in advertising. *Journal of Advertising, 34,* 85–98.

Christensen, A. J., Turner, C. W., Smith, T. W., Holman, J. M., Jr., & Gregory, M. C. (1991). Health locus of control and depression in end-stage renal disease. *Journal of Counseling and Clinical Psychology, 59,* 419–424.

Christensen, A., & Heavey, C. L. (1993). Gender differences in marital conflict: The demand/withdraw interaction pattern. In S. Oskamp & M. Costanzo (Eds.), *Gender issues in contemporary society* (pp. 113–141). Newbury Park, CA: Sage.

Christensen, L. (1988). Deception in psychological research: When is its use justified? *Personality and Social Psychology Bulletin, 14,* 664–675.

Christianson, S. (1992). Emotional stress and eyewitness memory: A critical review. *Psychological Bulletin, 112,* 284–309.

Chu, T. Q., Seery, M. D., Ence, W. A., Holman, E. A., & Silver, R. C. (2007). Ethnicity and gender in the face of a terrorist attack: A national longitudinal study of immediate responses and outcomes two years after September 11. *Basic and Applied Social Psychology,* in press.

Chun, W. Y., & Lee, H. K. (1999). Effects of the difference in the amount of group preferential information on illusory correlation. *Personality and Social Psychology Bulletin, 25,* 1463–1475.

Cialdini, R. B. (2001). *Influence: Science and practice* (4th ed.). Needham Heights, MA: Allyn & Bacon.

Cialdini, R. B. (2003). Crafting normative messages to protect the environment. *Current Directions in Psychological Science, 12,* 105–109.

Cialdini, R. B. (2007). *Influence: The psychology of persuasion.* New York: HarperCollins.

Cialdini, R. B., & Ascani, K. (1976). Test of a concession procedure for inducing verbal, behavioral, and further compliance with a request to give blood. *Journal of Applied Psychology, 61,* 295–300.

Cialdini, R. B., & De Nicholas, M. E. (1989). Self-presentation by association. *Journal of Personality and Social Psychology, 57,* 626–631.

Cialdini, R. B., & Fultz, J. (1990). Interpreting the negative mood-helping literature via "mega" analysis: A contrary view. *Psychological Bulletin, 107,* 210–214.

Cialdini, R. B., & Goldstein, N. J. (2004). Social influence: Compliance and conformity. *Annual Review of Psychology, 55,* 591–621.

Cialdini, R. B., Baumann, D. J., & Kenrick, D. T. (1981). Insights from sadness: A three-step model of the development of altruism as hedonism. *Developmental Review, 1,* 207–223.

Cialdini, R. B., Borden, R. J., Thorne, A., Walker, M. R., Freeman, S., & Sloan, L. R. (1976). Basking in reflected glory: Three (football) field studies. *Journal of Personality and Social Psychology, 34,* 366–375.

Cialdini, R. B., Cacioppo, J. T., Bassett, R., & Miller, J. A. (1978). Low-ball procedure for producing compliance: Commitment then cost. *Journal of Personality and Social Psychology, 36,* 463–476.

Cialdini, R. B., Kallgren, C. A., & Reno, R. R. (1991). A focus theory of normative conduct: A theoretical refinement and reevaluation of the role of norms in human behavior. *Advances in Experimental Social Psychology, 24,* 201–234.

Cialdini, R. B., Reno, R. R., & Kallgren, C. A. (1990). A focus theory of normative conduct: Recycling the concept of norms to reduce littering in public places. *Journal of Personality and Social Psychology, 58,* 1015–1026.

Cialdini, R. B., Schaller, M., Houlihan, D., Arps, K., Fultz, J., & Beaman, A. L. (1987). Empathy-based helping: Is it selflessly or selfishly motivated? *Journal of Personality and Social Psychology, 52,* 749–758.

Cialdini, R. B., Trost, M. R., & Newsom, J. T. (1995). Preference for consistency: The development of a valid measure and the discovery of surprising behavioral implications. *Journal of Personality and Social Psychology, 69,* 318–328.

Cialdini, R. B., Vincent, J. E., Lewis, S. K., Catalan, J., Wheeler, D., & Darby, B. L. (1975). Reciprocal concessions procedure for inducing compliance: The door-in-the-face technique. *Journal of Personality and Social Psychology, 31,* 206–215.

Cioffi, D., & Holloway, J. (1993). Delayed costs of suppressed pain. *Journal of Personality and Social Psychology, 64,* 274–282.

Clark, M. S. (1983). Reactions to aid in communal and exchange relationships. In J. D. Fisher, A. Nadler, & B. DePaulo. (Eds.), *New directions in helping: Vol. 1. Recipient reactions to aid* (pp. 281–304). New York: Academic Press.

Clark, M. S. (1984). Record keeping in two types of relationships. *Journal of Personality and Social Psychology, 47,* 549–557.

Clark, M. S., & Mills, J. (1979). Interpersonal attraction in exchange and communal relationships. *Journal of Personality and Social Psychology, 37,* 12–24.

Clark, M. S., & Mills, J. (1993). The difference between communal and exchange relationships: What it is and is not. *Personality and Social Psychology Bulletin, 19,* 684–691.

Clark, R. (2006). Perceived racism and vascular reactivity in black college women: Moderating effects of seeking social support. *Health Psychology, 25,* 20–25.

Clark, R. D., III, & Maass, A. (1990). The effects of majority size on minority influence. *European Journal of Psychology, 20,* 99–117.

Clark, R. D., III, & Word, L. E. (1972). Why don't bystanders help? Because of ambiguity? *Journal of Personality and Social Psychology, 24,* 392–400.

Clark, R. D., III. (2001). Effects of majority defection and multiple minority sources on minority influence. *Group Dynamics, 5,* 57–62.

Clark, S.E. (2005). A re-examination of the effects of biased lineup instructions in eyewitness identification. *Law and Human Behavior, 29,* 395–424.

Cleare, A. J., & Bond, A. J. (2000). Experimental evidence that the aggressive effect of tryptophan depletion is mediated via the 5-HT-sub-1A receptor. *Psychopharmacology, 147,* 439–441.

Clifford, M. M., & Walster, E. H. (1973). The effect of physical attractiveness on teacher expectations. *Sociology of Education, 46,* 248–258.

Cochran, S. D., Mays, V. M., Ciarletta, J., Caruso, C., & Mallon, D. (1992). Efficacy of the theory of reasoned action in predicting AIDS-related sexual risk reduction among gay men. *Journal of Applied Social Psychology, 22,* 1481–1501.

Coe, C. L. (1993). Psychosocial factors and immunity in nonhuman primates: A review. *Psychosomatic Medicine, 55,* 298–308.

Cohen, D., & Nisbett, R. E. (1997). Field experiments examining the culture of honor: The role of institutions in perpetuating norms about violence. *Personality and Social Psychology Bulletin, 23,* 1188–1199.

Cohen, D., Nisbett, R. E., Bowdle, B. F., & Schwarz, N. (1996). Insult, aggression, and the southern culture of honor: An "experimental ethnography." *Journal of Personality and Social Psychology, 70,* 945–960.

Cohen, D., Vandello, J., & Rantilla, A. K. (1998). The sacred and the social: Cultures of honor and violence. In P. Gilbert & B. Andrews (Eds.), *Shame: Interpersonal behavior, psychopathology, and culture* (pp. 261–282). Cambridge: Oxford University Press.

Cohen, G. L. (2003). Party over policy: The dominating impact of group influence on political beliefs. *Journal of Personality and Social Psychology, 85,* 808–822.

Cohen, G. L., Garcia, J., Apfel, N., & Master, A. (2006). Reducing the racial achievement gap: A social-psychological intervention. *Science, 313,* 1307–1310.

Cohen, G. L., Steele, C. M., & Ross, L. D. (1999). The mentor's dilemma: Providing critical feedback across the racial divide. *Personality and Social Psychology Bulletin, 25,* 1302–1318.

Cohen, S., & Herbert, T. (1996). Health psychology: Psychological factors and physical disease from the perspective of human psychoneuroimmunology. *Annual Review of Psychology, 47,* 113–142.

Cohen, S., & Williamson, G. (1991). Stress and infectious disease in humans. *Psychological Bulletin, 109,* 5–24.

Cohen, S., Doyle, W. J., Turner, R., Alper, C. M., & Skoner, D. P. (2006). Sociability and susceptibility to the common cold. *Psychological Science, 14,* 389–395.

Cohen, S., Frank, E., Doyle, W. J., Skoner, D. P., Rabin, B. S., & Gwaltney, J. M. (1998). Types of stressors that increase susceptibility to the common cold in healthy adults. *Health Psychology, 17,* 214–223.

Cohen, S., Kessler, R. C., & Gordon, L. U. (1995). *Measuring stress: A guide for health and social scientists.* New York: Oxford University Press.

Cohen, S., Tyrrell, D. A. J., & Smith, A. P. (1993). Negative life events, perceived stress, negative affect, and susceptibility to the common cold. *Journal of Personality and Social Psychology, 64,* 131–140.

Cohen, S., Underwood, L. G., & Gottlieb, B. H. (Eds.). (2000). *Social support measurement and intervention: A guide for health and social scientists.* New York: Oxford University Press.

Cohen-Kettenis, P. T., & Van Goozen, S. H. M. (1997). Sex reassignment of adolescent transsexuals: A follow-up study. *Journal of the American Academy of Child and Adolescent psychiatry, 36,* 263–271.

Cohn, E. G., & Rotton, J. (1997). Assault as a function of time and temperature: A moderator-variable time-series analysis. *Journal of Personality and Social Psychology, 72,* 1322–1334.

Cole, S. W., Kemeny, M. E., Taylor, S. E., Visscher, B. R., & Fahey, J. L. (1996). Accelerated course of human immunodeficiency virus infection in gay men who conceal their homosexual identity. *Psychosomatic Medicine, 58,* 219–231.

Cole, T. B. (2006). Rape at U.S. colleges often fueled by alcohol. *Journal of the American Medical Association, 296,* 504–505.

Collins, N. L., & Feeney, B. C. (2000). A safe haven: An attachment theory perspective on support seeking and caregiving in intimate relationships. *Journal of Personality and Social Psychology, 78,* 1053–1073.

Collins, N. L., & Miller, L. C. (1994). Self-disclosure and liking: a meta-analytic review. *Psychological Bulletin, 116,* 457–475.

Coltraine, S., & Messineo, M. (2000). The perpetuation of subtle prejudice: Race and gender imagery in 1990s television advertising. *Sex Roles, 42,* 363–389.

Colvin, C. R., Block, J., & Funder, D. C. (1995). Overly positive self-evaluations and personality: Negative implications for mental health. *Journal of Personality and Social Psychology, 68,* 1152–1162.

Conger, R. D., Reuter, M. A., & Elder, G. H., Jr. (1999). Couple resilience to economic pressure. *Journal of Personality and Social Psychology, 76,* 54–71.

Conger, R. D., Wallace, L. E., Sun, Y., Simons, R. L., McLoyd, V. C., & Brody, G. H. (2002). Economic pressure in African American families: A replication and extension of the family stress model. *Developmental Psychology, 38,* 179–193.

Conner, M., Norman, P., & Bell, R. (2002). The theory of planned behavior and healthy eating. *Health Psychology, 21,* 194–201.

Connors, E., Lundregan, T., Miller, N., & McEwen, T. (1996). *Convicted by juries, exonerated by science: Case studies in the use of DNA evidence to establish innocence after trial.* Washington, DC: U.S. Department of Justice.

Conway, L. G., III, & Schaller, M. (2005). When authorities' commands backfire: Attributions about consensus and effects on deviant decision making. *Journal of Personality and Social Psychology, 89,* 311–326.

Conway, J. M., & Huffcutt, A. I. (1997). Psychometric properties of multisource performance ratings: A meta-analysis of subordinate, supervisor, peer, and self-ratings. *Human Performance, 10,* 331–360.

Conway, L. G., Ryder, A. G., Tweed, R. G., & Sokol, B. W. (2001). Intranational cultural variation: Exploring further implications of collectivism within the United States. *Journal of Cross-Cultural Psychology, 32,* 681–697.

Conway, M. A. (1995). *Flashbulb memories.* Mahwah, NJ: Erlbaum.

Conway, M. A., & Pleydell-Pearce, C. W. (2000). The construction of autobiographical memories in the self-memory system. *Psychological Review, 107,* 261–288.

Cook, S. W. (1985). Experimenting on social issues: The case of school desegregation. *American Psychologist, 40,* 452–460.

Cook, S. W., & Pelfrey, M. (1985). Reactions to being helped in cooperating interracial groups: A context effect. *Journal of Personality and Social Psychology, 49,* 1231–1245.

Cook, T. D., & Campbell, D. T. (1979). *Quasi-experimentation: Design and analysis issues for field settings.* Chicago: Rand McNally.

Cooke, C. A. (2004). Young people's attitudes towards guns in America, Great Britain, and Western Australia. *Aggressive Behavior, 30,* 93–104.

Cooley, C. H. (1902). *Human nature and the social order.* New York: Schocken Books. (Reprinted in 1964)

Cooper, J., & Fazio, R. H. (1984). A new look at dissonance theory. In L. Berkowitz (Ed.), *Advances in experimental social psychology* (Vol. 17, pp. 229–267). New York: Academic Press.

Cooper, J., & Neuhaus, I. M. (2000). The "hired gun" effect: Assessing the effect of pay, frequency of testifying, and credentials on the perception of expert testimony. *Law and Human Behavior, 24,* 149–171.

Cooper, J., Zanna, M. P., & Goethals, G. R. (1974). Mistreatment of an esteemed other as a consequence affecting dissonance reduction. *Journal of Experimental Social Psychology, 10,* 224–233.

Cooper, M. L., Frone, M. R., Russell, M., & Mudar, P. (1995). Drinking to regulate positive and negative emotions: A motivational model of alcohol use. *Journal of Personality and Social Psychology, 69,* 990–1005.

Cooper, W. H. (1981). Ubiquitous halo. *Psychological Bulletin, 90,* 218–224.

Coopersmith, S. (1967). *The antecedents of self-esteem.* San Francisco: Freeman.

Copeland, J. T. (1994). Prophecies of power: Motivational implications of social power for behavioral confirmation. *Journal of Personality and Social Psychology, 67,* 264–277.

Corneille, O., Yzerbyt, V. Y., Rogier, A., & Buidin, G. (2001). Threat and the group attribution error: When threat elicits judgments of extremity and homogeneity. *Personality and Social Psychology Bulletin, 27,* 437–446.

Correll, J., Park, B., Judd, C. M., & Wittenbrink, B. (2002). The police officer's dilemma: Using ethnicity to disambiguate potentially threatening individuals. *Journal of Personality and Social Psychology, 83,* 1314–1329.

Correll, J., Park, B., Judd, C. M., Wittenbrink, B., Sadler, M. S., & Keesee, T. (2007). Across the Thin Blue Line: Police officers and racial bias in the decision to shoot. *Journal of Personality and Social Psychology,* in press.

Correll, J., Urland, G. R., & Ito, T. A. (2006). Event-related potentials and the decision to shoot: The role of threat perception and cognitive control. *Journal of Experimental Social Psychology, 42,* 120–128.

Corrigan, P. (2006, October 30). If a heart stops, will your office be prepared? *St. Louis Post-Dispatch,* p. H1.

Cose, E. (1997). *Color-blind: Seeing beyond race in a race-obsessed world.* New York: HarperCollins.

Cosmides, L., & Tooby, J. (2004). *What is evolutionary psychology? Explaining the new science of the mind.* New Haven, CT: Yale University Press.

Costa, R. M. (1982, March 6). Latin and Greek are good for you. *New York Times,* p. 23.

Costanzo, M. (1997). *Just revenge: Costs and consequences of the death penalty.* New York: St. Martin's Press.

Costanzo, M. (2004). *Psychology applied to law.* Belmont, CA: Wadsworth/Thomson.

Cota, A. A., Evans, C. R., Dion, K. L., Kilik, L., & Longman, R. S. (1995). The structure of group cohesion. *Personality and Social Psychology Bulletin, 21,* 572–580.

Cottrell, N. B., Wack, D. L., Sekerak, G. J., & Rittle, R. H. (1968). Social facilitation of dominant responses by the presence of an audience and the mere presence of others. *Journal of Personality and Social Psychology, 9,* 245–250.

Cousins, N. (1989). *Head first: The biology of hope.* New York: Dutton.

Covington, M. V. (2000). Intrinsic versus extrinsic motivation in schools: A reconciliation. *Current Directions in Psychological Science, 9,* 22–25.

Cowan, C. L., Thompson, W. C., & Ellsworth, P. C. (1984). The effects of death qualification on jurors' predisposition to convict and on the quality of deliberation. *Law and Human Behavior, 8,* 53–80.

Cowley, G. (1996, June 3). The biology of beauty. *Newsweek,* pp. 61–69.

Cox, M., & Tanford, S. (1989). An alternative method of capital jury selection. *Law and Human Behavior, 13,* 167–183.

Cox, T. H., Lobel, S. A., & McLeod, P. L. (1991). Effects of ethnic group cultural differences on cooperative and competitive behavior on a group task. *Academy of Management Journal, 34,* 827–847.

Coyne, J. C. (1994). Self-reported distress: Analog or ersatz depression? *Psychological Bulletin, 116,* 29–45.

Coyne, S. M., & Archer, J. (2004). Indirect aggression in the media: A content analysis of British television programs. *Aggressive Behavior, 30,* 254–271.

Coyne, S. M., Archer, J., & Eslea, M. (2004). Cruel intentions on television and in real life: Can viewing indirect aggression increase viewers' subsequent indirect aggression? *Journal of Experimental Child Psychology, 88,* 234–253.

Coyne, S. M., Archer, J., & Eslea, M. (2006). "We're not friends anymore! Unless . . .": The frequency and harmfulness of indirect, relational, and social aggression. *Aggressive Behavior, 32,* 294–307.

Craig, S. B., & Hannum, K. (2006). Research update: 360-degree performance assessment. *Consulting Psychology Journal: Practice and Research, 58,* 117–124.

Craig, W. M., Pepler, D., & Atlas, R. (2000). Observations of bullying in the playground and in the classroom. *School Psychology International, 21,* 22–36.

Cramer, R. E., McMaster, M. R., Bartell, P. A., & Dragna, M. (1988). Subject competence and the minimization of the bystander effect. *Journal of Applied Social Psychology, 18,* 1133–1148.

Crandall, C. S., & Eshleman, A. (2003). A justification-suppression of the expression and experience of prejudice. *Psychological Bulletin, 129,* 414–446.

Crano, W. D. (2000). Milestones in the psychological analysis of social influence. *Group Dynamics: Theory, Research, and Practice, 4,* 68–80.

Crano, W. D., & Prislin, R. (2006). Attitudes and persuasion. *Annual Review of Psychology, 57,* 345–374.

Crick, N. R., & Dodge, K. A. (1994). A review and reformulation of social information-processing mechanisms in children's social adjustment. *Psychological Bulletin, 115,* 74–101.

Crick, N. R., & Rose, A. J. (2000). Toward a gender-balanced approach to the study of social-emotional development: A look at relational aggression. In R. G. Geen & E. Donnerstein (Eds.), *Human aggression: Theories, research, and implications for social policy* (pp. 153–168). San Diego: Academic Press.

Crick, N. R., Casas, J. F., & Mosher, M. (1997). Relational and overt aggression in preschool. *Developmental Psychology, 33,* 579–588.

Crocker, J., & Park, L. E. (2004). The costly pursuit of self-esteem. *Psychological Bulletin, 130,* 392–414.

Crocker, J., & Quinn, D. M. (2000). Social stigma and the self: Meanings, situations, and self-esteem. In T. F. Heatherton & R. E. Kleck (Eds.), *The social psychology of stigma* (pp. 153–183). New York: Guilford.

Crocker, J., Voelkl, K., Testa, M., & Major, B. (1991). Social stigma: The affective consequences of attributional ambiguity. *Journal of Personality and Social Psychology, 60,* 218–228.

Croizet, J. C., & Claire, T. (1998). Extending the concept of stereotype and threat to social class: The intellectual underperformance of students from low socioeconomic backgrounds. *Personality and Social Psychology Bulletin, 24,* 588–594.

Croizet, J. C., Després, G., Gauzins, M. E., Huguet, P., Leyens, J.-P., & Meot, A. (2004). Stereotype threat undermines intellectual performance by triggering a disruptive mental load. *Personality and Social Psychology Bulletin, 30,* 721–731.

Cronbach, L. J. (1955). Processes affecting scores on "understanding of others" and "assumed similarity." *Psychological Bulletin, 52,* 177–193.

Cronin, P., & Reicher, S. (2006). A study of the factors that influence how senior officers police crowd events: On SIDE outside the laboratory. *British Journal of Social Psychology, 45,* 175–196.

Cropanzano, R. (Ed.). (1993). *Justice in the workplace: Approaching fairness in human resource management.* Hillsdale, NJ: Erlbaum.

Crosby, F. (1982). *Relative deprivation and working women.* New York: Oxford University Press.

Crosby, F. J. (1991). *Juggling.* New York: Free Press.

Crosby, F. J., Iyer, A., & Sincharoen, S. (2006). Understanding affirmative action. *Annual Review of Psychology, 57,* 585–611.

Crosby, F., Bromley, S., & Saxe, L. (1980). Recent unobtrusive studies of black and white discrimination and prejudice: A literature review. *Psychological Bulletin, 87,* 546–563.

Croyle, R., & Cooper, J. (1983). Dissonance arousal: Physiological evidence. *Journal of Personality and Social Psychology, 45,* 782–791.

Crozier, W. R. (Ed.). (2001). *Shyness: Development, consolidation, and change*. London: Routledge.

Crozier, W. R., & Alden, L. E. (Eds.). (2005). *The essential handbook of social anxiety for clinicians*. New York: John Wiley & Sons.

Crutchfield, R. S. (1955). Conformity and character. *American Psychologist, 10*, 195–198.

Csikszentmihalyi, M. (1999). If we are so rich, why aren't we happy? *American Psychologist, 54*, 821–827.

Csikszentmihalyi, M., & Figurski, T. J. (1982). Self-awareness and aversive experience in everyday life. *Journal of Personality, 50*, 15–28.

Cuddy, A. J. C., Norton, M. I., & Fiske, S. T. (2004). This old stereotype: The pervasiveness and persistence of the elderly stereotype. *Journal of Social Issues, 61*, 267–285.

Culbertson, F. M. (1997). Depression and gender: An international review. *American Psychologist, 52*, 25–31.

Cunningham, M. R. (1979). Weather, mood, and helping behavior: Quasi experiments with the sunshine Samaritan. *Journal of Personality and Social Psychology, 37*, 1947–1956.

Cunningham, M. R., Roberts, A. R., Wu, C., Barbee, A. P., & Druen, P. B. (1995). "Their ideas of beauty are, on the whole, the same as ours": Consistency and variability in the cross-cultural perception of female physical attractiveness. *Journal of Personality and Social Psychology, 68*, 261–279.

Cunningham, M. R., Steinberg, J., & Grev, R. (1980). Wanting to and having to help: Separate motivations for positive mood and guilt-induced helping. *Journal of Personality and Social Psychology, 38*, 181–192.

Cunningham, M. R., Wong, D. T., & Barbee, A. P. (1994). Self-presentation dynamics on overt integrity tests: Experimental studies of the Reid Report. *Journal of Applied Psychology, 79*, 643–658.

Cunningham, W. A., Johnson, M. K., Gatenby, J. C., Gore, J. C., & Banaji, M. R. (2003). Neural components of social evaluation. *Journal of Personality and Social Psychology, 85*, 639–649.

Cunningham, W. A., Johnson, M. K., Raye, C. L., Gatenby, J. C., Gore, J. C., & Banaji, M. R. (2004). Separable neural components in the processing of black and white faces. *Psychological Science, 15*, 806–813.

Cunningham, W. A., Johnson, M. K., Raye, C. L., Gatenby, J. C., Gore, J. C., & Banaji, M. R. (2004). Separable neural components in the processing of black and white faces. *Psychological Science, 15*, 806–813.

Cunningham, W. A., Johnson, W. A., Raye, C. L., Gatenby, J. C., Gore, J. C., & Banaji, M. R. (2004). Separable neural components in the processing of black and white faces. *Psychological Science, 15*, 806–813.

Curtis, R. C., & Miller, K. (1986). Believing another likes or dislikes you: Behaviors making the beliefs come true. *Journal of Personality and Social Psychology, 51*, 284–290.

Cutler, B. L., & Penrod, S. D. (1995). *Mistaken identification: The eyewitness, psychology, and the law*. New York: Cambridge University Press.

Cutler, B. L., Penrod, S. D., & Stuve, T. E. (1988). Juror decision making in eyewitness identification cases. *Law and Human Behavior, 12*, 41–55.

Cyranowski, J. M., Frank, E., Young, E., & Shear, M. K. (2000). Adolescent onset of the gender difference in lifetime rates of major depression. *Archives of General Psychiatry, 57*, 21–27.

Dabbs, J. M., & Dabbs, M. G. (2000). *Heroes, rogues, and lovers: Testosterone and behavior*. New York: McGraw-Hill.

Dabbs, J. M., Jr., Hargrove, M. F., & Heusel, C. (1996). Testosterone differences among college fraternities: Well-behaved vs. rambunctious. *Personality and Individual Differences, 20*, 157–161.

Daly, M., & Wilson, M. (1988). *Homicide*. New York: Aldine de Gruyter.

Daly, M., & Wilson, M. (1989). Homicide and cultural evolution. *Ethology and Sociobiology, 10*, 99–110.

Daly, M., & Wilson, M. (1996). Violence against stepchildren. *Current Directions in Psychological Science, 5*, 77–81.

Daly, M., & Wilson, M. (2005). The 'Cinderella effect' is no fairy tale: Comment. *Trends in Cognitive Sciences, 9*, 507–508.

Danheiser, P. R., & Graziano, W. G. (1982). Self-monitoring and cooperation as a self-presentational strategy. *Journal of Personality and Social Psychology, 42*, 497–505.

Dao, T. K., Kerbs, J. J., Potts, I., Gutierrez, R., Choi, K., Creason, A. H., Wolf, A., & Prevatt, F. (2006). The association between bullying dynamics and psychological distress. *Journal of Adolescent Health, 39*, 277–282.

Darby, B. L. (1975). Reciprocal concessions procedure for inducing compliance: The door-in-the-face technique. *Journal of Personality and Social Psychology, 31*, 206–215.

Darke, P. R., & Chaiken, S. (2005). The pursuit of self-interest: Self-interest bias in attitude judgment and persuasion. *Journal of Personality and Social Psychology, 89*, 864–883.

Darley, J. M., & Batson, C. D. (1973). From Jerusalem to Jericho: A study of situational and dispositional variables in helping behavior. *Journal of Personality and Social Psychology, 27*, 100–108.

Darley, J. M., & Fazio, R. (1980). Expectancy confirmation processes arising in the social interaction sequence. *American Psychologist, 35*, 867–881.

Darley, J. M., & Gross, P. H. (1983). A hypothesis-confirming bias in labeling effects. *Journal of Personality and Social Psychology, 44*, 20–33.

Darley, J. M., & Latané, B. (1968). Bystander intervention in emergencies: Diffusion of responsibility. *Journal of Personality and Social Psychology, 8*, 377–383.

Darley, J. M., & Latané, B. (1970). Norms and normative behavior: Field studies of social interdependence. In J. Macauley & L. Berkowitz (Eds.), *Altruism and helping behavior* (pp. 83–101). New York: Academic Press.

Darley, J. M., & Pittman, T. S. (2003). The psychology of compensatory and retributive justice. *Personality and Social Psychology Review, 7*, 324–336.

Darley, J. M., Carlsmith, K. M., & Robinson, P. H. (2000). Incapacitation and just deserts as motives for punishment. *Law and Human Behavior, 24*, 659–684.

Dar-Nimrod, I., & Heine, S. J. (2006). Exposure to scientific theories affects women's math performance. *Science, 314*, 435.

Darwin, C. (1872). *The expression of the emotions in man and animals*. London: John Murray.

Das, E. H. H. J., de Wit, J. B. F., & Stroebe, W. (2003). Fear appeals motivate acceptance of action recommendations: Evidence for a positive bias in the processing of persuasive messages. *Personality and Social Psychology Bulletin, 29*, 650–664.

Dasgupta, N., & Asgari, S. (2004). Seeing is believing: Exposure to counterstereotypic women leaders and its effect on the malleability of automatic gender stereotyping. *Journal of Experimental Social Psychology, 40*, 642–658.

David, N., Bewernick, B. H., Cohen, M. X., Newen, A., Lux, S., Fink, G. R., Shah, N. J., & Vogeley, K. (2006). Neural representations of self versus other: Visual-spatial perspective taking and agency in a virtual ball-tossing game. *Journal of Cognitive Neuroscience, 18*, 898–910.

Davidson, A. R., & Jaccard, J. J. (1979). Variables that moderate the attitude-behavior relation: Results of a longitudinal survey. *Journal of Personality and Social Psychology, 37*, 1364–1376.

Davidson, A. R., Yantis, S., Norwood, M., & Montano, D. E. (1985). Amount of information about the attitude object and attitude-behavior consistency. *Journal of Personality and Social Psychology, 49*, 1184–1198.

Davies, P. G., Spencer, S. J., Quinn, D. M., & Gerhardstein, R. (2002). Consuming images: How television commercials that elicit stereotype threat can restrain women academically and professionally. *Personality and Social Psychology Bulletin, 28,* 1615–1628.

Davies, P. T., & Cummings, E. M. (1994). Marital conflict and child adjustment: An emotional security hypothesis. *Psychological Bulletin, 116,* 387–411.

Davis, B. P., & Knowles, E. S. (1999). A Disrupt-Then-Reframe technique of social influence. *Journal of Personality and Social Psychology, 76,* 192–199.

Davis, J. H., Au, W. T., Hulbert, L., Chen, X., & Zarnoth, P. (1997). Effects of group size and procedural influence on consensual judgments of quantity: The example of damage awards and mock civil juries. *Journal of Personality and Social Psychology, 73,* 703–718.

Davis, J. H., Kameda, T., Parks, C., Stasson, M., & Zimmerman, S. (1989). Some social mechanics of group decision-making: The distribution of opinion, polling sequence, and implications for consensus. *Journal of Personality and Social Psychology, 57,* 1000–1012.

Davis, J. L., & Rusbult, C. E. (2001). Attitude alignment in close relationships. *Journal of Personality and Social Psychology, 81,* 65–84.

Davis, J. P., & Hall, J. W. (2003). A software-supported process for assembling evidence and handling uncertainty in decision-making. *Decision Support Systems, 35,* 415–433.

Davis, M. C., Matthews, K. A., & McGrath, C. (2000). Hostile attitudes predict elevated vascular resistance during interpersonal stress in men and women. *Psychosomatic Medicine, 62,* 17–25.

Davis, M. H., Mitchell, K. V., Hall, J. A., Lothert, J., Snapp, T., & Meyer, M. (1999). Empathy, expectations, and situational preferences: Personality influences on the decision to participate in volunteer helping behaviors. *Journal of Personality, 67,* 469–503.

Davis, M. H., Soderlund, T., Cole, J., Gadol, E., Kute, M., Myers, M., & Wiehing, J. (2004). Cognitions associated with attempts to empathize: How do we imagine the perspective of another? *Personality and Social Psychology Bulletin, 30,* 1625–1635.

Davis, S. (1990). Men as success objects and women as sex objects: A study of personal advertisements. *Sex Roles, 23,* 43–50.

Davison, K. P., Pennebaker, J. W., & Dickerson, S. S. (2000). Who talks? The social psychology of illness support groups. *American Psychologist, 55,* 205–217.

Dawes, R. M. (1980). Social dilemmas. *Annual Review of Psychology, 31,* 169–193.

Dawkins, R. (1989). *The selfish gene* (2nd ed.). Oxford: Oxford University Press.

Day, D. D., & Sulsky, L. M. (1995). Effects of frame-of-reference training and information configuration on memory organization and rating accuracy. *Journal of Applied Psychology, 80,* 158–167.

Day, D. V., Shleicher, D. J., Unckless, A. L., & Hiller, N. J. (2002). Self-monitoring personality at work: A meta-analytic investigation of construct validity. *Journal of Applied Psychology, 87,* 390–401.

Day, R.-F., Shyi, G. C.-W., & Wang, J.-C. (2006). The effects of flash banners on multiattribute decision making: Distractor or source of arousal? *Psychology and Marketing, 23,* 369–382.

De Cremer, D. (2004). The influence of accuracy as a function of leader's bias: The role of trustworthiness in the psychology of procedural justice. *Personality and Social Psychology Bulletin, 30,* 293–304.

De Cremer, D., & Leonardelli, G. J. (2003). Cooperation in social dilemmas and the need to belong: The moderating effect of group size. *Group Dynamics, 7,* 168–174.

De Cremer, D., & Van Lange, P. A. M. (2001). Why prosocials exhibit greater cooperation than proselfs: The roles of social responsibility and reciprocity. *European Journal of Personality, 15,* S5–S18.

De Dreu, C. K. W., & Carnevale, P. J. (2003). Motivational bases of information processing and strategy in negotiation and social conflict. In M. P. Zanna (Ed.), *Advances in experimental social psychology* (Vol. 35). New York: Academic Press.

De Dreu, C., & De Vries, N. (Eds.). (2001). *Group consensus and minority influence: Implications for innovation.* London: Blackwell.

De Drue, C. K. W., Beersma, B., Stroebe, K., & Euwema, M. C. (2006). Motivated information processing, strategic choice, and the quality of negotiated agreement. *Journal of Personality and Social Psychology, 90,* 927–943.

de Hoog, N., Stroebe, W., & de Wit, J. B. F. (2005). The impact of fear appeals on processing and acceptance of action recommendations. *Personality and Social Psychology Bulletin, 31,* 24–33.

de Kwaadsteniet, E. W., van Dijk, E., Wit, E., Wit, A., & de Cremer, D. (2006). Social dilemmas as strong versus weak situations: Social value orientations and tacit coordination under resource size uncertainty. *Journal of Experimental Social Psychology, 42,* 509–516.

De La Fuente, L., De La Fuente, E. I., & Garcia, J. (2003). Effects of pretrial juror bias, strength of evidence and deliberation process on juror decisions: New validity evidence of the Juror Bias Scale scores. *Psychology, Crime and Law, 9,* 197–209.

de Quervain, D. J.-F., Fischbacher, U., Treyer, V., Schellhammer, M., Schnyder, U., Buck, A., & Fehr, E. (2004). The neural basis of altruistic punishment. *Science, 305,* 1254–1258.

De Raad, B. (2000). *The big five personality factors: Theory and applications.* Germany: Hogrefe & Huber.

De Steno, D. M., Valdesolo, P., & Bartlett, M. Y. (2006). Jealousy and the threatened self: Getting to the heart of the green-eyed monster. *Journal of Personality and Social Psychology, 91,* 626–641.

De Veer, M. W., Gallup, G. G., Theall, L. A., van den Bos, R., & Povinelli, D. J. (2003). An 8-year longitudinal study of mirror self-recognition in chimpanzees (*Pan troglodytes*). *Neuropsychologia, 41,* 229–234.

de Waal, F. B. M. (1996). *Good natured: The origins of right and wrong in humans and other animals.* Cambridge, MA: Harvard University Press.

de Waal, F. B. M. (2003). The chimpanzee's service economy: Evidence for cognition-based reciprocal exchange. In E. Ostrom & J. Walker (Eds.), *Trust and reciprocity: Interdisciplinary lessons from experimental research* (pp. 128–143). New York: Russell Sage.

de Waal, F. B. M. (2006). Joint ventures require joint pay-offs: Fairness among primates. *Social Research, 73,* 349–364.

de Waal, F. B., & Berger, M. L. (2000). Payment for labor in monkeys. *Nature, 404,* 563.

DeAngelis, T. (1993, August). *APA Monitor,* p. 16.

Dear Abby. (2003, December 17). *The Berkshire Eagle,* p. C7.

Deater-Deckard, K., Dodge, K. A., Bates, J. E., & Pettit, G. S. (1998). Multiple-risk factors in the development of externalizing behavior problems: Group and individual differences. *Development and Psychopathology, 10,* 469–493.

Deaux, K., & Emswiller, T. (1974). Explanations for successful performance on sex-linked tasks: What is skill for the male is luck for the female. *Journal of Personality and Social Psychology, 29,* 80–85.

Deaux, K., & Lewis, L. L. (1984). The structure of gender stereotypes: Interrelationships among components and gender label. *Journal of Personality and Social Psychology, 46,* 991–1004.

Deaux, K., & Major, B. (1987). Putting gender into context: An interactive model of gender-related behavior. *Psychological Review, 94,* 369–389.

DeBono, K. G., Leavitt, A., & Backus, J. (2003). Product packaging and product evaluation: An individual difference approach. *Journal of Applied Social Psychology, 33,* 513–521.

Deci, E. L. (1971). Effects of externally mediated rewards on intrinsic motivation. *Journal of Personality and Social Psychology, 18,* 105–115.

Deci, E. L., & Ryan, R. M. (1985). *Intrinsic motivation and self-determination in human behavior.* New York: Plenum.

DeCramer, D. (2001). Relations of self-esteem concerns, group identification, and self-stereotyping to in-group favoritism. *Journal of Social Psychology, 141,* 389–400.

Deffenbacher, K. A., Bornstein, B. H., & Penrod, S. D. (2006). Mugshot exposure effects: Retroactive interference, mugshot commitment, source confusion, and unconscious transference. *Law and Human Behavior, 30,* 287–307.

DeKeseredy, W. S., Schwartz, M. D., & Tait, K. (1993). Sexual assault and stranger aggression on a Canadian university campus. *Sex Roles, 28,* 263–277.

Delahanty, D. L., Herberman, H. B., Fullerton, C. S., Ursano, R. J., Craig, K. J., Hayward, M. C., & Baum, A. (1997). Acute and chronic distress and posttraumatic stress disorder as a function of responsibility for serious motor vehicle accidents. *Journal of Consulting and Clinical Psychology, 65,* 560–567.

Demaré, D., Lips, H. M., & Briere, J. (1993). Sexually violent pornography, anti-women attitudes, and sexual aggression: A structural equation model. *Journal of Research in Personality, 27,* 285–300.

DeMarree, K. G., Wheeler, S. C., & Petty, R. E. (2005). Priming a new identity: Self-monitoring moderates the effects of nonself primes on self-judgments and behavior. *Journal of Personality and Social Psychology, 89,* 657–671.

Demoulin, S., Leyens, J.-P., & Yzerbyt, V. (2006). Lay theories of essentialism. *Group Processes and Intergroup Relations, 9,* 25–42.

DeNeve, K. M., & Cooper, H. (1998). The happy personality: A meta-analysis of 137 personality traits and subjective well-being. *Psychological Bulletin, 124,* 197–229.

Dennis, A. R., & Williams, M. L. (2003). Electronic brainstorming: Theory, research, and future directions. In P. B. Paulus & B. A. Nijstad (Eds.), *Group creativity: Innovation through collaboration* (pp. 160–178). New York: Oxford University Press.

Denrell, J. (2005). Why most people disapprove of me: Experience sampling in impression formation. *Psychological Review, 112,* 951–978.

DePaulo, B. M., & Kashy, D. A. (1998). Everyday lies in close and casual relationships. *Journal of Personality and Social Psychology, 74,* 63–79.

DePaulo, B. M., Charlton, K., Cooper, H., Lindsay, J. J., & Muhlenbruck, L. (1997). The accuracy-confidence correlation in the detection of deception. *Personality and Social Psychology Review, 1,* 346–357.

DePaulo, B. M., Lindsay, J. J., Malone, B. E., Muhlenbruck, L., Charlton, K., & Cooper, H. (2003). Cues to deception. *Psychological Bulletin, 129,* 74–112.

Deppe, R. K., & Harackiewicz, J. M. (1996). Self-handicapping and intrinsic motivation: Buffering intrinsic motivation from the threat of failure. *Journal of Personality and Social Psychology, 70,* 868–876.

Depret, E., & Fiske, S. T. (1999). Perceiving the powerful: Intriguing individuals versus threatening groups. *Journal of Experimental Social Psychology, 35,* 461–480.

Derakshan, N., & Eysenck, M. W. (2005). When the bogus pipeline interferes with self-deceptive strategies: Effects on state anxiety in repressors. *Cognition and Emotion, 19,* 83–100.

Derlega, V. J., Metts, S., Petronio, S., & Margulis, S. T. (1993). *Self-disclosure.* Newbury Park, CA: Sage.

Derlega, V. J., Wilson, M., & Chaikin, A. L. (1976). Friendship and disclosure reciprocity. *Journal of Personality and Social Psychology, 34,* 578–587.

Dershowitz, A. M. (1982). *The best defense.* New York: Vintage Books.

DeSteno, D. A., & Salovey, P. (1996). Evolutionary origins of sex differences in jealousy? Questioning the "fitness" model. *Psychological Science, 7,* 367–372.

Deutsch, F. M. (1989). The false consensus effect: Is the self-justification hypothesis justified? *Basic and Applied Social Psychology, 10,* 83–99.

Deutsch, M., & Gerard, H. B. (1955). A study of normative and informational social influences upon individual judgment. *Journal of Abnormal and Social Psychology, 51,* 629–636.

Deutsch, M., & Krauss, R. M. (1960). The effect of threat upon interpersonal bargaining. *Journal of Abnormal and Social Psychology, 61,* 181–189.

Devenport, J. L., Penrod, S. D., & Cutler, B. L. (1997). Eyewitness identification evidence: Evaluating commonsense evaluations. *Psychology, Public Policy, and Law, 3,* 338–361.

Devine, D. J., Clayton, L. D., Dunford, B. B., Seying, R., & Pryce, J. (2001). Jury decision making: 45 years of empirical research on deliberating groups. *Psychology, Public Policy, and Law, 7,* 622–727.

Devine, P. G. (1989). Stereotypes and prejudice: Their automatic and controlled components. *Journal of Personality and Social Psychology, 56,* 5–18.

Devine, P. G., Brodish, A. B., & Vance, S. L. (2005). Self-regulatory processes in interracial interactions: The role of internal and external motivation to respond without prejudice. In J. P. Forgas, K. D. Williams, & W. von Hippel (Eds.), *Social motivation: Conscious and unconscious processes* (pp. 249–273). New York: Psychology Press.

Devon, W. (2004). Improving race relations in higher education: The jigsaw classroom as a missing piece to the puzzle. *Urban Education, 39,* 316–344.

Devos-Comby, L., & Salovey, P. (2002). Applying persuasion strategies to alter HIV-relevant thoughts and behavior. *Review of General Psychology, 6,* 287–304.

DeWall, C. N., Altermatt, T. W., & Thompson, H. (2005). Understanding the structure of stereotypes of women: Virtue and agency as dimensions distinguishing female subgroups. *Psychology of Women Quarterly, 29,* 396–405.

Diamond, L. M. (2003). Was it a phase? Young women's relinquishment of lesbian/bisexual identities over a 5-year period. *Journal of Personality and Social Psychology, 84,* 352–364.

Diamond, M. (1993). Homosexuality and bisexuality in different populations. *Archives of Sexual Behavior, 22,* 291–310.

Diamond, S. S., Rose, M. R., & Murphy, B. (2006). Revisiting the unanimity requirement: The behavior of the non-unanimous civil jury. *Northwestern Law Review, 100,* 201–230.

Diamond, S., Vidmar, N., Rose, M. R., Ellis, L., & Murphy, E. (2003). Juror discussions during civil trials: Studying an Arizona innovation. *University of Arizona Law Review, 45,* 1.

Diehl, M., & Stroebe, W. (1987). Productivity loss in brainstorming groups: Toward the solution of a riddle. *Journal of Personality and Social Psychology, 53,* 497–509.

Diekman, A. B., Eagly, A. H., & Kulesa, P. (2002). Accuracy and bias in stereotypes about the social and political attitudes of women and men. *Journal of Experimental Social Psychology, 38,* 268–282.

Diekmann, K. A., Tenbrunsel, A. E., & Galinsky, A. D. (2003). From self-prediction to self-defeat: Behavioral forecasting, self-fulfilling prophecies, and the effect of competitive expectations. *Journal of Personality and Social Psychology, 85,* 672–683.

Diener, E. (1979). Deindividuation, self-awareness, and disinhibition. *Journal of Personality and Social Psychology, 37,* 1160–1171.

Diener, E. (1980). Deindividuation: The absence of self-awareness and self-regulation in group members. In P. B. Paulus (Ed.), *Psychology of group influence* (pp. 209–242). Hillsdale, NJ: Erlbaum.

Diener, E. (2000). Subjective well-being: The science of happiness, and a proposal for a national index. *American Psychologist, 55,* 34–43.

Diener, E., & Seligman, M. E. P. (2004). Beyond money: Toward an economy of well-being. *Psychological Science in the Public Interest, 5,* whole No. 1.

Diener, E., & Suh, E. M. (Eds.). (2000). Culture and subjective well-being. Cambridge, MA: MIT Press.

Diener, E., Emmons, R. A., Larsen, R. J., & Griffin, S. (1984). The Satisfaction with Life Scale. *Journal of Personality Assessment, 49,* 71–75.

Diener, E., Fraser, S. C., Beaman, A. L., & Kelem, R. T. (1976). Effects of deindividuation variables on stealing among Halloween trick-or-treaters. *Journal of Personality and Social Psychology, 33,* 178–183.

Diener, E., Suh, E. M., Lucas, R. E., & Smith, H. L. (1999). Subjective well-being: Three decades of progress. *Psychological Bulletin, 125,* 276–302.

Diener, E., Tamir, M., Scollon, C., Van Napa, L., & Paul, A. M. (Eds.). (2006). *Happiness, life satisfaction, and fulfillment: The social psychology of subjective well-being.* Mahwah, NJ: Erlbaum.

Diener, E., Wolsic, B., & Fujita, F. (1995). Physical attractiveness and subjective well-being. *Journal of Personality and Social Psychology, 69,* 120–129.

Dietz, T. L. (1998). An examination of violence and gender role portrayals in video games: Implications for gender socialization and aggressive behavior. *Sex Roles, 38,* 425–442.

Dietz-Uhler, B. (1996). The escalation of commitment in political decision-making groups: A social identity approach. *European Journal of Social Psychology, 26,* 611–629.

DiFonzo, N., & Bordia, P. (1997). Rumor and prediction: Making sense (but losing dollars) in the stock market. *Organizational Behavior and Human Decision Processes, 71,* 329–353.

Dijksterhuis, A., & Aarts, H. (2003). Of wildebeests and humans: The preferential detection of negative stimuli. *Psychological Science, 14,* 14–18.

Dijksterhuis, A., & Bargh, J. A. (2001). The perception-behavior expressway: Automatic effects of social perception on social behavior. *Advances in Experimental Social Psychology, 33,* 1–40.

Dijksterhuis, A., & van Knippenberg, A. (1996). The knife that cuts both ways: Facilitated and inhibited access to traits as a result of stereotype activation. *Journal of Experimental and Social Psychology, 32,* 271–288.

Dijkstra, P., & Buunk, B. P. (1998). Jealousy as a function of rival characteristics: An evolutionary perspective. *Personality and Social Psychology Bulletin, 24,* 1158–1166.

Dill, J. C., & Anderson, C. A. (1995). Effects of frustration justification on hostile aggression. *Aggressive Behavior, 21,* 359–369.

Dill, K. E., Anderson, C. A., Anderson, K. B., & Deuser, W. E. (1997). Effects of aggressive personality on social expectations and social perceptions. *Journal of Research in Personality, 31,* 272–292.

Dimberg, U. Thunberg, M., & Elmehed, K. (2000). Unconscious facial reactions to emotional facial expressions. *Psychological Science, 11,* 86–89.

Dimberg, U., & Ohman, A. (1996). Behold the wrath: Psychophysiological responses to facial stimuli. *Motivation and Emotion, 20,* 149–181.

Dindia, K., & Allen, M. (1992). Sex differences in self-disclosure: A meta-analysis. *Psychological Bulletin, 112,* 106–124.

Dion, K. K., & Dion, K. L. (1996). Cultural perspectives on romantic love. *Personal Relationships, 3,* 5–17.

Dion, K. K., Berscheid, E., & Walster, E. (1972). What is beautiful is good. *Journal of Personality and Social Psychology, 24,* 285–290.

Dion, K. L. (1979). Intergroup conflict and intragroup cohesiveness. In W. G. Austin & S. Worchel (Eds.), *The social psychology of intergroup relations* (pp. 211–224). Pacific Grove, CA: Brooks/Cole.

Dion, K. L. (2000). Group cohesion: From "field of forces" to multidimensional construct. *Group Dynamics, 4,* 7–26.

Dion, K. L., & Cota, A. A. (1991). The Ms. stereotype: Its domain and the role of explicitness in title preference. *Psychology of Women Quarterly, 15,* 403–410.

Dion, K. L., & Dion, K. K. (1976). Love, liking and trust in heterosexual relationships. *Personality and Social Psychology Bulletin, 2,* 187–190.

Dionisio, D. P., Granholm, E., Hillix, W. A., & Perrine, W. F. (2001). Differentiation of deception using pupillary responses as an index of cognitive processing. *Psychophysiology, 38,* 205–211.

Dittmann, M. (2005). After the wave. *APA Monitor on Psychology, 36,* No. 3, p. 36.

Dodd, D. K. (1985). Robbers in the classroom: A deindividuation exercise. *Teaching in Psychology, 12,* 89–91.

Doerr, E. D., & Doerr, V. A. (2006). Comparative demography of treecreepers: Evaluating hypotheses for the evolution and maintenance of cooperative breeding. *Animal Behaviour, 72,* 147–159.

Dolinski, D. (2000). On inferring one's beliefs from one's attempt and consequences for subsequent compliance. *Journal of Personality and Social Psychology, 78,* 260–272.

Dollard, J., Doob, L. W., Miller, N. E., Mowrer, O. H., & Sears, R. R. (1939). *Frustration and aggression.* New Haven, CT: Yale University Press.

Donne, J. (1975). Meditation, 17. In A. Raspa (Ed.), *Devotions upon emergent occasions* (p. 87). Montreal: McGill-Queen's University Press. (Original work published 1624)

Donnelly, M., & Straus, M. A. (Eds.). (2005). *Corporal punishment of children in theoretical perspective.* New Haven, CT: Yale University Press.

Donnerstein, E., & Berkowitz, L. (1981). Victim reactions in aggressive erotic films as a factor in violence against women. *Journal of Personality and Social Psychology, 41,* 710–724.

Donnerstein, E., & Donnerstein, M. (1976). Research in the control of interracial aggression. In R. G. Geen and E. C. O'Neal (Eds.), *Perspectives on aggression* (pp. 133–168). New York: Academic Press.

Donnerstein, E., & Hallam, J. (1978). Facilitating effects of erotica on aggression against women. *Journal of Personality and Social Psychology, 36,* 1270–1277.

Donnerstein, E., & Malamuth, N. (1997). Pornography: Its consequences on the observer. In L. B. Schlesinger & E. Revitch (Eds.), *Sexual dynamics of anti-social behavior* (2nd ed., pp. 30–49). Springfield, IL: Charles C Thomas.

Donnerstein, E., Linz, D., & Penrod, S. (1987). *The question of pornography.* New York: Free Press.

Dooley, P. A. (1995). Perceptions of the onset controllability of AIDS and helping judgments: An attributional analysis. *Journal of Applied Social Psychology, 25,* 858–869.

Dornbusch, S. M., Hastorf, A. H., Richardson, S. A., Muzzy, R. E., & Vreeland, R. S. (1965). The perceiver and the perceived: Their relative influence on categories of interpersonal perception. *Journal of Personality and Social Psychology, 1,* 434–440.

Dougherty, T. W., Turban, D. B., & Callender, J. C. (1994). Confirming first impressions in the employment interview: A field study of interviewer behavior. *Journal of Applied Psychology, 79,* 659–665.

Douglas, E. M., & Straus, M. A. (2006). Assault and injury of dating partners by university students in 19 countries and its relation to corporal punishment experienced as a child. *European Journal of Criminology, 7,* 293–318.

Douglas, E., & Straus, M. A. (2007). Discipline by parents and child psychopathology. In A. Felthous & H. Sass (Eds.), *International handbook of psychopathology and the law.* New York: Wiley.

Douglas, K. M., & McGarty, C. (2002). Internet identifiability and beyond: A model of the effects of identifiability on communicative behavior. *Group Dynamics, 6,* 17–26.

Dovidio, J. F., & Gaertner, S. L. (1998). On the nature of contemporary prejudice: The causes, consequences, and challenges of aversive racism. In J. L. Eberhardt & S. T. Fiske (Eds.), *Confronting racism: The problem and the response* (pp. 3–32). Thousand Oaks, CA: Sage.

Dovidio, J. F., & Gaertner, S. L. (1999). Reducing prejudice: Combating intergroup biases. *Current Directions in Psychological Science, 8,* 101–105.

Dovidio, J. F., & Gaertner, S. L. (2000). Aversive racism and selection decisions: 1989 and 1999. *Psychological Science, 11,* 319–323.

Dovidio, J. F., & Gaertner, S. L. (2004). Aversive racism. In M. P. Zanna (Ed.), *Advances in experimental social psychology* (Vol. 36, pp. 1–52). San Diego, CA: Elsevier.

Dovidio, J. F., Brigham, J. C., Johnson, B. T., & Gaertner, S. L. (1996). Stereotyping, prejudice, and discrimination: Another look. In C. N. Macrae, C. Stangor, & M. Hewstone (Eds.), *Stereotypes and stereotyping* (pp. 276–319). New York: Guilford.

Dovidio, J. F., Gaertner, S. E., Kawakami, K., & Hodson, G. (2002). Why can't we just get along? Interpersonal biases and interracial distrust. *Cultural Diversity and Ethnic Minority Psychology, 8,* 88–102.

Dovidio, J. F., Gaertner, S. L., Hodson, G., Houlette, M. A., & Johnson, K. M. (2005). Social inclusion and exclusion: Recategorization and the perception of intergroup boundaries. In D. Abrams, M. A. Hogg, & J. M. Marques (Eds.), *The social psychology of inclusion and exclusion* (pp. 245–264). New York: Psychology Press.

Dovidio, J. F., Kawakami, K., Johnson, C., Johnson, B., & Howard, A. (1997). On the nature of prejudice: Automatic and controlled processes. *Journal of Experimental Social Psychology, 33,* 510–540.

Dovidio, J. F., Piliavin, J. A., Schroeder, D. A., & Penner, L. A. (2006). *The social psychology of prosocial behavior.* Mahwah, NJ: Erlbaum.

Dovidio, J. F., Smith, J. K., Donnella, A. G., & Gaertner, S. L. (1997). Racial attitudes and the death penalty. *Journal of Applied Social Psychology, 27,* 1468–1487.

Dovidio, J. F., ten Vergert, M., Stewart, T. L., Gaertner, S. L., Johnson, J. D., Esses, V. M., Rick, B. M., & Pearson, A. R. (2004). Perspective and prejudice: Antecedents and mediating mechanisms. *Personality and Social Psychology Bulletin, 30,* 1537–1549.

Downs, A. C., & Lyons, P. M. (1991). Natural observations of the links between attractiveness and initial legal judgments. *Personality and Social Psychology Bulletin, 17,* 541–547.

Doyle, J. M. (2005). *True witness: Cops, courts, science, and the battle against misidentification.* New York: Palgrave MacMillan.

Dreher, G. F., & Cox, T. H., Jr. (1996). Race, gender, and opportunity: A study of compensation attainment and the establishment of mentoring relationships. *Journal of Applied Psychology, 81,* 297–308.

Drigotas, S. M., & Rusbult, C. E. (1992). Shall I stay or should I go? A dependence model of breakups. *Journal of Personality and Social Psychology, 62,* 62–87.

Drigotas, S. M., Rusbult, C. E., & Verette, J. (1999). Level of commitment, mutuality of commitment, and couple well-being. *Personal Relationships, 6,* 389–409.

Drizin, S. A., & Leo, R. A. (2004). The problem of false confessions in the post-DNA world. *North Carolina Law Review, 82,* 891–1007.

Druckman, D. (1994). Determinants of compromising behavior in negotiation: A meta-analysis. *Journal of Conflict Resolution, 38,* 507–556.

Duck, S., & Wright, P. H. (1993). Reexamining gender differences in same-gender friendships: A close look at two kinds of data. *Sex Roles, 28,* 709–727.

Duckitt, J. (2006). Differential effects of right wing authoritarianism and social dominance orientation on outgroup attitudes and their mediation by threat from and competitiveness to outgroups. *Personality and Social Psychology Bulletin, 32,* 684–696.

Duckitt, J., & Mphuthing, T. (1998). Group identification and intergroup attitudes: A longitudinal analysis in South Africa. *Journal of Personality and Social Psychology, 74,* 80–85.

Duckworth, K. L., Bargh, J. A., Garcia, M., & Chaiken, S. (2002). The automatic evaluation of novel stimuli. *Psychological Science, 13,* 513–519.

Duclos, S. E., Laird, J. D., Schneider, E., Sexter, M., Stern, L., & Van Lighten, O. (1989). Emotion-specific effects of facial expressions and postures on emotional experience. *Journal of Personality and Social Psychology, 57,* 100–108.

Dudley, N. M., Orvis, K. A., Lebiecki, J. E., & Cortina, J. M. (2006). A meta-analytic investigation of conscientiousness in the prediction of job performance: Examining the intercorrelations and the incremental validity of narrow traits. *Journal of Applied Psychology, 91,* 40–57.

Dueck, L. (2006, November 3). There's a lot we can learn from the Amish. *The Globe and Mail (Canada),* p. A25.

Duffy, M. K., & Shaw, J. D. (2000). The Salieri Syndrome: Consequences of envy in groups. *Small Group Research, 31,* 3–23.

Dulin, P. L., & Hill, R. D. (2003). Relationships between altruistic activity and positive and negative affect among low-income older adult service providers. *Aging and Mental Health, 7,* 294–299.

Dunning, D. (1999). A newer look: Motivated social cognition and the schematic representation of social concepts. *Psychological Inquiry, 10,* 1–11.

Dunning, D. (2002). The zealous self-affirmer: How and why the self lurks so pervasively behind social judgment. In S. J. Spencer, S. Fein, M. Zanna, & J. M. Olson (Eds.), *Motivated social perception: The Ontario symposium* (Vol. 9). Mahwah, NJ: Erlbaum.

Dunning, D. (2005). *Self-insight: Roadblocks and detours on the path to knowing thyself.* New York: Psychology Press.

Dunning, D., & Hayes, A. F. (1996). Evidence for egocentric comparison in social judgment. *Journal of Personality and Social Psychology, 71,* 213–229.

Dunning, D., & Perretta, S. (2002). Automaticity and eyewitness accuracy: A 10- to 12-second rule for distinguishing accurate from inaccurate positive identifications. *Journal of Applied Psychology, 87,* 951–962.

Dunning, D., & Sherman, D. A. (1997). Stereotypes and tacit inference. *Journal of Personality and Social Psychology, 73,* 459–471.

Dunning, D., & Stern, L. B. (1994). Distinguishing accurate from inaccurate eyewitness identifications via inquiries about decision processes. *Journal of Personality and Social Psychology, 67,* 818–835.

Dunning, D., Griffin, D. W., Milojkovic, J. D., & Ross, L. (1990). The overconfidence effect in social prediction. *Journal of Personality and Social Psychology, 58,* 568–581.

Dunning, D., Heath, C., & Suls, J. M. (2004). Flawed self-assessment: Implications for health, education, and the workplace. *Psychological Science in the Public Interest, 5,* 69–106.

Dunning, D., Johnson, K., Ehrlinger, J., & Kruger, J. (2003). Why people fail to recognize their own incompetence. *Current Directions in Psychological Science, 12,* 83–87.

Dunton, B. C., & Fazio, R. H. (1997). An individual difference measure of motivation to control prejudiced reactions. *Personality and Social Psychology Bulletin, 23,* 316–326.

Durantini, M. R., Albarracín, D., Mitchell, A. L., Earl, A. N., & Gillette, J. C. (2006). Conceptualizing the influence of social agents of behavior change: A meta-analysis of the effectiveness of HIV-prevention interventionists for different groups. *Psychological Bulletin, 132,* 212–248.

Dutton, D. G., & Aron, A. P. (1974). Some evidence for heightened sexual attraction under conditions of high anxiety. *Journal of Personality and Social Psychology, 30,* 510–517.

Duval, S., & Wicklund, R. A. (1972). *A theory of objective self-awareness.* New York: Academic Press.

Duval, S., Duval, V. H., & Mulilis, J. P. (1992). Effects of self-focus, discrepancy between self and standard, and outcome expectancy favorability on the tendency to match self to standard or to withdraw. *Journal of Personality and Social Psychology, 62,* 340–348.

Dweck, C. S., Chiu, C., & Hong, Y. (1995). Implicit theories and their role in judgments and reactions: A world from two perspectives. *Psychological Inquiry, 6,* 267–285.

Dysart, J. E., Lindsay, R. C. L., MacDonald, T. K., & Wicke, C. (2002). The intoxicated witness: Effects of alcohol on identification accuracy from showups. *Journal of Applied Psychology, 87,* 170–175.

Eagly, A. H, Mladinic, A., & Otto, S. (1994). Are women evaluated more favorably than men? An analysis of attitudes, beliefs, and emotions. *Psychology of Women Quarterly, 15,* 203–216.

Eagly, A. H. (1987). *Sex differences in social behavior: A social-role interpretation.* Hillsdale, NJ: Erlbaum.

Eagly, A. H. (2004). Few women at the top: How role incongruity produces prejudice and the glass ceiling. In D. van Knippenberg & M. A. Hogg (Eds.), *Leadership and power: Identity processes in groups and organizations* (pp. 79–93). London: Sage Publications.

Eagly, A. H., & Carli, L. L. (1981). Sex of researchers and sex-typed communications as determinants of sex differences in influenceability: A meta-analysis of social influence studies. *Psychological Bulletin, 90,* 1–20.

Eagly, A. H., & Crowley, M. (1986). Gender and helping behavior: A meta-analytic review of the social psychological literature. *Psychological Bulletin, 100,* 283–308.

Eagly, A. H., & Johnson, B. T. (1990). Gender and leadership style: A meta-analysis. *Psychological Bulletin, 108,* 233–256.

Eagly, A. H., & Karau, S. J. (2002). Role congruity theory of prejudice toward female leaders. *Psychological Review, 109,* 573–598.

Eagly, A. H., & Steffen, V. J. (1986). Gender and aggressive behavior: A meta-analytic review of the social psychology literature. *Psychological Bulletin, 100,* 309–330.

Eagly, A. H., Ashmore, R. D., Makhijani, M. G., & Longo, L. C. (1991). What is beautiful is good, but . . . : A meta-analytic review of research on the physical attractiveness stereotype. *Psychology Bulletin, 110,* 107–128.

Eagly, A. H., Chen, S., Chaiken, S., & Shaw-Barnes, K. (1999). The impact of attitudes on memory: An affair to remember. *Psychological Bulletin, 125,* 64–89.

Eagly, A. H., Johannesen-Schmidt, M. C., & van Engen, M. L. (2003). Transformational, transactional, and laissez-faire leadership styles: A meta-analysis comparing women and men. *Psychological Bulletin, 129,* 569–591.

Eagly, A. H., Karau, S. J., & Makhijani, M. G. (1995). Gender and effectiveness of leaders: A meta-analysis. *Psychological Bulletin, 117,* 125–145.

Eagly, A. H., Wood, W., & Chaiken, S. (1978). Causal inferences about communicators and their effect on opinion change. *Journal of Personality and Social Psychology, 36,* 424–435.

Eagly, A. H., Wood, W., & Johannesen-Schmidt, M. C. (2004). Social role theory of sex differences and similarities: Implications for the partner preferences of women and men. In A. H. Eagly, A. Beall, & R. J. Sternberg (Eds.), *The psychology of gender* (2nd ed.). New York: Guilford.

Eaton, J. (2001). Management communication: The threat of groupthink. *Corporate Communications, 6,* 183–192.

Eaton, J., & Struthers, C. W. (2006). The reduction of psychological aggression across varied interpersonal contexts through repentance and forgiveness. *Aggressive Behavior, 32,* 195–206.

Eberhardt, J. L., Davies, P. G., Purdie-Vaughns, V. J., & Johnson, S. L. (2006). Perceived stereotypicality of black defendants predicts capital-sentencing outcomes. *Psychological Science, 17,* 383–386.

Eberhardt, J. L., Davies, P. G., Purdie-Vaughns, V. J., & Johnson, S. L. (2006). Looking deathworthy: Perceived stereotypicality of black defendants predicts capital-sentencing outcomes. *Psychological Science, 17,* 383–386.

Eberhardt, J. L., Doty, N., & Goff, P. A. (2007). Keeping track of identity: Social identity cues direct eye movements on faces. *Perception,* in press.

Eberhardt, J. L., Goff, P. A., Purdie, V. J., & Davies, P. G. (2004). Seeing black: Race, crime, and visual processing. *Journal of Personality and Social Psychology, 87,* 876–893.

Eckes, T. (2002). Paternalistic and envious gender stereotypes: Testing predictions from the stereotype content model. *Sex Roles, 47,* 99–114.

Eden, D. (1990). Pygmalion without interpersonal contrast effects: Whole groups gain from raising manager expectations. *Journal of Applied Psychology, 75,* 394–398.

Eder, R. W., & Harris, M. M. (Eds.). (1999). *The employment interview handbook* (2nd ed.). Thousand Oaks, CA: Sage.

Edwards, K., & Smith, E. E. (1996). A disconfirmation bias in the evaluation of arguments. *Journal of Personality and Social Psychology, 71,* 5–24.

Eek, D., & Gärling, T. (2006). Prosocials prefer equal outcomes to maximizing joint outcomes. *British Journal of Social Psychology, 45,* 321–337.

Egan, J. (2003, November 23). Love in the time of no time. *New York Times Magazine,* Section 6, p. 66.

Egbert, B., & Weir, R. (2003, June 2). Bronx hero stops knife attack on woman. *New York Daily News,* p. 15.

Ehrlichman, H., & Eichenstein, R. (1992). Private wishes: Gender similarities and differences. *Sex Roles, 26,* 399–422.

Ehrlinger, J., Gilovich, T., & Ross, L. (2005). Peering into the bias blind spot: People's assessments of bias in themselves and others. *Personality and Social Psychology Bulletin, 31,* 680–692.

Eibach, R. P., & Keegan, T. (2006). Free at last? Social dominance, loss aversion, and white and black Americans' differing assessments of racial progress. *Journal of Personality and Social Psychology, 90,* 453–467.

Eichstaedt, J., & Silvia, P. J. (2003). Noticing the self: Implicit assessment of self-focused attention using word recognition latencies. *Social Cognition, 21,* 349–361.

Eisenberg, N., Guthrie, I. K., Cumberland, A., Murphy, B. C., Shepard, S. A., Zhou, Q., & Carlo, G. (2002). Prosocial development in early adulthood: A longitudinal study. *Journal of Personality and Social Psychology, 82,* 993–1006.

Eisenberg, N., Guthrie, I. K., Murphy, B. C., Shepard, S. A., Cumberland, A., & Carlo, G. (1999). Consistency and development of prosocial dispositions: A longitudinal study. *Child Development, 70,* 1360–1372.

Eisenberg, N., Spinrad, T. L., & Sadovsky, A. (2006). Empathy-related responding in children. In M. Killen & J. G. Smetana (Eds.), *Handbook of moral development* (pp. 517–549). Mahwah, NJ: Erlbaum.

Eisenberg, N., Valiente, C., & Champion, C. (2004). Empathy-related responding: Moral, social, and socialization correlates. In A. G. Miller (Ed.), *The social psychology of good and evil* (pp. 386–415). New York: Guilford.

Eisenberger, N. I., Lieberman, M. I., & Williams, K. D. (2003). Does rejection hurt? An fMRI study of social exclusion. *Science, 302,* 290–292.

Eisenberger, N. I., Way, B. M., Taylor, S. E., Welch, W. T., & Lieberman, M. D. (2007). Understanding genetic risk for aggression: Clues from the brain's response to social exclusion. *Biological Psychiatry,* in press.

Eisenberger, R., & Cameron, J. (1996). Detrimental effects of reward: Reality or myth? *American Psychologist, 51,* 1153–1166.

Eisenberger, R., & Rhoades, L. (2001). Incremental effects of reward on creativity. *Journal of Personality and Social Psychology, 81,* 728–741.

Eisenberger, R., Cotterell, N., & Marvel, J. (1987). Reciprocation ideology. *Journal of Personality and Social Psychology, 53,* 743–750.

Ekman, P., & Friesen, W. V. (1974). Detecting deception from the body or face. *Journal of Personality and Social Psychology, 29,* 288–298.

Ekman, P., & O'Sullivan, M. (1991). Who can catch a liar? *American Psychologist, 46,* 913–920.

Ekman, P., Friesen, W. V., O'Sullivan, M., Chan, A., Diacoyanni-Tarlatzis, I., Heider, K., Krause, R., LeCompte, W. A., Pitcairn, T., Ricci-Bitti, P., Scherer, K., Tomita, M., & Tzavaras, A. (1987). Universals and cultural differences in the judgments of facial expressions of emotion. *Journal of Personality and Social Psychology, 53,* 712–717.

El Leithy, S., Brown, G. P., & Robbins, I. (2006). Counterfactual thinking and posttraumatic stress reactions. *Journal of Abnormal Psychology, 115,* 629–635.

Elfenbein, H. A., & Ambady, N. (2002). On the universality and cultural specificity of emotion recognition: A meta-analysis. *Psychological Bulletin, 128,* 203–235.

Elfenbein, H. A., & Ambady, N. (2003). When familiarity breeds accuracy: Cultural exposure and facial emotion recognition. *Journal of Personality and Social Psychology, 85,* 276–290.

Elkin, R. A., & Leippe, M. R. (1986). Physiological arousal, dissonance, and attitude change: Evidence for a dissonance-arousal link and a "don't remind me" effect. *Journal of Personality and Social Psychology, 51,* 55–65.

Elliot, A. J., & Devine, P. G. (1994). On the motivational nature of cognitive dissonance: Dissonance as psychological discomfort. *Journal of Personality and Social Psychology, 67,* 382–394.

Elliott, M. A., Armitage, C. J., & Baughan, C. J. (2003). Drivers' compliance with speed limits: An application of the theory of planned behavior. *Journal of Applied Psychology, 88,* 964–972.

Elliott, R. (1991). Social science data and the APA: The Lockhart brief as a case in point. *Law and Human Behavior, 15,* 59–76.

Elloy, D. F., & Smith, C. R. (2003). Patterns of stress, work-family conflict, role conflict, role ambiguity and overload among dual-career and single-career couples: An Australian study. *Cross-Cultural Management, 10,* 55–66.

Ellsworth, P. C. (1991). To tell what we know or wait for Godot? *Law and Human Behavior, 15,* 77–90.

Elms, A., & Milgram, S. (1966). Personality characteristics associated with obedience and defiance toward authoritative command. *Journal of Experimental Research in Personality, 1,* 282–289.

Elwork, A., Sales, B. D., & Alfini, J. J. (1982). *Making jury instructions understandable.* Charlottesville, VA: Miche.

Englich, B., Mussweiler, T., & Strack, F. (2006). Playing dice with criminal sentences: The influence of irrelevant anchors on experts' judicial decision making. *Personality and Social Psychology Bulletin, 32,* 188–200.

English, P. W., & Sales, B. D. (1997). A ceiling or consistency effect for the comprehension of jury instructions. *Psychology, Public Policy, and Law, 3,* 381–401.

Enzle, M. E., & Anderson, S. C. (1993). Surveillant intentions and intrinsic motivation. *Journal of Personality and Social Psychology, 64,* 257–266.

Epley, N., & Huff, C. (1998). Suspicion, affective response, and educational benefit as a result of deception in psychology research. *Personality and Social Psychology Bulletin, 24,* 759–768.

Erber, R., & Tesser, A. (1992). Task effort and the regulation of mood: The absorption hypothesis. *Journal of Experimental Social Psychology, 28,* 339–359.

Erber, R., & Tesser, A. (1994). Self-evaluation maintenance: A social psychological approach to interpersonal relationships. In R. Erber & R. Gilmour (Eds.), *Theoretical frameworks for personal relationships* (pp. 211–233). Hillsdale, NJ: Erlbaum.

Ericksen, J. A., & Steffen, S. A. (1999). *Kiss and tell: Surveying sex in the twentieth century.* Cambridge, MA: Harvard University Press.

Eslea, M., Menesini, E., Morita, Y., O'Moore, M., Mora-Merchán, J. A., Pereira, B., & Smith, P. K. (2003). Friendship and loneliness among bullies and victims: Data from seven countries. *Aggressive Behavior, 30,* 71–83.

Esser, J. K. (1998). Alive and well after 25 years: A review of groupthink research. *Organizational Behavior and Human Decision Processes, 73,* 116–141.

Estrada-Hollenbeck, M., & Heatherton, T. F. (1998). Avoiding and alleviating guilt through prosocial behavior. In J. Bybee (Ed.), *Guilt and children* (pp. 215–231). San Diego: Academic Press.

Evans, G. W., & Lepore, S. J. (1993). Household crowding and social support: A quasiexperimental analysis. *Journal of Personality and Social Psychology, 65,* 308–316.

Evans, G. W., & Wener, R. E. (2006). Rail commuting duration and passenger stress. *Health Psychology, 25,* 408–412.

Evans, R. I., Smith, C. K., & Raines, B. E. (1984). Deterring cigarette smoking in adolescents: A psychosocial-behavioral analysis of an intervention strategy. In A. Baum, S. E. Taylor, & J. E. Singer (Eds.), *Handbook of psychology and health: Vol. 4. Social psychological aspects of health* (pp. 301–318). Hillsdale, NJ: Erlbaum.

Evers, A., Anderson, N., & Smit-Voskuijl, O. (Eds.). (2005). *Handbook of personnel selection.* Malden, MA: Blackwell.

Everson, S. A., et al. (1996). Hopelessness and risk of mortality and incidence of myorcardial infarction and cancer. *Psychosomatic Medicine, 58,* 133–121.

Everson, S. A., Goldberg, D. E., Kaplan, G. A., Julkunen, J., & Salonen, J. T. (1998). Anger expression and incident hypertension. *Psychosomatic Medicine, 60,* 730–735.

Exum, M. L. (2006). Alcohol and aggression: An integration of findings from experimental studies. *Journal of Criminal Justice, 34,* 131–145.

Fagan, A. A. (2005). The relationship between adolescent physical abuse and criminal offending: Support for an enduring and generalized cycle of violence. *Journal of Family Violence, 20,* 279–290.

Fairburn, C. G., & Brownell, K. D. (Eds.). (2002). *Eating disorders and obesity: A comprehensive handbook.* New York: Guilford Press.

Fay, R. E., Turner, C. F., Klassen, A. D., & Gagnon, J. H. (1989). Prevalence and patterns of same-gender sexual contact among men. *Science, 243,* 343–348.

Fazio, R. H. (1990). Multiple processes by which attitudes guide behavior: The MODE model as an integrative framework. In M. P. Zanna (Ed.), *Advances in experimental social psychology* (Vol. 23, pp. 75–109). New York: Academic Press.

Fazio, R. H., & Olson, M. A. (2003). Implicit measures in social cognition research: Their meaning and use. *Annual Review of Psychology, 54,* 297–327.

Fazio, R. H., & Towles-Schwen, T. (1999). The MODE model of attitude-behavior processes. In S. Chaiken & Y. Trope (Eds.), *Dual-process theories in social psychology* (pp. 97–116). New York: Guilford.

Fazio, R. H., & Zanna, M. P. (1981). Direct experience and attitude-behavior consistency. In L. Berkowitz (Ed.), *Advances in experimental social psychology* (Vol. 14, pp. 162–202). New York: Academic Press.

Fazio, R. H., Effrein, E. A., & Falender, V. J. (1981). Self-perceptions following social interactions. *Journal of Personality and Social Psychology, 41,* 232–242.

Fazio, R. H., Jackson, J. R., Dunton, B. C., & Williams, C. J. (1995). Variability in automatic activation as an unobtrusive measure of racial attitudes. A bona fide pipeline? *Journal of Personality and Social Psychology, 69,* 1013–1027.

Fazio, R. H., Ledbetter, J. E., & Towles-Schwen, T. (2000). On the costs of accessible attitudes: Detecting that the attitude object has changed. *Journal of Personality and Social Psychology, 78,* 197–210.

Fazio, R. H., Zanna, M. P., & Cooper, J. (1977). Dissonance and self perception: An integrative view of each theory's proper domain of application. *Journal of Experimental Social Psychology, 13,* 464–479.

Feeney, J. A., & Noller, P. (1990). Attachment style as a predictor of adult romantic relationships. *Journal of Personality and Social Psychology, 58,* 281–291.

Fehr, B., & Russell, J. A. (1991). The concept of love viewed from a prototype perspective. *Journal of Personality and Social Psychology, 60,* 425–438.

Fein, E., & Schneider, S. (1996). *The rules: Time-tested secrets for capturing the heart of Mr. Right.* New York: Warner Books.

Fein, S., & Eustis, E. F. (2001). *Effects of violent and sexist content in video games on men's sexist attitudes and judgments.* Paper presented at the second annual meeting of the Society of Personality and Social Psychology, San Antonio, TX.

Fein, S., & Spencer, S. J. (1997). Prejudice as self-image maintenance: Affirming the self through derogating others. *Journal of Personality and Social Psychology, 73,* 31–44.

Fein, S., Goethals, G. R., & Kassin, S. M. (2002). *Group influence on political judgments: The case of presidential debates.* Unpublished manuscript, Williams College.

Fein, S., Goethals, G. R., & Kugler, M. B. (2007). Social influence on political judgments: The case of presidential debates. *Political Psychology, 28,* 165–192.

Fein, S., Goethals, G. R., & Sandstrom, M. J. (Eds.). (2005). *Gender and aggression: Interdisciplinary perspectives.* Mahwah, NJ: Erlbaum.

Fein, S., Hoshino-Browne, E., Davies, P. G., & Spencer, S. J. (2003). Self-image maintenance goals and sociocultural norms in motivated social perception. In S. J. Spencer, S. Fein, M. P. Zanna, & J. M. Olson (Eds.), *Motivated social perception: The Ontario symposium* (Vol. 9, pp. 21–44). Mahwah, NJ: Erlbaum.

Fein, S., Morgan, S. J., Norton, M. I., & Sommers, S. R. (1997). Hype and suspicion: The effects of pretrial publicity, race, and suspicion on jurors' verdicts. *Journal of Social Issues, 53,* 487–502.

Fein, S., von Hippel, W., & Spencer, S. J. (1999). To stereotype or not to stereotype: Motivation and stereotype activation, application, and inhibition. *Psychological Inquiry, 10,* 49–54.

Feinberg, T. E., & Keenan, J. P. (Eds.). (2005). *The lost self: Pathologies of the brain and identity.* New York: Oxford University Press.

Feingold, A. (1988). Matching for attractiveness in romantic partners and same-sex friends: A meta-analysis and theoretical critique. *Psychological Bulletin, 104,* 226–235.

Feingold, A. (1992a). Gender differences in mate selection preferences: A test of the parental investment model. *Psychological Bulletin, 112,* 125–139.

Feingold, A. (1992b). Good-looking people are not what we think. *Psychological Bulletin, 111,* 304–341.

Fejfar, M. C., & Hoyle, R. H. (2000). Effect of private self-awareness on negative affect and self-referent attribution: A quantitative review. *Personality and Social Psychology Review, 4,* 132–142.

Fenigstein, A., & Abrams, D. (1993). Self-attention and the egocentric assumption of shared perspectives. *Journal of Experimental Social Psychology, 29,* 287–303.

Fenigstein, A., Scheier, M. F., & Buss, A. H. (1975). Public and private self-consciousness: Assessment and theory. *Journal of Consulting and Clinical Psychology, 43,* 522–527.

Ferrari, J. R. (1998). Procrastination. In H. S. Friedman (Ed.), *Encyclopedia of mental health* (pp. 5.1–5.7). San Diego: Academic Press.

Ferrari, J. R., Johnson, J. A., & McCowan, W. G. (1995). *Procrastination and task avoidance: Theory, research, and treatment.* New York: Plenum.

Ferreira, A., Picazo, O., Uriarte, N., Pereira, M., & Fernandez-Guasti, A. (2000) Inhibitory effect of buspirone and diazepam, but not of 8-OH-DPAT, on maternal behavior and aggression. *Pharmacology, Biochemistry and Behavior, 66,* 389–396.

Fershtman, M. (1997). Cohesive group detection in a social network by the segregation matrix index. *Social Networks, 19,* 193–208.

Festinger, L. (1950). Informal social communication. *Psychological Review, 57,* 271–282.

Festinger, L. (1954). A theory of social comparison processes. *Human Relations, 7,* 117–140.

Festinger, L. (1957). *A theory of cognitive dissonance.* Stanford, CA: Stanford University Press.

Festinger, L., & Carlsmith, J. M. (1959). Cognitive consequences of forced compliance. *Journal of Abnormal and Social Psychology, 58,* 203–210.

Festinger, L., Pepitone, A., & Newcomb, T. (1952). Some consequences of de-individuation in a group. *Journal of Abnormal and Social Psychology, 47,* 382–389.

Festinger, L., Schachter, S., & Back, K. W. (1950). *Social pressures in informal groups: A study of human factors in housing.* New York: Harper.

Fiedler, F. E. (1967). *A theory of leadership effectiveness.* New York: McGraw-Hill.

Fiedler, F. E., & Chemers, M. M. (1984). *Improving leadership effectiveness: The leader match concept* (2nd ed.). New York: Wiley.

Fiedler, F. E., & Garcia, J. E. (1987). *Leadership: Cognitive resources and performance.* New York: Wiley.

Fiedler, F. E., Murphy, S. E., & Gibson, F. W. (1992). Inaccurate reporting and inappropriate variables: A reply to Vecchio's (1990) examination of cognitive resource theory. *Journal of Applied Psychology, 77,* 372–374.

Fincham, F. D. (2003). Marital conflict, correlates, structure, and context. *Current Directions in Psychological Science, 12,* 23–27.

Fincham, F. D., Beach, S. R. H., & Davila, J. (2004). Forgiveness and conflict resolution in marriage. *Journal of Family Psychology, 18,* 72–81.

Fincham, F. D., Harold, G. T., & Gano-Phillips, S. (2000). The longitudinal association between attributions and marital satisfaction: Direction of effects and role of efficacy expectations. *Journal of Family Psychology, 14,* 267–285.

Fine, M. A., & Sacher, J. A. (1997). Predictors of distress following relationship termination among dating couples. *Journal of Social and Clinical Psychology, 16,* 381–388.

Fink, J. S., & Kensicki, L. J. (2002). An imperceptible difference: Visual and textual constructions of femininity in *Sports Illustrated* and *Sports Illustrated for Women. Mass Communication and Society, 5,* 317–339.

Finkel, E. J., Rusbult, C. E., Kumashiro, M., & Hannon, P. A. (2002). Dealing with betrayal in close relationships: Does commitment promote forgiveness? *Journal of Personality and Social Psychology, 82,* 956–974.

Finkel, N. J. (1995). *Commonsense justice: Jurors' notions of the law.* Cambridge, MA: Harvard University Press.

Fischer, C. S. (1976). *The urban experience.* New York: Harcourt Brace Jovanovich.

Fischer, P., & Greitemeyer, T. (2006). Music and aggression: The impact of sexual-aggressive song lyrics on aggression-related thoughts, emotions, and behavior toward the same and the opposite sex. *Personality and Social Psychology Bulletin, 32,* 1165–1176.

Fishbein, M. (1980). A theory of reasoned action: Some applications and implications. In H. E. Howe & M. M. Page (Eds.), *Nebraska Symposium on Motivation* (Vol. 27, pp. 65–116). Lincoln: University of Nebraska Press.

Fishbein, M., & Ajzen, I. (1972). Attitudes and opinions. In P. H. Mussen & M. R. Rosenzweig (Eds.), *Annual Review of Psychology, 23,* 487–544.

Fishbein, M., & Ajzen, I. (1975). *Beliefs, attitudes, intention, and behavior: An introduction to theory and research.* Reading, MA: Addison-Wesley.

Fisher, H. E. (2004). *Why we love: The nature and chemistry of romantic love.* New York: Henry Holt.

Fisher, J. D., Fisher, W. A., Bryan, A. D., & Misovich, S. J. (2002). Information-motivation-behavioral skills model-based HIV risk behavior change intervention for inner-city high school youth. *Health Psychology, 21,* 177–186.

Fisher, J. D., Fisher, W. A., Williams, S. S., & Malloy, T. E. (1994). Empirical tests of an information-motivation-behavioral skills model of AIDS-preventive behavior with gay men and heterosexual university students. *Health Psychology, 13,* 238–250.

Fisher, J. D., Nadler, A., & Whitcher-Alagna, S. (1982). Recipient reactions to aid. *Psychological Bulletin, 91,* 27–54.

Fiske, A. P. (1991). The cultural relativity of selfish individualism: Anthropological evidence that humans are inherently sociable. In M. S. Clark (Ed.), *Review of personality and social psychology: Vol. 12. Prosocial behavior* (pp. 176–214). Newbury Park, CA: Sage.

Fiske, A. P. (1992). The four elementary forms of sociality: Framework for a unified theory of social relations. *Psychological Review, 99,* 689–723.

Fiske, A. P. (2002). Using individualism and collectivism to compare cultures—A critique of the validity and measurement of the constructs: Comment on Oyserman et al. (2002). *Psychological Bulletin, 128,* 78–88.

Fiske, S. T. (2000). Interdependence reduces prejudice and stereotyping. In S. Oskamp (Ed.), *Reducing prejudice and discrimination* (pp. 115–135). Mahwah, NJ: Erlbaum.

Fiske, S. T., & Neuberg, S. L. (1990). A continuum model of impression formation: From category-based to individuating processes: Influence of information and motivation on attention and interpretation. In M. P. Zanna (Ed.), *Advances in experimental social psychology* (Vol. 23, pp. 1–74). San Diego, CA: Academic Press.

Fiske, S. T., Bersoff, D. N., Borgida, E., Deaux, K., & Heilman, M. E. (1991). Social science research on trial: Use of sex stereotyping research in *Price Waterhouse v. Hopkins. American Psychologist, 46,* 1049–1060.

Fiske, S. T., Lin, M., & Neuberg, S. L. (1999). The continuum model: Ten years later. In S. Chaiken & Y. Trope (Eds.), *Dual-process theories in social psychology* (pp. 231–254). New York: Guilford.

Fitzgerald, J. M. (1988). Vivid memories and the reminiscence phenomenon: The role of self-narrative. *Human Development, 31,* 261–273.

Fitzgerald, R., & Ellsworth, P. C. (1984). Due process vs. crime control: Death qualification and jury attitudes. *Law and Human Behavior, 8,* 31–52.

Fitzpatrick, J. L., Desjardins, J. K., Stiver, K. A., Montgomerie, R., Balshine, S., & Balshine, S. (2006). Male reproductive suppression in the cooperatively breeding fish *Neolamprologus pulcher. Behavioral Ecology, 17,* 25–33.

Fivush, R., Haden, C. A., & Dimmick, J. W. (Eds.). (2003). *Autobiographical memory and the construction of a narrative self: Developmental and cultural perspectives.* Mahwah, NJ: Erlbaum.

Fjermestad, J. (2004). An analysis of communication mode in group support systems research. *Decision Support Systems, 37,* 239–263.

Flack, W. F., Jr., Laird, J. D., & Cavallaro, L. A. (1999). Separate and combined effects of facial expressions and bodily postures on emotional feelings. *European Journal of Social Psychology, 29,* 203–217.

Fleming, M. A., Wegener, D. T., & Petty, R. E. (1999). Procedural and legal motivations to correct for perceived judicial biases. *Journal of Experimental Social Psychology, 35,* 186–203.

Fletcher, G. J. O. (2002). *The new science of intimate relationships.* Oxford, UK: Blackwell.

Fletcher, G. J. O., Danilovics, P., Fernandez, G., Peterson, D., & Reeder, G. D. (1986). Attributional complexity: An individual differences measure. *Journal of Personality and Social Psychology, 51,* 875–884.

Florian, V., Mikulincer, M., & Taubman, O. (1995). Does hardiness contribute to mental health during a stressful real-life situation? The roles of appraisal and coping. *Journal of Personality and Social Psychology, 68,* 687–695.

Flory, J. D., Raikkonen, K., Matthews, K. A., & Owens, J. F. (2000). Self-focused attention and mood during everyday social interactions. *Personality and Social Psychology Bulletin, 26,* 875–883.

Folger, R. (1986). Rethinking equity theory: A referent cognitions model. In H. W. Bierhoff, R. L. Cohen, & J. Greenberg (Eds.), *Justice in social relations* (pp. 145–162). New York: Plenum.

Folger, R., & Cropanzano, R. (1998). *Organizational justice and human resource management.* Thousand Oaks, CA: Sage.

Folger, R., & Greenberg, J. (1985). Procedural justice: An interpretive analysis of personnel systems. In K. Rowland & G. Ferris (Eds.), *Research in personnel and human resource management* (Vol. 3, pp. 141–183). Greenwich, CT: JAI Press.

Folger, R., Konovsky, M. A., & Cropanzano, R. (1992). A due process metaphor for performance appraisal. *Research in Organizational Behavior, 14,* 129–177.

Folkman, S., & Moskowitz, J. T. (2000). Positive affect and the other side of coping. *American Psychologist, 55,* 647–654.

Follett, M. P. (1942). Constructive conflict. In H. C. Metcalf & L. Urwick (Eds.), *Dynamic administration: The collected papers of Mary Parker Follett* (pp. 30–49). New York: Harper.

Forbes, G. B., Adams-Curtis, L. E., Pakalka, A. H., & White, K. B. (2006). Dating aggression, sexual coercion, and aggression-supporting attitudes among college men as a function of participation in aggressive high school sports. *Violence Against Women, 12,* 441–455.

Ford, T. E., & Tonander, G. R. (1998). The role of differentiation between groups and social identity in stereotype formation. *Social Psychology Quarterly, 61,* 372–384.

Ford, T. E., Ferguson, M. A., Brooks, J. L., & Hagadone, K. M. (2004). Coping sense of humor reduces effects of stereotype threat on women's math performance. *Personality and Social Psychology Bulletin, 30,* 643–653.

Forgas, J. P. (2006). Research on affect and social behavior: Links to cognitive, learning, and neuropsychology. In P. A. M. Van Lange (Ed.), *Bridging social psychology: Benefits of transdisciplinary approaches* (pp. 117–122). Mahwah, NJ: Erlbaum.

Forgas, J. P. (Ed.). (2000). *Feeling and thinking: Affective influences on social cognition.* New York: Cambridge University Press.

Forgas, J. P., & Bower, G. H. (1987). Mood effects on person perception judgments. *Journal of Personality and Social Psychology, 53,* 53–60.

Forgas, J. P., & Locke, J. (2005). Affective influences on causal inferences: The effects of mood on attributions for positive and negative interpersonal episodes. *Cognition and Emotion, 19,* 1071–1081.

Forgas, J. P., von Hippel, W. H., & Haselton, M. (Eds.). (2007). *Evolutionary psychology and social cognition.* New York: Psychology Press.

Forsterlee, L., Kent, L., & Horowitz, I. A. (2005). The cognitive effects of jury aids on decision-making in complex civil litigation. *Applied Cognitive Psychology, 19,* 867–884.

Forsyth, D. R. (1999). *Group dynamics* (3rd ed.). Belmont, CA: Wadsworth.

Forsythe, S. M. (1990). Effects of applicant's clothing on interviewer's decision to hire. *Journal of Applied Social Psychology, 20,* 1579–1595.

Foster, C. A., Witcher, B. S., Campbell, W. K., & Green, J. D. (1998). Arousal and attraction: Evidence for automatic and controlled processes. *Journal of Personality and Social Psychology, 74,* 86–101.

Fosterling, F. (1992). The Kelley model as an analysis of variance analogy: How far can it be taken? *Journal of Experimental Social Psychology, 28,* 475–490.

Fox, E., Russo, R., & Dutton, K. (2002). Attentional bias for threat: Evidence for delayed disengagement from emotional faces. *Cognition and Emotion, 16,* 355–379.

Fox, S., & Spector, P. E. (Eds.). (2004). *Counterproductive work behavior: Investigations of actors and targets.* Washington, DC: American Psychological Association.

Frable, D. E. S. (1989). Sex typing and gender ideology: Two facets of the individual's gender psychology that go together. *Journal of Personality and Social Psychology, 56,* 95–108.

Franck, K. A. (1980). Friends and strangers: The social experience of living in urban and non-urban settings. *Journal of Social Issues, 36*(3), 52–71.

Frank, J. (1949). *Courts on trial.* Princeton, NJ: Princeton University Press.

Frank, M. G., & Ekman, P. (1997). The ability to detect deceit generalizes across different types of high-stake lies. *Journal of Personality and Social Psychology, 72,* 1429–1439.

Frantz, C. M., Cuddy, A. J. C., Burnett, M., Ray, H., & Hart, A. (2004). A threat in the computer: The race Implicit Association Test as a stereotype threat experience. *Personality and Social Psychology Bulletin, 30,* 1611–1624.

Frattaroli, J. (2006). Experimental disclosure and its moderators: A meta-analysis. *Psychological Bulletin, 132,* 823–865.

Frazier, P. A. (2003). Perceived control and distress following sexual assault: A longitudinal test of a new model. *Journal of Personality and Social Psychology, 84,* 1257–1269.

Frazier, P., & Schauben, L. (1994). Causal attributions and recovery from rape and other stressful events. *Journal of Social and Clinical Psychology, 13,* 1–14.

Frazier, P., Steward, J., & Mortensen, H. (2004). Perceived control and adjustment to trauma: A comparison across events. *Journal of Social and Clinical Psychology, 23,* 303–324.

Frederickson, B. L., Maynard, K. E., Helms, M. J., Haney, T. L., Siegler, I. C., & Barefoot, J. C. (2000). Hostility predicts magnitude and duration of blood pressure response to anger. *Journal of Behavioral Medicine, 23,* 229–243.

Fredrickson, B. L., Roberts, T. A., Noll, S. M., Quinn, D. M., & Twenge, J. M. (1998). The swimsuit becomes you: Sex differences in self-objectification, restrained eating, and math performance. *Journal of Personality and Social Psychology, 75,* 269–284.

Fredrickson, B. L., Tugade, M. M., Waugh, C. E., & Larkin, G. R. (2003). What good are positive emotions in crisis? A prospective study of resilience and emotions following the terrorist attacks on the United States on September 11th, 2001. *Journal of Personality and Social Psychology, 84,* 365–376.

Freedman, J. L., & Fraser, S. C. (1966). Compliance without pressure: The foot-in-the-door technique. *Journal of Personality and Social Psychology, 4,* 195–202.

Freedman, J. L., & Sears, D. O. (1965). Warning, distraction, and resistance to influence. *Journal of Personality and Social Psychology, 1,* 262–266.

Freud, S. (1905). Fragments of an analysis of a case of hysteria. *Collected papers* (Vol. 3). New York: Basic Books. (Reprinted in 1959)

Freud, S. (1920). *Beyond the pleasure principle: A study of the death instinct in human aggression* (J. Strachey, Trans.). New York: Bantam Books. (Reprinted in 1959)

Frey, D., & Schulz-Hardt, S. (2001). Confirmation bias in group information seeking and its implications for decision making in administration, business and politics. In F. Butera & G. Mugny (Eds.), *Social influence in social reality: Promoting individual and social change* (pp. 53–73). Ashland, OH: Hogrefe & Huber.

Friedland, N., Keinan, G., & Regev, Y. (1992). Controlling the uncontrollable: Effects of stress on illusory perceptions of controllability. *Journal of Personality and Social Psychology, 63,* 923–931.

Friedman, H. S. (1991). *The self-healing personality.* New York: Henry Holt.

Friedman, H. S., & Booth-Kewley, S. (1987). The "disease-prone personality": A meta-analytic view of the construct. *American Psychologist, 42,* 539–555.

Friedman, H. S., & Silver, R. C. (2006). *Foundations of health psychology.* New York: Oxford University Press.

Friedman, M. S., Koeske, G. F., Silvestre, A. J., Korr, W. S., & Sites, E. W. (2006). The impact of gender-role nonconforming behavior, bullying, and social support on suicidality among gay male youth. *Journal of Adolescent Health, 38,* 621–623.

Friedrich, J., Fethersonhaugh, D., Casey, S., & Gallagher, D. (1996). Argument integration and attitude change: Suppression effects in the integration of one-sided arguments that vary in persuasiveness. *Personality and Social Psychology Bulletin, 22,* 179–191.

Friend, R., Rafferty, Y., & Bramel, D. (1990). A puzzling misinterpretation of the Asch "conformity" study. *European Journal of Social Psychology, 20,* 29–44.

Fritzsche, B. A., Finkelstein, M. A., & Penner, L. A. (2000). To help or not to help: Capturing individuals' decision policies. *Social Behavior and Personality, 28,* 561–578.

Frone, M. R. (2006). Prevalence and distribution of illicit drug use in the workforce and in the workplace: Findings and implications from a U.S. national survey. *Journal of Applied Psychology, 91,* 856–869.

Frye, N. E., & Karney, B. R. (2006). The context of aggressive behavior in marriage: A longitudinal study of newlyweds. *Journal of Family Psychology, 20,* 12–20.

Fuente-Fernandez, R., Ruth, T. R., Sossi, V., Schulzer, M., Calne, D. B., & Stoessl, A. J. (2001). Expectation and dopamine release: Mechanism of the placebo effect in Parkinson's disease. *Science, 293,* 1164–1166.

Funk, S. C. (1992). Hardiness: A review of theory and research. *Health Psychology, 11,* 335–345.

Furche, A., & Johnstone, D. (2006). Evidence of the endowment effect in stock market order placement. *Journal of Behavioral Finance, 7,* 145–154.

Furnham, A. (2003). Belief in a just world: Research progress over the past decade. *Personality and Individual Differences, 34,* 795–817.

Furnham, A., Pallangyo, A. E., & Gunter, B. (2001). Gender-role stereotyping in Zimbabwean television advertisements. *South African Journal of Psychology, 31,* 21–29.

Furnham, A., Simmons, K., & McClelland, A. (2000). Decisions concerning the allocation of scarce medical resources. *Journal of Social Behavior and Personality, 15,* 185–200.

Gabbert, F., Memon, A., & Allan, K. (2003). Memory conformity: Can eyewitnesses influence each other's memories for an event? *Applied Cognitive Psychology, 17,* 533–543.

Gabel, M., & Brunner, H. (2003). *Global Inc.: An atlas of the multinational corporation.* New York: New Press.

Gaertner, S. L., & Dovidio, J. F. (2000). *Reducing intergroup bias: The common ingroup identity model.* Philadelphia, PA: Psychology Press.

Gaertner, S. L., & Dovidio, J. F. (2005). Understanding and addressing contemporary racism: From aversive racism to the Common Ingroup Identity Model. *Journal of Social Issues, 61,* 615–639.

Gaertner, S. L., & Dovidio, J. F. (2005). Understanding and addressing contemporary racism: From aversive racism to the Common Ingroup Identity Model. *Journal of Social Issues, 61,* 615–639.

Gagne, F. M., & Lydon, J. E. (2001). Mindset and relationship illusions: The moderating effects of domain specificity and relationship commitment. *Personality and Social Psychology Bulletin, 27,* 1144–1155.

Gagnon, A., & Bourhis, R. Y. (1996). Discrimination in the minimal group paradigm: Social identity or self-interest? *Personality and Social Psychology Bulletin, 22,* 1289–1301.

Galanter, M. (1999). *Cults: Faith, healing, and coercion* (2nd ed.). New York: Oxford University Press.

Galea, S., Ahern, J., Resnick, H., Kilpatrick, D., Bucuvalas, M., Gold, J., & Vlahov, D. (2002). Psychological sequelae of the September 11 terrorist attacks in New York City. *New England Journal of Medicine, 346,* 982–987.

Galen, B. R., & Underwood, M. K. (1997). *Developmental Psychology, 33,* 589–600.

Galinsky, A. D., & Kray, L. J. (2004). From thinking about what might have been to sharing what we know: The role of counterfactual mind-sets in information sharing in groups. *Journal of Experimental Social Psychology, 40,* 606–618.

Galinsky, A. D., & Ku, G. (2004). The effects of perspective-taking in prejudice: The moderating role of self-evaluation. *Personality and Social Psychology Bulletin, 30,* 594–604.

Galinsky, A. D., & Moskowitz, G. B. (2000). Perspective-taking: Decreasing stereotype expression, stereotype accessibility, and in-group favoritism. *Journal of Personality and Social Psychology, 78,* 708–724.

Galinsky, A. D., Martorana, P. V., & Ku, G. (2003). To control or not to control stereotypes: Separating the implicit and explicit processes of perspective-taking and suppression. In J. P. Forgas, K. D. Williams, & W. von Hippel (Eds.), *Social judgments: Implicit and explicit processes* (pp. 343–363). New York: Cambridge University Press.

Galinsky, A. D., Stone, J., & Cooper, J. (2000). The reinstatement of dissonance and psychological discomfort following failed affirmations. *European Journal of Social Psychology, 30,* 123–147.

Gallo, L. C., & Matthews, K. A. (2003). Understanding the association between socioeconomic status and physical health: Do negative emotions play a role? *Psychological Bulletin, 129,* 10–51.

Gallup Poll Editors (2002). *Gallup poll of the Islamic world: Subscriber report.* Princeton, NJ: Gallup Press.

Gallup, G. G., Jr. (1977). Self-recognition in primates: A comparative approach to the bidirectional properties of consciousness. *American Psychologist, 32,* 329–337.

Game, F., Carchon, I., & Vital-Durand, F. (2003). The effect of stimulus attractiveness on visual tracking in 2- to 6-month-old infants. *Infant Behavior & Development, 26,* 135–150.

Gammie, S. C., Olaghere-da-Silva, U. B., & Nelson, R. J. (2000). 3-Bromo-7-nitroindazole, a neuronal nitric oxide synthase inhibitor, impairs maternal aggression and citrulline immunoreactivity in prairie voles. *Brain Research, 870,* 80–86.

Gamson, W. A., Fireman, B., & Rytina, S. (1982). *Encounters with unjust authority.* Homewood, IL: Dorsey.

Gan, S., Zillmann, D., & Mitrook, M. (1997). Stereotyping effect of Black women's sexual rap on White audiences. *Basic and Applied Social Psychology, 19,* 381–399.

Gangestad, S. W. (1993). Sexual selection and physical attractiveness: Implications for mating dynamics. *Human Nature, 4,* 205–235.

Gangestad, S. W., & Simpson, J. A. (2000). The evolution of human mating: Trade-offs and strategic pluralism. *Behavioral and Brain Sciences, 23,* 573–587.

Gangestad, S. W., & Snyder, M. (1991). Taxonomic analysis redux: Some statistical considerations for testing a latent class model. *Journal of Personality and Social Psychology, 61,* 141–146.

Gangestad, S. W., & Snyder, M. (2000). Self-monitoring: Appraisal and reappraisal. *Psychological Bulletin, 126,* 530–555.

Garcia, S. M., Weaver, K., Moskowitz, G. B., & Darley, J. M. (2002). Crowded minds: The implicit bystander effect. *Journal of Personality and Social Psychology, 83,* 843–853.

Gardner, W. L., Gabriel, S., & Hochschild, L. (2002). When you and I are "we," you are not threatening: The role of self-expansion in social comparison. *Journal of Personality and Social Psychology, 82,* 239–251.

Garland, H., & Conlon, D. E. (1998). Too close to quit: The role of project completion in maintaining commitment. *Journal of Applied Social Psychology, 28,* 2025–2048.

Gawronski, B., & Bodenhausen, G. V. (2006). Associative and propositional processes in evaluation: An integrative review of implicit and explicit attitude change. *Psychological Bulletin, 132,* 692–731.

Geary, D. C. (2000). Evolution and proximate expression of human paternal investment. *Psychological Bulletin, 126,* 55–77.

Geary, D. C. (2005). Evolution of life-history trade-offs in mate attractiveness and health: Comment on Weeden and Sabini. *Psychological Bulletin, 131,* 654–657.

Geen, R. G. (1981). Behavioral and physiological reactions to observed violence: Effects of prior exposure to aggressive stimuli. *Journal of Personality and Social Psychology, 40,* 868–875.

Geen, R. G. (1991). Social motivation. *Annual Review of Psychology, 42,* 377–399.

Geen, R. G. (1998). Aggression and antisocial behavior. In D. T. Gilbert, S. T. Fiske, & G. Lindzey (Eds.), *The handbook of social psychology* (4th ed., Vol. 2, pp. 317–356). New York: McGraw-Hill.

Geen, R. G., & Donnerstein, E. (Eds.). (1998). *Human aggression: Theories, research, and implications for social policy.* San Diego, CA: Academic Press.

Geen, R. G., & Quanty, M. B. (1977). The catharsis of aggression: An evaluation of a hypothesis. In L. Berkowitz (Ed.), *Advances in experimental social psychology* (Vol. 10, pp. 1–37). New York: Academic Press.

Geis, F. L., Brown, V., Jennings (Walstedt), J., & Porter, N. (1984). TV commercials as achievement scripts for women. *Sex Roles, 10,* 513–525.

Geiselman, R. E., Haight, N. A., & Kimata, L. G. (1984). Context effects in the perceived physical attractiveness of faces. *Journal of Experimental Social Psychology, 20,* 409–424.

Gelfand, M. J., Erez, M., & Aycan, Z. (2007). Cross-cultural organizational behavior. *Annual Review of Psychology, 58,* 479–514.

Gelles, R. J., & Cornell, C. P. (1990). *Intimate violence in families* (2nd ed.). Newbury Park, CA: Sage.

George, D. M., Carroll, P., Kersnick, R., & Calderon, K. (1998). Gender-related patterns of helping among friends. *Psychology of Women Quarterly, 22,* 685–704.

George, J. M., & Brief, A. P. (1992). Feeling good–doing good: A conceptual analysis of the mood at work–organizational spontaneity relationship. *Psychological Bulletin, 112,* 310–329.

Georgesen, J. C., & Harris, M. J. (1998). Why's my boss always holding me down? A meta-analysis of power effects on performance evaluations. *Personality and Social Psychology Review, 2,* 184–195.

Gerard, H. B., Whilhelmy, R. A., & Connolley, R. S. (1968). Conformity and group size. *Journal of Personality and Social Psychology, 8,* 79–82.

Gerbner, G., Gross, L., Morgan, M., & Signorielli, N. (1986). Living with television: The dynamics of the cultivation process. In J. Bryant & D. Zillmann (Eds.), *Perspectives on media effects* (pp. 17–40). Hillsdale, NJ: Erlbaum.

Gergen, K. J. (1973). Social psychology as history. *Journal of Personality and Social Psychology, 26,* 309–320.

Gerhart, B., & Rynes, S. (1991). Determinants and consequences of salary negotiations by male and female MBA graduates. *Journal of Applied Psychology, 76,* 256–262.

Gerrard, M., Gibbons, F. X., & Bushman, B. J. (1996). Relation between perceived vulnerability in HIV and precautionary sexual behavior. *Psychological Bulletin, 119,* 390–409.

Gershoff, E. T. (2002). Corporal punishment by parents and associated child behaviors and experiences: A meta-analytic and theoretical review. *Psychological Bulletin, 128,* 539–579.

Gersick, C. J. G. (1988). Time and transition in work teams: Toward a new model of group development. *Academy of Management Journal, 21,* 9–41.

Gersick, C. J. G. (1994). Pacing strategic change: The case of a new venture. *Academy of Management Journal, 37,* 9–45.

Gerson, J. (2006, September 21). Montreal shootings disturb Columbine game creator. *Toronto Star,* p. A12.

Gibbons, F. X. (1990). Self-attention and behavior: A review and theoretical update. In M. P. Zanna (Ed.), *Advances in experimental social psychology* (Vol. 23, pp. 249–303). New York: Academic Press.

Gibbons, F. X., & McCoy, S. B. (1991). Self-esteem, similarity, and reactions to active versus passive downward comparison. *Journal of Personality and Social Psychology, 60,* 414–424.

Gibbons, F. X., Gerrard, M., Cleveland, M. J., Wills, T. A., & Brody, G. (2004). Perceived discrimination and substance use in African American parents and their children: A panel study. *Journal of Personality and Social Psychology, 86,* 517–529.

Gibbons, F. X., Lane, D. J., Gerrard, M., Reis-Bergan, M., Lautrup, C., Pexa, N., & Blanton, H. (2002). Comparison level preferences after performance: Is downward comparison theory still useful? *Journal of Personality and Social Psychology, 83,* 865–880.

Gibbons, S. L., & Ebbeck, V. (1997). The effect of different teaching strategies on the moral development of physical education students. *Journal of Teaching in Physical Education, 17,* 85–98.

Gibbs, J. L., Ellison, N. B., & Heino, R. D. (2006). Self-presentation in online personals: The role of anticipated future interaction, self-disclosure, and perceived success in dating. *Communication Research, 33,* 152–177.

Gibson, B., & Sachau, D. (2000). Sandbagging as a self-presentational strategy: Claiming to be less than you are. *Personality and Social Psychology Bulletin, 26,* 56–70.

Giesler, R. B., Josephs, R. A., & Swann, W. B., Jr. (1996). Self-verification in clinical depression: The desire for negative evaluation. *Journal of Abnormal Psychology, 105,* 358–368.

Gigerenzer, G., Todd, P. M., & the ABC Research Group (1999). *Simple heuristics that make us smart.* New York: Oxford University Press.

Gigone, D., & Hastie, R. (1993). The common knowledge effect: Information sharing and group judgment. *Journal of Personality and Social Psychology, 65,* 959–974.

Gigone, D., & Hastie, R. (1997). The impact of information on small group choice. *Journal of Personality and Social Psychology, 72,* 132–140.

Gilbert, D. (2006). *Stumbling on happiness.* New York: Alfred A. Knopf.

Gilbert, D. T., & Hixon, J. G. (1991). The trouble of thinking: Activation and application of stereotypic beliefs. *Journal of Personality and Social Psychology, 60,* 509–517.

Gilbert, D. T., & Jones, E. E. (1986). Perceiver-induced constraint: Interpretations of self-generated reality. *Journal of Personality and Social Psychology, 50,* 269–280.

Gilbert, D. T., & Malone, P. S. (1995). The correspondence bias. *Psychological Bulletin, 117,* 21–38.

Gilbert, D. T., & Silvera, D. H. (1996). Overhelping. *Journal of Personality and Social Psychology, 70,* 678–690.

Gilbert, D. T., Giesler, R. B., & Morris, K. A. (1995). When comparisons arise. *Journal of Personality and Social Psychology, 69,* 227–236.

Gilbert, D. T., McNulty, S. E., Giuliano, T. A., & Benson, J. E. (1992). Blurry words and fuzzy deeds: The attribution of obscure behavior. *Journal of Personality and Social Psychology, 62,* 18–25.

Gilbert, D. T., Morewedge, C. K., Risen, J. L., & Wilson, T. D. (2004). Looking forward to looking backward: The misprediction of regret. *Psychological Science, 15,* 346–350.

Gilbert, D. T., Pelham, B. W., & Krull, D. S. (1988). On cognitive busyness: When person perceivers meet persons perceived. *Journal of Personality and Social Psychology, 54,* 733–740.

Gilbert, D. T., Pinel, E. C., Wilson, T. D., Blumberg, S. J., & Wheatley, T. (1998). Immune neglect: A source of durability bias in affective forecasting. *Journal of Personality and Social Psychology, 75,* 617–638.

Gilbert, S. J. (1981). Another look at the Milgram obedience studies: The role of the gradated series of shocks. *Personality and Social Psychology Bulletin, 7,* 690–695.

Giles, L. C., Glonek, G. F., Luszcz, M. A., & Andrews, G. R. (2005). Effect of social networks on 10 year survival in very old Australians: The Australian longitudinal study of aging. *Journal of Epidemiology and Community Health, 59,* 574–579.

Gillig, P. M., & Greenwald, A. G. (1974). Is it time to lay the sleeper effect to rest? *Journal of Personality and Social Psychology, 29,* 132–139.

Gilovich, T. (1991). *How we know what isn't so: The fallibility of human reason in everyday life.* New York: Free Press.

Gilovich, T., Grifin, D., & Kahneman, D. (Eds.). (2002). *Heuristics and biases: The psychology of intuitive judgment.* New York: Cambridge University Press.

Gilovich, T., Medvec, V. H., & Savitsky, K. (2000). The spotlight effect in social judgment: An egocentric bias in estimates of the salience of one's own actions and appearance. *Journal of Personality and Social Psychology, 78,* 211–222.

Giner-Sorolla, R., & Chaiken, S. (1997). Selective use of heuristic and systematic processing under defensive motivation. *Personality and Social Psychology Bulletin, 23,* 84–97.

Gintis, H., Bowles, S., Boyd, R., & Fehr, E. (2003). Explaining altruistic behavior in humans. *Evolution and Human Behavior, 24,* 153–172.

Gioia, D. A., & Longnecker, C. O. (1994). Delving into the dark side: The politics of executive appraisal. *Organizational Dynamics, 22,* 47–58.

Gladstone, G. L., Parker, G. B., & Malhi, G. S. (2006). Do bullied children become anxious and depressed adults? A cross-sectional investigation of the correlates of bullying and anxious depression. *Journal of Nervous and Mental Disease, 19,* 201–208.

Gladue, B. A., Boechler, M., & McCaul, K. D. (1989). Hormonal response to competition in human males. *Aggressive Behavior, 15,* 409–422.

Gladwell, M. (2005). *Blink: The power of thinking without thinking.* New York: Little, Brown, and Company.

Glanz, J., & Schwartz, J. (September 26, 2003). Dogged engineer's effort to assess shuttle damage. *New York Times,* p. A1.

Glasman, L. R., & Albarracín, D. (2006). Forming attitudes that predict future behavior: A meta-analysis of the attitude-behavior relation. *Psychological Bulletin, 132,* 778–822.

Glass, D. C., & Singer, J. E. (1972). *Urban stress.* New York: Academic Press.

Gledhill, L., & Lucas, G. (2000, September 19). Davis signs child assault "good Samaritan" bill: Death of 7-year-old girl in casino inspired legislation. *San Francisco Chronicle,* p. A3.

Gleicher, F., & Petty, R. E. (1992). Expectations of reassurance influence the nature of fear-stimulated attitude change. *Journal of Experimental Social Psychology, 28,* 86–100.

Gleick, E. (1997). The marker we've been waiting for. *Time,* April 7, 1997, pp. 31–36.

Glick, P., & Fiske, S. T. (2001a). Ambivalent sexism. In M. P. Zanna (Ed.), *Advances in experimental social psychology* (Vol. 33, pp. 115–188). San Diego, CA: Academic Press.

Glick, P., & Fiske, S. T. (2001b). Ambivalent stereotypes as legitimizing ideologies: Differentiating paternalistic and resentful prejudice. In J. T. Jost & B. Major (Eds.), *The psychology of legitimacy: Emerging perspectives on ideology, justice, and intergroup relations* (pp. 278–306). New York: Cambridge University Press.

Glick, P., Fiske, S. T., et al. (2000). Beyond prejudice as simple antipathy: Hostile and benevolent sexism across cultures. *Journal of Personality and Social Psychology, 79,* 763–775.

Godfrey, D. K., Jones, E. E., & Lord, C. G. (1986). Self-promotion is not ingratiating. *Journal of Personality and Social Psychology, 50,* 106–115.

Goethals, G. R. (2005). Presidential leadership. *Annual Review of Psychology, 56,* 545–570.

Goethals, G. R., & Darley, J. (1977). Social comparison theory: An attributional approach. In J. M. Suls & R. L. Miller (Eds.),

Social comparison processes: Theoretical and empirical perspectives (pp. 259–278). Washington, DC: Hemisphere.

Goethals, G. R., & Reckman, R. (1973). The perception of consistency in attitudes. *Journal of Experimental Social Psychology, 9,* 491–501.

Goethals, G. R., Cooper, J., & Naficy, A. (1979). Role of foreseen, foreseeable, and unforeseeable behavioral consequences in the arousal of cognitive dissonance. *Journal of Personality and Social Psychology, 37,* 1179–1185.

Goethals, G. R., Sorensen, G., & Burns, J. M. (Eds.). (2004). *Encyclopedia of leadership.* Thousand Oaks, CA: Sage.

Goffman, E. (1955). On face-work: An analysis of ritual elements in social interaction. *Psychiatry, 18,* 213–231.

Goffman, E. (1959). *The presentation of self in everyday life.* Garden City: Doubleday.

Goldberg, L. R. (1978). Differential attribution of trait-descriptive terms to oneself as compared to well-liked, neutral, and disliked others: A psychometric analysis. *Journal of Personality and Social Psychology, 36,* 1012–1028.

Goldberg, L. R., Grenier, J. R., Guion, R., Sechrest, L. B., & Wing, H. (1991). *Questionnaires used in the prediction of trustworthiness in pre-employment selection decisions: An A.P.A. task force report.* Washington, DC: American Psychological Association.

Goldberg, P. (1968). Are women prejudiced against women? *Transaction, 5,* 28–30.

Goldhagen, D. J. (1996). *Hitler's willing executioners: Ordinary Germans and the Holocaust.* New York: Knopf.

Goldin, C. (1990). *Understanding the gender gap: An economic history of American women.* New York: Oxford University Press.

Goldstein, A. G., Chance, J. E., & Schneller, G. R. (1989). Frequency of eyewitness identification in criminal cases: A survey of prosecutors. *Bulletin of the Psychonomic Society, 27,* 71–74.

Goldstein, D. G., & Gigerenzer, G. (2002). Models of ecological rationality: The recognition heuristic. *Psychological Review, 109,* 75–90.

Goleman, D., Boyatzis, R., & McKee, A. (2002). *Primal leadership: Realizing the power of emotional intelligence.* Cambridge, MA: Harvard Business School Press.

Gollwitzer, P. M., & Schaal, B. (2001). How goals and plans affect action. In J. M. Collis & S. Messick (Eds.), *Intelligence and personality: Bridging the gap in theory and measurement* (pp. 139–161). Mahwah, NJ: Erlbaum.

Golombok, S., & Hines, M. (2002). Sex differences in social behavior. In P. K. Smith & C. H. Hart (Eds.), *Blackwell handbook of childhood social development* (pp. 117–136). Malden, MA: Blackwell.

Gonsalkorale, K., & Williams, K. D. (2007). The KKK won't let me play: Ostracism even by a despised outgroup hurts. *European Journal of Social Psychology,* in press.

Gonzales, P. M., Blanton, H., & Williams, K. J. (2002). The effects of stereotype threat and double-minority status on the test performance of Latino women. *Personality and Social Psychology Bulletin, 28,* 659–670.

Goode, E. (2000, June 17). To Yankee second baseman, throwing is no idle thought. *New York Times,* p. A1.

Goodwin, S. A., Fiske, S. T., Rosen, L. D., & Rosenthal, A. M. (2002). The eye of the beholder: Romantic goals and impression biases. *Journal of Experimental Social Psychology, 38,* 232–241.

Gopnik, A., Meltzoff, A. N., & Kuhl, P. K. (1999). *The scientist in the crib: Minds, brains, and how children learn.* New York: Morrow.

Gordijn, E. H., Hindriks, I., Koomen, W., Dijksterhuis, A., & van Knippenberg, A. (2004). Consequences of stereotype suppression and internal suppression motivation: A self-regulation approach. *Personality and Social Psychology Bulletin, 30,* 212–224.

Gorenstein, G. W., & Ellsworth, P. C. (1980). Effect of choosing an incorrect photograph on a later identification by an eyewitness. *Journal of Applied Psychology, 65,* 616–622.

Gorman, C. (1994, September 19). Let's not be too hasty. *Time,* p. 71.

Gosling, P., Denizeau, M., & Oberlé, D. (2006). Denial of responsibility: A new mode of dissonance reduction. *Journal of Personality and Social Psychology, 90,* 722–733.

Gosling, S. D., Ko, S. J., Mannarelli, T., & Morris, M. E. (2002). A room with a cue: Personality judgments based on offices and bedrooms. *Journal of Personality and Social Psychology, 82,* 379–398.

Gossett, J. L., & Byrne, S. (2002). "CLICK HERE": A content analysis of Internet rape sites. *Gender and Society, 16,* 689–709.

Gottfredson, L. S. (2002). Where and why *g* matters: Not a mystery. *Human Performance, 15,* 25–46.

Gottman, J. M. (1994). *What predicts divorce?* Hillsdale, NJ: Erlbaum.

Gottman, J. M. (1998). Psychology and the study of marital processes. *Annual Review of Psychology, 49,* 169–197.

Gottman, J. M., & Levenson, R. W. (1992). Marital processes predictive of later dissolution: Behavior, physiology, and health. *Journal of Personality and Social Psychology, 63,* 221–233.

Gould, S. J. (1992, November 19). The confusion over evolution. *New York Review of Books,* pp. 47–54.

Gouldner, A. W. (1960). The norm of reciprocity: A preliminary statement. *American Sociological Review, 25,* 161–178.

Govorun, O., & Payne, B. K. (2006). Ego-depletion and prejudice: Separating automatic and controlled components. *Social Cognition, 24,* 111–136.

Graham, K., & Wells, S. (2001). The two worlds of aggression for men and women. *Sex Roles, 45,* 595–622.

Graham, K., Osgood, D. W., Wells, S., & Stockwell, T. (2006). To what extent is intoxication associated with aggression in bars? A multilevel analysis. *Journal of Studies on Alcohol, 67,* 382–390.

Graham, S. (1992). "Most of the subjects were white and middle class": Trends in published research on African Americans in selected APA journals, 1970–1989. *American Psychologist, 47,* 629–639.

Grammer, K., & Thornhill, R. (1994). Human facial attractiveness and sexual selection: The role of averageness and symmetry. *Journal of Comparative Psychology, 108,* 233–242.

Grammer, K., Fink, B., Moller, A. P., & Manning, J. T. (2005). Physical attractiveness and health: Comment on Weeden and Sabini. *Psychological Bulletin, 131,* 658–661.

Graña, J. L., Cruzado, J. A., Andreu, J. M., Muñoz-Rivas, M. J., Peña, M. E., & Brain, P. F. (2004). Effects of viewing videos of bullfights on Spanish children. *Aggressive Behavior, 30,* 16–28.

Granberg, D., & Bartels, B. (2005). On being a lone dissenter. *Journal of Applied Social Psychology, 35,* 1849–1858.

Granhag, P. A., & Strömwall. L. A. (Eds.). (2004). *Deception detection in forensic contexts.* Cambridge, England: Cambridge University Press.

Granhag, P., & Strömwall, L. (Eds.). (2004). *Deception detection in forensic contexts.* Cambridge, England: Cambridge University Press.

Graves, L. M., & Powell, G. N. (1988). An investigation of sex discrimination in recruiters' evaluations of actual applicants. *Journal of Applied Psychology, 73,* 20–29.

Gray, J. (1997). *Men are from Mars, women are from Venus.* New York: HarperCollins.

Gray, R. (2004). Attending to the execution of a complex sensorimotor skill: Expertise differences, choking, and slumps. *Journal of Experimental Psychology: Applied, 10,* 42–54.

Gray-Little, B., & Hafdahl, A. R. (2000). Factors influencing racial comparisons of self-esteem: A quantitative review. *Psychological Bulletin, 126,* 26–54.

Greatbatch, D., & Clark, T. (2003). Displaying group cohesiveness: Humour and laughter in the public lectures of management gurus. *Human Relations, 56,* 1515–1544.

Green, D. P., Glaser, J., & Rich, A. (1998). From lynching to gay bashing: The elusive connection between economic conditions and hate crime. *Journal of Personality and Social Psychology, 75,* 82–92.

Greenberg, D. L. (2004). President Bush's false "flashbulb" memory of 9/11/01. *Applied Cognitive Psychology, 18,* 363–370.

Greenberg, J. (1988). Equity and workplace status: A field experiment. *Journal of Applied Psychology, 73,* 606–613.

Greenberg, J. (1990). Employee theft as a reaction to underpayment inequity: The hidden costs of pay cuts. *Journal of Applied Psychology, 75,* 561–568.

Greenberg, J. (2006). Losing sleep over organizational injustice: Attenuating insomniac reactions to underpayment inequity with supervisory training in interactional justice. *Journal of Applied Psychology, 91,* 58–69.

Greenberg, J., & Pyszczynski, T. (1985). The effects of an overheard ethnic slur on evaluations of the target: How to spread a social disease. *Journal of Experimental Social Psychology, 21,* 61–72.

Greenberg, J., Pyszczynski, T., Solomon, S., Rosenblatt, A., et al. (1990). Evidence for terror management theory II: The effects of mortality salience on reactions to those who threaten or bolster the cultural worldview. *Journal of Personality and Social Psychology, 58,* 308–318.

Greenberg, J., Solomon, S., & Pyszczynski, T. (1997). Terror management theory of self-esteem and cultural worldviews: Empirical assessments and conceptual refinements. *Advances in Experimental Social Psychology, 29,* 61–139.

Greenberg, M. S., & Westcott, D. R. (1983). Indebtedness as a mediator of reactions to aid. In J. D. Fisher, A. Nadler, & B. M. DePaulo (Eds.), *New directions in helping: Vol. 1. Recipient reactions to aid* (pp. 85–112). New York: Academic Press.

Greene, E., & Bornstein, B. (2003). *Determining damages: The psychology of jury awards.* Washington, DC: American Psychological Association.

Greene, E., Heilbrun, K., Fortune, W. H., & Nietzel, M. T. (2006). *Wrightsman's psychology and the legal system* (6th ed.). Belmont, CA: Wadsworth.

Greenhause, S. (2001, September 1). Report shows Americans have more "Labor Days." *New York Times,* p. A6.

Greenwald, A. G. (1968). Cognitive learning, cognitive responses to persuasion, and attitude change. In A. Greenwald, T. Brock, & T. Ostrom (Eds.), *Psychological foundations of attitudes* (pp. 147–170). New York: Academic Press.

Greenwald, A. G. (1980). The totalitarian ego: Fabrication and revision of personal history. *American Psychologist, 35,* 603–618.

Greenwald, A. G. (1992). New look 3: Unconscious cognition reclaimed. *American Psychologist, 47,* 766–779.

Greenwald, A. G., & Farnham, S. D. (2000). Using the Implicit Association Test to measure self-esteem and self-concept. *Journal of Personality and Social Psychology, 79,* 1022–1038.

Greenwald, A. G., McGhee, D. E., & Schwartz, J. L. K. (1998). Measuring individual differences in implicit cognition: The implicit association test. *Journal of Personality and Social Psychology, 74,* 1464–1480.

Greenwald, A. G., Nosek, B. A., & Banaji, M. R. (2003). Understanding and using the Implicit Association Test: I. An improved scoring algorithm. *Journal of Personality and Social Psychology, 85,* 197–216.

Greenwald, A. G., Oakes, M. A., & Hoffman, H. G. (2003). Targets of discrimination: Effects of race on responses to weapons holders. *Journal of Experimental Social Psychology, 39,* 399–405.

Greenwald, A. G., Pratkanis, A. R., Leippe, M. R., & Baumgardner, M. H. (1986). Under what conditions does theory obstruct research progress? *Psychological Review, 93,* 216–229.

Greenwald, A. G., Spangenberg, E. R., Pratkanis, A. R., & Eskenazi, J. (1991). Double-blind tests of subliminal self-help audiotapes. *Psychological Science, 2,* 119–122.

Greitemeyer, T., Schulz-Hardt, S., Brodbeck, F. C., & Frey, D. (2006). Information sampling and group decision making: The effects of an advocacy decision procedure and task experience. *Journal of Experimental Psychology: Applied, 12,* 31–42.

Griffiths, R. A., Beumont, P. J. V., Giannakopoulos, E., Russell, J., Schotte, D., Thornton, C., Touyz, S. W., & Varano, P. (1999). Measuring self-esteem in dieting disordered patients: The validity of the Rosenberg and Coopersmith contrasted. *International Journal of Eating Disorders, 25,* 227–231.

Grisham, J. (1996). *The runaway jury.* New York: Bantam Books.

Griskevicius, V., Goldstein, N. J., Mortensen, C. R., Cialdini, R. B., & Kenrick, D. T. (2006). Going along versus going alone: When fundamental motives facilitate strategic (non)conformity. *Journal of Personality and Social Psychology, 91,* 281–294.

Gross, A. E., & Latané, J. G. (1974). Receiving help, reciprocation, and interpersonal attraction. *Journal of Applied Social Psychology, 4,* 210–223.

Gross, J. J., & Levenson, R. W. (1997). Hiding feelings: The acute effects of inhibiting negative and positive emotion. *Journal of Abnormal Psychology, 106,* 95–103.

Grossman, M., & Wood, W. (1993). Sex differences in intensity of emotional experience: A social role interpretation. *Journal of Personality and Social Psychology, 65,* 1010–1020.

Grote, N. K., & Clark, M. S. (2001). Perceiving unfairness in the family: Cause or consequence of marital distress? *Journal of Personality and Social Psychology, 80,* 281–293.

Grusec, J. E. (1991). The socialization of altruism. In M. S. Clark (Ed.), *Prosocial behavior. Review of personality and social psychology* (Vol. 12, pp. 9–33). Newbury Park, CA: Sage.

Gudjonsson, G. H. (2003). *The psychology of interrogations and confessions.* London: Wiley.

Gudykunst, W., & Bond, M. H. (1997). Intergroup relations across cultures. In J. W. Berry, M. H. Segall, & C. Kagitçibasi (Eds.), *Handbook of cross-cultural psychology: Social behavior and applications* (2nd ed., Vol. 3, pp. 119–161). Needham Heights, MA: Allyn & Bacon.

Guéguen, N., & Fischer-Lokou, J. (2005). Hitchhikers' smiles and receipt of help. *Psychological Reports, 94,* 756–760.

Guerin, B. (2003). Social behaviors as determined by different arrangements of social consequences: Diffusion of responsibility effects with competition. *Journal of Social Psychology, 143,* 313–329.

Guerra, N. G., Huesmann, L. R., Hanish, L., Font, E., & Henry, D. (1993). *Normative beliefs about aggression as a function of acculturation status among Hispanic children.* Toronto: American Psychological Association.

Guimond, S. (2000). Group socialization and prejudice: The social transmission of intergroup attitudes and beliefs. *European Journal of Social Psychology, 30,* 335–354.

Guion, R. M., & Highhouse, S. (2006). *Essentials of personnel assessment and selection.* Mahwah, NJ: Erlbaum.

Gully, S. M., Devine, D. J., & Whitney, D. J. (1995). A meta-analysis of cohesion and performance: Effects of level of analysis and task interdependence. *Small Group Research, 26,* 497–520.

Gump, B. B., & Kulik, J. A. (1997). Stress, affiliation, and emotional contagion. *Journal of Personality and Social Psychology, 72,* 305–319.

Gurin, P., Dey, E. L., Hurtado, S., & Gurin, G. (2002). Diversity and higher education: Theory and impact on educational outcomes. *Harvard Educational Review, 72,* 332–366.

Gurung, R. A. R. (2006). *Health psychology: A cultural approach.* Belmont, CA: Wadsworth.

Haberstroh, S., Oyserman, D., Schwarz, N., Kuehnen, U., & Ji, L. J. (2002). Is the interdependent self more sensitive to question context than the independent self? Self-construal and the observation of conversational norms. *Journal of Experimental Social Psychology, 38,* 323–329.

Hafer, C. L. (2000). Do innocent victims threaten the belief in a just world? Evidence from a modified Stroop task. *Journal of Personality and Social Psychology, 79,* 165–173.

Hagen, S., & Carouba, M. (2002). *Women at ground zero: Stories of courage and compassion.* Indianapolis, IN: Alpha Books.

Hagerty, M. R. (2000). Social comparisons of income in one's community: Evidence from national surveys of income and happiness. *Journal of Personality and Social Psychology, 78,* 761–771.

Haidt, J. (2006). *The happiness hypothesis: Finding modern truth in ancient wisdom.* New York: Basic Books.

Hajela, D. (2007, January 4). NYC subway savior: Someone had to help. http:news.yahoo.com/s/ap/20070104/ap_on_re_us/subway_rescue

Hakmiller, K. L. (1966). Threat as a determinant of downward comparison. *Journal of Experimental Social Psychology* (Suppl. 1), 32–39.

Halberstadt, J., & Rhodes, G. (2000). The attractiveness of non-face averages: Implications for an evolutionary explanation of the attractiveness of average faces. *Psychological Science, 11,* 285–289.

Halberstadt, J., & Rhodes, G. (2003). It's not just average faces that are attractive: Computer-manipulated averageness makes birds, fish, and automobiles attractive. *Psychonomic Bulletin and Review, 10,* 149–156.

Halberstam, D. (1972). *The best and the brightest.* New York: Random House.

Haley, H., & Sidanius, J. (2005). Person-organization congruence and the maintenance of group-based social hierarchy: A social dominance perspective. *Group Processes and Intergroup Relations, 8,* 187–203.

Haley, H., & Sidanius, J. (2006). The positive and negative framing of affirmative action: A group dominance perspective. *Personality and Social Psychology Bulletin, 32,* 656–668.

Hall, J. A., Coats, E. J., & LeBeau, L. S. (2005). Nonverbal behavior and the vertical dimension of social relations: A meta-analysis. *Psychological Bulletin, 131,* 898–924.

Hall, J. A., Herzberger, S. D., & Skowronski, K. J. (1998). Outcome expectancies and outcome values as predictors of children's aggression. *Aggressive Behavior, 24,* 439–454.

Hall, N. R., & Crisp, R. J. (2005). Considering multiple criteria for social categorization can reduce intergroup bias. *Personality and Social Psychology Bulletin, 31,* 1435–1444.

Hall, S., French, D. P., & Marteau, T. M. (2003). Causal attributions following serious unexpected negative events: A systematic review. *Journal of Social and Clinical Psychology, 22,* 515–536.

Hamer, D. H., Rice, G., Risch, N., & Ebers, G. (1999). Genetics and male sexual orientation. *Science, 285,* 803.

Hamermesh, D. S., & Biddle, J. E. (1994). Beauty and the labor market. *American Economic Review, 84,* 1174–1195.

Hamilton, D. L., & Gifford, R. K. (1976). Illusory correlation in interpersonal perception: A cognitive basis of stereotypic judgments. *Journal of Experimental Social Psychology, 12,* 392–407.

Hamilton, D. L., & Rose, T. L. (1980). Illusory correlation and the maintenance of stereotypic beliefs. *Journal of Personality and Social Psychology, 39,* 832–845.

Hamilton, W. D. (1964). The genetical evolution of social behavior: I and II. *Journal of Theoretical Biology, 7,* 1–52.

Hammersla, J. F., & Frease-McMahan, L. (1990). University students' priorities: Life goals vs. relationships. *Sex Roles, 23,* 1–14.

Hampson, R. B. (1984). Adolescent prosocial behavior: Peer-group and situational factors associated with helping. *Journal of Personality and Social Psychology, 46,* 153–162.

Hamrick, N., Cohen, S., & Rodriguez, M. S. (2002). Being popular can be healthy or unhealthy: Stress, social network diversity, and incidence of upper respiratory infection. *Health Psychology, 21,* 294–298.

Han, G., & Park, B. (1995). Children's choice in conflict: Application of the theory of individualism-collectivism. *Journal of Cross-Cultural Psychology, 26,* 298–313.

Han, S., & Shavitt, S. (1994). Persuasion and culture: Advertising appeals in individualistic and collectivistic societies. *Journal of Experimental Social Psychology, 30,* 326–350.

Hanc, J. (2006, September 12). Muscle men: Today's culture has produced fitness buffs obsessed with becoming muscular. But how much is too much? *Newsday (New York),* p. B12.

Haney, C. (1984). On the selection of capital juries: The biasing effects of the death-qualification process. *Law and Human Behavior, 8,* 121–132.

Haney, C., & Zimbardo, P. G. (1998). The past and future of U.S. prison policy: Twenty-five years after the Stanford Prison Experiment. *American Psychologist, 53,* 709–727.

Haney, C., Banks, C., & Zimbardo, P. (1973). Interpersonal dynamics in a simulated prison. *International Journal of Criminology and Penology, 1,* 69–97.

Haney, C., Hurtado, A., & Vega, L. (1994). "Modern" death qualification: New data on its biasing effects. *Law and Human Behavior, 18,* 619–633.

Hannaford, P. L., Hans, V. P., & Munsterman, G. T. (2000). Permitting jury discussions during trial: Impact on the Arizona reform. *Law and Human Behavior, 24,* 359–380.

Hans, V. P. (2000). *Business on trial: The civil jury and corporate responsibility.* New Haven, CT: Yale University Press.

Hans, V. P., & Vidmar, N. (1986). *Judging the jury.* New York: Plenum.

Hansen, C. H., & Hansen, R. D. (1988). Finding the face in the crowd: An anger superiority effect. *Journal of Personality and Social Psychology, 54,* 917–924.

Harachi, T. W., Fleming, C. B., White, H. R., Ensminger, M. E., Abbott, R. D., Catalano, R. F., & Haggerty, K. P. (2006). Aggressive behavior among girls and boys during middle childhood: Predictors and sequelae of trajectory group membership. *Aggressive Behavior, 32,* 279–293.

Harackiewicz, J. M., & Elliot, A. J. (1993). Achievement goals and intrinsic motivation. *Journal of Personality and Social Psychology, 65,* 904–915.

Hardin, C., & Banaji, M.R. (1993). The influence of language on thought. *Social Cognition, 11,* 277–308.

Hardin, G. (1968). The tragedy of the commons. *Science, 162,* 1243–1248.

Haritos-Fatouros, M. (2002). *Psychological origins of institutionalized torture.* London: Routledge.

Harkins, S. G., & Petty, R. E. (1981). Effects of source magnification of cognitive effort on attitudes: An information processing view. *Journal of Personality and Social Psychology, 40,* 401–413.

Harkins, S. G., & Petty, R. E. (1987). Information utility and the multiple source effect. *Journal of Personality and Social Psychology, 52,* 260–268.

Harkins, S. G., & Szymanski, K. (1987). Social loafing and social facilitation: New wine in old bottles. In C. Hendrick (Ed.), *Review of personality and social psychology: Group processes and intergroup relations* (Vol. 9, pp. 167–188). Beverly Hills, CA: Sage.

Harmon-Jones, E., & Mills, J. (Eds.). (1999). *Cognitive dissonance: Progress on a pivotal theory in social psychology.* Washington, DC: American Psychological Association.

Harmon-Jones, E., Brehm, J. W., Greenberg, J., Simon, L., & Nelson, D. E. (1996). Evidence that the production of aversive consequences is not necessary to create cognitive dissonance. *Journal of Personality and Social Psychology, 70,* 5–16.

Harré, N., Brandt, T., & Houkamau, C. (2004). An examination of the actor-observer effect in young drivers' attributions for their own and their friends' risky driving. *Journal of Applied Social Psychology, 34,* 806–824.

Harré, R., & Lamb, R. (1983). *The encyclopedic dictionary of psychology.* Oxford, England: Basil Blackwell.

Harris, C. R. (2002). Sexual and romantic jealousy in heterosexual and homosexual adults. *Psychological Science, 13,* 7–12.

Harris, C. R. (2003). A review of sex differences in sexual jealousy, including self-report data, psychophysiological responses, interpersonal violence, and morbid jealousy. *Personality and Social Psychology Review, 7,* 102–128.

Harris, C. R. (2005). Male and female jealousy: Still more similar than different: Reply to Sagarin. *Personality and Social Psychology Review, 9*, 76–86.

Harris, C. R., & Christenfeld, N. (1996). Gender, jealousy, and reason. *Psychological Science, 7*, 364–366.

Harris, M. B. (1995). Ethnicity, gender, and evaluations of aggression. *Aggressive Behavior, 21*, 343–357.

Harris, M. J., & Perkins, R. (1995). Effects of distraction on interpersonal expectancy effects: A social interaction test of the cognitive busyness hypothesis. *Social Cognition, 13*, 163–182.

Harris, M. J., & Rosenthal, R. (1985). Mediation of interpersonal expectancy effects. *Psychological Bulletin, 97*, 363–386.

Harris, R., Tobias, M., Jeffrey, M., Waldengrave, K., Karlsen, S., & Nazroo, J. (2006). Effects of self-reported racial discrimination and deprivation on Maori health and inequalities in New Zealand: Cross-sectional study. *Lancet, 367*, 2005–2009.

Harrison, A. A., & Connors, M. M. (1984). Groups in exotic environments. In L. Berkowitz (Ed.), *Advances in experimental social psychology* (Vol. 8, pp. 49–87). Orlando, FL: Academic Press.

Harrison, D. A., & Shaffer, M. A. (1994). Comparative examinations of self-reports and perceived absenteeism norms: Wading through Lake Wobegon. *Journal of Applied Psychology, 79*, 240–251.

Harrison, D. A., Kravitz, D. A., Mayer, D. M., Leslie, L. M., & Lev-Arey, D. (2006). Understanding attitudes toward affirmative action programs in employment: Summary and meta-analysis of 35 years of research. *Journal of Applied Psychology, 91*, 1013–1036.

Hart, A. J. (1995). Naturally occurring expectation effects. *Journal of Personality and Social Psychology, 68*, 109–115.

Hart, A. J., Whalen, P. J., Shin, L. M., McInerney, S. C., Fischer, H., & Rauch, S. L. (2000). Differential response in the human amygdala to racial outgroup vs ingroup face stimuli. *NeuroReport, 11*, 2351–2355.

Hart, J. W., Karau, S. J., Stasson, M. F., & Kerr, N. A. (2004). Achievement motivation, expected coworker performance, and collective task motivation: Working hard or hardly working? *Journal of Applied Social Psychology, 34*, 984–1000.

Hartwig, M., Granhag, P. A., Strömwall, L. A., & Vrij, A. (2005). Detecting deception via strategic disclosure of evidence. *Law and Human Behavior, 29*, 469–484.

Harvey, J. H., & Manusov, V. L. (Eds.). (2001). *Attribution, communication behavior, and close relationships.* New York: Cambridge University Press.

Harvey, J. H., & Omarzu, J. (2000). *Minding the close relationship: A theory of relationship enhancement.* New York: Cambridge University Press.

Hasel, L. E., & Wells, G. L. (2007). Catching the bad guy: Morphing composite faces helps. *Law and Human Behavior,* in press.

Haslam, N., & Levy, S. R. (2006). Essentialist beliefs about homosexuality: Structure and implications for prejudice. *Personality and Social Psychology Bulletin, 32*, 471–485.

Hass, R. G. (1981). Effects of source characteristics on the cognitive processing of persuasive messages and attitude change. In R. Petty, T. Ostrom, & T. Brock (Eds.), *Cognitive responses in persuasion* (pp. 141–172). Hillsdale, NJ: Erlbaum.

Hass, R. G. (1984). Perspective taking and self-awareness: Drawing an E on your forehead. *Journal of Personality and Social Psychology, 46*, 788–798.

Hass, R. G., & Eisenstadt, D. (1990). The effects of self-focused attention on perspective-taking and anxiety. *Anxiety Research, 2*, 165–176.

Hass, R. G., & Grady, K. (1975). Temporal delay, type of forewarning, and resistance to influence. *Journal of Experimental Social Psychology, 11*, 459–469.

Hass, R. G., Katz, I., Rizzo, N., Bailey, J., & Moore, L. (1992). When racial ambivalence evokes negative affect, using a disguised measure of mood. *Personality and Social Psychology Bulletin, 18*, 786–797.

Hassin, R. R., Uleman, J. S., & Bargh, J. A. (Eds.). (2005). *The new unconscious.* New York: Oxford.

Hassin, R., & Trope, Y. (2000). Facing faces: Studies on the cognitive aspects of physiognomy. *Journal of Personality and Social Psychology, 78*, 837–852.

Hastie, R. (1984). Causes and effects of causal attribution. *Journal of Personality and Social Psychology, 46*, 44–56.

Hastie, R. (Ed.). (1993). *Inside the juror: The psychology of juror decision making.* New York: Cambridge University Press.

Hastie, R., & Kameda, T. (2005). The robust beauty of majority rules in group decisions. *Psychological Review, 112*, 494–508.

Hastie, R., Penrod, S. D., & Pennington, N. (1983). *Inside the jury.* Cambridge, MA: Harvard University Press.

Hater, J. J., & Bass, B. M. (1988). Superiors' evaluations and subordinates' perceptions of transformational and transactional leadership. *Journal of Applied Psychology, 73*, 695–702.

Hatfield, E. (1988). Passionate and companionate love. In R. J. Sternberg & M. L. Barnes (Eds.), *The psychology of love* (pp. 191–217). New Haven, CT: Yale University Press.

Hatfield, E., & Rapson, R. L. (1993). *Love, sex, and intimacy: Their psychology, biology, and history.* New York: HarperCollins.

Hatfield, E., Greenberger, E., Traupmann, J., & Lambert, P. (1982). Equity and sexual satisfaction in recently married couples. *Journal of Sex Research, 18*, 18–32.

Hatfield, E., Rapson, R. L., & Martel, L. D. (2007). Passionate love. In S. Kitayama & D. Cohen (Eds.), *Handbook of cultural psychology.* New York: Guilford.

Hauber, M. E., & Sherman, P. W. (1998). Nepotism and marmot alarm calling. *Animal Behaviour, 56*, 1049–1052.

Haupt, A. L., & Leary, M. R. (1997). The appeal of worthless groups: Moderating effects of trait self-esteem. *Group Dynamics, 1*, 124–132.

Hawkins, D. L., Pepler, D. J., & Craig, W. M. (2001). Naturalistic observations of peer interventions in bullying. *Social Development, 10*, 512–527.

Hawkley, L. C., Bosch, J. A., Engeland, C. G., Marucha, P. T., & Cacioppo, J. T. (2007). Loneliness, dysphoria, stress and immunity: A role for cytokines. In N. P. Plotnikoff, R. E. Faith, & A. J. Murgo (Eds.), *Cytokines: Stress and immunity* (2nd ed.). Boca Raton, FL: CRC Press.

Hawkley, L. C., Masi, C. M., Berry, J. D., & Cacioppo, J. T. (2006). Loneliness as a unique predictor of age-related differences in systolic blood pressure. *Psychology and Aging, 21*, 152–164.

Hayes, T. C., & Lee, M. R. (2005). The southern culture of honor and violent attitudes. *Sociological Spectrum, 25*, 593–617.

Hays, R. B. (1985). A longitudinal study of friendship development. *Journal of Personality and Social Psychology, 48*, 909–924.

Hazan, C., & Diamond, L. M. (2000). The place of attachment in human mating. *Review of General Psychology, 4*, 186–204.

Hazan, C., & Shaver, P. (1987). Romantic love conceptualized as an attachment process. *Journal of Personality and Social Psychology, 52*, 511–524.

Hearold, S. (1986). A synthesis of 1043 effects of television on social behavior. In G. Comstock (Ed.), *Public communication and behavior* (Vol. 1, pp. 65–133). Orlando, FL: Academic Press.

Heatherton, T. F., & Polivy, J. (1991). Development and validation of a scale for measuring state self-esteem. *Journal of Personality and Social Psychology, 60*, 895–910.

Heatherton, T. F., & Vohs, K. D. (2000). Interpersonal evaluations following threats to self: Role of self-esteem. *Journal of Personality and Social Psychology, 78*, 725–736.

Heatherton, T. F., & Wyland, C. L. (2003). Assessing self-esteem. In S. J. Lopez & C. R. Snyder (Eds.), *Positive psychological assessment: A handbook of models and measures* (pp. 219–233). Washington, DC: American Psychological Association.

Hebl, M. R., & Heatherton, T. F. (1998). The stigma of obesity in women: The difference is black and white. *Personality and Social Psychology Bulletin, 24*, 417–426.

Hebl, M. R., & Turchin, J. M. (2005). The stigma of obesity: What about men? *Basic and Applied Social Psychology, 27,* 267–275.

Hechanova, R., Beehr, T. A., & Christiansen, N. D. (2003). Antecedents and consequences of employees' adjustment to overseas assignment: A meta-analytic review. *Applied Psychology: An International Review, 52,* 213–236.

Hedge, A., & Yousif, Y. H. (1992). Effects of urban size, urgency, and cost on helpfulness: A cross-cultural comparison between the United Kingdom and the Sudan. *Journal of Cross Cultural Psychology, 23,* 107–115.

Hedge, J. W., & Kavanagh, M. J. (1988). Improving the accuracy of performance evaluations: Comparison of three methods of performance appraiser training. *Journal of Applied Psychology, 73,* 68–73.

Heider, F. (1958). *The psychology of interpersonal relations.* New York: Wiley.

Heilman, M. E., & Alcott, V. B. (2001). What I think you think of me: Women's reactions to being viewed as beneficiaries of preferential selection. *Journal of Applied Psychology, 86,* 574–582.

Heilman, M. E., Battle, W. S., Keller, C. E., & Lee, R. A. (1998). Type of affirmative action policy: A determinant of reactions to sex-based preferential selection? *Journal of Applied Psychology, 83,* 190–205.

Heilman, M. E., Block, C. J., & Lucas, J. A. (1992). Presumed incompetent? Stigmatization and affirmative action efforts. *Journal of Applied Psychology, 77,* 536–544.

Heilman, M. E., McCullough, W. F., & Gilbert, D. (1996). The other side of affirmative action: Reactions of nonbeneficiaries to sex-based preferential selection. *Journal of Applied Psychology, 81,* 346–357.

Heilman, M. E., Rivero, J. C., & Brett, J. F. (1991). Skirting the competence issue: Effects of sex-based preferential selection on task choices of women and men. *Journal of Applied Psychology, 76,* 99–105.

Heilman, M. E., Simon, M. C., & Repper, D. P. (1987). Intentionally favored, unintentionally harmed? Impact of sex-based preferential selection on self-perceptions and self-evaluations. *Journal of Applied Psychology, 72,* 62–68.

Heine, S. J. (2005). Where is the evidence for pancultural self-enhancement? A reply to Sedikides, Gaertner, & Toguchi (2003). *Journal of Personality and Social Psychology, 89,* 531–538.

Heine, S. J. (2007). Culture and motivation. In S. Kitayama & D. Cohen (Eds.), *Handbook of cultural psychology.* New York: Guilford.

Heine, S. J., & Lehman, D. R. (1997). The cultural construction of self-enhancement: An examination of group-serving biases. *Journal of Personality and Social Psychology, 72,* 1268–1283.

Heine, S. J., Kitayama, S., & Hamamura, T. (in press). Different meta-analyses yield different conclusions: A comment on Sedikides, Gaertner, & Vevea (2005), Journal of Personality and Social Psychology. *Asian Journal of Social Psychology.*

Heine, S. J., Kitayama, S., Lehman, D. R., Takata, T., Ide, E., Lueng, C., & Matsumoto, H. (2001). Divergent consequences of success and failure in Japan and North America: An investigation of self-improving motivations and malleable selves. *Journal of Personality and Social Psychology, 81,* 599–615.

Heine, S. J., Lehman, D. R., Markus, H. R., & Kitayama, S. (1999). Is there a universal need for positive self-regard? *Psychological Review, 106,* 756–794.

Heine, S. J., Takata, T., & Lehman, D. R. (2000). Beyond self-presentation: Evidence for self-criticism among Japanese. *Personality and Social Psychology Bulletin, 26,* 71–78.

Helgesen, S. (1995). *Web of inclusion: A new architecture for building great organizations.* New York: Doubleday.

Helgeson, V. S. (1992). Moderators of the relation between perceived control and adjustment to chronic illness. *Journal of Personality and Social Psychology, 63,* 652–666.

Helgeson, V. S., Cohen, S., Schulz, R., & Yasko, J. (2000). Group support interventions for women with breast cancer: Who benefits from what? *Health Psychology, 19,* 107–114.

Helgeson, V. S., Reynolds, K. A., & Tomich, P. L. (2006). A meta-analytic review of benefit finding and growth. *Journal of Consulting and Clinical Psychology, 74,* 797–816.

Heller, J. F., Pallak, M. S., & Picek, J. M. (1973). The interactive effects of intent and threat on boomerang attitude change. *Journal of Personality and Social Psychology, 26,* 273–279.

Helweg-Larsen, M., & Shepperd, J. A. (2001). Do moderators of the optimistic bias affect personal or target risk estimates? A review of the literature. *Personality and Social Psychology Review, 5,* 74–95.

Henchy, T., & Glass, D. C. (1968). Evaluation apprehension and the social facilitation of dominant and subordinate responses. *Journal of Personality and Social Psychology, 10,* 446–454.

Henderlong, J., & Lepper, M. R. (2002). The effects of praise on children's intrinsic motivation: A review and synthesis. *Psychological Bulletin, 128,* 774–795.

Henderson, L., & Zimbardo, P. (1998). Shyness. In H. S. Friedman (Ed.), *Encyclopedia of mental health.* San Diego: Academic Press.

Henderson-King, D., Henderson-King, E., & Hoffman, L. (2001). Media images and women's self-evaluations: Social context and importance of attractiveness as moderators. *Personality and Social Psychology Bulletin, 27,* 1407–1416.

Henderson-King, E., & Henderson-King, D. (1997). Media effects on women's body esteem: Social and individual differences factors. *Journal of Applied Social Psychology, 27,* 399–417.

Hendrick, C., & Hendrick, S. S. (Eds.). (2000). *Close relationships: A sourcebook.* Thousand Oaks, CA: Sage.

Hendrick, S. S., & Hendrick, C. (1993). Lovers as friends. *Journal of Social and Personal Relationships, 10,* 459–466.

Hendrick, S. S., & Hendrick, C. (1995). Gender differences and similarities in sex and love. *Personal Relationships, 2,* 55–65.

Heneman, H. G., & Schwab, D. P. (1985). Pay satisfaction: Its multidimensional nature and measurement. *International Journal of Psychology, 20,* 129–141.

Henley, N. M. (1977). *Body politics: Power, sex, and nonverbal communication.* Englewood Cliffs, NJ: Prentice-Hall.

Henningsen, D. D., Henningsen, M. L. M., Eden, J., & Cruz, M. G. (2006). Examining the symptoms of groupthink and retrospective sensemaking. *Small Group Research, 37,* 36-64.

Henrich, J. (2004). Cultural group selection, coevolutionary processes and large-scale cooperation. *Journal of Economic Behavior and Organization, 53,* 3–35.

Heppner, P. P., Heppner, M. J., Lee, D., Wang, Y., Park, H., & Wang, L. (2006). Development and validation of a collectivist coping styles inventory. *Journal of Counseling Psychology, 53,* 107–125.

Herbert, T. B., & Cohen, S. (1993). Stress and immunity in humans: A meta-analytic review. *Psychosomatic Medicine, 55,* 364–379.

Herdt, G. (1998). *Same sex, different cultures: Exploring gay and lesbian lives.* Boulder, CO: Westview Press.

Herek, G. M. (2006). Legal recognition of same-sex relationships in the United States: A social science perspective. *American Psychologist, 61,* 607–621.

Herzberger, S. D. (1996). *Violence within the family: Social psychological perspectives.* Madison, WI: Brown & Benchmark.

Hewitt, P. L., Flett, G. L., Sherry, S. B., Habke, M., Parkin, M., Lam, R., McMurtry, B., Ediger, E., Fairlie, P., & Stein, M. B. (2003). The interpersonal expression of perfection: Perfectionistic self-presentation and psychological distress. *Journal of Personality and Social Psychology, 84,* 1303–1325.

Hewstone, M., & Lord, C. G. (1998). Changing intergroup cognitions and intergroup behavior: The role of typicality. In C. Sedikides, J. Schopler & C. A. Insko (Eds.), *Intergroup cognition and intergroup behavior* (pp. 367–392). Mahwah, NJ: Erlbaum.

Heyes, C. M., & Galef, B. G., Jr., (1996). *Social learning in animals: The roots of culture.* New York: Academic Press.

Heyman, R. E., & Slep, A. M. S. (2002). Do child abuse and interparental violence lead to adulthood family violence? *Journal of Marriage and Family, 64,* 864–870.

Higgins, C. A., & Judge, T. A. (2004). The effect of applicant influence tactics on recruiter perceptions of fit and hiring recommendations: A field study. *Journal of Applied Psychology, 89,* 622–632.

Higgins, E. T. (1989). Self-discrepancy theory: What patterns of self-beliefs cause people to suffer? In L. Berkowitz (Ed.), *Advances in experimental social psychology* (Vol. 22, pp. 93–136). New York: Academic Press.

Higgins, E. T. (1999). Self-discrepancy: A theory relating self and affect. In R. F. Baumeister (Ed.), *The self in social psychology* (pp. 150–181). Philadelphia, PA: Psychology Press/Taylor & Francis.

Higgins, E. T., & Rholes, W. S. (1978). "Saying is believing": Effects of message modification on memory and liking for the person described. *Journal of Experimental Social Psychology, 14,* 363–378.

Higgins, E. T., King, G. A., & Mavin, G. H. (1982). Individual construct accessibility and subjective impressions and recall. *Journal of Personality and Social Psychology, 43,* 35–47.

Higgins, E. T., Rholes, C. R., & Jones, C. R. (1977). Category accessibility and impression formation. *Journal of Experimental Social Psychology, 13,* 141–154.

Higgins, R. L., & Harris, R. N. (1988). Strategic "alcohol" use: Drinking to self-handicap. *Journal of Social and Clinical Psychology, 6,* 191–202.

Hill, C. A. (1987). Affiliation motivation: People who need people . . . but in different ways. *Journal of Personality and Social Psychology, 52,* 1008–1018.

Hills, P. J., & Lewis, M. B. (2006). Reducing the own-race bias in face recognition by shifting attention. *Quarterly Journal of Experimental Psychology, 59,* 996–1002.

Hilmert, C. J., Kulik, J. A., & Christenfeld, N. J. S. (2006). Positive and negative outcome modeling: The influence of another's similarity and dissimilarity. *Journal of Personality and Social Psychology, 90,* 440–452.

Hilton, J. L., & Darley, J. M. (1985). Constructing other persons: A limit on the effect. *Journal of Experimental Social Psychology, 21,* 1–18.

Hilton, J. L., & Darley, J. M. (1991). The effects of interaction goals on person perception. *Advances in Experimental Social Psychology, 24,* 235–267.

Hilton, J. L., & Fein, S. (1989). The role of typical diagnosticity in stereotype-based judgments. *Journal of Personality and Social Psychology, 57,* 201–211.

Hines, D. A., & Saudino, K. J. (2002). Intergenerational transmission of intimate partner violence: A behavioral genetic perspective. *Trauma Violence and Abuse, 3,* 210–225.

Hing, L. S. S., Li, W., & Zanna, M. P. (2002). Inducing hypocrisy to reduce prejudicial responses among aversive racists. *Journal of Experimental Social Psychology, 38,* 71–78.

Hinkle, S., Taylor, L. A., Fox-Cardamone, L., & Ely, P. G. (1998). Social identity and aspects of social creativity: Shifting to new dimensions of intergroup comparison. In S. Worchel & J. F. Morales (Eds.), *Social identity: International perspectives* (pp. 166–179). London: Sage.

Hinsz, V. B., Tindale, R. S., & Vollrath, D. A. (1997). The emerging conceptualization of groups as information processors. *Psychological Bulletin, 121,* 43–64.

Hinsz, V. B., Tindale, R. S., Nagao, D. H., Davis, J. H., & Robertson, B. A. (1988). The influence of the accuracy of individuating information on the use of base rate information in probability judgment. *Journal of Experimental Social Psychology, 24,* 127–145.

Hirt, E. R., Deppe, R. K., & Gordon, L. J. (1991). Self-reported versus behavioral self-handicapping: Empirical evidence for a theoretical distinction. *Journal of Personality and Social Psychology, 61,* 981–991.

Hirt, E. R., McCrea, S. M., & Boris, H. I. (2003). "I know you self-handicapped last exam": Gender differences in reactions to self-handicapping. *Journal of Personality and Social Psychology, 84,* 177–193.

Hirt, E. R., Zillman, D., Erickson, G. A., & Kennedy, C. (1992). Costs and benefits of allegiance: Changes in fans' self-ascribed competencies after team victory versus defeat. *Journal of Personality and Social Psychology, 63,* 724–738.

Hitler, A. (1933). *Mein Kampf* (E. T. S. Dugdale, Trans.). Cambridge, MA: Riverside.

Hixon, J. G., & Swann, W. B., Jr. (1993). When does introspection bear fruit? Self-reflection, self-insight, and interpersonal choices. *Journal of Personality and Social Psychology, 64,* 35–43.

Hobfoll, S. E., Canetti-Nisim, D., & Johnson, R. J. (2006). Exposure to terrorism, stress-related mental health symptoms, and defensive coping among Jews and Arabs in Israel. *Journal of Consulting and Clinical Psychology, 74,* 207–218.

Hochwarter, W. A., Witt, L. A., & Kacmar, K. M. (2000). Perceptions of organizational politics as a moderator of the relationship between conscientiousness and job performance. *Journal of Applied Psychology, 85,* 472–478.

Hodges, B. H., & Geyer, A. L. (2006). A nonconformist account of the Asch experiments: Values, pragmatics, and moral dilemmas. *Personality and Social Psychology Review, 10,* 2–19.

Hoffman, M. L. (2000). *Empathy and moral development: Implications for caring and justice.* New York: Cambridge University Press.

Hofling, C. K., Brotzman, E., Dalrymple, S., Graves, N., & Pierce, C. (1966). An experimental study of nurse-physician relations. *Journal of Nervous and Mental Disease, 143,* 171–180.

Hofstede, G. (1980). *Culture's consequences.* Beverly Hills, CA: Sage.

Hogan, R., Curphy, G. J., & Hogan, J. (1994). What we know about leadership: Effectiveness and personality. *American Psychologist, 49,* 493–504.

Hogg, M. A., Fielding, K. S., Johnson, D., Masser, B., Russell, E., & Svensson, A. (2006). Demographic category membership and leadership in small groups: A social identity analysis. *Leadership Quaterly, 17,* 335–350.

Hogg, M. A., Turner, J. C., & Davidson, B. (1990). Polarized norms and social frames of reference: A test of the self-categorization theory of group polarization. *Basic and Applied Social Psychology, 11,* 77–100.

Hoigaard, R., Såfvenbom, R., & Tonnessen, F. E. (2006). The relationship between group cohesion, group norms, and perceived social loafing in soccer teams. *Small Group Research, 37,* 217–232.

Hollander, E. P. (1958). Conformity, status, and idiosyncrasy credit. *Psychological Review, 65,* 117–127.

Hollander, E. P. (1985). Leadership and power. In G. Lindzey & E. Aronson (Eds.), *Handbook of social psychology* (3rd ed., Vol. 2, pp. 485–537). New York: Random House.

Holloway, R., & Johnston, L. (2007). Evaluating the evaluators: Perceptions of interviewers by rejected job applicants as a function of interviewer and applicant sex. *Journal of Applied Social Psychology,* in press.

Holmes, A., Murphy, D. L., & Crawley, J. N. (2003). Abnormal behavioral phenotypes of serotonin transporter knockout mice: Parallels with human anxiety and depression. *Biological Psychiatry, 54,* 953–959.

Holmes, J. (2005). Leadership talk: How do leaders 'do mentoring,' and is gender relevant? *Journal of Pragmatics, 37,* 1779–1800.

Holmes, T. H., & Rahe, R. H. (1967). The Social Readjustment Rating Scale. *Journal of Psychosomatic Research, 11,* 213–218.

Homans, G. C. (1961). *Social behavior*. New York: Harcourt, Brace & World.

Hönekopp, J. (2006). Once more: Is beauty in the eye of the beholder? Relative contributions of private and shared taste to judgments of facial attractiveness. *Journal of Experimental Psychology: Human Perception and Performance, 32,* 199–209.

Honeycutt, J. M., Woods, B. L., & Fontenot, K. (1993). The endorsement of communication conflict rules as a function of engagement, marriage and marital ideology. *Journal of Social and Personal Relationships, 10,* 285–304.

Hong, L. (2000). Toward a transformed approach to prevention: Breaking the link between masculinity and violence. *Journal of American College Health, 48,* 269–279.

Hong, Y., Chan, G., Chiu, C., Wong, R. Y. M., Hansen, I. G., Lee, S., Tong, Y., & Fu, H. (2004). How are social identities linked to self-conception and intergroup orientation? The moderating effect of implicit theories. *Journal of Personality and Social Psychology, 85,* 1147–1160.

Hong, Y., Morris, M. W., Chiu, C., & Benet-Martinez, V. (2000). Multicultural minds: A dynamic constructivist approach to culture and cognition. *American Psychologist, 55,* 709–720.

Honts, C. R. (1996). Criterion development and validity of the CQT in field application. *Journal of General Psychology, 123,* 309–324.

Honts, C. R., Raskin, D. C., & Kircher, J. C. (1994). Mental and physical countermeasures reduce the accuracy of polygraph tests. *Journal of Applied Psychology, 79,* 252–259.

Honts, C. R., Raskin, D. C., & Kircher, J. C. (2002). The scientific status of research on polygraph techniques: The case for polygraph tests (pp. 446–483). In D. L. Faigman, D. Kaye, M. J. Saks, & J. Sanders (Eds.), *Modern scientific evidence: The law and science of expert testimony*. St. Paul, MN: West.

Hoobler, J. M., & Brass, D. J. (2006). Abusive supervision and family undermining as displaced aggression. *Journal of Applied Psychology, 91,* 1125–1133.

Hoorens, V., & Nuttin, J. M. (1993). Overvaluation of own attributes: Mere ownership or subjective frequency? *Social Cognition, 11,* 177–200.

Hope, L., Memon, A., & McGeorge, P. (2004). Understanding pretrial publicity: Predecisional distortion of evidence by mock jurors. *Journal of Experimental Psychology: Applied, 10,* 111–119.

Hopthrow, T., & Hulbert, L. G. (2005). The effect of group decision making on cooperation in social dilemmas. *Group Processes and Intergroup Relations, 8,* 89–100.

Hornor, G. (2005). Domestic violence and children. *Journal of Pediatric Health Care, 19,* 206–212.

Hornsey, M. J., & Jetten, J. (2004). The individual within the group: Balancing the need to belong with the need to be different. *Personality and Social Psychology Review, 8,* 248–264.

Hornsey, M. J., & Jetten, J. (2005). Loyalty without conformity: Tailoring self-perception as a means of balancing belonging and differentiation. *Self and Identity, 4,* 81–95.

Hornsey, M. J., Jetten, J., McAuliffe, B. J., & Hogg, M. A. (2006). The impact of individualist and collectivist group norms on evaluations of dissenting group members. *Journal of Experimental Social Psychology, 42,* 57–68.

Horowitz, I. A., & ForsterLee, L. (2001). The effects of note-taking and trial transcript access on mock jury decisions in a complex civil trial. *Law and Human Behavior, 25,* 373–391.

Horowitz, I. A., & Willging, T. E. (1991). Changing views of jury power: The nullification debate, 1787–1988. *Law and Human Behavior, 15,* 165–182.

Horstmann, G., & Bauland, A. (2006). Search asymmetries with real faces: Testing the anger-superiority effect. *Emotion, 6,* 193–207.

Horvath, A. O., & Luborsky, L. (1993). The role of the therapeutic alliance in psychotherapy. *Journal of Consulting and Clinical Psychology, 61,* 561–573.

Hoshino-Browne, E., Zanna, A. S., Spencer, S. J.; Zanna, M. P., Kitayama, S., & Lackenbauer, S. (2005). On the cultural guises of cognitive dissonance: The case of Easterners and Westerners. *Journal of Personality and Social Psychology, 89,* 294–310.

Hosoda, M., Stone-Romero, E. F., & Coats, G. (2003). The effects of physical attractiveness on job-related outcomes: A meta-analysis of experimental studies. *Personnel Psychology, 56,* 431–462.

Houldsworth, C., & Mathews, B. P. (2000). Group composition, performance and educational attainment. *Education and Training, 42,* 40–53.

House, J. S., Landis, K. R., & Umberson, D. (1988). Social relationships and health. *Science, 241,* 540–545.

Houts, A. C., Cook, T. D., & Shadish, W. R., Jr. (1986). The person-situation debate: A critical multiplist perspective. *Journal of Personality, 54,* 52–105.

Hovland, C. I., & Sears, R. R. (1940). Minor studies in aggression: VI. Correlation of lynchings with economic indices. *Journal of Psychology, 9,* 301–310.

Hovland, C. I., & Weiss, W. (1951). The influence of source credibility on communication effectiveness. *Public Opinion Quarterly, 15,* 635–650.

Hovland, C. I., Janis, I. L., & Kelley, H. H. (1953). *Communication and persuasion: Psychological studies of opinion change*. New Haven, CT: Yale University Press.

Hovland, C. I., Lumsdaine, A. A., & Sheffield, F. D. (1949). *Experiments on mass communication*. Princeton, NJ: Princeton University Press.

Howard, D. J. (1990). The influence of verbal responses to common greetings on compliance behavior: The foot-in-the-mouth effect. *Journal of Applied Social Psychology, 20,* 1185–1196.

Hrobjartsson, A., & Gotzsche, P. C. (2001). Is the placebo powerless? An analysis of clinical trials comparing placebo with no treatment. *New England Journal of Medicine, 344,* 1594–1602.

Huang, W. W., Wei, K. K., Watson, R. T., & Tan, B. C. Y. (2003). Supporting virtual team-building with a GSS: An empirical investigation. *Decision Support Systems, 34,* 359–367.

Huesmann, L. R. (1988). An information processing model for the development of aggression. *Aggressive Behavior, 14,* 13–24.

Huesmann, L. R. (1998). The role of social information processing and cognitive schema in the acquisition and maintenance of habitual aggressive behavior. In R. G. Geen & E. Donnerstein (Eds.), *Human aggression: Theories, research, and implications for social policy* (pp. 73–109). San Diego: Academic Press.

Huesmann, L. R., & Eron, L. D. (Eds.). (1986). *Television and the aggressive child: A cross-national comparison*. Hillsdale, NJ: Erlbaum.

Huesmann, L. R., & Guerra, N. G. (1997). Children's normative beliefs about aggression and aggressive behavior. *Journal of Personality and Social Psychology, 72,* 408–419.

Huesmann, L. R., Moise-Titus, J., Podolski, C. P., & Eron, L. D. (2003). Longitudinal relations between children's exposure to TV violence and their aggressive and violent behavior in young adulthood: 1977–1992. *Developmental Psychology, 39,* 201–229.

Huey, S. J. Jr., Henggeler, S. W., Brondino, M. J., & Pickrel, S. G. (2000). Mechanisms of change in multisystemic therapy: Reducing delinquent behavior through therapist adherence and improved family and peer functioning. *Journal of Consulting and Clinical Psychology, 68,* 451–467.

Huffcutt, A. I., & Roth, P. L. (1998). Racial group differences in employment interview evaluations. *Journal of Applied Psychology, 83,* 179–189.

Huffcutt, A. I., Conway, J. M., Roth, P. L., & Stone, N. J. (2001). Identification and meta-analytic assessment of psychological constructs measured in employment interviews. *Journal of Applied Psychology, 86,* 897–913.

Huffman, T. (2006, August 2). Would you do the right thing? Action less likely if many present. *Toronto Star*, p. B1.

Hugenberg, K., & Bodenhausen, G. V. (2003). Facing prejudice: Implicit prejudice and the perception of facial threat. *Psychological Science, 14*, 640–643.

Hugenberg, K., & Bodenhausen, G. V. (2004). Ambiguity in social categorization: The role of prejudice and facial affect in race categorization. *Psychological Science, 15*, 342–345.

Huguet, P., Galvaing, M. P., Monteil, J. M., & Dumas, F. (1999). Social presence effects in the Stroop task: Further evidence for an attentional view of social facilitation. *Journal of Personality and Social Psychology, 77*, 1011–1025.

Hull, J. G., & Young, R. D. (1983). Self-consciousness, self-esteem, and success-failure as determinants of alcohol consumption in male social drinkers. *Journal of Personality and Social Psychology, 44*, 1097–1109.

Hull, J. G., Young, R. D., & Jouriles, E. (1986). Applications of the self-awareness model of alcohol consumption: Predicting patterns of use and abuse. *Journal of Personality and Social Psychology, 51*, 790–796.

Hunter, J. A., Cox, S. L., O'Brien, K., Stringer, M., Boyes, M., Banks, M., Hayhurst, J. G., & Crawford, M. (2005). Threats to group value, domain-specific self-esteem and intergroup discrimination amongst minimal and national groups. *British Journal of Social Psychology, 44*, 329–353.

Hur, M. H. (2006). Exploring the motivation factors of charitable giving and their value structure: A case study of Seoul, Korea. *Social Behavior and Personality, 34*, 661–680.

Hurtz, G. M., & Donovan, J. J. (2000). Personality and job performance: The Big Five revisited. *Journal of Applied Psychology, 85*, 869–879.

Huston, T. L., & Vangelisti, A. L. (1991). Socioemotional behavior and satisfaction in marital relationships: A longitudinal study. *Journal of Personality and Social Psychology, 61*, 721–733.

Iacono, W. G., & Lykken, D. T. (1997). The validity of the lie-detector test: Two surveys of scientific opinion. *Journal of Applied Psychology, 82*, 426–433.

Ickes, W., Bissonnette, V., Garcia, S., & Stinson, L. L. (1990). Implementing and using the Dyadic Interaction Paradigm. In C. Hendrick & M. S. Clark (Eds.), *Review of personality and social psychology: Vol. 11. Research methods in personality and social psychology* (pp. 16–44). Newbury Park, CA: Sage.

Imai, Y. (1991). Effects of influence strategies, perceived social power and cost on compliance with requests. *Japanese Psychological Research, 33*, 134–144.

Inbau, F. E., Reid, J. E., Buckley, J. P., & Jayne, B. C. (2001). *Criminal interrogation and confessions* (4th ed.). Gaithersburg, MD: Aspen.

Ingham, A. G., Levinger, G., Graves, J., & Peckham, V. (1974). The Ringelmann effect: Studies of group size and group performance. *Journal of Experimental Social Psychology, 10*, 371–384.

Ingoldsby, B. B. (1991). The Latin American family: Familism vs. machismo. *Journal of Comparative Family Studies, 23*, 47–62.

Ingram, R. E. (1990). Self-focused attention in clinical disorders: Review and a conceptual model. *Psychological Bulletin, 107*, 156–176.

Insko, C. A., Kirchner, J. L., Pinter, B., Efaw, J., & Wildschut, T. (2005). Interindividual-intergroup discontinuity as a function of trust and categorization: The paradox of expected cooperation. *Journal of Personality and Social Psychology, 88*, 365–385.

Insko, C. A., Sedlak, A. J., & Lipsitz, A. (1982). A two-valued logic or two-valued balance resolution of the challenge of agreement and attraction effects in p-o-x triads, and a theoretical perspective on conformity and hedonism. *European Journal of Social Psychology, 12*, 143–167.

Inzlicht, M., McKay, L., & Aronson, J. (2006). Stigma as ego depletion: How being the target of prejudice affects self-control. *Psychological Science, 17*, 262–269.

Inzlicht, M., McKay, L., & Aronson, J. (2006). Stigma as ego depletion: How being the target of prejudice affects self-control. *Psychological Science, 17*, 262–269.

Ip, G. W.-m., Chiu, C.-y., & Chang, C. (2006). Birds of a feather and birds flocking together: Physical versus behavioral cues may lead to trait- versus goal-based group perception. *Journal of Personality and Social Psychology, 90*, 368–381.

Irons, E. D., & Moore, G. W. (1985). *Black managers: The case of the banking industry.* New York: Praeger.

Irwin, M., Mascovich, S., Gillin, J. C., Willoughby, R., Pike, J., & Smith, T. L. (1994). Partial sleep deprivation reduces natural killer cell activity in humans. *Psychosomatic Medicine, 56*, 493–498.

Isen, A. M. (1984). Toward understanding the role of affect in cognition. In R. S. Wyer & T. K. Srull (Eds.), *Handbook of social cognition* (Vol. 3, pp. 179–236). Hillsdale, NJ: Erlbaum.

Isen, A. M., & Levin, P. A. (1972). Effect of feeling good on helping: Cookies and kindness. *Journal of Personality and Social Psychology, 21*, 384–388.

Ishii, K., Reyes, J., & Kitayama, S. (2003). Spontaneous attention to word content versus emotional tone: Differences among three cultures. *Psychological Science, 14*, 39–46.

Ito, T. A., Chiao, K. W., Devine, P. G., Lorig, T. S., & Cacioppo, J. T. (2006). The influence of facial feedback on race bias. *Psychological Science, 17*, 256–261.

Ito, T. A., Larsen, J. T., Smith, N. K., & Cacioppo, J. T. (1998). Negative information weighs more heavily on the brain: The negativity bias in evaluative categorizations. *Journal of Personality and Social Psychology, 75*, 887–900.

Ito, T. A., Miller, N., & Pollock, V. E. (1996). Alcohol and aggression: A meta-analysis on the moderating effects of inhibitory cues, triggering events, and self-focused attention. *Psychological Bulletin, 120*, 60–82.

Izard, C. E. (1990). Facial expressions and the regulation of emotions. *Journal of Personality and Social Psychology, 58*, 487–498.

Jacks, J. Z., & Cameron, K. A. (2003). Strategies for resisting persuasion. *Basic and Applied Social Psychology, 25*, 145–161.

Jackson, J. M. (1986). In defense of social impact theory: Comment on Mullin. *Journal of Personality and Social Psychology, 50*, 511–513.

Jackson, J. M., & Williams, K. D. (1985). Social loafing on difficult tasks: Working collectively can improve performance. *Journal of Personality and Social Psychology, 49*, 937–942.

Jackson, L. M., Esses, V. M., & Burris, C. T. (2001). Contemporary sexism and discrimination: The importance of respect for men and women. *Personality and Social Psychology Bulletin, 27*, 48–61.

Jackson, S. E., & Schuler, R. S. (1985). A meta-analysis and conceptual critique of research on role ambiguity and role conflict in work settings. *Organizational Behavior, 36*, 16–78.

Jackson, S. E., May, K. E., & Whitney, K. (1995). Understanding the dynamics of diversity in decision making teams. In R. A. Guzzo & E. Salas (Eds.), *Team effectiveness and decision making in organizations* (pp. 204–261). San Francisco: Jossey-Bass.

Jackson, T., Fritch, A., Nagasaka, T., & Gunderson, J. (2002). Towards explaining the association between shyness and loneliness: A path analysis with American college students. *Social Behavior and Personality, 30*, 263–270.

James, W. (1890). *Principles of psychology* (Vols. 1–2). New York: Holt.

James, W. H. (2005). Biological and psychosocial determinants of male and female human sexual orientation. *Journal of Biosocial Science, 37*, 555–567.

Janis, I. L. (1968). Attitude change via role playing. In R. Abelson, E. Aronson, W. McGuire, T. Newcomb, M. Rosenberg, & P. Tennenbaum (Eds.), *Theories of cognitive consistency: A sourcebook* (pp. 810–818). Chicago: Rand McNally.

Janis, I. L. (1982). *Groupthink* (2nd ed.). Boston: Houghton Mifflin.

Janis, I. L., & Feshbach, S. (1953). Effects of fear arousing communications. *Journal of Abnormal and Social Psychology, 48,* 78–92.

Janis, I. L., & King, B. T. (1954). The influence of role playing on opinion change. *Journal of Abnormal and Social Psychology, 49,* 211–218.

Janis, I. L., Kaye, D., & Kirschner, P. (1965). Facilitating effects of "eating while reading" on responsiveness to persuasive communications. *Journal of Personality and Social Psychology, 1,* 181–186.

Jankowiak, W. R., & Fischer, E. F. (1992). A cross-cultural perspective on romantic love. *Ethnology, 31,* 149–155.

Janoff-Bulman, R. (1979). Characterological versus behavioral self-blame: Inquiries into depression and rape. *Journal of Personality and Social Psychology, 37,* 1798–1809.

Janoff-Bulman, R. (1992). *Shattered assumptions: Towards a new psychology of trauma.* New York: Free Press.

Jansari, A., & Parkin, A. J. (1996). Things that go bump in your life: Explaining the reminiscence bump in autobiographical memory. *Psychology and Aging, 11,* 85–91.

Jarvis, W. B. G., & Petty, R. E. (1996). The need to evaluate. *Journal of Personality and Social Psychology, 70,* 172–194.

Jawahar, I. M., & Mattsson, J. (2005). Sexism and beautyism effects in selection as a function of self-monitoring level of decision maker. *Journal of Applied Psychology, 90,* 563–573.

Jayaratne, T. E., Ybarra, O., Sheldon, J. P., Brown, T. N., Feldbaum, M., Pfeffer, C. A., & Petty, E. M. (2006). White Americans' genetic lay theories of race differences and sexual orientation: Their relationship with prejudice toward Blacks, and gay men and lesbians. *Group Processes and Intergroup Relations, 9,* 77–94.

Jenkins, G. D., Jr., Mitra, A., Gupta, N., & Shaw, J. D. (1998). Are financial incentives related to performance? A meta-analytic review of empirical research. *Journal of Applied Psychology, 83,* 777–787.

Jennings (Walstedt), J., Geis, F. L., & Brown, V. (1980). Influence of television commercials on women's self-confidence and independent judgment. *Journal of Personality and Social Psychology, 38,* 203–210.

Jepson, C., & Chaiken, S. (1990). Chronic issue-specific fear inhibits systematic processing of persuasive communications. *Journal of Social Behavior and Personality, 5,* 61–84.

Jetten, J., & Hornsey, M. J. (2006). When group members admit to being conformist: The role of relative intragroup status in conformity self-reports. *Personality and Social Psychology Bulletin, 32,* 162–173.

Jetten, J., Hornsey, M. J., & Adarves-Yorno, I. (2006). When group members admit to being conformist: The role of relative intragroup status in conformity self-reports. *Personality and Social Psychology Bulletin, 32,* 162–173.

Jetten, J., Hornsey, M. J., & Adarves-Yorno, I. (2006). When group members admit to being conformist: The role of relative intragroup status in conformity self-reports. *Personality and Social Psychology Bulletin, 32,* 162–173.

Johansson, G., von Hofsten, C., & Jansson, G. (1980). Event perception. *Annual Review of Psychology, 31,* 27–53.

Johns, G. (1994). Absenteeism estimates by employees and managers: Divergent perspectives and self-serving perceptions. *Journal of Applied Psychology, 79,* 229–239.

Johns, M., Schmader, T., & Martens, A., (2005). Knowing is half the battle: Teaching stereotype threat as a means of improving women's math performance. *Psychological Science, 16,* 175–179.

Johnson v. Louisiana, 406 U.S. 356 (1972).

Johnson, A. (2000, April 27). Road-rage remedy? Flashing rear window message says "sorry." *Milwaukee Journal Sentinel,* p. 1A.

Johnson, B. T., & Eagly, A. H. (1989). Effects of involvement on persuasion: A meta-analysis. *Psychological Bulletin, 106,* 290–314.

Johnson, D. J., & Rusbult, C. E. (1989). Resisting temptation: Devaluation of alternative partners as a means of maintaining commitment in close relationships. *Journal of Personality and Social Psychology, 57,* 967–980.

Johnson, H. M., & Seifert, C. M. (1998). Updating accounts following a correction of misinformation. *Journal of Experimental Psychology: Learning, Memory, and Cognition, 24,* 1483–1494.

Johnson, R. D., & Downing, L. L. (1979). Deindividuation and valence of cues: Effects on prosocial and antisocial behavior. *Journal of Personality and Social Psychology, 37,* 1532–1538.

Johnson, R. W., Kelly, R. J., & LeBlane, B. A. (1995). Motivational basis of dissonance: Aversive consequences or inconsistency. *Personality and Social Psychology Bulletin, 21,* 850–855.

Johnson, W., & Krueger, R. F. (2006). How money buys happiness: Genetic and environmental processes linking finances and life satisfaction. *Journal of Personality and Social Psychology, 90,* 680–691.

Johnston, K. E., & Jacobs, J. E. (2003). Children's illusory correlations: The role of attentional bias in group impression formation. *Journal of Cognition and Development, 4,* 129–160.

Johnston, K. L., & White, K. M. (2003). Binge-drinking: A test of the role of group norms in the theory of planned behaviour. *Psychology and Health, 18,* 63–77.

Johnston, L. C., & Macrae, C. N. (1994). Changing social stereotypes: The case of the information seeker. *European Journal of Social Psychology, 24,* 581–592.

Jones, E. E. & Davis, K. E. (1965). From acts to dispositions: The attribution process in person perception. *Advances in Experimental Psychology, 2,* 219–266.

Jones, E. E. (1964). *Ingratiation: A social psychological analysis.* New York: Appleton-Century-Crofts.

Jones, E. E. (1990). *Interpersonal perception.* New York: Freeman.

Jones, E. E., & Harris, V. A. (1967). The attribution of attitudes. *Journal of Experimental Social Psychology, 3,* 1–24.

Jones, E. E., & Nisbett, R. E. (1972). The actor and the observer: Divergent perceptions of causality. In E. E. Jones, D. E. Kanouse, H. H. Kelley, R. E. Nisbett, S. Valins, & B. Weiner (Eds.), *Attribution: Perceiving the causes of behavior* (pp. 79–94). Morristown, NJ: General Learning Press.

Jones, E. E., & Pittman, T. S. (1982). Toward a general theory of strategic self presentation. In J. Suls (Ed.), *Psychological perspectives on the self.* Hillsdale, NJ: Erlbaum.

Jones, E. E., & Sigall, H. (1971). The bogus pipeline: A new paradigm for measuring affect and attitude. *Psychological Bulletin, 76,* 349–364.

Jones, E. E., Davis, K. E., & Gergen, K. (1961). Role playing variations and their informational value for person perception. *Journal of Abnormal and Social Psychology, 63,* 302–310.

Jones, E. E., Rhodewalt, F., Berglas, S., & Skelton, J. A. (1981). Effects of strategic self-presentation on subsequent self-esteem. *Journal of Personality and Social Psychology, 41,* 407–421.

Jones, E. E., Rock, L., Shaver, K. G., Goethals, G. R., & Ward, L. M. (1968). Pattern of performance and ability attribution: An unexpected primary effect. *Journal of Personality and Social Psychology, 10,* 317–340.

Jones, E. W. (1986). Black managers: The dream deferred. *Harvard Business Review, 64,* 84–93.

Jones, J. H. (1997). *Alfred C. Kinsey: A public/private life.* New York: Norton.

Jones, J. T., Pelham, B. W., Carvallo, M., & Mirenberg, M. C. (2004). How do I love thee? Let me count the Js: Implicit egotism and interpersonal attraction. *Journal of Personality and Social Psychology, 87,* 665–683.

Jones, T. F., et al. (2000). Mass psychogenic illness attributed to toxic exposure at a high school. *New England Journal of Medicine, 342,* 96–100.

Josephs, R. A., Bosson, J. K., & Jacobs, C. G. (2003). Self-esteem maintenance processes: When low self-esteem may be resistant to change. *Personality and Social Psychology Bulletin, 29,* 920–933.

Jost, J. T. (2007). The end of the end of ideology. *American Psychologist,* in press.

Jost, J. T. (2008). *A theory of system justification.* New York: Psychology Press/Taylor and Francis.

Jost, J. T., Banaji, M. R., & Nosek, B. A. (2004). A decade of system justification theory: Accumulated evidence of conscious and unconscious bolstering of the status quo. *Political Psychology, 25,* 881–920.

Joyce, C. (2005, May 16). Japanese women escape subway gropers: Transit officials tackle problems with women-only cars. *Ottawa Citizen,* p. A6.

Judd, C. M., Blair, I. V., & Chapleau, K. M. (2004). Automatic stereotypes versus automatic prejudice: Sorting out the possibilities in the Payne (2001) weapon paradigm. *Journal of Experimental Social Psychology, 40,* 75–81.

Judge, T. A., & Welbourne, T. M. (1994). A confirmatory investigation of the dimensionality of the Pay Satisfaction Questionnaire. *Journal of Applied Psychology, 79,* 461–466.

Judge, T. A., Bono, J. E., & Locke, E. A. (2000). Personality and job satisfaction: The mediating role of job characteristics. *Journal of Applied Psychology, 85,* 237–249.

Jussim, L., & Harber, K. D. (2005). Teacher expectations and self-fulfilling prophecies: Knowns and unknowns, resolved and unresolved controversies. *Personality and Social Psychology Review, 9,* 131–155.

Jussim, L., Eccles, J., & Madon, S. (1996). Social perception, social stereotypes, and teacher expectations: Accuracy and the quest for the powerful self-fulfilling prophecy. In M. P. Zanna (Ed.), *Advances in experimental social psychology* (Vol. 28, pp. 281–388). San Diego, CA: Academic Press.

Jussim, L., Harber, K. D., Crawford, J. T., Cain, T. R., & Cohen, F. (2005). Social reality makes the social mind: Self-fulfilling prophecy, stereotypes, bias, and accuracy. *Interaction studies: Social behavior and communication in biological and artificial systems, 6,* 85–102.

Juvonen, J., Graham, S., & Schuster, M. A. (2003). Bullying among young adolescents: The strong, the weak, and the troubled. *Pediatrics, 112,* 1231–1237.

Juvonen, J., Nishina, A., & Graham, S. (2006). Ethnic diversity and perceptions of safety in urban middle schools. *Psychological Science, 17,* 393–400.

Kagan, J. (1994). *Galen's prophecy: Temperament in human nature.* New York: Basic Books.

Kahneman, D., & Miller, D. T. (1986). Norm theory: Comparing reality to its alternatives. *Psychological Review, 93,* 136–153.

Kahneman, D., & Tversky, A. (1979). Prospect theory: An analysis of decisions under risk. *Econometrika, 47,* 263–291.

Kahneman, D., & Tversky, A. (1982). The simulation heuristic. In D. Kahneman, P. Slovic, & A. Tversky (Eds.), *Judgment under uncertainty: Heuristics and biases* (pp. 201–208). New York: Cambridge University Press.

Kahneman, D., Knetsch, J. L., & Thaler, R. H. (1990). Experimental tests of the endowment effect and the coase theorem. *Journal of Political Economy, 98,* 1325–1348.

Kahneman, D., Slovic, P., & Tversky, A. (Eds.). (1982). *Judgment under uncertainty: Heuristics and biases.* New York: Cambridge University Press.

Kalichman, S. C. (1998). *Understanding AIDS: Advances in research and treatment* (2nd ed.). Washington, DC: American Psychological Association.

Kallgren, C. A., & Wood, W. (1986). Access to attitude-relevant information in memory as a determinant of attitude-behavior consistency. *Journal of Experimental Social Psychology, 22,* 328–338.

Kalven, H., & Zeisel, H. (1966). *The American jury.* Boston: Little, Brown.

Kamen-Siegel, L., Rodin, J., Seligman, M. E. P., & Dwyer, J. (1991). Explanatory style and cell-mediated immunity in elderly men and women. *Health Psychology, 10,* 229–235.

Kampe, K. K. W., Frith, C. D., Dolan, R. J., & Frith, U. (2001). Reward value of attractiveness and gaze. *Nature, 413,* 589–590.

Kane, A. A., Argote, L., & Levine, J. M. (2005). Knowledge transfer between groups via personnel rotation: Effects of social identity and knowledge quality. *Organizational Behavior and Human Decision Processes, 96,* 56–71.

Kanetsuna, T., Smith, P. K., & Morita, Y. (2006). Coping with bullying at school: Children's recommended strategies and attitudes to school-based interventions in England and Japan. *Aggressive Behavior, 32,* 570–580.

Kaplan, M. F., & Schersching, C. (1981). Juror deliberation: An information integration analysis. In B. Sales (Ed.), *The trial process* (pp. 235–262). New York: Plenum.

Karau, S. J., & Williams, K. D. (1993). Social loafing: A meta-analytic review and theoretical integration. *Journal of Personality and Social Psychology, 65,* 681–706.

Karau, S. J., & Williams, K. D. (2001). Understanding individual motivation in groups: The collective effort model. In M. E. Turner (Ed.), *Groups at work: Theory and research. Applied social research* (pp. 113–141). Mahwah, NJ: Erlbaum.

Kark, R., Shamir, B., & Chen, G. (2003). The two faces of transformational leadership: Empowerment and dependency. *Journal of Applied Psychology, 88,* 246–255.

Karlsson, N., Juliusson, E. A., & Gärling, T. (2005). A conceptualisation of task dimensions affecting escalation of commitment. *European Journal of Cognitive Psychology, 17,* 835–858.

Karney, B. R., & Bradbury, T. N. (1995). The longitudinal course of marital quality and stability: A review of theory, method, and research. *Psychological Bulletin, 118,* 3–34.

Karney, B. R., & Bradbury, T. N. (1997). Neuroticism, marital interaction, and the trajectory of marital satisfaction. *Journal of Personality and Social Psychology, 72,* 1075–1092.

Karney, B. R., & Bradbury, T. N. (2000). Attributions in marriage: State or trait? A growth curve analysis. *Journal of Personality and Social Psychology, 78,* 295–309.

Karniol, R. (2003). Egocentrism versus protocentrism: The status of self in social prediction. *Psychological Review, 110,* 564–580.

Karpinski, A. T., & von Hippel, W. (1996). The role of the linguistic intergroup bias in expectancy maintenance. *Social Cognition, 14,* 141–163.

Kashima, Y., & Kerekes, A. R. Z. (1994). A distributed memory model of averaging phenomena in person impression formation. *Journal of Experimental Social Psychology, 30,* 407–455.

Kassin, S. M. (1997). The psychology of confession evidence. *American Psychologist, 52,* 221–233.

Kassin, S. M. (2002, November 1). False confessions and the jogger case. *New York Times,* p. A31.

Kassin, S. M. (2005). On the psychology of confessions: Does innocence put innocents at risk? *American Psychologist, 60,* 215–228.

Kassin, S. M., & Gudjonsson, G. H. (2004). The psychology of confession evidence: A review of the literature and issues. *Psychological Science in the Public Interest, 5,* 35–69.

Kassin, S. M., & Kiechel, K. L. (1996). The social psychology of false confessions: Compliance, internalization, and confabulation. *Psychological Science, 7,* 125–128.

Kassin, S. M., & Sommers, S. R. (1997). Inadmissible testimony, instructions to disregard, and the jury: Substantive versus procedural considerations. *Personality and Social Psychology Bulletin, 23,* 1046–1054.

Kassin, S. M., & Sukel, H. (1997). Coerced confessions and the jury: An experimental test of the "harmless error" rule. *Law and Human Behavior, 21,* 27–46.

Kassin, S. M., & Wrightsman, L. S. (1983). The construction and validation of a Juror Bias Scale. *Journal of Research in Personality, 17,* 423–442.

Kassin, S. M., & Wrightsman, L. S. (1985). Confession evidence. In S. Kassin & L. Wrightsman (Eds.), *The psychology of evidence and trial procedure.* Beverly Hills: Sage Books.

Kassin, S. M., & Wrightsman, L. S. (1988). *The American jury on trial: Psychological perspectives.* Washington, DC: Hemisphere.

Kassin, S. M., Goldstein, C. J., & Savitsky, K. (2003). Behavioral confirmation in the interrogation room: On the dangers of presuming guilt. *Law and Human Behavior, 27,* 187–203.

Kassin, S. M., Leo, R. A., Meissner, C. A., Richman, K. D., Colwell, L. H., Leach, A-M., & LaFon, D. (2007). Police interviewing and interrogation: A self-report survey of police practices and beliefs. *Law and Human Behavior,* in press.

Kassin, S. M., Meissner, C. A., & Norwick, R. J. (2005). "I'd know a false confession if I saw one": A comparative study of college students and police investigators. *Law and Human Behavior, 29,* 211–227.

Kassin, S. M., Tubb, V. A., Hosch, H. M., & Memon, A. (2001). On the "general acceptance" of eyewitness testimony research: A new survey of the experts. *American Psychologist, 56,* 405–416.

Katz, D., & Braly, K. W. (1933). Racial stereotypes of 100 college students. *Journal of Abnormal and Social Psychology, 28,* 280–290.

Kaufman, D. Q., Stasson, M. F., & Hart, J. W. (1999). Are the tabloids always wrong or is that just what we think? Need for cognition and perceptions of articles in print media. *Journal of Applied Social Psychology, 29,* 1984–1997.

Kawakami, K., Dion, K. L., & Dovidio, J. F. (1998). Racial prejudice and stereotype activation. *Personality and Social Psychology Bulletin, 24,* 407–416.

Kawakami, K., Dovidio, J. F., Moll, J., Hermsen, S., & Russin, A. (2000). Just say no (to stereotyping): Effects of training in the negation of stereotypic association on stereotype activation. *Journal of Personality and Social Psychology, 78,* 871–888.

Kawakami, K., Dovidio, J. F., & van Kamp, S. (2007). The impact of naïve theories related to strategies to reduce biases and correction processes on the application of stereotypes. *Group Processes and Intergroup Relations,* in press.

Kay, A. C., & Jost, J. T. (2003). Complementary justice: Effects of "poor but happy" and "poor but honest" stereotype exemplars on system justification and implicit activation of the justice motive. *Journal of Personality and Social Psychology, 85,* 823–837.

Kay, A. C., Jost, J. T., & Young, S. (2005). Victim derogation and victim enhancement as alternate routes to system justification. *Personality and Social Psychology Bulletin, 16,* 240–246.

Keelan, J. P. R., Dion, K. L., & Dion, K. K. (1994). Attachment style and heterosexual relationships among young adults: A short-term panel study. *Journal of Social and Personal Relationships, 11,* 201–214.

Keenan, J., Gallup, G. G., & Falk, D. (2003). *The face in the mirror: The search for the origins of consciousness.* New York: Ecco/HarperCollins.

Keillor, J. M., Barrett, A. M., Crucian, G. P., Kortenkamp, S., & Heilman, K. M. (2003). Emotional experience and perception in the absence of facial feedback. *Journal of the International Neurological Society, 8,* 130–135.

Keller, J. (2005). In genes we trust: The biological component of psychological essentialism and its relationship to mechanisms of motivated social cognition. *Journal of Personality and Social Psychology, 88,* 686–702.

Keller, J., & Dauenheimer, D. (2003). Stereotype threat in the classroom: Dejection mediates the disrupting threat effect on women's math performance. *Personality and Social Psychology Bulletin, 29,* 371–381.

Keller, P. A. (1999). Converting the unconverted: The effect of inclination and opportunity to discount health-related fear appeals. *Journal of Applied Psychology, 84,* 403–415.

Kelley, H. H. (1950). The warm-cold variable in first impressions of persons. *Journal of Personality, 18,* 431–439.

Kelley, H. H. (1967). Attribution in social psychology. *Nebraska Symposium on Motivation, 15,* 192–238.

Kelley, H. H., & Stahelski, A. J. (1970). Social interaction basis of cooperators' and competitors' beliefs about others. *Journal of Personality and Social Psychology, 16,* 66–91.

Kelley, M. W., Macrae, C. N., Wyland, C. L., Caglar, S., Inati, S., & Heatherton, T. F. (2002). Finding the self? An event-related fMRI study. *Journal of Cognitive Neuroscience, 14,* 785–794.

Kelly, A. E., & McKillop, K. J. (1996). Consequences of revealing personal secrets. *Psychological Bulletin, 120,* 450–465.

Kelly, A. E., & Rodriguez, R. R. (2006). Publicly committing oneself to an identity. *Basic and Applied Social Psychology, 28,* 185–191.

Kelly, J. (2002/2003, December 30/January 6). Persons of the year. *Time,* p. 8.

Kelly, J. A., St. Lawrence, J. S., Diaz, Y. E., Stevenson, L. Y., Hauth, A. C., Brasfield, T. L., Kalichman, S. C., Smith, J. E., & Andrew, M. E. (1991). HIV risk behavior reduction following intervention with key opinion leaders of a population: An experimental community-level analysis. *American Journal of Public Health, 81,* 168–171.

Kelman, H. C. (1961). Processes of opinion change. *Public Opinion Quarterly, 25,* 57–78.

Kelman, H. C. (1967). Human use of human subjects: The problem of deception in social psychology experiments. *Psychological Bulletin, 67,* 1–11.

Kelman, H. C., & Hamilton, V. L. (1989). *Crimes of obedience: Toward a social psychology of authority and responsibility.* New Haven, CT: Yale University Press.

Kelman, H. C., & Hovland, C. I. (1953). "Reinstatement" of the communicator in delayed measurement of opinion change. *Journal of Abnormal and Social Psychology, 48,* 327–335.

Kemmelmeier, M., Jambor, E. E., & Letner, J. (2006). Individualism and good works: Cultural variation in giving and volunteering across the United States. *Journal of Cross-Cultural Psychology, 37,* 327–344.

Kennedy, H. (2003). He takes fatal OD as internet pals watch: Chatroom vultures egged him to pop more Rx pills. *New York Daily News,* February 2, p. 5.

Kenny, D. A. (1994). *Interpersonal perception: A social relations analysis.* New York: Guilford.

Kenny, D. A., & Acitelli, L. K. (2001). Accuracy and bias of perceptions of the partner in close relationships. *Journal of Personality and Social Psychology, 80,* 439–448.

Kenny, D. A., & DePaulo, B. M. (1993). Do people know how others view them? An empirical and theoretical account. *Psychological Bulletin, 114,* 145–161.

Kenny, D. A., & Zaccaro, S. J. (1983). An estimate of variance due to traits in leadership. *Journal of Applied Psychology, 68,* 678–685.

Kenny, D. A., Albright, L., Malloy, T. E., & Kashy, D. A. (1994). Consensus in interpersonal perception: Acquaintance and the Big Five. *Psychological Bulletin, 116,* 245–258.

Kenny, D. A., Horner, C., Kashy, D. A., & Chu, L. (1992). Consensus at zero acquaintance: Replication, behavioral cues, and stability. *Journal of Personality and Social Psychology, 62,* 88–97.

Kenrick, D. T., & Keefe, R. C. (1992). Age preferences in mates reflect sex differences in human reproductive strategies. *Behavioral and Brain Sciences, 15,* 75–133.

Kenrick, D. T., & MacFarlane, S. W. (1986). Ambient temperature and horn honking: A field study of the heat/aggression relationship. *Environment and Behavior, 18,* 179–191.

Kenrick, D. T., Gabrielidis, C., Keefe, R. C., & Cornelius, J. S. (1996). Adolescents' age preferences for dating partners:

Support for an evolutionary model of life-history strategies. *Child Development, 67,* 1499–1511.

Kenrick, D. T., Gutierres, S. E., & Goldberg, L. L. (1989). Influence of popular erotica on judgments of strangers and mates. *Journal of Experimental Social Psychology, 25,* 159–167.

Kenrick, D. T., Montello, D. R., Gutierres, S. E., & Trost, M. R. (1993). Effects of physical attractiveness on affect and perceptual judgments: When social comparison overrides social reinforcement. *Personality and Social Psychology Bulletin, 19,* 195–199.

Kernis, M. H. (Ed.). (2007). *Self-esteem issues and answers: A sourcebook of current perspectives.* New York: Psychology Press.

Kernis, M. H., & Waschull, S. B. (1995). The interactive roles of stability and level of self-esteem: Research and theory. *Advances in Experimental Social Psychology, 27,* 93–141.

Kerr, N. L. (1981). Social transition schemes: Charting the group's road to agreement. *Journal of Personality and Social Psychology, 41,* 684–702.

Kerr, N. L. (1983). Motivation losses in small groups: A social dilemma analysis. *Journal of Personality and Social Psychology, 45,* 819–828.

Kerr, N. L., & Kaufman-Gilliland, C. M. (1994). Communication, commitment, and cooperation in social dilemma. *Journal of Personality and Social Psychology, 66,* 513–529.

Kerr, N. L., Harmon, D. L., & Graves, J. K. (1982). Independence of multiple verdicts by jurors and juries. *Journal of Applied Social Psychology, 12,* 12–29.

Kerr, N. L., Hymes, R. W., Anderson, A. B., & Weathers, J. E. (1995). Defendant-juror similarity in mock juror judgments. *Law and Human Behavior, 19,* 545–567.

Kerr, N. L., Kramer, G. P., Carroll, J. S., & Alfini, J. J. (1991). On the effectiveness of voir dire in criminal cases with prejudicial pretrial publicity: An empirical study. *American University Law Review, 40,* 665–701.

Kerr, N. L., Niedermeier, K. E., & Kaplan, M. F. (1999). Bias in jurors vs. bias in juries: New evidence from the SDS perspective. *Organizational Behavior and Human Decision Processes, 80,* 70–86.

Kessler, R. C., et al. (1994). Lifetime and 12-month prevalence of DSM-III-R psychiatric disorders in the United States. *Archives of General Psychiatry, 51,* 8–19.

Kessler, R. C., Sonnega, A., Bromet, E., Hughes, M., & Nelson, C. B. (1995). Posttraumatic stress disorder in the National Co-morbidity Survey. *Archives of General Psychiatry, 52,* 1048–1060.

Key, W. B. (1973). *Subliminal seduction.* Englewood Cliffs, NJ: Signet.

Key, W. B. (1989). *The age of manipulation.* New York: Holt.

Keysar, B., & Henly, A. S. (2002). Speakers' overestimation of their effectiveness. *Psychological Science, 13,* 207–212.

Kiecolt-Glaser, J. K., & Newton, T. L. (2001). Marriage and health: His and hers. *Psychological Bulletin, 127,* 472–503.

Kiecolt-Glaser, J. K., Marucha, P. T., Atkinson, C., & Glaser, R. (2001). Hypnosis as a modulator of cellular immune dysregulation during acute stress. *Journal of Consulting and Clinical Psychology, 69,* 674–682.

Kiecolt-Glaser, J. K., McGuire, L., Robles, T., & Glaser, R. (2002). Psychoneuroimmunology: Psychological influences on immune function and health. *Journal of Consulting and Clinical Psychology, 70,* 537–547.

Kiefer, A., Sekaquaptewa, D., & Barczyk, A. (2006). When appearance concerns make women look bad: Solo status and body image concerns diminish women's academic performance. *Journal of Experimental Social Psychology, 42,* 78–86.

Kierein, N. M., & Gold, M. A. (2000). Pygmalion in work organizations: A meta-analysis. *Journal of Organizational Behavior, 21,* 913–928.

Kiesler, C. A. (1971). *The psychology of commitment.* New York: Academic Press.

Kiesler, C. A., & Kiesler, S. B. (1969). *Conformity.* Reading, MA: Addison-Wesley.

Kilham, W., & Mann, L. (1974). Level of destructive obedience as a function of transmitter and executant roles in the Milgram obedience paradigm. *Journal of Personality and Social Psychology, 29,* 696–702.

Kilianski, S. E., & Rudman, L. A. (1998). Wanting it both ways: Do women approve of benevolent sexism? *Sex Roles, 39,* 333–352.

Kim, H., & Markus, H. R. (1999). Deviance or uniqueness, harmony or conformity? A cultural analysis. *Journal of Personality and Social Psychology, 77,* 785–800.

Kimmel, P. R. (1994). Cultural perspectives on international negotiations. *Journal of Social Issues, 50,* 179–196.

Kimmel, P. R. (2000). Culture and conflict. In M. Deutsch & P. T. Coleman (Eds.), *The handbook of conflict resolution: Theory and practice* (pp. 453–474). San Francisco, CA: Jossey-Bass.

Kinsey, A. C., Pomeroy, W. B., & Martin, C. E. (1948). *Sexual behavior in the human male.* Philadelphia: Saunders.

Kinsey, A. C., Pomeroy, W. B., Martin, C. E., & Gebhard, P. H. (1953). *Sexual behavior in the human female.* Philadelphia: Saunders.

Kinzer, S. (1999, September 13). A sudden friendship blossoms between Greece and Turkey. *New York Times* (http:www .nytimes.com/library/world/europe/091399greece-turkey .html).

Kirkpatrick, L. A., & Hazan, C. (1994). Attachment styles and close relationships: A four-year prospective study. *Personal Relationships, 1,* 123–142.

Kirkpatrick, S. A., & Locke, E. A. (1991). Leadership: Do traits matter? *Academy of Management Executive, 5,* 48–60.

Kitayama, S., & Uchida, Y. (2003). Explicit self-criticism and implicit self-regard: Evaluating self and friend in two cultures. *Journal of Experimental Social Psychology, 39,* 476–482.

Kitayama, S., Markus, H. R., Matsumoto, H., & Norasakkunkit, V. (1997). Individual and collective processes in the construction of the self: Self-enhancement in the United States and self-criticism in Japan. *Journal of Personality and Social Psychology, 72,* 1245–1267.

Kitayama, S., Snibbe, A. C., Markus, H. R., & Suzuki, T. (2004). Is there any "free" choice? Self and dissonance in two cultures. *Psychological Science, 15,* 527–533.

Kite, M. E. (1992). Age and the spontaneous self-concept. *Journal of Applied Social Psychology, 22,* 1828–1837.

Kitson, G. C., & Morgan, L. A. (1990). The multiple consequences of divorce: A decade review. *Journal of Marriage and the Family, 52,* 913–924.

Kivimäki, M., Vahtera, J., Elovainio, M., Helenius, H., Singh-Manoux, A., & Pentti, J. (2005). Optimism and pessimism as predictors of change in health after death or onset of severe illness in family. *Health Psychology, 24,* 413–421.

Klein, E. E., Clark, C. C., & Herskovitz, P. J. (2003). Ethical implications of social psychological consequences. *Computers in Human Behavior, 19,* 355–382.

Klein, J. G. (1991). Negativity effects in impression formation: A test in the political arena. *Personality and Social Psychology Bulletin, 17,* 412–418.

Klein, O., Licata, L., Azzi, A. E., & Durala, I. (2003). "How European am I?" Prejudice expression and the presentation of social identity. *Self and Identity, 2,* 251–264.

Klein, W. M. (1997). Objective standards are not enough: Affective, self-evaluative, and behavioral responses to social comparison information. *Journal of Personality and Social Psychology, 72,* 763–774.

Kleinke, C. L. (1986). Gaze and eye contact: A research review. *Psychological Bulletin, 100,* 78–100.

Kleinke, C. L., Paterson, T. R., & Rutledge, T. R. (1998). Effects of self-generated facial expressions of mood. *Journal of Personality and Social Psychology, 74,* 272–279.

Klinesmith, J., Kasser, T., & McAndrew, F. T. (2006). Guns, testosterone, and aggression: An experimental test of a mediational hypothesis. *Psychological Science, 17,* 568–571.

Kling, K. C., Hyde, J. S., Showers, C. J., & Buswell, B. N. (1999). Gender differences in self-esteem: A meta-analysis. *Psychological Bulletin, 125,* 470–500.

Kmec, J. A. (2005). Setting occupational sex segregation in motion: Sex traditional employment. *Work and Occupations, 32,* 322–354.

Knafo, A., & Plomin, R. (2006). Prosocial behavior from early to middle childhood: Genetic and environmental influences on stability and change. *Developmental Psychology, 42,* 771–786.

Kniffin, K., & Wilson, D. S. (2004). The effect of nonphysical traits on the perception of physical attractiveness: Three naturalistic studies. *Evolution and Human Behavior, 25,* 88–101.

Knight, G. P., Johnson, L. G., Carlo, G., & Eisenberg, N. (1994). A multiplicative model of the dispositional antecedents of a prosocial behavior: Predicting more of the people more of the time. *Journal of Personality and Social Psychology, 66,* 178–183.

Knobloch, S., Callison, C., Chen, L., Fritzsche, A., & Zillmann, D. (2005). Children's sex-stereotyped self-socialization through selective exposure to entertainment: Cross-cultural experiments in Germany, China, and the United States. *Journal of Communication, 55,* 122–138.

Knowles, E. S. (1983). Social physics and the effects of others: Tests of the effects of audience size and distance on social judgments and behavior. *Journal of Personality and Social Psychology, 45,* 1263–1279.

Knox, N. (2000, September 15). Wall Street battles sexual bias: Even as brokerage industry fights discrimination, women regularly make accusations. *USA Today,* p. 1B.

Knox, R. E., & Inskter, J. A. (1968). Postdecision dissonance at posttime. *Journal of Personality and Social Psychology, 8,* 319–323.

Knox, R. E., & Safford, R. K. (1976). Group caution at the race track. *Journal of Experimental Social Psychology, 12,* 317–324.

Ko, S. J., Judd, C. M., & Blair, I. V. (2006). What the voice reveals: Within- and between-category stereotyping on the basis of voice. *Personality and Social Psychology Bulletin, 32,* 806–819.

Kobasa, S. C., Maddi, S. R., & Kahn, S. (1982). Hardiness and health: A prospective study. *Journal of Personality and Social Psychology, 42,* 168–177.

Kohl, P. L., Edleson, J. L., English, D. J., & Barth, R. P. (2005). Domestic violence and pathways into child welfare services: Findings from the National Survey of Child and Adolescent Well-Being. *Children and Youth Services Review, 27,* 1167–1182.

Kohn, A. (1993). *Punished by rewards.* Boston: Houghton Mifflin.

Kohn, P. M., Lafreniere, K., & Gurevich, M. (1991). Hassles, health, and personality. *Journal of Personality and Social Psychology, 61,* 478–482.

Kolditz, T. A., & Arkin, R. M. (1982). An impression management interpretation of the self-handicapping strategy. *Journal of Personality and Social Psychology, 43,* 492–502.

Komorita, S. S., Chan, D. K-S., & Parks, C. (1993). The effects of reward structure and reciprocity in social dilemmas. *Journal of Experimental Social Psychology, 29,* 252–267.

Konecni, V. J., & Ebbesen, E. B. (1982). *The criminal justice system: A social-psychological analysis.* San Francisco: Freeman.

Korchmaros, J. D., Kenny, D. A., & Flory, K. (2006). An evolutionary and close-relationship model of helping. *Journal of Social and Personal Relationships, 23,* 21–43.

Korte, C. (1980). Urban-nonurban differences in social behavior and social psychological models of urban impact. *Journal of Social Issues, 36* (3), 29–51.

Korte, C., Ypma, I., & Toppen, A. (1975). Helpfulness in Dutch society as a function of urbanization and environmental input level. *Journal of Personality and Social Psychology, 32,* 996–1003.

Koslowsky, M., Kluger, A., & Reich, M. (1995). *Commuting stress.* New York: Plenum Press.

Kosonen, P., & Winne, P. (1995). Effects of teaching statistical laws of reasoning about everyday problems. *Journal of Educational Psychology, 87,* 33–46.

Kovacs, L. (1983). A conceptualization of marital development. *Family Therapy, 3,* 183–210.

Kovera, M. B. (2002). The effects of general pretrial publicity on juror decisions: An examination of moderators and mediating mechanisms. *Law and Human Behavior, 26,* 43–72.

Kovera, M. B. (2004). Psychology, law, and the workplace: An overview and introduction to the special issue. *Law and Human Behavior, 28,* 1–7.

Kovera, M. B., Penrod, S. D., Pappas, C., & Thill, D. L. (1997). Identification of computer-generated facial composites. *Journal of Applied Psychology, 82,* 235–246.

Kowalski, R. M. (1993). Inferring sexual interest from behavioral cues: Effects of gender and sexually relevant attitudes. *Sex Roles, 29,* 13–36.

Kowalski, R. M. (1996). Complaints and complaining: Functions, antecedents, and consequences. *Psychological Bulletin, 119,* 179–196.

Kozak, M. N., Marsh, A. A., & Wegner, D. M. (2006). What do I think you're doing? Action identification and mind attribution. *Journal of Personality and Social Psychology, 90,* 543–555.

Kozel, F. A., Padgett, T. M., & George, M. S. (2004). A replication study of the neural correlates of deception. *Behavioral Neuroscience, 118,* 852–856.

Kozlowski, S. W., Kirsch, M. P., & Chao, G. T. (1986). Job knowledge, ratee familiarity, conceptual similarity, and halo error: An exploration. *Journal of Applied Psychology, 71,* 45–49.

Kraines, D., & Kraines, V. (1995). Evolution of learning among Pavlov strategies in a competitive environment with noise. *Journal of Conflict Resolution, 39,* 439–466.

Kramer, G. P., Kerr, N. L., & Carroll, J. S. (1990). Pretrial publicity, judicial remedies, and jury bias. *Law and Human Behavior, 14,* 409–438.

Kramer, R. M. (1998). Revisiting the Bay of Pigs and Vietnam decisions 25 years later: How well has the groupthink hypothesis stood the test of time? *Organizational Behavior and Human Decision Processes, 73,* 236–271.

Kramer, R. M., & Brewer, M. B. (1984). Effects of group identity on resource use in a simulated commons dilemma. *Journal of Personality and Social Psychology, 46,* 1044–1057.

Krantz, D. S., & McCeney, M. K. (2002). Effects of psychological and social factors on organic disease: A critical assessment of research on coronary heart disease. *Annual Review of Psychology, 53,* 341–369.

Kraus, S. J. (1995). Attitudes and the prediction of behavior: A meta-analysis of the empirical literature. *Personality and Social Psychology Bulletin, 21,* 58–75.

Kravitz, D. A., & Martin, B. (1986). Ringelmann rediscovered: The original article. *Journal of Personality and Social Psychology, 50,* 936–941.

Kravitz, D. A., & Platania, J. (1993). Attitudes and beliefs about affirmative action: Effects of target and of respondent sex and ethnicity. *Journal of Applied Psychology, 78,* 928–938.

Kravitz, D. A., et al. (1997). *Affirmative action: A review of psychological and behavioral research.* Bowling Green, OH: Society for Industrial and Organizational Psychology.

Kray, L. J., & Galinsky, A. D. (2003). The debiasing effect of counterfactual mind-sets on group decisions: Increasing the search for disconfirmatory information in group decisions. *Organizational Behavior and Human Decision Processes, 91,* 69–81.

Kray, L. J., Galinsky, A. D., & Thompson, L. (2002). Reversing the gender gap in negotiations: An exploration of stereotype regeneration. *Organizational Behavior and Human Decision Processes, 87,* 386–409.

Krebs, D. (1987). The challenge of altruism in biology and psychology. In C. Crawford, M. Smith, & D. Krebs (Eds.), *Sociobiology and psychology: Ideas, issues, and applications* (pp. 81–118). Hillsdale, NJ: Erlbaum.

Krebs, D., & Rosenwald, A. (1994). Moral reasoning and moral behavior in conventional adults. In B. Puka (Ed.), *Fundamental research in moral development* (pp. 111–121). New York: Garland.

Kressel, N. J., & Kressel, D. F. (2002). *Stack and sway: The new science of jury consulting.* Boulder, CO: Westview Press.

Kroon, M. B. R., 't Hart, P., & van Kreveld, D. (1991). Managing group decision making processes: Individual versus collective accountability and groupthink. *International Journal of Conflict Management, 2,* 91–115.

Krueger, J. (1998). On the perception of social consensus. *Advances in Experimental Social Psychology, 30,* 163–240.

Krueger, J. (2000). The projective perception of the social world: A building block of social comparison processes. In J. Suls & L. Wheeler (Eds.), *Handbook of social comparison: Theory and research* (pp. 323–351). New York: Plenum/Kluwer.

Krueger, J. I., Hasman, J. F., Acevedo, M., & Villano, P. (2003). Perceptions of trait typicality in gender stereotypes: Examining the role of attribution and categorization processes. *Personality and Social Psychology Bulletin, 29,* 108–116.

Krueger, J., Rothbart, M., & Sriram, N. (1989). Category learning and change: Differences in sensitivity to information that enhances or reduces intercategory distinctions. *Journal of Personality and Social Psychology, 56,* 866–875.

Krueger, R. F., Hicks, B. M., & McGue, M. (2001). Altruism and antisocial behavior: Independent tendencies, unique personality correlates, distinct etiologies. *Psychological Science, 12,* 397–402.

Krug, E. G., Kresnow, M., Peddicord, J. P., Dahlberg, L. L., Powell, K. E., Crosby, A. E., & Annest, J. L. (1998). Suicide after natural disasters. *New England Journal of Medicine, 338,* 373–378.

Kruger, J., & Dunning, D. (1999). Unskilled and unaware of it: How difficulties in recognizing one's own incompetence lead to inflated self-assessments. *Journal of Personality and Social Psychology, 77,* 1121–1134.

Kruger, J., Wirtz, D., & Miller, D. T. (2005). Counterfactual thinking and the first instinct fallacy. *Journal of Personality and Social Psychology, 88,* 725–735.

Kruglanski, A. W. (2001). That "vision thing": The state of theory in social and personality psychology at the edge of the new millennium. *Journal of Personality and Social Psychology, 80,* 871–875.

Kruglanski, A. W., & Freund, T. (1983). The freezing and unfreezing of lay-inferences: Effects of impressional primacy, ethnic stereotyping, and numerical anchoring. *Journal of Experimental Social Psychology, 19,* 448–468.

Kruglanski, A. W., & Mayseless, O. (1988). Contextual effects in hypothesis testing: The role of competing alternatives and epistemic motivations. *Social Cognition, 6,* 1–20.

Kruglanski, A. W., & Webster, D. M. (1996). Motivated closing of the mind: "Seizing" and "freezing." *Psychological Review, 103,* 263–283.

Kubany, E. S., Leisen, M. B., Kaplan, A. S., Watson, S. B., Haynes, S. N., Owens, J. A., & Burns, K. (2000). Development and preliminary validation of a brief broad-spectrum measure of trauma exposure: The Traumatic Life Events Questionnaire. *Psychological Assessment, 12,* 210–224.

Kubzansky, L. D., Sparrow, D., Vokonas, P., & Kawachi, I. (2001). Is the glass half empty or half full? A prospective study of optimism and coronary heart disease in the Normative Aging Study. *Psychosomatic Medicine, 63,* 910–916.

Kugihara, N. (1999). Gender and social loafing in Japan. *Journal of Social Psychology, 139,* 516–526.

Kulik, J. A., & Mahler, H. I. M. (1989). Stress and affiliation in a hospital setting: Preoperative roommate preferences. *Personality and Social Psychology Bulletin, 15,* 183–193.

Kulik, J. A., Mahler, H. I. M., & Earnest, A. (1994). Social comparison and affiliation under threat: Going beyond the affiliate-choice paradigm. *Journal of Personality and Social Psychology, 66,* 301–309.

Kulik, J. A., Mahler, H. I. M., & Moore, P. J. (1996). Social comparison and affiliation under threat: Effects of recovery from major surgery. *Journal of Personality and Social Psychology, 71,* 967–979.

Kumkale, G. T., & Albarracín, D. (2004). The sleeper effect in persuasion: A meta-analytic review. *Psychological Bulletin, 130,* 143–172.

Kunda, Z. (1987). Motivated inference: Self-serving generation and evaluation of causal theories. *Journal of Personality and Social Psychology, 53,* 636–647.

Kunda, Z., & Sinclair, L. (1999). Motivated reasoning with stereotypes: Activation, application, and inhibition. *Psychological Inquiry, 10,* 12–22.

Kunda, Z., & Spencer, S. J. (2003). When do stereotypes come to mind and when do they color judgment? A goal-based theoretical framework for stereotype activation and application. *Psychological Bulletin, 129,* 522–544.

Kunda, Z., Adams, B., Davies, P. G., Hoshino-Browne, E., & Jordan, C. (2003). The impact of comprehension goals on the ebb and flow of stereotype activation during interaction. In Spencer, S. J., Fein, S., Zanna, M. P., & Olson, J. M. (Eds.), *Motivated social perception: The Ontario symposium* (Vol. 9: pp. 1–20). Mahwah, NJ: Erlbaum.

Kunda, Z., Davies, P. G., Adams, B. D., & Spencer, S. J. (2002). The dynamic time course of stereotype activation: Activation, dissipation, and resurrection. *Journal of Personality and Social Psychology, 82,* 283–299.

Kunda, Z., Sinclair, L., & Griffin, D. (1997). Equal ratings but separate meanings: Stereotypes and the construal of traits. *Journal of Personality and Social Psychology, 72,* 720–734.

Kuntz-Wilson, W., & Zajonc, R. B. (1980). Affective discrimination of stimuli that cannot be recognized. *Science, 207,* 557–558.

Kupers, T. A. (1999). *Prison madness: The mental health crisis behind bars and what we must do about it.* New York: Jossey-Bass.

Kurbat, M. A., Shevell, S. K., & Rips, L. J. (1998). A year's memories: The calendar effect in autobiographical recall. *Memory and Cognition, 26,* 532–552.

Kurdek, L. A. (1991a). Correlates of relationship satisfaction in cohabiting gay and lesbian couples: Interpretation of contextual, investment, and problem-solving models. *Journal of Personality and Social Psychology, 61,* 910–922.

Kurdek, L. A. (1991b). The dissolution of gay and lesbian couples. *Journal of Social and Personal Relationships, 8,* 265–278.

Kurdek, L. A. (1999). The nature and predictors of the trajectory of change in marital quality for husbands and wives over the first 10 years of marriage. *Developmental Psychology, 35,* 1283–1296.

Kurdek, L. A. (2000). Attractions and constraints as determinants of relationship commitment: Longitudinal evidence from gay, lesbian, and heterosexual couples. *Personal Relationships, 7,* 245–262.

Kurdek, L. A. (2005). What do we know about gay and lesbian couples? *Current Directions in Psychological Science, 14,* 251–254.

Kurzban, R., & Leary, M. R. (2001). Evolutionary origins of stigmatization: The functions of social exclusion. *Psychological Bulletin, 127,* 187–208.

Laird, J. D. (1974). Self-attribution of emotion: The effects of expressive behavior on the quality of emotional experience. *Journal of Personality and Social Psychology, 29,* 475–486.

Lakey, B., & Cassady, P. B. (1990). Cognitive processes in perceived social support. *Journal of Personality and Social Psychology, 59,* 337–343.

Lakin, J. L., & Chartrand, T. L. (2003). Using nonconscious behavioral mimicry to create affiliation and rapport. *Psychological Science, 14,* 334–339.

Lalwani, A. K., Shavitt, S., & Johnson, T. (2006). What is the relation between cultural orientation and socially desirable responding? *Journal of Personality and Social Psychology, 90,* 165–178.

Lambird, K. H., & Mann, T. (2006). When do ego threats lead to self-regulation failure? Negative consequences of defensive high self-esteem. *Personality and Social Psychology Bulletin, 32,* 1177–1187.

Lamm, H., & Myers, D. G. (1978). Group-induced polarization of attitudes and behavior. In L. Berkowitz (Ed.), *Advances in experimental social psychology* (Vol. 11, pp. 145–195). New York: Academic Press.

Landau, M. J., Solomon, S., Greenberg, J., Cohen, F., Pyszczynski, T., Arndt, J., Miller, C. H., Ogilvie, D. M., & Cook, A. (2004). Deliver us from evil: The effects of mortality salience and reminders of 9/11 on support for President George W. Bush. *Personality and Social Psychology Bulletin, 30,* 1136–1150.

Landau, T. (1989). *About faces: The evolution of the human face.* New York: Anchor Books.

Landy, F. J., & Farr, J. L. (1983). *The measurement of work performance: Methods, theory, and applications.* New York: Academic Press.

Lane, L. W., Groisman, M., & Ferreira, V. S. (2006). Don't talk about pink elephants! Speakers' control over leaking private information during language production. *Psychological Science, 17,* 273–277.

Langer, E. J. (1975). The illusion of control. *Journal of Personality and Social Psychology, 32,* 311–328.

Langer, E. J. (1989). *Mindfulness.* Reading, MA: Addison-Wesley.

Langer, E. J., & Rodin, J. (1976). The effects of choice and enhanced personal responsibility for the aged: A field experiment in an institutional setting. *Journal of Personality and Social Psychology, 34,* 191–198.

Langer, E. J., Blank, A., & Chanowitz, B. (1978). The mindlessness of ostensibly thoughtful action. *Journal of Personality and Social Psychology, 36,* 635–642.

Langer, G., Arnedt, C., & Sussman, D. (2004). Primetime Live poll: American sex survey. http:abcnews.go.com/Primetime/News/story?id=156921.

Langfred, C. W. (1998). Is group cohesiveness a double-edged sword? An investigation of the effects of cohesiveness on performance. *Small Group Research, 29,* 124–143.

Langlois, J. H., & Roggman, L. A. (1990). Attractive faces are only average. *Psychological Science, 1,* 115–121.

Langlois, J. H., Kalakanis, L., Rubenstein, A. J., Larson, A., Hallam, M., & Smoot, M. (2000). Maxims or myths of beauty? A meta-analytic and theoretical review. *Psychological Bulletin, 126,* 390–423.

Langlois, J. H., Ritter, J. M., Roggman, L. A., & Vaughn, L. S. (1991). Facial diversity and infant preferences for attractive faces. *Developmental Psychology, 27,* 79–84.

Langlois, J. H., Roggman, L. A., & Musselman, L. (1994). What is average and what is not average about attractive faces? *Psychological Science, 5,* 214–220.

Langton, S. R. H., Watt, R. J., & Bruce, V. (2000). Do the eyes have it? Cues to the direction of social attention. *Trends in Cognitive Sciences, 4,* 50–59.

Lanzetta, J. T. (1955). Group behavior under stress. *Human Relations, 8,* 29–52.

LaPiere, R. T. (1934). Attitudes vs. action. *Social Forces, 13,* 230–237.

Larrick, R. P., Morgan, J. N., & Nisbett, R. E. (1990). Teaching the use of cost-benefit reasoning in everyday life. *Psychological Science, 1,* 362–370.

Larsen, K. S. (1990). The Asch conformity experiment: Replication and transhistorical comparisons. *Journal of Social Behavior and Personality, 5,* 163–168.

Larsen, R. J., & Kasimatis, M. (1990). Individual differences in entrainment of mood to the weekly calendar. *Journal of Personality and Social Psychology, 58,* 164–171.

Larson, J. R., Jr., Foster-Fishman, P. G., & Franz, T. M. (1998). Leadership style and the discussion of shared and unshared information in decision-making groups. *Personality and Social Psychology Bulletin, 24,* 482–495.

Lassiter, G. D. (Ed.). (2004). *Interrogations, confessions, and entrapment.* New York: Kluwer Academic.

Lassiter, G. D. (Ed.). (2004). *Interrogations, confessions, and entrapment.* New York: Kluwer Academic.

Lassiter, G. D., Geers, A. L., Munhall, P. J., Handley, I. M., & Beers, M. J. (2001). Videotaped confessions: Is guilt in the eye of the camera? *Advances in Experimental Social Psychology, 33,* 189–254.

Lassiter, G. D., Stone, J. I., & Rogers, S. L. (1988). Memorial consequences of variation in behavior perception. *Journal of Experimental Social Psychology, 24,* 222–239.

Latané, B. (1981). The psychology of social impact. *American Psychologist, 36,* 343–356.

Latané, B., & Darley, J. M. (1968). Group inhibition of bystander intervention. *Journal of Personality and Social Psychology, 10,* 215–221.

Latané, B., & Darley, J. M. (1970). *The unresponsive bystander: Why doesn't he help?* New York: Appleton-Century-Crofts.

Latané, B., & L'Herrou, T. (1996). Spatial clustering in the conformity game: Dynamic social impact in electronic groups. *Journal of Personality and Social Psychology, 70,* 1218–1230.

Latané, B., & Werner, C. (1978). Regulation of social contact in laboratory rats: Time, not distance. *Journal of Personality and Social Psychology, 36,* 1128–1137.

Latané, B., & Wolf, S. (1981). The social impact of majorities and minorities. *Psychological Review, 88,* 438–453.

Latané, B., Liu, J. H., Nowak, A., Bonevento, M., & Zheng, L. (1995). Distance matters: Physical space and social impact. *Personality and Social Psychology Bulletin, 21,* 795–805.

Latané, B., Williams, K., & Harkins, S. (1979). Many hands make light the work: The causes and consequences of social loafing. *Journal of Personality and Social Psychology, 37,* 822–832.

Latimer, A. E., & Ginis, K. A. M. (2005). The importance of subjective norms for people who care what others think of them. *Psychology and Health, 20,* 53–62.

Lau, R. R. (1985). Two explanations for negativity effects in political behavior. *American Journal of Political Science, 29,* 119–138.

Laughlin, P. R., & Bonner, B. L. (1999). Collective induction: Effects of multiple hypotheses and multiple evidence in two problem domains. *Journal of Personality and Social Psychology, 77,* 1163–1172.

Laughlin, P. R., & Ellis, A. L. (1986). Demonstrability and social combination processes on mathematical intellective tasks. *Journal of Experimental Social Psychology, 22,* 177–189.

Laughlin, P. R., Bonner, B. L., & Miner, A. G. (2002). Groups perform better than the best individuals on Letters-to-Numbers problems. *Organizational Behavior and Human Decision Processes, 88,* 605–620.

Laughlin, P. R., Hatch, E. C., Silver, J. S., & Boh, L. (2006). Groups perform better than the best individuals on letters-to-numbers problems: Effects of group size. *Journal of Personality and Social Psychology, 90,* 644–651.

Lawson, E. (2001). Informational and relational meanings of deception: Implications for deception methods in research. *Ethics and Behavior, 11,* 115–130.

Lazarus, R. S., & Folkman, S. (1984). *Stress, appraisal, and coping.* New York: Springer.

Le Bon, G. (1895). *Psychologie des foules.* Paris: Félix Alcan.

Le, B., & Agnew, C. R. (2003). Commitment and its theorized determinants: A meta-analysis of the investment model. *Personal Relationships, 10,* 37–57.

Leana, C. R. (1985). A partial test of Janis' groupthink model: Effects of group cohesiveness and leader behavior on defective decision making. *Journal of Management, 11,* 5–17.

Leary, M. R. (Ed.). (2001). *Interpersonal rejection.* New York: Oxford University Press.

Leary, M. R., & Baumeister, R. F. (2000). The nature and function of self-esteem: Sociometer theory. *Advances in Experimental Social Psychology, 32,* 1-62.

Leary, M. R., & Kowalski, R. M. (1990). Impression management: A literature review and two-component model. *Psychological Bulletin, 107,* 34–47.

Leary, M. R., & Kowalski, R. M. (1995). *Social anxiety.* New York: Guilford Press.

Leary, M. R., & Tangney, J. P. (Eds.). (2003). *Handbook of self and identity.* New York: Guilford.

Leary, M. R., Kowalski, R. M., Smith, L., & Phillips, S. (2003). Teasing, rejection, and violence: Case studies of the school shootings. *Aggressive Behavior, 29,* 202–214.

Leary, M. R., Schreindorfer, L. S., & Haupt, A. L. (2004). The role of low self-esteem in emotional and behavioral problems: Why is low self-esteem dysfunctional? In R. M. Kowalski & M. R. Leary (Eds.), *The interface of social and clinical psychology: Key readings* (pp. 116–128). New York: Psychology Press.

Leary, M. R., Tchividjian, L. R., & Kraxberger, B. E. (1994). Self-presentation can be hazardous to your health: Impression management and health risk. *Health Psychology, 13,* 461–470.

Leary, M. R., Twenge, J. M., & Quinlivan, E. (2006). Interpersonal rejection as a determinant of anger and aggression. *Personality and Social Psychology Review, 10,* 111–132.

Lecci, L., & Myers, B. (2002). Examining the construct validity of the original and revised JBS: A cross-validation of sample and method. *Law and Human Behavior, 26,* 455–463.

Ledley, D. R., Storch, E. A., Coles, M. E., Heimberg, R. G., Moser, J., & Bravata, E. A. (2006). The relationship between childhood teasing and later interpersonal functioning. *Journal of Psychopathology and Behavioral Assessment, 28,* 33–40.

LeDoux, J. (2002). *The synaptic self: How our brains become who we are.* New York: Penguin Books.

LeDoux, J. E. (1996). *The emotional brain: The mysterious underpinnings of emotional life.* New York: Simon & Schuster.

Lee, J. A. (1977). A typology of styles of loving. *Personality and Social Psychology Bulletin, 3,* 173–182.

Lee, J. A. (1988). Love-styles. In R. J. Sternberg & M. L. Barnes (Eds.), *The psychology of love* (pp. 38–67). New Haven, CT: Yale University Press.

Lee, R. T., & Ashforth, B. E. (1996). A meta-analytic examination of the correlates of the three dimensions of job burnout. *Journal of Applied Psychology, 81,* 123–133.

Lee, S. Y., & Brand, J. L. (2005). Effects of control over office workspace on perceptions of the work environment and work outcomes. *Journal of Environmental Psychology, 25,* 323–333.

Lehman, D. R., Chiu, C.-Y., & Schaller, M. (2004). Psychology and culture. *Annual Review of Psychology, 55,* 689–714.

Lehman, D. R., Lempert, R. O., & Nisbett, R. E. (1988). The effects of graduate training on reasoning: Formal discipline and thinking about everyday-life events. *American Psychologist, 43,* 431–442.

Leichtman, M. D., & Ceci, S. J. (1995). The effects of stereotypes and suggestions on preschoolers' reports. *Developmental Psychology, 31,* 568–578.

Leigh, B. C., & Stacy, A. W. (1993). Alcohol outcome expectancies: Scale construction and predictive utility in higher-order confirmatory models. *Psychological Assessment, 5,* 216–229.

Leiker, M., & Hailey, B. J. (1988). A link between hostility and disease: Poor health habits? *Behavioral Medicine, 14,* 129–133.

Leinbach, M. D., & Fagot, B. I. (1993). Categorical habituation to male and female faces: Gender schematic processing in infancy. *Infant Behavior and Development, 16,* 317–332.

Leippe, M. R. (1995). The case for expert testimony about eyewitness memory. *Psychology, Public Policy, and Law, 1,* 909–959.

Leippe, M. R., & Eisenstadt, D. (1994). Generalization of dissonance reduction: Decreasing prejudice through induced compliance. *Journal of Personality and Social Psychology, 67,* 395–413.

Leland, J. (1995, December 11). "Copycat" crimes in New York's subways reignite the debate: Do TV and movies cause actual mayhem? *Newsweek,* p. 46.

Leo, R. A. (1996). Inside the interrogation room. *Journal of Criminal Law and Criminology, 86,* 266–303.

Leonard, K. E. (1989). The impact of explicit aggressive and implicit nonaggressive cues on aggression in intoxicated and sober roles. *Personality and Social Psychology Bulletin, 15,* 390–400.

Leonard, K. E., Collins, R. L., & Quigley, B. M. (2003). Alcohol consumption and the occurrence and severity of aggression: An event-based analysis of male-to-male barroom violence. *Aggressive Behavior, 29,* 346–365.

Lepore, L., & Brown, R. (1997). Category and stereotype activation: Is prejudice inevitable? *Journal of Personality and Social Psychology, 72,* 275–287.

Lepore, L., & Brown, R. (2002). The role of awareness: Divergent automatic stereotype activation and implicit judgment correction. *Social Cognition, 20,* 321–351.

Lepore, S. J., & Smyth, J. M. (2002). *The writing cure: How expressive writing promotes health and emotional well-being.* Washington, DC: American Psychological Association.

Lepore, S. J., Ragan, J. D., & Jones, S. (2000). Talking facilitates cognitive-emotional processes of adaptation to an acute stressor. *Journal of Personality and Social Psychology, 78,* 499–508.

Lepper, M. R., & Greene, D. (Eds.). (1978). *The hidden costs of reward.* Hillsdale, NJ: Erlbaum.

Lepper, M. R., Greene, D., & Nisbett, R. E. (1973). Undermining children's intrinsic interest with extrinsic reward: A test of the "overjustification" hypothesis. *Journal of Personality and Social Psychology, 28,* 129–137.

Lerner, M. J. (1980). *The belief in a just world: A fundamental delusion.* New York: Plenum.

Lerner, M. J. (1998). The two forms of belief in a just world: Some thoughts on why and how people care about justice. In L. Montada, & M. J. Lerner (Eds.), *Responses to victimization and belief in a just world: Critical issues in social justice* (pp. 247–269). New York: Plenum.

Lerner, M. J., & Simmons, C. H. (1966). Observers' reaction to the "innocent victim": Compassion or rejection? *Journal of Personality and Social Psychology, 4,* 203–210.

LeVay, S. (1991). A difference in hypothalamic structure between heterosexual and homosexual men. *Science, 253,* 1034–1037.

LeVay, S. (1993). *The sexual brain.* Cambridge, MA: MIT Press.

Leventhal, H. (1970). Findings and theory in the study of fear communications. In L. Berkowitz (Ed.), *Advances in experimental social psychology* (Vol. 5, pp. 119–186). New York: Academic Press.

Leventhal, H., Watts, J. C., & Pagano, F. (1967). Effects of fear and instructions on how to cope with danger. *Journal of Personality and Social Psychology, 6,* 313–321.

Levesque, M. J. (1997). Meta-accuracy among acquainted individuals: A social relations analysis of interpersonal perception and metaperception. *Journal of Personality and Social Psychology, 72,* 66–74.

Levesque, M. J., Nave, C. S., & Lowe, C. A. (2006). Toward an understanding of gender differences in inferring sexual interest. *Psychology of Women Quarterly, 30,* 150–158.

Levin, S. (2004). Perceived group differences and the effects of gender, ethnicity, and religion on social dominance orientation. *Political Psychology, 25,* 31–48.

Levin, S., Taylor, P. L., & Caudle, E. (2007). Interethnic and interracial dating in college: A longitudinal study of social psychological predictors and outcomes. *Journal of Social and Personal Relationships,* in press.

Levine, J. M. (1989). Reaction to opinion deviance in small groups. In P. B. Paulus (Ed.), *Psychology of group influence* (2nd ed., pp. 187–231). Hillsdale, NJ: Erlbaum.

Levine, J. M., & Moreland, R. L. (1990). Progress in small group research. *Annual Review of Psychology, 41*, 585–634.

Levine, J. M., & Moreland, R. L. (1998). Small groups. In D. T. Gilbert, S. T. Fiske, & G. Lindzey (Eds.), *The handbook of social psychology* (4th ed., Vol. 2, pp. 415–469). New York: McGraw-Hill.

Levine, J. M., & Moreland, R. L. (2004). Collaboration: The social context of theory development. *Personality and Social Psychology Review, 8*, 164–172.

Levine, J. M., Moreland, R. L., & Hausmann, L. R. M. (2004). Managing group composition: Inclusive and exclusive role transitions. In D. Abrams, J. M. Marques, & M.A. Hogg (Eds.), *The social psychology of inclusion and exclusion*. Philadelphia: Psychology Press.

Levine, J. M., Moreland, R. L., & Ryan, C. S. (1998). Group socialization and intergroup relations. In C. Sedikides, J. Schopler, & C. A. Insko (Eds.), *Intergroup cognition and intergroup behavior* (pp. 283–308). Mahwah, NJ: Erlbaum.

Levine, M., Prosser, A., Evans, D., & Reicher, S. (2005). Identity and emergency intervention: How social group membership and inclusiveness of group boundaries shape helping behavior. *Personality and Social Psychology Bulletin, 31*, 443–453.

Levine, R. A., & Campbell, D. T. (1972). *Ethnocentrism: Theories of conflict, ethnic attitudes, and group behavior*. New York: Wiley.

Levine, R. V., Martinez, T. S., Brase, G., & Sorenson, K. (1994). Helping in 36 U.S. cities. *Journal of Personality and Social Psychology, 67*(1), 69–82.

Levine, R. V., Norenzayan, A., & Philbrick, K. (2001). Cross-cultural differences in helping strangers. *Journal of Cross-Cultural Psychology, 32*, 543–560.

Levine, R., Sato, S., Hashimoto, T., & Verma, J. (1995). Love and marriage in eleven cultures. *Journal of Cross-Cultural Psychology, 26*, 554–571.

Levy, D. A., & Nail, P. R. (1993). Contagion: A theoretical and empirical review and reconceptualization. *Genetic, Social, and General Psychology Monographs, 119*, 233–284.

Levy, G. D., & Haaf, R. A. (1994). Detection of gender-related categories by 10-month-old infants. *Infant Behavior and Development, 17*, 457–459.

Levy, S. R., Chiu, C.-Y., & Hong, Y.-Y. (2006). Lay theories and intergroup relations. *Group Processes and Intergroup Relations, 9*, 5–24.

Levy, S. R., Freitas, A. L., & Salovey, P. (2002). Construing action abstractly and blurring social distinctions: Implications for perceiving homogeneity among, but also empathizing with and helping, others. *Journal of Personality and Social Psychology, 83*, 1224–1238.

Levy, S. R., Plaks, J. E., Hong, Y., Chiu, C., & Dweck, C. S. (2001). Static versus dynamic theories and the perception of groups: Different routes to different destinations. *Personality and Social Psychology Review, 5*, 156–168.

Levy, S. R., Plaks, J. E., Hong, Y., Chiu, C., & Dweck, C. S. (2001). Static versus dynamic theories and the perception of groups: Different routes to different destinations. *Personality and Social Psychology Review, 5*, 156–168.

Levy, S. R., Stroessner, S. J., & Dweck, C. S. (1998). Stereotype formation and endorsement: The role of implicit theories. *Journal of Personality and Social Psychology, 74*, 1421–1436.

Levy, S. R., West, T. L., Ramirez, L., & Karafantis, D. M. (2006). The Protestant work ethic: A lay theory with dual intergroup implications. *Group Processes and Intergroup Relations, 9*, 95–115.

Lewin, K. (1935). *A dynamic theory of personality*. New York: McGraw-Hill.

Lewin, K. (1947). Group decision and social change. In T. M. Newcomb & E. L. Hartley (Eds.), *Readings in social psychology* (pp. 330–344). New York: Holt.

Lewin, K. (1951). Problems of research in social psychology. In D. Cartwright (Ed.), *Field theory in social science* (pp. 155–169). New York: Harper & Row.

Lewis, B. P., & Linder, D. E. (1997). Thinking about choking? Attentional processes and paradoxical performance. *Personality and Social Psychology Bulletin, 23*, 937–944.

Lewis, K., Lange, D., & Gillis, L. (2005). Transactive memory systems, learning, and learning transfer. *Organization Science, 16*, 581–598.

Lewis, M. A., & Neighbors, C. (2004). Gender-specific misperceptions of college student drinking norms. *Psychology of Addictive Behaviors, 18*, 334–339.

Lewis, M., & Brooks-Gunn, J. (1979). *Social cognition and the acquisition of self*. New York: Plenum.

Leye, E., Powell, R. A., Nienhuis, G., Claeys, P., & Temmerman, M. (2006). Health care in Europe for women with genital mutilation. *Health Care for Women International, 27*, 362–378.

Leyens, J.-Ph., Cortes, B. P., Demoulin, S., Dovidio, J., Fiske, S. T., Gaunt, R., Paladino, M. P., Rodriguez-Perez, A., Rodriquez-Torres, R., & Vaes, V. (2003). Emotional prejudice, essentialism, and nationalism. *European Journal of Experimental Social Psychology, 23*, 704–717.

Li, D., Li, Y., Zong, A., & Ding, Y. (2005). The empathic responsiveness of children aged 2: Associations with child spontaneous helping, temperament, and parent-child interaction. *Psychological Science (China), 28*, 961–964.

Li, N. P., & Kenrick, D. T. (2006). Sex similarities and differences in preferences for short-term mates: What, whether, and why. *Journal of Personality and Social Psychology, 90*, 468–489.

Li, N. P., Bailey, J. M., Kenrick, D. T., & Linsenmeier, J. A. W. (2002). The necessities and luxuries of mate preferences: Testing the tradeoffs. *Journal of Personality and Social Psychology, 82*, 947–955.

Liden, R. C., Wayne, S. J., Jaworski, R. A., & Bennett, N. (2004). Social loafing: A field investigation. *Journal of Management, 30*, 285–304.

Lieberman, J. D. (1999). Terror management, illusory correlation, and perception of minority groups. *Basic and Applied Social Psychology, 21*, 13–23.

Lieberman, J. D., & Arndt, J. (2000). Understanding the limits of limiting instructions. *Psychology, Public Policy, and Law, 6*, 677–711.

Lieberman, J. D., & Sales, B. D. (2006). *Scientific jury selection*. Washington, DC: American Psychological Association.

Lieberman, M. D. (2007). Social cognitive neuroscience: A review of core processes. *Annual Review of Psychology, 58*, in press.

Lieberman, M. D., Gaunt, R., Gilbert, D. T., & Trope, Y. (2004). Reflection and reflexion: A social cognitive neuroscience approach to attributional inference. In M. P. Zanna (Ed.), *Advances in experimental social psychology* (Vol. 34, pp. 199–249). San Diego, CA: Academic Press.

Lieberman, M. D., Hariri, A., Jarcho, J. M., Eisenberger, N. I., & Bookheimer, S. Y. (2005). An fMRI investigation of race-related amygdala activity in African-American and Caucasian-American individuals. *Nature Neuroscience, 8*, 720–722.

Lieberman, M. D., Jarcho, J. M., & Obayashi, J. (2005). Attributional inferences across cultures: Similar automatic attributions and different controlled corrections. *Personality and Social Psychology Bulletin, 31*, 889–901.

Lieberman, M. D., Ochsner, K. N., Gilbert, D. T., & Schacter, D. L. (2001). Do amnesics exhibit cognitive dissonance reduction? The role of explicit memory and attention in attitude change. *Psychological Science, 12*, 135–140.

Lifton, R. J. (1986). *The Nazi doctors: Medical killing and the psychology of genocide.* New York: Basic Books.

Light, K. C., & Obrist, P. A. (1980). Cardiovascular response to stress: Effects of opportunity to avoid shock experience, and performance feedback. *Psychophysiology, 17,* 243–252.

Likert, R. (1932). A technique for the measurement of attitudes. *Archives of Psychology, 140,* 1–55.

Liljenquist, K. A., Galinsky, A. D., & Kray, L. J. (2004). The differential impact of individual and group level activation of counterfactual mind-sets on information sharing, group processes, and judgment accuracy. *Journal of Behavioral Decision Making, 17,* 263–279.

Lind, E. A., Erickson, B. E., Friedland, N., & Dickenberger, M. (1978). Reactions to procedural models for adjudicative conflict resolution: A cross national study. *Journal of Conflict Resolution, 22,* 318–341.

Lind, E. A., Kanfer, R., & Farley, P. C. (1990). Voice, control, and procedural justice: Instrumental and noninstrumental concerns in fairness judgments. *Journal of Personality and Social Psychology, 59,* 952–959.

Linde, J. A., Rothman, A. J., Baldwin, A. S., & Jeffery, R. W. (2006). The impact of self-efficacy on behavior change and weight change among overweight participants in a weight loss trial. *Health Psychology, 25,* 282–291.

Linder, D. E., Cooper, J., & Jones, E. E. (1967). Decision freedom as a determinant of the role of incentive magnitude in attitude change. *Journal of Personality and Social Psychology, 6,* 245–254.

Lindsay, R. C. L., & Bellinger, K. (1999). Alternatives to the sequential lineup: The importance of controlling the pictures. *Journal of Applied Psychology, 84,* 315–321.

Lindsay, R. C. L., & Wells, G. L. (1985). Improving eyewitness identifications from lineups: Simultaneous versus sequential lineup presentations. *Journal of Applied Psychology, 70,* 556–564.

Lindsay, R. C. L., Lea, J. A., & Fulford, J. A. (1991). Sequential lineup presentation: Technique matters. *Journal of Applied Psychology, 76,* 741–745.

Lindsay, R. C. L., Wells, G. L., & Rumpel, C. M. (1981). Can people detect eyewitness-identification accuracy within and across situations? *Journal of Applied Psychology, 66,* 79–89.

Lindskold, S., & Han, G. (1988). GRIT as a foundation for integrative bargaining. *Personality and Social Psychology Bulletin, 14,* 335–345.

Linville, P. (1998). The heterogeneity of homogeneity. In J. Cooper & J. Darley (Eds.), *Attribution processes, person perception, and social interaction: The legacy of Ned Jones.* Washington, DC: American Psychological Association.

Linville, P. W., & Jones, E. E. (1980). Polarized appraisals of outgroup members. *Journal of Personality and Social Psychology, 38,* 689–703.

Linville, P. W., Fischer, G. W., & Fischoff, B. (1992). Perceived risk and decision making involving AIDS. In J. B. Pryor & G. D. Reeder (Eds.), *The social psychology of HIV infection.* Hillsdale, NJ: Erlbaum.

Linville, P. W., Fischer, G. W., & Salovey, P. (1989). Perceived distributions of the characteristics of in-group and out-group members: Empirical evidence and a computer simulation. *Journal of Personality and Social Psychology, 57,* 165–188.

Linz, D., Donnerstein, E., & Penrod, S. (1987). The findings and recommendations of the Attorney General's Commission on Pornography: Do the psychological "facts" fit the political fury? *American Psychologist, 42,* 946–953.

Linz, D., Wilson, B. J., & Donnerstein, E. (1992). Sexual violence in the mass media: Legal solutions, warnings, and mitigation through education. *Journal of Social Issues, 48,* 145–171.

Lippa, R. A. (2006). Is high sex drive associated with increased sexual attraction to both sexes? *Psychological Science, 17,* 46–52.

Lipponen, J., Helkama, K., & Juslin, M. (2003). Subgroup identification, superordinate identification and intergroup bias between the subgroups. *Group Processes and Intergroup Relations, 6,* 239–250.

Liquori, S. A., Kreh, M. L., Holzapfel, L. L., & Fein, S. (2001). *Ad it up: Effects of sexy images of women in advertising on women's math performance in same-sex and mixed-sex groups.* Paper presented at the second annual meeting of the Society of Personality and Social Psychology, San Antonio, TX.

Liu, J. H., & Mills, D. (2006). Modern racism and neo-liberal globalization: The discourses of plausible deniability and their multiple functions. *Journal of Community and Applied Social Psychology, 16,* 83–99.

Livers, A. B., & Caver, K. A. (2003). *Leading in black and white: Working across the racial divide in corporate America.* San Francisco: Jossey-Bass.

Livingston, R. W., & Brewer, M. B. (2002). What are we really priming? Cue-based versus category-based processing of facial stimuli. *Journal of Personality and Social Psychology, 82,* 5–18.

Locke, E. A. (2000). *The prime movers: Traits of the great wealth creators.* New York: Amacomb.

Locke, E. A., & Latham, G. P. (1990). *A theory of goal setting and task performance.* Englewood Cliffs, NJ: Prentice-Hall.

Locke, E. A., & Latham, G. P. (2002). Building a practically useful theory of goal setting and task motivation: A 35-year odyssey. *American Psychologist, 57,* 705–717.

Lockhart v. McCree, 54 U.S.L.W. 4449 (1986).

Locksley, A., Borgida, E., Brekke, N., & Hepburn, C. (1980). Sex stereotypes and social judgment. *Journal of Personality and Social Psychology, 39,* 821–831.

Loewenstein, G. F., Weber, E. U., Hsee, C. K., & Welch, N. (2001). Risk as feelings. *Psychological Bulletin, 127,* 267–286.

Loftus, E. F. (1996). *Eyewitness testimony* (reprint ed.). Cambridge, MA: Harvard University Press.

Loftus, E. F., & Ketcham, K. (1991). *Witness for the defense: The accused, the eyewitness, and the expert who puts memory on trial.* New York: St. Martin's Press.

Loftus, E. F., & Palmer, J. C. (1974). Reconstruction of automobile destruction: An example of the interaction between language and memory. *Journal of Verbal Learning and Verbal Behavior, 13,* 585–589.

Loftus, E. F., Loftus, G. R., & Messo, J. (1987). Some facts about "weapon focus." *Law and Human Behavior, 11,* 55–62.

Loken, B. (2006). Consumer psychology: Categorization, inferences, affect, and persuasion. *Annual Review of Psychology, 57,* 453–485.

London, K., & Nunez, N. (2000). The effect of jury deliberations on jurors' propensity to disregard inadmissible evidence. *Journal of Applied Psychology, 85,* 932–939.

Long, E. C. J., & Andrews, D. W. (1990). Perspective taking as a predictor of marital adjustment. *Journal of Personality and Social Psychology, 59,* 126–131.

Lopata, C. (2003). Progressive muscle relaxation and aggression among elementary students with emotional or behavioral disorders. *Behavioral Disorders, 28,* 162–172.

Lopez, J. A. (1992, March 3). Study says women face glass walls as well as ceilings. *Wall Street Journal,* pp. B1, B8.

Lorenz, K. (1966). *On aggression.* New York: Harcourt, Brace & World.

Lorenzi-Cioldi, F., Deaux, K., & Dafflon, A. C. (1998). Group homogeneity as a function of relative social status. *Swiss Journal of Psychology, 57,* 255–273.

Lortie-Lussier, M. (1987). Minority influence and idiosyncrasy credit: A new comparison of the Moscovici and Hollander theories of innovation. *European Journal of Social Psychology, 17,* 431–446.

Losch, M. E., & Cacioppo, J. T. (1990). Cognitive dissonance may enhance sympathetic tonus, but attitudes are changed to reduce negative affect rather than arousal. *Journal of Experimental Social Psychology, 26,* 289–304.

Lott, A. J., & Lott, B. E. (1974). The role of reward in the formation of positive interpersonal attitudes. In T. L. Huston (Ed.), *Foundations of interpersonal attraction* (pp. 171–189). New York: Academic Press.

Lott, B. (1985). The devaluation of women's competence. *Journal of Social Issues, 41,* 43–60.

Lowe, K., Kroeck, K., & Sivasubramaniam, N. (1996). Effectiveness correlates of transformational and transactional leadership: A meta-analytic review of the MLQ literature. *Leadership Quarterly, 7,* 385–425.

Lubow, R. E., & Fein, O. (1996). Pupillary size in response to a visual guilty knowledge test: A new technique for the detection of deception. *Journal of Experimental Psychology: Applied, 2,* 164–177.

Lucas, R.E. (2005). Time does not heal all wounds: A longitudinal study of reaction and adaptation to divorce. *Psychological Science, 16,* 945–950.

Luo, S., & Klohnen, E. C. (2005). Assortative mating and marital quality in newlyweds: A couple-centered approach. *Journal of Personality and Social Psychology, 88,* 304–326.

Lüüs, C. A. E., & Wells, G. L. (1991). Eyewitness identification and the selection of distractors for lineups. *Law and Human Behavior, 15,* 43–58.

Lüüs, C. A. E., & Wells, G. L. (1994). The malleability of eyewitness confidence: Co-witness and perseverance effects. *Journal of Applied Psychology, 79,* 714–723.

Lykken, D. T. (1998). *A tremor in the blood: Uses and abuses of the lie detector* (2nd ed.). Cambridge, MA: Perseus.

Lykken, D. T. (2000). *Happiness: The nature and nurture of joy and contentment.* New York: St. Martin's Press.

Lykken, D. T., & Tellegen, A. (1993). Is human mating adventitious or the result of lawful choice? A twin study of mate selection. *Journal of Personality and Social Psychology, 65,* 56–68.

Lyness, K. S., & Thompson, D. E. (1997). Above the glass ceiling? A comparison of matched samples of female and male executives. *Journal of Applied Psychology, 82,* 359–375.

Lyness, K. S., & Thompson, D. E. (2000). Climbing the corporate ladder: Do female and male executives follow the same route? *Journal of Applied Psychology, 85,* 86–101.

Lynn, M., & Mynier, K. (1993). Effect of server posture on restaurant tipping. *Journal of Applied Social Psychology, 23,* 678–685.

Lyons, A., & Kashima, Y. (2001). The representation of culture: Communication processes tend to maintain cultural stereotypes. *Social Cognition, 19,* 372–394.

Lyubomirsky, S., Sheldon, K. M., & Schkade, D. (2005). Pursuing happiness: The architecture of sustainable change. *Review of General Psychology, 9,* 111–131.

Maass, A., & Clark, R. D., III. (1984). Hidden impact of minorities: Fifteen years of minority influence research. *Psychological Bulletin, 95,* 428–450.

Maass, A., & Kohnken, G. (1989). Eyewitness identification: Simulating the "weapon effect." *Law and Human Behavior, 13,* 397–408.

Maass, A., Volpato, C., & Mucchi-Faina, A. (1996). Social influence and the verifiability of the issue under discussion: Attitudinal versus objective items. *British Journal of Social Psychology, 35,* 15–26.

MacCoun, R. J., & Kerr, N. L. (1988). Asymmetric influence in mock jury deliberation: Jurors' bias for leniency. *Journal of Personality and Social Psychology, 54,* 21–33.

MacDonald, G., & Leary, M. R. (2005). Why does social exclusion hurt? The relationship between social and physical pain. *Psychological Bulletin, 131,* 202–223.

MacDonald, T. K., Fong, G. T., Zanna, M. P., & Martineau, A. M. (2000). Alcohol myopia and condom use: Can alcohol intoxication be associated with more prudent behavior? *Journal of Personality and Social Psychology, 78,* 605–619.

Macionis, J. J. (2003). *Sociology* (9th ed.). Upper Saddle River, NJ: Prentice-Hall.

Mackay, N., & Barrowclough, C. (2005). Accident and emergency staff's perceptions of deliberate self-harm: Attributions, emotions, and willingness to help. *British Journal of Clinical Psychology, 44,* 255–267.

Mackie, D. M., & Cooper, J. (1984). Attitude polarization: Effects of group membership. *Journal of Personality and Social Psychology, 46,* 575–585.

Mackie, D. M., & Worth, L. T. (1989). Processing deficits and the mediation of positive affect in persuasion. *Journal of Personality and Social Psychology, 57,* 27–40.

Mackie, D. M., Asuncion, A. G., & Rosselli, F. (1992). Impact of positive affect on persuasion processes. *Review of Personality and Social Psychology, 14,* 247–270.

Mackie, D. M., Worth, L. T., & Asuncion, A. G. (1990). Processing of persuasive in-group messages. *Journal of Personality and Social Psychology, 58,* 812–822.

MacLeod, C., & Campbell, L. (1992). Memory accessibility and probability judgments: An experimental evaluation of the availability heuristic. *Journal of Personality and Social Psychology, 63,* 890–902.

Macrae, C. N., Bodenhausen, G. V., & Milne, A. B. (1995). The dissection of selection in person perception: Inhibitory processes in social stereotyping. *Journal of Personality and Social Psychology, 69,* 397–407.

Macrae, C. N., Bodenhausen, G. V., Milne, A. B., & Jetten, J. (1994). Out of mind but back in sight: Stereotypes on the rebound. *Journal of Personality and Social Psychology, 67,* 808–817.

Madden, T. J., Ellen, P. S., & Ajzen, I. (1992). A comparison of the theory of planned behavior and the theory of reasoned action. *Personality and Social Psychology Bulletin, 18,* 3–9.

Maddox, K. B. (2004). Perspectives on racial phenotypicality bias. *Personality and Social Psychology Review, 8,* 383–401.

Maddux, J. E. (1995). *Self-efficacy, adaptation, and adjustment: Theory, research, and application.* New York: Perseus.

Maddux, J. E., & Rogers, R. W. (1980). Effects of source expertness, physical attractiveness, and supporting arguments on persuasion: A case of brains over beauty. *Journal of Personality and Social Psychology, 39,* 235–244.

Madey, S. F., Simo, M., Dillworth, D., Kemper, D., Toczynski, A., & Perella, A. (1996). They do get more attractive at closing time, but only when you are not in a relationship. *Basic and Applied Social Psychology, 18,* 387–393.

Madon, S., Guyll, M., Spoth, R., Cross, S. E., & Hilbert, S. J. (2003). The self-fulfilling influence of mother expectations on children's underage drinking. *Journal of Personality and Social Psychology, 84,* 1188–1205.

Madon, S., Jussim, L., Keiper, S., Eccles, J., Smith, A., & Palumbo, P. (1998). The accuracy and power of sex, social class, and ethnic stereotypes: A naturalistic study in person perception. *Personality and Social Psychology Bulletin, 24,* 1304–1318.

Madon, S., Willard, J., Guyll, M., Trudeau, L., & Spoth, R. (2006). Self-fulfilling prophecy effects of mothers' beliefs on children's alcohol use: Accumulation, dissipation, and stability over time. *Journal of Personality and Social Psychology, 90,* 911–926.

Maio, G., & Olson, J. M. (Eds.). (2000). *Why we evaluate: Functions of attitudes.* Mahwah, NJ: Erlbaum.

Major, B., & Crocker, J. (1993). Social stigma: The affective consequences of attributional ambiguity. In D. M. Mackie & D. L. Hamilton (Eds.), *Affect, cognition, and stereotyping: Interactive processes in intergroup perception* (pp. 345–370). New York: Academic Press.

Major, B., & Deaux, K. (1982). Individual differences in justice behavior. In J. Greenberg & R. L. Cohen (Eds.), *Equity and justice in social behavior* (pp. 13–76). New York: Academic Press.

Major, B., & Gramzow, R. H. (1999). Abortion as stigma: Cognitive and emotional implications of concealment. *Journal of Personality and Social Psychology, 77,* 735–745.

Major, B., & Konar, E. (1984). An investigation of sex differences in pay expectations and their possible causes. *Academy of Management Journal, 27,* 777–792.

Major, B., Carrington, P. I., & Carnevale, P. J. D. (1984). Physical attractiveness and self-esteem: Attributions for praise from an other-sex evaluator. *Personality and Social Psychology Bulletin, 10,* 43–50.

Major, B., Feinstein, J., & Crocker, J. (1994). Attributional ambiguity of affirmative action. *Basic and Applied Social Psychology, 15,* 113–142.

Major, B., McFarlin, D. B., & Gagnon, D. (1984). Overworked and underpaid: On the nature of gender differences in personal entitlement. *Journal of Personality and Social Psychology, 47,* 1399–1412.

Major, B., Quinton, W. J., & McCoy, S. K. (2002). Antecedents and consequences of attributions to discrimination: Theoretical and empirical advances. In M. Zanna (Ed.), *Advances in experimental social psychology* (Vol. 34, pp. 251–330). San Diego, CA: Academic Press.

Major, B., Quinton, W. J., & Schmader, T. (2003). Attributions to discrimination and self-esteem: Impact of group identification and situational ambiguity. *Journal of Experimental Social Psychology, 39,* 220–231.

Malamuth, N. M. (1983). Factors associated with rape as predictors of laboratory aggression against women. *Journal of Personality and Social Psychology, 45,* 432–442.

Malamuth, N. M. (1986). Predictors of naturalistic sexual aggression. *Journal of Personality and Social Psychology, 50,* 953–962.

Malamuth, N. M. (1996). The confluence model of sexual aggression: Feminist and evolutionary perspectives. In D. M. Buss & N. M. Malamuth (Eds.), *Sex, power, conflict: Evolutionary and feminist perspectives* (pp. 269–295). New York: Oxford University Press.

Malamuth, N. M., & Billings, V. (1986). The function and effects of pornography: Sexual communications versus the feminist model in light of research findings. In J. Bryant & D. Zillmann (Eds.), *Perspectives on media effects* (pp. 83–108). Hillsdale, NJ: Erlbaum.

Malamuth, N. M., & Donnerstein, E. I. (1982). The effects of aggressive-pornographic mass media stimuli. In L. Berkowitz (Ed.), *Advances in experimental social psychology* (Vol. 15, pp. 103–136). New York: Academic Press.

Malamuth, N. M., Addison, T., & Koss, M. (2000). Pornography and sexual aggression: Are there reliable effects and can we understand them? *Annual Review of Sex Research, 11,* 26–91.

Malinoski, P. T., & Lynn, S. J. (1999). The plasticity of early memory reports: Social pressure, hypnotizability, compliance, and interrogative suggestibility. International *Journal of Clinical and Experimental Hypnosis, 47,* 320–345.

Malkiel, B. G. (2007). *A random walk down Wall Street: The time-tested strategy for successful investing* (9th ed.). New York: Norton.

Malle, B. F., & Knobe, J. (1997). Which behaviors do people explain? A basic actor-observer asymmetry. *Journal of Personality and Social Psychology, 72,* 288–304.

Malle, B. F., Knobe, J., O'Laughlin, M. J., Pearce, G. E., & Nelson, S. E. (2000). Conceptual structure and social functions of behavior explanations: Beyond person-situation attributions. *Journal of Personality and Social Psychology, 79,* 309–326.

Malloy, T. E., & Albright, L. (1990). Interpersonal perception in a social context. *Journal of Personality and Social Psychology, 58,* 419–428.

Malpass, R. S., & Devine, P. G. (1981). Eyewitness identification: Lineup instructions and the absence of the offender. *Journal of Applied Psychology, 66,* 482–489.

Malpass, R. S., & Kravitz, J. (1969). Recognition for faces of own and other race. *Journal of Personality and Social Psychology, 13,* 330–334.

Man, D. C., & Lam, S. K. (2003). The effects of job complexity and autonomy on cohesiveness in collectivistic and individualistic work groups: A cross-cultural analysis. *Journal of Organizational Behavior, 24,* 979–1001.

Maner, J. K., Kenrick, D. T., Becker, D. V., Robertson, T. E., Hofer, B., Neuberg, S. L., Delton, A. W., Butner, J., & Schaller, M. (2005). Functional projection: How fundamental social motives can bias interpersonal perception. *Journal of Personality and Social Psychology, 88,* 63–78.

Maner, J. K., Luce, C. L., Neuberg, S. L., Cialdini, R. B., Brown, S., & Sagarin, B. J. (2002). The effects of perspective taking on motivations for helping: Still no evidence for altruism. *Personality and Social Psychology Bulletin, 28,* 1601–1610.

Mann, J. M. (1992). AIDS—The second decade: A global perspective. *Journal of Infectious Diseases, 165,* 245–250.

Mann, L. (1981). The baiting crowd in episodes of threatened suicide. *Journal of Personality and Social Psychology, 41,* 703–709.

Mannix, E., & Neale, M. A. (2005). What differences make a difference? The promise and reality of diverse teams in organizations. *Psychological Science in the Public Interest, 6,* whole No. 2 issue.

Marcus-Newhall, A., Pedersen, W. C., Carlson, M., & Miller, N. (2000). Displaced aggression is alive and well: A meta-analytic review. *Journal of Personality and Social Psychology, 78,* 670–689.

Mares, M.-L., & Woodard, E. (2005). Positive effects of television on children's social interactions: A meta-analysis. *Media Psychology, 7,* 301–322.

Margolin, G., & Wampold, B. E. (1981). A sequential analysis of conflict and accord in distressed and nondistressed marital partners. *Journal of Consulting and Clinical Psychology, 49,* 554–567.

Markey, P. M. (2000). Bystander intervention in computer-mediated communication. *Computers in Human Behavior, 16,* 183–188.

Markman, K. D., & Weary, G. (1996). The influence of chronic control concerns on counterfactual thought. *Social Cognition, 14,* 292–316.

Marks, J. (1995). *Human biodiversity: Genes, race, and history.* New York: Aldine de Gruyter.

Markus, H. (1977). Self-schemata and processing information about the self. *Journal of Personality and Social Psychology, 35,* 63–78.

Markus, H. R., & Kitayama, S. (1991). Culture and the self: Implications for cognition, emotion, and motivation. *Psychological Review, 98,* 224–253.

Markus, H. R., & Lin, L. R. (1999). Conflictways: Cultural diversity in the meanings and practices of conflict. In D. A. Prentice & D. T. Miller (Eds.), *Cultural divides: Understanding and overcoming group conflict* (pp. 302–333). New York: Russell Sage.

Markus, H. R., Uchida, Y., Omoregie, H., Townsend, S. M., & Kitayama, S. (2006). Going for the gold: Models of agency in Japanese and American contexts. *Psychological Science, 17,* 103–112.

Markus, H., Hamill, R., & Sentis, K. P. (1987). Thinking fat: Self-schemas for body weight and the processing of weight-relevant information. *Journal of Applied Social Psychology, 17,* 50–71.

Marlowe, C. M., Schneider, S. L., & Nelson, C. E. (1996). Gender and attractiveness biases in hiring decisions: Are more experienced managers less biased? *Journal of Applied Psychology, 81,* 11–21.

Marques, J. M., Yzerbyt, V. Y., & Rijsman, J. B. (1988). Context effects on intergroup discrimination: In-group bias as a function of experimenter's provenance. *British Journal of Social Psychology, 27,* 301–318.

Marshall, L. (1979). Sharing, talking, and giving: Relief of social tensions among !Kung Bushmen. In R. B. Lee & I. DeVore (Eds.), *Kalahari hunter-gatherers: Studies of the !Kung San and their neighbors* (pp. 349–372). Cambridge, England: Cambridge University Press.

Martin, C. L., Eisenbud, L., & Rose, H. (1995). Children's gender-based reasoning about toys. *Child Development, 66,* 1453–1471.

Martin, C. L., Wood, C. H., & Little, J. K. (1990). The development of gender stereotype components. *Child Development, 61,* 1891–1904.

Marx, B. P., Gross, A. M., & Adams, H. E. (1999). The effect of alcohol on the responses of sexually coercive and noncoercive men to an experimental rape analogue. *Sexual Abuse: Journal of Research and Treatment, 11,* 131–145.

Maslach, C. (1979). Negative emotional biasing of unexplained arousal. *Journal of Personality and Social Psychology, 37,* 953–969.

Maslach, C. (1982). *Burnout: The cost of caring.* Englewood Cliffs, NJ: Prentice-Hall.

Maslach, C., Schaufeli, W. B., & Leiter, M. P. (2001). Job burnout. *Annual Review of Psychology, 52,* 397–422.

Mason, M. F., Tatkow, E. P., & Macrae, C. N. (2005). The look of love: Gaze shifts and person perception. *Psychological Science, 16,* 236–239.

Masten, A. S. (2001). Ordinary magic: Resilience processes in development. *American Psychologist, 56,* 227–238.

Masten, A. S. (2001). Ordinary magic: Resilience processes in development. *American Psychologist, 56,* 227–238.

Masuda, T., & Kitayama, S. (2004). Perceiver-induced constraint and attitude attribution in Japan and the US: A case for the cultural dependence of the correspondence bias. *Journal of Experimental Social Psychology, 40,* 409–416.

Masuda, T., & Nisbett, R. E. (2001). Attending holistically vs. analytically: Comparing the context sensitivity of Japanese and Americans. *Journal of Personality and Social Psychology, 81,* 922–934.

Mathur, M., & Chattopadhyay, A. (1991). The impact of moods generated by TV programs on responses to advertising. *Psychology and Marketing, 8,* 59–77.

Matthews, K. A. (1988). Coronary heart disease and Type A behaviors: Update on and alternative to the Booth-Kewley and Friedman (1987) quantitative review. *Psychological Bulletin, 104,* 373–380.

Matthews, K. A. (2005). Psychological perspectives on the development of coronary heart disease. *American Psychologist, 60,* 783–796.

Matz, D. C., & Wood, W. (2005). Cognitive dissonance in groups: The consequences of disagreement. *Journal of Personality and Social Psychology, 88,* 22–37.

Mayberg, H. S., Silva, J. A., Brannan, S. K., Tekell, J. L., Mahurin, R. K., McGinnis, S., & Jerabek, P. A. (2002). The functional neuroanatomy of the placebo effect. *American Journal of Psychiatry, 159,* 728–737.

Maznevski, M. L. (1994). Understanding our differences: Performance in decision-making groups with diverse members. *Human Relations, 47,* 531–552.

Mazur, A., Booth, A., & Dabbs, J. M. (1992). Testosterone and chess competition. *Social Psychology Quarterly, 55,* 70–77.

McAdams, D. P. (1989). *Intimacy: The need to be close.* New York: Doubleday.

McAlister, A. L., Bandura, A., & Owen, S. V. (2006). Mechanisms of moral disengagement in support of military force: The impact of September 11. *Journal of Social and Clinical Psychology, 25,* 141–165.

McAlister, A. L., Bandura, A., & Owen, S. V. (2006). Mechanisms of moral disengagement in support of military force: The impact of Sept. 11. *Journal of Social & Clinical Psychology, 25,* 141–165.

McArthur, L. A. (1972). The how and what of why: Some determinants and consequences of causal attribution. *Journal of Personality and Social Psychology, 22,* 171–193.

McAuliffe, B. J., Jetten, J., Hornsey, M. J., & Hogg, M. A. (2003). Individualist and collectivist norms: When it's ok to go your own way. *European Journal of Social Psychology, 33,* 57–70.

McCabe, M. P., Ricciardelli, L. A., & Finemore, J. (2002). The role of puberty, media and popularity with peers on strategies to increase weight, decrease weight and increase muscle tone among adolescent boys and girls. *Journal of Psychosomatic Research, 52,* 145–154.

McCarty-Gould, C. (2000). *Crisis and chaos: Life with the combat veteran.* New York: Nova Kroshka Books.

McConahay, J. B. (1986). Modern racism, ambivalence, and the modern racism scale. In J. F. Dovidio & S. L. Gaertner (Eds.), *Prejudice, discrimination, and racism: Theory and research* (pp. 91–125). Orlando, FL: Academic Press.

McConnell, A. R. (2001). Implicit theories: Consequences for social judgments of individuals. *Journal of Experimental Social Psychology, 37,* 215–227.

McCowan, B., & Hooper, S. L. (2002). Individual acoustic variation in Belding's ground squirrel alarm chirps in the High Sierra Nevada. *Journal of the Acoustical Society of America, 111,* 1157–1160.

McCrae, R. R., & Costa, P. T., Jr. (2003). *Personality in adulthood: A five-factor theory perspective* (2nd ed.). New York: Guilford Press.

McCullough, M. E., Hoyt, W. T., Larson, D. B., Koenig, H. G., & Thoresen, C. (2000). Religious involvement and mortality: A meta-analytic review. *Health Psychology, 19,* 211–222.

McDougall, W. (1908). *An introduction to social psychology.* London: Methuen.

McElwee, R. O., Dunning, D., Tan, P. L., & Hollmann, S. (2001). Evaluating others: The role of who we are versus what we think traits mean. *Basic and Applied Social Psychology, 23,* 123–136.

McGarty, C., Turner, J. C., Hogg, M. A., David, B., et al. (1992). Group polarization as conformity to the prototypical group member. *British Journal of Social Psychology, 31,* 1–19.

McGillicuddy, N. B., Pruitt, D. G., & Syna, H. (1984). Perceptions of fairness and strength of negotiation. *Personality and Social Psychology Bulletin, 10,* 402–409.

McGrew, J. F., Bilotta, J. G., & Deeney, J. M. (1999). Software team formation and decay: Extending the standard model for small groups. *Small Group Research, 30,* 209–234.

McGuire, A. M. (1994). Helping behaviors in the natural environment: Dimensions and correlates of helping. *Personality and Social Psychology Bulletin, 20,* 45–56.

McGuire, W. J. (1964). Inducing resistance to persuasion. In L. Berkowitz (Ed.), *Advances in experimental social psychology* (Vol. 1, pp. 192–229). New York: Academic Press.

McGuire, W. J. (1967). Some impending reorientations in social psychology: Some thoughts provoked by Kenneth Ring. *Journal of Experimental Social Psychology, 3,* 124–139.

McGuire, W. J. (1968). Personality and susceptibility to social influence. In E. F. Borgatta & W. W. Lambert (Eds.), *Handbook of personality theory and research* (pp. 1130–1187). Chicago: Rand McNally.

McGuire, W. J. (1969). The nature of attitudes and attitude change. In G. Lindzey & E. Aronson (Eds.), *Handbook of social psychology* (2nd ed., Vol. 3, pp. 136–314). Reading, MA: Addison-Wesley.

McGuire, W. J., & McGuire, C. V. (1988). Content and process in the experience of self. In L. Berkowitz (Ed.), *Advances in experimental social psychology* (Vol. 20, pp. 97–144). New York: Academic Press.

McGuire, W. J., McGuire, C. V., & Winton, W. (1979). Effects of household sex composition on the salience of one's gender in the spontaneous self-concept. *Journal of Experimental Social Psychology, 15,* 77–90.

McIntyre, R. B., Paulson, R. M., & Lord, C. G. (2003). Alleviating women's mathematics stereotype threat through salience of group achievements. *Journal of Experimental Social Psychology, 39,* 83–90.

McKenna, K. Y. A., & Bargh, J. A. (1998). Coming out in the age of the Internet: "Demarginalization" through virtual group participation. *Journal of Personality and Social Psychology, 75*, 681–694.

McKenna, K. Y. A., & Bargh, J. A. (2000). Plan 9 from cyberspace: The implications of the Internet for personality and social psychology. *Personality and Social Psychology Review, 4*, 57–75.

McKenna, K. Y. A., & Bargh, J. A. (2002). The self, on-line: Motivated social perception on the Internet. In S. J. Spencer, S. Fein, M. Zanna, & J. M. Olson (Eds.), *Motivated social perception: The Ontario symposium* (Vol. 9). Mahwah, NJ: Erlbaum.

McKimmie, B. M., Terry, D. J., Hogg, M. A., Manstead, A. S. R., Spears, R., & Doosje, B. (2003). I'm a hypocrite, but so is everyone else: Group support and the reduction of cognitive dissonance. *Group Dynamics: Theory, Research, and Practice, 7*, 214–224.

McLeod, P. L., Lobel, S. A., & Cox, Jr., T. H. (1996). Ethnic diversity and creativity in small groups. *Small Group Research, 27*, 248–264.

McMullen, P. A., & Gross, A. E. (1983). Sex differences, sex roles, and health-related help-seeking. In B. M. DePaulo, A. Nadler, & J. D. Fisher (Eds.), *New directions in helping: Vol. 2. Help-seeking* (pp. 233–263). New York: Academic Press.

McNatt, D. B. (2000). Ancient Pygmalion joins contemporary management: A meta-analysis of the result. *Journal of Applied Psychology, 85*, 314–322.

McPherson, M., Smith-Lovin, L., & Cook, J. M. (2001). Birds of a feather: Homophily in social networks. *Annual Review of Sociology, 27*, 415–444.

McQuiston-Surrett, D., Malpass, R.S., & Tredoux, C.G. (2006). Sequential vs. simultaneous lineups: A review of methods, data, and theory. *Psychology, Public Policy, and Law, 12*, 137–169.

Mead, G. H. (1934). *Mind, self, and society.* Chicago: University of Chicago Press.

Mealey, L., Bridgstock, R., & Townsend, G. C. (1999). Symmetry and perceived facial attractiveness: A monozygotic co-twin comparison. *Journal of Personality and Social Psychology, 76*, 151–158.

Medvec, V. H., & Savitsky, K. (1997). When doing better means feeling worse: The effects of categorical cutoff points on counterfactual thinking and satisfaction. *Journal of Personality and Social Psychology, 72*, 1284–1296.

Medvec, V. H., Madey, S. F., & Gilovich, T. (1995). When less is more: Counterfactual thinking and satisfaction among olympic medalists. *Journal of Personality and Social Psychology, 69*, 603–610.

Medved, M. (1996, September 21). *Daily Telegraph*, p. 5.

Meeus, W. H. J., & Raaijmakers, Q. A. W. (1995). Obedience in modern society: The Utrecht studies. *Journal of Social Issues, 51*, 155–175.

Mehl, M. R., & Pennebaker, J. W. (2003). The sounds of social life: A psychometric analysis of students' daily social environments and natural conversations. *Journal of Personality and Social Psychology, 84*, 857–870.

Meiser, T., & Hewstone, M. (2006). Illusory and spurious correlations: Distinct phenomena or joint outcomes of exemplar-based category learning? *European Journal of Social Psychology, 36*, 315–336.

Meissner, C. A., & Brigham, J. C. (2001). 30 years of investigating the own-race bias in memory for faces: A meta-analytic review. *Psychology, Public Policy, and Law, 7*, 3–35.

Meissner, C. A., Brigham, J. C., & Butz, D. A. (2005). Memory for own- and other-race faces: A dual-process approach. *Applied Cognitive Psychology, 19*, 545–567.

Meissner, C. A., Brigham, J. C., & Pfeifer, J. E. (2003). Jury nullification: The influence of judicial instruction on the relationship between attitudes and juridic decision-making. *Basic and Applied Social Psychology, 25*, 243–254.

Melamed, S., Shirom, A., Toker, S., Berliner, S., & Shapira, I. (2006). Burnout and risk of cardiovascular disease: Evidence, possible causal paths, and promising research directions. *Psychological Bulletin, 132*, 327–353.

Mendes, W. B., Blascovich, J., Lickel, B., & Hunter, S. (2002). Challenge and threat during social interaction with white and black men. *Personality and Social Psychology Bulletin, 28*, 939–952.

Mendonca, P. J., & Brehm, S. S. (1983). Effects of choice on behavioral treatment of overweight children. *Journal of Social and Clinical Psychology, 1*, 343–358.

Merikle, P., & Skanes, H. E. (1992). Subliminal self-help audiotapes: A search for placebo effects. *Journal of Applied Psychology, 77*, 772–776.

Merritt, M. M., Bennett, G. G., Jr., Williams, R. B., Edwards, C. L., & Sollers, J. J., III. (2006). Perceived racism and cardiovascular reactivity and recovery to personally relevant stress. *Health Psychology, 25*, 364–369.

Merton, R. (1948). The self-fulfilling prophecy. *Antioch Review, 8*, 193–210.

Messick, D. M., & Cook, K. S. (Eds.). (1983). *Equity theory: Psychological and sociological perspectives.* New York: Praeger.

Messick, D. M., Wilke, H., Brewer, M. B., Kramer, R. M., Zemke, P. E., & Lui, L. (1983). Individual adaptation and structural change as solutions to social dilemmas. *Journal of Personality and Social Psychology, 44*, 294–309.

Meston, C. M., & Frohlich, P. F. (2003). Love at first sight: Partner salience moderates roller-coaster-induced excitation transfer. *Archives of Sexual Behavior, 32*, 537–544.

Metalsky, G. I., Joiner, T. E., Hardin, T. S., & Abramson, L. Y. (1993). Depressive reactions to failure in a naturalistic setting: A test of the hopelessness and self-esteem theories of depression. *Journal of Abnormal Psychology, 102*, 101–109.

Mezulis, A. H., Abramson, L. Y., Hyde, J. S., & Hankin, B. L. (2004). Is there a universal positivity bias in attributions? A meta-analytic review of individual, developmental, and cultural differences in the self-serving attributional bias. *Psychological Bulletin, 130*, 711–747.

Mezzacappa, E. S., Katkin, E. S., & Palmer, S. N. (1999). Epinephrine, arousal, and emotion: A new look at two-factor theory. *Cognition and Emotion, 13*, 181–199.

Michinov, N., & Primois, C. (2005). Improving productivity and creativity in online groups through social comparison process: New evidence for asynchronous electronic brainstorming. *Computers in Human Behavior, 21*, 11–28.

Mickelson, K. D., Kessler, R. C., & Shaver, P. R. (1997). Adult attachment in a nationally representative sample. *Journal of Personality and Social Psychology, 73*, 1092–1106.

Midlarsky, E., Fagan Jones, S., & Corley, R. P. (2005). Personality correlates of heroic rescue during the Holocaust. *Journal of Personality, 73*, 907–934.

Midlarsky, E., Kahana, E., Corley, R., Nemeroff, R., & Schonbar, R. A. (1999). Altruistic moral judgment among older adults. *International Journal of Aging and Human Development, 49*, 27–41.

Miles, D. R., & Carey, G. (1997). Genetic and environmental architecture on human aggression. *Journal of Personality and Social Psychology, 72*, 207–217.

Miles, J. A., & Greenberg, J. (1993). Using punishment threats to attenuate social loafing effects among swimmers. *Organizational Behavior and Human Decision Processes, 56*, 246–265.

Milgram, S. (1963). Behavioral study of obedience. *Journal of Abnormal and Social Psychology, 67*, 371–378.

Milgram, S. (1970). The experience of living in cities. *Science, 167*, 1461–1468.

Milgram, S. (1974). *Obedience to authority: An experimental view.* New York: Harper & Row.

Milgram, S., & Sabini, J. (1978). On maintaining urban norms: A field experiment in the subway. In A. Baum, J. E. Singer, & S. Valins (Eds.), *Advances in environmental psychology* (Vol. 1). Hillsdale, NJ: Erlbaum.

Milgram, S., & Toch, H. (1969). Collective behavior: Crowds and social movements. In G. Lindzey & E. Aronson (Eds.), *The handbook of social psychology* (2nd ed., Vol. 4, pp. 507–610). Reading, MA: Addison-Wesley.

Milgram, S., Bickman, L., & Berkowitz, L. (1969). Note on the drawing power of crowds of different size. *Journal of Personality and Social Psychology, 13,* 79–82.

Millar, M. (2002). Effects of guilt induction and guilt reduction on door in the face. *Communication Research, 29,* 666–680.

Miller, A. G. (1986). *The obedience experiments: A case study of controversy in social science.* New York: Praeger.

Miller, A. G., Gordon, A. K., & Buddie, A. M. (1999). Accounting for evil and cruelty: Is to explain to condone? *Personality and Social Psychology Review, 3,* 254–268.

Miller, A. G., Jones, E. E., & Hinkle, S. (1981). A robust attribution error in the personality domain. *Journal of Experimental Social Psychology, 17,* 587–600.

Miller, C. T. (2006). Social psychological perspectives on coping with stressors related to stigma. In S. Levin & C. van Laar (Eds.), *Stigma and group inequality: Social psychological perspectives* (pp. 21–44). Mahwah, NJ: Erlbaum.

Miller, C. T., & Myers, A. M. (1998). Compensating for prejudice: How heavyweight people (and others) control outcomes despite prejudice. In J. K. Swim & C. Stangor (Eds.), *Prejudice: The target's perspective* (pp. 191–218). San Diego: Academic Press.

Miller, D. T., & McFarland, C. (1987). Pluralistic ignorance: When similarity is interpreted as dissimilarity. *Journal of Personality and Social Psychology, 53,* 298–305.

Miller, D. T., Monin, B., & Prentice, D. A. (2000). Pluralistic ignorance and inconsistency between private attitudes and public behaviors. In D. J. Terry, M. A. Hogg, & K. M. White (Eds.), *Attitudes, behavior, and social context: The role of norms and group membership* (pp. 95–113). Mahwah, NJ: Erlbaum.

Miller, G. E., & Cohen, S. (2001). Psychological interventions and the immune system: A meta-analytic review and critique. *Health Psychology, 20,* 47–63.

Miller, J. G. (1984). Culture and the development of everyday social explanation. *Journal of Personality and Social Psychology, 46,* 961–978.

Miller, J. G., Bersoff, D. M., & Harwood, R. L. (1990). Perceptions of social responsibility in India and in the United States: Moral imperatives or personal decisions? *Journal of Personality and Social Psychology, 58,* 33–47.

Miller, M. L., & Thayer, J. F. (1989). On the existence of discrete classes in personality: Is self-monitoring the correct joint to carve? *Journal of Personality and Social Psychology, 57,* 143–155.

Miller, N. E. (1941). The frustration-aggression hypothesis. *Psychological Review, 48,* 337–342.

Miller, N., & Campbell, D. T. (1959). Recency and primacy in persuasion as a function of the timing of speeches and measurements. *Journal of Abnormal and Social Psychology, 59,* 1–9.

Miller, N., & Carlson, M. (1990). Valid theory-testing meta-analyses further question the negative state relief model of helping. *Psychological Bulletin, 107,* 215–225.

Miller, N., Pedersen, W. C., Earleywine, M., & Pollock, V. E. (2003). A theoretical model of triggered displaced aggression. *Personality and Social Psychology Review, 7,* 75–97.

Miller, P. A., & Eisenberg, N. (1988). The relation of empathy to aggressive and externalizing/antisocial behavior. *Psychological Bulletin, 103,* 324–344.

Miller, P. A., Eisenberg, N., Fabes, R. A., & Shell, R. (1996). Relations of moral reasoning and vicarious emotion to young children's prosocial behavior toward peers and adults. *Developmental Psychology, 32,* 210–219.

Miller, R., Perlman, D., & Brehm, S. S. (2006). *Intimate relationships.* New York: McGraw-Hill.

Miller, T. Q., Smith, T. W., Turner, C. W., Guijarro, M. L., & Hallet, A. J. (1996). A meta-analytic review of research on hostility and physical health. *Psychological Bulletin, 119,* 322–348.

Miller, T. Q., Turner, C. W., Tindale, R. S., Posavac, E. J., & Dugon, B. L. (1991). Reasons for the trend toward null findings in research on Type A behavior. *Psychological Bulletin, 110,* 469–485.

Miller, W. R. (1985). Motivation for treatment: A review with special emphasis on alcoholism. *Psychological Bulletin, 98,* 84–107.

Miller, W. R., & Thoresen, C. E. (2003). Spirituality, religion, and health: An emerging research field. *American Psychologist, 58,* 24–35.

Miranda, S. M. (1994). Avoidance of groupthink: Meeting management using group support systems. *Small Group Research, 25,* 105–136.

Mita, T. H., Dermer, M., & Knight, J. (1977). Reversed facial images and the mere exposure hypothesis. *Journal of Personality and Social Psychology, 35,* 597–601.

Mitchell, T. R. (1974). Expectancy models of job satisfaction, occupational preference, and effort: A theoretical, methodological, and empirical appraisal. *Psychological Bulletin, 81,* 1096–1112.

Miyamoto, Y., & Kitayama, S. (2002). Cultural variation in correspondence bias: The critical role of attitude diagnosticity of socially constrained behavior. *Journal of Personality and Social Psychology, 83,* 1239–1248.

Moghaddam, F. M., Taylor, D. M., & Wright, S. C. (1993). *Social psychology in cross-cultural perspective.* New York: W. H. Freeman.

Molleman, E., & Slomp, J. (2006). The impact of team and work characteristics on team functioning. *Human Factors and Ergonomics in Manufacturing, 16,* 1–15.

Mondschein, E. R., Adolph, K. E., & Tamis-LeMonda, C. S. (2000). Gender bias in mothers' expectations about infant crawling. *Journal of Experimental Child Psychology, 77,* 304–316.

Monin, B., & Miller, D. T. (2001). Moral credentials and the expression of prejudice. *Journal of Personality and Social Psychology, 81,* 33–43.

Monin, B., & Norton, M. I. (2003). Perceptions of a fluid consensus: Uniqueness bias, false consensus, false polarization, and pluralistic ignorance in a water conservation crisis. *Personality and Social Psychology Bulletin, 29,* 559–567.

Montada, L., & M. J. Lerner (Eds.). (1998). *Responses to victimizations and belief in a just world: Critical issues in social justice* (pp. 247–269). New York: Plenum.

Monteith, M. J., & Voils, C. I. (2001). Exerting control over prejudiced responses. In G. B. Moskowitz (Ed.), *Cognitive social psychology: On the future of social cognition* (pp. 375–388). Mahwah, NJ: Erlbaum.

Monteith, M. J., Ashburn-Nardo, L., Voils, C. I., & Czopp, A. M. (2002). Putting the brakes on prejudice: On the development and operation of cues for control. *Journal of Personality and Social Psychology, 83,* 1029–1050.

Monteith. M. J., Sherman, J. W., & Devine, P. G. (1998). Suppression as a stereotype control strategy. *Personality and Social Psychology Review, 2,* 63–82.

Montepare, J. M., & McArthur, L. Z. (1988). Impressions of people created by age-related qualities of their gaits. *Journal of Personality and Social Psychology, 55,* 547–556.

Moon, H. (2001). Looking forward and looking back: Integrating completion and sunk-cost effects within an escalation-of-commitment progress decision. *Journal of Applied Psychology, 86,* 104–113.

Moore, B. S., Underwood, B., & Rosenhan, D. L. (1973). Affect and altruism. *Developmental Psychology, 8,* 99–104.

Moore, D. A. (2005). Myopic biases in strategic social prediction: Why deadlines put everyone under more pressure than everyone else. *Personality and Social Psychology Bulletin, 31,* 668–679.

Moore, T. E. (1982). Subliminal advertising: What you see is what you get. *Journal of Marketing, 46,* 38–47.

Moorhead, G., Neck, C. P., & West, M. S. (1998). The tendency toward defective decision making within self-managing teams: The relevance of groupthink for the 21st century. *Organizational Behavior and Human Decision Processes, 73,* 327–351.

Mor, N., & Winquist, J. (2002). Self-focused attention and negative affect: A meta-analysis. *Psychological Bulletin, 128,* 638–662.

Moradi, B., Dirks, D., & Matteson, A. V. (2005). Roles of sexual objectification experiences and internalization of standards of beauty in eating disorder symptomatology: A test and extension of objectification theory. *Journal of Counseling Psychology, 52,* 420–428.

Moran, G., & Comfort, C. (1986). Neither "tentative" nor "fragmentary": Verdict preference of impaneled felony jurors as a function of attitude toward capital punishment. *Journal of Applied Psychology, 71,* 146–155.

Moran, G., & Cutler, B. L. (1991). The prejudicial impact of pretrial publicity. *Journal of Applied Social Psychology, 21,* 345–367.

Moreland, R. L., & Beach, S. R. (1992). Exposure effects in the classroom: The development of affinity among students. *Journal of Experimental Social Psychology, 28,* 255–276.

Moreland, R. L., Hogg, M. A., & Hains, S. C. (1994). Back to the future: Social psychological research on groups. *Journal of Experimental Social Psychology, 30,* 527–555.

Morgan, L. A., & Arthur, M. M. (2005). Methodological considerations in estimating the gender pay gap for employed professionals. *Sociological Methods and Research, 33,* 383–403.

Morgeson, F. P., Mumford, T. V., & Campion, M. A. (2005). Coming full circle: Using research and practice to address 27 questions about 360-degree feedback programs. *Consulting Psychology Journal: Practice and Research, 57,* 196–209.

Moriarty, D., & McCabe, A. E. (1977). Studies of television and youth sport. In *Ontario Royal Commission on Violence in the Communications Industry report* (Vol. 5). Toronto: Queen's Printer for Ontario.

Moriarty, T. (1975). Crime, commitment, and the responsive bystander: Two field experiments. *Journal of Personality and Social Psychology, 31,* 370–376.

Morrison, A. M., & Von Glinow, M. A. (1990). Women and minorities in management. *American Psychologist, 45,* 200–208.

Morrongiello, B. A., & Dawber, T. (2000). Mothers' responses to sons and daughters engaging in injury-risk behaviors on a playground: Implications for sex differences in injury rates. *Journal of Experimental Child Psychology, 76,* 89–103.

Morrongiello, B. A., Midgett, C., & Stanton, K. L. (2000). Gender biases in children's appraisals of injury risk and other children's risk-taking behaviors. *Journal of Experimental Child Psychology, 77,* 317–336.

Morse, B. J. (1995). Beyond the Conflict Tactics Scale: Assessing gender differences in partner violence. *Violence and Victims, 10,* 251–272.

Moscovici, S. (1980). Toward a theory of conversion behavior. In L. Berkowitz (Ed.), *Advances in Experimental Social Psychology, 6,* 149–202.

Moscovici, S., & Personnaz, B. (1991). Studies in social influence VI: Is Lenin orange or red? Imagery and social influence. *European Journal of Social Psychology, 21,* 101–118.

Moscovici, S., & Zavalloni, M. (1969). The group as a polarizer of attitudes. *Journal of Personality and Social Psychology, 12,* 125–135.

Moscovici, S., Lage, E., & Naffrechoux, M. (1969). Influence of a consistent minority on the responses of a majority in a color perception task. *Sociometry, 32,* 365–380.

Moscovici, S., Mugny, G., & Van Avermaet, E. (Eds.). (1985). *Perspectives on minority influence.* New York: Cambridge University Press.

Moskalenko, S., & Heine, S. J. (2003). Watching your troubles away: Television viewing as a stimulus for subjective self-awareness. *Personality and Social Psychology Bulletin, 29,* 76–85.

Moskowitz, G. B. (1996). The mediational effects of attributions and information processing in minority social influence. *British Journal of Social Psychology, 35,* 47–66.

Moskowitz, G. B. (2001). Preconscious control and compensatory cognition. In G. B. Moskowitz (Ed.), *Cognitive social psychology: The Princeton symposium on the legacy and future of social cognition* (pp. 333–358). Mahwah, NJ: Erlbaum.

Moskowitz, G. B. (2005). *Social cognition: Understanding the self and others.* New York: Guilford.

Moskowitz, G. B., Li, P., & Kirk, E. R. (2004). The implicit volition model: On the preconscious regulation of temporarily adopted goals. In M. P. Zanna (Ed.), *Advances in experimental social psychology* (pp. 317–413). San Diego, CA: Academic Press.

Mouton, J., Blake, R., & Olmstead, J. (1956). The relationship between frequency of yielding and the disclosure of personal identity. *Journal of Personality, 24,* 339–347.

Moynihan, J. A., & Ader, R. (1996). Psychoneuroimmunology: Animal models of disease. *Psychosomatic Medicine, 58,* 546–558.

Mueller, J. H. (1982). Self-awareness and access to material rated as self-descriptive and nondescriptive. *Bulletin of the Psychonomic Society, 19,* 323–326.

Mugny, G. (1982). *The power of minorities.* London: Academic Press.

Mugny, G., & Perez, J. A. (1991). *Social psychology of minority influence.* Cambridge: Cambridge University Press.

Mullen, B. (1983). Operationalizing the effect of the group on the individual: A self-attention perspective. *Journal of Experimental Social Psychology, 19,* 295–322.

Mullen, B. (1985). Strength and immediacy of sources: A meta-analytic evaluation of the forgotten elements of social impact theory. *Journal of Personality and Social Psychology, 48,* 1458–1466.

Mullen, B. (1986). Atrocity as a function of lynch mob composition: A self-attention perspective. *Personality and Social Psychology Bulletin, 12,* 187–197.

Mullen, B., & Copper, C. (1994). The relation between group cohesiveness and performance: An integration. *Psychological Bulletin, 115,* 210–227.

Mullen, B., Anthony, T., Salas, E., & Driskell, J. E. (1994). Group cohesiveness and quality of decision making: An integration of tests of the groupthink hypothesis. *Small Group Research, 25,* 189–204.

Mullen, B., Dovidio, J. F., Johnson, C., & Copper, C. (1992). In-group and out-group differences in social projection. *Journal of Experimental Social Psychology, 28,* 422–440.

Mullen, B., Johnson, C., & Salas, E. (1991). Productivity loss in brainstorming groups: A meta-analytic integration. *Basic and Applied Social Psychology, 12,* 3–23.

Muller, D., Atzeni, T., & Butera, F. (2004). Illusory conjunction effect: Support for distraction-conflict theory. *Journal of Experimental Social Psychology, 40,* 659–665.

Muraven, M., & Baumeister, R. F. (1998). Self-control as a limited resource: Regulatory depletion patterns. *Journal of Personality and Social Psychology, 74,* 774–789.

Muraven, M., & Baumeister, R. F. (2000). Self-regulation and depletion of limited resources: Does self-control resemble a muscle? *Psychological Bulletin, 126,* 247–259.

Murphy, K. R., & Balzer, W. K. (1986). Systematic distortions in memory-based behavior ratings and performance evaluation: Consequences for rating accuracy. *Journal of Applied Psychology, 71,* 39–44.

Murphy, K. R., Balzer, W. K., Lockhart, M. C., & Eisenman, E. J. (1985). Effects of previous performance on evaluations of present performance. *Journal of Applied Psychology, 70,* 72–84.

Murphy, K. R., Cronin, B. E., & Tam, A. P. (2003). Controversy and consensus regarding the use of cognitive ability testing in organizations. *Journal of Applied Psychology, 88,* 660–671.

Murray, C. B., Kaiser, R., & Taylor, S. (1997). The O. J. Simpson verdict: Predictors of beliefs about innocence or guilt. *Journal of Social Issues, 53,* 455–475.

Murray, S. L., & Holmes, J. G. (1999). The (mental) ties that bind: Cognitive structures that predict relationship resilience. *Journal of Personality and Social Psychology, 77,* 1228–1244.

Murray, S. L., Griffin, D. W., Rose, P., & Bellavia, G. M. (2003). Calibrating the sociometer: The relational contingencies of self-esteem. *Journal of Personality and Social Psychology, 85,* 63–84.

Murray, S. L., Holmes, J. G., & Collins, N. L. (2006). Optimizing assurance: The risk regulation system in relationships. *Psychological Bulletin, 132,* 641–666.

Murray, S. L., Holmes, J. G., & Griffin, D. W. (1996). The benefits of positive illusions: Idealization and the construction of satisfaction in close relationships. *Journal of Personality and Social Psychology, 70,* 79–98.

Murrell, A. R., Merwin, R. M., & Henning, K. R. (2005). When parents model violence: The relationship between witnessing weapon use as a child and later use as an adult. *Behavior and Social Issues, 14,* 128–133.

Murstein, B. I. (1986). *Paths to marriage.* Beverly Hills, CA: Sage.

Murstein, B. I. (1987). A clarification and extension of the SVR theory of dyadic pairing. *Journal of Marriage and the Family, 49,* 929–933.

Mussweiler, T., & Ruter, K. (2003). What friends are for! The use of routine standards in social comparison. *Journal of Personality and Social Psychology, 85,* 467–481.

Mussweiler, T., & Strack, F. (2000). The "relative self": Informational and judgmental consequences of comparative self-evaluation. *Journal of Personality and Social Psychology, 79,* 23–38.

Mussweiler, T., Rüter, K., & Epstude, K. (2004). The man who wasn't there: Subliminal social comparison standards influence self-evaluation. *Journal of Experimental Social Psychology, 40,* 689–696.

Myers, D. G., & Bishop, G. D. (1970). Discussion effects on racial attitudes. *Science, 169,* 778–779.

Myers, D. G., & Diener, E. (1995). Who is happy? *Psychological Science, 6,* 10–19.

Myers, D. G., & Lamm, H. (1976). The group polarization phenomenon. *Psychological Bulletin, 83,* 602–627.

Nabi, R. L., & Sullivan, J. L. (2001). Does television viewing relate to engagement in protective action against crime? A cultivation analysis from a theory of reasoned action perspective. *Communication Research, 28,* 802–825.

Nacoste, R. W. (1994). If empowerment is the goal . . . : Affirmative action and social interaction. *Basic and Applied Social Psychology, 15,* 87–112.

Nacoste, R. W. (1996). Social psychology and the affirmative action debate. *Journal of Social and Clinical Psychology, 15,* 261–282.

Nadler, A., & Fisher, J. D. (1986). The role of threat to self-esteem and perceived control in recipient reactions to help: Theory development and empirical validation. In L. Berkowitz (Ed.), *Advances in experimental social psychology* (Vol. 19, pp. 81–122). New York: Academic Press.

Narby, D. J., Cutler, B. L., & Moran, G. (1993). A meta-analysis of the association between authoritarianism and jurors' perceptions of defendant culpability. *Journal of Applied Psychology, 78,* 34–42.

National Center on Child Abuse and Neglect. (1988). *Study findings: Study of national incidence and prevalence of child abuse and neglect: 1988.* Washington, DC: U.S. Department of Health and Human Services.

National Law Journal (1990). Rock group not liable for deaths (September 10), p. 33.

National Research Council, Committee to Review the Scientific Evidence on the Polygraph, Division of Behavioral and Social Sciences and Education. (2003). *The polygraph and lie detection.* Washington, DC: National Academies Press.

National Television Violence Study, Vol. 2 (1998). Thousand Oaks, CA: Sage.

Nattinger, A. B., et al. (1998). Celebrity medical care decisions can influence others. *Journal of the American Medical Association, 279,* 788–789.

Neff, L. A., & Karney, B. R. (2005). To know you is to love you: The implications of global adoration and specific accuracy for marital relationships. *Journal of Personality and Social Psychology, 88,* 480–497.

Neisser, U. (1981). John Dean's memory: A case study. *Cognition, 9,* 1–22.

Nemeth, C. (1986). Differential contributions of majority and minority influence. *Psychological Review, 93,* 23–32.

Nemeth, C. J., & Nemeth-Brown, B. (2003). Better than individuals? The potential benefits of dissent and diversity for group creativity. In P. B. Paulus & B. A. Nijstad (Eds.), *Group creativity: Innovation through collaboration* (pp. 63–84). New York: Oxford University.

Nemeth, C. J., Connell, J. B., Rogers, J. D., & Brown, K. S. (2001). Improving decision making by means of dissent. *Journal of Applied Social Psychology, 31,* 48–58.

Nemeth, C., & Brilmayer, A. G. (1987). Negotiation versus influence. *European Journal of Social Psychology, 17,* 45–56.

Nemeth, C., & Kwan, J. (1987). Minority influence, divergent thinking, and detection of correct solutions. *Journal of Applied Social Psychology, 17,* 788–799.

Nemeth, C., Mayseless, O., Sherman, J., & Brown, Y. (1990). Exposure to dissent and recall of information. *Journal of Personality and Social Psychology, 58,* 429–437.

Nes, L. S., & Segerstrom, S. C. (2006). Dispositional optimism and coping: A meta-analytic review. *Personality and Social Psychology Review, 10,* 235–251.

Nesdale, D., & Naito, M. (2005). Individualism-collectivism and the attitudes to school bullying of Japanese and Australian students. *Journal of Cross-Cultural Psychology, 36,* 537–556.

Neumann, R., & Strack, F. (2000). "Mood contagion": The automatic transfer of mood between persons. *Journal of Personality and Social Psychology, 79,* 211–223.

Newby-Clark, I. R., McGregor, I., & Zanna, M. P. (2002). Thinking and caring about cognitive inconsistency: When and from whom does attitudinal ambivalence feel uncomfortable? *Journal of Personality and Social Psychology, 82,* 157–166.

Newcomb, T. M. (1943). *Personality and social change: Attitude formation in a student community.* Ft. Worth, TX: Dryden Press.

Newcomb, T. M. (1961). *The acquaintance process.* New York: Holt, Rinehart and Winston.

Newman, C. (2000, January). The enigma of beauty. *National Geographic,* pp. 94–121.

Newman, L. S., & Uleman, J. S. (1989). Spontaneous trait inference. In J. S. Uleman & J. A. Bargh (Eds.), *Unintended thought* (pp. 155–188). New York: Guilford.

Newman, R. S. (2005). The cocktail party effect in infants revisited: Listening to one's name in noise. *Developmental Psychology, 41,* 352–362.

Newtson, D. (1974). Dispositional inference from effects of actions: Effects chosen and effects foregone. *Journal of Experimental Social Psychology, 10,* 487–496.

Newtson, D., Hairfield, J., Bloomingdale, J., & Cutino, S. (1987). The structure of action and interaction. *Social Cognition, 5,* 191–237.

Nezlek, J. B., & Leary, M. R. (2002). Individual differences in self-presentational motives in daily social interaction. *Personality and Social Psychology Bulletin, 28,* 211–223.

Nezlek, J. B., & Smith, C. V. (2005). Social identity in daily social interaction. *Self and Identity, 4,* 243–261.

Ng, K. Y., & Van Dyne, L. (2005). Antecedents and performance consequences of helping behavior in work groups: A multi-level analysis. *Group and Organization Management, 30,* 514–540.

Nibler, R., & Harris, K. L. (2003). The effects of culture and cohesiveness in collectivistic and individualistic work groups: A cross-cultural analysis. *Journal of Organizational Behavior, 24,* 979–1001.

Nickerson, C., Schwarz, N., Diener, E., & Kahneman, D. (2003). Zeroing in on the dark side of the American dream: A closer look at the negative consequences of the goal for financial success. *Psychological Science, 14,* 531–536.

Niedermeier, K. E., Horowitz, I. A., & Kerr, N. L. (1999). Informing jurors of their nullification power: A route to a just verdict or judicial chaos? *Law and Human Behavior, 23,* 331–351.

Nieva, V. F., & Gutek, B. A. (1981). *Women and work: A psychological perspective.* New York: Praeger.

Nijstad, B. A., Diehl, M., & Stroebe, W. (2003). Cognitive stimulation and interference in idea-generating groups. In P. B. Paulus & B. A. Nijstad (Eds.), *Group creativity: Innovation through collaboration* (pp. 137–159). New York: Oxford University Press.

Nijstad, B. A., Stroebe, W., & Lodewijkx, H. F. M. (2006). The illusion of group productivity: A reduction of failures explanation. *European Journal of Social Psychology, 36,* 31–48.

Nisbett, R. E., & Cohen, D. (1996). *Culture of honor: The psychology of violence in the South.* Boulder, CO: Westview.

Nisbett, R. E., & Ross, L. (1980). *Human inference: Strategies and shortcomings of social judgment.* Englewood Cliffs, NJ: Prentice-Hall.

Nisbett, R. E., & Wilson, T. D. (1977). Telling more than we can know: Verbal reports on mental processes. *Psychological Review, 84,* 231–259.

Nisbett, R. E., Fong, G. T., Lehman, D. R., & Cheng, P. W. (1987). Teaching reasoning. *Science, 238,* 625–631.

Noel, J. G., Wann, D. L., & Branscombe, N. R. (1995). Peripheral ingroup membership status and public negativity toward outgroups. *Journal of Personality and Social Psychology, 68,* 127–137.

Nolen-Hoeksema, S., & Girgus, J. S. (1994). The emergence of gender differences in depression during adolescence. *Psychological Bulletin, 115,* 424–443.

Nolen-Hoeksema, S., & Morrow, J. (1991). A prospective study of depression and posttraumatic stress symptoms after a natural disaster: The 1989 Loma Prieta earthquake. *Journal of Personality and Social Psychology, 61,* 115–121.

Norenzayan, A., & Nisbett, R. E. (2000). Culture and causal cognition. *Current Directions in Psychological Science, 9,* 132–135.

North, A. C., Hargreaves, D. J., & McKendrick, J. (1999). The influence of in-store music on wine selections. *Journal of Applied Psychology, 84,* 271–276.

North, A. C., Tarrant, M., & Hargreaves, D. J. (2004). The effects of music on helping behavior: A field study. *Environment and Behavior, 36,* 266–275.

Northoff, G., & Bermpohl, F. (2004). Cortical midline structures and the self. *Trends in Cognitive Sciences, 8,* 102–107.

Northoff, G., Heinzel, A., de Greck, M., Bermpohl, F., Dobrowolny, H., & Panskepp, J. (2006). Self-referential processing in our brain—a meta-analysis of imaging studies on the self. *NeuroImage, 31,* 440–457.

Norton, K. I., Olds, T. S., Olive, S., & Dank, S. (1996). Ken and Barbie at life size. *Sex Roles, 34,* 287–294.

Norton, M. I., Monin, B., Cooper, J., & Hogg, M. A. (2003). Vicarious dissonance: Attitude change from the inconsistency of others. *Journal of Personality and Social Psychology, 85,* 47–62.

Norton, M. I., Sommers, S. R., Apfelbaum, E. P., Pura, N., & Ariely, D. (2006). Color blindness and interracial interaction: Playing the political correctness game. *Psychological Science, 17,* 949–953.

Norton, M. I., Sommers, S. R., Vandello, J. A., & Darley, J. M. (2006). Mixed motives and racial bias: The impact of legitimate and illegitimate criteria on decision making. *Psychology, Public Policy, and Law, 12,* 36–55.

Nosek, B. (2006). Personal communication.

Nosek, B. A., & Banaji, M. R. (2001). The Go/No-go Association Task. *Social Cognition, 19,* 625–666.

Nosek, B. A., Banaji, M. R., & Greenwald, A. G. (2002). Harvesting implicit attitudes and stereotype data from the Implicit Association Test website. *Group Dynamics, 6,* 101–115.

Nowack, M. A., Sasaki, A., Taylor, C., & Fudenberg, D. (2004). Emergence of cooperation and evolutionary stability in finite populations. *Nature, 428,* 646–650.

Nowak, M. A., & Sigmund, K. (2005). Evolution of indirect reciprocity. *Nature, 437,* 1291–1298.

Nowak, M., & Sigmund, K. (1993). A strategy of win-stay, lose-shift that outperforms tit-for-tat in the Prisoner's Dilemma game. *Nature, 364,* 56–58.

O'Brien, L. T., & Crandall, C. S. (2003). Stereotype threat and arousal: Effects on women's math performance. *Personality and Social Psychology Bulletin, 29,* 782–789.

O'Connor, S. C., & Rosenblood, L. K. (1996). Affiliation motivation in everyday experience: A theoretical comparison. *Journal of Personality and Social Psychology, 70,* 513–522.

O'Gorman, R., Wilson, D. S., & Miller, R. R. (2005). Altruistic punishing and helping differ in sensitivity to relatedness, friendship, and future interactions. *Evolution and Human Behavior, 26,* 375–387.

O'Keefe, D. J., & Figge, M. (1997). A guilt-based explanation of the door-in-the-face influence strategy. *Human Communication Research, 42,* 64–81.

O'Leary, K. D., & Smith, D. A. (1991). Marital interaction. *Annual Review of Psychology, 42,* 191–212.

O'Leary, K. D., Barling, J., Arias, I., Rosenbaum, A., Malone, J., & Tyree, A. (1989). Prevalence and stability of physical aggression between spouses: A longitudinal analysis. *Journal of Consulting and Clinical Psychology, 57,* 263–268.

O'Neil, K. M., Patry, M. W., & Penrod, S. D. (2004). Exploring the effects of attitudes toward the death penalty on capital sentencing verdicts. *Psychology, Public Policy, and Law, 10,* 443–470.

O'Neill, A. M., Green, M., & Cuadros, P. (1996, September 2). *People,* p. 72.

Ochsner, K. N. (2007). Social cognitive neuroscience: Historical development, core principles, and future promise. In A. W. Kruglanski & E. T. Higgins (Eds.), *Social psychology: Handbook of basic principles.* New York: Guilford.

Oddone-Paolucci, E., Genuis, M., & Violato, C. (2000). A meta-analysis of the published research on the effects of pornography. In C. Violato & E. Oddone-Paolucci (Eds.), *The changing family and child development* (pp. 48–59). Aldershot, England: Ashgate.

Oesterman, K., Bjorkqvist, K., Lagerspetz, K. M. J., Kaukiainen, A., Landau, S. F., Fraczek, A., & Caprara, G. V. (1998). Cross-cultural evidence of female indirect aggression. *Aggressive Behavior, 24,* 1–8.

Ofshe, R., & Watters, E. (1994). *Making monsters: False memories, psychotherapy, and sexual hysteria.* New York: Charles Scribner's Sons.

Ogilvy, D. (1985). *Ogilvy on advertising.* New York: Vintage Books.

Ogloff, J. R. P., & Vidmar, N. (1994). The impact of pretrial publicity on jurors: A study to compare the relative effects of television and print media in a child sex abuse case. *Law and Human Behavior, 18,* 507–525.

Ohbuchi, K., Kameda, M., & Agarie, N. (1989). Apology as aggression control: Its role in mediating appraisal of and response to harm. *Journal of Personality and Social Psychology, 56,* 219–227.

Olczak, P. V., Kaplan, M. F., & Penrod, S. (1991). Attorneys' lay psychology and its effectiveness in selecting jurors: Three empirical studies. *Journal of Social Behavior and Personality, 6,* 431–452.

Oliver, M. G., & Hyde, J. S. (1993). Gender differences in sexuality: A meta-analysis. *Psychological Bulletin, 114,* 29–51.

Olson, J. M., Vernon, P. A., Harris, J. A., & Jang, K. L. (2001). The heritability of attitudes: A study of twins. *Journal of Personality and Social Psychology, 80,* 845–860.

Olson, M. (1965). *The logic of collective action.* Cambridge, MA: Harvard University Press.

Olson, M. A., & Fazio, R. H. (2001). Implicit attitude formation through classical conditioning. *Psychological Science, 12,* 413–417.

Olson, M. A., & Fazio, R. H. (2006). Reducing automatically activated racial prejudice through implicit evaluative conditioning. *Personality and Social Psychology Bulletin, 32,* 421–433.

Olson, M. A., & Fazio, R. H. (2006). Reducing automatically activated racial prejudice through implicit evaluative conditioning. *Personality and Social Psychology Bulletin, 32,* 421–433.

Olweus, D. (2003). A profile of school bullying. *Educational Leadership, 60,* 12–18.

Olweus, D. (2003). Social problems in school. In A. Slater & G. Bremmer (Eds.), *An introduction to developmental psychology* (pp. 434–454). Malden, MA: Blackwell.

Olweus, D. (2004). The Olweus Bullying Prevention Programme: Design and implementation issues and a new national initiative in Norway. In P. K. Smith, D. Pepler, & K. Rigby (Eds.), *Bullying in schools: How successful can interventions be?* (pp. 13–36). New York: Cambridge University Press.

Omarzu, J. (2000). A disclosure decision model: Determining how and when individuals will self-disclose. *Personality and Social Psychology Review, 4,* 174–185.

Omoto, A. M., & Snyder, M. (1995). Sustained helping without obligation: Motivation, longevity of service, and perceived attitude change among AIDS volunteers. *Journal of Personality and Social Psychology, 68,* 671–686.

Omoto, A. M., & Snyder, M. (2002). Considerations of community: The context and process of volunteerism. *American Behavioral Scientist, 45,* 846–867.

Ones, D. S., Viswesvaran, C., & Schmidt, F. L. (1993). Comprehensive meta-analysis of integrity test validities: Findings and implications for personnel selection and theories of job performance. *Journal of Applied Psychology, 78,* 679–703.

Operario, D., & Fiske, S. T. (2001). Effects of trait dominance on powerholders' judgments of subordinates. *Social Cognition, 19,* 161–180.

Orbell, J., Dawes, R., & Schwartz-Shea, P. (1994). Trust, social categories, and individuals: The case of gender. *Motivation and Emotion, 18,* 109–128.

Ore, T. E. (2000). *The social construction of difference and inequality: Race, gender, and sexuality.* Mountain View, CA: Mayfield.

Orenstein, P. (1994). *Schoolgirls: Young women, self-esteem, and the confidence gap.* New York: Anchor Books.

Orne, M. T. (1962). On the social psychology of the psychological experiment: With particular reference to demand characteristics and their implications. *American Psychologist, 17,* 776–783.

Ortmann, A., & Hertwig, R. (1997). Is deception acceptable? *American Psychologist, 52,* 746–747.

Orwell, G. (1942). Looking back on the Spanish War. In S. Orwell & I. Angus (Eds.), *The collected essays, journalism and letters of George Orwell: Vol. 2. My country right or left, 1940–1943* (pp. 249–267). New York: Harcourt, Brace & World. (Reprinted in 1968)

Osbaldiston, R., & Sheldon, K. M. (2002). Social dilemmas and sustainability: Promoting peoples' motivation to "cooperate with the future." In P. Schmuck & W. P. Schultz (Eds.), *Psychology of sustainable development* (pp. 37–57). Dordrecht, Netherlands: Kluwer Academic.

Osborn, A. F. (1953). *Applied imagination.* New York: Scribner.

Osgood, C. E. (1962). *An alternative to war or surrender.* Urbana: University of Illinois Press.

Ostrom, T. M., & Sedikides, C. (1992). Out-group homogeneity effects in natural and minimal groups. *Psychological Bulletin, 112,* 536–552.

Oswald, D. L., & Harvey, R. D. (2000–2001). Hostile environments, stereotype threat, and math performance among undergraduate women. *Current Psychology: Developmental, Learning, Personality, Social, 19,* 338–356.

Otto, A. L., Penrod, S. D., & Dexter, H. R. (1994). The biasing impact of pretrial publicity on juror judgments. *Law and Human Behavior, 18,* 453–469.

Owens, L., Shute, R., & Slee, P. (2000) "Guess what I just heard!": Indirect aggression among teenage girls in Australia. *Aggressive Behavior, 26,* 67–83.

Oxley, N. L., Dzindolet, M. T., & Paulus, P. B. (1996). The effects of facilitators on the performance of brainstorming groups. *Journal of Social Behavior and Personality, 11,* 633–646.

Oyserman, D., Coon, H. M., & Kemmelmeier, M. (2002). Rethinking individualism and collectivism: Evaluation of theoretical assumptions and meta-analyses. *Psychological Bulletin, 128,* 3–72.

Oyserman, D., Coon, H. M., & Kemmelmeier, M. (2002). Rethinking individualism and collectivism: Evaluation of theoretical assumptions and meta-analyses. *Psychological Bulletin, 128,* 3–72.

Ozer, E. J., Best, S. R., Lipsey, T. L., & Weiss, D. S. (2003). Predictors of posttraumatic stress disorder and symptoms in adults: A meta-analysis. *Psychological Bulletin, 129,* 52–71.

Özgen, E. (2004). Language, learning, and color perception. *Current Directions in Psychological Science, 13,* 95–98.

Packard, V. (1957). *The hidden persuaders.* New York: Pocket Books.

Páez, D., Martinez-Taboada, C., Arrospide, J. J., Insua, P., & Ayestaran, S. (1998). Constructing social identity: The role of status, collective values, collective self-esteem, perception and social behaviour. In S. Worchel, J. F. Morales, D. Páez, & J. C. Deschamps (Eds.), *Social identity: International perspectives* (pp. 211–229). London: Sage.

Paik, H., & Comstock, G. (1994). The effects of television violence on antisocial behavior: A meta-analysis. *Communication Research, 21,* 516–546.

Palazzolo, E. T., Serb, D. A., & She, Y. (2006). Coevolution of communication and knowledge networks in transactive memory systems: Using computational models for theoretical development. *Communication Theory, 16,* 223–250.

Panee, C. D., & Ballard, M. E. (2002). High versus low aggressive priming during video-game training: Effects on violent action during game play, hostility, heart rate, and blood pressure. *Journal of Applied Social Psychology, 32,* 2458–2474.

Parducci, A. (1995). *Happiness, pleasure, and judgment: The contextual theory and its applications.* Mahwah, NJ: Erlbaum.

Parents Television Council (2003). TV bloodbath: Violence on prime time broadcast TV.

Park, B. (1986). A method for studying the development of impressions of real people. *Journal of Personality and Social Psychology, 51,* 907–917.

Parker, C. P., Baltes, B. B., & Christiansen, N. D. (1997). Support for affirmative action, justice perceptions, and work attitudes: A study of gender and racial-ethnic group differences. *Journal of Applied Psychology, 82,* 376–389.

Parkinson, S. (1994). Scientific or ethical quality? *Psychological Science, 5,* 137–138.

Parks, C. D. (1994). The predictive ability of social values in resource dilemmas and public goods games. *Personality and Social Psychology Bulletin, 20,* 431–438.

Parks, C. D., Sanna, L. J., & Posey, D. C. (2003). Retrospection in social dilemmas: How thinking about the past affects future cooperation. *Journal of Personality and Social Psychology, 84,* 988–996.

Parsons, H. M. (1974). What happened at Hawthorne? *Science, 183,* 922–932.

Partridge, A., & Eldridge, W. B. (1974). *The second circuit sentencing study: A report to the judges of the second circuit.* Washington, DC: Federal Judicial Center.

Patzer, G. L. (2006). *The power and paradox of physical attractiveness.* Boca Raton, FL: Brown Walker Press.

Paulhus, D. L. (1998). Interpersonal and intrapsychic adaptiveness of trait self-enhancement: A mixed blessing? *Journal of Personality and Social Psychology, 74,* 1197–1208.

Paulhus, D., Graf, P., & Van Selst, M. (1989). Attentional load increases the positivity of self-presentation. *Social Cognition, 7,* 389–400.

Paulus, P. B. (1988). *Prison crowding: A psychological perspective.* New York: Springer-Verlag.

Paulus, P. B. (2000). Groups, teams, and creativity: The creative potential of idea-generating groups. *Applied Psychology: An International Review, 49,* 237–262.

Paulus, P. B., & Brown, V. R. (2003). Enhancing ideational creativity in groups: Lessons from research on brainstorming. In P. B. Paulus & B. A. Nijstad (Eds.), *Group creativity: Innovation through collaboration* (pp. 110–136). New York: Oxford University Press.

Paulus, P. B., & Paulus, L. E. (1997). Implications of research on group brainstorming for gifted education. *Roeper Review, 19,* 225–229.

Paulus, P. B., Dzindolet, M. T., Poletes, G., & Camacho, L. M. (1993). Perception of performance in group brainstorming: The illusion of group productivity. *Personality and Social Psychology Bulletin, 19,* 78–89.

Paulus, P. B., Larey, T. S., Putman, V. L., & Leggett, K. L. (1996). Social influence processes in computer brainstorming. *Basic and Applied Social Psychology, 18,* 3–14.

Paulus, P. B., Nakui, T., Putman, V. L., & Brown, V. (2006). Effects of task instructions and brief breaks on brainstorming. *Group Dynamics: Theory, Research, and Practice, 10,* 206–219.

Pavitt, C. (1994). Another view of group polarizing: The "reasons for" one-sided oral argumentation. *Communication Research, 21,* 625–642.

Pavot, W., & Diener, E. (1993). Review of the Satisfaction with Life Scale. *Psychological Assessment, 5,* 164–172.

Pawlowski, B., Dunbar, R. I. M., & Lipowicz, A. (2000). Evolutionary fitness: Tall men have more reproductive success. *Nature, 403,* 156.

Payne, B. K. (2001). Prejudice and perception: The role of automatic and controlled processes in misperceiving a weapon. *Journal of Personality and Social Psychology, 81,* 181–192.

Payne, B. K., Cheng, C. M., Govorun, O., & Stewart, B. D. (2005). An inkblot for attitudes: Affect misattribution as implicit measurement. *Journal of Personality and Social Psychology, 89,* 277–293.

Pedersen, W. C., Gonzales, C., & Miller, N. (2000). The moderating effect of trivial triggering provocation on displaced aggression. *Journal of Personality and Social Psychology, 78,* 913–927.

Pedersen, W. C., Miller, L. C., Putch-Bhagavatula, A. D., & Yang, Y. (2002). Evolved sex differences in the number of partners desired? The long and the short of it. *Psychological Science, 13,* 157–161.

Pelham, B. W. (1995). Self-investment and self-esteem: Evidence for a Jamesian model of self-worth. *Journal of Personality and Social Psychology, 69,* 1141–1150.

Pelham, B. W., & Swann, W. B., Jr. (1989). From self-conceptions to self-worth: The sources and structure of self-esteem. *Journal of Personality and Social Psychology, 57,* 672–680.

Pelham, B. W., Mirenberg, M. C., & Jones, J. T. (2002). Why Susie sells seashells by the seashore: Implicit egotism and major life decisions. *Journal of Personality and Social Psychology, 82,* 469–487.

Pendry, L. F., & Macrae, C. N. (1994). Stereotypes and mental life: The case of the motivated but thwarted tactician. *Journal of Experimental Social Psychology, 30,* 303–325.

Pendry, L. F., & Macrae, C. N. (1996). What the disinterested perceiver overlooks: Goal-directed social categorization. *Personality and Social Psychology Bulletin, 22,* 249–256.

Peng, K., & Knowles, E. D. (2003). Culture, education, and the attribution of physical causality. *Personality and Social Psychology Bulletin, 29,* 1272–1284.

Pennebaker, J. W. (1997). *Opening up: The healing power of expressing emotions.* New York: Guilford Press.

Pennebaker, J. W. (1997). Writing about emotional experiences as a therapeutic process. *Psychological Science, 8,* 162–166.

Pennebaker, J. W., Colder, M., & Sharp, L. K. (1990). Accelerating the coping process. *Journal of Personality and Social Psychology, 58,* 528–537.

Pennebaker, J. W., Dyer, M. A., Caulkins, R. J., Litowitz, D. L., Ackreman, P. L., Anderson, D. B., & McGraw, K. M. (1979). Don't the girls get prettier at closing time: A country and western application to psychology. *Personality and Social Psychology Bulletin, 5,* 122–125.

Penner, L. A. (2004). Volunteerism and social problems: Making things better or worse? *Journal of Social Issues, 60,* 645–666.

Penner, L. A., & Fritzsche, B. A. (1993). Magic Johnson and reactions to people with AIDS: A natural experiment. *Journal of Applied Social Psychology, 23,* 1035–1050.

Penner, L. A., Dovidio, J. F., Piliavin, J. A., & Schroeder, D. A. (2005). Prosocial behavior: Multiple perspectives. *Annual Review of Psychology, 56,* 365–392.

Pennington, N., & Hastie, R. (1992). Explaining the evidence: Tests of the story model for juror decision making. *Journal of Personality and Social Psychology, 62,* 189–206.

Penrod, S. D., & Cutler, B. (1995). Witness confidence and witness accuracy: Assessing their forensic relation. *Psychology, Public Policy, and Law, 1,* 817–845.

People (1996, December 30). She gave a helping hand to a distant—very distant—relation. p. 66.

Peplau, L. A. (2003). Human sexuality: How do men and women differ? *Current Directions in Psychological Science, 12,* 37–40.

Peplau, L. A., & Fingerhut, A. W. (2007). The close relationships of lesbians and gay men. *Annual Review of Psychology, 58,* 405–424.

Peplau, L. A., & Perlman, D. (Eds.). (1982). *Loneliness: A sourcebook of current theory, research, and therapy.* New York: Wiley.

Peplau, L. A., Garnets, L. D., Spalding, L. R., Conley, T. D., & Veniegas, R. C. (1998). A critique of Bem's "Exotic becomes erotic" theory of sexual orientation. *Psychological Review, 105,* 387–394.

Pepler D., Craig, W., Yuile, A., & Connolly, J. (2004). Girls who bully: A developmental and relational perspective. In M. Putallaz & K. L. Bierman (Eds.), *Aggression, antisocial behavior, and violence among girls: A developmental perspective* (pp. 90–109). New York: Guilford.

Pepler, D. J., & Craig, W. M. (1995). A peek behind the fence: Naturalistic observations of aggressive children with remote audiovisual recording. *Developmental Psychology, 31,* 548–553.

Pepler, D. J., Craig, W. M., Connolly, J. A., Yuile, A., McMaster, L., & Jiang, D. (2006). A developmental perspective on bullying. *Aggressive Behavior, 32,* 376–384.

Perdue, C. W., Dovidio, J. F., Gurtman, M. B., & Tyler, R. B. (1990). Us and them: Social categorization and the process of intergroup bias. *Journal of Personality and Social Psychology, 59,* 475–486.

Perloff, R. M. (2003). *The dynamics of persuasion: Communication and attitudes in the 21st century.* Mahwah, NJ: Erlbaum.

Persky, V. W., Kempthorne-Rawson, J., & Shekelle, R. B. (1987). Personality and risk of cancer: 20-year follow-up of the Western Electric Study. *Psychosomatic Medicine, 49,* 435–449.

Peruche, B. M., & Plant, E. A. (2006). The correlates of law enforcement officers' automatic and controlled race-based responses to criminal suspects. *Basic and Applied Social Psychology, 28,* 193–199.

Peters, T. J., & Waterman, R. H. (1982). *In search of excellence: Lessons from America's best-run companies.* New York: Warner.

Peterson, C. (2000). The future of optimism. *American Psychologist, 55,* 44–55.

Peterson, C., Seligman, M. E. P., & Vaillant, G. E. (1988). Pessimistic explanatory style is a risk factor for physical illness: A thirty-five-year longitudinal study. *Journal of Personality and Social Psychology, 55,* 23–27.

Peterson, K. S. (1997, November 3). For today's teens, race "not an issue anymore." *USA Today,* p. 1A.

Peterson, R. S., Owens, P. D., Tetlock, P. E., Fan, E. T., & Martorana, P. (1998). Group dynamics in top management teams: Groupthink, vigilance, and alternative models of organizational failure and success. *Organizational Behavior and Human Decision Processes, 73,* 272–305.

Petrie, K. J., Booth, R. J., & Pennebaker, J. W. (1998). The immunological effects of thought suppression. *Journal of Personality and Social Psychology, 75,* 1264–1272.

Pettigrew, T. F. (1958). Personality and sociocultural factors in intergroup attitudes: A cross-national comparison. *Journal of Conflict Resolution, 2,* 29–42.

Pettigrew, T. F. (1998a). Intergroup contact theory. *Annual Review of Psychology, 49,* 65–85.

Pettigrew, T. F. (1998b). Reactions toward the new minorities of Western Europe. *Annual Review of Sociology, 24,* 77–103.

Pettigrew, T. F., & Martin, J. (1987). Shaping the organizational context for black American inclusion. *Journal of Social Issues, 43,* 41–78.

Pettigrew, T. F., & Meertens, R. W. (1995). Subtle and blatant prejudice in western Europe. *European Journal of Social Psychology, 25,* 57–75.

Pettigrew, T. F., & Tropp, L. R. (2000). Does intergroup contact reduce prejudice: Recent meta-analytic findings. In S. Oskamp (Ed.), *Reducing prejudice and discrimination: The Claremont Symposium on Applied Social Psychology* (pp. 93–114). Mahwah, NJ: Erlbaum.

Pettigrew, T. F., & Tropp, L. R. (2006). A meta-analytic test of intergroup contact theory. *Journal of Personality and Social Psychology, 90,* 751–783.

Petty, R. E., & Cacioppo, J. T. (1983). The role of bodily responses in attitude measurement and change. In J. Cacioppo & R. Petty (Eds.), *Social psychophysiology: A sourcebook* (pp. 51–101). New York: Guilford.

Petty, R. E., & Cacioppo, J. T. (1984). The effects of involvement on response to argument quantity and quality: Central and peripheral routes to persuasion. *Journal of Personality and Social Psychology, 46,* 69–81.

Petty, R. E., & Cacioppo, J. T. (1986). *Communication and persuasion: Central and peripheral routes to attitude change.* New York: Springer-Verlag.

Petty, R. E., & Chaiken, S. (Eds.). (2004). *Key readings in attitudes and persuasion.* London: Taylor & Francis.

Petty, R. E., & Krosnick, J. A. (Eds.). (1995). *Attitude strength: Antecedents and consequences.* Mahwah, NJ: Erlbaum.

Petty, R. E., & Wegener, D. T. (1999). The Elaboration Likelihood Model: Current status and controversies. In S. Chaiken & Y. Trope (Eds.), *Dual-process theories in social psychology* (pp. 41–72). New York: Guilford.

Petty, R. E., Cacioppo, J. T., & Goldman, R. (1981). Personal involvement as a determinant of argument-based persuasion. *Journal of Personality and Social Psychology, 41,* 847–855.

Petty, R. E., Fazio, R. H., & Brinol, P. (Eds.). *Attitudes: Insights from the new wave of implicit measures.* Mahwah, NJ: Erlbaum, in press.

Petty, R. E., Schumann, D. W., Richman, S. A., & Strathman, A. J. (1993). Positive mood and persuasion: Different roles for affect under high- and low-elaboration conditions. *Journal of Personality and Social Psychology, 64,* 5–20.

Petty, R. E., Wegener, D. T., & Fabrigar, L. R. (1997). Attitudes and attitude change. *Annual Review of Psychology, 48,* 609–647.

Petty, R. E., Wegener, D. T., & White, P. (1998). Flexible correction processes in persuasion. *Social Cognition, 16,* 93–113.

Pezdek, K., Blandon-Gitlin, I., & Moore, C. (2003). Children's face recognition memory: More evidence for the cross-race effect. *Journal of Applied Psychology, 88,* 760–763.

Pfau, M., Kenski, H. C., Nitz, M., & Sorenson, J. (1990). Efficacy of inoculation strategies in promoting resistance to political attack messages: Application to direct mail. *Communication Monographs, 57,* 25–43.

Phelps, E. A., O'Connor, K. J., Cunningham, W. A., Funayama, E. S., Gatenby, J. C., Gore, J. C., & Banaji, M. R. (2000). Performance on indirect measures of race evaluation predicts amygdala activation. *Journal of Cognitive Neuroscience, 12,* 729–738

Philippot, P. (2005). Stereotyping and action tendencies attribution as a function of available emotional information. *European Journal of Social Psychology, 35,* 517–536.

Phillips, A. G., & Silvia, P. J. (2005). Self-awareness and the emotional consequences of self-discrepancies. *Personality and Social Psychology Bulletin, 31,* 703–713.

Phillips, A. P., & Dipboye, R. L. (1989). Correlational tests of predictions from a process model of the interview. *Journal of Applied Psychology, 74,* 41–52.

Pickel, K. L. (1999). The influence of context on the "weapon focus" effect. *Law and Human Behavior, 23,* 299–311.

Pickett, C. L., & Brewer, M. B. (2001). Assimilation and differentiation needs as motivational determinants of perceived ingroup and out-group homogeneity. *Journal of Experimental Social Psychology, 37,* 341–348.

Piferi, R. L., Jobe, R. L., Jones, W. H., & Gaines, S. O., Jr. (2006). Giving to others during national tragedy: The effects of altruistic and egoistic motivations on long-term giving. *Journal of Social and Personal Relationships, 23,* 171–184.

Pihl, R. O., Lau, M. L., & Assaad, J. M. (1997). Aggressive disposition, alcohol, and aggression. *Aggressive Behavior, 23,* 11–18.

Piliavin, J. A. (2003). Doing well by doing good: Benefits for the benefactor. In C. L. M. Keyes & J. Haidt (Eds.), *Flourishing: Positive psychology and the life well-lived* (pp. 227–247). Washington, DC: American Psychological Association.

Piliavin, J. A., & Callero, P. L. (1991). *Giving blood: The development of an altruistic identity.* Baltimore: Johns Hopkins.

Piliavin, J. A., Dovidio, J. F., Gaertner, S. L., & Clark, R. D., III. (1981). *Emergency intervention.* New York: Academic Press.

Piliavin, J. A., Grube, J. A., & Callero, P. L. (2002). Role as a resource for action in public service. *Journal of Social Issues, 58,* 469–485.

Pillai, R., & Willams, E. A. (2004). Transformational leadership, self-efficacy, group cohesiveness, commitment, and performance. *Journal of Organizational Change Management, 17,* 144–159.

Pillemer, D. B., Picariello, M. L., Law, A. B., & Reichman, J. S. (1996). Memories of college: The importance of educational episodes. In D. C. Rubin (Ed.), *Remembering our past: Studies in autobiographical memory* (pp. 318–337). New York: Cambridge University Press.

Pinderhughes, E. E., Dodge, K. A., Bates, J. E.. Pettit, G. S., & Zelli, A. (2000). Discipline responses: Influences of parents' socioeconomic status, ethnicity, beliefs about parenting, stress, and cognitive-emotional processes. *Journal of Family Psychology, 14,* 380–400.

Pinel, E. C., Long, A. E., Landau, M. J., Alexander, K., & Pyszczynski, T. (2006). Seeing I to I: A pathway to interpersonal connectedness. *Journal of Personality and Social Psychology, 90,* 243–257.

Pittman, T. S. (1975). Attribution of arousal as a mediator of dissonance reduction. *Journal of Experimental Social Psychology, 11,* 53–63.

Pittman, T. S., & Heller, J. F. (1987). Social motivation. *Annual Review of Psychology, 38,* 461–489.

Plaks, J. E., & Higgins, E. T. (2000). Pragmatic use of stereotyping in teamwork: Social loafing and compensation as a function of inferred partner-situation fit. *Journal of Personality and Social Psychology, 79,* 962–974.

Plant, E. A. (2004). Responses to interracial interactions over time. *Personality and Social Psychology Bulletin, 30,* 1458–1471.

Plant, E. A., & Butz, D. A. (2006). The causes and consequences of an avoidance-focus for interracial interactions. *Personality and Social Psychology Bulletin, 32,* 833–846.

Plant, E. A., & Devine, P. G. (1998). Internal and external motivation to respond without prejudice. *Journal of Personality and Social Psychology, 75,* 811–832.

Plant, E. A., Devine, P. G., & Brazy, P. C. (2003). The bogus pipeline and motivations to respond without prejudice: Revisiting the fading and faking of racial prejudice. *Group Processes and Intergroup Relations, 6,* 187–200.

Plant, E. A., Peruche, B. M., & Butz, D. A. (2005). Eliminating automatic racial bias: Making race non-diagnostic for responses to criminal suspects. *Journal of Experimental Social Psychology, 41,* 141–156.

Platek, S. M., et al. (2006). Neural substrates for functionally discriminating self-face from personally familiar faces. *Human Brain Mapping, 27,* 91–98.

Platow, M. J., Byrne, L., & Ryan, M. K. (2005). Experimentally manipulated high in-group status can buffer personal self-esteem against discrimination. *European Journal of Social Psychology, 35,* 599–608.

Platz, S. J., & Hosch, H. M. (1988). Cross-racial/ethnic eyewitness identification: A field study. *Journal of Applied Social Psychology, 18,* 972–984.

Polivy, J., Garner, D. M., & Garfinkel, P. E. (1986). Causes and consequences of the current preference for thin female physiques. In C. P. Herman, M. P. Zanna, & E. T. Higgins (Eds.), *The Ontario symposium: Vol. 3. Physical appearance, stigma, and social behavior* (pp. 89–112). Hillsdale, NJ: Erlbaum.

Pontari, B. A., & Schlenker, B. R. (2000). The influence of cognitive load on self-presentation: Can cognitive busyness help as well as harm social performance? *Journal of Personality and Social Psychology, 78,* 1092–1108.

Poole, D. A., & Lamb, M. E. (1998). *Investigative interviews of children: A guide for helping professionals.* Washington, DC: American Psychological Association.

Poole, D. A., & White, L. T. (1991). Effects of question repetition on the eyewitness testimony of children and adults. *Developmental Psychology, 27,* 975–986.

Poole, D., & Lindsay, D. S. (2001). Children's eyewitness reports after exposure to misinformation from parents. *Journal of Experimental Psychology: Applied, 7,* 27–50.

Pooley, E. (1997, June 16). Death or life? *Time,* pp. 30–36.

Pope, H. G., Jr., Phillips, K. A., & Olivardia, R. (2000). *The Adonis complex: The secret crisis of male body obsession.* New York: Free Press.

Poppen, P. J., & Segal, N. J. (1988). The influence of sex and sex role orientation on sexual coercion. *Sex Roles, 19,* 689–701.

Pornpitakpan, C. (2004). The persuasiveness of source credibility: A critical review of five decades' evidence. *Journal of Applied Social Psychology, 34,* 243–281.

Porter, D. P., & Smith, V. L. (2003). Stock market bubbles in the laboratory. *Journal of Behavioral Finance, 4,* 7–20.

Posavac, H. D., Posavac, S. S., & Posavac, E. J. (1998). Exposure to media images of female attractiveness and concern with body weight among young women. *Sex Roles, 38,* 187–201.

Post, S. G. (2005). Altruism, happiness, and health: It's good to be good. *International Journal of Behavioral Medicine, 12,* 66–77.

Postmes, T., & Spears, R. (2002). Behavior online: Does anonymous computer communication reduce gender inequality? *Personality and Social Psychology Bulletin, 28,* 1073–1083.

Postmes, T., Spears, R., & Cihangir, S. (2001). Quality of decision making and group norms. *Journal of Personality and Social Psychology, 80,* 918–930.

Postmes, T., Spears, R., & Lea, M. (2002). Intergroup differentiation in computer-mediated communication: Effects of depersonalization. *Group Dynamics, 6,* 3–16.

Povinelli, D. J., Gallup, G. G., Jr., Eddy, T. J., Bierschwale, D. T., Engstrom, M. C., Perilloux, H. K., & Toxopeus, I. B. (1997). Chimpanzees recognize themselves in mirrors. *Animal Behaviour, 53,* 1083–1088.

Powell, L. H., Shahabi, L., & Thoresen, C. E. (2003). Religion and spirituality: Linkages to physical health. *American Psychologist, 58,* 36–52.

Powers, S. I., Pietromonaco, P. R., Gunlicks, M., & Sayer, A. (2006). Dating couples' attachment styles and patterns of cortisol reactivity and recovery in response to a relationship conflict. *Journal of Personality and Social Psychology, 90,* 613–628.

Powlishta, K. K. (1995). Intergroup processes in childhood: Social categorization and sex role development. *Developmental Psychology, 31,* 781–788.

Prapavessis, H., & Carron, A. V. (1997). Sacrifice, cohesion, and conformity to norms in sport teams. *Group Dynamics, 1,* 231–240.

Pratkanis, A. R. (1992). The cargo-cult science of subliminal persuasion. *Skeptical Inquirer, 16,* 260–272.

Pratkanis, A. R., & Turner, M. E. (1994). Nine principles of successful affirmative action: Mr. Branch Rickey, Mr. Jackie Robinson, and the integration of baseball. *Nine: A Journal of Baseball History and Social Policy Perspectives, 3,* 36–65.

Pratkanis, A. R., & Turner, M. E. (1996). The proactive removal of discriminatory barriers: Affirmative action as effective help. *Journal of Social Issues, 52,* 111–132.

Pratkanis, A. R., Greenwald, A. G., Leippe, M. R., & Baumgardner, M. H. (1988). In search of reliable persuasion effects: III. The sleeper effect is dead. Long live the sleeper effect. *Journal of Personality and Social Psychology, 54,* 203–218.

Pratto, F., & John, O. P. (1991). Automatic vigilance: The attention-grabbing power of negative social information. *Journal of Personality and Social Psychology, 61,* 380–391.

Pratto, F., Stallworth, L. M., Sidanius, J., & Sieres, B. (1997). The gender gap in occupational attainment: A social dominance approach. *Journal of Personality and Social Psychology, 72,* 37–53.

Prentice, D. A., & Carranza, E. (2002). What women should be, shouldn't be, are allowed to be, and don't have to be: The contents of prescriptive gender stereotypes. *Psychology of Women Quarterly, 26,* 269–281.

Prentice, D. A., & Miller, D. T. (1996). Pluralistic ignorance and the perpetuation of social norms by unwitting actors. *Advances in Experimental Social Psychology, 28,* 161–209.

Prentice-Dunn, S., & Rogers, R. W. (1982). Effects of public and private self-awareness on deindividuation and aggression. *Journal of Personality and Social Psychology, 43,* 503–513.

Prentice-Dunn, S., & Rogers, R. W. (1983). Deindividuation in aggression. In R. G. Geen & E. I. Donnerstein (Eds.), *Aggression:*

Theoretical and empirical reviews: Vol. 2. Issues in research (pp. 155–171). New York: Academic Press.

President's Commission on Law Enforcement and Administration of Justice. (1967). *The challenge of crime in a free society.* Washington, DC: U.S. Government Printing Office.

Pressman, S. D., Cohen, S., Miller, G. E., Barkin, A., Rabin, B. S., & Treanor, J. J. (2005). Loneliness, social network size, and immune response to influenza vaccination in college freshmen. *Health Psychology, 24,* 297–306.

Preston, S. D., & de Waal, F. B. M. (2002). Empathy: Its ultimate and proximate bases. *Behavioral and Brain Sciences, 25,* 1–72.

Price, S. L. (1997, December 8). What ever happened to the White athlete? *Sports Illustrated,* pp. 30–55.

Priester, J. R., & Petty, R. E. (1995). Source attributions and persuasion: Perceived honesty as a determinant of message scrutiny. *Personality and Social Psychology Bulletin, 21,* 637–654.

Priester, J. R., Cacioppo, J. T., & Petty, R. E. (1996). The influence of motor processes on attitudes toward novel versus familiar semantic stimuli. *Personality and Social Psychology Bulletin, 22,* 442–447.

Principe, G. F., & Ceci, S. J. (2002). "I saw it with my own ears": The effects of peer conversations on preschoolers' reports of nonexperienced events. *Journal of Experimental Child Psychology, 83,* 1–25.

Principe, G. F., Ornstein, P. A., Baker-Ward, L., & Gordon, B. N. (2000). The effects of intervening experiences on children's memory for a physical examination. *Applied Cognitive Psychology 14,* 59–80.

Prioleau, L., Murdock, M., & Brody, N. (1983). An analysis of psychotherapy versus placebo studies. *Behavioral and Brain Sciences, 6,* 275–310.

Pronin, E., Gilovich, T., & Ross, L. (2004). Objectivity in the eye of the beholder: Divergent perceptions of bias in self versus others. *Psychological Review, 111,* 781–799.

Pronin, E., Steele, C. M., & Ross, L. (2004). Identity bifurcation in response to stereotype threat: Women and mathematics. *Journal of Experimental Social Psychology, 40,* 152–168.

Pronin, E., Wegner, D. M., McCarthy, K., & Rodriguez, S. (2006). Everyday magical powers: The role of apparent mental causation in the overestimation of personal influence. *Journal of Personality and Social Psychology, 91,* 218–231.

Proto-Campise, L., Belknap, J., & Wooldredge, J. (1998). High school students' adherence to rape myths and the effectiveness of high school rape-awareness programs. *Violence Against Women, 4,* 308–328.

Pruitt, D. G. (1998). Social conflict. In D. T. Gilbert, S. T. Fiske, & G. Lindzey (Eds.), *The handbook of social psychology* (4th ed., Vol. 2, pp. 410–503). New York: McGraw-Hill.

Pryor, J. B., & Merluzzi, T. V. (1985). The role of expertise in processing social interaction scripts. *Journal of Experimental Social Psychology, 21,* 362–379.

Pryor, J.B., & McKinney, K. (1995). Research advances in sexual harassment: Introduction and overview. *Basic and Applied Social Psychology, 17,* 605–611.

Putnam, R. D. (2001). *Bowling alone: The collapse and revival of American community.* New York: Simon & Schuster.

Putnam, R. D. (2006). You gotta have friends. *Time,* July 3, 2006, p. 36.

Pyszczynski, T. A., Solomon, S., & Greenberg, J. (2002). *In the wake of 9/11: The psychology of terror.* Washington, DC: American Psychological Association.

Pyszczynski, T., & Greenberg, J. (1987). Self-regulatory preservation and the depressive self-focusing style: A self-awareness theory of reactive depression. *Psychological Bulletin, 201,* 122–138.

Pyszczynski, T., & Greenberg, J. (1992). *Hanging on and letting go.* New York: Springer-Verlag.

Pyszczynski, T., Greenberg, J., Solomon, S., Arndt, J., & Schimel, J. (2004). Why do people need self-esteem? A theoretical and empirical review. *Psychological Bulletin, 130,* 435–468.

Qualter, T. H. (1962). *Propaganda and psychological warfare.* New York: Random House.

Quattrone, G. A. (1986). On the perception of a group's variability. In S. Worchel & W. G. Austin (Eds.), *Psychology of intergroup relations* (2nd ed., pp. 25–48). Chicago: Nelson Hall.

Quigley, B. M., & Leonard, K. E. (2006). Alcohol expectancies and intoxicated aggression. *Aggression and Violent Behavior, 11,* 484–496.

Quinn, D. M., Kahng, S. K., & Crocker, J. (2004). Discreditable: Stigma effects of revealing a mental illness history on test performance. *Personality and Social Psychology Bulletin, 30,* 803-815.

Radar Online. (2006). http:www.radaronline.com/features/misc_content/060908_japan/index.php.

Ragins, B. R., & Sundstrom, E. (1989). Gender and power in organizations: A longitudinal perspective. *Psychological Bulletin, 105,* 51–88.

Rains, S. A. (2005). Leveling the organizational playing field—virtually: A meta-analysis of experimental research assessing the impact of group support system use on member influence behaviors. *Communication Research, 32,* 193–234.

Rajecki, D. W., Bledsoe, S. B., & Rasmussen, J. L. (1991). Successful personal ads: Gender differences and similarities in offers, stipulations, and outcomes. *Basic and Applied Social Psychology, 12,* 457–469.

Raskin, D. C. (1986). The polygraph in 1986: Scientific, professional, and legal issues surrounding application and acceptance of polygraph evidence. *Utah Law Review, 1,* 29–74.

Ray, O. (2004). How the mind hurts and heals the body. *American Psychologist, 59,* 29–40.

Read, S. J. (1987). Constructing causal scenarios: A knowledge structure approach to causal reasoning. *Journal of Personality and Social Psychology, 52,* 288–302.

Read, S. J., & Urada, D. I. (2003). A neural network simulation of the outgroup homogeneity effect. *Personality and Social Psychology Review, 7,* 146–159.

Reeder, G. D. (1993). Trait-behavior relations and dispositional inference. *Personality and Social Psychology Bulletin, 19,* 586–593.

Reeder, G. D., & Brewer, M. B. (1979). A schematic model of dispositional attribution in interpersonal perception. *Psychological Review, 86,* 61–79.

Reeder, G. D., Davison, D. M., Gipson, K. L., & Hesson-McInnis, M. S. (2001). Identifying the motivations of African American volunteers working to prevent HIV/AIDS. *AIDS Education and Prevention, 13,* 343–354.

Regan, D. T. (1971). Effects of a favor and liking on compliance. *Journal of Experimental Social Psychology, 7,* 627–639.

Regan, D. T., & Kilduff, M. (1988). Optimism about elections: Dissonance reduction at the ballot box. *Political Psychology, 9,* 101–107.

Regan, P. C., & Berscheid, E. (1997). Gender differences in characteristics desired in a potential sexual and marriage partner. *Journal of Psychology and Human Sexuality, 9,* 25–37.

Regan, P. C., & Berscheid, E. (1999). *Lust: What we know about human sexual desire.* Thousand Oaks, CA: Sage.

Regan, P. C., Kocan, E. R., & Whitlock, T. (1998). Ain't love grand! A prototype analysis of the concept of romantic love. *Journal of Social and Personal Relationships, 15,* 411–420.

Reicher, S. D. (2001). The St. Pauls' riot: An explanation of the limits of crowd action in terms of a social identity model. In M. A. Hogg & D. Abrams (Eds.), *Intergroup relations: Essential readings. Key readings in social psychology* (pp. 302–315). Philadelphia: Psychology Press.

Reifman, A. S., Larrick, R. P., & Fein, S. (1991). Temper and temperature on the diamond: The heat-aggression relationship in major-league baseball. *Personality and Social Psychology Bulletin, 17,* 580–585.

Reifman, A., Klein, J. G., & Murphy, S. T. (1989). Self-monitoring and age. *Psychology and Aging, 4,* 245–246.

Reinhard, M-A., Messner, M., & Sporer, S. L. (2006). Explicit persuasive intent and its impact on success at persuasion: The determining roles of attractiveness and likeableness. *Journal of Consumer Psychology, 16,* 249–259.

Reisenzein, R. (1983). The Schachter theory of emotion: Two decades later. *Psychological Bulletin, 94,* 239–264.

Reiss, D., & Marino, L. (2001). Mirror self-recognition in the bottlenose dolphin: A case of cognitive convergence. *Proceedings of the National Academy of the Sciences, 98,* 5937–5942.

Remley, A. (1988, October). The great parental value shift: From obedience to independence. *Psychology Today,* 56–59.

Rendell, L., & Whitehead, H. (2001). Culture in whales and dolphins. *Behavioral and Brain Sciences, 24,* 309–382.

Renfrew, J. W. (1997). *Aggression and its causes: A biopsychosocial approach.* New York: Oxford University Press.

Renteln, A. D. (2004). *The Cultural Defense.* New York: Oxford University Press.

Rentfrow, P. J., & Gosling, S. D. (2006). Message in a ballad: The role of music preferences in interpersonal perception. *Psychological Science, 17,* 236–242.

Report of the Presidential Commission on the Space Shuttle Challenger Accident. (1986, June 6). Washington, D.C., U.S. Government Printing Office.

Responsible citizenship. (2002, December 31). *Ottawa Citizen,* p. A14.

Reynolds, B., & Karraker, K. (2003). A "Big Five" model of disposition and situation interaction: Why a "helpful" person may not always behave helpfully. *New Ideas in Psychology, 21,* 1–13.

Rhatigan, D. L., & Axsom, D. K. (2006). Using the investment model to understand battered women's commitment to abusive relationships. *Journal of Family Violence, 21,* 153–162.

Rhee, E., Uleman, J. S., Lee, H. K., & Roman, R. J. (1995). Spontaneous self-descriptions and ethnic identities in individualistic and collectivistic cultures. *Journal of Personality and Social Psychology, 69,* 142–152.

Rhoden, W. C. (1996, December 24). A two-hour psychological test turns into Giants' lightning rod. *New York Times,* pp. B1, B10.

Rhodes, G. (2006). The evolutionary psychology of facial beauty. *Annual Review of Psychology, 57,* 199–226.

Rhodes, G., Simmons, L. W., & Peters, M. (2005). Attractiveness and sexual behavior: Does attractiveness enhance mating success? *Evolution and Human Behavior, 26,* 186–201.

Rhodes, G., Sumich, A., & Byatt, G. (1999). Are average facial configurations attractive only because of their symmetry? *Psychological Science, 10,* 52–58.

Rhodes, G., Zebrowitz, L. A., Clark, A., Kalick, S. M., Hightower, A., & McKay, R. (2001). Do facial averageness and symmetry signal health? *Evolution and Human Behavior, 22,* 31–46.

Rhodes, N., & Wood, W. (1992). Self-esteem and intelligence affect influenceability: The mediating role of message reception. *Psychological Bulletin, 111,* 156–171.

Rhodewalt, F. (1990). Self-handicappers: Individual differences in the preference for anticipatory, self-protective acts. In R. L. Higgins, C. R. Synder, & S. Berglas (Eds.), *Self-handicapping: The paradox that isn't* (pp. 69–106). New York: Plenum.

Rhodewalt, F., & Agustsdottir, S. (1986). Effects of self-presentation on the phenomenal self. *Journal of Personality and Social Psychology, 50,* 47–55.

Rhodewalt, F., Sandonmatsu, D. M., Tschanz, B., Feick, D. L., & Waller, A. (1995). Self-handicapping and interpersonal trade-offs: The effects of claimed self-handicaps on observers' performance evaluations and feedback. *Personality and Social Psychology Bulletin, 21,* 1042–1050.

Rholes, W. S., & Simpson, J. A. (Eds.). (2004). *Adult attachment: Theory, research, and clinical implications.* New York: Guilford.

Ricciardelli, L. A., McCabe, M. P., & Banfield, S. (2000). Sociocultural influences on body image and body change methods. *Journal of Adolescent Health, 26,* 3–4.

Richardson, M. J., Marsh, K. L., & Schmidt, R. C. (2005). Effects of visual and verbal interaction on unintentional interpersonal coordination. *Journal of Experimental Psychology: Human Perception and Performance, 31,* 62–79.

Richeson, J. A., & Shelton, J. N. (2003). When prejudice does not pay: Effects of interracial contact on executive function. *Psychological Science, 14,* 287–290.

Richeson, J. A., & Trawalter, S. (2005). Why do interracial interactions impair executive function? A resource depletion account. *Journal of Personality and Social Psychology, 88,* 934–947.

Richeson, J. A., Baird, A. A., Gordon, H. L., Heatherton, T. F., Wyland, C. L., Trawalter, S., & Shelton, J. N. (2003). An fMRI investigation of the impact of interracial contact on executive function. *Nature Neuroscience, 6,* 1323–1328.

Richeson, J. A., Trawalter, S., & Shelton, J. N. (2005). African Americans' implicit racial attitudes and the depletion of executive function after interracial interactions. *Social Cognition, 23,* 336–352.

Rieger, G., Chivers, M. L., & Bailey, J. M. (2005). Sexual arousal patterns of bisexual men. *Psychological Science, 16,* 579–584.

Rilling, J. K., Gutman, D. A., Zeh, T. R., Pagnoni, G., Berns, G. S., & Kilts, C. D. (2002). A neural basis for social cooperation. *Neuron, 35,* 395–405.

Rind, B., & Strohmetz, D. B. (2001). Effect on restaurant tipping of a helpful message written on the back of customers' checks. *Journal of Applied Social Psychology, 31,* 1379–1384.

Ringelmann, M. (1913). Recherches sur les moteurs animés: Travail de l'homme. *Annales de l'Institut National Agronomique,* 2e série, tom XII, 1–40.

Riniolo, T. C., Johnson, K. C., Sherman, T. R., & Misso, J. A. (2006). Hot or not: Do professors perceived as physically attractive receive higher student evaluations? *Journal of General Psychology, 133,* 19–35.

Roane, K. R. (2000, February 28). Boston's big-bucks highway to hell. *U.S. News and World Report,* p. 34.

Robins, R. W., Hendin, H. M., & Trzesniewski, K. H. (2001). Measuring global self-esteem: Construct validation of a single-item measure and the Rosenberg self-esteem scale. *Personality and Social Psychology Bulletin, 27,* 151–161.

Robins, R. W., Mendelsohn, G. A., Connell, J. B., & Kwan, V. S. Y. (2004). Do people agree about the causes of behavior? A social relations analysis of behavior ratings and causal attributions. *Journal of Personality and Social Psychology, 86,* 334–344.

Robinson, I., Ziss, K., Ganza, B., Katz, S, & Robinson, E. (1991). Twenty years of the sexual revolution, 1965–1985: An update. *Journal of Marriage and the Family, 53,* 216–220.

Robinson, J. P., Shaver, P. R., & Wrightsman, L. S. (Eds.). (1991). *Measures of personality and social psychological attitudes.* New York: Academic Press.

Robinson, J. P., Shaver, P. R., & Wrightsman, L. S. (Eds.). (1998). *Measures of political attitudes.* New York: Academic Press.

Robles, T. F., Glaser, R., & Kiecolt-Glaser, J. K. (2005). Out of balance. A new look at chronic stress, depression, and immunity. *Current Directions in Psychological Science, 14,* 111–115.

Roccas, S. (2003). Identification and status revisited: The moderating role of self-enhancement and self-transcendence values. *Personality and Social Psychology Bulletin, 29,* 726–736.

Rodin, J. (1986). Aging and health: Effects of the sense of control. *Science, 233,* 1271–1276.

Rodkin, P. C., Farmer, T. W., Pearl, R., & van Acker, R. (2000). Heterogeneity of popular boys: Antisocial and prosocial configurations. *Developmental Psychology, 36,* 14–24.

Rodrigues, A., Assmar, E. M. L., & Jablonski, B. (2005). Social-psychology and the invasion of Iraq. *Revista de Psicologia Social, 20,* 387–398.

Roesch, S. C., & Amirkhan, J. H. (1997). Boundary conditions for self-serving attributions: Another look at the sports pages. *Journal of Applied Social Psychology, 27,* 245–261.

Roese, N. J. (1997). Counterfactual thinking. *Psychological Bulletin, 121,* 133–148.

Roese, N. J., & Jamieson, D. W. (1993). Twenty years of bogus pipeline research: A critical review and meta-analysis. *Psychological Bulletin, 114,* 363–375.

Roese, N. J., & Olson, J. M. (Eds.). (1995). *What might have been: The social psychology of counterfactual thinking.* Hillsdale, NJ: Erlbaum.

Roese, N. J., & Summerville, A. (2005). What we regret most . . . and why. *Personality and Social Psychology Bulletin, 31,* 1273–1285.

Roethlisberger, F. J., & Dickson, W. J. (1939). *Management and the worker.* Cambridge, MA: Harvard University Press.

Rofé, Y. (1984). Stress and affiliation: A utility theory. *Psychological Review, 91,* 235–250.

Rogers, M., Miller, N., Mayer, F. S., & Duval, S. (1982). Personal responsibility and salience of the request for help: Determinants of the relation between negative affect and helping behavior. *Journal of Personality and Social Psychology, 43,* 956–970.

Rogers, R. W. (1983). Cognitive and psychological processes in fear appeals and attitude change: A revised theory of protection motivation. In J. Cacioppo & R. Petty (Eds.), *Social psychophysiology: A sourcebook* (pp. 153–176). New York: Guilford.

Rogers, R. W., & Mewborn, R. C. (1976). Fear appeals and attitude change: Effects of a threat's noxiousness, probability of occurrence, and the efficacy of coping responses. *Journal of Personality and Social Psychology, 34,* 54–61.

Rohrer, J. H., Baron, S. H., Hoffman, E. L., & Swander, D. V. (1954). The stability of autokinetic judgments. *Journal of Abnormal and Social Psychology, 49,* 595–597.

Roney, J. R. (2003). Effects of visual exposure to the opposite sex: Cognitive aspects of mate attraction in human males. *Personality and Social Psychology Bulletin, 29,* 393–404.

Rook, K. S. (1984). The negative side of social interaction: Impact on psychological well-being. *Journal of Personality and Social Psychology, 46,* 1097–1108.

Rook, K. S. (1987). Reciprocity of social exchange and social satisfaction among older women. *Journal of Personality and Social Psychology, 52,* 145–154.

Rook, K. S., & Peplau, L. A. (1982). Perspectives on helping the lonely. In L. A. Peplau & D. Perlman (Eds.), *Loneliness: A sourcebook of current theory, research and therapy* (pp. 351–378). New York: Wiley.

Rose, V. G., & Ogloff, J. R. P. (2001). Evaluating the comprehensibility of jury instructions: A method and an example. *Law and Human Behavior, 25,* 409–431.

Rosenbaum, M. E. (1986). The repulsion hypothesis: On the nondevelopment of relationships. *Journal of Personality and Social Psychology, 51,* 1156–1166.

Rosenberg, M. (1965). *Society and the adolescent self-image.* Princeton, NJ: Princeton University Press.

Rosener, J. B. (1995). *America's competitive secret: Utilizing women as a management strategy.* New York: Oxford University Press.

Rosenman, R. H., Brand, R. J., Jenkins, C. D., Friedman, M., Strau, R., & Wurm, M. (1975). Coronary heart disease in the Western Collaborative Group Study: Final follow-up experience of 8 1/2 years. *Journal of the American Medical Association, 233,* 872–877.

Rosenthal, E. (2006, June 2). Genital cutting raises by 50% likelihood mothers or their newborns will die, study finds. *New York Times,* p. A10.

Rosenthal, H. E. S., & Crisp, R. J. (2006). Reducing stereotype threat by blurring intergroup boundaries. *Personality and Social Psychology Bulletin, 32,* 501–511.

Rosenthal, R. (1976). *Experimenter effects in behavioral research.* New York: Irvington.

Rosenthal, R. (1985). From unconscious experimenter bias to teacher expectancy effects. In J. B. Dusek, V. C. Hall, & W. J.

Meyer (Eds.), *Teacher expectancies* (pp. 37–65). Hillsdale, NJ: Erlbaum.

Rosenthal, R. (2002). Covert communication in classrooms, clinics, courtrooms, and cubicles. *American Psychologist, 57,* 839–849.

Rosenthal, R., & Jacobson, L. (1968). *Pygmalion in the classroom: Teacher expectation and pupils' intellectual development.* New York: Holt, Rinehart and Winston.

Rosnow, R. L., & Rosenthal, R. (1993). *Beginning behavioral research: A conceptual primer.* New York: Macmillan.

Ross, E. A. (1908). *Social psychology: An outline and source book.* New York: Macmillan.

Ross, J., & Staw, B. M. (1986). Expo 86: An escalation prototype. *Administrative Science Quarterly, 31,* 274–297.

Ross, L. (1977). The intuitive psychologist and his shortcomings: Distortions in the attribution process. In L. Berkowitz (Ed.), *Advances in experimental social psychology* (Vol. 10, pp. 174–221). New York: Academic Press.

Ross, L., Amabile, T. M., & Steinmetz, J. L. (1977). Social roles, social control, and biases in social-perception processes. *Journal of Personality and Social Psychology, 35,* 485–494.

Ross, L., Bierbrauer, G., & Hoffman, S. (1976). The role of attribution processes in conformity and dissent. *American Psychologist, 31,* 148–157.

Ross, L., Greene, D., & House, P. (1977). The false consensus phenomenon: An attributional bias in self-perception and social-perception processes. *Journal of Experimental Social Psychology, 13,* 279–301.

Ross, M. (1989). The relation of implicit theories to the construction of personal histories. *Psychological Review, 96,* 341–357.

Ross, M., & Sicoly, F. (1979). Egocentric biases in availability and attribution. *Journal of Personality and Social Psychology, 37,* 322–336.

Ross, M., Heine, S. J., Wilson, A. E., & Sugimori, S. (2005). Cross-cultural discrepancies in self-appraisals. *Personality and Social Psychology Bulletin, 31,* 1175–1188.

Rosse, J. G., Miller, J. L., & Stecher, M. D. (1994). A field study of job applicants' reactions to personality and cognitive ability testing. *Journal of Applied Psychology, 79,* 987–992.

Roth, P. L., Huffcutt, A. I., & Bobko, P. (2003). Ethnic group differences in measures of job performance: A new meta-analysis. *Journal of Applied Psychology, 88,* 694–706.

Rothbaum, F., & Tsang, B. Y. (1998). Lovesongs in the United States and China: On the nature of romantic love. *Journal of Cross-Cultural Psychology, 29,* 306–319.

Rothman, D. J., & Rothman, S. M. (2006). *Trust is not enough: Bringing human rights to medicine.* New York: New York Review Books.

Rowatt, W. C., Cunningham, M. R., & Druen, P. B. (1999). Lying to get a date: The effect of facial physical attractiveness on the willingness to deceive prospective dating partners. *Journal of Social and Personal Relationships, 16,* 209–223.

Rozin, P., & Royzman, E. B. (2001). Negativity bias, negativity dominance, and contagion. *Personality and Social Psychology Review, 5,* 296–320.

Ruback, R. B., & Weiner, N. A. (Eds.). (1995). *Interpersonal violent behaviors: Social and cultural aspects.* New York: Springer Publishing.

Ruback, R. B., & Wroblewski, J. (2001). The federal sentencing guidelines: Psychological and policy reasons for simplification. *Psychology, Public Policy, and Law, 7,* 739–775.

Rubenowitz, S., Norrgren, F., & Tannenbaum, A. S. (1983). Some social psychological effects of direct and indirect participation in ten Swedish companies. *Organization Studies, 4,* 243–259.

Rubenstein, S. (1996, August 29). Letting Binti just be herself. *San Francisco Chronicle,* p. A17.

Rubin, D. C. (Ed.). (1996). *Remembering our past: Studies in autobiographical memory.* New York: Cambridge University Press.

Rubin, J. Z., Provenzano, F. J., & Luria, Z. (1974). The eye of the beholder: Parents' views on sex of newborns. *American Journal of Orthopsychiatry, 44*, 512–519.

Rubin, J. Z., Pruitt, D. G., & Kim, S. H. (1994). *Social conflict: Escalation, stalemate, and settlement.* New York: McGraw-Hill.

Rubin, M., & Hewstone, M. (1998). Social identity theory's self-esteem hypothesis: A review and some suggestions for clarification. *Personality and Social Psychology Review, 2*, 40–62.

Rubin, Z. (1973). *Liking and loving.* New York: Holt, Rinehart and Winston.

Ruble, D. N., & Martin, C. L. (1998). Gender development. In W. Damon & N. Eisenberg (Eds.), *Handbook of child psychology, 5th edition: Volume 3: Social, emotional, and personality development* (pp. 933–1016). Hoboken, NJ: Wiley.

Rubonis, A. V., & Bickman, L. (1991). Psychological impairment in the wake of disaster: The disaster-psychopathology relationship. *Psychological Bulletin, 109*, 384–399.

Rudman, L. A., & Borgida, E. (1995). The afterglow of construct accessibility: The behavioral consequences of priming men to view women as sexual objects. *Journal of Experimental Social Psychology, 31*, 493–517.

Rudman, L. A., & Glick, P. (2001). Prescriptive gender stereotypes and backlash toward agentic women. *Journal of Social Issues, 57*, 743–762.

Ruffle, B. J., & Sosis, R. (2006). Cooperation and the in-group-out-group bias: A field test on Israeli kibbutz members and city residents. *Journal of Economic Behavior and Organization, 60*, 147–163.

Rule, B. G., Taylor, B. R., & Dobbs, A. R. (1987). Priming effects of heat on aggressive thoughts. *Social Cognition, 5*, 131–143.

Rusbult, C. E., & Buunk, B. P. (1993). Commitment processes in close relationships: An interdependence analysis. *Journal of Social and Personal Relationships, 10*, 175–204.

Rusbult, C. E., Martz, J. M., & Agnew, C. R. (1998). The investment model scale: Measuring commitment level, satisfaction level, quality of alternatives, and investment size. *Personal Relationships, 5*, 357–391.

Ruscher, J. B. (1998). Prejudice and stereotyping in everyday communication. In M. P. Zanna (Ed.), *Advances in experimental social psychology* (Vol. 30, pp. 241–307). San Diego: Academic Press.

Rushton, J. P. (1981a). Television as a socializer. In J. P. Rushton & R. M. Sorrentino (Eds.), *Altruism and helping behavior: Social, personality, and developmental perspectives* (pp. 91–108). Hillsdale, NJ: Erlbaum.

Rushton, J. P. (1981b). The altruistic personality. In J. P. Rushton & R. M. Sorrentino (Eds.), *Altruism and helping behavior: Social, personality, and developmental perspectives* (pp. 251–266). Hillsdale, NJ: Erlbaum.

Rushton, J. P., Russell, R. J. H., & Wells, P. A. (1984). Genetic similarity theory: Beyond kin selection. *Behavior Genetics, 14*, 179–193.

Russano, M. B., Meissner, C. A., Narchet, F. M., & Kassin, S. M. (2005). Investigating true and false confessions within a novel experimental paradigm. *Psychological Science, 16*, 481–486.

Russell, D., Peplau, L. A., & Cutrona, C. E. (1980). The revised UCLA Loneliness Scale: Concurrent and discriminant validity evidence. *Journal of Personality and Social Psychology, 39*, 472–480.

Russell, G. W., Arms, R. L., & Bibby, R. W. (1995). Canadians' belief in catharsis. *Social Behavior and Personality, 23*, 223–228.

Russell, J. A. (1994). Is there universal recognition of emotion from facial expression? A review of cross-cultural studies. *Psychological Bulletin, 115*, 102–141.

Rutkowski, G. K., Gruder, C. L., & Romer, D. (1983). Group cohesiveness, social norms, and bystander intervention. *Journal of Personality and Social Psychology, 44*, 545–552.

Ryan, C. S., & Bogart, L. M. (1997). Development of new group members' ingroup and outgroup stereotypes: Changes in perceived group variability and ethnocentrism. *Journal of Personality and Social Psychology, 73*, 719–732.

Rynes, S. L., & Connerly, M. L. (1993). Applicant reactions to alternative selection procedures. *Journal of Business and Psychology, 4*, 261–277.

Sackett, P. R., & DuBois, C. L. Z. (1991). Rater-ratee race effects on performance evaluation: Challenging meta-analytic conclusions. *Journal of Applied Psychology, 76*, 873–877.

Sackett, P. R., & Wilson, M. A. (1982). Factors affecting the consensus judgment process in managerial assessment centers. *Journal of Applied Psychology, 67*, 10–17.

Sackett, P. R., Burris, L. R., & Callahan, C. (1989). Integrity testing for personnel selection: An update. *Personnel Psychology, 42*, 491–525.

Sacks, O. (1985). *The man who mistook his wife for a hat.* New York: Summit.

Saenz, D. S. (1994). Token status and problem-solving deficits: Detrimental effects of distinctiveness and performance monitoring. *Social Cognition, 12*, 61–74.

Sagar, H. A., & Schofield, J. W. (1980). Racial and behavioral cues in black and white children's perceptions of ambiguously aggressive acts. *Journal of Personality and Social Psychology, 39*, 590–598.

Sagarin, B. J. (2005). Reconsidering evolved sex differences in jealousy: Comment on Harris (2003). *Personality and Social Psychology Review, 9*, 62–75.

Saks, M. J. (1974). Ignorance of science is no excuse. *Trial, 10*, 18–20.

Saks, M. J., & Marti, M. W. (1997). A meta-analysis of the effects of jury size. *Law and Human Behavior, 21*, 451–468.

Saldana, L., & Henggeler, S. W. (2006). Multisystemic therapy in the treatment of adolescent conduct disorder. In W. M. Nelson, III, A. J. Finch, Jr., & K. J. Hart (Eds.), *Conduct disorders: A practitioner's guide to comparative treatments* (pp. 217–258). New York: Springer.

Salgado, J. F. (1997). The five factor model of personality and job performance in the European community. *Journal of Applied Psychology, 82*, 30–43.

Salovey, P. (1992). Mood-induced focus of attention. *Journal of Personality and Social Psychology, 62*, 699–707.

Salovey, P., & Rodin, J. (1984). Some antecedents and consequences of social-comparison jealousy. *Journal of Personality and Social Psychology, 47*, 780–792.

Salovey, P., Mayer, J. D., & Rosenhan, D. L. (1991). Mood and helping: Mood as a motivator of helping and helping as a regulator of mood. In M. S. Clark (Ed.), *Prosocial behavior* (Vol. 12, pp. 215–237). Newbury Park, CA: Sage.

Salvemini, N. J., Reilly, R. R., & Smither, J. W. (1993). The influence of rater motivation on assimilation effects and accuracy in performance ratings. *Organizational Behavior and Human Decision Processes, 55*, 41–60.

Salzer, M. S. (2000). Toward a narrative conceptualization of stereotypes: Contextualizing perceptions of public housing residents. *Journal of Community and Applied Social Psychology, 10*, 123–137.

Sampson, E. E. (2000). Reinterpreting individualism and collectivism: Their religious roots and monologic versus dialogic person-other relationship. *American Psychologist, 55*, 1425–1432.

Sanchez, J. I., & De La Torre, P. (1996). A second look at the relationship between rating and behavioral accuracy in performance appraisal. *Journal of Applied Psychology, 81*, 3–10.

Sanchez-Burks, J., Nisbett, R. E., & Ybarra, O. (2000). Relational schemas, cultural styles, and prejudice against outgroups. *Journal of Personality and Social Psychology, 79*, 174–189.

Sanders, G. S. (1981). Driven by distraction: An integrative review of social facilitation theory and research. *Journal of Experimental Social Psychology, 17,* 227–251.

Sanders, G. S., & Baron, R. S. (1977). Is social comparison irrelevant for producing choice shifts? *Journal of Experimental Social Psychology, 13,* 303–314.

Sanders, S. A., & Reinisch, J. M. (1999). Would you say you "had sex" if . . . ? *Journal of the American Medical Association, 281,* 275–277.

Sanderson, C. A., & Evans, S. M. (2001). Seeing one's partner through intimacy-colored glasses: An examination of the processes underlying the intimacy goals-relationship satisfaction link. *Personality and Social Psychology Bulletin, 27,* 463–473.

Sanderson, D. W. (1997). *Smileys.* Sebastopol, CA: O'Reilly.

Sani, F., & Todman, J. (2002). Should we stay or should we go? A social psychological model of schisms in groups. *Personality and Social Psychology Bulletin, 28,* 1647–1655.

Sanna, L. J. (1992). Self-efficacy theory: Implications for social facilitation and social loafing. *Journal of Personality and Social Psychology, 62,* 774–786.

Sanna, L. J., Parks, C. D., & Chang, E. C. (2003). Mixed-motive conflict in social dilemmas: Mood as input to competitive and cooperative goals. *Group Dynamics, 7,* 26–40.

Sanoff, A. P., & Leight, K. (1994). Altruism is in style. *U.S. News and World Report* (America's Best Colleges: 1994 College Guide), pp. 25–28.

Sansone, C., & Harackiewicz, J. M. (Eds.). (2000). *Intrinsic and extrinsic motivation: The search for optimal motivation and performance.* New York: Academic Press.

Santos, M. D., Leve, C., & Pratkanis, A. R. (1994). Hey buddy, can you spare seventeen cents? Mindful persuasion and the pique technique. *Journal of Applied Social Psychology, 24,* 755–764.

Sapolsky, B. S. (1984). Arousal, affect, and the aggression-moderating effect of erotica. In N. M. Malamuth & E. I. Donnerstein (Eds.), *Pornography and sexual aggression* (pp. 85–113). New York: Academic Press.

Sapolsky, R. M. (1994). *Why zebras don't get ulcers: A guide to stress, diseases, and coping.* New York: Freeman.

Sapolsky, R. M. (2004). *Why zebras don't get ulcers* (3rd ed.). New York: Owl Books.

Sarason, I. G., Levine, H. M., Basham, R. B., & Sarason, B. R. (1983). Assessing social support: The social support questionnaire. *Journal of Personality and Social Psychology, 44,* 127–139.

Sarason, I. G., Sarason, B. R., & Pierce, G. R. (1994). Social support: Global and relationship-based levels of analysis. *Journal of Social and Personal Relationships, 11,* 295–312.

Sarason, I. G., Sarason, B. R., Pierce, G. R., Shearin, E. N., & Sayers, M. H. (1991). A social learning approach to increasing blood donations. *Journal of Applied Social Psychology, 21,* 896–918.

Sarat, A. (Ed.). (2005). *Dissent in dangerous times.* Ann Arbor: University of Michigan Press.

Sargent, M. J., & Bradfield, A. L. (2004). Race and information processing in criminal trials: Does the defendant's race affect how the facts are evaluated? *Personality and Social Psychology Bulletin, 30,* 995–1008.

Sarnoff, I., & Zimbardo, P. (1961). Anxiety, fear, and social affiliation. *Journal of Abnormal and Social Psychology, 62,* 356–363.

Sassenberg, K. (2002). Common bond and common identity groups on the Internet: Attachment and normative behavior in on-topic and off-topic chats. *Group Dynamics, 6,* 27–37.

Saucier, D. A., Miller, C. T., & Doucet, N. (2005). Differences in helping whites and blacks: A meta-analysis. *Personality and Social Psychology Review, 9,* 2–16.

Saulnier, K., & Perlman, D. (1981). The actor-observer bias is alive and well in prison: A sequel to Wells. *Personality and Social Psychology Bulletin, 7,* 559–564.

Saulny, S. (2002). Why confess to what you didn't do? *New York Times,* December 8, Section 4.

Savin, H. B. (1973). Professors and psychological researchers: Conflicting values in conflicting roles. *Cognition, 2,* 147–149.

Savitsky, K., Epley, N., & Gilovich, T. (2001). Do others judge us as harshly as we think? Overestimating the impact of our failures, shortcomings, and mishaps. *Journal of Personality and Social Psychology, 81,* 44–56.

Savitsky, K., Gilovich, T., Berger, G., & Medvec, V. H. (2003). Is our absence as conspicuous as we think? Overestimating the salience and impact of one's absence from a group. *Journal of Experimental Social Psychology, 39,* 386–392.

Schachter, S. (1951). Deviation, rejection, and communication. *Journal of Abnormal and Social Psychology, 46,* 190–207.

Schachter, S. (1959). *The psychology of affiliation: Experimental studies of the sources of gregariousness.* Stanford, CA: Stanford University Press.

Schachter, S. (1964). The interaction of cognitive and physiological determinants of emotional state. In L. Berkowitz (Ed.), *Advances in experimental social psychology* (Vol. 1, pp. 49–80). New York: Academic Press.

Schachter, S., & Singer, J. (1962). Cognitive, social, and physiological determinants of the emotional state. *Psychological Review, 69,* 379–399.

Schachter, S., & Singer, J. (1979). Comments on the Maslach and Marshall-Zimbardo experiments. *Journal of Personality and Social Psychology, 37,* 989–995.

Schachter, S., Hood, D., Gerin, W., Andreasson, P. B., & Rennert, M. (1985). Some causes and consequences of dependence and independence in the stock market. *Journal of Economic Behavior and Organization, 6,* 339–357.

Schachter, S., Ouellette, R., Whittle, B., & Gerin, W. (1987). Effects of trends and of profit or loss on the tendency to sell stock. *Basic and Applied Social Psychology, 8,* 259–271.

Schafer, R. B., & Keith, P. M. (1980). Equity and depression among married couples. *Social Psychology Quarterly, 43,* 430–435.

Schaller, M. (1991). Social categorization and the formation of social stereotypes: Further evidence for biased information processing in the perception of group-behavior correlations. *European Journal of Social Psychology, 21,* 25–35.

Schaller, M., & Conway, L. G., III (1999). Influence of impression-management goals on the emerging contents of group stereotypes: Support for a social-evolutionary process. *Personality and Social Psychology Bulletin, 25,* 819–833.

Schaller, M., & Conway, L. G., III (2001). From cognition to culture: The origins of stereotypes that really matter. In G. Moscowitz (Ed.), *Cognitive social psychology: On the tenure and future of social cognition* (pp. 163–176). Mahwah, NJ: Erlbaum.

Schaller, M., Conway, L. G., & Tanchuk, T. L. (2002). Selective pressures on the once and future contents of ethnic stereotypes: Effects of the communicability of traits. *Journal of Personality and Social Psychology, 82,* 861–877.

Schaller, M., Simpson, J. A., & Kenrick, D. T. (Eds.). (2006). *Evolution and social psychology.* New York: Taylor & Francis.

Scharfe, E., & Bartholomew, K. (1994). Reliability and stability of adult attachment patterns. *Personal Relationships, 1,* 23–43.

Scheck, B., Neufeld, P., & Dwyer, J. (2000). *Actual innocence: Five days to execution and other dispatches from the wrongly convicted.* New York: Doubleday.

Scheepers, D., & Ellemers, N. (2005). When the pressure is up: The assessment of social identity threat in low and high status groups. *Journal of Experimental Social Psychology, 41,* 192–200.

Scheier, M. F., & Carver, C. S. (1983). Two sides of the self: One for you and one for me. In J. Suls and A. G. Greenwald (Eds.), *Psychological perspectives on the self* (Vol. 2, pp. 123–157). Hillsdale, NJ: Erlbaum.

Scheier, M. F., & Carver, C. S. (1985). Optimism, coping, and health: Assessment and implications of generalized outcome expectancies. *Health Psychology, 4,* 219–247.

Scheier, M. F., & Carver, C. S. (1992). Effects of optimism on psychological and physical well-being: Theoretical overview and empirical update. *Cognitive Therapy and Research, 16,* 201–228.

Scher, S. J., & Cooper, J. (1989). Motivational basis of dissonance: The singular role of behavioral consequences. *Journal of Personality and Social Psychology, 56,* 899–906.

Schimel, J., Arndt, J., Pyszczynski, T., & Greenberg, J. (2001). Being accepted for who we are: Evidence that social validation of the intrinsic self reduces general defensiveness. *Journal of Personality and Social Psychology, 80,* 35–52.

Schimmack, U., Oishi, S., & Diener, E. (2005). Individualism: A valid and important dimension of cultural differences between nations. *Personality and Social Psychology Review, 9,* 17–31.

Schlagman, S., Schulz, J., & Kvavilashvili, L. (2006). A content analysis of involuntary autobiographical memories: Examining the positivity effect in old age. *Memory, 14,* 161–175.

Schlenger, W. E., et al. (2002). Psychological reactions to terrorist attacks: Findings from the National Study of Americans' Reactions to September 11. *Journal of the American Medical Association, 288,* 581–588.

Schlenker, B. R. (1982). Translating actions into attitudes: An identity-analytic approach to the explanation of social conduct. In L. Berkowitz (Ed.), *Advances in experimental social psychology* (Vol. 15, pp. 193–247). New York: Academic Press.

Schlenker, B. R. (2003). Self-presentation. In M. R. Leary & J. P. Tangney (Eds.), *Handbook of self and identity* (pp. 492–518). New York: Guilford.

Schlenker, B. R., & Trudeau, J. V. (1990). The impact of self-presentations on private self-beliefs: Effects of prior self-beliefs and misattribution. *Journal of Personality and Social Psychology, 58,* 22–32.

Schlenker, B. R., Weigold, M. F., & Hallam, J. R. (1990). Self-serving attributions in social context: Effects of self-esteem and social pressure. *Journal of Personality and Social Psychology, 58,* 855–863.

Schmader, T., & Johns, M. (2003). Converging evidence that stereotype threat reduces working memory capacity. *Journal of Personality and Social Psychology, 85,* 440–452.

Schmidt, F. L. (2002). The role of general cognitive ability and job performance: Why there cannot be a debate. *Human Performance, 15,* 187–210.

Schmidt, F. L., & Rader, M. (1999). Exploring the boundary conditions for interview validity: Meta-analytic validity findings for a new interview type. *Personnel Psychology, 52,* 445–464.

Schmitt, D. P. (2003). Universal sex differences in the desire for sexual variety: Tests from 52 nations, 6 continents, and 13 islands. *Journal of Personality and Social Psychology, 85,* 85–104.

Schmitt, D. P., International Sexuality Description Project. (2004). Patterns and universals of mate poaching across 53 nations: The effects of sex, culture, and personality on romantically attracting another person's partner. *Journal of Personality and Social Psychology, 86,* 560–584.

Schmitt, M. T., & Maes, J. (2002). Stereotypic ingroup bias as self-defense against relative deprivation: Evidence from a longitudinal study of the German unification process. *European Journal of Social Psychology, 32,* 309–326.

Schmitt, M. T., Branscombe, N. R., Silvia, P. J., Garcia, D. M., & Spears, R. (2006). Categorizing at the group-level in response to intragroup social comparisons: A self-categorization theory integration of self-evaluation and social identity motives. *European Journal of Social Psychology, 36,* 297–314.

Schmitt, M. T., Branscrombe, N. R., Kobrynowicz, D., & Owen, S. (2002). Perceiving discrimination against one's gender group has different implications for well-being in women and men. *Personality and Social Psychology Bulletin, 28,* 197–210.

Schmitt, M. T., Spears, R., & Branscombe, N. R. (2003). Constructing a minority group identity out of shared rejection: The case of international students. *European Journal of Social Psychology, 33,* 1–12.

Schmitt, N., & Oswald, F. L. (2006). The impact of corrections for faking on the validity of noncognitive measures in selection settings. *Journal of Applied Psychology, 91,* 613–621.

Schneider, D. J. (1973). Implicit personality theory: A review. *Psychological Bulletin, 79,* 294–309.

Schneider, D. M., & Watkins, M. J. (1996). Response conformity in recognition testing. *Psychonomic Bulletin and Review, 3,* 481–485.

Schneider, M. E., Major, B., Luhtanen, R., & Crocker, J. (1996). Social stigma and the potential costs of assumptive help. *Personality and Social Psychology Bulletin, 22,* 201–209.

Schneider, S. G., Taylor, S. E., Hammen, C., Kemeny, M. E., & Dudley, J. (1991). Factors influencing suicide intent in gay and bisexual suicide ideators: Differing models for men with and without human immunodeficiency virus. *Journal of Personality and Social Psychology, 61,* 776–778.

Schneiderman, N., Antoni, M. H., Saab, P. G., & Ironson, G. (2001). Health psychology: Psychosocial and biobehavioral aspects of chronic disease management. *Annual Review of Psychology, 52,* 555–580.

Schoeneman, T. J., & Rubanowitz, D. E. (1985). Attributions in the advice columns: Actors and observers, causes and reasons. *Personality and Social Psychology Bulletin, 11,* 315–325.

Schofield, P. E., Pattison, P. E., Hill, D. J., & Borland, R. (2001). The influence of group identification on the adoption of peer group smoking norms. *Psychology and Health, 16,* 1–16.

Schofield, P. E., Pattison, P. E., Hill, D. J., & Borland, R. (2003). Youth culture and smoking: Integrating social group processes and individual cognitive processes in a model of health-related behaviours. *Journal of Health Psychology, 8,* 291–306.

Schonert-Reichl, K. A. (1999). Relations of peer acceptance, friendship adjustment, and social behavior to moral reasoning during early adolescence. *Journal of Early Adolescence, 19,* 249–279.

Schoorman, F. D. (1988). Escalation bias in performance appraisals: An unintended consequence of supervisor participation in hiring decisions. *Journal of Applied Psychology, 73,* 58–62.

Schopler, J. (1970). An attribution analysis of some determinants of reciprocating a benefit. In J. R. Macaulay & L. Berkowitz (Eds.), *Altruism and helping behavior* (pp. 231–238). New York: Academic Press.

Schroots, J. J. F., van Dijkum, C., & Assink, M. H. J. (2004). Autobiographical memory from a life span perspective. *International Journal of Aging and Human Development, 58,* 69–85.

Schulman, J., Shaver, P., Colman, R., Emrick, B., & Christie, R. (1973, May). Recipe for a jury. *Psychology Today,* pp. 37–44, 77, 79–84.

Schultheiss, O. C., & Brunstein, J. C. (2000). Choice of difficult tasks as a strategy of compensating for identity-relevant failure. *Journal of Research in Personality, 34,* 269–277.

Schultz, B., Ketrow, S. M., & Urban, D. M. (1995). Improving decision quality in the small group: The role of the reminder. *Small Group Research, 26,* 521–541.

Schulz, R. (1976). Effects of control and predictability on the physical and psychological well-being of the institutionalized aged. *Journal of Personality and Social Psychology, 33,* 563–573.

Schuster, M. A., Stein, B. D., Jaycox, L. H., Collins, R. L., Marshall, G. N., Elliott, M. N., Zhou, A. J., Kanouse, D. E., Morrison, J. L., & Berry, S. H. (2001). A national survey of stress reactions after the September 11, 2001, terrorist attacks. *New England Journal of Medicine, 345,* 1507–1512.

Schwartz, C., Meisenhelder, J. B., Ma, Y., & Reed, G. (2003). Altruistic social interest behaviors are associated with better mental health. *Psychosomatic Medicine, 65,* 778–785.

Schwartz, S. H. (1990). Individualism-collectivism: Critique and proposed refinements. *Journal of Cross-Cultural Psychology, 21,* 139–157.

Schwartz, S. H., & Gottlieb, A. (1980). Bystander anonymity and reaction to emergencies. *Journal of Personality and Social Psychology, 39,* 418–430.

Schwarz, N. (1990). Feelings as information: Information and motivational functions as affective states. In E. T. Higgins et al. (Eds.), *Handbook of motivation and cognition: Foundations of social behavior* (Vol. 2, pp. 527–561). New York: Guilford.

Schwarz, N. (1999). Self-reports: How the questions shape the answers. *American Psychologist, 54,* 93–105.

Schwarz, N. (2007). Retrospective and concurrent self-reports: The rationale for real-time data capture. In A. A. Stone, S. S. Shiffman, A. Atienza, & L. Nebeling (Eds.), *The science of real-time data capture: Self-reports in health research.* New York: Oxford University Press.

Schwarz, N., & Oyserman, D. (2001). Asking questions about behavior: Cognition, communication and questionnaire construction. *American Journal of Evaluation, 22,* 127–160.

Schwarz, N., Bless, H., & Bohner, G. (1991). Mood and persuasion: Affective states influence the processing of persuasive communications. In M. P. Zanna (Ed.), *Advances in experimental social psychology* (Vol. 24, pp. 161–199). New York: Academic Press.

Schwarz, N., Strack, F., Hilton, D., & Naderer, G. (1991). Base rates, representativeness, and the logic of conversation: The contextual relevance of "irrelevant" information. *Social Cognition, 9,* 67–84.

Schwarzwald, J., Raz, M., & Zvibel, M. (1979). The applicability of the door-in-the-face technique when established behavioral customs exist. *Journal of Applied Social Psychology, 9,* 576–586.

Scourfield, J., John, B., Martin, N., & McGuffin, P. (2004). The development of prosocial behaviour in children and adolescents: A twin study. *Journal of Child Psychology and Psychiatry, 45,* 927–935.

Scullen, S. E., Mount, M., & Goff, M. (2000). Understanding the latent structure of job performance ratings. *Journal of Applied Psychology, 85,* 956–970.

Searcy, E., & Eisenberg, N. (1992). Defensiveness in response to aid from a sibling. *Journal of Personality and Social Psychology, 62,* 422–433.

Sears, D. O. (1986). College sophomores in the laboratory: Influences of a narrow data base on social psychology's view of human nature. *Journal of Personality and Social Psychology, 51,* 515–530.

Sears, D. O., & Henry, P. J. (2005). Over thirty years later: A contemporary look at symbolic racism. In M. P. Zanna (Ed.), *Advances in experimental social psychology, Vol. 37,* (pp. 95–150). San Diego: Elsevier.

Sears, D. O., & Kinder, D. R. (1985). Whites' opposition to busing: On conceptualizing and operationalizing group conflict. *Journal of Personality and Social Psychology, 48,* 1141–1147.

Sedikides, C. (1992). Attentional effects on mood are moderated by chronic self-conception valence. *Personality and Social Psychology Bulletin, 18,* 580–584.

Sedikides, C. (1993). Assessment, enhancement, and verification determinants of the self-evaluation process. *Journal of Personality and Social Psychology, 65,* 317–338.

Sedikides, C., & Anderson, C. A. (1994). Causal perceptions of intertrait relations: The glue that holds person types together. *Personality and Social Psychology Bulletin, 20,* 294–302.

Sedikides, C., & Brewer, M. B. (Eds.). (2001). *Individual self, relational self, collective self.* Philadelphia: Psychology Press.

Sedikides, C., & Jackson, J. M. (1990). Social impact theory: A field test of source strength, source immediacy and number of targets. *Basic and Applied Social Psychology, 11,* 273–281.

Sedikides, C., & Skowronski, J. J. (1997). The symbolic self in evolutionary context. *Personality and Social Psychology Review, 1,* 80–102.

Sedikides, C., Gaertner, L., & Toguchi, Y. (2003). Pancultural self-enhancement. *Journal of Personality and Social Psychology, 84,* 60–79.

Sedikides, C., Gaertner, L., & Vevea, J. L. (2005). Pancultural self-enhancement reloaded: A meta-analytic reply to Heine (2005). *Journal of Personality and Social Psychology, 89,* 539–551.

See, Y. H. M., & Petty, R. E. (2006). Effects of mortality salience on evaluation of ingroup and outgroup sources: The impact of pro- versus counterattitudinal positions. *Personality and Social Psychology Bulletin, 32,* 405–416.

Seeman, T. E., Dubin, L. F., & Seeman, M. (2003). Religiosity/spirituality and health: A critical review of the evidence for biological pathways. *American Psychologist, 58,* 53–63.

Segal, N. L. (1993). Twin, sibling, and adoption methods: Tests of evolutionary hypotheses. *American Psychologist, 48,* 943–956.

Segerstrom, S. C. (2006a). *Breaking Murphy's law: How optimists get what they want from life and pessimists can too.* New York: Guilford Press.

Segerstrom, S. C. (2006b). How does optimism suppress immunity? Evaluation of three affective pathways. *Health Psychology, 25,* 653–657.

Segerstrom, S. C., & Miller, G. E. (2004). Psychological stress and the human immune system: A meta-analytic study of 30 years of inquiry. *Psychological Bulletin, 130,* 601–630.

Segerstrom, S. C., Taylor, S. E., Kemeny, M. E., & Fahey, J. L. (1998). Optimism is associated with mood, coping, and immune change in response to stress. *Journal of Personality and Social Psychology, 74,* 1646–1655.

Seijts, G. H., & Latham, G. P. (2000). The effects of goal setting and group size on performance in a social dilemma. *Canadian Journal of Behavioural Science, 32,* 104–116.

Sekaquaptewa, D., & Thompson, M. (2003). Solo status, stereotype threat, and performance expectancies: Their effects on women's performance. *Journal of Experimental Social Psychology, 39,* 68–74.

Sekaquaptewa, D., Espinoza, P., Thompson, M., Vargas, P., & von Hippel, W. (2003). Stereotypic explanatory bias: Implicit stereotyping as a predictor of discrimination. *Journal of Experimental Social Psychology, 39,* 75–82.

Seligman, M. E. P. (1975). *On depression, development, and death.* San Francisco: Freeman.

Seligman, M. E. P. (1991). *Learned optimism.* New York: Knopf.

Sellers, R. M., & Shelton, J. N. (2003). The role of racial identity in perceived racial discrimination. *Journal of Personality and Social Psychology, 84,* 1079–1092.

Seltzer, R. (2006). Scientific jury selection: Does it work? *Journal of Applied Social Psychology, 36,* 2417–2435.

Selvan, M. S., Ross, M. W., Kapadia, A. S., Mathai, R., & Hira, S. (2001). Study of perceived norms, beliefs and intended sexual behaviour among higher secondary school students in India. *AIDS Care, 13,* 779–788.

Selye, H. (1936). A syndrome produced by diverse nocuous agents. *Nature, 138,* 32.

Serbin, L. A., Poulin-Dubois, D., & Eichstedt, J. A. (2002). Infants' response to gender-inconsistent events. *Infancy, 3,* 531–542.

Sergeant, M. J. T., Dickins, T. E., Davies, M. N. O., & Griffiths, M. D. (2006). Aggression, empathy and sexual orientation in males. *Personality and Individual Differences, 40,* 475–486.

Seta, J. J., Seta, C. E., & McElroy, T. (2003). Attributional biases in the service of stereotype maintenance: A schema-maintenance through compensation analysis. *Personality and Social Psychology Bulletin, 29,* 151–163.

Seto, M. C., Marc, A., & Barbaree, H. E. (2001). The role of pornography in the etiology of sexual aggression. *Aggression and Violent Behavior, 6,* 35–53.

Seyfarth, R. M., & Cheney, D. L. (1984). Grooming, alliances and reciprocal altruism in vervet monkeys. *Nature, 308,* 541–543.

Seyle, D. C., & Newman, M. L. (2006). A house divided? The psychology of red and blue America. *American Psychologist, 61,* 571–580.

Seyle, D. C., & Newman, M. L. (2006). A house divided? The psychology of red and blue America. *American Psychologist, 61,* 571–580.

Seymour, T. L., Seifert, C. M., Shafto, M. G., & Mosmann, A. L. (2000). Using response-time measures to assess "guilty knowledge." *Journal of Applied Psychology, 85,* 30–47.

Shackelford, T. K. (2001). Cohabitation, marriage, and murder: Woman-killing by male romantic partners. *Aggressive Behavior, 27,* 284–291.

Shackelford, T. K., & Goetz, A. T. (2005). When we hurt the ones we love: Predicting violence against women from men's mate retention tactics. In S. M. Platek & T. K. Shackelford (Eds.), *Human paternal uncertainty and anti-cuckoldry tactics: How males deal with female infidelity.* Cambridge: Cambridge University Press.

Shackelford, T. K., & Larsen, R. J. (1999). Facial attractiveness and physical health. *Evolution and Human Behavior, 20,* 71–76.

Shackelford, T. K., Buss, D. M., & Euler, H. A. (2005). When we hurt the ones we love: Predicting violence against women from men's mate retention. *Personal Relationships, 12,* 447–463.

Shackelford, T. K., Weekes-Shackelford, V. A., & Schmitt, D. P. (2005). An evolutionary perspective on why some men refuse or reduce their child support payments. *Basic and Applied Social Psychology, 27,* 297–306.

Shaffer, D. R., Smith, J. E., & Tomarelli, M. (1982). Self-monitoring as a determinant of self-disclosure reciprocity during the acquaintance process. *Journal of Personality and Social Psychology, 43,* 163–175.

Shakun, M. F. (1999). An ESD computer culture for intercultural problem solving and negotiation. *Group Decision and Negotiation, 8,* 237–249.

Shanab, M. E., & Yahya, K. A. (1977). A behavioral study of obedience in children. *Journal of Personality and Social Psychology, 35,* 530–536.

Shanab, M. E., & Yahya, K. A. (1978). A cross cultural study of obedience. *Bulletin of the Psychonomic Society, 11,* 267–269.

Shapiro, P. N., & Penrod, S. (1986). Meta-analysis of facial identification studies. *Psychological Bulletin, 100,* 139–156.

Shaver, K. G. (1970). Defensive attribution: Effects of severity and relevance on the responsibility assigned for an accident. *Journal of Personality and Social Psychology, 14,* 101–113.

Shaver, P., & Rubenstein, E. (1980). Childhood attachment experience and adult loneliness. In L. Wheeler (Ed.), *Review of personality and social psychology* (Vol. 1, pp. 42–73). Beverly Hills, CA: Sage.

Shavit, Y., Fischer, C. S., & Koresh, Y. (1994). Kin and nonkin under collective threat: Israeli networks during the Gulf War. *Social Forces, 72,* 1197–1215.

Shavitt, S., Sanbonmatsu, D. M., Smittipatana, S., & Posavac, S. S. (1999). Broadening the conditions for illusory correlation formation: Implications for judging minority groups. *Basic and Applied Social Psychology, 21,* 263–279.

Shaw, J. S., III (1996). Increases in eyewitness confidence resulting from postevent questioning. *Journal of Experimental Psychology: Applied, 2,* 126–146.

Shaw, J. S., III., Garven, S., & Wood, J. M. (1997). Co-witness information can have immediate effects on eyewitness memory reports. *Law and Human Behavior, 21,* 503–523.

Shea, C. (1996, January 12). New students uncertain about racial preferences. *Chronicle of Higher Education,* p. A33.

Shefrin, H. (2006). *Greed and fear: Understanding behavioral finance and the psychology of investing.* New York: Oxford University Press.

Shefrin, H. M., & Statman, M. (1985). The disposition to sell winners too early and ride losers too long: theory and evidence. *Journal of Finance, 40,* 777–790.

Shefrin, H. M., & Statman, M. (1986, February). How not to make money in the stock market. *Psychology Today,* pp. 52–57.

Shell, R. M., & Eisenberg, N. (1992). A developmental model of recipients' reactions to aid. *Psychological Bulletin, 111,* 413–433.

Shelton, J. N. (2003). Interpersonal concerns in social encounters between majority and minority group members. *Group Processes and Intergroup Relations, 6,* 171–185.

Shelton, J. N., & Richeson, J. A. (2005). Intergroup contact and pluralistic ignorance. *Journal of Personality and Social Psychology, 88,* 91–107.

Shelton, J. N., & Richeson, J. A. (2007). Interracial interactions: A relational approach. In M. P. Zanna (Ed.), *Advances in experimental social psychology.* San Diego: Elsevier.

Shelton, J. N., Richeson, J. A., Salvatore, J., & Trawalter, S. (2005). Ironic effects of racial bias during interracial interactions. *Psychological Science, 16,* 397–402.

Shepela, S. T., Cook, J., Horlitz, E., Leal, R., Luciano, S., Lutfy, E., Miller, C., Mitchell, G., & Worden, E. (1999). Courageous resistance: A special case of altruism. *Theory and Psychology, 9,* 787–805.

Sheppard, B. H. (1985). Justice is no simple matter: Case for elaborating our model of procedural fairness. *Journal of Personality and Social Psychology, 49,* 953–962.

Shepperd, J. A. (1993a). Productivity loss in performance groups: A motivation analysis. *Psychological Bulletin, 113,* 67–81.

Shepperd, J. A. (1993b). Student derogation of the Scholastic Aptitude Test: Biases in perceptions and presentations of college board scores. *Basic and Applied Social Psychology, 14,* 455–473.

Shepperd, J. A., & Taylor, K. M. (1999). Social loafing and expectancy-value theory. *Personality and Social Psychology Bulletin, 25,* 1147–1158.

Sherif, M. (1936). The psychology of social norms. New York: Harper.

Sherif, M. (1966). *In common predicament: Social psychology of intergroup conflict and cooperation.* Boston: Houghton Mifflin.

Sherif, M., Harvey, L. J., White, B. J., Hood, W. R., & Sherif, C. W. (1961). *The Robbers Cave experiment: Intergroup conflict and cooperation.* Middletown, CT: Wesleyan University Press. (Reprinted in 1988)

Sherman, J. W., Conrey, F. R., & Groom, C. J. (2004). Encoding flexibility revisited: Evidence for enhanced encoding of stereotype-inconsistent information under cognitive load. *Social Cognition, 22,* 214–232.

Sherman, J. W., Stroessner, S. J., Conrey, F. R., & Azam, O. A. (2005). Prejudice and stereotype maintenance processes: Attention, attribution, and individuation. *Journal of Personality and Social Psychology, 89,* 607–622.

Shih, M., Pittinsky, T. L., & Ambady, N. (1999). Stereotype susceptibility: Identity salience and shifts in quantitative performance. *Psychological Science, 10,* 80–83.

Shore, T. H., Shore, L. M., & Thornton, G. C., III. (1992). Construct validity of self- and peer evaluations of performance dimensions in an assessment center. *Journal of Applied Psychology, 77,* 42–54.

Shorr, D. N., & McClelland, S. E. (1993). Children's recognition of pride and guilt as consequences of helping and not helping. *Child Study Journal, 28,* 123–136.

Shorr, D. N., & McClelland, S. E. (1998). Children's recognition of pride and guilt as consequences of helping and not helping. *Child Study Journal, 28,* 123–136.

Shotland, R. L., & Heinold, W. D. (1985). Bystander response to arterial bleeding: Helping skills, the decision-making process, and differentiating the helping response. *Journal of Personality and Social Psychology, 49,* 347–356.

Shotland, R. L., & Stebbins, C. A. (1980). Bystander response to rape: Can a victim attract help? *Journal of Applied Social Psychology, 10*, 510–527.

Shotland, R. L., & Straw, M. K. (1976). Bystander response to an assault: When a man attacks a woman. *Journal of Personality and Social Psychology, 34*, 990–999.

Shrauger, J. S., & Schoeneman, T. (1979). Symbolic interactionist view of the self-concept: Through the looking-glass darkly. *Psychological Bulletin, 86*, 549–573.

Sidanius, J., Levin, S., Federico, C. M., & Pratto, F. (2001). Legitimizing ideologies: The social dominance approach. J. T. Jost & B. Major (Eds.), *The psychology of legitimacy: Emerging perspectives on ideology, justice, and intergroup relations* (pp. 307–331). New York: Cambridge University Press.

Sidebotham, P., & Heron, J. (2006). Child maltreatment in the 'children of the nineties': A cohort study of risk factors. *Child Abuse and Neglect, 30*, 497–522.

Siegler, I. C. (1994). Hostility and risk: Demographic and lifestyle variables. In A. W. Siegman & T. W. Smith (Eds.), *Anger, hostility, and the heart* (pp. 199–214). Hillsdale, NJ: Erlbaum.

Siegman, A. W., & Smith, T. W. (1994). *Anger, hostility, and the heart.* Hillsdale, NJ: Erlbaum.

Silke, A. (2003). Deindividuation, anonymity, and violence: Findings from Northern Ireland. *Journal of Social Psychology, 143*, 493–499.

Silverstein, B., Perdue, L., Peterson, B., & Kelly, E. (1986). The role of the mass media in promoting a thin standard of bodily attractiveness for women. *Sex Roles, 14*, 519–532.

Silvia, P. J., & Duval, T. S. (2001). Objective self-awareness theory: Recent progress and enduring problems. *Personality and Social Psychology Review, 5*, 230–241.

Simon, H. A. (1956). Rational choice and the structure of the environment. *Psychological Review, 63*, 129–138.

Simonson, I., & Staw, B. W. (1992). Deescalation strategies: A comparison of techniques for reducing commitment to losing courses of action. *Journal of Applied Psychology, 77*, 419–426.

Simpson, J. A. (1987). The dissolution of romantic relationships: Factors involved in relationship stability and emotional distress. *Journal of Personality and Social Psychology, 53*, 683–692.

Simpson, J. A., & Gangestad, S. W. (1992). Sociosexuality and romantic partner choice. *Journal of Personality, 60*, 31–51.

Simpson, J. A., & Kenrick, D. T. (Eds.). (1997). *Evolutionary social psychology.* Mahwah, NJ: Erlbaum.

Simpson, J. A., Campbell, B., & Berscheid, E. (1986). The association between romantic love and marriage: Kephart (1967) twice revisited. *Personality and Social Psychology Bulletin, 12*, 363–372.

Simpson, J. A., Gangestad, S. W., & Lerma, M. (1990). Perception of physical attractiveness: Mechanisms involved in the maintenance of romantic relationships. *Journal of Personality and Social Psychology, 59*, 1192–1201.

Simpson, J. A., Rholes, W. S., & Phillips, D. (1996). Conflicts in close relationships: An attachment perspective. *Journal of Personality and Social Psychology, 71*, 899–914.

Sinclair, L., & Kunda, Z. (1999). Reactions to a black professional: Motivated inhibition and activation of conflicting stereotypes. *Journal of Personality and Social Psychology, 77*, 885–904.

Sinclair, L., & Kunda, Z. (2000). Motivated stereotyping of women: She's fine if she praised me but incompetent if she criticized me. *Personality and Social Psychology Bulletin, 26*, 1329–1342.

Sinclair, R. C., Hoffman, C., Mark, M. M., Martin, L. M., & Pickering, T. L. (1994). Construct accessibility and the misattribution of arousal: Schachter and Singer revisited. *Psychological Science, 5*, 15–19.

Sinervo, B., Chaine, A., Clobert, J., Calsbeek, R., Hazard, L., Lancaster, L., McAdam, A. G., Alonzo, S., Corrigan, G., & Hochberg, M. E. (2006). Self-recognition, color signals, and cycles of greenbeard mutualism and altruism. *Proceedings of the National Academy of Sciences, 103*, 7372–7377.

Singelis, T. M. (1994). The measurement of independent and interdependent self-construals. *Personality and Social Psychology Bulletin, 20*, 580–591.

Singh, D. (1993). Adaptive significance of female physical attractiveness: Role of waist-to-hip ratio. *Journal of Personality and Social Psychology, 65*, 293–307.

Singh, D. (1995). Female judgment of male attractiveness and desirability for relationships: Role of waist-to-hip ratio and financial status. *Journal of Personality and Social Psychology, 69*, 1089–1101.

Sistrunk, F., & McDavid, J. W. (1971). Sex variable in conforming behavior. *Journal of Personality and Social Psychology, 17*, 200–207.

Siu, A. M. H., Cheng, H. C. H., & Leung, M. C. M. (2006). Prosocial norms as a positive youth development construct: Conceptual bases and implications for curriculum development. *International Journal of Adolescent Medicine and Health, 18*, 451–457.

Skarlicki, D. P., & Folger, R. (1997). Retaliation in the workplace: The roles of distributive, procedural, and interactional justice. *Journal of Applied Psychology, 82*, 434–443.

Skinner, E. A. (1996). A guide to constructs of control. *Journal of Personality and Social Psychology, 71*, 549–570.

Skinner, E. A., Edge, K., Altman, J., & Sherwood, H. (2003). Searching for the structure of coping: A review and critique of category systems for classifying ways of coping. *Psychological Bulletin, 129*, 216–269.

Skitka, L. J. (1999). Ideological and attributional boundaries on public compassion: Reactions to individuals and communities affected by a natural disaster. *Personality and Social Psychology Bulletin, 25*, 793–808.

Skitka, L. J., Mullen, E., Griffin, T., Hutchinson, S., & Chamberlin, B. (2002). Dispositions, scripts, or motivated correction? Understanding ideological differences in explanations for social problems. *Journal of Personality and Social Psychology, 83*, 470–487.

Sklar, L. S., & Anisman, H. (1981). Stress and cancer. *Psychological Bulletin, 89*, 369–406.

Skov, R. B., & Sherman, S. J. (1986). Information-gathering processes: Diagnosticity, hypothesis confirmatory strategies, and perceived hypothesis confirmation. *Journal of Experimental Social Psychology, 22*, 93–121.

Skowronski, J. J., & Carlston, D. E. (1989). Negativity and extremity biases in impression formation: A review of explanations. *Psychology Bulletin, 105*, 131–142.

Slamecka, N. J., & Graff, P. (1978). The generation effect: Delineation of a phenomenon. *Journal of Experimental Psychology: Human Learning and Memory, 4*, 592–604.

Sloan, R., Bagiella, E., & Powell, T. (1999). Religion, spirituality, and medicine. *Lancet, 353*, 664–667.

Slovic, P. (2000). *The perception of risk.* London: Earthscan.

Smeaton, G., Byrne, D., & Murnen, S. K. (1989). The repulsion hypothesis revisited: Similarity irrelevance or dissimilarity bias? *Journal of Personality and Social Psychology, 56*, 54–59.

Smeesters, D., Warlop, L., van Avermaet, E., Corneille, O., & Yzerbyt, V. (2003). Do not prime hawks with doves: The interplay of construct activation and consistency of social value orientation on cooperative behavior. *Journal of Personality and Social Psychology, 84*, 972–987.

Smith, A., & Williams, K. D. (2004). RU there? Ostracism by cell phone text messages. *Group Dynamics: Theory, Research, and Practice, 8*, 291–301.

Smith, A., Jussim, L., & Eccles, J. (1999). Do self-fulfilling prophecies accumulate, dissipate, or remain stable over time? *Journal of Personality and Social Psychology, 77*, 548–565.

Smith, B. N., Kerr, N. A., Markus, M. J., & Stasson, M. F. (2001). Individual differences in social loafing: Need for cognition as a motivator in collective performance. *Group Dynamics, 5*, 150–158.

Smith, E. R., & Semin, G. R. (2006). Socially situated cognition as a bridge. In P. A. M. Van Lange (Ed.), *Bridging social psychology:*

Benefits of transdisciplinary approaches (pp. 145–150). Mahwah, NJ: Erlbaum.

Smith, E. R., Jackson, J. W., & Sparks, C. W. (2003). Effects of inequality and reasons for inequality on group identification and cooperation in social dilemmas. *Group Processes and Intergroup Relations, 6,* 201–220.

Smith, H. J., & Tyler, T. R. (1997). Choosing the right pond: The impact of group membership on self-esteem and group-oriented behavior. *Journal of Experimental Social Psychology, 33,* 146–170.

Smith, H. J., Spears, R., & Hamstra, I. J. (1999). Social identity and the context of relative deprivation. In N. Ellemers, R. Spears, & I. J. Hamstra (Eds.), *Social identity: Context, commitment, content* (pp. 205–229). Oxford, England: Blackwell.

Smith, K. D., Keating, J. P., & Stotland, E. (1989). Altruism reconsidered: The effect of denying feedback on a victim's status to empathic witnesses. *Journal of Personality and Social Psychology, 57,* 641–650.

Smith, M. L., Glass, G. V., & Miller, T. I. (1980). *The benefits of psychotherapy.* Baltimore: Johns Hopkins University Press.

Smith, N. K., Cacioppo, J. T., Larsen, J. T., & Chartrand, T. L. (2003). May I have your attention, please: Electrocortical responses to positive and negative stimuli. *Neuropsychologia, 41,* 171–183.

Smith, P. B., & Bond, M. H. (1993). *Social psychology across cultures: Analysis and perspective.* New York: Harvester/Wheatsheaf.

Smith, P. K., Morita, Y., Junger-Tas, J., Olweus, D., Catalano, R. F., & Slee, P. (Eds.). (1998). *The nature of school bullying: A cross-national perspective.* New York: Routledge.

Smith, S. M., McIntosh, W. D., & Bazzani, D. G. (1999). Are the beautiful good in Hollywood? An investigation of the beauty-and-goodness stereotype on film. *Basic and Applied Social Psychology, 21,* 69–80.

Smith, S. S., & Richardson, D. (1983). Amelioration of deception and harm in psychological research: The important role of debriefing. *Journal of Personality and Social Psychology, 44,* 1075–1082.

Smith, T. W., Snyder, C. R., & Perkins, S. C. (1983). The self-serving function of hypochondriacal complaints: Physical symptoms as self-handicapping strategies. *Journal of Personality and Social Psychology, 44,* 787–797.

Smith, V. L., & Kassin, S. M. (1993). Effects of the dynamite charge on the deliberations of deadlocked mock juries. *Law and Human Behavior, 17,* 625–643.

Smither, J. W., Reilly, R. R., & Buda, R. (1988). Effect of prior performance information on ratings of present performance: Contrast versus assimilation revisited. *Journal of Applied Psychology, 73,* 487–496.

Smitherman, H. O. (1992). Helping: The importance of cost/reward considerations on likelihood to help. *Psychological Reports, 71,* 305–306.

Smurda, J. D., Wittig, M. A., & Gokalp, G. (2006). Effects of threat to a valued social identity on implicit self-esteem and discrimination. *Group Processes and Intergroup Relations, 9,* 181–197.

Smyth, J., & Lepore, S. J. (2002). *The writing cure: How expressive writing promotes health and emotional well-being.* Washington, DC: American Psychological Association.

Snibbe, A. C., Kitayama, S., Markus, H. R., & Suzuki, T. (2003). They saw a game: A Japanese and American (football) field study. *Journal of Cross-Cultural Psychology, 34,* 581–595.

Snyder, C. R. (Ed.). (2001). *Coping with stress: Effective people and processes.* New York: Oxford University Press.

Snyder, C. R., & Higgins, R. L. (1988). Excuses: Their effective role in the negotiation of reality. *Psychological Bulletin, 104,* 23–35.

Snyder, C. R., Higgins, R. L., & Stucky, R. J. (1983). *Excuses: Masquerades in search of grace.* New York: Wiley.

Snyder, C. R., Lassegard, M. A., & Ford, C. E. (1986). Distancing after group success and failure: Basking in reflected glory and cutting off reflected failure. *Journal of Personality and Social Psychology, 51,* 382–388.

Snyder, M. (1974). The self-monitoring of expressive behavior. *Journal of Personality and Social Psychology, 30,* 526–537.

Snyder, M. (1987). *Public appearances private/realities: The psychology of self-monitoring.* New York: Freeman.

Snyder, M. (1993). Basic research and practical problems: The promise of a "functional" personality and social psychology. *Personality and Social Psychology Bulletin, 19,* 251–264.

Snyder, M., & Clary, E. G. (2004). Volunteerism and the generative society. In E. de St. Aubin & D. P. McAdams (Eds.), *The generative society: Caring for future generations* (pp. 221–237). Washington, DC: American Psychological Association.

Snyder, M., & DeBono, K. (1985). Appeals to image and claims about quality: Understanding the psychology of advertising. *Journal of Personality and Social Psychology, 49,* 586–597.

Snyder, M., & Gangestad, S. (1986). On the nature of self-monitoring: Matters of assessment, matters of validity. *Journal of Personality and Social Psychology, 51,* 125–139.

Snyder, M., & Monson, T. C. (1975). Persons, situations, and the control of social behavior. *Journal of Personality and Social Psychology, 32,* 637–644.

Snyder, M., & Stukas, A. A. (1999). Interpersonal processes: The interplay of cognitive, motivational, and behavioral activities in social interaction. *Annual Review of Psychology, 50,* 273–303.

Snyder, M., & Swann, W. B., Jr. (1978). Behavioral confirmation in social interaction: From social perception to social reality. *Journal of Personality and Social Psychology, 36,* 1202–1212.

Snyder, M., Tanke, E. D., & Berscheid, E. (1977). Social perception and interpersonal behavior: On the self-fulfilling nature of social stereotypes. *Journal of Personality and Social Psychology, 35,* 656–666.

Sober, E., & Wilson, D. S. (1998). *Unto others: The evolution and psychology of unselfish behavior.* Cambridge, MA: Harvard University Press.

Sommer, K. L., & Baumeister, R. F. (2002). Self-evaluation, persistence, and performance following implicit rejection: The role of trait self-esteem. *Personality and Social Psychology Bulletin, 28,* 926–938.

Sommers, S. (2006). On racial diversity and group decision making: Identifying multiple effects of racial composition on jury deliberations. *Journal of Personality and Social Psychology, 90,* 597–612.

Sommers, S. R. (2006). On racial diversity and group decision making: Identifying multiple effects of racial composition on jury deliberations. *Journal of Personality and Social Psychology, 90,* 597–612.

Sommers, S. R. (2006). On racial diversity and group decision making: Identifying multiple effects of racial composition on jury deliberations. *Journal of Personality and Social Psychology, 90,* 597–612.

Sommers, S. R., & Ellsworth, P. C. (2001). White juror bias: An investigation of racial prejudice against Black defendants in the American courtroom. *Psychology, Public Policy, and Law, 7,* 201–229.

Sommers, S. R., & Norton, M. I. (2006). Lay theories about white racists: What constitutes racism (and what doesn't). *Group Processes and Intergroup Relations, 9,* 117–138.

Son Hing, L. S., Bobocel, D. R., & Zanna, M. P. (2002). Meritocracy and opposition to affirmative action: Making concessions in the face of discrimination. *Journal of Personality and Social Psychology, 83,* 493–509.

Son Hing, L. S., Chung-Yan, G. A., Grunfeld, R., Robichaud, L. K., & Zanna, M. P. (2005). Exploring the discrepancy between implicit and explicit prejudice: A test of aversive racism theory. In J. P. Forgas, K. D. Williams, & S. M. Laham (Eds.), *Social motivation: Conscious and unconscious processes* (pp. 274–293). New York: Cambridge University Press.

Souweidane, V., & Huesmann, L. R. (1999). The influence of American urban culture on the development of normative beliefs about aggression in Middle-Eastern immigrants. *American Journal of Community Psychology, 27*, 239–254.

Spears, R. (2002). Four degrees of stereotype formation: Differentiation by any means necessary. In C. McGarty, V. Y. Yzerbyt, & R. Spears (Eds.), *Stereotypes as explanations: The formation of meaningful beliefs about social groups* (pp. 127–156). Cambridge, UK: Cambridge University Press.

Spears, R., Postmes, T., Lea, M., & Watt, S. E. (2001). A SIDE view of social influence. In J. P. Forgas & K. D. Williams (Eds.), *Social influence: Direct and indirect processes. The Sydney symposium of social psychology* (pp. 331–350). Philadelphia: Psychology Press.

Special report: A crime as American as a Colt .45. (1995, August 15). *Newsweek*, 22–23, 45.

Spencer, S. J., Fein, S., Wolfe, C. T., Fong, C., & Dunn, M. A. (1998). Automatic activation of stereotypes: The role of self-image threat. *Personality and Social Psychology Bulletin, 24*, 1139–1152.

Spencer, S. J., Fein, S., Zanna, M., & Olson, J. M. (Eds.). (2003). *Motivated social perception: The Ontario symposium* (Vol. 9). Mahwah, NJ: Erlbaum.

Spencer, S. J., Steele, C. M., & Quinn, D. M. (1999). Stereotype threat and women's math performance. *Journal of Experimental Social Psychology, 35*, 4–28.

Spiegel, D. (1993). Social support: How friends, family, and groups can help. In D. Goleman & J. Gurin (Eds.), *Mind body medicine: How to use your mind for better health* (pp. 331–350). Yonkers, NY: Consumer Reports Books.

Spivey, C. B., & Prentice-Dunn, S. (1990). Assessing the directionality of deindividuated behavior: Effects of deindividuation, modeling, and private self-consciousness on aggressive and prosocial responses. *Basic and Applied Social Psychology, 11*, 387–403.

Sporer, S. L. (1993). Eyewitness identification accuracy, confidence, and decision times in simultaneous and sequential lineups. *Journal of Applied Psychology, 78*, 22–33.

Sporer, S. L., Malpass, R. S., & Koehnken, G. (Eds.). (1996). *Psychological issues in eyewitness identification*. Mahwah, NJ: Erlbaum.

Sporer, S. L., Penrod, S. D., Read, J. D., & Cutler, B. L. (1995). Choosing, confidence, and accuracy: A meta-analysis of the confidence-accuracy relation in eyewitness identification studies. *Psychological Bulletin, 118*, 315–327.

Spradley, J., & McCurdy, D. W. (2006). *Conformity and conflict: Readings in cultural anthropology* (12th ed.). Boston: Allyn & Bacon.

Sprafkin, J. N., Liebert, R. M., & Poulos, R. W. (1975). Effects of a prosocial televised example on children's helping. *Journal of Experimental Child Psychology, 20*, 119–126.

Sprecher, S. (1994). Two sides to the breakup of dating relationships. *Personal Relationships, 1*, 199–222.

Sprecher, S. (1999). "I love you more today than yesterday": Romantic partners' perceptions of changes in love and related affect over time. *Journal of Personality and Social Psychology, 76*, 46–53.

Sprecher, S. (2001). Equity and social exchange in dating couples: Associations with satisfaction, commitment, and stability. *Journal of Marriage and the Family, 63*, 599–613.

Sprecher, S., & Hendrick, S. S. (2004). Self-disclosure in intimate relationships: Associations with individual and relationship characteristics over time. *Journal of Social and Clinical Psychology, 23*, 857–877.

Sprecher, S., & Regan, P. C. (1998). Passionate and companionate love in courting and young married couples. *Sociological Inquiry, 68*, 163-185.

Sprecher, S., Sullivan, Q., & Hatfield, E. (1994). Mate selection preferences: Gender differences examined in a national sample. *Journal of Personality and Social Psychology, 66*, 1074–1080.

Sraus, M. A. (1999). The controversy over domestic violence by women: A methological, theoretical, and sociology of science analysis. In X. B. Arriaga & S. Oskamp (Eds.), *Violence in intimate relationships* (pp. 17–44). Thousand Oaks, CA: Sage.

Staats, A. W., & Staats, C. K. (1958). Attitudes established by classical conditioning. *Journal of Abnormal and Social Psychology, 57*, 37–40.

Stalans, L. J., & Diamond, S. S. (1990). Formation and change in lay evaluations of criminal sentencing: Misperception and discontent. *Law and Human Behavior, 14*, 199–214.

Stangor, C., & Lange, J. E. (1994). Mental representations of social groups: Advances in understanding stereotypes and stereotyping. In M. P. Zanna (Ed.), *Advances in experimental social psychology* (Vol. 26, pp. 357–416). San Diego, CA: Academic Press.

Stangor, C., Lynch, L., Changming, D., & Glass, B. (1992). Categorization of individuals on the basis of multiple social features. *Journal of Personality and Social Psychology, 62*, 207–218.

Stangor, C., Sechrist, G. B., & Jost, J. T. (2001). Changing racial beliefs by providing consensus information. *Personality and Social Psychology Bulletin, 27*, 486–496.

Stanton, A. L., Kirk, S. B., Cameron, C. L., & Danoff-Berg, S. (2000). Coping through emotional approach: Scale construction and validation. *Journal of Personality and Social Psychology, 78*, 1150–1169.

Stapel, D. A., & Koomen, W. (2000). How far do we go beyond the information given? The impact of knowledge activation on interpretation and inference. *Journal of Personality and Social Psychology, 78*, 19–37.

Stasser, G. (1992). Pooling of unshared information during group discussions. In S. Worchel, W. Wood, & J. A. Simpson (Eds.), *Group process and productivity* (pp. 48–67). Newbury Park, CA: Sage.

Stasser, G., & Birchmeier, Z. (2003). Group creativity and collective choice. In P. B. Paulus & B. A. Nijstad (Eds.), *Group creativity: Innovation through collaboration* (pp. 85-109). New York: Oxford University Press.

Stasser, G., & Davis, J. H. (1981). Group decision making and social influence: A social interaction sequence model. *Psychological Review, 88*, 523–551.

Stasser, G., Kerr, N. L., & Bray, R. M. (1982). The social psychology of jury deliberations: Structure, process, and product. In N. Kerr & R. Bray (Eds.), *The psychology of the courtroom* (pp. 221–256). New York: Academic Press.

Stasser, G., Stewart, D. D., & Wittenbaum, G. M. (1995). Expert roles and information exchange during discussion: The importance of knowing who knows what. *Journal of Experimental Social Psychology, 31*, 244–265.

Stasson, M. F., & Bradshaw, S. D. (1995). Explanations of individual-group performance differences: What sort of "bonus" can be gained through group interaction? *Small Group Research, 26*, 296–308.

Staub, E. (1996). Cultural-societal roots of violence: The examples of genocidal violence and of contemporary youth violence in the United States. *American Psychologist, 51*, 117–132.

Staub, E. (2004). Understanding and responding to group violence: Genocide, mass killing, and terrorism. In F. M. Moghaddam, & A. J. Marsella (Eds.), *Understanding terrorism: Psychosocial roots, consequences, and interventions* (pp. 151–168). Washington, DC: American Psychological Association.

Stauffer, J. M., & Buckley, M. R. (2005). The existence and nature of racial bias in supervisory ratings. *Journal of Applied Psychology, 90*, 586–591.

Staw, B. M. (1997). The escalation of commitment: An update and appraisal. In Z. Shapira (Ed.), *Organizational decision making. Cambridge series on judgement and decision making* (pp. 191–215). New York: Cambridge University Press.

Staw, B. M., & Hoang, H. (1995). Sunk costs in the NBA: Why draft order affects playing time and survival in professional basketball. *Administrative Science Quarterly, 40,* 474–493.

Staw, B. M., Barsade, S. G., & Koput, K. W. (1997). Escalation at the credit window: A longitudinal study of bank executives' recognition and write-off of problem loans. *Journal of Applied Psychology, 82,* 130–142.

Steblay, N. M. (1987). Helping behavior in rural and urban environments: A meta-analysis. *Psychological Bulletin, 102,* 346–356.

Steblay, N. M. (1992). A meta-analytic review of the weapon-focus effect. *Law and Human Behavior, 16,* 413–424.

Steblay, N. M. (1997). Social influence in eyewitness recall: A meta-analytic review of lineup instruction effects. *Law and Human Behavior, 21,* 283–297.

Steblay, N., Besirevic, J., Fulero, S., & Jiminez-Lorente, B. (1999). The effects of pretrial publicity on juror verdicts: A meta-analytic review. *Law and Human Behavior, 23,* 219–235.

Steblay, N., Hosch, H. M., Culhane, S. E., & McWethy, A. (2006). The impact on juror verdicts of judicial instruction to disregard inadmissible evidence: A meta-analysis. *Law and Human Behavior, 30,* 469–492.

Steele, C. M. (1988). The psychology of self-affirmation: Sustaining the integrity of the self. In L. Berkowitz (Ed.), *Advances in experimental social psychology* (Vol. 21, pp. 261–302). New York: Academic Press.

Steele, C. M. (1997). A threat in the air: How stereotypes shape intellectual identity and performance. *American Psychologist, 52,* 613–629.

Steele, C. M. (1999). Thin ice: "Stereotype threat" and black college students. *Atlantic Monthly, 284,* 44–47, 50–54.

Steele, C. M., & Aronson, J. (1995). Stereotype vulnerability and the intellectual test performance of African Americans. *Journal of Personality and Social Psychology, 69,* 797–811.

Steele, C. M., & Josephs, R. A. (1990). Alcohol myopia: Its prized and dangerous effects. *American Psychologist, 45,* 921–933.

Steele, C. M., Spencer, S. J., & Aronson, J. (2002). Contending with group image: The psychology of stereotype and social identity threat. In M. P. Zanna (Ed.), *Advances in experimental social psychology* (Vol. 34, pp. 379–440). San Diego, CA: Academic Press.

Steele, C. M., Spencer, S. J., & Lynch, M. (1993). Self-image resilience and dissonance: The role of affirmational resources. *Journal of Personality and Social Psychology, 64,* 885–896.

Stein, M. B., Walker, J. R., & Forde, D. R. (1996). Public-speaking fears in a community sample. *Archives of General Psychiatry, 53,* 169–174.

Steiner, I. D. (1966). Models for inferring relationships between group size and potential group productivity. *Behavioral Science, 11,* 273–283.

Steiner, I. D. (1972). *Group process and productivity.* New York: Academic Press.

Stempfle, J., Huebner, O., & Badke-Schaub, P. (2001). A functional theory of task role distribution in work groups. *Group Processes and Intergroup Relations, 4,* 138–159.

Stephan, W. G. (1986). The effects of school desegregation: An evaluation 30 years after Brown. In M. J. Saks & L. Saxe (Eds.), *Advances in applied social psychology* (Vol. 3, pp. 181–206). Hillsdale, NJ: Erlbaum.

Stephan, W. G., & Finlay, K. (1999). The role of empathy in improving intergroup relations. *Journal of Social Issues, 55,* 729–743.

Stephan, W. G., Renfro, C. L., Esses, V. M., Stephan, C. W., & Martin, T. (2005). The effects of feeling threatened on attitudes toward immigrants. *International Journal of Intercultural Relations, 29,* 1–19.

Stephan, W. G., Ybarra, O., & Bachman, G. (1999). Prejudice toward immigrants. *Journal of Applied Social Psychology, 29,* 2221–2237.

Stepper, S., & Strack, F. (1993). Proprioceptive determinants of emotional and nonemotional feelings. *Journal of Personality and Social Psychology, 64,* 211–220.

Sternberg, R. J. (1986). A triangular theory of love. *Psychological Review, 93,* 119–135.

Sternberg, R. J. (1997). *Successful intelligence: How practical and creative Intelligence determine success in life.* New York: Plume.

Sternberg, R. J. (1999). *Cupid's arrow: The course of love through time.* New York: Cambridge University Press.

Sternberg, R. J., & Hedlund, J. (2002). Practical intelligence, *g,* and work psychology. *Human Performance, 15,* 143–160.

Sternberg, R. J., & Weis, K. (Eds.). (2006). *The new psychology of love.* New Haven, CT: Yale University Press.

Stets, J. E., & Straus, M. A. (1989). The marriage license as a hitting license: A comparison of assaults in dating, cohabiting, and married couples. *Journal of Family Violence, 41,* 33–52.

Stevens, C. K., & Kristof, A. L. (1995). Making the right impression: A field study of applicant impression management during job interviews. *Journal of Applied Psychology, 80,* 587–606.

Stewart, A. J., Sokol, M., Healy, J. M., Jr., & Chester, N. L. (1986). Longitudinal studies of psychological consequences of life changes in children and adults. *Journal of Personality and Social Psychology, 50,* 143–151.

Stine, G. J. (2007). *AIDS Update 2007.* New York: McGraw-Hill Science.

Stinson, V., Devenport, J. L., Cutler, B. L., & Kravitz, D. A. (1996). How effective is the presence-of-counsel safeguard? Attorney perceptions of suggestiveness, fairness, and correctability of biased lineup procedures. *Journal of Applied Psychology, 81,* 64–75.

Stinson, V., Devenport, J. L., Cutler, B. L., & Kravitz, D. A. (1997). How effective is the motion-to-suppress safeguard? Judges perceptions of the suggestiveness and fairness of biased lineup procedures. *Journal of Applied Psychology, 82,* 26–43.

Stogdill, R. (1972). Group productivity, drive, and cohesiveness. *Organizational Behavior and Human Performance, 8,* 26–43.

Stoltzfus, N. (1996). *Resistance of the heart: Intermarriage and the Rosenstrasse protest in Nazi Germany.* New York: Norton.

Stone J., Perry, Z. W., & Darley, J. M. (1997). "White men can't jump": Evidence for the perceptual confirmation of racial stereotypes following a basketball game. *Basic and Applied Social Psychology, 19,* 291–306.

Stone, A. A., Neale, J. M., Cox, D. S., Napoli, A., Valdimarsdottir, H., & Kennedy-Moore, E. (1994). Daily events are associated with a secretory immune response to an oral antigen in men. *Health Psychology, 13,* 440–446.

Stone, J. (2002). Battling doubt by avoiding practice: The effects of stereotype threat on self-handicapping in white athletes. *Personality and Social Psychology Bulletin, 28,* 1667–1678.

Stone, J. (2003). Self-consistency for low self-esteem in dissonance processes: The role of self-standards. *Personality and Social Psychology Bulletin, 29,* 846–858.

Stone, J., Lynch, C. I., Sjomeling, M., & Darley, J. M. (1999). Stereotype threat effects on black and white athletic performance. *Journal of Personality and Social Psychology, 77,* 1213–1227.

Stone, J., Wiegand, A. W., Cooper, J., & Aronson, E. (1997). When exemplification fails: Hypocrisy and the motive for self-integrity. *Journal of Personality and Social Psychology, 72,* 54–65.

Stone, W. F., Lederer, G., & Christie, R. (Eds.). (1993). *Strength and weakness: The authoritarian personality today.* New York: Springer-Verlag.

Stoner, J. A. F. (1961). *A comparison of individual and group decisions involving risk.* Unpublished manuscript, Massachusetts Institute of Technology, Cambridge, MA.

Stotland, E. (1969). Exploratory investigations of empathy. In L. Berkowitz (Ed.), *Advances in experimental social psychology* (Vol. 4, pp. 271–313). New York: Academic Press.

Stouten, J., De Cremer, D., & van Dijk, E. (2006). Violating equality in social dilemmas: Emotional and retributive reactions as a function of trust, attribution, and honesty. *Personality and Social Psychology Bulletin, 32,* 894–906.

Strahan, E. J., Spencer, S. J., & Zanna, M. P. (2002). Subliminal priming and persuasion: Striking while the iron is hot. *Journal of Experimental Social Psychology, 38,* 556–568.

Strauman, T. J. (1992). Self-guides, autobiographical memory, and anxiety and dysphoria: Toward a cognitive model of vulnerability to emotional distress. *Journal of Abnormal Psychology, 101,* 87–95.

Strauman, T. J., Lemieux, A. M., & Coe, C. L. (1993). Self-discrepancy and natural killer cell activity: Immunological consequences of negative self-evaluation. *Journal of Personality and Social Psychology, 64,* 1042–1052.

Strauman, T. J., Woods, T. E., Schneider, K. L., Kwapil, L., & Coe, C. L. (2004). Self-regulatory cognition and immune reactivity: Idiographic success and failure feedback effects on the natural killer cell. *Brain, Behavior and Immunity, 18,* 544–554.

Straus, M. A. (1999). The controversy over domestic violence by women: A methodical, theoretical, and sociology of science analysis. In X. B. Arriaga & S. Oskamp (Eds.), *Violence in intimate relationships* (pp. 17–44). Thousand Oaks, CA: Sage.

Straus, M. A. (2000). *Beating the devil out of them: Corporal punishment in American families and its effects on children* (2nd ed.). New Brunswick, NJ: Transaction Publishers.

Straus, M. A. (2006). Future research on gender symmetry in physical assaults on partners. *Violence Against Women, 12,* 1086–1097.

Straus, M. A., & Mouradian, V. E. (1998). Impulsive corporal punishment by mothers and antisocial behavior and impulsiveness of children. *Behavioral Sciences and the Law, 16,* 353–374.

Straus, M. A., & Ramirez, I. L. (2005). Gender symmetry in prevalence, severity, and chronicity of physical aggression against dating partners by university students in Mexico and the USA. In S. Fein, G. R. Goethals, & M. J. Sandstrom (Eds.), *Gender and aggression: Interdisciplinary perspectives.* Mahwah, NJ: Erlbaum.

Strawbridge, W. J., Shema, S. J., Cohen, R. D., & Kaplan, G. A. (2001). Religious attendance increases survival by improving and maintaining good health behaviors, mental health, and social relationships. *Annals of Behavioral Medicine, 23,* 68–74.

Strentz, T., & Auerbach, S. M. (1988). Adjustment to the stress of simulated captivity: Effects of emotion-focused versus problem-focused preparation on hostages differing in locus of control. *Journal of Personality and Social Psychology, 55,* 652–660.

Strier, F. (1999). Wither trial consulting: Issues and projections. *Law and Human Behavior, 23,* 93–115.

Strodtbeck, F. L., & Hook, L. (1961). The social dimensions of a twelve-man jury table. *Sociometry, 24,* 397–415.

Strodtbeck, F. L., James, R., & Hawkins, C. (1957). Social status in jury deliberations. *American Sociological Review, 22,* 713–719.

Stroebe, W., & Diehl, M. (1994). Why groups are less effective than their members: On productivity losses in idea generating groups. In W. Stroebe & M. Hewstone (Eds.), *European Review of Social Psychology* (Vol. 5, pp. 272–303). Chichester, England: Wiley.

Stroessner, S. J., & Plaks, J. E. (2001). Illusory correlation and stereotype formation: Tracing the arc of research over a quarter century. In G. B. Moskowitz (Ed.), *Cognitive social psychology: The Princeton symposium on the legacy and future of social cognition* (pp. 247–259). Mahwah, NJ: Erlbaum.

Strohmetz, D. B., Rind, B., Fisher, R., & Lynn, M. (2002). Sweetening the till: The use of candy to increase restaurant tipping. *Journal of Applied Social Psychology, 32,* 300–309.

Struck, D. (2006, September 15). Gunman's writings presaged rampage; blog described fascination with death, laid out events that would unfold in Montreal. *Washington Post,* p. A12.

Struckman-Johnson, C., & Struckman-Johnson, D. (1994). Men pressured and forced into sexual experience. *Archives of Sexual Behavior, 23,* 93–114.

Strupp, H. H. (1996). The tripartite model and the Consumer Reports study. *American Psychologist, 51,* 1017–1024.

Studebaker, C. A., & Penrod, S. D. (1997). Pretrial publicity: The media, the law, and common sense. *Psychology, Public Policy, and Law, 3,* 428–460.

Stuhlmacher, A. F., & Walters, A. E. (1999). Gender differences in negotiation outcome: A meta-analysis. *Personnel Psychology, 52,* 653–677.

Stürmer, S., Snyder, M., & Omoto, A. M. (2005). Prosocial emotions and helping: The moderating role of group membership. *Journal of Personality and Social Psychology, 88,* 532–546.

Stutzer, A. (2004). The role of income aspirations in individual happiness. *Journal of Economic Behavior and Organization, 54,* 89–109.

Suarez, E. C., & Krishnan, K. R. R. (2006). The relation of free plasma tryptophan to anger, hostility, and aggression in a nonpatient sample of adult men and women. *Annals of Behavioral Medicine, 31,* 254–260.

Sue, S., Smith, R. E., & Caldwell, C. (1973). Effects of inadmissible evidence on the decisions of simulated jurors: A moral dilemma. *Journal of Applied Social Psychology, 3,* 345–353.

Suh, E., Diener, E., & Fujita, F. (1996). Events and subjective well-being: Only recent events matter. *Journal of Personality and Social Psychology, 70,* 1091–1102.

Suls, J. M., & Wheeler, L. (Eds.). (2000). *Handbook of social comparison: Theory and research.* New York: Plenum.

Suls, J., & Green, P. (2003). Pluralistic ignorance and college student perceptions of gender-specific alcohol norms. *Health Psychology, 22,* 479–486.

Suls, J., & Wallston, K. A. (Eds.). (2003). *Social psychological foundations of health and illness.* London: Blackwell.

Sundstrom, E. (1986). *Work places.* New York: Cambridge University Press.

Sunstein, C. R., Hastie, R., Payne, J. W., Schkade, D. A., & Viscusi, W. K. (2002). *Punitive damages: How juries decide.* Chicago: University of Chicago Press.

Surowiecki, J. (2005). *The wisdom of crowds.* New York: Anchor Books.

Susskind, J. (2003). Children's perception of gender-based illusory correlations: Enhancing preexisting relationships between gender and behavior. *Sex Roles, 48,* 483–494.

Sutker, P. B., Uddo, M., Brailey, K., & Allain, A. N., Jr., (1993). War-zone trauma and stress-related symptoms in Operation Desert Shield/Storm (ODS) returnees. *Journal of Social Issues, 49,* 33–49.

Swann, W. B., Jr. (1984). Quest for accuracy in person perception: A matter of pragmatics. *Psychological Review, 91,* 457–477.

Swann, W. B., Jr. (1987). Identity negotiation: Where two roads meet. *Journal of Personality and Social Psychology, 53,* 1038–1051.

Swann, W. B., Jr. (1997). The trouble with change: Self-verification and allegiance to the self. *Psychological Science, 8*, 177–180.

Swann, W. B., Jr. (1999). *Resilient identities: Self, relationships, and the construction of social reality.* New York: Basic Books.

Swann, W. B., Jr., & Bosson, J. K. (2007). Identity negotiation: A theory of self and social interaction. In O. John, R. Robins, & L. Pervin (Eds.), *Handbook of personality psychology: Theory and research.* New York: Guilford.

Swann, W. B., Jr., & Ely, R. J. (1984). A battle of wills: Self-verification versus behavioral confirmation. *Journal of Personality and Social Psychology, 46*, 1287–1302.

Swann, W. B., Jr., & Hill, C. A. (1982). When our identities are mistaken: Reaffirming self-conceptions through social interaction. *Journal of Personality and Social Psychology, 43*, 59–66.

Swann, W. B., Jr., Hixon, J. G., & De La Ronde, C. (1992). Embracing the bitter "truth": Negative self-concepts and marital commitment. *Psychological Science, 3*, 118–121.

Swann, W. B., Jr., Kwan, V. S. Y., Polzer, J. T., & Milton, L. P. (2003). Fostering group identification and creativity in diverse groups: The role of individuation and self-verification. *Personality and Social Psychology Bulletin, 29*, 1396–1406.

Swann, W. B., Jr., Polzer, J. T., Seyle, D. C., & Ko, S. J. (2004). Finding value in diversity: Verification of personal and social self-views in diverse groups. *Academy of Management Review, 29*, 9–27.

Swann, W. B., Jr., Stein-Seroussi, A., & Giesler, B. J. (1992). Why people self-verify. *Journal of Personality and Social Psychology, 62*, 392–401.

Swim, J. K., & Sanna, L. J. (1996). He's skilled, she's lucky: A meta-analysis of observers' attributions for women's and men's successes and failures. *Personality and Social Psychology Bulletin, 22*, 507–519.

Swim, J. K., Aikin, K. J., Hall, W. S., & Hunter, B. A. (1995). Sexism and racism: Old-fashioned and modern prejudices. *Journal of Personality and Social Psychology, 68*, 199–214.

Swim, J. K., Borgida, E., Maruyama, G., & Myers, D. G. (1989). Joan McKay versus John McKay: Do gender stereotypes bias evaluations? *Psychological Bulletin, 105*, 409–429.

t'Hart, P. (1998). Preventing groupthink revisited: Evaluating and reforming groups in government. *Organizational Behavior and Human Decision Processes, 73*, 306–326.

t'Hart, P., Stern, E., & Sundelius, B. (1995). *Beyond groupthink.* Stockholm: Stockholm Center for Organizational Research.

Tajfel, H. (1982). Social psychology of intergroup relations. *Annual Review of Psychology, 33*, 1–39.

Tajfel, H., Billig, M. G., Bundy, R. P., & Flament, C. (1971). Social categorization and intergroup behavior. *European Journal of Social Psychology, 1*, 149–178.

Tan, H. T., & Yates, J. F. (2002). Financial budgets and escalation effects. *Organizational Behavior and Human Decision Processes, 87*, 300–322.

Tanford, S., & Penrod, S. (1984). Social influence model: A formal integration of research on majority and minority influence processes. *Psychological Bulletin, 95*, 189–225.

Tang, S., & Hall, V. C. (1995). The overjustification effect: A meta-analysis. *Applied Cognitive Psychology, 9*, 365–404.

Tangney, J. P., Wagner, P. E., Hill-Barlow, D., Marschall, D. E., & Gramzow, R. (1996). Relation of shame and guilt to constructive versus destructive responses to anger across the lifespan. *Journal of Personality and Social Psychology, 70*, 797–809.

Tannen, D. (1990). *You just don't understand: Women and men in conversation.* New York: Morrow.

Tapper, K., & Boulton, M. J. (2004). Sex differences in levels of physical, verbal, and indirect aggression amongst primary school children and their associations with beliefs about aggression. *Aggressive Behavior, 30*, 123–145.

Tapper, K., & Boulton, M. J. (2005). Victim and peer group responses to different forms of aggression among primary school children. *Aggressive Behavior, 31*, 238–253.

Tarde, G. (1890). *Les lois de l'imitation. Étude sociologique.* Paris: Félix Alcan.

Tassinary, L. G., & Cacioppo, J. T. (1992). Unobservable facial actions and emotion. *Psychological Science, 3*, 28–33.

Tate, D. C., Reppucci, N. D., & Mulvey, E. P. (1995). Violent juvenile delinquents: Treatment effectiveness and implications for future action. *American Psychologist, 50*, 777–781.

Taubman-Ben-Ari, O., Findler, L., & Mikulincer, M. (2002). The effects of mortality salience on relationship strivings and beliefs: The moderating role of attachment style. *British Journal of Social Psychology, 41*, 419–441.

Tauer, J. M., & Harackiewicz, J. M. (2004). The effects of cooperation and competition on intrinsic motivation and performance. *Journal of Personality and Social Psychology, 86*, 849–861.

Tay, C., Ang, S., & Linn, V. (2006). Personality, biographical characteristics, and job interview success: A longitudinal study of the mediating effects of interviewing self-efficacy and the moderating effects of internal locus of causality. *Journal of Applied Psychology, 91*, 446–454.

Taylor, D. (2006, September 13). Get fit now, pay later: More and more men want a body like David Beckham's—even if they have to take dangerous short cuts to get them. *The Guardian (London)*, p. 16.

Taylor, R. B. (2000). *Breaking away from broken windows: Baltimore neighborhoods and the nationwide fight against crime, grime, fear, and decline.* Boulder, CO: Westview Press.

Taylor, S. E. (1989). *Positive illusions: Creative self-deceptions and the healthy mind.* New York: Basic Books.

Taylor, S. E. (1990). Health psychology: The science and the field. *American Psychologist, 45*, 40–50.

Taylor, S. E. (1991). Asymmetrical effects of positive and negative events: The mobilization-minimization hypothesis. *Psychological Bulletin, 110*, 67–85.

Taylor, S. E. (2002). *The tending instinct: Women, men, and the biology of nurturing.* New York: Times Books.

Taylor, S. E. (2006a). *Health psychology* (6th ed.). New York: McGraw-Hill.

Taylor, S. E. (2006b). Tend and befriend: Biobehavioral bases of affiliation under stress. *Current Directions in Psychological Science, 15*, 273–277.

Taylor, S. E., & Brown, J. D. (1988). Illusion and well-being: A social psychological perspective on mental health. *Psychological Bulletin, 103*, 193–210.

Taylor, S. E., & Fiske, S. T. (1975). Point of view and perceptions of causality. *Journal of Personality and Social Psychology, 32*, 439–445.

Taylor, S. E., & Lobel, M. (1989). Social comparison activity under threat: Downward evaluation and upward contacts. *Psychological Review, 96*, 569–575.

Taylor, S. E., Klein, L. C., Lewis, B. P., Gruenewald, T. L., Guring, R. A. R., & Updegraff, J. A. (2000). Biobehavioral responses to stress in females: Tend-and-befriend, not fight-or-flight. *Psychological Review, 107*, 411–429.

Taylor, S. E., Lerner, J. S., Sherman, D. K., Sage, R. M., & McDowell, N. K. (2003). Portrait of the self-enhancer: Well adjusted and well liked or maladjusted and friendless? *Journal of Personality and Social Psychology, 84*, 165–176.

Taylor, S. E., Sherman, D. K., Kim, H. S., Jarcho, J., Takgi, K., & Dunagan, M. S. (2004). Culture and social support: Who seeks it and why? *Journal of Personality and Social Psychology, 87*, 354–362.

Taylor, S. P., & Hulsizer, M. R. (1998). Psychoactive drugs and human aggression. In R. G. Geen & E. Donnerstein (Eds.), *Human aggression: Theories, research, and implications for social policy* (pp. 139–165). San Diego: Academic Press.

Tazelaar, M. J. A., Van Lange, P. A. M., & Ouwerkerk, J. W. (2004). How to cope with 'noise' in social dilemmas: The benefits of communication. *Journal of Personality and Social Psychology, 87,* 845–859.

Tedeschi, J. T. (Ed.). (1981). *Impression management theory and social psychological research.* New York: Academic Press.

Tedeschi, J. T., & Bond, M. H. (2001). Aversive behavior and aggression in cultural perspective. In R. M. Kowalski (Ed.), *Behaving badly: Aversive behaviors in interpersonal relationships* (pp. 257–293). Washington, DC: American Psychological Association.

Tedeschi, J. T., & Quigley, B. M. (2000). A further comment on the construct validity of laboratory aggression paradigms: A response to Giancola and Chermack. *Aggression and Violent Behavior, 5,* 127–136.

Tedeschi, J. T., Schlenker, B. R., & Bonoma, T. V. (1971). Cognitive dissonance: Private ratiocination or public spectacle? *American Psychologist, 26,* 685–695.

Teger, A. (1980). *Too much invested to quit.* New York: Pergamon Press.

Tenenbaum, H. R., & Leaper, C. (2002). Are parents' gender schemas related to their children's gender-related cognitions? A meta-analysis. *Developmental Psychology, 38,* 615–630.

Tepper, B. J. (2001). Health consequences of organizational injustice: Tests of main and interactive effects. *Organizational Behavior and Human Decision Processes, 86,* 197–215.

Terkel, S. (1992). *Race: How blacks and whites think and feel about the American obsession.* New York: New Press.

Tesser, A. (1978). Self-generated attitude change. In L. Berkowitz (Ed.), *Advances in experimental social psychology* (Vol. 11, pp. 288–338). New York: Academic Press.

Tesser, A. (1988). Toward a self-evaluation maintenance model of social behavior. In L. Berkowitz (Ed.), *Advances in experimental social psychology* (Vol. 21, pp. 181–227). New York: Academic Press.

Tesser, A. (1993). The importance of heritability in psychological research: The case of attitudes. *Psychological Review, 100,* 129–142.

Tesser, A., & Collins, J. E. (1988). Emotion in social reflection and comparison situations: Intuitive, systematic, and exploratory approaches. *Journal of Personality and Social Psychology, 55,* 695–709.

Tesser, A., & Smith, J. (1980). Some effects of task relevance and friendship on helping: You don't always help the one you like. *Journal of Experimental Social Psychology, 16,* 582–590.

Tesser, A., Pilkington, C. J., & McIntosh, W. D. (1989). Self-evaluation maintenance and the mediational role of emotion: The perception of friends and strangers. *Journal of Personality and Social Psychology, 57,* 442–456.

Tesser, A., Wood, J. V., & Stapel, D. A. (Eds.). (2005). *On building, defending, and regulating the self: A psychological perspective.* New York: Psychology Press.

Tetlock, P. E. (1998). Social psychology and world politics. In D. T. Gilbert, S. T. Fiske, & G. Lindzey (Eds.), *The handbook of social psychology* (4th ed., Vol. 2, pp. 868–912). New York: McGraw-Hill.

Thaler, R. (1980). Toward a positive theory of consumer choice. *Journal of Economic Behavior and Organization, 1,* 39–60.

The Daily Telegraph (Australia). (2006, October 30). Heartless drivers hit. p. 2.

The Herald (Glasgow). (2005, February 16). Lawsuit claims video game developed by Edinburgh company inspired police killings, p. 2.

Thibaut, J. W., & Kelley, H. H. (1959). *The social psychology of groups.* New York: Wiley.

Thibaut, J., & Walker, L. (1975). *Procedural justice: A psychological analysis.* Hillsdale, NJ: Erlbaum.

Thibaut, J., & Walker, L. (1978). A theory of procedure. *California Law Review, 66,* 541–566.

Thibodeau, R. (1989). From racism to tokenism: The changing face of blacks in New Yorker cartoons. *Public Opinion Quarterly, 53,* 482–494.

Thomas, A. K., & Loftus, E. F. (2002). Creating bizarre false memories through imagination. *Memory and Cognition, 30,* 423–431.

Thomas, D. A., & Gabarro, J. J. (1999). *Breaking through: The making of minority executives in corporate America.* Cambridge, MA: Harvard Business School Press.

Thomas, S. L., Skitka, L. J., Christen, S., & Jurgena, M. (2002). Social facilitation and impression formation. *Basic and Applied Social Psychology, 24,* 67–70.

Thompson, C. P., Herrmann, D. J., Read, J. D., Bruce, D., Payne, D. G., & Toglia, M. P. (Eds.). (1998). *Autobiographical memory: Theoretical and applied perspectives.* Mahwah, NJ: Erlbaum.

Thompson, C. P., Herrmann, D. J., Read, J. D., Bruce, D., Payne, D. G., & Toglia, M. P. (Eds.). (1998). *Eyewitness memory: Theoretical and applied perspectives.* Mahwah, NJ: Erlbaum.

Thompson, J. K. (Ed.). (2003). *Handbook of eating disorders and obesity.* New York: Wiley.

Thompson, L. (1990). Negotiation behavior and outcomes: Empirical evidence and theoretical issues. *Psychological Bulletin, 108,* 515–532.

Thompson, L. (1991). Information exchange in negotiation. *Journal of Experimental Social Psychology, 27,* 161–179.

Thompson, L. (1995). "They saw a negotiation": Partisanship and involvement. *Journal of Personality and Social Psychology, 68,* 839–853.

Thompson, L. L. (Ed.). (2006). *Negotiation theory and research.* Madison, CT: Psychological Press.

Thompson, L., & Hrebec, D. (1996). Lose-lose agreements in interdependent decision making. *Psychological Bulletin, 120,* 396–409.

Thompson, L., Gentner, D., & Loewenstein, J. (2000). Avoiding missed opportunities in managerial life: Analogical training more powerful than individual case training. *Organizational Behavior and Human Decision Processes, 82,* 60–75.

Thompson, S. C. (1999). Illusions of control: How we overestimate our personal influence. *Current Directions in Psychological Science, 8,* 187–190.

Thompson, S. C., Sobolew-Shubin, A., Galbraith, M. E., Schwankovsky, L., & Cruzen, D. (1993). Maintaining perceptions of control: Finding perceived control in low-control circumstances. *Journal of Personality and Social Psychology, 64,* 293–304.

Thompson, W. M., Dabbs, J. M., Jr., & Frady, R. L. (1990). Changes in saliva testosterone levels during a 90-day shock incarceration program. *Criminal Justice and Behavior, 17,* 246–252.

Thornhill, R., & Gangestad, S. W. (1993). Human facial beauty: Averageness, symmetry, and parasite resistance. *Human Nature, 4,* 237–269.

Thornton, B. (1992). Repression and its mediating influence on the defensive attribution of responsibility. *Journal of Research in Personality, 26,* 44–57.

Thornton, G. C., & Rupp, D. E. (2006). *Assessment centers in human resource management: Strategies for prediction, diagnosis, and development.* Mahwah, NJ: Erlbaum.

Thorsteinsson, E. B., James, J. E., & Gregg, M. E. (1998). Effects of video-relayed social support on hemodynamic reactivity and salivary cortisol during laboratory-based behavioral challenge. *Health Psychology, 17,* 436–444.

Thurstone, L. L. (1928). Attitudes can be measured. *American Journal of Sociology, 33,* 529–544.

Tice, D. M. (1991). Esteem protection or enhancement? Self-handicapping motives and attributions differ by trait self-esteem. *Journal of Personality and Social Psychology, 60,* 711–725.

Tice, D. M., & Baumeister, R. F. (1997). Longitudinal study of procrastination, performance, stress, and health: The costs and benefits of dawdling. *Psychological Science, 8,* 454–458.

Tice, D. M., & Wallace, H. M. (2003). The reflected self: Creating yourself as (you think) others see you. In M. R. Leary & J. P. Tangney (Eds.), *Handbook of self and identity* (pp. 91–105). New York: Guilford.

Tilker, H. A. (1970). Socially responsible behavior as a function of observer responsibility and victim feedback. *Journal of Personality and Social Psychology, 14,* 95–100.

Time (1994, June 27). p. 26.

Timmons-Mitchell, J., Bender, M. B., Kishna, M. A., & Mitchell, C. C. (2006). An independent effectiveness trial of multisystemic therapy with juvenile justice youth. *Journal of Clinical Child and Adolescent Psychology, 35,* 227–236.

Tjaden, P., & Thoennes, N. 2000. *Extent, nature, and consequences of intimate partner violence.* Washington, DC: U.S. Department of Justice.

Tobin, A. M. (2006, October 3). "Copycat effect" may explain cluster. *Toronto Star,* p. A7.

Todorov, A., & Uleman, J. S. (2004). The person reference process in spontaneous trait inferences. *Journal of Personality and Social Psychology, 87,* 482–493.

Tolin, D. F., & Foa, E. B. (2006). Sex differences in trauma and posttraumatic stress disorder: A quantitative review of 25 years of research. *Psychological Bulletin, 132,* 959–992.

Tolstedt, B. E., & Stokes, J. P. (1984). Self-disclosure, intimacy, and the depenetration process. *Journal of Personality and Social Psychology, 46,* 84–90.

Tomada, G., & Schneider, B. H. (1997). Relational aggression, gender, and peer acceptance: Invariance across culture, stability over time, and concordance among informants. *Developmental Psychology, 33,* 601–609.

Toobin, J. (1996, September 9). The Marcia Clark verdict. *New Yorker,* pp. 58–71.

Tooby, J., & Cosmides, L. (1988). *The evolution of war and its cognitive foundations.* Institute for Evolutionary Studies, Technical Report No. 88-1.

Top, T. J. (1991). Sex bias in the evaluation of performance in the scientific, artistic, and literary professions: A review. *Sex Roles, 24,* 73–106.

Tormala, Z. L., & Petty, R. E. (2002). What doesn't kill me makes me stronger: The effects of resisting persuasion on attitude certainty. *Journal of Personality and Social Psychology, 83,* 1298–1313.

Tormala, Z. L., Clarkson, J. J., & Petty, R. E. (2006). Resisting persuasion by the skin of one's teeth: The hidden success of resisted persuasive messages. *Journal of Personality and Social Psychology, 91,* 423–435.

Törngren, G., & Montgomery, H. (2004). Worse than chance? Performance and confidence among professionals and laypeople in the stock market. *Journal of Behavioral Finance, 5,* 148–153.

Tosi, H. L., & Einbender, S. W. (1985). The effects of the type and amount of information in sex discrimination research: A meta-analysis. *Academy of Management Journal, 28,* 712–723.

Tougas, F., Brown, R., Beaton, A. M., & Joly, S. (1995). Neosexism: Plus ça change, plus c'est pareil. *Personality and Social Psychology Bulletin, 21,* 842–849.

Tourangeau, R., Rips, L. J., & Rasinksi, K. (2000). *The psychology of survey response.* New York: Cambridge University Press.

Trafimow, D., Silverman, E. S., Fan, R. M. T., & Law, J. S. F. (1997). The effects of language and priming on the relative accessibility of the private self and collective self. *Journal of Cross-Cultural Psychology, 28,* 107–123.

Trafimow, D., Triandis, H. C., & Goto, S. G. (1991). Some tests of the distinction between the private and collective self. *Journal of Personality and Social Psychology, 60,* 649–655.

Trawalter, S., & Richeson, J. A. (2006). Regulatory focus and executive function after interracial interactions. *Journal of Experimental Social Psychology, 42,* 406–412.

Triandis, H. C. (1994). *Culture and social behavior.* New York: McGraw-Hill.

Triandis, H. C. (1995). *Individualism and collectivism.* Boulder, CO: Westview.

Triandis, H., Chen, X. P., & Chan, D. K. (1998). Scenarios for the measurement of collectivism and individualism. *Journal of Cross-Cultural Psychology, 29,* 275–289.

Triplett, N. (1897–1898). The dynamogenic factors in pacemaking and competition. *American Journal of Psychology, 9,* 507–533.

Tripp, C., Jensen, T. D., & Carlson, L. (1994). The effects of multiple product endorsements by celebrities on consumers' attitudes and intentions. *Journal of Consumer Research, 20,* 535–547.

Trivers, R. L. (1971). The evolution of reciprocal altruism. *Quarterly Review of Biology, 46,* 35–57.

Trivers, R. L. (1972). Parental investment and sexual selection. In B. Campbell (Ed.), *Sexual selection and the descent of man* (pp. 136–179). Chicago: Aldine-Atherton.

Trivers, R. L. (1985). *Social evolution.* Menlo Park, CA: Benjamin/Cummings.

Troll, L. E., & Skaff, M. M. (1997). Perceived continuity of self in very old age. *Psychology and Aging, 12,* 162–169.

Trope, Y. (1986). Identification and inferential processes in dispositional attribution. *Psychological Review, 93,* 239–257.

Trope, Y., & Alfieri, T. (1997). Effortfulness and flexibility of dispositional judgment processes. *Journal of Personality and Social Psychology, 73,* 662–674.

Trope, Y., & Thompson, E. P. (1997). Looking for truth in all the wrong places? Asymmetric search of individuating information about stereotyped group members. *Journal of Personality and Social Psychology, 73,* 229–241.

Trope, Y., Bassock, M., & Alon, E. (1984). The questions lay interviewers ask. *Journal of Personality, 52,* 90–106.

Trzesniewski, K. H., Donnellan, M. B., & Robins, R. W. (2003). Stability of self-esteem across the life span. *Journal of Personality and Social Psychology, 84,* 205–220.

Tubre, T. C., & Collins, J. M. (2000). Jackson and Schuler (1985) revisited: A meta-analysis of the relationships between role ambiguity, role conflict, and job performance. *Journal of Management, 26,* 155–169.

Tucker, P., & Aron, A. (1993). Passionate love and marital satisfaction at key transition points in the family life cycle. *Journal of Social and Clinical Psychology, 12,* 135–147.

Tuckman, B. W. (1965). Developmental sequence in small groups. *Psychological Bulletin, 63,* 384–399.

Tuckman, B. W., & Jensen, M. A. (1977). Stages of small-group development revisited. *Group and Organization Studies, 2,* 419–427.

Turner, J. C. (1987). *Rediscovering the social group: A self-categorization theory.* Oxford, England: Basil Blackwell.

Turner, J. C. (1991). *Social influence.* Pacific Grove, CA: Brooks/Cole.

Turner, J. C., & Oakes, P. J. (1989). Self-categorization theory and social influence. In P. B. Paulus (Ed.), *Psychology of group influence* (2nd ed., pp. 233–275). Hillsdale, NJ: Erlbaum.

Turner, M. E., & Pratkanis, A. R. (1994). Affirmative action as help: A review of recipient reactions to preferential selection and affirmative action. *Basic and Applied Social Psychology, 15,* 43–70.

Tversky, A., & Kahneman, D. (1973). Availability: A heuristic for judging frequency and probability. *Cognitive Psychology, 5,* 207–232.

Tversky, A., & Kahneman, D. (1974). Judgment under uncertainty: Heuristics and biases. *Science, 185,* 1124–1131.

Twenge, J. M., & Crocker, J. (2002). Race and self-esteem: Meta-analyses comparing Whites, Blacks, Hispanics, Asians, and American Indians. *Psychological Bulletin, 128,* 371–408.

Tyler, T. R. (2006a). Viewing *CSI* and the threshold of guilt: Managing truth and justice in reality and fiction. *Yale Law Journal, 115,* 1050–1085.

Tyler, T. R. (2006b). *Why people obey the law.* Princeton, NJ: Princeton University Press.

Tyler, T., Lind, E. A., Ohbuchi, K., Sugawara, I., & Huo, Y. J. (1998). Conflict with outsiders: Disputing within and across cultural boundaries. *Personality and Social Psychology Bulletin, 24,* 137–146.

Tyson, P. D. (1998). Physiological arousal, reactive aggression, and the induction of an incompatible relaxation response. *Aggression and Violent Behavior, 2,* 143–158.

U.S. Bureau of the Census. (1994). *Statistical Abstract of the United States: 1994.* Washington, DC: The Reference Press.

U.S. Department of Health, Education, and Welfare. (1974, May 30). Protection of human subjects. *Federal Register, 39*(105): 18914–20 (45CFR, part 46).

U.S. Department of Justice (1999). *Eyewitness evidence: A guide for law enforcement.* Washington, DC: U.S. Department of Justice.

U.S. Department of Justice. (1998). *Prevalence, incidence, and consequences of violence against women: Findings from the national violence against women survey, U.S.* Washington, DC: U.S. Government Printing Office.

Uchino, B. N. (2006). Social support and health: A review of physiological processes potentially underlying links to disease outcomes. *Journal of Behavioral Medicine, 29,* 377–387.

Uchino, B. N., Cacioppo, J. T., & Kiecolt-Glaser, J. K. (1996). The relationship between social support and physiological processes: A review with emphasis on underlying mechanisms and implications for health. *Psychological Bulletin, 119,* 488–531.

Uleman, J. S., Rhee, E., Bardoliwalla, N., Semin, G., & Toyama, M. (2000). The relational self: Closeness to ingroups depends on who they are, culture, and the type of closeness. *Asian Journal of Social Psychology, 3,* 1–17.

Underwood, J., & Pezdek, K. (1998). Memory suggestibility as an example of the sleeper effect. *Psychonomic Bulletin and Review, 5,* 449–453.

United States v. Hines, 55 F.Supp.2d 62 (D.Mass.1999).

United States v. Scheffer (1998), 188 S.Ct. 1261.

USA Today (1998, January 16). p. 1A.

USA Today (1999, February 3).

Vaes, J., Paladino, M. P., Castelli, L., Leyens, J.-P., & Giovanazzi, A. (2003). On the behavioral consequences of infrahumanization: The implicit role of uniquely human emotions in intergroup relations. *Journal of Personality and Social Psychology, 85,* 1016–1034.

Vaillancourt, T., & Hymel, S. (2006). Aggression and social status: The moderating roles of sex and peer-valued characteristics. *Aggressive Behavior, 32,* 396–408.

Valacich, J. S., Dennis, A. R., & Connolly, T. (1994). Idea generation in computer-based groups: A new ending to an old story. *Organizational Behavior and Human Decision Processes, 57,* 448–467.

Vallacher, R. R., Read, S. J., & Nowak, A. (2002). The dynamical perspective in personality and social psychology. *Personality and Social Psychology Review, 6,* 264–273.

van Anders, S. M., & Watson, N. V. (2006). Social neuroendocrinology: Effects of social contexts and behaviors on sex steroids in humans. *Human Nature, 17,* 212–237.

van Baaren, R. B., Holland, R. W., Kawakami, K., & Knippenberg, A. (2004). Mimicry and prosocial behavior. *Psychological Science, 15,* 71–74.

van Bokhoven, I., van Goozen, S. H. M., van Engeland, H., Schaal, B., Arseneault, L., Séguin, J. R., Assaad, J.-M., Nagin, D. S., Vitaro, F., & Tremblay, R. E. (2006). Salivary testosterone and aggression, delinquency, and social dominance in a population-based longitudinal study of adolescent males. *Hormones and Behavior, 50,* 118–125.

Van Dyne, L., & Saavedra, R. (1996). A naturalistic minority influence experiment: Effects on divergent thinking, conflict, and originality in work-groups. *British Journal of Social Psychology, 35,* 151–167.

Van Eerde, W., & Thierry, H. (1996). Vroom's expectancy models and work-related criteria: A meta-analysis. *Journal of Applied Psychology, 81,* 575–586.

Van Goozen, S. H. M., Cohen-Kettenis, P. T., Gooren, L. J. G., & Frijda, N. H., et al. (1995). Gender differences in behaviour: Activating effects of cross-sex hormones. *Psychoneuroendocrinology, 20,* 343–363.

Van Iddekinge, C. H., Raymark, P. H., & Roth, P. L. (2005). Assessing personality with a structured employment interview: Construct-related validity and susceptibility to response inflation. *Journal of Applied Psychology, 90,* 536–552.

van Knippenberg, D., & Schippers, M. C. (2007). Work group diversity. *Annual Review of Psychology, 58,* 515–541.

Van Lange, P. A. M. (Ed.). (2006). *Bridging social psychology: Benefits of transdisciplinary approaches.* Mahwah, NJ: Erlbaum.

Van Lange, P. A. M., Van Vugt, M., Meertens, R. M., & Ruiter, R. A. C. (1998). A social dilemma analysis of commuting preferences: The roles of social value orientation and trust. *Journal of Applied Social Psychology, 28,* 796–820.

Van Prooijen, J.-W., Van den Bos, K., Lind, E. A., & Wilke, H. (2006). How do people react to negative procedures? On the moderating role of authority's biased attitudes. *Journal of Experimental Social Psychology, 42,* 632–645.

Vandello, J. A., & Cohen, D. (1999). Patterns of individualism and collectivism across the United States. *Journal of Personality and Social Psychology, 77,* 279–292.

Vandello, J. A., & Cohen, D. (2003). Male honor and female fidelity: Implicit cultural scripts that perpetuate domestic violence. *Journal of Personality and Social Psychology, 84,* 997–1010.

Vandello, J. A., & Cohen, D. (2004). When believing is seeing: Sustaining norms of violence in cultures of honor. In M. Schaller & C. S. Crandall (Eds.), *The psychological foundations of culture* (pp. 281–304). Mahwah, NJ: Erlbaum.

VanderStoep, S. W., & Shaughnessy, J. J. (1997). Taking a course in research methods improves reasoning about real-life events. *Teaching of Psychology, 24,* 122–124.

VanderZee, K. I., Buunk, B. P., DeRuiter, J. H., Tempelaar, R., VanSonderen, E., & Sanderman, R. (1996). Social comparison and the subjective well-being of cancer patients. *Basic and Applied Social Psychology, 18,* 453–468.

Vandevelde, L., & Miyahara, M. (2005). Impact of group rejections from a physical activity on physical self-esteem among university students. *Social Psychology of Education, 8,* 65–81.

Vasquez, E. A., Denson, T. F., Stenstrom, D. M., & Miller, N. (2005). The moderating effect of trigger intensity on triggered displaced aggression. *Journal of Experimental Social Psychology, 41,* 61–67.

Vazire, S., & Gosling, S. D. (2004). E-perceptions: Personality impressions based on personal websites. *Journal of Personality and Social Psychology, 87,* 123–132.

Vecchio, R. P. (2002). Leadership and the gender advantage. *Leadership Quarterly, 13,* 643–671.

Veenhoven, R. (1993). *Happiness in nations.* Rotterdam, The Netherlands: Risbo.

Verona, E., Patrick, C. J., & Lang, A. R. (2002). A direct assessment of the role of state and trait negative emotion in aggressive behavior. *Journal of Abnormal Psychology, 111,* 249–258.

Vescio, T. K., Gervais, S. J., Heidenreich, S. P., & Snyder, M. (2006). The effects of prejudice level and social influence strategy on powerful people's responding to racial out-group members. *European Journal of Social Psychology, 36,* 435–450.

Vescio, T. K., Hewstone, M., Crisp, R. J., & Rubin, M. (1999). Perceiving and responding to multiply categorizable individuals: Cognitive processes and affective intergroup bias. In D. Abrams & M. Hogg (Eds.), *Social identity and social cognition* (pp. 111–140). Oxford: Blackwell.

Vierikko, E., Pulkkinen, L., Kaprio, J., & Rose, R. J. (2006). Genetic and environmental sources of continuity and change in teacher-rated aggression during early adolescence. *Aggressive Behavior, 32,* 308–320.

Vierikko, E., Pulkkinen, L., Kaprio, J., & Rose, R. J. (2006). Genetic and environmental sources of continuity and change in teacher-rated aggression during early adolescence. *Aggressive Behavior, 32,* 308–320.

Vinokur, A., & Burnstein, E. (1974). Effects of partially shared persuasive arguments on group-induced shifts: A group-problem-solving approach. *Journal of Personality and Social Psychology, 29,* 305–315.

Visintainer, M., Volpicelli, J., & Seligman, M. (1982). Tumor rejection in rats after inescapable or escapable shock. *Science, 216,* 437–439.

Visser, P. S., & Mirabile, R. R. (2004). Attitudes in the social context: The impact of social network composition on individual-level attitude strength. *Journal of Personality and Social Psychology, 87,* 779–795.

Viswesvaran, C., Sanchez, J. I., & Fisher, J. (1999). The role of social support in the process of work stress: A meta-analysis. *Journal of Vocational Behavior, 54,* 314–334.

Vittengl, J. R., & Holt, C. S. (2000). Getting acquainted: The relationship of self-disclosure and social attraction to positive affect. *Journal of Social and Personal Relationships, 17,* 53–66.

Vogel, D. L., Wester, S. R., & Heesacker, M. (1999). Dating relationships and the demand/withdraw pattern of communication. *Sex Roles, 41,* 297–306.

Vohs, K. D., & Finkel, E. J. (Eds.). (2006). *Self and relationships: Connecting intrapersonal and interpersonal processes.* New York: Guilford.

Vohs, K. D., & Heatherton, T. F. (2000). Self-regulatory failure: A resource-depletion approach. *Psychological Science, 11,* 249–252.

Vohs, K. D., Baumeister, R. F., & Ciarocco, N. J. (2005). Self-regulation and self-presentation: Regulatory resource depletion impairs impression management and effortful self-presentation depletes regulatory resources. *Journal of Personality and Social Psychology, 88,* 632–657.

Vohs, K. D., Mead, N. L., & Goode, M. R. (2006). The psychological consequences of money. *Science, 314,* 1154–1156.

von der Pahlen, B., Lindman, R., Sarkola, T., Maekisalo, H., & Eriksson, C. J. P. (2002). An exploratory study on self-evaluated aggression and androgens in women. *Aggressive Behavior, 28,* 273–280.

von Hippel, C., Yeung, J., Zouroudis, A., & Walsh, A. (2005). *Stereotype threat in the real world.* Paper presented at the Society for Australasian Social Psychology, Townsville, Qld.

von Hippel, W., Lakin, J. L., & Shakarchi, R. J. (2005). Individual differences in motivated social cognition: The case of self-serving information processing. *Personality and Social Psychology Bulletin, 31,* 1347–1357.

Von Hippel, W., Lakin, J. L., & Shakarchi, R. J. (2005). Individual differences in motivated social cognition: The case of self-serving information processing. *Personality and Social Psychology Bulletin, 31,* 1347–1357.

von Hippel, W., Sekaquaptewa, D., & Vargas, P. (1995). On the role of encoding processes in stereotype maintenance. In M. P. Zanna (Ed.), *Advances in experimental social psychology* (Vol. 27, pp. 177–254). San Diego, CA: Academic Press.

von Hippel, W., Silver, L. A., & Lynch, M. E. (2000). Stereotyping against your will: The role of inhibitory ability in stereotyping and prejudice among the elderly. *Personality and Social Psychology Bulletin, 26,* 523–532.

Von Lang, J., & Sibyll, C. (Eds.). (1983). *Eichmann interrogated* (R. Manheim, Trans.). New York: Farrar, Straus & Giroux.

Vonk, R. (1998). The slime effect: Suspicion and dislike of likeable behavior toward superiors. *Journal of Personality and Social Psychology, 74,* 849–864.

Voracek, M., & Fisher, M. L. (2002). Shapely centrefolds? Temporal change in body measures: Trend analysis. *British Medical Journal, 325,* 1447–1448.

Vorauer, J. D. (2003). Dominant group members in intergroup interaction: Safety or vulnerability in numbers? *Personality and Social Psychology Bulletin, 29,* 498–511.

Vorauer, J. D., & Claude, S. D. (1998). Perceived versus actual transparency of goals in negotiation. *Personality and Social Psychology Bulletin, 24,* 371–385.

Vorauer, J. D., Cameron, J. J., Holmes, J. G., & Pearce, D. G. (2003). Invisible overtures: Fears of rejection and the signal amplification bias. *Journal of Personality and Social Psychology, 84,* 793–812.

Vrij, A. (1997). Wearing black clothes: The impact of offenders' and suspects' clothing on impression formation. *Applied Cognitive Psychology, 11,* 47–53.

Vrij, A. (2000). *Detecting lies and deceit: The psychology of lying and the implications for professional practice.* Chichester, New York: John Wiley.

Vroom, V. H. (1964). *Work and motivation.* New York: Wiley.

Vroom, V. H., & Jago, A. G. (1988). *Managing participation in organizations.* Englewood Cliffs, NJ: Prentice-Hall.

Vroom, V. H., & Jago, A. G. (2007). The role of the situation in leadership. *American Psychologist, 62,* 17–24.

Vroom, V. H., & Yetton, P. W. (1973). *Leadership and decision-making.* Pittsburgh: University of Pittsburgh Press.

Waldman, D. A., & Avolio, B. J. (1991). Race effects in performance evaluations: Controlling for ability, education, and experience. *Journal of Applied Psychology, 76,* 897–901.

Walker, I., & Smith, H. J. (2002). *Relative deprivation: Specification, development, and integration.* Cambridge, UK: Cambridge University Press.

Walker, L., LaTour, S., Lind, E. A., & Thibaut, J. (1974). Reactions of participants and observers to modes of adjudication. *Journal of Applied Social Psychology, 4,* 295–310.

Walster, E. (1966). Assignment of responsibility for important events. *Journal of Personality and Social Psychology, 3,* 73–79.

Walster, E., & Festinger, L. (1962). The effectiveness of "overheard" persuasive communications. *Journal of Abnormal and Social Psychology, 65,* 395–402.

Walster, E., Aronson, V., Abrahams, D., & Rottman, L. (1966). The importance of physical attractiveness in dating behavior. *Journal of Personality and Social Psychology, 4,* 508–516.

Walster, E., Walster, G. W., & Berscheid, E. (1978). *Equity: Theory and research.* Boston: Allyn & Bacon.

Walster, E., Walster, G. W., & Traupmann, J. (1978). Equity and premarital sex. *Journal of Personality, 36,* 82–92.

Walster, E., Walster, G. W., Piliavin, J., & Schmidt, L. (1973). "Playing hard-to-get": Understanding an elusive phenomenon. *Journal of Personality and Social Psychology, 26*, 113–121.

Walther, E. (2002). Guilty by mere association: Evaluative conditioning and the spreading attitude effect. *Journal of Personality and Social Psychology, 82*, 919–934.

Walther, E. (2002). Guilty by mere association: Evaluative conditioning and the spreading attitude effect. *Journal of Personality and Social Psychology, 82*, 919–934.

Walton, G., & Cohen, G. (2003). Stereotype lift. *Journal of Experimental Social Psychology, 39*, 456–467.

Wampold, B. E., Mondin, G. W., Moody, M., Stich, F., Benson, K., & Ahn, H. (1997). A meta-analysis of outcome studies comparing bona fide psychotherapies: Empirically, "all must have prizes." *Psychological Bulletin, 122*, 203–215.

Wang, H., Liu, Y., & Zhang, K. (2003). The effects of group decision support system (GDSS) and group discussion on group decision making. *Acta Psychologica Sinica, 35*, 190–194.

Wang, S. (2006). Contagious behavior. *APS Observer, 19*, 2.

Wann, D. L., & Grieve, F. G. (2005). Biased evaluation of in-group and out-group spectator behavior at sporting events: The importance of team identification and threats to social identity. *Journal of Social Psychology, 145*, 531–545.

Warburton, W. A., Williams, K. D., & Cairns, D. R. (2006). When ostracism leads to aggression: The moderating effects of control deprivation. *Journal of Experimental Social Psychology, 42*, 213–220.

Ward, L. M., & Friedman, K. (2006). Using TV as a guide: Associations between television viewing and adolescents' sexual attitudes and behavior. *Journal of Research on Adolescence, 16*, 133–156.

Ward, M. L., & Friedman, K. (2006). Using TV as a guide: Associations between television viewing and adolescents' sexual attitudes and behavior. *Journal of Research on Adolescence, 16*, 133–156.

Ward, M. L., Hansbrough, E., & Walker, E. (2005). Contributions of music video exposure to black adolescents' gender and sexual schemas. *Journal of Adolescent Research, 20*, 143–166.

Warneken, F., & Tomasello, M. (2006). Altruistic helping in human infants and young chimpanzees. *Science, 311*, 1301–1303.

Warren, B. L. (1966). A multiple variable approach to the assortive mating phenomenon. *Eugenics Quarterly, 13*, 285–298.

Watson, D. (1982). The actor and the observer: How are their perceptions of causality divergent? *Psychological Bulletin, 92*, 682–700.

Watson, D., Wiese, D., Vaidya, J., & Tellegen, A. (1999). The two general activation systems of affect: Structural findings, evolutionary considerations, and psychobiological evidence. *Journal of Personality and Social Psychology, 76*, 820–838.

Wayment, H. A. (2004). It could have been me: Vicarious victims and disaster-focused distress. *Personality and Social Psychology Bulletin, 30*, 515–528.

Weary, G., & Edwards, J. A. (1994). Individual differences in causal uncertainty. *Journal of Personality and Social Psychology, 67*, 308–318.

Weber, R., & Crocker, J. C. (1983). Cognitive processes in the revision of stereotypic beliefs. *Journal of Personality and Social Psychology, 45*, 961–967.

Webster, D. M., Richter, L., & Kruglanski, A. W. (1996). On leaping to conclusions when feeling tired: Mental fatigue effects on impressional primacy. *Journal of Experimental Social Psychology, 32*, 181–195.

Weeden, J., & Sabini, J. (2005). Physical attractiveness and health in Western societies: A review. *Psychological Bulletin, 131*, 635–653.

Wegener, D. T., & Petty, R. E. (1994). Mood management across affective states: The hedonic contingency hypothesis. *Journal of Personality and Social Psychology, 66*, 1034–1048.

Wegener, D. T., Petty, R. E., & Smith, S. M. (1995). Positive mood can increase or decrease message scrutiny: The hedonic contingency view of mood and message processing. *Journal of Personality and Social Psychology, 69*, 5–15.

Wegge, J. (2000). Participation in group goal setting: Some novel findings and a comprehensive model as a new ending to an old story. *Applied Psychology: An International Review, 49*, 498–516.

Wegge, J., & Haslam, S. A. (2005). Improving work motivation and performance in brainstorming groups: The effects of three group goal-setting strategies. *European Journal of Work and Organizational Psychology, 14*, 400–430.

Wegner, D. M. (1980). The self in prosocial action. In D. M. Wegner & R. R. Vallacher (Eds.), *The self in social psychology* (pp. 131–157). New York: Oxford University Press.

Wegner, D. M. (1994). Ironic processes of mental control. *Psychological Review, 101*, 34–52.

Wegner, D. M. (1997). When the antidote is the poison: Ironic mental control processes. *Psychological Science, 8*, 148–153.

Wegner, D. M., Ansfield, M., & Pilloff, D. (1998). The putt and the pendulum: Ironic effects of the mental control of action. *Psychological Science, 9*, 196–199.

Wegner, D. M., Erber, R., & Raymond, P. (1991). Transactive memory in close relationships. *Journal of Personality and Social Psychology, 61*, 923–929.

Wegner, D. M., Lane, J. D., & Dimitri, S. (1994). The allure of secret relationships. *Journal of Personality and Social Psychology, 66*, 287–300.

Weiner, B. (1985). "Spontaneous" causal thinking. *Psychological Bulletin, 97*, 74–84.

Weinstein, N. D. (1980). Unrealistic optimism about future life events. *Journal of Personality and Social Psychology, 39*, 806–820.

Weinstein, N. D. (1989). Effects of personal experience on self-protective behavior. *Psychological Bulletin, 105*, 31–50.

Weiss, D. E. (1991). *The great divide.* New York: Simon & Schuster.

Weldon, M. S., Blair, C., & Huebsch, D. (2000). Group remembering: Does social loafing underlie collaborative inhibition? *Journal of Experimental Psychology: Learning, Memory, and Cognition, 26*, 1568–1577.

Wells, G. L., & Bradfield, A. L. (1998). "Good, you identified the suspect": Feedback to eyewitnesses distorts their reports of the witnessing experience. *Journal of Applied Psychology, 83*, 360–376.

Wells, G. L., & Bradfield, A. L. (1999). Distortions in eyewitnesses' recollections: Can the postidentification-feedback effect be moderated? *Psychological Science, 10*, 138–144.

Wells, G. L., & Murray, D. M. (1984). Eyewitness confidence. In G. Wells & E. Loftus (Eds.), *Eyewitness testimony: Psychological perspectives* (pp. 155–170). New York: Cambridge University Press.

Wells, G. L., & Olson, E. A. (2003). Eyewitness testimony. *Annual Review of Psychology, 54*, 277–295.

Wells, G. L., & Petty, R. E. (1980). The effects of overt head-movements on persuasion: Compatibility and incompatibility of responses. *Basic and Applied Social Psychology, 1*, 219–230.

Wells, G. L., Charman, S. D., & Olson, E. A. (2005). Building face composites can harm lineup identification performance. *Journal of Experimental Psychology: Applied, 11*, 147–156.

Wells, G. L., Lindsay, R. C. L., & Ferguson, T. J. (1979). Accuracy, confidence, and juror perceptions in eyewitness identification. *Journal of Applied Psychology, 64*, 440–448.

Wells, G. L., Malpass, R. S., Lindsay, R. C. L., Fisher, R. P., Turtle, J. W., & Fulero, S. M. (2000). From the lab to the police station: A successful application of eyewitness research. *American Psychologist, 55*, 581–598.

Wells, G. L., Olson, E. A., & Charman, S. D. (2003). Distorted retrospective eyewitness reports as functions of feedback and delay. *Journal of Experimental Psychology: Applied, 9,* 42–52.

Wells, G. L., Small, M., Penrod, S., Malpass, R. S., Fulero, S. M., & Brimacombe, C. A. E. (1998). Eyewitness identification procedures: Recommendations for lineups and photospreads, *Law and Human Behavior, 22,* 603–648.

Wenzlaff, R. M., & Wegner, D. M. (2000). Thought suppression. *Annual Review of Psychology, 51,* 59–91.

Whatley, M. A., Webster, J. M., Smith, R. H., & Rhodes, A. (1999). The effect of a favor on public and private compliance: How internalized is the norm of reciprocity? *Basic and Applied Social Psychology, 21,* 251–259.

Wheeler, L., & Kim, Y. (1997). What is beautiful is culturally good: The physical attractiveness stereotype has different content in collectivist cultures. *Personality and Social Psychology Bulletin, 23,* 795–800.

Wheeler, L., & Miyake, K. (1992). Social comparison in everyday life. *Journal of Personality and Social Psychology, 62,* 760–773.

Wheeler, L., Koestner, R., & Driver, R. E. (1982). Related attributes in the choice of comparison others. *Journal of Experimental Social Psychology, 18,* 489–500.

Wheeler, M. E., & Fiske, S. T. (2005). Controlling racial prejudice and stereotyping: Social cognitive goals affect amygdala and stereotype activation. *Psychological Science, 16,* 56–3.

Wheeler, M. E., & Fiske, S. T. (2005). Controlling racial prejudice: Social-cognitive goals affect amygdala and stereotype activation. *Psychological Science, 16,* 56–63.

Whitbeck, L. B., & Hoyt, D. R. (1994). Social prestige and assortive mating: A comparison of students from 1956 and 1988. *Journal of Social and Personal Relationships, 11,* 137–145.

White, G. L., Fishbein, S., & Rutstein, J. (1981). Passionate love: The misattribution of arousal. *Journal of Personality and Social Psychology, 41,* 56–62.

Whiteside, K. (2006, June 2). Pockets of intolerance raise Cup concerns: Players feel the reality of racism in soccer as tensions continue to boil in Europe. *USA Today,* p. 12C.

Whittaker, J. O., & Meade, R. D. (1967). Social pressure in the modification and distortion of judgment: A cross-cultural study. *International Journal of Psychology, 2,* 109–113.

Whorf, B.L. (1956). Science and linguistics. In J. B. Carroll (Ed.), *Language, thought, and reality: Selected writings of Benjamin Lee Whorf* (pp. 207–219). Canbridge, MA: MIT Press.

Whyte, G. (1993). Escalating commitment in individual and group decision making: A prospect theory approach. *Organizational Behavior and Human Decision Processes, 54,* 430–455.

Whyte, G. (1998). Recasting Janis's groupthink model: The key role of collective efficacy in decision fiascoes. *Organizational Behavior and Human Decision Processes, 73,* 185–209.

Wicker, A. W. (1969). Attitudes versus actions: The relationship between verbal and overt behavioral responses to attitude objects. *Journal of Social Issues, 25*(4), 41–78.

Wicklund, R. A. (1975). Objective self-awareness. In L. Berkowitz (Ed.), *Advances in experimental social psychology* (Vol. 8, pp. 233–275). New York: Academic Press.

Widmeyer, W. N., & Loy, J. W. (1988). When you're hot, you're hot! Warm-cold effects in first impressions of persons and teaching effectiveness. *Journal of Educational Psychology, 80,* 118–121.

Wiedenfeld, S. A., O'Leary, A., Bandura, A., Brown, S., Levine, S., & Raska, K. (1990). Impact of perceived self-efficacy in coping with stressors on components of the immune system. *Journal of Personality and Social Psychology, 59,* 1082–1094.

Wiener, R. L., Hackney, A., Kadela, K., Rauch, S., Seib, H., Warren, L., & Hurt, L. E. (2002). The fit and implementation of sexual harassment law to workplace evaluations. *Journal of Applied Psychology, 87,* 747–764.

Wiener, R. L., Prichard, C. C., & Weston, M. (1995). Comprehensibility of approved jury instructions in capital murder cases. *Journal of Applied Psychology, 80,* 455–467.

Wiesner, W. H., & Cronshaw, S. F. (1988). A meta-analytic investigation of the impact of interview format and degree of structure on the validity of the employment interview. *Journal of Occupational Psychology, 61,* 275–290.

Wigboldus, D. H. J., Sherman, J. W., Franzese, H. L., & van Knippenberg, A. (2004). Capacity and comprehension: Spontaneous stereotyping under cognitive load. *Social Cognition, 22,* 292–309.

Wiggins, J. S. (Ed.). (1996). *The five-factor model of personality: Theoretical perspectives.* New York: Guilford.

Wilder, D. A. (1977). Perception of groups, size of opposition, and social influence. *Journal of Experimental Social Psychology, 13,* 253–268.

Wilder, D. A., Simon, A. F., & Myles, F. (1996). Enhancing the impact of counterstereotypic information: Dispositional attributions for deviance. *Journal of Personality and Social Psychology, 71,* 276–287.

Wildschut, T., Pinter, B., Vevea, J. L., Insko, C. A., & Schopler, J. (2003). Beyond the group mind: A quantitative review of the interindividual intergroup discontinuity effect. *Psychological Bulletin, 129,* 698–722.

Wilkenfeld, J., Young, K., Asal, V., & Quinn, D. (2003). Mediating international crises: Cross-national and experimental perspectives. *Journal of Conflict Resolution, 47,* 279–301.

Willer, R. (2004). The effects of government-issued terror warnings on presidential approval ratings. *Current Research in Social Psychology, 10,* 1–12.

Williams v. Florida, 399 U.S. 78 (1970).

Williams, D. R., Neighbors, H. W., & Jackson, J. S. (2003). Racial/ethnic discrimination and health: Findings from community studies. *American Journal of Public Health, 93,* 200–208.

Williams, J. E., & Best, D. L. (1982). *Measuring sex stereotypes: A thirty nation study.* Beverly Hills, CA: Sage.

Williams, K. D. (2003). Ostracism: The power of silence. *Journal of Social and Personal Relationships, 20,* 141–142.

Williams, K. D. (2007). Ostracism. *Annual Review of Psychology, 58,* 425–452.

Williams, K. D., Cheung, C., & Choi, W. (2000). Cyberostracism: Effects of being ignored over the internet. *Journal of Personality and Social Psychology, 79,* 748–762.

Williams, K. D., Govan, C. L., Croker, V., Tynan, D., Cruickshank, M., & Lam, A. (2002). Investigations into differences between social- and cyberostracism. *Group Dynamics: Theory, Research, and Practice, 6,* 65–77.

Williams, K. D., Forgas, J. P., & von Hippel, W. (Eds.). (2005). *The social outcast: Ostracism, social exclusion, rejection, and bullying.* New York: Psychology Press.

Williams, K. Y., & O'Reilly, C. A. (1998). Demography and diversity in organizations: A review of 40 years of research. *Research in Organizational Behavior, 20,* 77–140.

Williams, R. (1993). *Anger kills.* New York: Times Books.

Williamson, G. M., & Clark, M. S. (1992). Impact of desired relationship type on affective reactions to choosing and being required to help. *Personality and Social Psychology Bulletin, 18,* 10–18.

Williamson, G. M., Clark, M. S., Pegalis, L. J., & Behan, A. (1996). Affective consequences of refusing to help in communal and exchange relationships. *Personality and Social Psychology Bulletin, 22,* 34–47.

Willis, J., & Todorov, A. (2006). First impressions: Making up your mind after a 100-ms exposure to a face. *Psychological Science, 17,* 592–598.

Wills, T. A. (1981). Downward comparison principles in social psychology. *Psychological Bulletin, 90,* 245–271.

Wills, T. A. (1992). The helping process in the context of personal relationships. In S. Spacapan & S. Oskamp (Eds.), *Helping* and being helped: Naturalistic studies (pp. 17–48). Newbury Park, CA: Sage.

Wills, T. A. (Ed.). (1990). Social support in social and clinical psychology. *Journal of Social and Clinical Psychology, 9*.

Wills, T. A., & DePaulo, B. M. (1991). Interpersonal analysis of the help-seeking process. In C. R. Snyder & D. R. Forsyth (Eds.), *Handbook of social and clinical psychology: The health perspective* (pp. 350–375). New York: Pergamon Press.

Wilson, A. E., & Ross, M. (2000). The frequency of temporal and social comparisons in people's personal appraisals. *Journal of Personality and Social Psychology, 78*, 928–942.

Wilson, D. S., & Sober, E. (1994). Reintroducing group selection to the human behavioral sciences. *Behavioral and Brain Sciences, 17*, 585–654.

Wilson, J. P. (1976). Motivation, modeling, and altruism: A person x situation analysis. *Journal of Personality and Social Psychology, 34*, 1078–1086.

Wilson, M. I., & Daly, M. (1996). Male sexual proprietariness and violence against wives. *Current Directions in Psychological Science, 5*, 2–7.

Wilson, T. D. (2002). *Strangers to ourselves: Discovering the adaptive unconscious*. Cambridge, MA: Belknap Press.

Wilson, T. D., & Gilbert, D. T. (2003). Affective forecasting. *Advances in Experimental Social Psychology, 35*, 345–411.

Wilson, T. D., & Gilbert, D. T. (2005). Affective forecasting: Knowing what to want. *Current Directions in Psychological Science, 14*, 131–134.

Wilson, T. D., Lindsey, S., & Schooler, T. Y. (2000). A model of dual attitudes. *Psychological Review, 107*, 101–126.

Wilson, T. D., Wheatley, T., Meyers, J. M., Gilbert, D. T., & Axsom, D. (2000). Focalism: A source of durability bias in affective forecasting. *Journal of Personality and Social Psychology, 78*, 821–836.

Winch, R. F., Ktsanes, I., & Ktsanes, V. (1954). The theory of complementary needs in mate selection: An analytic and descriptive study. *American Sociological Review, 19*, 241–249.

Winter, D. G. (1987). Leader appeal, leader performance, and the motive profiles of leaders and followers: A study of American presidents and elections. *Journal of Personality and Social Psychology, 52*, 41–46.

Wise, R. A., & Safer, M. A. (2004). What U.S. judges know and believe about eyewitness testimony. *Applied Cognitive Psychology, 18*, 427–443.

Wishman, S. (1986). *Anatomy of a jury: The system on trial*. New York: Times Books.

Wisloski, J., & Melago, C. (2006, July 20). Straphanger hero! Queens woman risks life, helps pull man to safety after he falls onto subway tracks. *Daily News (New York)*, p. 5.

Wissler, R. L., & Saks, M. J. (1985). On the inefficacy of limiting instructions: When jurors use prior conviction evidence to decide on guilt. *Law and Human Behavior, 9*, 37–48.

Wittenbrink, B., & Schwarz, N. (Eds.). (2007). *Implicit measures of attitudes*. New York: Guilford.

Wittenbrink, B., Judd. C. M., & Park, B. (1997). Evidence for racial prejudice at the implicit level and its relationship with questionnaire measures. *Journal of Personality and Social Psychology, 72*, 262–274.

Wolf, S., & Montgomery, D. A. (1977). Effects of inadmissible evidence and level of judicial admonishment to disregard on the judgments of mock jurors. *Journal of Applied Social Psychology, 7*, 205–219.

Wolfe, C., & Crocker, J. (2003). What does the self want? Contingencies of self-worth and goals. In S. J. Spencer, S. Fein, M. P. Zanna, & J. M. Olson (Eds.), *Motivated social perception: The Ontario symposium* (Vol. 9., pp. 147–170). Mahwah, NJ: Erlbaum.

Wong, J. (2006, September 16). "Get under the desk": Last Wednesday was just like any other at Montreal's Dawson College. Then all hell broke loose. Kimveer Gill was walking the hallways, spraying students with gunfire. *The Globe and Mail (Canada)*, p. A8.

Wong, K. F. E., Yik, M., & Kwong, J. Y. Y. (2006). Understanding the emotional aspects of escalation of commitment: The role of negative affect. *Journal of Applied Psychology, 91*, 282–297.

Wong, P. T. P., & Wong, L. C. J. (Eds.). (2006). *Handbook of multicultural perspectives on stress and coping*. New York: Springer.

Wong, R. Y.-m., & Hong, Y.-y. (2005). Dynamic influences of culture on cooperation in the prisoner's dilemma. *Psychological Science, 16*, 429–434.

Wood, J. V. (1989). Theory and research concerning social comparisons of personal attributes. *Psychological Bulletin, 106*, 231–248.

Wood, J. V., Saltzberg, J. A., & Goldsamt, L. A. (1990). Does affect induce self-focused attention? *Journal of Personality and Social Psychology, 58*, 899–908.

Wood, N., & Cowan, N. (1995). The cocktail party phenomenon revisited: How frequent are attention shifts to one's name in an irrelevant auditory channel? *Journal of Experimental Psychology: Learning, Memory, and Cognition, 21*, 255–260.

Wood, W., & Eagly, A. H. (2007). Social structural origins of sex differences in human mating. In S. W. Gangestad & J. A. Simpson (Eds.), *Evolution of the mind*. New York: Guilford.

Wood, W., & Quinn, J. M. (2003). Forewarned and forearmed? Two meta-analysis syntheses of forewarnings of influence appeals. *Psychological Bulletin, 129*, 119–138.

Wood, W., Kallgren, C. A., & Preisler, R. M. (1985). Access to attitude-relevant information in memory as a determinant of persuasion: The role of message attributes. *Journal of Experimental Social Psychology, 21*, 73–85.

Wood, W., Lundgren, S., Ouellette, J. A., Busceme, S., & Blackstone, T. (1994). Minority influence: A meta-analytic review of social influence processes. *Psychological Bulletin, 115*, 323–345.

Wood, W., Pool, G. J., Leck, K., & Purvis, D. (1996). Self-definition, defensive processing, and influence: The normative impact of majority and minority groups. *Journal of Personality and Social Psychology, 71*, 1181–1193.

Woodward, B. (2006). *State of denial: Bush at war, Part III*. New York: Simon & Schuster.

Word, C. O., Zanna, M. P., & Cooper, J. (1974). The nonverbal mediation of self-fulfilling prophecies in interracial interaction. *Journal of Experimental Social Psychology, 10*, 109–120.

Worth, L. T., & Mackie, D. M. (1987). Cognitive mediation of positive affect in persuasion. *Social Cognition, 5*, 76–94.

Wright, D. B., Boyd, C. E., & Tredoux, C. G. (2003). Inter-racial contact and the own-race bias for face recognition in South Africa and England. *Applied Cognitive Psychology, 17*, 365–373.

Wright, L., von Bussman, K., Friedman, A., Khoury, M., & Owens, F. (1990). Exaggerated social control and its relationship to the Type A behavior pattern. *Journal of Research in Personality, 24*, 258–269.

Wright, P. H. (1982). Men's friendships, women's friendships and the alleged inferiority of the latter. *Sex Roles, 8*, 1–20.

Wright, R. A., & Contrada, R. J. (1986). Dating selectivity and interpersonal attraction: Toward a better understanding of the "elusive phenomenon." *Journal of Social and Personal Relationships, 3*, 131–148.

Wright, R. A., Wadley, V. G., Danner, M., & Phillips, P. N. (1992). Persuasion, reactance, and judgments of interpersonal appeal. *European Journal of Social Psychology, 22*, 85–91.

Wright, S. C., Aron, A., McLaughlin-Volpe, T., & Ropp, S. A. (1997). The extended contact effect: Knowledge of cross-group friendships and prejudice. *Journal of Personality and Social Psychology, 73*, 73–90.

Wrightsman, L. S. (2006). *The psychology of the Supreme Court*. New York: Oxford University Press.

Wrightsman, L. S., & Fulero, S. M. (2004). *Forensic psychology* (2nd ed.). Belmont, CA: Wadsworth.

Wrightsman, L. S., & Kassin, S. M. (1993). *Confessions in the courtroom*. Newbury Park, CA: Sage.

Wuthnow, R. (1991). *Acts of compassion*. Princeton, NJ: Princeton University Press.

Wyer, N. A. (2004). Not all stereotypic biases are created equal: Evidence for a stereotype disconfirmation bias. *Personality and Social Psychology Bulletin, 30*, 706–720.

Wyer, N. A., Sadler, M. S., & Judd, C. M. (2002). Contrast effects in stereotype formation and change: The role of comparative context. *Journal of Experimental Social Psychology, 38*, 443–458.

Wyer, N. A., Sherman, J. W., & Stroessner, S. J. (2000). The roles of motivation and ability in controlling the consequences of stereotype suppression. *Personality and Social Psychology Bulletin, 26*, 13–25.

Yamagishi, T., Kanazawa, S., Mashima, R., & Terai, S. (2005). Separating trust from cooperation in a dynamic relationship: Prisoner's Dilemma with variable dependence. *Rationality and Society, 17*, 275–308.

Yopyk, D. J. A., & Prentice, D. A. (2005). Am I an athlete or a student? Identity salience and stereotype threat in student-athletes. *Basic and Applied Social Psychology, 27*, 329–336.

Young, R. K., Kennedy, A. H., Newhouse, A., Browne, P., & Thiessen, D. (1993). The effects of names on perceptions of intelligence, popularity, and competence. *Journal of Applied Social Psychology, 23*, 1770–1788.

Yu, D. W., & Shepard, G. H. (1998). Is beauty in the eye of the beholder? *Nature, 296*, 321–322.

Yuille, J. C., & Tollestrup, P. A. (1990). Some effects of alcohol on eyewitness memory. *Journal of Applied Psychology, 75*, 268–273.

Yuki, M. (2003). Intergroup comparison versus intragroup relationships: A cross-cultural examination of social identity theory in North American and East Asian cultural contexts. *Social Psychology Quarterly, 66*, 166–183.

Yzerbyt, V. Y., Dardenne, B., & Leyens, J.-Ph. (1998). Social judgeability concerns in impression formation. In V. Y. Yzerbyt, G. Lories, & B. Dardenne (Eds.), *Metacognition: Cognitive and social dimensions* (pp. 126–156). London: Sage.

Zaccaro, S. J. (2007). Trait-based perspectives of leadership. *American Psychologist, 62*, 6–16.

Zajonc, R. B. (1965). Social facilitation. *Science, 149*, 269–274.

Zajonc, R. B. (1968). Attitudinal effects of mere exposure. *Journal of Personality and Social Psychology Monograph Supplement, 9*(2), 1–27.

Zajonc, R. B. (1980). Compresence. In P. B. Paulus (Ed.), *Psychology of group influence* (pp. 35–60). Hillsdale, NJ: Erlbaum.

Zajonc, R. B. (1993). Brain temperature and subjective emotional experience. In M. Lewis & J. M. Haviland (Eds.), *Handbook of emotions* (pp. 209–220). New York: Guilford.

Zajonc, R. B. (2001). Mere exposure: A gateway to the subliminal. *Current Directions in Psychological Science, 10*, 224–228.

Zajonc, R. B., Heingartner, A., & Herman, E. M. (1969). Social enhancement and impairment of performance in the cockroach. *Journal of Personality and Social Psychology, 13*, 82–92.

Zajonc, R. B., Murphy, S. T., & Inglehart, M. (1989). Feeling and facial efference: Implications of the vascular theory of emotion. *Psychological Review, 96*, 395–416.

Zanna, M. P., & Cooper, J. (1974). Dissonance and the pill: An attribution approach to studying the arousal properties of dissonance. *Journal of Personality and Social Psychology, 29*, 703–709.

Zárate, M. A., & Sanders, J. D. (1999). Face categorization, graded priming, and the mediating influences of similarity. *Social Cognition, 17*, 367–389.

Zárate, M. A., Garcia, B., Garza, A. A., & Hitlan, R. T. (2004). Cultural threat and perceived realistic group conflict as dual predictors of prejudice. *Journal of Experimental Social Psychology, 40*, 99–105.

Zebrowitz, L. A., & McDonald, S. M. (1991). The impact of litigants' babyfacedness and attractiveness on adjudications in small claims courts. *Law and Human Behavior, 15*, 603–624.

Zebrowitz, L. A., & Montepare, J. M. (2005). Appearance DOES Matter. *Science, 308*, 1565–1566.

Zebrowitz, L. A., Fellous, J. M., Mignault, A., & Andreoletti, C. (2003). Trait impressions as overgeneralized responses to adaptively significant facial qualities: Evidence from connectionist modeling. *Personality and Social Psychology Review, 7*, 194–215.

Zebrowitz, L. A., Tenenbaum, D. R., & Goldstein, L. H. (1991). The impact of job applicants' facial maturity, gender, and academic achievement on hiring recommendations. *Journal of Applied Social Psychology, 21*, 525–548.

Zeisel, H., & Diamond, S. (1978). The effect of peremptory challenges on jury and verdict: An experiment in a federal district court. *Stanford Law Review, 30*, 491–531.

Zentall, T. R. (2003). Imitation by animals: How do they do it? *Current Directions in Psychological Science, 12*, 91–95.

Zhang, J., & Shavitt, S. (2003). Cultural values in advertisements to the Chinese X-generation. *Journal of Advertising, 32*, 23–33.

Zhang, L., & Baumeister, R. F. (2006). Your money or your self-esteem: Threatened egotism promotes costly entrapment in losing endeavors. *Personality and Social Psychology Bulletin, 32*, 881–893.

Zillmann, D. (1979). *Hostility and aggression*. Hillsdale, NJ: Erlbaum.

Zillmann, D. (1983). Arousal and aggression. In R. G. Geen & E. I. Donnerstein (Eds.), *Aggression: Theoretical and empirical reviews: Vol. l. Theoretical and methodological issues* (pp. 75–101). New York: Academic Press.

Zillmann, D. (1984). *Connections between sex and aggression*. Hillsdale, NJ: Erlbaum.

Zillmann, D. (1996). Sequential dependencies in emotional experience and behavior. In R. D. Kavanaugh, B. Zimmerberg, & S. Fein (Eds.), *Emotion: Interdisciplinary perspectives* (pp. 243–272). Mahwah, NJ: Erlbaum.

Zillmann, D. (2003). Theory of affective dynamics: Emotions and moods. In J. Bryant, D. Roskos-Ewoldsen, & J. Cantor (Eds.), *Communication and emotion: Essays in honor of Dolf Zillmann* (pp. 533–567). Mahwah, NJ: Erlbaum.

Zillmann, D., & Bryant, J. (1984). Effects of massive exposure to pornography. In N. M. Malamuth & E. I. Donnerstein (Eds.), *Pornography and sexual aggression* (pp. 115–138). New York: Academic Press.

Zillmann, D., & Weaver, J. B., III. (1997). Psychoticism in the effect of prolonged exposure to gratuitous media violence on the acceptance of violence as a preferred means of conflict resolution. *Personality and Individual Differences, 22*, 613–627.

Zillmann, D., Bryant, J., Cantor, J. R., & Day, K. D. (1975). Irrelevance of mitigating circumstances in retaliatory behavior at high levels of excitation. *Journal of Research in Personality, 9*, 282–293.

Zimbardo, P. G. (1969). The human choice: Individuation, reason, and order versus deindividuation, impulse, and chaos. *Nebraska Symposium on Motivation, 17*, 237–307.

Zimbardo, P. G. (1985, June). Laugh where we must, be candid where we can. *Psychology Today*, pp. 43–47.

Zimbardo, P. G., Banks, W. C., Haney, C., & Jaffe, D. (1973, April 8). The mind is a formidable jailer: A Pirandellian prison. *New York Times Magazine*, pp. 38–60.

Zimbardo, P. G., LaBerge, S., & Butler, L. D. (1993). Psychophysiological consequences of unexplained arousal: A posthypnotic suggestion paradigm. *Journal of Abnormal Psychology, 102*, 466–473.

Zimbardo, P.G. (1967, June). The psychology of police confessions. *Psychology Today, 1,* 17–27.

Zuckerman, M., DePaulo, B. M., & Rosenthal, R. (1981). Verbal and nonverbal communication of deception. In L. Berkowitz (Ed.), *Advances in experimental social psychology* (Vol. 14, pp. 1–59). New York: Academic Press.

Zuckerman, M., Knee, C. R., Hodgins, H. S., & Miyake, K. (1995). Hypothesis confirmation: The joint effect of positive test strategy and acquiescence response set. *Journal of Personality and Social Psychology, 68,* 52–60.

Zuwerink, J. R., & Devine, P. G. (1996). Attitude importance and resistance to persuasion: It's not just the thought that counts. *Journal of Personality and Social Psychology, 70,* 931–944.

CREDITS

Photo Credits

Chapter 1

p. 2 (*Opener*) IT Stock/Jupiter Images. **p. 3:** Alexander Tamargo/Getty Images. **p. 4 (left):** AP/Wide World Photos. **p. 4 (right):** Courtesy CNN. **p. 5:** Randy Faris/Corbis. **p. 6:** Vince Bucci/Getty Images. **p. 10:** Michael Newman/Photo Edit Inc. **p. 12:** Vincent Kessler/Reuters/Landov. **p. 13:** Mike Greenslade/Alamy. **p. 14:** Courtesy of The National Archives and Records Administration. **p. 15:** Lorne Resnick/Stone/GETTY IMAGES. **p. 16:** © The New Yorker Collection 1997 Robert Mankoff from cartoonbank.com. All rights reserved. **p. 19:** Ingo Wagner/dpa/Landov.

Chapter 2

p. 22 (*Opener*) Spencer Grant/Photo Edit Inc. **p. 24:** Atlantide Phototravel/Corbis. **p. 25:** Matthew Cavanaugh/epa/Corbis. **p. 28:** Kate Connell. **p. 29:** Reuters/CORBIS. **p. 29:** © The New Yorker Collection 1997 Dean Vietor from cartoonbank.com. All rights reserved. **p. 31:** Joanne Pasila/one². **p. 32:** Joanne Pasila/one². **p. 33:** © The New Yorker Collection 2003 Matthew Diffee from cartoonbank.com. All rights reserved. **p. 33:** Richard Lord/Photo Edit Inc. **p. 34:** UPI/Corbis–Bettmann. **p. 35:** Mike Watson Images/Corbis. **p. 40:** Gideon Mendel/Corbis. **p. 44:** Fabian Cevallos/CORBIS SYGMA. **p. 47:** © The New Yorker Collection 2004 Mike Twohy from cartoonbank.com. All rights reserved.

Chapter 3

p. 52 (*Opener*) Gail Mooney/Corbis. **p. 55:** PBWPIX/ Alamy. **p. 56:** © The New Yorker Collection 1998 Robert Mankoff from cartoonbank.com. All rights reserved. **p. 58:** © The New Yorker Collection 1991 Ed Frascino from cartoonbank.com. All rights reserved. **p. 63 (left):** Classmates.com. **p. 63 (right):** Ciniglio Lorenzo/CORBIS SYGMA. **p. 65 (left):** J.P. Laffont/CORBIS/SYGMA. **p. 65 (right):** Jeffrey Cadge/The Image Bank/Getty. **p. 68:** © The New Yorker Collection 1996 Mike Twohy from cartoonbank.com. All rights reserved. **p. 75 (left):** AP/Wide World Photos. **p. 75 (right):** Anatoly Maltsev/epa/Corbis. **p. 77:** Royalty Free/CORBIS Images. **p. 79:** J.L. Atlan/CORBIS SYGMA. **p. 84:** © The New Yorker Collection 1992 Mischa Richter from cartoonbank.com. All rights reserved.

Chapter 4

p. 92 (*Opener*) Ali Kabas/ Alamy. **p. 94 (left):** FIFA/Infront Sports & Media AG. **p. 94 (right):** JOHN MACDOUGALL/AFP/Getty Images. **p. 95 (left):** Liaison/Newsmakers/OnlineUSA. **p. 95 (right):** AP/Wide World Photos. **p. 96:** CORBIS/Bettmann. **p. 97 (upper left):** Guido Alberto Rossi/Tips Images. **p. 97 (upper middle):** Alan S. Weiner. **p. 97 (upper right):** Peter Dazeley/zefa/Corbis. **p. 97 (lower left):** Courtesy of Paramount Pictures. **p. 97 (lower middle):** M. Thomsen/zefa/Corbis. **p. 97 (lower right):** Carl Durocher/Creative Stock. **p. 100:** STEVE MARCUS/Las Vegas Sun/Reuters/Corbis. **p. 101:** © 2004 Robert Mankoff from cartoonbank.com. All Rights Reserved. **p. 102:** © The New Yorker Collection 2000 Robert Mankoff from cartoonbank.com. All Rights Reserved. **p. 109:** "Jeopardy!" courtesy King World/Sony Pictures Television. **p. 111:** James T. Spencer/PhotoResearchers. **p. 113:** AP/Wide World Photos. **p. 115:** © The New Yorker Collection 1994 Bernard Schoenbaum from cartoonbank.com. All rights reserved. **p. 118 (left):** Bill Ross/CORBIS Images. **p. 118 (right):** Francoise de Mulder/CORBIS Images.

Chapter 5

p. 130 (*Opener*) Ariel Skelley/CORBIS. **p. 131:** Courtesy Red Cross. **p. 132:** Chris Hondros/Getty Images. **p. 135:** Richard Pasley/Stock Boston. **p. 136:** Courtesy of Harvey Hutter & Company. **p. 137:** Mark Ludak/The Image Works, Inc. **p. 139:** VALDRIN XHEMAJ/epa/Corbis. **p. 144:** Los Angeles County Sheriff's Department/Handout/epa/Corbis. **p. 146 (left):** Correll et al, 2002. **p. 146 (middle):** Correll et al, 2002. **p. 146 (right):** Correll et al, 2002. **p. 147:** Annie Tritt/Polaris. **p. 149:** Will Hart. **p. 152:** Mark Graham/AP/Wide World Photos. **p. 155:** Colin Woodbridge/Alamy. **p. 155:** Jeff Greenberg/Alamy. **p. 157 (left):** Kevin Dodge/Corbis. **p. 157 (right):** Frank Trapper/Corbis. **p. 159:** Jodi Hilton/The New York Times/Redux. **p. 163:** Courtesy Jennifer Eberhardt. **p. 164:** Courtesy of Jennifer Richeson. **p. 166:** © The New Yorker Collection 2000 David Sipress from cartoonbank.com. All Rights Reserved. **p. 167:** Louise Gubb/CORBIS SABA. **p. 171:** Otto Greule Jr/Getty Images. **p. 173 (left):** AP/Wide World Photos. **p. 173 (right):** AP/Wide World Photos. **p. 175:** Paul Mounce/Corbis.

Chapter 6

p. 180 (*Opener*) Paul Hardy/Corbis. **p. 183:** AP/Wide World Photos. **p. 184:** © The New Yorker Collection 2000 Dana Fradon from cartoonbank.com. All Rights Reserved. **p. 187:** T.K. Wanstal/The Image Works. **p. 190 (left):** David Klee. **p. 190 (right):** Digital Focus/Alamy. **p. 195 (left):** Allen Einstein/Getty Images. **p. 195 (right):** David N. Berkwitz/NewSport/Corbis. **p. 196:** Jean Catuffe/SIPA Press. **p. 199: p. 200:** Courtesy The National Campaign to Prevent Teen Pregnancy. **p. 201:** Homeland Security – Public Document. **p. 202:** Courtesy of American Association of Advertising Agencies. **p. 206:** © Apple Inc. Used with permission. All rights reserved. Apple® and the Apple logo are registered trademark of Apple Inc. **p. 207:** UPI/CORBIS Bettmann. **p. 209:** From the Wall Street Journal. Permission, Cartoon Features Syndicate. All rights reserved. **p. 211:** Shannon Stapleton/Reuters/Corbis.

Chapter 7

p. 220 (*Opener*) Tim Davis/CORBIS. **p. 222:** Glen Tepke. **p. 223:** The New Yorker Collection 2000 Mick Stevens from cartoonbank.com. All rights reserved. **p. 225:** William Vandevert. **p. 227:** Kevin Winter/AMA/Getty Images for AMA. **p. 228:** Courtesy Gregory Berns. **p. 230 (left):** David Frazier/Photo Researchers. **p. 230 (right):** Bob Glasheen. **p. 235 (top left):** Robert van der Hilst/CORBIS. **p. 235 (right):** RAJ PATIDAR/Reuters/Corbis. **p. 235:** Reuters NewMedia Inc./CORBIS. **p. 236 (left):** Peter Ginter/Peter Menzel/Material World. **p. 236 (right):** Peter Ginter/Peter Menzel/Material World. **p. 237:** © 2004 Robert Mankoff from cartoonbank.com. All Rights Reserved. **p. 240:** Nonstock/Stephen Black. **p. 243:** Syndicated Features Limited/The Image Works,Inc. **p. 243:** Syndicated Features Limited/The Image Works,Inc. **p. 244 (left):** From the film *Obedience* by Stanley Milgram copyright 1965 and distributed by The Penn. State University Audio

Text Credits

Chapter 1
p. 18 *Figure 1.2:* Ross, M. Heine, S.J., Wilson, A.E. Sugimori, S. (2005). Cross–cultural discrepancies in self–appraisals. *Personality and Social Psychology Bulletin, 31,* 1175–1188.

Chapter 3
p. 60 *Figure 3.1:* From M.R. Lepper, D. Greene, and K.E. Nisbett, "Undermining children's intrinisic interest with extrinsic reward: A test of the 'overjustification' hypothesis," *Journal of Personality and Social Psychology, 28,* (1973): 129–137. Copyright © 1973 by the American Psychological Association. Reprinted with permission. **p. 64 *Figure 3.2:*** From Bahrick et al., *Psychological Science,* 1996, Vol. 7, pp. 266–271. Copyright © 1996 Blackwell Publishing. Reprinted with permission. **p. 66 *Figure 3.3:*** From H.R. Markus and S. Kitayama, "Culture and the self: Implications for cognition, emotion, and motivation," *Psychological Review, 98* (1991): 226. Copyright © 1991 by the American Psychological Association. Reprinted with permission. **p. 66 *Figure 3.4:*** From H. Kim and H.R. Marcus, "Deviance or Uniqueness, Harmony or Conformity? A Cultural Analysis" (1999) from *Journal of Personality and Social Psychology, 77,* 785–800.Copyright © 1999 by the American Psychological Association. Reprinted with permission. **p. 69 *Figure 3.5:*** From Twenge, J.M., and Crocker, J. (2002). Race and Self–Esteem: Meta–Analysis Comparing Whites, Blacks, Hispanics, Asians, and American Indians. *Psychological Bulletin, 128,* 371–408. Copyright © 2002 by the American Psychological Association. Reprinted with permission. **p. 72 *Table 3.1*** Copyright © 1975 by the American Psychological Association. Reproduced with permission. From A. Fenigstein, M.F. Scheier, and A.H. Buss, "Public and Private Self-Consciousness: Assessment and Theory," *Journal of Consulting and Clinical Psychology, 43,* 522–527, 1975. **p. 86 *Table 3.3*** Copyright © 1986 by the American Psychological Association. Reproduced with permission. From M. Snyder and S. Gangestad, "On the Nature of Self-Monitoring: Matters of Assessment, Matters of Validity," *Journal of Personality and Social Psychology, 51,* 125–139, 1986.

Chapter 4
p. 99 *Figure 4.1:* From Elfenbein, H. A. and Ambady, N. (2002). How Good are People at Identifying Emotions in the Face? *Psychological Bulletin, 128,* 203–235. **p. 100 *Figure 4.2:*** Reprinted with permission from "Smileys" © 1996, O'Reilly & Associates, Inc. All rights reserved. Orders and Information: 800–998–9938, www.oreilly.com. **p. 103 *Figure 4.3:*** Reprinted from *Journal of Experimental Social Psychology,* Vol. 3, E.G. Jones and K.E. Harris, "The Attribution of Attitudes," pp. 1–24, Copyright © 1967, with permission from Elsevier. **p. 108 *Figure 4.5:*** From L. Ross, T.M. Amabile, and J.L. Steinmetz, "Social Roles, Social Control, and Biases in Social Perception Process," *Journal of Personality and Social Psychology,* Vol. 35, 485–494, 1977. Copyright © 1977 American Psychological Association. Adapted with permission. **p. 111 *Figure 4.7:*** From J.G. Miller, "Culture and the Development of Everyday Social Explanation," *Journal of Personality and Social Psychology,* Vol. 46, 961–978, 1984. Copyright © 1984 American Psychological Association. Adapted with permission.

p. 112 *Figure 4.8:* From Y. Hong, M.W. Morris, C. Chiu and V. Benet–Martinez, "Multicultural Minds: A Dynamic Constructivist Approach to Culture and Cognition," *American Psychologist,* Vol. 55, 709–720, 2000. Copyright © 2000 American Psychological Association. Reprinted with permission. **p. 117 *Figure 4.9:*** From J.A. Bargh, M. Chen and L. Burrows, "Automaticity of Social Behavior: Direct Effects of Trait Construct and Stereotype Activation on Action," *Journal of Personality and Social Psychology,* Vol. 71, 230–244, 1996. Copyright © 1996 American Psychological Association. Reprinted with permission. **p. 101 *Table 4.2:*** From P. Ekman and M. O'Sullivan, "Who Can Catch a Liar?" *American Psychologist,* Vol. 46, 913–920, 1991. Copyright © 1991 American Psychological Association. Reprinted with permission.

Chapter 5
p. 132 (top): American Skin – (41 Shots) by Bruce Springsteen. Copyright © 2000 by Bruce Springsteen (ASCAP). Reprinted by permission. **p. 143 *Figure 5.3:*** From L. Sinclair and Z. Kunda, "Reactions to a Black Professional: Motivated Inhibition and Activation of Conflicting Stereotypes," *Journal of Personality and Social Psychology,* Vol. 77, 885–904. Copyright © American Psychological Association. Reprinted with permission. **p. 169 *Figure 5.11:*** From Claude Steele, *Journal of Personality and Social Psychology, 69,* 797–811, 1995. Copyright © 1995 by the American Psychological Association. Reprinted with permission. **p. 170 *Figure 5.12:*** From B.L. Fredrickson, T.A. Roberts, S.M. Noll, D.A. Quinn and J.M. Twenge, "That Swimsuit Becomes You: Sex Differences in Self–Objectification, Restrained Eating, and Math Performance," *Journal of Personality and Social Psychology,* 1998. Copyright © 1998 by the American Psychological Association. Reprinted with permission.

Chapter 6
p. 185 *Figure 6.2:* From J.T. Cacioppo and R.E. Petty, "Electromyograms as Measures of Extent and Affectivity of Information Processing," *American Psychologist, 36,* 441–456, 1981. Copyright © 1981 American Psychological Association. Reprinted with permission. **p. 186 *Figure 6.3:*** From Essentials of Psychology by Saul Kassin, Copyright © 2004. Reprinted by permission of Pearson Education, Inc., Upper Saddle River, NJ. **p. 188 *Figure 6.4:*** Reprinted from *Organizational Behavior, and the Human Decision Process,* Vol. 50, Professor Ajzen, pp. 179–211, Copyright © 1991, with permission from Elsevier. **p. 197 *Figure 6.6:*** Reprinted by permission from Richard E. Petty. **p. 204 *Figure 6.9:*** From J.M. Snyder and K.G. DeBono, "Appeals to Image and Claims About Quality: Understanding the Psychology of Advertising," *Journal of Personality and Social Psychology, 49,* 586–597, 1985. Copyright © 1985 American Psychological Association. Adapted with permission. **p. 210 *Figure 6.10:*** From L. Festinger and J.M. Carlsmith, "Cognitive Consequences of Forced Compliance," *Journal of Abnormal and Social Psychology, 58,* 203–210, 1959. Copyright © 1959 by the American Psychological Association. Reprinted with permission. **p. 204 *Table 6.3:*** Copyright © 1982 by the American Psychological Association. Reproduced with permission. From J.T. Cacioppo and R.E. Petty "The Need for Cognition," *Journal of Personality and Social Psychology, 42,* 116–131, 1982.

Chapter 7
p. 223 *Figure 7.2:* From Psychology, 3rd Edition by Saul Kassin. Copyright © 1997. Reprinted by permission of Prentice–Hall, Inc., Upper Saddle River, NJ. **p. 229 *Figure 7.6:*** From Robert Baron et al., *Journal of Personality and Social Psychology, 71,* 915–927, 1996. Copyright © 1996 by the American Psychological Association. Adapted with permission. **p. 247 *Figure 7.7:*** Based on Stanley Milgram, Obedience to Authority, 1974. **p. 251 *Figure 7.8:*** From B. Latane, "The Psychology of

Psychological Association. Reprinted with permission. **p. 423 Table 11.4:** From M. C. Burt, "Cultural myths and supports for rape," *Journal of Personality and Social Psychology, 38* (1980): 217–230. Copyright © 1980 by the American Psychological Association. Reprinted with permission.

Chapter 12

p. 449 Figure 12.3: (Top Portion) Adapted from E.F. Loftus and J.C. Palmer, "Reconstruction of Automobile Destruction: An Example of the Interaction Between Language and Memory," *Journal of Verbal Learning and Verbal Behavior, Vol. 13,* 1974, pp. 585–589. (Bottom Portion) From G.R. Loftus and E.F. Loftus, Human Memory: The Processing of Information. Copyright © 1976 by Lawrence Erlbaum Associates, Inc. Reprinted with permission. **p. 456 Figure 12.6:** From N.I. Kerr, G.P. Kramer, J.S. Carroll and J.J. Alfinin, (1982), "On the Effectiveness of Voir Dire in Criminal Cases with Prejudicial Pretrial Publicity: An Empirical Study," *American University Law Review, 40,* pp. 665–701. Reprinted with permission. **p. 438 Table 12.1:** From S.M. Kassin and L.S. Wrightsman (1983), "The Construction and Validation of a Juror Bias Scale," From *Journal of Research in Personality, 17,* 423–442. Reprinted by permission of Academic Press. **p. 444 Table 12.3:** From S. M. Kassin and K. L. Kiechel, "The Social Psychology of False Confessions: Compliance, Internalization, and Confabulation," Psychological Science (1996). Reprinted by permission from Blackwell Publishers. **p. 453 Table 12.5:** From R. Malpass and P. Devine. "Eyewitness identification: Lineup instructions and the absence of the offender." *Journal of Applied Psychology, 66,* 482–489, 1981. Copyright © 1981 by the American Psychological Association. Reprinted with permission. **p. 455 Table 12.6:** From "On The 'General Acceptance' Of Eyewitness Testimony Research: A New Survey of the Experts" by S. M. Kassin, V.A. Tubb, H.M. Hosch, and A. Memon. From American Psychologist, May 2001. Copyright © 2001 by the American Psychological Assoication. Reprinted with permission.

Chapter 13

p. 476 Figure 13.1: From C.M. Marlowe, S.L. Schenider, and C.E. Nelson. "Gender and attractiveness biases in hiring decisions: Are more experienced managers less biased?" *Journal of Applied Psychology, 81,* 11–21, 1996. Copyright © 1996 by the American Psychological Association. Reprinted with permission. **p. 478 Figure 13.3:** From Alliger, G. M., Lillienfeld, S. O., & Mitchell, K. E. (1996). The susceptibility of overt and covert integrity tests to coaching and faking," from *Psychological Science,*

7, pp. 32–39. Reprinted by permission from Blackwell Publishers. **p. 481 Figure 13.5:** From "Social psychology and the affirmative action debate" by R.W. Nacoste, *Journal of Social and Clinical Psychology, 15,* 261–282, © 1996. Reprinted by permission from The Guildford Press. **p. 496 Figure 13.8:** From E.L. Deci. "Effects of externally mediated rewards on intrinsic motivation." *Journal of Personality and Social Psychology, 18,* 105–115, 1971. Copyright © 1971 by the American Psychological Association. Reprinted with permission. **p. 497 Figure 13.9:** From J. Greenberg, "Equity and Workplace Status: A Field Experiment" *Journal of Applied Psychology, 73,* 606–613, 1988. Copyright © 1988 by the American Psychological Association. Reprinted with permission.

Chapter 14

p. 514 Figure 14.2: From A. Baum and S. Valins, Architecture and Social Behavior: Psychological Studies of Social Density. Copyright © 1977 by Lawrence Erlbaum Associates, Inc. Reprinted with permission. **p. 522 Figure 14.6:** From Psychology, 3rd Edition by Saul Kassin. Copyright © 1997. Reprinted by permission of Prentice–Hall, Inc., Upper Saddle River, NJ. **p. 524 Figure 14.7:** From S.A. Everson, et al., "Hopelessness and Risk of Mortality and Incidence of Myocardial Infarction and Cancer," *Psychosomatic Medicine, Vol. 58,* 121–133. Reprinted with permission of Lippincott, Williams & Wilkins. **p. 532 Figure 14.8:** From Aspinwall and Taylor. A stitch in time: self–regulation and proactive coping. *Psychological Bulletin, 121,* 417–436, 1997. Copyright © 1997 by the American Psychological Association. Reprinted with permission. **p. 533 Figure 14.9:** From N. Hamrick, S. Cohen, and M.S. Rodriguez, "Being Popular Can Be Healthy or Unhealthy: Stress, Social Network Diversity, and Incidence of Upper Respiratory Infection," *Health Psychology, 21,* 294–298, 2002. Copyright © 2002 by the American Psychological Association. Reprinted with permission. **p. 541 Figure 14.12:** From Psychology, 3rd Edition by Saul Kassin. Copyright © 1997. Reprinted by permission of Prentice-Hall, Inc., Upper Saddle River, NJ. **p. 542:** Reprinted with permission of WebMD.com. **p. 518 Table 14.1:** From Anger Kills: 17 Strategies by Redford B. Williams and Virginia Williams. Copyright © 1993 by Redford B. Williams, M.D., and Virginia Williams, Ph.D. Used by permission of Times Books, a division of Random House, Inc. **p. 526 Table 14.2:** From Carver, C.S., M.F. Scheier, and J.K. Weintraub (1989). "Assessing Coping Strategies: A Theoretically Based Approach." *Journal of Personality and Social Psychology, 56,* 267–283. Copyright © 1989 by the American Psychological Association. Reprinted with permission.

NAME INDEX

Subject Index

Page numbers followed by *c* indicate captions; page numbers followed by *f* indicate figures; page numbers followed by *t* indicate tables.

Academic performance, and stereotype threat, 167–171
Acceptance
  in coping, 526*t*, 535*t*
  of persuasive message, 190–191
Accountability cues, 267
Acquaintance rape, 423–424
Acquisition stage, of memory, 447–449
Actor-observer effect, 110
Actual self, 69, 72
Adaptation-level theory, 541–542
Additive group tasks, 278–279
Adjourning stage, of groups, 270
Adventures of Tom Sawyer, The (Twain), 59
Adversarial model of justice, 467
Advertising
  celebrity endorsement, 193, 195, 196*c*
  gender stereotypes, 156–157
  negative, 200, 201
  overheard communicator trick, 194
  public service, 200–201
  and sexual aggression, 10*c*
  subliminal messages, 201–203
  use of physical attractiveness, 195
  See also Media; Persuasive communication
Affect. *See* Emotions; Negative affect; Positive emotions
Affective forecasting, 57
Affiliation, need for, 302–303
Affirmative action, 479–482, 483*t*
Affluence, and cultural orientation, 235
Agape love style, 326
Age
  and loneliness, 305
  and self-monitoring, 86
  and violent crime, 395
Ageism, 153
Age of Manipulation, The (Key), 202
Aggression
  and alcohol, 28, 44, 413, 428
  and arousal, 408, 410–411, 421–423
  arousal-affect model of, 410–411
  behavior genetics on, 400
  biological factors in, 400–401
  bullying behavior, 32, 394
  child abuse, 425–426
  cognitive factors in, 411–413
  cultural differences in, 392–395, 404–405
  cycle of violence, 426
  defined, 391–392
  displacement of, 406–408
  emotional, 391–392
  evolutionary perspective on, 398–400

examples of, 389–391
  and frustration, 406–408
  gender differences in, 18, 395–397, 399, 400–401, 403–404, 424–425
  indirect vs. direct, 396, 419
  individual differences in, 397
  instinct theories of, 398
  instrumental, 391–392
  in intimate relationships, 423–426, 427–428
  as learned behavior, 401–405
  media effects on, 414–423, 426–427
  methods for reducing, 426–429
  nature vs. nurture debate on, 398, 406
  and negative affect, 408–410, 411
  origins of, 397–406
  and pornography, 420–423
  and punishment, 402
  regional differences in, 395, 404–405
  retaliatory, 410, 413, 421
  situational factors in, 406–414
  socialization of, 403–405, 426
  social learning theory on, 402–403
  temperature and, 408–410
  weapons effect on, 411–412
  See also Sexual aggression; Violence
AIDS
  prevention of, 537, 538, 539–540
  treatment research for, 42
  and volunteerism, 358, 377–378
Alarm reaction, to stress, 515–516
Alcohol
  and aggression, 28, 44, 413, 428
  for coping, 526*t*
  and eyewitness testimony, 448, 455*t*
  for reducing self-awareness, 71–72
  and sexual aggression, 424
  and stereotype activation, 144
Alcohol myopia, 413
Alice's Adventures in Wonderland (Carroll), 119
Altruism
  defined, 353–354
  vs. egoism, 353–358
  and empathy, 354–356, 376
  limits of, 357
  reciprocal, 348–349
Altruistic personality, 374, 375–376
Ambivalent racism, 161–162
Ambivalent sexism, 157–158
American Academy of Child and Adolescent Psychiatry, 418
American Academy of Family Physicians, 418
American Academy of Pediatrics, 418
American Jury, The (Kalven, Zeisel), 461
American Medical Association, 418
American Psychiatric Association, 418
American Psycho, 416*t*

American Psychological Association (APA), 9, 46, 418, 442
Amish, 25*c*, 350*c*, 394–395
Amnesty International, 248
"Anchoring effect," 464
Anger
  and aggression, 391
  and heart disease, 518
  identifying from face, 98–99
"Anger superiority effect," 99
Anonymity
  and deviant behavior, 266–268
  and diffusion of responsibility, 363
Anorexia nervosa, 312
Antisocial behavior
  and corporal punishment, 402
  and deindividuation, 266–268
Anxious attachment style, 325–326
Apodaca v. *Oregon,* 462
Appearance. *See* Physical appearance; Physical attractiveness
Applied research, 27
Appraisal, 521–525
  and capacity for resilience, 522–525
  defined, 510
  dispositional optimism, 524–525
  explanatory styles, 521–522
  negative attributions, 522
  perceptions of control, 523–524
Arbitrators, 293
Archival studies, 32–33
Arousal
  and aggression, 408, 410–411, 421–423
  in cognitive dissonance, 212
  effect on memory, 448
  and lie detection, 446
  in passionate love, 328–329
  physiological, measures of, 184
  in social facilitation, 259–262, 265
  and stress response, 516
  in two-factor theory of emotion, 62–63, 328
Arousal-affect model, of aggression, 410–411, 421
Arousal: cost-reward model, 350–351
Assertions of confidence, 205*t*
Assertiveness, vs. compliance, 222*f*, 241–242, 250
Assessment centers, 479, 486
As You Like It (Shakespeare), 83
Attachment styles, 324–326
Attentional cues, 267
Attitude bolstering, 204, 205*t*
Attitude change. *See* Persuasive communication; Self-persuasion
Attitude discrepant behavior, 206–209. *See also* Cognitive dissonance